The Legal, Ethical and International Environment of Business

Second Edition

The Legal, Ethical and International Environment of Business
Second Edition

Herbert M. Bohlman
Associate Professor
Arizona State University
Judge Pro Tempore, Maricopa County Superior Court

Mary Jane Dundas
Associate Professor
Arizona State University

West Publishing Company
Minneapolis/St. Paul   New York   Los Angeles   San Francisco

Composition: Parkwood Composition Services
Copyeditor: Nancy Palmer Jones
Artwork: Miyake Illustration

Cover: Comstock

WEST'S COMMITMENT TO THE ENVIRONMENT

In 1906, West Publishing Company began recycling materials left over from the production of books. This began a tradition of efficient and responsible use of resources. Today, up to 95 percent of our legal books and 70 percent of our college texts are printed on recycled, acid-free stock. West also recycles nearly 22 million pounds of scrap paper annually—the equivalent of 181,717 trees. Since the 1960s, West has devised ways to capture and recycle waste inks, solvents, oils, and vapors created in the printing process. We also recycle plastics of all kinds, wood, glass, corrugated cardboard, and batteries, and have eliminated the use of styrofoam book packaging. We at West are proud of the longevity and the scope of our commitment to our environment.

Production, Prepress, Printing and Binding by West Publishing Company

COPYRIGHT ©1989   By WEST PUBLISHING COMPANY
COPYRIGHT ©1993   By WEST PUBLISHING COMPANY
                  610 Opperman Drive
                  P.O. Box 64526
                  St. Paul, MN 55164-0526

Printed in the United States of America
00 99 98 97 96 95 94 93   8 7 6 5 4 3 2 1 0

Library of Congress Cataloging-in-Publication Data

Bohlman, Herbert M.
    The legal, ethical and international environment of business / Herbert
M. Bohlman, Mary Jane Dundas. — 2nd Ed.
    Includes index.
    ISBN 0-314-00905-1 (hard)
    1. Industrial laws and legislation—United States.   2. Commercial
law—United States.   3. Business enterprises—United States.
I. Dundas, Mary Jane. II. Title.
KF1600.B64 1992
346.73'07—dc20
[347.3067]

Contents in Brief

v

Unit III
Business Formation   395

Unit IV
Business and Government Regulation   471

Appendices

Contents

UNIT II
BUSINESS AND PRIVATE LAW   181

UNIT IV
BUSINESS AND GOVERNMENT REGULATION   471

Appendices

Preface

The American legal scene has changed tremendously during the last quarter century and even more changes are expected as we approach the 21st century. As a result, the effect of the legal environment in which business operates has changed dramatically. THE LEGAL, ETHICAL AND INTERNATIONAL ENVIRONMENT OF BUSINESS, SECOND EDITION was written with two goals in mind—to present to the student the breadth of the legal, ethical and international environment of business and to provide a legal foundation that can be used in his or her business or government career.

To accomplish these goals, we have presented materials that cover both the private and public regulation of business. Legal topics discussed in the first area include contracts, sales, secured transactions, negotiable instruments, property, agency, partnerships, and corporations. Legal topics covered in the second area—public regulation—are labor law, securities law, antitrust, consumer rights, and environmental law. The second edition includes revised chapters on ethics and international law and integrates into all chapters both ethical and international considerations. The text integrates the American Assembly of Collegiate Schools of Business (AACSB) curriculum standards to cover ethical, global, political, social, legal, regulatory, environmental, and technological issues.

Total Learning/Teaching Package

This text constitutes what we believe to be a total learning/teaching package. It contains numerous pedagogical aids and high-interest additions.

Case Selection and Presentation

Each chapter has several cases to illustrate the application of the law to specific business problems. We have tried to create a balance between classic cases that are well recognized and recent cases that have changed the law significantly. Each case starts with the citation that includes the court, the date, the federal or state reporter (if available), and the West reporter. The Background and Facts focuses on the setting in which the case arose and identifies the plaintiffs and defendants. The actual court case is presented in an edited manner. Finally, the Decision and Remedy clearly states who won the case and why. When appropriate, we have a Comment section that presents additional material not available from the case itself or that indicates future trends.

Features of Each Chapter

Each chapter has an example of one or more of the following special sections that are designed to instruct as well as to interest the student.

Quotations

Each chapter opens with a brief quotation that is appropriate to the chapter material.

Exhibits

Most chapters have at least one exhibit to illustrate important aspects of the law. Some exhibits are charts, such as the one setting out the federal court system; others focus on classifications or summaries; and others set out forms used in the legal or business world, such as the one presenting a sample credit sale contract.

Legal Highlights

Nearly all chapters have legal highlights in which the student is presented with practical advice, such as how to check on a social security account, or with examples of how the law was applied in an unusual situation, such as the one on the cross-cultural conflict on the Texas Gulf Coast.

Ethical Considerations

Disclosures of criminal activity by businesses shook the business world and public confidence. Old, established Wall Street brokerage houses were found guilty of securities law violations, the savings and loan institutions were destroyed by those who looted them, businesses were found guilty of criminal violations of environmental laws. As public confidence waned, businesses turned to incorporating ethics into their daily activities. The emphasis on ethics in academic studies is reflected in the standards set by the American Assembly of Collegiate Schools of Business (AACSB). The new standards require that ethics be integrated into the study of business. This text likewise integrates ethics into each chapter. Chapter 2 covers ethical theories and provides a basis for class discussion of the ethical problems set out at the end of each chapter.

International Considerations

The economic future of the United States is dependent upon international trade. People involved with international business will need a working knowledge as to how international trade functions and the legal problems that may arise. The AACSB is also concerned with integrating global issues into the academic studies of business. Each chapter has an International Consideration that discusses international aspects of the chapter's subject matter. Chapter 24 covers various aspects of doing business in the global environment.

Facing a Legal Issue

Located at the end of each chapter is material entitled Facing a Legal Issue. In each discussion, we have attempted to present a factual situation which a business person could confront in his or her career. These situations concern problems that are collateral to the rest of the material contained within the chapter. They are an attempt to give students practical factual advice on how to apply the law.

Key Terms

Each chapter ends with a list of key terms first identified by bold-faced type in the text.

Questions and Case Problems

At the end of each chapter, five to ten Questions and Case problems are set out. The questions are a mix of hypotheticals and problems taken from actual cases for which full citations are given. Complete answers to all of the Questions and Case Problems are found in a separate booklet entitled Answers to Questions and Case Problems.

Appendices

So that this book can serve as a reference, we have included a full set of appendices. They are as follows:

A The Constitution of the United States of America

B   The Uniform Commercial Code (Excerpts)
C   Restatement of Torts, Second (Excerpts)
D   The Sherman Antitrust Act (Excerpts)
E   The Clayton Act (Excerpts)
F   The Federal Trade Commission Act (Excerpts)
G   National Labor Relations Act (Excerpts)
H   The Federal Civil Rights Laws (Excerpts)
I   The Uniform Partnership Act (Excerpts)
J   Spanish Equivalents for Important Legal Terms in English

Supplements

Study Guide

The Study Guide was written by Thomas Brierton of the University of the Pacific. Each chapter reinforces what the text has presented. The Study Guide consists of descriptions of general principles discussed in each chapter, chapter summaries in sentence outline form, and true-false, fill-in-the-blank, and multiple-choice questions to test students' comprehension.

Instructor's Manual with Test Bank

The Instructor's Manual and Test Bank was written by Larry D. Strate of the University of Nevada at Las Vegas. Each chapter includes a chapter overview, chapter outline, case comments, discussion questions, ethical and international considerations comments, and instructional suggestions. Each chapter of the Test Bank has a minimum of 15 true-false questions and 50 multiple-choice questions with many chapters having more items.

The Test Bank is available on WESTEST, which offers computerized testing for IBM-PC and compatible microcomputers or the Macintosh. WESTEST allows instructors to create new tests, modify existing tests, change the questions from West's original Test Bank, and print tests in a variety of formats. Instructors can add questions of their own to the Test Bank. Instructors should contact their West sales representative to inquire about acquiring WESTEST.

Educational Legal Software

LEGAL CLERK®—A Software Package for Research and Learning is the highly acclaimed West Publishing LEGAL CLERK® Research Software System. LEGAL CLERK® is a user-friendly, interactive software package that simultaneously introduces students to the rudiments of computer-aided legal research and reinforces the underlying concepts of business law. LEGAL CLERK® provides a valuable learning tool to help your school meet AACSB recommendations for using microcomputers in business legal courses.

LEGAL CLERK® enables students with access to IBM-PC and compatible personal computers to retrieve specific cases found in THE LEGAL, ETHICAL AND INTERNATIONAL ENVIRONMENT OF BUSINESS, SECOND EDITION, for extensive study. To provide instructors with maximum flexibility, LEGAL CLERK® covers three major subject areas of business law and legal environment—UCC Article 2 Sales; Government Regulations and the Legal Environment of Business; and Contracts. Instructors may select one or all three versions for their classes. Cases appearing in LEGAL CLERK® are clearly identified in the text with a computer logo. The logos are color coded to help users easily identify which version of LEGAL CLERK® contains specific cases.

 Uniform Commercial Code Article 2 Sales—Version 1.0

 Government Regulation and The Legal Environment of Business—Version 1.0

Contracts—Version 1.0

A site license for all three versions of LEGAL CLERK® is free to qualified adopters. Each version is accompanied by an Instructor's Resource Guide and, for student purchase, a Student User's Guide.

Answers to Questions and Case Problems

This manual provides solutions to the questions and case problems found in the text. It is available free to adopters of the text.

LEGAL Review

For those who would not utilize the legal research capabilities of LEGAL CLERK®, West Publishing now offers LEGAL Review. It provides reference material from the tutorial portion of LEGAL CLERK®. This software is divided into three topic menus: UCC, Contracts, and Legal Environment. A Student User's Guide contains questions for the topic areas. The software can be used to learn the answers.

West's Book of Forms

West's Book of Legal Forms, prepared by Robert McNutt, California State University at Northridge, is also available for student purchase. It provides 40 samples of often-used business forms.

Transparency Acetates

The supplements package contains a set of approximately 40 transparency acetates.

Acknowledgments

Many people are involved in the production of a textbook. The initial impetus for THE LEGAL, ETHICAL AND INTERNATIONAL ENVIRONMENT OF BUSINESS, SECOND EDITION came from Clyde Perlee, Jr., who has been a strong supporter of this project. A hearty thanks to Carole Balach, our production editor, who kept the project moving in a timely manner, and to Jan Lamar, our developmental editor, who coordinated all the reviews and provided expert analysis. We thank Rose Gruenhagen who also helped us on this project.

A number of reviewers were kind enough to give us their ideas and comments on various drafts of the manuscript. They are listed below for both the first and second editions.

Reviewers for the First Edition:

David L. Baumer, North Carolina State University
Katherine Beebe, Salt Lake Community College
Thomas H. Brucker, University of Washington
Mark A. Buchanan, St. Cloud State University
Daylin J. Butler, Kansas State University

Lawrence S. Clark, Louisiana State University in Shreveport
Gamewell D. Gantt III, Idaho State University
John Geary, Appalachian State University
Amy Zoe Gershenfeld, University of Kentucky
Martin F. Grace, Georgia State University
Gerard Halpern, University of Arkansas
Marsha E. Hass, College of Charleston
James P. Hill, Central Michigan University
E. C. Hipp, Clemson University
David D. Jaeger, University of Cincinnati
Marianne M. Jennings, Arizona State University
Jack E. Karns, University of North Dakota
Nancy P. Klintworth, University of Central Florida
Paul Lansing, University of Iowa
Andrew Laviano, University of Rhode Island
F. Raymond Lewis, Northeastern Illinois University
Nancy R. Mansfield, Georgia State University
S. Scott Massin, Emory University
John E. McDonald, Jr., University of North Carolina at Charlotte
Sheel P. Pawar, Idaho State University
Jordan B. Ray, University of Florida
Lim Razook, University of Oklahoma
Daniel L. Reynolds, Middle Tennessee State University
Rene Sacasas, University of Miami, Florida
Scott Sibray, California State University, Chino
Lou Ann Simpson, Drake University
S. Jay Sklar, Temple University
Lucy L. Spalding, Illinois State University
Larry Strate, University of Nevada at Las Vegas
Donald J. Swanz, St. Bonaventure University
Irvin Tankersley, Memphis State University
Bernard F. Thiemann, Bellarmine College
Daphney Thomas, James Mason University
Wayne R. Wells, St. Cloud State University

Reviewers for the Second Edition:

Thomas M. Apke, California State University, Fullerton
Thomas D. Brierton, University of the Pacific
Frank J. Cavaliere, Lamar University
Michael P. Litka, University of Akron
Paul Lyons, Frostburg State University
Charles W. McGuire, De Vry Institute
Dinah Payne, University of New Orleans

Jeffrey R. Pittman, Arkansas State University
Martha Sartoris, North Hennepin Community College
Darryl L. Webb, University of Alabama
Kay Wilburn, The University of Alabama at Birmingham

We thank our fellow colleagues who encouraged us, supported us, and spent hours reviewing our rough drafts: Professors Louie Aranda, Marianne M. Jennings, Ethan Lock, Claude Olney, and Peter Reiss of Arizona State University. They were extremely helpful with our initial drafts and giving us their creative ideas and thoughts. They also gave us the motivation to keep going on both editions.

As careful as we have attempted to be, there are, no doubt, errors in this text for which we take full responsibility. We welcome comments from all users of the text, for it is by incorporating such comments that we can make this text even better in future editions.

Mary Jane Dundas
Herbert M. Bohlman

Dedication

M.J.D. dedicates this book to the memory of her parents, R.J. and Marie A. Dundas, and her sisters, Jean and Marilyn, and their families.

H.M.B. dedicates this book to his wife, Mimi, and his children, Bill, Patti, Mike, and Laura.

UNIT I   INTRODUCTION TO LAW

INTRODUCTION

Ignorance of the law excuses no man; not that all men know the law, but because 'tis an excuse every man will plead, and no man can tell how to confute him.

Table Talk,
p. 99, (1892).

OUTLINE

The Need to Know the Law

Why should you study law when you are majoring in business? Read a newspaper or magazine, turn on the television or listen to the radio, and you will find the business news full of legal issues. These issues impact not only the owners of businesses but their employees, customers, suppliers, and the community at large. The congressional decision to deregulate the savings and loan industry in the late 1970s cost taxpayers billions of dollars, sent dozens of corporations into receivership, caused thousands of employees to lose their jobs, devastated various communities by depressing real estate markets, and resulted in criminal prosecution of corporate owners and managers. This is just one example of how the law and business interrelate.

Business exists in the economic, social, technological, and political environments. In all of these areas, the law has a profound impact on business. In the economic arena, for example, the Federal Reserve Board regulates the money supply and interest rates. In the area of social concerns, a business is legally liable for its employees who become intoxicated at the company's annual picnic. In the technological arena, the inventor-employee may have a right to royalties earned from patents granted while working for a university.

In the political arena, legislators face competing demands from various groups. The laws these legislators pass then affect business operations. In 1964, for example, Congress passed the Civil Rights Act, which has since been amended several times. Over the years, this act has been interpreted by the Supreme Court of the United States in ways that affect sex and racial discrimination in the workplace. This statute has caused businesses to change their employment and personnel policies.

Businesses face new and sometimes conflicting regulations coming from federal and state regulatory agencies. The Occupational Health and Safety Administration inspector requires a meat packing plant to have dry floors so employees will not slip and fall. The Department of Agriculture meat inspector requires the floors to be washed down to clear debris in order to control the spread of any bacteria. Businesses are often caught between conflicting regulations.

These and other legal issues challenge people in the business community on a daily basis. The stakes are high, for a legal mistake can be costly; judgments against a business found at fault can add up to multimillion-dollar losses. Thus, to pursue a business career, you must have at least some familiarity with the law and the legal system.

This book, then, presents a brief overview of how law and business interface. It is not an in-depth study of the law, for any single area of the law can merit a semester or more of study at law school. Bankruptcy law, for example, is so complicated that it is generally handled only by a lawyer who specializes in this particular field. This book presents an overview of various areas of the law affecting businesses of which students should be aware.

To illustrate the relationship between business and the law, this textbook includes many specific cases, statutes, and regulatory rules. You need to know where these examples come from and how to read case and statute citations. The following sections cover these topics. We also provide here a sample case and offer suggestions on how to analyze and understand the cases in this book.

Locating Case Law

Except for the federal courts, New York, and California, few states publish their trial court opinions in book form. Decisions of trial courts are filed in the offices of the clerks of the courts and are available for public inspection. Of the thousands of trial court decisions made each year, less than 10% are appealed to higher courts, which are called **appellate courts.**

Appellate Court Decisions

Most decisions by courts of appeals are published and distributed in book form and are available in computer data banks. These reported cases make up the common law. The published appellate court cases are those that are concerned with legal issues of great importance to society. The other appellate court decisions (approximately 40 percent of all decisions) are not reported, although they are available to the public. The cases in this book have been taken from reported appellate court decisions. Thus, you need to understand the system for reporting these cases.

Reporter Systems for Case Decisions   The reported appellate decisions are published in volumes called *Reports* or *Reporters,* which are numbered consecutively. Many state appellate court decisions are published by the state governments. These state-published *Reports* are called "official reports"; however, they usually are about a year behind in publication. State cases also appear in regional units of the *National Reporter System,* published privately by West Publishing Company. These are called "unofficial reporters."

Most lawyers and libraries have the West reporters because these cases are published more quickly and are distributed more widely than the state-published reports. Because of the completeness of the *National Reporter System* and the quick publication of the latest cases (usually two weeks), many states have eliminated their own reports in favor of West's *National Reporter System.* These states have designated the *National Reporter System* as the official reports for their state cases.

West Publishing Company has divided the states into geographic areas (see Exhibit I–1): Atlantic (A. or A.2d), South Eastern (S.E. or S.E.2d), South Western (S.W. or S.W.2d), North Western (N.W. or N.W.2d), North Eastern (N.E. or N.E.2d), Southern (So. or So.2d), and Pacific (P. or P.2d). The first set of initials in each pair represents the first series; the initials that have 2d behind them are known as the second series. All of the regional *Reporters* are now in the second series, where all the new cases appear.

In addition, West Publishing Company distributes a number of specialized *Reporters.* United States court of appeals decisions are found in the *Federal Reporter* (F. or F.2d), while federal district court decisions are printed in the *Federal Supplement* (F.Supp.). Decisions concerning the federal rules of procedure are given in the *Federal Rules Decisions* (F.R.D.). Bankruptcy cases are reported in West's *Bankruptcy Reporter* (B.R.).

Decisions made by the United States Supreme Court are found in the official reports printed by the United States Government Printing Office and called *United States Reports* (U.S.). Two unofficial reporters publish these same decisions privately: *Supreme Court Reporter* (S.Ct.), published by West Publishing Company, and *Lawyers' Edition of the United States Supreme Court Reports* (L.Ed.), published by Lawyers Co-Operative Publishing Company and Bancroft-Whitney Company.

How to Read a Citation   After appellate decisions are published, they are normally referred to

(or cited) by giving the name of the case; the volume, name, and page of the state report (if any); the volume and page of the *National Reporter;* the volume, name, and page of any other selected case series; and the year the decision was filed (see Exhibit I–2). For example, consider the following case: *Blazovic v. Andrich,* 124 N.J. 90, 590 A.2d 222 (1991). After the names of the parties, we see that the opinion in this case may be found in volume 124 of the official New Jersey *Reports* (published by the state of New Jersey) beginning on page 90 and in volume 590 of the *Atlantic Reporter,* second series (published by West Publishing Company), beginning on page 222. The year of filing of the appellate court decision is 1991.

In the title of a case, such as *Blazovic v. Andrich,* the *v.* or *vs.* stands for "versus," which means against. When the case is appealed, the appellate court will sometimes place the name of the party appealing the decision first. In some states, however, the appellate courts retain the trial court order of names; thus, it is impossible to distinguish the plaintiff from the defendant in the title of a reported appellate court decision. The facts of each case must be read carefully in order to identify each party; otherwise, the discussion by the appellate court will be difficult to understand.

Statute Publications

A **statute** is a law that has been passed by a legislative body and signed by the President or Governor. Statutes are also published, but they are published by topic, while cases are published in chronological order. The citations for statutes are also different from those for cases. In a case citation, the first number is the volume number, and the last number is the page where the case is found. In a statutory citation, the first number is the title number, and the second number is the section number (see Exhibit I–3).

Federal statutes are found in the *United States Code* (U.S.C., published by the United States Government Printing Office) and the *United States Code Annotated* (U.S.C.A., published by West Publishing Company). The annotated statutes provide a summary and a list of cases decided under that statute.

For example, the federal criminal statutes are found in Title 18, which consists of eighteen vol-

Exhibit I–1 *National Reporter System*—Regional and Federal

Regional Reporters	Coverage Beginning	Coverage
Atlantic Reporter	1885	Connecticut, Delaware, Maine, Maryland, New Hampshire, New Jersey, Pennsylvania, Rhode Island, Vermont, and District of Columbia Municipal Court of Appeals.
North Eastern Reporter	1885	Illinois, Indiana, Massachusetts, New York, and Ohio.
North Western Reporter	1879	Iowa, Michigan, Minnesota, Nebraska, North Dakota, South Dakota, and Wisconsin.
Pacific Reporter	1883	Alaska, Arizona, California, Colorado, Hawaii, Idaho, Kansas, Montana, Nevada, New Mexico, Oklahoma, Oregon, Utah, Washington, and Wyoming
South Eastern Reporter	1887	Georgia, North Carolina, South Carolina, Virginia, and West Virginia.
South Western Reporter	1886	Arkansas, Kentucky, Missouri, Tennessee, and Texas.
Southern Reporter	1887	Alabama, Florida, Louisiana, and Mississippi.
Federal Reporters		
Federal Reporter	1880	United States Circuit Court from 1880 to 1912; Commerce Court of the United States from 1911 to 1913; United States District Courts from 1880 to 1932; United States Court of Claims from 1929 to 1932 and since 1960; United States Court of Appeals since 1891; United States Court of Customs and Patent Appeals since 1929; and the United States Emergency Court of Appeals since 1943.
Federal Supplement	1932	United States Court of Claims from 1932 to 1960; United States District Courts since 1932; United States Customs Court since 1956.
Federal Rules Decisions	1939	United States District Courts involving the Federal Rules of Civil Procedure since 1939 and Federal Rules of Criminal Procedure since 1946.
Supreme Court Reporter	1882	United States Supreme Court since the October term of 1882.
Bankruptcy Reporter	1960	Bankruptcy decisions of United States Bankruptcy Courts, United States District Courts, United States Courts of Appeals, and United States Supreme Court.
Military Justice Reporter	1978	United States Court of Military Appeals and Courts of Military Review for the Army, Navy, Marine Corps, Air Force, and Coast Guard.

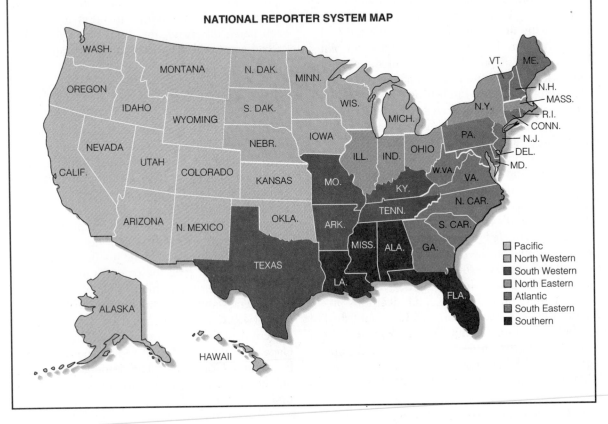

NATIONAL REPORTER SYSTEM MAP

Exhibit I–2 **Case Citation Examples**

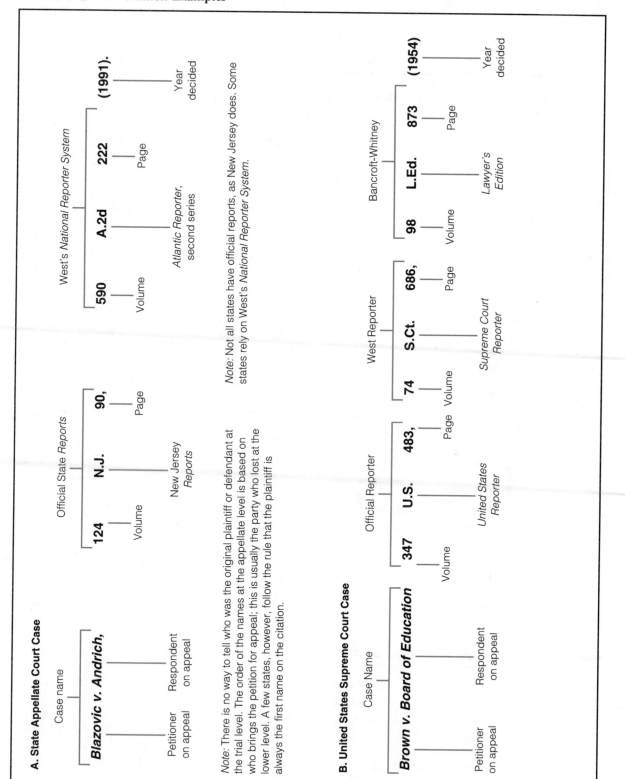

A. State Appellate Court Case

Case name   Official State *Reports*

Blazovic v. Andrich, 124 **N.J.** 90,

Petitioner   Respondent   Volume   New Jersey   Page
on appeal   on appeal   *Reports*

West's *National Reporter System*

590 **A.2d** 222 **(1991)**.

Volume   *Atlantic Reporter,*   Page   Year
         second series   decided

Note: There is no way to tell who was the original plaintiff or defendant at the trial level. The order of the names at the appellate level is based on who brings the petition for appeal; this is usually the party who lost at the lower level. A few states, however, follow the rule that the plaintiff is always the first name on the citation.

Note: Not all states have official reports, as New Jersey does. Some states rely on West's *National Reporter System.*

B. United States Supreme Court Case

Case Name

Brown v. Board of Education

Petitioner
on appeal

Respondent
on appeal

Official Reporter

347 **U.S.** 483,

Volume   *United States   Page
         Reporter*

West Reporter

74 **S.Ct.** 686,

Volume   *Supreme Court   Page
         Reporter*

Bancroft-Whitney

98 **L.Ed.** 873 **(1954)**

Volume   *Lawyer's   Page   Year
         Edition*   decided

Exhibit I–3 Statute Citation

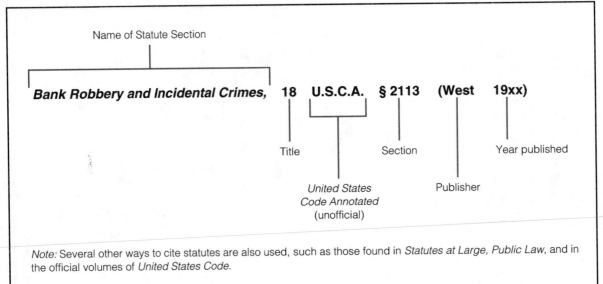

Name of Statute Section

Bank Robbery and Incidental Crimes,   18   U.S.C.A.   § 2113   (West   19xx)

Title

United States
Code Annotated
(unofficial)

Section

Publisher

Year published

Note: Several other ways to cite statutes are also used, such as those found in *Statutes at Large, Public Law,* and in the official volumes of *United States Code.*

umes. A citation to a particular statute reads 18 U.S.C.A. § 2113 (West, 1984). The number 18 is the title number, not the volume number. The citation indicates that West is the publisher and provides the year this statute was published. Section numbers are printed on the binding of statute volumes. You look for the volume that contains Section 2113, which is the federal criminal statute entitled "Bank Robbery and Incidental Crimes." The statute itself takes up only two pages; a one-paragraph discussion of the appellate court cases that have been decided involving Section 2113 follows the statute. Then, it takes 258 pages to list all the cases that have been decided under this particular statute. In contrast, some statutes do not have any related cases because these laws are not controversial; the state statutes requiring a birth certificate are examples.

Administrative Agency Regulations

An **administrative agency** is created when the executive or legislative branch of the government delegates some of its authority to an appropriate administrative body. Since the days of President Franklin Roosevelt's New Deal, government agencies have proliferated in the United States. Federal agencies include the Federal Commu-

nications Commission, the Federal Aviation Administration, the National Labor Relations Board, the Occupational Safety and Health Administration, the Environmental Protection Agency, the Internal Revenue Service, the Food and Drug Administration, and the Interstate Commerce Commission. State and local agencies include highway commissions, public utility commissions, and pardon and parole boards. Many agencies are found in the executive branch of government.

These agencies exercise legislative, executive, and judicial power. In making rules, the agencies are using legislative power; in enforcing their rules, they are using executive power; and in their adjudication procedures, they are using judicial power. Unlike legislators, presidents, governors, and many judges, administrative agency personnel are rarely chosen by popular elections, and most do not serve fixed terms. As a result, great power is given to people who may not be responsive to the public.

Federal, state, and local administrative agencies have expanded the number of their rulings at what appears to be an exponential rate. Some observers and citizens believe that the United States is in danger of having an overly bureaucratic government. We will examine administrative agencies in more detail in Chapter 6.

Legal Research by Computers

Technology has developed computers large enough to handle the memory and the storage data bases (collections of information) necessary for computerized legal research. The two most widely used high-speed data-delivery systems are WESTLAW and LEXIS. WESTLAW is a computer-assisted legal research service of West Publishing Company. LEXIS, provided by Mead Data Central, Inc., provides a similar service. Each system has data-base-access software that allows researchers to interact with the delivery system.

In the WESTLAW data-delivery system, data are stored at West's headquarters in Saint Paul, Minnesota. User interaction with the data-delivery system can be initiated anywhere in the world from a computer terminal or a personal computer running a special WESTLAW access program. The WESTLAW user sends a query, or message, to the computer. The query is processed, and information stored in the computer is identified to answer the message. The information is transmitted back to the user where it is seen on a video display terminal (VDT) and can be printed as "hard copy" on paper. The information displayed on the VDT can also be stored on the user's storage equipment, such as a diskette.

WESTLAW, LEXIS, and similar computerized data-search systems are able to access virtually every case, statute, or regulation in the United States with a minimum of time and effort. Today, the latest cases are available within three days on the computer, far in advance of the printed copies that are sent to law libraries and subscribers.

Analyzing Case Law:
A Supreme Court Case

The study of reported cases requires an understanding and application of legal analysis. The following excerpt is part of a case that was decided by the Supreme Court in 1985. Each of the different sections of the case are described in order to help you read the other cases in this book. All the cases have been edited. Three asterisks (* * *) indicate that part of the opinion within a paragraph or sentence has been deleted to make the case more concise and readable. Four asterisks

(* * * *) mean that one or more paragraphs have been omitted. Any references by the court to other cases have been omitted to make the case more readable.

The following case involves a federal question. The Supreme Court granted a **writ of *certiorari*.** This writ is the decision by an appellate court to hear an appeal. In this case, the Supreme Court had the discretion to decide whether it would hear the appeal. (Writs of *certiorari* are discussed in more detail in Chapter 1).

The Supreme Court had to determine whether a student had the right to retake an examination that he had failed. He was required to pass the examination in order to continue his studies toward a medical degree. The student took the legal position that he had a property right in his continued enrollment. He further argued that his dismissal was arbitrary and capricious and therefore his substantive due process rights were violated.

In its analysis, the Supreme Court used prior case decisions (precedent) to resolve the issues before the Court: what authority did a university have in dismissing students, and what procedure did the university have to follow?

REGENTS OF THE UNIVERSITY OF MICHIGAN v. EWING
Supreme Court of the United States, 1985.
474 U.S. 214, 106 S.Ct. 507, 88 L.Ed.2d 523.

Justice *STEVENS* delivered the opinion of the Court.

Respondent Scott Ewing was dismissed from the University of Michigan after failing an important written examination. The question presented is whether the University's action deprived Ewing of property without due process of law because its refusal to allow him to retake the examination was an arbitrary departure from the University's past practice. The Court of Appeals held that his constitutional rights were violated. We disagree.

In the fall of 1975 Ewing enrolled in a special 6-year program of study, known as "Inteflex," offered jointly by the undergraduate college and the Medical School. An undergraduate degree and a medical degree are awarded upon successful completion of the program. * * *

In the spring of 1981, after overcoming certain academic and personal difficulties, Ewing successfully completed the courses prescribed for the first four years of the Inteflex program and thereby qualified to take the NBME Part I. Ewing failed five of the seven subjects on that examination, receiving a total score of 235 when the passing score was 345. (A score of 380 is required for state licensure and the national mean is 500.) Ewing received the lowest score recorded by an Inteflex student in the brief history of that program.

On July 24, 1981, the Promotion and Review Board individually reviewed the status of several students in the Inteflex program. After considering Ewing's record in some detail, the nine members of the Board in attendance voted unanimously to drop him from registration in the program.

In response to a written request from Ewing, the Board reconvened a week later to reconsider its decision. Ewing appeared personally and explained why he believed that his score on the test did not fairly reflect his academic progress or potential. After reconsidering the matter, the nine voting members present unanimously reaffirmed the prior action to drop Ewing from registration in the program.

In August, Ewing appealed the Board's decision to the Executive Committee of the Medical School. After giving Ewing an opportunity to be heard in person, the Executive Committee unanimously approved a motion to deny his appeal for a leave of absence status that would enable him to retake Part I of the NBME examination. In the following year, Ewing reappeared before the Executive Committee on two separate occasions, each time unsuccessfully seeking readmission to the Medical School. On August 19, 1982, he commenced this litigation in the United States District Court for the Eastern District of Michigan.

*   *   *   *

The District Court held a 4-day bench trial at which it took evidence on the University's claim that Ewing's dismissal was justified as well as on Ewing's allegation that other University of Michigan medical students who had failed the NBME Part I had routinely been given a second opportunity to take the test. *   *   *

Ewing discounted the importance of his own academic record by offering evidence that other students with even more academic deficiencies were uniformly allowed to retake the NBME Part I. *   *   * The statistical evidence indicated that of the 32 standard students in the Medical School who failed Part I of the NBME since its inception, all 32 were permitted to retake the test, 10 were allowed to take the test a third time, and 1 a fourth time. Seven students in the Inteflex program were allowed to retake the test, and one student was allowed to retake it twice. Ewing is the only student who, having failed the test, was not permitted to retake it. Dr. Robert Reed, a former Director of the Inteflex program and a member of the Promotion and Review Board, stated that students were "routinely" given a second chance. *   *   *

*   *   *   *

*   *   * The District Court, however, found no violation of Ewing's due process rights. The trial record, it emphasized, was devoid of any indication that the University's decision was "based on bad faith, ill will or other impermissible ulterior motives"; to the contrary, the "evidence demonstrate[d] that the decision to dismiss plaintiff was reached in a fair and impartial manner, and only after careful and deliberate consideration." To "leave no conjecture" as to his decision, the District Judge expressly found that "the evidence demonstrate[d] no arbitrary or capricious action since [the Regents] had good reason to dismiss Ewing from the program."

Without reaching the state-law breach-of-contract and promissory-estoppel claims, the Court of Appeals reversed the dismissal of Ewing's federal constitutional claim. *   *   *

[I]t concluded that the University had arbitrarily deprived him of that property in violation of the Fourteenth Amendment because (1) "Ewing was a 'qualified' student, as the University defined that term, at the time he sat for NBME Part I"; (2) "it was the consistent practice of the University of Michigan to allow a qualified medical student who initially failed the NBME Part I an opportunity for a retest"; and (3) "Ewing was the only University of Michigan medical student who initially failed the NBME Part I between 1975 and 1982, and was not allowed an opportunity for a retest." *   *   *

We granted the University's petition for certiorari to consider whether the Court of Appeals had misapplied the doctrine of "substantive due process." We now reverse.

* * * *

Ewing's claim, therefore, must be that the University misjudged his fitness to remain a student in the Inteflex program. The record unmistakably demonstrates, however, that the faculty's decision was made conscientiously and with careful deliberation, based on an evaluation of the entirety of Ewing's academic career. When judges are asked to review the substance of a genuinely academic decision, such as this one, they should show great respect for the faculty's professional judgment. Plainly, they may not override it unless it is such a substantial departure from accepted academic norms as to demonstrate that the person or committee responsible did not actually exercise professional judgment.

* * * *

This narrow avenue for judicial review precludes any conclusion that the decision to dismiss Ewing from the Inteflex program was such a substantial departure from accepted academic norms as to demonstrate that the faculty did not exercise professional judgment. Certainly his expulsion cannot be considered aberrant when viewed in isolation. The District Court found as a fact that the Regents "had good reason to dismiss Ewing from the program." Before failing the NBME Part I, Ewing accumulated an unenviable academic record characterized by low grades, seven incompletes, and several terms during which he was on an irregular or reduced course load. Ewing's failure of his medical boards, in the words of one of his professors, "merely culminate[d] a series of deficiencies. . . . In many ways, it's the straw that broke the camel's back." Moreover, the fact that Ewing was "qualified" in the sense that he was eligible to take the examination the first time does not weaken this conclusion, for after Ewing took the NBME Part I it was entirely reasonable for the faculty to reexamine his entire record in the light of the unfortunate results of that examination. Admittedly, it may well have been unwise to deny Ewing a second chance. Permission to retake the test might have saved the University the expense of this litigation and conceivably might have demonstrated that the members of the Promotion and Review Board misjudged Ewing's fitness for the medical profession. But it nevertheless remains true that his dismissal from the Inteflex program rested on an academic judgment that is not beyond the pale of reasoned academic decision making when viewed against the background of his entire career at the University of Michigan, including his singularly low score on the NBME Part I examination.

The judgment of the Court of Appeals is reversed, and the case is remanded for proceedings consistent with this opinion.

Review of the Case

1. The name of the case is *Regents of the University of Michigan v. Ewing*. The names are in this order because the case was appealed to the United States Supreme Court by the regents of the University of Michigan after they lost in the lower appellate court. You can never be sure what the role of the party is unless you read the case. The only exception is that all lawsuits filed at the trial court level will have the plaintiff listed first.

2. The Supreme Court of the United States heard this case in 1985. This court is the highest appellate court in the United States. The citation (the information below the case name) discloses the name and level of the court. The numbers and letters found below the court name indicate to lawyers and researchers how to find the case in the library or computer. This case can be found in volume 474 of *United States Reports* beginning on page 214; it can also be found in volume 106 of the *Supreme Court Reporter* beginning on page 507; and it can be found in volume 88 of the *Lawyer's Edition* beginning on page 523.

3. Justice Stevens delivered the opinion of the Supreme Court. The United States Supreme Court has a chief justice and eight associate justices.

4. The opinion begins with a recital of the facts, followed by a discussion of the law.

5. In this opinion, the Court first reviews the procedure followed by the university before Ewing filed a lawsuit in federal district court (the trial court).

6. Then the Court discusses what transpired during the trial in district court. Normally, the trial court decides all the facts that are being contested.

7. The United States Supreme Court states in a very brief summary on what basis the court of appeals reversed the trial court's decision.

8. The loser of that decision, the regents, petitioned the United States Supreme Court for a writ of *certiorari*. The Court granted the writ, which means that the Court agreed to review the lower court's decision. At this point, the Supreme Court gives its **holding**—that is, the decision of the case. The decision of the appeals court was reversed, and the district court's decision was affirmed.

9. The Supreme Court gives the legal reasoning that supports its decision. The Court reasons that, in reviewing an academic decision, courts must give great respect to faculty judgment. A substantial departure from academic norms must exist to warrant a reversal of a faculty decision.

10. The Court applies its rule of law to the facts of the case. The findings of fact by the district court were very persuasive in the Supreme Court's reversal of the court of appeals' decision.

11. Appellate courts generally do not have the power to enter a judgment for either party. Judgments are rendered by trial courts. This is why the Supreme Court remands (sends back) the case to the district court and does not enter a judgment. If the case had not been reversed but had been affirmed, no further action would be required and the original judgment would be enforced.

How to Brief a Case

In order to understand the law and its implications with respect to business, you must be able to read and understand court decisions. One method of case analysis, often referred to as a briefing, facilitates such an understanding. There is a fairly standard procedure that may be followed when briefing a case in this book or in any other book. First, read the case carefully. When you believe that you understand the case, you can prepare a brief of it. Briefing a case while reading the case for the first time does little to enhance your legal education.

Although the format of a brief may vary, it will typically contain the following essentials:

1. Full case citation, including the name of the case and the date it was decided
2. Facts
3. Issue(s)
4. Holding
5. Reasoning (including policy).

In preparing a brief, you should incorporate all the important facts, but a brief should, of course, be short. The following illustrates a brief of the case we have just analyzed.

CASE CITATION:

REGENTS OF THE UNIVERSITY OF MICHIGAN v. EWING
Supreme Court of the United States, 1985.
474 U.S. 214, 106 S.Ct. 507, 88 L.Ed.2d 523.

FACTS:

Ewing was disqualified from continuing his education because he failed an examination. His prior academic record was weak. He was, however, the only one out of 33 students not allowed to retake the examination.

ISSUE:

Did the university action deprive Ewing of his property without due process of law?

HOLDING:

A court cannot override a university decision concerning academic affairs unless it is such a substantial departure from academic norms as to demonstrate an absence of professional judgment.

REASONING:

The Supreme Court held that the university had handled Ewing's dismissal in a professional manner. His academic record was very weak, and this fact could be taken into consideration when deciding not to allow him to retake the examination.

Traditional Versus Environmental Approach to the Law

We can begin to understand something about the nature of law by looking at two approaches to the study of it. The traditional approach sees law as a body of principles and rules that courts apply in deciding disputes. The study of law, then, is the study of these rules and the general principles of right and wrong on which the rules are based. Reason and logic tell how the rules should be applied in specific cases. The traditional approach is based on the idea that the principles of right and wrong change, if at all, less rapidly than society changes. This approach fulfills one of the important functions of law—to provide stability, predictability, and continuity so that people can conduct their business affairs more effectively.

The environmental approach sees law as only one part of the total environment of society. Law is the institution that specializes in social control, and other parts of society act on and influence it. Studying the process by which the broader society shapes the rules to govern itself is part of the study of law. In the legal world, this approach is known as sociological jurisprudence. The legal environmentalist emphasizes how social change is accomplished by using the legal system and how law functions to provide an orderly process for social change. The environmentalist believes that, if law fails to adapt to changes in technology, attitudes, and organization, social change may become violent.

In this book, you will be using the legal environmental approach to study business. You will be studying the breadth of the law as it applies to business as opposed to studying business law, which focuses in depth on only certain laws. The business world and the principles on which it is based are shaped in part by the legal environment. Other outside forces also help to shape the rules by which business is conducted. The interplay between logic and social pressure, the tension between stability and change, and the strain between predictability and flexibility—all affect both the legal and business worlds. Neither world is wholly independent of the other.

Key Terms

administrative agency (8)	holding (12)	writ of *certiorari* (9)
appellate courts (4)	statute (5)	

Chapter 1   Sources of the Law

The educated citizen has an obligation to uphold the law. This is the obligation of every citizen in a free and peaceful society—but the educated citizen has a special responsibility by the virtue of his greater understanding. For, whether he has ever studied history or current events, ethics or civics, the rules of a profession or the tools of a trade, he knows that only a respect for the law makes it possible for free men to dwell together in peace and progress.

He knows that law is the adhesive force of the cement of society, creating order out of chaos and coherence in place of anarchy. He knows that for one man to defy a law or court order he does not like is to invite others to defy those which they do not like, leading to a breakdown of all justice and all order.

He knows, too, that every fellow man is entitled to be regarded with decency and treated with dignity. Any educated citizen who seeks to subvert the law, to suppress freedom, or to subject other human beings to acts that are less than human degrades his inheritance, ignores his learning, and betrays his obligations.

Certain other societies may respect the rule of force—we respect the rule of law.

John F. Kennedy,
Speech at Vanderbilt University,
Nashville, Tennessee, May 13, 1963,
quoted in the *New York Times*, May 19, 1963, p. 62.

OUTLINE

Introduction

Law pervades all of our lives. The law affects an individual in many ways, but its effect on the business world is multiplied many times. This book provides an overview of the multiple and complex laws with which businesses must contend. Understanding the basic concepts of the law is essential to being a good businessperson.

In this chapter we will examine the definitions of law and discuss the various schools of legal philosophy. The history and sources of American law and the various classifications of law are reviewed. We will also look at the distinction between courts of law and courts of equity.

Definition of Law

The word **law** defies a simple definition. Unfortunately, when the English language evolved, only one word was developed to cover three different concepts: First, law means a system designed to give order to society. Second, it means a system of moral conduct that attempts to ensure justice in society. Third, it means a principle represented by a rule or rules. When we speak of *the* law, we are using the first and second meanings, and when we say *a* law, we are using the third meaning.

Roscoe Pound, an early twentieth-century legal philosopher, thought that human beings established an ordered society using two fundamental sets of ideas. Society's moral ideas are taken from ethics; its political ideas are taken from political science. Moral ideas give us *the* law, while political ideas give us *a* law or *a* rule. A sovereign political authority is needed to enforce rules, while the principles of law (that is, the moral ideas) need judges who interpret the law based on experience, reason, and prior case law.

Schools of Legal Philosophy

Jurisprudence is the science or philosophy of law. The cases you will read in this book reflect the judge's opinion. But what is the judge's opinion based on? It is based in part on a person's philosophy of law, his or her reasoning abilities, and his or her personality, as well as on custom, logic,

and history. Other than personality, all these components of decision making can be developed through study. Such study includes the discovery of the various legal philosophies.

The Natural Law School

The **natural law school** holds that there is an ideal state of being that is either part of human nature or that comes from a divine source. This ideal state presupposes a definite right or wrong that constitutes natural law. Society does not create this natural law; it is discovered through the use of reason and the knowledge of good and evil. The natural law school emphasizes ethics as the source of law's authority. Basic ethical values are used to make legal decisions.

Documents such as the Magna Charta, the Declaration of Independence, the United States Constitution (see Appendix A for the complete text), and the United Nations Declaration of Human Rights reflect natural law ideals in phrases like: "We hold these truths to be self-evident, that all men are created equal, that they are endowed by their Creator with certain unalienable Rights * * *."

An example of the natural law school of philosophy is the civil rights movement. In the 1960s, when African Americans sat at lunch counters or sat in the front of buses—areas that had been reserved for whites only—they were arrested. At their trials, the defense was that segregation is inherently wrong. Therefore, the defendants' acts of defiance could not be wrong because a higher law gives real meaning to the words of the United States Constitution. Although these African Americans were convicted, society eventually changed the laws about segregation, as we will see later.

The Historical and Sociological Schools

The **historical school** concentrates on the origin and history of the legal system and looks to the past to discover what the principles of contemporary law should be. The legal principles that have withstood the passage of time are best suited for shaping present laws. Thus, law develops in and with the social environment.

Tied to the historical school is the **sociological school.** This philosophy depends on observation of which laws work, according to the principles of social science. The sociological school emphasizes how people ought to conduct themselves within society. While the historical school is descriptive in nature, the sociological school is based on observation.

The legal field of **probate** uses the philosophy of the historical school. Probate is the court process of settling a person's estate by collecting all the debts owed to the deceased person (also called the decedent), paying all the debts the deceased person owed, and transferring ownership of the decedent's property to the heirs. The probate court will follow the deceased person's wishes expressed in his or her will, or if there is no will, the court will follow the state statutes that determine who will receive the property.

The right to determine through a will who will receive a person's estate after death was granted by the English parliament in 1540 in a law known as the statute of wills. Some version of this English law has been adopted through statutes in each of the fifty states. In making determinations in probate law, a probate judge relies almost exclusively on the rules that have developed historically and not on what she or he believes to be right or wrong in a particular case.

For example, in many states if you are married to someone for one hour and die before you can make out a will, your spouse will inherit everything. On the other hand, you may have lived happily with your lover as if you were husband and wife for fifty years. If you die without a will in a state that does not recognize a common-law marriage (if you live together as husband and wife you are deemed by law to be married), your lover will not inherit anything because you were not legally married. The historical approach is used here because our legal system does not recognize a change in probate law in the absence of a legislative act.

The Analytical School

Logic shapes the law. A member of the **analytical school** examines the structure and subject matter of a legal code and analyzes it logically to extract the underlying principles. By analyzing cases and rules, the analytical school formulates general principles. These principles are the starting points for legal reasoning.

The American Law Institute (ALI), through its **Restatements,** represents this philosophy. The ALI has written Restatements of various areas of the law, such as torts, trusts, contracts, and agency law. The people who developed and wrote the Restatements have reviewed the thousands of cases decided in the last 200 years to establish the **common law** in a particular area. Common law is a body of law developed from custom and from judicial decisions (that is, from cases) in English and American courts.

Although the Restatements themselves are not the law, they are statements of what the majority law is. They, in effect, have pulled together the cases on a particular topic and placed them in logical order in a series of volumes. The ALI sets out a particular law and gives the reason for it. Today, judges rely on the Restatements and cite them in case opinions.

The Legal Realists

Law is shaped by social forces and is an instrument of social control. **Legal realists** stress the pragmatic and empirical sides of law; because they see law as a means to a social end, they try to predict and influence lawmaking. In the legal realist school, despite moral law, historical development, and logical analysis, the same set of facts will not always result in the same conclusion. A reviewing court often views the law differently than a lower court, for example. For the legal realist, the legitimacy of law and of legal institutions is measured by how well they serve the needs of society.

The Economic School

The **economic school** of thought was developed in the 1970s by Richard A. Posner.[1] This theory holds that most laws may be evaluated in accordance with economic theory. This theory assumes that everyone in the legal system is rational and will act in order to maximize his or her welfare. For example, a person who has been injured in an automobile accident, although he or she may

---

1. A former law professor at the University of Chicago Law School, Mr. Posner was appointed by President Reagan as a judge to the United States Court of Appeals, Seventh Circuit, on December 4, 1981.

file a lawsuit, will usually settle the claim because a settlement is faster and less costly than waiting for a courtroom trial.

Sources of American Law

American law has been evolving ever since the first landings of English settlers at Jamestown, Virginia, in 1607 and at Plymouth Rock, Massachusetts, in 1620. At first, the colonies relied heavily on the English legal system, but during the early decades of the new nation the Americans also borrowed from the French and the German legal systems. These borrowed ideas and philosophies helped to shape the current sources of American law: the Constitution, the statutes passed by the legislatures, and the common law.

Constitutions

Each state and the federal government has a constitution. The constitution is the highest source to which a court will look when deciding law. The United States Constitution is the supreme law of the land. A law in violation of the Constitution, no matter what its source, will be declared unconstitutional if tested in court and, thus, will not be enforced. Similarly, each state constitution, although supreme within the respective state's borders, cannot conflict with the United States Constitution. The United States Constitution has two functions, described in the sections that follow.

Creation of Powers, Structure, and Limitations of the Federal Government The Constitution creates the powers, structure, and limitations of the federal government. All powers not retained by the federal government reside in the states or the people. For example, the Constitution gives the federal government the power to regulate interstate commerce—that is, the commerce among the various states or foreign nations. The states retain the power to regulate intrastate commerce—commerce that is strictly within each state's geographic boundaries. Another example is that the federal government is given the exclusive right to coin money; the states cannot make their own money.

The Constitution outlines the structure of the federal government. It establishes three branches of government, creating a system of **checks and balances** in which each branch ensures that the other two branches do not abuse their powers. The legislative branch (Congress) passes statutes; the executive branch (the president) enforces the laws; and the judicial branch (the courts) determines the validity of the laws and applies them to specific cases. Even though these three branches of government are separate, their powers do overlap at times.

The limitations of the powers of the federal and state governments are also contained in the Constitution. For example, no titles of nobility may be granted. Another section of the Constitution limits a state from imposing export and import taxes. (See Article I, Sections 9 and 10 of the United States Constitution.)

Guarantee of Freedoms The Constitution guarantees the citizens of the United States (and often aliens) various individual freedoms. Most individual rights are set out in the first ten amendments, now called the **Bill of Rights.** The government is prohibited from infringing on these freedoms by specific restrictions expressed in the Bill of Rights. For example, the Fourth Amendment ensures that every person is free from unreasonable (but not all) searches.

Congress may on rare occasions pass a statute contrary to the Constitution, or, indeed, the president may act counter to the Constitution. The process of deciding whether a law is in conflict with the mandates of the Constitution is known as **judicial review.** The power of judicial review was first established in 1803 in the case of *Marbury v. Madison.*[2] The Supreme Court determined that it had the power to decide whether a law passed by Congress violated the Constitution. Thus, the power of judicial review, residing in the judicial branch, is part of the system of checks and balances. Judicial review is examined in more detail in Chapter 4.

Statutes and Ordinances

Laws enacted by Congress or a state legislature are called **statutes. Ordinances** are laws enacted by cities and counties. Both statutes and ordinances must be in compliance with the United

---

2. 5 U.S. 137, 2 L.Ed. 135 (1803). See Chapter 4 for the case.

States Constitution and the relevant state constitution.

Because the states have retained many powers, Congress can pass only the legislation that falls within the range of powers granted to it by Article I of the United States Constitution.[3] Many of the cases coming before the courts today involve statutes. Much of the work of the courts involves interpreting what the legislators meant when the law was passed and applying that interpretation to a present set of facts. In many instances, statutory law has replaced common law. In a particular controversy, the court looks first for a statute, ordinance, or regulation on which to base its decision. If none is found, the court looks to common law.

Common Law

The origins of common law lie in the ancient unwritten law of England. In 1066 the Normans, led by William the Conqueror, were the last invaders to conquer England. William and his successors began the process of unifying the country. One of the means used was the king's court. Before the Norman Conquest, disputes were settled locally according to local custom. The king's court sought to establish a common or uniform set of customs for the whole country and gave a person the right to appeal a local decision to the king.

The body of rules that evolved under the king's court was the beginning of the common law. As the number of courts and cases increased, the more important decisions of each year were recorded in year books. Judges, settling disputes similar to ones that had been decided before, used the year books as the basis for their decisions. If a case was unique, judges had to create new laws, but they based their decisions on the general principles suggested by earlier cases. The body of judge-made law that developed under this system is still used today in England and the United States and is known as the common law.

Today, common law is derived from the usages and customs of society and from the judgments of the courts recognizing, affirming, enforcing, and sometimes changing those usages and cus-

toms. These judgments constitute case law. If the legislature believes it necessary, it can pass statutes that embody the common law; it can also pass statutes that completely change—or modify—the common law.

If a case before the court involves an issue for which no legislation exists, the court will refer to the common law to make its decision. Where it does not conflict with a statute, common law has the same force as statutory law. Even where statutes have been substituted for common law, courts often rely on common law to interpret the legislation, on the theory that the people who drafted the statute intended to codify a previous common-law rule.

Most states have adopted common law by legislative decree. For example, the California Civil Code, Section 22.1, states that the "common law of England, so far as it is not repugnant to or inconsistent with the Constitution of the United States, or the Constitution or laws of this State, is the rule of decision in all the courts of this State." Louisiana is the only state that did not adopt the common-law system. Based on its French background, it adopted the civil-law system. The civil-law system is strictly based upon statutory provisions and originated in continental Europe.

Stare Decisis

The practice of deciding new cases with reference to former decisions is a cornerstone of the American judicial system. This practice is called **stare decisis** ("let the decision stand"). The use of a prior case decision, similar in facts or legal principles, in deciding a present case is referred to as **precedent.** Judges usually follow the precedent established by the decisions of previous courts. *Stare decisis* reflects the experience and wisdom of the past.

Functions of *Stare Decisis*   The rule of *stare decisis* performs many useful functions. First, it allows the courts to be more efficient. A judge needs only to look at previous court decisions that set out the policies for a particular law; if other judges have confronted the same issue as that before the court and if they have reasoned through the case carefully, their opinions can serve as guides. This process saves the valuable time it would take for judges to reason out each and every case as if no other case like it had ever been decided.

---

3. Article I, Section 8, gives eighteen specific powers to Congress. The Tenth Amendment reserves all other powers to the states or to the people.

Legal Highlight

Common-Law Writs

The common law developed through the issuance of writs. Historically, a writ was a command. Originally, only the king of England or his emissaries could issue writs. There are two main categories of writs: substantive and procedural.

Most of our modern legal rights have developed from substantive writs. You are injured in an automobile accident caused by someone else. At common law you would have brought this action under a writ called "trespass on the case." Today, you would bring a legal action for negligence. All modern negligence laws developed from this writ.

Courts no longer use substantive writs. The procedural writs, however, are still important in federal and many state courts. Following are examples of some procedural writs.

WRIT	MEANING	PURPOSE
Habeas corpus	You have the body	Used in criminal law and child custody cases; requires that the person held or detained be brought before the court.
Mandamus	We command	Requires public officials to do their jobs.
Quo warranto	By what authority	Used to revoke corporation charters if the corporation is involved in illegal conduct.
Replevin	Redeliver	Directs sheriff to seize personal property.
Certiorari	Review or inquiry	Enables a higher court to review a lower court's decision.

Second, *stare decisis* results in a more just and uniform system of decision making. The rule of precedent works to neutralize the personal prejudices of individual judges. Judges are not required to but usually do use precedent as the basis for their decisions. Some variations in rules of law still occur, however, because judges in different states and regions will apply different precedents in accordance with local law. Reasonable judges can differ in their interpretation and application of the law.

Third, precedent makes the law more stable and predictable. If the law on a particular subject is well settled, people will abide by the law and not bring cases involving that law to court. For example, no one today would think of bringing a lawsuit to have schools segregated on the basis of race. A law that is stable encourages people to settle their differences peaceably without using the court system.

Flexibility of *Stare Decisis* *Stare decisis* gives the law stability, but it is also flexible. Judges depart occasionally from the rule of precedent because the precedent is incorrect or no longer applicable. For example, changes in technology, business practices, or society's attitudes necessitate changes in the law.

If courts were not able to depart from precedent, all legal thinking and reasoning would be frozen in time. Judges are reluctant to overthrow precedent; whether they do or not depends on the subject of the case, the number and prestige of prior decisions, the degree of social change that has occurred, and the identity of the deciding court. The Supreme Court of the United States is the highest authority in the land and is, therefore, freer to reverse the direction of the law than a lower court.

Judges sometimes find themselves faced with making a decision on a case of first impression. In this type of case, no precedent exists because there is no law on the topic. For example, in the 1960s judges were uncertain about how a person could steal time from a computer. Some courts held that the unauthorized use of the computer was not a crime. Today, many states have statutes that make the theft of computer time a crime.

At other times, judges find conflicting precedents or no precedents. In these situations, courts use one or more of the following to aid in making a decision: First, they refer to previous decisions that are similar in nature to the current case, and they use analogies to decide the case. Second, courts look at social factors and develop a policy. For example, state legislatures in the mid 1980s had not developed statutes concerning surrogate mothers; this left it up to the courts to develop policy concerning the contracts and legal relations involved among the biological or adoptive mother, the surrogate mother, the child, and the biological father. Third, courts balance the interests of the parties involved.

Cases that overturn precedent often receive a lot of publicity. For example, the case of *Brown v. Board of Education* overruled *Plessy v. Ferguson* and ended sixty years of segregation, thus setting the stage for integration of all peoples into U.S. society on an equal basis. The publicity that surrounds major cases makes it seem that case law is frequently overturned. In reality, the majority of cases are decided according to precedent by the rule of *stare decisis*.

BACKGROUND AND FACTS *Petitioner, Plessy, was a resident of Louisiana and was of mixed descent, in the proportion of seven-eighths Caucasian and one-eighth African blood. He purchased a first-class ticket on the East Louisiana Railway to travel from New Orleans to Covington, Louisiana. He sat in a vacant seat in a coach where passengers of the white race were accommodated. The conductor requested that he take a seat in another coach for persons who were not of the white race. The only reason Plessy was asked to move was that he was deemed under Louisiana law not to be a white person. Upon his refusal to move, he was forcibly ejected from the coach, arrested, and jailed. He was charged with violation of the 1890 Louisiana criminal statute providing for separate railroad coaches for the white and black races.*

Plessy brought a petition against the criminal court judge to prevent him from enforcing the statute. Plessy argued that the statute violated his federal constitutional rights.

Case 1.1
PLESSY v. FERGUSON
Supreme Court of the United States, 1896.
163 U.S. 537, 16 S.Ct. 1138, 41 L.Ed. 256.

Justice BROWN delivered the opinion of the Court.
*   *   *   *

So far, then, as a conflict with the fourteenth amendment is concerned, the case reduces itself to the question whether the statute of Louisiana is a reasonable regulation, and with respect to this there must necessarily be a large discretion on the part of the legislature. In determining the question of reasonableness, it is at liberty to act with reference to the established usages, customs, and traditions of the people, and with a view to the promotion of their comfort, and the preservation of the public peace and good order. Gauged by this standard, we cannot say that a law which authorizes or even requires the separation of the two races in public conveyances is unreasonable, or more obnoxious to the fourteenth amendment than the acts of congress requiring separate schools for colored children in the District of Columbia, the constitutionality of which does not seem to have been questioned, or the corresponding acts of state legislatures.
*   *   *   *

Justice HARLAN dissenting.
*   *   *   *

The white race deems itself to be the dominant race in this country. And so it is, in prestige, in achievements, in education, in wealth, and in power. So, I doubt not, it will continue to be for all time, if it remains true to its great heritage, and holds fast to the principles of constitutional liberty. But in view of the constitution, in the eye of the law, there is in this country no superior, dominant, ruling class of citizens. There is no caste here. Our constitution is color-blind, and neither knows nor tolerates classes among citizens. In respect of civil rights, all citizens are equal before the law. The humblest is the peer of the most powerful. The law regards man as man, and takes no account of his surroundings or of his color when his civil rights as guarantied by the supreme law of the land are involved. It is therefore to be regretted that this high tribunal, the final expositor of the fundamental law of the land, has reached the conclusion that it is competent for a state to regulate the enjoyment by citizens of their civil rights solely upon the basis of race.

In my opinion, the judgment this day rendered will, in time, prove to be quite as pernicious as the decision made by this tribunal in the Dred Scott Case.

*　　*　　*　　*

DECISION AND REMEDY   *In 1896 the United States Supreme Court upheld the right of individual states to have separate but equal facilities based solely upon race. The decision legitimized an era of racial segregation.*

The Dred Scott *case, to which the Court referred, was a decision made in 1857. In that case, Dred Scot, an African American, was a slave. His owner took him to a state that prohibited slavery. Later he was returned to a slave state. He brought a lawsuit in St. Louis, Missouri, to obtain his freedom based on previous decisions that residence in free territory, conferred freedom. The United States Supreme Court refused to recognize the earlier lower court decisions and found that Dred Scott was still a slave. Many historians claim that this case was one of the major causes of the Civil War.*

The next case, *Brown v. Board of Education*, exemplifies the flexibility of the common law to adapt to changing social mores. During the 58 years from *Plessy* in 1896 to *Brown* in 1954, two World Wars had been fought, African Americans in large numbers had moved from the rural South to Northern industrialized urban centers, and women had been granted the right to vote by constitutional amendment. Fundamental structures and attitudes in our society had changed. Normally the law lags behind such societal changes, but when these changes are momentous, the law adapts to them as we shall see in the following case.

Brown v. Board of Education was first argued in 1952, but the Court decided it needed more information and set the case for reargument in 1953. Before the second hearing, Chief Justice Fred Vinson died, and President Eisenhower appointed Earl Warren as chief justice of the United States. The case was then argued a second time before the Court.

Case 1.2

BROWN v. BOARD OF EDUCATION

Supreme Court of the United States, 1954.
347 U.S. 483, 74 S.Ct. 686,
98 L.Ed. 873.

BACKGROUND AND FACTS   *Five cases, from Kansas, South Carolina, Virginia, Delaware, and the District of Columbia, were joined together because of the common legal issues involved. The lead case was from Kansas. The plaintiff, Linda Brown, was an African-American child living in Topeka. Her father brought this action on her behalf in the United States District Court to prohibit enforcement of a Kansas statute that permitted cities with a population of more than 15,000 to maintain separate school facilities for African-American students.*

The Topeka Board of Education had elected to establish segregated elementary schools. The three-judge district court found that segregation in public education had a detrimental effect on African-American children, but it denied a remedy on the grounds that the African-American and white schools were substantially equal with respect to buildings, transportation, curricula, and the educational qualifications of their teachers.

Chief Justice WARREN delivered the opinion of the Court.
* * * *

It is true that public school education at the time of the [Fourteenth] Amendment had advanced further in the North, but the effect of the Amendent on Northern States was generally ignored in the congressional debates. Even in the North, the conditions of public education did not approximate those existing today. The curriculum was usually rudimentary; ungraded schools were common in rural areas; the school term was but three months a year in many states; and compulsory school attendance was virtually unknown. As a consequence, it is not surprising that there should be so little in the history of the Fourteenth Amendment relating to its intended effect on public education.
* * * *

Here, * * * there are findings below that the Negro and white schools involved have been equalized, or are being equalized, with respect to buildings, curricula, qualifications and salaries of teachers, and other "tangible" factors. Our decision, therefore, cannot turn on merely a comparison of these tangible factors in the Negro and white schools involved in each of the cases. We must look instead to the effect of segregation itself on public education.

In approaching this problem, we cannot turn the clock back to 1868 when the Amendment was adopted, or even to 1896 when Plessy v. Ferguson was written. We must consider public education in the light of its full development and its present place in American life throughout the Nation. Only in this way can it be determined if segregation in public schools deprives these plaintiffs of the equal protection of the laws.

Today, education is perhaps the most important function of state and local governments. Compulsory school attendance laws and the great expenditures for education both demonstrate our recognition of the importance of education to our democratic society. It is required in the performance of our most basic public responsibilities, even service in the armed forces. It is the very foundation of good citizenship. Today it is a principal instrument in awakening the child to cultural values, in preparing him for later professional training, and in helping him to adjust normally to his environment. In these days, it is doubtful that any child may reasonably be expected to succeed in life if he is denied the opportunity of an education. Such an opportunity, where the state has undertaken to provide it, is a right which must be made available to all on equal terms.

We come then to the question presented: Does segregation of children in public schools solely on the basis of race, even though the physical facilities and other "tangible" factors may be equal, deprive the children of the minority group of equal educational opportunities? We believe that it does.
* * * *

We conclude that in the field of public education the doctrine of "separate but equal" has no place. Separate educational facilities are inherently unequal. Therefore, we hold that the plaintiffs and others similarly situated for whom the actions have been brought are, by reason of the segregation complained of, deprived of the equal protection of the laws guaranteed by the Fourteenth Amendment.
* * * *

DECISION AND REMEDY *The United States Supreme Court held that separate but equal public school facilities where the segregation was based on race were inherently unconstitutional. This decision laid the foundation for the desegregation of all public facilities. Ten years later the Civil Rights Act of 1964, which attempted to end all overt discrimination, was passed. Thus, Plessy v. Ferguson is no longer valid law.*

COMMENT *This decision was pivotal. The Court understood the impact that its decision would have on the country; thus, the justices came together in a nine-to-zero vote. The decision itself is only three and a half pages long. To add to the prestige of the occasion, Chief Justice Warren read the decision in open Court, a procedure which is rarely done.*

The short opinion was reproduced in magazines and newspapers across the country. With no satellites to help speed transmission of this decision, the Voice of America, a broadcasting company, translated Brown into thirty-four languages and by the end of an hour was broadcasting it around the world.[a]

But the Brown case included no remedy. Instead, the Court set the case for another hearing, and in 1955, in the case known as Brown II, it ordered the remedy to desegregate with "all deliberate speed." Unfortunately, desegregation did not mean automatic integration of the races.

Thurgood Marshall represented the Browns and the other plaintiffs. During his years of litigation, he won 29 of the 32 cases he argued before the Court. In 1967 Mr. Marshall was appointed to the Supreme Court by President Johnson. He served on the Court until 1991.

a.   Source: 18 University of Detroit Law Journal 64 (1954).

At first glance, the cases of *Plessy v. Ferguson* and *Brown v. Board of Education* may seem out of place in a textbook concerning the legal environment of business. Each of these cases, however, had an important impact on the business world. *Plessy v. Ferguson* promoted an era of segregation. Businesses provided separate facilities for whites and nonwhites: separate entrances, rest rooms, and drinking fountains. There was a tremendous cost of building and maintaining separate facilities. Such segregation applied to other ethnic and religious groups besides African Americans. Groups often discriminated against included Native Americans, Asians, Hispanics, Irish, Jews, and Catholics, to name just a few. Often who was discriminated against depended on the area of the country in which they lived.

Brown v. Board of Education began the long journey toward desegregation; along the way, Congress has passed a whole series of civil rights acts. Businesses have spent billions of dollars attempting to comply with federal regulations on affirmative action and equal opportunity, such as recruiting and training programs for minorities. Large sums have been spent on legal defense in lawsuits where businesses have been charged with violating people's right to be treated equally. The segregated system as permitted by *Plessy v. Ferguson* caused enormous economic losses, but the losses due to wasted and unused talent have been incalculable.

Classification of Law

The law is classified by its various topics, although there is no way to prevent the overlapping of various aspects of the law. For example, contracts are generally classified as private law; a contract with a government agency, however, is classified as public law. These classifications are, of necessity, somewhat arbitrary.

Legal Highlight

A Paddling Precedent

In 1837 the state of North Carolina prosecuted and convicted a schoolteacher of assault and battery for whipping a student with a switch. The switching left marks, but these disappeared after a few days. The teacher appealed her conviction.[a]

The appeals court reversed the teacher's conviction. The court found that the welfare of the child was the main purpose for which the pain was inflicted. Any punishment that would endanger life, limb, or health, would disfigure the child, or would result in permanent injury would be unnecessary and inconsistent with the purpose of the switching. The teacher's judgment was presumed to be correct.

According to the appellate court, a jury could find that the pain inflicted was too severe and was disproportionate to the offense for the age of the child. If the jury also found that the switching did not leave any permanent marks and if they found that the teacher was acting in accordance with her sense of right, the teacher should be acquitted. The appellate court reasoned that it could not decide otherwise, or it would be interfering with the authority necessary to preserve discipline. If the teacher acted beyond her power, the parents and the public would act as a check. If they failed to act, the punishment "must be tolerated as part of the imperfections and inconveniences, which no human laws can wholly remove or redress."

Has our thinking on this matter changed in the last 150 years? What would the United States Supreme Court have to say about corporal punishment today? Would the Supreme Court follow the thinking of the North Carolina court?

In 1977 the United States Supreme Court had a chance to review a Florida statute that permitted corporal punishment of students in school.[b] The court said:

The use of corporal punishment in this country as a means of disciplining schoolchildren dates back to the colonial period. It has survived the transformation of primary and secondary education from the colonials' reliance on optional private arrangements to our present system of compulsory education and dependence on public schools. * * * [W]e can discern no trend toward its elimination.

At common law a single principle has governed the use of corporal punishment since before the American Revolution: Teachers may impose reasonable but not excessive force to discipline a child. * * * * * * *

Because it is rooted in history, the child's liberty interest in avoiding corporal punishment while in the care of public school authorities is subject to historical limitations. * * *

* * * *

Florida has continued to recognize, and indeed has strengthened by statute, the common-law right of a child not to be subjected to excessive corporal punishment in school. * * * [T]he teacher and principal * * * decide in the first instance whether corporal punishment is reasonably necessary under the circumstances in order to discipline a child who has misbehaved. But they must exercise prudence and restraint. For Florida has preserved the traditional judicial proceedings for determining whether the punishment was justified. If the punishment inflicted is later found to have been excessive * * * [those] inflicting it may be held liable in damages, and if malice is shown, they may be subject to criminal penalties.

Notice how the United States Supreme Court's reasoning followed closely that of the North Carolina Supreme Court. Although the North Carolina decision was not binding on the United States Supreme Court, the latter followed the precedent established by the earlier court. Common law was used to uphold the Florida statute.

a. State v. Pendergrass, 19 N.C. 365, 31 Am.Dec. 416 (1837).
b. Ingraham v. Wright, 430 U.S. 651, 97 S.Ct. 1401, 51 L.Ed.2d 711 (1977).

Substantive Law Versus Procedural Law

Substantive law defines, describes, regulates, and creates legal rights and obligations. An example of substantive law is the contract law that determines whether a minor can enter into a contractual agreement. Although a minor may enter into many types of contracts, he or she still cannot sell real estate without the help of a legal guardian or the court. Another example of substantive law is the rule that a person who, through his or her own fault, injures another must pay damages.

Procedural law establishes the methods of enforcing the rights created by substantive law. For example, how a lawsuit begins, how to select the court in which the lawsuit should be filed, how a jury is selected, how judgments are enforced, and which legal papers need to be filed are all questions of procedural law. Substantive law sets out our legal rights; procedural law sets out the process to enforce our legal rights.

Public Law Versus Private Law

Public and private law are both subdivisions of substantive law. **Public law** addresses the relationship between people and their government; **private law** addresses direct dealings among individuals. **Criminal law** is classified as public law because, although a criminal act may involve only one victim, it is also an offense against society as a whole; thus, these acts are prohibited by governments in order to protect the public. The criminal act usually violates a civil right, as well. For example, drunk driving is a criminal act; if an accident occurs, the injured person can sue in civil court and recover damages.

Constitutional law is classified as public law since it involves questions of whether the government—federal, state, or local—has the power to act. The United States Constitution empowers the government to perform certain acts. Often the issue is whether the government—that is, the legislative or the executive branch—has exceeded the limits set by the Constitution. In addition, constitutional law limits the exercise of governmental power in ways usually designed to protect a person's life, liberty, or property from improper governmental action. For example, the Fourth and Fifth Amendments to the United States Constitution protect individuals from unreasonable searches and coerced confessions.

Administrative law is another example of public law; it governs the activities of various businesses. Whether a regulated business may stop a proposed regulation by the Occupational Safety and Health Administration (OSHA) that will require all noise to be reduced to very low decibels but that will raise costs excessively is an administrative law problem.

Other areas of the law, such as contract rights and duties, fall within the private law category. A businessperson who sues a supplier for breaking a contract or a pedestrian who sues a motorist for running into her or him is using private law. If a state government contracts to have a classroom building erected at the state university, this contract will fall under public law because the government is involved. Public law is involved if a gardener employed by a state university, while driving a university truck, hits a pedestrian. See Exhibit 1–1 for some examples of public and private law.

Exhibit 1–1 **Examples of Public Law and Private Law**

PUBLIC LAW	PRIVATE LAW
Administrative law and procedure	Computer law
Appellate procedure	Contract law
Civil procedure	Corporation law
Constitutional law	Domestic relations law
Criminal law and procedure	Media law
International treaties	Mining law
Rules of evidence	Partnership law
Tax law	Property law
Traffic law	Tort law
	Uniform Commercial Code

Civil Law Versus Criminal Law

Civil law encompasses the legal rights and duties that exist among persons or between citizens and their governments. Corporation law, partnership law, and contract law, for example, are part of civil law. Civil law is concerned with a person's legally recognized rights and duties in relationship with others.

Criminal law involves a violation or wrong committed against society as a whole. Acts that are criminal are defined by statutes enacted by the local, state, or federal government. Criminal law is always public law, whereas civil law is sometimes public and sometimes private. In a criminal case, the government seeks to impose a penalty, such as a fine, a term of imprisonment, or even the death penalty, on an accused person. In civil law the person is seeking damages and/or other remedies. All law that is not classified as criminal is civil.

Courts of Law Versus Courts of Equity

Today the distinction between law and equity is primarily of historical interest, but understanding the differences between these two concepts is essential to understanding the modern court system and its remedies.

Courts of Law: Remedies at Law

The difference between **courts of law** and **courts of equity** evolved over a long period of time. The early English courts were severely restricted in the kinds of **remedies** (legal means to recover a right or redress a wrong) that they could grant. The **plaintiff** (the person seeking relief from a harm) would sue the **defendant** (the person accused of causing harm) by going to court to claim what was rightly his or hers.

The court could award land, items of value, money, or any combination of these three as compensation to the plaintiff. The courts that awarded these compensations became known as courts of law, and the three remedies were called **remedies at law.** Over the centuries, the courts of law became so strict that the only means of appeal was to petition the king.

Courts of Equity: Equitable Remedies

Unable to hear all the appeals, the king appointed an adviser, called a **chancellor,** to hear the petitions. The chancellor had the ability to grant new and unique remedies that fit the facts of the particular case. Eventually, a new body of rules and remedies was established. These courts in time became known as courts of equity and the relief granted as **equitable remedies.** Equity courts were grounded in justice and fair dealing; these courts furnished more equitable and adequate remedies than the remedies available in courts of law.

Plaintiffs had to decide whether they were going to file a lawsuit in a court of law or in a court of equity based on the remedy they were seeking. Courts of law could grant only damages. Courts of equity could force a person to do or not to do something. The effect of the strictness of the courts of law several centuries ago still lingers in the consciousness of society through such adages as "You must cross every *t* and dot every *i*" when dealing with legal matters.

Merging of the Two Court Systems

In most states the courts of law and the courts of equity have merged. In these states most distinctions between the two have disappeared. A plaintiff may request both legal and equitable remedies in the same action, and the trial court judge may grant either or both forms of relief.

Yet the merging of the courts of law and equity has not diminished the importance of distinguishing legal remedies from equitable remedies. Let's turn now to the distinctions between the two remedies.

Distinctions

Three distinctions exist between courts of law and courts of equity. First, courts of law award money damages while courts of equity grant other types of relief, such as **specific performance** (the contract must be specifically performed according to its terms) and **injunctions** (usually to prohibit someone from doing something, such as going on strike). In the end, the person seeking equity may end up with a money award, but that was not the primary relief he or she originally sought.

Second, a jury is allowed in a court of law, while in an equity court the judge makes the de-

Legal Highlight

Equitable Maxims

When making a decision with regard to equitable remedies, judges are guided by equitable principles. These principles were developed over the past centuries and are based on common sense. Examples of equitable maxims are:

1. Whoever seeks equity must do equity.
2. Equality is equity.
3. Where there is equal equity, the law must prevail.

4. One seeking the aid of an equity court must come to the court with clean hands.
5. Equity will not suffer a right to exist without a remedy.
6. Equity aids the vigilant, not those who rest on their rights.

The last maxim means that individuals who fail to look out for their rights until after a reasonable time has passed will not be helped. It forms the doctrine of laches discussed in the text.

---

cision. Historically, juries were never used in courts of equity. Today, an advisory jury is available when equitable relief is sought, but its decision is not binding. The right to a jury in a court of law in a civil suit is preserved by the Seventh Amendment of the Constitution.

Third, the courts of law are bound by the **statute of limitations,** which sets out a specific time period during which a lawsuit must be filed or forever barred. The statute of limitations is measured in specific years. For example, if a contract has been broken, the person may be able to sue anytime during a four-year period. If the person sues one day after the four years have passed, his or her case will not be heard by a court.

Courts of equity are bound by the **doctrine of laches.** This doctrine holds that individuals who fail to act promptly to protect their rights will not be helped by the court. (See Legal Highlight, "Equitable Maxims," number six.) In other words, a person must sue within a reasonable time period or be forever barred from suing. For example, if a business is seeking an injunction to prevent the labor union from striking, the management must act within a reasonable time, usually a few days. Because of the nature of the cases heard, it is impossible to set specific time limits. A reasonable time may range from a few days to several decades.

Specific Types of Equitable Remedies

Equitable remedies try to correct a situation so that the harmed party may find relief.

Specific Performance   A plaintiff may ask a court of equity to issue a decree of specific performance, which orders a defendant to perform the acts that he or she promised in a contract. The subject matter of the contract must be unique before a court will order specific performance. For example, in most states, land is considered to be unique. So is personal property that is considered one of a kind, like the Hope diamond. A court of law can only order payment of money or property for damages; in many cases, this is not a satisfactory remedy. The buyer of the Hope diamond, for instance, wants the gem, not money damages. A court of equity can order the seller of the diamond to turn over the diamond to the buyer.

On the other hand, a court cannot issue an order for specific performance of personal services because this would be considered involuntary servitude. Besides, such an order would be unenforceable in a practical sense. If a court ordered a football player to play football, for example, how could anyone force him or her to play?

Injunctions   A plaintiff may want to prevent or to stop a certain activity from happening. For example, a corporation may want to stop a union from striking. The corporation can file a lawsuit in a court of equity requesting that the union be ordered not to strike. The order is called a negative injunction. A negative injunction is an order to any person to refrain from or to stop doing a particular act.

Ethical Considerations

Ethical Attitudes

Ethics can be thought of as the study and science of morals; thus, it encompasses both the legal and political arenas. Ethics provide the foundation for our entire legal system, for this system attempts to set minimum moral standards. But to behave ethically requires more than simply meeting minimum legal standards.

Many businesses have recognized that to ensure long-term profits they must strive for integrity and ethical conduct not only by setting corporate policies but by implementing those policies in their day-to-day operations. Corporate policies must ensure ethical conduct toward all the business's audiences: customers, employees, unions, government, competitors, and suppliers. One method businesses use to ensure ethical conduct is the adoption of a formal code of ethics.

By having and enforcing a code of ethics, businesses hope to gain a reputation for integrity and honesty, thus attracting investors, employees, and customers. A good reputation also helps a company when unexpected problems arise, as it did for Johnson & Johnson, Inc., when someone tampered with its product, Tylenol. Johnson & Johnson immediately pulled all Tylenol products off the market. Months later the Tylenol products were returned to the shelves with new packaging, which would prevent tampering. Johnson & Johnson during this time period kept its good reputation by ensuring that the tampering had not occurred during manufacturing and by structuring an advertising campaign, to keep the public informed.

You may want to write several companies for their code of ethics. How do these companies implement and follow their codes of ethics?

Rescission A person signs and performs a contract because of the other party's misrepresentations. Once the misrepresentation is discovered, the injured party wants to return to the position she or he had before signing the contract. The equitable remedy of **rescission** is available. Rescission cancels the agreement and reinstates the parties to the contract to the status quo. Before rescission will be granted, the injured party must show that she or he relied on the misrepresentations when signing the contract. If the equity court grants rescission, the plaintiff is entitled to have returned to him or her any property or money that changed hands because of the contract. All duties created by the agreement are rescinded.

For example, a sales agreement is made because the seller misrepresents the quality of goods. If the fraud is discovered before any money changes hands, the buyer will want to have the agreement rescinded—an equitable remedy. If, however, money has been exchanged and the buyer has already resold some of the goods, the buyer will want a remedy at law and will seek money damages for harm suffered.

International Considerations

Treaties, Conventions and Agreements

In today's competitive world, the financial future of the United States depends on international trade. In order to compete effectively, an American businessperson must have some knowledge of international law. Every sovereign state has its own body of law (for example, we can speak of Japanese law, German law, Egyptian law, or Mexican law). International law, however, does not exist as a unified set of codes. Instead, the relationships among nations are established through treaties, conventions, and agreements.

In the United States, a treaty is made by the president acting with the heads of a foreign country or countries; it must be ratified by two-thirds of the Senate to become binding on our government. Treaties are always between nations. Treaties may create, among other things, an international organization, such as the European Community.

A convention is the code adopted by an international organization such as the United Nations. This code is circulated among the organization's member states. A nation that signs a treaty or a convention is known as a signatory.

No international organization can dictate a nation's adherence to the organization's code without that nation's permission. This permission can only be obtained through a treaty with the sovereign nation; the ability to withdraw that permission is usually built into the treaty provisions.

A treaty may provide for the formation of an international organization, such as the 1945 **Charter of the United Nations,** which created the **United Nations,** or the 1957 **Treaty of Rome,** which created the **European Community** (EC).[a] Within these organizations, if granted by the treaty and approved by the individual sovereign states, laws can be passed that are binding on the member nations. No nation has ever given up complete sovereignty to an international organization.

An American businessperson must have a working knowledge of the laws of the United States, the laws of the country where his or her business is being conducted, and the international laws that govern the relationship between the countries. Businesspeople should always obtain independent legal advice from someone who knows not only the laws of the other country but also the laws contained within the treaties and lower-level agreements, such as a protocol.

The General Assembly of the United Nations has declared the period of 1990–1999 the U.N. Decade of International Law. During this decade, nations will be encouraged to develop and codify various proposals for international law that will deal with subjects ranging from the protection, security, and safety of diplomatic personnel and premises to the newly emerging commercial transactions based on computer-assisted methods.

a.   Prior to 1992, the European Community was called the European Economic Community (EEC).

FACING A LEGAL ISSUE

How To Find An Attorney

How do you find a competent attorney when you need one? The best method is the oldest one: Ask your friends and acquaintances. A good attorney has a good reputation; word-of-mouth recommendations, even in this age of high technology, are still very reliable.

The yellow pages of your telephone directory provide a second method. Most attorneys specialize in a certain legal area, such as real estate, bankruptcy, or taxation. Many lawyers indicate their bar–specialty in advertisements. Unfortunately, very few bar-certified specialties are actually authorized. A licensed attorney can place his or her name under most of the headings without having passed any special examinations and without having any length of experience in that particular field. You will have a better chance of finding a knowledgeable attorney if you find a lawyer who is bar certified or who is not listed under any other heading than the specialty you need.

Most local bar associations have a referral service. Attorneys register their area of expertise with the bar association. For a small fee you can have an initial interview with these attorneys. Last, certain books, such as the *Martindale-Hubbell Law Directory*, list attorneys and their specialties. These books are found in local libraries, and they list the lawyer's specialty, age, sex, years of practice, the schools from which the lawyer graduated, and a list of the partners in the law firm.

Lawyers may be hired on a contingent-fee basis for certain types of cases, such as automobile accidents. If the lawyer wins the case for the clients, his or her fee is taken from the amount of the award. Thus, the fee is contingent on the lawyer winning an award, either in court or through negotiations, for the client. Often this is the only way a person can afford an attorney. Lawyers may also be hired on an hourly rate or for a fixed fee (such as $500 for handling a noncontested divorce without property settlement).

A good practice is to speak with several attorneys before deciding which one you want to retain. It is very important that you and the attorney have a good working relationship. Ask about the attorney's fees and the costs involved, the time required to resolve the case, whether the case will go to court or be settled, and what the settlement terms should be. Go prepared with a list of questions, just as you would for any other business appointment.

Summary

What is law? No one definition of the law exists, and law is only one part of the total environment of society.

Several schools of legal philosophy exist. The natural school presupposes an ideal state of being in which there is a definite right or wrong on which law is based, while the historical school emphasizes the evolution of the law based on its origins and history. The sociological school emphasizes discovery of the law through observation of society. The analytical school uses logic to shape the law, while legal realists view the law as a means to a social end. The economic school holds that laws may be evaluated in accordance with economic theory.

The courts examine various sources of the law when making a decision. If applicable, the state or federal constitution, statutes, and regulations are examined. In addition, the courts review the case law.

The law can also be classified in several ways: substantive law or procedural law, public law or private law, and civil law or criminal law. Finally, the remedies that a court can apply can be divided into remedies at law and equitable remedies. Courts of law allow monetary damages, use juries, and apply the statute of limitations. Courts of equity are able to grant remedies other than monetary damages, have no right to use a jury, and apply the doctrine of laches.

Key Terms

administrative law (26)
analytical school (17)
Bill of Rights (18)
chancellor (27)
charter of the United
      Nations (30)
checks and balances (18)
civil law (27)
common law (17)
constitutional law (26)
courts of equity (27)
courts of law (27)
criminal law (26)
defendant (27)
doctrine of laches (28)

economic school (17)
equitable remedies (27)
European Community (30)
historical school (16)
injunctions (27)
judicial review (18)
jurisprudence (16)
law (16)
legal realist (17)
natural law school (16)
ordinances (18)
plaintiff (27)
precedent (19)
private law (26)
probate (17)

procedural law (26)
public law (26)
remedies (27)
remedies at law (27)
rescission (29)
Restatements (17)
sociological school (16)
specific performance (28)
stare decisis (19)
statute of limitations (28)
statutes (18)
substantive law (26)
Treaty of Rome (30)
United Nations (30)

Questions and Case Problems

1. Define the word *law*.

2. What is the difference between common law and statutory law? Judges are able to overrule common law by making a different decision in a later case based on similar facts. Should judges have the same authority to overrule statutory law?

3. Explain the following philosophies of law:
a. Natural law school
b. Historical school
c. Sociological school
d. Analytical school
e. Legal realists
f. Economic school

4. What are three differences between courts of law and courts of equity?

5. What are remedies at law? What are equitable remedies?

6. Discuss fully which of the following breach-of-contract situations warrants specific performance or only money damages as a remedy.
a. Norma signs a contract to sell her house and lot to Jethro. A few days later she finds another buyer who is willing to pay a higher price. Norma now refuses to sell to Jethro. What remedies are available to Jethro?

b. Y—U, a rock-and-roll group, contracts to appear for a week at a Las Vegas hotel showroom. Two days before the scheduled engagement, the group informs the management that it refuses to appear. What remedies are available to the Las Vegas hotel?

c. Ronald signs a contract to purchase a rare stamp owned by George, who is breaking up his stamp collection. Before the stamp is turned over to Ronald, George decides to keep the stamp collection and refuses to deliver the stamp to Ronald. What remedies are available to Ronald?

7. Laurel offers to sell his automobile to Hardy. Laurel tells Hardy that the car has been driven only 25,000 miles and has never been in an accident. Hardy hires Mike, a mechanic, to appraise the condition of the car. Mike believes that the car has been driven at least 50,000 miles and appears to have been in an accident. In spite of Mike's report, Hardy decides the car is a good buy for the price and purchases the car. Later, the car develops numerous mechanical problems. Hardy seeks to rescind the contract on the basis of Laurel's misrepresentations of the car's condition. Will Hardy be able to rescind the contract? Please explain your answer.

Chapter 2 Ethics and Corporate Social Responsibility

*There is one and only one social responsibility of business[:] * * * to increase its profits.*

Milton Friedman

If you want to read about Tammy Bakker, read Sinclair Lewis. If you want to read about insider trading, read Ida Tarbell.

Daniel Patrick Moynihan

OUTLINE

Introduction

Corporate business executives have a responsibility to their shareholders and employees to make decisions that help their business to make a profit. A company's bottom-line goal, after all, is to minimize costs and maximize profits. All businesspeople also have a responsibility to the public and to themselves to behave ethically. How a business analyzes its goals, particularly its goal to make profits, can influence the decisions that are made and can have an impact on the business's ethical standards. When short-term profits are emphasized, the temptation may be greater to act unethically—although, certainly, when a business makes substantial short-term profits, it does not mean that the business has been unethical. Still, when a business considers profits over the long term rather than on an annual basis, ethical considerations and socially responsible actions are enhanced.

For example, a business may fund scholarships at a university with the expectation that some of the recipients, on graduation, will actually become employees of the firm. The company may not see any profits from these scholarships for years. It has no guarantee that the recipients will become employees, yet it is for the long-term benefit of the business to give these scholarships. In this case, the business's decision makers are not only fulfilling their responsibility to benefit the education community, but also enhancing the possible future profit making of the business; the fulfillment of these responsibilities constitutes ethical and socially responsible behavior.

In this chapter, we will look at ethical theories and the concept of **ethics.** We will examine how ethics relates to what is legal or illegal, and we will look at the different forms of ethical and social responsibility in the business world. Finally, we will discuss briefly the issue of ethics in the legal profession.

Theories of Ethical Conduct

Ethics is the study of human behavior as it relates to right and wrong conduct. Ethics is a Greek word, while **morals** is a Latin word. Both evolved from the Greek word *ethos*, which means "custom" or "habitual mode of conduct." In the English language, the two words have become interchangeable.

Ethics is a system of moral standards that serve as guidelines for right behavior, or **ethical conduct.** Although ethics provides general knowledge as to what is right and wrong, it is for us to apply this knowledge in making decisions. Business ethics is not a separate theory of ethics; rather, it is one application of ethics.

Over the centuries, philosophers have developed different theories as to what constitutes ethical conduct. The Western foundations of the study of ethics lie in the writings of the ancient Greek philosophers, such as Socrates, Plato, Aristotle, the Epicureans, and the Stoics. The following subsections look briefly at a few Western theories of ethics.

Normative Ethics

One of the basic theories is called **normative ethics.** Under this theory, you evaluate a situation by asking which behavior is morally right or good and which is morally wrong or bad. Normative ethics has two main divisions: deontology and teleology.

Deontology   A **deontologist** believes that a person knows the difference between right and wrong. The term comes from the Greek *deontos*, which means "of the obligation." This theory treats moral values as absolutes; there are no exceptions. For example, a deontologist believes that you may never kill another person, no matter what the circumstances. A deontologist does not consider the ultimate consequences of an action. A person following the Ten Commandments without exception is a deontologist.

Teleology   The **teleologist** looks at the consequences of a person's conduct. The word teleologist comes from the Greek *teleios*, which means "that which is brought to its end or purpose." These philosophers look at the goodness of the result in judging the morality of a particular behavior. In other words, teleologists recognize exceptions to ethical rules depending on the results.

The two theories can result in different codes of ethics. Should a person look at a certain mode of conduct and say this is always right or always wrong? Or should a person consider the shades of gray that exist between such black and white distinctions? Philosophers have confronted this dilemma for centuries.

Utilitarianism

Utilitarianism is based on the idea that what is useful is good. This standard of usefulness can be applied both to the conduct of individuals and to that of the government. Jeremy Bentham (1748–1832), the founder of this theory, summed up utilitarianism as valuing "the greatest happiness of the greatest number." The basic tenet is that whatever brings happiness has utility. Underlying this theory is the idea that all humans want to obtain happiness or pleasure and to refrain from pain.

The problem with utilitarian theory is that it is impossible to measure success, failure, or the utility of certain behavior. In some situations, this problem can be overcome by using profits or the accumulation of wealth as a measure of success or failure. Another problem with utilitarian theory is that attention is directed to society as a whole and not to individuals. One individual might suffer more as a result of behavior that brings society greater happiness. For example, the payment of substandard wages to illegal immigrants enables society to have less expensive food and other products.

A Scenario

Theories of ethics allow a person to analyze his or her own moral conduct. The following scenario is a practical example of how to apply these theories. Perhaps it will inspire you to think of other examples where the results might conflict when the different theories are applied.

You are a high-level manager in a company that sells a drug that is 90 percent effective in curing a very contagious, but not a deadly disease. The other 10 percent who have used the drug have died. As a result, this drug is not for sale in the United States. Other countries have not banned the sale of this drug. Should you, as a manager, allow the sale of this product in other countries?

If you are a deontologist, you would not allow any sales because accelerating a person's death is never permitted.

The teleologist would look at the consequences of making these sales. What is the goodness of the end result? One person might argue that because 90 percent of the people are helped, the product should be sold. Yet another person, using the same theory, might conclude that the

death of 10 percent of the users is not good, and thus the product should not be sold.

Utilitarians would allow the sale. After all, 90 percent of the effected group would be helped or cured. The end result for the greatest number justifies the selling of this drug.

Ethical Behavior and Legal Behavior

Despite the differences in these ethical theories, all of us would readily agree that certain conduct is or is not ethical. In almost all cases, what is illegal is also unethical. Generally, the converse is true in our society—that is, what is legal is also considered to be ethical. Sometimes, however, conduct that is legal is considered unethical.

Many managers confuse legality and ethics, thinking that if an act is legal (or, at least, not forbidden), it is also ethical. Although legality and ethics often coincide, they are not one and the same.

The law has developed through ratification of constitutions, through court cases, and through statutes passed by legislative bodies. This development of the law is a reactive process. For example, specific laws forbidding computer crimes were not written before the first crime was committed. They were written only after computer crime became rampant; legislatures then passed statutes defining this "new" type of crime. During the period when there were no specific laws forbidding theft by computer, were those thefts ethical? Of course not. Thus, the law is imperfect. There may be no law where there needs to be one; where there is a law, it may not always be obeyed or even enforced. The law cannot necessarily cure a particular problem in business behavior. For this reason, businesspeople must make ethical and legal decisions a priority in deciding how to operate their business.

Areas of Ethical Responsibility

A business corporation must take into consideration five basic groups of people when dealing with the ethical issues of its responsibilities. These groups are: (1) the shareholders, (2) the employees,

(3) the customers, (4) the suppliers, and (5) the community or public at large. Emphasizing any one of these groups in making decisions sometimes has the ultimate effect of harming one or more of the other groups; thus, business managers must balance the interests of all five groups in order to make decisions that are ethical.

Shareholders and Ethics

One of the prime objectives of our capitalist society is for a business, over the long run, to maximize its profits. Without a profit, a business cannot survive. The owners, and the primary investors in a business corporation, are the shareholders. As an owner and investor, the shareholder expects a monetary return from the activities of the corporation. This return basically comes from the profits made by the corporation. Therefore, any decisions by the management of the corporation to increase employee wages and benefits, to lower the price or improve the quality and safety of the product for the consumer, or to contribute improvements for the well-being of the community, could mean lower profits.

Obviously shareholders expect that their interests will be fully protected by corporate management. This protection is expected by both majority and minority shareholders, and when shareholders believe corporate management has acted improperly, shareholders have the right to file a lawsuit to correct any such mismanagement activity. Corporate management, however, is given wide latitude in setting aside shareholder demands, including the board of directors' right to refuse to pay dividends.

Numerous reasons exist for a board's decision to refuse to pay dividends to shareholders. Obviously, if those reasons are to improve the welfare of the corporation's employees and lower the cost to customers, an ethical conflict arises between management behavior toward these groups and its behavior toward the shareholders. The following case, decided in 1919, illustrates the court's dilemma in resolving the conflict between what is ethical behavior toward shareholders versus what is ethical behavior toward employees and customers.

Case 2.1
DODGE v. FORD MOTOR CO.
Supreme Court of Michigan, 1919.
204 Mich. 459, 170 N.W. 668.

BACKGROUND AND FACTS *Ford Motor Company was formed in 1903. Henry Ford, the president and majority shareholder, attempted to run the corporation as if it were a one-man operation. The business expanded rapidly and, in addition to regular quarterly dividends, often paid special dividends. Sales and profits were:*

- *1910 18,664 cars; $4,521,509 profit*
- *1911 34,466 cars; $6,275,031 profit*
- *1912 68,544 cars; $13,057,312 profit; $14,475,095 surplus*
- *1913 168,304 cars; $25,046,767 profit; $28,124,173 surplus*
- *1914 248,307 cars; $30,338,454 profit; $48,827,032 surplus*
- *1915 264,351 cars; $24,641,423 profit; $59,135,770 surplus*

By 1919, surplus above capital was $111,960,907.

Originally, the Ford car sold for more than $900. From time to time, the price was reduced, and in 1916 it sold for $440. For the year beginning August 1, 1916, the price was reduced again, to $360. In the interests of setting aside money for future investment and expansion, Ford Motor Company paid no special dividend after October 1915. The plaintiffs were mi-

nority stockholders, who owned one-tenth of the shares of the corporation. They petitioned the court to compel the directors to declare a dividend.

Chief Justice OSTRANDER.

*   *   *   *

*   *   * [I]t is charged that notwithstanding the earnings for the fiscal year ending July 31, 1916, the Ford Motor Company has not since that date declared any special dividends:

"And the said Henry Ford, president of the company, has declared it to be the settled policy of the company not to pay in the future any special dividends, but to put back into the business for the future all of the earnings of the company, other than the regular dividend of five per cent (5%) monthly upon the authorized capital stock of the company—two million dollars ($2,000,000)."

This declaration of the future policy, it is charged in the [complaint,] was published in the public press in the city of Detroit and throughout the United States in substantially the following language:

" 'My ambition,' declared Mr. Ford, 'is to employ still more men; to spread the benefits of this industrial system to the greatest possible number, to help them build up their lives and their homes. To do this, we are putting the greatest share of our profits back into the business.' "

It is charged further that the said Henry Ford stated to plaintiffs personally, in substance, that as all the stockholders had received back in dividends more than they had invested they were not entitled to receive anything additional to the regular dividend of 5 per cent a month, and that it was not his policy to have larger dividends declared in the future, and that the profits and earnings of the company would be put back into the business for the purpose of extending its operations and increasing the number of its employe[e]s, and that, inasmuch as the profits were to be represented by investment in plants and capital investment, the stockholders would have no right to complain. *   *   *

*   *   *   *

"It is a well-recognized principle of law that the directors of a corporation, and they alone, have the power to declare a dividend of the earnings of the corporation, and to determine its amount. Courts of equity will not interfere in the management of the directors unless it is clearly made to appear that they are guilty of fraud or misappropriation of the corporate funds, or refuse to declare a dividend when the corporation has a surplus of net profits which it can, without detriment to its business, divide among its stockholders, and when a refusal to do so would amount to such an abuse of discretion as would constitute a fraud, or breach of that good faith which they are bound to exercise towards the stockholders."

*   *   *   *

There is committed to the discretion of directors, a discretion to be exercised in good faith, the infinite details of business, including the wages which shall be paid to employees, the number of hours they shall work, the conditions under which labor shall be carried on, and the price for which products shall be offered to the public.

*   *   * [I]t is not within the lawful powers of a board of directors to shape and conduct the affairs of a corporation for the merely incidental benefit of shareholders and for the primary purpose of benefiting others, and no one will contend that, if the avowed purpose of the defendant directors was to sacrifice the interests of shareholders, it would not be the duty of the courts to interfere.

*   *   *   *

Defendants say, and it is true, that a considerable cash balance must be at all times carried by such a concern. But, as has been stated, there was a large daily, weekly, monthly, receipt of cash. The output was practically continuous and was continuously, and within a few days, turned into cash. Moreover, the contemplated expenditures were not to be immediately made. The large sum appropriated for the smelter plant was payable over a considerable period of time. *So that, without going further, it would appear that, accepting and approving the plan of the directors, it was their duty to distribute on or near the 1st of August, 1916, a very large sum of money to stockholders.* [Emphasis added.]

In reaching this conclusion, we do not ignore, but recognize, the validity of the proposition that plaintiffs have from the beginning profited by, if they have not lately, officially, participated in, the general policy of expansion pursued by this corporation. We do not lose sight of the fact that it had been, upon an occasion, agreeable to the plaintiffs to increase the capital stock to $100,000,000 by a stock dividend of $98,000,000. These things go only to answer other contentions now made by plaintiffs, and do not and cannot operate to stop them to demand proper dividends upon the stock they own. It is obvious that an annual dividend of 60 per cent upon $2,000,000 or $1,200,000 is the equivalent of a very small dividend upon $100,000,000, or more.

DECISION AND REMEDY

The defendant, Ford, was ordered by the court to declare a dividend.

COMMENT

The two Dodge brothers received enough money from their share of the dividends and the sale of their stock to Henry Ford to establish their own automobile company, which produced Dodge automobiles. This company became part of the Chrysler Corporation in 1928.

Henry Ford was, at times, a farsighted business leader. He had a real concern for his employees. In 1914, when most of his competitors were requiring twelve-hour workdays, he instituted the eight-hour workday. When his competitors were paying $1 a day for unskilled labor and $2.50 for skilled workers, Henry Ford increased his minimum wage to $5 a day. This type of management resulted in more dedicated and efficient workers at Ford Motor Company.

As a result of the court decision, Ford purchased back all the outstanding stock and took the company private. The corporation went public again in 1956 after his death.

Currently, Congress and the media are discussing the amount of income chief executive officers (CEOs) should earn from their corporations. Is it fair and ethical to a corporation's shareholders for the CEO to make millions of dollars a year? For example, Steven J. Ross, CEO of Time Warner recently earned $78.2 million in one year. At the same time, Time Warner had a debt of $11.2 billion. Obviously, the large earnings of the CEO decreased the earnings of the corporation. Do CEOs perform better if they are paid another million dollars when they are already earning several million a year?

The Securities Exchange Commission did not regulate this area in the past because salaries were and still are set by a corporation's board of direc-

tors. The members of these boards are normally selected in part by the CEO. Currently the SEC rules allow anyone who owns $1,000 or one percent of a company stock to submit the executive's compensation package to the shareholders for a vote. The vote is not binding, but will put pressure on the board to review the package. Institutional shareholders, such as insurance companies and pension funds, are also in a position to demand reform or to elect boards that will tie salaries to performance.

Employees and Ethics

What are a corporation's duties to its employees? The answer to this ethical question is not an easy one because of the trade-offs involved. To the extent that the corporation provides higher than competitive wages, better than "reasonable" working conditions, and other benefits, its costs per unit of production will be higher. This means that the price of the product will be higher. Who has a greater "right," the employee or the consumer? In addition, this presents a conflict between the shareholder and the employee. The more employees receive, presumably the less shareholders will receive. No easy solution to such conflicts is available.

An employer has the duty to the employee of providing adequate compensation, reimbursement and safe working conditions. Think about the ethical implications of the last point. To what extent does a businessperson have an ethical mandate to provide a safe working environment for employees? To what extent, for example, should a company use its own resources to eliminate health risks from some airborne by-product of production? Should individual employees, who are willing to work in spite of possible exposure to dangerous chemicals, bear such a responsibility, or should businesses be constrained by government to eliminate such risks?

To ensure that employers provide safe working conditions for their employees, government regulation of the workplace has increased dramatically in the last decade. Such government regulation, mostly carried out by the Occupational Safety and Health Administration (OSHA), was a result of inadequate action on the part of employers. Even so, not everyone agrees with OSHA's operating methods; some argue that there is "too much" safety in the workplace and that the regulations upset the balance between economic and ethical concerns. For many employers, the safer the workplace, the higher the cost related to labor in the production process. That higher cost is paid for by consumers in the form of higher prices, by stockholders in the form of lower dividends, or by employees in the form of lower wages. Once again, a conflict exists among the responsibilities of a business toward these groups of people.

Employers have an ethical and a legal duty to treat employees fairly in hiring, training, compensating, and dismissing them. To do otherwise is costly, as it invites lawsuits. These suits have become more frequent in recent years. To minimize losing in a lawsuit, employers develop and maintain documented records on their employees. The extent and detail of these records create a conflict between the potential legal liability of the employer and the employee's right of privacy. The environment of trust between employer and employee can easily become strained. Thus the employer has an ethical conflict: developing detailed records (sometimes through "spying") to protect the business from legal liability versus retaining the employee's privacy and trust. Such a dilemma was faced in the situation described in the Legal Highlight entitled "It Takes Guts."

Sometimes the ethical problem for an employee becomes whether to be a "whistle-blower" or to keep quiet in order to hold onto a job. (A **whistle-blower** is one who informs public officials or the news media of an unsafe or illegal activity conducted covertly by a business.) This can be a major ethical dilemma, for keeping quiet compromises a person's own ethical standards and may require his or her participation in unethical or illegal actions. Choosing the alternative, however, may lead to undesirable results: Employees who blow the whistle often find themselves disciplined or even fired by their employers.

As will be discussed in Chapter 16, the common law holds that an employee normally can be hired and discharged at will by an employer. Except where limited by contract or statute, employers are free to determine the conditions and terms of employment and to conduct their affairs without judicial or administrative interference. Some states have passed special laws with respect to workers and whistle-blowing, and federal legislation covers employees in certain areas. Many states, however, still uphold the common-law at-will doctrine; in such states, whistle-blowers have little protection.

Customers and Ethics

What is the nature of a corporation's duty to the consumer? This issue often dominates discussions of product quality, pricing, and advertising. The customer often believes that he or she has absolutely no effect on the pricing, quality, and nature of the products and services offered by today's giant corporations. Some consumers believe, therefore, that corporations should be heavily regulated by the government and the courts in order to ensure protection of their rights.

Legal Highlight

It Takes Guts

We have never seen a (business) form or manual that couldn't be reduced by 50 to 75 percent. But it does take guts to give up on the paper. Paper is a form of security, and something is lost when it's given up, something that must be replaced by mushy old trust (abetted by prior training and development). And it takes guts of another sort, as well: A friend runs a forty-person establishment. Someone is fired (for, it seems to us, just causes), and for a while it appeared that the separated employee might file a suit, which, though frivolous, would have been expensive and time-consuming to defend. One day her lawyer sat our friend down and took her through the routine she must follow, he said, in order to avoid such eventualities in the future. It turned out that if she followed through exactly, she would have to accumulate an FBI-like dossier on each of her people. She refused flatly, because to do so would be in complete contradiction to the people-oriented philosophy behind her fine and spirited (and profitable) business. "I'd rather be sued and lose than become an undercover agent spying on our people" was her conclusion. And it took guts.

Source: A Passion for Excellence by Thomas J. Peters and Nancy K. Austin. Copyright (©) 1985 by Thomas J. Peters and Nancy K. Austin. Reprinted by permission of Random House, Inc.

The critics of modern-day corporations assert that these corporations consider profit maximization to be basically their only duty. The supporters of these corporations, however, claim that it is impossible for the well-being of the consumer to be ignored. In fact, they assert that ultimate control of a corporation actually lies in the hands of the consumer. After all, the consumer freely chooses to buy a corporation's product. Even in the absence of effective competition, the consumer can purchase a smaller quantity of the product being offered. Thus, it is in the corporation's best interest to attempt to satisfy, rather than defraud, the consumer.

Other ethical issues remain. If corporate leaders know or suspect that certain of their products may have long-run deleterious effects on the consumer, do the corporate leaders have an ethical responsibility to inform the consumer? Eli Lilly, for example, failed to recognize an ethical responsibility that resulted in the death of an 81-year-old woman who had taken Lilly's arthritis drug, Oraflex. Lilly had had Oraflex approved for sale in the United States without informing the Food and Drug Administration of 32 overseas deaths associated with the use of this drug. In a subsequent lawsuit, a $6 million judgment was entered against Lilly.

The issue of disclosing or not disclosing problems in product quality places a great deal of pressure on the middle manager in a corporation. In fact, middle managers are often the ones who face such ethical dilemmas, for they must be concerned with the needs and reactions of upper management as well as with the needs and reactions of lower-level employees. In addition, the profitability of the middle manager's department may be directly affected by customer satisfaction or dissatisfaction. Is it the middle manager's ethical responsibility, then, to disclose quality problems, even if the situation is clearly under someone else's control and that person seems content to ignore the problems? Is it the corporation's ethical responsibility to ensure that ethical problems are openly discussed and guidance provided for managers?

What ethical responsibility does a corporation have to citizens in other countries? If the Food and Drug Administration has prohibited the sale of a particular substance in the United States because it might have long-run carcinogenic effects, should the manufacturer sell it in those countries where it is still legal? This is an example of an ethical conflict between short-term profits for shareholders and concern for the well-being of customers. When such a conflict arises, ethical businesses consider the effects of their products on customers and do not consider only the short-range profit picture.

The following case represents a situation in which a corporation was concerned about its short-term profit. No doubt it utilized what is commonly known as high-pressure sales techniques. In reviewing the case, you should ask yourself whether these sales practices best serve the long-term interests of the corporation.

BACKGROUND AND FACTS *Audrey E. Vokes, 51 years old, was a widow who wanted to become an accomplished dancer. On several occasions, an instructor and other salespersons for Arthur Murray told her that she had great dance potential and would reach her goal; in reality, the plaintiff had difficulty hearing the beat in the music. With continued assurance of her progress, she contracted for over $31,000 in dance lessons; at one time, she had over 1,200 unused hours of credit when she was induced to buy an additional 175 hours of instruction at a cost of $2,472.75 in order to obtain a free trip to Mexico. In total, she contracted for well over 2,000 hours of instruction. The lower court dismissed the case because the plaintiff failed to state in her complaint a proper cause of action. Vokes appealed.*

**Case 2.2
VOKES v. ARTHUR
MURRAY, INC.**
Court of Appeal of Florida,
1968.
212 So.2d 906.

Judge PIERCE.
*   *   *   *

The material allegations of the complaint must, of course, be accepted as true for the purpose of testing its legal sufficiency. Defendants contend that contracts can only be rescinded for fraud or misrepresentation when the alleged misrepresentation is as to a material fact, rather than an opinion, prediction or expectation, and that the statements and representations set forth at length in the complaint were in the category of "trade puffing", within its legal orbit.

It is true that "generally a misrepresentation, to be actionable, must be one of fact rather than of opinion." But this rule has significant qualifications, applicable here. It does not apply where there is a fiduciary relationship between the parties, or where there has been some article or trick employed by the representor, or where the parties do not in general deal at "arm's length" as we understand the phrase, or where the representee does not have equal opportunity to become apprised of the truth or falsity of the fact represented.
*   *   *   *

It could be reasonably supposed here that defendants had "superior knowledge" as to whether plaintiff had "dance potential" and as to whether she was noticeably improving in the art of terpsichore. And it would be a reasonable inference from the undenied averments of the complaint that the flowery eulogiums heaped upon her by defendants as a prelude to her contracting for 1944 additional hours of instruction in order to attain the rank of the Bronze Standard, thence to the bracket of the Silver Standard, thence to the class of the Gold Bar Standard, and finally to the crowning plateau of a Life Member of the Studio, proceeded as much or more from the urge to "ring the cash register" as from any honest or realistic appraisal of her dancing prowess or a factual representation of her progress.

Even in contractual situations where a party to a transaction owes no duty to disclose facts within his knowledge or to answer inquiries respecting such facts, the law is if he undertakes to do so he must disclose the *whole truth*. From the face of the complaint, it should have been reasonably apparent to defendants that her vast outlay of cash for the many hundreds of additional hours of instruction was not justified by her slow and awkward progress, which she would have been made well aware of if they had spoken the "whole truth."

*   *   *   *

[W]here parties are dealing on a contractual basis at arm's length with no inequities or inherently unfair practices employed, the Courts will in general "leave the parties where they find themselves." But in the case sub judice, from the allegations of the unanswered complaint, we cannot say that enough of the accompanying ingredients *   *   * were not present which otherwise would have barred the equitable arm of the Court to her. In our view, from the showing made in her complaint, plaintiff is entitled to her day in Court.

It accordingly follows that the order dismissing plaintiff's last amended complaint with prejudice should be and is reversed.

DECISION AND REMEDY   *The decision of the lower court was reversed. Mrs. Vokes's right to pursue the lawsuit was restored. The appellate court held that the defendant owed a duty to the plaintiff to be truthful, even in expressions of opinion. A person cannot knowingly misrepresent his or her opinion in order to profit from misleading another.*

COMMENT   *This case illustrates how a court will handle an ethical problem in legal terms. The defendant took unfair advantage of the plaintiff. Our legal system attempts to control this type of overreaching by one party in relationship to another.*

Suppliers and Ethics

All businesses are dependent on suppliers in obtaining everything from major inventory purchases to paper clips. A business has an ethical responsibility to its current supplier when the business is considering obtaining supplies from a different source. Often such a decision is based on finances: For example, a business may have located a less expensive supplier, it may have decided to produce the item itself, or a different supplier may offer better service. This type of major change, however, may have an adverse effect on the former supplier and its employees. Often the former supplier has assisted the company when business was difficult, and many times these relationships have spanned a considerable period of time. To terminate them suddenly does not seem fair. On the other hand, is it fair for a new supplier who offers a better or less expensive product or who provides better service not to be able to increase his or her market share? Switching to a new supplier may lower expenses and thus increase profits for the shareholders and lower prices to customers, but you may be terminating economic relationships that have been built over years.

The United States government is one of the largest customers in the world. Often it has been cheated and defrauded by its suppliers. To counteract this situation, Congress adopted the Federal False Claims Act[1] in 1986. This statute is an example of how the government uses regulations for dual purposes: in this case, to protect whistle-blowers and to establish penalties for fraud. Any employee who is discharged or suffers discrimination because of informing the federal government of his or her employer's fraudulent activities may sue and win double his or her back pay and attorney's fees and costs. If fired, the employee must be reinstated with the same seniority.

The act also allows private persons, i.e., anyone, to bring a legal action in the name of the United States against any party who has filed a fraudulent claim for payment for products or services. As an incentive, the person is allowed to collect from 15 to 25 percent of any damages or fines collected by the government. If the United States does not proceed with the litigation but the person continues with it and prevails, he or she

---

1.   31 U.S.C.A. §§ 3729–3730

is entitled to 25 to 30 percent of the damages awarded. In the future, consumer watchdog groups or retired employees may use this act to enforce the law and legitimately earn compensation for their efforts. Naturally, the law does not allow anyone to collect under the Federal False Claims Act if he or she helped to plan and execute the fraud against the government.

Businesses that have the federal government as a customer must make certain that no fraud is committed. Ethically, this has always been true, but as a result of being overcharged and defrauded by businesses, the government has made it explicitly illegal.

The Community and Ethics

A considerable number of corporations include moral and political concerns in their decision making. In 1983 the Bank of America announced that no loans would be made to the Union of South Africa and its governmental entities until concrete steps had been taken to dismantle the apartheid laws. Other businesses continued doing business in South Africa despite apartheid laws. Now that the last apartheid statutes have been repealed, will businesses be willing to invest in South Africa?

Making loans is one way to interact with the community and making gifts is another method. Despite criticisms of a lack of corporate social responsiveness, most major corporations engage in philanthropic activities. Corporations routinely donate to hospitals, the arts, and universities by giving money, employee time, and access to special assets. Most major corporations employ one or more individuals to screen charitable requests and to determine which organizations should be the recipients of charitable contributions. B. Dalton Bookseller, for example, put up $3 million to launch a massive drive against functional illiteracy. Over the succeeding years, this contribution will help support 50,000 volunteer literacy tutors. The Bank of America has created a $10 million revolving loan program in which funds are loaned to community development groups at a 3 percent interest rate.

The following subsections describe two situations in which businesses have faced ethical, political, and legal problems in their relationships with a community.

Exxon Valdez   In 1989, Valdez, Alaska, became an instantly recognizable name and place after the tanker *Exxon Valdez* spilled more than 11 million gallons of crude oil (out of the 53 million aboard ship) into Prince William Sound.[2] The long-term environmental effects are still unknown, but in the short term, the spill spoiled the natural beauty of over 1,200 miles of Alaskan shoreline and killed or maimed over 100,000 migratory birds and unknown numbers of fish, including prized pink salmon. It halted the thriving fishing industry, forcing thousands of people out of work. How did such a cataclysmic event occur?

The huge ship was guided through the Valdez Narrows (seven miles from Valdez) by a harbor pilot, who commanded the ship for another seven miles before departing and turning the ship over to Captain Joseph J. Hazelwood. The captain set a course to avoid icebergs and notified the Coast Guard of his action. The ship, however, strayed from the outbound shipping lane, went through the separation lane, crossed through the inbound shipping lane, and traveled several more miles before hitting Bligh Reef. The captain was trying to keep the ship clear of an ice floe, yet he had ordered the ship to accelerate, placed the ship on automatic pilot with the third mate in charge (who allegedly was not qualified for this type of duty), and left the bridge. While the captain's actions clearly were irresponsible, other factors arguably contributed to the resulting environmental tragedy.[3]

To cut expenses, Exxon had reduced the number of employees who manned its tankers. Did this decision jeopardize the ship's safety? Further,

---

2.   In 1989, three other large oil spills occurred where 850,000 gallons of oil were spilled in Houston Ship Channel near Galveston Bay, Texas; the Delaware River; and off the coast of Rhode Island. Although the *Exxon Valdez* was the largest single oil spill in U.S. waters, according to the National Academy of Sciences, Washington, D.C., the world's waters are polluted annually with 540 million gallons of oil, i.e., the equivalent of 50 *Exxon Valdez* accidents every year.

3.   On March 22, 1990, a jury in Anchorage, Alaska, found Captain Hazelwood not guilty of being drunk and reckless while in command of the *Exxon Valdez*. He was found guilty of a lesser charge of negligent discharge of oil. He was sentenced to pay $50,000 restitution and to spend 1,000 hours assisting in the oil cleanup. His conviction was overturned in 1992 by the Alaska Court of Appeals on the grounds that his report of the oil spill could not be used in a criminal trial under federal law.

Have You Gotten Our Letter Yet?

A colleague, Pat Townsend, reports an example of Perdue Farms' response to a customer (remember, this is a three-quarter-billion-dollar company): "A friend of mine mentioned last week that he once bought a Perdue chicken that, he discovered after getting home, was all dry and nasty. He took it back to the store and got an immediate refund. Then he decided to write Frank [Perdue, president of Perdue Farms]—having seen him on TV—and tell him that he had bought one of his damn quality chickens and it was all dry and nasty. By return mail he got a letter from Frank that not only included profuse apologies and a certificate for a free chicken but also enlisted his help to make sure it never happened again by asking a whole list of specific questions. Where did he buy it? When? Exactly what was wrong? What did he think had happened? What exactly did the store say when he returned it? Etc., etc. Two days later an executive of Perdue Chickens called to make sure he'd gotten the letter, to make sure that all was well, and to ask some more specific questions. My friend will never buy anything but Perdue Chicken."

Source: A Passion for Excellence by Thomas J. Peters and Nancy K. Austin. Copyright (©) 1985 by Thomas J. Peters and Nancy K. Austin. Reprinted by permission of Random House, Inc.

Exxon was criticized for failing to have a double-hulled ship. Should Exxon have had this type of ship? Three-fourths of the oil tankers docking at Valdez have single hulls, because in 1975 the federal government refused to require tankers to have double hulls.[4]

Should Alyeska Pipeline Service Company[5] share the blame because it failed in its specific promises to the Department of the Interior and to Congress to have trained personnel and equipment ready to meet such accidents? What were the failures of the Coast Guard, which tracked the ship on radar only as far as the Valdez Narrows? The Coast Guard had not informed the oil companies that ships were no longer tracked beyond the narrows. Nor were pilots required to accompany these tankers out to the open sea. The Coast Guard also failed to install an additional radar site (at a cost of $100,000) further out to sea, a rec-

ommendation made in 1981. Its old larger radar had been replaced with one half the size. Finally, the Coast Guard had no method of independent observation of the ice packs.[6]

Did the state of Alaska also fail by not having trained personnel and equipment ready for this type of disaster? The state earned an annual average of $1.5 billion[7] from this venture, yet it failed to fund any staff position for oil-spill contingency planning and funded only 10 percent of what the state Department of Environmental Conservation had requested for oil regulation and monitoring.[8]

By the fall of 1990, 185 civil suits had been filed in state and federal courts as a result of the *Exxon Valdez* disaster. Over 75 law firms represented thousands of plaintiffs. Among the defen-

---

4. The Oil Pollution Act of 1990 requires double hulls on all new tankers. All single-hulled tankers are to be phased out by 2010.

5. Alyeska Pipeline consists of seven oil companies: British Petroleum (50.01 percent), ARCO (20 percent), Exxon (20 percent); Mobil, Amerada Hess, Unocal, and Phillips Petroleum share the remaining 10 percent.

6. The Oil Pollution Act of 1990 gave the Coast Guard the statutory authority and funding needed to improve the policing of tanker activity. Specific references are made in the act to Bligh Reef.

7. From 1969 to 1987, Alaska earned over $29 billion in oil income. Alaska set aside part of this fund, about $400 million a year, to pay people a dividend for being residents.

8. The Oil Pollution Act of 1990 created the Oil-Spill Recovery Institute to study and evaluate oil spills and cleanup measures.

dants were Exxon Corporation, Exxon Shipping Company, and Alyeska Pipeline Service Company and each of its members. It would have been one of the most complex litigations ever, but most state and federal suits were settled in 1991 for $1 billion.

Congress established the Trans-Alaska Pipeline Liability Fund in 1973. The fund received five cents on each barrel of North Slope crude oil. By 1989 the fund balance was $100 million. Over 28,000 claimants sought more than $50 billion in compensation from the fund. The claims were settled for approximately $20 million.

Whatever the business and governmental management decisions that led to the spill, it has cost Exxon financially. Earnings fell; Exxon's reputation suffered. Was the incident the result of a combination of unethical, illegal, and poor management decisions in a tight economy? The answers may have been revealed if the matters had been litigated in a courtroom. Since Exxon settled out of court, many questions remain unanswered.

Bhopal This town in India was unknown in the United States until 1984 when 40 tons of toxic gases were released from a Union Carbide pesticide factory, killing approximately 1,800.[9] The plant was located in a heavily populated urban area; slums surrounded the plant. What actually happened on the night of the accident is not clear. What is known is that safety information was never distributed to the surrounding public, and the alarm that sounded that night was the same alarm that signaled practice drills, which occurred about 30 times a week.

In 1986, the government of India, on behalf of the families harmed, filed a lawsuit against Union Carbide for $3.3 billion. In 1989, the case was settled. Union Carbide paid $470 million to the Indian government on behalf of the families. Yet through 1991, less than $5 million had been distributed, and the Indian government was reconsidering criminal charges.

Was this disaster a result of a poorly constructed physical plant or of poorly trained indigenous personnel working in a highly sophisticated

factory? Did the company fail to heed warnings by experts that a serious accident could occur? Union Carbide asserts that the event was caused by sabotage. Or was it caused by a combination of poor management decisions and negligent acts? Again, unless fully investigated or litigated in open court, the ethical and legal questions will remain unanswered.

Legal Ethics

Some mention of **legal ethics** and the practice of law should be made in a course involving the legal environment of business. Although the legal profession is the butt of many jokes concerning ethical issues, most lawyers are ethical. Lawyers face legal ethical issues every day. The unanswered ethical issue, "Should a lawyer defend a criminal defendant the lawyer knows is guilty?", is just one example. What the public often does not understand is that a lawyer cannot prejudge legal guilt. It is the prosecutor's job to prove the defendant guilty "beyond a reasonable doubt" in a courtroom. The accused is presumed innocent and has a constitutional right to assistance of counsel and a right to trial by jury under the Sixth Amendment. The lawyer's role is to ensure that a person's constitutional rights are respected by the government.

Courts are becoming increasingly irritated by the "frivolous" lawsuit. It is true that a few lawyers, just to earn a fee, will take cases knowing there is no chance of winning on the merits, while leading the clients to believe otherwise. Bar associations have the authority to suspend or disbar attorneys who engage in this conduct. Further, courts today will force the lawyer to bear all the expenses of such frivolous suits.

The following United States Supreme Court case involves the issue of whether an attorney or his firm was personally liable for instituting a groundless action. Federal court rules and many states permit the recovery of expenses when an attorney or a client brings a worthless claim; this is commonly called a Rule 11 sanction. The following case looks at whether an attorney or his firm should pay the Rule 11 sanction.

---

9. The actual number is not known, but estimates range from 2,000 to 10,000. The number 1,800 was determined by the Indian government.

Legal Highlight

Supplier As "Customer"

It seems that one of the half-dozen traits that we hear exemplify Japanese management (in contrast to management in the United States) is the long-term, almost familial relations between suppliers and producers. But there's no Japanese magic about it; it can happen in the United States—and does in many of the best companies. . . .

Domino's Pizza Distribution Company (Domino's ingredients and equipment supplier) just says, "Thanks." They regularly stage Vendor Appreciation Days. A horde of Domino's people will descend on a Wisconsin cheese maker or a California olive grower and shower the supplier with attention. Distribution executive Jeff Smith can't imagine it any other way. "They're part of the family, aren't they," he says, with surprise that anyone could conceive of a different position on the issue. (Interestingly, family relations with vendors are an explicit part of Domino's Distribution statement of its mission. Now, that is rare. But why not?)

Source: A Passion for Excellence by Thomas J. Peters and Nancy K. Austin. Copyright (©) 1985 by Thomas J. Peters and Nancy K. Austin. Reprinted by permission of Random House, Inc.

Case 2.3

PAVELIC & LeFLORE v. MARVEL ENTERTAINMENT GROUP

Supreme Court of the United States, 1989.
493 U.S. 120, 110 S.Ct. 456, 107 L.Ed.2d 438.

BACKGROUND AND FACTS *Calloway sued Marvel Entertainment Group for willful copyright infringement of his motion picture script. The original complaint—signed and filed by Calloway's attorney, Ray. L. LeFlore—alleged that Calloway had developed an idea for a motion picture and had written a script. Further, the complaint alleged that Marvel had begun to develop Calloway's work without his permission. Marvel filed a motion to dismiss, pointing to a series of documents annexed to the complaint that gave the production company the right to develop the work commercially. The district court dismissed the complaint (with leave to refile), not on the ground that the documents authorized the alleged infringement, but on the ground that Calloway's complaint had failed to specify the registration number of his copyright and the dates on which the alleged acts of infringement had occurred.*

Several weeks later an amended complaint, again signed by LeFlore, was filed. At the trial the jury found in favor of Marvel on all the claims. After the original case was completed, Marvel brought a Rule 11 motion and sought sanctions in the amount of $100,000 against both the law firm and Ray L. LeFlore. The Supreme Court took jurisdiction to decide whether a Rule 11 sanction should apply to the law firm or only to the individual lawyer.

Justice SCALIA delivered the opinion of the Court.

*   *   *   *

But in any event it is not at all clear that respondents' strained interpretation would better achieve the purposes of the Rule. It would, to be sure, better guarantee reimbursement of the innocent party for expenses caused by the Rule 11 violation, since the partnership will normally have more funds than the individual signing attorney. The purpose of the provision in question, however, is not reimbursement but "sanction"; and the purpose of Rule 11 as a whole is to bring home to the individual signer his personal, nondelegable responsibility. It is at least arguable that *these* purposes are better served by a provision which makes clear that, just as the court expects the signer personally—and not some nameless person within his law firm—to validate the truth and legal reasonableness of the papers filed, so also it will visit upon him personally—and not his law firm—its retribution for failing in that responsibility. The message thereby conveyed to the attorney, that this is not a "team effort" but in the last analysis *yours alone,* is precisely the point of Rule 11. Moreover, psychological effect aside, there will be greater economic deterrence upon the signing attorney, who will know for certain that the district court will impose its sanction entirely upon him, and not divert part of it to a partnership of which he may not (if he is only an associate) be a member, or which (if he is a member) may not choose to seek recompense from him. To be sure, the partnership's knowledge that it was subject to sanction might induce it to increase "internal monitoring," but one can reasonably believe that more will be achieved by directly increasing the incentive for the individual signer to take care. Such a belief is at least not so unthinkable as to compel the conclusion that the Rule does not mean what it most naturally seems to say.

*   *   *   *

The United States Supreme Court found that an attorney, not his or her law firm, is individually liable when a groundless action is instituted.   **DECISION AND REMEDY**

Lawyers' fees are continuing to increase. The very nature of how lawyers charge creates ethical issues. Is the contingency fee (a fee based generally on a percentage—typically between 20 and 40 percent—of an award granted by a court) ethical? It may seem sensible that if the lawyer cannot obtain a judgment for the client, the client does not owe the lawyer a fee, but it can cause ethical concerns. For example, if the judgment includes only medical expenses, should the lawyer receive a percentage of this amount?

When a lawyer charges by the hour, law firms frequently divide the hour into segments. At $200–$300 per hour, this can add up. Some firms use fifteen-minute segments. Thus, if you consult with your lawyer for ten minutes, you are charged for fifteen. Is this ethical?

The American Bar Association drafted a code of ethics for attorneys. This code is in effect in almost every state. Attorneys must follow the code's standards of professional ethics, or they will not be allowed to practice law. Bar associations have ethics boards that investigate complaints of alleged attorney misconduct and recommend to the appropriate authorities any corrective action that might be needed.

It has been suggested that a similar approach might be applied to the business community—a separate code of ethics could be adopted by the states for different business endeavors. As with attorneys, if a business did not follow the ethical code, it would be unable to continue its operations in those states.

International Considerations

Codes and Guidelines that Emphasize Ethical Conduct

The United Nations has drafted a code of conduct to regulate the relations among transnational corporations, multinational corporations, host countries, and home countries. These relationships face a dynamic combination of economic, political, historical, sociological, and cultural issues. Underdeveloped countries are seeking protection from predatory business practices of multinational or transnational corporations, while the corporations in turn want protection from arbitrary government seizures in underdeveloped nations.

The **Organization for Economic Cooperation and Development (OECD)** adopted the **Guidelines for Multinational Enterprises,** which is being used as a model by the United Nations. The multinational enterprise is to operate within the general policy objectives of the OECD members and to refrain from interfering with the host country's political activities. The needs of the developing nation must be considered as an important factor in decisions that businesses make when investment opportunities arise.

The transfer of technology from developed nations to underdeveloped or third-world countries is one example of an ethical issue facing the international community. In the past, large investments that transferred advanced technology to areas where people were impoverished have often failed to assist the host country because the local people did not benefit from the technology. A steel manufacturing plant in Egypt might give jobs to a few thousand people, for example, but not enough would be earned for the employees to stimulate the country's economy.

Would it not be better to target business opportunities that would improve conditions for the general population? Devices such as low-cost water pumps, windmills, solar heaters, and steam-driven turbines would benefit far more people in most underdeveloped countries than would factories involving advanced technology.

FACING A LEGAL ISSUE

When Should You Blow the Whistle?

Ethics consists of a person's basic moral values. No doubt you have been tempted at times, either in school or in the workplace, to act in a manner contrary to your basic moral values.

In our society we have been taught not to inform against another person. This concept is instilled at an early age, when we are told not to "tattle" on another child, and it is reinforced throughout our lives. It raises many problems for employees and for the businesses that employ them, however. For example, assume that you are employed by a wholesaler who sells a large number of consumer goods from toys to small appliances. You have always been honest and fair in your dealings with your employer. You discover, however, that one of your fellow employees is stealing small quantities of items to use as Christmas gifts. What should you do? If you inform your employer about these thefts, are you not "tattling" on a fellow employee? If you do not inform the employer, are you not, morally speaking, as guilty as the dishonest employee? The legal system can give you direction here: In most states it is a crime not to disclose this type of situation. This means that either you inform your employer about it or you will face the possibility of being criminally prosecuted.

Summary

This chapter has addressed the subject of ethics. Because each individual has a different background and different values, there can be no one definition of ethical conduct. A person's ethics consists of his or her basic moral values as established by cultural background, experiences, religious and political beliefs, and ideas about what is fair. Most activity that is illegal is also unethical, but ethical conduct addresses broader issues than simply the question of what is legal.

Ethical issues arise because of competing interests in the business world among buyers, sellers, managers, nonmanagers, and others. Many times these issues arise over the question of how to make a profit in the short run versus how to maximize profits over a period of time.

What is considered ethical conduct does change over time. As society changes, so does society's concept of what is ethical.

Whistle-blowing is a major ethical dilemma confronted by employees. They must choose between condoning unethical, unsafe, and illegal activities and coming forth to blow the whistle on their employers. The first choice requires unethical conduct, while the second choice may mean termination of employment.

Businesses are ethically responsible to competing interest groups. In particular, the following five groups occasionally have conflicting interests: the shareholders or owners of a business, its employees, customers, suppliers, and the community or public at large.

All attorneys are bound by rules of professional conduct. An attorney who does not follow these rules is subject to censure and disbarment. But even attorneys who operate within the rules face ethical issues and considerations daily.

Key Terms

deontologist (34)
ethical conduct (34)
ethics (34)

Guidelines for Multinational Enterprises (48)
legal ethics (45)

morals (34)
normative ethics (34)

Organization for Economic Cooperation and Development (OECD) (48)

teleologist (34)
utilitarianism (35)
whistle-blower (39)

Questions and Case Problems

1. Define ethics and distinguish among ethics, morals, and law.

2. Should businesses be concerned with ethics? In other words, should companies have social or ethical goals in addition to profit-making goals, and if so, who in the company should set these goals?

3. Should the decision about who sets a company's goals depend on the type of business conducted or on the current political and environmental climate?

4. Should ethics be solely a concern of top management, or should it be a shared concern of all employees, distributors, suppliers, and so on?

5. United States automobile manufacturers have recently been attempting to produce higher-quality cars. Did this result from an ethical concern of the companies? If so, why did this concern not exist before? Alternatively, is the attempt to produce higher quality cars merely a result of Japanese competition, and will such an attempt cease if and when the Japanese competition disappears?

6. To what extent does competition in the marketplace obviate the need for standards of business ethics?

7. Can a human life be subjected to a cost-benefit analysis? For example, consider the following situation: A rule is proposed that will require all commercial airlines to use jets that have two additional emergency exit doors. Given the average number of airline crashes per year and the average number of individuals injured or killed in such crashes, it is estimated that the new safety standard will save an additional ten lives per year. Should the standard therefore be instituted? What if it costs $10 million? $50 million? $3 billion? To what extent, if any, is cost relevant where human life is concerned?

8. Should conservation of natural resources and other environmental considerations become ethical concerns to which businesses should address themselves?

9. Michael Hauck was a deckhand for Sabine Pilot Service, Inc. He was employed at will. One of his duties each day was to pump the bilges (the inner hulls) of one of his employer's boats into the waterways. Hauck had noticed a sign on the boat that stated it was illegal to empty the bilges into the water. He had also called the United States Coast Guard concerning this, and a Coast Guard officer had confirmed that it was indeed illegal. Hauck thereafter refused to perform this illegal act for his employer, and he was fired because of this refusal. Hauck brought an action against Sabine for wrongful discharge. Texas was an employment-at-will state, and the Texas courts had steadfastly refused to grant any exception to this doctrine. On what basis might the Texas court to which this case was appealed create an exception to the at-will doctrine? Discuss your answer. [Sabine Pilot Service, Inc. v. Hauck, 687 S.W.2d 733 (Tex. 1985)].

Chapter 3   The Judicial System and Litigation

Litigation is a contest authorized by law in a court of Justice for the purpose of enforcing a right.

Summerour v. Fortson,
174 Ga. 862, 164 S.E. 809 (1932).

Introduction

Why does a businessperson need to understand the judicial system and to appreciate how cases are litigated? First, everyone should have a basic working knowledge of the structure of the court system, both at the state and federal level. This knowledge leads to a better understanding not only of how the system operates but also of the flaws in the system that need correction. Second, basic knowledge of how a trial proceeds is necessary in order to understand the reports of trials covered in the newspapers and on television.

Third, as taxpayers, businesspeople have an interest in whether the system works as efficiently as possible without sacrificing the protections it should provide. Finally, the businessperson needs to understand what he or she will confront when involved in litigation. In our society, almost all businesspeople will be involved in litigation at some point in their careers.

This chapter will look at both the state and federal court systems and will follow a sample case from beginning to end. In studying the courts and their procedures, the first question is which court has the power to decide a particular case—that is, which court has jurisdiction.

Jurisdiction

Juris means law; *diction* means to speak. Thus, the power to speak the law is the literal meaning of the term **jurisdiction.** Before any court can legally hear a case, it must have jurisdiction. Having jurisdiction means a court has the power to decide a case. When a court exercises jurisdiction, it has power over the person against whom the suit is brought and over the subject matter of the case. Without jurisdiction, a court has no power to act, and any judgment it enters is null and void.

Proper jurisdiction ensures that a judgment obtained in one state is enforceable in all other states where the defendant may be located or owns property. The **full faith and credit clause** of the Constitution (Article IV, Section 1) mandates the enforcement of judgments made in sister states.

Jurisdiction over the Person

In order to consider a case, a court must have power over the person or, in some cases, the property of the person against whom a suit is brought. A state court's power is limited to the territorial boundaries of the state in which the court is located. Therefore, a court has jurisdiction over anyone who can be served with a summons within those boundaries, unless that person's presence was obtained by fraudulent means. Jurisdiction over the person is known as *in personam* jurisdiction.

A court has personal jurisdiction in the following situations. First, the court has jurisdiction over any resident of the state and over any person who does business within the state. Second, the court has jurisdiction over a nonresident who has committed a wrong within the state, such as being at fault in an automobile accident or having sold defective goods within the state. The court can exercise jurisdiction over the nonresident person by using the authority of a **long-arm statute.** A long-arm statute allows a state, through its courts, to obtain jurisdiction over a defendant who lives beyond its geographical boundaries when two conditions are met: The person committed the wrongful act within the state, and the traditional notions of fair play and substantial justice are met.

Third, a court can exercise jurisdiction over any corporation that has been incorporated in that state, even if the corporation has its main plant or office in another state. The state also has jurisdiction over any corporation that does substantial business within the state, even if the corporation does not have an office in that state.

In all cases where a court exercises personal jurisdiction, the defendants must be served with actual notice that they are being sued (usually by service of a summons and complaint). If the defendants are out of state, they may be served either by a person or by a certified letter which the defendant must sign and which contains the summons and complaint.

In the following case, the United States Supreme Court was confronted by the question of whether a state obtains jurisdiction over a person when the defendant in the past had very limited contact within that state but was physically present for the summons. The Court also discusses when a state has jurisdiction over defendants who are not present within that state.

BACKGROUND AND FACTS *Dennis and Francie Burnham were married in 1976 in West Virginia. In 1977 the couple moved to New Jersey, where their children were born. In July 1987, the Burnhams decided to separate. They agreed that Francie, who was moving to California, would have custody of the children. She filed for divorce on grounds of irreconcilable differences.*

In late January 1988, Dennis visited Southern California on business, after which he went to the San Francisco Bay Area to visit his children. Dennis was served there with a California court summons and a copy of Francie's divorce petition. He then returned to New Jersey.

Later that year, Dennis made a special appearance in the California Superior Court, moving to quash the service of process on the ground that the court lacked personal jurisdiction over him because his only contacts with California were a few short visits to the state for the purposes of conducting business and visiting his children. The superior court denied the motion.

The California Court of Appeal rejected his contention that the federal due process clause prohibited California courts from asserting jurisdiction over him because he lacked minimum contacts with the state. Burnham appealed to the Supreme Court.

Case 3.1
BURNHAM v. SUPERIOR COURT OF CALIFORNIA
Supreme Court of the United States, 1990.
495 U.S. 604, 110 S.Ct. 2105, 109 L.Ed.2d 631.

Justice SCALIA delivered the opinion of the Court.

*   *   *   *

Among the most firmly established principles of personal jurisdiction in American tradition is that the courts of a State have jurisdiction over nonresidents who are physically present in the State. The view developed early that each State had the power to hale before its courts any individual who could be found within its borders, and that once having acquired jurisdiction over such a person by properly serving him with process, the State could retain jurisdiction to enter judgment against him, no matter how fleeting his visit.

*   *   *   *

Despite this formidable body of precedent, petitioner contends, in reliance on our decisions applying the *International Shoe* standard, that in the absence of "continuous and systematic" contacts with the forum, a nonresident defendant can be subjected to judgment only as to matters that arise out of or relate to his contacts with the forum. This argument rests on a thorough misunderstanding of our cases.

*   *   *   *

Our opinion in *International Shoe* made explicit the underlying basis of these decisions: Due process does not necessarily *require* the States to adhere to the unbending territorial limits on jurisdiction. The validity of assertion of jurisdiction over a nonconsenting defendant who is not present in the forum depends upon whether "the quality and nature of [his] activity" in relation to the forum renders such jurisdiction consistent with " 'traditional notions of fair play and substantial justice.' " Subsequent cases have derived from the *International Shoe* standard the general rule that a State may dispense with in-forum personal service on nonresident defendants in suits arising out of their activities in the State. As *International Shoe* suggests, the defendant's litigation-related "minimum contacts" may take the place of physical presence as the basis for jurisdiction:

*   *   *   *

Nothing in *International Shoe* or the cases that have followed it, however, offers support for the very different proposition petitioner seeks to establish today: that a defendant's presence in the forum is not only unnecessary to validate novel, nontraditional assertions of jurisdiction, but is itself no longer sufficient to establish jurisdiction. That proposition is unfaithful to both elementary logic and the foundations of our due process jurisprudence. The distinction between what is needed to support novel procedures and what is needed to sustain traditional ones is fundamental.

DECISION AND REMEDY

The Supreme Court upheld an old but continuing practice of all the state and federal courts that if a nonresident is personally served within a state, generally that state has jurisdiction over the person. The Court held that this practice meets the due process clause requirements of the Fourteenth Amendment, even though the defendant is only temporarily within the state.

Subject-Matter Jurisdiction

Subject-matter jurisdiction imposes a limitation on the types of cases a court can hear. The limitation is set by the constitution or statute creating the court. A court's subject-matter jurisdiction can be limited not only by the subject of the lawsuit but also by the amount of money in controversy, by the type of criminal case, or by whether the proceeding is a trial or an appeal. Probate courts (courts that handle only matters relating to wills and estates) and small-claims courts (courts that handle cases involving small amounts of money) are examples of courts with limited subject-matter jurisdiction.

Jurisdiction Over Property

In *Shaffer v. Heitner*,[1] the United States Supreme Court distinguished between *in personam* and *in rem* or *quasi in rem* jurisdiction. When a court's jurisdiction is based on its authority over the defendant's person, the action and judgment are called *in personam* jurisdiction. With this kind of jurisdiction, a court can impose a personal obligation on the defendant in favor of the plaintiff.

If jurisdiction is based on the court's power over property within its territory, the action is called *in rem* or *quasi in rem* jurisdiction. The effect of a judgment in such a case is limited to the property that supports the jurisdiction, and no personal liability can be imposed on the property owner since he or she is not before the court.

A judgment *in rem* affects the interests of all persons in the designated property. A judgment *quasi in rem* affects the interest of particular persons in the property. Take the following example: A person purchases property that is sold by the government for unpaid taxes. The purchaser wants to be certain that no one else has an interest in the property. He or she can determine who previously owned the property by looking at public records. The records contain addresses that were valid at the time the entry was made, but these addresses may be out of date when the records are searched years later.

These owners are specific persons. Their current whereabouts may be unknown. They might be deceased and their heirs may have a claim to the property. The new owner wants to clear title to the property and would file a suit. The court has *quasi in rem* jurisdiction over the specified persons, the prior owners. As to the unknown heirs, the court has *in rem* jurisdiction. In either case when the person's whereabouts is unknown, the jurisdiction is obtained by publishing appropriate notices in a newspaper of general circulation.

Venue

Jurisdiction is concerned with whether a court has authority over a specific subject matter or individual. **Venue** is concerned with the particular geographic area within a judicial district where a suit should be brought. The concept of venue reflects the policy of convenience. A trial court should be in the geographic neighborhood where the incident leading to the suit occurred or where the parties involved in the suit reside. Pretrial publicity or other factors may require a change of venue—that is, moving the trial to another community. A change of venue is used frequently in criminal cases if the defendant's right to a fair and impartial jury is impaired.

---

1.   433 U.S. 186, 97 S.Ct. 2569, 53 L.Ed.2d 683 (1977).

Court Systems in the United States

Today in the United States, at least 52 separate court systems are functioning. Each of the 50 states, the District of Columbia, and the federal government have their own fully developed and independent court systems.

The federal court system is authorized by Article III, Section 1, of the United States Constitution. The federal courts are not superior to the state courts; they are simply an independent system. The United States Supreme Court is the final controlling voice over all the court systems when questions concerning the Constitution, federal statutes, or treaties are involved.

A Typical State Court System

Most court systems, including the federal system, are based on a three-tiered model. Any person who is a party to a lawsuit typically has the opportunity to **plead** (or present) the case before a trial court and then, if he or she loses, before two levels of appellate courts. In other words, a case first proceeds through a trial court, which is, as its name implies, where trials are held and testimony is taken. The loser has the legal right to appeal the case to an appellate court. These courts review the decision of the lower court only on points of law; the facts of the case are not retried.

The loser of the decision by the appellate court may appeal to the state supreme court. If a federal issue is involved in the decision of the state supreme court, that decision may be appealed to the United States Supreme Court.

Exhibit 3–1 depicts a typical state court system. It has three main tiers: (1) the trial court of either general or limited jurisdiction, (2) the appellate court, and (3) the supreme court.

General and Limited Jurisdiction Trial Courts Trial courts that have **general jurisdiction** can hear cases on a variety of subject matters. Other trial courts have **limited jurisdiction** and can hear only cases on a specific subject matter. For example, a probate court, family court, criminal court, municipal court, or small-claims court cannot hear cases that go beyond its stated jurisdiction. A criminal court can hear only criminal cases; the judge has no authority to make decisions in a divorce case, which must be heard by a family court. Trial courts have **original jurisdiction**—that is, cases in trial courts are coming before a court for the first time to be resolved.

The state constitution and statutes determine how a court system will work in that particular state. Trial courts are called by many names, such as county, district, superior, or circuit courts. For example, in Ohio the trial court is called the court of common pleas, while in New York the trial court is called the supreme court.

Exhibit 3–1 **Hypothetical State Court System**

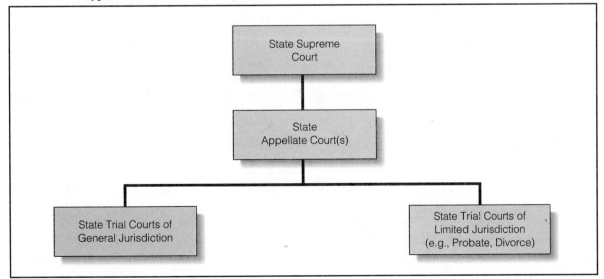

Appellate Courts In some states, trial courts of general jurisdiction also have limited jurisdiction to hear appeals from the lower judiciary, such as small-claims courts or traffic courts. Generally, the term appellate court refers to the higher reviewing courts and not to trial courts.

Appellate courts are also called courts of appeal or courts of review. Every state has at least one appellate court. The appellate court has **appellate jurisdiction**—that is, the court hears appeals only on issues of law. Many states have intermediate reviewing courts and one supreme court. The intermediate appellate court is often called the court of appeals, while the highest court of the state is normally called the supreme court. New York, however, calls its highest court the court of appeals.

Appellate courts do not try cases that they are reviewing. Examination of the written record of the case on appeal is made by the justices to determine whether the trial court committed an error of law. The appellate courts look at questions of law and procedure, not questions of fact. The only time an appellate court disagrees with a trial court's findings of fact is when the finding is clearly erroneous—that is, when it is contrary to the evidence presented at trial or when there is no evidence to support the finding. Otherwise, the trial court determines all questions of fact.

The decisions of each state's highest court in all questions of state law are final. It is only when questions of federal law are involved that a decision by the state's highest court can be reviewed by the United States Supreme Court.

The Federal Court System

The federal court system is similar in many ways to most state court systems. Also three-tiered, it consists of: (1) trial courts, (2) intermediate courts of appeal, and (3) the Supreme Court. The federal government also has special courts. Exhibit 3–2 shows the organization of the federal court system in some detail.

Article III of the United States Constitution establishes the one Supreme Court. Congress is empowered to create such other inferior courts as it deems necessary. Inferior courts include the United States courts of appeal, the district courts, and the other courts of limited, or specialized, jurisdiction.

District Courts At the federal level, the trial court of general jurisdiction is the district court. Every state has at least one federal district court located within its boundaries. Congress has divided the states and territories into 95 federal judicial districts, a number that will be reduced to 94 when the district court in the Canal Zone is phased out in 2000. The number of judicial districts varies over time primarily because of population changes and corresponding caseloads.

Most federal cases originate in the United States district courts. Whenever there are two or more district courts within a single state, there is limited geographical jurisdiction in each court. The state of Florida, for example, has district courts for northern, middle, and southern Florida; thus, a case that arises in the southern Florida district cannot be tried by a court in the northern district, unless a motion for a change of venue has been granted.

United States district courts have original jurisdiction in federal matters—that is, federal cases start in the district courts. Other trial courts with original, albeit special or limited, jurisdiction are the United States Tax Court, the United States Bankruptcy Court, and the United States Claims Court (which hears claims against the United States on federal contracts). Certain administrative agencies and departments with quasi-judicial power also have original jurisdiction. These agencies and departments are listed in Exhibit 3–2.

Courts of Appeal Congress has established twelve judicial circuits; each hears appeals from the district courts located within its respective circuit, or region. There is also a thirteenth circuit, the Federal Circuit, which has national jurisdiction limited by subject matter. Exhibit 3–3 shows these judicial circuits. The courts located within a judicial circuit are called courts of appeal or circuit courts. The decision of a court of appeal is final unless the Supreme Court accepts the case. Appeals from decisions made by federal administrative agencies, such as the Federal Trade Commission, are also heard by the United States courts of appeals.

Supreme Court of the United States The highest level of the federal court system is the Supreme Court of the United States. The Supreme Court consists of nine justices. This number is not set

Exhibit 3–2　Organization of the Federal Court System

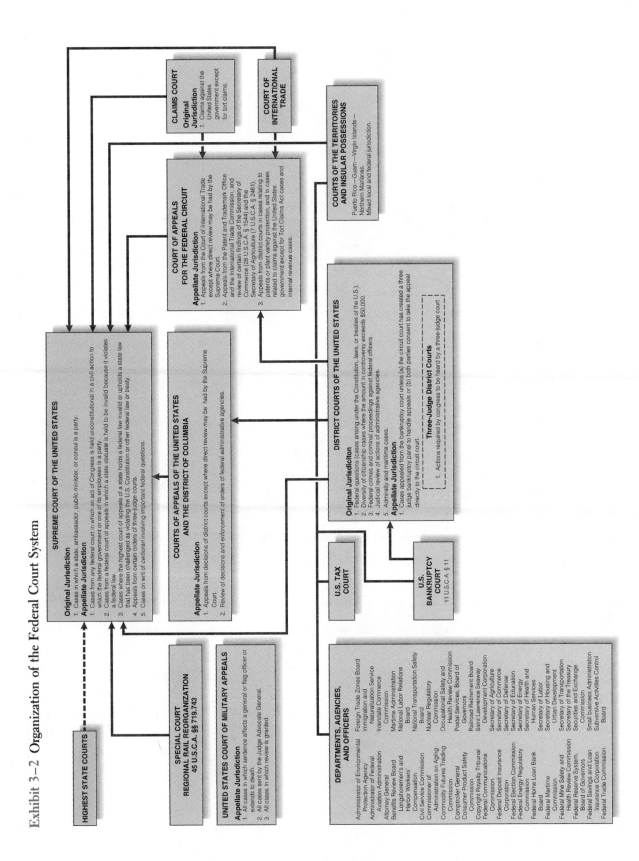

Exhibit 3–3 Judicial Circuits for the United States Courts of Appeals

Source: **Administrative Office of The United States Courts,** January 1983

by the Constitution, but it has been nine ever since the Civil War. All federal judges are appointed by the president of the United States and confirmed by the Senate. Under Article III, they "hold their Offices during Good Behavior;" Congress does have the power to impeach judges but rarely has this been done. All federal judges (with few exceptions—such as Bankruptcy Court judges) hold virtual lifetime appointments.

The Supreme Court has original, or trial, jurisdiction in rare instances as set forth in Article III, Section 2. Most of the time it operates as an appellate court. The Supreme Court can review any case decided by any of the federal courts of appeals; it also has appellate authority over cases decided in the state courts that involve a federal issue.

Jurisdiction of Federal Courts

Because the federal government is a government of limited powers, the jurisdiction of the federal courts is limited. Although the Constitution sets the outer limits of federal judicial power, Congress sets other limits on federal jurisdiction. The courts themselves can also establish rules that limit the types of cases that have certain characteristics, which the following subsections examine.

Federal Question Lawsuits   Whenever a plaintiff's cause of action is based, at least in part, on the United States Constitution, a treaty, or a federal law, a **federal question** arises, and the federal courts have jurisdiction over the case. Some lawsuits involving a federal question must originate in a federal court. For example, all bankruptcy cases must be brought in federal court. No minimum dollar amount in controversy is required where a case involves a federal question.

Diversity of Citizenship Lawsuits   **Diversity of citizenship** cases involve: (1) citizens of different states, (2) a foreign country as plaintiff and citizens of the same or different states, and (3) citizens of a state and citizens of a foreign country. In diversity of citizenship cases, however, the amount in controversy must be $50,000 or more before a federal court can have jurisdiction. Diversity of citizenship lawsuits need not involve a federal question.

Consider this example: Smith is driving from his home state, New York, to Florida. In Georgia

he runs into a car owned by Able, a citizen of Georgia. Able's new Mercedes is demolished, and, as a result of the personal injuries she sustained in the accident, Able is unable to work for six months. The property damage is $35,000, and her loss of income for the six months is $18,000. Thus, this case involves more than $50,000 worth of damages. Able can sue Smith either in Georgia or in the federal district court. Georgia has *in personam* jurisdiction through its long-arm statute. By driving on the Georgia highways, Smith has consented to Georgia jurisdiction. If Smith is sued in Georgia, Smith can have the suit removed to a federal district court on the basis of diversity of citizenship.

Concurrent Versus Exclusive Jurisdiction

When both federal and state courts have the power to hear a case (such as in diversity of citizenship cases), there is **concurrent jurisdiction**. When cases can be tried only in federal or only in state courts, there is **exclusive jurisdiction**. Federal courts have exclusive jurisdiction in cases involving federal crimes, bankruptcy, patents, copyrights, and lawsuits against the United States. States have exclusive jurisdiction in some other types of legal matters, such as divorce, probate, or adoption cases.

Writ of *Certiorari*

The United States Supreme Court has appellate jurisdiction over cases involving a federal question "with such Exceptions, and such Regulations as the Congress shall make" (Article III of the U.S. Constitution). Thousands of cases are filed with the Supreme Court each year, but it is only able to hear on the average of 125 to 150 cases annually. To bring a case before the Supreme Court, a party requests the Court to issue a **writ of *certiorari*.**

When a writ of *certiorari* is granted, the Supreme Court orders a lower court to send the record of a case to it for review. Whether the Court will issue the writ is entirely at its discretion; it is not required under any circumstances to issue a writ of *certiorari*.

The Court is more inclined to issue a writ in the following situations:

Legal Highlight

The Friday Conference

On Friday mornings promptly at 9:30, a buzzer summons the nine justices to an all-day meeting. Entering the conference room, each justice shakes hands with the other eight, a ritual started in the 1880s to symbolize harmony. The nine justices are Byron R. White (1962), Harry A. Blackmun (1970), William H. Rehnquist, chief justice of the United States (1972), John Paul Stevens (1975), Sandra Day O'Connor (1981), Antonin Scalia (1987), Anthony Kennedy (1988), David H. Souter (1990), and Clarence Thomas (1991).

Once the door is shut, no one else is allowed in the room—no law clerks, no secretaries, no pages, no security personnel—another custom, started in 1907. The junior justice takes care of the coffee, answers the door (should anyone dare to knock), and handles all messages and documents.

The justices have assigned seats based on seniority; the chief justice sits at the east end of the table, and the senior associate justice sits at the west end. Behind each justice is a cart that holds his or her books and papers. The volumes of the *United States Reports*, containing every decision made by the body since its first decision, line the walls.

The conference has two purposes: to vote on the cases already argued during the week and to select new cases for the Court to review. Only a few cases make it to the "Discuss List." Every justice has already screened each case, so the cases are processed quickly. Of the cases originally on the Discuss List, rarely more than six survive to be heard by the Court. During these conferences, each justice tries to persuade the others of his or her point of view; in effect, the other justices serve as a jury. It is this persuasion process that eventually produces the consensus for a coherent Court decision.

Although much is known about the procedure of the Friday conference, the heart of the conference—the exchange of ideas and arguments among the justices—is not revealed. The justices customarily destroy their conference papers, and they rarely talk about the sessions.

■ When a state supreme court has decided a substantial federal question that has not been determined by the Supreme Court
■ When two federal courts of appeal are in disagreement with each other
■ When a federal court of appeals has decided an important federal question not yet addressed by the Court but that should be decided by the Court, or has decided a federal question in conflict with applicable decisions of the Court, or has departed from the accepted and usual course of judicial proceedings
■ When a federal court of appeals holds a state statute invalid because it violates federal law
■ When a federal court holds an act of Congress unconstitutional and the federal government or one of its employees is a party.

Most petitions for writs of *certiorari* are denied. A denial is not a decision on the merits of a case, nor does it indicate agreement with the lower court's opinion. Denial of the writ has no value as precedent. The court will not issue a writ unless at least four justices approve it. Typically, only the petitions for cases that may raise important constitutional questions are granted writs of *certiorari*.

Judicial Review

Very early in the history of our country, the United States Supreme Court decided that it had the power of judicial review, as mentioned in Chapter 1. The Constitution does not provide for the courts to declare a statute unconstitutional; through the decision in the following case, the Supreme Court decided it had such power.

BACKGROUND AND FACTS *As a result of the national elections of 1800, the political party controlling the White House and Congress changed from the Federalist to the Republican-Democrat Party, and President John Adams lost his bid for reelection to Thomas Jefferson. Believing that the Republican-Democrats would weaken the national government, Adams, during the final hours of his administration, made 59 midnight appointments to the judiciary. He hoped to "pack" the courts with loyal Federalists before Jefferson took office.*

Adams nominated William Marbury as a justice of the peace for Washington, D.C. The United States Senate ratified the appointment, and the commission was signed by Adams. Adams's secretary of state, John Marshall, delivered 42 of the 59 appointments before he left office. Under Jefferson's administration, however, the new secretary of state, James Madison, refused to deliver the commission to Marbury. Marbury, along with three others, decided to sue.

Before the government changed, the Federalist Congress had passed a law (the Judiciary Act of 1789) concerning, in part, the issuance of a **writ of mandamus**—*that is, a writ to enforce the performance of a public duty. The writ was to be issued directly by the United States Supreme Court, effectively making it a trial court. This statute greatly expanded the powers of the United States Supreme Court. It was on the basis of this new law that Marbury sued.*

In an unusual turn of events, John Marshall had gone from being secretary of state under Adams to chief justice of the United States (appointed by Adams). Today, any judge would remove himself or herself from the case because of conflict of interest, but Marshall heard the Marbury *case and wrote the opinion.*

Case 3.2
MARBURY v. MADISON
Supreme Court of the United
States, 1803.
5 U.S. (1 Cranch) 137,
2 L.Ed. 60.

Chief Justice MARSHALL delivered the opinion of the Court.
* * * * *

The act to establish the judicial courts of the United States authorizes the supreme court, "to issue writs of *mandamus*, in cases warranted by the principles and usages of law, to any courts appointed or persons holding office, under the authority of the United States." The secretary of state, being a person holding an office under the authority of the United States, is precisely within the letter of this description; and if this court is not authorized to issue a writ of *mandamus* to such an officer, it must be because the law is unconstitutional.
* * * *

The question, whether an act, repugnant to the constitution, can become the law of the land, is a question deeply interesting to the United States; but, happily, not of an intricacy proportioned to its interest. It seems only necessary to recognize certain principles, supposed to have been long and well established, to decide it. That the people have an original right to establish, for their future government, such principles, as, in their opinion, shall most conduce to their own happiness is the basis on which the whole American fabric has been erected.
* * * *

It is emphatically the province and duty of the judicial department to say what the law is. Those who apply the rule to particular cases, must of necessity expound and interpret that rule. If two laws conflict with each other, the courts must decide on the operation of each.

So if a law be in opposition to the constitution; if both the law and the constitution apply to a particular case, so that the court must either decide that case conformably to the law, disregarding the constitution; or conformably to the constitution, disregarding the law; the court must determine which of these conflicting rules governs the case. This is of the very essence of judicial duty.

If, then, the courts are to regard the constitution, and the constitution is superior to any ordinary act of the legislature, the constitution, and not such ordinary act, must govern the case to which they both apply.

Those, then, who controvert the principle that the constitution is to be considered, in court, as a paramount law, are reduced to the necessity of maintaining that courts must close their eyes on the constitution, and see only the law.

This doctrine would subvert the very foundation of all written constitutions. It would declare that an act which, according to the principles and theory of our government, is entirely void, is yet, in practice, completely obligatory. It would declare that if the legislature shall do what is expressly forbidden, such act, notwithstanding the express prohibition, is in reality effectual. It would be giving to the legislature a practical and real omnipotence, with the same breath which professes to restrict their powers within narrow limits. It is prescribing limits, and declaring that those limits may be passed at pleasure.

* * * *

Thus, the particular phraseology of the constitution of the United States confirms and strengthens the principle, supposed to be essential to all written constitutions, that a law repugnant to the constitution is void; and that courts, as well as other departments, are bound by that instrument.

The rule must be discharged.

DECISION AND REMEDY

The Court held unconstitutional the provision of the Judiciary Act of 1789 that gave original jurisdiction to the U.S. Supreme Court to issue writs of mandamus. Thus, Marbury never became a justice of the peace.

COMMENT

Marshall was faced with a dilemma. If he exercised the authority given the Court by Congress to issue the writ of mandamus and thus ordered Madison, the new secretary of state, to deliver the commissions, Madison could refuse. The Court has no way to enforce its orders because it has no enforcement machinery. If Marshall did not issue the order, the secretary of state would end up being allowed to choose which acts he would perform.

Marshall took another approach altogether: He found the act of Congress unconstitutional. The Constitution clearly sets out the cases over which the Court has original jurisdiction. No power was given to Congress to expand the Court's original jurisdiction. Since Congress did not have that power, the congressional act was declared unconstitutional by the Supreme Court. Marshall went on to say that Jefferson and Madison had acted incorrectly in refusing to deliver Marbury's commission, but the Supreme Court did not issue any order because it found that it did not have that power.

The Court's decision was a masterpiece of judicial navigation. Marshall avoided a confrontation with the president by not ordering him to do anything, found that the president had acted incorrectly, and firmly established the doctrine of judicial review. Marshall did not create this doctrine; it was based on previous English and American legal decisions. The case also illustrates that a situation revolving around an insignificant fact, such as an appointment as justice of the peace, can lead to a monumental judicial decision, in this case the establishment of judicial review.

Judicial Procedures: Following a Case Through the Courts

American courts use the **adversary system** of justice. The judge plays an unbiased and mostly passive role. The lawyer functions as the client's advocate; he or she presents the client's version of the facts in order to convince the judge or the jury (or both) that the client's version is true.

Judges do not have to be entirely passive. They are responsible for the appropriate application of the law. They do not have to accept the legal reasoning of the attorneys; they can base a ruling and a decision on their own study of the law. Judges sometimes ask questions of witnesses and even suggest types of evidence to be presented. For example, if an indigent defendant chooses to act as her or his own counsel, the judge will often play more of an advocate role, intervening during the trial proceedings to help the defendant.

Procedure

Procedure involves the way disputes are handled in the courts. Procedural law establishes the rules and standards for resolving these disputes. The rules are very complex and vary from court to court. There is a set of federal rules of procedure, and there are various sets of procedural rules in the state courts. In addition, rules of procedure differ between criminal and civil cases.

A Sample Case

We will now follow a civil case through the state court system. The case involves a standard collection account by Acme Copiers, Inc. Lakin, the owner of a small accounting firm, has used Acme copiers for several years. Acme believes that Lakin owes it money on a copier that it sold to Lakin. Lakin and Acme are unable to agree on a settlement through an alternative dispute resolution method, which we will discuss in Chapter 4. As a result, Acme files a lawsuit against Lakin; this makes Acme the plaintiff and Lakin the defendant in the case. Both parties have lawyers.

Pleadings and Process   A **pleading** is a document that is written by one of the parties to the lawsuit and is sent to the other party (or parties) and to the court to be included in the judge's case file.

The purpose of a pleading is to provide information to the other parties. The following are the more well-known pleadings:

1. A complaint or petition
2. An answer or response
3. A counterclaim
4. A cross-claim
5. A reply
6. A third-party complaint.

Process is an order that comes from the court and is signed by the judge or judge's representative, such as the clerk of the court. A piece of process (the actual document) goes through three steps: issued, served, and filed. A judge *issues* a piece of process that orders a person affiliated with the case to do something. A copy of the process is *served* on the person by a process server, usually a marshal or sheriff, or an authorized private party. A party to the lawsuit cannot personally serve any papers involved with that suit. The process server *files* the process by returning it to the court case file with a notation as to when, where, and how the process was served.

The following is a partial list of documents that are known as process:

1. Summons—allows the defendant to defend against the claim of the plaintiff (pretrial)
2. Subpoena—requires the attendance of a witness (pretrial or during trial)
3. Subpoena *duces tecum*—requires evidence to be brought to court (pretrial or during trial)

4. Writs of attachment
5. Writs of garnishment
6. Writs of execution.

These writs are issued to assist a party in the collection of his or her claim after that party has received a favorable judgment.

A **complaint** is one type of pleading, while a **summons** is one type of process. In our case, Acme's lawsuit (or action) against Lakin will start when Acme's lawyer files a complaint (sometimes called a petition or declaration). The complaint is filed with the clerk of the trial court in the appropriate geographical area (the proper venue). The summons will then be issued by the court. The complaint informs the defendant why he or she is being sued. The summons notifies the defendant where, when, and how many days he or she has to file an answer or response.

Legal Highlight

Singing the Courthouse Blues

Appearing at a concert in Portland, Oregon, on November 9, 1981, the Beach Boys—Al Jardine, Bruce Johnston, Mike Love, and Dennis Wilson—were provided security by off-duty deputies. Three of these deputies—Fred Byler, Donald Kerr, and Kevin McVicker—later sued the Beach Boys for $5.4 million. The deputies claimed they were battered and falsely imprisoned when they tried to take photographs of the musicians.

The Beach Boys were properly served with a summons and a copy of the complaint at another concert they were playing in Portland in February 1983. No appearance was made or answer filed, and in August 1984 a default judgment was entered against the Beach Boys for $5.4 million. Each deputy was granted an award of $300,000 in general damages and $1.5 million in punitive damages. That award was upheld in December 1985 by a judge in the Multnomah County Circuit Court.

The lesson: Never ignore a summons and complaint. If you do, you may be liable for the full amount of damages alleged in the plaintiff's complaint.

The complaint contains: (1) a statement alleging the facts necessary for the court to take jurisdiction, (2) a short statement of the facts necessary to show that the plaintiff has been harmed by the defendant and is entitled to a remedy, and (3) a statement of the remedy the plaintiff is seeking. A typical complaint is shown in Exhibit 3–4.

The complaint states that Acme is a duly organized corporation within the state and that Lakin is a resident of that county and state. Next, the facts are recited: Lakin agreed to purchase the copier, and he has not paid the monies he owes for it. The complaint goes on to state that Acme is entitled to $3,500 to cover the cost of the copier.

After the complaint has been filed, the process server will serve a summons and a copy of the complaint on the defendant, Lakin. This is the only time a pleading is served by a process server. Usually pleadings are mailed by the parties to each other or are personally delivered by messenger service.

A typical summons is shown in Exhibit 3–5. It notifies Lakin that he is allowed to prepare an answer to the complaint. Lakin also knows that failure to file an answer will result in a judgment by default for the plaintiff. A copy of the answer must be filed with the court and sent to the plaintiff's attorney within a specified time period, usually 20 to 30 days after the summons has been served. If Lakin does not file an answer within the time period, Acme may obtain a **default judgment.**

Rules governing the service of a summons vary, but usually service is made by handing the summons to the defendant personally or by leaving it at the defendant's residence or place of business. In a few states, a summons and complaint can be served by mail. When the defendant cannot be reached, special rules sometimes permit serving the summons by publishing it in the newspaper or by leaving it with a designated person, such as the secretary of state. If service is obtained in this manner, the court usually will not have personal jurisdiction over the defendant but will have authority over the defendant's property located within the court's jurisdiction.

Choices Available After Receipt of the Summons and Complaint   Once the defendant is served with a copy of the summons and complaint, the defendant should file a responsive pleading. This filing must be done within the stipulated time period. Among the choices are (1) to file a **motion to dismiss,** (2) to file an **answer** containing an **affirmative defense,** (3) to file a **counterclaim,** or (4) to file an answer containing both an affirmative defense and a counterclaim. If the defendant does nothing, a default judgment may be entered against him or her.

Exhibit 3–4   **Typical Complaint**

IN THE SUPERIOR COURT OF THE STATE OF ARIZONA
IN AND FOR THE COUNTY OF MARICOPA

ACME COPIERS, INC., an
Arizona corporation,
 	
       Plaintiff,
 	
vs.
 	
PAUL L. LAKIN, a single
person,
 	
       Defendant.
	No. _____
	
	C O M P L A I N T
	
	(Contract)

    COMES NOW, the Plaintiff, ACME COPIERS, INC., by and through its attorney, I. M. GOODGUY, and for its cause of action against the Defendant claims and alleges as follows:

I

    The Defendant, PAUL L. LAKIN, is a resident of Maricopa County, Arizona. The said Defendant caused events to occur within Maricopa County, Arizona, which gave rise to this Complaint. The Plaintiff is a duly organized corporation within the State of Arizona.

II

    The Defendant, PAUL L. LAKIN, contracted with the Plaintiff to purchase a copy machine for $3,500.00. The copy machine was delivered by Plaintiff to the Defendant. Plaintiff then billed the Defendant on May 16, 1992, in the amount of $3,500.00. No payments have been received, which conduct constitutes breach of contract by the Defendant, PAUL L. LAKIN.

III

    Plaintiff has made all demands or performed all other acts necessary to mature or accelerate the aforesaid amount. The Defendant is liable for the Plaintiff's reasonable attorney fees under Arizona Revised Statutes, Section 12-341.01.

    WHEREFORE, Plaintiff respectively demands judgment against Defendant as follows:

1. For the sum of $3,500.00 as compensatory damages.
2. For reasonable attorney fees under Arizona Revised Statutes, Section 12-341.01, plus Court costs in bringing this action.
3. For interest on all said sums from May 16, 1992, until paid.
4. For such other relief as the Court deems just and proper.

    DATED this _____ day of January, 1993.

                                      _____

                                      I. M. GOODGUY
                                      2001 N. Winning Trial Lane
                                      Tempe, Arizona 85281
                                      Attorney for Plaintiff

Exhibit 3–5 A Typical Summons

IN THE SUPERIOR COURT OF THE STATE OF ARIZONA
IN AND FOR THE COUNTY OF MARICOPA

ACME COPIERS, INC., an
Arizona corporation,   )   No. _____

                Plaintiff,   )   S U M M O N S

vs.   )

PAUL L. LAKIN, a single
person,   )
                Defendant.   )

THE STATE OF ARIZONA TO THE DEFENDANT:

PAUL L. LAKIN

If served within Arizona, you shall appear and defend within 20 days after the service of the Summons and Complaint upon you, exclusive of the day of service. If served, out of the State of Arizona—whether by direct service, by registered or certified mail or by publication—you shall appear and defend within 30 days after the service of the Summons and Complaint upon you is complete, exclusive of the day of service. Where process is served upon the Arizona Director of Insurance as an insurer's attorney to receive service of legal process against it in this state, the insurer shall not be required to appear, answer to plead until expiration of 40 days after date of such service upon the Director. Service by registered or certified mail without the State of Arizona is complete 30 days after the date of filing the receipt and affidavit of service with the Court. Service by publication is complete 30 days after the date of first publication. Direct service is complete when made. Service upon the Arizona Motor Vehicle Superintendent is complete 30 days after filing the Affidavit of Compliance and return receipt or Officer's Return.

YOU ARE HEREBY NOTIFIED that in case of your failure to appear and defend within the time application, judgment by default will be rendered against you for the relief demanded in the Complaint.

YOU ARE CAUTIONED that in order to appear and defend, you must either appear in person or file an Answer or proper response in writing with the Clerk of this Court, accompanied by the necessary filing fee within the time required, and you are required to serve a copy of any Answer or response upon the Plaintiff's attorney. Rules of Civil Procedure 10(d), Arizona Revised Statutes, Section 12-311; Rules of Civil Procedure 5, Arizona Revised Statutes, Sections 22-215, 22-216.

The name and address of the Plaintiff's attorney is:

        I. M. GOODGUY
        2001 N. Winning Trial Lane
        Tempe, Arizona 85281

SIGNED AND SEALED this date: _____

        JUDITH ALLEN
        Clerk Superior Court

        By _____
            Deputy Clerk

Motion to Dismiss   If the defendant decides to challenge the plaintiff's complaint, the defendant can present to the court a motion to dismiss, also called a demurrer. The motion to dismiss contends that, even if the facts presented in the complaint were true, the legal consequences are such that no reason exists to go further with the suit and there is no need for the defendant to file an answer. If, for example, Acme's complaint alleges facts that exclude the possibility of any breach of contract by Lakin, he can move to dismiss. If his motion is granted, he will not be required to file an answer.

If the court grants the motion to dismiss, the judge is saying that the plaintiff has failed to state a recognized cause of action. The plaintiff generally is given time to correct the problem and file an amended complaint.

If the plaintiff does not file an amended complaint, a judgment will be entered against the plaintiff solely on the basis of the pleadings, and the plaintiff will not be allowed to bring suit on the matter again. On the other hand, if the court denies the motion to dismiss, the judge is indicating that the plaintiff has stated a recognized cause of action, and the defendant is given an extension of time to file a further pleading. If the defendant does not file an answer, a default judgment normally will be entered for the plaintiff.

Answer and Counterclaim   If the defendant does not choose to file a motion to dismiss or has filed a motion to dismiss that has been denied, an answer must be filed with the court. This document either admits the allegations set out in the complaint or denies them and sets out any defenses that the defendant may have. In most answers, the defendant admits to part of the allegations, such as admitting venue, and denies other parts of the complaint, such as denying any breach of contract.

If Lakin admits all of Acme's allegations in his answer, a judgment will be entered for Acme. If Lakin denies Acme's allegations, the matter will proceed to trial. Lakin may admit the facts, but deny owing the money, in which case no actual trial will take place. A trial is to determine the facts; since no facts are in dispute, the judge hears only arguments on the legal issues—in this case, the legal determination of whether there was a breach of contract by Lakin. If a breach of contract occurred, he owes the money. On the other hand, Lakin can prevail in the case by successfully raising an affirmative defense.

Lakin can admit the truth of Acme's complaint but raise new facts that will result in dismissal of the action. This is called raising an affirmative defense. For example, Lakin could admit that he was liable, but plead that the time period for raising the claim has passed. Acme's complaint must therefore be dismissed because it is barred by the statute of limitations. The factor that determines whether there will be a trial is whether both parties agree to the facts. If they do, no trial will be held; the judge will only need to determine the law as to whether the money is owed.

Lakin can deny Acme's allegations and set forth his own claim against Acme, alleging that Acme's copy machine never functioned properly. This is called, appropriately, a counterclaim. If Lakin files a counterclaim, Acme will have to answer it with a pleading, normally called a reply, that has the same characteristics as an answer.

Discovery   Before a trial begins, the parties can use a number of procedural devices to obtain information and to gather evidence about the case. Acme, for example, will want to know whether Lakin admits he received the copier, what malfunctioned on the copier, and why a rental unit was necessary. The process of obtaining information from the opposing party or from other witnesses is known as **discovery**. Discovery includes gaining access to witnesses, documents, records, and other types of evidence. The rules governing discovery are designed to make sure that a witness or party is not unduly harassed, that privileged material is safeguarded, and that only matters relevant to the case at hand are subject to the discovery.

Discovery serves several purposes. Evidence is preserved from witnesses who might not be available at the time of the trial or whose memories will fade as time passes. A witness's testimony is established so that the witness's credibility can be challenged at trial if that testimony changes. If discovery reveals that both parties agree on all the facts, a motion for a summary judgment may be made. If one party finds that the opponent's case is too strong to challenge, discovery can lead to an out-of-court settlement. Even if the case does go to trial, discovery prevents surprises by giving parties access to evidence that might otherwise be hidden. Also, discovery serves to narrow the issues so that trial time is spent on the main questions in the case.

Discovery can involve the use of **depositions, interrogatories,** or both. Depositions are sworn oral testimony by the opposing party or any witness, recorded by a court official. The person being deposed appears before a court officer and is sworn in. The person answers questions asked by the attorneys from both sides. The questions and answers are taken down and later transcribed by the court official. Today depositions may sometimes be videotaped. Even satellite transmission is used to allow a busy witness to stay on her or his job while answering questions for attorneys a continent away.

Interrogatories consist of a series of written questions normally sent to the opposing party. The person, with the aid of an attorney, prepares written answers that are then signed under oath. The scope of interrogatories is broader than that of depositions; parties are obligated to answer questions even if the answer involves the disclosure of information from their records and files. Uniform interrogatories for specific types of cases, such as automobile accidents, have been developed to make the process more efficient.

Other discovery procedures exist. A party may file a **request to produce,** which requires the other party to make available specified physical evidence it has in its possession. For example, if the defendant claims it paid the debt by a check, a request to produce the check may be sought by the plaintiff. **Requests for physical or mental examination** are often used in such cases as automobile accidents if the health of one of the parties is at issue.

Dismissals and Judgments Before Trial   After the pleadings and discovery process are finished, either of the parties can file pretrial motions. A lawsuit can be shortened or a trial can be avoided by the use of motions. In fact, most lawsuits that are filed never come to trial. Numerous procedural avenues are available for disposing of a case without a trial. Usually a party attempts to have the case dismissed through the use of pretrial motions.

Motion for Summary Judgment   Either party may move for a **summary judgment.** When the court considers such a motion, it can take into account evidence outside the pleadings. Most of the time, the lawyers submit written legal briefs (arguments) that set out the law.

Lakin, for example, can bring in the sworn statement of a witness that Lakin did not purchase a copier or that Acme has served the wrong person. Unless Acme can bring in other statements raising the possibility that Lakin was the purchaser, Lakin will be entitled to dismissal on a motion for summary judgment. Motions for summary judgment can be made before a trial, but they will be granted only if it is truly obvious that there are no factual disputes.

In order for a judge to grant a pretrial motion that would avoid a trial, there cannot be any genuine issues of fact in the case; the only question must be one of law. If there are any facts in dispute, there must be a trial. Only a fact finder, a jury, or a judge sitting alone (if the parties do not want a jury) can decide the facts of the case. If the motion to dismiss is denied by the judge, the case proceeds to trial.

Pretrial Hearing   Either party or the court can request a **pretrial hearing,** sometimes called a conference. Usually the hearing consists of an informal discussion between the judge and the opposing attorneys after discovery has taken place. The purpose of the hearing is to identify and narrow the amount of subject matter that is in dispute and to plan the course of the trial. The pretrial hearing is not intended to compel the parties to settle their case before trial, although judges may encourage them to settle out of court if circumstances suggest that a trial would be a waste of time.

The Trial   A trial procedurally consists of several steps from start to finish; it results when the parties are unable to reach a settlement. Although many lawsuits are filed, a large percentage are settled prior to their conclusion. About 95 percent of the lawsuits filed are settled out of court, mainly because of the time and expense of trying a case. Furthermore, of those cases that do finally go to trial, about 97 percent are resolved at the trial court level; relatively few trial court decisions are appealed, and even fewer are changed on appeal.

Jury Selection A trial can be held with or without a jury. If there is no jury, the judge determines the truth of the facts alleged in the case. The right to a trial by jury does not have to be exercised, and many cases are tried without one. In most states and in federal courts, one of the parties in a civil trial must request a jury or else the right to a jury is waived.

If a jury is requested, the jury members are selected from a panel of citizens who have been ordered by the court to jury duty. The jury panel is subject to **voir dire** (questions) from the judge and from the attorneys for the parties. The questions are asked to determine if any potential jury member has a bias toward one side, has any connection with the parties, or is unable to serve for the whole time of the trial. In significant cases, attorneys may use a psychologist to help them select members of the jury. Jurors who are selected to hear the case are paid a small daily fee and mileage. The losing party normally must pay these costs.

As a result of the questions asked during *voir dire*, jury members may be dismissed from serving on a jury for a particular trial. For example, if a jury member admits he or she has read about the case in the newspaper and has formed an opinion about it, the juror may be **challenged for cause.** Unlimited challenges for cause are allowed for each party.

A **peremptory challenge** occurs when a juror is dismissed without any reason being given. The number of peremptory challenges allowed varies from state to state, but is usually around three. Each side is limited to the same number of peremptory challenges.

In the case between Acme and Lakin, both parties want a jury trial. After the jurors are selected, they are impaneled, sworn in, and the trial is ready to begin.

Opening Statements Both attorneys are allowed to make opening statements concerning the facts that they expect to prove during the trial. The plaintiff's attorney gives the first opening statement, followed by the defendant's opening statement.

Rules of Evidence Adopted by the courts, formal rules of evidence ensure a fair hearing. The judge rules on the admissibility of all evidence, which must be *material, relevant,* and *reliable.* For example, Acme cannot introduce evidence that Lakin has been married five times, has fifteen children, and was convicted of jaywalking twenty years ago. None of this information is material or relevant to the issue of whether Lakin purchased and paid for the copier.

Cases are decided by both direct and circumstantial evidence. *Direct evidence* shows the existence of facts in question without the need for any additional evidence. A witness may testify that he or she saw Lakin using the copier. *Circumstantial evidence* consists of facts or circumstances from which the existence or nonexistence of a fact in issue may be inferred. Proof that Lakin mailed out 100,000 copies of an advertisement produced on a copy machine would be circumstantial evidence that the copier was functioning properly.

Information can be kept out of the trial if it qualifies as one of several types of exceptions, such as *hearsay evidence* or *privileged information.* Hearsay evidence is out-of-court "evidence" given by someone other than the witness to prove the truth of a contested fact. For example, Joe is a witness for Acme. He may be asked while he is on the stand to testify that he had a conversation with Liz, Lakin's neighbor, who said that Lakin told her that he was "going to get the copier without having to pay for it." Liz's words, as quoted by Joe, are hearsay. The proper person to call as a witness is Liz, who can testify as to her own conversation with Lakin.

Information can also be kept out of a trial if it can be categorized by the court as privileged information. By recognizing a privilege, the court protects a relationship in which confidential communication is very important. The best example of privileged information is the attorney-client relationship. Most communications between a person and his or her lawyer cannot be disclosed in court or anywhere else. Only the client may waive this right. This privilege encourages full communication between the lawyer and client, so the attorney can represent the client to the best of his or her ability during any legal proceedings.

The physician-patient privilege has been recognized in common law for centuries, as have the husband-wife privilege and the priest-penitent privilege. Other privileges are based on rules adopted by the court or by statute, such as the accountant-client or the media reporter-informer privilege. Over the past decade, many exceptions to the privilege rules have been made by statutory provisions or court rules.

Now that we have examined some rules of evidence, let's turn to see how the trial proceeds.

Plaintiff's Case   Since Acme is the plaintiff, it has the burden of proving that its case is correct. After opening statements, Acme's attorney calls the first witness for the plaintiff and then examines the witness in what is called *direct examination*. After Acme's attorney has finished, the witness may be cross-examined by Lakin's attorney. After *cross-examination*, Acme's attorney has an opportunity to ask the witness further questions called *redirect examination*, and Lakin's attorney can follow with *recross-examination*. When both attorneys have finished with the first witness, Acme's attorney calls the succeeding witnesses in the plaintiff's case; each is examined first by Acme's attorney and then is subject to cross-examination by Lakin's attorney (and redirect and recross, if necessary). For both attorneys, the type of question asked and the way in which it is asked are governed by the rules of evidence. After the last of the plaintiff's witnesses has been examined, the plaintiff rests its case.

Defendant's Case   Lakin's attorney then presents the evidence and witnesses for Lakin's case. Witnesses for the defense are called and examined, and the attorney for Acme has a right to cross-examine them. There is also the right to redirect and recross-examine each witness. Evidence favorable to Lakin is introduced. After all evidence has been presented and all witnesses dismissed, the defendant rests its case.

When the defendant's attorney has finished the presentation of evidence, the plaintiff's attorney can present additional evidence to refute the defendant's case in a rebuttal. The defendant's attorney can meet that evidence in a rejoinder.

Burden of Proof   During any trial, the plaintiff generally has the burden of proof. There are three standards of proof. If Acme is seeking monetary damages, the plaintiff's burden is to establish its case with a *preponderance of the evidence*. If, however, Acme were seeking an equitable remedy, it would be required to prove its case with a higher degree of evidence, sometimes called *clear and convincing evidence*. In order to prove a defendant guilty in a criminal case, the prosecution must prove its case *beyond a reasonable doubt*.

Motions for Directed Verdicts   After the plaintiff's case has been presented, the defendant's attorney may ask the judge to direct a verdict on the grounds that the plaintiff has failed to present a sufficient case for jury consideration; thus, there can only be one verdict as a matter of law—for the defendant. This is referred to as a motion for a directed verdict. It is rarely granted at this stage of the trial.

After the defendant's case has been presented, either attorney may move for a directed verdict. If the judge determines that the evidence presented by either side is so persuasive that a reasonable jury could only decide for that party, the motion will be granted. Frequently these motions are denied and the case proceeds to a jury verdict.

Closing Arguments   After both sides have rested their cases, each attorney presents a closing argument, urging a verdict in favor of his or her client. The judge instructs the jury (if it is a jury trial) in the law that applies to the case. The instructions to the jury are called charges. Then the jury retires to the jury room to deliberate and deliver a verdict (that is, to make the decision).

Jury Verdict and Judgment   In the *Acme v. Lakin* case, the jury will have to weigh the evidence and not only decide the case but also, if it finds for the plaintiff, decide the amount of money owed. The jury's decision is called a verdict. The verdict is converted into a judgment once the judge signs the document that states who prevailed and what amount is to be paid, if an award was made.

Motion for a Judgment Notwithstanding the Verdict (j.n.o.v.)   After the jury verdict is returned, a motion can be filed with the trial judge to overturn the jury's verdict. This is in the form of a motion for a judgment notwithstanding the verdict rendered by the jury. This gives the judge the opportunity to decide as a matter of law that after consideration of all the evidence the jury erred in its decision. This motion is usually denied by the trial judge, but if granted, a judgment will be entered for the party filing the motion.

Legal Highlight

The Legacy

All federal judges are nominated by the president and confirmed by the senate. Through the nominating process, a president can have a long-term effect on the judiciary and in turn on how the law is interpreted since the judges nominated almost always represent the philosophy of the appointing president; an appointment thus has the effect of continuing the president's legacy. The following shows the number of appointees still serving on the judiciary, listed by the president who appointed them.

- Bush 103
- Reagan 377
- Carter 241
- Ford 51
- Nixon 156
- Johnson 107
- Kennedy 48
- Eisenhower 36
- Truman 8

Motion for New Trial   At the end of the trial, the loser can move to set aside the adverse verdict and to have a new trial. The motion will be granted if the trial judge is convinced, after looking at all the evidence, that the verdict was in error. A new trial can also be granted on the grounds of newly discovered evidence, misconduct by the participants during the trial, or error by the judge.

The Appeal   A notice of appeal must be filed within the prescribed time. If Acme loses at the trial and decides to appeal, Acme becomes the appellant and Lakin becomes the respondent, or appellee. Acme's attorney files in the court of appeals the record on appeal, which contains the following: (1) the pleadings, (2) a transcript of the trial testimony and copies of the exhibits, (3) the judge's rulings on motions made by the parties, (4) the arguments of counsel, (5) the instructions to the jury, (6) the verdict, (7) the posttrial motions, and (8) the judgment or order being appealed. Acme may be required to post a bond for the appeal.

Appellate courts do not hear any evidence. Their decision concerning a case is based on the abstracts, the record, and the briefs. The attorneys can present oral arguments, after which the case is taken under advisement. When the court has reached a decision, the decision is written. It contains the opinion (the court's reasons for its decision) and the rules of law that apply.

In general, the appellate courts do not reverse findings of fact unless the findings are unsupported or contradicted by the evidence. Rather, these courts review the record for errors of law. If the reviewing court believes that an error was committed during the trial or that the jury was improperly instructed, the judgment will be reversed. Sometimes the case will be remanded (sent back to the court that originally heard the case) for a new trial. Most decisions of the lower court are affirmed, resulting in enforcement of that court's judgment.

Enforcement of Judgments   Once a judgment has been finalized, the party who has been awarded the judgment wants to be able to collect or enforce it. Several procedures exist for the successful party to enforce the judgment against the losing party, if he or she does not pay up willingly. These procedures are discussed in Chapter 13.

The Judiciary

On center stage in any trial or appeal is the judge, the person responsible for overseeing the proceedings and for making the final decision in the case.

State Judicial Selection Procedures

Judicial selection varies from state to state; however, all judges are selected either by election or by merit. Many states still elect judges to the bench. Opponents of this process claim that it introduces politics into the judiciary.

Judicial merit systems were created as an alternative to elections in order to ensure a more independent judiciary. Under a judicial merit selection system, applicants apply for an opening on the bench. After a committee reviews the applications, several names are sent to the governor, who then appoints one person from the list. State judges, whether elected or selected by the merit system, serve for specific time periods. Judges who are appointed under the merit system must stand for retention at regular elections.

Federal Judicial Selection Procedures

When a vacancy occurs in the federal court system, the United States Senators and others recommend candidates for the position to the president. No formal requirement, such as being a lawyer, exists for a person who wants to serve as a judge at the federal level. The president nominates a person for the vacancy from the list of candidates. The name is sent to the Senate, which will either confirm or deny the appointment.

A federal judge holds office for as long as he or she exhibits good behavior. Since it is very rare for a federal judge to be impeached, confirmation is in effect a lifetime appointment.

United States Magistrate Judges

The concept of a magistrate was established in the federal judiciary with the Judiciary Act of 1789. Today, a United States magistrate judge is a special-jurisdiction judge, and he or she holds a position created by the Federal Magistrates Act of 1968. The act was amended in 1990, and a magistrate is now officially called a magistrate judge.

A magistrate judge is a judicial officer appointed by the federal district court to assist in administering some of its functions. The magistrate judge has the authority to conduct many pretrial proceedings and to try minor federal criminal offenses and certain civil cases. For example, a person arrested for speeding in a national park would fall under a magistrate judge's jurisdiction.

Ethical Considerations

Are Contingent Fees Ethical?

Litigation is very expensive. A normal two- to three-day trial with limited discovery can cost as much as $10,000. Assuming a person prevails at the trial, should that person recover his or her total attorneys' fees and costs from the losing party? Other countries have adopted the rule that the loser pays all of the court costs and both sets of attorneys' fees. But is this procedure always ethical and fair?

Situations do occur where this procedure is unfair. In the United States, many cases are brought to court through the retention of an attorney on a contingency fee basis. Under this arrangement, a plaintiff can retain a very competent attorney. The plaintiff is not responsible for compensating the attorney if the case is lost. The attorney stands to lose his or her time and effort, if he or she is not successful. Even under the contingency fee arrangement, however, the plaintiff is liable for court costs, such as filing fees and discovery costs. If the plaintiff is successful at trial, a percentage of the judgment is then paid to the attorney. Normally this percentage is one-third of the amount awarded.

Contingency fee arrangements are used particularly in negligence lawsuits, such as those involving an automobile accident. The defendant who may have caused the accident is normally represented by attorneys hired by the defendant's insurance company. These attorneys are paid by the hour. Assuming that the defendant in the automobile accident case prevails at the trial, should his or her insurance company be compensated for its attorneys' fees? But what about the plaintiff who brought the case with

reason to believe that the case was winnable? If this person is a blue-collar worker earning the minimum wage, is it ethical or even economically feasible to have him or her pay the attorneys' fees for the insurance company? How many cases would be pursued if people knew that, even though they might have a valid claim, they would be financially responsible for all court costs and for all attorneys' fees for both sides if they lose the case? This harsh financial burden would probably prevent most people from filing a lawsuit to protect their rights.

This is not to say that the convenience of the contingency fee for employing attorneys has not been abused in the past, such as filing fraudulent insurance lawsuits. But should society prohibit the contingency fee arrangement, in the light of abuses? Many people have benefited from being able to hire attorneys on a contingency fee basis. Under this system, even the poorest person can afford competent legal assistance.

Think back to Chapter 1. It was clear that unless the law changed, Brown would lose the case involving the segregation of the races based on the precedent *Plessy v. Ferguson*. It was not at all clear when the lawsuit started that Brown would win at the Supreme Court level. If you had been Brown, would you have started down the legal path if you knew that if you lost the case, you would be held responsible for all court costs and attorneys' fees?

Contingency fees were not involved in the *Brown* case. There, each party was responsible for its own attorney's fees no matter who prevailed. But would anyone bring a court action to protect his or her basic constitutional or legal rights if there were a question about the outcome?

International Considerations

Different Legal Systems in Foreign Trade

Procedures to enforce your legal rights internationally differ greatly from country to country. The civil-law system is based on statutes that can be traced back to the Roman emperor, Justinian I, in 500 A.D. Most European countries,[a] including those formerly in the Eastern bloc, today operate under the civil-law system.

If no statute covers a given topic, the result is no law on the topic. The judge in a civil-law system acts more like an attorney in developing a case. The legislature—or, in some countries, the executive—is dominant in a civil-law system. A civil-law judge cannot create law as judges do under the common-law system.

The common-law system developed in England and is now the legal system in many of the former English colonies, such as Australia and Nigeria as well as the United States. Under the common-law system, the judge is neutral and independent of the parties suing before the court. The judge makes law that must be followed. The legislature also adopts statutes, but these statutes are subject to judicial interpretation.

Other countries, such as Iran and Saudi Arabia, follow Islamic law. These countries have adopted commercial law codes, but these laws must be interpreted by the Koran, a religious document similar in comprehensiveness to the Bible, and by the Sharià. The Sharià interprets the Koran. These interpretations have not been changed in nearly a thousand years. Non-Islamic businesspeople must be sensitive to the role religion plays in Islamic countries.

American businesspeople must appreciate that other cultures have different ways of making, deciding, and applying laws. In addition, the laws may be applied differently to foreigners than to natives before the court. Foreign legislative and judicial bodies often operate completely differently from those of the American legal system. However, there is one international court that any country in the world community may utilize: the **International Court of Justice** (ICJ).

The ICJ is the principal judicial organ of the United Nations. Located at The Hague in the Netherlands, it is separated from the U.N.'s main headquarters in New York and from the headquarters of the European office and the offices of specialized agencies found in Geneva, Switzerland. The ICJ decides cases submitted by United Nations members and renders opinions on legal questions at the request of authorized international organizations. The court is composed of fifteen judges elected by the U.N. General Assembly and the Security Council. Judges serve a nine-year term, with one-third of the judges elected every three years. The jurisdiction of the court depends on the consent of the nations that are the parties to the cases before it. The ICJ has jurisdiction over a sovereign nation only if and only to the extent that the nation has agreed that the ICJ shall have jurisdiction covering that particular factual situation.

a. The civil-law system is used in Germany, France, Spain, and their former colonies, such as Algeria and Mexico.

FACING A LEGAL ISSUE   Using a Small-Claims Court

Many times disputes occur over small sums of money. For example, your former roommate owes you for the last month's rent or for a telephone bill. Lawyers are expensive; it is not practical to hire one for such a small sum. Most states have small-claims courts. The amounts that can be in controversy will vary from one state to another, but small-claims courts offer an expeditious way to seek these smaller sums.

You can bring an action against your former roommate by filing a complaint. The service of the complaint and summons normally can be accomplished by certified mail. This alleviates the need to pay for a process server. The defendant must file a written answer to your complaint; otherwise, you can obtain a default judgment.

If an answer is filed, the case proceeds to trial before a judge. In some small-claims courts, a jury is not allowed, nor are lawyers allowed to represent either party. The hearing is usually very informal, with each party presenting his or her side of the case. The judge makes his or her decision based on the facts.

Small-claims courts provide a quick and inexpensive way to resolve minor disputes involving money damages.

Summary

Before a court can act, it must have jurisdiction. Personally serving a defendant grants a court *in personam* jurisdiction over that individual. Occasionally a defendant cannot be located, and service must be accomplished in some other way. This grants a court *in rem* jurisdiction but does not allow a judgment to be rendered against an individual for money damages.

Within the United States, there are 52 separate court systems: one for each of the fifty states, for the District of Columbia, and for the federal government. The United States Constitution provides for the Supreme Court and such other federal courts as Congress shall designate. Congress has created a federal system with at least one federal district court in each state and U.S. courts of appeal to handle their appeals. To fall under the jurisdiction of the federal courts, a case must involve either a federal question or diversity of citizenship involving $50,000 or more in controversy.

Actions are instituted by filing a complaint and having a summons issued by the court. Once these are served on the defendant, the defendant must file an answer within a specific period of time or have a default judgment rendered against him or her. The defendant may also bring a counterclaim against the plaintiff, which, in turn, requires a reply. During the course of the lawsuit, either party may bring appropriate motions.

Prior to trial, discovery occurs by either oral depositions or written interrogatories. The plaintiff must carry the burden of proof at the time of trial. The plaintiff always introduces evidence first. Once both parties have presented all the evidence, the case is submitted to the jury for a verdict or to the judge if there is no jury. The jury or judge is the trier of fact. The losing party may appeal the decision. The reviewing court usually will not reverse the trial court unless there has been an error of law in the trial process.

Two methods are used to select state judges: election or merit. Federal judges are nominated by the president and are confirmed by the Senate. The conduct of a state judge is monitored by the population and through peer review. If any judge fails to perform as mandated, she or he may be removed from office.

Key Terms

adversary system (63)
affirmative defense (64)
answer (64)
appellate jurisdiction (56)
challenge for cause (69)
complaint (63)
concurrent jurisdiction (59)
counterclaim (64)
default judgment (64)
depositions (68)
discovery (67)
diversity of citizenship (59)
exclusive jurisdiction (59)
federal question (59)
full faith and credit clause (52)

general jurisdiction (55)
in personam jurisdiction (52)
in rem jurisdiction (54)
International Court of Justice (74)
interrogatories (68)
jurisdiction (52)
limited jurisdiction (55)
long-arm statute (52)
motion to dismiss (64)
original jurisdiction (55)
peremptory challenge (69)
plead (55)
pleading (63)
pretrial hearing (68)
process (63)

quasi in rem jurisdiction (54)
request for physical or mental examination (68)
request to produce (68)
subject-matter jurisdiction (54)
summary judgment (68)
summons (63)
venue (54)
voir dire (69)
writ of *certiorari* (59)
writ of *mandamus* (61)

Questions and Case Problems

1. The American court system has two types of courts—courts with original jurisdiction and those with appellate jurisdiction. What is the difference between the two court systems?

2. Discuss the difference between pleadings and process.

3. Discuss the method of appellate review that the Supreme Court exercises.

4. Discuss judicial review.

5. In state judicial systems, judges serve specific terms in office, while federal judges serve for a term of good behavior. Should both systems be the same? Which system is better on constitutional and public policy grounds?

6. Before the two parties go to trial, pleadings must be exchanged and discovery must take place. Until recently, pleadings were very formal, and trials frequently turned on elements of surprise. Often the plaintiff would not know the nature of the defendant's case or who the witnesses would be. Should there be an exchange of information, gathered through the discovery process, prior to trial to eliminate surprises during the trial from either side? Please explain your answer.

7. Marvin, a resident of Alabama, was walking near a busy street in Birmingham when a large crate fell off a passing truck and hit him. Marvin suffered from numerous injuries that resulted in large medical expenses, a great deal of pain and suffering, and he was off work for six months. He wants to sue the trucking firm for $300,000. The firm's headquarters are in Mississippi, although the company does business in Alabama. Where should Marvin bring his lawsuit—in an Alabama state court, a Mississippi state court, or a federal district court located in Alabama or Mississippi?

8. Colleen Cote, who lived in Wisconsin, brought a lawsuit in the federal district court located in Wisconsin. She sued Peter Wadel, a lawyer in Michigan, for legal malpractice in representing her in a case she had in Michigan. Wadel claimed that the federal court in Wisconsin did not have jurisdiction over him. Wadel did not have an office in Wisconsin. At this point, Cote could not file a lawsuit in the federal district court in Michigan because the statute of limitations had run out, and the Wisconsin court refused to transfer the case to Michigan. Should the case be dismissed? Please explain your answer. [Cote v. Wadel, 796 F.2d 981 (7th Cir. 1986)]

9. Rudzewicz, an experienced and sophisticated businessperson, signed a twenty-year franchise contract in 1979 with Burger King to operate a restaurant in Michigan. He obligated himself to pay $1 million over the twenty-year period. At first business was steady, but after the recession hit, patronage declined. Rudzewicz fell behind in his payments. After extended negotiations, Burger King filed a lawsuit in 1981. Burger King is a Florida corporation with principal offices in Miami. The franchise contract provided that the franchise relationship was established in Miami and governed by Florida law. All fees and notices were to be sent to the Miami headquarters. Rudzewicz claimed that he was a Michigan resident, that he had not been to Florida, and that the claim did not arise in Florida, thus the district court lacked personal jurisdiction over him. Should the case be dismissed in Florida? Please explain your answer. [Burger King Corp. v. Rudzewicz, 471 U.S. 462, 105 S.Ct. 2174, 85 L.Ed. 528 (1985)]

Chapter 4 **Alternative Dispute Resolution Procedures**

All disputes (if unhappily any should arise) shall be decided by three impartial and intelligent men, known for their probity and good understanding, two to be chosen by the disputants, each having the choice of one, and the third by those two, which three men thus chosen shall, unfettered by law or legal constructions, declare their sense of the testator's intention, and such decision is, to all intents and purposes, to be binding on the parties as if it had been given in the Supreme Court of the United States.

George Washington's last will and testament

OUTLINE

Introduction

Many lawsuits are unwieldy in terms of money and time, for both the litigants and the taxpayers. Money is expended by the litigants on attorneys' fees, court fees, and the development of evidence. The taxpayers, however, pay most of the costs since the litigants' fees do not cover the real cost of running the judicial system. The time from the filing of a lawsuit to the final disposition of the case is always uncertain and usually is measured in years. As a result, the memories of the witnesses fade and evidence may be destroyed or lost. As long as the litigation is in progress, the litigants will often harbor very negative feelings about both the opposition and the judicial system. Litigation is a stressful ordeal.

Many persons have arrived at the conclusion that less expensive and more expeditious methods must be found to settle disputes. Various advocates of **alternative dispute resolution** (ADR) **procedures** have different interests, but all have the same basic goal: a speedy and just determination of the dispute at a reasonable cost to both parties.

Advocates of Alternative Dispute Resolution Procedures

Who in society is advocating the use of alternative dispute resolution procedures and why?

Today the judiciary is one of the strong advocates of alternative dispute resolution procedures. Former Chief Justice of the United States Warren E. Burger advocates the development of "mechanisms that can produce an acceptable result in the shortest possible time, with the least possible expense and with a minimum of stress on the participants." He has spoken continuously on the topic.

The judiciary recognizes that the average citizen does not have his or her rights protected when he or she must spend thousands of dollars and several years in litigation to reach a decision, especially for such routine cases as those following an automobile accident. More often than not, the case is settled literally in front of the courtroom door after considerable expense, frustration, and years in the judicial system.

The business sector is another strong proponent of alternative dispute resolution procedures.

Businesspersons need expeditious justice at a reasonable cost, but they also need to be able to maintain a business relationship with the opponent while resolving a particular dispute. Most disputes between businesses involve a contractual problem. People in business accept the fact that disputes are inevitable. Even when the written contract was carefully drawn, problems will arise over the interpretation of a clause or over a disputed set of facts. Delays in manufacturing, disputes over the quality of merchandise, problems with the performance of the contract, and other such misunderstandings are bound to arise.

Once a dispute occurs, most businesspersons like to resolve the dispute quickly, privately, inexpensively, and informally. Maintaining a business relationship while involved in litigation is very difficult, if not impossible. To preserve goodwill, most businesspersons are in favor of alternative dispute resolution procedures that will be fair, inexpensive, and quick, but that will also arrive at a just result.

The public has a great interest in reducing the caseload handled by the judiciary. Most cases in court are routine in nature and rarely involve great legal issues. Like businesspersons, the public wants fair, inexpensive, and quick procedures to settle routine legal problems.

Comparisons Between Alternative Dispute Resolution Procedures and the Judicial System

The Institute for Civil Justice, established within the Rand Corporation, has developed data from its studies of the judicial system. The Institute for Civil Justice has performed one of the few research projects that critically examines the problems within the court system. With this data a comparison can be made between the judicial system and ADR procedures. Six factors that can be reviewed are money, time, privacy, formality, selection of the decision maker, and the forum.

Financial Costs

The first comparison is the cost in terms of money. Government expenditures vary widely in running the judicial system. The cost of a jury trial including judge, jury members, court reporter, bailiff, clerk, and secretary averages about $8,300 in California. In Los Angeles County the cost is high: $10,500 for a jury trial. Perhaps because of these costs, only about 1 percent of the civil lawsuits filed in all of California end up in a jury trial. In Florida the cost is much less, around $3,000 for a jury trial. At a daily cost of $2,700 to use a federal court, the cost of the average federal trial is more than $10,800.

What did the plaintiff win? The plaintiff did not obtain a money judgment in 43 percent of the cases when the defendant disputed liability. The average award over the twenty-year period was $84,000. However, the Rand study discovered that one-fourth of the jury awards were less than $8,000, and in one-half of the cases, the awards were less than $21,000. Only in 19 percent of the cases did the plaintiff equal or exceed the $84,000 average. Ten percent of the awards were over $181,000 and only 1 percent exceeded $1,000,000. The plaintiffs in the automobile accident cases received the smallest awards; over 50 percent were under $15,000. Thus, most of the money went to only a few plaintiffs.

Another way of stating these facts is that in one-fourth of the cases decided, the cost to the public of the trial was more than the amount recovered by the plaintiff. Not all types of lawsuits should be judged strictly by the cost, but in terms of the sheer numbers of cases filed on routine matters (such as automobile accident cases), there should be and can be a better method of resolving the dispute between the two parties. The amount in controversy in routine cases does not justify the public expense of the trial.

The costs of alternative dispute resolution procedures also have a wide range, but all are on the lower end of the cost scale. The American Arbitration Association estimates the average cost of a private arbitration to be as low as $275. If the arbitration is private, the cost is paid by the disputing parties, not the taxpayers. Over 50,000 cases are arbitrated each year, and the number is increasing.

Time Costs

The second comparison is the cost factor measured in time. Extremes exist in the processing time of a case, which is measured from the date a lawsuit is filed to the date of its final disposition.

In Arizona, this time period is less than twelve months, but in Connecticut the courts were recently backlogged beyond a five-year period, with over 60,000 tort cases alone waiting for trial. Half of these cases were pending before the courts in just four cities.

In Los Angeles County a 41-month delay exists from the time of filing to the time of final disposition. This time lag exists even though judicial arbitration is required. In Los Angeles County only 10 percent of the cases filed ever go to trial. Forty percent of the cases were disposed of by the court, and 50 percent were either settled or dropped by the litigants.

Reasons for Time Lag Why is the time lag so long in a lawsuit? During a lawsuit a continuing debate takes place between the attorney representing the plaintiff and the attorney representing the defendant. For example, in a personal injury case, the plaintiff's attorney argues that he or she has little reason to encourage delay. An injured plaintiff must receive and pay for medical care and is usually off work while recovering. A plaintiff's attorney receives compensation from the amount recovered on behalf of the client. It is in his or her best interest to dispose of the case quickly. But a practice has developed in which, once the plaintiff's medical condition has stabilized and the attorneys have finished the discovery stage, the plaintiff's attorney will wait and see what the defense attorney will do.

Unless the judge forces the case to move along, it will stall at this stage until the plaintiff's attorney or the court sets the trial date. Even if the trial date is set early in the case, it will not have preference, because of all the other lawsuits (including criminal proceedings) ahead of it that must be tried. Most courts have a rule that a lawsuit must go to trial within a specific time period. As cases pile up, many are in danger of going beyond that time period; thus those cases have a preference on the trial calendar.

Both sides have a tendency to polarize their positions as the case is being processed through the court system. As the case proceeds, the attorneys for the plaintiff and the defendant will evaluate the evidence. Quite often one attorney will make an offer to settle the case. The other attorney will consider the settlement offer and make a recommendation to the client. The party must weigh the settlement offer (that is, the given amount of money paid now) against the potential of winning or losing more in a trial at a later time.

Typically the first offer is rejected and a counteroffer is made. In between each offer there is usually a waiting period. Only when faced with the decision of actually getting ready for trial is a settlement seriously pursued, and even then attorneys usually wait to see if the judge will force early case preparation. A judge can force early case preparation by controlling the court calendar, refusing to allow continuances of the case, limiting discovery to a reasonable level, and promoting pretrial settlement conferences.

ADR Time Periods   Statistics on the time it takes for alternative dispute resolution procedures are hard to find because of the wide range of different procedures that may be used. The time spent in the court system, however, may be contrasted with the time spent in arbitration, which is a specific type of ADR procedure. In private arbitration, the average commercial case takes 145 days from the time of the filing until the arbitrator makes the decision.

California has two types of judicially mandated arbitration: volunteer and court-ordered. Those litigants who volunteer to have their lawsuit arbitrated have a decision within seven months. Those litigants who are ordered by the court to have their case arbitrated wait 22 months for a decision. Thus in California either type of arbitration is faster than the judicial system.

Privacy Factor

A third comparison is the privacy factor. Civil court procedures are of public record. Anyone can observe many of the pretrial procedures and all of the trial. As a result, information that people or businesses would prefer to keep private is available for anyone to read. The disclosure factor becomes critical when a business must reveal trade secrets, budget planning, marketing strategies, or other sensitive information in court.

Most alternative dispute resolution procedures are private and not open to the public. Nonjudicial procedures allow for confidentiality of most information, whereas judicial proceedings, by law, are rarely closed to the public.

Formality

A fourth comparison is the difference in formality. A judicial proceeding is very formal in nature. The judge wears a black robe, and his or her entry into the courtroom is announced in a formal manner by the bailiff. Only attorneys and the litigants are allowed beyond the railing that separates the public area from the formal courtroom area. Courtroom decorum has developed through the centuries and is strictly adhered to by judges. During the trial itself, court rules and the rules of evidence are closely followed. Although the rules have a definite purpose, the application often seems meaningless and confusing to the litigants.

Alternative dispute resolution procedures are informal in their setting. This allows the parties to be more relaxed, reducing stress from the level the parties would feel in a courtroom. Do not confuse an informal setting with a sloppy or inadequate presentation of material—as in a courtroom, the better prepared the parties are in presenting their cases, the better the chance of resolving the dispute in a manner acceptable to both sides.

Selection of the Decision Maker

A fifth comparison is the selection of the decision maker. In the judicial system the parties have very little control as to which judge is selected for their case. Most alternative dispute resolution procedures allow the participants to play a role in deciding who will be the decision maker. When people have a voice in choosing the decision maker, they usually are more ready to accept the final decision.

Choice of Forum

A sixth comparison is the choice of the forum. The parties in a lawsuit have little control over where the case will be heard. The judicial system has limited the ability of the parties to "forum shop."

Arbitration will allow the disputing parties the opportunity to select a common forum in advance. This selection opportunity is particularly important when there are business arrangements between the parties in more than one state. Because the disputing parties are not subject to a court system, they can decide the best place to hold the arbitration hearing. The American Arbitration Association operates in all states and in foreign countries. As a result, the disputing parties are not restricted by the jurisdictional limits they would encounter in a particular court system.

Alternative Dispute Resolution Procedures

Before examining various alternative dispute resolution procedures, negotiations need to be studied. Negotiations are an integral part of the dispute resolution process, for both alternative dispute resolution procedures and judicial procedures.

Negotiation

Negotiation is the process in which two or more persons meet to discuss their differences and attempt to arrive at a settlement acceptable to both. Negotiation is a technique used to resolve a dispute, not win an argument. Although reasonableness cannot be ensured by using negotiation, people can use it to engage in joint problem solving through cooperative behavior and to arrive at a mutually acceptable agreement.

All parties should win in a successful negotiation. If only one party gains and the other loses completely, the loser has no vested interest in making sure that the agreement will work. In fact, it is human nature to try to sabotage a forced agreement. Negotiation is at the same time both a skill that can be learned and an art form to be practiced.

Negotiation is an integral part of all alternative dispute resolution procedures. It is not, by itself, an alternative dispute resolution procedure in any formal sense. No alternative dispute resolution procedure, however, could exist without negotiation. In fact, the act of filing a lawsuit may in itself be a negotiating technique. Negotiation is by far the best dispute resolution technique, because the parties arrive at a solution that they design themselves.

Negotiation Skills As important a skill as negotiation is, many persons are inexperienced at it.

People generally have poorly developed negotiating skills. Bargaining or negotiating is rarely taught at primary or secondary schools and is not often found at the college or university level. In addition, the business level at which consumers purchase merchandise or services is not geared to constant negotiation. For example, the price of clothing at a department store is not subject to negotiation. The same is true of other items, such as food in a grocery store or restaurant, or a night's stay in a motel room.

Negotiating skills are necessary in the business world. For example, a customer purchases merchandise, becomes dissatisfied with it, and desires to return it. The customer would like a full cash refund. The businessperson must decide whether to accept the merchandise back and, if the merchandise is returnable, whether credit toward the purchase of additional products from the store or a full refund will be offered. Both parties want different results, but will normally settle for something less than what they initially thought would be appropriate.

When Negotiation Occurs Negotiation may occur at any stage of a dispute. This time period ranges from the moment the customer purchases the merchandise to the time immediately before the judge renders a decision if a lawsuit has resulted. In fact, sometimes negotiation of a settlement will occur even after a case has been tried and the judge has entered a judgment.

Most cases filed in any court system are settled through negotiation by the attorneys. Rarely do lawsuits end in a full trial where the judge or jury makes the decision. In other words, comparatively few cases are fully litigated. Good-faith negotiation is a necessity—without it, the judicial system would collapse if even one-fifth of the lawsuits filed ever went to trial.

Conciliation

Conciliation occurs whenever a third party successfully brings together the conflicting parties. A conciliator does not take an active part in the negotiations but rather attempts to limit all parties' passions and negative rhetoric. Conciliation is one method for obtaining a negotiated settlement from the parties.

Code of Ethics for Arbitrators

Arbitrators operate under a code of ethics. The persons who act as arbitrators undertake a serious responsibility to the public as well as to the parties involved. If the arbitrators do not discharge their duties in good faith and in a diligent manner, the whole system becomes suspect and the public could lose faith in arbitration. There are seven canons in the code of ethics developed by the American Arbitration Association.

First, the arbitrator will uphold the integrity and fairness of the arbitration process. Second, if the arbitrator has an interest or relationship that is likely to affect his or her impartiality or that

might create an appearance of partiality or bias, it must be disclosed. Third, an arbitrator, in communicating with the parties, should avoid impropriety or the appearance of it. Fourth, the arbitrator should conduct the proceedings fairly and diligently. Fifth, the arbitrator should make decisions in a just, independent, and deliberate manner. Sixth, the arbitrator should be faithful to the relationship of trust and confidentiality inherent in that office. Finally, in a case where there is a board of arbitrators, each party may select an arbitrator. That arbitrator must ensure that he or she follows all the ethical considerations in this type of situation.

Conciliation has not been used as extensively in this country as it has in other cultures. It is, however, widely used in labor disputes and is part of the federal labor law. Also, many states have statutory provisions relating to conciliation in divorce actions. When a divorce is filed, one of the parties may request a conciliation hearing, which is similar to marriage counseling.

Judges use conciliation in many other types of litigated cases besides divorce. For example, when a judge holds a pretrial conference and attempts to bring the two parties together in a negotiated settlement, he or she is using conciliation.

The Better Business Bureau uses conciliation techniques when it handles complaints between businesses and customers. It attempts to bring the two parties together to reach a settlement of their differences.

Newspaper and radio and television stations may have a team devoted to resolving disputes involving its readers or listeners. Often a reader or listener will contact the media, informing them of the problem. A person from the media will then contact the business with whom the client has a dispute. Because the media have extensive resources and are very visible, reporters can often reach the person who has the power to resolve the dispute. Most businesses want to avoid bad publicity and they are willing to participate when approached in this way.

Mediation

The terms *mediation* and *conciliation* are used interchangably. A conciliator brings the parties together and assists them with their discussion. It is a voluntary process.

The essence of mediation is compromise. In **mediation,** an impartial third person first persuades the parties to discuss their issues. The mediation process is completely voluntary.

If the parties cannot agree on the issues, the mediator will assist in clarifying them. The mediator will also make suggestions as to possible settlement parameters. Having no formal position, the mediator can be discharged at any time by either party. The mediator does not have the power to make a decision or to force the parties to accept any suggestions or recommendations. Only when the parties come to a final settlement of their differences is mediation successful.

The American Arbitration Association has developed mediation rules. Early mediation intervention allows for a quick solution to the problem before the positions taken by the parties become polarized. Mediation is a first step that allows the parties to fall back to arbitration or even a lawsuit if they cannot work out their differences. Often a contract requires that money be deposited to cover the expenses of arbitration or litigation, in case a dispute should reach that stage. Mediation does not require the setting aside of these funds; thus the parties have another incentive to attempt to resolve their differences using this process.

Arbitration

Arbitration is a procedure where the parties to a dispute submit it to an impartial third person called an **arbitrator.** An arbitrator is a person who frequently specializes in an area, such as real estate or labor, and arbitrates disputes in that area. This person is selected by the parties to make a decision based upon evidence they both submit. The decision of the arbitrator usually is binding.

American Arbitration Association   The **American Arbitration Association** (AAA) was founded in 1926 as a private, nonprofit organization. The AAA was an outgrowth of two earlier arbitration associations. Within both associations were two groups that held different philosophies concerning arbitration. One group was comprised of business leaders and trade association executives. They viewed arbitration as a businessperson's court, much like the trade and guild courts of the Middle Ages. The other group was comprised of attorneys who, although they believed in arbitration, also be-

lieved in the fundamental concepts of due process and fairness.

As a result, to satisfy these two groups, the AAA adopted as its purpose "to foster the study of arbitration in all of its aspects, to perfect its techniques under arbitration law, and to advance generally the science of arbitration for the prompt and economical settlement of disputes."

Besides the administration of arbitration, the AAA's other functions are education, promotion, and research into the uses of arbitration for settling all types of disputes. Its slogan is "Speed, Economy, and Justice," and AAA's performance has repeatedly shown that justice does result when there is speed and economy.

Federal Legislation   Congress passed the **Federal Arbitration Act** in 1925 and by doing so declared a federal policy favoring arbitration. The act withdraws from states the power to require a judicial forum for the resolution of disagreements if the parties have agreed by contract to solve the problem by arbitration. In the following case the Supreme Court upholds the intent of Congress to have parties abide by their contract when it requires the arbitration of any subsequent disputes.

BACKGROUND AND FACTS   *McMahon and others were customers of Shearson/American Express, Inc. The customer agreements provided for arbitration of any controversy relating to their accounts. The customers filed suit in federal district court for violations of the Securities Exchange Act of 1934 and the Racketeer Influenced and Corrupt Organizations Act (RICO). Shearson/American Express, Inc., moved to have the case arbitrated. The trial court granted the motion to have the alleged Securities Exchange Act violations arbitrated but denied the motion as to the RICO violations. The court of appeals upheld the trial court as to the RICO but reversed as to the Exchange Act claims. Shearson/American Express, Inc., appealed to the Supreme Court.*

Case 4.1 ✦
SHEARSON/AMERICAN EXPRESS, INC. v. McMAHON

Supreme Court of the United States, 1987.
482 U.S. 220, 107 S.Ct. 2332, 96 L.Ed.2d 185.

Justice O'CONNOR delivered the opinion of the Court.

This case presents two questions regarding the enforceability of predispute arbitration agreements between brokerage firms and their customers. The first is whether a claim brought under § 10(b) of the Securities Exchange Act of 1934 (Exchange Act) must be sent to arbitration in accordance with the terms of an arbitration agreement. The second is whether a claim brought under the Racketeer Influenced and Corrupt Organizations Act (RICO) must be arbitrated in accordance with the terms of such an agreement.

*   *   *   *

The Federal Arbitration Act provides the starting point for answering the questions raised in this case. *   *   * The Arbitration Act *   *   * provid[es] that arbitration agreements "shall be valid, irrevocable, and enforceable, save upon such grounds as exist at law or in equity for the revocation of any contract." The Act also provid[es] that a court must stay [stop or delay] its proceedings if it is satisfied that an issue before it is arbitrable under the agreement, and it authorizes a federal district court to issue an order compelling arbitration if there has been a "failure, neglect, or refusal" to comply with the arbitration agreement.

The Arbitration Act thus establishes a "federal policy favoring arbitration."
*   *   *

The Arbitration Act *   *   * mandates enforcement of agreements to arbitrate statutory claims. Like any statutory directive, the Arbitration Act's mandate may be overridden by a contrary congressional command. The burden is on the party opposing arbitration, however, to show that Congress intended to preclude a waiver of judicial remedies for the statutory rights at issue. *   *   *
*   *   *   *

*   *   * Since the 1975 amendments to the Exchange Act, *   *   * the [Securities and Exchange] Commission (SEC) has had expansive power to ensure the adequacy of the arbitration procedures employed by the SROs [self-regulatory organizations]. No proposed rule change may take effect unless the SEC finds that the proposed rule is consistent with the requirements of the Exchange Act, and the Commission has the power, on its own initiative, to "abrogate, add to, and delete from" any SRO rule if it finds such changes necessary or appropriate to further the objectives of the Act. In short, the Commission has broad authority to oversee and to regulate the rules adopted by the SROs relating to customer disputes, including the power to mandate the adoption of any rules it deems necessary to ensure that arbitration procedures adequately protect statutory rights.

In the exercise of its regulatory authority, the SEC has specifically approved the arbitration procedures of the New York Stock Exchange, the American Stock Exchange, and the National Association of Securities Dealers, the organizations mentioned in the arbitration agreement at issue in this case. We conclude that where, as in this case, the prescribed procedures are subject to the Commission's authority, an arbitration agreement does not effect a waiver of the protections of the Act. *   *   *
*   *   *   *

*   *   * Accordingly, we hold the McMahons' agreements to arbitrate Exchange Act claims "enforce[able] . . . in accord with the explicit provisions of the Arbitration Act." *   *   *

Unlike the Exchange Act, there is nothing in the text of the RICO statute that even arguably evinces congressional intent to exclude civil RICO claims from the dictates of the Arbitration Act. This silence in the text is matched by silence in the statute's legislative history. *   *   *

Because RICO's text and legislative history fail to reveal any intent to override the provisions of the Arbitration Act, the McMahons must argue that there is an irreconcilable conflict between arbitration and RICO's underlying purposes. Our decision in *Mitsubishi Motors Corp. v. Soler Chrysler-Plymouth, Inc.*, however, already has addressed many of the grounds given by the McMahons to support this claim. In *Mitsubishi*, we held that nothing in the nature of the federal antitrust laws prohibits parties from agreeing to arbitrate antitrust claims arising out of international commercial transactions. Although the holding in *Mitsubishi* was limited to the international context, much of its reasoning is equally applicable here. Thus, for example, the McMahons have argued that RICO claims are too complex to be subject to arbitration. We determined in *Mitsubishi*, however, that "potential complexity should not suffice to ward off arbitration." Antitrust matters are every bit as complex as RICO claims, but we found that the "adaptability and access to expertise" characteristic of arbitration rebutted the view "that an arbitral tribunal could not properly handle an antitrust matter."
*   *   *   *

The legislative history *   *   * reveals the same emphasis on the remedial role of the treble-damages provision. In introducing the treble-damages provision to the

House Judiciary Committee, Representative Steiger stressed that "those who have been wronged by organized crime should at least be given access to a legal remedy." The policing function * * *, although important, was a secondary concern.

* * *

* * * *

In sum, we find no basis for concluding that Congress intended to prevent enforcement of agreements to arbitrate RICO claims. The McMahons may effectively vindicate their RICO claim in an arbitral forum, and therefore there is no inherent conflict between arbitration and the purposes underlying [RICO]. Moreover, nothing in RICO's text or legislative history otherwise demonstrates congressional intent to make an exception to the Arbitration Act for RICO claims. Accordingly, the McMahons, "having made the bargain to arbitrate," will be held to their bargain. Their RICO claim is arbitrable under the terms of the Arbitration Act.

The federal law establishes a policy favoring arbitration. This policy is not reduced when a person raises a claim founded upon statutory rights. The Supreme Court held that when parties have an agreement to arbitrate, it includes statutory rights under the securities laws and for RICO violations. An arbitrator has the authority to grant punitive damages in the amount of three times the original damages for violations of RICO.

DECISION AND REMEDY

State Legislation   The **Uniform Arbitration Act** was drafted by the National Conference of Commissioners on Uniform State Laws in 1955. The American Bar Association has approved it. The act is designed to make legislation on arbitration more uniform throughout the country. Covering standards of procedure and rules to be used in the arbitration process, the act also provides for judicial enforcement of the agreements to arbitrate.

The stated purpose of the act is to "validate voluntary, written arbitration agreements, make the arbitration process effective, provide necessary safeguards, and provide an efficient procedure when judicial assistance is necessary." This act has been adopted in 34 states and the District of Columbia (see Exhibit 4–1). The states that have not yet adopted the act normally follow many of the procedures suggested by it.

Contractual Arbitration   Arbitration occurs in one of two settings: contractual or judicial. The **contractual agreement to arbitrate** may be reached before or after the dispute arises. The parties may include a future dispute arbitration clause in their initial contract, ensuring that they will submit any future disputes to arbitration. If a dispute arises, the party making the complaint serves the Demand for Arbitration notice upon the opposing party. See Exhibit 4–2.

Exhibit 4–1 **Chart of States that Have Adopted the Uniform Arbitration Act**

Alaska	Missouri
Arizona	Montana
Arkansas	Nebraska
Colorado	Nevada
Delaware	New Mexico
District of Columbia	North Carolina
Florida	North Dakota
Idaho	Oklahoma
Illinois	Pennsylvania
Indiana	South Carolina
Iowa	South Dakota
Kansas	Tennessee
Kentucky	Texas
Maine	Utah
Maryland	Vermont
Massachusetts	Virginia
Michigan	Wyoming
Minnesota	

If the parties fail to include an arbitration clause in the contract, however, when a dispute arises they may still mutually agree to submit the problem to arbitration. This agreement is called a Submission to Arbitration and is signed by both parties. See Exhibit 4–3.

Exhibit 4–2 Sample Demand for Arbitration

COMMERCIAL ARBITRATION RULES

DEMAND FOR ARBITRATION

DATE: _____

To: (Name) _____
                         (of party upon whom the demand is made)

(Address) _____

(City and State) _____ (ZIP Code) _____

(Telephone) _____

Named claimant, a party to an arbitration agreement contained in a written contract,

dated _____, providing for arbitration, hereby

demands arbitration thereunder.

(Attach arbitration clause or quote hereunder.)

NATURE OF DISPUTE:

CLAIM OR RELIEF SOUGHT: (amount, if any)

TYPE OF BUSINESS:

Claimant _____ Respondent _____

HEARING LOCALE REQUESTED: _____
                                          (City and State)

You are hereby notified that copies of our arbitration agreement and of this demand are being filed with the American Arbitration Association at its _____ regional office, with the request that it commence the administration of the arbitration. Under Section 7 of the Commercial Arbitration Rules, you may file an answering statement within seven days after notice from the administrator.

Signed _____ Title _____
                   (may be signed by attorney)

Name of Claimant _____

Home or Business Address of Claimant _____

City and State _____ ZIP Code _____

Telephone _____

Name of Attorney _____

Attorney's Address _____

City and State _____ ZIP Code _____

Telephone _____

To institute proceedings, please send three copies of this demand and the administrative fee, as provided in Section 48 of the rules, to the AAA. Send the original demand to the respondent.

Form C2–AAA–7/87

Note Reprinted with permission of the American Arbitration Association.

Exhibit 4–3 Sample Submission to Arbitration

American Arbitration Association

SUBMISSION TO ARBITRATION

Date:

The named Parties hereby submit the following dispute to arbitration under the COMMERCIAL ARBITRATION RULES of the American Arbitration Association:

Amount of money involved:

Place of Hearing:

We agree that we will abide by and perform any Award rendered hereunder and that a judgment may be entered upon the Award.

Name of Party

Telephone

Address

Signed by

Name of Party

Telephone

Address

Signed by

PLEASE FILE TWO COPIES
Consult counsel about valid execution

Note: Reprinted with permission of the American Arbitration Association.

The Agreement to Arbitrate Two requirements exist for voluntary arbitration: First, the agreement must be entered voluntarily; and second, it must be in writing to be enforceable in a court. Initially this last requirement may seem like a contradiction, but even though there is a written agreement to arbitrate, one of the parties may refuse to participate in the arbitration proceedings or may file a lawsuit, as in the *Shearson* case. The other party may request the court to order the first party to arbitrate. An oral agreement to arbitrate will not suffice. The reason that the agreement is required to be in writing is that the parties are giving up a federal constitutionally guaranteed right. The Seventh Amendment preserves the right to a trial by jury for civil cases at common law exceeding $20.

The modern view is that arbitration is binding upon the parties once they have agreed to it. In other words, a legal action cannot be brought if the parties have agreed to submit a controversy to arbitration. The arbitration procedures must be utilized to the fullest extent prior to filing a court action. The only exception would be when both parties refuse to arbitrate after initially agreeing to it.

If one party refuses to arbitrate, the other party may file a lawsuit and seek a court order to compel arbitration. The only defense is that there was no written agreement to arbitrate. The court will order arbitration and stay any other proceedings if it finds there was an agreement to arbitrate. An arbitration agreement is a contractual obligation into which the parties have voluntarily entered. The terms will be enforced as long as they are not illegal or contrary to public policy. Although the court may now be ordering both parties to arbitrate, the initial contract clause to submit disputes to arbitration was agreed to voluntarily.

The following case illustrates the court's attitude toward arbitration in a domestic relations case. Although the court allowed the arbitrator's award to stand, it made sure that the state's interest in this matter was protected.

✈ **Case 4.2**
FAHERTY v. FAHERTY
Supreme Court of New Jersey,
1984.
97 N.J. 99, 477 A.2d 1257.

BACKGROUND AND FACTS *Susan and Roger Faherty were divorced. Prior to their divorce, both parties, represented by attorneys, entered into a property settlement agreement. The agreement, which mandated that any financial dispute arising out of it must be arbitrated before any court action could be taken, was incorporated into the final divorce decree. The rules of the American Arbitration Association were to be used in any such arbitration and the arbitrator's decision would be binding on the parties.*

Roger fell behind in alimony and child support payments. Susan went to court to seek enforcement of the agreement and payment of what he owed. Roger made a motion to have the court compel arbitration, and the court issued such an order. The arbitration took seven months. The arbitrator's award fixed alimony arrearages at $37,648 and child support arrearages at $12,284. The arbitrator made no written findings of fact. Susan moved the court to confirm the award. Roger made a cross-motion and, although he originally petitioned the court to compel arbitration, now challenged the validity of the arbitration clause in alimony and child support matters. He contended that as a matter of public policy, these matters should not be permitted to be settled outside the courts.

J. GARIBALDI
*   *   *   *

[Court's discussion on arbitrating disputes over alimony]
     *   *   * Since the parties may settle spousal support rights and obligations by contract there is no policy reason to prohibit their submitting disputes arising out of such contracts to binding arbitration. *   *   * Rather than frowning on arbitration of alimony disputes, public policy supports it. We recognize that in many

cases arbitration of matrimonial disputes may offer an effective alternative method of dispute resolution. As commentators have noted, the advantages of arbitration of domestic disputes include reduced court congestion, the opportunity for resolution of sensitive matters in a private and informal forum, reduction of the trauma and anxiety of marital litigation, minimization of the intense polarization of parties that often occurs, and the ability to choose the arbitrator. In this sensitive and intensely private area of domestic disputes, arbitration expressly contracted for by the spouses is highly desirable. We accordingly hold today that under the laws of New Jersey, parties may bind themselves in separation agreements to arbitrate disputes over alimony. *   *   *
*   *   *   *

[Court's discussion on arbitrating disputes over child support]

*   *   * [T]here has been a growing tendency to recognize arbitration in child support clauses. We do not agree with those who fear that by allowing parents to agree to arbitrate child support, we are interfering with the judicial protection of the best interests of the child. We see no valid reason why the arbitration process should not be available in the area of child support; the advantages of arbitration in domestic disputes outweigh any disadvantages.

Nevertheless, we recognize that the courts have a nondelegable, special supervisory function in the area of child support that may be exercised upon review of an arbitrator's award. We therefore hold that whenever the validity of an arbitration award affecting child support is questioned on the grounds that it does not provide adequate protection for the child, the trial court should conduct a special review of the award. This review should consist of a two-step analysis. First, as with all arbitration awards, the courts should review child support awards[.] *   *   * Second, the courts should conduct a *de novo* review unless it is clear on the face of the award that the award could not adversely affect the substantial best interests of the child.

*   *   * Thus, only an arbitrator's award that either reduced child support or refused a request for increased support could be subject to court review beyond the review provided by statute, because only such an award could adversely affect the interests of the child. *   *   *
*   *   *   *

*   *   * [W]e note that the arbitrator made no written findings of fact. The AAA [American Arbitration Association] rules do not require such findings, but because alimony and child support are always subject to modification for changed circumstances, we suggest, but do not mandate, that the arbitrator in all future domestic dispute arbitrations make reasonably detailed findings of fact upon which she or he bases the arbitration award. Such findings will aid not only the court's review of the award but also will aid later arbitrators in determining requests for modification. *   *   *

DECISION AND REMEDY

The court approved the arbitrator's award as having satisfied the statutory and public policy requirements. The state's interest in the welfare of the children was protected. Roger had to pay Susan the amounts awarded by the arbitrator.

COMMENT

Although the matters of child custody and visitation rights were not before the court, it noted that the development of a fair and workable mediation or arbitration process to resolve these issues would be more beneficial for children than the present system of courtroom confrontation. The court went on to state that the policy reasons for its holding with respect to child support may be equally applicable in child custody and visitation rights in any future cases.

Judicial Arbitration   **Judicial arbitration** is compulsory (court-mandated) arbitration. In some courts, after the parties have started a lawsuit they can volunteer to have their case arbitrated and the judge will issue an order to that effect. Even if the parties do not volunteer, they may be ordered by the judge to submit their case to arbitration. In some jurisdictions, cases under a certain amount, such as $50,000, must be arbitrated. The types of civil disputes required to be submitted to arbitration are those in which money damages are sought.

The actual hearing is the same as if the arbitration were a contractual one. No judge or jury is involved, and the arbitrator does not submit a written decision that sets out the reasons for the decision. Instead, only an award is issued, which is similar to a judgment. In the hearing, the parties may use depositions, interrogatories, and certified documents to save the cost of a person testifying at the hearing. Because the time spent to resolve the case is shorter than if the case went to court, the attorneys' fees are usually less.

Differences   Nine differences exist between a contractual arbitration and a judicial arbitration. First, under the contract arrangement the proceedings are private, but they are public for a judicial arbitration. Second, under judicial arbitration full discovery rights are preserved, while discovery is usually very limited under the contract arrangement. Third, subpoena power is fully preserved under the court arbitration, while none exists in the contract arrangement unless provided by statute. A subpoena is issued by a court, not an arbitrator. Fourth, the rules of evidence apply in a judicial arbitration but not in the contract arrangement.

Fifth, the award is binding under the AAA arbitration rules, while in the judicial arbitration the award is binding only if it is not appealed. Judicial arbitration cannot be binding because the Seventh Amendment to the Constitution guarantees the right to a jury trial. Sixth, the appeal rights are fully preserved in a judicial arbitration, and if the appeal is granted the parties have a right to a trial in the court. Under the AAA arrangement, the arbitrator's decision is binding and final. Appeals may be made only on very limited grounds. Seventh, in the judicial arbitration setting the arbitrator is usually an attorney with little or no experience in arbitration, selected at random from

the legal community. Under the contractual arrangement, the arbitrator is selected because of subject-matter expertise. Eighth, the cost to the client is less under the contract arrangement because no lawsuit has been filed. Under the judicial arrangement, the cost is more because the case is pending before the courts. The cost, however, is usually less than that of a full court trial. Ninth, the stress on the parties is greater under judicial arbitration because the case is already in the court system. The stress level is less under the contract arrangement because the arbitration has been mutually agreed to by both parties.

Contractual Arbitration Procedure   Just as a lawsuit has a series of steps to be followed, so does arbitration. Some of the procedure is similar to a judicial proceeding while other parts are unique to arbitration. To describe the process, however, a set of terms exists that is peculiar to arbitration.

Tribunal Administrator   The American Arbitration Association maintains offices around the country. The regional office has the responsibility of providing a **tribunal administrator.** This person manages the administrative matters and all communications between the parties and the arbitrator. The advantage is that the administrative burden of managing details and arrangements is not placed on the arbitrator, who may be located some distance from the parties and the place of the hearing. The arbitrator will not be in direct communication with either of the parties except at the hearing. This arrangement prevents one side from making any arguments, presenting evidence, or making suggestions to the arbitrator without the other side having an opportunity to be heard.

Selection of the Arbitrator   If the parties have thought about arbitration, they will have determined the method of appointing arbitrators in the arbitration agreement. The arbitration agreement can specify the procedure to be followed in selecting arbitrators because it is a contractual arrangement. In the judicial system this control cannot be exercised in selecting a judge—usually the parties must accept any judge assigned to the case.

Generally the parties do not have the foresight to include the method of selecting the arbitrator in the contract. The American Arbitration Association has a simple system for selecting an arbitrator. Each party receives a prepared list of proposed arbitrators that has been specifically drawn for a controversy of the nature of their dispute. Every arbitrator on the list is technically qualified to resolve a dispute on that particular subject. Each party examines the list, crossing off the names of the arbitrators not wanted, and then lists the remaining names in order of preference.

The two lists are then compared by the tribunal administrator to determine which arbitrators are mutually acceptable and the order of preference. This process can be repeated until a mutually acceptable choice is selected. If the parties cannot agree upon an arbitrator, the AAA can appoint one. The arbitrator will not be one whose name was crossed out by either party. If this is a case where a lawsuit has been filed and the dispute is subject to compulsory arbitration, the court has the authority to appoint an arbitrator.

Preparation for the Hearing The parties determine a mutually convenient day and time for the hearing. Written notice of the hearing must be given to each party. Each side will prepare for the hearing as it would for a trial. All documents and papers to be submitted into evidence will be assembled and placed in a logical order. Proper arrangements will be made if the arbitrator needs to visit a place for an on-the-spot investigation. Before the hearing all the witnesses should be interviewed by each party. The case must be studied from the opposing party's viewpoint, so the opposition's evidence and arguments can be answered. If a transcript of the hearings is needed, arrangements will be made with the tribunal administrator for a court reporter to be present.

The Hearing An arbitration proceeding is very similar in form to a trial, but it is not quite the adversarial proceeding that a trial is. A cooperative attitude is necessary for effective arbitration. Ordinary rules of courtesy and decorum are encouraged. Exaggeration, overemphasis, concealing of facts, and use of legal technicalities to disrupt or delay the hearing are not encouraged and may have an adverse effect on the arbitrator.

Each party presents his or her case to the arbitrator in an orderly and logical manner. Just as in a trial, each side starts out with a clear but concise opening statement. The complaining party usually starts first and tells the arbitrator what rem-

edy is sought. After the second party's opening statement, documents, depositions, and other materials are presented to the arbitrator by both parties. If there are witnesses, they are examined to help each party establish his or her case. Finally, each side makes a closing argument. The closing argument includes a summary of the evidence, a refutation of the points made by the other side, and an argument as to why the arbitrator should decide in favor of that person. At the conclusion of the closing arguments, the arbitrator will declare the hearing closed.

The arbitrator may hear and determine the controversy upon the evidence produced, even if one party failed to appear after being notified of the hearing. A party to the case may have an attorney present, but it is not required. Witnesses can be compelled to appear at an arbitration hearing through the use of subpoenas issued by the arbitrator.

The technical judicial rules of evidence are not followed in arbitration hearings. Often an arbitrator will hear evidence that would not be allowed in a courtroom; usually an arbitrator will listen to most evidence. This aspect of arbitration has been criticized. The technical rules of evidence used in court were developed to make certain there is a fair hearing. Evidence must not be based upon gossip or prejudices and must not include irrelevant material. The arbitrator must be especially careful to consider only evidence that has a bearing on the case. The hearing can be adjourned to another time if the first meeting is not sufficient to hear all the evidence.

The Award The arbitrator must make his or her decision within 30 days after the hearing. If there are two or more arbitrators on the case, the majority decision is the binding one. The parties may agree beforehand that only a unanimous decision will be binding. The arbitrator's decision is called the **award**. The award is based upon the facts presented at the hearing. The purpose is to dispose of the controversy in a final and complete manner. The arbitrator must rule on each claim that has been submitted for a decision.

Once the award is made, the arbitrator cannot change it. Only if the parties both agree to reopen the proceedings and restore power to the arbitrator can the award be changed. The award merely states the decision of the arbitrator with no written support for it. The award is final and binding upon the parties. If the arbitration were court-ordered, the award is submitted to the court. Once the court accepts the award, it becomes the judgment of the court.

The Appeal   The following are the grounds upon which the losing party may appeal the award in contractual arbitration:

1. The award was obtained by corruption, fraud, or other undue means.
2. Misconduct or partiality was exhibited by the arbitrator.
3. The arbitrator exceeded his or her powers.
4. There was a refusal to postpone the hearing or a refusal to hear evidence material to the controversy that substantially prejudiced the rights of one of the parties.
5. The parties did not have a written arbitration agreement and the issue of whether to take the dispute to arbitration was not determined in a court action to compel arbitration.

If the court does find one of the above grounds applicable to the case, it orders either a rehearing in front of the same arbitrator or a new hearing with a different arbitrator. The court does have the right to modify the award in the event of an evident miscalculation of figures, an evident mistake in the description of any person or property referred to in the award, or if the matters determined by the arbitrator were not those submitted to arbitration or the award was not in the proper form. A court is not allowed to modify an award on any other grounds.

In judicial arbitration, either party may appeal to the court. Normally, no grounds are required for the appeal other than that the appealing party does not accept the decision of the arbitrator. The appeal is treated by the court as a completely new case, and a new trial will be ordered. In legal language, this is called a trial *de novo*. The arbitration is treated as if it never happened. The case proceeds as a lawsuit, as it normally would have without the arbitration hearing.

Arbitration does have certain inherent disadvantages when it is compared to a judicial proceeding. First, the arbitrator's background is probably not well known to a party when a case is first submitted to arbitration. All persons have their own bias or prejudice that may affect the outcome of a case, even when serving as an arbitrator and attempting to be neutral. Judges in lawsuits, however, also have biases and prejudices. But with formal judicial proceedings a record is maintained, and an appeal can be based upon a judge's prejudicial behavior, while normally a record is not maintained in an arbitration hearing. The bias or prejudice of a judge that wrongfully affects the outcome of a case can be reversed. The same cannot be said about a contractual arbitration proceeding.

Second, it has been argued that arbitrators tend to compromise in making awards, rather than making clear-cut decisions for either party. Therefore justice is also being compromised. Judicial decisions most often decide for or against one of the parties based on the merits of the case. Third, future parties lose the use of prior decisions as precedent. Written judicial opinions are one of the foundations of the development of American law.

The following case spells out the power of an arbitrator's award and how it may not be appealed.

✗ **Case 4.3**
HEMBREE v. BROADWAY REALTY AND TRUST COMPANY, INC.

Court of Appeals of Arizona, 1986.
151 Ariz. 418, 728 P.2d 288.

BACKGROUND AND FACTS   *Broadway Realty and Trust Company sold Hembree a home. The purchase contract had an arbitration clause requiring arbitration of any controversy or claim between the parties. The home had a defective roof. The case was arbitrated, and an award was given to Hembree based upon breach of implied warranty. The decision was appealed on the basis that (1) the arbitrator acted beyond his scope of authority and (2) the law of implied warranty should not have been applied. The trial court confirmed the award, and Broadway Realty appealed.*

Chief Judge HATHAWAY.
* * * *

I. SCOPE OF AUTHORITY

* * * [T]he superior court will not confirm an arbitrator's award if the arbitrator exceeded his authority. An arbitrator's powers are defined by the agreement of the parties. The contract between appellees and appellants states that arbitration will be available for any controversy or claim "arising out of or *relating to this contract.*" (Emphasis added) * * * [O]nce an implied warranty comes into existence by reason of the circumstances of the sale, the law conceives such a warranty as being a term of the contract. Appellants argue that appellees' implied warranty claim does not arise out of or relate to "this contract." The gist of appellant's argument is that implied warranty can only apply to the sale of a home by a builder/vendor, and since appellant is a developer/vendor, the arbitration clause does not encompass this breach of implied warranty allegation. Appellants' argument, however, is legal rather than jurisdictional. The dispute between these parties relates to the sale of the home and the allegedly defective roof. In their lawsuit, appellees alleged a number of theories including implied warranty. Whether or not that theory was viable under these circumstances was a legal question for the arbitrator. The dispute, however, clearly arose out of and related to this contract for the sale of a home. Therefore, we find the arbitrator was within his authority in addressing the implied warranty claim.

II. MISTAKE OF LAW

As stated above, appellants argue that parties who are not builders may not be held liable for breach of an implied warranty of habitability. It is settled case law that upon application to confirm an arbitration award, the superior court may not inquire as to whether errors of law were made by the arbitrator in reaching his decision. The power of this court is likewise severely circumscribed. Therefore this court may not review whether or not the arbitrator was correct in his application of the law. * * *

DECISION AND REMEDY

The court upheld the award of the arbitrator. Although noting that the arbitrator might have been mistaken as to the legal issues on the implied warranty, the court held it could not inquire into errors of law made by an arbitrator.

COMMENT

Possibly one of the major reasons why some lawyers do not like arbitration is that an error of law cannot be appealed. An award from a trial judge who makes an error of law can be reversed on appeal. But arbitration allows the dispute to be expedited even though the award may be based upon incorrect legal doctrine.

Hybrid Mediation and Arbitration

Commercial agreements today have a hybrid system of combining mediation and arbitration to resolve disputes. If a dispute arises, mediation is used first. The mediator will attempt to help the parties find their own solution to the problem. Meeting with the parties separately, the mediator suggests various solutions. The effect is to guide the parties to a resolution by building momentum in that direction. The resolution is an agreement mutually reached by the disputing parties.

The parties know that if they do not resolve their differences by mutual agreement, the next step is arbitration. The arbitrator's award is binding on both parties. It is, in effect, a forced solution.

Mediation is used in many different legal areas. Mediation and arbitration are used extensively in labor disputes. The Federal Mediation and Conciliation Service has experienced mediators available who serve in disputes between labor and management. If direct negotiations between management and labor break down, the mediators are sent by the service to mediate the dispute.

The Magnuson-Moss Product Warranty Act of 1975 authorizes mediation when a dispute occurs between a consumer and a business over a malfunctioning consumer product. A business may establish a mediation procedure on its own to resolve disputes that customers may have; this procedure has been used by automobile manufacturers when customers have had disputes with dealerships, and a combination of mediation and arbitration is used extensively in the construction industry.

Exhibit 4–4 sums up the distinctions among the different kinds of dispute resolution procedures discussed thus far.

Fact Finding

Used in complex commercial disputes, **fact finding** is an investigative process in which an independent third party will investigate the issues and make findings of fact. Courts use fact finders when confronted with a highly technical and involved fact situation requiring a high degree of expertise in a given area.

Frequently a fact finder's role is solely that of making a recommendation. Having an independent person determine certain facts often assists parties in reaching a settlement. If nothing else, the conclusions reached by the fact finder give the parties an indication as to what might occur if the dispute were litigated in a judicial system. This indication by itself will often assist the parties in reaching a negotiated settlement.

Minitrial

The **minitrial** is a procedure recently utilized as an alternative dispute resolution mechanism. Its name possibly misstates its purpose and the procedures involved with it. A minitrial is another voluntary procedure in which all parties must agree to its use and to what will transpire. The primary purpose in initiating a minitrial is to resolve questions of fact and law in complex, commercial disputes. It may be used in addition to fact finding.

In a minitrial, there is no judge. Instead, the parties agree on an adviser. Normally the adviser is a person who has had considerable experience with the subject matter that is the basis of the dispute. The parties determine the amount of authority that can be exercised by the adviser.

Upon being appointed, the adviser will establish an abbreviated discovery process. This process requires exchanging the documents, exhibits, written arguments, and names of witnesses that will be used by the parties. Upon conclusion of the discovery phase the adviser will meet with the parties, issue rulings on discovery matters, and attempt to resolve questions of procedure.

When all parties know what facts actually exist, settlement of the case is facilitated. Many lawyers and judges believe that one major reason for trials is the lack of discovery in arbitration. When the parties have full knowledge of what the facts are and what the case entails, the parties will be better able to reach a settlement. Minitrials attempt to expedite discovery of the facts.

Another advantage of the minitrial is the confidentiality of its procedures. Many businesses do not want to disclose information to the general public. The minitrial provides a procedure that limits the amount of information made public.

Minitrials have been used in cases of patent infringement, product liability, unfair competition, and antitrust violations. It is not considered an appropriate mechanism for cases involving constitutional law issues or where there are a large number of multiple parties, when novel questions about the law need to be answered.

Private Judge

A few states, particularly California, will allow the parties in a dispute privately to hire a judge, who is called a *referee*. Normally the referee is a person who has retired from the judiciary. The parties attempt to obtain a referee with expertise in the subject matter of the litigation. The referee is given the full powers of a judge, except the power to find someone in contempt of court.

When this procedure is utilized, it is the same as a regular courtroom proceeding. The proceedings are in front of the referee, no jury is allowed, and all trial procedures and rules of evidence are

Exhibit 4–4 Dispute Resolution Process Comparison Chart

Distinguishing Features	Voluntary Mediation	Contractual Arbitration	Court-Ordered/Judicial Arbitration	Court Litigation
Dispute types	Any negotiable matter	Civil matters of any type or complexity, unless prohibited by law, but only what parties provide for/agree to in writing	Civil matters for monetary relief only; usually a limit on the monetary amount of the claim	Civil and criminal cases heard; money damages and equitable remedies available
Private or public proceedings	Private	Private	Public	Public
Discovery rights	None provided by statute	Usually none or very limited under arbitration statutes; parties can provide for/agree to discovery in writing	Full rights as available under law or statute	Full rights as available under law or statute
Subpoena power	None provided by statute	Arbitrator has power to issue subpoenas in accordance with arbitration statutes; enforcement power rests with the court	Court has power to issue and enforce subpoenas	Court has power to issue and enforce subpoenas
Formal rules of evidence	None provided by statute	Do not apply unless provided by statute or unless parties provide for/agree to in writing	Do apply as provided for by statute and by court rules of procedure	Do apply as provided by statute and by court rules of procedure
Decision maker	The parties; the mediator facilitates further negotiations and settlement by the parties	An impartial arbitrator selected and/or empowered by the parties, who has special subject-matter expertise	An impartial attorney usually chosen by the parties	A judge appointed by the court or an impartial jury chosen by the parties
Decision finality and enforcement	Verbal or written settlement agreement may be enforceable through a judicial process	Final and binding; enforceable by an appropriate court upon the entering of a judgment upon the award	Final and binding, unless appealed; if not appealed, enforceable by the court upon the entering of a judgment based upon the award	Final unless reversed on appeal
Appeal rights	Only available through a judicial process	Usually very limited under arbitration statutes unless parties provide/agree otherwise	Trial de novo (new trial) and full appeal rights as available under law	Full appeal rights as available under law
Relative speed from initiation to settlement or decision (not including appeal time)	Fastest (days to weeks to months); settlement occurs in 60% to 90% of cases mediated depending on the type of case surveyed	Faster or fast (weeks to months to year); settlement occurs in 50% of all cases submitted to AAA arbitration; parties can agree to how fast or slow process will be	Fast (months to year); settlement occurs in 50% of these cases; the percentage of cases going to trial de novo is not known	Slowest (year to years); settlement occurs in 95% of all civil cases and generally right before trial date
Who pays cost?	Parties	Parties	Taxpayers and parties	Taxpayers and parties

Source: American Arbitration Association

Cross-Cultural Conflict on the Texas Gulf Coast[a]

Since 1975, over 800,000 Southeast Asians have migrated to the United States. As of June 1987, an estimated 62,700 Southeast Asians had made their home in the state of Texas. A large number earn their living through fishing, shrimping, and/or crabbing in the Gulf of Mexico, making their homes in small coastal towns with names like Palacios, Seabrook, and Rockport, some with populations numbering around 4,000.

During the past decade, the Community Relations Services (CRS) has built a significant body of conflict resolution casework responding to tensions between Vietnamese fishermen, shrimpers, and crabbers and their white counterparts along the Texas Gulf Coast. More recently, CRS has been working to improve interaction between the Vietnamese fishermen and the institutions governing their livelihood.

Early on, tensions among whites arose as a result of Vietnamese's violations of traditional Gulf Coast fishing customs. These unknowing violations of local customs often made complete sense in the Vietnamese cultural context. White reactions to these behavioral differences resulted in boat burnings, followed by a killing of a white by a Vietnamese, and serious but less violent tension on a number of different fronts.

The CRS interventions, aimed at building bridges between disputing parties, employed Asian individuals who were more acculturated to American society and/or more conversant in English as intermediaries. To decrease tension levels between white and Vietnamese groups and individuals, CRS met with each separately and was able to identify and clarify areas of key tension. Bringing the groups together, CRS assisted them to present their perceptions to each other. Some of the differences they discovered were:

One Side: White fishermen whose boats had broken down out on the water were incensed

when Vietnamese fishermen smiled and waved as they passed by. The white Texans felt that they were being mocked and laughed at by foreigners.

And the Other: The "universal" sign for a fisherman in distress on the Gulf waters is for him to raise both arms in front of his body, fists closed, and to make a motion as if breaking a pencil. The Vietnamese thought that the white fishermen were waving to them, smiled and waved back.

One Side: White shrimpers along the Texas Gulf Coast were angered that groups of Vietnamese shrimpers would work their nets in the same area, overfishing the waters.

And the Other: When a white shrimper discovered a good harvesting spot, other white shrimpers would pass, leaving the lucky individual alone to reap the rewards of his labor. Vietnamese shrimpers on the other hand, upon discovering a good spot, would invite everyone else to the area to share in the good fortune.

One Side: White fishermen were irate that the federal government was subsidizing the success of the Vietnamese, helping them to buy newer and bigger boats.

And the Other: Vietnamese were borrowing money from family members, working together in large family units, and limiting living expenses in order to put more money back into their business. After buying their first boat from Americans, Vietnamese fishermen learned how to construct their own—using the same pattern and through group efforts similar to the old American pioneer barn raisings.

Through this process of facilitated cross-cultural education, each of the disputing parties learned about the different priorities and values that guided the behavior of the other. They were better able to understand and to adapt to each other, decreasing tension-producing interactions.

Evidence of CRS success in the process of their party intervention was follow-on requests for assistance. For example, a series of requests from community leaders and a local Parks and Wildlife game warden led CRS to develop a seminar for the Vietnamese fishermen, which featured the following:

- the Parks and Wildlife Regional Director provided an updated copy of the Texas fishing laws translated into Vietnamese,
- the city's mayor presented a list of local customs allegedly violated by Vietnamese during the previous shrimping season which were the most irritating to Anglo shrimpers,
- the local Parks and Wildlife game warden participated in the seminar and led the presentation on the current laws, and
- an interpreter was present for the seminar and served as an intermediary in order to convey accurately both the words used and the nuances intended.

As part of a follow-through, CRS has focused on increasing the direct communication between Vietnamese and institutional representatives. For example, state agencies and local Vietnamese groups have begun to work together to build a network providing translations and dissemination of both emergency weather information and the changing regulations guiding sport and commercial fishing and shrimping.

Note: Reprinted with permission of the National Institute for Dispute Resolution.
a. The Community Relations Services (CRS) work along the Texas Gulf Coast described in this case study was conducted by Efram Martinez, a conciliator working out of the Houston Field Office. This excerpt from CRS experience has been contributed by Barbara Huie, CRS program analyst, to provide examples of cross-cultural conflict and resolution. This excerpt first appeared in National Institute for Dispute Resolution, *Dispute Resolutions Forum*, "Culture's Consequences in Dispute Resolution" (September 1987).

---

followed. A record is maintained for appeal purposes. The formality of the proceedings and the judicial nature of this procedure set it apart from arbitration.

The advantage of a **private judge** is the fact that the parties are not controlled by the local court calendar. The case will be heard prior to cases filed earlier because it will not be heard by the judges in the local court system. This procedure allows expeditious treatment of the case before a referee who has both experience as a judge and special expertise in the subject matter.

The parties pay most, if not all, of the cost of this type of litigation. It can be expensive and is, therefore, available only to parties who can afford it. Because of this expense, the use of private judges has been criticized as creating a legal system for the wealthy that may result in a dual system of justice (that is, one for the rich and one for the less advantaged). The wealthy are able to have their cases decided rather quickly in front of judges who have specialized experience and will devote full time to their cases, while the thousands of other parties to lawsuits must wait for months and often years before their cases are placed on the court calendar.

Recently, relatively low-cost alternative private courts have been created as a for-profit business. These business private courts allow both parties to decide on the date of the hearing, where the hearing will be held, who will be the presiding judge, and whether the judge's decision is binding. Each party is charged a filing fee, as well as a set fee for each halfday hearing session. Obviously, the longer the hearing, the more costly the procedure becomes.

Ethical Considerations

Ethical Issues in Arbitration

One of the major benefits of contractual arbitration is that all information provided during the process is kept private and away from the public and other competitors. Another benefit is the fast resolution of the matter. But the major trade-off for these benefits is that an arbitrator is not required to follow any rules of evidence during the hearing. In addition, discovery procedures prior to the arbitration hearing are either nonexistent or are very limited in scope.

Let's assume that you are involved as a claimant in an arbitration case. You know that the other side has no knowledge of your exhibits, nor does the other side know that you have obtained sworn statements from witnesses that are beneficial to your case. Assume that the witnesses' statements would be considered hearsay in a regular court and would not be allowed there as evidence. In arbitration they might be admitted at the discretion of the arbitrator. If this matter were before a regular court, you would have been required in most jurisdictions to give copies of your exhibits to the other side weeks before the trial. The exchange of exhibits reduces the chance of surprise at the time of trial.

Is it ethical for you to use the exhibits or witnesses' statements without giving the other side a copy of them prior to the hearing?

What if you were on the other side? If you knew about the witnesses' statements, you might be able to obtain contradictory ones from other witnesses. How do you defend against information presented to the arbitrator if you do not have any advance knowledge of the contents of the exhibits or statements? Obviously you want to prevail at the hearing. But is it not ethical to disclose this information prior to the hearing? Should disclosure make a difference as to which side prevails at the hearing?

One of the major criticisms of arbitration is the lack of discovery procedures in which the exhibits and documents to be used during the hearing are disclosed to the other party ahead of time. On the other hand, the discovery process is one of the reasons that handling a dispute through the judicial system takes longer than handling it through arbitration. Can you think of any procedures that might be implemented that would keep arbitration a desirable alternative to a trial, but that would also include ethical conduct?

International Considerations

Arbitration in International Situations

Judicial procedures are used frequently in the United States to resolve disputes at all levels. In other cultures, it is considered a personal failure if a dispute must be resolved by a court. Thus, many international contracts provide for mediation, arbitration, or both.

The world community favors alternative dispute resolution procedures to the judicial forum. In 1958, the **United Nations Convention on the Recognition and Enforcement of Foreign Arbitral Awards,** commonly called the **New York Convention,** was sent out to various countries for signatures. Today 73 countries, including the United States, have signed the agreement. This convention allows the enforcement of arbitrated awards in any of the signature countries. When business associates have a dispute, it may be decided by arbitration, and that arbitral award may be enforced in the country where the loser resides. A few defenses may be raised when the prevailing party tries to have the award enforced. The loser may raise the defense of incapacity to contract—that is, one of the parties did not have the authority to enter into the contract; the loser may claim that the illegality of the contract or the enforcement of the award would violate public policy; the loser may raise the defense that no notice was given concerning the arbitration procedure; or the defense may be raised that the matter before the arbitrator was not included in the original agreement and thus the arbitrator had no jurisdiction to make the award.

Several organizations worldwide handle arbitration matters. The American Arbitration Association, the United Nations Commission on International Trade Law, the London Court of International Arbitration, the Euro-Arab Chamber of Commerce, and the International Chamber of Commerce (Paris) are among the better-known organizations.

FACING A
LEGAL ISSUE

Arbitration of Disputes Involving "Lemons"

You have purchased your first new automobile. On the way home it suddenly stops. This event is just the beginning of your nightmare. After twelve trips to the dealership in a six-week period, you come to the realization that you have a true lemon.

You could bring a judicial action against the manufacturer and dealer to compensate you for your loss. But you know this will be very expensive and it will be months or years before you finally have your day in court. Because of this, the majority of states have enacted "lemon laws." These laws generally allow a purchaser to go through an alternative dispute resolution procedure, such as arbitration, to resolve the purchaser's problem. This is usually a modified arbitration procedure, and if the vehicle meets the criteria for the "lemon" classification, the consumer is entitled to a replacement auto or an appropriate cash refund. If the consumer is not satisfied with the decision of the arbitrator, the consumer can take his or her case to court. The automobile manufacturer, however, is bound by the decision. Many of these cases are handled through the local Better Business Bureau.

You should check your state law or contact your dealership to see if this procedure is available. Most regional offices of the manufacturer can also give you this information. In many states you are not bound by the arbitration, but the manufacturer is. You have nothing to lose in using this alternative dispute mechanism.

Summary

The judicial system is overburdened with litigation that results in long and expensive delays from the time of filing a complaint to the final conclusion of the case. The judiciary, businesspersons, and the public have a real interest in alternatives to formal court procedures. These alternative dispute resolution procedures include informal negotiation, arbitration, conciliation, and mediation.

Arbitration is very similar to a judicial trial because the arbitrator makes a decision, called an *award*, that is binding. The award can be made into a judgment by a court, if necessary. Arbitration is an alternative to a judicial trial, where an independent third-party decision is binding upon the disputing parties.

Arbitration is ordered by a court, judicial arbitration, or is authorized by a written contractual agreement. An arbitration hearing is conducted more informally than a judicial trial. The parties limit the grounds of appeal when they contractually agree to arbitration. Both a judicial arbitration award and a contractual arbitration award can be appealed to a court.

Business problems have increased because of the complexity of our modern society. More formal complaints among businesses and between businesses and the general public occur. Alternative dispute resolution procedures have assisted in limiting the number of cases handled by the judiciary. These procedures save considerable expense and time for the litigants. In the future it is anticipated that alternative dispute resolution procedures will be used more extensively as they gain greater acceptance from the legal system, businesspersons, and the public.

Key Terms

alternative dispute resolution
    procedures (78)

American Arbitration
    Association (83)

arbitration (83)
arbitrator (83)

award (91)
conciliation (81)
contractual agreement to
    arbitrate (85)
fact finding (94)
Federal Arbitration Act (83)

judicial arbitration (90)
mediation (82)
minitrial (94)
negotiation (81)
New York Convention (99)
private judge (97)

tribunal administrator (90)
Uniform Arbitration Act (85)
United Nations Convention
    on the Recognition and
    Enforcement of Foreign
    Arbitral Awards (99)

Questions and Case Problems

1. Do you think that mediation should be used before a civil case goes to trial? If so, should the judge trying the case be the mediator? What advantages and disadvantages do you see in such a situation?

2. With a few exceptions, parties arbitrate their disputes because they have agreed to do so. Even with an agreement to arbitrate, one of the parties frequently has a change of mind and decides not to arbitrate the dispute. Why do you think a person would want to avoid arbitration?

3. You are the president of a medium-sized company manufacturing air conditioners. Recently you have noticed a substantial increase in legal expenses due to legal actions being brought against your firm. Most, if not all, are being brought by former employees, customers, and suppliers of inventory. In all cases you believe the actions are not justified, but you want to decrease the cost of formal litigation. What types of cases would you allow to be handled through alternative dispute resolution procedures? What types of cases would you not allow to be handled through alternative dispute resolution procedures? Which alternative dispute resolution procedures would you use?

4. The Southland Corporation is the owner and franchiser of 7-Eleven convenience stores. Within its franchise agreement there is an arbitration clause requiring arbitration for any controversy or claim arising out of it. California has a franchise statute that allows legal actions to be brought in the court. Some of the franchisees brought action against Southland Corporation based upon violations of the California franchise law, along with other claims for fraud, misrepresentation, and breach of contract. Southland moved to force arbitration. What should the court hold? [Southland Corp. v. Keating, 465 U.S. 1, 104 S.Ct. 852, 79 L.Ed.2d 1 (1984)]

5. Alexander lost his job. He argued that he had been discharged because of his race. He had his case arbitrated but lost because the arbitrator found that Alexander's discharge was for just cause. Alexander appealed to a federal court to have the arbitration award overturned. On appeal his employer argued that Alexander had waived his rights under federal law to have the case heard by a court. Do you think Alexander should have a new trial over the same issues and facts decided by the arbitrator? [Alexander v. Gardner-Denver Co., 415 U.S. 36, 94 S.Ct. 1011, 39 L.Ed.2d 147 (1974)]

6. Lamar Byrd sold his medical practice and invested $160,000 in securities through Dean Witter Reynolds, Inc. The value of his investments declined to about $60,000. Because of this, Byrd brought an action to recover his investment under the Securities Exchange Act of 1934 and also stated causes of action to recover under state law. There have been numerous decisions holding that actions under the Securities Exchange Act of 1934 could not be subject to arbitration because of federal statute. The question presented to the United States Supreme Court was whether arbitration of the state law claims had to occur prior to any action being taken concerning the alleged federal violations. What do you think was the result? Explain your answer. [Dean Witter Reynolds, Inc. v. Byrd, 470 U.S. 213, 105 S.Ct. 1238, 84 L.Ed.2d 158 (1985)]

Chapter 5   The Constitution and the Regulation of Business

The Constitution of 1789 deserves the veneration with which the Americans have been accustomed to regard it. It is true that many criticisms have been passed upon its arrangements, upon its omissions, upon the artificial character of some of the institutions it creates. * * * Yet, after all deductions, it ranks above every other written constitution for the intrinsic excellence of its scheme, its adaptation to the circumstances of the people, the simplicity, brevity, and precision of its language, its judicious mixture of definiteness in principle with elasticity in details.

Lord Bryce,
The American Commonwealth, 1888.

OUTLINE

Introduction

Why does a businessperson or an individual need to know and understand the United States Constitution? First, it governs our personal and business lives as the supreme law in this country. All statutes passed by Congress or by any state legislature, all decisions made by judges in the federal and state courts, and all actions by the president or by the governor of a state must be in accordance with the Constitution. If there is any conflict, the United States Constitution will prevail. The Constitution serves as a limitation on the power of the government.

Second, we must read the Constitution in order to understand court decisions and why Congress acts or does not act in different situations. Third, every businessperson should appreciate the impact on business of the interstate commerce clause contained in the Constitution.

Articles of the Constitution

The Constitution has two functions: It creates the government, and it sets out an individual's rights in relation to that government. The first three articles of the Constitution establish the framework of the government. Article IV gives direction to the states through the full faith and credit clause. This clause requires that each state respect the laws of the other states. Article V sets out the methods of amending the Constitution. Article VI ranks the order of the laws, giving highest priority to the Constitution itself and lowest priority to the laws of a local government. Article VII, the last article, provides for the ratification of the Constitution.

The Supremacy Clause

Article VI provides that the Constitution, laws, and treaties of the United States are "the supreme Law of the Land." The **supremacy clause** governs the relationship between the states and the federal government. When the Constitution specifically delegates a power to the federal government, any state law that conflicts with a federal law in that area is prohibited. If the conflict in the laws is taken to court, the state law will be rendered in-

valid. For example, only the federal government can coin money or pass naturalization laws.

In other areas, however, the state and federal governments may share powers—that is, they have **concurrent powers.** If Congress chooses to act exclusively in one of these areas, the federal government has preempted the area. For example, the federal government has preempted the areas of aviation and nuclear power.

Congress rarely preempts an entire subject area by prohibiting state regulation. If a state law and a federal law conflict in an area of concurrent powers and if Congress has not been clear as to its intent, the courts must determine whether Congress intended to exercise exclusive dominion over the given area.

Federalism is the organizational system of the United States government. Under this system, state governments share powers with the federal government, and neither government is superior to the other except within the particular area of authority granted to it by the Constitution. Federalism appreciates that society is best served by distributing various functions among local governments and the national government based on which government is best able to perform each function. For instance, the federal government can best handle national defense and foreign relations, while state and local governments are best able to handle traffic tickets, domestic relations, and probate.

Exhibit 5–1 depicts this division of powers.

Separation of Powers

The main body of the Constitution creates the federal government by dividing it into three branches: the **executive branch,** the **legislative branch,** and the **judicial branch.** The rights, duties, and powers of the legislative branch are set forth in Article I. Article II creates the executive branch and establishes the powers of the president. The federal judicial system is created by Article III.

Each branch of the government fulfills a separate function. Although no branch may exercise the authority of another branch, each branch has some power to limit the actions of the other two branches. This scheme creates a system of checks and balances, as mentioned in Chapter 1, so that no one branch of government is able to accumulate too much power. For example, the ex-

Exhibit 5–1 The American Federal System: Division of Powers Between the National Government and the State Governments

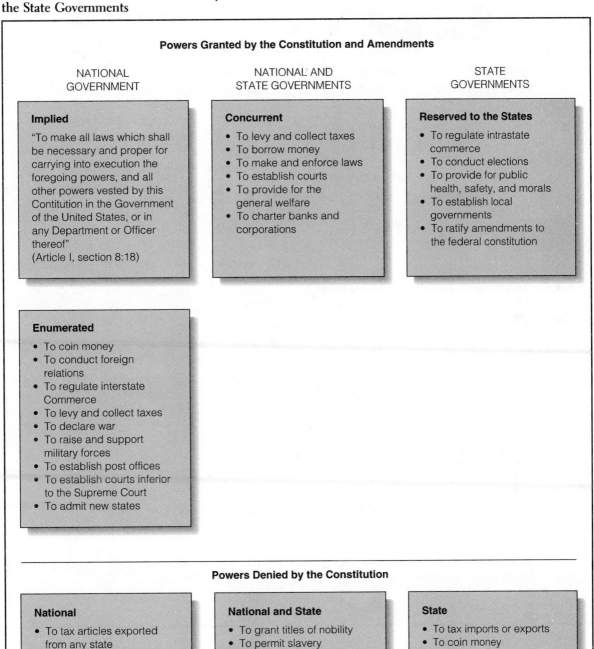

A Funny Thing Happened on the Way to Amend the Articles of Confederation

The Articles of Confederation, in effect since 1781, were not working. Although there was a federal government, all the power was held by the states. Unfortunately, the states were not working together; each state based its decisions on its own best interests and not on the best interests of a unified thirteen colonies. After extended deliberations, Congress, meeting on Wall Street in New York City, called a federal convention to amend the Articles. If anyone had called this meeting a constitutional convention, no meeting would have taken place. The delegates were to meet only to amend a couple of sections of the Articles of Confederation. Many people were vehemently opposed to the idea of a strong central government.

Seventy-four delegates were named to the convention. Fifty-five delegates from twelve states attended. Rhode Island disagreed with the whole procedure and did not send any delegates. The convention started on May 14, 1787, in Philadelphia. These men labored through a hot, humid Pennsylvania summer. Working secretly, they wrote guarded letters to friends and rarely spoke of the business at hand during their leisure hours.

Instead of amending the Articles of Confederation, the delegates drafted a completely new constitution that would replace the Articles. The document created the strong central government so feared by many. Of the 55 delegates who started the work, 41 were present when the convention ended on September 17, 1787, and only 39 signed the document, the Constitution of the United States of America.

The Constitution was then submitted to the states. Heated debate in the newspapers and in meetings followed. Arguing for the adoption of the Constitution was a series of newspaper articles that have become known as the *Federalist Papers*. These articles were written by James Madison, Alexander Hamilton, and John Jay. Before the Constitution could take effect, it had to be ratified by three-fourths of the states (nine out of thirteen).

After intense debate, the ninth state, New Hampshire, ratified the Constitution on June 21, 1788. Article VII of the proposed constitution stipulated that the Constitution would become effective (for those who ratified) when ratified by nine states. By 1790 all thirteen states had ratified the Constitution. This document is now the oldest constitution in the world in continuous use. The genius of the writers lay in creating a mechanism that could translate theory into reality.

Many people observed that the Constitution did not list any personal freedoms. Before ratifying the Constitution, a number of states made it clear that amendments containing the rights of the people in relation to the government would be necessary. The first ten amendments, known as the Bill of Rights, were adopted in 1791.

ecutive branch is responsible for foreign affairs, but treaties with foreign governments require the advice and consent of the Senate. Congress has the power to tax, but the president can veto a tax bill. Congress determines the jurisdiction of the federal courts, but the Supreme Court has the power to hold acts of the other branches of the federal government unconstitutional.

The specific powers granted to Congress are listed in Article I, Section 8. Among those powers are the power to regulate commerce, the taxing power, and the spending power.

The Commerce Clause

Congress has the power "to regulate Commerce with foreign Nations, and among the several States, and with the Indian Tribes" (Article I, Section 8). No other clause in the Constitution has a greater impact on business. Because the federal government is able to regulate commerce, the rules governing the movement of goods through the states are uniform.

Congress has the power to regulate any activity, interstate or intrastate, that substantially affects interstate commerce. For example, wheat that a farmer grows strictly for his or her own consumption is still subject to federal regulation. The federal regulation allows only so many acres of wheat to be grown. A farmer cannot grow the allowed acreage of wheat *plus* enough for his or her own consumption. If enough farmers grew excess wheat for home consumption, it would reduce the overall demand for wheat because these farmers would not need to buy it. Thus, even one farmer may have a substantial economic effect on interstate commerce; if he or she could grow excess wheat, others could, too, and the goal of the federal regulation would be defeated.[1]

---

1. Wickard v. Filburn, 317 U.S. 111, 63 S.Ct. 82, 87 L.Ed. 122 (1942).

State Regulation of Commerce   States have a strong interest in regulating activities within their borders. States are sovereign governments; as part of their inherent sovereignty, they possess **police powers**. The police power gives the states the authority to regulate private activities in order to protect or to promote the health, safety, morals, or general welfare of their citizens. States, for example, have a strong interest in making sure that the trucks and automobiles on state highways are safe. Most state regulations place some burden on interstate commerce.

When a state regulation encroaches on interstate commerce, the courts must balance the state's interest, reflected in the merits and purposes of the regulation, against the burden it places on interstate commerce. A state law enacted pursuant to a state's police powers and affecting the health, safety, and welfare of local citizens carries a strong presumption of validity. Because courts balance the interests between the state and federal governments, the outcome in a particular case cannot be predicted. In the following case, the United States Supreme Court considered whether Nebraska could impose taxes and fees on out-of-state trucks.

BACKGROUND AND FACTS   *In 1984 Nebraska adopted a statute that imposed taxes and fees on out-of-state trucks when the trucks were operated within Nebraska. No equivalent taxes and fees were required to be paid by Nebraska residents who operated trucks within the state. Dennis owned a trucking business located in Ohio. His trucks were driven within several states including Nebraska. He filed a lawsuit against Higgins, the director of the Department of Motor Vehicles, claiming that a statute of this type violates the commerce clause of the Constitution. Prior to filing the action, Dennis paid the taxes. This case was appealed up through the Supreme Court of Nebraska.*

Case 5.1
DENNIS v. HIGGINS
Supreme Court of the United States, 1991.
498 U.S. ____, 111 S.Ct. 865, 112 L.Ed.2d 969.

Justice WHITE delivered the opinion of the Court.

*   *   *   *

The Commerce Clause provides that "Congress shall have Power . . . [t]o regulate Commerce with foreign Nations, and among the several States, and with the Indian Tribes." US Const, Art I, § 8, cl 3. Although the language of that Clause speaks only of Congress' power over commerce, "the Court long has recognized that it also limits the power of the States to erect barriers against interstate trade. *   *   *

There is no doubt that the Commerce Clause is a power-allocating provision, giving Congress pre-emptive authority over the regulation of interstate commerce. It is also clear, however, that the Commerce Clause does more than confer power on the Federal Government; it is also a substantive "restriction on permissible state regulation" of interstate commerce. *   *   * The Commerce Clause has long been recognized as a selfexecuting limitation on the power of the States to enact laws imposing substantial burdens on such commerce. *   *   * In addition, individuals injured by state action that violates this aspect of the Commerce Clause may sue and obtain injunctive and declaratory relief. *   *   * Indeed, the trial court in the case before us awarded petitioner such relief, and respondents do not contest that decision. We have also recently held that taxpayers who are required to pay taxes before challenging a state tax that is subsequently determined to violate the Commerce Clause are entitled to retrospective relief that will cure any unconstitutional discrimination against interstate commerce during the contested tax period. *   *   * This combined restriction on state power and entitlement to relief under the Commerce Clause amounts to a "right, privilege, or immunity" under the ordinary meaning of those terms.

*   *   *   *

As Justice Jackson, writing for the Court [in 1949], eloquently explained: "Our system, fostered by the Commerce Clause, is that every farmer and every craftsman shall be encouraged to produce by the certainty that he will have free access to every market in the Nation, that no home embargoes will withhold his exports, and no foreign state will by customs duties or regulations exclude them. Likewise, every consumer may look to the free competition from every producing area in the Nation to protect him from exploitation by any. Such was the vision of the Founders; such has been the doctrine of this Court which has given it reality.

DECISION AND REMEDY   *The Court held that the Nebraska statute unduly interfered with interstate commerce and declared the statute unconstitutional.*

The Taxing Power

Congress has the "Power to lay and collect Taxes, Duties, Imposts and Excises *   *   * but all Duties, Imposts and Excises shall be uniform throughout the United States" (Article I, Section 8). Congress may not tax some states while exempting others. All states must be treated in an equal manner. The courts examine whether Congress is actually attempting to regulate an area indirectly through taxation. If Congress is empowered to regulate the area, the tax is valid. On the other hand, if Congress is attempting to regulate an area over which it has no authority, the tax law is void.

Federal taxes can be supported as a valid exercise of federal regulation. The Supreme Court has upheld taxes imposed on the transfer of firearms, on the transfer of marijuana, and on the income of persons who are gambling. Taxes can also be upheld if they comprise a revenue-raising measure; that is, when a tax produces revenues, it is generally held to be within the national **taxing power.** Moreover, the expansive interpretation of the commerce clause usually provides a basis for sustaining a federal tax.

The Spending Power

Congress has the power "to pay the Debts and provide for the common Defense and general welfare of the United States" (Article I, Section 8). In other words, Congress can spend the monies collected under the taxing power. The **spending power** unavoidably involves policy choices. Some taxpayers object to the government spending money on a particular program. For example, some people object to Congress spending money to support national defense. It is, however, nearly impossible to object to specific government spending through the legal system because of the **standing to sue** requirement.

The doctrine of standing to sue requires a litigant to demonstrate a direct and immediate personal injury due to the challenged action. A litigant must show that the injury is directly related to the particular government spending program and that the court can give the litigant relief from the harm alleged. Rarely is a taxpayer directly harmed by any government spending program. As a result, the spending power is seldom challenged. Communicating directly with members of Congress is a more efficient method of influencing

Legal Highlight

The Rising Sun

On Monday, September 17, 1787, the delegates met for the last time at Independence Hall in Philadelphia, Pennsylvania. James Madison penned an eloquent paragraph concerning that day:

> Whilst the last members were signing, Doctor Franklin, looking toward the President's chair, at the back of which a rising sun happened to be painted, observed to a few members near

him that painters had found it difficult to distinguish in their art, a rising, from a setting, sun. I have, said he, often and often in the course of the session, and the vicissitudes of hopes and fears as to its issue, looked at that behind the President, without being able to tell whether it was rising or setting; but now at length I have the happiness to know, that it is a rising, and not a setting, sun.

spending policies. The voters can speak through the ballot box.

Bill of Rights and the Other Amendments

The Bill of Rights was added to the Constitution in 1791. Specific protections for the individual from the federal government were set out in these first ten amendments.

Among the guarantees provided by the Bill of Rights are:

1. The First Amendment protections of religion, speech, and assembly
2. The Fourth Amendment provisions regarding arrest and unreasonable search and seizure
3. The Fifth Amendment
   a. Protection from **double jeopardy**—a person cannot be tried by the same level of government more than once for the same crime
   b. Freedom from **self-incrimination**—a person cannot be forced to testify against himself or herself
   c. Right to **due process**—a person has the right to timely notice of a trial and to a fair hearing
4. The Sixth Amendment rights to a speedy and public trial, to an attorney, to confront witnesses, and to cross-examination in criminal prosecutions
5. The Seventh Amendment guarantee of jury trials in civil suits

6. The Eighth Amendment provisions for bail and prohibitions against cruel and unusual punishment.

The Fourteenth Amendment was passed after the Civil War. This amendment includes a due process clause, like the one found in the Fifth Amendment; it also includes an **equal protection clause,** not found in any other part of the Constitution. Under the Fourteenth Amendment, people are protected from specific actions by the state governments.

Over a long series of cases, the Supreme Court adopted the **doctrine of selective incorporation.** Through the use of this doctrine and the due process clause of the Fourteenth Amendment, specific individual rights guaranteed by the first ten amendments are now applicable to the state governments as well as to the federal government. Those guarantees of individual liberty that are fundamental to the American system of law must now also be protected by the states.

Delegated Powers

The Tenth Amendment delegates certain **enumerated powers** to the federal government and reserves all other powers to the states or to the people. This amendment limits the power of the federal government by stating that "the powers not delegated to the United States by the Constitution, nor prohibited by it to the States, are reserved to

Twenty-Seven of 10,000 Proposed Amendments

The delegates to the constitutional convention did not believe that any protections of individual freedoms should be included in the document. Very shortly it became evident that the people had other ideas; indeed, they demanded constitutional protections.

Over the past 200 years, more than 10,000 amendments have been proposed. The first ten amendments came as a package, but the next seventeen amendments span the years from 1798 to 1992. Of those seventeen amendments, one canceled an earlier one: The 21st Amendment repealed the Eighteenth Amendment on liquor prohibition. One early proposed amendment was intended to ban constitutionally the act of dueling. Another attempted to prohibit Congress from abolishing slavery—ironically, it would have been the Thirteenth Amendment. Instead, the Thirteenth Amendment does abolish slavery. Over 200 proposed amendments attempted to stop the Civil War. More recent proposals include the Equal Rights Amendment, Right to Life Amendment, and a Balanced Budget Amendment.

the States respectively, or to the people." The federal government has no powers apart from those specified in the Constitution; it holds only enumerated powers, since it can exercise only those powers that are expressly or implicitly granted to it.

The term *expressly* was not included in the Tenth Amendment. This word was found in the Articles of Confederation in a similar provision. By not having the word *expressly* in the amendment, the federal government is able to find *implied* federal powers. Thus, it is implicit in the Constitution that the federal government may do whatever is necessary to follow through on the specific powers it has been granted.

Bill of Rights in a Business Context

A business may be conducted by one person operating under her or his own name, a common name, or a fictitious name. Other types of businesses are conducted by partnerships or by corporations. Corporations and some types of partnerships exist as separate legal entities. As a legal entity, a business is entitled to some of the same rights and privileges as an individual citizen. For example, a legal entity can sue and be sued in a court, pays taxes under the legal entity status, and holds title to property. The Bill of Rights guarantees persons certain protections. The Supreme Court has recognized corporations as persons in very specific areas of the Constitution, while in other areas corporations do not qualify for constitutional protection.

Business and the First Amendment

The First Amendment to the Constitution states:

> Congress shall make no law respecting an establishment of religion, or prohibiting the free exercise thereof; or abridging the freedom of speech, or of the press; or the right of the people peaceably to assemble, and to petition the government for redress of grievances.

Freedom of expression is one of the foundations of our society. Our forefathers believed that the ability and the right to exchange ideas allow for the development of a free and open society. Armed with knowledge, the citizen has the ability to make better decisions.

The freedom of speech is not an absolute right. No one has a basic right to speak to another about planning a murder. A person does not have a right to spread lies about others, nor does anyone have a right to yell "fire" in a crowded theater if there is no fire. Although we have the basic right of freedom of speech, there are limits to it.

The problem lies in establishing these limits. Everyone is in favor of freedom of speech for himself or herself. The difficulty occurs when an attempt is made to limit the freedom of speech of others. Should the American Nazi Party be allowed to hold a parade in a predominantly Jewish neighborhood? Should antinuclear demonstrators be allowed to block the entrance to nuclear plants?

The limitations on freedom of speech have varied over the years. This book focuses on defamation and commercial speech in looking at how these limitations affect businesses. You must recognize, however, that this is an extremely wide-ranging issue. Almost 200 years after the adoption of this amendment in 1791, society is still deciding what is meant by freedom of speech and what limits should be placed on that freedom.

Defamation **Defamation** is discussed in greater detail in Chapter 8. It is defined as the act of making any untrue statements that impinge on the integrity or character of another person or corporation.

Historically, defamation has never been protected by the First Amendment. During the civil rights actions of the early 1960s, the *New York Times* printed articles of a defamatory nature against an elected Southern official. The United States Supreme Court held that public officials seeking to recover for defamation relating to their performance of official duties must prove **actual malice**.[2] Actual malice means that a statement must be made with the knowledge that it is false or with reckless disregard of whether it is false or not.

Public figures and officials are covered by the First Amendment. A public official is a person who is elected or appointed to government service. A public figure is a person, such as an actor or an athletic coach, who seeks public recognition or a person who is thrust into the limelight, such as a person accused of a crime or a survivor of an airline crash.

Commercial Speech In the past, the United States Supreme Court drew a distinction between freedom of speech as to political views or individual expression and freedom of speech in commercial statements. For example, political speech could not be restrained, but commercial advertising was subject to government control. This view continued until the case of *Virginia State Board of Pharmacy v. Virginia Citizens Consumer Council, Inc.*[3] This case, along with several others, challenged a legal ban on advertising the price of prescription drugs. Justice Blackmun held, "It is clear * * * that speech does not lose its First Amendment protection because money is spent * * * as in a paid advertisement."

After this case, several cases arose confronting the issue of **commercial speech**. One of the leading cases was *Bates v. State Bar of Arizona.*[4] The State Bar of Arizona refused to allow any attorney to advertise for services or to advertise the price of those services. Advertising was not considered professional. Two attorneys advertised, quoting prices for routine legal work. The advertisements did not include anything that might commonly be called trade puffing. Because of this advertisement, the State Bar of Arizona suspended the attorneys from the practice of law. The United States Supreme Court held that the attorneys' freedom of speech had been violated.

Eventually the United States Supreme Court was confronted with additional problems of fact. How far should professionals be allowed to go in advertising? How much information must be contained within the advertisement? In the following case, the United States Supreme Court discussed commercial speech as it applies to advertising legal services.

2. New York Times Co. v. Sullivan, 376 U.S. 254, 84 S.Ct. 710, 11 L.Ed.2d 686 (1964).

3. 425 U.S. 748, 96 S.Ct. 1817, 48 L.Ed.2d 346 (1976).
4. 433 U.S. 350, 97 S.Ct. 2691, 53 L.Ed.2d 810 (1977).

Case 5.2

ZAUDERER v. OFFICE OF DISCIPLINARY COUNCIL OF THE SUPREME COURT OF OHIO

Supreme Court of the United States, 1985.
471 U.S. 626, 105 S.Ct. 2265, 85 L.Ed.2d 652.

BACKGROUND AND FACTS *Zauderer was a licensed attorney in Ohio. He placed several advertisements in the local media advising readers that his firm would represent defendants in drunk driving cases and that his clients' full legal fees would be refunded if they were convicted of drunk driving. He did not disclose in the advertisements that many cases would be plea-bargained to a lesser offense. Later, Zauderer ran another newspaper advertisement publicizing his willingness to represent women who had suffered injuries resulting from their use of the Dalkon Shield. The advertisement featured a line drawing of the device and stated that the cases would be handled on a contingency fee basis and that, if there were no recovery, no legal fees would be owed. Nothing was mentioned about the client being responsible for court costs. This advertisement attracted 106 clients. A complaint was filed with the state bar association claiming that Zauderer's advertisements were deceptive.*

Justice WHITE delivered the opinion of the Court.

*   *   *   *

*   *   * [T]he decision in *Virginia Pharmacy Board v. Virginia Citizens Consumer Council, Inc.*, held for the first time that the First Amendment precludes certain forms of regulation of purely commercial speech. *   *   * This case presents additional unresolved questions regarding the regulation of commercial speech by attorneys: whether a State may discipline an attorney for soliciting business by running newspaper advertisements containing nondeceptive illustrations and legal advice, and whether a State may seek to prevent potential deception of the public by requiring attorneys to disclose in their advertising certain information regarding fee arrangements.

*   *   *   *

There is no longer any room to doubt that what has come to be known as "commercial speech" is entitled to the protection of the First Amendment, albeit to protection somewhat less extensive than that afforded "noncommercial speech." More subject to doubt, perhaps, are the precise bounds of the category of expression that may be termed commercial speech, but it is clear enough that the speech at issue in this case—advertising pure and simple—falls within those bounds. Our commercial speech doctrine rests heavily on "the 'common-sense' distinction between speech proposing a commercial transaction *   *   * and other varieties of speech," and appellant's advertisements undeniably propose a commercial transaction. *   *   *

Our general approach to restrictions on commercial speech is also by now well settled. The States and the Federal Government are free to prevent the dissemination of commercial speech that is false, deceptive, or misleading, or that proposes an illegal transaction. Commercial speech that is not false or deceptive and does not concern unlawful activities, however, may be restricted only in the service of a substantial governmental interest, and only through means that directly advance that interest. Our application of these principles to the commercial speech of attorneys has led us to conclude that blanket bans on price advertising by attorneys and rules preventing attorneys from using nondeceptive terminology to describe their fields of practice are impermissible. To resolve this appeal, we must apply the teachings of these cases to three separate forms of regulation Ohio has imposed on advertising by its attorneys: prohibitions on soliciting legal business through advertisements containing advice and information regarding specific legal problems; restrictions on the use of illustrations in advertising by lawyers; and disclosure requirements relating to the terms of contingent fees. *   *   *

The interest served by the application of the Ohio self-recommendation and solicitation rules to appellant's advertisement is not apparent. The advertisement's information and advice concerning the Dalkon Shield were * * * neither false nor deceptive: in fact, it was entirely accurate. The advertisement did not promise readers that lawsuits alleging injuries caused by Dalkon Shield would be successful, nor did it suggest that appellant had any special expertise in handling such lawsuits other than his employment in other such litigation. Rather, the advertisement reported the indisputable fact that the Dalkon Shield has spawned an impressive number of lawsuits and advised readers that appellant was currently handling such lawsuits and was willing to represent other women asserting similar claims.

* * * *

* * * The application of * * * [Ohio's r]estriction on illustrations in advertising by lawyers to appellant's advertisement fails for much the same reasons as does the application of the self-recommendation and solicitation rules. The use of illustrations or pictures in advertisements serves important communicative functions: it attracts the attention of the audience to the advertiser's message, and it may also serve to impart information directly.

* * * *

Appellant, however, overlooks material differences between disclosure requirements and outright prohibitions on speech. In requiring attorneys who advertise their willingness to represent clients on a contingent-fee basis to state that the client may have to bear certain expenses even if he loses, Ohio has not attempted to prevent attorneys from conveying information to the public; it has only required them to provide somewhat more information than they might otherwise be inclined to present.

* * * *

The Supreme Court of Ohio issued a public reprimand. That judgment is affirmed to the extent that it is based on appellant's advertisement involving his terms of representation in drunken driving cases and on the omission of information regarding his contingent-fee arrangements in his Dalkon Shield advertisement. But insofar as the reprimand was based on appellant's use of an illustration in his advertisement and his offer of legal advice in his advertisement the judgment is reversed.

The Supreme Court held that Zauderer did violate disciplinary rules by not disclosing material information concerning costs and plea bargaining. The Supreme Court continued to allow commercial speech to be protected by the First Amendment. Within the legal profession, however, a high disclosure requirement of all material facts exists.

DECISION AND REMEDY

Today, there is no question that commercial speech is protected by the First Amendment; however, advertisements must not be deceptive, misleading, or fraudulent. In addition to advertisements, corporations may also want to make known their positions on various topics. At times it is difficult to determine when a corporation is advocating a public or political position and when it is using commercial speech. For example, a bank wants to spend money to present its views opposing a referendum that would allow a graduated personal income tax. A corporation has as much right to publicize its views as an individual, even though these views promote the corporation's own profit or some other benefit. Moreover, the public is enriched by being exposed to all views, whether they are those of an individual or of a corporation.

On the other hand, should a corporation be allowed to fund the political campaigns of specific candidates? The following case looks at the right of a corporation to express its views as opposed to its right to support specific candidates for elected office.

Case 5.3

AUSTIN v. MICHIGAN CHAMBER OF COMMERCE

Supreme Court of the United States, 1990.
494 U.S. 652, 110 S.Ct. 1391, 108 L.Ed.2d 652.

BACKGROUND AND FACTS *Michigan adopted a statute that prohibited corporations from making contributions to candidates for state office. The Michigan Chamber of Commerce wanted to support certain candidates for elected office. The violation of the statute was a felony. The Michigan Chamber of Commerce sought an injunction against the enforcement of this statute.*

Justice MARSHALL delivered the opinion of the Court.

* * * *

To determine whether Michigan's restrictions on corporate political expenditures may constitutionally be applied to the Chamber, we must ascertain whether they burden the exercise of political speech and, if they do, whether they are narrowly tailored to serve a compelling state interest. * * * Certainly, the use of funds to support a political candidate is "speech"; independent campaign expenditures constitute political expression at the core of our electoral process and of the First Amendment freedoms. * * * The mere fact that the Chamber is a corporation does not remove its speech from the ambit of the First Amendment.

* * * *

The State contends that the unique legal and economic characteristics of corporations necessitate some regulation of their political expenditures to avoid corruption or the appearance of corruption. * * * [P]reventing corruption or the appearance of corruption are [sic] the only legitimate and compelling government interests thus far identified for restricting campaign finances. State law grants corporations special advantages—such as limited liability, perpetual life, and favorable treatment of the accumulation and distribution of assets—that enhance their ability to attract capital and to deploy their resources in ways that maximize the return on their shareholders' investments. These state-created advantages not only allow corporations to play a dominant role in the nation's economy, but also permit them to use resources amassed in the economic marketplace to obtain an unfair advantage in the political marketplace. * * * [T]he political advantage of corporations is unfair because

[t]he resources in the treasury of a business corporation . . . are not an indication of popular support for the corporation's political ideas. They reflect instead the economically motivated decisions of investors and customers. The availability of these resources may make a corporation a formidable political presence, even though the power of the corporation may be no reflection of the power of its ideas. * * *

We therefore have recognized that the compelling governmental interest in preventing corruption support[s] the restriction of the influence of political war chests funneled through the corporate form.

* * * *

We emphasize that the mere fact that corporations may accumulate large amounts of wealth is not the justification for [the statute], rather, the unique state-conferred corporate structure that facilitates the amassing of large treasuries warrants the limit on independent expenditures. Corporate wealth can unfairly influence elections when it is deployed in the form of independent expenditures, just as it can when it assumes the guise of political contributions. We therefore hold that the State has articulated a sufficiently compelling rationale to support its restriction on independent expenditures by corporations.

DECISION AND REMEDY *The Court determined that the state has the power to prohibit corporations from making political contributions to specific candidates.*

Freedom of Religion

The government cannot establish any religion nor can it prohibit the free exercise of religious practices. Any government action, both federal and state, must be neutral toward religion. Although a statute may have some impact on religion, as long as it does not promote or place a significant burden on religion, the statute is constitutional.

Sunday closing laws, for example, forbid the performance of certain business activities on Sunday. The closing laws have been found to be constitutional because the government has a legitimate interest in providing workers a day of rest. Although closing laws originally were religious in character, they have taken on the secular purpose of promoting the health and welfare of workers. Even though closing laws admittedly make it easier for Christians to attend religious services, the United States Supreme Court has viewed this effect as an incidental, not a primary, purpose of Sunday closing laws. Today, the few closing laws that still remain generally allow the businesses of people of other religious faiths to be open on Sunday so long as they observe a day of rest.

Title VII of the Civil Rights Act of 1964 prohibits government and private employers and unions from discriminating against individuals because of their religion. Businesses must accommodate and not discriminate against their employees on the basis of religious beliefs.

The United States Supreme Court addressed this issue in *Estate of Thornton v. Caldor, Inc.*[5] In this case, the Court held that a Connecticut statute granting employees the absolute right not to work on their Sabbath had the effect of advancing religious practices in violation of the establishment clause of the First Amendment. This type of statute discriminated against employees who might want a day off during the weekend for secular reasons.

In *Trans World Airlines, Inc. v. Hardison,*[6] the United States Supreme Court reviewed the case of a former airline clerk who brought a lawsuit against the airline and the union, claiming religious discrimination. He sought to have Saturday, his Sabbath, off. Neither the union nor the airline could work out a solution to the problem because he had low seniority, while those of higher seniority also wanted Saturdays off. Eventually he was fired for refusing to work on Saturday. The Supreme Court held the airline and the union had made reasonable efforts to accommodate his religious beliefs and that all the proposed solutions to his problem worked an undue hardship on the airline, the union, and his fellow employees. The operation of the seniority system was agreed to by both the airline and the union. As long as the seniority system did not have a discriminatory purpose, it was not an unlawful employment practice, even though the operation of the seniority system was discriminatory in its effect.

Search and Seizure

Before any governmental agency may search a place, that agency must obtain a search warrant from the court. The Supreme Court has found some exceptions, such as limited searches of automobiles or any place where the suspect may reach for a weapon. The search warrant must be based on **probable cause.** The Fourth Amendment states that the "right of the people to be secure in their persons, houses, papers, and effects, against unreasonable searches and seizures, shall not be violated, and no Warrants shall issue, but upon probable cause * * *." Probable cause requires law enforcement officials to have objective evidence that would convince a neutral magistrate that the proposed search is justified.

The warrant must particularly describe the place to be searched and the persons to be arrested or the things to be seized. General search warrants are prohibited. For example, a general search through a person's belongings is impermissible. Nothing is left to the discretion of the officer executing a search warrant; the search cannot extend beyond what is described in the warrant.

Constitutional protection against searches and seizures is extremely important to businesses and professionals. With increased federal and state regulation of commercial activities, frequent and unannounced government inspection to ensure

5.   472 U.S. 703, 105 S.Ct. 2914, 86 L.Ed.2d 557 (1985).
6.   432 U.S. 63, 97 S.Ct. 2264, 53 L.Ed.2d 113 (1977).

compliance with the law would be extremely disruptive. In *Marshall v. Barlow's, Inc.*,[7] the Supreme Court held that the government inspectors do not have the right to enter business premises without a warrant. In this case, the purpose of the law (Occupational Safety and Health Act of 1970) was to provide a safe workplace. If the business

---

7. 436 U.S. 307, 98 S.Ct. 1816, 56 L.Ed.2d 305 (1978).

was found to be in violation of the government requirements, the government could impose fines for violations. Businesses have a right to require the government to obtain a warrant from a neutral magistrate. This case is discussed in greater detail in Chapter 6.

The Supreme Court reviewed the following case, which involved a public employer's search of the office of an employee.

Case 5.4

O'CONNOR v. ORTEGA

Supreme Court of the United
States, 1987.
480 U.S. 709, 107 S.Ct. 1492,
94 L.Ed.2d 714.

BACKGROUND AND FACTS *Dr. Ortega was a physician and psychiatrist. He was chief of professional education at Napa State Hospital for seventeen years, until his dismissal in 1981. In July 1981, Dr. O'Connor, the executive director of the hospital, became concerned with possible improprieties in Dr. Ortega's work. In particular, he was concerned with whether Dr. Ortega had acquired an Apple II computer by donation or whether the funds were raised by coercion of the residents in Dr. Ortega's program. Dr. O'Connor was also concerned with possible sexual harassment of two female employees.*

Dr. Ortega was placed on paid administrative leave pending the investigation of these charges. He was not allowed into his office. The hospital searched Dr. Ortega's office. The specific reason for the entry was unclear, but the hospital claimed it was to inventory and secure state property. At first the hospital claimed it was a routine inventory, but later it admitted having no policy of inventorying the offices of those employees placed on administrative leave. The hospital finally ended up seizing several items from Dr. Ortega's desk, including a Valentine's Day card, a photograph, and a book of poetry, all sent to Dr. Ortega by a former resident physician. These items were used against Dr. Ortega in the administrative personnel hearing. Attempts to separate Dr. Ortega's personal property from state property were given up, and no inventory of his office was ever made. His papers were placed in a box and put in storage for Dr. Ortega to retrieve. As a result of the personnel hearing, Dr. Ortega was discharged.

He brought this lawsuit alleging that the search of his office violated his Fourth Amendment rights and that he had a reasonable expectation of privacy in his office.

Justice O'CONNOR delivered the opinion of the Court.
*   *   *   *

The strictures of the Fourth Amendment, applied to the States through the Fourteenth Amendment, have been applied to the conduct of governmental officials in various civil activities. Thus, we have held in the past that the Fourteenth Amendment governs the conduct of school officials, building inspectors, *   *   * and Occupational Safety and Health Act inspectors. *   *   * As we observed, *   *   * "[b]ecause the individual's interest in privacy and personal security 'suffers whether the government's motivation is to investigate violations of criminal laws or breaches of other statutory or regulatory standards,' . . . it would be anomalous to say that the individual and his private property are fully protected by the Fourth Amendment only when the individual is suspected of criminal behavior.' " *   *   *
Searches and seizures by government employers or supervisors of the private prop-

erty of their employees, therefore, are subject to the restraints of the Fourth Amendment.

* * * Our cases establish that Dr. Ortega's Fourth Amendment rights are implicated only if the conduct of the Hospital officials at issue in this case infringed "an expectation of privacy that society is prepared to consider reasonable." * * *
* * * *

Within the workplace context, this Court has recognized that employees may have a reasonable expectation of privacy against intrusions by police. As with the expectation of privacy in one's home, such an expectation in one's place of work is "based upon societal expectations that have deep roots in the history of the Amendment." * * *
* * * *

Given the societal expectations of privacy in one's place of work * * * we reject the contention made by the Solicitor General and petitioners that public employees can never have a reasonable expectation of privacy in their place of work. Individuals do not lose Fourth Amendment rights merely because they work for the government instead of a private employer. The operational realities of the workplace, however, may make *some* employees' expectations of privacy unreasonable when an intrusion is by a supervisor rather than a law enforcement official. Public employees' expectations of privacy in their offices, desks, and file cabinets, like similar expectations of employees in the private sector, may be reduced by virtue of actual office practices and procedures, or by legitimate regulation. * * *
* * * *

The legitimate privacy interests of public employees in the private objects they bring to the workplace may be substantial. Against these privacy interests, however, must be balanced the realities of the workplace, which strongly suggest that a warrant requirement would be unworkable. While police, and even administrative enforcement personnel, conduct searches for the primary purpose of obtaining evidence for use in criminal or other enforcement proceedings, employers most frequently need to enter the offices and desks of their employees for legitimate work-related reasons wholly unrelated to illegal conduct. Employers and supervisors are focused primarily on the need to complete the government agency's work in a prompt and efficient manner. An employer may have need for correspondence, or a file or report available only in an employee's office while the employee is away from the office. Or, as is alleged to have been the case here, employers may need to safeguard or identify state property or records in an office in connection with a pending investigation into suspected employee misfeasance.

In our view, requiring an employer to obtain a warrant whenever the employer wished to enter an employee's office, desk, or file cabinets for a work-related purpose would seriously disrupt the routine conduct of business and would be unduly burdensome. Imposing unwieldy warrant procedures in such cases upon supervisors, who would otherwise have no reason to be familiar with such procedures, is simply unreasonable. * * *
* * * *

* * * We hold, therefore, that public employer intrusions on the constitutionally protected privacy interests of government employees for noninvestigatory, work-related purposes, as well as for investigations of work-related misconduct, should be judged by the standard of reasonableness under all the circumstances.

DECISION AND REMEDY

The Court concluded that a search of an employee's office by a supervisor will be justified at its inception when there are reasonable grounds for suspecting that the search will turn up evidence that the employee is guilty of work-related misconduct or when a search is necessary for a noninvestigatory work-related purpose such as retrieving a needed file. The Court sent the case back to the district court to determine the justification for the search and seizure and to evaluate the reasonableness of both the inception of the search and the scope of the search that included the seizure of Dr. Ortega's personal belongings.

Self-Incrimination

The Fifth Amendment guarantees that no person "shall be compelled in any criminal case to be a witness against himself." An accused person cannot be made to confess or to give any evidence that might be used against him or her in any criminal prosecution. An accused person is protected by the Fifth Amendment from the actions of the federal government. The Fourteenth Amendment due process clause incorporates the Fifth Amendment provision against self-incrimination and protects an accused from any illegal action by the state government. The accused, however, has this protection only for himself or herself. He or she may be forced to testify against others.

The Fifth Amendment's guarantee against self-incrimination extends only to natural persons and not to legal entities. Corporations and partnerships are legal entities; therefore, they do not have the protection of that clause of the Fifth Amendment. When records of these organizations are ordered by the court to be produced, the information must be given even if the evidence is incriminating.

The protection from self-incrimination does not apply to an individual's business records if they are being sought by the government through the use of a warrant. As discussed previously, before a warrant will be issued, probable cause must be established. The items must be produced under the warrant even though they might incriminate the person. What are the rights of a businessperson when she or he has turned over incriminating papers to an accountant or lawyer? This question was answered in the following case.

Case 5.5
FISHER v. UNITED STATES
Supreme Court of the United States, 1976.
425 U.S. 391, 96 S.Ct. 1569, 48 L.Ed.2d 39.

BACKGROUND AND FACTS   *In two cases, taxpayers were under investigation for possible civil or criminal liability under the federal income tax laws. The taxpayers obtained from their accountants certain documents relating to the accountants' preparation of their tax returns and transferred these documents to their attorneys. The Internal Revenue Service attempted to obtain these documents by serving summonses on the taxpayers' attorneys. The attorneys refused to comply based on their clients' Fifth Amendment rights after self-incrimination and the attorney-client privilege.*

Justice WHITE delivered the opinion of the Court.
   In these two cases we are called upon to decide whether a summons directing an attorney to produce documents delivered to him by his client in connection with the attorney-client relationship is enforceable over claims that the documents were constitutionally immune from summons in the hands of the client and retained that immunity in the hands of the attorney.
*   *   *   *

   *   *   * [P]etitioners' appeal raised only their Fifth Amendment claim, but they argued in connection with that claim that enforcement of the summons would involve a violation of the taxpayers' reasonable expectation of privacy and particularly so in light of the confidential relationship of attorney to client. *   *   *
*   *   *   *

   All of the parties in these cases have concurred in the proposition that if the Fifth Amendment would have excused a taxpayer from turning over the accountant's papers had he possessed them, the attorney to whom they are delivered for the purpose of obtaining legal advice should also be immune from subpoena. Although we agree with this proposition, we are convinced that it is not the taxpayer's Fifth Amendment privilege that would excuse the attorney from production.

The relevant part of that Amendment provides:

"No person * * * shall be *compelled* in any criminal case to be a *witness against himself.*" (Emphasis added.)

The taxpayer's privilege under this Amendment is not violated by enforcement of the summonses involved in these cases because enforcement against a taxpayer's lawyer would not "compel" the taxpayer to do anything—and certainly would not compel him to be a "witness" against himself. The Court has held repeatedly that the Fifth Amendment is limited to prohibiting the use of "physical or moral compulsion" exerted on the person asserting the privilege. In *Couch v. United States,* we recently ruled that the Fifth Amendment rights of a taxpayer were not violated by the enforcement of a documentary summons directed to her accountant and requiring production of the taxpayer's own records in the possession of the accountant. We did so on the ground that in such a case "the ingredient of personal compulsion against an accused is lacking."

Here, the taxpayers are compelled to do no more than was the taxpayer in *Couch.* The taxpayers' Fifth Amendment privilege is therefore not violated by enforcement of the summonses directed toward their attorneys. * * *

* * * *

Confidential disclosures by a client to an attorney made in order to obtain legal assistance are privileged. As a practical matter, if the client knows that damaging information could more readily be obtained from the attorney following disclosure than from himself in the absence of disclosure, the client would be reluctant to confide in his lawyer and it would be difficult to obtain fully informed legal advice. However, since the privilege has the effect of withholding relevant information from the factfinder, it applies only where necessary to achieve its purpose. Accordingly it protects only those disclosures—necessary to obtain informed legal advice—which might not have been made absent the privilege. This Court and the lower courts have thus uniformly held that pre-existing documents which could have been obtained by court process from the client when he was in possession may also be obtained from the attorney by similar process following transfer by the client in order to obtain more informed legal advice. * * * It is otherwise if the documents are not obtainable by subpoena *duces tecum* [subpoena used to obtain evidence in the hands of another] or summons while in the exclusive possession of the client, for the client will then be reluctant to transfer possession to the lawyer unless the documents are also privileged in the latter's hands. * * *

* * * *

A subpoena served on a taxpayer requiring him to produce an accountant's workpapers in his possession without doubt involves substantial compulsion. But it does not compel oral testimony; nor would it ordinarily compel the taxpayer to restate, repeat, or affirm the truth of the contents of the documents sought. Therefore, the Fifth Amendment would not be violated by the fact alone that the papers on their face might incriminate the taxpayer, for the privilege protects a person only against being incriminated by his own compelled testimonial communications. The accountant's workpapers are not the taxpayer's. They were not prepared by the taxpayer, and they contain no testimonial declarations by him. * * *

* * * *

Whether the Fifth Amendment would shield the taxpayer from producing his own tax records in his possession is a question not involved here; for the papers demanded here are not his "private papers[.]" * * *

The Supreme Court held that nontestimonial business records not prepared by the taxpayer in the custody of third parties, including lawyers and accountants, must be surrendered when a search warrant is issued for them.

DECISION AND REMEDY

COMMENT *This case did not confront the issue of whether the individual would have to produce his or her own records. Other tangible evidence, such as a blood sample, sperm sample, or clothing, must be surrendered when a warrant is issued. But would personal business records prepared solely by the taxpayer be required to be surrendered? The Supreme Court has not yet answered this question.*

Due Process

Under our Constitution, no person shall be deprived "of life, liberty, or property, without due process of law." This clause is contained in both the Fifth and the Fourteenth Amendments and thus is applicable to both the federal and state governments.

Due process is a basic principle that requires fairness in the government's dealing with persons. Because the Supreme Court interprets this clause on a case-by-case basis, it has generated more cases than any other clause in the Constitution. Most of the basic rights discussed in this chapter are applicable to both government and private employers. But because the Fifth and Fourteenth Amendments apply explicitly to both federal and state governments, public employees have more due process rights than private employees.

The due process clause has two aspects: procedural and substantive. **Procedural due process** requires safeguards before any government decision can be made to take a person's life, liberty, or property.

Substantive due process focuses on the content, or substance, of legislation. Every statute and regulation and every government act must be in compliance with the Constitution; otherwise, substantive due process has been violated. For example, Congress passes a statute imposing a $1 million fine and mandatory five-year prison term without a trial on any university professor who appears as an expert on a television news program. This law would be unconstitutional on both substantive and procedural grounds.

A court would invalidate this legislation because it abridges freedom of speech, a violation of the First Amendment. A denial of substantive due process requires a court to overrule any state or federal law that violates the Constitution. Procedurally, the law is unfair because the penalty is imposed without giving the accused a chance to defend her or his actions. A court will invalidate any statute or court decision because of the lack of procedural due process.

Equal Protection

Under the Fourteenth Amendment, a state may not "deny to any person within its jurisdiction the equal protection of the laws." The Supreme Court has used the due process clause of the Fifth Amendment to make the equal protection guarantee applicable to the federal government. Equal protection means that the government must treat similarly situated individuals in a similar manner.

Equal protection is concerned with whether there is a rational and legitimate purpose for applying different rules to people. For example, Congress passes a law that provides employment benefits for pregnant women for two weeks prior to delivery and for six months after the baby's arrival. The court would have to determine if there is a rational basis for this law. Similarly, if Congress passed a statute that exempted all men who play football from paying personal taxes, the courts would examine the facts to determine whether there was a rational basis for the law.

Full Faith and Credit

Article IV, Section 1, reads, "Full Faith and Credit shall be given in each State to the public Acts, Records, and judicial Proceedings of every other State." The Constitution requires every state through the **full faith and credit clause** to recognize and enforce the judgments and other public actions of sister states. For example, if you obtain a divorce in one state, all other states must recognize your divorce. Limitations do apply; for instance, if the original court did not have jurisdiction, the judgment may be challenged in the state where the plaintiff is trying to enforce the judgment.

Ethical Considerations

Conflicts between Freedom of Speech and Ethics

This chapter discusses one of our most important rights, freedom of speech. Included within free speech is the publication of books. Books cover a wide range of topics, some of which may be considered immoral by many members of society. If the topic is immoral, is it ethical for a person to write a book or article on the topic and for the publisher to print it? Let's look at three examples.

What are the ethics of writing and publishing a book on various methods of suicide? Persons who are in favor of euthanasia may argue that a person has a fundamental right to commit suicide, especially if he or she is suffering great pain from a fatal disease. Others would argue that it is never moral to commit suicide and thus to write or publish books on the topic is inherently immoral.

What about a book on how to construct a bomb? Some people believe they have a right to know this information in order to protect the country from a foreign takeover. The other argument is that the task of defending the country belongs to the president and the Department of Defense and not to paramilitary organizations. Thus, it is inherently immoral to put information on bomb making in the hands of private parties. Under the First Amendment a person has the right to write and read a book on this topic, but is it ethical to do so?

Another topic involves a conflict with our environment. All states have caves, most of which are not well known to the general public. A great deal of care must be taken to preserve the cave and the animal, insect, and plant life within it. So sensitive is this life that a single film wrapper contains sufficient chemicals to kill all life within the cave. In addition, it takes stalactites and stalagmites hundreds, indeed thousands, of years to develop. Is it ethical or moral to publish a book that gives the location of every cave in the state? Laypersons, not recognizing the damage they are doing, may break off a piece of these rock formations to take home with them. In one state every cave mentioned in a book was extensively damaged and all life destroyed.

Is it ethical to write and publish books on these subjects? Should courts stop the publication? If so, which books should be printed and which ones banned? Is it ever the court's responsibility to legislate morality? You may not agree with a particular position, but do you think you should impose your ethical position on a person who has a contrary view? Are there ways to achieve consensus on whether a subject is moral? Where do you draw the line?

Privileges and Immunities

Article IV, Section 2, provides that "The citizens of each State shall be entitled to all Privileges and Immunities of Citizens in the several States." As a result of the **privileges and immunities clause**, one state cannot discriminate against the citizens of another state solely on that basis. Limitations on this clause have been developed by the courts over the past 200 years. A state may pass a statute that protects "legitimate local interest." Under this protection, state-supported colleges and univer-sities may charge higher tuition to nonresident students than to resident students. This is because the state's residents pay taxes that support the public university system.

In addition, the Supreme Court has held that corporations are not "citizens" within the meaning of Section 2, so a state may subject a non-resident corporation to higher tax rates and user fees as long as the rates are reasonable and not of a confiscatory nature.

International Considerations

Must a Court Recognize a Foreign Judgment

Over the decades, the Supreme Court of the United States has implemented various well-recognized principles of international law. Among these principles are those of **comity,** the **act of state,** and **sovereign immunity.**

Comity means courtesy or a willingness to grant a privilege, not as a matter of right but out of deference and goodwill. The *principle of comity* means that one nation recognizes the legislative, executive, or judicial acts of another nation. This doctrine is not based upon any international legal obligations but rather on respect for the laws of another country. Under the principle of comity, a judgment from a foreign country is enforceable within the courts of the United States.[a] The foreign judgment must be based upon having proper jurisdiction. The effect of comity is similar to the full faith and credit clause of the Constitution, which requires states to recognize the judgments coming from sister states.

The *act of state* doctrine means not interfering with the acts of another nation within its boundaries. Courts in the United States are not allowed to question these actions. The effect of this doctrine is that courts in the United States are normally precluded from hearing cases where a sovereign nation has expropriated or confiscated the assets of an American business. **Expropriation** occurs when a government seizes privately owned goods or a privately owned business for a proper public purpose, and it awards just compensation. A **confiscation** occurs when the other country takes the privately owned goods or business without a proper public purpose and with no award of just compensation. The only exception to the principle regarding an act of state is when a treaty exists between the two countries that allows a legal action in the United States.

In 1976, Congress passed the **Foreign Sovereign Immunities Act** (FSIA), which codifies the doctrine of sovereign immunity. Sovereign immunity means you cannot sue the government without its permission. For the purposes of this doctrine, a "foreign state" includes both the political subdivision that comprises the state and any instrumentality of the foreign state, such as a state-owned bank.

The FSIA exclusively governs the circumstances under which an action may be brought against a foreign state in the United States. Attachment of a foreign nation's property, for example, is provided for by the FSIA. One of the primary purposes of the FSIA is to ensure that federal courts, rather than the Department of State, determine claims of foreign sovereign immunity. By removing the claims to federal court, the Department of State is relieved from political pressures to make diplomatic decisions that might be legally correct but politically unpopular.

Section 1605 of the FSIA sets out the major exceptions to the jurisdictional immunity of a country. A foreign state is not immune from the jurisdiction of the courts of the United States when the foreign government has waived its immunity. Nor is the foreign country immune when the action is based on a commercial activity carried out by the foreign nation within the jurisdictional limits of the United States.

a. Chapter 4 described how the New York Convention requires nations that have signed it to recognize foreign arbitration awards; the principle of comity refers to judgments coming from courts.

FACING A LEGAL ISSUE

Stopping Employee Theft

You are in a business that employs a large number of people. You have recently noticed big increases in lost inventory, which often indicates that employees are pilfering items. You have no idea who these employees may be or how many are involved. After considering this problem, you decide to listen to your employees' telephone conversations.

In absence of state law to the contrary, it is generally recognized that a business may listen to conversations of their employees. The business owns the telephone service and may have a wiretap that is not considered illegal because the business is consenting to the tap. A wiretap becomes illegal when a third party listens to a conversation without consent from either one of the persons speaking or from one of the owners of the telephone service.

You also decide that, once the number of employees under suspicion is narrowed, you will administer a polygraph test to the suspected ones. Whether the use of polygraphs by businesses is legal is a more difficult question. Most courts will not allow the results of a polygraph into evidence because of the unreliability of the tests. The results depend greatly on the analysis of the person giving the test.

Estimations show an error rate of 16 percent in polygraph tests given. In other words, nearly two out of every ten persons will fail the test when they should have passed it. In the past, these tests were utilized by many businesses. Today, 21 states prohibit polygraphs and in 1988, Congress adopted the Employee Polygraph Protection Act which strictly governs the use of polygraphs. As a result of the restrictions contained in the Act, most businesses no longer use polygraph tests.

Summary

The United States Constitution is the oldest active constitution in the modern world. The reason it has lasted so long is that our founders had the insight to produce a document that accomplishes three major objectives. First, the Constitution creates three branches of government, each independent of the other but with the ability to limit the powers of the other two branches through a system of checks and balances.

Second, it creates a central government that derives its power from the states but that is supreme. Federalism is the basic structure of our government. Certain powers are given to the federal government while other powers are shared with the states. The Constitution delegates certain powers or rights to the federal government; these are called enumerated powers. For example, the

commerce clause of the Constitution allows the federal government to regulate all interstate and foreign commerce. Any commerce, considered cumulatively, that has a substantial economic effect will be considered interstate commerce and subject to regulation. Occasionally, there can be conflicts between federal and state law. The federal law will be upheld under the supremacy clause of the Constitution.

Third, it guarantees the people certain basic rights that neither local nor federal governments can abridge. These rights are set out in detail in the first ten amendments to the Constitution, called the Bill of Rights. These amendments have particular applications to business. For example, under the First Amendment, commercial speech is protected as long as it is not false, deceptive, or misleading. Under the Fourth Amendment, businesses are protected from illegal search and seizures in the absence of a valid warrant. However, corporations or partnerships are not protected from self-incrimination under the Fifth Amendment.

Businesses are also protected by the due process clause in the Fifth and Fourteenth Amendments. There is a distinction between substantive and procedural due process. Procedural due process involves the methods used in protecting legal rights, while substantive due process involves protecting the basic legal rights themselves. The equal protection clause applies to both federal and state governments, which must give equal protection of the laws to all persons.

Key Terms

act of state (122)
actual malice (111)
comity (122)
commercial speech (111)
concurrent powers (104)
confiscation (122)
defamation (111)
doctrine of selective
    incorporation (109)
double jeopardy (109)
due process (109)
enumerated powers (109)

equal protection clause (109)
executive branch (104)
expropriation (122)
federalism (104)
Foreign Sovereign Immunities
    Act (122)
full faith and credit clause
    (120)
judicial branch (104)
legislative branch (104)
police powers (107)

privileges and immunities
    clause (121)
procedural due process (120)
probable cause (115)
self-incrimination (109)
sovereign immunity (122)
spending power (108)
standing to sue (108)
substantive due process (120)
supremacy clause (104)
taxing power (108)

Questions and Case Problems

1. A business has a backlog of orders. In order to meet its deadlines, management is considering running the firm seven days a week, eight hours a day. What issues of constitutional law might the management consider in making this decision? Is it possible to terminate someone for refusing to work more than 40 hours a week? Is it possible to terminate employees for refusing to work on their religious holy day?

2. Unlike all other states in the West and Midwest, Iowa prohibited by statute the use of 65-foot, double-trailer trucks on its highways. Use of 55-foot trailer trucks and 60-foot double-trailer trucks was allowed. Consolidated Freightways, a Delaware corporation, owned 65-foot double-trailer trucks. These trucks, which carried commodities, could not use the interstate highways that passed through Iowa. Consequently, Consolidated filed suit, alleging that Iowa's statutory scheme unconstitutionally burdened interstate commerce. Does Consolidated have a valid case? Please explain your answer. [Kassel v. Consolidated Freightways Corporation of Delaware, 450 U.S. 662, 101 S.Ct. 1309, 67 L.Ed.2d 580 (1981)]

3. A Wisconsin statute prohibits persons or firms that have violated the National Labor Relations Act (NLRA) three times within a five-year period from doing business with the state. Gould, Inc., was not allowed to do business with the state after having three violations of the NLRA within a five-year period. The NLRA has substantive requirements that are in conflict with the Wisconsin statute. Is this statute constitutional under the supremacy clause? Is the Wisconsin statute displaced by the NLRA? [Wisconsin Department of Industry v. Gould, Inc., 475 U.S. 282, 106 S.Ct. 1057, 89 L.Ed.2d 223 (1986)]

4. Puerto Rico passed a statute and regulations restricting casino gambling advertisements that were aimed at Puerto Rican residents. The operator of one of the casinos sought a declaratory judgment to have these restrictions declared null and void as violating freedom of speech. Puerto Rico took the position that it had a "substantial governmental interest" and the restrictions on such advertising "directly advance[d]" the Commonwealth's asserted interest. How would you hold in this situation? [Posadas de Puerto Rico Associates v. Tourism Co. of Puerto Rico, 478 U.S. 328, 106 S.Ct. 2968, 92 L.Ed.2d 266 (1986)]

5. The owner of a motel who refused to rent rooms to African Americans, despite the Civil Rights Act of 1964, brought an action to have the act declared unconstitutional. The motel owner alleged that Congress, in passing

the act, had exceeded its power to regulate commerce. The statute was upheld. What legal arguments were used to validate it? [Heart of Atlanta v. United States, 379 U.S. 241, 85 S.Ct. 348, 13 L.Ed.2d 258 (1964)]

6. Pacific Gas and Electric Company (P.G.&E.) has distributed a newsletter in its monthly billing statement for many years. The newsletter has included such items as political editorials, feature stories of public interest, and tips on energy conservation. The state regulatory commission decided that the envelope space was the ratepayers' property and ordered the company to allow an independent organization to publicize information there that was contrary to P.G.&E.'s position. P.G.&E. filed a lawsuit alleging that its First Amendment rights had been violated. Does P.G.&E. have a valid argument? Please explain your answer. [Pacific Gas and Electric Company v. Public Utilities Commission of California, 475 U.S. 1, 106 S.Ct. 903, 89 L.Ed.2d 1 (1986)]

7. In the early 1970s, an oil pipeline was being built across Alaska. In 1972 the Alaska legislature passed an act that became known as the Alaska Hire. The act had a provision that required the employment of qualified Alaska residents in preference to nonresidents. A person had to live in Alaska for one year before he or she could qualify for the preference. The reason for the act was to reduce unemployment. The plaintiffs were individuals who wanted jobs but who did not qualify for preference as residents of Alaska. The act was challenged under the privileges and immunities clause. Who should win this case—the plaintiffs seeking jobs or Alaska seeking to reduce unemployment—and why? [Hicklin v. Orbeck, 437 U.S. 518, 98 S.Ct. 2482, 57 L.Ed.2d 397 (1978)]

8. The plaintiffs, Americans United for Separation of Church and State, Inc., as taxpayers, brought an action to challenge a conveyance of land from the Department of Health, Education, and Welfare (HEW) to Valley Forge Christian College, the defendant. The plaintiffs alleged that such a conveyance violated the establishment clause of the First Amendment to the Constitution. The district court dismissed the complaint on the ground that the plaintiffs lacked standing to sue. What was the result on appeal? [Valley Forge Christian College v. Americans United for Separation of Church and State, Inc., 454 U.S. 464, 102 S.Ct. 752, 70 L.Ed.2d 700 (1982)]

9. Congress passed a law making it a federal crime for a person to steal any merchandise from any commercial truck that is part of an interstate shipment. Faulkner was a truck driver. In San Diego, California, he picked up 105 refrigerators that he was supposed to drive to Hartford, Connecticut. In Las Vegas, Nevada, he attempted to sell them to an undercover agent and was arrested. He claimed that he was innocent because the refrigerators never left his truck, and, therefore, no theft took place. Is he correct? Please explain your answer. [United States v. Faulkner, 638 F.2d 129 (9th Cir. 1981)]

10. New Jersey enacted a law prohibiting the importation of most wastes into the state. Some of the landfill operators in New Jersey, however, had agreements with out-of-state residents to dispose of their solid and liquid waste. Philadelphia brought an action claiming that this statute violated the commerce clause because it discriminated against interstate commerce. New Jersey asserted that its statute was justified since its landfills were inadequate to dispose of its own waste and importation had a significant and adverse potential effect on the environment. Is this state regulation of interstate commerce permissible? [Philadelphia v. New Jersey, 437 U.S. 617, 98 S.Ct. 2531, 57 L.Ed.2d 475 (1978)]

Chapter 6   Administrative Agencies and the Regulation of Business

The rise of administrative bodies probably has been the most significant legal trend of the last century and perhaps more values today are affected by their decisions than by those of all the courts, review of administrative decisions apart. They also have begun to have important consequences on personal rights. * * * They have become a veritable fourth branch of the Government, which has deranged our three-branch legal theories as much as the concept of a fourth dimension unsettles our three-dimensional thinking.

**Federal Trade Commission
v. Ruberoid Co.,**
343 U.S. 470, 487,
70 S.Ct. 800,
96 L.E.D.2d 1081 (1952).

OUTLINE

Introduction

Why should businesspeople know about administrative agencies? When most people think about enforcement of the law, they think about the courts. In actuality, most will never see the inside of a courtroom, and if they do, it will probably be for a traffic ticket. In contrast, most people have already dealt with an administrative agency.

Today's business decisions are restrained by congressional statutes and by the interpretation and enforcement of those statutes through rules made and enforced by administrative agencies. The study of the powers, procedures, and practices of these administrative agencies is called **administrative law.** Since the late 1960s, the regulation of business has dramatically shifted from the courts applying statutory and common law in order to resolve problems to the more direct and comprehensive controls of administrative agencies. The current constraints placed on business transactions by regulatory authorities have a great impact on the economy. (See Exhibit 6–1 which shows how administrative agencies fit into the organizational structure of the federal government.)

In this chapter, we will first review the areas of business that administrative agencies regulate. Second, we will look at the features embodied in administrative agencies that allow them to handle problems more effectively than the legislature or the courts can. Third, we will study the Administrative Procedure Act, its amendments, and the three types of power of an administrative agency: quasi-legislative, quasi-judicial, and quasi-executive. Fourth, we will discuss the constitutional, statutory, and judicial limits of an administrative agency's power. Fifth, we will briefly review the deregulation process.

Areas of Regulation

Administrative agencies handle two areas of public concern: **economic regulation** and **public welfare,** which in turn is broken into two parts—protection and **entitlement programs.** (See Exhibit 6–2 for some examples of different types of regulation.)

Economic Regulation

Economic regulation covers the following areas, among others. First, administrative agencies ap-

prove the entry into certain types of business; the Federal Aviation Administration, for example, certifies airlines and airports for operation. Second, administrative agencies regulate securities and financial businesses; for instance, the Federal Reserve System regulates the banking industry. Third, agencies regulate rate control, as when the Federal Energy Regulatory Commission oversees the setting of rates for natural gas and electricity. Fourth, some business activities are entirely subject to regulation, such as the broadcast media, which are regulated by the Federal Communications Commission.

Other agencies have regulatory powers that cut across all types of businesses. For example, the Equal Employment Opportunity Commission has responsibility for all compliance and enforcement activities that work to eliminate discrimination in business, in labor unions, and in government.

Public Welfare

For regulation purposes, the term *public welfare* refers to programs that benefit the public at large; it does not mean only government aid to lower-income people. For example, the Occupational Health and Safety Administration (OSHA) protects all workers in the workplace. OSHA provides for the public welfare of all by ensuring safety in the work area. All citizens benefit if workers have a safe workplace because the time and money lost from injuries and death decrease.

An example of an agency that handles entitlement programs for the public welfare is the Social Security Administration. Employed persons contribute to social security; if they become disabled or if they retire and they meet the eligibility criteria, they are entitled to receive social security benefits. Social security benefits are not based on income; even millionaires may receive social security if they have contributed to it during their working days.

Features of Administrative Agencies

Several features allow regulatory agencies to deal with problems more effectively than the legislature can. First, because an agency regulates only a specific subject-matter area, it develops expertise in that area and is able to adopt detailed regula-

Exhibit 6–1 Organization Chart of THE GOVERNMENT OF THE UNITED STATES

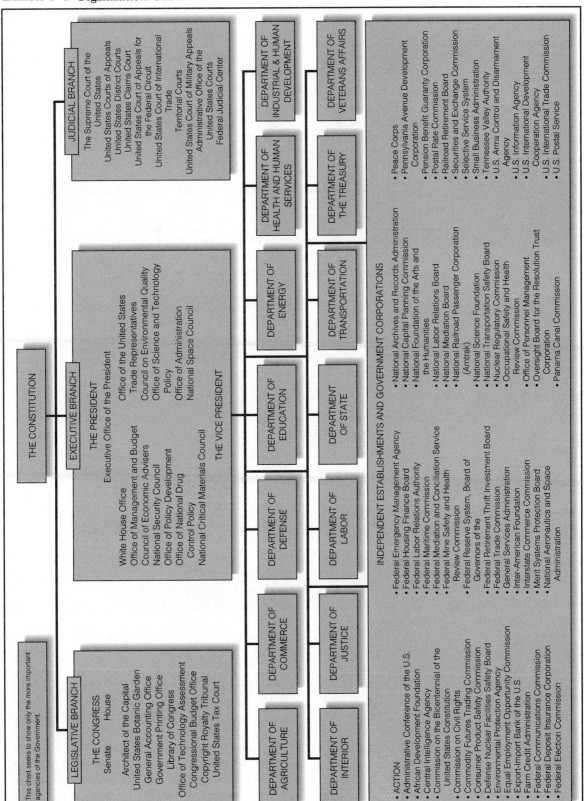

Source: U.S. Government Manual, 1991/92, Government Printing Office, (Washington, D.C.: 1991) p. 21.

Exhibit 6–2 **Types of Regulation**

Advertising Regulation	Cigarette, cigar, and liquor advertisements and sexually explicit material are controlled for the broadcast media.
Contract Regulation	Private contracts must follow certain regulations, such as the format for interest-rate disclosures, language requirements, and the consumer's right to rescind the contract within three days in some situations.
Disclosure Regulation	These regulations require health and nutritional information on food labels, fuel consumption labels on automobiles, and warning labels on dangerous products; in addition, information on securities must be filed with the Securities and Exchange Commission.
Licensing Regulation	Bank charters are issued by the state banking departments; insurance business charters are issued by the state insurance departments; and certificates of operation to railroads, trucking companies, and bus lines are issued by the Interstate Commerce Commission.
Material and Process Regulation	Materials and processes of manufacture are regulated. The Food and Drug Administration can ban the use of additives to food. The Environmental Protection Agency regulates the use and disposal of hazardous chemicals.
Quota Regulation	The importation or exportation of certain products is limited. The sale of computer components to terrorist countries is not allowed. The importation of oil is subject to quotas.
Rate Regulation	Where the government has granted a monopoly, it controls the profit returned. Utilities, electric, gas, water, and nuclear energy rates are controlled. Rates charged by common carriers are regulated by the Department of Transportation when buses, railroads, or trucks are involved. The Federal Maritime Commission governs rates charged by common carriers using the waters.
Standard Regulation	Standards are set by various agencies. The Department of Agriculture sets the standards for meat and poultry. The Federal Aviation Administration sets the standards for airplane certification.

tions. The legislature, with its limited resources and competing demands, is simply unable to develop the detailed plans needed to implement and monitor all the policies it establishes.

Second, a regulatory agency consists of a very well-developed hierarchy. A government employee generally will work for a particular agency for long periods of time, if not her or his entire career. The employee is promoted and rewarded within that structured bureaucracy. In contrast, the legislature consists of elected representatives and thus does not have continuity in its personnel.

Third, an agency has more flexibility than the legislature. If a business wants Congress to pass a certain law, the process is tedious and the results tenuous at best. Agencies, on the other hand, have been granted by Congress the ability to change regulations in a quick and efficient manner. Some regulations may be redrafted by the agency as soon as it sees the need for the change. Other regulations take longer to change because of the requirement to hold formal, public hearings, but even with this requirement, it is a faster method than the procedure Congress must follow in adopting or amending statutes.

Criticisms

Some observers believe that the growth of administrative agencies has limited the ability of elected officials to effect change. In the past, political power and influence were in the hands of the legislative and executive branches of government, but recently they have been moving into the bureaucracy. Thus, political power and influence are, to a substantial degree, wielded by quasi-permanent, unelected, nonpartisan administrative officials. The existing constraints on agencies' powers are generally seen as ineffective. The administrative agencies are now recognized by some as the fourth branch of the government. (See Exhibit 6–3, which shows the growing number and distribution of federal employees for the years 1980 and 1988.)

The Nature of Administrative Agencies

Administrative agencies are the primary interpreters and enforcers of congressional statutes that focus on business regulation. Created by Congress, an agency derives its authority from its enabling legislation. Four types of agencies can be created.

Line Agencies, Independent Agencies, Government Agencies, and Quasi-Official Agencies

When an agency is under the direct control of the president, it is known as a **line agency.** A line agency is headed by one person who is appointed by and serves at the pleasure of the president but who must be confirmed by the Senate. The members of the president's cabinet are heads of line agencies. For example, the secretary of the Department of Labor (a line agency) is a member of the cabinet who serves at the pleasure of the president. Exhibit 6–4 shows the structure of a sample line agency.

Congress also has established administrative agencies that are independent of the executive branch. If an agency is freestanding from the president and Congress, it is known as an **independent agency.** Many independent agencies have a com-

Exhibit 6–3 **Distribution of Employees in the Federal Government**

Branch of Government	1980	1988
Legislative (total)	**39,710**	**37,547**
Judicial (total)	**15,178**	**21,502**
Executive Office of the President	**1,886**	**1,554**
Executive Departments (total)	**1,945,255**	**2,049,424**
Agriculture	129,139	120,869
Commerce	48,563	52,819
Defense	960,116	1,049,619
Education	7,364	4,542
Energy	21,557	17,031
Health and Human Services	155,662	123,270
Housing and Urban Development	16,964	13,242
Interior	77,357	78,216
Justice	56,327	76,515
Labor	23,400	18,178
State	23,497	25,634
Transportation	72,361	63,506
Treasury	124,663	160,516
Veterans Administration	228,285	245,467
Independent Agencies (total)	**879,839**	**1,017,812**
Federal Reserve System	1,498	1,520
Environmental Protection Agency	14,715	15,309
Equal Employment Opportunity Commission	3,515	3,229
Federal Deposit Insurance Corporation	3,520	8,249
Federal Trade Commission	1,846	1,079
National Aeronautics and Space Administration	23,714	23,130
U.S. Postal Service	660,014	831,956
All Others	171,017	133,340

Source: U.S. Bureau of the Census, *Statistical Abstract of the United States,* 1990 (110th edition), Washington, D.C., 1989.

Exhibit 6–4 A Line Agency: DEPARTMENT OF COMMERCE

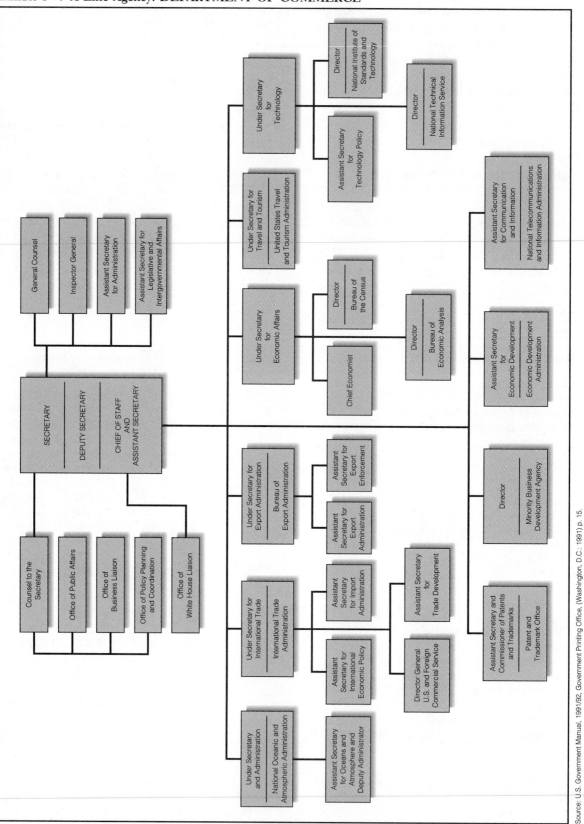

Source: U.S. Government Manual, 1991/92, Government Printing Office, (Washington, D.C.: 1991) p. 15.

mission created by Congress. The chair of the commission runs the daily operations. The Federal Trade Commission and the National Aeronautics and Space Administration are independent agencies.

The commission is a group usually ranging in size from three to fifteen people; the number is determined by Congress. When appointing people to the commission, the president is required to be bipartisan, which means that both political parties must be represented. The length of service on the commission varies from agency to agency, but all terms are staggered and are longer than the four-year term served by the president. Each commissioner is equal to each of the other members, with the chair of the commission having additional administrative duties. Although commissioners are appointed by the president, they act independently of the president and cannot be removed unilaterally by the president. See Exhibit 6–5 for the structure of a sample independent agency.

A **government agency** is created by Congress to administer a quasi-business venture. These agencies have three similar elements: (1) Each conducts a businesslike activity that (2) produces revenue to continue its own existence and, as a result, (3) needs greater flexibility than is usually given to other types of agencies. The major government agencies are the Tennessee Valley Authority (TVA), the Federal Deposit Insurance Corporation (FDIC), the Pension Benefit Guaranty Corporation, the Resolution Trust Corporation (RTC), and the United States Postal Service.

A **quasi-official agency** is created by Congress but does not have the same authority as other agencies. These agencies must publish notice and information about certain types of activities in the *Federal Register*. The members of the agency are appointed by the president, subject to approval by the Senate. Only four quasi-official agencies exist: Legal Services Corporation, National Railroad Passenger Corporation (Amtrak), Smithsonian Institute, and United States Railway Association.

Enabling Legislation

Most administrative agencies are created by Congress when it passes an **enabling act.** This act creates the agency; sets out its structure; gives it the authority to make rules, investigate problems,

and adjudicate cases; and defines what other powers it will have. Congress decides whether the agency will be a line agency in the executive branch, whether it will be an independent agency, or a government corporation.

Congress has control over the agencies. First, Congress creates and defines the powers of the agency. Second, the Senate must confirm the appointments of the head of the agency and the commissioners. Third, although the president sends to Congress the budget, only Congress, through its constitutional ability to tax and spend, controls the appropriations to the agency. Fourth, Congress may reorganize or abolish the agency. For example, Congress passed the Airline Deregulation Act of 1978. Part of the act abolished the Civil Aeronautics Board, effective January 1985.

After the agency has been created, it must adopt a **general policy statement.** The statement sets out, in broad terms, the philosophy of that particular agency; it describes the mission and objectives of the agency. For example, the general policy statement for the Federal Trade Commission reads that "[i]t is responsible for the administration of a variety of statutes which, in general, are designed to promote competition and to protect the public from unfair and deceptive acts and practices in the advertising and marketing of goods and services."[1]

The statement must also be politically astute; it must satisfy both the political atmosphere that created the agency and those who might curb its powers, if not abolish the agency outright. The authority of different agencies occasionally overlaps. The courts allow this overlapping as long as the actions taken by the agencies are consistent with their respective enabling statutes.

Administrative Procedure Act

The **Administrative Procedure Act (APA)** of 1946 standardized many practices of the agencies and now governs how all federal agencies must conduct their business. The APA does allow for differences among the agencies, however, because each agency has a different enabling act. The APA sets out the procedures that an agency must follow when making rules, when acquiring and investigating information, and when adjudicating. The

---

1.   16 C.F.R. § 0.1 (1991 edition).

Exhibit 6–5 An Independent Agency: FEDERAL TRADE COMMISSION

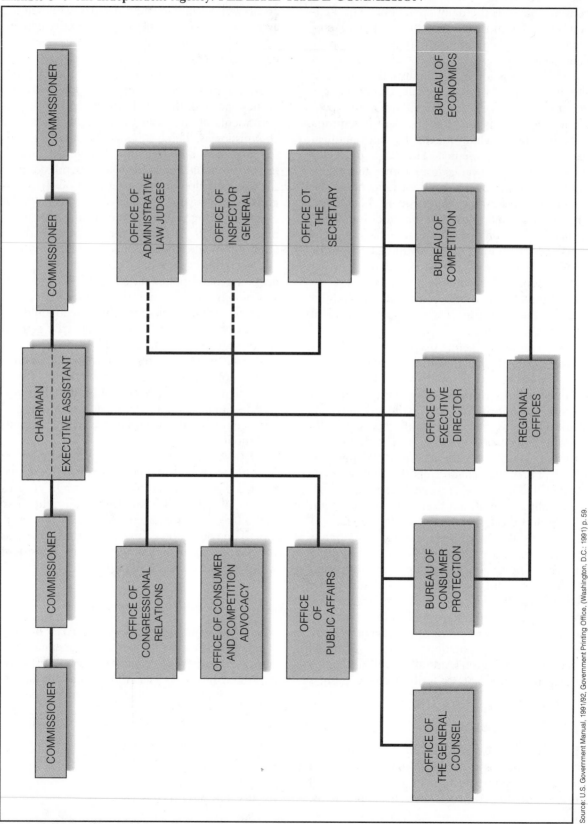

Source: U.S. Government Manual, 1991/92, Government Printing Office, (Washington, D.C.: 1991) p. 59.

APA ensures that the agency adheres to constitutional requirements.

Three Areas of Power

Administrative agencies have three prime areas of activity: to make rules, to acquire and act on information, and to judge cases. These activities are carried out through the legislative, executive, and judicial powers that an agency possesses. Any one agency may possess a combination of all three types of power. These powers are really quasi-powers. For example, an agency with quasi-legislative power does not have the actual power to pass legislation; only Congress has legislative power. The agency does, however, have a power to adopt rules that is very similar to legislative power—thus the name "quasi-legislative power."

Agencies are able to promulgate rules that have the effect of law (a **quasi-legislative function**). They have policing powers to ensure compliance with those rules by acquiring information through record keeping and investigations (a **quasi-executive function**). They prosecute violators, render judgments, and impose penalties in an administrative hearing (a **quasi-judicial function**). Congress, however, has not given all three powers to every agency.

Legislative Function The first function of an administrative agency is the legislative function. Operating in a similar manner to a legislative body, the administrative agency must adopt rules so the public knows how to conduct itself when dealing with the items regulated by the agency. For example, if the Environmental Protection Agency has set out rules on how to dispose of asbestos found in a building, any contractor who agrees to remodel a building containing asbestos must follow those rules or face possible fines.

Purpose of Rule Making A rule adopted by an administrative agency is like a statute passed by Congress. A rule is designed to implement, interpret, or prescribe a law, policy, or practice of an agency. When an agency announces a broadly applicable, prospective policy, the agency uses the mechanism of a rule. Based on future standards of conduct rather than a past or current act, a rule is more appropriate and efficient than applying regulations in a case-by-case approach. A rule is

often more specific and easier to follow than agency case decisions.

Ministerial Powers The ministerial powers are a very important part of an agency's activities. Most members of the public have their only contact with an agency when it is exercising its ministerial powers. For example, when a person visits a social security office for information, the agency is using its ministerial powers. Often a business will request an agency's opinion as to whether an action contemplated by the business will be legal under a certain regulation. The agency will give an opinion and offer the business informal advice.

Misinformation Members of the public rely on the agency to give them correct information. Based on that information, individuals and businesses carry out plans, knowing that their action complies with the agency rules. What happens, however, if an agency employee gives out inaccurate or wrong information? Public policy dictates that an agency is not bound by or liable for the incorrect information given by its employees. The real meaning of this statement is that a person cannot successfully sue the government.

Why is an agency not liable for the misinformation given by an employee? If it were, an agency could assume powers that Congress had not authorized nor did Congress want the agency to have. If the agency were held liable, the courts would be ordering monies to be spent in a manner not authorized by Congress. Under the Constitution only Congress has the power to appropriate monies.

The agency is also responsible for spending the public monies entrusted to it in accordance with the law; the agency has no authority to do otherwise. Therefore, even if one individual is devastated by incorrect information given by the agency, the government's duty is to the public and to the protection of the public's trust and monies.

The agency rules are available to the public through the *Federal Register* and through the **Freedom of Information Act (FOIA)** of 1966 (discussed later in this chapter). The courts have held that ignorance of the agency's rules or reliance on the agency's information is no excuse for not knowing, not understanding, or not complying with those rules. A person may be able to alleviate the harshness of the rule that ignorance of the law is no excuse if she or he fits into one of the following categories.

First, Congress can authorize an agency to stand behind the advice it gives in specific situations. For example, the Internal Revenue Service (IRS) may issue a binding-opinion letter to a business about a question on a specific tax issue. The IRS must stand by the advice given in that type of letter.

Second, a person may incur a debt to the government because he or she relied on incorrect information given by an agency employee. The harmed person is not able to sue the government, but in certain types of cases the government has the power to grant a remission of indebtedness if the person is qualified. In other words, the person may ask the government to forgive the debt based on hardship and poor advice.

Third, a person who has been harmed by incorrect advice given by a government employee may also apply to Congress for a private bill of relief. The person's congressional representative drafts and submits a bill to Congress to compensate the person for the error of the government. This route is long and difficult and not often successful.

Discretionary Rule-Making Powers   Congress has authorized administrators to formulate rules and guidelines under a general (discretionary) authority granted to administrative agencies. For example, the commissioner of Social Security has the discretionary authority to make rules that specify who is eligible for Medicare benefits. This rule-making authority, authorized by Congress, grants quasi-legislative powers to administrators.

The three types of agency rules are **procedural rules, interpretive rules,** and **substantive rules.** Procedural rules govern the internal practices of an agency. An agency inherently has the power to determine its own governance. In accordance with the APA, procedural rules must be published in the *Federal Register,* but no other hearings need be held. An agency must follow its own procedural rules; a court may overturn any action that violates a procedural rule.

Remember that an agency is created by a statute. An interpretive rule allows the agency to interpret the statute that it is charged with administering. When an agency issues an interpretive rule, the only public action it must take is to publish the rule in the *Federal Register.* For example, the Federal Reserve Board is charged with enforcing the Truth-in-Lending Act. The Federal Reserve Board published in the *Federal Register* an interpretation of the criteria for determining when a late charge would be considered a "finance charge." No prior notice or opportunity to comment was given. An agency's definition of a term is considered an interpretive rule.

A substantive rule is based on a specific statutory authority to issue rules that create and manage programs. All rules that are not procedural or interpretive in nature are deemed substantive. APA procedural requirements for rule making vary, depending on whether an agency engages in **informal** or **formal rule making.**

Informal or formal rule making is used when an agency adopts a substantive rule. In informal rule making, the agency must publish notice of the proposed rule, give interested persons an opportunity to participate in the rule making, and incorporate in the rule a concise general statement of its basis and purpose. Informal rule making is frequently referred to as notice-and-comment rule making.

In formal rule making, an agency must conduct a hearing before it can adopt a rule. The parties for and against the rule are entitled to present their case or defense, to submit oral and documentary evidence, to present witnesses, and to conduct examinations of the various witnesses who testify before the agency. Although the parties do not have a right to an attorney, most parties, more often than not, employ an attorney to represent them. In many respects, a formal rule-making hearing is similar to a trial.

Agency rules have the same legal effect as a statute; in other words, these rules are the law. Ignorance of these rules is no excuse when a person is accused of violating an administrative rule. These rules are made available to the public in the *Federal Register* and in the *Code of Federal Regulations.*

Once a rule has been adopted, the agency can rescind the rule. The agency's action is reviewable by a court, as seen in the following case. The rescission cannot be arbitrary or illogical and cannot be contrary to the will of Congress.

BACKGROUND AND FACTS *Congress enacted the National Traffic and Motor Vehicle Safety Act in 1966. The purpose was to reduce the number of deaths and personal injuries resulting from traffic accidents. The act directed the secretary of transportation to issue motor vehicle safety standards. Under the congressional guidelines, the Department of Transportation (DOT) issued a regulation in 1967 that required seat belts in all cars. By 1969 DOT had concluded that the level of seat-belt use was too low to reduce traffic injuries. DOT issued a notice of proposed rule making to consider the development and installation of passive restraint systems. In 1972, after extensive hearings and modifications of the original proposed rule, DOT adopted the final standard (Standard 208). The standard called for complete passive restraint protection on vehicles manufactured after 1975. The standard was changed after a further series of hearings and modifications. Now called Modified Standard 208, it extended the deadline to 1984.*

In February 1981, only one month after taking office, the new secretary of transportation, appointed by President Reagan, reopened discussion of the standard. In April, DOT announced it had rescinded the standard through what became known as Notice 25. The reasons given were that the automobile industry was not in good shape economically, sales were depressed, and unemployment high. State Farm and other insurance companies petitioned the court for review of the rescission of the standard.

Case 6.1
STATE FARM MUTUAL AUTOMOBILE INSURANCE v. DEPARTMENT OF TRANSPORTATION
United States Court of Appeals, District of Columbia Circuit, 1982.
680 F.2d 206.

Circuit Judge MIKVA
* * * *

* * * NHTSA [National Highway Transportation Safety Administration] artificially narrowed its analysis of Modified Standard 208. Although that regulation is a performance standard, the agency offered no evidence that certain technology would fail to perform. More important, it then rescinded the standard without analyzing it in terms of technology that clearly would comply.

By any measure of reasoned decisionmaking, NHTSA's action was arbitrary and capricious. Despite carefully issuing notice on an array of possible changes to Modified Standard 208, NHTSA proceeded as though the only question were whether to implement or rescind the safety standard exactly as that standard was first written five years ago. "It is easy enough for an administrator to ban everything."
* * *

On balance, it is difficult to find anything positive to say about NHTSA's decisionmaking in this case. After conducting an elaborate quantitative analysis in a 280-page Regulatory Impact Analysis, NHTSA essentially rejected much of this analysis as "hypothetical[.]" * * *

In other words, the analysis to support Notice 25 has not yet been undertaken. Moreover, several of the explanations stated in Notice 25 fly directly in the face of the agency's own analysis. In stating that the standard would raise equity problems, for example, because current users of manual belts would "subsidize" the nonusers who "will generate all of the benefits that result directly and solely from this regulation," * * * NHTSA ignored the fact that high insurance savings could be realized *even by regular users of manual belts.* * * * It is difficult to avoid the conclusion that NHTSA's analysis in Notice 25 has been distorted by solicitude for the economically depressed automobile industry—which is not the agency's mandate—at the expense of consideration of traffic safety, which is.

We do not hold, of course, that an agency charged with promulgating safety standards may never rescind those regulations once promulgated. But rescission must be supported by rational explanations, after a reasoned and good-faith effort to consider alternative means of advancing the agency's purpose. If Congress chooses, it has the authority to override Modified Standard 208 or any other regulation. * * * But NHTSA may not confuse its role with that of Congress. Based on the record and the statements in Notice 25, we must conclude that NHTSA has acted capriciously, wearing blinders that prevented it from reasoned evaluation of methods to fulfill the purposes of the Safety Act.

* * * *

At the same time, we should not simply remand this petition to the agency so that recalcitrance might succeed where rational decisionmaking might not. The implementation of a passive restraint standard has already been delayed without acceptable reasons, perhaps unconscionably so. Our decision does not foreclose rescission, but requires simply that the agency analyze obvious technological alternatives for compliance before doing so. * * *

DECISION AND REMEDY   *The Court remanded (returned) the case to DOT. Its decision to rescind the safety standard was arbitrary and capricious and not supported by the evidence in the record.*

Judicial Function Any problems that a person has with an agency can usually be resolved within the agency's administrative courts. The ability of the administrative agency to resolve internally most of the disputes that arise relieves the judicial court system of many cases. Not all agencies have this function.

Purpose of Adjudication Administrative agencies develop policy through adjudication as well as through rule making. Adjudication is often appropriate when a decision relates to specific facts and to particular parties or when an agency is not ready to announce a rule and wants to take a more cautious, case-by-case approach. The number of adjudications each year is substantial.

Rule making is a legislative power, whereas adjudication is a judicial power. Agencies use either rule making or adjudication depending on the circumstances. If the future consequences of conduct are to be prescribed and the application will be general, rule making is proper. If liability is to be determined based on present or past acts concerning a specific individual, the case should be subject to adjudication.

Administrative Law Judge An administrative agency adjudicates an individual case in a hearing conducted by an administrative law judge (ALJ)

assigned to the agency. As an employee of the agency, an ALJ is not a member of the federal judiciary. The ALJ is authorized to perform a variety of judgelike functions in the judicial hearing. The ALJ issues subpoenas, administers oaths to witnesses, conducts hearing conferences, regulates the conduct and course of the hearing, rules on admissibility of evidence, and makes other procedural rulings.

Outside the hearing, an ALJ may not talk with anyone on any issues before him or her in order to remain as insulated as possible from all external influences. After the hearing, the ALJ issues a decision with the findings and conclusions that support it, just as in a court judgment.

Procedures for Administrative Adjudication Administrative adjudication begins with the issuance of a complaint to a business that the agency believes has violated a particular rule or standard. After a complaint is served on an alleged wrongdoer, the party is given an opportunity to answer. Eventually, the complaint is heard by an administrative law judge, who conducts the hearing, rules on all motions, and decides both the facts and the law. In an agency hearing, no right to a jury exists.

After considering all the evidence and law, the ALJ issues an **order** that is subject to review by the head of the administrative agency. An order is defined as the final disposition of the case be-

Legal Highlight

"Governmentese" and Plain English

The contorted language used by the regulators has jokingly been called "governmentese." For instance, in the 1970s the Occupational Safety and Health Administration published standards concerning the ability of a ladder to hold a "live load unit ascending and descending the ladder with additional weights." Translated, this passage was referring to a person—the "live load unit"—climbing up and down the ladder with something in his or her hand. Regulators are now required to write in "plain English." Here is the Consumer Product Safety Commission's description of a book of matches.

§ 1202.3 Definitions.

In addition to the definitions given in section 3 of the Consumer Product Safety Act (15 U.S.C. 2052), the following definitions apply for the purpose of this standard:

(a) "Bookmatch" means a single splint, with a matchhead attached, that comes from a matchbook.

(b) "Bridge" means the matchhead material held in common by two or more splints.

(c) "Broken bridge" means a bridge that has become separated.

(d) "Caddy" means a package of two or more matchbooks wrapped or boxed together at a production plant.

(e) "Comb" means a piece of wood, paper, or other suitable material that has been formed into splints, that remain joined at their base, and that are designed to have matchheads attached to their tips.

(f) "Cover" means the paperboard or other suitable material that is wrapped around and fastened to the comb(s).

(g) "Friction" means the dried chemical mixture on the matchbook cover used to ignite the bookmatch.

(h) "Match" means a single splint with matchhead attached.

(i) "Matchbook" means one or more combs with matchheads attached and a cover that is wrapped around and fastened to those combs.

(j) "Matchhead" means the dried chemical mixture on the end of a splint.

(k) "Splint" means the support for the matchhead or that portion normally held when using the bookmatch.

§ 1202.4 Matchbook general requirements.

A matchbook shall meet the following general requirements:

(a) The friction shall be located on the outside back cover near the bottom of the matchbook.

(b) The cover shall remain closed without external force.

(c) No friction material shall be located on the inside of the cover where possible contact with the matchheads may occur during ordinary use.

(d) There shall be no bridge(s) or broken bridge(s).

(e) No matchhead in the matchbook shall be split, chipped, cracked, or crumbled.

(f) No portion of any matchhead shall be outside the matchbook cover when the cover is closed.

(g) No part of a staple or other assembly device for securing the cover and combs shall be within or touching the friction area.

(h) A staple used as an assembly device for securing the cover and combs shall be fully clinched so that the ends are flattened or turned into the cover.

§ 1202.5 Certification.

Certification shall be in accordance with section 14(a) of the Consumer Product Safety Act (15 U.S.C. 2063(a)). Under this provision, manufacturers and private labelers of products subject to safety standards must certify that their products conform to the standard, based on either a test of each product or on a reasonable testing program.

Legal Highlight

§ 1202.6 Marking.

(a) The manufacturer's or private labeler's name and city or a symbol which will identify the name and city shall appear on the matchbook. In addition, every private labeler must label the matchbook with a code which enables it to identify, if requested, the manufacturer of the product.

(b) Boxes or cartons in which two or more caddies are shipped shall be marked "For safety, store in a cool, dry place."

Source: 16 C.F.R. §§ 1202.3–1202.6, Ch. II (1-1-87 edition).

---

tween the government and the party. An order is similar to a judgment by a court.

Most agencies have an appeal route built into the system. For example, a person audited by the Internal Revenue Service may appeal the auditor's decision to the Tax Court, a quasi-judicial court within the Internal Revenue Service. In some cases, the party can engage in an informal settlement process or agree to a **consent decree**—an agreement by the parties that carries the sanction of the court. After the final hearing, the affected party can appeal to the judicial courts. The courts will uphold the administrative agency's decision if there is substantial evidence on the record to support the order.

Executive Function Through the executive function, administrative agencies are able to ensure that their rules are followed.

Acquisition of Information The bureaucracy is an information-gathering instrument of the government. The acquisition of information enables an agency to become an expert on the subject matter it regulates.

Most of the information the agency gathers is obtained voluntarily. On occasion, information must be obtained through compulsion. Agencies gather the information in one of three ways: record keeping and periodic reports, subpoena power, and power to conduct physical inspections. The first method obtains information through voluntary cooperation, while the latter two methods use compulsion to obtain the information.

Record-Keeping and Reporting Requirements Federal agencies that regulate businesses require those businesses to keep specific records and to make periodic mandatory reports based on those records. For example, a whiskey manufacturer must keep and maintain records for the Bureau of Alcohol, Tobacco, and Firearms. This information allows the agency to study problems and to promulgate, amend, or delete rules as necessary.

Investigatory Powers Other executive functions performed by an administrative agency are investigations and prosecutions. When performing these functions, an agency follows procedural rules prescribing its conduct. Sometimes an agency fails to take any action. The following case concerns the refusal of an administrative agency to conduct an investigation.

Case 6.2
CENTER FOR AUTO SAFETY v. DOLE
United States Court of Appeals, District of Columbia Circuit, 1987.
828 F.2d 799.

BACKGROUND AND FACTS *The National Traffic and Motor Vehicle Safety Act of 1966 states that if the secretary of transportation makes a determination that a safety-related defect exists, the secretary, through the National Highway Transportation Safety Administration (NHTSA) must order the manufacturer to recall and remedy the defect. It was alleged that between 1966 and 1979 defects in automatic transmissions built by the Ford Motor Company caused cars to disengage from "Park" and to roll without warning.*

A 1982 NHTSA investigation ended without a final determination on the existence of a defect because NHTSA and Ford entered a settlement agreement that required Ford to notify owners about the possibility of a defect. NHTSA explicitly reserved the right to commence a new proceeding on the alleged defect if additional facts warranted. In March 1985, the Center for Auto Safety petitioned NHTSA to reopen the hearing because of additional evidence. The NHTSA administrator denied the petition after reviewing the administrative record. She was not convinced that a final defect determination would be warranted even if a further investigation was undertaken. The Center for Auto Safety appealed the denied petition. The district court denied the review, and the center appealed to the court of appeals.

Chief Judge WALD
*   *   *   *

Because this case involves "informal agency action," *   *   * judicial review of NHTSA's denial of appellants' petition under the APA [Administrative Procedure Act] is limited to whether the decision was "arbitrary, capricious, or abuse of discretion, or otherwise not in accordance with the law." *   *   * Judicial review *   *   * determines whether the reasons for the agency's decision were legally permissible and reasoned ones, and whether there was adequate factual support for the decision. *   *   * The reviewing court may not consider new evidence that was not before the agency when it made its decision.

Here, we can identify no congressional objectives of the Motor Vehicle Safety Act with which the normal level of judicial review would interfere. The basic congressional objective underlying the Motor Vehicle Safety Act is stated simply and clearly in the Act's first section: "Congress hereby declares that the purpose of this chapter is to reduce traffic accidents and deaths and injuries to persons resulting from traffic accidents." *   *   * To the extent that judicial review helps to assure that factual support exists for NHTSA decisions denying enforcement petitions, it helps to reduce the threat of traffic accidents, and aids, not hinders, the basic congressional purpose of the statute.

Moreover, the Motor Vehicle Safety Act expressly contemplates extensive citizen involvement in enforcement of the Act by providing for citizen petitions for enforcement of safety standards, by expressly authorizing public hearings on allegations of safety-related defects, and by requiring the agency to publish a statement of reasons for denying a petition.
*   *   *   *

By contrast, the administrative decision in this case concerns the possibility that certain kinds of cars are defective and unsafe. This possibility, in turn, depends on an evaluation of "technical" evidence about the cars which the agency's own regulations prescribe. *   *   * Of course, the reviewing court may not substitute its judgment for the agency's but it certainly is possible for the court to review the administrative decision for factual support without an impermissible substitution of judgment, in the same way we review agency factual determinations *   *   * thousands of times every year.
*   *   *   *

While this court cannot, and should not, second-guess the agency's safety determinations, this court can and should assure that the agency has *some* factual support for those safety determinations. Making sure that the agency's stated reason for denying an enforcement petition is in truth the lack of a "substantial safety issue" guarantees that the responsible administrative agency has given at least a minimum amount of consideration to the citizens whose safety Congress has entrusted to the agency.

Our holding then is this: When Congress grants citizens the right to petition administrative agencies for enforcement on an issue of public safety, and the relevant substantive statute sends out no identifiable signals on the availability or scope of judicial review of an agency's denial of that petition, but the agency has bound itself by a legal rule to grant the petition unless it makes a finding of "no reasonable possibility" of a safety defect, then a petitioner is entitled under the APA to judicial review of a decision denying the petition to assure that the agency had some factual support for its "no reasonable possibility" finding. In such circumstances, the arbitrary or capricious standard of review in * * * the APA functions as usual, and is not limited to examining merely the stated reasons for the agency's decision. Therefore, * * * we hold that NHTSA's determination that no "reasonable possibility" of a safety-related defect exists in this case is subject to judicial review on the basis of the evidence that the Administrator had before her when she made her decision.

DECISION AND   *The court reversed the decision of the district court and remanded the case*
REMEDY   *to the district court. The court of appeals held that the Motor Vehicle Safety Act allows judicial review of NHTSA decisions, even those denying a citizen's petition. The district court has the "reasonable possibility" standard with which to review the decisions. The reviewing court must examine the administrative record in order to make its decision.*

Enforcement Powers   Enforcement powers are also delegated to agencies. All final orders issued by an ALJ may result in civil or criminal penalties if violated. These penalties are enforceable, unless a reviewing court reverses the agency decision. Failure to comply with the penalties is treated like any other violation of the law.

In most cases, violations are considered to be a civil matter. A business is held liable for money damages or is required to take some specific action, such as the installation of pollution-control equipment. In recent years, there has been a trend toward issuing civil penalties, such as fines.

The following case examines the right to a jury trial when fines may be levied as punishment.

Case 6.3
ATLAS ROOFING CO., INC. v. OSHA

Supreme Court of the United States, 1977.
430 U.S. 422, 97 S.Ct. 1261, 51 L.Ed.2d 464.

BACKGROUND AND FACTS   *Two firms were cited by Occupational Safety and Health Administration (OSHA) inspectors for having unsafe workplaces. The first firm was cited for failing to have the sides of trenches shored and was fined $7,500. The second firm was cited for failing to have roof-opening covers installed to prevent accidents. The fine was $600. Both firms appealed the fines. They were given a hearing before an administrative law judge, who affirmed the findings of the OSHA inspectors. The fine of $7,500 was reduced to $5,000, but the second fine was affirmed at $600. Both firms appealed to the court of appeals, challenging the constitutionality of OSHA's enforcement procedures. The court of appeals affirmed the decision of the administrative law judge and found the enforcement procedures to be constitutional. Both firms appealed to the United States Supreme Court. The defendants argued that they were entitled to a jury trial under the Constitution.*

Justice WHITE delivered the opinion of the Court.

*   *   *   *

We granted the petitions for writs of certiorari limited to the important question whether the Seventh Amendment prevents Congress from assigning to an administrative agency, under these circumstances, the task of adjudicating violations of OSHA. *   *   *

The Seventh Amendment provides that "[i]n Suits at common law, where the value in controversy shall exceed twenty dollars, the right of trial by jury shall be preserved. *   *   *" The phrase "Suits at common law" has been construed to refer to cases tried prior to the adoption of the Seventh Amendment in courts of law in which jury trial was customary as distinguished from courts of equity or admiralty in which jury trial was not. *   *   * Petitioners claim that a suit in a federal court by the Government for civil penalties for violation of a statute is a suit for a money judgment which is classically a suit at common law, *   *   * and that the defendant therefore has a Seventh Amendment right to a jury determination of all issues of fact in such a case. *   *   *

*   *   * [W]hen Congress creates new statutory "public rights," it may assign their adjudication to an administrative agency with which a jury trial would be incompatible, without violating the Seventh Amendment's injunction that jury trial is to be "preserved" in "suits at common law." Congress is not required by the Seventh Amendment to choke the already crowded federal courts with new types of litigation or prevented from committing some new types of litigation to administrative agencies with special competence in the relevant field. This is the case even if the Seventh Amendment would have required a jury where the adjudication of those rights is assigned to a federal court of law instead of an administrative agency. *   *   *

More to the point, it is apparent from the history of jury trial in civil matters that factfinding, which is the essential function of the jury in civil cases, was never the exclusive province of the jury under either the English or American legal systems at the time of the adoption of the Seventh Amendment; and the question whether a fact would be found by a jury turned to a considerable degree on the nature of the forum in which a litigant found himself. Critical factfinding was performed without juries in suits in equity, and there were no juries in admiralty, nor were there juries in the military justice system. The jury was the factfinding mode in most suits in the common-law courts, but it was not exclusively so: Condemnation was a suit at common law but constitutionally could be tried without a jury[.] *   *   *

Thus, history and our cases support the proposition that the right to a jury trial turns not solely on the nature of the issue to be resolved but also on the forum in which it is to be resolved. Congress found the common-law and other existing remedies for work injuries resulting from unsafe working conditions to be inadequate to protect the Nation's working men and women. It created a new cause of action, and remedies, therefor, unknown to the common law, and placed their enforcement in a tribunal supplying speedy and expert resolutions of the issues involved. The Seventh Amendment is no bar to the creation of new rights or to their enforcement outside the regular courts of law.

DECISION AND REMEDY

The decision of the court of appeals was affirmed, and the fines for both firms were upheld. More importantly, the Supreme Court found that Congress had the power to create statutory rights without providing that juries be available to decide the facts. Congress is free to create new methods to resolve problems between disagreeing parties.

Limitations on Administrative Agencies' Powers

Most limitations on administrative agencies' powers arise from one of three sources: (1) the Constitution, (2) congressional statutes, and (3) judicial review. Constitutional limitations typically relate to the substance of administrative agency behavior; any procedural inadequacies are subject to judicial review.

Major Constitutional Limitations

Amendments to the Constitution provide the most important limitations on administrative agency actions. Although most constitutional rights, such as due process and unreasonable search and seizure, are regarded primarily as rights of individuals, businesses also have some constitutional rights.

Both procedural and substantive due process protect businesses against arbitrary, capricious, and unreasonable administrative agency actions. Substantive due process applies when issues arise that involve property or other rights affected by government. Procedural due process focuses on notice and hearing procedures. Enforcement of due process rights through the Fifth and Fourteenth Amendments, however, follows a double standard. Whenever government action directly affects economic activity, courts usually find it to be constitutional. On the other hand, courts are generally suspicious of government actions that might limit basic human freedoms.

Fourth Amendment Limitations People are protected from unwarranted intrusions into their personal privacy by the Constitution. In civil and criminal cases, businesses are also protected from unreasonable searches. The Fourth Amendment has been used to prohibit building inspectors from looking for building-code violations against the desires of the owner of the premises when the inspectors do not have a warrant. On the other hand, an agency may make an unannounced inspection of those businesses that traditionally have been heavily regulated, such as the alcoholic beverage industry, the firearm industry, the fishing industry, and the meat-packing industry.

In the case that follows, the United States Supreme Court held that government safety inspectors must have a warrant to make a routine inspection of work areas in a private business.

Case 6.4
MARSHALL v. BARLOW'S, INC.
Supreme Court of the United States, 1978.
436 U.S. 307, 98 S.Ct. 1816, 56 L.Ed.2d 305.

BACKGROUND AND FACTS *Prior to this case, inspectors of the Occupational Safety and Health Administration (OSHA) were not required to obtain permission to enter the work areas of firms under OSHA's jurisdiction. In 1975, an OSHA inspector entered the customer service area of Barlow's, Inc., an electrical and plumbing installation business. After showing his credentials, the inspector informed the president and general manager, Barlow, that he would be conducting an inspection of the working areas of the business.*

On inquiry, Barlow learned that no complaint had been received about his company. The inspection was simply the result of random selection. The inspector did not have a search warrant. Barlow refused to permit the inspector to enter the working area of his business, relying on his rights guaranteed by the Fourth Amendment.

OSHA filed suit in the United States District Court, which issued an order compelling Barlow to admit the OSHA inspector for purposes of conducting an occupational safety and health inspection.

The OSHA inspector, now armed with a court order, went back to Barlow's, Inc., and Barlow again refused admission. This time, Barlow went to the same district court seeking an injunction to prohibit the inspector from making a warrantless search on the ground that the OSHA inspection violated the Fourth Amendment.

This time the district court ruled in Barlow's favor. The district court held that the Fourth Amendment required a warrant for the type of search involved and that the authorization for warrantless inspections under the OSHA statute was unconstitutional. A permanent injunction against such searches or inspections was entered on the behalf of Barlow. The appeal by OSHA to the Supreme Court challenged the validity of that injunction.

Justice WHITE delivered the opinion of the Court.
* * * *

The Warrant Clause of the Fourth Amendment protects commercial buildings as well as private homes. To hold otherwise would belie the origin of that Amendment, and the American colonial experience. * * *

* * * [U]nless some recognized exception to the warrant requirement applies, * * * a warrant [is required] to conduct the inspection sought in this case.

* * * Certain industries have such a history of government oversight that no reasonable expectation of privacy could exist for a proprietor over the stock of such an enterprise. Liquor and firearms are industries of this type; when an entrepreneur embarks upon such a business, he has voluntarily chosen to subject himself to a full arsenal of governmental regulation.

* * * The element that distinguishes these enterprises from ordinary businesses is a long tradition of close government supervision, of which any person who chooses to enter such a business must already be aware. * * *

The clear import * * * is that the closely regulated industry * * * is the exception. * * *
* * * *

The critical fact in this case is that entry over Mr. Barlow's objection is being sought by a Government agent. Employees are not being prohibited from reporting OSHA violations. What they observe in their daily functions is undoubtedly beyond the employer's reasonable expectation of privacy. The Government inspector, however, is not an employee. Without a warrant he stands in no better position than a member of the public. What is observable by the public is observable, without a warrant, by the Government inspector as well. The owner of a business has not, by the necessary utilization of employees in his operation, thrown open the areas where employees alone are permitted to the warrantless scrutiny of Government agents. That an employee is free to report, and the Government is free to use, any evidence of noncompliance with OSHA that the employee observes furnishes no justification for federal agents to enter a place of business from which the public is restricted and to conduct their own warrantless search.
* * * *

Whether the Secretary proceeds to secure a warrant or other process, with or without prior notice, his entitlement to inspect will not depend on his demonstrating probable cause to believe that conditions in violation of OSHA exist on the premises. Probable cause in the criminal law sense is not required. For purposes of an administrative search such as this, probable cause justifying the issuance of a warrant may be based not only on specific evidence of an existing violation but also on a showing that "reasonable legislative or administrative standards for conducting an . . . inspection are satisfied with respect to a particular [establishment]."

A warrant showing that a specific business has been chosen for an OSHA search on the basis of a general administrative plan for the enforcement of the Act derived from neutral sources such as, for example, dispersion of employees in various types of industries across a given area, and the desired frequency of searches in any of the lesser divisions of the area, would protect an employer's Fourth Amendment rights. We doubt that the consumption of enforcement energies in the obtaining of such warrants will exceed manageable proportions.
* * * *

* * * The authority to make warrantless searches devolves almost unbridled discretion upon executive and administrative officers, particularly those in the field, as to when to search and whom to search. A warrant, by contrast, would provide assurances from a neutral officer that the inspection is reasonable under the Constitution, is authorized by statute, and is pursuant to an administrative plan containing specific neutral criteria. Also, a warrant would then and there advise the owner of the scope and objects of the search, beyond which limits the inspector is not expected to proceed. These are important functions for a warrant to perform, functions which underlie the Court's prior decisions that the Warrant Clause applies to inspections for compliance with regulatory statutes. We conclude that the concerns expressed by the Secretary do not suffice to justify warrantless inspections under OSHA or vitiate the general constitutional requirement that for a search to be reasonable a warrant must be obtained.

✳   ✳   ✳   ✳

DECISION AND REMEDY   *The permanent injunction was upheld. OSHA inspections conducted without warrants were held to be unconstitutional when the business to be inspected is not one that is otherwise regulated by close government supervision.*

Fifth Amendment Applications   Under the Fifth Amendment, a person cannot be forced to testify against himself or herself in a criminal case. The Supreme Court has held that a corporation is not a person within the meaning of the Constitution, and thus corporations are not eligible for Fifth Amendment protection.

Administrative agencies may require businesses to make and maintain records. Because corporations are not persons, the records that they must maintain are not included under the self-incrimination clause and, therefore, may be disclosed in criminal or civil cases. These types of corporate records become, in effect, quasi-public records. An agency has the right to inspect these records to ensure the accuracy of the reports it receives on a periodic basis.

Although these records are quasi-public, the disclosure requirement is not tantamount to public disclosure. Businesses legitimately have secrets concerning the product or service sold; they may have secret marketing strategies or trade secrets, as well as sensitive personal records. Congress has provided protection in two ways. First, the enabling act may specifically prohibit the records from being made public and prohibit the agency's employees from disclosing the information. Second, in 1966 Congress passed the Freedom of Information Act. Although this act promotes access and availability of information to the public and individuals, certain information is restricted from disclosure. This act will be examined in detail in

the next section. In short, business records are protected from public disclosure under certain restricted circumstances.

Congressional Statutes

When Congress creates an agency, its statutory scheme includes congressional limitations on that agency. Although certain general rules apply to all agencies, a person dealing with a specific agency must be aware of these congressional limitations. Some statutes amend the Administrative Procedure Act and thus affect all agencies, while other statutes apply only to one agency.

Freedom of Information Act   The Freedom of Information Act (FOIA) is an amendment to the Administrative Procedure Act. All administrative agencies are subject to FOIA. FOIA makes all the information held by federal agencies available to the public. Exemptions do exist if the information falls within certain categories.

Information may be disclosed under FOIA in one of three ways. First, the *Federal Register* publishes information, such as policy statements and procedural and substantive rules, from the agencies. Second, agencies must make available for public inspection and copying certain information that is not printed in the *Federal Register*. Reprints of the opinions of the administrative law judges, public statements, interpretive rules, staff manuals, and directives are all sold to the public for a nominal fee. Third, if the information is not published under either of these methods and it is not exempt, each agency has established reasonable procedures for the public to follow when requesting a copy of that information.

The important exempt categories are those that contain information in the following areas: information relating to national defense or foreign policy; internal personnel rules; information protected by another statute that prohibits disclosure; business trade secrets and privileged or confidential business information; and any information that violates personal privacy. Even though certain information may be classified in one of the exempt

categories, the agency is not automatically prohibited from disclosing that information. FOIA gives the agency discretion as to whether or not to disclose the information.

When an agency decides not to disclose information under FOIA, the agency must disclose its reasons to the requester. After exhausting the administrative remedies, the requester has the right to file a lawsuit in district court to force the agency to disclose the information. The agency has the burden of proof to support its action. The following case examines FOIA from a different perspective.

BACKGROUND AND FACTS   *This case is known as a reverse Freedom of Information Act (FOIA) case. In this type of case, the submitter of information (usually a business) seeks to prevent the government from releasing the information to a third party in response to its FOIA request. The government must still follow the FOIA rules in determining whether to release the information.*

CNA Financial Corporation is an insurance company that does business with the federal government. As part of the contract, CNA had to report its affirmative action performance on an Equal Employment Opportunity (EEO) form. In 1977 a group called Women Employed requested from the government the affirmative action programs, EEO forms, and government documents concerning CNA's compliance with the affirmative action requirements.

CNA objected to the disclosures under the Trade Secrets Act. CNA argued that the act qualified as a statute that authorized the withholding of information under the FOIA exemption. Claiming substantial competitive harm, CNA asserted that if the information was released, the disclosure would facilitate the raiding of its employees, demoralize its employees, generate adverse publicity if the data were misconstrued, and reveal to competitors CNA's plans to enter, expand, or contract different markets and product lines.

The Office of Federal Contract Compliance Programs (OFCCP) hired an expert to evaluate the data submitted by CNA. After careful examination of the report and of other evidence that had been submitted, the OFCCP hearing officer determined that the Trade Secrets Act was not a withholding statute within the meaning of Exemption 4 of FOIA. The hearing officer ordered the information to be disclosed. The district court affirmed OFCCP's decision.

Circuit Judge ROBINSON

*   *   *   *

FOIA is itself the product of a most thoughtful and deliberate weighing process, in which Congress considered the views of those who submit information, those who collect it, and those who desire it. *   *   * To the extent that commercial

Case 6.5
CNA FINANCIAL CORPORATION v. DONOVAN
United States Court of Appeals, District of Columbia Circuit, 1987.
830 F.2d 1132.

and financial data within the ambit of the Trade Secrets Act do not fall within one of the FOIA exemptions, * * * the decision has been made that on balance it ought to be unmasked in the interest of informing the public of the bases for governmental action. To the extent that such data as trade secrets and confidential financial information are excepted from mandatory disclosure by one or more of the exemptions that Congress has incorporated into FOIA, the Trade Secrets Act will bar a discretionary release unless, after notice and comment, an agency, possessing delegated power to do so, promulgates a contrary rule having the force of law. Clearly, this resolution does not undermine the foundation of the Trade Secrets Act by throwing open the door to wholesale, haphazard revelation of private financial and business data in the possession of governmental agencies.
* * * *

CNA and OFCCP disagree on what material is within the purview of Exemption 4. The data that OFCCP proposes to release can be grouped into three principal types: statistics on the racial and sexual composition of the workforce within various CNA departments; goals developed for equal employment purposes; and "applicant flow information" showing the percentage, by race and sex, of applications hired from without and employees promoted from within.

CNA's objections and the responses thereto by OFCCP may also be arranged in three occasionally overlapping categories. First, OFCCP says that much of the information sought by CNA to be confined is already publicly available, and this assertion has not been contested before this court. To the extent that any data requested under FOIA are in the public domain, the submitter is unable to make any claim to confidentiality—a *sine qua non* of Exemption 4. We do not further consider CNA's arguments regarding these data.

Second, several of CNA's claims with respect to other information relate not to alleged competitive harm but rather to anticipated displeasure of its employees or to adverse public reaction. CNA has protested, for example, that release of information on the number of women and minorities hired might result in unfavorable publicity. It also fears that its employees may become "demoralized" following disclosure of data showing the percentage of individuals promoted. We have previously found such complaints unrelated to the policy behind Exemption 4 of protecting submitters from external injury. These proffered objections simply do not amount to "harm flowing from the affirmative use of proprietary information by competitors."

The remaining disagreements between CNA and OFCCP concern the long-range consequences of the release of the data at issue. CNA submitted affidavits predicting a number of harmful effects; OFCCP, while offering no independent evidence, has answered these contentions with its own predictions of the repercussions of disclosure. One noteworthy objection by CNA to revelation of applicant flow data is that it would enable competitors more easily to direct their recruiting efforts to the best sources of potential employees. OFCCP counters with the logical rejoinder that these data will not be of any particular help to competitors since the employee-source and employee-position categories are broad, and the applicant pool is a function of the labor market and beyond an individual competitor's control.

These and other similar contentions presented no more than two contradictory views of what likely would ensue upon release of information that CNA sought to protect. In each case, OFCCP retorted with reasonable and thorough prognoses of its own. We thus are confronted by the type of judgments and forecasts courts traditionally leave largely to agency expertise, with judicial review limited by the narrow standard sanctioned. After careful consideration of OFCCP's decision, we are satisfied that it cannot in any way be characterized as arbitrary, capricious, or an abuse of discretion. CNA's objections were answered fully, and OFCCP's explanations of anticipated effects were certainly no less plausible than those advanced by CNA. Each of OFCCP's explanations is well reasoned, logical and consistent, and predictive judgments are not capable of exact proof. We find OFCCP's application of Exemption 4 entirely rational, and therefore legally permissible.

The court of appeals affirmed the decision of the district court. The Trade Secrets Act does not qualify as a statute that authorizes the withholding of this type of information under the FOIA exemption. OFCCP presented a reasoned and detailed basis for its decision, and it was legally sufficient to be upheld after judicial review.

DECISION AND REMEDY

Privacy Act   The **Privacy Act** was a result of a 1974 amendment of the Administrative Procedure Act. The Privacy Act protects only individuals who are citizens or legal aliens. By statutory definition, corporations or other business entities are not covered.

Agencies accumulate tremendous amounts of information on individuals. If a person requests it, agencies are required to give the person all the information that it has on him or her. The information maintained must be correct, accurate, and current. If this information is stale, inaccurate, or incomplete, the individual is able to make corrections. The Privacy Act does not require an agency to disclose the information it has on that individual under certain circumstances. For example, if a person is being investigated for a crime, the investigating agency does not have to disclose that information even if it is requested.

On the other hand, the agency is not allowed to disclose this information to others unless the conditions under the statute are met. For example, a newspaper requests information from an agency on a particular person. The agency cannot provide that information because it is protected under the Privacy Act; no exceptions to the act exist for newspapers.

Equal Access to Justice Act   An individual or a small business does not have the financial resources to defend against an unjustified action by a governmental agency. In 1982 Congress passed the **Equal Access to Justice Act.** It allows an administrative law judge or a court to award to the small business legal fees (limited to $75 an hour), expert witness fees, or reasonable cost of studies and engineering reports. These fees cannot be awarded if the judge decides that the agency was substantially justified in bringing the action.

The act applies to individuals whose net worth does not exceed $2 million and to small for-profit and nonprofit organizations with no more than 500 employees and a net worth of $7 million dollars. This act allows an ordinary person to challenge an incorrect legal position held by the government.

Sunshine Act   The **Sunshine Act** of 1976 also amended the Administrative Procedure Act. This act prohibits agencies from holding secret meetings. An agency must give notice of the time and place of the meeting and list the matters to be discussed. Not all meetings are open to the public. Even though the meeting is closed to the public, the meeting notice must post the fact that there will be a meeting and whether the meeting is open or closed. The Sunshine Act prevents secret, not closed, meetings.

If a person believes that the agency was in error in its decision to close the meeting, the person can sue the agency in district court. The court may grant an injunction against future violations of the Sunshine Act. The court may not, however, overturn the action taken by the agency behind closed doors solely because the Sunshine Act was violated. Any basis for overturning the agency act must be established on other legal grounds.

Regulatory Flexibility Act   In 1980 Congress again amended the Administrative Procedure Act. The **Regulatory Flexibility Act** takes into account the differences among the various businesses subject to regulation. A regulation may have a different effect on a small business than it has on a large corporation. The act requires a special regulatory flexibility agenda to be printed in the *Federal Register* twice a year, in April and October. An agency must publish a list of all rules that the agency is considering or may consider during the next few months. The rules listed are the ones likely to have a significant economic impact on a substantial number of small businesses.

Sunset Acts

Sunset acts are included in the statutes that create specific agencies. A sunset act sets an automatic expiration date for the agency in order to force regular legislative review. In the past, some administrative agencies have outlived their purpose or usefulness but have continued to exist because the agency's enabling act has not been repealed. If an agency is to continue, Congress must take affirmative action. When Congress reviews an agency periodically, the agency is more likely to be responsive to the public will. At reviewing time, Congress can make known its concerns about the agency through manipulating its budget or by threatening to reorganize or dismantle the agency.

Judicial Review

Administrative decisions can be appealed to the courts because the judiciary has the power and the duty to interpret the law. The province of Congress is to formulate legislative policy, to mandate programs and projects, and to establish their relative priority for the nation. Once Congress has exercised its legislative power by creating a new administrative agency and giving it a mandate, then the agency is to administer the law, and the judiciary is to interpret and enforce the law.

In a judicial review of an agency's decision, the courts investigate first whether that agency has any authority for rule making. If the court finds that the agency has the authority, the court then determines whether the agency has exceeded its properly delegated authority.

In other words, the court first focuses on whether the delegation from Congress was proper. Then it focuses on whether the exercise of that power by the agency was proper.

Congress has delegated broad discretionary powers over a specialized subject matter to each administrative agency. As a result, a court gives **judicial deference** to agency decisions and does not reverse an agency action unless it finds the agency violated a condition set out by the Administrative Procedure Act.

Each agency has a series of procedures that a person must follow before an appeal may be made to the courts. The requirement that the appealing party must follow these procedures is called the **doctrine of exhaustion of remedies.** This doctrine is deeply rooted in history and provides a reasonable balance between a person's rights and the rights of the government.

Deregulation

The federal government has imposed restraints on agencies by limiting the number of ineffective or potentially harmful rules. In 1978 President Carter issued an order requiring agencies to determine the possible impact of various government regulations that affect the economy.

Although in office for only four years, President Carter's administration made dramatic strides toward deregulation. Congress passed many deregulatory acts that took effect after President Reagan took office. The deregulation has taken place mainly in the agencies responsible for economic regulation.

President Reagan issued two executive orders that further limited administrative regulations. These executive orders had several purposes: to establish regulatory priorities, to increase the accountability of agency officials, to provide for presidential oversight of the regulatory process, to reduce the burdens of existing and future regulations, to minimize duplication and conflict of regulations, and to enhance public and congressional understanding of the regulatory objectives.

Each agency must submit to the Office of Management and Budget (OMB) each year a statement of its regulatory policies, goals, and objectives for the coming year, along with information concerning all significant regulatory action under way or planned. Each agency must prepare a regulatory impact analysis of major rules. These executive orders apply only to the agencies in the executive branch and not to independent agencies, but many independent agencies have chosen to comply voluntarily.

Ethical Considerations

Your Friend, the Government Buyer

One continuing problem confronted by businesses occurs when their employees become socially involved with employees of administrative agencies. Let's assume that you are a salesperson employed on a commission basis. Your employer sells light fixtures as its primary product line. On your own time, you become involved with a charitable organization. Among the active members is Pat, who is a purchasing agent for an administrative agency. In time you become good friends.

Most administrative agencies are allowed to make purchases of items under a specified amount, let's say $5,000, without requesting competitive bids. Talking with Pat, you discover that the agency is in need of $3,000 worth (retail price) of light fixtures. You recognize that your competition does not know about this business opportunity. Should you take advantage of it? If you think you can ethically do so, what price should you charge? Do you reduce the price because you are dealing with a government agency as well as with a friend? If the price is reduced, your own commission will be less. On the other hand, you could increase the price to the amount you charge some of your customers. Then, obviously, your commission will be more. How would you handle this ethical problem? Should your company have ethical guidelines to cover this situation, and if so, what should they be?

International Considerations

Use of Administrative Law in Assisting International Transactions

The United Nations has developed various administrative agencies to help it function. The six major agencies created to carry out the U.N.'s work are (1) the General Assembly, (2) the Security Council, (3) the Secretariat, (4) the Economic and Social Council, (5) the International Court of Justice, and (6) the Trusteeship Council. Other agencies help the United Nations carry out its mission; these include the United Nations Development Program, the United Nations Educational, Scientific, and Cultural Organization (UNESCO), and the United Nations International Children's Emergency Fund (UNICEF).

The United Nations also has developed an international civil service based on administrative rules. These rules cover such diverse subjects as conditions of service and reasons for dismissal. Administrative tribunals interpret these staff rules and develop case law. These decisions protect employees from such arbitrary actions as dismissal because of alleged disloyalty to their home country.

The United States has established several administrative agencies that are concerned with international trade. The **Export-Import Bank (Eximbank)** encourages exports of American products. It makes loans in the form of dollar credits directly to purchasers of U.S. goods. The **International Trade Commission** (ITC) and **International Trade Administration** (ITA) investigate unfair trade practices and prepare extensive reports for Congress and the president concerning trade. For example, the ITC will conduct hearings to determine if certain increases in imports have resulted in substantial injury to a domestic industry. It will issue a published opinion and make recommendations to the president. The president may grant relief, including increasing tariffs up to 50 percent, restricting the number of imports of a given product, or granting import licenses to a limited number of enterprises.

The ITC operates under the provisions of the **General Agreement on Tariffs and Trade (GATT)** treaty. This agreement is based on the ideas that nations should eventually reduce all tariffs, quotas, and restrictions; that they should grant certain countries the *most-favored-nation* status; and that they should ensure that treatment of imported products is equal to that accorded domestic goods in the home market.

FACING A LEGAL ISSUE

Administrative Law: Facing Zoning Problems

You want to open a small video rental store that offers movies appealing to college students. You find a perfect location with a low monthly rent near the dormitories and other student housing. Before signing the lease, however, your prospective landlord insists that you contact the local municipal zoning agency to make certain that this type of business activity is permitted.

Wanting to open the store as soon as possible, you go to the proper city office and discover that the zoning ordinance does not allow the rental of products, only the sale of products. You ask whether there are any exceptions to this ordinance. The zoning official states that you can either obtain a use permit or a variance to the zoning ordinance, or you can attempt to have city council change the zoning ordinance.

This venture is your first contact with administrative law. In order to obtain a variance or use permit, you must submit an application to the zoning board. An appointed official will grant or deny your application in a summary manner. If it is denied, you have a right to appeal his or her decision to a board of adjustment. Normally, the members of the board of adjustment are appointed by the elected officials, either the members of the city council or the mayor. If your request is denied by the board of adjustment, you can then take your appeal to the judicial system.

You may try another administrative route. You can file a petition for a zoning change with the city planning department. The department will make a recommendation to the planning and zoning commission. This body is also appointed by elected officials; however, unlike the board of adjustment, which has the power to make a final administrative decision, the actions of the planning and zoning commission are simply advisory to the city council. Once a recommendation is made, it must be adopted by the city council, which acts in a legislative manner when deciding zoning issues.

You probably should file a petition for a change because the ordinance seems to be rather arbitrary in excluding rental businesses but allowing commercial sales. No doubt it was just an oversight when the ordinance was initially adopted, and it needs to be changed.

Summary

Administrative agencies handle two areas of public concern: economic regulation and public welfare. Economic regulation takes several forms. An agency may control entry into the marketplace through licensing procedures, setting rates, or setting standards. Public welfare includes the protection of the public as well as entitlement programs. Public welfare has two meanings; the broad meaning covers regulation that is for the benefit of the public at large, while the second meaning covers programs for lower-income people. Entitlement programs, such as Social Security, benefit those people who meet the programs' eligibility requirements.

Federal regulatory agencies have several features that allow them to deal with certain problems more effectively than the legislatures or the courts. First, an agency develops expertise in a particular area. Second, a regulatory agency consists of a very well-developed hierarchy that helps ensure continuity of personnel and experience. Third, an agency has more flexibility than the legislature.

When an agency is under the direct control of the president, it is known as a line agency. The members of the president's cabinet are heads of line agencies. Congress has also established independent agencies, which are freestanding from the president and from Congress. Government agencies are created by Congress to administer a quasi-business venture. Quasi-official agencies are also created by Congress but do not have the same authority as other agencies.

Administrative agencies engage in three prime areas of activity: They make rules, they acquire and act on information, and they judge cases. These activities are carried out through the quasi-legislative, quasi-executive, and quasi-judicial powers that an agency possesses. The Administrative Procedure Act (APA) standardized the procedures that agencies must use in exercising their powers. In addition, agencies must not violate a person's constitutional rights.

The APA has been amended several times. The Freedom of Information Act makes all the information held by federal agencies available to the public unless the information falls within one of the exempt categories. The important exempt categories are information relating to national defense or foreign policy; internal personnel rules; information protected by another statute that prohibits disclosure; business trade secrets and privileged or confidential business information; and any information that violates personal privacy.

The Privacy Act protects U.S. citizens and legal aliens but not corporations. A person is entitled to see the information that an agency has concerning him or her. The Equal Access to Justice Act allows recovery of legal fees and court costs by individuals and small businesses when the government is wrong. The Sunshine Act prohibits agencies from holding secret, not closed, meetings. If the topics before the meeting do not qualify for a closed meeting, the meeting must be open.

The Regulatory Flexibility Act takes into account differences in the way a regulation affects a small business versus a large business. The rules that will affect small businesses must be published in the *Federal Register*.

The sunset acts are not part of the APA but are included in the statutes that create the agencies. A sunset act sets an automatic expiration date for the agency.

Actions taken by administrative agencies can be appealed to the courts. The courts investigate first whether the authority delegated by Congress to that agency is valid. If the court finds that the agency has the authority, the court then determines whether the agency has exceeded its properly delegated authority.

Because an agency is given broad discretionary powers over a specialized subject matter, a court will give judicial deference to agency decisions. A court will not reverse an agency action unless it finds that the agency violated a condition set out by the Administrative Procedure Act.

Deregulation has taken place since the late 1970s. Two executive orders limit administrative regulations of line agencies. Each agency must submit to the Office of Management and Budget a statement of the goals of the upcoming year and set out major planned programs. Each agency must also prepare a regulatory impact analysis of major rules.

Key Terms

administrative law (128)
Administrative Procedure Act (APA) (133)
consent decree (140)
doctrine of exhaustion of remedies (150)
economic regulation (128)
enabling act (133)
entitlement programs (128)
Equal Access to Justice Act (149)

Export-Import Bank (Eximbank) (152)
formal rule making (135)
Freedom of Information Act (FOIA) (135)
General Agreement on Tariffs and Trade (GATT) (152)
general policy statement (152)
government agency (133)
independent agency (131)
informal rule making (135)

International Trade Administration (152)
International Trade Commission (152)
interpretive rules (135)
judicial deference (150)
line agency (131)
order (138)
Privacy Act (149)
procedural rules (135)
public welfare (128)

quasi-executive function **(135)**
quasi-judicial function **(135)**
quasi-legislative function
    (135)

quasi-official agency **(133)**
Regulatory Flexibility Act
    (149)

substantive rules **(135)**
sunset acts **(149)**
Sunshine Act **(149)**

Questions and Case Problems

1. In what way is administrative law related to the United States Constitution and to both the legislative and judicial branches of government?

2. Administrative agency law has been described as the "headless fourth branch" of the government. What does this expression mean? Do you agree or disagree? Why?

3. An appellate court will affirm the findings of the administrative law judge if those findings are supported by "substantial evidence on the record." When an administrative agency conducts a quasi-judicial hearing, a record is made of all the evidence and testimony presented at the hearing. The Adolph Coors Company was accused by the Federal Trade Commission (FTC) of engaging in certain price-fixing agreements in violation of the Sherman Antitrust Act. After a hearing, the FTC concluded that Coors had in fact engaged in illegal price fixing. Substantial evidence was presented at the hearings in support of the findings. Coors also presented substantial evidence that it had never entered into any price-fixing arrangements. Should an appellate court uphold the FTC's findings? [Adolph Coors Co. v. Federal Trade Commission, 497 F.2d 1178 (10th Cir. 1974)]

4. An agency must provide notice and a hearing before it can deprive a party of his or her property or rights. New York state and New York City officials administered various federally assisted welfare programs. Some of those on welfare filed a complaint in court alleging that the state and city terminated, or were about to terminate, the aid without prior notice and a hearing, thereby denying the plaintiffs due process of law. The state and the city, however, adopted procedures, posted notice, and had a hearing *after* these suits were brought. Does the failure to provide a welfare recipient with a notice of termination before the aid is stopped violate procedural due process? [Goldberg v. Kelly, 397 U.S. 254, 90 S.Ct. 1011, 25 L.Ed.2d 287 (1970)]

5. Thompson Medical Company produced an over-the-counter analgesic medicine that was sold under the name Aspercreme. The product did not contain any aspirin. The Federal Trade Commission (FTC) brought action against Thompson, claiming that the name of the product was false and misleading. Thompson took the position that the Food and Drug Administration (FDA) was the agency entrusted with the authority to evaluate and regulate over-the-counter medicine and that the FDA had exclusive regulatory authority. Was Thompson correct in its position? [Thompson Medical Co. v. Federal Trade Commission, 791 F.2d 189 (D.C. Cir. 1986)]

6. Congress passed the Marine Mammal Protection Act (MMPA) to protect porpoises during commercial fishing operations. Captains of fishing boats are allowed to take porpoises only if the captains comply with certain conditions. The MMPA requires that captains allow government observers to board and accompany vessels on regular fishing trips either to do research or to observe and collect data on the fishing operations for enforcement proceedings by the National Marine Fisheries Service. The captains of two fishing vessels object. You are the judge. On what will you base your decision as to whether government scientific observers should be required aboard the fishing vessel to collect data and conduct research? These inspectors will collect data on the captain's fishing practices for later inclusion in any quasi-judicial proceeding against the captain if he or she has failed to follow the government regulations. Will your decision be different if the fishing boat is out for one day or for a six-month trip? [Balelo v. Baldrige, 724 F.2d 753 (9th Cir. 1984)]

7. Regulations were published under the Federal Food, Drug, and Cosmetic Act that established the standard for farina and enriched farina. Quaker Oats could not sell its product under either label because the product did not meet the regulations for farina or enriched farina. The product was not farina because it contained vitamin D, and the product was not enriched farina because it did not contain the minimum quantities of vitamin B-1, riboflavin, nicotinic acid, or iron. Quaker Oats sues the government. You are the hearing officer. Will you uphold the regulations? State your reasons. [Federal Security Administration v. Quaker Oats Co., 318 U.S. 218, 63 S.Ct. 589, 87 L.Ed. 724 (1943)]

8. Eldridge received disability benefits under the Social Security Act. He was informed that there was a determination that he no longer qualified and that his benefits were being stopped. After the benefits were terminated, he was allowed a hearing. Eldridge filed a lawsuit claiming that he had been denied due process. You are the judge. Give your decision and support it with your reasons. [Mathews v. Eldridge, 424 U.S. 319, 96 S.Ct. 893, 47 L.Ed.2d 18 (1976)]

Chapter 7 The Regulation of Business Through Criminal Law

Small crimes always precede great ones. Never have we seen timid innocence pass suddenly to extreme licentiousness.

Jean Baptiste Racine (1639–1699)

OUTLINE

Introduction

At first, the subject of criminal law may seem out of place in a discussion of the legal environment of business. Businesspeople, for the most part, are basically honest and truthful, and their integrity is beyond question. Certain business activities, however, once considered legal, are now deemed to be criminal. Both Congress and state legislatures have regulated specific corporate activities by passing criminal statutes.

For example, not until 1911 was there an attempt by a state to regulate the sale of securities through criminal statutes. Two decades later, the federal government passed the first federal statute, the Securities Act of 1933, which regulates the sale of new securities. Today, stockbrokers, accountants, lawyers, and others are being convicted of violating the securities laws.

Before discussing specific criminal acts, we need to emphasize the distinction between civil and criminal law. When a person brings an action against another for an alleged violation of the law, he or she is seeking legal redress through a civil case of a harm committed against himself or herself. If the plaintiff wins the lawsuit, he or she usually obtains a monetary award.

When there is a violation of criminal law, only the government—city, county, state, or federal—can prosecute the accused person. All criminal actions are brought in the name of the government—for example, *The United States of America v. John Doe, Defendant*. The defendant must have violated a specific law for which a punishment is generally prescribed. The accused may be incarcerated, fined, or both. The harm here is not to a specific individual but to society as a whole.

The same wrongful act may give rise to both criminal and civil litigation. For example, a person who intentionally kills another is guilty of the crime of murder. He or she is also liable to the victim's estate for the civil tort of wrongful death. Two major differences exist between a criminal trial and a civil trial: First, the burden of proof is higher in the criminal case (**beyond a reasonable doubt**) than in the civil case (**preponderance of the evidence**). Second, the Fifth Amendment right against self-incrimination does not apply in a civil case. With the exception of these two issues, the procedures involved in a criminal action and a civil action are similar in many respects.

In this chapter we will discuss the classification of crimes and the elements of crimes in general. Then we will focus on criminal activity that has a direct application to the business world, frequently referred to as white-collar crime.

Classification of Crimes

A crime is classified as a **felony, misdemeanor,** or **petty offense** according to its seriousness. The definitions of these classifications vary greatly among the states and the federal government.

A felony is more serious than a misdemeanor or a petty offense and is punishable by imprisonment in a federal or state penitentiary for more than a year, by a fine, or even by death. The Model Penal Code drafted by the American Bar Association makes the following four distinctions among felonies, based on their seriousness: Capital offenses are punishable by death; first-degree felonies are punishable by a maximum penalty of life imprisonment; second-degree felonies are punishable by a maximum of ten years' imprisonment; and third-degree felonies are punishable by up to five years' imprisonment. These classifications set the maximum penalties; an actual sentence is usually less.

A misdemeanor is a crime punishable by a fine or by confinement for up to a year. People convicted of a misdemeanor are incarcerated in a city or county jail instead of in the state penitentiary. Disorderly conduct and trespassing are common misdemeanors. Misdemeanors are tried in city or county courts, while felonies are tried in state or federal courts.

A petty offense is often not classified as a crime but as a civil offense. These offenses include many traffic violations or violations of building codes. Even for petty offenses, a guilty party can be put in jail for a few days, fined, or both.

Crimes can also be classified according to their nature. For example, there are crimes against the person (murder, assault, rape), crimes against property (theft, burglary, arson), and crimes against the government (perjury, bribery). These classifications are used to group crimes within a statutory code. The criminal code is structured to punish acts, not classifications of people, despite the popular use of such terms as white-collar crimes.

Criminal Statutory Law

Originally, criminal acts were defined by the judiciary under common law and not by legislative statutes. Today, all crimes are based on statutes, but judges still use the original common-law definitions when interpreting these criminal statutes.

Every criminal statute prohibits certain behavior. The statute sets out the specific elements of the crime. The prosecutor must prove each element of the crime before a person can be convicted. Most crimes require an act of commission—that is, a person must *do* something in order to commit a crime. In some cases, an act of omission can be a crime, but only if the person has failed to carry out a legal duty. Failure to file a tax return is an example of an omission that is a crime.

Statutes in criminal law are narrowly interpreted by the courts. Courts take into consideration the statutory language, legislative history, and the purpose of the statute in order to determine what type of behavior is prohibited. In the following case, the United States Supreme Court interpreted a criminal statute passed by Congress.

BACKGROUND AND FACTS *Dowling and others had an extensive bootleg record operation involving the manufacture and distribution by mail of recordings of vocal performances by Elvis Presley. In 1976 Dowling, an avid collector of Presley recordings, began to manufacture phonograph records, or "phonorecords," of unreleased Presley recordings. He used material from a variety of sources, including studio outtakes, soundtracks from Presley motion pictures, and tapes of Presley concerts and television appearances. Dowling never obtained authorization from or paid royalties to the owners of the copyrights of the musical compositions. Dowling mailed several hundred packages per week and regularly spent $1,000 per week on postage.*

The Federal Bureau of Investigation started investigating Dowling. Eventually, he was arrested and tried. He was convicted of one count of conspiracy to transport stolen property in interstate commerce, eight counts of interstate transportation of stolen property, three counts of mail fraud, and nine counts of copyright infringement. He appealed all the convictions except those for copyright infringement. The Supreme Court considered whether this activity, which did not involve Dowling stealing physical items, was covered by the National Stolen Property Act.

Case 7.1
DOWLING v. UNITED STATES
Supreme Court of the United States, 1985.
473 U.S. 207, 105 S.Ct. 3127, 87 L.Ed.2d 152.

Justice BLACKMUN delivered the opinion of the Court.
*   *   *   *

Federal crimes, of course, "are solely creatures of statute." Accordingly, when assessing the reach of a federal criminal statute, we must pay close heed to language, legislative history, and purpose in order strictly to determine the scope of the conduct the enactment forbids. Due respect for the prerogatives of Congress in defining federal crimes prompts restraint in this area, where we typically find a "narrow interpretation" appropriate. *   *   *

Applying that prudent rule of construction here, we examine at the outset the statutory language. [18 U.S.C. § 2314] requires, first, that the defendant have transported "goods, wares, [or] merchandise" in interstate or foreign commerce; second, that those goods have a value of $5,000 or more"; and, third, that the defendant "kno[ws] the same to have been stolen, converted or taken by fraud." *   *   * [Dowling] argues *   *   * that the goods shipped were not "stolen, converted or taken by fraud." *   *   * The Government argues, however, that the shipments come within the reach of § 2314 because the phonorecords physically embodied performances of musical compositions that Dowling had no legal right to distribute. According to the Government, the unauthorized use of the musical compositions rendered the phonorecords "stolen, converted or taken by fraud" within the meaning of the statute. We must determine, therefore, whether phono-records that include the performance of copyrighted musical compositions for the use of which no authorization has been sought nor royalties paid are consequently "stolen, converted or taken by fraud" for purposes of § 2314. We conclude that they are not.

* * * [C]ases * * * prosecuted under § 2314 have always involved physical "goods, wares, [or] merchandise " that have themselves been "stolen, converted or taken by fraud." This basic element comports with the common-sense meaning of the statutory language: by requiring that the "goods, wares, [or] merchandise" be "the same" as those "stolen, converted or taken by fraud," the provision seems clearly to contemplate a physical identity between the items unlawfully obtained and those eventually transported, and hence some prior physical taking of the subject goods.

*   *   *   *

* * * There is no dispute in this case that Dowling's unauthorized inclusion on his bootleg albums of performances of copyrighted compositions constituted infringement of those copyrights. It is less clear, however, that the taking that occurs when an infringer arrogates the use of another's protected work comfortably fits the terms associated with physical removal employed by § 2314. The infringer invades a statutorily defined province guaranteed to the copyright holder alone. But he does not assume physical control over the copyright; nor does he wholly deprive its owner of its use. While one may colloquially link infringement with some general notion of wrongful appropriation, infringement plainly implicates a more complex set of property interests than does run-of-the-mill theft, conversion, or fraud. As a result, it fits but awkwardly with the language Congress chose—"stolen, converted or taken by fraud"—to describe the sorts of goods whose interstate shipment § 2314 makes criminal. "And, when interpreting a criminal statute that does not explicitly reach the conduct in question, we are reluctant to base an expansive reading on inferences drawn from subjective and variable 'under-standing.' "

*   *   *   *

No more than other legislation do criminal statutes take on straightjackets upon enactment. In sanctioning the use of § 2314 in the manner urged by the Govern-ment here, the Courts of Appeals understandably have sought to utilize an existing and readily available tool to combat the increasingly serious problem of bootlegging, piracy, and copyright infringement. Nevertheless, the deliberation with which Congress over the last decade has addressed the problem of copyright infringement for profit, as well as the precision with which it has chosen to apply criminal penalties in this area, demonstrates anew the wisdom of leaving it to the legislature to define crime and prescribe penalties. Here, the language of § 2314 does not "plainly and unmistakably" cover petitioner Dowling's conduct. * * * In sum, Congress has not spoken with the requisite clarity. Invoking the "time-honored interpretive guideline" that " 'ambiguity concerning the ambit of criminal statutes should be resolved in favor of lenity,' " * * * we reverse the judgment of the Court of Appeals.

DECISION AND   *The Supreme Court narrowly interpreted the National Stolen Property Act.*
REMEDY   *The phonorecords were made by Dowling; therefore, they were not physical items "stolen, converted, or taken by fraud"; it was the nonphysical item of the copyright that was stolen. The statutory language required the item unlawfully obtained and the item unlawfully transported to be the same*

physical item. The Court in reviewing the history of the statute found that Congress did not intend to include copyright infringement under this act. Dowling's convictions were reversed.

Three of the justices dissented. They believed that the act was too narrowly interpreted and noted that it does not make any distinction between tangible and intangible property. As the dissenting opinion observed, Dowling "could not have had any doubt that he was committing a theft as well as defrauding the copyright owner." He had no right to reproduce the copyrighted Elvis Presley performances, and it was that same property that Dowling transported across state lines. Dowling did steal the intangible copyrighted material, even if he could not physically carry it away.

Congress to date has not amended the National Stolen Property Act to include intangible goods.

COMMENT

Constitutional Safeguards

The criminal justice system operates on the premise that it is far worse for an innocent person to be punished than for a guilty person to go free. A person is innocent until proved guilty, and guilt must be proved beyond a reasonable doubt. The procedures of the criminal legal system are designed to protect the rights of the individual and to preserve the presumption of innocence.

Criminal law brings the weighty force of the government, with all its resources, to bear against the individual. The Fourth, Fifth, Sixth, and Eighth Amendments of the Constitution provide the safeguards for all persons including those accused of crimes. The United States Supreme Court has ruled that most of these safeguards apply not only in federal but also in state courts by virtue of the due process clause of the Fourteenth Amendment.

In past years, the Supreme Court has been active in interpreting these constitutional rights. The *Miranda v. Arizona*[1] case, for example, established the rule that a person who is arrested must be given his or her rights. The *Miranda* warnings include the right to remain silent because anything said can be used against the accused in court, the right to have a lawyer present, and, if the accused cannot pay for a lawyer, the right to have the state provide one.

Criminal Procedure

A criminal prosecution differs procedurally from a civil case in several respects. These differences reflect the desire to safeguard the rights of the individual against the state. Before a warrant for arrest can be issued, probable cause must exist for believing that the individual in question has committed a crime. Probable cause can be defined as involving a substantial likelihood that the individual has committed a crime. Note that probable cause involves a likelihood, not just a possibility. Arrests may sometimes be made without a warrant when there is no time to get one, but the action of the arresting officer is still judged by the standard of probable cause.

Individuals must be formally charged with having committed specific crimes before they can be brought to trial. This charge is called an **indictment**, if issued by a grand jury, or a **bill of information**, if issued by a magistrate. Before a charge can be issued, the grand jury or the magistrate must determine that sufficient evidence exists to justify bringing the individual to trial based upon probable cause.

At the trial, the accused person does not have to prove anything. The entire burden of proof is on the prosecution (the government). The prosecution must show that, based on all the evidence, the defendant's guilt is established beyond a reasonable doubt. A verdict of not guilty is not the same as a statement that the defendant is innocent. It merely means that not enough evidence was

---

1. 384 U.S. 436, 86 S.Ct. 1602, 16 L.Ed.2d 694 (1966).

Legal Highlight

Film Recovery Systems, Inc.

Three managers of Film Recovery were convicted in 1985 of murder, and Film Recovery and its parent company, Metallic Marketing Systems, Inc., were found guilty of involuntary manslaughter and reckless conduct. An employee had died of acute cyanide poisoning while working at the plant.

The company reclaimed silver from exposed X-ray film. Workers stirred the cyanide solution in large, open vats with wooden paddles. The cyanide would splash on the employees and enter their bodies through their pores; the workers also breathed the hydrogen cyanide gas and were frequently ill as a result of this exposure. The judge found that the managers knew of the substantial possibility of cyanide poisoning and were aware that they had failed to provide safe working conditions.

---

properly presented to the court to prove criminal guilt beyond a reasonable doubt.

Courts have complex rules about the types of evidence allowed and how that evidence may be presented, especially in jury trials. These rules are designed to ensure that evidence in the trial is relevant, reliable, and not unfairly prejudicial to the defendant. The defense attorney will cross-examine the witnesses who present evidence against his or her client in an attempt to show that their evidence is not reliable. Of course, the government may also cross-examine any witnesses presented by the defendant.

Basic Elements of Criminal Responsibility

Common law developed the twin requirements of criminal intent (*mens rea)* and criminal conduct (*actus reus)*. Thinking about embezzling funds or about stealing a computer program may be morally wrong, but these thoughts in themselves are not criminal until they are translated into action. A person can be punished for attempting to commit a crime, but only if substantial steps toward the criminal objective have been taken.

The Model Penal Code recognizes four categories of *mens rea:*

1. Purpose: What did the accused intend to be doing, or what was his or her conscious objective?
2. Knowledge: Did the accused act with knowl-edge of what he or she was doing, or did he or she act knowingly with respect to the result?
3. Recklessness: Did the accused act in such a wanton manner—that is, with knowledge and conscious disregard—that he or she created a considerable and unjustifiable risk to others?
4. Negligence: Did the accused act so negligently—that is, deviate so substantially from the standard of care a reasonable person would exercise under the circumstances—that he or she created a substantial and unnecessary risk to others?

In most cases, a wrongful mental state is required along with the wrongful act to establish criminal liability. In these cases, the mental state of the accused is important in determining the degree of wrongfulness of the crime. For example, the same criminal act that causes the death of another can be committed by different defendants with varying mental states. One person may kill in a cold-blooded manner with premeditation: This is murder in the first degree. A second person may kill in the heat of passion: This is voluntary manslaughter. A third person may kill as the result of negligence: This is involuntary manslaughter, as when someone dies as a result of extreme carelessness involving an automobile accident. In each of these situations, the law recognizes a different degree of wrongfulness, and the punishment differs accordingly. The greater the degree of *mens rea,* the more reprehensible the crime and thus the greater the punishment.

Some statutes do not require any criminal intent, only criminal conduct. For example, a person shoots a rifle in the air to help the neighborhood celebrate the New Year. The person does not intend any harm, but his or her conduct, the shooting of a rifle, was in violation of a statute, and that conduct constitutes the crime.

Criminal statutes in recent years have targeted corporate behavior by not requiring any criminal intent, only criminal conduct by the corporation. These statutes avoid the problem found in the past—namely, that a corporation cannot form a mental intent and, therefore, cannot be guilty of a crime. Likewise, the statutes apply to responsible individuals who manage a business. The following case involves a statute that does not require *mens rea*.

BACKGROUND AND FACTS *The defendant was the president of Acme Markets, Inc. As a large national food chain, Acme employed 36,000 employees and had 874 retail outlets, twelve general warehouses, and four special warehouses. During 1970, the president received a letter from the Food and Drug Administration (FDA) concerning rodents in a Baltimore warehouse where his firm stored a considerable amount of food. The rodents caused the food to become adulterated and not fit for consumption. The vice-president in charge of the warehouse responded to the FDA letter.*

In 1971 and 1972, similar conditions were observed. The defendant did not have direct control over the Baltimore warehouse but was convicted on five counts of causing adulteration of food that had been in interstate commerce. He was fined $50 for each of the five convictions under the Federal Food, Drug, and Cosmetic Act.

Case 7.2
UNITED STATES v. PARK
Supreme Court of the United States, 1975.
421 U.S. 658, 95 S.Ct. 1903, 44 L.Ed.2d 489.

Chief Justice BURGER delivered the opinion of the Court.

* * * *

The Act does not * * * make criminal liability turn on "awareness of some wrongdoing" or "conscious fraud." The duty imposed by Congress on responsible corporate agents is, we emphasize, one that requires the highest standard of foresight and vigilance, but the Act, in its criminal aspect, does not require that which is objectively impossible. The theory upon which responsible corporate agents are held criminally accountable for "causing" violations of the Act permits a claim that a defendant was "powerless" to prevent or correct the violation to "be raised defensively at a trial on the merits." If such a claim is made, the defendant has the burden of coming forward with evidence, but this does not alter the Government's ultimate burden of proving beyond a reasonable doubt the defendant's guilt, including his power, in light of the duty imposed by the Act, to prevent or correct the prohibited condition. Congress has seen fit to enforce the accountability of responsible corporate agents dealing with products which may affect the health of consumers by penal sanctions cast in rigorous terms, and the obligation of the courts is to give them effect so long as they do not violate the Constitution.

* * * *

Although we need not decide whether this testimony would have entitled respondent to an instruction as to his lack of power had he requested it, the testimony clearly created the "need" for rebuttal evidence. That evidence was not offered to show that respondent had a propensity to commit criminal acts[;] its purpose was to demonstrate that respondent was on notice that he could not rely on his system of delegation to subordinates to prevent and correct insanitary conditions at Acme's warehouses, and that he must have been aware of the deficiencies of this system before the Baltimore violations were discovered. The evidence was therefore relevant since it served to rebut respondent's defense that he had justifiably relied upon subordinates to handle sanitation matters.

DECISION AND REMEDY *Even though the defendant had no actual criminal intent, he was still convicted of a crime. All that was required was the wrongful conduct of producing adulterated food that was in interstate commerce.*

The trend today is to hold corporations criminally responsible for the conduct of their employees. The Model Penal Code recognizes that a corporation can be guilty of a criminal offense through the actions of its employees if one of three situations occurs: First, the legislative purpose of the statute in question is to impose criminal liability on corporations for the acts of its employees when those acts are committed within the scope of the employment. Second, the corporation has a legal statutory duty to perform a specific function, and it fails to perform that function, such as keeping accurate accounting records. Third, the criminal act has been authorized, requested, commanded, performed, or recklessly tolerated by the higher echelons of corporate management.

Crimes Affecting Business

Two categories of crimes that affect businesses directly are offenses against property and white-collar crimes.

Offenses Against Property

Businesses are most often involved in crimes against property. In this section, we examine the following offenses against property: (1) burglary, (2) larceny, (3) robbery, (4) receiving stolen goods, (5) arson, (6) forgery, (7) obtaining goods by false pretenses, and (8) embezzlement.

Burglary **Burglary** is defined as entering into or remaining in the building of another with the intent to commit a crime. For example, Ace breaks into a warehouse and intends to steal a truckload of video tape recorders. Before he can load his truck, the burglar alarm goes off, and he flees the scene. Ace is guilty of burglary because he intended to commit the felony of theft. Aggravated burglary, which is defined as burglary with the use of a deadly weapon or burglary of a dwelling place, incurs a heavier penalty.

Larceny The wrongful or fraudulent taking and carrying away by any person of the personal property of another is **larceny**. Generally, the person must also have had the intent to deprive the owner of her or his property permanently. Many business-related larcenies entail fraudulent conduct. The place from which physical property is taken is generally immaterial, although statutes usually prescribe a stiffer sentence for property taken from such buildings as banks or warehouses. Larceny differs from robbery in that robbery involves force or fear, and larceny does not. Therefore, picking pockets is larceny, not robbery.

As society has become more complex, the question often arises as to what is property. In most states, the definition of the property that is subject to larceny statutes has been expanded. Stealing computer programs may constitute larceny even though the programs consist of magnetic impulses. Trade secrets can be subject to larceny statutes. Stealing the use of telephone wires by the device known as a blue box is subject to larceny statutes. The theft of natural gas or electricity is often covered by special larceny statutes.

Robbery **Robbery** is defined as taking personal property of another from the other's person or in his or her presence by force or intimidation with the intent permanently to deprive the other of it. The use of force or fear is necessary for an act of theft to be considered a robbery. Thus, picking pockets is not robbery because the action is unknown to the victim. Typically, states have more severe penalties for aggravated robbery—robbery with the use of a deadly weapon. Liquor stores, all-night convenience stores, and banks are especially vulnerable to being robbed.

Receiving Stolen Goods In the crime of **receiving stolen goods,** the recipient of the goods does not need to know the true identity of the owner or of the thief. All that is necessary is that the recipient knows or should have known that the

Ford

Ford designed the Pinto to meet the Volkswagen competition. A decision was made not to include an $11 safety improvement that would have lessened the likelihood of an automobile fire in case of collision. Injury and death lawsuits totaled more than $1 billion. Losing several lawsuits, Ford made headlines when a judgment was awarded against it of $128.5 million, later reduced to $2.5 million.[a] By 1980 Ford had spent more than $50 million on litigation and recalls involving the Pinto.

In 1980 Ford went on trial in Indiana for reckless homicide as a result of the deaths of three people. Ford was eventually acquitted after it had spent $1 million to defend itself.

a. Grimshaw v. Ford Motor Company, 119 Cal.App.3d 757, 175 Cal.Rptr. 348 (1981). See Chapter 11.

goods were stolen. This knowledge implies an intent to deprive the owner of those goods.

Arson   The willful and malicious burning of a building (and, in some states, of personal property) owned by another is the crime of **arson.** Arson statutes apply to all kinds of buildings. If someone is killed as a result of arson, the act is felony murder.

Every state has a special statute that covers burning a building in order to collect insurance. If Akin owns an insured apartment building that is falling apart and burns it himself or pays someone else to set fire to it, Akin is guilty of arson to defraud insurers. Of course, the insurer need not pay the claim when insurance fraud has been proved.

Forgery   The fraudulent making or altering of any writing that changes the legal liability of another is **forgery.** If Smith signs Brown's name without authorization to the back of a check made out to Brown, Smith has committed forgery. Forgery also includes changing trademarks, falsifying public records, counterfeiting, and the altering of any legal document.

Most states have a special statute, often called a credit card statute, to cover the illegal use of credit cards. Thus, the state attorney can prosecute a person who uses a forged credit card for violating either the forgery statute or the special credit card statute.

Obtaining Money or Goods by False Pretenses   The crime of **obtaining goods by false pretenses** consists of obtaining title to another's property by a knowing false statement of a past or existing fact with intent to defraud the other. Statutes covering such illegal activities vary widely from state to state. Almost all states have created a separate crime prohibiting the giving of a no-account or insufficient-funds check with the intent to defraud.

Congress, in 1984, passed the **Trademark Counterfeiting Act,** which makes it a federal crime to deal in goods or services under a trademark that is a counterfeit. The federal **False Statement Act** makes it a crime to make a false statement intentionally to the United States government in order to obtain a monetary return.

In the following case, the United States Supreme Court was confronted with the question of whether the term *falsely made* prohibited the introduction into commerce of valid automobile titles that were obtained under false pretenses.

Case 7.3
MOSKAL v. UNITED STATES

Supreme Court of the United States, 1990.
498 U.S. ____, 111 S.Ct. 461,
112 L.Ed.2d 449.

BACKGROUND AND FACTS *Moskal was accused by the federal government of participating in a "title-washing" scheme in which automobile titles were altered to show rolled-back mileage figures on each car's odometer. Moskal's confederates purchased used cars in Pennsylvania, rolled back the cars' odometers, and altered the titles to reflect the new mileage figures. The altered titles were then sent to an accomplice in Virginia, who submitted the titles to Virginia authorities. Unaware of the alterations, the officials issued Virginia titles incorporating the false mileage figures. The "washed" titles were then sent back to Pennsylvania, where they were used in connection with used-car sales to unsuspecting buyers. Moskal played two roles in this scheme; he sent the altered titles from Pennsylvania to Virginia, and he received washed titles when they were returned.*

Moskal was convicted of receiving two washed titles, each recording a mileage figure that was 30,000 miles lower than the true number. The federal statute, 18 U.S.C. § 2314, prohibits the knowing transportation of "falsely made, forged, altered or counterfeited securities" in interstate commerce. Moskal appealed, contending that although he participated in a fraud (and thus had the intent under § 2314), the washed titles themselves were not "falsely made." When a title is issued by the appropriate state authorities who do not know of its falsity, Moskal claimed, the title is "genuine" or valid. It is the state document it purports to be and, therefore, is not "falsely made."

The Court uses the word "scienter," which means guilty knowledge.

Justice MARSHALL delivered the opinion of the Court.

The issue in this case is whether a person who knowingly procures genuine vehicle titles that incorporate fraudulently tendered odometer readings receives those titles "knowing [them] to have been *falsely made.*" 18 USC § 2314 (emphasis added). We conclude that he does.

*   *   *   *

In determining the scope of a statute, we look first to its language, *   *   * giving the words used their ordinary meaning. *   *   * We think that the words of § 2314 are broad enough, on their face, to encompass washed titles containing fraudulently tendered odometer readings. Such titles are "falsely made" in the sense that they are made to contain false, or incorrect, information.

Moskal resists this construction of the language on the ground that the state officials responsible for issuing the washed titles did not know that they were incorporating false odometer readings. We see little merit in this argument. As used in § 2314, "falsely made" refers to the character of the securities being transported. In our view, it is perfectly consistent with ordinary usage to speak of the security as *being* "falsely made" regardless of whether the party responsible for the physical production of the document *knew* that he was making a security in a manner that incorporates false information. Indeed, we find support for this construction in the nexus between the actus reus and mens rea elements of § 2314. Because liability under the statute depends on *transporting* the "falsely made" security with unlawful or fraudulent intent, there is no reason to infer a scienter requirement for the act of falsely making itself.

Short of construing "falsely made" in this way, we are at a loss to give *any* meaning to this phrase independent of the other terms in § 2314, such as "forged" or "counterfeited." By seeking to exclude from § 2314's scope any security that is "genuine" or valid, Moskal essentially equates "falsely made" with "forged" or "counterfeited." His construction therefore violates the established principle that a court should " 'give effect, if possible, to every clause and word of a statute.' "

*   *   *   *

We think that "title washing" operations are a perfect example of the * * * frauds that Congress sought to halt in enacting § 2314. As Moskal concedes, his title-washing scheme is a clear instance of fraud involving securities. And as the facts of this case demonstrate, title washes involve precisely the sort of fraudulent activities that are dispersed among several States in order to elude state detection.

Moskal's conviction was upheld. The Supreme Court held that a person who receives genuine vehicle titles knowing that they incorporate fraudulently tendered odometer readings receives those titles knowing them to have been falsely made within the plain meaning of the statute.

DECISION AND REMEDY

Embezzlement   The fraudulent conversion of property or money of another by a person in lawful possession of that property is **embezzlement.** Typically, this crime involves an employee who fraudulently appropriates money. Banks and other businesses face this problem where corporate officers or accountants "jimmy" the books to cover up the fraudulent conversion of money for their own benefit. Embezzlement is not larceny because the wrongdoer does not physically take the property from the possession of another, and it is not robbery because there is no taking by use of force or fear.

Whether the accused takes the money from the victim or from a third person is immaterial. If, as the comptroller of a large corporation, Saunders pockets a certain number of checks from third parties that were given to her to deposit into the account of another company, she has committed embezzlement.

Often the owner of a property will give money to a contractor specifically to pay various people who have worked on the owner's building. The contractor who does not use the money for this purpose commits a special form of embezzlement called **misapplication of trust funds.** The funds are entrusted to the contractor for a specific purpose, and that trust is violated. The fact that the accused may intend eventually to replace the embezzled property does not constitute a sufficient defense.

White-Collar Crime

The concept of **white-collar crime** distinguishes those crimes that involve offenses for monetary gain from crimes committed by physical means, such as the crimes described earlier in this chapter. Crimes, however, cannot be easily pigeon-holed; for example, forgery, obtaining goods by false pretenses, and embezzlement could also be called white-collar crimes. Today, over 30 percent of the criminal filings in federal district courts involve white-collar crimes.

White-collar crime consists of two categories: occupational and corporate. Occupational crime is committed by people through their work. Businesspeople, labor union leaders, politicians, and such professionals as medical doctors, lawyers, accountants, and stockbrokers may commit crimes in the course of doing their jobs. Insider trading, tax evasion, defrauding Medicare, check kiting, kickbacks, and bribes are a few examples of occupational crimes.

Corporate crime is committed by a complex organization. Because of its large size, the delegation of decisions, and the need to specialize, a corporation can compete effectively in the marketplace; these elements also result in the ability of employees to disavow any personal responsibility for corporate decisions. The executives at higher levels can distance themselves from criminal responsibility by claiming ignorance of the illegal activities of lower-echelon employees. At the same time, the lower-echelon employees can also disclaim criminal liability. They may be given goals that they believe must be achieved by almost any means if they want to keep their jobs; since the decision on how to achieve the goals is made by various groups, no one person is responsible. Each subgroup participates, and eventually an activity results that is criminal in nature and that has potentially dangerous ramifications in civil court if the harmed individuals also sue the corporation.

Legal Highlight

E. F. Hutton & Co.[a]

From July 1980 to February 1982, E. F. Hutton and Company engaged in check kiting. This crime involves depositing a check drawn on one bank into an account held at another bank, usually one located across the country. The balance of the account is inflated by the amount of the deposit, which is as yet uncollected by the deposit bank from the bank on which the check is drawn. The party then has use of this money, which is known as the float, during the time it takes for the deposited check to make it back to the original bank and for the funds actually to be transferred. The party can invest the money during the two to seven days it takes the check to clear the banking system without really having any actual cash involved. The interest income can be considerable.

Over a period of two years, senior employees at Hutton wrote at least $4 billion in overdrafts, which created the float, thus cheating 400 banks

out of millions of dollars. The Securities Exchange Commission estimates that Hutton earned $4 million on floats in 1980, $9 million in 1981, and $4.7 million in 1982 when the scheme was stopped. Approximately 15.8 percent of the $22 million increase in interest income was a result of the check-kiting scheme. Hutton pled guilty to 2,000 counts of mail and wire fraud and paid over $2.5 million in fines and settlements.

In a separate criminal action in 1988, Hutton pled guilty to concealing at least $532,000 from the Internal Revenue Service. The income came from a money-laundering scheme in which cash transactions of over $10,000 from 1981 to 1984 were not reported as required by federal disclosure rules. As a result, Hutton faced up to $1 million in fines.

a. E. F. Hutton was acquired in 1987 by Shearson Lehman Brothers, Inc. The company is now known as Shearson Lehman Hutton, Inc.

Since it is impossible to cover the range of what are considered to be white-collar crimes, the rest of this chapter will center on five areas: (1) computer crimes, (2) use of the mails to defraud, (3) RICO crimes, (4) bribery, (5) bankruptcy fraud, and (6) corporate crimes.

Computer Crimes   Computers have been used by governments and businesses since the 1940s, but the real explosion of computers for government, business, and home use took place in the late 1970s through the 1980s. This growth will continue. **Computer crimes** are an unfortunate result of this widespread use.

Computers can be used to commit a wide range of crimes and can do so in record time—as little as three milliseconds. Detection is often difficult. Companies, and even the government, have discovered multimillion-dollar electronic thefts, but only after a significant amount of time has elapsed. These electronic thefts are made by causing a computer to write extra paychecks, transfer

monies, or shave cents off interest accounts and place them into personal accounts.

The law involving computer crime is still in its formative state. To counter the rising computer crime activity, Congress passed the **Counterfeit Access Device and Computer Fraud and Abuse Act** in 1985 and the **Electronic Communications Privacy Act** in 1986. These statutes make it a crime for anyone without proper authorization to seek entrance into other computer systems, including electronic mail, computer-to-computer data transmissions, remote computing services, and private video conferences; they also prohibit the establishment of bulletin boards that list the passwords of individuals or businesses. The acts apply to governmental computers, computers of federally insured institutions, cellular car telephones, and computer access that crosses state lines. The penalties vary but can be as much as ten years in prison plus a $100,000 fine.

The full extent of computer crime in business is not known. Firms victimized by computer crime rarely publicize the fact. They are afraid that their customers will then doubt the accuracy of their computer-generated material. Trials of apprehended perpetrators of computer crimes are rare. The affected business usually allows the case to be plea-bargained instead of going to a trial. Some-times, for fear of publicity, the business will not even report the crime and may be blackmailed into giving the person who committed the crime a reference for another job.

In the following case, the court adopted the modern view of computer theft.

BACKGROUND AND FACTS *McGraw was charged with unlawfully exerting control over the property of the city of Indianapolis through the unauthorized use of the city's computer. It was undisputed at the trial that McGraw had used the computer to operate a business involving the sale of a dietary product known as NaturSlim. Employees had no authority to use the computers for private business. McGraw was convicted by the jury, but the trial judge dismissed the conviction because he thought that the use of the computer could not be theft.*

Case 7.4
INDIANA v. McGRAW
Indiana Court of Appeals,
Second District, 1984.
459 N.E.2d 61.

Judge NEAL
*   *   *   *

No Indiana case under the modern theft statute exists which addresses this question. We view McGraw's arguments as derived from old common law concepts which do not control the much broader definition of property and theft contained in modern statutes. *   *   *
*   *   *   *

The view that under modern theft statutes unauthorized use of computer services is theft is supported by the analysis of Michael Gemignani, J.D., Acting Chairman of the Computer Sciences section of Indiana University-Purdue University at Indianapolis, in his article on computer crime in 13 Indiana Law Review 681.

We deem McGraw's interpretation of the statutes overly restrictive. In short, he is arguing old common law precepts pertaining to larceny. In our view his contentions are inapposite to the plain meaning of the statutory sections involved herein.

Computer services, leased or owned, are a part of our market economy in huge dollar amounts. Like cable television, computer services are ". . . anything of value". Computer time is "services" for which money is paid. Such services may reasonably be regarded as valuable assets to the beneficiary. Thus, computer services are property within the meaning of the definition of property subject to theft. When a person "obtains" or "takes" those services, he has exerted control. *   *   * Taking without the other person's consent is unauthorized taking. Depriving the other person of any part of the services' use completes the offense.

Property must be shown to have a value, however slight, but the monetary value of property is of no concern, and the jury may under proper instructions infer some value. The theft statute comprehends a broad field of conduct, and does not limit the means or methods by which unauthorized control of property may be obtained. *   *   *
*   *   *   *

The court of appeals reversed the trial court's order to dismiss the two counts of theft for the unauthorized use of computer services. The definition of property and theft is no longer restricted to the old common-law concept of larceny, which is the actual taking and carrying away of an item. The statute was worded broadly enough to include the theft of computer services.

DECISION AND REMEDY

Criminal Schemes

Although all criminal acts have some cost to society, some types of criminal schemes involve millions of dollars. The following lists some examples of these illegal practices:

1. Charles Ponzi developed a loan-investment system that has become known as the Ponzi Scheme. He promised people who gave him money 50 percent interest on their money if he could keep it for 30 days and 100 percent if he could keep it for 90 days. By word of mouth, news of this fantastic investment spread, and people invested large sums of money. He paid the first people with the money coming in from the later investors. Eventually, he disappeared with most of the money. Today, similar scams exist as multilevel marketing schemes.

2. Glen W. Turner had a firm called Dare to Be Great. His company sold motivation self-improvement material by using another multilevel scheme. When a person sold one of Turner's courses, he or she kept some of the money and forwarded the rest up the pyramid, with each person at a higher level taking a cut. The seller would, in turn, work his or her way up the pyramid by recruiting others into the scheme; they would purchase the materials through him or her, and the recruiter would also take a cut when the new people had resold the materials. Money went to the top of the pyramid where people no longer had to recruit or to sell the courses through their own efforts. Turner was finally tried and convicted after earning millions of dollars.

3. The pigeon drop is a standard confidence game. One person will allegedly discover, in front of the victim (who is usually elderly), a billfold containing a large sum of money. The victim is told he or she can share the money, but he or she has to put up security. An accomplice offers to take the victim to the bank to withdraw money to be used as the security to show good faith. The victim gives the accomplice the money. The "lost" billfold is switched with one that has no money in it. The switched billfold is given to the victim to hold as an act of good faith by the two accomplices. They disappear leaving the victim with nothing.

4. Various schemes involve enticing someone to give out his or her credit card number over the telephone. In one scheme, the caller claims to be an agent of the telephone company. The agent tells the victim that a large number of telephone calls have been placed on his or her credit card. To verify and cancel these charges, the caller requests that the victim read out the credit card number. Later this credit card number is used to place numerous long-distance telephone calls throughout the world. In another scheme, the caller may announce that the victim has won a trip to Hawaii. The victim won this prize because his or her credit card number was randomly selected in a promotion by the credit card company. To verify the win, the con artist requests that the victim repeat the credit card numbers. Later the credit card bill reflects thousands of dollars of purchases made by these criminals.

5. The bank examiner scheme is successful because most people are honest and want to work with the authorities. A victim is contacted by telephone; the caller claims to be a bank examiner who suspects a bank teller of embezzling money. The caller requests that the victim go to the bank and remove a large sum of money. A very respectable-looking person then goes to the victim's residence, claims to be the bank examiner, gives the victim a receipt, takes the money, and disappears. In actuality, bank examiners never use laypeople in any type of investigation.

Use of the Mails to Defraud   **Use of the mails** (or telegrams) **to defraud** the public is a federal crime. Illegal use of the mails involves (1) mailing a writing for the purpose of executing a scheme to defraud and (2) an organized scheme to defraud by false pretenses. If, for example, Daniel Webster

Equity Funding

Equity Funding started operations in 1960, primarily selling mutual fund shares and life insurance policies. Listed on the New York Stock Exchange, it was audited by independent accounting firms and by government regulators. Still, for over a decade, it carried out complicated schemes of both insurance fraud and securities fraud. The Equity Funding scandal was broken by Ray Dirks, a financial analyst who was given information by a fired Equity employee. From 1964 to 1972, $143 million in fictitious income was reported. In one fraudulent maneuver, more than 64,000 insurance policies, of the 97,000 that Equity claimed on its reports to have issued, were bogus. Equity's fraud cost investors over $2 billion, making it to that date the largest single company fraud.

---

sends in the mail an advertisement offering for sale a cure for baldness that he knows to be fraudulent, he can be prosecuted for use of the mails to defraud.

RICO Crimes   Congress passed an amendment to the Organized Crime Control Act of 1970, known as the **Racketeer Influenced and Corrupt Organizations Act** of 1970 (**RICO**). The policy behind the amendment was to control organized crime's investments in legitimate business and to force forfeiture of any profits made as a result of criminal activity. Any offenses that violate this statute are called **RICO crimes**. RICO has two major sections: criminal and civil. Many states have followed the federal example and have adopted what are known as "Little RICOs," which are very similar to the federal statute.

Criminal RICO   Criminal RICO requires that a person show a "pattern of racketeering activity," which is defined as two or more racketeering acts within ten years of each other. The federal statute lists specific federal and state crimes that constitute these acts, such as mail fraud, wire fraud, fraud in the sale of securities, bankruptcy fraud, extortion, interference with interstate commerce by violence or by threats of violence, interstate transportation of stolen property, arson, murder, gambling, robbery, and drug dealing.

More than 30 offenses are listed, and a conviction of any two individual offenses within ten years can lead to a conviction under criminal RICO. A person convicted under this act can be fined $25,000, sentenced to twenty years in prison, and must forfeit to the federal government the property obtained through the criminal activity.

Civil RICO   The unique aspects of this section are the civil remedies for its violation and the triple-damage awards. Treble damages equal the amount of the actual damages multiplied by three. The RICO civil action section has resulted in cases being filed against such firms as General Motors, Merrill Lynch, American Express, and Prudential Insurance Company of America.

The inclusion of acts of fraud and of securities violations under the RICO statutes accounts for the increase in civil RICO suits. These violations establish a pattern of racketeering. Most lawyers, when bringing civil actions, ignored this statute until the last few years.

All though more lawsuits are being filed under RICO statutes, the chance of being sued under RICO is still very slight. In 1989 less than one-half of 1 percent of the federal courts' entire caseload involved RICO allegations. Even so, many groups (manufacturers, various chambers of commerce, and certified public accountants among them) wanted the law changed. Legislation was moving through Congress to lessen substantially the impact of RICO when the scandal with the savings and loan associations became public. Congress quickly and quietly let the proposed change to the statute drop in an effort to appear strong against business crime. Nevertheless, RICO cases, both civil and criminal, will continue to expand in the future.

In the following case, the United States Supreme Court considerably broadened the effect of

RICO. Injured parties are not required to show a prior criminal conviction against the defendant

before a civil lawsuit can be brought, and they do not need to show a distinct racketeering injury.

Case 7.5
**H. J. INC. v.
NORTHWESTERN
BELL TELEPHONE CO.**
Supreme Court of the United
States, 1989.
492 U.S. 229, 109 S.Ct. 2893,
106 L.Ed.2d 195.

BACKGROUND AND FACTS *Customers, including H. J. Inc., instituted this action against Northwestern Bell Telephone Company alleging that the company had paid numerous bribes to the Minnesota Public Utilities Commission. These bribes were paid in order to have the utility rates raised unreasonably. Plaintiffs sought an injunction and triple damages under RICO. Both the trial court and the Eighth Circuit Court of Appeals held that all of the bribes were committed in furtherance of a single scheme; RICO requires at least two racketeering acts.*

Justice BRENNAN delivered the opinion of the Court.

The Racketeer Influenced and Corrupt Organizations Act (RICO or the Act), * * * 18 U.S.C. §§ 1961–1968, * * * imposes criminal and civil liability upon those who engage in certain prohibited activities. Each prohibited activity is defined * * * to include, as one necessary element, proof either of "a pattern of racketeering activity" or of "collection of an unlawful debt." Racketeering activity is defined in RICO to mean "any act or threat involving" specified state-law crimes, any "act" indictable under various specified federal statutes, and certain federal "offenses," * * * but of the term "pattern" the statute says only that it "requires at least two acts of racketeering activity" within a 10-year period. * * * We are called upon in this civil case to consider what conduct meets RICO's pattern requirement.

* * * *

RICO provides for drastic remedies: conviction for a violation of RICO carries severe criminal penalties and forfeiture of illegal proceeds, * * * and a person found in a private civil action to have violated RICO is liable for treble damages, costs, and attorney's fees.

* * * *

In *Sedima, S.P.R.L. v. Imrex Co.*, 473 U.S. 479, 105 S.Ct. 3275, 87 L.Ed.2d 346 (1985), this Court rejected a restrictive interpretation * * * that would have made it a condition for maintaining a civil RICO action both that the defendant had already been convicted of a predicate racketeering act or of a RICO violation, and that plaintiff show a special racketeering injury. In doing so, we acknowledged concern in some quarters over civil RICO's use against "legitimate" businesses, as well as "mobsters and organized criminals." * * * But we suggested that RICO's expansive uses "appear to be primarily the result of the breadth of the predicate offenses, in particular the inclusion of wire, mail, and securities fraud, and the failure of Congress and the courts to develop a meaningful concept of 'pattern' "— both factors that apply to criminal as well as civil applications of the Act. * * * Congress has done nothing in the interim further to illuminate RICO's key requirement of a pattern of racketeering; and as the plethora of different views expressed by the Courts of Appeals since *Sedima* demonstrates, * * * developing a meaningful concept of "pattern" within the existing statutory framework has proved to be no easy task.

It is, nevertheless, a task we must undertake in order to decide this case. Our guides in the endeavor must be the text of the statute and its legislative history. We find no support in those sources for the proposition, espoused by the Court of Appeals for the Eighth Circuit in this case, that predicate acts of racketeering may form a pattern only when they are part of separate illegal schemes. Nor can we agree with those courts that have suggested that a pattern is established merely by proving two predicate acts, * * * or with *amici* in this case who argue that the word "pattern" refers only to predicates that are indicative of a perpetrator involved in organized crime or its functional equivalent. In our view, Congress had a more natural and commonsense approach to RICO's pattern element in mind, intending a more stringent requirement than proof simply of two predicates, but also envisioning a concept of sufficient breadth that it might encompass multiple predicates within a single scheme that were related and that amounted to, or threatened the likelihood of, continued criminal activity.

*   *   *   *

Whether the predicates proved establish a threat of continued racketeering activity depends on the specific facts of each case. Without making any claim to cover the field of possibilities—preferring to deal with this issue in the context of concrete factual situations presented for decision—we offer some examples of how this element might be satisfied. A RICO pattern may surely be established if the related predicates themselves involve a distinct threat of long-term racketeering activity, either implicit or explicit. Suppose a hoodlum were to sell "insurance" to a neighborhood's storekeepers to cover them against breakage of their windows, telling his victims he would be reappearing each month to collect the "premium" that would continue their "coverage." Though the number of related predicates involved may be small and they may occur close together in time, the racketeering acts themselves include a specific threat of repetition extending indefinitely into the future, and thus supply the requisite threat of continuity. In other cases, the threat of continuity may be established by showing that the predicate acts or offenses are part of an ongoing entity's regular way of doing business. Thus, the threat of continuity is sufficiently established where the predicates can be attributed to a defendant operating as part of a long-term association that exists for criminal purposes. Such associations include, but extend well beyond, those traditionally grouped under the phrase "organized crime." The continuity requirement is likewise satisfied where it is shown that the predicates are a regular way of conducting defendant's ongoing legitimate business (in the sense that it is not a business that exists for criminal purposes), or of conducting or participating in an ongoing and legitimate RICO enterprise.

The Supreme Court returned the case to the district court for trial. The Court held that in order to prove a pattern of racketeering activity, the plaintiffs must prove two elements: First, at a minimum there must be two racketeering acts that are related. Second, these acts must amount to, or threaten to continue the likelihood of, criminal activity. In other words, a plaintiff does not have to prove two separate unrelated criminal acts. In the case at hand, each act of bribery was a separate criminal act that fit into a pattern of racketeering.

DECISION AND REMEDY

Bribery   Three types of actions called **bribery** are considered crimes: (1) bribery of foreign officials, (2) bribery of public officials, and (3) commercial bribery.

Bribery of Foreign Officials   Until the 1970s, bribery of foreign officials to obtain business contracts was rarely, if ever, discussed. Indeed, payments in cash or in-kind benefits to government officials for such purposes were considered normal business practice. This is not to say that the practice was legal. In order to reduce the amount of bribes given to foreign government officials by

representatives of American corporations, in 1977 Congress passed the **Foreign Corrupt Practices Act (FCPA)**.

The act is divided into two major parts. The first part applies to all American companies, their directors, officers, shareholders, employees, or agents. The act prohibits bribes (offering something of value in return for official action) to foreign government officials where the purpose is to obtain or retain business for the American company.

The second part applies to all businesses registered with the Securities and Exchange Commission (SEC), even if the business operates only in the United States. In fact, the second part does not have anything to do with bribery or foreign corrupt practices. This part of the FCPA is directed toward accountants and financial officers, because previous bribes were often concealed in corporate financial records. All registered companies are required to keep detailed records that "accurately and fairly" reflect the company's financial activities, and these companies must have an accounting system that provides "reasonable assurance" that all transactions entered into by the company are accounted for and are legal.

Any person in the company is prohibited from making false statements to accountants and no person can make any false entry in any record or account. Any violation of the act may result in a fine of up to $1 million and the incarceration of convicted officers or directors for up to a maximum of five years. Those officers and directors can also be fined up to $10,000, and the fine cannot be paid with company funds.

Bribery of Public Officials   The attempt to influence a public official to act in a way that serves a private interest is a crime. As an element of this crime, intent must be present and proved. The bribe offered can be anything that the recipient of the offer considers to be valuable. The act of bribery is committed when the bribe is offered or when the recipient accepts the bribe.

Commercial Bribery   Kickbacks and payoffs from an individual working for one company to an individual working for another company are crimes. No public official need be involved. Such commercial bribes are typically given with the intent of obtaining proprietary information, covering up an inferior product, or securing new business. Industrial espionage sometimes involves this kind of activity—for example, a payoff of some type may be made to an employee in a competing firm in exchange for trade secrets and pricing schedules.

Bankruptcy Fraud   Today, individuals or businesses can be relieved of oppressive debt under the federal Bankruptcy Reform Act of 1978 as amended. This act is discussed in more detail in Chapter 13. **Bankruptcy fraud** takes place when a person is involved in bankruptcy and is not hon-

est with the bankruptcy court. The following are examples of white-collar crimes that can be perpetrated during a bankruptcy proceeding.

False Claims of Creditors   Creditors are required to file their individual claims against a debtor who is in bankruptcy proceedings. A creditor who files a false claim commits a crime.

Transfer of Property   Obviously, a debtor, knowing that he or she will be in bankruptcy proceedings, has an incentive to transfer assets to favored parties before or after the petition for bankruptcy is filed. For example, a company-owned automobile worth $15,000 can be sold at a bargain price of $1,000 to a trusted friend or relative. Closely related to the crime of fraudulent transfer of property is fraudulent concealment of property. The number of ways in which debtors have fraudulently, but cleverly, concealed assets would require several books to outline.

Scam Bankruptcies   The term *scam bankruptcy* has been used to indicate a swindle in which a bankruptcy is planned in advance. The perpetrators purchase a legitimate business that sells highly movable goods, such as jewelry or electronic home entertainment equipment. Numerous items are purchased on credit by the new owners. The creditors are paid off within a relatively short period of time.

This activity continues until the creditors are willing to offer larger and larger amounts of credit to the new owners. Finally, the new owners order a very large amount of merchandise on credit, sell it at whatever price is necessary to unload it quickly for cash, and then close down the business. Of course, the business is bankrupt. The amount that those creditors will recover, however, is typically very small, and the scam operators are nowhere to be found.

Corporate Crimes   Criminal statutes do not have specific crimes that are called **corporate crimes.** The term is generic and covers many types of crimes that are related to corporations. Corporate criminal liability has been expanding over the last decade to include more than the traditional monetary crime. Statutes are now drafted in such a manner that corporations can be held criminally liable for their acts.

For example, a corporation may be held criminally liable for antitrust violations (such as price fixing), for failing to meet securities standards in the issuing of stock in the corporation, or for failing to meet statutory safety standards. Corporations may also fail to pay their taxes and be held criminally liable. In addition, the corporate officers and directors who were in a position to prevent the crime can be prosecuted and, if found guilty, can be fined and/or incarcerated.

Regulatory Offenses   Congress has passed statutes that regulate businesses. Among these statutes are the Occupational Safety and Health Act, the Clean Water Act, the Clean Air Act, the Environmental Protection Act, the Securities Act of 1933, the Securities Exchange Act of 1934, the Sherman Antitrust Act, the Clayton Act, and the Food, Drug, and Cosmetic Act. These acts have created regulatory agencies that monitor business activities. If the agency finds that a business is in violation of a statute, the business may be criminally prosecuted by the Justice Department.

These same violations may be pursued through the use of administrative law courts. In fact, in the past decade, more violators have been assessed civil and administrative penalties than have been criminally prosecuted. The burden of proof is less in an administrative court, no right to a jury exists, and settlements can be reached more easily. At the same time, administrative penalties may amount to more than $1 million a day. All of these factors make administrative law courts an attractive alternative in cases involving regulatory violations.

Breach of Fiduciary Duty   The federal government can prosecute executives for breach of their fiduciary duty under the federal mail fraud statute. The government needs to prove that the executives failed to disclose material information that they had a duty to disclose and that the misleading information was sent to others through the mails.

Obstruction of Justice   Executives may be prosecuted for destroying or hiding corporate records that they have a duty to turn over to a grand jury, to the court, or to the investigative agency. The crime of obstruction of justice is independent of any other criminal violation. Even if the corporation is not guilty of any other criminal act, it can be found guilty of obstruction of justice.

Conspiracy or Aiding and Abetting   A corporation can be found criminally liable under several federal statutes if it aids, abets, counsels, commands, induces, procures, or conspires to commit a crime. Two distinct crimes exist: aiding and abetting, and conspiracy. Aiding and abetting does not require proof of an agreement to carry out a criminal act, while a conspiracy needs an agreement with others in order for this crime to have been committed.

Ethical Considerations

Conduct Toward Victims of Crime

In this chapter you have seen how criminal law regulates business activity. What is illegal is usually unethical. But what ethical repercussions do the effects of the criminal act on the victims have?

Does a business owe an ethical duty to the victims of a crime that the business itself did not commit? For example, what obligation is owed to employees and customers who are present during an armed robbery? Heart attacks and miscarriages have occurred among those who have witnessed a robbery. Should the business that was robbed pay for the resulting emergency medical treatment or psychological treatment, particularly for its employees?

Other examples exist where the law is inadequate to protect the victim. What about a financial institution that sells worthless securities to retired people, who lose their entire life savings? The judicial system may put the perpetrators in prison for many years, but this will not return the money. Should society compensate these victims? In considering this question, you should recognize that a compensation fund from the government will result in higher taxes for everyone.

What are the victims' rights while the legal action against the accused is pending? Remember, everyone is presumed innocent until proved guilty beyond a reasonable doubt. Should a victim be required to give an interview to the defendants' attorney prior to the trial? In cases involving sexual violence, should the alleged victim be required to give blood or other physical evidence? After a person is convicted, should the victim's feelings or those of the victim's family be considered by the judge in determining the perpetrator's sentence? If so, how much weight should be given to a victim's testimony? Should it make any difference if the victim is a judge, minister, police officer, mayor, child, or just a person who happens to be in the wrong place at the wrong time? If the victim is a person who is prominent in the community and he or she testifies, might the victim's social standing have an undue impact on the final sentence? Is this ethical?

International Considerations

The World Community Versus International Criminals

International criminal law as a definitive body of law is very limited in scope, but it is a growing area. In 1951, the United Nations drafted a proposal for an international criminal court that has been revised recently in the light of international narcotics trade and terrorism. Political considerations, constitutional prohibitions, and divergent cultural backgrounds have kept the proposal in various stages of draft form.

The United Nations Committee on Crime Prevention and Control has adopted various resolutions including recommendations that the U.N. conduct surveys of criminal justice more often, promote technical cooperation in crime prevention and criminal justice, redress the victims of crime and human rights violations, and address illicit drug production and trafficking. It has drafted five model treaties covering prevention of crimes that infringe on the cultural heritage of peoples, extradition, mutual assistance, and transfer of supervision of foreign offenders.

The Commission on Narcotic Drugs (CND) is responsible for drafting policy concerning illicit drugs. It places drafts and resolutions before the U.N. General Assembly. The U.N. also has other agencies working in this area. The U.N. Division of Narcotic Drugs (DND) provides practical, technical, and scientific assistance to member states. It operates the Drug Abuse Assessment System, which enables DND to analyze drug abuse data at national, regional, and international levels and to facilitate worldwide cooperation. The International Narcotics Control Board (INCB) assesses the adverse national security aspects of drug trafficking; it looks at the direct threat to political institutions and economics from the illicit production, trafficking, and abuse of drugs and from escalating drug-related violence.

Economic crime is a relatively new category of crime. The policies of various nations on this topic thus far remain divergent. The United States was the first country to define antitrust activities as both a criminal and a civil offense. Over the decades many other countries have come to recognize antitrust as a criminal act, but still other nations officially encourage their businesses to participate in antitrust activities. Even the United States now allows some form of antitrust activities by businesses when they have dealings overseas.

Extradition has been recognized as a very political topic for centuries. Extradition means the delivery of an accused or convicted person to the country where the crime allegedly occurred. For extradition to be required, a treaty outlining the extradition rules must exist between the two countries involved. Often these treaties will provide that a person cannot be executed if extradited or that a person cannot be extradited if accused of a political crime. What constitutes a political crime is a matter of definition. Are persons who plant bombs in Northern Ireland involved in a criminal act or a political crime? What if innocent persons are injured or killed? Defining a political crime is difficult even for one country acting alone, let alone for two nations striving to reach an agreement on extradition.

FACING A LEGAL ISSUE

Bad Checks

All states have a statute that makes it a crime to write a check when there are insufficient funds in the account or when the account is closed. Many times these crimes constitute a felony, and a defendant, if convicted, is sentenced to prison. Each year, businesses lose millions of dollars because of bad checks. The following are some of the ways a business might reduce these losses:

1. Most bad checks are written on new accounts. If the printed number of the check on the upper right-hand corner is low or is a handwritten number, this should signal that the check might not be good.

2. A business should never accept a postdated check, even though it is not illegal to postdate a check. To convict a person of writing bad checks requires proof that the defendant at the time of giving the check intended to defraud the business. When a merchant accepts a postdated check, she or he acknowledges that presently there is not enough money in the account to cover the check; in effect, the merchant is granting credit by accepting a postdated check. The check cannot be dishonored until the date on the check, which makes it very difficult to prove the fraudulent intent at the time that the check was written.

3. The person writing the check may write a figure different in numbers than in longhand on a check. If the figures do not match, a bank is supposed to return the check to the business.

Check processors, however, review hundreds of checks an hour and often look only at the numbers; they may not take time to verify that the words written out are a match. Generally, the figure written in words is the amount legally posted to the bank account.

4. For identification of the check writer at trial, merchants, when accepting a check, should require picture identification, such as a driver's license, and should record the identifying driver's license number on the check.

5. Forged checks may be spotted in several ways. First, each geographic area has a specific two-digit federal reserve number that appears twice on the check: as the first two digits of the nine-digit series at the bottom and as the denominator of the fraction at the upper right. If these are not the same, the check is forged. A businessperson should know the federal reserve number for his or her area. Second, the nine-digit number has a special magnetic ink that has a dull finish. Third, checks should have one edge that is perforated. Most forgers use a regular paper cutter that leaves all four sides of the check smooth.

6. A businessperson should never threaten criminal prosecution after receiving a bad check. Making such a threat could result in the merchant being charged with extortion. The crook might go free, and the businessperson might end up serving time! If the businessperson believes a crime has taken place, he or she should report it to the police or to the county or district attorney's office.

Summary

This chapter has stressed criminal law and how it relates to the business community. A wrongful act may be both a criminal and a civil wrong. When criminal conduct occurs, society is harmed. All criminal actions are brought in the name of the government—for example, *United States of America v. John Worthless*. Many criminal acts

also give rise to a private civil action by the injured party.

Crimes may be classified as felonies, misdemeanors, and petty offenses. A person convicted of a felony may serve a sentence of one year or more in a state or federal prison, be fined, or be put to death. A person convicted of a misdemeanor may serve time of less than one year in a local jail and/or be fined. If convicted of a petty offense, a person usually is fined.

Historically, most crimes require both criminal intent (*mens rea*) and criminal conduct (*actus reus*). For murder, the *mens rea* is the intent to take life. Many modern crimes require only criminal conduct and not criminal intent, which allows corporations incapable of criminal "intent" to be convicted of crimes.

When a person is charged with a crime, the government must prove the defendant guilty beyond a reasonable doubt. The guarantees found in the Constitution protect individuals and businesses when accused of crimes.

We have discussed generally the requirements for some of the more important crimes, such as burglary, larceny, robbery, receiving stolen goods, arson, forgery, obtaining goods or money by false pretenses, and embezzlement. This chapter emphasized white-collar crimes, including computer crimes, use of the mails to defraud, bribery, bankruptcy fraud, and corporate crimes.

One of the most important additions to federal law was the passage of the Racketeer Influenced and Corrupt Organizations Act. This act has both criminal and civil provisions. A business that has committed more than two acts of racketeering in ten years may be criminally prosecuted and may be liable for treble damages to the injured party in a civil lawsuit. Racketeering acts consist of such criminal activity as mail fraud, wire fraud, fraud in the sale of securities, bankruptcy fraud, extortion, interference with interstate commerce, interstate transportation of stolen property, arson, murder, gambling, and robbery.

Key Terms

actus reus (162)
arson (165)
bankruptcy fraud (174)
beyond a reasonable doubt (158)
bill of information (161)
bribery (173)
burglary (164)
computer crimes (168)
corporate crimes (174)
Counterfeit Access Device and Computer Fraud and Abuse Act (168)
Electronic Communications Privacy Act (168)

embezzlement (167)
extradition (177)
False Statement Act (165)
felony (158)
Foreign Corrupt Practices Act (FCPA) (173)
forgery (165)
indictment (161)
larceny (164)
mens rea (162)
misapplication of trust funds (167)
misdemeanor (158)
obtaining goods or money by false pretenses (165)

petty offense (158)
preponderance of the evidence (158)
Racketeer Influenced and Corrupt Organizations Act (RICO) (171)
receiving stolen goods (164)
RICO crimes (171)
robbery (164)
Trademark Counterfeiting Act (165)
use of the mails to defraud (170)
white-collar crime (167)

Questions and Case Problems

1. Civil trials and criminal trials follow essentially the same format. There are, however, several important differences. In criminal trials, the defendant must be proved guilty beyond a reasonable doubt, whereas in civil trials, the defendant need only be proved guilty by a preponderance of the evidence. Can you see any reason for this difference? Explain.

2. The following fact situations are similar (all involve the theft of Jean's television set), yet three different crimes are described. Identify the three crimes, noting the differences among them.

a. While passing Jean's house one night, Sam sees a portable television set left unattended on Jean's lawn. Sam takes the television set, carries it home, and tells everyone he owns it.

b. While passing Jean's house one night, Sam sees Jean outside with a portable television set. Holding Jean at gunpoint, Sam forces her to give up the set, and he runs away with it.

c. While passing Jean's house one night, Sam sees a portable television set in a window. Sam breaks the front door lock, enters, and leaves with the set.

3. Two basic elements are needed for a person to be convicted of a crime. The first element is called criminal intent, and the second is called criminal conduct. Explain what these terms mean, and discuss how each is applied to the following:
   a. Murder
   b. Forgery
   c. Arson

4. The plaintiff, Sedima, and defendant, Imrex, entered into a joint-venture agreement in which Imrex would provide electronic components to Sedima. They were to split the net proceeds when Sedima sold the product. Although $8 million in orders were processed, Sedima became convinced that Imrex was inflating the bill and cheating Sedima out of profits. Sedima filed a lawsuit alleging RICO claims based on mail fraud and wire fraud because Imrex had used the mails and wires allegedly to overbill Sedima. Imrex's defense was that it had never been criminally convicted of any RICO violations. Should Sedima have to prove that Imrex was criminally prosecuted or could have been criminally prosecuted in order to recover civil damages under RICO? [Sedima S.P.R.L. v. Imrex Co., 473 U.S. 479, 105 S.Ct. 3275, 87 L.Ed.2d 346 (1985)]

5. Joseph Russello was involved with committing arson on a building he owned. Prior to being charged and convicted, he had been able to collect the insurance on the building. What type of crime has Russello committed under these circumstances? [Russello v. United States, 464 U.S. 16, 104 S.Ct. 296, 78 L.Ed.2d 17 (1983)]

6. Faulknor was a seaman on the ship *Zemindar*. One night, while on duty, Faulknor went in search of the rum that he knew the ship was carrying. He found it and opened one of the kegs, but because he was holding a match at the time, he inadvertently ignited the rum and set fire to the ship. At the trial, it was determined that even though he had not intended to set fire to the rum, he had been engaged in the unlawful act of stealing it. Does Faulknor's theft of the rum make him criminally liable for setting fire to the ship? [Regina v. Faulknor, 13 Cox Crim. Cas. 550 (Ireland 1877)]

7. Defendants Petullo and Argentiere were convicted of conspiracy and of making false statements in violation of federal law. In 1979, they had devised a scheme to obtain money by submitting false claims for snow removal work in Chicago. Although the claims were submitted to the city of Chicago and not to a federal agency, they were charged with the federal crime because federal disaster relief funds were used to pay for snow removal. The defendants argued that the government failed to prove all of the necessary elements for a violation of the law. Should the prosecutor have to prove that the defendants obtained the money directly from the United States, or can the defendants be convicted of a federal crime on the basis that they had been paid from monies that originally came from the federal government? [United States v. Petullo, 706 F.2d 1178 (1983)]

8. Lund was working on his doctoral dissertation in statistics at Virginia Polytechnic Institute in Blacksburg, Virginia. He was required to use the computer facilities at the university. His faculty adviser neglected to arrange for the use of the computer. Lund, nonetheless, went ahead and used it without obtaining proper authorization. At the trial, Lund was convicted of grand larceny for obtaining approximately $30,000 worth of computer services without authorization. Four faculty members testified that computer time "probably would have been" or "would have been" assigned to Lund if properly requested. Lund appealed his conviction. What was the result? [Lund v. Commonwealth, 217 Va. 688, 232 S.E.2d 745 (1977)]

UNIT II   BUSINESS AND PRIVATE LAW

Chapter 8   **Torts**

I am charmed with many points of the Turkish law; when proved the authors of any notorious falsehood, they are burned on the forehead with a hot iron.

Lady Montague

OUTLINE

Introduction

Tort is a French word for wrong. Society recognizes an interest in one's personal physical safety and in the prevention of damage to property. Tort law provides remedies for those acts that cause harm. Society also recognizes other more intangible interests in such things as personal privacy, family relations, reputation, and dignity; tort law provides a remedy for the invasion of these protected interests, too.

Tort law is a part of the civil law. Injured parties may file civil lawsuits hoping to be compensated for their injuries. An act that is a tort can also be a crime; thus, criminal law and tort law overlap. For example, Cal drives an automobile while under the influence of alcohol. He runs a red light and has an accident that wrecks Tex's automobile and injures the driver. Cal has committed a crime, driving under the influence of alcohol, and has committed a tort, negligent driving. Tex will decide whether to retain an attorney and sue Cal in a civil court. The local prosecuting attorney will decide whether to prosecute Cal for any criminal acts, such as driving under the influence of alcohol, running a red light, and reckless driving.

Some tort actions result solely in civil lawsuits; there is no criminal prosecution. The burden of proof in a criminal action is higher (beyond a reasonable doubt) than the burden of proof in a civil tort case (by a preponderance of the evidence). (Preponderance means that the greater weight of the evidence was presented by the plaintiff and was more convincing than the evidence presented by the defendant.) Thus, a person might be found innocent of a crime but still be liable to an injured party in a civil lawsuit.

In this chapter we will examine those situations where the law imposes liability on a person or a business through tort law.

Types of Torts

Torts are traditionally divided into three categories. **Intentional torts,** as the name implies, are injuries caused by intentional acts. For example, when a movie star hits a photographer, this is the intentional tort of assault and battery. **Negligence** consists of harm caused by careless acts or failure

to perform a legal duty. Most automobile accidents are the result of negligence. **Strict liability** requires someone to compensate the injured party without regard to fault; generally, this liability is imposed by law.

The following sections examine these three types of torts in more detail.

Intentional Torts

An intentional tort arises from an act that the defendant consciously performs. He or she either intends to harm another or knows with substantial certainty that injury to another could result. The intent to perform the act is the important element. The actual nature of the damage ultimately caused is irrelevant in determining whether there was intent.

For example, if Sean intentionally pushes Lil and she falls to the ground and breaks her arm, it does not matter that Sean never intended to break Lil's arm. Sean did intend to push Lil, and that in itself is a tortious act of battery; Sean is liable for the consequences, including injury to Lil's arm. If the push was accidental, no intentional tort would exist, but liability might be imposed for negligent conduct.

Intentional torts are subdivided into two categories: wrongs against the person and wrongs against property.

Wrongs Against the Person

Intentional torts against a person include assault, battery, false imprisonment, infliction of mental distress, invasion of privacy, defamation (including disparagement of goods, slander of title, and defamation by computer), and fraud or deceit. In any of these torts, if the person suffers an injury it is often referred to as a personal injury or PI.

Assault and/or Battery   An intentional act (that is not excused or privileged on grounds of self-defense or defense of others) that creates in another person a reasonable apprehension or fear of harm is an **assault;** if there is physical contact injuring that person, a **battery** occurs.

For example, Foster threatens to hit Heise with a baseball bat during an argument. The threat is an assault, and if Foster strikes Heise, a battery has occurred.

Physical injury does not have to occur. An unwelcome kiss or escorting a person out of your apartment by holding his or her arms can constitute an assault and/or battery.

False Imprisonment **False imprisonment**, frequently associated with false arrest, is the intentional confinement or restraint of a person without justification and interferes with the person's ability to move about freely. Physical barriers, physical restraint, or threats of physical force can be used to confine someone. It is essential that the person being restrained not comply with the restraint willingly. On the other hand, a person is under no duty to risk personal harm in trying to escape.

The loss to business from shoplifting is estimated to exceed $10 billion a year. Almost all states have adopted **merchant protection legislation** that allows a merchant to detain any suspected shoplifter, provided that there is reasonable cause for suspicion and provided that the confinement is carried out in a reasonable way. The merchants are given statutory protection from being sued successfully for false imprisonment. The following case provides a good discussion of whether a merchant's actions in a particular situation were reasonable.

BACKGROUND AND FACTS *Mrs. Gathers, a schoolteacher and the plaintiff in this case, went to Harris Teeter Supermarket, the defendant, to purchase a particular brand of cigarettes and some other items. Mrs. Gathers searched the cigarette displays at each cash register. Unable to find the particular brand, she went to the rack containing cartons of cigarettes. She found one package of this brand, picked it up, examined it, and replaced it on the shelf because it was crushed. She picked up the other items in the store, went to the checkout stand, purchased the items, and left.*

During this time, she was observed by Ackerman, who was on duty as a police officer. Ackerman's second job was as a security officer for another Harris Teeter store. On his normal break from his duties as a police officer, he had gone to the office of Harris Teeter's assistant manager, Steven Marks.

There he observed Mrs. Gathers through the glass wall of the office. With Marks's full knowledge of what he was about to do, Ackerman asked the cashier if Mrs. Gathers had purchased any cigarettes. She said no. Ackerman then detained Mrs. Gathers outside the store and asked her to return inside with him.

After he had detained Mrs. Gathers, he interrogated her in the glass-walled office (with Marks's permission) in full view of the store's customers. Mrs. Gathers was not given her Miranda warnings.[a] She was not allowed to call her husband or her attorney. Her three requests that he check the cigarette display rack were refused. Ackerman told her she would be searched. She was subjected to a pat-down body search, including the breast and groin areas, by a female store employee, not a female police officer. Ackerman searched her grocery bag, pocketbook, and raincoat. The searches did not produce any stolen goods. She was then told she was free to go.

Case 8.1
GATHERS v. HARRIS TEETER SUPERMARKET
Court of Appeals of South Carolina, 1984.
282 S.C. 220, 317 S.E.2d 748.

---

a. *Miranda v. Arizona*, 384 U.S. 436, 86 S.Ct. 1602, 16 L.Ed.2d 694 (1966). The *Miranda* warnings are:
  1. You have a right to remain silent.
  2. If you say anything, it may be used against you in a court of law.
  3. You have a right to an attorney.
  4. If you cannot afford an attorney, one will be appointed for you.

She sued for slander, assault and battery, and false imprisonment. She was awarded a $20,000 judgment. Harris Teeter appealed. The trial court had found that Ackerman was an agent of Harris Teeter. Although he was employed as a police officer and in uniform at the time, he was off duty and taking a coffee break. He specifically told Marks he was about to catch a shoplifter, and Marks was aware of what he was going to do.

In its review of the case, the appellate court examined the merchant protection statute, Section 16-13-140 of the 1976 South Carolina Code of Laws. The court had to decide whether Ackerman was acting as a police officer or as an agent of Teeters. If he were acting as an agent of Teeters, the question was whether Ackerman's action violated the merchant protection statute in such a manner that Teeters lost the protection of the statute.

Judge SHAW

*   *   *   *

Section 16-13-140 [of the South Carolina Code of Laws] reads

In any action brought by reason of having been delayed by a merchant or merchant's employee or agent on or near the premises of a mercantile establishment for the purpose of investigation concerning the ownership of any merchandise, it shall be a defense to such action if: (1) the person was delayed in a reasonable manner and for a reasonable time to permit such investigation, and (2) reasonable cause existed to believe that the person delayed had committed the crime of shoplifting.

In *Faulkenberry v. Spring Mills, Inc.,* the S.C. Supreme Court stated that probable cause is now a defense under Section 16-13-140 to actions arising from a merchant's delay of suspected shoplifters. Probable cause is defined as a good faith belief that a person is guilty of a crime when this belief rests on such grounds as would induce an ordinarily prudent and cautious man, under the circumstances, to believe likewise. The issue of probable cause is essentially a question of fact and ordinarily for the determination of the jury.

The trial judge properly submitted the issues of probable cause and reasonable delay to the jury. As there is evidence which supports the jury's findings, we are bound to uphold them. In *Faulkenberry*, the good faith belief of guilt resulted from two reports from an eyewitness that the plaintiff was seen placing cloth in her purse. Here, Ackerman admitted that he never saw Mrs. Gathers put anything in her pockets. In *Faulkenberry*, the restraint was for only about twenty minutes, and the investigation consisted solely of requests that the plaintiff open her purse. These requests were refused and no further searches were attempted. Here, Mrs. Gathers was delayed for about one hour and subject to a full pat-down body search. We cannot say as a matter of law that probable cause existed or that Mrs. Gathers' delay was reasonable.

Harris Teeter claims that Mrs. Gathers consented to all of the actions taken against her. It is true that no one can enforce a right arising out of a transaction which he has voluntarily assented to. This rule applies to intentional acts which would otherwise be tortious. Where the evidence as to whether consent was given is conflicting, ambiguous, or inconsistent, it becomes a question of fact for the jury.

Mrs. Gathers allowed the search by [the store employee] but only because she was in a custodial situation, did not know her rights, and was afraid that she would be taken to jail if she refused. From this evidence, the jury could have reasonably concluded that the consent was a product of duress or coercion, express or implied, and not voluntarily given. Again, we cannot say as a matter of law that Mrs. Gathers consented to the search.

Harris Teeter takes exception to the jury charges made by the trial judge. Initially, the store claims that the defense of probable cause was not charged to the causes of action for slander and assault and battery. This argument is without merit. Prior to charging the law on false imprisonment, the trial judge listed all of the defenses Harris Teeter has raised, including probable cause. The trial judge then stated, "And so as not to have to repeat it each time, I'll cover it all in the next cause of action, each of those defenses." He then later instructed the jury on probable cause.

* * * *

Mrs. Gathers prayed for actual damages of $300,000 and was awarded $20,000. The proper amounts to be rendered as actual or punitive damages are left almost entirely to the jury and trial judge. An appellate court cannot reduce a verdict and will only strike down a verdict *in toto* in those rare cases where the amount is so shockingly excessive as to indicate it was the result of passion, partiality, prejudice, or corruption.

We see no evidence of passion, partiality, prejudice or corruption.

The trial court's judgment was affirmed. Sending the issue of probable cause to detain Mrs. Gathers to the jury was proper. The judgment of $20,000 was not so shockingly excessive as to indicate that it was the result of passion, partiality, prejudice, or corruption, and, therefore, it was not struck down.

Often merchants carry insurance to protect against legal actions. Such insurance, however, covers only unintentional risks; thus, intentional torts are not usually covered by insurance. In this case, Harris Teeter—and not the insurance company—would have to pay the $20,000.

DECISION AND REMEDY

Infliction of Mental Distress   People have a right to be free from mental distress. The tort of **infliction of mental distress** is defined as an intentional act that amounts to extreme and outrageous conduct resulting in severe emotional distress. For example, a creditor telephones Paul every hour during the night attempting to collect a debt. As a result, Paul suffers intense mental anxiety. The courts have found such acts by the creditor to be extreme and outrageous conduct that exceeds the bounds of decency accepted by society. The person committing these acts may be liable in a tort action. These acts are also in violation of the Fair Debt Collection Practices Act, which is described in Chapter 13.

Right of Privacy   Closely allied to intentional infliction of mental distress is the separate tort of the intentional invasion of a person's privacy. A lawsuit based on **invasion of privacy** does not involve an injury to a person's property or character but rather concerns an invasion of a person's intangible right to be left alone. The use of two-way mirrors in women's fitting rooms that allow the store manager and others to observe women changing clothes has led to liability under this tort. The unauthorized use of a person's picture for commercial use is another example of invasion of privacy.

Defamation   **Defamation** of character involves wrongfully hurting a person's good reputation. The law imposes a general duty on all people to refrain from making false, defamatory statements about others. Breaching this duty verbally involves the tort of **slander**; breaching it in writing involves the tort of **libel**. These torts were reviewed in Chapter 5 under free speech.

The basis of the tort is the publication of a statement or statements that hold an individual up to contempt, ridicule, or hatred. Publication means that the defamatory statements are made to or within the hearing of people other than the defamed party. If Thompson writes Andrews a private letter accusing him of embezzling funds, that letter does not constitute libel. If Peters calls Gordon dishonest, unattractive, and incompetent when no one else is around, that act does not constitute slander. In neither case was the message communicated to a third party.

A person who is sued for defamation may assert several defenses. First, truth is normally a complete defense against a defamation charge. Second, under the defense of **privilege of im-**

Legal Highlight

Can the Dead Be Defamed?

Errol Flynn was a flamboyant movie star of the 1940s and 1950s. In the book, *Errol Flynn: The Untold Story*, Charles Higham described the popular celebrity as a homosexual and Nazi spy. His family was outraged and brought a civil lawsuit against the publisher.[a]

Both the trial court and the court of appeals held that, no matter how egregious or disturbing the material, California law does not allow the surviving family members, who were not defamed, to bring a lawsuit. A California law that made libel tending to blacken the memory of one who is dead a crime had been declared unconstitutional by a California court in 1976.

Essentially, at least in California, the surviving family members cannot sue to protect their beloved deceased from any defamation.

The family, however, can prevent others from making economic gains from the use of the name or likeness of the deceased person whose fame and, occasionally, earning power continue after death. Many families have formed corporations that have the right to all the mascots, logos, likenesses, licensing and distribution rights, and even trademarks associated with their deceased relatives.

a. Flynn v. Higham, 149 Cal.App.3d 677, 197 Cal.Rptr. 145 (1983).

---

munity, even if the statement is false, no action can be brought against the speaker or writer. Privileged communications are of two types: absolute and qualified. In general, these privileges are granted where there is some important and overriding social value in sanctioning a person's conduct, even though the conduct may result in defamation.

Absolute privilege applies to judicial and legislative proceedings, but only when it is relevant to the activities of either governmental body. For example, statements made by an elected representative on the floor of Congress are absolutely privileged communications. These same statements, if made in a different arena, such as a newsletter or a press conference, are not so privileged. **Qualified privilege** is a common-law concept based on the philosophy that a person's right to know or to speak is of equal importance to another person's right not to be defamed. If the communication has a qualified privilege, the plaintiff must show that the privilege was abused in order to recover.

An example of a qualified privilege is found in letters of recommendation and in written evaluations of employees. Generally, if the communicated statements are made in good faith and the publication is limited to those who have a legit-

imate interest in the communication, the statement falls within the qualified privilege.

Disparagement of Goods, Slander of Title, and Defamation by Computer These three torts involve defamation and directly involve business. A false statement made about a person's product is a tort called **disparagement of goods.** For example, a salesperson might lie about a competitor's product.

Defaming the title (proof of ownership) that a person has to his or her property may prevent a person from being able to sell the property. This tort is called **slander of title.**

Erroneous information from a computer about a person's credit standing or business reputation can impair that person's ability to obtain further credit. If the company that owns the computer information fails to correct the information in a timely manner, it may be liable to the victim. This tort is called **defamation by computer.** The company is also responsible, under the Fair Credit Reporting Act discussed in Chapter 13, for making sure that the information is correct.

Fraud or Deceit The tort of **fraud** or **deceit** involves (1) a misrepresentation of material facts, (2) made with the intent to deceive or with reckless disregard as to the truthfulness of the facts, (3) made with the knowledge that they are false, (4) justifiable reliance on these facts by the victim, and (5) damages. Sometimes failure to disclose material facts is a form of deceit. For example, the owner of a house knows that the roof has started to leak even though it is not evident. The house is for sale. The owner should inform any potential buyer of this latent (hidden) defect. If he or she fails to disclose this fact to any potential buyer, he or she may be held liable for any damages that the buyer suffers in the future as a result of the leaky roof.

Wrongs Against Property

Intentional torts that are wrongs against property include trespass, conversion, and nuisance. In these types of torts, the property is said to be damaged.

Trespass to Land   Any time a person enters upon another's land or causes something to enter onto the land or to remain there without consent or privilege, a tort of trespass to land has been committed.

Once established as a trespasser, certain rights, duties, and privileges flow to both the owner and the trespasser. Some of these are:

1. A trespasser is liable for any damage he or she causes to the property.
2. A trespasser can be removed from the premises by use of *reasonable force* without the property owner being liable for assault and/or battery.
3. The trespasser generally assumes the risks of the premises (that is, a trespasser cannot complain of personal injuries that occur as a result of the condition of the premises). This rule does not permit the owner to lay traps and even may require a warning of dangers to be found on the property, such as guard dogs. Under the "attractive nuisance doctrine," young children do not assume the risks of premises if it is the condition of the premises that attracts them to it (such as a swimming pool, large sandpiles on construction sites, and the like).

Conversion   Whenever personal property is taken from its rightful owner or possessor and placed in the service of another, the tort of **conversion** occurs. Conversion is the civil side of those crimes relating to stealing. A store clerk who steals mer-

chandise from the store commits a crime of embezzlement and the tort of conversion at the same time. Of course, when conversion occurs, the lesser offense of trespass to personal property usually occurs as well.

If the initial taking of the property was unlawful, there is trespass. The retention of that property is conversion. Even if the initial taking of the property was permitted by the owner, failure to return the property may be conversion.

Nuisance   It is possible to commit a tort through the unreasonable use of your own property. A **nuisance** is an improper activity (which may involve the use of your own property) that interferes with another's enjoyment or use of his or her property. Nuisances can be either public or private. This topic is discussed in Chapter 23.

A **public nuisance** disturbs or interferes with the public and is generally a crime. A **private nuisance** interferes with the property interest of a limited number of individuals and is a tort. Reasonable limitations are placed on the use of property; such limitations prevent the owner from unreasonably interfering with the health and comfort of neighbors or with their right to enjoy their own private property.

For example, Rick cannot keep chickens in his townhouse because this would constitute a nuisance, even if there were no city ordinances prohibiting such activity. Hal cannot set up a speaker system in his backyard and play rock-and-roll or symphonic music at such volume that his neighbors are disturbed. This may also be a crime (public nuisance) as a typical city ordinance specifies that no sound exceeding 100 decibels shall be audible within 100 feet of one's property between the hours of 11 P.M. and 7 A.M.

Negligence

Intentional torts involve a particular mental state. In negligence, however, the actor neither intends to bring about the consequences of the act nor believes that the consequences will occur. The actor's conduct merely creates the risk of such consequences. Without the creation of a risk, there can be no negligence. Moreover, the risk must be foreseeable; that is, it must be such that a reasonable person would anticipate it and guard against it.

Many of the actions discussed in the section on intentional torts would constitute negligence if they were committed carelessly and without intent. For instance, carelessly bumping into someone who then falls and breaks an arm constitutes negligence. Likewise, carelessly (as opposed to intentionally) flooding someone's land constitutes negligence. In a sense, negligence describes a *way* of committing a tort rather than constituting a distinct *category* of torts.

Negligence occurs when a person is injured or his or her property is damaged because someone else's conduct falls below the required duty of care. Three elements are involved: (1) breach (failure) of duty of care, (2) injury, and (3) causation. Various defenses may be available to the person accused of negligence.

Breach of Duty of Care

[handwritten: Applies to other duties as well]

The first element of negligence can be broken into a two-part question:

1. Is there a duty of care?

[handwritten: Causes { Actual → Direct cause of damages / Proximate → Foreseeability of the result]

2. Did the defendant's action breach (fail to live up to) that duty?

Tort law recognizes several standards for the duty of care depending on the particular fact situation. First, the standard of care may be measured by an **objective standard** of reasonableness—the "reasonable person" standard. In determining whether a tort has been committed, the courts ask: How would a reasonable person have acted in the same or similar circumstances?

The reasonable person standard is objective. It is not necessarily how a particular person would act, but it is society's judgment as reflected by a jury as to how people should act in the same situation. If the reasonable person existed, he or she would be careful, conscientious, even-tempered, and honest. This hypothetical reasonable person is frequently used in discussions of law.

Common carriers, such as trucking firms, and innkeepers are held to a higher standard of care than that of reasonableness. In the following case, the court reviews the standard of care based on a reasonably prudent motel operator.

Case 8.2
KVERAGAS v. SCOTTISH INNS, INC.
United States Court of Appeals, Sixth Circuit, 1984.
733 F.2d 409.

BACKGROUND AND FACTS *Charles and Esther Kveragas, the plaintiffs, rented a motel room at the Scottish Inns in Knoxville, Tennessee. That night three intruders kicked open the door, shot Charles, injured Esther, and robbed them of $3,000. The Kveragases filed a lawsuit alleging that the motel owners and operators failed to make adequate provisions for the safety of the motel guests.*

The evidence at trial showed that the room was equipped with a hollow-core door that fit poorly into the door frame. The only door lock was that incorporated into the handle, described as a grade-three lock, although a security chain was also provided. The plaintiffs had both locked and chained the door. A single kick, however, was the only force applied to the door, and all that was necessary to open it.

Evidence showed that dead-bolt locks and other security devices were easily available and in use throughout the motel industry. Dead-bolt locks are considerably stronger than the type of lock employed at this motel. Evidence also showed that a dead-bolt lock could withstand the force that was applied to the door.

The trial court directed the jury to return a verdict for the defendants, which the jury did, on the grounds that the motel owners and operators had no duty to protect their guests from sudden criminal acts. The plaintiffs appealed.

Judge MERRITT
*   *   *   *

The common law has long recognized the special legal relationship between innkeepers and registered guests. Historically, innkeepers operated under an extreme standard of liability, approaching that of an insurer against all dangers save acts of God. The Supreme Court of New York long ago offered an explanation for the emergence of the innkeeper's special responsibility:

> This rigorous rule had its origin in the feudal conditions which were the outgrowth of the Middle Ages. In those days there was little safety outside of castles and fortified towns for the wayfaring traveler, who, exposed on his journey to the depredations of bandits and brigands, had little protection when he sought at night temporary refuge at the wayside inns, established and conducted for his entertainment and convenience. Exposed as he was to robbery and violence, he was compelled to repose confidence, when stopping on his pilgrimages over night, in landlords who were not exempt from temptation; and hence there grew up the salutary principles that a host owed to his guest the duty, not only of hospitality, but also of protection.

Although castles and fortified towns are no longer part of our landscape, bandits and brigands remain. The common law has responded to these cultural changes by lessening, but not removing, the innkeeper's liability for criminal acts committed by third parties.

*   *   *   *

[In *Zang v. Leonard*, the] *Zang* court *   *   * set out the standard of care which we believe the Tennessee Supreme Court would apply in cases such as the instant one: the duty placed on innkeepers to protect registered guests from the misconduct of third persons is a duty of due care under all the circumstances. Put differently, the "reasonable person" standard, the cornerstone of common law tort jurisprudence, is the standard that applies to innkeepers in the protection of their guests, just as it governs countless other relationships.

The *Zang* court did not leave the application of the general due care standard to the unfettered discretion of the jury, and neither do we. The *Zang* court addressed the factors which a jury should consider in assessing due care:

> The measure of the liability of the possessor of land to invitees is due care under all the circumstances including the nature and use of the land, the nature of the invitation, the nature of the relationship with the invitee, the opportunity of the possessor and the invitee to know and avoid existing or probable dangers, and any and all other factors which would challenge the attention of the possessor and/or invitee to the probability of danger to the invitee and produce the precautions which a reasonably prudent person would instigate under the same or similar circumstances.

Under the *Zang* rule, the first responsibility of the factfinder is to determine "what, if any, protective measures would have been employed by a reasonably prudent motel operator under the same circumstances" which the factfinder finds existed at the time of the injury. The finding of fact as to the protective measures which a reasonably prudent motel operator would have employed is to be based on a comprehensive study of *all* relevant conditions. The *Zang* court listed some of the appropriate considerations: whether the motel is advertised as an unusual establishment which offers better than ordinary facilities; whether the location of the motel is such as to be convenient to criminals; and whether prior assaults or other criminal acts have occurred on the premises.

*   *   *   *

Once the factfinder determines what, if any, protective measures would have been employed by a reasonably prudent motel operator under the same circumstances, the factfinder next should determine "whether the actions of the responsible defendants conform to the actions of a reasonably prudent motel operator" as found by the factfinder. If the factfinder determines that the responsible defendants did not comply with this standard of care, then it should find the defendants negligent; otherwise, it should find them not negligent.

* * * *

Turning now to the facts of the case, * * * we conclude that under the *Zang* rule plaintiffs have presented sufficient proof to survive a motion for a directed verdict. The evidence that the assailants gained entry to the room by kicking open the door, that the door fit poorly and had a grade three lock with no deadbolt lock; that other types of doors and locks were available and in use in the motel industry which could withstand the force applied to the door in this case; this evidence, together with the inferences that arise therefrom, is sufficient to permit a jury to find that a reasonably prudent motel operator would, under the circumstances of this case, have employed a more substantial door and lock; that the responsible defendants failed to adopt these protective measures; and that if the protective measures had been adopted the assailants would not have been able to gain entry into the plaintiffs' room. These facts, if found by the jury, are sufficient to establish a cause of action under the *Zang* standard. Hence, it was error to direct a verdict for the defendants.

DECISION AND REMEDY   *The appellate court reversed the judgment of the trial court and remanded the case to the trial court for a new trial. At the new trial, the jury would decide the standard of care for a reasonably prudent motel operator under these circumstances.*

A second standard of care may be imposed by a statute. Everyone driving a vehicle has a **statutory duty** not to proceed through an intersection when the traffic light is red. Reasonableness is not involved under this standard of care. For example, a person receives a traffic ticket for running a red light. He may tell the judge that at 3:00 A.M. he was rushing his pregnant wife to the hospital, that he stopped at the red light, that he looked both ways and determined that no cross traffic was coming from either direction, and that he then proceeded through the signal. The judge in his or her wisdom may dismiss the ticket. If the driver had hit someone in the intersection, reasonableness as to his action could not be used as a defense. The statutory duty to stop at the red light is the standard of care. Because someone was harmed, the judge does not have the discretion to dismiss the ticket.

Injury

The plaintiff must suffer some loss, harm, wrong, or invasion of a protected interest in order to recover damages for a negligent act. The reason for the requirement of injury is obvious. Without an injury of some kind, the defendant is not required to give the plaintiff compensation. Compensation is paid in an effort to make the plaintiff "whole" again. Essentially, the purpose of the tort of negligence is to compensate the victim for legally recognized injuries resulting from acts of the wrongdoer; its intent is not to punish those acts.

Causation

Causation is the last element necessary to prove negligence. If a person breaches her or his duty of care, that breach must cause harm, and the person's negligent act must be closely linked with the harm for the person to be liable. The courts have imposed limits on the amount of a person's liability if the negligent act is not wholly responsible for the harm that results.

In deciding whether there is causation, the court must address two questions: First, is there *causation in fact?* Did the injury occur because of the defendant's act, or would it have occurred anyway? Causation in fact can usually be determined by the *but for* test: But for the wrongful act, the injury would not have occurred. If Carl carelessly leaves a campfire burning and the fire burns down the forest, causation in fact exists. The forest would not have burned but for Carl's negligent act; therefore, Carl may be liable for the damages he caused.

If Carl carelessly leaves a campfire burning, but it burns out, and lightning causes a fire that burns down the forest, there is no causation in fact. In both examples, there is a wrongful act (Carl leaving the campfire burning), and there is damage, but in the second example, no causal connection exists between the wrongful act and the damage, and thus Carl is not liable.

The second question is: Was the act the *proximate cause* of the injury? How far should a defendant's liability extend for a wrongful act that was a *substantial* factor in causing injury? For example, Carl's fire not only burns down the forest but also sets off an explosion in a nearby ammunition plant that levels the entire plant, destroys the marshmallow factory located next door, and severely damages houses and businesses in the nearby community. Should Carl be liable to the ammunition plant owners, the marshmallow plant owners, and the people harmed in the nearby community?

The limitations on a person's liability are the issue when the courts consider proximate cause. Proximate cause is a question of public policy; the courts must ask whether the connection between an act and an injury is strong enough to justify imposing liability.

The courts use **foreseeability** as the test for proximate cause. If the consequences of the harm done or the victims of the harm were unforeseeable, there is no proximate cause. Carl was negligent, but how far does his liability go? Is this the chain of events that a reasonable person would usually guard against? In the next case, the court reviews the issue of foreseeability.

BACKGROUND AND FACTS *Charles Bigbee, the plaintiff, was in a telephone booth on Century Boulevard. Looking up, he saw an automobile coming toward him and realized that it was going to hit the telephone booth. He attempted to flee, but the door to the booth jammed, trapping Bigbee inside. The evidence at the trial showed that the driver of the automobile was intoxicated. Evidence also showed that the telephone booth had been demolished by an automobile twenty months before.*

Bigbee sued the driver and the companies that served the driver alcoholic beverages. The case was settled as to those defendants. Bigbee also sued Pacific Telephone and Telegraph Company for negligence and strict liability for the design, location, installation, and maintenance of the telephone booths. Pacific Telephone was granted a summary judgment that, in effect, dismissed the case. Bigbee appealed.

Case 8.3
BIGBEE v. PACIFIC TELEPHONE AND TELEGRAPH CO.
Supreme Court of California, 1983.
34 Cal.3d 49, 665 P.2d 947, 192 Cal.Rptr. 857.

Chief Justice BIRD
*   *   *   *

[The] defendants contend that their duty to use due care in the location, installation, and maintenance of telephone booths does not extend to the risk encountered by plaintiff and that neither their alleged negligence in carrying out these activities nor any defect in the booth was a proximate cause of plaintiff's injuries. These contentions present the same issue in different guises. Each involves this question—was the risk that a car might crash into the phone booth and injure plaintiff reasonably foreseeable in this case?

Ordinarily, foreseeability is a question of fact for the jury. It may be decided as a question of law only if, "under the undisputed facts there is no room for a reasonable difference of opinion." Accordingly, this court must decide whether foreseeability remains a triable issue in this case.

If any triable issue of fact exists, it is error for a trial court to grant a party's motion for summary judgment.
*   *   *   *

Turning to the merits of this case, the question presented is a relatively simple one. Is there room for a reasonable difference of opinion as to whether the risk that a car might crash into the phone booth and injure an individual inside was reasonably foreseeable under the circumstances set forth above?

In pursuing this inquiry, it is well to remember that "foreseeability is not to be measured by what is more probable than not, but includes whatever is likely enough in the setting of modern life that a reasonably thoughtful [person] would take account of it in guiding practical conduct." One may be held accountable for creating even " 'the risk of a slight possibility of injury if a reasonably prudent [person] would not do so.' " Moreover, it is settled that what is required to be foreseeable is the general character of the event or harm—e.g., being struck by a car while standing in a phone booth—not its precise nature or manner of occurrence.

Here, defendants placed a telephone booth, which was difficult to exit, in a parking lot 15 feet from the side of a major thoroughfare and near a driveway. Under these circumstances, this court cannot conclude as a matter of law that it was unforeseeable that the booth might be struck by a car and cause serious injury to a person trapped within. A jury could reasonably conclude that this risk was foreseeable. This is particularly true where, as here, there is evidence that a booth at this same location had previously been struck.

Indeed, in light of the circumstances of modern life, it seems evident that a jury could reasonably find that defendants should have foreseen the possibility of the very accident which actually occurred here. Swift traffic on a major thoroughfare late at night is to be expected. Regrettably, so too are intoxicated drivers. Moreover, it is not uncommon for speeding and/or intoxicated drivers to lose control of their cars and crash into poles, buildings or whatever else may be standing alongside the road they travel—no matter how straight and level that road may be.
* * * *

It is of no consequence that the harm to plaintiff came about through the negligent or reckless acts of Roberts. "If the likelihood that a third person may act in a particular manner is the hazard or one of the hazards which makes the actor negligent, such an act whether innocent, negligent, intentionally tortious, or criminal does not prevent the actor from being liable for harm caused thereby." Here, the risk that a car might hit the telephone booth could be found to constitute one of the hazards to which plaintiff was exposed.
* * * *

Since the foreseeability of harm to plaintiff remains a triable issue of fact, the judgment is reversed and the case is remanded to the trial court for further proceedings consistent with the views expressed in this opinion.

DECISION AND REMEDY *Bigbee was entitled to have a trial. The Supreme Court of California held that there was a substantial fact issue as to the foreseeability of risk for the user of the telephone booth. The booth was difficult to exit, placed in a parking lot fifteen feet from the side of a major thoroughfare, near a driveway, and the booth had been struck before. The court's decision gives Bigbee a right to have a trial; the decision does not guarantee any recovery.*

Defenses to Negligence

Defenses to negligence are (1) superseding intervening forces, (2) assumption of risk, and (3) contributory and comparative negligence. A superseding or intervening force may break the causal connection between a wrongful act and injury to another. If so, it cancels out the wrongful act.

For example, Jed takes his automobile to a mechanic to have his brakes repaired. After repair of the brakes, on replacing the tires, the mechanic fails to tighten two bolts. Jed is driving along when he hears a terrible rattle coming from the automobile. As he is stopping his car along the shoulder of the freeway, the wheel comes off. Just then a drunk driver comes along, hits the car, and

Legal Highlight

Mass Torts

Often the media talk about mass torts. Just what is a mass tort? In this type of tort, an act has harmed a number of plaintiffs, with the numbers sometimes in the hundreds or even thousands. Some recent examples of mass disaster litigation include the following cases:

■ In 1981, the skywalks in the Hyatt Regency Hotel in Kansas City collapsed. The federal court certified two class-action suits. Over 100 people were killed, and hundreds were injured.
■ A. H. Robins manufactured the Dalkon Shield, an IUD product, from 1971 to 1974. Between 1974 and 1986 over 12,000 women filed damage

suits. Robins went into bankruptcy court in 1986. Over 130,000 claims were filed against Robins.
■ In 1979, a fire swept through the lobby of the MGM Grand Hotel in Las Vegas, Nevada. The final settlement was in excess of $205 million.
■ In 1992 Pfizer, Inc., established a $500 million settlement plan to compensate 55,000 people who received defective heart valves that had a history of fracturing.
■ Since the 1950s, over 2 million women received breast implants with an estimated 40% complication rate. Most are from silicone gel manufactured by Dow Corning, Bristol-Myers Squibb, McGhan Medical, and Heyer Schulte corporations.

---

injures Jed. The drunk driver is an intervening force and may break the connection between the mechanic's wrongful act and the damage to Jed and his automobile that resulted from the accident.

A plaintiff who voluntarily enters into a risky situation, knowing the risk involved, will not be allowed to recover. This defense is called **assumption of risk.** For example, a driver who enters a race knows that there is a risk of being killed or injured in a crash. The driver has assumed the risk of injury. Knowledge of the risk and voluntary assumption of that risk are the two requirements for this defense.

All individuals are expected to exercise a reasonable degree of care in looking out for themselves. In some jurisdictions, recovery for injury resulting from negligence is prevented when the injured person has failed to exercise such care over himself or herself. The defense of **contributory negligence** is available where both parties have been negligent, and their combined negligence has contributed to cause the injury. When one party sues the other in tort for damages from negligence, the defendant can claim contributory negligence, which is a complete defense under common-law rules.

The modern legal trend is toward narrowing the scope of this defense. Instead of allowing con-

tributory negligence to negate a cause of action completely, an increasing number of states allow recovery based on the doctrine of **comparative negligence.** This doctrine enables computation of both the plaintiff's and the defendant's negligence. The plaintiff's damages are reduced by a percentage that represents the degree of his or her contributing fault.

For example, Mario is driving his automobile. Although it is equipped with safety belts, he is not wearing his. Mario is approaching an intersection with a green light. Peter, approaching in his car from the opposite direction, turns left in front of Mario's automobile. The cars collide, and Mario is thrown from his automobile and severely injured.

Subsequently, Mario files a lawsuit against Peter alleging negligence. Peter defends by using the comparative negligence theory. Through expert witnesses, Peter can show the jury that Mario's nonuse of his seatbelt is a factor which the jury may use to reduce Mario's claim to damages. Mario may not recover for the full extent of his injuries. His failure to wear safety belts was an act of negligence that contributed to the extent of his injuries. Several states have now adopted this view because the data demonstrate that the frequency and severity of injuries are lessened when motorists wear seat belts.

Strict Liability

The final category of torts is called strict liability, or liability without fault. Negligent torts involve an act that departs from a standard of care and causes an injury. Under the doctrine of strict liability, liability for injury is imposed for reasons other than fault.

When a person engages in abnormally dangerous activities, that person will be liable under strict liability if any harm occurs to others. Abnormally dangerous activities have three characteristics:

1. The activity involves potential harm of a serious nature to persons or to property.
2. The activity involves a high degree of risk that cannot be completely guarded against by exercising reasonable care.
3. The activity is not commonly performed in the community.

Strict liability is applied because of the extreme risk of the activity. Although an activity such as blasting with dynamite is performed with all reasonable care, there is still a risk of injury to in-nocent persons. Thus, unless a person voluntarily and with knowledge enters a posted work site in which blasting is occurring, the dynamiter is liable for any damage to property or injury to a person caused by the blasting.

Because of the risk of harm, public policy requires that the person engaged in the activity must be held liable for injuries caused by the activity. Although fault does not exist, responsibility is imposed because of the nature of the activity. It is reasonable to require the person engaged in the activity to carry insurance or otherwise be prepared to compensate anyone who suffers harm.

In the past, strict liability was thought to apply basically to ultrahazardous activities, such as blasting. In the next case, the court applies strict liability for a hidden defect in a common everyday item, a shower door made of untempered glass. The courts are expanding the application of strict liability. In this case, the court is faced with deciding who will be responsible when two innocent parties are involved: the landlord who did not have any actual knowledge of the hidden defect or the tenant who did not have knowledge or control over the type of glass in the shower door.

Case 8.4
BECKER v. IRM CORP.
Supreme Court of California,
1985.
38 Cal.3d 454, 698 P.2d 116,
213 Cal.Rptr. 213.

BACKGROUND AND FACTS   *George Becker, plaintiff, rented an apartment from IRM Corporation (IRM), the defendant. The apartment complex was built in 1962 and 1963 and sold to IRM in 1974. The shower doors in the apartments were of untempered frosted glass. No visible difference exists between tempered and untempered glass. In 1978 when Becker was taking a shower, he slipped and fell against the shower door, breaking the glass and severely lacerating his arm. He sued IRM in strict liability and in negligence, asserting that it was liable for a latent defect. Undisputed evidence showed that the risk of serious injury is reduced if the shower door is of tempered glass rather than untempered glass.*

The trial court granted the defendant's motion for a summary judgment that it was not liable to a tenant for a latent defect of the rented premises absent concealment of a known danger or an expressed contractual or statutory duty to repair.

Justice BROUSSARD
*   *   *   *

In *Greenman v. Yuba Power Products, Inc.* we established the rule: "A manufacturer is strictly liable in tort when an article he places on the market, knowing that it is to be used without inspection for defects, proves to have a defect that causes injury to a human being. Recognized first in the case of unwholesome food products, such liability has now been extended to a variety of other products that create as great or greater hazards if defective." The court recognized that the cases imposing strict liability had "usually been based on the theory of an express or implied warranty running from the manufacturer to the plaintiff." The justification for departing from warranty theory and for establishing a doctrine of strict liability in tort was the recognition that the liability was imposed by law and the refusal to permit the manufacturer to define the scope of its own liability for defective products.

*　*　*　*

Greenman also noted that the purpose of strict liability in tort is "to insure that the costs of injuries resulting from defective products are borne by the manufacturers that put such products on the market rather than by the injured persons who are powerless to protect themselves."

We follow a stream of commerce approach to strict liability in tort and extend liability to all those who are part of the "overall producing and marketing enterprise that should bear the cost of injuries from defective products." The doctrine of strict liability in tort has been applied not only to manufacturers but to the various links in the commercial marketing chain including a retailer, a wholesale-retail distributor, personal property lessors and bailors, and a licensor of personalty. In holding that strict liability in tort was applicable to lessors and bailors in *Price v. Shell Oil Co.*, it was pointed out that strict liability does not apply to isolated transactions such as the sale of a single lot.

*　*　*　*

A similar development appears with respect to the landlord-tenant relationship.

*　*　*　*

We are satisfied that the rationale of the foregoing cases, establishing the duties of a landlord and the doctrine of strict liability in tort, requires us to conclude that a landlord engaged in the business of leasing dwellings is strictly liable in tort for injuries resulting from a latent defect in the premises when the defect existed at the time the premises were let to the tenant. It is clear that landlords are part of the "overall producing and marketing enterprise" that makes housing accommodations available to renters. A landlord, like defendant owning numerous units, is not engaged in isolated acts within the enterprise but plays a substantial role. The fact that the enterprise is one involving real estate may not immunize the landlord. Our courts have long recognized that contracts relating to realty may give rise to implied warranties.

Absent disclosure of defects, the landlord in renting the premises makes an implied representation that the premises are fit for use as a dwelling and the representation is ordinarily indispensable to the lease. The tenant purchasing housing for a limited period is in no position to inspect for latent defects in the increasingly complex modern apartment buildings or to bear the expense of repair whereas the landlord is in a much better position to inspect for and repair latent defects. The tenant's ability to inspect is ordinarily substantially less than that of a purchaser of the property.

*　*　*　*

Landlords are an integral part of the enterprise of producing and marketing rental housing. *　*　* They have more than a random or accidental role in the marketing enterprise. In addition, landlords have a continuing relationship to the property following the renting in contrast to the used machinery dealer who sells. As we have seen, in renting property the landlord *　*　* makes representations of habitability and safety.

*　*　*　*

We conclude that the absence of a continuing business relationship between builder and landlord does not preclude application of strict liability in tort for latent defects existing at the time of the lease because landlords are an integral part of the enterprise and they should bear the cost of injuries resulting from such defects rather than the injured persons who are powerless to protect themselves.

DECISION AND REMEDY *The Supreme Court of California decided that IRM could be held strictly liable for injuries resulting from latent defects on its premises. The landlord had a duty to exercise due care in inspecting for dangerous conditions in connection with the purchase of rental premises. The fact that the landlord was not aware of the dangerous condition did not necessarily preclude liability. The trial court's judgment was reversed.*

Other applications of the strict liability principle are found in workers' compensation acts and in the area of product liability. Product liability is discussed in Chapter 11. In workers' compensation and product liability, the liability is borne by either the employer or the manufacturer as a matter of public policy. Such liability is based on two factors:

1. The employer and manufacturer are better able to bear the cost of injury than the injured person because they can spread it out to society through an increase in the cost of goods and services. For example, a toy manufacturer would normally sell a toy to a million customers for $20. The price can be raised to $21 (an increase of 5 percent) in order to pay for the liability claim ($1 million) of one customer.
2. The employer and manufacturer are making a profit from their activities and, therefore, as a matter of public policy, should bear the cost of injury as an operating expense.

Specific Torts Related to Business

Some torts that have a direct application to the business environment include:

1. Wrongful interference with a contractual or business relationship
2. Infringement of trademarks, trade names, patents, and copyrights
3. Theft of trade secrets.

Wrongful Interference with a Contractual or Business Relationship

The application of tort law relating to intentional **interference with a contractual or business relationship** has increased greatly in recent years. In such a case, the plaintiff must prove that the defendant intentionally induced the breach of a valid contractual or business relationship, not merely that the defendant reaped the benefits of the broken relationship.

For example, Alicia has a one-year requirements contract to deliver to Eat-Rite Restaurants all the doughnuts Eat-Rite requires for its breakfast menu. Frank's Doughnut Hole had unsuccessfully bid for the contract earlier. Frank offers Eat-Rite a special price, much lower than Alicia's, if Eat-Rite will change suppliers immediately and further offers to pay for any costs Eat-Rite incurs in making the change. Eat-Rite breaks its contract with Alicia.

This is clearly a wrongful interference with a contractual relationship. Suppose, however, that Frank merely advertises a special price and further states it will beat any valid price offered by a competitor. Eat-Rite reads the advertisement, breaks its contract with Alicia, and contracts with Frank's Doughnut Hole. Although Frank will reap the benefits of Eat-Rite's breach of contract with Alicia, Frank will not be liable for the tort of wrongful interference with a contractual relationship.

The best-known case of wrongful interference is *Texaco v. Pennzoil.*[1] The trial jury found that Texaco wrongfully interfered with a planned merger (the contract) between Pennzoil and Getty Oil Company. The jury found that the three elements required for a wrongful interference with a contract relationship were present, as follows:

1. A *valid contract* existed between Pennzoil and Getty.
2. Texaco *knew* that this contract existed.
3. Texaco *intentionally induced* the breach of the contract by Getty resulting in an economic or pecuniary gain.

---

1.   729 S.W.2d 768 (Tex.Ct.App. 1987).

The trial judgment was the largest in United States history—$7.53 billion in actual damages and $3 billion in punitive damages.[2]

Infringement of Trademarks, Trade Names, Patents, and Copyrights

A **trademark** is a distinctive mark, motto, device, or implement that a manufacturer stamps, prints, or otherwise affixes to the goods it produces. For example, WordPerfect, a software word-processing program, is a trademark owned by WordPerfect Corporation. The trademark allows goods to be identified on the market; it vouches for their origin. At common law, the person who owns a trademark is protected. Clearly, if a person uses the trademark of another, consumers will be misled into believing that the goods were made by someone else. The law seeks to avoid this kind of confusion.

A **service mark** is similar to a trademark but is used to distinguish the services of one person from those of another. For example, each airline has a particular mark or symbol associated with its name. Titles or character names used in radio and television are frequently registered as service marks.

Once a trademark or service mark has been registered, a firm is entitled to the exclusive use of it for marketing purposes. Whenever that trademark or service mark is copied to a substantial degree or used in its entirety by another, intentionally or unintentionally, the trademark or service mark has been infringed. The trademark need not be registered with the state or with the federal government in order to obtain protection from the tort of trademark infringement, but registration does furnish proof of the date of inception of its use.

A **patent** is a grant from the government that conveys and secures to an inventor the exclusive right to make, use, and sell an invention for a period of seventeen years. Patents for a lesser period are given for designs, as opposed to inventions. For either a regular patent or a design patent, the applicant must demonstrate to the satisfaction of the United States Patent Office that the invention, discovery, or design is genuine, novel, useful, and not obvious in the light of the technology of the time. A patent holder gives notice to all that an article or design is patented by placing on it the word "Patent" or the abbreviation "Pat.," plus the patent number.

If a firm uses a device that is substantially similar to someone else's patented device, the tort of patent infringement exists. Patent infringement may exist even though not all features or parts of an invention are copied.

A **copyright** is a right granted by statute to the author or originator of certain literary or artistic productions. Works created after January 1, 1978, are automatically given statutory copyright protection for the life of the author plus 50 years. Note that it is not possible to copyright an idea. What is copyrightable is the particular way in which an idea is expressed. Recent legislation permits the copyright of computer programs.

Whenever the form of expression of an idea is copied, an infringement of copyright has occurred. The production does not have to be exactly the same as the original, nor does it have to reproduce the original in its entirety. If a substantial part of the original is reproduced, a copyright infringement exists. Limited copying is permitted under the "fair use" doctrine, such as copying a page of this text for classroom use. The following case shows how the fair use doctrine has been applied in the music world.

---

2. The case was settled in 1988 for $3 billion. The day of the payment, Texaco completed its reorganization and emerged from twelve months of bankruptcy proceedings.

BACKGROUND AND FACTS *Roy Orbison and William Dees co-authored "Oh, Pretty Woman" and assigned their rights in the song to Acuff-Rose Music in 1964. Acuff-Rose copyrighted the song the same year. On July 5, 1989, 2 Live Crew's manager wrote Gary Teifer of Opryland U.S.A., Inc. and Acuff-Rose, informing them that 2 Live Crew was going to parody "Oh, Pretty Woman." Full credit would be given to Orbison and Dees as owners and authors, and Acuff-Rose would be paid the statutorialy required rate*

Case 8.5
ACUFF-ROSE MUSIC, INC. v. CAMPBELL
United States Court of Appeals, Sixth Circuit, 1992.
___ F.2d ___.

for use of the song. Teifer responded on July 17, denying the license because "we cannot permit the use of a parody of 'Oh, Pretty Woman.' "

On July 5, two days before Teifer's letter, 2 Live Crew released its version of "Oh, Pretty Woman" on record albums, tapes, and compact discs, all entitled "As Clean As They Wanna Be." Both the compact disc cover and compact disc itself acknowledged Orbison and Dees as the authors of "Oh, Pretty Woman" and Acuff-Rose as the publisher.

On June 18, 1990, Acuff-Rose sued 2 Live Crew and their record company, Luke Skywalker Records, for copyright infringement among other allegations. Acuff-Rose contended that the lyrics of "Oh, Pretty Woman" as sung by 2 Live Crew "are not consistent with good taste or would disparage the future value of the copyright." Moving for summary judgment, 2 Live Crew argued that "Pretty Woman" was a parody that constitutes fair use under the Copyright Act. The district court granted the summary judgment which was appealed.

Judge JOINER
*   *   *   *

Section 107 of the Copyright Act states:
*   *   * In determining whether the use made of a work in any particular case is a fair use the factors to be considered shall include—

(1) the purpose and character of the use, including whether such use is of a commercial nature or is for nonprofit educational purposes;

(2) the nature of the copyrighted work;

(3) the amount and substantiality of the portion used in relation to the copyrighted work as a whole; and

(4) the effect of the use upon the potential market for or value of the copyrighted work.

In this case 2 Live Crew defends against a charge of copyright infringement by arguing that "Pretty Woman" falls within the exceptions spelled out in section 107.
*   *   * Section 107 takes from a copyright owner the exclusive rights to his work insofar as a derivative, or allegedly infringing work, is a "fair use" of the copyrighted work. Traditionally, fair use is defined as " 'a privilege in others than the owner of the copyright to use the copyrighted material in a reasonable manner without his consent.' " Fair use is the only exception to a copyright holder's exclusive rights in his work, but section 107 explains that the overreaching concept of fair use embraces use of a copyrighted work for the purpose of "criticism, comment, news reporting, teaching, scholarship, or research."
*   *   *   *

Unfortunately, the terminology of the fair use analysis has evolved in such a way that the popular definition of parody and the statutory definition of parody as a form of criticism have become somewhat confused. Popularly, the term parody may be described as "when one artist, for comic effect or social commentary, closely imitates the style of another artist and in so doing creates a new artwork that makes ridiculous the style and expression of the original." *   *   * Much of entertainment involves parodies in the popular sense, but section 107 does not direct the courts to conclude that all such parodies are fair uses. For the purposes of this opinion, we will assume that 2 Live Crew's song is a parody of Acuff-Rose's copyrighted song, and proceed to determine whether the calculus of section 107 results in a determination of fair use. That determination requires careful application of the four statutory factors.

[I.] Purpose and Character of Use
*   *   *   *

*   *   * The Supreme Court explained that "the crux of the profit/nonprofit distinction is not whether the sole motive of the use is monetary gain, but whether the user stands to profit from exploitation of the copyrighted material without paying the customary price."

* * * " 'Every commercial use of copyrighted material is presumptively an unfair exploitation of the monopoly privilege that belongs to the owner of the copyright.' " Therefore, in analyzing the purpose and character of 2 Live Crew's use of the copyrighted song, the facts in the record require that we start from the position that the use is unfair. We are asked to then consider whether 2 Live Crew met its burden to rebut the presumption by a defense, we note, requiring the court to be convinced that the "parody does not unfairly diminish the economic value of the original."

[II.] Nature of Copyrighted Work

* * * As a general rule, creative works—literary works of fiction or artistic works—are afforded greater protection from the fair use determination than are works of fact. The status of "Oh, Pretty Woman" as a creative work is not contested. In determining whether this factor should weigh in favor of the copyright holder we also ask whether the work "represented a substantial investment of time and labor made in anticipation of financial return." The record amply supports a finding in favor of Acuff-Rose on this factor.

[III.] Portion Used

The third factor we consider is the amount and substantiality of the portion of the copyrighted work used in the derivative work in relation to the copyrighted work as a whole. As applied to alleged parodies, this factor has historically turned on analysis of the "conjure up" test. The test asks "whether the parodist has appropriated a greater amount of the original work than is necessary to 'recall or conjure up' the object of his satire."

* * * *

* * *While it may not be inappropriate to find that no more was taken than necessary, the copying was qualitatively substantial. Both of defendants' affiants [persons who are sworn and signed an affidavit] stated that 2 Live Crew's version tracks the music and meter of the original. * * * Near verbatim taking of the music and meter of a copyrighted work without the creation of a parody is excessive taking. Most importantly, defendants' affiants stated that the song is built upon the recognizable base or guitar riff of the original by repeating that riff eight times. * * * We conclude that taking the heart of the original and making it the heart of a new work was to purloin a substantial portion of the essence of the original. * * *

[IV.] Effect of Potential Market

This factor has been characterized as "undoubtedly the single most important element of fair use." * * *

Actual present harm need not be shown; such a requirement would leave the copyright holder with no defense against predictable damage. Nor is it necessary to show with certainty that future harm will result. What is necessary is a showing by a preponderance of evidence that some meaningful likelihood of future harm exists. If the intended use is for commercial gain, that likelihood may be presumed. But if it is for a noncommercial purpose, the likelihood must be demonstrated.

The focus is on potential harm, and the "inquiry must take account not only of harm to the original but also of harm to the market for derivative works."

In the instant case, the use of the copyrighted work is wholly commercial, so that we presume that a likelihood of future harm to Acuff-Rose exists. * * * *

[V.] Conclusion

* * * * The four factors set forth in section 107 of the Act support the conclusion that 2 Live Crew's use of Acuff-Rose's copyrighted song was not a fair use.

The court found that the blatantly commercial purpose of the derivative work by 2 Live Crew prevented the parody of the Acuff-Rose song from being a fair use.

DECISION AND REMEDY

Ethical Considerations

Ultimate Ethical Conduct: The Good Samaritan

As you are walking along, you see a person in obvious distress, possibly suffering from a heart attack. Do you have an ethical or moral duty to help? Most people would answer yes. But do you have a legal duty? The courts have said that individuals do not have a legal duty to help unless a special legal relationship exists between the parties. If you are directly involved in an automobile accident, for example, most states require you to give aid to the injured.

Many states have Good Samaritan laws. Under this doctrine, if you render aid in an emergency situation, you will not be held liable for any negligence, unless you are *reckless*. A person would be reckless, if he or she attempts to move a person with back or neck injuries without proper training and equipment. Good Samaritan laws were designed to encourage people to stop and give aid to their fellow human beings.

You see a fellow employee who has stopped breathing and is possibly suffering from a heart attack. Do you have an ethical or moral duty to render aid? Again, most people would respond affirmatively. Should you be concerned about whether the person has a communicable disease? Should it make any difference if you suspect the person has such a disease? What would your reaction be if you knew the person had a communicable disease? Is there a legal duty?

Theft of Trade Secrets

Some processes or items of information that are not patented or are not patentable are nevertheless protected by law against appropriation by a competitor. Businesses that have trade secrets generally protect themselves by having all employees who use the process or information agree in their contracts never to divulge it. If a salesperson tries to solicit the company's customers for noncompany business or if an employee copies the employer's unique method of manufacture, he or she has appropriated a trade secret and has also broken a contract—two separate wrongs.

When confidential data are stolen through industrial espionage, as when a business taps into a competitor's computer, this constitutes a **theft of trade secrets** without any contractual violations, and the wrong is actionable in itself.

Current Tort Controversy

During President Bush's term in office, the Council on Competitiveness targeted the legal system for "unrestrained litigation" that has exacted a "terrible toll" on the U.S. economy. The cost, it charged, deterred U.S. manufacturers from product innovation, impeded competition with foreign companies, and cost consumers up to $300 billion. Congress is considering bills that would place a cap on pain and suffering, as well as punitive damages; force the loser to pay all the court costs and the attorneys' fees for the prevailing party; and abolish the contingent fee system which is the current method by which plaintiffs can afford attorneys.

What does an analysis of court statistics reveal? State courts handle more than 98 percent of all litigation in the United States. A study conducted by the National Center for State Courts (NCSC)

International Considerations

Combining Criminal and Civil Law

Two primary differences exist between the common-law system and the civil-law system regarding tort liability. In the common-law system, a wrong must be covered by a specific body of law in order for an injured party to bring a legal action and possibly recover damages. The civil-law system allows great latitude in compensating victims of wrongs. The French civil code, which is followed by a large number of countries, reads "every human act that causes damages to another obliges the one through whose fault it has occurred to pay damages."

This French act gives the courts greater authority to decide cases on an individual basis. Usually, in the civil-law system, if there are no statutory provisions covering specific subject matters, then there are no rights. Tort law is a major exception to this theory.

In the civil-law system, it is relatively common to find a combination of civil and criminal proceedings. The victim of a crime will be represented by an attorney in criminal proceedings. In the same procedure, the court can determine criminal guilt, establish the sentence, and calculate civil liability.

Recently, some jurisdictions in the United States have begun to take the same approach. For example, if a person is assaulted and has medical expenses, he or she may be granted restitution in a criminal proceeding after the accused has been found guilty. Restitution covers actual expenses and lost income; it does not include damages for pain and suffering. It appears that gradually the common-law and civil-law systems are coming together.

shows that 98 million new cases were filed, of which 17.3 million were civil cases. Civil cases were defined as all contract cases, estate and probate matters, small claims court filings, and domestic relations. The actual number of tort cases filed in that year was 447,374, less than half of one percent of all cases filed. Included in the tort filings were all motor vehicle cases, which is the majority of tort cases.

When the NCSC compared the tort filings with previous years, it found that tort cases were increasing at more modest rates than in previous years. The conclusion was that tort filings were not increasing at a faster rate than other major categories of civil filings.

The NCSC findings were consistent with research conducted by the University of Wisconsin Law School. The project examined federal court data for nearly 20 years. The major change found was a major increase in lawsuits among corporations. The federal courts are where most national and multinational corporate lawsuits are filed.

The RAND Corporation's Institute for Civil Justice also conducted a similar study. It surveyed 70,000 individuals who had been injured. Most were injured on the job or in motor vehicle accidents. Only 10 percent received compensation through the court system. Only a few people injured through defective products sought compensation through litigation.

The Council on Competitiveness also contended that the United States has 70 percent of the world's lawyers. This figure is based on the number of lawyers in England, Germany, Japan, Wales, and the United States. A recent study that compared figures for 100 countries showed that the United States is 35th in ranking and had only 9.4 percent of the world's 7.3 million lawyers.[3]

The message from the Council on Competitiveness is not borne out by the facts. Various studies have demonstrated that the tort system is not out of control. If any tort reform is needed, it must be based on facts, not perceived inequities.

---

3.   78 American Bar Association Journal 72 (Sept. 1992).

FACING A LEGAL ISSUE

Liability Attaches to the Employer

You own a small business. Over the years, you have maintained detailed records on every incident that might result in a claim against your business. Because your insurance rates have increased considerably in recent years, you asked your insurance company how you could reduce risks.

The insurance risk-analysis team made suggestions that you have followed. One suggestion was for you to write out a detailed list of all activities that are prohibited for employees. For example, employees are prohibited from picking up hitchhikers while driving a company vehicle, and they are prohibited from having a gun with them while working. Mandatory workshops are held regularly to review these written instructions.

Contrary to these instructions, an employee named Lucky picks up a hitchhiker. While riding in the company vehicle, the hitchhiker attempts to rob Lucky with a gun. During the struggle, Lucky pulls out his own gun, and it discharges. The bullet misses the hitchhiker but strikes and injures a passing bicyclist. The police are called, and the hitchhiker is arrested for armed robbery. Should your company have any liability to the bicyclist for Lucky's actions, which were contrary to the written instructions provided to the employees? Your records show that Lucky attended two workshops on these issues.

The answer is that your firm will most likely be held liable to the bicyclist. This liability is based on a social policy that all employers are liable for the acts of their employees when committed within the scope of the employment and furthering the employers' business. Most jurisdictions impose strict liability when firearms are involved. Your insurance company will probably cover liability under these circumstances.

Summary

This chapter has discussed tort liability. Three general forms of tort were examined. First, intentional torts are injuries caused by intentional acts. Second, negligence is a tort theory under which careless acts can result in liability. Third, strict liability is imposed by law without regard for fault.

Intentional torts can be caused by wrongs against the person, such as false imprisonment, intentional infliction of mental distress, defamation (including slander of title and disparagement of goods), invasion of privacy, and fraud. Intentional torts can also be wrongs against property, such as trespass to real and personal property, conversion, and nuisance. All of these actions are based on the concept that the person or property was intentionally harmed.

The concept underlying negligence is that the defendant did not intend to harm another, but through his or her carelessness, a person was injured or there was property damage.

The first element of negligence is a breach of the duty of care. This duty is the objective standard of care that each of us owes one another. The duty of care is breached when someone fails to act as a reasonable and prudent person would act when confronted with similar circumstances or fails to act in accordance with the duties defined by statutes. The second requirement for negligence is that there is an injury or damage. The last requirement is causation—in other words, did the breach of the duty of care cause the damages?

A limiting factor to liability based on negligence is the doctrine of foreseeability—could the defendant foresee the injury or damages to persons in the plaintiff's position when he or she breached the duty of care? Defenses to negligence include superseding intervening forces, assumption of risk, and contributory negligence.

Strict or absolute liability is based on the idea that certain dangerous activities automatically create liability if there are damages or injuries. The law imposes this liability because of public policy.

Certain torts apply only in a business situation. For example, a business cannot wrongfully interfere with other businesses' contractual or business relationships. A business cannot infringe on another's trademark, trade name, patent or copyright, nor may a business use another's trade secrets.

Key Terms

absolute privilege (188)
assault (184)
assumption of risk (195)
battery (184)
causation (192)
comparative negligence (195)
contributory negligence (195)
conversion (189)
copyright (199)
deceit (188)
defamation (187)
defamation by computer (188)
disparagement of goods (188)
false imprisonment (185)

foreseeability (193)
fraud (188)
infliction of mental distress (187)
intentional tort (184)
interference with a contractual or business relationship (198)
invasion of privacy (187)
libel (187)
merchant protection legislation (185)
negligence (184)
nuisance (189)

objective standard (190)
patent (199)
private nuisance (189)
privilege of immunity (187)
public nuisance (189)
qualified privilege (188)
service mark (199)
slander (187)
slander of title (188)
statutory duty (192)
strict liability (184)
theft of trade secrets (202)
tort (184)
trademark (199)

Questions and Case Problems

1. In what ways are intentional and unintentional torts alike? How are they different?

2. Rural Telephone Service Company provides telephone service to rural communities in Kansas. Feist Publications, Inc., is a publishing company that specializes in areawide telephone directories covering a much larger geographical range than Rural. The Feist directories are distributed free of charge; both companies compete for yellow-pages advertising. Feist approached Rural and offered to pay for the right to use its white pages. Rural refused. Feist then used them without Rural's consent. Is this a violation of the Copyright Act? Please give reasons to support your answer. [Feist Publications, Inc. v. Rural Telephone Service, 499 U.S. ____, 111 S.Ct. 1282, 113 L.Ed.2d 358 (1991)]

3. Mr. and Mrs. Bhattal checked into the Grand Hyatt–New York. Shortly after arriving at their room with their luggage, they left to have lunch. They remembered to lock the door. On returning to their room, they discovered that their luggage was missing. As a result of a computer error made at the front desk, the plaintiff's luggage had been taken from their room and sent to the airport along with the luggage of the previous occupants of the room, who were crew members of a Saudi Arabian airline. The Bhattal's luggage was never recovered. The Bhattals sued for conversion and intentional infliction of mental anguish. Who should prevail and why? [Bhattal v. Grand Hyatt–New York, 563 F.Supp. 277 (1983)]

4. Plaintiffs are tenants in an apartment complex located in New Jersey, which had rent control. Sheva Gardens purchased the apartments with the intent to rehabilitate them. The company had the mistaken impression that if it started the rehabilitation, it could increase the rents. The tenants were notified that the rent would be substantially increased, and Sheva started the project. The tenants contacted public officials, who denied the increase. Sheva was informed that it had to wait one year to request the increases. In the meantime, Sheva had removed furnaces and many of the water pipes. When the rent increase was denied, Sheva could not pay for the renovations and ceased work, leaving tenants without heat or water. The city condemned the property, and all the tenants had to move. The tenants sued for intentional infliction of mental distress. Who should prevail and why? [49 Prospect Street Tenants Association v. Sheva Gardens, Inc., 547 A.2d 1134 (N.J.Super.A.D. 1988)]

5. Over a ten-year period, a series of break-ins occurred at a farm home that was used to store miscellaneous items. No one lived in this home during that time period. The couple that owned it decided to place a twenty-gauge

shotgun in such a manner that it would discharge when the interior door was opened. Katko knew the place was not lived in and thought it had been abandoned. He had collected old bottles around the area. He decided to enter the house by pulling off a panel covering a window that did not have glass. He looked around the inside of the house for old bottles. When he pulled the interior door open to leave, the gun went off and injured his leg severely. He was convicted later of misdemeanor larceny and paid a $50 fine. He sued the owners for his leg injury. Who should prevail and why? [Katko v. Briney, 183 N.W. 2d 657 (Iowa, 1971)]

6. Lehigh Corporation was engaged in selling real property in a development known as Lehigh Acres. As part of its promotional campaign, the company brought prospective purchasers to Lehigh Acres where they were provided accommodations and an opportunity to view the property. Azar, a competitor, would follow the prospective customers to the only motel in town and persuade them to rescind their signed, written contracts with Lehigh and purchase property from him at a lower price. Lehigh brought an action for an injunction on the basis of malicious interference with a business relationship. Azar defended by stating that the customers had a right under federal law to rescind their contracts within three days of signing and that he provided them with an opportunity to obtain similar property at a lower price. Who should prevail and why? [Azar v. Lehigh Corp., 364 So. 2d 860 (Fla. App. 1978)]

7. K-Mart sold a rifle to William Knuck, who was a heavy user of marijuana and was under indictment for a felony. Federal law prohibits the sale of any firearm to such a person. K-Mart was supposed to ask the question about marijuana use or felony indictments prior to the sale. This was not accomplished. William Knuck's brother, a heroin addict and alcoholic, took the rifle while drunk and assaulted his estranged wife and a police officer. The police officer brought a negligence action against K-Mart, who defended on the grounds of intervening circumstances. Was K-Mart successful? [K-Mart Enterprises v. Keller, 439 So. 2d 283 (Fla. Dist. Ct. App. 1983)]

Chapter 9   Contract Formation

An acre of performance is worth the whole world of promise.

J. B. Howell, *Familiar Letters, 1650*

OUTLINE

Introduction

Millions of contracts are entered into and performed daily. Few people go through even one day without making or acting on a contract. A **contract** is an agreement between two or more parties that can be enforced in a court of law or equity. In the legal environment of business, questions and disputes about contracts arise daily; answering those questions and resolving those disputes are the essence of contract law.

The legal framework provides the stability and the structure within which businesses can plan and carry out their contracts. When adverse business conditions occur, a businessperson cannot rely on the good faith that the other party to the contract will perform simply out of a sense of duty. The enforceability of contracts in courts of law and equity ensures the promised performance or entitles the person harmed to some form of relief.

Businesspeople need to have a working knowledge of contract law because the fundamental method of exchanging goods, services, property, and money is through contracts. It is the businessperson who negotiates and frequently drafts contracts. Contract law is a complicated topic that can be reviewed only briefly in a legal environment course.

In this chapter, we will look at the sources of commercial law, at the formation of a contract, at the Uniform Commercial Code and its effect on contract law, and at some unique contractual terms.

Sources of Commercial Law

Commercial, or business, law is the body of law that governs commercial transactions. Commercial law covers such topics as contracts, partnerships, corporations, and agencies. Many of the principles of business law were developed centuries ago from what was known as the **law merchant**.

The Law Merchant

A system of mercantile courts existed in England and the rest of Europe well before the advent of the common-law courts. These mercantile courts administered the law merchant, which was developed from the uniform customs of the merchants, many of whom traveled from place to place to do business. The law merchant was important during the Middle Ages when the fair, or market, was the primary commercial event. In fact, the Magna Charta made special provisions for merchants. Section 41, for example, states that all merchants should "have safe and secure conduct, to go out of, and to come into England, and to stay there, and to pass as well by lands as by water, for buying and selling by the ancient and allowed customs." The law merchant eventually became part of the common law and was incorporated into American law.

Codification of Commercial Law

The United States from its very beginning as a nation adopted the English common law covering commercial transactions. In the early days, when commerce was just beginning to develop, there were many gaps in the body of this law. Different states took opposing positions on many commercial issues, leaving businesspeople in New York, for example, uncertain as to what the law would be in another state. Both the legal and the business professions over the years realized that uniform laws covering commercial transactions were necessary.

In order to achieve this uniformity, the legal profession, through the National Conference of Commissioners on Uniform State Laws in conjunction with the American Law Institute (ALI), has developed model codes of commercial law. Once a model code is completed, it is sent to each state. The state may choose to adopt the model code completely, may change parts of it to make it compatible with local law, or may choose not to consider or adopt the model code. Today, these codes are continually being developed as business needs change. Of all the model codes, the most important to businesses is the **Uniform Commercial Code** (UCC).

Uniform Commercial Code

During the 1930s, in order to create uniform commercial laws, some members of Congress proposed a statutory scheme that would cover all interstate commercial transactions. The bills were never passed. Congress realized that this area really belonged to the individual states, since Congress cannot control intrastate commerce. The National Conference and the ALI began work on the Uniform Commercial Code in 1942 and in 1952 completed the final draft of a uniform act that would apply to both intrastate and interstate transactions. All 50 states, the District of Columbia, and the Virgin Islands have adopted the Uniform Commercial Code.[1]

The UCC consists of these articles:

1. General Provisions
2. Sales
2A. Leases of Goods
3. Commercial Paper
4. Bank Deposits and Collections
4A. Funds Transfers
5. Letters of Credit
6. Bulk Transfers
7. Documents of Title
8. Investment Securities
9. Secured Transactions
10. Effective Date and Repealer
11. Effective Date and Transition Provisions.

The UCC generally does not cover transactions involving real estate or personal services.

The code does not greatly change the basic principles of commercial law derived from the law merchant or common law. Instead, the UCC expands these principles and places them in a comprehensive order to modernize, clarify, and standardize the rules. The UCC also clarifies the legal relationship of the parties in modern commercial transactions. The code is designed to help determine the intentions of the parties to a commercial contract and to give force and effect to their agreement. Businesspeople are assured that their contracts, if validly entered into, will be enforced; this, in turn, encourages further business transactions.

The courts, when reviewing a contract case, look first to the subject matter of the contract. Once the subject matter is determined, the court reviews any applicable statutes, such as the UCC. If no statute exists, the principles of common law are applied.

Of the articles that make up the UCC, only three have importance in this and the next three chapters. Article 2 (Sales), Article 3 (Commercial Paper), and Article 9 (Secured Transactions; Sales of Accounts and Chattel Paper) are the three articles used most frequently in contractual situations. In this chapter, we will cover the common law, statutes, and several provisions of Article 2, Sales. We will review Articles 3 and 9 in the chapters that follow.

Contract Terms

A contract is an agreement between two or more parties to perform—or refrain from performing—some act now or in the future, and when valid, this agreement is enforceable in a court of law or equity. A contract is based on a promise, but not all promises are legally enforceable. A contract is developed by an offer and an acceptance of that offer.

An **offer** presents a promise that can be met with **acceptance** (a return promise) or with **rejection.** Every offer involves at least two parties. The **offeror** is the party making the offer. The offeror is promising to do—or not to do—an act. The **offeree** is the party to whom the offer is made and who has the power to accept or reject the offer. If the offeree accepts (by performing an act or by returning a promise), the contract is formed because promises have been exchanged. A rejection terminates the offer.

The offer stage is when negotiations occur. Negotiations may take years, as in the purchase of a large tract of land, or may be over quickly, as in the decision to purchase a soft drink.

Terms Used with Contracts

Contract law uses specific terms to describe different contractual situations. Three sets of terms describe the formation of the contract, the enforceability of the contract in a court, and the performance of the contract.

Formation These terms define the various situations in which a contract is formed.

Unilateral and Bilateral Contracts Whether the contract is unilateral or bilateral depends on what the offeror requires the offeree to do in order to accept the offer. If the offeror makes a promise

---

1. Louisiana has adopted only Articles 1, 3, 4, and 5.

that requires the offeree to complete his or her performance of the contract with a return act (not with a promise), the contract is called a **unilateral contract.** The person making the promise wants the other person to perform an act in return. An example is the reward situation; the promisor offers a cash amount for the return of a lost dog: REWARD . . . *for return of two-year-old male basset hound. Responds to name Useless.* The person offering the reward wants action, the return of Useless, not promises.

A **bilateral contract** is created when the offeror wants the offeree to give her or his promise to perform. The offeree's return promise is the acceptance. A bilateral contract is a "promise for a promise." Most contracts are bilateral. For example, Miguel offers to sell his residence for $100,000. When someone agrees (gives a return promise) to purchase Miguel's residence at that price, a bilateral contract is the result. In a sale of land, a statute (called the statute of frauds) requires that this type of contract must be in writing in order to be enforceable.

Express and Implied Contracts In an **express contract,** the terms of the offer on acceptance are specially stated, whether orally or in writing. If the terms are not exactly set out but are implied, a valid contract exists, but it is called an **implied-in-fact contract.** Implied contracts are created by the conduct of the parties. When individuals act as if there is a contract, even though no words have been spoken or written to that effect, the law will imply that there is one. For example, when a person visits the doctor's office to be treated for a cold, the person by her or his conduct is agreeing to pay for the doctor's services.

Quasi-Contracts Occasionally a person will be unjustly enriched at the expense of another. No express contract exists, and no conduct has happened to imply a contract, yet it is unjust for the one individual to be enriched at the expense of the other. The law will imply a promise to pay. This type of conduct creates a contract by operation of law, an implied-in-law contract. More commonly called **quasi-contracts,** the parties did not make any promise by word or conduct, but the law will impose a promise on the party who benefited.

A quasi-contract is distinguishable from an implied-in-fact contract. An implied-in-fact contract is a true contract made between the parties and is enforceable in court. In contrast, only a court can declare that a quasi-contract exists, because it is a legal fiction. The court creates a quasi-contract (that is, a fictional contract) for reasons of social policy—that is, to prevent a person from being enriched unjustly at the expense of another. Quasi-contracts are equitable, rather than contractual, in nature.

Here is an example of a quasi-contract. Joel is a salesperson. He returns home at 10:00 A.M. to find a work crew ready to paint his house. He knows that they are supposed to be painting his neighbor's house. He does not say anything and leaves. When he returns to his house at 5:00 P.M., the house is painted. Under a quasi-contract, the painting company will be able to collect a reasonable amount for the paint job from Joel. He has received a benefit, and it would be unjust for him to retain that benefit without paying for it. Joel had a chance to stop the painting, and he failed to do so. Until he pays, he has been unjustly enriched at the expense of the paint company.

The following case represents another application of this doctrine.

Case 9.1
PETRIE v. LeVAN
Missouri Court of Appeals,
1990.
799 S.W.2d 632.

BACKGROUND AND FACTS *The Petries purchased a house from LeVan. The deed to the house was transferred on September 24, 1986. Unknown to either party, the roof was damaged by a severe storm the night before the deed was recorded. LeVan was asked by the Petries to make a claim against his homeowner's insurance policy. The insurance company issued him a check in the amount of $2,176.22. He refused to turn the money over to the Petries, who had made the repairs to the roof at a cost in excess of the $2,176.22. The Petries filed this lawsuit against LeVan, claiming that LeVan was unjustly enriched.*

Judge SHANGLER

* * * *

A person who has been unjustly enriched at the expense of another is required to make restitution to the other. The principle against unjust enrichment emerged against the grain of the common law forms of action then available for remedy and with the aid of the restitution devices of the equity court. The common law courts overcame this limitation on remedies imposed by the forms of action through the fiction of *quasi contract*. The law gave to a plaintiff against a defendant under an obligation, from the ties of natural justice, to refund, an action as if it were upon a contract. The equity courts independently developed restitution remedies against unjust enrichment. The fiction of constructive trust was used in cases of fraud or breach of fiduciary duty to reach the gains that, in conscience, belonged to another by treating the fraudulent procurer as a trustee. The constructive trust also became the means for restitution from one unjustly enriched by the mistake of another, even though the mistake was not induced by fraud or misrepresentation.

* * * *

The right to restitution for unjust enrichment presupposes: (1) that the defendant was enriched by the receipt of a benefit; (2) that the enrichment was at the expense of the plaintiff; (3) that it would be unjust to allow the defendant to retain the benefit.

* * * *

In that assessment, it is not the power of equity to order specific performance, injunction, or some variant of equitable conversion by contract as to the insurance proceeds that is invoked. It is equitable principle and good conscience that govern. In this case, it is the equitable principle against double recovery that disallows LeVan from retention of both the insurance proceeds and the full purchase price of the property and that good conscience requires that LeVan pay over to the Petries. If LeVan may keep the proceeds of the insurance and also the full purchase price, he has a windfall. LeVan is compensated for that which he did not lose and the Petries pay for that which they did not receive.

The court found that LeVan was unjustly enriched at the expense of the Petries. The trial court was directed to enter a judgment in the amount of $2,176.22 against LeVan. **DECISION AND REMEDY**

Formal and Informal Contracts Statutes set out the provisions for a **formal contract** requiring it to be in a special form to be valid. All formal contracts must be written, but not all written contracts are classified as formal contracts. An example of a formal contract is a bail bond, which is a bond to obtain the release of someone from jail. Other examples are negotiable instruments and letters of credit. (See Chapter 12.) Most contracts do not require a specified form or formality for their validity and, therefore, almost all contracts today are classified as **informal contracts** and can be oral or written.

Enforceability The following terms describe the enforceability of a contract by a court.

Valid, Void, Voidable, and Unenforceable Contracts Most contracts are valid. A **valid contract** meets all the elements required for the contract to be enforced in a court. (These elements are discussed in detail in the next section.) A void contract, on the other hand, is a misnomer. Whenever a contract is rendered void, the law will not enforce the agreement. For example, if the purpose of the contract is illegal, it is a **void agreement**. In these cases, the word *agreement* is used because by definition a contract is a legal situation.

A **voidable contract** means that one party to the contract is bound, but the other party may disaffirm (or avoid) it. For example, a minor has the right to disaffirm most contracts—that is, he

Legal Highlight

The Tow Truck and the Implied-In-Fact Contract

In Maryland, Ron's car got stuck in the mud in a swampy area behind the local bait shop. He called a tow truck to haul the car out of the mud; then he went fishing. The tow truck came and got stuck in the mud. The driver called another tow truck, which promptly got stuck in the mud in front of the first tow truck. The two drivers called a third tow truck, which also got stuck.

A bulldozer was called in. It too got stuck in the mud. Next called was a construction company, which, with the help of four dump trucks, constructed a dirt road. With a solid base now in place, the bulldozer, the three tow trucks, and Ron's car were rescued from the mud. The bill was $4,740. Who pays? Ron says he will pay for one tow truck. The first tow truck driver says Ron told him to get the car out and that Ron's father would pay for it. Ron's father says, "No way."

As in many cases of this type, the dispute was settled out of court, and only the parties know how it ended. All in all, it is a muddled contract case.

or she can avoid performing the contract. Occasionally both parties may have the right to disaffirm the contract, such as when two minors have entered into a contract.

An **unenforceable contract** is one that started out as a valid contract, but, for some legal reason, it now cannot be enforced in court against the other party. In other words, statutes forbid the courts to enforce the contract. Consider this example: A person enters into a valid contract to buy a stereo system on credit. Later the person goes into bankruptcy, and the contract debt is discharged (forgiven) by the bankruptcy court. The valid contract has been converted into an unenforceable contract by the bankruptcy statute as applied by the bankruptcy court. Now the creditor cannot sue the debtor to collect the money owed on the contract.

Performance The following terms describe the contract based on the performance status of each of the parties.

Executed or Executory Contracts These terms can refer to one of two situations. First, they can refer to the status of the contract seen as a whole. An **executed contract** is a fully performed contract, while an **executory contract** is one that has not been performed. Second, these terms can refer to the state of performance by one party in relationship to the other. For example, Ann hands over a textbook to a friend with the understanding that she will receive $20 for it. Ann's performance is fully executed while the friend's performance is executory. In this case, the contract is partially performed.

Exhibit 9–1 summarizes the contract terms covered here.

Elements of a Contract: Part 1

All legally enforceable contracts must satisfy these requirements:

1. **Offer:** An offer (promise) must be made.
2. **Acceptance:** An acceptance to the offer must be given, whether by return promise or an act. (The offer and acceptance constitute mutual assent.)
3. **Consideration:** Promises must be bargained for and exchanged, have legal value, and be sufficient to support the offer and acceptance.
4. **Capacity:** The parties must have the legal capacity to form a contract.
5. **Legality:** The subject matter of the contract must be legal.
6. **Writing:** Certain agreements must be in writing to be enforceable in court. (Not all contracts need to meet this requirement.)

Exhibit 9–1 **Contract Terms**

CONTRACT FORMATION	1. The manner by which the offeree is required to respond (accept the offer) determines this classification of contract. a. *Unilateral*—A promise for an act (completed act is acceptance) b. *Bilateral*—A promise for a promise. 2. The parties' manner of expression determines this classification of contract. a. *Express*—Formed by words (oral, written, or both) b. *Implied-in-fact*—Formed by the conduct of the parties. 3. A court decision determines this classification of contract. a. *Quasi-contract*—Imposed by law to prevent unjust enrichment. 4. Form determines this classification of contract. a. *Formal*—Required by law to be in special written form to be valid b. *Informal*—No special form. May be oral or written.
ENFORCEABILITY	1. *Valid*—The contract has the necessary contractual elements of offer, acceptance, consideration, parties with capacity, and it is made for a legal purpose. 2. *Voidable*—A contract exists, but one party by law has the right to avoid the contractual obligation. 3. *Unenforceable*—A contract exists, but it cannot be enforced because of a legal defense. 4. *Void*—No contract exists. There is an agreement without legal obligations.
PERFORMANCE	1. *Executed*—A fully performed contract. 2. *Executory*—A contract not fully performed.

The first three elements are discussed in this chapter, and the last three are examined in the next chapter.

Requirements of the Offer

An offer is a promise to do—or to refrain from doing—some specified thing now or in the future. Three elements are necessary for an offer to be effective: (1) There must be *objective intent* by the offeror to be bound by his or her offer; (2) the terms of the offer must be *reasonably definite*; and (3) the offer must be *communicated* to the offeree. For a valid contract to exist, the first question to be answered is the following: Is there an offer?

Intention An offeror must objectively intend to be bound by his or her offer. Objective intent is determined from the words and actions of the parties as interpreted by a reasonable person. The issue is whether the offeror intends to be bound to his or her offer if the offeree accepts it. Offers made in obvious anger, jest, or excitement do not meet the objective intent test. Since these offers are not effective, the offeree's acceptance does not create a valid contract.

In the following case, the court must decide whether a statement was a joke, as the officer of a corporation contended, or whether it met the objective intent test and was a valid offer.

Case 9.2

BARNES v. TREECE

Court of Appeals of the State
of Washington, 1976.
15 Wash.App. 437,
549 P.2d 1152.

BACKGROUND AND FACTS *Treece, the defendant, was a vice president of Vend-A-Win, Inc., a corporation that was in the business of distributing punchboards (a gambling device). The Washington State Gambling Commission was investigating various aspects of gambling. Treece spoke before the commission on behalf of Vend-A-Win's application for a temporary license to distribute punchboards. During his appearance, which was televised, he stated, "I'll pay a hundred thousand dollars to anyone to find a crooked board. If they find it, I'll pay it." The statement brought laughter from the audience.*

Barnes, the plaintiff, watched a television news report of Treece's statement and also read a newspaper account. Barnes telephoned Treece, asking him if his statement was serious. Treece restated that he meant it and that the money was being held in escrow. Barnes was in possession of two crooked punchboards. Following Treece's instructions, Barnes brought one of the punchboards into Vend-A-Win's offices for inspection. He turned the other board over to the Washington State Gambling Commission.

Treece and Vend-A-Win each refused to pay Barnes. Barnes filed a lawsuit. The trial court held Treece personally liable for the $100,000. The case against Vend-A-Win was dismissed because the court found that Treece never inquired of Vend-A-Win whether he had the authority to bind the corporation on this matter and that Vend-A-Win did not have time to deny that Treece had this authority. The case was appealed. The issue was whether the statement was an offer for a unilateral contract.

Judge CALLOW
* * * *

The first issue is whether the statement of Treece was the manifestation of an offer which could be accepted to bind the offeror to performance of the promise. Treece contends that no contract was formed. He maintains that his statement was made in jest and lacks the necessary manifestation of a serious contractual intent.

When expressions are intended as a joke and are understood or would be understood by a reasonable person as being so intended, they cannot be construed as an offer and accepted to form a contract. However, if the jest is not apparent and a reasonable hearer would believe that an offer was being made, then the speaker risks the formation of a contract which was not intended. It is the objective manifestations of the offeror that count and not secret, unexpressed intentions. As stated in *Wesco Realty, Inc. v. Drewry*:

> If a party's words or acts, judged by a reasonable standard, manifest an intention to agree in regard to the matter in question, that agreement is established, and it is immaterial what may be the real but unexpressed state of the party's mind on the subject.

The trial court found that there was an objective manifestation of mutual assent to form a contract. This was a matter to be evaluated by the trier of fact. The record includes substantial evidence of the required mutual assent to support the finding of the trial court. Although the original statement of Treece drew laughter from the audience, the subsequent statements, conduct, and the circumstances show an intent to lead any hearer to believe the statements were made seriously. There was testimony, though contradicted, that Treece specifically restated the offer over the telephone in response to an inquiry concerning whether the offer was serious. Treece, when given the opportunity to state that an offer was not intended, not only reaffirmed the offer but also asserted that $100,000 had been placed in escrow and directed Barnes to bring the punchboard to Seattle for inspection. The parties met, Barnes was given a receipt for the board, and he was told that the board would be taken to Chicago for inspection. In present day society it is known that gambling generates a great deal of income and that large sums are spent on its advertising and promotion. In that prevailing atmosphere, it was a credible statement that $100,000 would be paid to promote punchboards. The statements of the defendant and the surrounding circumstances reflect an objective manifestation of a contractual intent by Treece and support the finding of the trial court.

The trial court properly categorized Treece's promise of $100,000 as a valid offer for a unilateral contract. The offer made promised that a contract would result upon performance of the act requested. Performance of the act with the intent to accept the offer constituted acceptance. The trial judge entered a specific finding that Barnes performed the requested act of acceptance when he produced a rigged and fraudulent punchboard. We concur with the trial court's holding that a binding unilateral contract was formed between Barnes and Treece and uphold the conclusions of the trial court in that regard.

Barnes won a $100,000 judgment against Treece. Under other circumstances, Treece's statement might have been a joke, but Treece made the statement before an official state commission that was investigating a multi-million-dollar business, he knew that the statement was being reported on television and in the newspapers, and he repeated the statement over the telephone to Barnes. The court found the objective intent standard had been met. The statement was an offer calling for an action; thus, when Barnes produced the crooked boards, a unilateral contract resulted.

DECISION AND REMEDY

Definiteness An offer must have reasonably definite terms. The parties must be able to determine what they must do in order to perform the contract. If a dispute arises, a court must be able to determine if the contract promises have been broken and, if so, to decide on an appropriate remedy.

Even prior to the adoption of the Uniform Commercial Code, the courts were reluctant to declare a contract invalid based on the indefiniteness of its terms if, during the trial, the evidence showed a clear intention by both parties to enter into the contract. The courts inserted reasonable terms wherever possible to resolve ambiguous or missing terms.

UCC Article 2, Sales, covers the sale of goods. Article 2 of the UCC has liberalized the requirement of definiteness. Under the UCC, even though one or more of the contract's terms are left open, a contract for the sale of goods may be enforced by a court. If it is clear that the parties intended to make a contract and if a reasonably certain basis exists for giving an appropriate remedy, the court will supply the missing terms [UCC 2-204(3)]. The missing terms are provided in some of the following ways.

If no price is stated, the price is the reasonable price at the time the goods were delivered [UCC 2-305(1)]. If no place of delivery is specified, delivery is at the seller's (not the buyer's) home or business [UCC 2-308(a)]. If the time for shipment or delivery is not provided, the deadline is a reasonable period after the contract is formed [UCC 2-309]. If the time for payment is not specified, payment is due at the time and place of delivery [UCC 2-310(a)]. This means that unless you have arranged to pay for the goods on credit, you must pay in cash (currency or check) at the time and place that the goods are delivered to you.

Communication The third requirement for an effective offer is communication. A person cannot agree to a contract without knowing that the contract exists. Suppose Emerman advertises a reward of $100 for the return of her lost dog. Garcia, not knowing of the reward, finds the dog and returns it to Emerman. Garcia cannot recover the $100 in a court because he did not know it was offered, and, therefore, no contract existed to be enforced. Emerman may still give the reward to Garcia, but Emerman cannot be forced by a court to do so.

Exhibit 9–2 summarizes the requirements for an effective offer.

Exhibit 9–2 **Requirements for an Effective Offer**

1. *Intent*—A serious, objective intent by the offeror to become bound by the offer.

2. *Definiteness*—The terms of the offer must be sufficiently definite to be ascertainable by the parties or by a court. Under the UCC, the court can supply missing terms if it is clear the parties intended to make a contract for the sale of goods and if a reasonably certain basis exists for giving an appropriate remedy [UCC 2-204]:
   a. No price: reasonable price at time of delivery [2-305]
   b. No delivery place: seller's place of business or, if none, seller's home [2-308(a)]
   c. No time set to ship or deliver: reasonable time after contract formed [2-310(a).
   d. No time set for payment: money to be paid on delivery [2-310(a)].

3. *Communication*—The offer must be communicated to the offeree.

Termination of the Offer

An effective offer gives the offeree the power to transform that offer into a contract by accepting it. This power of acceptance, however, does not continue forever. An offer can be terminated either by an action of one of the parties or by the law. First, the offer can be ended in three ways by an action of one of the parties: (1) **revocation** of the offer *by the offeror*, (2) **rejection** of the offer *by the offeree*, or (3) **counteroffer** *by the offeree*. Second, an offer can be terminated by **operation of law** (lapse of time, destruction of the specific subject matter of the offer, death or incompetence of either party, and illegality of the offer). The second question then, in determining the validity of a contract is: Is the offer still open?

Revocation of the Offer by the Offeror Revocation is the withdrawal of the offer by the offeror. Even if the offeror promises to keep the offer open, he or she can inform the offeree of the revocation before the offeree accepts. Revocation may be achieved (1) by expressly repudiating the offer ("I withdraw my previous offer of October 17") or (2) by an act inconsistent with the existence of the offer such as selling the item and the offeree knows about the sale.

The offeree must be informed of the revocation before she or he accepts the offer. If the revocation comes after the offeree has accepted the offer, the revocation is not normally effective. A valid contract has already been formed because an acceptance is usually effective at the time it is made. The general rule followed by most states is that a revocation is effective only on actual receipt of the revocation by the offeree.

For example, an offer is made on April 1. When the offeree accepts the offer on April 3, a contract is formed. If the offeror sends a revocation on April 2 that is delivered to the offeree on April 4, the revocation is not effective. But if the revocation had reached the offeree on April 2, the offer would have been terminated.

Although most offers are revocable, certain offers can be made irrevocable. Three types of irrevocable offers are (1) those involved in option contracts, (2) firm offers under the UCC, and (3) those made irrevocable by virtue of promissory estoppel. The third question is: Is this type of offer revocable?

Option Contract An **option contract** is a separate contract that takes away the offeror's right to revoke the offer for the period of time specified in the option. If an offeror promises to hold an offer open for a specific time period and the offeree pays for the promise, an option contract has been created. If no time is specified, a reasonable period of time is implied.

For example, Beverly plans to purchase twelve acres at a prime location. She needs time to determine if she can obtain financing. If she cannot obtain financing, she does not want to buy the property. Beverly pays the landowner $1,000 to give up his right to sell the land to someone else and to take the property off the market for a specified period of time, such as 180 days. An option contract has been created. During the 180 days, the landowner cannot revoke his offer to Beverly. At the end of the 180 days, the option expires. If she does not obtain financing, Beverly will not be obligated to purchase the land under this option contract.

Firm Offer Created by the UCC, a **firm offer** occurs when a **merchant** (a person who regularly deals in a particular type of goods) makes a written, signed offer to buy or sell goods and states in the offer words to the effect that it is not revocable. The merchant's offer is irrevocable without the payment of consideration by the offeree [UCC 2-205]. The offer remains open for the stated period of time; if no time is specified, the offer remains open for a reasonable period, but the period cannot exceed three months.

Promissory Estoppel Estoppel means to bar, to impede, or to stop. **Promissory estoppel** means that the promisor (the offeror) is prevented from revoking the offer. Increasingly, courts are refusing to allow an offeror to revoke an offer when the offeree has changed his or her position by relying on the offer. In such cases, revocation is considered unjust to the offeree.

For example, Dan (the offeree) owns a grocery business and the store. Big Chain (the offeror) offers him a manager's position in a new store that it plans to build, but Dan is told by Big Chain that he will have to sell his business in order to be hired as manager. Relying on this offer, Dan sells his store; then Big Chain says that it no longer plans to build its store and thus does not plan to employ Dan. Had the offer not been made, Dan still would have his store and grocery business. Dan has a case based on promissory estoppel: Big Chain cannot revoke its offer because the offeree, relying on the offer, has changed his situation.

Rejection of the Offer by the Offeree An offeree may reject the offer, in which case the offer ends. A rejection, by conduct or by words, shows an intent not to accept the offer. Any other words or conduct by the offeree does not terminate the offer. Rejection is not effective as a termination of the offer until the offeror learns of the rejection.

For example, Mary makes an offer to sell her used personal computer printer to David for $450. On May 1, David responds that the offer appears to be a little high and asks if Mary would lower her price. Mary cannot treat these words as a rejection because David's words did not indicate an intent not to accept but only to make an inquiry as to whether Mary would modify her offer. Mary, however, refuses to modify her offer. On May 3 David mails to Mary a letter of rejection. Before Mary receives David's letter, David calls Mary and accepts her offer. Since David's rejection was not received by Mary before David's call accepting the offer, David and Mary have a valid and enforceable contract.

Counteroffer by the Offeree A counteroffer is a rejection of the original offer, and at the same time, it constitutes a new offer. Any subsequent attempt to accept the expired offer by the offeree (now the offeror) will be construed as a new offer, giving the original offeror (now the offeree) the power of acceptance. Suppose Arnold offers to sell his computer to Dale for $1,000. Dale responds, "Your price is too high. I'll offer to purchase your computer for $650." Dale's response is termed a counteroffer, since it constituted a rejection, ended Arnold's offer to sell at $1,000, and at the same time created a new offer by Dale to purchase at $650. Exhibit 9–3 illustrates how the relationships of offeror and offeree change when a counteroffer is made.

Exhibit 9–3 **The Dynamics of a Rejection and Counteroffer**

Mirror-Image Rule   At common law, the **mirror-image rule** requires the offeree's acceptance to match the offeror's offer exactly; in other words, the acceptance must mirror the offer. Any change in, or addition to, the terms of the original offer automatically ends that offer and constitutes a counteroffer. The original offeror (now the offeree) can accept the terms of the counteroffer and thus create a valid contract.

UCC Rules on Acceptances and Exceptions
Slight variations in terms between the offer and the acceptance that violate the mirror-image rule have caused considerable problems in commercial transactions. In the business world, when goods are bought and sold, the buyer usually uses his or her standard *purchase order* form and the seller accepts on her or his standard *confirmation* form. Chances are high that the two forms will vary to some degree. For example, the confirmation form contains a requirement that any disputes must be submitted to arbitration (see Chapter 4), while the purchase order form is silent on this topic. Such a conflict is referred to as the "battle of the forms." Under the common law's mirror-image rule, no contract results when different terms in the standardized forms do not mirror the terms in the offer.

If, however, a contract falls under the UCC's rules concerning the sale of goods and both parties are *merchants*, the contract is formed when the offeree "accepts" the offer, even though the terms of the acceptance (the confirmation form) modify or add to the terms of the original offer [UCC 2-207(1)]. When the contract is between merchants, the new terms become part of the contract automatically. For example, if the confirmation form requires disputes to be arbitrated, this new term becomes part of the contract, unless an exception exists.

The UCC has three *exceptions* to this rule as it applies to merchants: First, the offer clearly requires the acceptance to be the same as the offer with no variations. The purchase form can include a statement ("Acceptance to be on these terms only") that any additional terms in the confirmation order will not become part of the contract. Second, if the new or changed terms of the contract materially change the other party's duties, the new terms in the confirmation order will not be part of the contract. In our example, the issue

is whether submitting disputes to arbitration materially alters the right of the offeror to go to a judicial court. If so, the arbitration clause addition does not become a part of the contract. Third, the offeror reads the new or changed terms and objects to (rejects) those terms within a reasonable period of time.

The UCC rule is different if one or both parties are *nonmerchants*. In these cases, the contract is formed according to the terms of the offer, not according to the additional terms of the acceptance. The additional terms are considered to be proposals for addition to the contract.

Termination of the Offer by Operation of Law   The offeree's power to accept the offer and form a contract can be ended by operation of law. Four conditions can end the offer:

1. *Lapse of time*—In other words, either the time to accept the offer has expired or the offeree has failed to accept the offer within a reasonable time.
2. The *specific subject matter* of the offer is destroyed.
3. *Death or incompetence* of the offeror or offeree is established. Death or incompetence does not terminate, however, an irrevocable offer (such as an option).
4. After the offer is made, the legislature or court makes that type of offer *illegal*. For example, Congress passes a law making it illegal to sell computer chips to any terrorist countries. Any outstanding offers to sell computer chips to a firm in Iraq now ends by operation of law.

Exhibit 9–4 summarizes the ways in which an offer may be terminated.

Acceptance

Acceptance is a voluntary act by the offeree; it can be either words or conduct that shows assent (agreement) to the terms of an offer. The acceptance must be unequivocal and communicated to the offeror.

Except in certain special circumstances, only the person to whom the offer is made or that person's authorized agent can accept the offer and create a binding contract. Part of the offer identifies the offeree and is one of the conditions of the offer. For example, Jones offers to sell his

Exhibit 9-4 **Termination of an Offer**

---

1. *By acts of the parties:*
   a. Revocation—Unless the offer is irrevocable, it can be revoked at any time before acceptance without liability; not effective until *known* by the offeree. Irrevocable offers are (i) a merchant's firm offer [UCC 2-205], (ii) those made irrevocable by virtue of promissory estoppel, or (iii) those involved in option contracts.
   b. Rejection—Accomplished by words or actions that demonstrate a clear intent not to accept or consider the offer further; not effective until *known* by the offeror.
   c. Counteroffer—A rejection of the original offer and the making of a new offer.

2. *By operation of law:*
   a. Lapse of time—The offer terminates (i) at the end of the time period specified in the offer, or (ii) , if no time period is stated in the offer, at the end of a reasonable time period.
   b. Destruction of the specific subject matter of the offer—Automatically terminates the offer.
   c. Death or mental incompetence—Terminates the offer unless the offer is irrevocable.
   d. Illegality—Supervening illegality terminates the offer.

---

motorcycle to Hanley. Hanley rejects the offer, but Hanley's friend, Smith, attempts to accept the offer. No contract is formed.

Silence as an Act of Acceptance   Ordinarily, silence does not constitute acceptance, even if the offeror states, "By your silence and inaction you will be deemed to have accepted this offer." An offeree does not have the burden of performing some act in order to reject an offer unless the offeree has a "duty to speak," such as by agreement or where the offeree solicited the offer.

Book and record clubs have an agreement with their members that a book or record selection will be sent out automatically unless the member returns a card indicating that no selection is wanted in the upcoming month. Silence acts as an acceptance because the contract between the club and the member sets out silence as a method of acceptance. These clubs fall under the Federal Trade Commission's Negative Option Rule, which requires the clubs to give the members enough time to respond if they do not want the monthly selection.

Communication of Acceptance   At common law, whether the offeror must be notified of the acceptance depends on the nature of the offer. In a unilateral contract, generally it is not necessary to notify the offeror because the act of acceptance is evident [see, however, UCC 2-206(2)]. The offer calls for the full performance of the act; therefore, acceptance is not completed until the act has been

fully performed. For example, only when someone returns the lost dog for the reward, in the example used previously to illustrate a unilateral contract, is the contract complete.

In a bilateral contract, communication of acceptance is necessary because acceptance takes the form of a promise (not an act), and the contract is formed when the promise is made (rather than when the act is performed). Acceptance takes effect when *sent* if the offeree uses a method of communication authorized by the offeror. This is known as the mailbox rule. The method of communication can be expressly stated by the offeror in the offer. If the offeror does not state any specific method of responding, such as by telegram, the rule is to mail the acceptance. It will be effective when mailed.

Under the UCC, an offer may be accepted in any manner and by any medium reasonable under the circumstances [UCC 2-206(1)(a)]. This is a practical rule for business transactions, and the acceptance is effective when sent; under these rules a contract can be formed even though the offeror never receives the message of acceptance.

The UCC also provides that an order to buy goods may be treated as either a bilateral or a unilateral offer. The offer can be accepted through a promise to ship or through actual shipment [UCC 2-206(1)(b)]. For example, Peters receives a telegram that he is to ship red shirts to Johnson. Peters can accept either by promptly shipping the red shirts or by sending a telegram to Johnson, saying that he is going to ship the goods. If the shipment will take a considerable amount of time, Peters

Exhibit 9–5 **Acceptance of a Contract**

1. Can be made only by the offeree or the offeree's authorized agent.

2. Must be unequivocal.
   a. Mirror-image rule—Under common law, terms of acceptance must be same as terms of offer.
   b. UCC rule—A definite acceptance of an offer is not a counteroffer, even if new terms modify the terms of the original offer [UCC 2-207]. If either party is a *nonmerchant,* additional terms are proposals for addition to the contract but not part of it. Between *merchants,* the additional terms become a part of the contract with these exceptions:
      i. Offer limits acceptance to its terms, or
      ii. New terms materially change offer, or
      iii. New terms are rejected.

3. Acceptance of a bilateral offer can be communicated to the offeror by authorized mode of communication and is effective upon dispatch. Unless the mode of communication is expressly specified by the offeror, the following methods are implicitly authorized:
   a. The same mode used by the offeror, or a faster mode, or
   b. By mail, when the two parties are at a distance, or
   c. Under the UCC, in acceptance of offers for the sale of goods, any medium that is reasonable under the circumstances.

4. Under the UCC, acceptance of an offer to buy goods for prompt shipment:
   a. By prompt shipment of conforming goods, or
   b. By prompt promise to ship.

would be wise to telegraph Johnson that the goods are in transit.

Exhibit 9–5 summarizes the requirements for acceptance of a contract.

To summarize, the offeror and the offeree must have a meeting of the minds, called **mutual assent.** In other words, the offer made by one person must be the offer accepted by another person; the terms of the offer must be the terms of the acceptance. Mutual assent means that both sides are contracting for the same item or service, for example.

Genuineness of Mutual Assent

Factual disputes occur when it seems as if there was a meeting of the minds but in reality the parties did not reach an understanding. No genuine assent exists as to the terms of the contract when there is **fraud, misrepresentation,** certain forms of mistake, **duress,** or **undue influence.** These situations are defenses a party to the contract can

use to show why he or she should not be ordered by a court to perform the contract.

Fraud and Misrepresentation   When fraud occurs, the contract is voidable by the injured party. The five requirements that establish fraud are (1) a misrepresentation of a material fact exists; (2) the contract is made with the knowledge by the guilty party that the material fact is false; (3) the guilty party has the intent to deceive; (4) the innocent party has justifiably relied on the misrepresentation; and (5) the innocent party has suffered damages.

Fraud is difficult to prove because the knowledge and wrongful intent of the other party must be established. Because of the difficulty in proving fraud, many injured parties sue for misrepresentation instead. To establish a claim for misrepresentation, one need not prove intent to deceive or knowledge. Obviously, this makes misrepresentation much easier to prove. The following case discusses misrepresentation.

BACKGROUND AND FACTS *Alabi wanted to ship $15,000 in currency to his cousin in London, England. He had shipped frequently with DHL Airways and had been given a supply of DHL bills of lading to use. He inquired about obtaining insurance coverage in the amount of $15,000. DHL informed him that the maximum was $10,000. Alabi completed the bill of lading. Under description of goods, he wrote "documents regarding school bills" and placed $15,000 in currency in the package. Alabi took the package to DHL for shipment, but the $15,000 never reached his cousin. DHL would not accept currency for shipment if they knew the package contained money.*

Case 9.3
ALABI v. DHL AIRWAYS, INC.
Superior Court of Delaware, 1990.
583 A.2d 1358.

Judge HERLIHY
❊   ❊   ❊   ❊

DHL seeks summary judgment claiming plaintiff's contracts with it are voidable due to his alleged misrepresentation of the contents of the envelope. A contract may be voidable on the basis of misrepresentation, be it a fraudulent or an innocent misrepresentation.

❊   ❊   ❊

The *Restatement (Second) of Contracts* provides probably the clearest discussion of the elements that need be shown to prevail when asserting misrepresentation as a defense. In order for a contract to be voidable, a party must show all four of the following elements: (1) that there was a misrepresentation; (2) that the misrepresentation was either fraudulent or material; (3) that the misrepresentation induced the recipient to enter into the contract; and (4) that the recipient's reliance on the misrepresentation was reasonable.

The first issue is whether the labeling of the envelope, allegedly containing $15,000 in cash, as documents regarding school bills constitutes a misrepresentation. A misrepresentation is an assertion that is not in accordance with the facts.

❊   ❊   ❊

The term "documents regarding school bills" does not indicate that the contents are inherently valuable to third-party interlopers or others in DHL's position. Plaintiff's description is not in accord with the now alleged fact that there was cash in the envelope and, consequently, is a misrepresentation of the contents.

The second element is whether the misrepresentation was fraudulent or material. If the misrepresentation was nonfraudulent or innocent, it must be material for the contract to be voidable.

❊   ❊   ❊

The plaintiff claims that the description was as accurate as he felt it could be without inviting theft. By making such an assertion, to some extent plaintiff purposely mislead [sic] DHL about the contents of the shipment. However, plaintiff also claims that he was unaware that DHL would not ship cash. In considering the requirement to view the record in a light most favorable to the non-moving party, the Court is simply unwilling at this point to rule that the misrepresentation was fraudulent as a matter of law.

The alternative factor to be considered under the second element is, if the misrepresentation is not fraudulent, is it, nevertheless, material. A misrepresentation is material if it would be likely to induce a reasonable person to manifest his assent, or if the maker knows that it would be likely to induce the recipient to do so.

❊   ❊   ❊

In the instant case, plaintiff had in his possession airbills which are bills of lading. Further, plaintiff had frequently utilized DHL's services for two years prior to the shipment at issue in this case. There is nothing contained in the record that indicates the Airway bill form changed in those two years. Based on this long-time use of DHL's services, plaintiff cannot now be heard to complain that he was unaware of the terms and conditions contained on the Airway bill. Therefore, plaintiff is bound by those terms and conditions, as he signed the Airway bill.

Given that plaintiff must be charged with the knowledge that DHL does not accept cash for delivery, the misrepresentation becomes material. It is material because "the maker [plaintiff] knows that for some special reason it is likely to induce the particular recipient [DHL] to manifest his assent." * * * Put simply, the plaintiff had reason to know DHL would not accept cash and describing the shipment as otherwise, he induced DHL to enter into a contract to which it would not otherwise assent to.

The third element to be considered is whether the misrepresentation induced DHL to enter into the contract. "A misrepresentation induces a party's manifestation of assent if it substantially contributes to his decision to manifest his assent." * * *

In the instant case, the misrepresentation was material. Further, there is nothing in the record to indicate that DHL did not attach importance to the misrepresentation. In fact, it is just the opposite. As noted before, the shipper's signature block of the Airway bill contains the following statement, "I warrant that all details given herein are true and correct", plus paragraph 2 on the back of the bill, relating to giving an accurate description of the contents, reflects DHL's concern as to the accuracy of the description of the shipment, as does the blank the shipper uses to describe the contents. Therefore, it is clear that the misrepresentation was a substantial factor in DHL's decision to enter into the contracts at issue.

The fourth element to be considered is whether DHL's reliance on the misrepresentation is reasonable. A misrepresentation will have no legal effect unless the recipient's reliance is justified. Prior to shipping and giving the envelope to DHL, plaintiff twice inquired as to the availability of $15,000 worth of insurance. This would indicate that the documents' value belied the description on the Airway bill. DHL argues that plaintiff attempts to impose a duty to inspect every envelope. This may or may not be plaintiff's intent but that is of no moment. What is important is the fact that DHL does reserve the right to inspect the envelopes it accepts for delivery. DHL would not reserve such a right if it did not believe that at some point or on some occasion it would want to check the contents because it has reason to believe the description is inaccurate. DHL realizes that it is not always reasonable to rely on the description supplied by a shipper. Where that point or occasion falls is a question of fact that should be left to the trier of fact. * * * Therefore, the Court finds that a material issue of fact exists as to the reasonableness of DHL's reliance on the description supplied by plaintiff.

DECISION AND REMEDY   *The trial court judge found that not all of the four elements of misrepresentation had been established as a matter of law. The motion for a summary judgment was not granted, thereby allowing the plaintiff to have his day in court.*

Mistake, Duress, and Undue Influence
Mistakes occur in two forms: A **unilateral mistake** is made by only one of the contracting parties, while a **mutual mistake** is made by both of them.

Unilateral Mistake   A unilateral mistake does not affect the contract, which is still valid and en-

forceable, unless the mistake is so obvious that the other party should have known it was a mistake.

For example, Jean runs a retail camera store. Jim, a salesperson for a printing company, obtains an order from Jean for return address labels. Jean was busy at the time she filled out the form and wrote "$4,000 m.m." Jim returns to the office with this order, elated that he has a sale for 4 billion labels. Neither he nor his company has ever had such a large order. In fact, a special press run has to be made, and delivery must be made by a freight company rather than by the usual method of sending the labels through the mails. Jean refuses delivery because she wanted only 4,000 labels. In this case, Jim should have known there was a mistake. He could have easily telephoned Jean to recheck before going to all the trouble and expense of having these labels printed.

On the other hand, had Jean filled out the form for "4,900" labels (with intent only to order 4,000), her unilateral mistake would fall on her, and she would be held liable for the purchase of 4,900 address labels. The mistake would not have been so obvious, and thus, Jim would not have known of it.

Mutual Mistake No contract is formed when there is a mutual mistake in a couple of circumstances: (1) when the parties are in disagreement as to the identity of the subject matter of the contract or (2) when they are mistaken as to the existence of the subject matter. If one of these two events occurs, there is no meeting of the minds and a court will not find a binding contract. If a court finds that a mutual mistake has occurred as to the value of the subject matter of the contract, the contract generally will be fully enforceable against both parties.

For example, Gary contracts to sell Kathy a painting for $5,000. Both believe the artist of the painting is Rory. They now learn that the artist is Lori. Since the mutual mistake went to the identity of the subject matter, there is no meeting of the minds and neither can enforce the contract. Had the mistake been as to the value—not the artist—of the painting, the contract would be fully enforceable.

In the following case, the court was confronted with the issue of whether the jury should have been instructed about the requirement for a meeting of the minds.

BACKGROUND AND FACTS *The plaintiff, Flo-Products Company, gave a quote over the telephone of "fifteen thirty-six" for certain cylinders to be used in the defendant's dairy packaging machine. The defendant's maintenance supervisor testified that the oral quote was "fifteen thirty-six," which he thought was $15.36. The cylinders were shipped to the defendant billed at $1,536. The defendant refused to accept delivery because of the question as to price.*

Flo-Products sued Valley Farms. The trial court did not instruct the jury to consider whether the parties had ever had a meeting of the minds. The plaintiff won a judgment in the trial court. Valley Farms appealed because the jury was not given instructions concerning the "meeting of the minds" element.

Case 9.4
FLO-PRODUCTS CO. v. VALLEY FARMS DAIRY CO.
Court of Appeals of Missouri, 1986.
718 S.W.2d 207.

Judge DOWD

*   *   *   *

*   *   * The jury was instructed *   *   * to find for plaintiff if they believe[d] plaintiff furnished the cylinders at defendant's request and that the charges for the cylinders were reasonable. Defendant requested the court to instruct the jury that "meeting of the minds" was a necessary element of plaintiff's case but the court refused the instruction.

Defendant alleges the trial court erred: in refusing to give defendant's requested instruction on "meeting of the minds."

*   *   * "Meeting of the minds" is a necessary element to the making of a contract[.] *   *   * [A] "meeting of the minds" as to price was a controverted issue. For a verdict-directing instruction in favor of plaintiff to be acceptable, it must require the jury to find all the necessary elements of plaintiff's case except for uncontroverted facts. It is reversible error for an instruction to assume or ignore a controverted fact.

The discrepancy in the parties' understanding of the price term remained a controverted fact throughout the trial. Plaintiff Flo-Products Co. chose to submit its case to the jury[.] * * * [T]he jury [is required] to find for plaintiff if they believe: 1) Defendant requested plaintiff to furnish the goods, 2) Plaintiff furnished the goods to defendant, and 3) Plaintiff's charges were reasonable. Instructing the jury * * * under these circumstances resulted in a directed verdict for plaintiff without the only controverted issue of the case ever being before the jury.

DECISION AND REMEDY   *The trial court erred in not giving the jury an instruction on the requirement that the parties must have a meeting of the minds to have a valid contract. The discrepancy in the parties' understanding of the price remained the contested issue throughout the trial, yet the jury never made a decision on these contested facts. The trial court's judgment was reversed and the case was remanded to the trial court.*

Duress   Duress occurs when one of the parties is forced into the contract by fear. The courts allow the party who was under duress to rescind the contract. For example, if Piranha Loan Company threatens to harm Chang unless he signs over to Piranha his $10,000 car in order to secure a $100 loan, Piranha is guilty of using duress.

Duress may involve the threat of physical harm or economic harm, such as the loss of a job. The threatened act must be wrongful or illegal. In a lawsuit, the party who was under duress (whose free will was overcome) can choose to carry out the contract or to avoid the entire transaction.

Undue Influence   Undue influence arises from special kinds of relationships in which one party can greatly influence another party, thus overcoming that party's free will. Minors and elderly people are often under the influence of close relatives. If Shady influences an elderly person who is under his legal care to enter into a contract that benefits Shady, undue influence has been exerted.

Undue influence can arise from a number of fiduciary (that is, founded on trust) or confidential relationships: attorney-client, doctor-patient, guardian-ward, parent-child, husband-wife, or trustee-beneficiary. The essential feature of undue influence is that the party being taken advantage of does not, in reality, exercise free will when entering into the contract. This contract is voidable by the person who was unduly influenced.

Exhibit 9–6 summarizes the defenses a party to a contract can use to show that mutual assent was not obtained.

Consideration

The third requirement of a legally enforceable agreement is consideration. Consideration is broken into two elements: (1) Something of **legal value** must be given in exchange for a promise, and (2) the promises must be **bargained for and exchanged.** The "something of legal value" may consist of a return promise or a performance.

Requirements of Consideration   In order to create a binding contract, the elements of consideration must not only exist but must also be legally sufficient. To be legally sufficient, consideration for a promise must be legally detrimental to the promisee—the one receiving the promise—or legally beneficial to the promisor—the one making the promise. In every bilateral contract, each party (offeror and offeree) is treated as both a promisor and a promisee. **Legal detriment** or **legal benefit** is not synonymous with actual economic detriment or benefit.

Note the change in language from offeror and offeree to promisor and promisee. The former two words describe the parties during the formation of the contract; once the parties have exchanged promises, they are called the promisor and promisee.

Legal detriment occurs when a person does or promises to do something that he or she did not have a prior legal duty to do or when the person gives up a legal right. Conversely, legal benefit occurs when a person obtains something that he or she had no prior legal right to obtain.

Exhibit 9–6 **Problems of Assent**

MISTAKE	1. *Mutual*—When both parties' mistake goes to a material fact, such as identity, either party can avoid the contract. If the mistake goes to value or quality, either party can enforce the contract.
	2. *Unilateral*—Generally, the mistaken party is bound by the contract *unless* the other party knows or should have known of the mistake.
FRAUD	1. *Fraud*—When fraud occurs, usually the innocent party can enforce or avoid the contract. The five elements necessary to establish fraud are: a. Misrepresentation of a material fact exists, b. Contract is made with knowledge that fact is false, c. Contract is made with the intent to deceive, d. Innocent party justifiably relies on the misrepresentation, and e. Innocent party is damaged.
MISREPRESENTATION	2. *Other*—Both b. and c. above are not required to find misrepresentation. Usually in such cases, the innocent party can rescind the contract but cannot seek damages.
INFLUENCE/COERCION	1. *Undue influence*—Arises from special relationships, such as fiduciary or confidential relationships, in which one party's free will has been overcome by the undue influence exerted by the other party. Usually, the contract is voidable.
	2. *Duress*—Defined as forcing a party to enter a contract under fear induced by a threat; for example, the threat of violence or economic pressure. The party forced to enter the contract can rescind the contract.

For example, Fine Gravel Company owns and mines a gravel pit. The land owned by Fine Gravel is adjacent to a school, but the actual mining takes place on the land furthest from the school. The school is one mile away from that mining site. After many years, Fine Gravel decides to mine within a few hundred yards of the school. It also plans to build a road for its trucks next to the school fence. The school board objects because of the danger to the children and the noise that will be produced. The school board offers $150,000 to Fine Gravel Company to refrain from building the road and from mining near the school. The

gravel company agrees. The consideration flowing from the gravel company is the promise to refrain from an act that it is legally entitled to do—that is, to earn a living by mining gravel. The consideration flowing from the school board to Fine Gravel is the promise to pay a sum of money that it is not otherwise legally required to pay.

In the following case, one of the classics of contract law, the court found that refraining from certain behavior at the request of another was sufficient consideration to support a promise to pay a sum of money.

BACKGROUND AND FACTS *William E. Story, Sr., was the uncle of William E. Story II. In the presence of family members and guests at a family gathering, Story, Sr., promised to pay his nephew $5,000 if he would refrain from drinking, using tobacco, swearing, and playing cards or billiards for money until he reached the age of 21.*

The nephew agreed and fully performed his part of the bargain. When he reached age 21, he wrote his uncle that he had kept his part of the agreement and was entitled to $5,000. The uncle replied that he was pleased with his nephew's performance and that he was keeping the nephew's money

Case 9.5
HAMER v. SIDWAY
Court of Appeals of New York,
Second Division, 1891.
124 N.Y. 538, 27 N.E. 256.

in the bank to earn interest. The nephew agreed that his uncle should keep the money according to the terms and conditions of the letter.

The uncle died about twelve years later without having paid his nephew any part of the $5,000 and interest. Sidway, the executor of the uncle's estate (the defendant in this action), did not want to pay the $5,000 and interest to the nephew, claiming that the nephew had not given valid consideration for the promise. In the meantime, the nephew sold his interest (his right to collect the $5,000 if the court ruled in his favor) to Hamer. Hamer sued Sidway to collect the $5,000. The court disagreed with the executor and reviewed the doctrine of detriment-benefit as valid consideration under the law.

Justice PARKER

*   *   * The defendant contends that the contract was without consideration to support it, and therefore invalid. He asserts that the promisee, by refraining from the use of liquor and tobacco, was not harmed, but benefited; that which he did was best for him to do, independently of his uncle's promise,—and insists that it follows that, unless the promisor was benefited, the contract was without consideration,—a contention which, if well founded, would seem to leave open for controversy in many cases whether that which the promisee did or omitted to do was in fact of such benefit to him as to leave no consideration to support the enforcement of the promisor's agreement. Such a rule could not be tolerated, and is without foundation in the law. The exchequer chamber [a type of court] in 1875 defined "consideration" as follows: "A valuable consideration, in the sense of the law, may consist either in some right, interest, profit, or benefit accruing to the one party, or some forbearance, detriment, loss, or responsibility given, suffered, or undertaken by the other." Courts "will not ask whether the thing which forms the consideration does in fact benefit the promisee or a third party, or is of any substantial value to any one. It is enough that something is promised, done, forborne, or suffered by the party to whom the promise is made as consideration for the promise made to him. In general a waiver of any legal right at the request of another party is a sufficient consideration for a promise." *   *   * Now, applying this rule to the facts before us, the promisee used tobacco, occasionally drank liquor, and he had a legal right to do so. That right he abandoned for a period of years upon the strength of the promise of the testator that for such forbearance he would give him $5,000. We need not speculate on the effort which may have been required to give up the use of those stimulants. It is sufficient that he restricted his lawful freedom of action within certain prescribed limits upon the faith of his uncle's agreement, and now, having fully performed the conditions imposed, it is of no moment whether such performance actually proved a benefit to the promisor, and the court will not inquire into it; but, were it a proper subject of inquiry, we see nothing in this record that would permit a determination that the uncle was not benefited in a legal sense. *   *   *

DECISION AND REMEDY *The court ruled that the nephew had provided legally sufficient consideration by giving up smoking, drinking, swearing, and playing cards or billiards for money until he became 21, and, therefore, he was entitled to the money promised him. A minor in the late 1800s, when this case took place, could legally do all these things.*

COMMENT *The* Hamer v. Sidway *case is a good illustration of the distinction between a benefit to the promisor and a detriment to the promisee. Here the court did not inquire as to whether a benefit flowed to the promisor but required only that there was a legally sufficient detriment to the promisee.*

Legal Highlight

Opera, Dinner, and Court?

In San Francisco, Bill, a certified public accountant, asked Ann to join him in attending the opera and to have dinner afterward. The date was made three months in advance. Late on the afternoon of the date, Ann called Bill to tell him that she would have to break the date because her old boyfriend was in town. Because it was late in the afternoon, Bill was unable to find anyone else to accompany him.

He sued Ann for breach of contract and asked for the following damages:

- The cost of one ticket to the opera
- One-half of the cost of the mileage to purchase and pick up the ticket in advance
- The cost of his time to find someone else to take her place.

The small-claims court dismissed the case, stating that a promise to go on a date was not a legally enforceable contract.

Adequacy of Consideration Adequacy of consideration refers to the fairness of the bargain. A court will not normally question the adequacy of the consideration if it is legally sufficient. If a person buys an item at too high a price, he or she may have buyer's remorse, but the court will not set the contract aside unless a reason, such as fraud or mistake, exists.

Exhibit 9–7 summarizes the legal elements of consideration.

In the next chapter we will discuss the other elements of a contract and possible defenses.

Exhibit 9–7 **Consideration**

ELEMENTS OF CONSIDERATION	1. *Legal value*—not economic value.
	  a. Legal detriment—to promisee who promises to do (or refrain from doing). No prior legal duty to perform (or refrain from doing).
	  b. Legal benefit—to promisor.
	
	2. *Bargained for and Legally Sufficient*—The promisee's performance or promises to perform must be given in exchange for the promisor's promise. Adequacy of consideration relates to "how much" consideration is given and whether a fair bargain was reached. Courts will inquire into the adequacy of consideration (if the consideration is legally sufficient) only when fraud, undue influence, or duress may be involved.

Ethical Considerations

Advertising Mistakes

The general rule is that advertisements are not offers, but are usually invitations to negotiate. If advertisements were treated as offers, a business would have to sell the item at the advertised price to everyone who came in to shop until the business revoked its offer. Most advertisements are not definite and certain but are merely invitations to the public to come to the business premises. If an advertisement is very certain and definite, the courts have treated these advertisements as offers.

Consider this example. A certain citizens band (CB) radio normally costs $400. In the Sunday paper, a company runs an advertisement that lists many items for sale. Among those items is a picture of the $400 CB radio with its model number, listed for a sale price of $40. The business intended to sell a lower-priced CB radio in this sale. The business did not catch the error when the original layout was sent over to the newspaper nor when it reviewed the advertisement prior to its being published.

Ethically, should the business sell the $400 CB radio for $40? Should it sell out only the number of $400 CB radios it has in stock? What should the business do when people use their CB radios to notify other radio owners of the sale and over 1,500 people stop at the store to make this fantastic purchase?

Legally, the store would probably not be required to sell at the advertised price. Although the advertisement is a unilateral mistake, the other parties should have realized it was a mistake.

International Considerations

Variations in Terms of Sale when Dealing Internationally

International commerce depends upon contracts. What terms should be included in a contract? Should contracts be in writing, and what is "in writing"? Would a videotape or a fax qualify, or is only the conventional method considered to be "in writing"? Many problems of this type confront the people who negotiate, draft, and adopt treaties and conventions.

The **United Nations Commission on International Trade Law (UNCITRAL)** has developed model laws that cover commercial transactions. These codes include the 1974 **Convention on the Limitation Period in the International Sale of Goods.** This convention establishes unified rules for determining the statute of limitations in a lawsuit. It attempts to reconcile the differences between the common-law and the civil-law approaches of various countries. It sets four years as the maximum period within which a party to an international sales contract may bring a lawsuit.

In 1980 the **Convention on Contracts for the International Sale of Goods (CISG)** was adopted. The 101-article document is structured in a manner similar to that of the UCC, Article 2, Sale of Goods. This code has been ratified by the United States and many of the major trading nations. The rules provide guidance for forming and interpreting contracts, for contract performance, for warranty provisions, and for remedies.

In the Western countries, in a sale of goods, the price is usually left open. This practice allows the market to set the price when the goods are delivered. The market price is assumed to be the reasonable price. Other nations insist on having the price stated within a detailed written contract. The CISG has adopted the market price for an open-price sale, unless the parties put in their contract a price or some other method of setting the price.

The CISG also sets out the time period for acceptance. This period begins the moment the telegram stating the offer is handed in for dispatch, or on the date shown on the letter, or if there is no date, then on the date on the envelope. If the offer is made by telephone, telex, or other means of instantaneous communications, the period begins at the time the offer reaches the offeree. The acceptance is effective when it reaches the offeror. The contract is made at the moment when the acceptance of an offer becomes effective. Please note that this time when the acceptance becomes effective is very different from the time set out in the UCC. Under the UCC, the acceptance is effective, under most conditions, when it is sent.

Making Sure You Are Insured

A common problem confronted by businesses involves consumer complaints about the provided product or service. For example, you go to Jim Onest Insurance Agency to purchase automobile liability insurance coverage. Mr. Onest obtains all the necessary information to bind your vehicle for coverage and records this information in his computer. You pay the initial premium and leave his office. Shortly after you leave, a power failure causes all the information contained in the computer to be lost.

As you are driving down the street, you overlook a stop sign and collide with a vehicle that had the right of way. No personal injuries are sustained, but extensive property damage does occur to the other vehicle. You contact Mr. Onest to inform him of the accident. He attempts to verify coverage but cannot do so because the information in the computer has been lost. He forgets about your check and informs you that there is no coverage.

This simple example illustrates all of the aspects of contract law. When you went to the insurance agency, you made an offer to purchase insurance, which was accepted. Legal consideration was present because the promises were bargained for and exchanged, and each party received a legal benefit and suffered a legal detriment. Lack of capacity or having an illegal contract is not at issue here. In most states, this type of contract does not have to be in writing to be enforceable. You have proof of this contract in your canceled check. By not recognizing your contract, Mr. Onest has breached it.

You should have done several things, however, in order to protect yourself. While you were in his office, you should have asked for the name of the company that was insuring you, obtained the policy number, and requested a receipt instead of relying on your check as your receipt.

If you filed a lawsuit, you would seek compensatory damages amounting to the cost of repairs to the other vehicle. In most states, you could also recover your attorney's fees and court costs. On the other hand, if you had obtained the specifics of who, what, when, where, and how much before you left the office, this lawsuit could have been avoided.

Summary

This chapter has emphasized basic contract law. The old law merchant has been replaced by uniform laws for the states to adopt. The most important is the Uniform Commercial Code (UCC). The UCC Article 2, Sales, covering the sale of goods, is the important article for contract law.

Contracts are divided into three elements: formation, enforceability, and performance. The following terms describe the types of formation of a contract: formal and informal contracts, unilateral and bilateral contracts, express and implied-in-fact contracts, and quasi-contracts (implied-in-law) contracts. Enforceability of a contract is described as valid, void, voidable, or unenforceable. The performance status of the contract is either executed or executory.

To have a valid and enforceable contract, the parties must ensure that the following items are present:

1. Offer: An offer must be made.
2. Acceptance: An acceptance must be given by return promise or by an act.
3. Consideration: Promises must be bargained for and exchanged, have legal value, and be legally sufficient to support the offer and acceptance.
4. Capacity: The parties must have the capacity to form a contract.

5. Legality: The subject matter of the contract must be legal.

6. Writing: Certain agreements must be in writing to be enforceable.

An offer and an acceptance represent the concept of mutual assent or a meeting of the minds. To have a valid offer: (1) the offeror must have an objective intent to contract, (2) the terms must be reasonably definite (the UCC liberalizes this rule), and (3) the terms must be communicated. An offer may be terminated by revocation, rejection (including a counteroffer), and by operation of law.

Acceptance is a voluntary act by which the offeree agrees to the terms of the offer. Silence normally does not constitute acceptance. The UCC includes specific rules as to when an acceptance is valid for a contract for the sale of goods. Sometimes there is an appearance of a meeting of the minds because an offer and an acceptance have been made, but in reality, mutual consent has not been given because of fraud, mistake, duress, or undue influence.

Legal consideration has two elements: bargained for and exchanged promises and the giving of something of legal value and sufficiency (that is, a legal benefit to the promisor or a legal detriment to the promisee). The courts normally are not concerned with the adequacy of consideration, only with the sufficiency.

Key Terms

acceptance (**209**)
bargained for and exchanged (**224**)
bilateral contract (**210**)
capacity (**212**)
consideration (**212**)
contract (**208**)
Convention on Contracts for the International Sale of Goods (CISG) (**229**)
Convention on the Limitation Period in the International Sale of Goods (**229**)
counteroffer (**216**)
duress (**220**)
executed contract (**212**)
executory contract (**212**)
express contract (**210**)
firm offer (**216**)

formal contract (**211**)
fraud (**220**)
implied-in-fact contract (**210**)
informal contract (**211**)
law merchant (**208**)
legal benefit (**224**)
legal detriment (**224**)
legality (**212**)
legal value (**224**)
merchant (**216**)
mirror-image rule (**218**)
misrepresentation (**220**)
mutual assent (**220**)
mutual mistake (**222**)
offer (**209**)
offeree (**209**)
offeror (**209**)
operation of law (**216**)
option contract (**216**)

promissory estoppel (**217**)
quasi-contract (**210**)
rejection (**209**)
revocation (**216**)
undue influence (**220**)
unenforceable contract (**212**)
Uniform Commercial Code (**208**)
unilateral contract (**210**)
unilateral mistake (**222**)
United Nations Commission on International Trade Law (UNCITRAL) (**229**)
valid contract (**211**)
void agreement (**211**)
voidable contract (**211**)
writing (**212**)

Questions and Case Problems

1. James is confined to his bed. He calls a friend who lives across the street and offers to sell her his watch next week for $100. If his friend wants to accept, she is to put a red piece of paper in her front window. The next morning, she places a red piece of paper in her front window. Is this contract bilateral or unilateral? Explain.

2. Douros entered into discussions with Hoehne about purchasing his property. Hoehne was not willing to sell. Upon Hoehne's death, Douros contacted the children, who were willing to sell. He typed up a contract that indicated the seller was to pay Douros a commission. Douros also had discussions with Kelley Properties and told it about the prime location that Douros had found. He would reveal the location if Kelley would sign an agreement and pay a commission if a sale of the property resulted. Kelley and Douros signed an agreement. In the

meantime, the children questioned Douros about the commission and by letter refused to pay it. Douros gave Kelley the letter. Later, Kelley sent Williams to meet with the Hoehne children, and eventually a sales contract between Kelley and the Hoehne children was signed. Douros filed a lawsuit against Kelley for refusing to pay the commission. Who should prevail and why? [Douros Realty v. Kelley Properties, 799 S.W.2d 179 (Mo.App. 1990)

3. Ingram started to work for Central Adjustment Bureau, Inc. (CABI). A week after starting work, his supervisor gave him an employment contract for him to sign. The contract contained a provision that restrained him from competing against CABI if he quit the company. He signed the contract after he was told that he would be fired if he did not sign. Seven years later, he quit and started a competing business. CABI sued Ingram to prevent him from competing. Ingram defended on the basis that the contract lacked consideration, since he signed it after he was working. [Central Adjustment Bureau, Inc. v. Ingram, 678 S.W.2d 28 (Tenn. 1984)]

4. Conrad purchased a farm in 1945 for $23,500. He had thirteen children. In 1975 he conveyed his farm to his eldest son for the same amount as he had paid. The farm was worth about $150,000. At the time of the conveyance, Conrad, 82, was in extremely poor health and had been hospitalized often for various ailments. A lawsuit was filed to rescind the conveyance. At the trial, the eldest son testified that his father trusted and relied on him. Should this conveyance be set aside and if so, why? [Schaneman v. Schaneman, 206 Neb. 113, 291 N.W.2d 412 (1980)]

5. The Olivers were planning to sell off some of their ranch land and mentioned this fact to Southworth, a neighbor. Southworth expressed interest in purchasing the property and later notified the Olivers that he had the money available to buy it. The Olivers told Southworth they would let him know shortly about the details concerning the sale. The Olivers later sent a letter to Southworth—and (unknown to Southworth) to several other neighbors—giving information about the sale, including the price, the location of the property, and the amount of acreage involved. When Southworth received the letter, he sent a letter to the Olivers "accepting" their offer. The Olivers stated that the information letter had not been intended as an "offer" but merely as a starting point for negotiations. Southworth brought suit against the Olivers to enforce the "contract." Did a contract exist? [Southworth v. Oliver, 284 Or. 361, 587 P.2d 994 (1978)]

6. James owned timber that he desired to sell. Notices were sent to numerous potential buyers for bids (offers) for the timber. Eames responded by submitting the highest bid (offer), but James refused to go through with the transaction and Eames sued. What are the legal arguments for James and Eames? [Eames v. James, 452 So.2d 384 (La.App. 1984)]

7. Laemmar was an employee of J. Walter Thompson Company. During the years of his employment, he purchased shares of common stock from the company. Laemmar's stock was to be subject to repurchase by the company if Laemmar's employment was terminated for any reason. The officers and directors of the company decided to increase their control and demanded that Laemmar and several other employees sell their stock back to the company or lose their jobs. Although Laemmar did not want to sell his stock, he did so in order to keep his job. The officers and directors never made any physical threats or suggestions of physical harm to Laemmar. Later, Laemmar instituted a lawsuit to rescind his sale of the stock on the basis of duress. Can Laemmar rescind? Explain. [Laemmar v. J. Walter Thompson Co., 435 F.2d 680 (7th Cir. 1970)]

Chapter 10 Contract Defenses and Remedies

If a man owe a debt and Adad, the storm god, inundate his field and carry away the produce, or, through lack of water, grain has not grown in the field, in that year he shall not make any return of grain to the creditor, he shall alter his contract tablet, and he shall not pay the interest for that year.

Hammurabi, *Floruit,*
2100 B.C.

OUTLINE

Introduction

In the last chapter we discussed three of the elements for a binding contract: offer, acceptance, and consideration. This chapter looks at the other two elements: legal capacity and legality. These two requirements can be used as defenses to a contract. The other potential defenses, such as the statute of frauds, are also included in this chapter. A defense to a contract is a legal excuse as to why a person does not have to perform his or her promise.

We have studied the two original parties to a contract. In this chapter, we will examine when a third party becomes involved and what that party's rights and defenses are on a contract.

Although most contracts are discharged because they are fully performed, we will study other ways for contracts to be discharged. Finally, when a party to a contract has been harmed, we will review the types of damages and remedies a person may request in a lawsuit.

Elements of a Contract: Part 2

Contractual Capacity

Contractual capacity—that is, the competence (or legal ability) of the parties—is the fourth requirement for a valid contract. Full competence exists when both parties have full legal capacity to enter into a contract and to have the contract enforced against them. No competence exists when a party has been judged by a court to be mentally incompetent; such a person has no legal capacity to form a contract, and any contract into which he or she enters is void.

Limited competence exists when one or both parties are minors, are intoxicated, or are mentally incompetent but not yet officially judged to be mentally incompetent by a court. These parties have full and legal capacity to enter into a contract, but, if they want, they can avoid liability under the contract. This type of contract is said to be voidable. We will emphasize the contracts of minors here because this is the area that involves the most litigation.

Minors　The **age of majority** (when a person is no longer a minor) for contractual purposes varies from state to state. For the sake of discussion in this text, we will use 18 years as the age when a person becomes an adult. The general rule of law is that a minor can enter into any contract that an adult can enter into, provided that the contract is not one prohibited by law. For example, in most states a person must be 21 years old to purchase any alcoholic beverages.

Although minors can enter into contracts, they also have the right to **disaffirm** (or avoid) their liabilities under the contracts, subject to certain exceptions such as necessaries. A minor may disaffirm a contract any time prior to age eighteen or during a reasonable period of time thereafter. If, however, by the time the minor becomes an adult, he or she has failed to disaffirm an *executed* contract, the contract is ratified. **Ratification** is the act of accepting and giving legal force to any contract that the minor had a right to disaffirm. Only after minors reach adulthood can they ratify (adopt) contracts made when they were minors.

A contract to purchase necessaries (that is, goods or services needed for the sustenance of the minor, such as food, clothing, or shelter) may not be totally disaffirmed by a minor. The rule applicable to contracts for the purchase of necessaries is that the minor is liable to the other contracting party for the *reasonable value* of the property or services *actually used*. This imposes a quasi-contractual liability on the minor to pay for purchases needed to fulfill the basic needs of the minor where no parent or guardian is *willing* and *able* to furnish or provide the required necessity.

Under the UCC, dealing with the sale of goods, a minor cannot recover the goods transferred by the adult purchaser to a third party who is a bona fide purchaser (a good-faith purchaser for value). The buyer needs to know that the items he or she buys in good faith will not be taken as the result of a dispute between the seller and a minor from whom the seller purchased the item. For example, Minor owns a car at age sixteen. He sells the car to Al Adult. Al drives the car for six months and then sells it to Susan. Minor now decides he wants the car back. He could disaffirm the contract with Al, but Minor cannot recover the car from Susan.

When disaffirmance occurs, the adult must give back to the minor whatever she or he has received as a result of the contract. If the property itself cannot be returned, the adult must pay the minor its equivalent value.

When disaffirmance occurs, the minor is also required to give back whatever he or she has received and still possesses as a result of the contract. In most states, the minor's duty of restoration is only to return the goods (or other consideration).

If this condition is met, the minor is not liable for depreciation or nonwillful damage to the goods. In the following case, for example, a minor was not liable for damages to an automobile.

BACKGROUND AND FACTS *Halbman, the plaintiff, contracted with Lemke, the defendant, to purchase a 1968 Oldsmobile for $1,250, of which Halbman paid $1,100 to Lemke. Halbman was a minor when he purchased the vehicle. A connecting rod broke, and Halbman took it to a garage for repairs. He did not pay the repair bill. The mechanic, therefore, placed a lien (called an artisan's lien) on the car for his repairs. This lien was foreclosed, and the engine was sold to another person to pay for the repairs. The car was towed to Halbman's residence.*

Halbman disaffirmed the contract. He contacted Lemke to come get the car and to return the $1,100. Lemke claimed he did not have a legal obligation to take back the car. Eventually the car was vandalized, making it unsalvageable. Halbman sued Lemke for the return of his $1,100. The trial court entered a judgment for Halbman. Lemke appealed.

Case 10.1
HALBMAN v. LEMKE
Supreme Court of Wisconsin, 1980.
99 Wis.2d 241,
298 N.W.2d 562.

Justice CALLOW
*   *   *   *

The sole issue before us is whether a minor, having disaffirmed a contract for the purchase of an item which is not a necessity and having tendered the property back to the vendor, must make restitution to the vendor for damage to the property prior to the disaffirmance. Lemke argues that he should be entitled to recover for the damage to the vehicle up to the time of disaffirmance, which he claims equals the amount of the repair bill.

Neither party challenges the absolute right of a minor to disaffirm a contract for the purchase of items which are not necessities. That right, variously known as the doctrine of incapacity or the "infancy doctrine," is one of the oldest and most venerable of our common law traditions. Although the origins of the doctrine are somewhat obscure, it is generally recognized that its purpose is the protection of minors from foolishly squandering their wealth through improvident contracts with crafty adults who would take advantage of them in the marketplace. Thus it is settled law in this state that a contract of a minor for items which are not necessities is void or voidable at the minor's option.

Once there has been a disaffirmance, however, as in this case between a minor vendee and an adult vendor, unresolved problems arise regarding the rights and responsibilities of the parties relative to the disposition of the consideration exchanged on the contract. As a general rule a minor who disaffirms a contract is entitled to recover all consideration he has conferred incident to the transaction. In return the minor is expected to restore as much of the consideration as, at the time of disaffirmance, remains in the minor's possession.

The minor's right to disaffirm is not contingent upon the return of the property, however, as disaffirmance is permitted even where such return cannot be made. *   *   * In this case we have a situation where the property cannot be returned to the vendor in its entirety because it has been damaged and therefore diminished in value, and the vendor seeks to recover the depreciation. Although this court has been cognizant of this issue on previous occasions, we have not heretofore resolved it.

The law regarding the rights and responsibilities of the parties relative to the consideration exchanged on a disaffirmed contract is characterized by confusion, inconsistency, and a general lack of uniformity as jurisdictions attempt to reach a fair application of the infancy doctrine in today's marketplace. * * *
* * * *

The principal problem is the use of the word "restitution." * * * When the contract is disaffirmed, title to that part of the purchased property which is retained by the minor revests in the vendor; it no longer belongs to the minor. The rationale for the rule is plain: a minor who disaffirms a purchase and recovers his purchase price should not also be permitted to profit by retaining the property purchased. The infancy doctrine is designed to protect the minor, sometimes at the expense of an innocent vendor, but it is not to be used to bilk merchants out of property as well as proceeds of the sale. Consequently, it is clear that, when the minor no longer possesses the property which was the subject matter of the contract, the rule requiring the return of property does not apply. The minor will not be required to give up what he does not have. We conclude that the word "restitution" * * * is limited to the return of the property to the vendor.

Here Lemke seeks restitution of the value of the depreciation by virtue of the damage to the vehicle prior to disaffirmance. Such a recovery would require Halbman to return more than that remaining in his possession. It seeks compensatory value for that which he cannot return. Where there is misrepresentation by a minor or willful destruction of property, the vendor may be able to recover damages in tort. But absent these factors, as in the present case, we believe that to require a disaffirming minor to make restitution for diminished value is, in effect, to bind the minor to a part of the obligation which by law he is privileged to avoid.

DECISION AND REMEDY

The trial court's decision was affirmed. The court did not require restitution by the minor in order for him to recover what he had paid. When Halbman disaffirmed the contract, the title went back to Lemke; thus, when the automobile was vandalized, the automobile was owned by Lemke. Because Lemke failed to remove the automobile from Halbman's yard when first called by Halbman, it was rendered unsalvageable. Naturally, Halbman cannot now make actual restitution; Halbman did, however, attempt to make restoration, and the law will not make him return what he no longer has—especially in this case, when it was not his fault.

What happens if a minor lies about his or her age? The courts have not been uniform in handling this troublesome area, but they have created four different approaches: The traditional view allows the minor to disaffirm his or her contract on the theory that a lack of capacity cannot be forfeited by misstating one's age. The adult who contracts with a minor who has lied can suffer severe consequences because the minor is allowed to return to the adult only what remains of the item purchased, if anything is left. The second approach also allows the minor to disaffirm, but he or she must return to the adult everything the adult had transferred to the minor. The third method of handling this problem does not allow a minor

to disaffirm. The last approach allows disaffirmance but holds the minor liable for fraud.

Legality

The fifth requirement for a valid contract is legality; the contract must be for the performance of a legal act. An agreement is illegal if either its formation or its performance is criminal, tortious, or otherwise opposed to public policy. The reasoning for this is quite simple: If a civil court requires a person to perform a contract that involves the commission of an illegal act, a criminal court could punish that person for committing a crime as a result of a civil court order. This is not

"Blue" Sabbath

As a result of the Puritan spirit, nearly all contracts were at one time considered to be illegal if made on Sunday. Eventually the types of contracts that could or could not be made on Sunday became a hodgepodge. Called blue laws, the restrictions have eased significantly over the years. Court challenges have struck down the blue laws in Virginia, North Carolina, Tennessee, Mississippi, Arkansas, and, as recently as in 1984, in Louisiana. That last court decision came in time for tourists to be able to buy souvenirs anywhere in Louisiana, without being restricted on Sundays to the 1984 World's Fair or the French Quarter in New Orleans.

In the past, the hodgepodge of restrictions included the following:

- You could go to the grocery store and buy such "necessities" as *Playboy* (deemed literature) but not meat (not deemed necessary to survive the day).
- You could buy a house but not any furniture.
- You could buy a battery but not a car.
- In South Carolina, you could go to a movie only in the eight largest cities, not in the rural areas.

Only one blue law is still enforced in almost every state: Liquor still cannot be sold on Sunday mornings.

only illogical, but it is also against public policy for the courts to be a party to a crime.

The general effect of an illegal agreement is that it is void, and the court leaves the parties where they are found. Neither party has rights against the other when the agreement has an illegal purpose.

The following subsections look at areas where the court has found illegality.

Licenses Most businesses need some type of license from the government to operate. Licenses can be divided into two categories: regulatory or revenue raising. Regulatory licensing statutes govern the qualifications of the person or business to conduct specific types of operations; real estate and construction licenses are examples. If a person lacks this type of license, any business contract he or she enters into is normally declared null and void. If an unlicensed pool builder constructs a swimming pool, for instance, the homeowner is not required to pay for it because the agreement is void.

A good business practice is to verify that the person is properly licensed before contracting with him or her. Most states have a consumer protection law setting up a recovery fund for consumers. A consumer may recover damages from the fund if a licensed business fails to perform appropriately. Most states do not protect consumers if they have dealt with an unlicensed business.

Revenue-raising licensing statutes, as the name implies, establish licensing requirements solely to raise revenues. Most states have a sales or use tax, for example. When people operate a business, they are required to collect the sales tax on their gross receipts. In order to keep track of these businesses, the state or local government requires them to secure a license. Generally, if this type of business is not licensed, it has no effect on contracts into which the business may enter.

Usury Usury statutes set the maximum rate of interest that may be charged for loaning money. Any higher rate of interest is considered usurious and may result in severe consequences. If the interest rate is 10 percent per annum, any rate above 10 percent is illegal, and the creditor must forfeit both principal and interest. Many states abolished usury laws or have set a very high rate of interest in response to economic conditions of the 1970s and 1980s. The harsh consequence of total forfeiture has also been modified. Today, in many states, the business may forfeit all interest but not the principal. Other states merely require the forfeiture of the amount of interest deemed to be usurious.

Blue Sky Laws Blue sky laws were passed by states to prevent fraud in the sale of investments. These laws apply to the sale of securities within a state—that is, intrastate sales. The basic purposes are to prevent dishonest sales practices and to require full truthful disclosure. Chapter 19 covers this topic in more detail.

Restraints of Trade Competition is the basis of our economic system. Common law has long prohibited restraints of trade. For example, if Haught owns a shopping center and agrees with O'Brian, who operates a record store, not to allow any other record stores in the mall, this agreement is void because it is in restraint of trade.

Although a restraint-of-trade agreement is void by itself, a restraint may be made part of a contract. These clauses are allowed as part of a contract in two situations: sale of a business and employment contracts. When a business is sold, one of the major assets is the seller's goodwill, especially in a small business. The last thing a buyer needs is for the seller to open a new business near the original one.

The second situation, involving employment contracts, is not as easily defendable. In this case, the employee signs a contract and agrees not to compete against the employer after termination of the employment relationship. Both of these types of restrictions have been upheld by courts if the restrictions are reasonable as to time and area. The theory upholding both restrictions is that the buyer and the employer are protecting their valuable property rights.

Other restraints of trade may be illegal under the Sherman Antitrust Act, the Clayton Act, and other federal or state antitrust statutes. These acts are discussed in Chapter 20.

Unconscionable Bargain The law has long been concerned about the balance of power between the strong and weak parties to a contract. In Chapter 1, we discussed the concept of equity, which is applied by the courts to obtain fairness. Today this concept has been adopted by the UCC in Section 2-302, which is concerned with **unconscionable contracts.** It provides that a court may refuse to enforce a contract or a provision of a contract if it is found to be unconscionable.

The legal test for unconscionability is whether, in the light of the general commercial background and the business needs of the particular trade or case, the clauses involved are so one-sided as to be unconscionable under the circumstances. Consider this example: A school purchases catsup in large quantities. In the sale contract is a provision that requires the school to reject each shipment within ten days, if the goods do not meet the contract specifications. After this rejection period, the school finds that a shipment of catsup is contaminated. This contamination could be not discovered except by microscopic analysis of the catsup bottles after the shipping container had been opened. The court in this case would find the ten-day rejection clause to be unconscionable.

In the following case, the court was faced with determining whether a contract was unconscionable.

Case 10.2
PIEHL v. NORWEGIAN OLD PEOPLES' HOME SOCIETY OF CHICAGO

Appellate Court of Illinois, 1984.

469 N.E.2d 705 (Ill.App. 1 Dist.).

BACKGROUND AND FACTS *Cheryl L. Piehl was appointed to administer the estate of Mabel Finn, who was deceased. Six months prior to Finn's death, Finn had signed a contract with the defendant, Norwegian Old Peoples' Home Society, a nursing home. The contract required Finn to transfer all of her assets to the defendant in return for a promise of continuing care for the rest of her life. The defendant reserved the right to cancel the contract for medical or safety reasons or if Finn became ineligible for old-age benefits once her assets had been exhausted for her maintenance.*

Justice WHITE
*   *   *   *

Plaintiff maintains that the "continuing care contract" was oppressive and unconscionable in that, although it purports to provide care for Mrs. Finn's lifetime, the contract allowed the Home to terminate such care upon exhaustion of the transferred assets or for medical or safety reasons. An unconscionable contract has been defined as a one-sided contract or one which no man in his senses, not under delusion, would make, on the one hand, and which no fair and honest man would accept on the other. The term unconscionability encompasses an absence of a meaningful choice on the part of one of the parties together with contract terms which are unreasonably favorable to the other party. Where a contract is found to be unconscionable, courts will refuse to give full effect to it as written. We are of the opinion that the terms of the "continuing care contract" were not unreasonably favorable to the Home. The contract provided that the Home would care for decedent until she left the facility voluntarily, involuntarily, or by reason of death. In the event Mrs. Finn left the facility voluntarily she was entitled to recover the balance then remaining in the account paid or deposited with the facility on her behalf less charges properly allocated to her stay in the facility. Mrs. Finn was also entitled to a refund should the Home request that she leave the facility for medical reasons, safety reasons or for other reasons permitted by law. Lastly, the Home reserved the right to terminate the contract should Mrs. Finn not be eligible for old age assistance benefits. However, the Home incorporated certain safeguards in the contract to insure Mrs. Finn's eligibility for old age assistance benefits. Most importantly, the Home's option could only be exercised once all assets transferred to the Home had been used in the care of Mrs. Finn. Accordingly, we conclude that the "continuing care contract" signed by Mrs. Finn was not unconscionable.

The court found that the contract was not unconscionable, even though the defendant reserved the right to cancel the contract under certain conditions, after all Finn's assets had been expended.

DECISION AND REMEDY

Writing

Certain valid contracts, by statute, must be in writing to be legally enforceable by a court. This statute is called the Statute Against the Perpetuation of Fraud, or the **statute of frauds** for short. The writing must be signed by the person against whom it is being enforced. Good business practice requires a written contract.

The statute of frauds varies from state to state. The major types of business contracts required to be in writing are:

1. Contracts involving interests in land, such as leases and sales
2. Contracts that, by their terms, cannot be performed within one year from the date that the contract was formed
3. **Collateral contracts,** such as promises to pay the debt or perform the duties of someone else

4. Contracts for the sale of goods priced at $500 or more, under the UCC.

The statute of frauds allows other methods to substitute for a written contract. For example, the UCC requires that contracts involving the sale of goods for the price of $500 or more must be in writing and signed by the party against whom enforcement is sought [UCC 2-201]. But if the signed writing is insufficient because it omits or incorrectly states a term, the UCC provides that the contract is still valid. (In any case, however, a contract is not enforceable under the UCC for any amount of goods greater than that stated in the writing.) If there is an oral agreement between merchants and if one of them sends the other a written confirmation, the confirmation is the written evidence of the oral contract. The receiver has ten days to give her or his written objection; if this is not sent, the terms of the oral contract are en-

Exhibit 10–1 Contracts Covered by the Statute of Frauds

Contracts to Guarantee the Debt of Another	*Application*—Applies only to express contracts made between the guarantor and the creditor, whose terms make the guarantor secondarily liable for the debt of another.
Contracts Involving an Interest in Realty	*Application*—Applies to any contract for an interest in realty, such as sale or lease.
Contracts Whose Terms Cannot Be Performed Within One Year	*Application*—Applies only to contracts objectively impossible to perform fully within one year from the date of the contract's formation.

Contracts for the Sale of Goods Priced at $500 or More	1. *Application*—Applies only to the sale of goods whose purchase price (excluding taxes) is $500 or more [UCC 2-201(1)].
	
	 2. *Exceptions:*
	   a. Between merchants, where one sends a written confirmation and the recipient does not object in writing within ten days.
	   b. Admission under oath of an oral contract.
	   c. Partial performance by buyer's payment or possession, at least to the extent paid or quantity possessed [UCC 2-201(2)(3)].

Exception to Contracts Otherwise Unenforceable Under the Statute of Frauds	*Memorandum*—Written evidence of an oral contract signed by the party against whom enforcement is sought. Generally, the writing must name the parties and identify the subject matter of the contract. In the sale of goods, the quantity must be stated. In the sale of realty, the contract requires a land description and price. Exceptions exist under each section.

forceable and are presumed to be those contained in the written confirmation. The contract is binding on both parties even though not signed by both parties.

The UCC allows oral contracts to be enforced up to the amount to which the parties admit in any court action. Also, the UCC allows courts to enforce oral contracts up to the amount of payment that has been made or up to the quantity of the goods already received and accepted by the buyer. Any other parts of the oral contract remain unenforceable.

Exhibit 10–1 summarizes the contracts covered by the statute of frauds.

The following case discusses whether an oral contract was primarily for the sale of goods or of services. The UCC is concerned with the sale of goods and not services.

Case 10.3
COLORADO CARPET INSTALLATION v. PALERMO

Supreme Court of Colorado, 1983.
668 P.2d 1384.

BACKGROUND AND FACTS *Colorado Carpet Installation filed this lawsuit to collect on an alleged oral contract in which the Palermos (husband and wife) agreed to pay $4,775.75 for the purchase and installation of carpeting, other flooring materials, and bathroom tile. The Palermos denied that they ever ordered anything beyond the tile for the bathroom.*

Justice QUINN
*   *   *   *

We address the court of appeals' determination that the contract was one for the sale of goods, rather than for the performance of labor or services. We conclude that the agreement in question involved a contract for the sale of goods[.] *   *   *
*   *   * The Uniform Commercial Code defines "goods" to mean "all things
*   *   * which are movable at the time of identification to the contract for sale

other than the money in which the price is to be paid, investment securities . . . and things in action." * * * A "sale," by statutory definition, "consists in the passing of title from the seller to the buyer for a price[.]" * * *

In this case the subject of the contract involved "goods" because the carpeting and other materials were movable at the time that Colorado Carpet procured them for installation pursuant to the agreement. Since the agreement contemplated that title to the carpeting and other materials would pass to the Palermos, it constituted a "contract for sale." The scope of the contract, however, included not only the sale of goods but also the performance of labor or service. Thus, we must determine whether such a mixed contract qualified as a contract for the sale of goods or, instead, constituted a contract for labor or service outside the scope of [the UCC].

The performance of some labor or service frequently plays a role in sales transactions. "Goods," however, are not the less "goods" merely because labor or service may be essential to their ultimate use by the purchaser. The mere furnishing of some labor or service, in our view, should not determine the ultimate character of a contract for purposes * * * of the Uniform Commercial Code. Rather, the controlling criterion should be the primary purpose of the contract—that is, whether the circumstances underlying the formation of the agreement and the performance reasonably expected of the parties demonstrate the primary purpose of the contract as the sale of goods or, in contrast, the sale of labor or service. * * *

[The] "primary purpose" test, we believe, is designed to promote one of the expressed statutory policies of the Uniform Commercial Code—"[t]o simplify, clarify, and modernize the law governing commercial transactions." * * * Useful factors to consider in determining whether "goods" or "service" predominates include the following: the contractual language used by the parties[;] whether the agreement involves one overall price that includes both goods and labor or, instead, calls for separate and discrete billings for goods on the one hand and labor on the other[;] the ratio that the cost of goods bears to the overall contract price[;] and the nature and reasonableness of the purchaser's contractual expectations of acquiring a property interest in goods * * *.

Considering the contract under these guidelines, we are satisfied that, as a matter of law, its primary purpose was the sale of goods and not the sale of labor or service. The language in Colorado Carpet's proposal referred to the parties as "seller" and "customer." In addition, the agreement called for an overall contract price that included both the cost of goods and labor, and, as the trial evidence established, the charge for labor was slight in relation to the total contractual price. Finally, the carpeting and other materials were movable when Colorado Carpet procured them for the purpose of selling them to the Palermos. The fact that these materials might later be installed in the Palermo home and assume the character of fixtures does not undermine the primary purpose of the contract as one for a sale of goods. * * *

The court found that this contract was for the sale of goods, not services. The oral agreement was not enforceable because the statute of frauds requires a written contract for the sale of goods priced at $500 or more.

DECISION AND REMEDY

Parol Evidence Rule The **parol** (oral) **evidence rule** is also known as the best evidence rule. The courts will not allow into evidence any oral statements made prior to or at the time of the signing of a written contract. It is believed that the best evidence is the written contract. Oral evidence is not allowed to change or add to a fully integrated contract.

This rule does allow for some oral testimony. For example, oral testimony is allowed to explain terms used in the contract or to clarify an ambiguity. Parol evidence may be used to show misrepresentation, fraud, duress, undue influence, mistake, and lack of contractual capacity. Oral testimony is also used if there is a gross typographical or clerical error that, when corrected, allows the court to reform the contract to the true intentions of the parties.

Other Contractual Issues

After all the requirements of a valid contract have been met, other problems may arise. First, third parties may have rights based on the contract even though they did not participate in its original formation. Second, if a contract dispute arises, the parties need to know the available remedies.

Assignments and Delegations

Sometimes people not directly connected with the initial contract become involved in it. Third parties can acquire an interest in a contract by assuming the rights or duties arising from it. An original party to a contract can transfer his or her rights or duties to a third person (that is, someone who was not an original party) after the original contract has been made.

Each party to the contract has rights and duties. One party has the right to the performance that the other party has promised; the other party has a duty to perform it. The transfer of duties to another person is called a **delegation**. When a party to a contract transfers her or his rights to a third person, it is known as an **assignment**, and the original party is known as the **assignor**. The third party who takes the assignment is known as the **assignee**. The assignee steps into the shoes of the original party to the contract. If the other party to the contract has a defense to the contract, the defense may also be used against the assignee.

For example, Nancy contracts to purchase a computer for $4,000. She is going to pay Computer Company $200 a month. Computer Company (the assignor) assigns the right to receive the $4,000 to Finance Company (the assignee). Nancy is now required to pay the $200 a month to Finance Company until she has paid the $4,000 and the contract ends. If the computer fails to work or Nancy has a good defense, such as fraud, against the contract with Computer Company, that defense may also be used against the assignee, Finance Company.

A contractual duty can be delegated to someone else to perform unless the duty of performance is personal and must be performed by the original party. For example, Vic has a house for sale. Alex wants to buy the house. He can assume the **mortgage** (the amount owed) that Vic has on the house. Vic is under a duty to pay, but his duty can be delegated to Alex if Alex is financially qualified. Now Alex is primarily liable on the mortgage, but Vic is still liable if Alex fails to pay. A person who owes a duty is not relieved of the duty if he delegates it to someone else to perform. If the performance is personal in nature, such as a contract with a surgeon to perform a heart transplant, the surgeon has no right to delegate this duty to a third person, even another surgeon, without the consent of the patient.

Exhibit 10–2 summarizes third-party rights.

The following case emphasizes the distinction between a personal-service contract and other contracts. Sometimes such distinctions must be based on fine lines.

Exhibit 10–2 **Assignment and Delegation**

Assignment	An assignment is the transfer of *rights* under a contract to a third party whereby the rights of the assignor (the person making the assignment) may be extinguished, and the assignee (the person to whom the rights are assigned) has a right to demand performance from the other original party to the contract. Generally all rights are assignable except where the law prohibits such, the contract prohibits assignment, or where the assignment would materially alter or increase the duties of the original party to the contract.
Delegation	A delegation is the transfer of *duties* under a contract to a third party whereby the delegate (the third party) assumes the obligation of performing the contractual duties previously held by the delegator (the one making the delegation). Generally duties cannot be delegated because most duties are personal or because their delegation is prohibited by contract.

BACKGROUND AND FACTS *McClendon Kennels entered into a booking contract with Investment Corporation of South Florida (ICSF), the owner and operator of the Hollywood Dog Track (the track). Under the contract, McClendon was to provide greyhounds to the track for the 1983–1985 racing seasons. In March 1984, Leo Green approached McClendon to purchase McClendon Kennels, including the contract with the track. The value of the kennels was much higher if the sale of the business included the contract with the track. An officer for the track allegedly refused to allow the assignment of the contract to the potential purchaser, Green. Later this refusal was denied by the track. Green decided not to purchase the McClendon Kennels. Later Green bought another kennel and entered into a separate booking contract with the track.*

McClendon Kennels brought action against the track under several theories, including tortious interference with a business relationship, and requested a declaratory judgment to determine if the track had a right of refusal of the assignment of the booking contract and, if so, whether such a right was absolute or limited. The trial court granted the track its motion for summary judgment; McClendon appealed.

Judge NESBITT
* * * *

Though the contract obviously contemplates a delegation of rights * * *, it is silent as to the right of assignment. Thus, the contract, by its terms, does not prohibit an assignment.

ICSF claims that the booking contract involves obligations for the personal services of McClendon Kennels, and therefore an assignment of it is forbidden. However, the Florida supreme court in *Wilson v. Sandstrom*, held that a contract to supply greyhounds to a racing track is not a personal service contract. Though ICSF urges us to distinguish *Wilson* from the present case, we find its argument unpersuasive and hold that the proposed assignment of this booking contract was not invalid as one involving a personal service.
* * * *

ICSF is required to exercise discretion in granting a booking contract so as to maintain the highest level of integrity in greyhound racing. In a contract in which one party selects the other party through the exercise of discretion based upon the qualifications and fitness of the selected party, the selected party may not assign the contract at his pleasure. * * * Since ICSF grants booking contracts based upon the qualifications of the kennels, McClendon Kennels' right of assignment must be subject to ICSF's right of refusal. ICSF may only refuse consent to a proposed assignment through the exercise of its discretion based upon an assignee's qualifications and fitness. Its refusal may not be arbitrary and unreasonable. * * * Based upon the foregoing analysis, the trial court's entry of a summary final judgment was erroneous, as it failed to even reach the issue of whether McClendon Kennels possessed a limited right of assignment. Since there remain disputed issues of material fact concerning ICSF's refusal and whether the refusal was commercially reasonable, the trial court should have allowed this case to go to trial.

The court found that a booking contract was not a contract involving personal services. It did find, however, that the track had a right to select a party based upon the other party's qualifications and fitness. The question remained whether the refusal was solely based upon Green's qualification and fitness. This question had to be decided by the trial court and could not be determined through the use of summary judgment procedures.

Case 10.4
L. V. McCLENDON KENNELS v. INVESTMENT CORP.
District Court of Appeal, 1986. 490 S.2d 1374 (Fla.App. 3 Dist.).

DECISION AND REMEDY

Third-Party Beneficiaries

Normally when parties contract, they do not intend third persons to have any rights in the contract. However, there are times when the original parties will consider other persons to be included in the benefits of the contract. At other times, third persons who were not considered at the time of contracting may benefit by the actual performance of the contract. These third parties are called third-party beneficiaries.

Third-party beneficiaries fall into two general categories: **intended beneficiaries** and **incidental beneficiaries.** Whether a person is included in one or the other category depends upon whether the original parties, at the time of contracting, intended to benefit a third person. If so, that party is an intended beneficiary; if not, the party is an incidental beneficiary. For example, commuters on a train are the incidental beneficiaries of the contract between the union and the railroad.

Intended beneficiaries generally are either a **creditor beneficiary** or a **donee beneficiary** (although, in some situations, the intended beneficiary may not fall under the heading of creditor or donee). A creditor beneficiary exists when the performance of the contract will discharge a duty owed by one of the original parties to the creditor. For example, you owe Alice $100. You are hired to work at a music performance, and you will earn $100 for the evening. You request your employer to pay the $100 to Alice and not to you. Alice is a creditor beneficiary of your contract for services with the music company.

A person is a donee beneficiary when the main purpose of the contract is to make a gift to someone who is not a party to the contract. The best example is the standard life insurance contract. The contract is between the life insurance company and the insured, but the party who is designated to receive the insurance proceeds after the insured has died is the donee beneficiary.

What rights does a creditor or donee beneficiary have? Generally, an intended beneficiary may bring a lawsuit on the contract, but an incidental beneficiary may not.

The following case represents the court's determination as to when a person is an intended beneficiary to a contract. Please note that the plaintiffs were neither creditor nor donee beneficiaries.

Case 10.5
CONCERNED TENANTS ASSOCIATION OF FATHER PANIK VILLAGE v. PIERCE
United States District Court, 1988.
685 F.Supp. 316 (D.Conn.).

BACKGROUND AND FACTS *The Concerned Tenants Association of Father Panik Village (Concerned Tenants), along with others filed a class-action suit against Samuel Pierce, then secretary of the Department of Housing and Urban Development (HUD), and Bridgeport Housing Authority (BHA). The lawsuit sought to correct allegedly dangerous, indecent, and unsanitary living conditions at Father Panik Village, a low-income housing project in Bridgeport, Connecticut. In particular, plaintiffs alleged that HUD failed to repair broken windows, doors, electrical fixtures, appliances, radiators, pipes, showers, stairway railings, floors, walls, and ceilings. HUD also failed to provide adequate security, including door locks, hallway lighting, and smoke alarms. The hallways and stairs were filled with garbage and refuse, and apartments were infested with rodents and insects. This neglect resulted in frequent robberies of the tenants and the use of vacant apartments by drug addicts and drug sellers.*

The plaintiffs claimed that BHA had breached the Annual Contributions Contract (ACC) into which it had entered with HUD. The ACC is an agreement between HUD and the local public housing authority by which HUD disburses federal funds on the condition that the local housing authority comply with the requirements of the federal Housing Act and with HUD's regulations. The ACC at issue in this case required the BHA to maintain Father Panik Village in proper condition. The plaintiffs asserted that, as third-party beneficiaries of the ACC, they could enforce its terms and conditions.

Chief Judge DALY

The first question the Court must resolve is what law governs the third-party beneficiary claim. State law usually controls the interpretation and enforcement of contractual obligations between private parties. However, federal common law applies when an overriding federal interest is implicated, for example, when substantial rights and duties of the United States are at stake in the litigation. Because the resolution of the issue of plaintiffs' status as a third-party beneficiary requires a uniform rule, because the outcome of this action could directly affect significant obligations of the United States, and because the Secretary of HUD is a party to the action, federal common law must govern the issue.

Federal common law provides that a third party has enforceable rights under a contract that was intended to benefit directly that third party. The analysis of whether plaintiffs are intended beneficiaries or merely incidental beneficiaries with no cognizable rights under the ACC turns on a consideration of the intentions of the parties to the agreement, which is evinced in part in the language and legislative history of the statute pursuant to which the ACC was executed. * * *

The ACC, which is entered into pursuant to the Housing Act, does exhibit an intention to benefit the tenants directly. The provisions of the ACC make clear that it was executed primarily for the purpose of benefiting the tenants. The ACC requires that defendant BHA * * * provide decent, safe, and sanitary housing. Moreover, the language of the Housing Act and its legislative history demonstrate the Congress intended that the regulatory contracts entered into pursuant to the Act were designed to benefit the tenants as a mechanism for ensuring they receive decent and safe housing. Indeed, it is difficult to imagine any purpose for the Contract other than to benefit the tenants of public housing.

The court found that the Concerned Tenants had enforceable rights as third-party beneficiaries and could require the ACC to obtain decent and safe housing.

DECISION AND REMEDY

Discharge

A contract is usually discharged because it has been fully performed, but contracts can also be discharged in other ways.

Discharge by Agreement   If the contract has not been fully performed, the parties may agree to discharge the contract. An understanding of the enforceability of agreements that settle claims or discharge debts is important in the business world. The following agreements are the most frequent transactions: (1) accord and satisfaction, (2) covenant (agreement) not to sue, and (3) novation. See Exhibit 10–3.

Accord and Satisfaction   The concept of **accord and satisfaction** involves a debtor's offer to settle a debt he or she owes by a performance different from that originally agreed on and a creditor's acceptance of the offer. An accord is an agreement where the parties decide to modify their contract or to settle a disputed debt. Satisfaction takes place when the accord has been executed—that is, when the agreed performance has been completed. At that point, the accord and satisfaction are concluded and the debtor's obligation is discharged.

Covenant Not to Sue   A **covenant not to sue** is a contract between the two parties agreeing that one person will give up his or her right to sue, usually in return for a settlement. For example, Brian is involved in an automobile accident because of Kay's negligence. Kay offers Brian $500 if he will release her from any further liability resulting from the accident. Brian believes that the damages to his car will not exceed $400 and agrees to the release by signing a covenant not to sue. Later Brian discovers that the damage to his car is $600. Can Brian collect the balance of $100? The answer is no; Brian is limited to the $500 by the covenant not to sue. He no longer has the right to file a negligence lawsuit.

Exhibit 10–3 **Discharge of a Contract by Agreement**

1. *Accord and satisfaction*—The agreement by one party to a contract to give or perform, and the other party to accept, something different from that which is purportedly owed, in satisfaction of a contractual claim; the agreement is the accord, and the execution of the agreement is the satisfaction.

2. *Covenant not to sue*—An agreement not to sue on a present, valid claim.

3. *Novation*—A valid contract that substitutes a new party for one of the original parties, thereby discharging the original contract.

Novation   A **novation** is a contract entered into by the parties whereby one party is substituted for another party; that is, one party is completely discharged from the contract, and another is substituted. The discharged party is no longer liable under the original contract.

Discharge by Operation of Law   A contract may also be discharged by operation of law. If the terms of the contract have been altered by one party without the knowledge of the other party, the contract may be discharged because there was no meeting of the minds on the part of the contract that has been changed. If a contract has been breached, the harmed party must file his or her lawsuit during the time period set out in a statute of limitations. If the time period during which the harmed party could have sued has passed, the contract is discharged. If one of the parties goes into bankruptcy and receives a discharge from the court, the contract is ended. If he or she dies or becomes mentally incompetent, and if that person's performance is essential to completion of the contract, then the contract ends. If the specific subject matter of the contract is destroyed, the contract is also discharged under these circumstances.

Remedies and Damages

Breach of contract is the failure to perform what a party to a contract is under an absolute duty to perform—in other words, to do what he or she promised to do. Once a party fails to perform or performs inadequately, the other party (the nonbreaching party) can choose one or more of several remedies. A **remedy,** in contract law, is the relief provided for an innocent party when the other party has breached the contract. A remedy enforces a right or gives redress to an injury. Strictly speaking, the remedy is not a part of a lawsuit; it is the end result of the lawsuit.

The most common remedies available to a nonbreaching party are the equitable remedies of rescission and restitution, specific performance of the contract, and reformation of the contract, and the legal remedy of money damages.

Equitable Remedies   **Rescission** of the contract means that the parties are restored to their original positions before the contract was made. Rescission is available when fraud, a mistake, duress, or failure of consideration occurs. If the contract is rescinded, each party must return any money or items that he or she received from the other party under the contract. Giving back the items is called **restitution.** Restitution prevents unjust enrichment.

Specific performance of a contract is not allowed very often. If money damages would be an inadequate remedy and a contract involves land or a piece of unique personal property, the court may grant the equitable remedy of specific performance by ordering each party to perform the specific promises in the contract. Specific performance can be ordered for contracts relating to unique goods and real estate but not for those relating to personal services.

Reformation of the contract occurs when the contract needs to be rewritten (reformed) because of errors in the written document. The court orders the contract to be reformed in accordance with the true intentions of the parties.

Legal Remedies   Nonbreaching parties most often seek the legal remedy of money damages. The three most common damages sought in a contract case are **compensatory damages, consequential damages,** and **liquidated damages.**

Exhibit 10–4 **Remedies for Breach of Contract**

LEGAL REMEDY	
Damages	A legal remedy designed to compensate the nonbreaching party for the loss of the bargain. By awarding money damages, the court tries to place the parties in the position they would have occupied had the contract been fully performed. The nonbreaching party frequently has a duty to *mitigate* (lessen or reduce) the damages incurred as a result of the contract's breach. There are two broad categories of damages: 1. *Compensatory Damages*—Compensate the nonbreaching party for injuries actually sustained and proved to have arisen directly from the loss of the bargain, which resulted from the breach of contract. 2. *Consequential Damages*—Damages resulting from special circumstances beyond the contract itself; they flow only from the consequences of a breach. For a party to recover consequential damages, the damages must be the foreseeable result of a breach of contract, and the breaching party must have known at the time the contract was formed that special circumstances existed and that the nonbreaching party would incur additional loss upon breach of the contract. Also called *special* damages. 3. *Liquidated Damages*—Compensate nonbreaching party by setting out amount of damages in the contract.
EQUITABLE REMEDIES	
Rescission and Restitution	1. *Rescission*—An action to cancel the contract and return the parties to the positions they occupied prior to the transaction. Available when fraud, a mistake, duress, or failure of consideration is present. 2. *Restitution*—When a contract is rescinded, both parties must make restitution to each other by returning goods, property, or money previously conveyed. Restitution prevents the unjust enrichment of the defendant.
Specific Performance	An equitable remedy calling for the performance of the act promised in the contract. Only available in special situations—such as contracts for the sale of unique goods or land, and where monetary damages would be an inadequate remedy. Specific performance is not available as a remedy in breached contracts for personal services.
Reformation	An equitable remedy allowing a contract to be "reformed" or rewritten to reflect the parties' true intentions. Available when an agreement is imperfectly expressed in writing.

Compensatory Damages Compensatory damages make up for the money lost by the injured party because the other party has breached the contract. The damages place the party, as nearly as possible, where he or she would have been if the contract had been performed.

Consequential Damages Consequential damages, on the other hand, are foreseeable damages that result when a party breaches the contract. The damages arise, not directly out of the contract, but as a consequence of it.

For example, TV Systems Manufacturer contracts to sell for $40,000 four wide-screen television sets with full Dolby sound to Stereo Systems. The delivery date is December 1. Stereo Systems plans immediately to resell the television sets and to make a profit of $15,000. TV Systems Man-

Ethical Considerations

Unfair Dealing Equals Unconscionability

The concept underlying unconscionability is that the law should not consist of inflexible rules if those rules allow one person to take great unfair advantage of another. The term *unconscionable* has purposely not been specifically defined. The drafters of the UCC wanted the concept to apply whenever there was overreaching by one party against another. The section in the UCC makes it possible for the courts to police contracts by giving the courts the statutory authority to conclude as a matter of law that certain actions by one party are unconscionable.

Should the court have examined the contract between Mrs. Finn and the Norwegian Old Peoples' Home Society more closely? How much money did Finn pay for the life care? Should there have been provisions for periodic payments to the Home Society instead of turning over her total assets at one time? Since Mrs. Finn paid for her lifetime care up front, should the Home Society have included a provision to reimburse her estate for the amount not actually used for her care?

Can you think of specific circumstances when the court should find that conduct by a business is unconscionable?

---

ufacturer is aware of Stereo Systems' resell plans. On November 25, TV calls up Stereo Systems to say that the television sets will not be delivered and that the contract has been canceled. Stereo Systems purchases from another manufacturer equivalent televisions for $50,000. Stereo Systems can sue TV for compensatory damages in the amount of $10,000—the difference between the open market price, $50,000, and the contract price, $40,000 (plus any costs incurred because of the breach). In addition, Stereo Systems is entitled to any foreseeable loss it can prove, which in this illustration would be lost profits.

Liquidated Damages   The parties in a contract may provide for the amount of damages in the event that one party breaches the contract. These clauses are called liquidated damage provisions.

They are very common, for example, in the construction industry. The contractor will promise to complete a building on a specified date. In the event he or she fails, the contractor will owe the owner a certain sum for every day that he or she is late.

These provisions will be upheld if they meet two requirements: First, the amount of liquidated damages must be difficult to assess at the time the contract is signed. Second, the damages specified in the contract must bear some reasonable relationship to the actual damages incurred. A contract will be declared null and void if it does not satisfy both requirements. The amount of damages contained in the liquidated damages clause cannot be punitive in nature.

Exhibit 10–4 summarizes the remedies available for a breach of contract.

International Considerations

Selling Goods Internationally

As discussed in Chapter 9, the Convention on Contracts for the International Sale of Goods (CISG) is a comprehensive document covering all aspects of the sales of goods. Articles in the CISG cover the delivery of the goods and the handing over of the shipping documents or warehouse receipts so the seller can take possession of the goods.

The seller must deliver goods that are of the quantity, quality, and description required by the contract. The seller is liable when the goods fail to conform. The buyer must inspect the goods promptly after receipt and must give notice of any problems with conformity within a reasonable period of time. The buyer loses the right to rely on the lack of conformity if he or she does not give the seller notice within two years after the goods were "actually handed over to the buyer."

The remedies under the CISG are money damages, avoidance of the contract, and specific performance. This last remedy is rarely allowed in contracts for the sale of goods under American law unless the good is unique, such as the Hope diamond.

Contractual Capacity

There are several ways in which a businessperson may become involved with parties who lack contractual capacity (such as minors or those judged to be mentally incompetent). For example, a minor might earn millions of dollars on a successful recording and need to invest this money. Another example is a person who has had a successful business career but now has Alzheimer's disease and is unable to manage his or her affairs.

In all states, procedures exist to appoint a person to manage these assets. This person is called either a guardian or conservator. In many states, the appointed guardian arranges for the personal care of the incompetent person, while a conservator is appointed to manage the assets of the protected party. The same person may serve in both roles, or two different people may be appointed. Before appointment, the conservator must post a bond with the court in the amount of the total assets that will be managed. If no bond is posted, all assets must be held in restricted, fully insured bank accounts. No funds can be removed from these restricted accounts except by specific court order. In the states that have not established the concept of a conservator, the appointed person is called a guardian and handles both the personal care and the finances of the protected person.

You, as a businessperson, can contract with individuals who are under a legal restraint through their guardian or conservator, but care should be exercised. If you know or should have known that the guardian was embezzling monies and using the funds for his or her own personal benefit, you will be required to pay back anything that you have obtained. But you need not be hesitant to deal with the court-appointed official. Verify that the person has authority to enter into a contract on behalf of the protected party and do not participate in any wrongdoing.

Summary

In this chapter and the last, we have covered all of the requirements for a contract. This chapter described the last two elements, legal capacity and legality, needed for a binding contract.

Parties to a contract must have the capacity to contract. Minors and most mentally incompetent people can enter into contracts, but these contracts are voidable at their option. A minor is liable for necessary items but only to the extent of the reasonable value of the property or services actually used. When disaffirmance occurs, a minor must return any items obtained under the contract. Only if a court has determined a person to be mentally incompetent, are the contracts made afterwards void.

A valid contract must have a legal object or subject matter. The general rule is that an illegal agreement is void. In addition, the law requires certain contracts to be in writing to be enforceable.

Contractual rights and duties can be transferred to a third person through assignment of the rights or delegation of the duties. Third parties may be given benefits under a contract. These beneficiaries are called either incidental or intended beneficiaries.

Contracts can be discharged by acts or agreement of the parties, such as full performance, accord and satisfaction, covenant not to sue, or novation. Contracts may be ended by operation of the law, such as unilateral alteration of a written contract; passing of the period set out in a statute of limitations; discharge in bankruptcy; or objective impossibility of performance because of death or insanity of a party or because of the destruction of the specific subject matter of the contract.

Whenever a party breaches her or his contractual commitments, she or he is liable for the damages caused. The injured party may recover the legal remedy of money damages or the equitable remedies of rescission and restitution, specific performance, or reformation.

Key Terms

accord and satisfaction (245)
age of majority (234)
assignee (242)
assignment (242)
assignor (242)
breach of contract (246)
collateral contracts (239)
compensatory damages (246)
consequential damages (246)
covenant not to sue (245)

creditor beneficiary (244)
delegation (242)
disaffirm (234)
donee beneficiary (244)
incidental beneficiary (244)
intended beneficiary (244)
liquidated damages (246)
mortgage (242)
novation (246)
parol evidence rule (241)

ratification (234)
reformation (246)
remedy (246)
rescission (246)
restitution (246)
specific performance (246)
statute of frauds (239)
usury (237)
unconscionable contracts (238)

Questions and Case Problems

1. As an employee of a major corporation, you are required to sign a contract as a condition of your employment. The contract contains certain restrictions. It states that you cannot compete directly or indirectly with the employer for a period of one year after your termination. Are these provisions legal? Why or why not? Does this type of covenant constitute duress?

2. Ahern, plaintiff, called Knecht, defendant, to repair her central air-conditioning unit. On April 19, a new blower assembly and motor were installed, and on May 30, more service was rendered. On June 23, the unit was not cooling, and Knecht was called again. He repeated the same work previously performed but failed to fix the cooling problem. He charged $762. The next day Ahern called another repair shop, and the unit was fixed for $72. Ahern sued Knecht, alleging that his charges were outrageously exorbitant and unconscionable. Who should prevail and why? [Ahern v. Knecht, 563 N.E.2d 787 (Ill.App. 2 Dist. 1990)]

3. Leydet entered into a written contract with the city of Mountain Home for delivery of treated wastewater over a twenty-year period to irrigate his farmland. Delivery started in 1982, and Leydet paid. The city was never capable of delivering the amount set out in the contract, and Leydet was never able to use more than what the city delivered from 1982 to 1987. A drought for two years prevented the city from delivering the amount of water previously delivered. Leydet sued seeking damages. The city defended that the drought excused the city from fully performing on the contract. Any other steps taken would have been prohibitively expensive, thus performing was impracticable and nonperformance was excused. Who should prevail and why? [Leydet v. City of Mountain Home, 812 P.2d 755 (Idaho App. 1991)]

4. Six Industries, Inc., is a general contractor for the construction of an insurance building. Six Industries entered into a subcontract with Kirk Williams Company for heating and air-conditioning the building. As a standard practice on projects of this size, the contract between the parties was changed by formal written change orders on several occasions. Near completion of the building, Six Industries submitted two last change orders. Kirk Williams refused to sign or complete the change orders because it claimed that Six Industries had delayed the project to the detriment of Kirk Williams. Six Industries issued a check to Kirk Williams for $14,850.04. On the check, the following language appeared: "Endorsement and/or negotiation of the check constitutes a full and complete release of Six Industries, Inc., and acknowledges full payment of all monies due." Kirk Williams received the check in the normal course of business and deposited it. Is there an accord and satisfaction through the cashing of the check?

Explain. [Kirk Williams Co. v. Six Industries, Inc., 11 Ohio. App. 3d 152, 463 N.E. 2d 1266 (1983)]

5. In 1982, Webster Street Partnership, Ltd. (Webster) entered into a lease agreement with Matthew Sheridan and Pat Wilwerding. Webster was aware that both Sheridan and Wilwerding were minors. Both tenants were living away from home, apparently with the understanding that they could return home at any time. Sheridan and Wilwerding paid the first month's rent, but then failed to pay the rent for the next month and vacated the apartment. Webster sued them for breach of contract. They claimed that the lease agreement was voidable since they were minors. Who will win, and why? [Webster Street Partnership, Ltd. v. Sheridan, 220 Neb. 9, 368 N.W. 2d 439 (1985)]

6. Vrgora, a general contractor, entered into a contract with the Los Angeles Unified School District (LAUSD) to construct an automotive service shed and a specifically enclosed room outfitted with an electronic vehicle performance tester. The contract called for damages of $100 per day if the project was not completed within 250 days. Vrgora was responsible for purchasing and installing the tester. A dispute between the manufacturer of the tester and Vrgora arose. The tester was finally delivered over six months later. As a result, Vrgora completed the project several months late. LAUSD now wants Vrgora to pay $20,700 in damages for failing to complete the contract within 250 days. Who should win and why? [Vrgora v. Los Angeles Unified School District, 152 Cal. App. 3d 1178, 200 Cal. Rptr. 130 (1984)]

7. Alchem, an Israeli corporation, manufactures and sells lightweight, small-sized, halogenated aerosol fire extinguishers. Alchem entered into a contract with Gerard that made Gerard its exclusive distributor outside of Israel. A condition in the contract required the approval of the Underwriters Laboratories (UL). A UL approval in the United States is an indication of safety, quality control, and reliability, and is required by almost all purchasers. Approval by the UL is essential if the product is to be marketed in the United States, but it means very little, if anything, outside the United States. UL approval takes a long time, ranging from a minimum of three years to a maximum of fifteen years. After seven years, Alchem still had not obtained UL approval. Naturally, Gerard did not sell any extinguishers in the United States. Alchem, however, did sell some fire extinguishers in territories to which it had given exclusive dealership to Gerard. Alchem and Gerard ended up in a lawsuit. Alchem argued that Gerard could have sold the product outside the United States and, by not doing so, it had acted in bad faith. Gerard argued that it did not have a duty to sell any products prior to UL approval. Which company is correct? Was there a mutual mistake? Please explain your answer. [Gerard v. Almouli, 746 F. 2d 936 (2d Cir. 1984)]

Chapter 11   Sales Law and Product Liability

To things of sale, a seller's praise belongs.

Shakespeare
Love's Labour's Lost, 1595

OUTLINE

Introduction

In the last two chapters, we examined contract law, along with a few basic provisions for the sale of goods. In this chapter, we will be looking at many provisions of the Uniform Commercial Code (UCC or Code), Article 2, Sale of Goods. This article governs the sale of goods, while the sale of services and real estate law are governed by other statutory provisions and common law. When examining a contract, you must determine if the subject matter of the contract is goods, services, or real estate. Once you determine the subject matter of the contract, you then know which set of statutes to read or whether you must look to the common law.

Why study the special area of the law governing the sale of goods? Our entire economic system is based upon the sale of goods, services, and real estate. As you read the text and the cases, notice that Article 2 provisions tend to protect the interests of the buyer over those of the seller. The laws covering the sale of services or the sale of real estate, on the other hand, follow common law, which tends to favor the seller.

Leasing goods instead of purchasing them has become very popular in recent years. No specific law is available to handle problems that arise out of leasing contracts. Obviously, a lease is not a sale, but the courts have had to apply the analogy of the UCC sale of goods provisions to leasing situations. For example, the problems arising out of leasing an automobile are similar to those involved with the purchase of an automobile. The UCC has a draft called Article 2A that provides legal guidance in the lease of goods. The draft is currently available to the states for their consideration and possible adoption. It basically treats the long-term lease of goods in the same manner as a sale.

This chapter will examine specific contract and warranty sections of Article 2. We will study the meaning of various terms under the UCC. We will then look at the legal theories of product liability.

Theory of the Uniform Commercial Code

The UCC gives guidance to parties who are in a contract for the sale and purchase of goods. The drafters of the UCC wanted it to be a practical guideline for businesspeople to use. The Code is flexible enough to provide for expansion of commercial practices under the interpretation of the courts, while the statutory aspects provide a framework of stability.

The UCC respects the principle of the freedom of contract. The parties to the contract may make whatever arrangements suit them. The obligations of good faith, diligence, and reasonableness are the standards set by the UCC for the courts to use when asked to review a contract. Many UCC sections include the words "unless otherwise agreed." This means the parties may set the terms.

If the parties fail to place in the contract certain terms, the UCC encourages application of the rules of a particular trade to fill in the missing term or to give guidance to a court in interpreting a clause. This principle is called **usage of trade** [UCC 1-205]. A baker's dozen, for example, means thirteen items, not twelve. A contract for the sale of a baker's dozen jelly-filled rolls would mean that thirteen rolls should be in the box sold.

The UCC also defers to the parties' previous **course of dealing.** In other words, the previous conduct between the parties establishes a basis for understanding and interpreting their expressions in the contract and their other conduct [UCC 1-205]. Here again, the UCC honors the principle of freedom of contract.

If the parties fail to include a term in the contract and no trade usage rules exist, the parties may turn to the UCC to provide guidance for filling in the missing term. In Chapter 9, for example, you learned that if the contract fails to provide for the place of delivery, the UCC states that the place of delivery is the seller's place of business or, if the seller does not have a place of business, the seller's home.

Often the sheer number of UCC rules may seem overwhelming, but most are based on common sense. When you purchase a new automobile, for example, you pick it up at the car dealership (seller's place of business). Yet if you were to purchase a used automobile from a private party, you would go to the seller's home to take delivery of the automobile (if the seller does not have a business, the place of delivery is the seller's home) [UCC 2-308]. Under the UCC, you are also free to agree that the automobile will be delivered at a place other than the seller's place of business or home.

A **merchant** is a person who deals in goods and holds himself or herself out as having knowledge or skill peculiar to the practices or goods involved in the contract. A contract "between merchants" means that both parties to the contract are chargeable with the knowledge or skill of merchants [UCC 2-104]. Merchants are subject to special rules under the UCC. All of these sections will not be included in this chapter, but you should be aware that under certain circumstances special rules do exist for merchants.

Goods

Under the UCC 2-105, **goods** are defined as all things that are movable at the time they are identified to this specific contract. Goods also include growing crops and the unborn young of animals, plus any other item that may be severed from real estate by the seller. Money, negotiable instruments, and investment securities, are not classified as goods.

Identification

Goods must exist and be identified to the contract. The terms *existing* and *identification* have separate meanings under the UCC. Existing means just that: The goods have been manufactured and are now in a tangible form. **Identified goods** are existing goods that have been identified to this contract. Often in a store, an appliance will have a sign saying, for example, "SOLD to Mr. & Mrs. J. B. Flick." This existing good, the appliance, has now been identified to a particular contract. Identification can be made in any manner to which the parties explicitly agree.

For parties who fail to place in their contract the manner in which the identification will occur, the UCC has provided guidelines [UCC 2-501]. If the goods are existing, they are automatically identified to the contract at the time the contract was made. If you purchase a coat in a store, the coat is existing and was identified to the contract at the time you made the purchase.

A contract may be made for the sale of goods that do not yet exist. This agreement is called a **contract for future goods.** After these goods are manufactured, they are identified to the contract when they are shipped, marked, or otherwise designated by the seller as the goods belonging to this particular contract.

May the seller substitute other goods if the seller has already identified particular goods to the contract? The UCC does allow the seller to substitute other goods until he or she notifies the buyer that the identification is final.

The seller retains the risk of loss until he or she has completed all duties with respect to the goods under the contract. (We will look at the risk of loss in more detail later in this chapter.) As long as the seller has a risk of loss, he or she has the right to obtain insurance to protect himself or herself against such a risk. Likewise, the buyer has an insurable risk in the goods once they are existing and identified to the contract. The reason for the UCC rules concerning the manner of identifying the goods is to determine who has an insurable interest in the goods.

Title

Three concerns arise around the issue of the title to goods. The first is **warranty of title**—that is, whether the seller's statement concerning his or her title is a true statement. (Warranties in general will be discussed in detail later in this chapter.) The second issue concerns when the title passes from the seller to the buyer. The third problem involves voidable titles—that is, when is the title subject to legal challenge?

Warranty of Title

The UCC requires sellers to **warrant** that they have good title to the goods they are selling [UCC 2-312]. The seller must tell the truth as to the type of title he or she has. Perhaps the seller has only a half interest in the goods, and the other half interest is owned by someone else. Thus, the seller can only sell his or her half interest. The seller must also fully disclose any **liens** that are held against the goods, unless this disclosure is exempt by law. We will be discussing liens in the next chapter. For now, liens are placed against the seller's title by a creditor who has lent the seller money and wants to make sure that the loan is repaid. By placing a lien on the goods, the creditor must be notified of the pending sale and is thus able to protect his or her interest.

The following case involves a warranty of title in the sale of an automobile.

Case 11.1
BOYER v. TRINITY
UNIVERSAL
INSURANCE CO.
Court of Appeal of Louisiana,
1990.
564 So.2d 384 (La.App. 3 Cir.).

BACKGROUND AND FACTS   *Edward J. Cop purchased a 1982 BMW from Sunbelt Auto Imports, Inc. He received a Louisiana certificate of title. Cop sold the BMW to Wade B. Randolph, who likewise obtained a Louisiana title. Randolph sold the BMW to James Boyer, who also secured a Louisiana title. Approximately two years later, the vehicle was repossessed by Reimer-Oberst, a German BMW dealership. Reimer-Oberst claimed that they were never paid for the BMW and had never released the original title.*

Boyer reported this situation to his insurance company, Trinity Universal Insurance Company. He filed a claim to be reimbursed the cost of the BMW. Failing to reach a negotiated settlement, Boyer sued Trinity, and Trinity in turn sued Randolph. The trial court granted a judgment in favor of Boyer against Trinity. It dismissed the action by Trinity against Randolph. Trinity appealed.

Judge KNOLL

*   *   *   *

We first look at the legal relationship between Boyer and his immediate predecessor in title, Randolph. A seller is bound to two principal obligations, that of delivering and that of warranting the thing which he sells. The warranty respecting the seller has two objects: the buyer's peaceable possession of the thing sold, and the second is the hidden defects of the thing sold, or its redhibitory vices.

The peaceable possession of a buyer is disturbed when he is evicted from the totality or a part of the thing purchased, due to the right or claims of a third person. Moreover, Civil Code Article 2501 defines the buyer's warranty against eviction:

"Although at the time of the sale no stipulations have been made respecting the warranty, the seller is obliged, of course, to warrant the buyer against the eviction suffered by him from the totality or part of the thing sold, and against the charges claimed on such thing, which were not declared at the time of the sale."

Louisiana law is clear that an evicted buyer is entitled to the restitution of the purchase price from the seller.

*   *   *   *

We now turn our attention to Trinity's indemnity claim against Randolph. In *Bewley Furniture Co., Inc. v. Maryland Casualty Co.*, the Louisiana Supreme Court characterized indemnification as follows:

"It has long been held in Louisiana that a party not actually at fault, whose liability results from the faults of others, may recover by way of indemnity from such others. The cases have referred to this imposed liability variously as technical, constructive, vicarious and derivative.

*   *   *   *

The rule of indemnity . . . is founded upon the general obligation to repair the damage caused by one's fault and the moral maxim that 'no one ought to enrich himself at the expense of another.' "

Applying this jurisprudence to the case *sub judice*, we find that Trinity, who was found vicariously liable to Boyer under its contract of insurance, sought indemnification from Randolph on the basis that the cause of Boyer's eviction was Randolph's defective title to the BMW. Under this analysis, it is clear that Randolph was the real party at fault, and ultimately should bear the burden for Boyer's loss. Therefore, we find that the trial court clearly erred when it failed to grant Trinity's third-party demand for indemnification against Randolph.

The court found that the insurance company was liable to Boyer, who lost his vehicle. The court allowed the insurance company to recover from Randolph, who had sold the BMW to Boyer, for breach of warranty of title.

DECISION AND REMEDY

Passing of Title

Passing of title from the seller to the buyer and passing the risk of loss for the goods from the seller to the buyer are not the same thing. Different rules apply as to when a buyer comes into title and when he or she assumes risk of loss. The UCC deals with these issues between the seller and buyer in terms of their performance under the contract.

The buyer and seller can always agree as to when the title is to pass from the seller to the buyer. Most of the time, the parties do not even consider who has the title when making a contract. In the absence of an agreement as to when the title passes, UCC 2-401 outlines several situations to be discussed in the following text. Title cannot change from the seller to the buyer prior to the goods being identified to a particular contract [UCC 2-401(1)].

Shipping Contracts When the goods are to be moved, title passes at the time the seller completes his or her duty with respect to the physical delivery of the goods. The moving of goods involves several types of shipping contracts: **free on board—point of shipment** (designated as **F.O.B.**), and **free on board—destination (F.O.B. destination)**. In an F.O.B. situation, if the contract requires the seller to ship ten computers to the buyer, the title passes to the buyer at the time and place that the seller physically delivers the goods to the shipper for the shipment. F.O.B. is the most common way to ship goods [UCC 2-401(2)(a)].

If the contract requires the ten computers to be shipped and delivered at the buyer's place of business, the title changes when the shipper **tenders** delivery of the computers at the buyer's location. This is an example of an F.O.B. destination contract. The act of the shipper notifying the buyer that the goods are ready to be delivered is called the tender of the goods. Think of the word tender as meaning "to offer." The shipper is tendering (offering) the goods for delivery to the buyer at the

buyer's location [UCC 2-401(2)(b)]. Exhibit 11-1 summarizes the terms of these agreements.

Documents of Title Let's assume the goods do not need to be shipped. Two scenarios may occur. First, the title will change when the seller gives the buyer a **document of title** [UCC 2-401(3)(a)]. The two most common documents of title are **bill of lading** and **warehouse receipts**. The buyer, for example, knows the videotapes she has purchased are in a warehouse ten miles away. The seller gives her a warehouse receipt. She is able to drive to the warehouse, present the warehouse receipt, and the videotapes will be turned over to her. Title passed to her when the seller delivered the warehouse receipt to her. See Exhibit 11-2.

But what happens if there are no documents of title controlling the goods that are held by a third party? In this second scenario, title passes at the time and place of contracting once the goods are identified to the contract [UCC 2-401(3)(b)]. In the situation just described, suppose the seller does not have a document of title controlling the videotapes. The seller calls down to the warehouse, gives the attendant the buyer's description, and authorizes the warehouse to release the videotapes to her. Here, title passed at the time the buyer contracted with the seller to purchase the videotapes.

If the buyer rejects the goods or otherwise refuses to perform and if the title has passed to the buyer, the title now reverts back to the seller. This revestment occurs by operation of law and is not considered a sale [UCC 2-401(4)].

Voidable Title

The original seller can reclaim the goods from the buyer if the buyer committed illegal acts. Although the seller can reclaim the goods from the original buyer, what happens if the buyer sells the goods to an unsuspecting third party? In certain situations, the buyer may transfer good title to a

Exhibit 11–1 **Types of Transportation Contracts**

I. Point-of-shipment contract:
  A. Seller has duty to:
    1. Contract with a transportation company
    2. Deliver the goods to the transportation company.
  B. Buyer has duty to pay shipping costs.
  C. Terms:
    1. Free on board (F.O.B.) [UCC 2-319(1)(a)]. Used in ground or air transportation.
    2. Free alongside (F.A.S.) [UCC 2-319(2)]. Used in marine transportation.
    3. F.O.B. vessel, car, or other vehicle [UCC 2-319(1)(c)]. The seller, at his own expense and risk, must load the goods on board. After loading, the goods are treated as F.O.B.
  D. Most contracts are point-of-shipment contracts.
II. Destination contract:
  A. Seller has duty to:
    1. Contract with a transportation company
    2. Deliver the goods to the transportation company
    3. Pay for shipment to destination
    4. Retain the risk of loss and the right to insure.
  B. Terms
    1. Free on board, destination (F.O.B. destination) [UCC 2-319(1)(b)].
    2. Cost, insurance, and freight (C.I.F.) [UCC 2-320(1)].
    3. Cost and freight (C. & F.) [UCC 3-320(1)].
    4. Ex-ship [UCC 2-322].
    5. No arrival, no sale [UCC 2-324].

---

new buyer in the ordinary course of business if the new buyer does not have knowledge of the illegal conduct of the original buyer.

For example, assume that an original buyer pays for a lamp with a check that eventually is dishonored by the bank because of insufficient funds. The lamp is in the possession of the buyer. If the buyer sells the lamp to an innocent purchaser who has no knowledge of the bad check, the new buyer will obtain valid title to the lamp.

Title can be transferred when the seller is mistaken as to the identity of the buyer and turns over possession of the goods to an impostor. An order to purchase a dining-room set is received from Judy Pivon, who is well known and has excellent credit. You turn over the dining-room set to an impostor, thinking she is Judy Pivon. The impostor sells the dining-room set to a third party who knows nothing about this fraudulent transaction. The new purchaser will have good title. The only thing the original seller may do is to locate the impostor and bring a civil legal action against her. The seller may also file a criminal complaint against the impostor with the local prosecuting attorney's office.

The seller, instead of the original buyer, can at times be the one at fault. If a person leaves goods with a business that sells similar merchandise, the UCC allows the business to transfer good title. For example, you take your lawn mower in to be repaired. The repair shop also sells new and used lawn mowers. Accidentally, your lawn mower is sold to a person who has no knowledge that you own it. That purchaser has good title to your lawn mower. You can, however, bring a civil action against the repair shop.

The reasoning behind these rules is simple. When both parties are innocent, the person who could have controlled the loss must incur the loss. Review the examples just cited, and note that this underlying principle applies to each of them [UCC 2-403].

Risk of Loss

At one time the question as to who had title was of prime importance in determining who incurred the risk of loss. The old rule was that whoever had title was also responsible for the goods in the

Exhibit 11–2 **Documents of Title**

I. Documents of title are covered by UCC 1-201(15) and Article 7, Warehouse Receipts, Bills of Lading, and Other Documents of Title.

    A. *Document of title* is a paper representing ownership in the goods. The paper or document represents that the person in possession or named in the document has the right to receive, hold, and dispose of the goods listed on the document of title.

    B. The document of title may be *negotiable* or *nonnegotiable*. (Negotiability is discussed in Chapter 12.)

II. *Warehouse receipt:*

    A. Goods are in a warehouse [UCC 1-201(45) and 7-201 through 7-210].

III. *Bill of lading:*

    A. Goods are in transportation [UCC 1-201(6) and 7-302 through 7-309].

    B. Bill of lading: used in marine or rail transportation.

    C. Air bill, air consignment note, or airway bill: used in air transportation.

IV. *Miscellaneous terms:*

    A. *Bill of sale:* method of transferring ownership in goods.

    B. *Certificate of title:* method of transferring ownership in goods. Used in titles for motor vehicles.

    C. *Deed:* method of conveying ownership in real property.

---

event they were damaged. Today that rule is no longer valid.

A buyer and seller can always bargain over who has the risk of loss in the event the merchandise is damaged or destroyed. Normally, the parties will bargain over price, quality of goods, shipment terms, and credit terms. Seldom do they consider the consequences if the merchandise is damaged or lost. If risk of loss is not covered in the agreement, the Uniform Commercial Code will supply the rules as to who must stand the loss. These rules were drafted with the view that whoever would have insurance would assume the risk of loss. This underlying principle applies even in situations when the buyer or seller has breached his or her contractual obligations.

In the absence of breach of contract by either the buyer or seller and if the contract does not require the seller to deliver the goods to a particular place, the risk of loss passes to the buyer when the goods are delivered F.O.B. to the carrier. This is true even when the goods are shipped on the basis of **collect on delivery (C.O.D.).** If the seller is required to deliver the goods at a particular destination (F.O.B. destination), the risk of loss passes to the buyer when the goods are tendered, enabling the buyer to take delivery [UCC 2-319].

If the goods are held by a third person and there is a document of title, the risk of loss transfers to the buyer upon his or her receipt of the document of title. If there is no document of title,

risk of loss passes to the buyer when the third person is informed of the sale [UCC 2-509(2)].

In all other cases, if no breach of contract is involved and if the seller is a businessperson, the risk of loss is transferred to the buyer when the buyer takes possession of the goods. If the seller is not in business, the risk of loss is transferred to the buyer upon the tender of delivery [UCC 2–509(3)]. Let's say that you purchase a desk at a yard sale, but you are on your bicycle and have no way of getting the desk to your home. The seller, who is not a merchant, tells you that you can have immediate delivery of the desk. You ride home to get your automobile. While you are gone, a rainstorm occurs and lightning strikes your desk. In this situation, you have the risk of loss. If the seller had been a merchant, on the other hand, the seller would have retained the risk of loss.

What happens when either the buyer or seller breaches his or her contractual obligation? If the seller ships goods whose condition makes it possible for the buyer to reject them, the risk of loss remains with the seller [UCC 2-510(1)]. Many times a buyer will accept goods even though they are not what was ordered and then will revoke the acceptance. In that event, the buyer, to the extent of any deficiency in his or her insurance coverage, may treat the risk of loss as resting on the seller [UCC 2-510(2)].

The seller may look to the buyer when goods have been identified to the contract but the buyer

Legal Highlight

The Midas Touch

Advance technology makes possible the recovery of treasures from ships sunk centuries ago. Who has title to these riches? Is it the person who studies history, makes careful calculations, raises money for the project, risks his or her life to search underwater, and recovers the gold, silver, and artifacts? Or is it the original owner, or even the government? Consider the *Nuestra Señora de Atocha*, which sunk off the Marquesas Keys in 1622 while en route to Spain, heavily laden with $250 million in cargo (contemporary value). Or the SS *Central America*, carrying three tons of gold (worth $1 billion today), lost in 1857 during a hurricane off the South Carolina coast.

The law was not clearly established when these cases reached the courts. In the case of the Spanish galleon, the court ruled that the persons who recovered the treasure could treat the treasure as abandoned and thus had good title. The rule applied is called the "American rule." The court noted that, under the "English rule," the treasure would belong to the United States government.

In the case of the SS *Central America* 39 insurance companies claim ownership of the gold because they paid the claims of the original owners after the ship was lost. They contended that the gold was never abandoned and that salvage attempts were made over the years. Under salvage laws, the insurance companies showed that title was never divested. Factors beyond the control of the owners caused the ship to be destroyed and the cargo to be lost, but the gold was never abandoned. The insurance companies were able to share the gold with the salvagers.

At times the courts have protected the rights of the original owner while compensating the party who recovered the cargo. Called *salvage law*, these decisions are based on the principle of equity. The person taking the risk to recover the cargo is paid a reasonable amount (based on the difficulty and hazardousness of the salvage efforts), while the owner retains title and ownership.

---

repudiates the contract and the goods are later damaged. In such cases, the seller, to the extent of any deficiency in the seller's insurance coverage, may treat the risk of loss as the buyer's responsibility for a commercially reasonable length of time [UCC 2-510(3)].

There are other delivery terms that affect risk of loss. For example, **cost, insurance, and freight (C.I.F.)** means that part of the purchase price includes insurance. In this situation, the insurance company has the risk of loss once the goods are shipped. If the contract is **cost and freight (C. & F.)**, the rules of F.O.B. contracts, already stated, apply [UCC 2-320].

Sometimes it is not easy to ascertain which party has the risk of loss, as the following case illustrates.

Case 11.2
COMMONWEALTH PETROLEUM CO. v. PETROSOL INTERNATIONAL, INC.
United States Court of Appeals, Sixth Circuit, 1990.
901 F.2d 1314 (6th Cir.).

BACKGROUND AND FACTS *Petrosol was a wholesale marketer and distributor of petroleum products but did not have any storage facilities. Commonwealth Petroleum was also a marketer and distributor but did have storage facilities. Both companies acted as the middle person between gasline producers and gas distributors. Petrosol entered into a contract to purchase 10,000 barrels of propane from Cal Gas at $0.56 per gallon. On the same day Petrosol sold this propane to Commonwealth for $0.58 per gallon. This propane was stored at Lake Underground Storage facility in Painsville,*

Ohio. The propane was to be delivered in place, i.e., the goods were not to be moved, over a period between November 1982 and March 1983 and in quantities left to the discretion of Commonwealth.

A contract entitled "Sales Acknowledgment" was signed between Petrosol and Commonwealth on November 22, 1982. It stated in part that the delivery point was Painsville, Ohio, that storage was to be at no charge, and it specified when full payment was due. Besides the "to be delivered to" caption on the front of the form, the form included five boxes indicating different types of delivery methods (buyer's tank trucks or cars, seller's tank trucks or cars, or pipeline), none of which applied since the propane was in an underground facility and was not to be moved. The boxes on the form were left unchecked since the propane was to be an inventory transfer. Commonwealth, in its projection figures during this time period, treated the propane as inventory for future use.

The Sales Acknowledgment also made specific reference to the passage of title and of risk of loss. The standard language referred to the normal situation, in which the propane would be shipped. The title would pass to the buyer upon completion of the loading and delivery of the propane into the trucks, cars, or pipeline. The risk of loss would be transferred when the title passed.

In February 1983, a wall in the cavern of Lake Underground Storage collapsed and the propane was lost before Commonwealth was able to remove it. Commonwealth sued Petrosol for breach of contract. The trial court found for Petrosol on the basis that the risk of loss had passed to Commonwealth.

Circuit Judge JONES
*　*　*　*

Under Ohio law, the risk of loss would be on Commonwealth if the transactions were inventory transfers unless there was an agreement to the contrary by the parties. Ohio Rev. Code § 1302.53 (UCC 2-509) provides:

(B) Where the goods are held by a bailee to be delivered without being moved, the risk of loss passes to the buyer.

(1) on his receipt of a negotiable document of title covering the goods; or

(2) on acknowledgement by the bailee of the buyer's right to possession of the goods; or

(3) after his receipt of a non-negotiable document of title or other written direction to deliver. . . .

*　*　*　*

(D) The provisions of this section are subject to contrary agreement of the parties and to the provisions of sections 1302.40 and 1302.54 of the Revised Code.

The district court found that the parties intended the transactions to be inventory transfers based on several factors: (1) Tkachuk of Petrosol testified that he did not check any of the five boxes on the Sales Acknowledgement relating to methods of delivery because the transactions were inventory transfers, for which no box existed; (2) Williams of Commonwealth made no changes in the method of delivery in the Sale Acknowledgement, even though he had a practice of making changes in a written contract that did not conform to his understanding of the deal; (3) Commonwealth knew at the time of the contract the propane was in storage at Lake Underground, as it received the two confirmations of distribution stating that the product flow was from Cal Gas to Petrosol to Commonwealth; (4) Williams admitted that upon receipt of the confirmations, Commonwealth had the right to pick up the propane at any time—in fact, during the winter of 1982 and 1983, Commonwealth treated the propane as a reserve in its own projection figures because it was "counting on it to be part of its supply"; (5) as part of the transactions, Petrosol provided Commonwealth "free storage," evidence that the propane was in the hands of a bailee to be delivered without being moved; (6) Petrosol invoiced Commonwealth promptly after each contract was signed, and each invoice described the transaction as an "inventory transfer" and one was initialed by Commonwealth; and (7) Commonwealth entered into another transaction to purchase propane at Lake Underground, similar to the purchase from Petrosol, and treated it as "inventory."

Commonwealth argues that the district court's finding was improper for three reasons. First, it contends that the evidence of an intended inventory transfer is inadequate. It notes that the Sales Acknowledgement forms make no mention of an inventory transfer. Commonwealth also alleges that Williams' initialing of the invoices was not an admission that they were "inventory transfers" as mentioned on the form; instead, it was signed solely for the purpose of paying the invoices. Moreover, Commonwealth relies upon the testimony of Stan Smith, the President of Petrosol, who admitted that an inventory transfer would not have a delivery term providing for delivery over a period of months, as in the instant case. Second, Commonwealth argues that Petrosol previously established a different course of dealing between the parties. In a similar sale of propane in Bath, New York by Petrosol to Commonwealth in October 1982, Tkachuk checked the box "PTO Pipeline" in a transaction which both parties agreed was an inventory transfer. Tkachuk testified that he could use the "PTO Pipeline" box for inventory transfers. Commonwealth asserts that the absence of any checked box on either Sales Acknowledgement form in the instant case indicates that an inventory transfer was not intended. Third, Commonwealth contends that it could not have intended an inventory transfer because it did not have an inventory account at Lake Underground in October 1982.

Commonwealth's arguments do not provide us with sufficient basis for reversing the district court's finding. That Tkachuk checked the box in one case and not in another does not establish any course of dealing; it only proves that the five boxes on the form were not adequate, which is why Petrosol later changed its form so that the fifth box was "PTO Pipeline/Inventory Transfers." Additionally, the evidence indicates that Commonwealth did establish an account with Lake Underground, although ostensibly for another deal. The fact that Commonwealth did not have the transfer noted on its records at Lake Underground is not conclusive, for it might not have wanted such a transfer recorded during the time in which it received free storage. After hearing testimony from Tkachuk, Williams, and many other witnesses, the district court decided that the intent of the parties was for an inventory transfer, based upon its assessment of the evidence and the credibility of witnesses. This court will not disturb that finding.

DECISION AND REMEDY *The court found that this was not an F.O.B. contract. Thus, the risk of loss was upon the buyer, Commonwealth, once Lake Underground Storage had recognized the transfer from Petrosol to Commonwealth.*

Performance

Normally, the parties to a contract negotiate the terms of its performance. As we have seen, the UCC will supply many of the necessary terms if the parties neglect to cover certain areas. The UCC also assists both the seller and the buyer by giving

them certain rights when the contract is silent on a particular issue.

First, a buyer is given a right to inspect the goods before they are accepted or before there is payment. The buyer is allowed a chance to make certain that the goods conform to the contract. This right of inspection is not available when the goods are sent C.O.D. In such cases, the inspection can only occur after payment. The buyer then has a right to revoke his or her acceptance if the breach of contract substantially impairs the value of the goods [UCC 2-513].

Second, the UCC gives both parties the right of obtaining adequate assurance for future performance. Each party to a contract expects the other person to perform fully. At times, one party may feel insecure about the other person's ability to perform fully. As long as this concern is based on good faith and fair treatment of the other party, then the buyer or seller can request further assurances of full performance from the other. For example, you have ordered 100,000 computer chips from Johnson Industries. In a recent trade journal, an article implies that Johnson's quality control has not been fully effective and that many defective chips have resulted. You could insist that Johnson post a performance bond prior to your accepting future chips. Another example is when you have granted credit to a buyer of your product. Later you find out that your buyer is considering filing bankruptcy. At that point, you could decide to send future shipments C.O.D., or you could request payment before shipment [UCC 2-609].

If a buyer of goods has paid part or all of the purchase price and the seller declares bankruptcy, the buyer is given the right to obtain possession of the goods. The seller must file for bankruptcy within ten days after the buyer's payment. To obtain possession of the goods, the buyer is required to pay any outstanding balance [UCC 2-502].

At the time of contracting, the parties believe certain conditions exist that will allow the seller to perform fully on the contract. What happens when certain products cannot be delivered as promised by the seller because of factors beyond the seller's control? The UCC allows allocation of the goods by the seller to the buyer in any manner that is fair and reasonable. At the time of contracting, the event that now makes it impracticable to perform fully on the contract must not have been foreseeable [UCC 2-615].

In the following case, both parties at the time of contracting thought the tomato production would be higher than it actually turned out to be. Notice how the court handled this problem when the buyer brought an action for damages.

BACKGROUND AND FACTS *Riverbend processes and sells tomato paste; its processing plants are located in California and Arizona. Cliffstar ordered 3.2 million pounds of tomato paste from Riverbend. Delivery was to be spread out over the following year. Thereafter, Riverbend obtained total orders for 78 million pounds from all of its customers. A severe shortage of tomatoes developed because of poor weather conditions. Shortages also developed in other parts of the country. Riverbend was short 3.2 million pounds of paste needed to fulfill all its contracts. Riverbend chose to allocate its available supply among its customers. Cliffstar and Riverbend negotiated but failed to reach a settlement. Riverbend delivered less than 1 million pounds of tomato paste on the Cliffstar contract. Cliffstar sued and moved for a summary judgment.*

Case 11.3
CLIFFSTAR CORPORATION v. RIVERBEND PRODUCTS
United States District Court, 1990.
750 F.Supp. 81 (W.D.N.Y.).

District Judge CURTIN
* * * *

Under § 2-615, the first question is whether the 1988 tomato crop shortage was a contingency the non-occurrence of which was a basic assumption on which the contract was made. This question, in turn, hinges on whether the crop shortage was foreseeable at the time the contract was made. If a contingency is foreseeable, it and its consequences are taken outside the scope of U.C.C. § 2-615, because the party disadvantaged by fruition of the contingency might have protected himself in his contract. However, non-foreseeability is not an absolute requirement. * * * [P]ractically any occurrence can be foreseen but whether the foreseeability is sufficient to render unacceptable the defense of impossibility is one of degree.

*   *   *   *

Plaintiff's second argument is that Riverbend's failure to deliver the tomato paste was not caused by the 1988 crop shortfall but by oversale of its contracted-for supply. To successfully assert the affirmative defense of commercial impracticability, the party must show that the unforeseen event upon which excuse is predicated is due to factors beyond the party's control. Defendant may not have caused the event that prevents performance.

Plaintiff's third argument is that Riverbend has failed under § 2-615(b) to make a fair and reasonable allocation of the shortfall. Plaintiff admits that in making its allocation Riverbend considered such factors as customer loyalty, past performance, needs, the relationship between Riverbend and the customer, and Riverbend's projections of potential future sales to the customer. Plaintiff argues, however, that Riverbend did not treat it *equally*. Riverbend does not contest this. Riverbend argues instead that § 2-615 does not require equal allocation. *   *   *

The court finds that the question whether Riverbend's allocation to Cliffstar was fair and reasonable is one of fact to be decided by the jury.

Finally, plaintiff argues that Riverbend failed to seasonably notify it of its allocation amount. Riverbend sent a letter on September 27, 1988 informing Cliffstar they were being forced by the crop shortage to reevaluate all contracts. Riverbend did not, however, inform Cliffstar of its allocation quota at that time. This did not take place formally by letter until November 21, 1988.

Although plaintiff is correct that § 2-615(c) requires notification not only of the facts of delay or non-delivery but also, where allocation is contemplated, of the estimated quota that will be delivered to buyer, as a practical matter, a seller may not be able to provide this notice instantaneously.

*   *   *   *

In this case, Riverbend was not fully aware of the extent of the tomato crop shortage until mid-to-late September. A short time later, [Riverbend] informed Cliffstar that it would have difficulty filling the order completely. Thereafter, Riverbend was in regular contact with Cliffstar discussing the tomato paste contract. Although its final, formal notification of the amount Cliffstar would be allocated did not come until November 21, 1988, the court does not agree with plaintiff that, as a matter of law, this notice was unseasonable.

DECISION AND REMEDY   *The court held that triable issues of fact existed. The trial court will now have to determine (1) whether the tomato crop shortage was foreseeable at the time the contract was made, (2) whether the failure to perform was caused by the crop shortage, and (3) whether the allocation of the tomato paste by Riverbend was fair and reasonable.*

Remedies

What are your rights in the event the other party should breach his or her contractual obligations with you? The same basic rules apply here as for the breach of a contract, discussed in Chapter 10. We will see which specific rights the parties have when a breach occurs, but keep in mind that the rules are really not that different from those that apply to the breach of an ordinary contract.

Remedies of Buyers

Let's assume that you have ordered 100,000 bushels of wheat to be delivered in 60 days from Growers Market. The agreed price was the current market price on the day that you entered into your contract. The market price then increases substantially. Because of this, Growers notifies you that it will not send you the 100,000 bushels of wheat. What can you do?

Wheat is the type of product that is easily purchased on the open market. Thus, you can secure what is called **cover**. This means that you can obtain similar goods as required by the contract from other available sources. You may then recover from the original seller the difference between the contract and current market price, plus incidental or consequential damages [UCC 2-712].

The incidental damages would include such items as costs for transportation, reasonable charges, and expenses or commissions incurred in connection with obtaining cover. Consequential damages would include loss of profits from your business being closed because of the seller's breach. For consequential damages to be available, the seller must have known at the time of contracting that if he or she breached the contract, it would result in a closure of your business [UCC 2-712, 2-713, 2-715].

Occasionally, a seller will be forced to perform the contract. This result will occur where the goods are very unique or it is not possible to obtain cover. For example, one of the best indicators of the overall state of the economy is the health of the construction industry. Concrete is one construction item normally available. When the economy is sharply expanding, a shortage of concrete may exist. To produce concrete takes large investments in capital goods and plants. It is not very easy to start a new plant, nor is this process a quick one. Under certain conditions, a concrete manufacturer might refuse to deliver the amount of concrete for which it contracted. This refusal may be an attempt to secure a higher price from you. You can bring action in court to force this manufacturer to deliver the contracted amount of concrete if you cannot obtain cover from any other reasonable source. In such an action, the court may also award you appropriate damages [UCC 2-716].

Remedies of Sellers

The major problem confronted by a seller is nonpayment for goods accepted by the buyer. In this situation, the seller is entitled to be paid the contract price.

A more complicated problem occurs when the goods have not been accepted by the buyer and the buyer repudiates the contract. Normally, the seller may recover the difference between the market price and the unpaid contract price together with incidental damages, less any expenses saved by the buyer's breach. If this rule fails to place the seller in as good a position as if the contract had been performed, the measure of damages is the profit, including overhead, that the seller would have earned from full performance of this contract by the buyer, plus any incidental expenses [UCC 2-708].

A third kind of problem occurs when the seller cannot sell the goods identified to the contract at a reasonable price in the market. In this situation, the measure of damages is the contract price [UCC 2-709].

Some people are able to obtain a remedy because of a malfunctioning product. The legal theories involved include breach of warranty, negligence, and strict liability. The remainder of this chapter looks at these theories and discusses the liability a business may incur when a malfunctioning product harms someone.

Product Liability

Increasingly, the courts are combining tort law and contract law when the lawsuit involves products that malfunction and cause injuries. Consumers buy beer, medicine, microwave ovens, hair dryers, sporting goods, automobile tires, and thousands of other items with the complete faith that the product is properly designed and manufactured for its intended use, is safe for consumption, and is correctly labeled. The Product Safety Commission, however, reported 21,600 deaths and 30 million consumer-product-related injuries from defective products in a recent one-year period.

How should the losses from injury and death because of defective products be allocated? The distribution of these losses and of what is called "economic loss"—the loss suffered because a product did not perform as expected—makes up an area of the law called **product liability**. It does not fit squarely into any one body of law.

Common law rules of torts and contracts once set the parameters of product safety, but the common law standards applicable to product liability vary greatly from state to state. The Uniform Commercial Code helps the courts to give some degree of uniformity when determining potential liability for products through warranty law.

Historical Development

A long-established rule holds that the seller of goods has a duty to exercise the care of a reasonable person in ensuring that the goods do not harm the buyer. In the past, this rule was enforced by using negligence as a basis for liability. Even in applying negligence principles, however, earlier courts required privity of contract in product liability cases. The privity requirement meant that the injured party who sued in negligence also had to prove that there was a contract—that is, that he or she had bought the defective item from the defendant.

This same requirement was found in contract and warranty law. A warranty is a legally binding guarantee. Contract, warranty, and tort laws were insufficient by themselves to protect the consumer completely from unsafe products. Because of the requirement of privity, the ultimate consumer frequently was not covered. The courts eventually resorted to the law of torts, specifically negligence, and abandoned the privity requirement. Yet negligence, too, proved to be inadequate because the manufacturer could avoid liability by proving that he or she had exercised reasonable care in producing the goods.

In the absence of a legal theory that fully compensated victims of defective products, a new theory developed. To deal with the dilemma of the injured but uncompensated victim, the common law extended the theories of contracts and torts, finally blending them to develop a cohesive restraint. This new doctrine, known as strict liability, permits an injured plaintiff to recover even though the manufacturer exercised reasonable care.

Product Liability Based on Negligence

As previously discussed in Chapter 8, negligence is defined as failure to use that degree of care that a reasonable, prudent person would have used under similar circumstances. The manufacturer of a product must exercise due care to make that product safe to be used as it was intended. Due care must be exercised in designing the product, in selecting the materials, in using the appropriate production process, in assembling and testing the product, and in placing adequate warnings on the label of dangers of which an ordinary person might not be aware. The duty of care extends to the inspection and testing of purchased products that are used in the final product sold by the manufacturer.

The defendant-manufacturer can prove it used due care in the manufacture of its product as an appropriate defense against a negligence suit. A major problem of the plaintiff is to tie the defendant-manufacturer's failure to exercise due care to the plaintiff's injury. Numerous events, involving different people, take place between the time a product is manufactured and the time the plaintiff uses the product. Often a retailer, for example, will have to assemble a product before it can be sold to the consumer. If any of these events can be shown to have caused or contributed to the injury, the manufacturer will claim no liability on the basis of this intervening cause. Other defenses may also be used, but their application varies from state to state.

Defenses discussed in Chapter 8 are contributory negligence, comparable negligence, and assumption of risk. For example, when a person plugs an electric cord into an outlet, plugs the other end into the plug-in of an electric lawn mower that has a bare metal pushbar, and tries to mow wet grass, he or she may be electrocuted. The bare metal pushbar may be a negligent design, but mowing a wet lawn may be contributory negligence.

Likewise, any time a plaintiff misuses, modifies, or alters a product, the manufacturer will claim that the plaintiff contributed to the cause of the injuries. The defense is that the plaintiff's comparable negligence offsets the negligence of the manufacturer.

Product Liability Based on Strict Liability

In early English history, people were liable for the results of their act regardless of their intentions or their exercise of reasonable care. A person whose conduct resulted in the injury of another was held liable for damages, even if he or she had not intended to injure anyone and had exercised reasonable care. This approach was abandoned around 1800 in favor of the fault approach (negligence), in which the act became a tort only if it was wrongful or blameworthy in some respect. Dissatisfaction with the product liability cases led to a return to the English doctrine of strict liability.

Requirements of Strict Product Liability The difference between negligence and strict liability is that negligence evaluates the conduct of a supplier, processor, or manufacturer, while strict liability focuses entirely on the condition of the product. The five basic requirements of strict product liability are:

1. The defendant must sell the product in a defective condition.
2. The defendant must be engaged in the business of manufacturing that product. *or selling*
3. The product must be unreasonably dangerous to the user or consumer because of its defective condition.
4. The defective condition must be the proximate cause of the injury or damage.
5. The goods must not have been substantially changed from the time the product was sold to the time the injury was sustained.

In any action against a manufacturer or seller, the plaintiff does not have to show why or in what manner the product became defective. The plaintiff does, however, have to show that, at the time the injury was sustained, the condition of the product was essentially the same as it was when it left the hands of the defendant-manufacturer. In addition, all states have extended strict liability's protection to "bystanders." Thus, the injured party does not have to be a consumer or user of the product. In the following case, the court reviews the use of an expert witness to show management's attitude toward safety and the use of documentary evidence to show that management knew the product was unsafe but decided not to correct the defect because of cost considerations.

BACKGROUND AND FACTS *In November 1971, the Grays purchased a new 1972 Pinto hatchback. The Grays had trouble with the car from the beginning. The car was returned for repairs a number of times, including excessive gas and oil consumption, downshifting of the automatic transmission, lack of power, and stalling. The stalling and excessive fuel consumption were caused by a heavy carburetor float.*

On May 28, 1972, Mrs. Gray and thirteen-year-old Richard Grimshaw set out on a trip in the Pinto, which was then six months old and had 3,000 miles on it. Getting on the freeway, Mrs. Gray was driving at 60 miles per hour. As she approached a major exit ramp where the traffic was congested, she moved from the outer fast lane to the middle lane of the freeway. Shortly after this lane change, the Pinto suddenly stalled and coasted to a halt in the middle lane. It was later established that the carburetor float had become so saturated with gasoline that it suddenly sank, opening the float chamber and causing the engine to flood and stall. The Pinto erupted into flames when it was rear-ended by a car proceeding in the same direction. Mrs. Gray suffered fatal burns, and Grimshaw suffered severe and permanently disfiguring burns on his face and entire body.

Grimshaw and the heirs of Mrs. Gray, the plaintiffs, sued Ford Motor Company, the defendant. Following a six-month jury trial, verdicts were returned in favor of the plaintiffs. The Gray family was awarded $559,680 in compensatory damages. Grimshaw was awarded $2,516,000 in compensatory damages and $125 million in punitive damages. The trial court reduced the punitive damages to $3.5 million. Ford appealed the judgment on seven major grounds.

Case 11.4
GRIMSHAW v. FORD MOTOR CO.
Court of Appeal of California, Fourth District, 1981.
119 Cal.App.3d 757,
174 Cal.Rptr. 348.

Acting Presiding Justice TAMURA
* * * *

Ford seeks reversal of the judgment as a whole * * *.

In the ensuing analysis (ad nauseam) of Ford's wideranging assault on the judgment, we have concluded that Ford has failed to demonstrate that any errors or irregularities occurred during the trial which resulted in a miscarriage of justice requiring reversal.

*   *   *   *

[Court's discussion of expert witness who was a former Ford employee]

A party offering an expert witness is entitled to examine him "as to his qualifications and experience so that the full weight to be accorded his testimony will become apparent." Such examination "should not be limited by narrow and stringent rules." It was therefore within the court's discretion to permit plaintiffs to elicit from Mr. Copp testimony as to when he left Ford and why. Evidence as to why he left Ford was part of the background information concerning the witness's professional experience which would assist the fact finder in determining the weight to be given to his testimony. While the evidence may also have tended to enhance the witness' credibility, the purpose of permitting a party producing an expert to question him as to his educational background, training, and experience in his area of expertise is not only to establish "the competency of the witness to the satisfaction of the court, but also for the purpose of making plain the strength of the witness's [sic] grounds of knowledge and the reason for trusting his belief." Therefore, the fact that the evidence may have enhanced the witness' credibility did not render it inadmissible.

*   *   *   *

*   *   * The fact that Ford fired a high ranking engineering executive for advocating automotive safety was indicative of Ford management's attitude towards safety in automobile production and was thus relevant to the issue of malice. It had a tendency in reason to prove that Ford's failure to correct the Pinto's fuel system design defects, despite knowledge of their existence, was deliberate and calculated. Ford's argument that firing Mr. Copp in 1976 for speaking out on safety does not reasonably tend to show that Ford disregarded safety in designing the Pinto some five years earlier lacks merit. The evidence was not that Mr. Copp first took his stand on safety in 1976; he testified that he had been outspoken on auto safety during all the many years he worked for Ford.

Ford complains that since Mr. Copp was permitted to testify to the circumstances surrounding his termination, Ford was compelled to cross-examine him to show that the reason for his dismissal was unexplained absences from work and unsatisfactory work performance; that if the court had not permitted Mr. Copp to give his version of the reason for termination, Ford would have had little or no reason to examine him about his retirement and plaintiffs would not have been able to adduce rehabilitation testimony highly prejudicial to Ford. The record discloses that Mr. Copp testified only briefly concerning the circumstances of his early retirement from Ford but that on cross-examination Ford engaged in extensive questioning to show that the reason for his termination was not his safety views but unsatisfactory work and absenteeism. Plaintiffs thereafter introduced rehabilitating testimony. Mr. Copp was permitted to testify to his campaign for automotive safety during his entire period of employment with Ford, including a conversation he had with Henry Ford II on the subject, his testimony before a United States Senate Committee concerning the Chevrolet Corvair's unsafe design and his role in exposing Ford's conduct in connection with the emission control program. Ford argues that but for the court's erroneous initial ruling and its consequent cross-examination on the reason for Mr. Copp's retirement, the damaging rehabilitation evidence would not have come in. Since we find no error in the court's initial ruling and since Ford has not advanced any independent reason why the rehabilitating evidence should have been excluded, Ford's complaint concerning the prejudicial nature of that evidence must be rejected.

*   *   *   *

[Court's discussion of documentary evidence]

Ford contends that the court erroneously admitted irrelevant documentary evidence highly prejudicial to Ford. We find the contention to be without merit.

(1) *Exhibit No. 125:*

Exhibit No. 125 was a report presented at a Ford production review meeting in April 1971, recommending action to be taken in anticipation of the promulgation of federal standards on fuel system integrity. The report recommended * * * deferral from 1974 to 1976 of the adoption of "flak suits" or "bladders" in all Ford cars, including the Pinto, in order to realize a savings of $20.9 million. The report stated that the cost of the flak suit or bladder would be $4 to $8 per car. The meeting at which the report was presented was chaired by Vice President Harold MacDonald and attended by Vice President Robert Alexander and occurred sometime before the 1972 Pinto was placed on the market. A reasonable inference may be drawn from the evidence that despite management's knowledge that the Pinto's fuel system could be made safe at a cost of but $4 to $8 per car, it decided to defer corrective measures to save money and enhance profits. The evidence was thus highly relevant and properly received.

* * * *

(2) *Exhibits Nos. 95 and 122:*

Ford urges that a report (Exhibit No. 95) and a motion picture depicting Ford's crash test No. 1616 (Exhibit No. 122) should have been excluded because they were irrelevant and highly prejudicial to Ford in that they showed that in a 21.5-mile-per-hour crash of a 1971 Pinto prototype into a fixed barrier the filler neck of the fuel tank separated allowing fluid to spill from the tank, whereas no such filler neck separation occurred in the Gray vehicle. Under the test for ascertaining relevancy of evidence to which we have previously alluded, we find no abuse of discretion in the court's ruling. Not only did the filler neck separation show the vulnerability of the Pinto fuel system in a 21.5-mile-per-hour fixed barrier test, but crash test No. 1616, as Ford conceded, resulted in a puncture of the fuel tank from the exposed bolt heads on the differential housing. Thus, the exhibits showed the defect in the Pinto's gas tank location and design, the hazard created by the protrusions on the differential housing, and, in addition, they served as evidence of Ford's awareness of those defects. Exhibits Nos. 95 and 122 were properly received in evidence.

* * * *

Ford contends that Grimshaw's counsel committed prejudicial misconduct in referring to Ford's executives meeting in the "glass house" and deciding to approve the Pinto's fuel tank design with knowledge that it was unsafe and would result in the loss of many lives. Ford argues that although there was evidence that the corporate headquarters of Ford was referred to as the "glass house" there was no evidence of management meetings held there in connection with the Pinto design. The record contains substantial evidence from which it reasonably may be inferred that Ford's management knew that the Pinto was unsafe but nevertheless decided not to alleviate the problem because of cost considerations, and thus that those decisions were made in Ford's corporate headquarters.

The court of appeals, in a 41-page opinion, found against Ford on every issue on appeal. The trial court's judgment was affirmed.   **DECISION AND REMEDY**

Defenses to Strict Product Liability   The traditional defense of contributory fault has frequently been rejected in strict tort liability actions even though it remains a defense in a negligence action. In principle, negligence and contributory negligence are immaterial in any action based on the theory of strict liability in tort. After all, strict liability assumes that the danger presented was foreseeable by the manufacturer of the product.

The exclusion of the defense of contributory fault has forced courts to utilize assumption of risk as a defense in product liability suits. Assumption of risk can be used as a defense in an action based on strict liability in tort. The defendant must show: (1) that the plaintiff voluntarily proceeded while recognizing the risk; (2) that the plaintiff knew and appreciated the risk created by the defect; and (3) that the plaintiff's decision to undertake the known risk was unreasonable. The doctrine of comparable negligence may apply here.

Most courts allow the application of the strict liability doctrine to cases even when no personal injuries have occurred. When a defective product causes only property damage, the seller also may be liable under the theory of strict liability.

Product Liability Based on Warranty

Warranty liability is applied in product liability cases. A warranty is the seller's assurance to the buyer that goods will meet certain standards. If the goods fail to meet those standards, the warranty is breached and the defendant will be liable. The UCC designates several types of warranties that can arise: express warranties [UCC 2-313], implied warranties of merchantability [UCC 2-314], and implied warranties of fitness for a particular purpose [UCC 2-315].

Express Warranties A seller can create an **express warranty** by making representations concerning the quality, condition, description, or performance potential of the goods. Express warranties arise when a seller suggests that:

1. The goods will conform to the seller's affirmation of fact or promise. (Such affirmations or promises are usually made during the bargaining process through such statements as "these drill bits will easily penetrate stainless steel without dulling.")
2. The goods will conform to a description of them. (For example, the description states, "Crate contains one 150-horsepower diesel engine," or the contract calls for delivery of a "camel hair coat.")
3. The goods will conform to a sample or model.

For any express warranty to be created, the seller's affirmation or promise must become part of the basis of the bargain. If the seller merely makes a statement that relates to the value or worth of the goods or makes a statement of opinion or recommendation about the goods, the seller is not creating an express warranty. For example, a seller claims, "This is the best used car to come along in years; it has four new tires and a 350-horsepower engine just rebuilt this year." The seller has stated several facts that create a warranty: The automobile has an engine; it is a 350-horsepower engine; the engine was rebuilt this year; there are four tires on the automobile; the tires are new.

The seller's opinion that it is "the best used car to come along in years" is known as "puffing" and creates no warranty. Puffing is the expression of an opinion by a seller that is not made as a representation of fact. A statement relating to the value of the goods, such as "it's worth a fortune" or "anywhere else you'd pay $10,000 for it," will not normally create a warranty.

Implied Warranties Implied warranties are created by law from the facts of the case and are not expressly stated by the parties.

An **implied warranty of merchantability** automatically arises in every sale of goods made by a merchant who deals in goods of that kind. A retailer of ski equipment makes an implied warranty of merchantability every time the retailer sells a pair of skis, but a neighbor selling skis at a garage sale does not.

Goods that are merchantable must be reasonably fit for the ordinary purposes for which such goods are used. They must be of at least average, fair, or medium-grade quality. The quality must be comparable to the quality of similar goods on the market. In addition, the goods, to be merchantable, must be adequately packaged and labeled, and they must conform to their labels.

Some examples of nonmerchantable goods include light bulbs that explode when switched on, pajamas that burst into flames on slight contact with a stove burner, high heels that break off during normal use, or shotgun shells that explode prematurely.

The implied warranty of merchantability also imposes liability on the merchant for the safe performance of the product; it makes no difference whether the merchant knew of or could have discovered a defect that makes the product unsafe. Merchants, however, are not absolute insurers against all accidents arising in connection with the goods. For example, a bar of soap will not be unmerchantable merely because a user can slip and fall by stepping on it.

The **implied warranty of fitness for a particular purpose** arises when any seller (merchant or nonmerchant) knows the particular purpose for which a buyer will use the goods and knows that the buyer is relying on the seller's skill and judgment to select suitable goods. A "particular purpose of the buyer" differs from the "ordinary purpose for which goods are used" (merchantability). Goods can be merchantable but still not fit for the buyer's particular purpose. For example, house paints suitable for outside wooden siding are not suitable for painting over stucco walls.

A contract can include both a warranty of merchantability and a warranty of fitness for a particular purpose, which relates to a specific use or to a special situation in which a buyer intends to use the goods. For example, a merchant-seller recommends a particular pair of shoes, knowing that a customer is looking for mountain-climbing shoes. The buyer purchases the shoes relying on the seller's judgment. If the shoes are found to be not only improperly made but also suitable only for walking, not for mountain climbing, the seller has breached both the warranty of merchantability and the warranty of fitness for a particular purpose.

Exhibit 11–3 summarizes the three types of warranty covered by the Uniform Commercial Code.

Disclaimers or Defenses Against Implied Warranty Liability

The Uniform Commercial Code permits a seller to disclaim implied warranties or to have certain defenses against implied warranty liability. Some of these disclaimers or defenses are as follows:

1. The seller (manufacturer) can specifically disclaim either or both implied warranties. To specifically disclaim *any* implied warranty of fitness, the disclaimer must be in writing and conspicuous. The UCC gives an example: "There are no warranties which extend beyond the description on the face hereof." To specifically disclaim the implied warranty of merchantability, the disclaimer can be oral or written, but must "mention merchantability" and if in writing, must be conspicuous [UCC 2-316(2)].

2. The seller can disclaim both implied warranties by selling the goods with expressions such as "with all faults" or sold "as is" [UCC 2-316(3)(a)].

3. A defense may be available to the seller if the buyer actually examines the goods. The defense is that the buyer cannot complain of any defect he or she found or should have found [UCC 2–316(3)(b)].

4. Implied warranties can also be excluded or modified by usage of trade or previous course of performance or dealings between the parties [UCC 2–316(3)(c)].

Because of the availability of these defenses and disclaimers, implied warranties may have limited

Exhibit 11–3 **Three Warranties Under the UCC**

TYPE	HOW CREATED
Express Warranty UCC 2-313	As part of a sale or bargain— 1. An affirmation of fact or promise 2. A sale by description 3. A sample shown as conforming to bulk.
Warranty of Merchantability UCC 2-314	1. Where the seller is a merchant, and 2. Deals in goods of the kind.
Warranty of Fitness for a Particular Purpose UCC 2-315	1. The buyer's particular purpose or use must expressly or implicitly be known by the seller, and 2. The buyer must purchase in reliance on the seller's selection.

importance to a buyer in seeking recovery under the warranty theory of product liability.

Magnuson-Moss Warranty Act The **Magnuson-Moss Warranty Act** of 1975 is designed to prevent deception in warranties by making them easier to understand. The Magnuson-Moss Warranty Act is enforced mainly by the Federal Trade Commission (FTC). To some degree, the Magnuson-Moss Warranty Act modifies the UCC warranty rules where consumer sales transactions are involved. The UCC remains the primary statute of warranty rules for commercial (business-to-business) transactions.

No seller is required to give a written warranty for consumer goods, but if a seller chooses to make an express written warranty and the cost of the consumer goods is more than $10, the warranty must be labeled as "full" or "limited." In addition, if the cost of the goods is more than $15 (FTC regulation), the warrantor is required to make certain disclosures fully and conspicuously in a single document in "readily understood language." These disclosures include the names and addresses of the warrantor(s), what specifically is warranted, procedures for enforcement of the warranty, any limitations on warranty relief, and the fact that the buyer has legal rights.

Although a **full warranty** may not cover every aspect of the consumer product sold, what it covers ensures some type of buyer satisfaction in case the product is defective. Full warranty requires free repair or replacement of any defective part; if it cannot be repaired within a reasonable time, the consumer has the choice of either a refund or a replacement without charge. The full warranty frequently does not have a time limit on it.

The warrantor need not perform warranty services if the problem with the product was caused by damage to the product or by unreasonable use by the consumer. A **limited warranty** arises when the written warranty fails to meet one of the minimum requirements for a full warranty.

Implied warranties do not arise under the Magnuson-Moss Warranty Act, only under the UCC provisions. Where an express warranty is made in a sales contract, however, the Magnuson-Moss Warranty Act prevents sellers from disclaiming or modifying the implied warranties of merchantability and fitness for a particular purpose. Sellers can impose a time limit on the duration of an implied warranty, but such a time limit has to correspond to the duration of the express warranty.

Federal Preemption in Product Liability Cases Congress has passed legislation requiring information to be disclosed when certain products may be unsafe. The question presented is whether these statutes have preempted state laws under the Supremacy Clause of the federal Constitution. The problem of exemption has confronted the courts in deciding cases concerning the health hazards in smoking of tobacco products. Congress has passed legislation that requires health and safety warnings on all tobacco products and restricts the advertising of these products. The tobacco industry has taken the position that these federal statutory provisions have preempted all state laws that might create liability. The following case discusses preemption and several different theories of product liability.

Case 11.5 **CIPOLLONE v.** **LIGGETT GROUP, INC.** Supreme Court of the United States, 1992. 505 U.S. _____, 112 S.Ct. 2608, 120 L.Ed.2d 407.	BACKGROUND AND FACTS *Rose Cipollone began smoking in 1942 and died of lung cancer in 1984. Before she died she brought a lawsuit against the manufacturers of tobacco products based on several theories. First, the manufacturers had breached express warranties contained in their advertising because they failed to warn consumers about the hazards of smoking. Second, that the hazards had been fraudulently misrepresented to consumers. Third, that the manufacturers conspired to deprive the public of medical and scientific information about smoking. Cipollone's son continued the litigation after her death.*

Justice STEVENS delivered the opinion of the Court.

"WARNING: THE SURGEON GENERAL HAS DETERMINED THAT CIGARETTE SMOKING IS DANGEROUS TO YOUR HEALTH." A federal statute enacted in 1969 requires that warning (or a variation thereof) to appear in a conspicuous place on every package of cigarettes sold in the United States. The questions presented to us by this case are whether that statute, or its 1965 predecessor which required a less alarming label, pre-empted Cipollone's common law claims against the cigarette manufacturers.

* * * *

Although physicians had suspected a link between smoking and illness for centuries, the first medical studies of that connection did not appear until the 1920s. The ensuing decades saw a wide range of epidemiologic and laboratory studies on the health hazards of smoking. Thus, by the time the Surgeon General convened an advisory committee to examine the issue in 1962, there were more than 7,000 publications examining the relationship between smoking and health.

In 1964, the advisory committee issued its report, which stated as its central conclusion: "Cigarette smoking is a health hazard of sufficient importance in the United States to warrant appropriate remedial action."

* * * *

In July 1965, Congress enacted the Federal Cigarette Labeling and Advertising Act. The 1965 Act effectively adopted half of the FTC's regulation: the Act mandated warnings on cigarette packages [under] § 5(a), but barred the requirement of such warnings in cigarette advertising [under] § 5(b).

* * * *

It was in this context that Congress enacted the Public Health Cigarette Smoking Act of 1969, which amended the 1965 Act in several ways. First, the 1969 Act strengthened the warning label, in part by requiring a statement that cigarette smoking "is dangerous" rather than that it "may be hazardous." Second, the 1969 Act banned cigarette advertising in "any medium of electronic communication subject to [FCC] jurisdiction." Third, and related, the 1969 Act modified the pre-emption provision by replacing the original § 5(b) with a provision that reads:

"(b) No requirement or prohibition based on smoking and health shall be imposed under State law with respect to the advertising or promotion of any cigarettes the packages of which are labeled in conformity with the provisions of this Act."

* * *

Article VI of the Constitution provides that the laws of the United States "shall be the supreme Law of the Land; . . . any Thing in the Constitution or Laws of any state to the Contrary notwithstanding." Art. VI, cl. 2. [I]t has been settled that state law that conflicts with federal law is "without effect." Consideration of issues arising under the Supremacy Clause "start[s] with the assumption that the historic police powers of the states [are] not to be superseded by . . . Federal Act unless that [is] the clear and manifest purpose of Congress." Accordingly, " '[t]he purpose of Congress is the ultimate touchstone' " of pre-emption analysis.

Congress' intent may be "explicitly stated in the statute's language or implicitly contained in its structure and purpose." In the absence of an express congressional command, state law is pre-empted if that law actually conflicts with federal law, or if federal law so thoroughly occupies a legislative field " 'as to make reasonable the inference that Congress left no room for the States to supplement it.' "

* * * *

Compared to its predecessor in the 1965 Act, the plain language of the pre-emption provision in the 1969 Act is much broader. First, the later Act bars not simply "statements" but rather "requirement[s] or prohibition[s] . . . imposed under State law." Second, the later Act reaches beyond statements "in the advertising" to obligations "with respect to the advertising or promotion" of cigarettes.

* * *

The 1969 Act worked substantial changes in the law: rewriting the label warning, banning broadcast advertising, and allowing the FTC to regulate print advertising. In the context of such revisions and in light of the substantial changes in wording, we cannot accept the parties' claim that the 1969 Act did not alter the reach of § 5(b).

*   *   *   *

[T]here is no "good reason to believe" that Congress meant less than what it said; indeed, in light of the narrowness of the 1965 Act, there is "good reason to believe" that Congress meant precisely what it said in amending that Act.

*   *   *   *

As explained above, the 1965 version of § 5 was precise and narrow on its face; the obviously broader language of the 1969 version extended that section's pre-emptive reach.

*   *   *   *

Nor does the statute indicate that any familiar subdivision of common law claims is or is not pre-empted. We therefore cannot follow [Cipollone's] passing suggestion that § 5(b) pre-empts liability for omissions but not for acts, or that § 5(b) pre-empts liability for unintentional torts but not for intentional torts. Instead we must fairly but—in light of the strong presumption against pre-emption— narrowly construe the precise language of § 5(b) and we must look to each of [Cipollone's] common law claims to determine whether it is in fact pre-empted. The central inquiry in each case is straightforward: we ask whether the legal duty that is the predicate of the common law damages action constitutes a "requirement or prohibition based on smoking and health . . . imposed under State law with respect to . . . advertising or promotion," giving that clause a fair but narrow reading. As discussed below, each phrase within that clause limits the universe of common law claims pre-empted by the statute.

We consider each category of damages actions in turn. In doing so, we express no opinion on whether these actions are viable claims as a matter of state law; we assume *arguendo* that they are.

Failure to Warn

To establish liability for a failure to warn, [Cipollone] must show that "a warning is necessary to make a product . . . reasonably safe, suitable and fit for its intended use," that respondents failed to provide such a warning, and that that failure was a proximate cause of petitioner's injury. In this case, [Cipollone] offered two closely related theories concerning the failure to warn: first, that respondents "were negligent in the manner [that] they tested, researched, sold, promoted, and advertised" their cigarettes; and second, that respondents failed to provide "adequate warnings of the health consequences of cigarette smoking."

Petitioner's claims are pre-empted to the extent that they rely on a state law "requirement or prohibition . . . with respect to . . . advertising or promotion." Thus, insofar as claims under either failure to warn theory require a showing that respondents' post–1969 advertising or promotions should have included additional, or more clearly stated, warnings, those claims are pre-empted. The Act does not, however, pre-empt [Cipollone's] claims that rely solely on [defendants'] testing or research practices or other actions unrelated to advertising or promotion.

Breach of Express Warranty

[Cipollone's] claim for breach of an express warranty arises under [New Jersey statute] which provides:

> "Any affirmation of fact or promise made by the seller to the buyer which relates to the goods and becomes part of the basis of the bargain creates an express warranty that the goods shall conform to the affirmation or promise."

[Cipollone's] evidence of an express warranty consists largely of statements made in respondents' advertising.

*   *   *

A manufacturer's liability for breach of an express warranty derives from, and is measured by, the terms of that warranty. Accordingly, the "requirements" imposed by an express warranty claim are not "imposed under State law," but rather imposed *by the warrantor*. If, for example, a manufacturer expressly promised to pay a smoker's medical bills if she contracted emphysema, the duty to honor that promise could not fairly be said to be "imposed under state law," but rather is best understood as undertaken by the manufacturer itself. While the general duty not to breach warranties arises under state law, the particular "requirement . . . based on smoking and health . . . with respect to the advertising or promotion [of] cigarettes" in an express warranty claim arises from the manufacturer's statements in its advertisements. In short, a common law remedy for contractual commitment voluntarily undertaken should not be regarded as a "requirement . . . *imposed under State law*" within the meaning of § 5(b).

*   *   *   *

Fraudulent Misrepresentation

*   *   *   *

Section 5(b) pre-empts only the imposition of state law obligations "with respect to the advertising or promotion" of cigarettes. [Cipollone's] claims that [defendants] concealed material facts are therefore not pre-empted insofar as those claims rely on a state law duty to disclose such facts through channels of communication other than advertising or promotion. Thus, for example, if state law obliged [defendants] to disclose material facts about smoking and health to an administrative agency, § 5(b) would not pre-empt a state law claim based on a failure to fulfill that obligation.

Moreover, [Cipollone's] fraudulent misrepresentation claims that do arise with respect to advertising and promotions (most notably claims based on allegedly false statements of material fact made in advertisements) are not pre-empted by § 5(b). Such claims are not predicated on a duty "based on smoking and health" but rather on a more general obligation—the duty not to deceive.

*   *   *   *

Conspiracy to Misrepresent or Conceal Material Facts

[Cipollone's] final claim alleges a conspiracy among [defendants] to misrepresent or conceal material facts concerning the health hazards of smoking. The predicate duty underlying this claim is a duty not to conspire to commit fraud. For the reasons stated in our analysis of [Cipollone's] intentional fraud claim, this duty is not pre-empted by § 5(b) for it is not a prohibition "based on smoking and health"

Ethical Considerations

Dangerous Product: Who to Tell?

What is your ethical duty if you know a product to be dangerous? Should you report it to the government, to the manufacturer, to the retailer, or do nothing? At the present time, insurance carriers often have such knowledge. Carriers insure manufacturers, for example, against product liability. When the manufacturer has a claim filed against it or is sued on a product liability basis, this information is reported to the manufacturer's insurance carrier.

Ethically, what should the insurance company do with this information? Should insurance companies become quasi-governmental officials and report the claims to the appropriate agency? Should the information be released to the media to warn the public of the potential danger? What is the ethical duty owed by the insurance carrier to its client, the manufacturer, on the insurance contract?

On the other hand, what is the ethical duty owed by the manufacturer to the insurance company when the manufacturer declares bankruptcy, leaving the insurance company to defend all the lawsuits? These are troubling questions that need to be resolved in both the ethical and legal worlds.

as that phrase is properly construed. Accordingly, we conclude that the 1969 Act does not pre-empt [Cipollone's] conspiracy claim.

VI

To summarize our holding: The 1965 act did not pre-empt state law damages actions; the 1969 Act pre-empts [Cipollone's] claims based on a failure to warn and the neutralization of federally mandated warnings to the extent that those claims rely on omissions or inclusions in [defendants'] advertising or promotions; the 1969 Act does not pre-empt [Cipollone's] claims based on express warranty, intentional fraud and misrepresentation, or conspiracy.

DECISION AND REMEDY   *The Supreme Court held that the 1965 Act did not preempt state law damages actions since she had started smoking prior to the Act. The 1969 Act, also, did not preempt her claims based on express warranty, intentional fraud and misrepresentation, or conspiracy. The 1969 Act did, however, preempt Cipollone's claims based on a failure to warn.*

International Considerations

Foreign Products: Who Can You Sue?

Often sales of goods between two parties from different countries are informal; thus, a negotiated, written contract is not made. How the contract comes into being is through correspondence, catalogs, brochures, or even television advertisements. Whenever the seller is communicating with the buyer, no matter what the method, the seller is making representations about that product.

Implied warranties are not prevalent among sophisticated merchants who deal internationally. The United Nations Convention on Contracts for the International Sale of Goods (CISG) addresses implied warranties by setting out four areas. The goods must (1) be fit for ordinary purposes for which the product is used, (2) be fit for any particular purpose expressly or implicitly made known to the seller, (3) possess the qualities that the seller used in a sample or model, and (4) be contained or packaged in the manner usual for such goods. These warranties are similar to the ones set out in the UCC.

The issue of product liability and of where a legal action may be instituted in the event the product causes harm have not been fully resolved. What happens when a foreign-made toy injures a child in the United States? For example, a doll that is manufactured overseas has asbestos in its stuffing. A shipment of 10,000 dolls is purchased and imported by a domestic corporation, Super Sales Company. One of the dolls is sold to Mr. and Mrs. Parent, who give the toy to their child. The child rips the poorly manufactured doll apart, eats the stuffing, and is injured. Mr. and Mrs. Parent try to settle the case against Super Sales Company, but before the case is settled, Super Sales Company goes into bankruptcy.

Can Mr. and Mrs. Parent sue the foreign manufacturer for the defective doll? Where should the lawsuit be brought? Questions such as these have not been answered by international law adopted by the United Nations. If the United States has a treaty concerning jurisdiction with the country where the manufacturer is located, Mr. and Mrs. Parent may be able to sue in the United States. Otherwise, the action will have to be brought in the foreign country.

When a Retailer Becomes Liable

You are the chief executive officer (CEO) for a chain of stores that sells retail toys and hobby supplies. Your segment of the market is directed toward older children and adults. Your firm does not manufacture products but rather purchases inventory directly from manufacturers located throughout the world.

Recently, one of your competitors lost a case and was held liable for $1.5 million involving a miniature radio-controlled automobile kit. The customer had bought a kit; it exploded because of a short circuit and caused the customer to suffer severe eye damage.

Your firm sells the same type of product, and you become concerned that your firm might be confronted with a similar case. You have sampled your product and have not found a similar problem. You wonder, however, what legal theories might be used in this type of case or similar ones. You contact your attorney for general information about product liability.

To your surprise, she lists several different legal theories that could be used. If you are a retailer, you may be liable to the consumer even though you did not manufacture or package the product.

First, a plaintiff may bring action based on a breach of express warranty because the product must conform to the description on the box or to the model that you use for demonstration purposes.

Second, a plaintiff may rely on the theory of breach of the implied warranties of merchantability and of fitness for a particular purpose.

Third, a plaintiff may base his or her action on the legal theory of strict liability. This theory applies whenever a product is unreasonably dangerous and causes an injury.

An action for negligence might be brought, but normally this will be used against the manufacturer.

Fraud might also exist if you intended to deceive the customer about a material fact. The deception must be made with the knowledge of its falsity and must be relied on by the customer to his or her injury.

How can you limit your potential liability? Obviously, one way would be through the use of liability insurance. The cost of insurance, however, has greatly increased during the last few years. Your firm has decided to be a self-insured organization. This means that your firm has no insurance to protect itself from legal action and has decided to assume this potential liability.

What else can you do to give the maximum protection to your firm in the absence of insurance coverage? Two possible legal routes might be used.

First, you could obtain from each customer a signed written statement that would disclaim any liability for your firm. This approach might be applicable to a small service business such as a Go-Kart Track. As a practical matter, this is not an acceptable business practice for most retail concerns. The disclaimer of liability also does not prevent a consumer who was not the original purchaser from filing a lawsuit.

The second procedure is to use the Uniform Commercial Code. The retailer is allowed to bring into the lawsuit the manufacturer if the lawsuit is brought for breach of warranty. The manufacturer must either defend the lawsuit or be bound by the court decision. The practical effect is that the manufacturer is ultimately held liable.

Note, however, that this provision applies only to warranties and not to strict product liability. Remember, too, that your firm purchases inventory from international sources. It is not possible to enforce a judgment against a manufacturer outside of the United States on inventory bought from Asia, South America, or other parts of the world.

In other words, in your type of business, no foolproof method exists to protect your firm from lawsuits brought by consumers based on malfunctioning products. Even though insurance rates are high, insurance may be the only reliable method of protecting your firm. The cost of this protection will have to be passed on to the consumer in the form of higher prices.

Summary

The UCC provides rules that govern the sale of goods. Often the buyer and seller neglect to provide details in their contracts. When a court is asked to examine the agreement in a lawsuit, the court first looks to see whether particular rules of the trade exist or if the parties have a history of prior dealings in order to supply missing terms. If neither exists, the court applies the rules found in the UCC.

Before any of these rules are applied, the goods must be existing and identified to this particular contract. Placing the customer's name on an existing item is one way of identifying goods. Other UCC rules apply to future goods.

Title to goods is important. Unless excluded by specific terms of the contract or by circumstances, the seller always warrants that the goods do not have any liens against them. Specific rules are set out in the UCC as to when the title is transferred from the seller to the buyer. Under certain circumstances, the seller may transfer voidable title to a bona fide purchaser in the ordinary course of business.

Risk of loss is another important area. The UCC sets out rules that determine whether the seller or the buyer has the risk of loss when this clause is not included in the contract. In addition, the buyer has the right to inspect goods on delivery. This right is not available when the goods are sent C.O.D.

If either side believes that the other may not perform on its promise, the UCC provides for adequate assurances for future performance. The buyer's or the seller's doubt as to whether the other side will perform must be based on good faith and fair dealing. The UCC also provides rules for performance and for breach of contract by either party.

Product liability causes specific legal problems for a business. Several legal doctrines apply when a product malfunctions. Negligence can be used, but the difficulty is establishing the point when the breach of the duty of care occurred. Under limited circumstances, strict liability may be used. Warranties provided by the seller, such as an express warranty, implied warranty of merchantability, or implied warranty of fitness for a particular purpose, may also provide the basis for liability.

Key Terms

bill of lading (257)
contract for future goods (255)
cost and freight (C. & F.) (260)
cost, insurance, and freight (C.I.F.) (260)
collect on delivery (C.O.D.) (259)
course of dealing (254)
cover (265)
document of title (257)

express warranty (270)
free on board, destination (F.O.B. destination) (257)
free on board, point of shipment (F.O.B.) (257)
full warranty (272)
goods (255)
identified goods (255)
implied warranty of fitness for a particular purpose (271)
implied warranty of merchantability (270)

lien (255)
limited warranty (272)
Magnuson-Moss Warranty Act (272)
merchant (255)
product liability (265)
tender (257)
usage of trade (254)
warehouse receipt (257)
warrant (255)
warranty of title (255)

Questions and Case Problems

1. Kerly is standing on a street corner waiting for a ride to work. Beyer has just purchased a new car manufactured by Able Motors. Beyer is driving down the street when suddenly the steering mechanism breaks, causing Beyer to run over Kerly. Kerly suffers permanent injuries. Beyer's total income per year has never exceeded $15,000. Kerly files suit against Able under the theory of strict liability in tort. Able pleads no liability because: (1) due care was used in the manufacture of the car, and (2) Able is not the manufacturer of the steering mechanism (Smith is). What is the outcome of Kerly's lawsuit?

2. Baxter manufactures electric hair dryers. Garza purchases a Baxter dryer from her local Ace Drugstore. Green, a friend and guest in Garza's home, has taken a shower and wants to dry her hair. Garza tells Green to use the new Baxter hair dryer. As Green plugs in the dryer, sparks fly out from the motor and continue to do so as she operates it. Despite this, Green begins drying her hair. Suddenly, the entire dryer ignites into flames, severely burning Green's scalp. Green sues Baxter on the basis of the torts of negligence and strict liability. Baxter denies liability, particularly since Green did not purchase the dryer. Discuss the validity of Green's actions and any defense claimed by Baxter.

3. Beech Aircraft Corporation manufactured airplanes. Some of the parts could be installed backwards, which would cause a plane to crash. George Nesselrode was a passenger in a plane that did crash; everyone on board was killed. The crash was caused by the reverse installation of parts. His estate brought an action against Beech Aircraft. Beech Aircraft argued that they were not at fault because they had not installed the parts. Were they correct? [Nesselrode v. Executive Beechcraft, Inc., 707 S.W.2d 371 (Mo. 1986)]

4. Ford Motor Company manufactured and distributed the Ford Cortina, which had only a cardboard shield separating the fuel tank from the passenger compartment. Nanda suffered severe disabling burns when the gas tank in his car exploded on being struck in the rear by another car. In a strict liability action by Nanda against Ford Motor Company, Nanda argued that the absence of a fire wall or metal shield between the fuel tank and passenger compartment constituted an unreasonably dangerous defect in the product and that his injuries were caused by this defect. What was the result? [Nanda v. Ford Motor Co., 509 F.2d 213 (7th Cir. 1974)]

5. A two-year-old child lost his leg when he became entangled in a grain auger on his grandfather's farm. The auger had a safety guard that prevented any item larger than four and five-eighths inches from coming into contact with the machine's moving parts. The child's foot was smaller than the openings in the safety guard. Was such an injury reasonably foreseeable? [Richelman v. Kewanee Machinery & Conveyor Co., 59 Ill.App.3d 578, 375 N.E.2d 885, 16 Ill.Dec. 778 (1978)]

6. Larry Colvin, an ironworker, was setting a steel truss on a concrete column while in a squatting position. He reached above his head to pull himself up and grabbed an I-beam, known as a purlin, which was eight or ten feet long and was not yet welded into place. The purlin failed to support Colvin's weight, and he fell. The plans for the building called for the purlins to be over 40 feet long, but only seven were that length. The remaining purlins were substantially shorter and were welded together to serve their purpose as spacers between the trusses and the roof. The purlins were supplied by Red Steel Company. Explain whether Red Steel is strictly liable for Colvin's injury due to the short length of the purlins. [Colvin v. Robert E. McKee, Inc., 671 S.W.2d 556 (Tex.Civ.App.—Dallas 1984)]

7. Block and Company was in the mail-order business. It entered into a contract with Alden Press for Alden to print 125,000 copies of a catalog. Later Block discovered that the covers of the catalogs with the address labels were falling off. Alden Press attempted to solve this problem, but Block believed that the entire catalog had to be reprinted. Block had Alden Press mail out 20,000 catalogs anyway because he had no other choice in order to stay in the mail-order business. Block ordered catalogs from another source and refused to pay anything to Alden Press. Alden alleged the catalogs had been accepted. How would you decide this case? [Alden Press, Inc. v. Block and Co., Inc., 527 N.E.2d 489 (Ill.App. 1 Dist. 1988)]

8. Crysen entered into a long-term contract to supply fuel oil to Con Edison. The contract provided for an independent inspector to determine the quantity of fuel oil delivered by gauging the amount of oil received in Con Edison's shore tanks. If these measurements were unavailable, the contract provided for gauging according to the ship's discharge figures. Crysen contracted to purchase the oil from Con Edison. During one delivery, the independent inspector observed 113,255 barrels being discharged from the vessel, but another independent inspector observed that only 99,719 barrels were received in the shore tank. This represented $300,000 in lost oil. Under these circumstances, who should have the risk of loss and why? [In Re Crysen/Montenay Energy Co. 902 F.2d 1098 (2nd Cir. 1990)]

Chapter 12 Commercial Paper and Secured Transactions

We promise according to our hopes, we perform according to our selfishness and our fears.

François de la Rochefoucauld
(1613–1680)

Introduction

Contracts are essential for the existence of a market economy. Many contracts are completed simply by the exchange of an item for money; for example, you purchase a textbook and pay the cashier. Other contracts, especially those involving large sums of money, are not completed so quickly. For example, people generally do not purchase automobiles with cash. How does the buyer (debtor) purchase expensive goods or real estate, and how does the seller (creditor) protect himself, herself, or itself to ensure that the money loaned is paid back?

The answer is found in two concepts that the law has developed over the centuries: **commercial paper** and **secured transactions.**

Commercial paper has a very long history, going back to the age of Hammurabi, around 2100 B.C. In Europe, starting in the thirteenth century, traveling merchants used some form of commercial paper because of the problems of transporting and guarding gold and silver. In the early 1700s, the English parliament adopted the first commercial paper statutes; these, in turn, have led to the present law of commercial paper. Today, in the United States, the law of commercial paper is found in the Uniform Commercial Code (UCC), Article 3. Under Article 3 of the UCC, commercial paper consists of negotiable instruments (signed writings that contain an unconditional promise or order to pay an exact sum of money either on demand or at a specified time in the future) in the form of drafts, checks, notes, or certificates of deposits.

Secured transactions are nearly as old as commercial paper; they date back to Roman times. A secured transaction has two parts: First, a debtor and a creditor have a contract in which the debtor agrees to repay the creditor the money he or she has lent the debtor or to repay the credit extended to the debtor. Second, the debtor promises the creditor that he or she can take specific property (personal or real) that belongs to the debtor if the debtor fails to repay the debt. If the debtor is in default, the creditor can then repossess and sell the property, using the proceeds to pay the debt. The law of secured transactions is found in the Uniform Commercial Code, Article 9.

In this chapter, we will review some of the more important provisions of the law concerning commercial paper, the banking system, and secured transactions. Each of these areas is very complex and can only be reviewed briefly in a legal environment textbook.

Functions of Commercial Paper

Commercial paper has the dual purposes of substituting for currency and serving as a credit device.

A Substitute for Currency

The financial system does not have enough currency to meet all the needs of society. For centuries commercial paper has been used, as it still is today, as a substitute for currency. Seldom does anyone in our society actually use currency to purchase an automobile, a residence, a business, or to make any other large purchase. Commercial paper is used because it is convenient and safe.

A Credit Device

Commercial paper is one method by which credit is extended to debtors. For example, Ed Foster wants to purchase an automobile but needs to borrow money to finance the purchase. When Ed borrows money from a financial institution, the Anywhere Bank of Iowa, he signs a type of commercial paper called a **promissory note.** In it, Ed promises to repay the money he owes. See Exhibit 12–1 for a sample note.

The terms referring to the parties to commercial paper are confusing at first because two types of commercial paper exist. One type has only two parties and involves a promise to pay. Examples include notes and certificates of deposits. The other type involves orders to pay and has three parties. Checks and drafts are examples of orders to pay.

Parties to Commercial Paper

Makers and Payees

The first type of commercial paper (called a "promise to pay") has two parties: the **maker** and the **payee.** A maker is the person who signs and

Exhibit 12–1 **A Sample Note**

SAVINGS

INSURANCE

SEC. AGREEMENT

2. CONSUMER GOODS

SECURITIES

OTHER

1. INV. & ACCTS.

3. EQUIP.

$ 6,000.00   Anywhere, Iowa   April 30 , 19 94 Due 6/29/94

Sixty days _____ after date

for value received, the undersigned jointly and severally promise to pay to the order of THE FIRST NATIONAL BANK OF ANYWHERE at its office in Anywhere, Iowa, $ Six thousand

Dollars with interest thereon from date hereof at the rate of -14- percent per annum (computed on the basis of actual days and a year of 360 days) indicated in No. 7 below.

Payee

7 INTEREST IS PAYABLE AT MATURITY
8 INTEREST IS PAID TO MATURITY
9 INTEREST IS PAYABLE_____ BEGINNING ON _____ 19 ___

SIGNATURE *Ed Foster*   SIGNATURE _____

SIGNATURE _____   SIGNATURE _____

Maker

NO.	
OFFICER	
BY	Clark
ACCRUAL	
☐ NEW	☐ RENT
☐ SECURED	
☐ UNSECURED	

issues an instrument with a *promise* to pay a certain sum of money to a payee. To **issue** means to deliver the instrument involved for the first time. The maker's signature must appear on the face of the commercial paper if the maker is to be liable. The payee is the person to whom an instrument is made payable. The maker is usually the debtor to the payee.

For example, Gary Ross goes to Citizen's Bank, where he has an account, to purchase a **certificate of deposit (CD)**. Ross is lending the bank his money, and he expects to earn interest on it. Ross is considering the purchase of one of three lake lots within the next six months and may need the CD as a down payment. Therefore, Ross wants the CD payable to **bearer** (person who has physical possession of the instrument). Citizen's Bank signs the certificate of deposit as a maker and issues the CD to Ross payable to bearer. See Exhibit 12–2 for a sample certificate of deposit.

Drawers, Drawees, and Payees

The second type of commercial paper (called an "order to pay") has three parties: **drawers, drawees, and payees**. One party (the drawer) creates an instrument that *orders* another party (the drawee) to pay money, usually to a third party (the payee). The payee can be either a specific person or anyone who is the bearer of the instrument. The drawee is a debtor of the drawer.

Exhibit 12–2 **A Sample Small Certificate of Deposit**

Citizen's Bank of Whiteacre
NEGOTIABLE CERTIFICATE OF DEPOSIT

22-1
960

NUMBER 332

Whiteacre, Minnesota   February 15   19 94

THIS CERTIFIES to the deposit in the Bank the sum of $ 5,000.00

----- Five thousand and no/100 ------ _____ Dollars

Payee
(bearer)

which is payable to bearer on the 15th day of July 19 94 against presentation and surrender of this certificate and bears interest at the rate of 9 3/4 % per annum, to be computed (on the basis of 360 days and actual days elapsed) to, and payable at, maturity. No payment may be made prior to, and no interest runs after, that date. Payable at maturity in federal funds, and if desired, at Manufacturers Hanover Trust Company, New York.

THE FIRST NATIONAL BANK OF ANYWHERE

By *Kathy Holland, President*

Signature

Maker

A **draft** (historically referred to as a bill of exchange) is an instrument drawn on a drawee (not necessarily a bank) that orders the drawee to pay money, usually to a third party. In the business world, a trade acceptance is a form of a draft frequently used in the payment for the sale of goods.

For example, Travis Lake Fabrics sells $50,000 worth of fabric to Quilts Plus, Inc., each fall on terms requiring payment to be made in 90 days. One year Travis Lake needs cash, so it draws a *trade acceptance* that orders Quilts Plus to pay $50,000 to the order of Travis Lake Fabrics 90 days hence. Travis Lake presents the paper to Quilts Plus. Quilts Plus *accepts* by signing the face of the paper and returns it to Travis Lake Fabrics. Quilts Plus's acceptance creates an enforceable promise to pay the instrument when it comes due in 90 days. Travis Lake can sell the trade acceptance in the commercial money market more easily than it can assign the $50,000 account receivable. Trade acceptances are the standard credit instruments in sales transactions. See Exhibit 12–3 for a sample trade acceptance.

A **check** is the most commonly used three-party instrument. For example, Marilyn Hicks has a checking account at the First National Bank of Anytown. She plans to pay for her new automobile by check. She signs the check as the drawer and issues it to Car Company, the payee. On the face of the check, she orders the drawee, First National Bank, to pay the amount written on the face of the check to the payee, Car Company. See Exhibit 12–4 for a sample check.

Indorsers and Indorsees

If commercial paper is to be used as a substitute for currency, a method to transfer an order instrument from the payee to a third person must exist. This method of transfer is simple. The payee indorses (signs) the instrument on the back and delivers it to another person. The payee is the **indorser,** and the person who receives the instrument is the **indorsee.** Thus, indorsement means to sign on the back of the instrument for the purpose of transferring the ownership. The various types of indorsements will be explored later in this chapter.

For example, Marie Holland, a medical doctor, receives a check for $125 from a patient. Marie wants to purchase some software for her computer from Positive Logic Computer Company. She indorses (signs her name) on the back of the check and delivers it to Positive Logic. Marie is both the payee on the check and the indorser on the back of the check. Positive Logic is the indorsee and is entitled to the $125. Positive Logic can then indorse the check to someone else and become an indorser in turn.

Bearers

A bearer is any person who has physical possession of an instrument that either is payable to anyone without designation or is indorsed in blank. The maker or drawer controls whether the instrument will have a named payee or whether a bearer is entitled to payment. Often the instrument will be

Exhibit 12–3 A Sample Time Draft—Trade Acceptance

TRADE ACCEPTANCE	Mytown, California			March 15 19 94
	To **Quilts Plus, Inc.** ◄— Drawee–Acceptor			
	On **June 15, 1994** PAY TO THE ORDER OF **Travis Lake Fabrics** ◄— Payee			
	————Fifty thousand and no/100———— DOLLARS ——50,000.00——			
	The obligations of the acceptor hereof arise out of the purchase of goods from the drawer. The drawee my accept this bill payable at any bank or trust company in the United Sates which drawee may designate.			
	Accepted at **Blackacre, N.Y.** on **March 15** 19 **94**			
	Payable at **Bank of Blackacre**		**Travis Lake Fabrics**	
	Blackacre, New York			
	Buyer's Signature **Quilts Plus, Inc.**	Drawer —►		
	By Agent or Officer *Tom Smith, Pres.*	By *Joe Jones/Pres*		

Exhibit 12–4 **A Sample Check**

made out as "payable to bearer," which means that any person who physically has possession of the commercial paper is entitled to the payment. At other times, a maker or a drawer will not name a payee but will make the commercial paper out to "Cash." Again, whoever has possession is entitled to the payment.

An instrument can also become a bearer instrument through the action of the indorser. When the payee indorses the instrument on the back, as Marie did (see Exhibit 12–5), this indorsement is called a **blank indorsement.** This type of indorsement makes the instrument payable to any bearer because the indorser, Marie, did not name another payee in her indorsement, although she had the right to do so.

Holders and Holders in Due Course

Commercial paper can be held by one of two designees: the **holder** or the **holder in due course (HDC).** Legally the two have very different rights.

Holder A holder is a person who possesses a commercial paper "drawn, issued, or indorsed to him or his order or to bearer or in blank" [UCC 1-201(20)]. A holder is one of two people: First, the holder may be the original payee. Second, if the payee has transferred the commercial paper to another, that person (also called the transferee) is a holder and has the status of an assignee of a contract right. As an assignee, the holder obtains only those rights that his or her predecessor-transferor had in the instrument. If there is a con-

flicting, superior claim or defense to the instrument, an ordinary holder is not able to collect payment.

The holder is usually the owner of the commercial paper but not necessarily. For example, Valdez takes a check made payable to him. He indorses the check on the back in blank, anticipating that he will deposit the check in his bank in the afternoon. He misplaces the check, and someone steals it. The thief is a holder under the law; even though, obviously, he or she is not the owner, the thief can legally transfer the check (a bearer instrument because of Valdez's blank indorsement) to another person and that person can collect the money. This third person now becomes the holder.

Holder in Due Course A holder in due course is a special-status transferee of negotiable commercial paper. An HDC has a very special and protected standing within the law. If a holder has acquired the instrument in a manner that meets the UCC requirements, the holder transforms his or her position from that of ordinary holder to that of holder in due course. An HDC is *normally* immune to any defenses (excuses) asserted by the drawer or maker against paying the instrument. As we will see later in this chapter, the Federal Trade Commission has modified the HDC doctrine as it applies to consumer transactions.

The reason that an HDC is protected by the law is that commercial paper is used as a substitute for currency. If people are going to accept com-

Exhibit 12–5 Indorsements

A. Checks

Checks deposited must be indorsed in a specific area on the back side of each check. The entire indorsement (whether a signature or a stamp), along with any other indorsements, identification information, driver's license number, etc., must fall within 1 1/2 inches of the trailing edge of a check. As you look at the front of a check, the trailing edge is the left edge. When you flip the check over, be sure to keep all indorsement information within 1 1/2 inches of the edge.

B. Other negotiable instruments

On the other types of negotiable instruments, an indorsement may legally be placed anywhere.

A Sample Blank Indorsement

A Sample Qualified Blank Indorsement

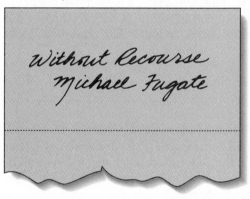

A Sample Special Indorsement

A Sample Restrictive Indorsement

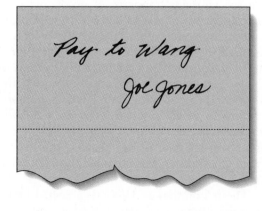

mercial paper as a substitute, they must have some protection. The law, therefore, does not allow the drawer or maker many reasons for not paying the instrument that he or she signed.

In order to become an HDC, a holder of a negotiable instrument must meet three requirements. The holder must take the instrument (1) for value, (2) in good faith, and (3) without notice that it is overdue or is defective [UCC 3-302]. The underlying requirement of due-course status is, of course, that a person must first be an ordinary holder of that instrument.

Value An HDC must give value for the instrument [UCC 303]. A person who receives an instrument as a gift or who inherits the instrument has not met the requirement of value. In these situations, the person remains an ordinary holder and does not possess the rights of an HDC. The concept of value in the law of negotiable instruments is not the same as the concept of consideration in the law of contracts. For example, under contract law a promise to pay a debt the person already owes is not consideration, but a holder taking an instrument in payment of a prior debt has given value.

Likewise, an executory promise (a promise to perform or pay in the future) is valid consideration to support a contract but does not constitute value to qualify a holder as an HDC. Therefore, a holder takes the instrument for value only to the extent that the consideration has been actually performed or paid. For example, Lori makes out a check for $500 payable to Rory on Sunday. Rory is in need of funds but cannot cash the check until Monday. Rory negotiates the check to Gary who pays Rory $200 in cash and promises Rory he will pay the balance on Friday when he gets his paycheck. Gary has only given value in the amount of $200 and can only qualify as an HDC for that amount.

Good Faith An HDC must take the instrument in good faith [UCC 3-302(1)(b)]. The purchaser-holder must act honestly in the process of acquiring the instrument. "Good faith" is defined as honesty in fact in the conduct of the transaction concerned [UCC 1-201(19)]. The good-faith requirement applies only to the holder; whether the transferor acted in good faith is immaterial. Thus, a person who in good faith takes a negotiable instrument from a thief can be an HDC.

Without Notice HDC protection is not given to a person who acquires an instrument knowing, or having reason to know, that it is defective in any one of the following ways: It is overdue, it has been dishonored, there is a defense against it, or there is another claim to it [UCC 3-302(1)(c)]. Before taking the instrument, a person should examine it to see if there is anything wrong with it (any erasures or words crossed out) and to see if the time for payment has passed. The following case emphasizes this issue.

BACKGROUND AND FACTS *Chalfont Industries was a manufacturer of an automotive product. Kutner Buick was an automobile dealer. Chalfont Industries and Kutner Buick maintained a close relationship: Kutner Buick was wholly owned by Jules Kutner, and Chalfont Industries was wholly owned by Jules's son, Jerome. From December 1981 to February 1982, Chalfont negotiated with Stuart Crawford concerning the possible purchase of a distributorship. During the negotiations, Chalfont made a number of false representations to Crawford relating to the product and the distributorship. Chalfont drafted a contract and sent the draft to Crawford. Crawford's attorney redrafted the contract.*

Crawford went to the Chalfont's office to sign the redrafted contract. Crawford presented the contract and wrote a check in the amount of $42,023 to Chalfont. One of Chalfont's employees took the contract and check into Jerome's office for him to sign, while Crawford was made to wait in the outer office. The employee came out and gave Crawford the signed contract, but that contract was not the one Crawford had presented; it was, rather,

Case 12.1
BANKERS TRUST COMPANY OF WESTERN NEW YORK v. CRAWFORD
United States Court of Appeals, Third Circuit, 1986.
781 F.2d 39.

a substitute one. Immediately after Crawford left Chalfont's offices, Jerome indorsed and delivered the check to Kutner Buick, which immediately deposited the check.

On discovering the fraud, Crawford successfully stopped payment on the check. When the check was presented to Crawford's bank for payment out of Crawford's account, the bank refused to pay because of the stop-payment order. Crawford's bank sent the check back to Kutner Buick's bank, which withdrew the amount out of Kutner Buick's account; thus, Kutner Buick was out of pocket $42,023.

Crawford reentered negotiations with Chalfont. Finally, Crawford had a cashier's check drawn in the amount of $50,023. He mailed the check to Chalfont. Later, however, Crawford had misgivings after Chalfont's national sales manager called and warned Crawford to stop payment on his check. Crawford instructed his lawyer to try to stop payment while he went to Chalfont's office to intercept the check. Crawford's attorney went to court and obtained a restraining order that prohibited the bank from paying the check.

Crawford waited for two days in Chalfont's offices after Chalfont's employee told him that he could have the check on its arrival. He was told the check had not arrived. In fact, the check had been received, and Chalfont already had indorsed and delivered it to Kutner Buick. Kutner Buick deposited the check into its bank account.

Crawford's bank was caught in a legal bind. The bank could not refuse to pay a cashier's check, but it could not disobey the judicial restraining order that prohibited payment. The bank did not pay the check, but filed an interpleader naming Chalfont, Kutner Buick, and Crawford as defendants. (An interpleader means that the bank has paid the money to the court and is asking the court to decide who is entitled to the money.) The trial court ordered the bank to pay the check to Kutner Buick.

Judge ROSENN

* * * *

Crawford * * * argues that Kutner Buick was under a "duty to inquire" into the transactional circumstances surrounding the receipt of the check and, because it failed to do so, did not take the check in good faith. * * *

In Pennsylvania, a holder in due course is a person "who takes the instrument: (1) for value; (2) in good faith; and (3) without notice that it is overdue or has been dishonored or of any defense or claim to it on the part of any person." * * * A holder in due course takes an instrument free of all defenses except for fraud in factum and such illegality as would render the obligation of the party a nullity. * * * Therefore, if Kutner Buick was a holder in due course, it is not subject to defenses arising from the underlying transaction, and properly received the check proceeds regardless of any defenses Crawford has against Chalfont.

* * * *

Crawford * * * argues, as he did in the trial court, that Kutner Buick was not a holder in due course because it did not take the check in good faith. In order to have taken in good faith, Crawford maintains, Kutner Buick had a duty to inquire into the circumstances surrounding transfer of the check. The district court held that the proper test for determining good faith is to ascertain whether the transferee exhibited willful dishonesty or actual knowledge, and that the evidence did not demonstrate that Kutner Buick was guilty of either.

* * * *

* * * In this case * * * the district court made three insurmountable findings of fact that are supported by the record and are not clearly erroneous.

There is no evidence that Jules Kutner or any employee of Kutner Buick knew or had reason to know of Crawford's attempt to stop or reclaim the cashier's check.

There is no evidence that Jules Kutner or any employee of Kutner Buick knew or had reason to know of the occurrence of substance of any conversations between Crawford and employees of Chalfont.

There is no evidence that the failure of Jules Kutner or any employee of Kutner Buick to make any inquiries about the cashier's check stemmed from any desire to evade knowledge of Crawford's efforts to stop the check.

These findings contrast sharply with the facts of *Normal v. World Wide Distributors, Inc.*, also cited by appellant. In *Norman*, the appellate court found that the transferee of the note had been previously purchasing similar notes from the seller and its suspicions had been aroused sufficiently concerning the honesty of the underlying transaction as to prompt a call to the maker of the note in question "whether they were satisfied with the transaction." Moreover, the court concluded that the frequency with which the transferors changed their operating name—three times in one year—and the sale of the note made payable three days after the date of its execution to the transferee at a substantial discount were circumstances that imposed a duty upon the transferee of the note to have inquired further into the sales operation of the seller of the notes. Thus, in *Norman*, there were circumstances in the negotiation of the note itself, as well as other strong circumstances, suggesting irregularities in the underlying transaction for the note.

Thus, it appears from an analysis of the foregoing case that Pennsylvania consistently follows the common law rule adopted by * * * the Uniform Commercial Code that there is no affirmative duty of inquiry on the part of one taking a negotiable instrument, and there is no constructive notice from the circumstances of the transaction, unless the circumstances are so strong that if ignored they will be deemed to establish bad faith on the part of the transferee.

The close relationship between the father and son, the unusual financial transactions between Kutner Buick and Chalfont, the extensive loans and guarantees of the father personally and of Kutner Buick and the advance of the bankruptcy filing fee, may raise questions as to how much Kutner Buick knew of the frauds practiced by Chalfont. The district court, however, found no evidence from the circumstances of the negotiation of the Crawford cashier's check or from the face of the instrument as would impose an affirmative duty on Kutner Buick to inquire into the underlying transaction. Kutner Buick apparently received the cashier's check in substitution for the check of February 10 on which Crawford had stopped payment. We have carefully reviewed the record and we can find nothing in the circumstances pertaining to the actual negotiation of the Crawford check or from the face of the check to put Kutner Buick on notice of any infirmity in the underlying transaction to suggest an affirmative duty of inquiry by Kutner Buick.

Although the detestable fraud practiced upon Crawford by Chalfont commands a searching inquiry into the validity of the negotiation of the check, we are confronted by very broad principles of public policy that support the circulation and credit of negotiable instruments. We are constrained to conclude that under Pennsylvania law Kutner Buick accepted the cashier's check as a holder in due course.

DECISION AND REMEDY

The court affirmed the judgment of the trial court. Crawford was a victim of Chalfont's fraud. Crawford could not collect the amount of the check from Chalfont because Chalfont filed for bankruptcy, nor can Crawford collect the amount from Kutner Buick because it is a holder in due course. Crawford is out the money.

COMMENT

The court upheld the law of negotiable instruments and, by doing so, upheld the policy behind it. If negotiable instruments are to be treated as substitutes for currency, even in a case such as this one where a hardship is imposed on one party, the public's faith in the use of negotiable instruments must be maintained.

Types of Commercial Paper

Four types of instruments (commercial paper) are set out in UCC 3-104: certificates of deposit, notes, drafts, and checks. All of these instruments fall into one of two categories: **promises to pay** or **orders to pay.**

Generally, instruments classified as promises to pay are two-party instruments, such as notes and certificates of deposit, and they are used as credit devices. Instruments that are classified as orders to pay are three-party instruments and are used in lieu of currency, such as checks and drafts.

Promises to Pay

The two most common types of promises to pay are promissory notes and certificates of deposit.

Promissory Notes   The promissory note is a written promise to pay (other than a certificate of deposit) made between two parties [UCC 3-104(2)(d)]. One party is the maker of the promise to pay and the other is the payee, the one to whom the promise is made. A promissory note, commonly referred to as a *note*, can be made payable at a definite time or on demand. Notes are commonly used by banks and by other financial institutions to document a loan of money.

Various types of credit transactions use notes. Often the name of the type of loan appears in the name of the note. For example, a promissory note to repay money lent to purchase real property is called a **mortgage note.** A mortgage is a separate document by which the debtor agrees to repay the money lent on the note; if he or she fails to repay, the creditor can take the property, sell it, and use the proceeds to pay what is owed on the mortgage note. Although the note is not the mortgage, it lets others know that payment on it is secured (or backed up) by a mortgage.

Similarly, a **collateral note** indicates that money was lent to a debtor to purchase personal property. The item purchased, such as an automobile, is used to secure the repayment; that is, the automobile serves as collateral (hence the name of the note) to secure repayment of the loan. An **install-**ment note** means that the note is payable by installments, such as when you pay for a stereo over a 24-month period. The names of these contracts overlap frequently. For example, if the stereo was given as collateral to secure repayment over the 24 months, the contract may be called a "collateral installment note."

Certificate of Deposit   A certificate of deposit (CD) is an acknowledgment by a bank of the receipt of money with an agreement to repay it [UCC 3-104(2)(c)]. Certificates of deposit pay interest and are either negotiable or nonnegotiable instruments. Most large CDs ($100,000 or more) are negotiable. Their negotiability allows them to be sold, to be used to pay debts, or to serve as security (collateral) for a loan.

Orders to Pay

When an instrument is an order to pay, three parties are on the document. The drawer creates an instrument that orders the drawee to pay money, usually to a third party who is either a specific payee or a bearer. The drawer can make the instrument payable to himself or herself—for example, you can make a check out to yourself. The drawer "orders" the instrument to be paid by the drawee. The drawer does not "make" a promise to pay, which is the language used in instruments that have only two parties. The two most common orders to pay are drafts and checks.

Drafts   A draft is an unconditional written order [UCC 3-104(2)(a)]. The draft represents a debt owed by the drawee to the drawer. The debt has been made either by agreement or through a debtor-creditor relationship. Two types of drafts are recognized: **time drafts** and **sight drafts.** A time draft is a draft that is payable at a definite future time. The trade acceptance in Exhibit 12–3 was an example of a time draft. A sight (or demand) draft is payable on sight. When the holder presents for payment a sight draft, such as a share draft used by a credit union, the draft is paid. Insurance companies use sight drafts to pay claims.

Checks A check is drawn on a bank or financial institution, ordering it to pay a sum of money on demand [UCC 3-104(2)(b)]. The person who writes the check is called the drawer and is a depositor in the bank on which the check is drawn. The person to whom the check is payable is the payee. The bank on which the check is drawn is the drawee. If Dominic writes a check on his checking account to pay for his boat, he is the drawer, his bank is the drawee, and the boat seller is the payee.

Requirements for a Negotiable Instrument

Commercial paper is either **negotiable** or non-negotiable. Both the form and content determine whether the instrument is negotiable. In order for an instrument to be negotiable, according to UCC 3-104(1), it must:

1. Be in writing
2. Be signed by the maker or drawer
3. Be an unconditional promise or order to pay
4. Be stated in a specific sum of money
5. Be payable on demand or at a definite time
6. Be payable to order or to bearer.

In Writing

Negotiable instruments must be written and they must be written on something that has permanence and on something that is portable so it can be freely transferred. It is impossible to transfer to a third party an oral promise with its danger of fraud and with the difficulty of determining liability. Having the negotiable instrument in writing makes it possible for it to be used as a substitute for currency.

Signed by the Maker or the Drawer

For an instrument to be negotiable, it must be signed by the maker of a note or certificate of deposit or by the drawer of a check or draft [UCC 3-104(1)(a)]. Extreme latitude is granted in determining what constitutes a signature. The word "signed" includes any symbol used by the party with the intention of authenticating the instrument. Various symbols can be used in lieu of the traditional written signature. Initials, an "X," a thumbprint, or anything else will suffice if it is intended to be a signature.

Unconditional Promise or Order to Pay

The terms of payment must be included in the writing on the face of a negotiable instrument. The party who is holding the instrument must be able to look only at the instrument and determine what the terms are. These terms cannot be conditioned on an event or agreement [UCC 3-104(1)(b)]. The instrument cannot be controlled by events beyond the instrument itself [UCC 3-105]. If conditional promises had to be investigated by the holder, the use of these documents as a substitute for currency would be dramatically reduced.

For an instrument to be negotiable, it must contain an express order or promise to pay a specific sum of money. A mere acknowledgment of the debt, which might logically imply a promise, is not sufficient. For example, the traditional note (IOU) is only an acknowledgment of indebtedness. The IOU is a written instrument, but it is not a negotiable one.

To Pay a Specific Sum of Money

A specific sum of money must be stated—at least in such a manner that the debtor can calculate the amount he or she must pay [UCC 3-106]. If the instrument's value was stated in terms of goods or services, it would be too difficult to ascertain the market value. For example, if the value in a ten-year promissory note was stated in computer chips, what value does a 64-bit chip have today as compared to its value in ten years?

Payable on Demand or at a Definite Time

A negotiable instrument must be payable on demand or at a definite time [UCC 3-104(1)(c)]. Clearly, the maker or drawee must know when he or she is required to pay. With an interest-bearing instrument, one must know the exact interval during which the interest will accrue in order to determine the present value of the instrument.

The very nature of the instrument may indicate that it is payable on demand [UCC 3-108]. For example, a check, by definition, is payable on demand [UCC 3-104(2)(b)]. Negotiable time drafts, on the other hand, are payable at a definite time that is specified on the face of the instrument [UCC 3-109]. The maker or drawee is under no obligation to pay until the specified time has arrived or elapsed.

Payable to Order or to Bearer

Because one function of a negotiable instrument is to substitute for currency, freedom to transfer the instrument is an essential requirement. A negotiable instrument requires that it be "payable to order or to bearer" [UCC 3-104(1)(d)]. These words acknowledge that another person, unknown at the time that the instrument is issued and thus not the immediate payee, may eventually be the owner. These words or their equivalents must be present on both the three-party order-to-pay instruments and the two-party promise-to-pay instruments. If these words are not present, the instrument is non-negotiable, and, therefore, it is only assignable and would be governed by contract law.

An instrument that states "payable to order" and that names a *specific payee* (named with certainty) is often referred to as **order paper** [UCC 3-110]. When no specific payee is designated so that essentially the instrument is payable to any person, the paper is called **bearer paper** [UCC 3-111].

Assignment or Negotiation

Once issued, a negotiable instrument can be transferred by assignment or by negotiation. The critical distinction is this: Contract rights are *assigned* to a third party who has the status of an assignee and who has no better rights than the transferor-assignor, while a negotiable instrument is *negotiated* to a third person who, if he or she has the status of an HDC, can have better rights than the transferor. Again, because negotiable instruments are used as substitutes for currency, a person who accepts an instrument wants to be reasonably certain that he or she can collect on it free from any defenses that may be asserted against the holder of a normal contract assignment.

Assignment

Assignment is a transfer of rights under a contract. Recall from Chapter 10 that, under general contract principles, a transfer by assignment from an assignor (the original party to the contract) to an assignee (the person buying the contract right) gives the assignee only those rights that the assignor has possessed. Any defenses to the contract that can be raised against the assignor can also be raised against the assignee. Nonnegotiable commercial paper cannot be negotiated but can be assigned. Furthermore, when a transfer fails to qualify as a negotiation, it becomes an assignment.

Negotiation

Negotiation is the transfer of a negotiable instrument in a manner such that the transferee becomes a holder [UCC 3-202(1)]. The holder, at the very least, receives the rights of the previous possessor [UCC 3-201(1)]. Unlike an assignment, a transfer by negotiation makes it possible for a holder to become a holder in due course and to receive more rights in the instrument than the prior possessor [UCC 3-305]. Two methods of negotiating an instrument exist that allow the receiver to become qualified as a holder or as an HDC.

Negotiating Order Paper   Order paper initially names a specific payee who is then able to indorse the instrument.

Two steps are required to negotiate (transfer) order paper: indorsement and delivery. For example, the Transco Company issues a payroll check "to the order of Wang." Wang takes the check to the supermarket, signs her name on the back (a blank indorsement), gives it to the cashier (a delivery), and receives currency. Wang has negotiated the check (an order instrument) by a blank indorsement and delivery to the supermarket [UCC 3-202(1)]. The supermarket is now an HDC because it took the check for value, in good faith, and without notice of any problems with the check.

Negotiating Bearer Paper   Bearer paper is negotiated by delivery alone. No indorsement is necessary [UCC 3-202(1)]. In an actual situation, the bank may require a person cashing a check indorsed in blank (now a bearer instrument) to sign the back of the check, but, technically, this signature on the back is not required for negotiation. The bank may require it for purposes of identification and verification that this person received the money [UCC 3-505]. The use of bearer paper involves more risk through loss or theft than does the use of order paper.

Legal Highlight

Telemarketing Fraud

One often-used telemarketing scheme is the following: You receive a postcard announcing that you have won cash, an appliance, a diamond, or even an automobile. You call the toll-free number to check on the prize. The postcard represents the items as free but states that a small shipping fee is charged. You are asked to give the operator the numbers on the bottom of your check.

Without your knowledge, the outfit you have called sends a demand draft to your bank. A demand draft is similar to a check, but the customer's signature is not needed. Banks do not normally check for authorized signatures; thus, you will not discover the theft until your checks start bouncing or until you receive your monthly statement. In the meantime, the thief who has posed as a telemarketer has changed locations. The moral of the story is never give anyone your checking account number. Treat it as a secret.

Assume Bob Brown writes a check "payable to cash" and hands it (a delivery) to Mary Maack. Brown has negotiated the check (bearer paper) to Maack by delivery alone. Maack places the check in her wallet, which is subsequently stolen. The thief has possession of the check. At this point, negotiation has not occurred, because delivery must be voluntary on the part of the transferor. If the thief "delivers" the check to an innocent party, negotiation will have occurred. All rights to the check will be passed absolutely to that party, and Maack will lose all rights to recover the proceeds of the check from that party [UCC 3-305]. Of course, she can recover her money from the thief, if the thief can be found.

Converting Order to Bearer Paper and Vice Versa The method used for negotiation depends on the character of the instrument at the time the negotiation takes place. Once the payee has negotiated the instrument to a holder, the indorsement on the back determines whether the instru-ment is now order or bearer paper. For example, a check originally payable to "Cash" is bearer paper and is negotiated by delivery. If the check is subsequently indorsed "Pay to Jones," it now must be negotiated as order paper (by indorsement and delivery) because it now names a specific payee [UCC 3-204(1)]. Bearer paper may be converted to order paper if the back of the paper has a **special indorsement** (payable to a specific person), such as "pay to Wang. [signed] Joe Jones." See Exhibit 12–5 for a sample special indorsement. An instrument originally payable to the order of a named payee (order paper) and indorsed in blank (the payee signs only her or his name) becomes a bearer instrument [UCC 3-204(2)].

The following case discusses the difference between an assignment of a contract and the negotiation of an instrument. You will see that the transfer of an instrument that is not negotiable makes the new holder subject to all the defenses that the maker may have against the original payee.

BACKGROUND AND FACTS *A promissory note and purchase money mortgage (a lien taken by the seller or lender of the realty to secure the unpaid purchase price) were executed by the appellant, Holly Hill Acres, as maker in favor of Rogers and Blythe as payees. Subsequently, Rogers and Blythe pledged the promissory note and mortgage in question to the appellee, Charter Bank of Gainesville, to secure their own note. Charter Bank took the note and mortgage either under an assignment-of-a-contract theory or under the negotiation theory if the note was a negotiable instrument. Ul-*

Case 12.2
HOLLY HILL ACRES, LTD. v. CHARTER BANK OF GAINESVILLE
District Court of Appeal, Florida, 1975.
314 So.2d 209.

timately, both Rogers and Blythe and Holly Hill Acres defaulted (failed to pay) on their notes.

Charter Bank sued both Rogers and Blythe and Holly Hill to recover payment on the promissory note executed by Holly Hill Acres. Charter Bank alleged that the note was a negotiable instrument and that the bank was a holder in due course. As a holder in due course, the bank claimed that it was entitled to collect on the note from Holly Hill Acres despite any underlying disputes between Rogers and Blythe and Holly Hill Acres.

Holly Hill Acres answered the complaint by alleging that Rogers and Blythe had defrauded it and that the note was not a negotiable instrument because the note incorporated by reference the terms of the purchase money mortgage. If the note was not negotiable, any defenses that Holly Hill had against Rogers and Blythe were also available against any assignee of Rogers and Blythe, such as Charter Bank.

The trial court ruled in a summary judgment that the note was negotiable and allowed the bank to recover. Holly Hill Acres appealed the decision.

Judge SCHEB

*   *   *   *

*   *   * The note *   *   * contains the following stipulation:

This note with interest is secured by a mortgage on real estate, of even date herewith, made by the maker hereof in favor of the said payee, and shall be construed and enforced according to the laws of the State of Florida. *The terms of said mortgage are by this reference made a part hereof.* (Emphasis supplied.)

*   *   *   *

The note having incorporated the terms of the purchase money mortgage was not negotiable. The appellee Bank was not a holder in due course, therefore, the appellant was entitled to raise against the appellee any defenses which could be raised between the appellant and Rogers and Blythe. Since appellant asserted an affirmative defense of fraud, it was incumbent on the appellee to establish the nonexistence of any genuine issue of any material fact or the legal insufficiency of appellant's affirmative defense. Having failed to do so, appellee was not entitled to a judgment as a matter of law; hence, we reverse.

The note, incorporating by reference the terms of the mortgage, did not contain the unconditional promise to pay required by [UCC 3-104(1)(b)]. Rather, the note falls within the scope of [UCC 3-105(2)(a)]. *   *   *

*   *   * Mere reference to a note being secured by mortgage is a common commercial practice and such reference in itself does not impede the negotiability of the note. There is, however, a significant difference in a note stating that it is "secured by a mortgage" from one which provides, "the terms of said mortgage are by this reference made a part hereof." In the former instance the note merely refers to a separate agreement which does not impede its negotiability, while in the latter instance the note is rendered non-negotiable. *   *   *

As a general rule the assignee of a mortgage securing a non-negotiable note, even though a bona fide purchaser for value, takes subject to all defenses available as against the mortgagee. *   *   *

DECISION AND REMEDY

The appellate court ruled that the note was conditional on its face. A holder of the note had to look at the mortgage to determine all the terms of the note. As a result, the note was nonnegotiable, and Charter Bank was not a holder in due course. The court set aside the summary judgment and ordered a new trial. At the new trial, Holly Hill can assert the affirmative defense of fraud on the contract, note, and mortgage against both the bank and Rogers and Blythe.

Defenses

Defenses by a party to avoid payment fall into two general categories: **real defenses** and **personal defenses.** Real defenses are used to avoid payment to all holders of a negotiable instrument including an HDC [UCC 3-305(2)]. Personal defenses are used to avoid payment to an ordinary holder of a negotiable instrument [UCC 3-306].

Real Defenses

Real (or universal) defenses are valid against all holders, including HDCs or holders who take an instrument through an HDC. (A holder who does not qualify as an HDC but who derives his or her title through an HDC acquires the rights and privileges of an HDC [UCC 3-201]. This is sometimes referred to as the "shelter principle.") The following are some of these defenses.

Forgery   Forgery of a maker's or a drawer's signature cannot bind the person whose name is used unless that person ratifies the signature [UCC 3-401 and 3-404(1)].

Fraud in Execution   A person may be deceived into signing a negotiable instrument, as when a person believes that she or he is signing something other than a negotiable instrument (for example, a receipt). This is called fraud in execution. For instance, a consumer unfamiliar with the English language signs a paper presented by a salesperson as a request for an estimate. In fact, it is a promissory note. Even if the note is negotiated to an HDC, the consumer may have a valid defense based on the real defense of fraud in execution. This defense cannot be used if a reasonable person would not or should not have been deceived as to the character of the instrument being signed.

Alteration   An alteration is material if it changes the contract terms between any two parties in any way. Examples of material alterations are changing the number or relations of the parties, completing the instrument in an unauthorized manner, or adding to or removing something from the writing after it has been signed [UCC 3-407(1)]. Material alteration is a complete defense against an ordinary holder but is at best only a partial defense against an HDC. A holder cannot recover anything on an instrument if it has been materially

altered [UCC 3-407(2)]. If the original terms have been altered, such as the amount payable, the HDC can collect the original amount from the maker or drawer. If the instrument was incomplete and later completed in an unauthorized manner, alteration cannot be used as a defense against an HDC, and the HDC can enforce the instrument up to the amount written in [UCC 3-407(3)].

Bankruptcy   When a debt represented by a negotiable instrument has been discharged (forgiven) in bankruptcy, that discharge is an absolute defense against paying the instrument to either a holder or an HDC. The purpose of bankruptcy is to settle and forgive all of the insolvent party's debts [UCC 3-305(2)(d)].

Operation of Law   When illegal conduct renders an instrument void, no payment can be made to either a holder or an HDC. If a person is declared mentally incompetent by state proceedings, any instrument issued by that person thereafter is null and void. The instrument is void from the beginning (time of issue) and unenforceable by any holder or an HDC [UCC 3-305(2)(a)].

When a person signs and issues a negotiable instrument under such extreme duress as an immediate threat of force or violence (for example, at gunpoint), the instrument is void and unenforceable by any holder or HDC [UCC 3-305(2)(a)].

Personal Defenses

All other defenses that are valid in a contract setting, such as breach of contract, breach of warranty, misrepresentation, mistake, undue influence, and economic duress, are considered personal defenses. These defenses are not valid against an HDC but only against an ordinary holder.

For example, Penny owns a bar and wants to install a big-screen television for the patrons. Penny agrees to purchase from an acquaintance a big-screen television for $2,800. Slick, knowing his statements to be false, tells Penny that the television is only six months old and is in good working order. In addition, he tells Penny that he owns the television free and clear of all claims. Penny pays Slick $500 in cash and issues a negotiable promissory note for the balance. As it turns out, Slick still owes the original seller $500 on the purchase of the television, and the television is subject to a filed security interest (lien). In addition, the television is three years old. Penny can refuse to pay the note if it is held by an ordinary holder; but if Slick has negotiated the note to an HDC, Penny must pay the HDC. Of course, Penny can then sue Slick. (Penny cannot use the FTC rule described in the next section because she owns a business and therefore does not qualify as a consumer.)

Federal Limitations on Holder-in-Due-Course Rights

A Federal Trade Commission (FTC) rule has severely limited the preferential position enjoyed by an HDC in a **consumer credit transaction.** Payment by check is not a credit transaction for purposes of this FTC rule.

Prior to the FTC rule, the law giving preferential treatment to an HDC worked a severe hardship on consumers. For example, Ron, a consumer, buys a new wide-screen television from Shady TV Dealers for $2,500. Ron signs a promissory note to pay for the television; the payee is Shady TV Dealers. Shady turns around and sells the note (negotiates it) at a discounted amount to Better Bank. The bank, having paid value, taken the note in good faith, and taken it without notice of any problems with the note, qualifies as an HDC. Ron discovers the television is defective and will never work properly. This is a personal defense, and naturally, he does not want to pay for the TV. The note, however, is now held by the bank, an HDC. Ron is forced to pay the bank on the note. The defenses Ron has on the contract for the purchase of the defective television are valid only against Shady TV Dealers, not the bank.

Today, under the FTC rule, this type of note is given as a part of a consumer credit contract. The note must contain a warning to any holder who may qualify as an HDC. It states that the holder of the note is subject to all contract defenses that the original purchaser may have against the original seller. In other words, in a consumer credit contract even personal defenses are valid against an HDC. Ron can now use the defenses he has against both Shady TV Dealers and Better Bank.

Indorsements

As previously discussed, indorsements are required whenever the instrument being negotiated is classified as order paper. An indorsement is the signature of the person, known as the indorser, and is used to transfer ownership of the instrument to someone else. The indorsement may or may not include additional words or statements limiting liability, and it is written on the back of the instrument itself. The indorsement should be identical to the name that appears on the instrument. The payee or indorsee whose name is misspelled can indorse with the misspelled name, the correct name, or both [UCC 3-203].

Categories

Four categories of indorsements are recognized: blank, special, qualified, and restrictive.

Blank and Special Indorsements—Signature and Transfer Warranty Liability Unless a bank or special indorser can claim a valid defense against the holder demanding payment, the indorser may be held liable by the holder on the instrument either on the basis of his or her signature (guaranty of payment) or on breach of warranties made on transfer of the instrument.

For signature liability, the blank and special indorsers have what is called *secondary* liability. What this means is that their signature liability is dependent upon the instrument being properly presented to the person with the responsibility of paying it, that the instrument has been dishonored, and that the indorser received timely notice of dishonor [UCC 3-414].

Proper presentment requires the holder to present the instrument to the party responsible for its payment (for example, a note to the maker), in a proper manner (for example, a check at the drawee's bank or at the holder's bank to go through a clearing house), and on or before the date the instrument is due [UCC 3-503, 3-504]. Most improper presentments are the result of the holder's failure to present the instrument within a proper time. Time instruments must be presented on or before the due date, and demand instruments (other than domestic checks) within a reasonable period after date or issue. For domestic checks, to hold blank and special indorsers liable on their signatures, the holder must present the check within seven days of the indorser's indorsement [UCC 3-503(2)].

Dishonor usually occurs when the party responsible for payment fails to do so upon presentment. Once dishonored, the holder is required to give notice (in any reasonable manner) to any secondary party the holder wants to hold on signature liability. This notice must be given by a bank before midnight of the next banking day after receipt. For those other than a bank, the notice must be given before midnight of the third business day. Written notice is effective when sent even though it is not received [UCC 5-308].

Should the holder fail to make proper presentment or to give the blank or special indorser proper notice of dishonor, the indorser is *completely discharged* from contract signature liability [UCC 3-502].

In addition to possible signature liability of the blank and special indorser, these indorsers, if they receive consideration from the transferee, make five transfer warranties [UCC 3-417(2)]. These warranties flow to all subsequent holders of the instrument. The five warranties are:

1. The transferor has good title to the instrument or is otherwise authorized to obtain payment or acceptance on behalf of one who does have good title.
2. All signatures are genuine or authorized.
3. The instrument has not been materially altered.
4. No defense of any party is good against the transferor.
5. The transferor has no knowledge of any insolvency proceedings against the maker, the acceptor, or the drawer of an unaccepted instrument.

Should any of these warranties be breached at the time of the indorser's transfer, a subsequent holder can hold the indorser liable. This action is independent of presentment and notice of dishonor (signature liability). Thus, a holder could sue for breach of warranty even if the instrument was improperly presented.

Nonindorsers also transfer an instrument and as such make the same transfer warranties as a blank or special indorser. There is one exception to the extent of liability, however: These warranties only flow to the nonindorsers' immediate transferee, not to all subsequent holders.

Qualified Indorsement   Generally, an indorser, merely by indorsing, promises to pay the holder, or any subsequent indorser, the amount of the instrument in the event that the drawee (on behalf of the drawer) or maker defaults on the payment [UCC 3-414(1)]. A **qualified indorsement** is used

by an indorser to disclaim or limit this liability on the instrument. This form of indorsement commonly includes the notation "without recourse."

Blank and special indorsements are unqualified indorsements; that is, the blank or special indorser is guaranteeing payment of the instrument in addition to transferring title to it. The qualified indorser is not guaranteeing any payment, but the qualified indorsement still transfers title to the indorsee or holder, and an instrument bearing a qualified indorsement can be further negotiated. See Exhibit 12–5 for a sample blank qualified indorsement.

A qualified indorser, who receives consideration, also makes transfer warranties. These warranties are the same as those made by a blank or special indorser (with one exception), and these warranties also flow to all subsequent holders. The one exception is that a qualified indorser warrants only that he or she has no *knowledge* of a defense good against the transferor, rather than the broad warranty that there are no defenses [UCC 3-417(2)(3)].

Restrictive Indorsement   The **restrictive indorsement** requires future indorsees or holders to comply with certain instructions regarding the funds involved.

Types of restrictive indorsements are conditional indorsements ("Pay to Rosemary Porter on condition of her delivery of her blue truck at 100 Green Street by August 7, 1993"), prohibiting indorsements ("Pay to Regina Heise only"), and trust indorsements ("Pay to Katherine Burns in trust for David Burns") [UCC 3-205]. As a general rule, restrictive indorsements do not prevent the further transfer or negotiation of the instrument [UCC 3-206(1)]. A common type of restrictive indorsement is one that makes the indorsee (almost always a bank) a collecting agent of the indorser. For example, "For Deposit Only" is a very common indorsement (see Exhibit 12–5). This type of indorsement has the effect of locking the instrument into the bank collection process. A restrictive indorser cannot be held liable unless the restriction (instruction) has been met.

Signature Liability of Makers, Acceptors, and Drawers

Makers and acceptors (an acceptor is a drawee who by signature has agreed to pay the drawer's instrument or is a bank's certification of a check) are *primarily* liable on the instrument [UCC 3-413(1)]. This means that the maker or acceptor is absolutely required to pay the face amount of the instrument (assuming there is no valid defense) at the time he or she signs it. There is no requirement for the holder to make proper presentment or give the maker or acceptor any notice.

A drawer is a party *secondarily* liable (much the same as a blank or general indorser) [UCC 3-413(2)]. Thus, to hold the drawer absolutely liable on his or her signature requires the holder to make proper presentment (for example, for a domestic check, within 30 days of date or issue) and to give the drawer proper notice of dishonor. There is one difference, however, in the liability of the drawer if the holder fails to make a proper presentment or give proper notice of dishonor and the drawee is a bank. The drawer is excused from liability only if the drawee bank is insolvent, and such insolvency caused the drawer to suffer a loss [UCC 3-502(1)(b)].

Discharge

Discharge from liability on an instrument can come from payment, cancellation, or material alteration. If the drawer or maker pays the instrument, it is discharged [UCC 3-603]. The payee or holder may cancel the instrument by intentionally marking it paid or by destroying it [UCC 3-605]. If the instrument has been materially altered as previously discussed, liability on the instrument may be totally, partially, or not at all discharged [UCC 3-407].

Checks and the Banking System

Checks are the most common kind of commercial paper regulated by the Uniform Commercial Code. Checks, credit cards, and charge accounts are rapidly replacing currency as a means of payment in almost all transactions for goods and services. Approximately 62 billion personal and commercial checks are written each year in the United States. Checks are more than a daily convenience; "checkbook money" is an integral part of the economic system. A check is a credit instrument treated as if it were cash.

The Bank-Customer Relationship

Modern bank deposit and collection procedures

are governed by Article 4 of the UCC. This article governs the relationship of banks with one another as they process checks for payment, and it establishes a framework for deposit and checking agreements between a bank and its customers.

The extent to which any party is either liable or not liable on a check is established according to the provisions of Article 3 of the UCC. A check can fall within the scope of Article 3 as a negotiable instrument and yet be subject to the provisions of Article 4 while it is in the course of collection. In the case of a conflict between Articles 3 and 4, Article 4 controls [UCC 4-102(1)]. See Exhibit 12–6.

Duties of the Bank

A commercial bank serves its customers primarily in two ways:

1. By honoring checks for the withdrawal of funds deposited in the customer's account
2. By accepting deposits in United States currency and collecting checks written to or indorsed to its customers that are drawn on other banks.

Honoring Checks   When a commercial bank provides checking services, it agrees to honor the checks written by its customers, if sufficient funds are available in the account to pay each check. When a drawee bank wrongfully fails to honor a check, it is liable to its customer, not the holder of the check, for damages resulting from its refusal to pay. The bank has a contract with the customer, not the holder of the check [UCC 4-402].

The bank may agree with the customer to accept overdrafts. An overdraft charges the customer's account for the amount of the check, even though the account contains insufficient funds to cover the check [UCC 4-401(1)]. Once a bank makes special arrangements with a customer to accept overdrafts on an account, the bank may be liable to the customer for damages caused by any wrongful dishonoring of overdrafts. Today, overdrafts are treated as loans to the customer, and interest is often charged from the day the overdraft is paid until funds are deposited to cover the overdraft plus the fees for handling the overdraft.

The following case discusses the potential liability of a bank when it wrongfully dishonors a customer's check.

Exhibit 12–6 A Simple Route of a Check

Case 12.3
**BUCKLEY v. TRENTON
SAVINGS FUND
SOCIETY**
Superior Court of New Jersey,
1987.
524 A.2d 886 (N.J.Super.A.D.).

BACKGROUND AND FACTS   *Trenton Savings Fund Society (Trenton)
wrongfully dishonored two checks written by Joseph Buckley to his estranged
wife while divorce proceedings were pending. Soon after the checks were
dishonored, Buckley received calls from his wife, sister, parents, children,
and his best friend inquiring why he was not providing support to his family.
Mrs. Buckley did not have an account with Trenton. Trenton was trying
to induce people to open new accounts and refused to cash checks drawn on
other accounts unless the holder also had an account with Trenton. Buckley
claimed he suffered great emotional stress because of this refusal by Trenton
to cash his checks. He sought both compensatory and punitive damages. The
jury returned a $25,000 verdict for Buckley, which was appealed by Trenton.*

Judge STERN
*   *   *   *

A bank's liability for wrongful dishonor of a customer's check is defined in
§ 4-402 of the Uniform Commercial Code (UCC) which was adopted in this State:
*   *   *

> A payor bank is liable to its customer for damages proximately caused by the wrongful
> dishonor of an item. When the dishonor occurs through mistake liability is limited
> to actual damages proved. If so proximately caused and proved damages may include
> damages for an arrest or prosecution of the customer or other consequential damages.
> Whether any consequential damages are proximately caused by the wrongful dis-
> honor is a question of fact to be determined in each case.

The UCC does not indicate the theory or basis for a bank's liability for wrongful
dishonor. As explained in the UCC official comment to § 4-402, "The liability
of the drawee for dishonor has sometimes been stated as one for breach of contract,
sometimes as for negligence or other breach of a tort duty, and sometimes as for
defamation. This section does not attempt to specify a theory." *   *   * The drafters
of the UCC did not intend to exclude the possibility of mental distress damages
upon a wrongful dishonor by a bank. *   *   * Since § 4-402 is silent "[o]n any
restriction of damages when the dishonor is grounded on an action other than
mistake . . .," *   *   * it implies that these damages are not precluded by the
Code. Thus, out-of-state courts interpreting § 4-402 have concluded that mental
suffering is compensable under this section.
*   *   *   *

In this case the judge's instructions failed to delineate the distinction between
mistake and an intentional breach or wilful, wanton or reckless misconduct. Moreover, the judge neglected to adequately address the subject of proximate cause.
The jury may well have determined that there was an intentional breach or wilful
misconduct but that plaintiff's emotional distress was not proximately caused by,
or the "natural and probable consequences" of, the bank's conduct, as opposed to
the result of intervention of independent factors including the unforeseeable conduct
and overreaction of Linda Buckley following the dishonor. *   *   * As a result,
the matter must be remanded for a new trial and for a determination of damages
based on appropriate instructions.

We preclude an award of punitive damages, however. Punitive damages are
not generally recoverable for breach of contract, *   *   * at least when the breach
of contract does not also constitute a tort for which punitive damages are recoverable.

**DECISION AND
REMEDY**
*The court returned the case to the trial court for a new trial. The jury had
to be instructed on the difference between mistake and intentional breach
or reckless misconduct as these relate to awarding damages. No punitive
damages were allowed.*

Honoring Stop-Payment Orders   Only a customer can order his or her bank to pay a check, and only a customer can order the payment of the check to be stopped. This right does not extend to holders (such as payees or indorsees) because the drawee bank's contract is only with its customer-drawers. A **stop-payment order** can be given orally, usually by phone, and it is binding on the bank for 14 calendar days unless confirmed in writing. A written stop-payment order is effective for six months, unless renewed in writing [UCC 4-403(2)]. When the customer uses her or his bank guarantee card in writing a check, the customer gives up the right to stop payment on that check.

The bank must be given a reasonable time to permit the bank to put the stop-payment order in effect. Until such time, the bank is not liable to its customer if the bank honors the check. If the drawee bank pays a check after the customer has instituted a proper stop-payment order, the bank is liable for the actual loss suffered by the customer-drawer because of the wrongful payment. This amount might be much less than the amount of the check. For example, JoAnn orders six plants priced at $50 each from Frank's Greenhouse. JoAnn pays Frank $300 in advance. Frank delivers only five plants and tells JoAnn it will be six months before the other plant will be delivered. JoAnn immediately stops payment on her $300 check. Inadvertently the bank honors the $300 check over her stop-payment order. JoAnn can only establish a loss of $50, having received five plants, and the bank is liable for only that amount.

The bank has a duty to inform its customers of the requirements for a stop-payment order. This issue is presented in the next case.

BACKGROUND AND FACTS   *Staff Service Associates, Inc. (Staff Service), the plaintiff, had a checking account with the Midlantic National Bank, the defendant. Staff Service issued a check in the amount of $4,117.12 on July 2, 1982. On July 7, 1982, Staff Service executed a stop-payment order but incorrectly wrote the amount of the check as $4,117.72. The employee acknowledged that he had read the statement on the bottom of the stop-payment order, which stated:*

> IMPORTANT: *The information on this Stop Payment Order must be correct, including the exact amount of the check to the penny, or the bank will not be able to stop payment and this Stop Payment Order will be void.*

The computer could not stop payment on the check unless the exact amount was indicated, but it could honor a stop payment if other information was not correct. The check was paid by the bank. Staff Service filed this lawsuit, and the bank filed a motion for a summary judgment. The trial court refused to grant the bank a summary judgment, and the bank appealed.

Case 12.4
STAFF SERVICE ASSOCIATES, INC. v. MIDLANTIC NATIONAL BANK
Superior Court of New Jersey, Law Division, Essex County, 1985.
207 N.J.Super. 237, 504 A.2d 148.

J.S.C. HIGGINS CASS
*   *   *   *

*   *   * Staff Service's representative did not know that Midlantic utilized a computer to effect stop payment of a check. In addition, Midlantic never informed Staff Service that the exact amount of the check is necessary for the computer to pull the check. It chose a computerized system which searches for stopped checks by amount alone. By electing this system Midlantic assumed the risk that it would not be able to stop payment of a check despite the customer's accurate description of the account number, the payee's name, the number and date of the check and a *de minimis* error in the check amount. Midlantic should not be permitted to relieve itself of this risk unless it calls attention to its computerized system and the necessity for the exact check amount to meet computer requirements.

The court is not persuaded by the clause in the stop payment order which states that Midlantic cannot stop payment unless the information provided by the customer is correct, including the exact amount of the check to the penny. Indeed this clause is inaccurate since, as Midlantic's representative explained in his certification, "if the amount of the check is correct, the check will be stopped, although a discrepancy may exist in the remaining elements of the stop payment order, unless and until the customer instructs otherwise." Consequently, notwithstanding the clause, it appears that a check will be stopped even if all the information on the stop payment order is incorrect except the check amount.

Implicated also is the question of how said clause is affected by [the UCC] which provides that a bank and its customers may vary by agreement the effect of the provisions of Article 4, but that

> [N]o agreement can disclaim a bank's responsibility for its own lack of good faith or failure to exercise ordinary care or can limit the measure of damages for such lack or failure; but the parties may by agreement determine the standards by which such responsibility is to be measured if such standards are not manifestly unreasonable.

Did the bank exercise good faith in the placement of a clause on the stop payment order which did not focus on the single critical item which it required? Moreover, in these circumstances, it is manifestly unreasonable to measure a bank's responsibility by a term not brought to the customer's attention with such specificity as to permit him to give the bank notice "in such manner as to afford the bank a reasonable opportunity to act."

Therefore, the court holds that a bank has a reasonable opportunity to stop payment on a check when a customer accurately describes the check in all respects except for a single digit error in the check amount. The result would be different only if the bank specifically informed the customer that its computer requires the exact check amount for stop payment.

The Uniform Commercial Code must be liberally construed and applied to promote its underlying purposes. The purpose of [the UCC] is expressed in comment 2 following the section:

> The position taken by this section is that stopping payment is a service which depositors expect and are entitled to receive from banks notwithstanding its difficulty, inconvenience and expense. The inevitable occasional losses through failure to stop should be borne by the banks as a cost of the business of banking.

Accordingly, defendant's motion for summary judgment is denied.

DECISION AND REMEDY *The appellate court denied the motion by the bank for a summary judgment because the facts were contested. The court held that, if the bank is not to be held liable for an improperly filled out stop payment, it must show the court that it specifically notified the customer that the exact amount of the check is necessary for the computer to pull the check and stop payment.*

Paying on a Forged Signature of the Drawer A forged drawer signature on a check has no legal effect [UCC 3-404(1)]. Banks require signature cards from each customer who opens a checking account. The bank is responsible for determining whether the signature on a customer's check is genuine. The general rule is that the bank must recredit the customer's account when it pays on a forged signature unless the customer's negligence substantially contributed to the making of the forgery, or the customer breached his or her duty to discover and report the forgery to the bank.

Customer Duties

When the customer's negligence substantially contributes to a forgery, the bank is not obliged to recredit the customer's account for the amount of the check [UCC 3-406]. Further, a customer has a duty to examine his or her monthly statements and canceled checks promptly and, if there is a series of forgeries, report any forged signatures within 14 days [UCC 4-406(1)]. Failure to examine and report or any carelessness by the customer that results in a loss to the bank makes the customer liable for the loss [UCC 4-406(1), (2)(a)(b)].

New Law: Amendments to Article 3

Most states adopted the UCC into statute 20 to 30 years ago. The UCC has worked very well to meet the problems of business. Over time, however, deficiencies in the UCC have become apparent, and new amendments of the code have been developed. These new provisions have been sent to the states, and by 1991 seven states had adopted these changes into law. The following are the major changes that have been made:

1. A check is still a negotiable instrument even if the words *Payable to order or bearer* have been crossed out. People were marking out these words when writing a check. Without these words, the check became a nonnegotiable instrument and destroyed the possibility of anyone being a holder in due course. The new provisions ensure that persons who take a check in good faith and for value can become holders in due course.
2. Many notes contained variable interest rates. In order to find the rate, however, one needed to look at external data such as the prime rate of a given bank or the Federal Reserve discount rate; this destroyed the negotiability of the note. The amendment allows a reference to external data to set a variable interest rate.
3. Under the new provisions, a conditional indorsement on a check, such as "Pay to John Doe only if the HMS *Pinafore* arrives in port by September 30, 1993," is no longer effective against the banks. Banks process thousands of checks an hour and cannot be held responsible to research whether the conditions in an indorsement have been met.
4. Under the new rules, a person can still be an HDC if he or she takes a check up to 90 days after it is issued. The old rule set the limit at 30 days.
5. The accord and satisfaction doctrine has been modified. Few businesses inspect all checks sent to them prior to deposit. Occasionally, a customer may send a check marked "Paid in full" in order to settle a disputed debt. Now a business can insist that their customers send a "payment in full" check to a specified address. If a business does not provide this notice, it can still avoid the accord and satisfaction doctrine by reimbursing the customer

within 90 days after it has cashed the "paid in full" check.
6. Comparative negligence rules may be applied when a bank pays on a forged signature on a check under the new rules.
7. Under the new rules, a customer must give advance notice to a bank if the customer is writing a postdated check. Under current law, a customer can write a postdated check without any notice.
8. The new rules make a payor bank liable to its customer for damages proximately caused by wrongful dishonor. Under the old rules, mistake and other situations were treated differently in the award of damages. This was part of the problem in the case of *Buckley v. Trenton Savings Fund Society*; under the new rules, this case probably would have been settled out of court.

Electronic Funds Transfer Systems

The present basis of the payment-collection process is the check, but banks are finding it increasingly difficult to cope with these billions of pieces of paper. **Electronic funds transfer systems** (EFTs)[1] have assisted the banks by removing the mountains of paperwork formerly necessary to transfer money.

An EFT system has:

1. Teller machines: Located conveniently and connected on-line to the bank's computers, these machines receive payments on loans, receive deposits for or dispense cash from checking or savings accounts, and make credit card advances.
2. Point-of-sale systems: Located in the merchant's store and connected on-line to the bank's computers, a point-of-sale system immediately debits the customer's checking account and transfers the funds to the merchant's account.
3. Automatic payments and direct deposits: Advance authorization allows regular electronic transfers of funds from an account (for the automatic payment of bills) or into an account (for a direct deposit).
4. Telecommunications systems: A customer can order by telephone or through the use of a computer the transfer of money to and from her or his accounts or for payment of a bill.

---

1. The terms *electronic funds transfer system* (EFT) and *electronic transfer of funds system* (ETF) are used interchangeably in business.

Consumers, Paper, and Electronic Banking

Visionaries in the 1960s foresaw a paperless, checkless society by the mid-1980s. All-electronic business would prevail. What has happened instead is that:

- The average person writes 25 checks per month, a rate that has steadily increased.
- By the early 1990s, over 62 billion checks a year were written.
- Consumers pay their bills:
  - First with checks (almost 90 percent of the time)
  - Second with credit cards (over 50 percent of the time)
- Third and trailing far behind, alas, the debit card is used less than 5 percent of the time.

What went wrong? Consumers are a suspicious lot. They fear the computer. They know that a computer can mess up their bank accounts thoroughly. They fear the loss of security if the computer breaks down. Worse, they lose the float time that occurs between the time the check is written and the time the amount is actually debited from their account, which can sometimes amount to days.

Who is happy? Check manufacturers, printers of paper charge slips, and, of course, printers of monthly statements, otherwise known as bills.

---

5. Automatic clearinghouses: Entries are made in the form of electronic signals; no checks are used. Clearinghouses are used by businesspeople for recurrent payments, such as payroll, social security, or pension funds.

This new technology, however, has aroused some serious consumer concerns. With the speed of the transmissions, it is difficult to issue stop-payment orders. Precisely because the transmissions are electronic, fewer paper records are available. These systems allow more opportunities for an unauthorized person to tamper with an account, and there is a resulting decrease in privacy. The time between the writing of a check and its deduction from an account (the float time) is lost.

A Bank's Liability in EFTs

Federal statutes such as the Electronic Fund Transfer Act (EFTA) govern electronic funds transfer accounts that are operated by telephone or by the presentation of a debit card to merchants when making purchases. The information concerning the consumer's rights under federal law must be given to every customer who opens an EFT account.

A monthly statement must be made for every month in which there is an electronic transfer of funds; otherwise, statements must be made every quarter. The statement must show the amount and date of the transfer, the names of the retailers involved, the location or identification of the terminal, the fees, and an address and telephone number for inquiries and error notices. The bank must furnish receipts for transactions made through computer terminals, but it is not obliged to do so for telephone transfers. The customer has the duty to reconcile his or her receipts against the statements.

New Law: Article 4A

All banks, other financial institutions, and the federal government electronically transfer funds. Between $1 billion and $2 trillion are transferred on any given day. The law failed to cover a number of problems that arose during the 1980s involving bank transfers. Thus, the drafters of the UCC have prepared a new section. Called Article 4A, Funds Transfers, it sets out a comprehensive scheme that covers the relationship of the bank with the originator of the funds and with the payee. Typically, the originator sends money via electronic transfer through the bank to the customer (payee). Article 4A has been distributed to the states for possible adoption into the UCC statutory scheme.

Secured Transactions

The concept of a secured transaction is as basic to modern business practice as the concept of credit. Few purchasers (manufacturers, wholesalers, retailers, or consumers) have the resources to pay cash for major goods being purchased. Lenders are reluctant to lend money to a debtor based solely on the debtor's promise to repay the debt. The simple fact is that sellers and lenders want to minimize the risk of loss because of nonpayment. The seller will not sell goods or lend money unless the promise of payment is somehow guaranteed.

To minimize the risk of loss, the creditor often requires the debtor to provide some type of security. When this security takes the form of personal property or real property that is owned by the debtor or in which the debtor has a legal interest, the transaction becomes known as a secured transaction, more commonly called a lien.

Business today cannot exist without secured transactions. Secured creditors are generally not subject to state exemption laws that exist to protect debtors. Secured creditors under federal bankruptcy laws have a favored position over unsecured creditors should the debtor become bankrupt.

The underlying philosophy of secured transaction laws deals with two major concerns of the creditor should the debtor default on the obligation: First, the debt will be satisfied from specific property (collateral) of the debtor. Second, the creditor's debt will have priority over the claims of other creditors to and purchasers of that specific collateral.

Article 9 of the UCC applies to any transaction that is intended to create a security interest in *personal property*. Transactions involving real property are excluded from Article 9 [UCC 9-104].

Exhibit 12–7 shows a sample security agreement.

Exhibit 12–7 A Sample Security Agreement

				June 30, 1993
				Date
William M. Smith	1306 - 37th Street	Des Moines,	Polk	Iowa
Name	No. and Street	City	County	State

(hereinafter called "Debtor") hereby grants to ___ **Janet Johnson Appliance Corporation**

			Name	
706 Grand Avenue		**Des Moines**	**Polk**	**Iowa**
No. and Street		City	County	State

(hereinafter called "Security Party") a security interest in the following property (hereinafter called the "Collateral"):
One 1993 Zenith 27" screen television set, Serial No. AZ22478

to secure payment and performance of obligations identified or set our as follows (hereinafter called the "Obligations"):
$50.00 per month for the next 60 months to be paid on the first day of every month beginning on the first day of August, 1993.

Default in payment or performance of any of the Obligations or default under any agreement evidencing any of the Obligations is a default under this agreement. Upon such default Secured Party may declare all Obligations immediately due and payable and shall have the remedies of a secured party under the ___**Iowa**___ Uniform Commercial Code.
Signed in (duplicate) triplicate.

William M Smith
Debtor

Janet Johnson Appliance Corp.
Secured Party
By *Janet Johnson, President*

Creating a Security Interest

In order for a creditor to become a secured party, the creditor must have a security interest in the collateral of the debtor. Three requirements must be met before a creditor has an enforceable security interest. First, unless the creditor has possession of the collateral, there must be a written security agreement signed by the debtor. Second, the creditor must give something of value to the debtor. Normally, the value given by a secured party is in the form of a direct loan, or it involves a commitment to sell goods on credit.

Third, the debtor must have rights in the property used as collateral; that is, the debtor must have some ownership interest or right to obtain possession of that collateral. The debtor's rights can represent either a current or a future legal interest in the collateral. For example, a retail seller-debtor can give a secured party a security interest not only in existing inventory owned by the retailer but also in future inventory to be acquired by the retailer.

Once these requirements are met, the creditor's rights are said to "attach to" the collateral. Attachment means that the creditor has an enforceable security interest against the debtor. The attachment of the security interest establishes the rights and liabilities of the debtor and creditor [UCC 9-203].

Perfection

Even though the creditor's security interest has attached to the debtor's property, the secured creditor must take steps in order to protect his or her claim to the collateral over claims that third parties may have to the same property. The procedures to protect the creditor's rights are called **perfection**. The third parties may be other secured creditors, general creditors, trustees in bankruptcy, or purchasers of the collateral.

There are three methods of perfection:

1. Upon attachment: If there is a purchase-money security interest in consumer goods (goods used or bought primarily for personal, family, or household purposes), perfection occurs automatically upon creation of the security interest without a filing or the secured party taking possession.
2. Upon possession: A secured party's possession of a debtor's collateral is notice of a possible lien and thus perfection. Negotiable instruments can only be perfected by possession.
3. Upon filing: The most common method is for the secured party to file with the appropriate government office a **financing statement** [UCC 9-402].

As a general rule, first in time of perfection is first in priority right to the collateral. There is one group of purchasers who will prevail regardless of a secured party's perfection and even if the purchaser knows of the secured party's interest at the time of purchase. Those are any purchasers who purchase goods in the ordinary course of business [UCC 9-307(1)].

For example, Last Bank has a perfected security interest in the inventory of Gary's retail TV store. Joan purchases one of the TV sets from Gary subject to Last Bank's perfected security interest. Joan takes the TV set free of Last Bank's security interest (if Gary goes into default, Last Bank cannot repossess the TV from Joan), even if Joan knew of it at the time of sale.

Default

Article 9 of the UCC defines the rights, duties, and remedies in case a debtor defaults on a secured loan. When a debtor defaults, a secured creditor can protect his or her claim to the collateral and enforce his or her security interest by a court judgment, by foreclosure, or by any available judicial process [UCC 9-501].

Secured Party's Remedies   A secured party's remedies can be divided into two basic categories. First, a secured party can forgo his or her security interest and proceed to a court judgment on the debt. Once the secured party has the judgment, he or she can use it to take other assets of the debtor to satisfy the judgment debt. This procedure is used when the value of the secured collateral has been greatly reduced below the amount of the debt, such as a wrecked automobile, and the debtor has other assets available to satisfy the debt [UCC 9-501(1)].

Second, a secured party can take possession, called repossession, of the collateral covered by the security agreement [UCC 9-503]. On repossession, the secured party can retain the collateral covered by the security agreement for satisfaction of the debt [UCC 9-505(2)] or can resell the goods and apply the proceeds toward the debt. The sale

Legal Highlight

A Tale of Woe!

During the recession of the early 1990s, many people lost their jobs. Arthur, a former computer engineer, owned two cars and owed money on both. Hoping to cut back on his expenses now that he was unemployed, he decided to turn one car over to the bank, an act called voluntary repossession. Just as many people do, Arthur believed that he did not now owe the unpaid amount of the loan.

This belief is wrong. Not only does Arthur lose his car but he also still owes the difference between the debt still to be repaid and what the bank receives when it sells his car.

Arthur originally purchased the car for $30,000, paid $5,000 down, and financed the remaining $25,000. Over the past year, he has paid the balance of the principal down to $20,000. The blue-book value is $17,000.

If the bank is able to sell the car for the $20,000 plus costs of resale, Arthur will owe nothing. If the bank sells it for more, Arthur receives the surplus. Unfortunately, most cars in this type of situation are sold for less than the amount still owed the bank. If the bank is able to obtain $13,000, Arthur will still owe the deficiency of $7,000.

If Arthur fails to pay the $7,000, the bank can go to court and obtain a deficiency judgment (that is, a judgment for the amount still deficient to have the contract paid in full).

---

must be conducted in a commercially reasonable manner [UCC 9-504].

The creditor's rights and remedies under the UCC are cumulative; therefore, if a creditor is unsuccessful in enforcing his or her rights by one method, another method can be pursued. The UCC does not require the creditor to choose between remedies—that is, between a lawsuit to obtain a judgment and repossession of the collateral.

The secured party has the right to take peaceful possession of the collateral on default. As long as there is no breach of the peace, the secured party can simply repossess the collateral. Otherwise, the secured party must resort to the judicial process [UCC 9-503].

What constitutes a breach of the peace is of prime importance to both parties, for such an act can open the secured party (the party repossessing) to tort liability. The UCC does not define breach of the peace; the parties must look to the state laws to determine it.

In most states the secured party must be able to obtain the collateral without breaking and entering, committing assault or battery, or trespassing.

Generally, the creditor or the creditor's agent cannot enter a debtor's home, garage, or place of business without permission. For example, say that an automobile is the collateral on a defaulted loan. If the repossessing party walks onto the debtor's premises, proceeds up the driveway, enters the vehicle without entering the garage, and drives off, this probably will not amount to a breach of the peace. In some states, however, an action for wrongful trespass could be the basis for the debtor to file a breach-of-the-peace lawsuit. Thus, most car repossessions occur when the car is parked on a street or in a parking lot.

Proceeds from the Disposition of Collateral If the secured party sells the collateral upon the debtor's default, proceeds from the sale of the collateral are applied in the following order. First, reasonable expenses stemming from the retaking, holding, or preparing for sale are paid. These expenses can include reasonable attorneys' fees and legal expenses. Second, satisfaction of the balance of the debt owed to the secured party is made. Third, subordinate security interests whose written demands have been received prior to the completion of distribution of the proceeds are paid. Subordinate security interests are for loans that are second or third liens on the property.

For example, Bill buys an expensive antique automobile, one that is known to appreciate in value, and signs a security agreement. He has the car nearly paid off but has to use the car (equity) as collateral for a loan to start a small business. Unfortunately, the business fails, and Bill defaults on the original car loan and on the second (business) loan. When the creditor repossesses the car and sells it, first the costs of the whole process of repossession are paid, then the original loan balance is paid, and finally the second (business) loan balance is paid assuming that the business loan secured party gave written notice [UCC 9-504(1)].

If there is any surplus, it is paid to the debtor. If the loan balances are not paid, the creditor may go to court and obtain a deficiency judgment. The following case represents a creditor seeking to collect on a deficiency judgment.

BACKGROUND AND FACTS *The plaintiff, Poti Holding Company, a secured creditor, sold Piggott, the defendant, a wire-insulating machine. Poti Holding in return took a collateral note—that is, a promissory note that was secured with a lien on the wire-insulating machine (the collateral). Piggott defaulted on paying the note. Poti Holding repossessed and sold the machinery. The proceeds from the sale did not cover the amount owed on the note. Poti Holding sued Piggott for a deficiency judgment on a promissory note.*

The trial court appointed a special master to determine whether the sale of the machine was commercially reasonable. A special master investigates the facts and makes findings for the court. The lower court found for the defendant because the plaintiff had not proved that the sale was conducted in a commercially reasonable manner.

Case 12.5
POTI HOLDING COMPANY, INC. v. PIGGOTT

Appeals Court, Massachusetts, 1983.
15 Mass.App.Ct. 275,
444 N.E.2d 1311.

Justice DREBEN
❖   ❖   ❖   ❖

After sale or disposition of the collateral held by a secured party, the debtor, unless otherwise agreed, "is liable for any deficiency." The defendant argues, however, that a creditor who missteps in conducting a sale automatically loses his right to a deficiency judgment.

In concluding that the plaintiff had not sustained its burden of proving that the sale had been conducted in a commercially reasonable manner, the master did not find that the plaintiff had engaged in sharp or unconscionable practices. Rather, he relied on the plaintiff's failure to submit evidence on a number of matters such as: the normal commercial practices in disposing of collateral of this type; the experience of the auctioneer in auctioning this kind of machinery; the areas of circulation of the newspapers in which the advertisements were placed; and whether there were experienced brokers available to sell goods of this type. He also noted that although the plaintiff had placed advertisements in the Boston Herald American, the Wall Street Journal and a local newspaper, and had notified between 210 and 235 parties, including the defendant, it had only notified two of the nine or more companies in the high temperature wire business in the eastern United States, and had not advertised in any publication of the wire industry. These findings underscore the lack of precision in the meaning of the term "commercially reasonable;" its determination depends on the particular facts in each case.
❖   ❖   ❖   ❖

We think more consistent with Massachusetts law and the provisions for remedies in the Uniform Commercial Code are those authorities which provide for a balancing of equities between the parties and allow the "remedy and the recovery . . . [to] be adjusted to the particular situation."

Although we have found no case in the Supreme Judicial Court or this court on the precise issue before us, our cases frown on forfeitures and penalties. In addition, where violations of the Code are not involved, wrongdoings of a creditor do not normally preclude a deficiency. * * *

The Code does not require automatic forfeiture. Specific remedies are provided * * * against a secured creditor who, among other misdeeds, fails to sell collateral in a commercially reasonable manner. A debtor may restrain an improper sale and also "has a right to recover from the secured party any loss caused by [the] failure to comply" with the Code. There is no mention of a forfeiture of the right to a deficiency and, in addition, the Code remedies are to be "liberally administered to the end that the aggrieved party may be put in as good a position as if the other party had fully performed but neither consequential or special nor penal damages may be had except as specifically provided in this chapter or by other rule of law."

In view of the specific remedies provided, the reluctance of Massachusetts to impose forfeitures, and the explicit statement in [the UCC] against penalties, "[w]e are unwilling to assume that the Legislature intended to effect such a forfeiture of private contractual rights."

DECISION AND REMEDY

The appellate court reversed the trial court. Poti Holding could recover the deficiency. The courts do not like forfeitures or penalties. In this case, the term "commercially reasonable manner" does not have a precise meaning. Since the statute does not authorize a forfeiture—that is, forfeiting the right to sue for a deficiency judgment by failing to sell an item in a commercially reasonable manner—the court would not allow a forfeiture under the facts in this case.

Termination

When a debt is paid, the secured party must send a **termination statement** to the debtor or must file such a statement in the same place where the original financing statement is located. The termination statement shows that the debt has been paid. If the secured party fails to file a termination statement at the proper time, the secured party may be liable to the debtor for $100. Additionally, the secured party is liable for any loss caused to the debtor for failing to file the appropriate release-of-debt documents.

Ethical Considerations

Bought a Lemon?
Will You Pay?

A holder in due course has many advantages over an assignee of a contract. Defenses that can be asserted against an assignee cannot be used against an HDC. If you had purchased a consumer item, such as an automobile, 20 years ago, you would have signed a contract and a promissory note. The note would have been immediately sold to a financial institution. If the automobile turned out to be a lemon, you had little recourse but to file a lawsuit against the seller of the automobile. You could not stop payment on the note because the holder of the note (usually a bank) qualified as a holder in due course. Two distinct legal forces were at play here: You had to find a way to make the seller live up to the promise of an automobile that worked in a reasonable manner under contract law, while you were forced to pay the holder in due course on the note under commercial paper law.

Today you can stop making payments until the automobile is repaired or you are provided with a new automobile under the Federal Trade Commission rules that took away the holder-in-due-course status from those who purchase commercial paper involved in a consumer transaction. But is this fair to banks or lending institutions? They have no way of knowing whether an automobile is a lemon. Should you take advantage of the FTC rule when confronted

with this type of situation? Lending institutions do not emphasize this rule at all to their borrowers, even though the language required by the FTC is clearly printed on the documents. Few consumers have any idea of the import of the language. Is it ethical for the lending institutions not to inform their borrowers in plain language of their rights in case the borrower has purchased a lemon? Is it ethical for a lender not to inform the borrower that if he or she legitimately stops payment on the note and the automobile is fixed or a new one furnished, then he or she must immediately restart the payments and make up all the back payments?

The HDC doctrine is still used when a check is involved. For example, you give a check for a new computer that must be special ordered by the store. The retailer cashes your check with its bank. The bank is now a holder in due course, assuming it has met all the other requirements. You never receive your new computer. You go back to the retailer but find to your dismay that the retailer has left town with no forwarding address. You will still be liable to the retailer's bank, if it is an HDC. This is true even if you place a stop-payment order on the check at your bank. Your bank will return the check to the retailer's bank, which will then seek payment from you. Is it ethical for the retailer's bank to seek repayment from you? Since you are both innocent parties, why should the bank prevail over you?

International Considerations

So You Want to Sell Overseas: How Do You Get Your Money?

The United States has signed the **United Nations Convention on International Bills of Exchange and Promissory Notes.** Basically, the convention covers both orders to pay and promises to pay. Bills of exchange were developed during the Middle Ages. Article 3 of the UCC, Commercial Paper, does not use the term *bill of exchange* but rather the term *draft*.

Bills of exchange and bills of lading are commonly used in international trade. Bills of lading are used by common carriers such as ocean vessels, airline companies, and railroad companies to keep track of goods being shipped. The shipping company issues a multipart bill of lading; one part stays with the goods while another part is turned over to the seller. Whoever has control of the seller's copy of the bill of lading controls the goods. The seller's bill of lading must be surrendered to the transport company before the buyer may have possession of these goods. How does the buyer obtain possession of the seller's bill of lading?

A bill of exchange is essentially like a check, but it is not drawn on a bank. It is drawn on the buyer by the seller. The bill of exchange is signed by the drawer (seller) who orders the drawee (buyer) to pay the money to the payee (usually a financial institution).

The seller sends the seller's copy of the bill of lading and the bill of exchange to its financial institution, typically a bank. The seller's bank forwards the documents to the buyer's bank, which notifies the buyer that the documents are available to be picked up. The buyer accepts (pays for) the bill of exchange and in return is provided the bill of lading. The buyer is now able to obtain possession of the goods from the transportation company. The buyer's bank sends the money, minus a service fee, to the seller's bank.

The U.N. convention provides unified rules on this complex topic. While the Western world has had centuries of experience in this field, many developing countries have not. This convention helps provide guidance and ensure uniformity for the creation, interpretation, and performance of bills of exchange and promissory notes.

Normally, a letter of credit issued by a financial institution is associated with the transaction just described. Letters of credit will be discussed in more detail in Chapter 24. The rules covering letters of credit are based upon treaties. The International Chamber of Commerce originally adopted the **Uniform Customs and Practices for Documentary Credits (UCP)** in the 1930s. It has since been modified to reflect changes in business. The UCP has many provisions involving letters of credit.

FACING A LEGAL ISSUE

The Problem with Postdating a Check

On Wednesday, Sally sees an advertisement to join a health club, stating "today only for one-half price." After work, she stops by to check out the club. A salesperson shows her all the club features and reminds her of the one-half price sale. Payday is Monday, five days away, but she wants to get the bargain rate. The salesperson agrees to accept a postdated check and assures her that the check will not be deposited until Monday.

Arriving home on Tuesday after work, she receives a notice from her bank that her account is overdrawn. Two minutes later, she has a call from the health club concerning her bounced check. On Wednesday, she checks with the bank and finds out that the postdated check was deposited on the previous Thursday. The health club is threatening criminal action. Has Sally committed a crime?

Most people believe that postdating or antedating a check is illegal. No date is required on a check to make it negotiable because it is a demand instrument; thus, to postdate or antedate a check is not illegal. The act of postdating or antedating the check becomes illegal when the drawer intends to defraud the payee by not having the money in his or her account. It is difficult to prove fraud under these circumstances, however. As you may remember from Chapter 9, to prove fraud you must prove an objective intent to deceive at the time of the act. Intent is difficult to prove with a postdated check.

In Sally's case, the district attorney will not prosecute because it was clear on the face of the check that the funds were not available until Monday. If Sally can show that the money (her paycheck) was in the account on Monday, the district attorney cannot show intent to deceive.

Many payees, such as the health club, will require a date to be inserted on the check. Under UCC 4-404 a check is "stale" if it is not presented to the bank for payment within six months after the date on the check. Thus, after six months, the bank is not obligated to pay the check but can do so in good faith. Wanting to make sure that the bank will pay the check, the payee may require the date to be filled in.

A check is a credit instrument (conditional on being honored) even though banks treat it as a cash instrument. A merchant accepting a check may have signed up for a bank's guarantee protection program and may have paid the bank a fee for the service. In this case, if the customer's bank account does not have enough cash to honor the check, the bank, not the merchant, is responsible for collecting the amount from the customer. The bank pays the merchant, who does not even know that the check has bounced, if he or she has signed up for the guarantee program. A merchant who has not signed up for a bank's guarantee protection program may require a person writing a check to produce a bank guarantee card in an attempt to limit losses caused by bad checks.

The lessons Sally learned include:

- Never write a postdated check.
- Never rely on the oral assurances of a salesperson.

Summary

Commercial paper serves two purposes: as a substitute for currency and as a credit device. The UCC recognizes four basic types of commercial paper: drafts, checks, notes, and certificates of deposit. These instruments, in turn, fall into one of two categories: orders to pay or promises to pay. In order for these instruments to be negotiable, six requirements must be met. A negotiable instrument must be (1) in writing, (2) signed by the maker or drawer (3) contain an unconditional promise or order to pay, (4) stated in a specific sum of money, (5) payable on demand or at a definite time, (6) payable to order or to bearer.

A distinction exists between an assignment and a negotiation. An assignment of a contract right does not transfer to the assignee any greater rights in the contract than the original party had. If an instrument is negotiated, the holder of the instrument may have greater rights than the original party. Such a holder is known as a holder in due course. Only those defenses known as real defenses (defenses that apply to the document itself) may be asserted against a holder in due course and will preclude payment of the instrument to the HDC.

The relationship between a bank and its customers is governed by the UCC. The bank has a duty to pay checks drawn on a customer's account and to accept deposits. The customer has a duty to check her or his statements every month and to check for forged signatures. The banking system has been revolutionized by electronic funds transfer systems, which include teller machines, point-of-sale systems, and automated clearinghouses. Federal laws govern many aspects of electronic funds transfers.

When a merchant extends credit, he or she wants to make sure that the debt is secured by some type of collateral. If the seller extends credit for the purchase of an item or if the debtor borrows money to purchase an item and the debt is secured by the item purchased, this transaction is called a purchase-money security interest. The creditor's security interest must be valid against the debtor's right to the item and must have priority over any claims by third parties.

Key Terms

bearer (283)
bearer paper (292)
blank indorsement (285)
certificate of deposit (CD) (283)
check (284)
collateral note (290)
commercial paper (282)
consumer credit transaction (296)
draft (284)
drawees (283)
drawers (283)
electronic funds transfer systems (303)
financing statement (306)

holder (285)
holder in due course (HDC) (285)
indorsee (284)
indorser (284)
installment note (290)
issue (283)
maker (282)
mortgage note (290)
negotiable (291)
order paper (292)
orders to pay (290)
payee (282)
personal defenses (295)
promises to pay (290)
promissory note (282)

qualified indorsement (297)
real defenses (205)
restrictive indorsement (207)
secured transactions (282)
sight drafts (290)
special indorsement (293)
stop-payment order (301)
termination statement (309)
time drafts (290)
Uniform Customs and Practices for Documentary Credits (UCP) (311)
United Nations Convention on International Bills of Exchange and Promissory Notes (311)

Questions and Case Problems

1. The following note is written by Gloria Natale on the back of an envelope: "I, Gloria Natale, promise to pay to Perry Wilson or bearer $1,000 on demand." Is this note a negotiable instrument? Please discuss fully.

2. A check is drawn by Jeff for $500 and made payable to the order of Kelley. Jeff turns the check over to Kelley. Kelley owes her landlord $500 in rent and transfers the check to her landlord with the following indorsement: "For rent paid, [Signed] Kelley." Kelley's landlord has contracted to have Eric repair the electrical wiring in several apartments. Eric insists on immediate payment. The landlord transfers the check to Eric without indorsement. Later, in order to pay for the electrical supplies at Supply Store, Eric transfers the check with the following indorsement: "Pay to Supply Store, without recourse [Signed] Eric." Supply sends the check to its bank indorsed "For deposit only. [Signed] Supply Store."

a. Classify each of these indorsements.

b. Was the transfer from Kelley's landlord to Eric without indorsement an assignment or a negotiation? Explain.

3. Mansfield issues a 90-day negotiable promissory note payable to the order of Eastwood. The amount of the note is left blank until the price of the diamond Mansfield plans to buy from Eastwood is determined. Mansfield orally authorizes Eastwood to fill in the blank, but the amount is not to exceed $10,000. Eastwood, without authority, fills in the note in the amount of $200,000 and 30 days later sells the note to the First National Bank for $16,000. Eastwood does not buy the diamond and leaves the state. First National Bank had no knowledge that the instrument was incomplete when issued or that Eastwood had no authority to complete the instrument in an amount over $10,000. Does the bank qualify as a holder in due course and, if so, for what amount? Explain fully.

4. On June 1, Jesse draws a check payable to George for $2,000 to reroof his house by July 1. George indorses the check in blank to Ronald on June 15 as payment for a debt he owed (value). Ronald, on July 5, negotiates the check to Peter, without indorsement, as payment for fireworks that he bought for the July 4 celebration. George never reroofs the house and Jesse stops payment on the check on July 3. Peter attempts to cash the check. Jesse claims that his defense—that George never performed the agreed-on services (reroofing the house)—is valid against Peter. Peter claims that the check must be honored. Who is right? Explain fully.

5. A business advertises freezers with an incentive: the right to purchase frozen food, including meat, at substantial discounts. You visit the business and discover the cost of the freezer is twice the cost offered by other retailers, but you can finance the freezer by signing a promissory note and security agreement. You are promised that upon signing the documents you are entitled to purchase all the meat you need over the next year for only 99 cents a pound. You decide to purchase the freezer and sign the documents. The retailer the next day takes the note to the local bank and sells the bank the note by discounting it. The bank sends you a notice that it now holds the note and that you should make your payments to it. The freezer arrives a week later, and it works. When the meat arrives, it is spoiled. Can you stop making payments to the bank until the retailer supplies meat that is edible?

6. Roberts executed a promissory note that was made payable to the order of Baines. Baines gave this note to Duxbury along with a separate document stating that he was transferring it to Duxbury. Roberts refused to pay the note to Duxbury because it had not been indorsed. What rights does Duxbury have, if any? Is he a holder of the note or a holder in due course? Explain. [Duxbury v. Roberts, 388 Mass. 385, 446 N.E.2d 401 (1983)]

7. Money Mart cashed a paycheck for an employee of Epicycle. Epicycle had placed a stop payment on this check because of claims it had against the employee. Was Money Mart required to verify the validity of this check before cashing it? [Money Mart Check Cashing Center, Inc. v. Epicycle Corp., 667 P.2d 1372 (Colo. 1983)]

8. Wade purchased a Ford automobile that was financed by Ford Motor Credit. Wade fell behind in her monthly payment. The vehicle was repossessed from Wade's driveway at 2:00 A.M. by an agent of Ford Motor Credit. Wade testified that she heard a car burning rubber, looked outside, and saw her vehicle was missing. No other confrontation occurred. Wade claims that this repossession was a breach of the peace and was wrongful. She sought damages from Ford Motor Credit while Ford Motor Credit sought $2,900 as a deficiency. Was this repossession wrongful? Was Ford Motor Credit entitled to a deficiency judgment? [Wade v. Ford Motor Credit Co., 8 Kan.App.2d 737, 668 P.2d 183 [1983]

9. Trans World Airlines (TWA) entered into a sale and lease-back agreement with Connecticut National Bank (CNB). The sale was for $312 million, which included ten aircraft. TWA agreed to pay back $100 million on January 31, 1991. The Persian Gulf conflict in early 1991 resulted in decreased air travel and increased oil prices. This curtailed the cash flow, and TWA was unable to pay the $100 million on January 31. CNB filed a lawsuit for the return of the aircraft. TWA argued that the aircraft should not be repossessed because the Persian Gulf conflict was an intervening cause excusing TWA from its agreed performance. Who should prevail and why? [Connecticut National Bank v. Trans World Airlines, Inc., 762 F.Supp. 76 (S.D.N.Y. 1991)]

Chapter 13 Rights of Consumers, Debtors, and Creditors

Creditors have better memories than debtors; they are a superstitious sect, great observers of set days and times.

Benjamin Franklin

OUTLINE

Introduction

Purchase on credit is the foundation of our business community. In the last 50 years, we have converted from a cash to a credit society. Credit card use by consumers has led this transformation. Consumer credit has increased from $2.5 billion at the end of World War II to $500 billion by 1991. Major consumer products, such as automobiles, stereos, televisions, and furniture are almost always purchased on credit. Consumer credit rests on two assumptions: the debtor's willingness to pay and the debtor's ability to pay.

By the mid 1960s, the tremendous increase in credit had unfortunately also led to a rise in the abuse of consumers. Consumers were not informed sufficiently in order to shop comparatively for interest rates, they were misled into signing installment contracts, debt collectors were harassing them, they were denied access to their credit reports, and, worst of all, if the computer said they owed a bill, the poor consumers had no one with whom to talk. Consumers were not adequately protected by state law.

The United States Congress became concerned and, in 1968, adopted the **Consumer Credit Protection Act,** which has been amended several times. These amendments are known by their popular names. In this chapter, we will review the following acts:

1. **Consumer Credit Cost Disclosure Act,** commonly known as the **Truth-in-Lending Act (TILA)**
2. **Fair Credit Billing Act**
3. **Fair Credit Reporting Act**
4. **Equal Credit Opportunity Act**
5. **Fair Debt Collection Practices Act.**

The Electronic Fund Transfer Act is also part of the Consumer Credit Protection Act and is discussed in Chapter 12. To finish the chapter, we will discuss the rights of creditors and review some of the bankruptcy laws.

Consumer Credit Protection Act

The Consumer Credit Protection Act (CCPA) is the primary source of federal law covering credit transactions, and numerous federal agencies enforce the CCPA. Individual consumers can also use the act to protect their rights when a business does not fully comply with the CCPA's provisions. The legal consequences vary for each provision violated, but both criminal and civil sanctions exist if a business fails to comply.

Consumer Credit Cost Disclosure: Truth-in-Lending Act

During hearings in 1968, Congress discovered that financial institutions were using a variety of ways to state rates of interest and the total dollar cost of a loan. Rates of interest were based on recognized, but varying, financial methods of calculation. No uniform method of stating an interest rate existed. Congress heard considerable debate as to whether charges for insurance, credit reports, discount points, and other items should be classified as interest charges. Prior to 1968, a consumer could not shop for credit because of the difficulties in comparing one lending institution's charges with another.

To resolve this problem, Congress passed Title I of the Consumer Credit Protection Act. Title I is commonly known as the Truth-in-Lending Act (TILA). The TILA deals with deceptive credit practices and requires notice and disclosure to prevent sellers and creditors from taking unfair advantage of consumers. Through disclosure, the purchaser can more easily compare the credit terms that are available. The act applies to most consumer credit transactions.

Disclosure Requirements of the TILA   The disclosure requirements apply to credit transactions in which a finance charge is imposed or in which payment is to be made in more than four installments. The most important information that a lender must disclose includes: (1) the cash price; (2) the down payment or trade-in allowance, if any; (3) the unpaid cash price (the cash price minus the down payment) that is to be financed; (4) the **finance charge** (the total amount of interest and other charges such as filing fees and insurance premiums); and (5) the **annual percentage rate** (the true rate of interest charged on a yearly basis) by which the finance charge is calculated.

The creditor must also tell the debtor the date that the finance charge starts; the number, amounts, and due dates of payments; the late-payment charges; and if there is a prepayment penalty. A prepayment penalty is an amount that the debtor must pay if he or she wants to pay off the debt early. In the past, the prepayment penalty often was a substantial amount of the debt. For example, say that Harris borrowed $5,000 and that over time he has paid back $4,000. He now wants to pay the remaining $1,000 in order to complete the loan payments. The prepayment penalty, however, might be $2,000; in other words, he would have to pay a total of $3,000 in order to pay off the loan early. Today, many states do not allow prepayment penalties.

The provisions of the Truth-in-Lending Act apply to both sales and leases of personal and real property. Two key terms summarize the disclosure philosophy of the act: finance charge and annual percentage rate. Armed with this information, the consumer can now comparison shop for a loan or for credit.

The Federal Reserve Board issues the administrative rules that implement the TILA. Known as Regulation Z, these rules include model forms for businesses to follow when selling goods. The forms, if used correctly by a business, are in full compliance with the statute. Examples are found in Exhibits 13–1 and 13–2.

The **Consumer Leasing Act** requires full disclosure of all financial terms in consumer leasing contracts. The Federal Reserve Board's Regulation M governs this area. Regulation M requires similar disclosures to consumers as those required by Regulation Z.

Creditors Subject to the TILA   The Truth-in-Lending Act does not apply to everyone. It applies to businesses that, in the ordinary course of their operations, lend money, sell on credit, or arrange for the extension of credit to consumers. For this reason, sales or loans made between two consumers do not come under the act. Only debtors who are individuals (natural persons) are protected by this law; corporations or other legal entities (including governmental agencies) are not.

Transactions involving purchases of property (real or personal) for personal, family, household, or agricultural use come under the terms and provisions of the act if the amount being financed is less than $25,000. Transactions covered by the act typically include retail and installment sales, installment loans, car loans, home improvement loans, and certain real estate loans. Real estate loans of more than $25,000 on a debtor's residence are not covered by the act.

Penalties   A creditor who fails to comply with the disclosure requirements may be liable to the consumer for any actual damages plus twice the amount of the finance charge, plus attorneys' fees. In no event may damages exceed $1,000, however. The consumer has one year from the date of the violation to bring suit against a creditor who has failed to provide the disclosure statement. A person who willfully and knowingly violates these provisions is liable criminally and may be fined $5,000 and/or imprisoned for up to one year. In addition, the debtor is entitled to rescind the transaction at any time up to three years from the date of the transaction.

Other Provisions of the CCPA

Over the years, other statutes have been adopted that add to the CCPA's initial provisions. These provisions cover real estate improvements, credit card usage, credit billing errors, equal credit opportunities, and debt collection practices.

Real Estate   Often when a creditor forms a contract to improve a consumer's residence, the consumer will, in turn, give the creditor a security interest in the residence to secure payment for the improvement. Under the TILA, each consumer has the right to rescind the transaction by midnight of the third business day following the signing of the transaction even if all disclosure provisions of the TILA have been followed. A consumer must be given notice of this right to rescind along with the material disclosures of annual percentage rate, the finance charge, the amount financed, the total payments, and the payment schedule.

For example, Sandy wants to have a pool built. She signs a contract with Pool Company to have the pool built in return for $15,000. Sandy does not have $15,000, so she signs a note to repay the $15,000 and gives Pool Company a security interest in her home. If she fails to pay the note, Pool Company will still have its interest in the $15,000 secured under its contract. The company may be able to force the sale of the house to recover the $15,000. To have this right, however, the security contract must clearly state Sandy's

Exhibit 13–1 Sample Credit Sale Contract Supplied by the Federal Reserve Board

Big Wheel Auto   Alice Green

ANNUAL PERCENTAGE RATE The cost of your credit as a yearly rate.	FINANCE CHARGE The dollar amount the credit will cost you.	Amount Financed The amount of credit provided to you or on your behalf.	Total of Payments The amount you will have paid after you have made all payments as scheduled.	Total Sale Price The total cost of your purchase on credit, including your downpayment of $ _1500 –_
14.84 %	$1496.80	$6107.50	$7604.30	$9129.30

You have the right to receive at this time an itemization of the Amount Financed.

☐ I want an itemization.   ☒ I do not want an itemization.

Your payment schedule will be:

Number of Payments	Amount of Payments	When Payments Are Due
36	$211.23	Monthly beginning 6-1-81

Insurance

Credit life insurance and credit disability insurance are not required to obtain credit, and will not be provided unless you sign and agree to pay the additional cost.

Type	Premium	Signature	
Credit Life	$120 –	I want credit life insurance.	*alice Green* Signature
Credit Disability		I want credit disability insurance.	Signature
Credit Life and Disability		I want credit life and disability insurance.	Signature

Security: You are giving a security interest in:

☒ the goods being purchased.

☐ _____.

Filing fees $ _12.50_   **Non-filing insurance $** _____

Late Charge: If a payment is late, you will be charged $10.

Prepayment: If you pay off early, you

☐ may   ☐ will not   have to pay a penalty.

☒ may   ☐ will not   be entitled to a refund of part of the finance charge.

See your contract documents for any additional information about nonpayment, default, any required repayment in full before the scheduled date, and prepayment refunds and penalties.

I have received a copy of this statement.

alice Green   _5-1-81_

Signature   Date

_____

e means an estimate

Source: 12 Code of Federal Regulations, Section 226, Appendix H-10, 1991

Exhibit 13–2 Sample Installment Loan Contract Supplied by the Federal Reserve Board

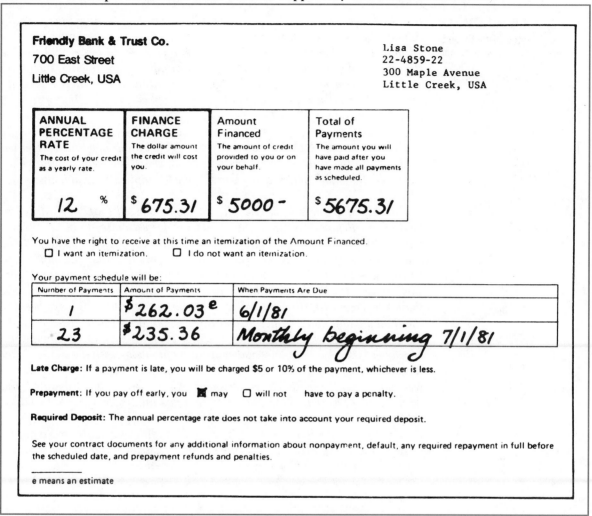

Source: 12 *Code of Federal Regulations,* Section 226, Appendix H-11, 1991

right to rescind the contract, must include all disclosure requirements, and Sandy must be notified of her right to rescind the contract within three days, and she must not have rescinded it.

If the consumer rescinds the transaction, the security interest in the residence is void, and no finance charge may be charged. The creditor must return any money or property that was received, and the consumer must give back whatever she or he has received. If this is impracticable, she or he must give back the reasonable value of what has been received.

Two exceptions to the three-day right of rescission have primary importance. The first exception involves an emergency situation in which the customer needs to have her or his home repaired immediately, as in the case of damage resulting from a fire or storm.

The second major exception is when a consumer purchases a house and grants the lender a first lien (mortgage).

The following case illustrates the need for businesses to comply with the requirements of the Truth-in-Lending Act.

Case 13.1
COLE v. LOVETT
United States District Court,
Southern District, Mississippi,
1987.
672 F.Supp. 947.

BACKGROUND AND FACTS *In November 1982, plaintiffs Norman and Judy Cole were visited by two salespeople, Stepp and Smith, from Capitol Roofing, who were selling siding for homes. After a sales pitch, it was estimated that the cost to cover the Coles' house would be $4,900. Before the salespeople left, the Coles had signed a number of documents, including a work order, a home improvement retail installment contract, a security agreement and disclosure statement, a loan application, a notice of right to cancel, and a deed of trust.*

The only document the Coles really saw was the work order; they only saw the signature block on the other papers. The salespeople misrepresented to the Coles the real nature of the paperwork that they were signing. They were told they had signed a work order, credit application, and insurance papers.

Shortly after the salespeople left, the Coles decided that they wanted to hold off on the work order so they could ask for estimates from other companies. Mrs. Cole called Capitol Roofing the next morning and told the salesperson that they had decided to wait. She was told that the papers had been processed, the workers would be out at the end of the week, and there was nothing she could do. She went to work and, when she returned, she found the crew installing the siding. She did not tell them to leave because she thought that she and her husband were bound by the contract.

The contract was assigned by Capitol Roofing to United Companies Mortgage (UCM). The Coles had continuing problems with the siding. After repeated unsuccessful calls by Mrs. Cole to Capitol Roofing, the problems were not remedied. After eleven payments, the Coles became frustrated and discontinued payment to UCM. They retained an attorney, who, by letter, informed both Capitol Roofing and UCM that the Coles were exercising their right of rescission under the Truth-in-Lending Act. After receiving no answer, the Coles filed this lawsuit seeking rescission, and UCM counterclaimed, alleging the Coles' default under the contract.

Judge LEE
* * * *

[Court's discussion of security interest]

The first violation which plaintiffs contend entitles them to rescind the transaction under TILA is the failure of Capitol Roofing to disclose the security interest that was being acquired in their home. Under TILA, the right to rescind is available in any "credit transaction in which a security interest is or will be retained or acquired in the consumer's principal dwelling." The testimony of the parties regarding the deed of trust signed by the Coles was in direct contradiction. Stepp testified that he explained to the Coles that they were granting a security interest in their home, and further said that either he or Smith completed the relevant portions of the deed of trust, with the exception of the property description, before the Coles signed the document. * * * According to Stepp, both the Coles knew they were granting a second mortgage on their home. Plaintiffs, on the other hand, testified that neither Smith nor Stepp informed them that their home would be security for the siding contract. Neither of them recalled having signed a deed of trust. The disclosure statement signed by the Coles did not mention a deed of trust but contained the following language:

Security: Buyers are giving a security interest in:

___ the goods or property being purchased.

_X_ land located at *P.O. Box D'Lo, MS.*

[The TILA] requires the creditor to disclose "the fact that the creditor has or will acquire a security interest in the property purchased as part of the transaction, or in other property identified by item or type." * * * [B]oth Norman and Judy Cole denied any knowledge of the existence of a deed of trust against their home and stated affirmatively that they did not learn of the deed of trust until approximately a year later when they applied for credit to make interior improvements on their home and the deed of trust was discovered in the land records. * * * The court credits the testimony of the Coles and is of the opinion that Capitol Roofing did not disclose to them the fact that a security interest was being acquired in their home. Therefore, * * * this constituted a material violation of TILA and Regulation Z, * * * and plaintiffs are entitled to rescind.

[Court's discussion of notice to rescind]

The plaintiffs next charge that Capitol Roofing failed to furnish them with notice of their right to rescind as required by TILA. TILA and Regulation Z expressly require the creditor in a consumer credit transaction, in which a security interest is being conveyed in the property used by the consumers as their principal dwelling, to provide each consumer who own[s] an interest in the property two copies of a notice of the right to rescind. At trial, Stepp testified that he verbally informed the Coles of their right to rescind the transaction and gave them each two copies of a notice of right to cancel form which contained the required information. Capitol Roofing introduced a document entitled "notice of right to cancel" with an acknowledgement of receipt of form signed by both plaintiffs and dated November 9, 1982. However, the Coles claimed that they had never seen the notice of right to cancel and that, despite their having signed the acknowledgement portion of the document, neither of them ever received copies of the notice form. Moreover, both testified that Stepp never explained the right of rescission and, in fact, after her discussion with Stepp on November 10, Judy Cole was under the impression that she and her husband were bound by having signed the contract. The effect of the Coles' signatures on the acknowledgement * * * "does no more than create a rebuttable presumption of delivery thereof." As it appears from the testimony that the Coles were unaware of any right of rescission and did not learn of their right until much later upon consulting with an attorney, the court is of the opinion that the Coles have effectively rebutted the presumption of delivery. The court finds that plaintiffs were not informed of their right to rescind and that, notwithstanding their signing an acknowledgement of receipt of forms, they never received copies of the notice. The failure by Capitol Roofing to provide each of the plaintiffs with the required notice constituted a violation of TILA and entitled them to rescind the transaction. As they were never given proper notice of their right to rescind, they timely exercised this right, having notified defendants of their rescission within three years following consummation of the transaction. * * * *

As a result of Capitol Roofing's violations of TILA, plaintiffs were entitled to rescind the transaction. After the Coles served notice on defendants of their election to cancel the transaction, defendants were required to "return to the [Coles] any money or property given as earnest money, down payment, or otherwise, and [were required to] take any action necessary or appropriate to reflect the termination of any security interest created under the transaction." Plaintiffs' attempt at cancellation was met with total inaction by defendants. Consequently, the Coles are entitled to the cancellation of the finance charges in their transaction, and to have the security interest in their home voided.

The district court found that Capitol Roofing had violated the Truth-in-Lending Act. First, the Coles were not informed that they were granting Capitol Roofing a security interest in their home.

DECISION AND REMEDY

Second, the Coles were not furnished with notice of their right to rescind the contract. Since Capitol Roofing had not complied with the TILA, the Coles had three years to rescind the contract. The Coles notified Capitol Roofing in a timely manner of their problems and of their decision to rescind the contract. Capitol Roofing failed to demand possession of the siding within a reasonable time after the Coles had canceled the contract. The end results were that the Coles retained the siding free of any further payment, the finance charges were canceled, and the security interest in the Coles' house was released.

Credit Cards   The TILA has specific provisions that cover the issuance and use of credit cards. First, an initial credit card cannot be sent to an individual or a business unless it is requested. Any unauthorized use of such a card cannot be charged to the named cardholder. Renewal credit cards can be sent without a specific request. Second, if a credit card is lost or stolen, $50 is the limit of the cardholder's liability for the unauthorized use of the card. The $50 limit is for each card, so if a consumer loses ten cards, the actual loss to the consumer could be $500.

Debit Cards   These cards are used to debit the bank account of the user through the use of electronic transfer of funds. People often use debit cards at teller machines or in stores when making purchases. The consumer is liable for an unauthorized transfer up to $50 if he or she takes reasonable steps to notify the financial institution within two business days after learning of the loss or theft. After the two-day period, the consumer's liability goes up to $500. If a person is unable to notify the institution of the loss or of the theft because of extended travel or hospitalization, he or she has a reasonable time to notify the institution and the two-day rule is waived.

Fair Credit Billing Act   Even with computers, errors are made on charge accounts. It can be an unnerving experience to try to correct these errors. An amendment to the TILA, the Fair Credit Billing Act, requires creditors to correct errors promptly and without damage to a person's credit rating.

A person who believes his or her statement is in error must notify the creditor in writing with a statement explaining the perceived error. The customer must pay the *undisputed* amount while waiting for an answer from the business on the amount in question. Within 30 days the creditor must acknowledge the inquiry, and within 90 days either the account must be corrected or an explanation must be given as to why the creditor believes the account is correct. During this time, the creditor is not allowed to give an unfavorable credit report or to attempt to collect the amount in dispute.

Fair Credit Reporting Act   At one time, consumers did not have access to the contents of credit and investigative reports kept on them by others, and they could not control the use of these reports. Inaccuracies, once reported, were almost impossible to uncover, much less to correct.

In 1970, Congress enacted the Fair Credit Reporting Act. Consumers are entitled, on request, to be informed of the nature and scope of a credit investigation, the kind of information that is being compiled, and the names of people who will be receiving the report.

Any inaccurate or misleading material must be reinvestigated and, if not verified, removed from the file. If there is a dispute about the accuracy of certain parts of the report, consumers have the right to include in the file their own 100-word statement describing their position with regard to disputed matters. The law also provides for updating information. Information over seven years old must be deleted, and information regarding any bankruptcy more than ten years old must be removed.

A consumer credit reporting agency that fails to comply with the terms of the act can be held liable for actual damages, for punitive damages, and for attorneys' fees and court costs.

The following case involves a credit reporting agency and one of its reports.

Legal Highlight

Earth Calling Computer, Earth Calling Computer, Do You Read Me?

When Congress was considering passing the Fair Credit Billing Act, the members of Congress heard horror stories such as the following about computers that sent bills to consumers:

- A woman in Yonkers, New York, bought furniture from Gimbels. One piece arrived damaged beyond repair and was returned. The replacement piece did not match and was returned. The third piece had not arrived after five months. Payment was made for the delivered pieces but not for the undelivered piece. The woman was in constant contact with the Gimbels credit department, but apparently no one talked to the computer. It billed her for one year, then turned the unpaid bill over to a debt collection agency. The letter to her read, "The good things of life are obtainable by many people through their recorded credit reputation." In frustration, she wrote to the debt collection agency, three Gimbels executives, the attorney general for New York, the Federal Trade Commission, Consumers Union, Senator Proxmire, and the New York State Consumer Protection Board. She had

replies from all except the debt collection agency and Gimbels.

- BankAmericard sent an unsolicited credit card to a man in the Bronx, New York. He never received the card because it was stolen, but that did not stop the computer from sending him the bill, plus interest, plus late-payment charges, despite his repeated efforts to inform the computer that these charges were not his.

- A couple from Monaghan, New York, ordered furniture from Macy's. They owed $1,217, but the furniture delivered was not what they had ordered. It was sent back twice. After ten months, the correct furniture was finally delivered, and the couple paid what was owed. They were in contact with Macy's during this period, but no one told the computer. It billed them for finance charges for the ten months, plus 6 percent sales tax, although the sales tax in that area was only 3 percent. Finally, they wrote the chairman of the board of Macy's. He expressed concern, but within three days an attorney for Macy's wrote them, giving them five days to pay up or be taken to court. They contacted the New York State Consumer Protection Board, which resolved the problem. In the meantime, they could not buy a house because of this "unpaid" bill.

BACKGROUND AND FACTS *In 1976 the plaintiff, Zeller, and the defendant, Samia, jointly purchased a beach cottage. Zeller signed a note promising to pay the defendant $3,333.33, which was his share of the $10,000 down payment. In 1985 the relationship between the two parties deteriorated. In 1986, in another lawsuit separate from this reported one, Samia sued Zeller for partition of the cottage property and demanded that Zeller pay the balance due on the note. In 1987, after Zeller failed to pay, Samia reported a charge-off to Credit Data of New England. The charge-off totaled approximately $11,000, which included the unpaid principal, interest, and costs. A charge-off occurs when a creditor believes the debt is no longer collectible. It is a bookkeeping entry.*

Later in 1987, Samia made inquiries to Credit Data to verify that the charge-off he had reported had been received and recorded by Credit Data. Zeller contends that Samia not only used the report to verify the recording

Case 13.2
ZELLER v. SAMIA
United States District Court, 1991.
758 F.Supp. 775 (D.Mass.).

of the charge-off, but also used the credit information against him in the previous lawsuit. Samia had obtained from Credit Data Zeller's two-page credit report which contained his entire history. As a result of Samia's placement of the charge-off and his subsequent inquiries, Zeller was rejected for credit with two mortgage companies and a credit card company. Zeller filed this action alleging violations of the Fair Credit Reporting Act (FCRA) and sought actual and punitive damages.

Senior District Judge CAFFREY
*   *   *   *

FCRA defines a consumer report as:
[A]ny written, oral, or other communication of any information by a consumer reporting agency bearing a consumer's creditworthiness, credit standing, credit capacity, character, general reputation, personal characteristics, or mode of living which *is used or expected to be used or collected in whole or in part for the purpose* of serving as a factor in establishing the consumer's eligibility for (1) credit or insurance to be used primarily for personal, family, or household purposes, or (2) employment purposes, or (3) other purposes authorized under 1681b. . . .
*   *   * Section 1681b, which completes the definition of a consumer report, provides in relevant part:
A consumer reporting agency may furnish a consumer report under the following circumstances and no other:
*   *   *   *

(3) To a person it has reason to believe—
(A) intends to use the information in connection with a credit transaction involving the consumer on whom the information is to be furnished and involving the extension of credit to, or review or collection of an account of, the consumer; or
*   *   *   *

(E) . . . has a legitimate business need for the information in connection with a business transaction involving the consumer.
*   *   *   *

In this case, the plaintiff has not introduced any evidence indicating that the defendant's use of the information was for any other reason than "in connection with" a business arrangement involving the plaintiff. It is undisputed that defendant's inquiry and use of the plaintiff's credit information was limited to the transaction involving the [cottage] property which was the subject of the [this] proceeding. Therefore, the evidence shows that the defendant had a legitimate business need for the information in connection with a "business transaction" involving the plaintiff.

DECISION AND REMEDY *Zeller did not introduce any evidence indicating that Samia's use of the information was for any other reason than "in connection with" a business arrangement involving Zeller. Samia's inquiry and use of the information from Credit Data were limited to the transaction involving the cottage property in the other lawsuit. Thus, no violation of the Fair Credit Reporting Act had occurred.*

Equal Credit Opportunity Act In 1974, Congress enacted the Equal Credit Opportunity Act. The Equal Credit Opportunity Act forbids certain forms of discrimination. If a person has the ability to repay the loan, he or she cannot be denied credit on the basis of race, color, religion, national origin, sex, marital status, age, or a person's income being derived from public assistance. To

Legal Highlight

Gossip, Gossip, Gossip

What type of information was placed in people's credit files prior to the passage of the Fair Credit Reporting Act? Here are a few examples:

■ A man who applied for automobile insurance was denied. He later found this statement in his file: "Subject's son is a hippie type."

■ A woman's application for automobile insurance was denied. In her file was a notation that she was a topless dancer who was divorced.

■ A man who applied for life insurance was denied. In his record was a statement based on hearsay that his former boss had "suspected him of taking money from the till." No charges had ever been filed.

■ Another man was fortunate. In his file was found this statement: "We learn of no connection with any Peace movement or other serversice [sic] type organization. He is regarded as a normal loyal american [sic]."

■ A man who applied for life insurance was denied. In his file was a false statement that he kept "unsavory company." The second statement, over fifteen years old, was that he had destroyed property. The truth was that he had accidentally broken a neighbor's plate-glass window while playing softball. When he went to the credit bureau and told his story, the credit bureau agreed to correct his file for a fee. The fee to check out his story was $10 a hour, with a fifteen-hour minimum, payable in advance.

■ A man in Atlanta had immigrated to the United States from his native Hungary. He arrived in the United States penniless and knowing little English. Twelve years later he had a thriving business. When he went to borrow money, however, he was denied credit again and again. Finally he found that his record noted that he had been involved in a $200 lawsuit, had bad debts, had gone bankrupt, and had skipped town. In fact he had a business, had lived in the same house for twelve years, was not involved in a $200 lawsuit, had no bad debts, and had never filed for bankruptcy.

After two personal visits to the credit reporting bureau and letters to the Justice Department, the Federal Trade Commission, President Nixon, and his hometown newspaper—and with lawyers talking directly to the credit reporting bureau—he still had not cleared the false information from his file. This problem began in 1966. He was finally told that the incorrect information had been expunged from his file in March 1972, but, when he applied for credit cards from Standard Oil and Sears in May 1972, credit was denied. Both companies cited the same source of their negative information: the credit reporting agency that he had been fighting for years.

---

discriminate against a person by denying him or her credit on any of these bases is illegal. The civil liabilities for violation of this act include actual damages as well as punitive damages up to $10,000, plus attorneys' fees and court costs.

Fair Debt Collection Practices Act In 1977 Congress passed the Fair Debt Collection Practices Act. This act applies to anyone who is in the *business* of consumer debt collection for others (collection agencies). Even without federal statutory provisions, however, it is not legal to invade a person's privacy or intentionally to cause emotional distress.

For example, under the Fair Debt Collection Practices Act, Ace, a debt collector, cannot contact Dan, a debtor, before 8 A.M. or after 9 P.M. Repeatedly calling Dan on the telephone is prohibited. Dan cannot be reached at his place of employment if his employer has a policy against debt collectors contacting employees at work. Ace can contact a third party one time for Dan's address but cannot tell the third party that a debt is owed. Dan can tell (write) Ace to stop communicating with him. If Dan has an attorney, and Ace knows it, subsequent communications must be made with Dan's attorney. On postcards or

Women and the Credit Revolution

The Equal Credit Opportunity Act was passed in 1974. Until this act was adopted, most single working women could not obtain credit or buy homes or automobiles in their own names without a cosigner.

A woman whose marriage had ended either in divorce or by the death of her husband also found it impossible to obtain credit. A married couple's credit was kept in the name of the husband, even though the wife may have been the only person working. When the marriage was over, the woman had no credit rating. She would discover that no financial institution would grant her a loan, credit cards, or a bank card. Worse, although an ex-husband's good credit rating did not follow her, the bad credit rating of an ex-husband did. The following are further examples:

■ A woman received $250,000 in a divorce settlement. From 1970 to 1972 she repeatedly applied for a bank card with a $500 limit; she was denied credit because she was divorced.
■ In 1973, a married woman attorney who had a ten-year law practice was denied a department store credit card in her own name.
■ In 1969, a widow of six years found it easier to get a credit card in her deceased husband's name than in her own name.

Congress heard many similar stories. Recognizing that women had become a stable part of the nation's work force, Congress passed the Equal Credit Opportunity Act.

As a side note, prior to this law, both single women and single men found it nearly impossible to purchase a house. Single people were deemed unstable by financial institutions. Today, over one-fourth of all houses, condominiums, and townhouses are sold to single people.

envelopes that Ace uses, the return address cannot indicate that Ace is a debt collector. Ace cannot threaten to use physical violence and cannot threaten to harm Dan's reputation or his property. Use of obscene or profane language is forbidden.

Ace cannot imply that he is collecting the debt under the authority of the government and cannot use a badge or uniform. Ace cannot misrepresent that nonpayment of the debt will result in Dan's arrest or imprisonment. The threats of the seizure, garnishment, attachment, or sale of any of Dan's property or his wages is forbidden unless Ace intends to file a lawsuit against Dan and informs Dan of the remedies that Ace may use to collect if Ace wins the suit.

If a provision of the act is violated, the collection agency must pay actual damages, plus additional damages up to $1,000 and attorneys' fees. The following case illustrates two ways in which a debt collection agency can violate the act.

Case 13.3
KIMBER v. FEDERAL FINANCIAL CORP.
United States District Court, Middle District, Alabama, 1987.
668 F.Supp. 1480.

BACKGROUND AND FACTS In 1976, W. T. Grant Stores assigned its accounts receivable (debts owed to Grant) to Federal Financial Corporation (FFC), a debt collection agency. In 1985, FFC filed a lawsuit against Kimber to collect a debt she owed. In an independent lawsuit, plaintiff Kimber sued FFC for violations of the Fair Debt Collection Practices Act.

Kimber alleged that FFC had sued her for a debt while knowing that it was not entitled to recover because the time limitation imposed by the statute of limitations had passed. FFC, therefore, had sued her on stale debts, or, in the language of the court, the debts were "time-barred." Kimber also alleged that FFC had attempted to collect a debt against her by falsely *claiming it could win the lawsuit, although FFC knew the debt was time-barred; thus, FFC's conduct was false and deceptive.*

Judge THOMPSON
*   *   *   *   *

*   *   * To help ensure the most complete protection possible, determinations as to whether conduct violates the Act are made in keeping with the standard of the "least sophisticated consumer." Thus, in applying the law to this case, the court must decide whether FFC's actions were unfair or unconscionable, or whether the least sophisticated of consumers would have been deceived, misled, or harassed by such practices.
*   *   *   *   *

[Court's discussion of time-barred debts]

The court agrees with Kimber that a debt collector's filing of a lawsuit on a debt that appears to be time-barred, without the debt collector having first determined after a reasonable inquiry that limitations period has been or should be tolled, is an unfair and unconscionable means of collecting the debt. *   *   * [T]ime-barred lawsuits are *   *   * unjust and unfair as a matter of public policy, and this is no less true in the consumer context. As with any defendant sued on a stale claim, the passage of time not only dulls the consumer's memory of the circumstances and validity of the debt, but heightens the probability that she will no longer have personal records detailing the status of the debt. Indeed, the unfairness of such conduct is particularly clear in the consumer context where courts have imposed a heightened standard of care—that sufficient to protect the least sophisticated consumer. Because few unsophisticated consumers would be aware that a statute of limitations could be used to defend against lawsuits based on stale debts, such consumers would unwittingly acquiesce to such lawsuits. And, even if the consumer realizes that she can use time as a defense, she will more than likely still give in rather than fight the lawsuit because she must still expend energy and resources and subject herself to the embarrassment of going into court to present the defense; this is particularly true in light of the costs of attorneys today.
*   *   *   *   *

The court must therefore conclude that FFC violated [the Act] when it filed suit against Kimber. There is no question that the debt FFC sought from Kimber was barred as stale. *   *   *

[Court's discussion of misrepresentation]

Kimber argues next that FFC made false, deceptive and misleading representations in violation of the Fair Debt Collection Practices Act by threatening to sue her on a claim the corporation knew was barred. *   *   *
*   *   *   *

*   *   * She alleges that by threatening her with a lawsuit which the corporation knew or reasonably should have known was time-barred, the corporation falsely represented the legal status of her debt, misled her as to what action might be legally taken against her, and deceptively used this threat in attempting to collect on her alleged debt. In so doing, Kimber argues, FFC preyed upon the ignorance of an unsophisticated consumer. Threats to sue communicated through an attorney would only naturally represent to the least sophisticated consumer that a lawsuit was viable, even when in fact it was not, Kimber contends.

FFC answers that since it was clearly possible to *file* a lawsuit against Kimber— whether or not it was possible to *win* one—there was no deception as to the legal status of the debt, nor any false threat of legal action used to coerce payment. FFC asserts that ordinary statutes of limitations bar only the remedy, not the underlying right.

Whether it is true that a statute of limitations defense does not erase the right underlying a lawsuit but rather prevents success on a claim is immaterial, for the court cannot agree with FFC that this legal principle, even if true, lends approval to the practice of threatening and undertaking lawsuits for which the statute of limitations has clearly run and for which there is no evidence that would warrant tolling. The dispositive fact is that a debt collector could not legally prevail in such lawsuit, and for the debt collector to represent otherwise is fraudulent.

* * * *

Here, it is obvious to the court that by employing the tactics it did, FFC played upon and benefited from the probability of creating a deception. Honest disclosure of the legal unenforceability of the collection action due to the time lapsed since the debt was incurred would have foiled FFC's efforts to collect on the debt. So instead, the corporation implicitly misrepresented to Kimber the status of the debt, and thereby misled her as to the viability of legal action to collect. As such, FFC's conduct was false and deceptive[.] * * *

DECISION AND REMEDY *The court found that FFC had violated the Act when it filed a lawsuit against Kimber because the lawsuit had not been filed within the time limits established by the statute of limitations. The court also found that FFC had misrepresented its ability to win a lawsuit in a false and deceptive manner. The case, however, was sent back to the trial court on another issue.*

Other Consumer-Oriented Laws

At the federal and state levels, a variety of consumer protection laws exist. These laws regulate a range of activities from the operation of dance studios and health clubs to used automobile sales and even the sale of funerals. We will review three major laws here.

Uniform Consumer Credit Code

In 1968, the National Conference of Commissioners on the Uniform State Laws promulgated the **Uniform Consumer Credit Code** (UCCC). The UCCC has been controversial, and only a few states have adopted it. It is a comprehensive body of rules governing the most important aspects of consumer credit. Sections of the UCCC, for example, focus on truth in lending, door-to-door sales, referral sales, and maximum credit interest rate ceilings.

The UCCC is also concerned with creditor remedies, including deficiency judgments and **garnishments** (proceedings where property, money, or wages controlled by a third person are transferred to the court to satisfy a judgment). The UCCC applies to most types of sales, including real estate. It also covers installment loans, retail installment sales, and **usury** (charging more than the maximum rate of interest allowed by state law).

Real Estate Settlement Procedures Act

The **Real Estate Settlement Procedures Act** (RESPA) was passed by Congress in 1974. It governs the purchase of a house and the borrowing of money to pay for it. RESPA requires that all closing costs be specifically outlined before a person buys a home.

After a person applies for a mortgage loan, the lender must, within three business days, send a booklet, prepared by the United States Department of Housing and Urban Development, that outlines the applicant's rights and explains settlement procedures and costs. The lender must give an estimate of most of the settlement costs within that three-day period. If the loan is approved, the lender must provide a truth-in-lending statement that shows the annual percentage rate on the mortgage loan.

Creditors' Rights

A creditor has the right to payment. When the debtor does not fulfill his or her obligation to make timely payments, state laws establish procedures by which a creditor can secure payment of the debt or recovery of the goods for which the debt was incurred.

Writ of Execution

A debt must be past due in order for a creditor to commence legal action against a debtor. If the creditor is successful, the court awards the creditor a judgment against the debtor (usually for the amount of the debt plus any interest and legal costs incurred in obtaining the judgment). If the debtor still does not or cannot pay the judgment, the creditor is entitled to go back to the court and obtain a **writ of execution.**

A writ of execution is an order, issued by a judge or the clerk of the court, directing the sheriff to seize and sell any of the debtor's *nonexempt* real or personal property that is within the court's geographic jurisdiction (usually the county in which the courthouse is located). The proceeds of the sale are used to pay off the judgment and the costs of the sale itself. This procedure is known as a **judicial sale.** Any excess is paid to the debtor.

At any time before the sale takes place, the debtor can pay the judgment and redeem the non-exempt property. **Exempt property** is property that, according to a statute, can be kept by the debtor and is protected from the creditor; such property may include the debtor's home, furniture, and other essentials for living.

Attachment

Writ of attachment is the court-ordered seizure and taking into custody property of the defendant. Attachment rights are created by state statutes. Attachment is normally a prejudgment remedy. It occurs either at the time of or immediately after the commencement of a lawsuit but before the entry of a final judgment. By statute, the restrictions and requirements concerning a creditor's right to attachment before judgment are very specific. The due process clause of the Fourteenth Amendment to the Constitution limits a court's power to authorize seizure of a debtor's property without notice to the debtor or a hearing on the facts.

In order to use attachment as a remedy, the creditor must follow certain procedures. He or she must file with the court an affidavit stating that

the debtor is in default and stating the statutory grounds under which attachment is sought. A bond must be posted by the creditor to cover court costs, the value of the loss of the use of the goods as suffered by the debtor, and the value of the property attached. When the court is satisfied that all the requirements have been met, it issues a writ of attachment. This writ directs the sheriff or other officer to seize nonexempt property. If the creditor prevails at trial, the seized property can then be sold to satisfy the judgment.

Garnishment

A garnishment is a statutory procedure in which a debtor's property, currently in another's possession, is applied to the payment of that person's debts. An example might be the wages owed to a debtor by his or her employer; a writ of garnishment for these wages is issued by the court and addressed to the employer requiring that a portion of the employee's paycheck be paid to the creditor.

Garnishments are regulated by federal and state law. Before the federal law was passed, many states allowed the creditor to garnish (that is, to take) the debtor's entire paycheck. The lack of laws protecting debtors encouraged lenders to extend credit to people who could not afford the payments. But many employers fired the employee if his or her paycheck was garnished.

Congress determined that debtors needed some limited protection. The federal law sets out the maximum amounts that can be garnished. State laws frequently set even lower limits on the amounts that can be garnished. Now the employee has at least some of his or her paycheck to take home. One exception is when the government is owed taxes. In this case, the government can garnish the entire paycheck until all the taxes owed are paid. An employer cannot discharge an employee for garnishment of the employee's paycheck. If the debtor is fired, the employer may be fined $1,000, imprisoned for one year, or both.

In addition to the protections offered by federal or state statutes, the United States Supreme Court has declared that a consumer has a right to a hearing before wages can be garnished. The following case established this right. This decision was based in part on the due process clause in the Constitution.

Case 13.4
SNIADACH v. FAMILY FINANCE CORP.

Supreme Court of the United
States, 1969.
395 U.S. 337, 89 S.Ct. 1820,
23 L.Ed.2d 349.

BACKGROUND AND FACTS *Family Finance Corporation attempted under Wisconsin law to garnish the wages of Mrs. Sniadach after she failed to make timely payments on a loan. No trial or hearing was ever held to determine that Mrs. Sniadach had defaulted on the debt or that the garnishment was otherwise authorized. Her only notice was served on her at the same time that her wages were garnished.*

Mrs. Sniadach contended that the finance company's failure to give her notice that the wages would be seized violated her right to due process. Both the trial court and the Wisconsin Supreme Court upheld the procedure allowed by Wisconsin law to garnish wages without prior notice to the consumer. Mrs. Sniadach took her case to the United States Supreme Court.

Justice DOUGLAS delivered the opinion of the Court.

[Family Finance Corp.] instituted a garnishment action against [Sniadach] as defendant and Miller Harris Instrument Co., her employer, as garnishee. The complaint alleged a claim of $420 on a promissory note. * * *

* * * * *

* * * She * * * claims that the Wisconsin garnishment procedure violates that due process required by the Fourteenth Amendment, in that notice and an opportunity to be heard are not given before the *in rem* seizure of the wages. What happens in Wisconsin is that the clerk of the court issues the summons at the request of the creditor's lawyer; and it is the latter who by serving the garnishee sets in motion the machinery whereby the wages are frozen. They may, it is true, be unfrozen if the trial of the main suit is ever held and the wage earner wins on the merits. But in the interim the wage earner is deprived of his enjoyment of earned wages without any opportunity to be heard or to tender any defense he may have, whether it be fraud or otherwise.

Such summary procedure may well meet the requirements of due process in extraordinary situations. But in the present case, no situation requiring special protection to a state or creditor interest is presented by the facts; nor is the Wisconsin statute narrowly drawn to meet any such unusual condition. [Sniadach] was a resident of this Wisconsin community and *in personam* jurisdiction was readily obtainable.

* * * In this case, the sole question is whether there has been a taking of property without that procedural due process that is required by the Fourteenth Amendment. We have dealt over and over again with the question of what constitutes "the right to be heard" within the meaning of procedural due process. * * * [W]e said that the right to be heard "has little reality or worth unless one is informed that the matter is pending and can choose for himself whether to appear or default, acquiesce or contest." * * *

A prejudgment garnishment of the Wisconsin type is a taking which may impose tremendous hardship on wage earners with families to support. Until a recent Act of Congress which forbids discharge of employees on the ground that their wages have been garnished, garnishment often meant loss of a job. Over and beyond that was the great drain on family income. As stated by Congressman Reuss:

> The idea of wage garnishment in advance of judgment, of trustee process, of wage attachment, or whatever it is called is a most inhuman doctrine. It compels the wage earner, trying to keep his family together, to be driven below the poverty level.

* * * * *

The result is that a prejudgment garnishment of the Wisconsin type may as a practical matter drive a wage-earning family to the wall. Where the taking of one's property is so obvious, it needs no extended argument to conclude that absent notice and a prior hearing this prejudgment garnishment procedure violates the fundamental principles of due process.

The court ruled that the Wisconsin statute was unconstitutional. As a result of this decision, today a court must determine that a valid debt exists before wages can be garnished, and there must be proper notice and a hearing available to the debtor before garnishment can take place.

DECISION AND REMEDY

Mortgage Foreclosure on Real Property

In Chapter 12, we reviewed how a secured party (a creditor) repossesses personal property. The basic format is the same for the repossession of real property, but some differences do exist. Various methods exist to create a lien on real estate. For this discussion, we will group all of them under the term *mortgage*.

Creation of the Mortgage A real estate mortgage is a lien against the realty to secure payment of a loan given usually to secure the purchase of real property. For example, Jane wants to purchase a house. After entering into a purchase agreement (contract) to buy a house, she arranges with a lender to borrow money over a 30-year period at a 9 percent interest rate. She must sign a note with the lender in which she, the debtor-borrower, agrees to pay back the money in monthly installments to the creditor-lender over the next 30 years. At this point, the unsecured note is the only evidence of the debt, and if Jane were to default on the note, all the creditor could do would be to sue her in court on the note.

What the creditor wants is something to back up the note; that is, the creditor wants a secured note. In real estate, the note is secured by a lien against the home, known as a mortgage. Jane, the debtor-borrower, creates a mortgage on the real estate; thus, she is called the **mortgagor.** This creator-lender is the beneficiary of the mortgage and is called the **mortgagee.** Once the mortgage is created to back up (secure) the note, the note is usually called a mortgage note.

Default and Foreclosure Let's say that Jane now defaults by failing to pay the note. The real estate mortgage agreement provides that, if the mortgagor (debtor-borrower) defaults in making the payments, the mortgagee (creditor-lender) can declare that the entire mortgage debt is due immediately. The mortgagee can obtain payment in full by a lawsuit called a foreclosure.

In this suit, the real estate that is covered by the mortgage is usually sold at a court-ordered sale (a judicial sale) under the authority of a writ of execution. If the proceeds of the sale are sufficient to cover both the costs of the foreclosure and the mortgaged debt, any surplus is paid to the debtor. Jane is entitled to this money since she is the owner of the property. The creditor holds only a lien against her property; thus, the creditor is entitled to have only the lien paid back and is not entitled to make a profit. All the creditor can collect is the amount of the unpaid debt.

Deficiency Judgment If, on the other hand, the sale proceeds are insufficient to cover the foreclosure costs and the mortgaged debt, the mortgagee can seek to recover the difference from Jane (the mortgagor) by obtaining a deficiency judgment in most states. A deficiency judgment represents the deficiency amount—that is, the difference between the mortgaged debt and costs of foreclosure and the amount actually received from the proceeds of the foreclosure sale.

A deficiency judgment is normally obtained in a separate legal action that is filed after the foreclosure, because the creditor does not know until after the sale if there is a surplus or a deficiency. The creditor can recover the deficiency judgment from other property owned by the debtor. Only nonexempt property (property that is subject to execution or garnishment) can be used to satisfy the deficiency judgment. In many states, the creditor cannot obtain a deficiency judgment at all against a debtor when the foreclosure involves the debtor's residence.

From the time of default until the time of the foreclosure sale, Jane can redeem her property by paying the full amount of the debt, plus any interest and other costs that have accrued. In some states, Jane may even be able to redeem her property within a statutory period after the judicial sale.

Protection for the Debtor

In most states, certain types of real and personal property are exempt from execution or attachment. Probably the most familiar of these exemptions is the **homestead exemption.** Each state permits the debtor to retain the family home, either in its entirety or up to a specified dollar amount, free from unsecured creditors or trustees in bankruptcy claims. The purpose is to ensure that the debtor will retain or be able to obtain some form of shelter. A homestead exemption is not valid against the first mortgage.

For example, Daniels owes Carey $40,000. The debt is the subject of a lawsuit, and the court awards Carey a judgment of $40,000 against Daniels. At some time before, during, or in some states even after the judgment, Daniels can file a homestead exemption. Daniels's home is valued at $50,000. To satisfy the judgment debt, Daniels's family home is sold at public auction for $45,000. Assume that the state law allows a homestead exemption of $25,000. The proceeds of the sale are distributed as follows:

1. Daniels is paid $25,000 as his homestead exemption.
2. Carey is paid $20,000 toward the judgment debt.
3. A $20,000 debt is still owed.

Carey now obtains a deficiency judgment for $20,000. This deficiency judgment can be satisfied from any other nonexempt property (personal or real) that Daniels may have, if allowed by state law.

Personal property that is most often exempt from satisfaction of judgment debts includes:

1. Household furniture, such as beds, dining tables and chairs, usually up to a specified dollar amount
2. Clothing and certain personal possessions, such as family pictures, books, tools, and Bibles
3. A vehicle for transportation (at least up to a specific dollar amount).

Bankruptcies and Reorganizations

The United States Constitution, Article I, Section 8, provides that "the Congress shall have Power

. . . To establish . . . uniform Laws on the subject of Bankruptcies throughout the United States." Congress has adopted a series of bankruptcy statutes; the latest are the Bankruptcy Reform Acts of 1978, 1984, and 1986. Federal law governs bankruptcy proceedings. Bankruptcy courts are special federal courts, and the bankruptcy judges are appointed for fourteen-year terms by the United States Courts of Appeals.

Goals of Bankruptcy

Bankruptcy law is designed to accomplish two main goals. The first is to provide relief and protection (a fresh start) to debtors who are deeply in debt and cannot recover financially without help. The second major goal of bankruptcy is to provide a fair means of distributing a debtor's assets among all creditors. Although the bankruptcy acts are federal law, state laws on secured transactions, liens, judgments, and exemptions play a role in federal bankruptcy proceedings.

The Bankruptcy Reform Acts of 1978, 1984, and 1986

The Bankruptcy Reform Acts of 1978, 1984, and 1986 are contained in Title 11 of the United States Code and have several chapters. Chapters 1, 3, and 5 include general definitions and provisions governing the case administration, the creditors, the debtor, and the estate. These three chapters apply generally to all bankruptcies. Several chapters set forth different types of bankruptcy relief. Chapter 7 provides for liquidations. Chapter 9 governs the adjustment of debts of a municipality. Chapter 11 allows for reorganizations of individual and business debtors. Chapter 12 provides for bankruptcy relief of family farmers, and Chapter 13 provides for the adjustment of debts of individuals with regular income. The following sections deal with Chapter 7, Liquidations; Chapter 11, Reorganizations; Chapter 13, Adjustment of Debts of Individuals; and Chapter 12, Adjustment of Debts of Family Farmers.

The 1986 act created the position of U.S. trustee in each federal judicial district. U.S. trustees monitor the administrative side of bankruptcies.

Chapter 7: Liquidations   The most familiar type of bankruptcy proceedings is often referred to as a **straight bankruptcy.** Put simply, a debtor in a straight bankruptcy lists his or her debts and turns his or her assets over to a trustee. The trustee sells the assets and distributes the proceeds to creditors. Most of the balance of the debts are then discharged (extinguished), and the debtor is relieved from the obligation to pay these debts.

Any person—defined here to include individuals, partnerships, and corporations—may be a debtor under Chapter 7. "Corporation" as used here includes unincorporated companies and associations; it also covers labor unions. Chapter 7 does not apply to railroads, insurance companies, banks, savings and loan associations, and governmental units. Other chapters of the Bankruptcy Act or other federal and state statutes apply to them.

Bankruptcy Procedure   A straight bankruptcy is started by the filing of a petition on the official forms of the bankruptcy court. The debtor can file a voluntary petition, or unsecured creditors whose aggregate claims equal $5,000 or more can file an involuntary petition against the debtor. The petition contains a list of both secured and unsecured creditors, their addresses, and the amount of debt owed to each; a statement of the financial affairs of the debtor; and a list of all property owned by the debtor, including property claimed by the debtor to be exempt. The official forms must be completed accurately, sworn to under oath, and signed by the debtor. To conceal assets or knowingly supply false information on these schedules is a federal crime and can be grounds for denying the debtor a discharge in bankruptcy.

The filing of a petition operates as an **automatic stay** that stops or suspends all civil litigation against the debtor. In other words, creditors cannot start or continue legal actions against the debtor to recover claims they have against him or her, nor can creditors take any action to repossess property in the hands of the debtor. All actions against the debtor must now go through the bankruptcy court.

Trustees   A court-appointed trustee is to be distinguished from a U.S. trustee. The U.S. trustee is an administrative position within the bankruptcy court. A regular trustee (interim or permanent) is appointed by the court to represent the creditors.

The court appoints an interim trustee to preside over the debtor's property until the first meeting of creditors. At this first meeting, a permanent trustee is elected. The trustee's principal duty is to collect the debtor's property, reduce it to money, and close up the estate as soon as possible, keeping in mind the best interests of all parties. Trustees are entitled to compensation for services rendered plus reimbursement for expenses.

A trustee steps into the shoes of the debtor, and the trustee has specific powers to rescind obligations of the debtor. This power is called avoidance. Any reason that a debtor can use to obtain return of his or her property can be used by the trustee as well. These grounds include fraud, duress, incapacity, and mutual mistake. For example, Ben sells his boat to Frank. Frank gives Ben a check, knowing that there are insufficient funds in the bank account to cover the check. Frank has committed fraud. Ben has the right to cancel the contract and to recover the boat from Frank. If Ben has filed for bankruptcy, the trustee for Ben can exercise the same right to recover the boat from Frank. The trustee's power of avoidance includes setting aside preferences (payments made by the debtor to a creditor while insolvent) and setting aside certain statutory liens, such as a landlord's lien.

Exemptions   An individual debtor is entitled to exempt certain property from bankruptcy. An individual debtor can choose between the exemptions provided under the state law or under the federal law, if the state law allows this choice. The following lists some of the property that is exempt under federal law:

1. Equity interest in a debtor's residence up to $7,500
2. One motor vehicle up to $1,200
3. Household furnishings and apparel up to $4,000 with no one item being worth more than $200
4. Jewelry up to $500
5. Professional books or tools of no more than $750
6. Life insurance contracts
7. Professionally prescribed health aids
8. Miscellaneous property up to $400
9. Social security, profit sharing, disability, alimony, and other funds for the support of the debtor or of his or her dependents

10. Amounts paid to the debtor under a crime victims law, wrongful death award, and up to $7,500 not including pain and suffering for a personal injury.

Property Distribution The trustee, after reducing the debtor's available estate to money, is obligated to pay the debts of those unsecured creditors who appropriately file claims. Bankruptcy law establishes an order of priority for certain classes of debts owed these unsecured creditors. Each class must be fully paid before the next class on the list is entitled to any proceeds. If there are insufficient proceeds to pay a class, the proceeds are prorated among the creditors of that class and all classes lower in priority receive nothing. If all classes are fully paid and there is a remaining balance, it goes to the debtor.

Examples of the order of priority among classes of unsecured creditors are as follows:

1. All bankruptcy costs have top priority.
2. Claims for unpaid wages, salaries, or commissions due employees earned within 90 days of the bankruptcy petition, limited to $2,000 per employee.
3. Claims for funds prepaid by creditors to the debtor for goods or services not delivered by the debtor up to $900 for each claim.
4. Certain taxes (and penalties) owed to government entities.

All of these creditors and others must be paid before any unsecured general creditor is entitled to any proceeds from the debtor's estate.

Nondischargeable Debts From the debtor's point of view, the primary purpose of a Chapter 7 liquidation is to obtain a fresh start through the **discharge** of debts. There are circumstances, however, in which a debt will not be discharged.

Debts that are not dischargeable include claims for back taxes accruing within three years prior to bankruptcy; claims against property or money obtained by the debtor under false representations; claims for alimony and child support; claims for certain student loans; and judgments or consent decrees awarded against a debtor for liability incurred as a result of the debtor's operation of a motor vehicle while legally intoxicated. Discharges are granted only to "individuals" as debt-

ors, not to corporations or partnerships. The latter may use Chapter 11 or, where appropriate, Chapter 12 bankruptcy proceedings.

Reaffirmation Under previous bankruptcy acts, it was very common for a creditor to convince the debtor to **reaffirm** (renew) his or her debts. For example, a finance company would offer a debtor a loan of $1,000 if he or she would reaffirm the debt that had been owed to the finance company, but that had been discharged by bankruptcy. Creditors knew that the debtor could not file for bankruptcy again for six more years. Reaffirmation tended to defeat one of the purposes of bankruptcy: to give a debtor a fresh start.

As a result, Congress has restricted the procedure of reaffirmations. Since 1984, to be enforceable, reaffirmation agreements must be made before a debtor is granted a discharge. The agreement must be filed with the court. The debtor must be counseled by his or her attorney, and a declaration must be filed stating that the debtor knows the consequences of the voluntary agreement and that it does not impose a hardship on the debtor or on his or her dependents. If the debtor is not represented by an attorney, court approval is required except for the debtor's real property. Here the court must find that the agreement presents no undue hardship and that it is in the best interests of the debtor.

The debtor has the ability to rescind the agreement at any time prior to discharge or within 60 days of the filing of the agreement, whichever is later. This rescission period must be stated clearly and conspicuously in the reaffirmation agreement.

Chapter 11: Reorganizations Chapter 11 reorganization is used most commonly by a corporate debtor. Essentially, in a reorganization the creditors and the debtor formulate a plan under which the debtor pays a portion of his or her debts and is discharged of the remainder. The debtor is allowed to continue in business. Although this type of bankruptcy is commonly a corporate reorganization, debtors who are eligible for Chapter 7 relief and railroads are also eligible for Chapter 11 relief. Proceedings may be initiated by either a voluntary or involuntary petition.

The same principles that govern the filing of a Chapter 7 petition apply to Chapter 11 proceedings and to the court's entry of the order for relief. The automatic stay and adequate protection provisions previously discussed are applicable in reorganizations.

The debtor generally continues to operate his or her business as a "debtor in possession." The court may appoint a trustee to operate the debtor's business if gross mismanagement of the business is shown or if it is in the best interests of the debtor.

The debtor files a Chapter 11 plan that must be "fair and equitable." Classes of claims, such as secured and unsecured creditors, under the plan must be designated, and each claim within a particular class must be provided the same treatment.

Once the plan has been developed, it is submitted to each class of creditors for acceptance. Acceptance of a plan is required by each class.

The plan must be in the best interests of the creditors. On confirmation, the debtor is given a Chapter 11 discharge for all claims not protected under the plan. Those debts protected by the plan are paid in part according to the plan, but the remainder of those debts is also discharged.

The following case examines whether unsecured creditors can have a fund established for them when the fund was not part of the reorganization plan.

BACKGROUND AND FACTS *A. H. Robins Company is a pharmaceutical firm. From 1971 to 1974, it sold the Dalkon Shield intrauterine device (IUD) to physicians and clinics. Over 2.2 million women were fitted with the Dalkon Shield. From the start, Robins received complaints. Eventually more than 12,000 women filed lawsuits. They sought damages for debilitating pain, severe bleeding, perforated uteri, unplanned pregnancies, spontaneous miscarriages, septic abortions, chronic pelvic inflammatory disease, and for being rendered sterile. Over twenty women died. Although Robins won the initial lawsuits, as more information was disclosed about Robins's negligence in designing, testing, and marketing the Dalkon Shield, more women won their lawsuits, some receiving judgments of over $1 million.*

Robins, in 1985, filed a petition for relief under Chapter 11. The United States District Court for the Eastern District of Virginia, where Robins's headquarters are located, took jurisdiction over certain aspects of the bankruptcy, including all the lawsuits filed by the women. The district court ordered a notice of claim to be advertised worldwide so that any woman who had a Dalkon Shield claim against Robins could file a claim with the court. The court expected fewer than 30,000 notices of claims to be filed; over 325,000 notices of claims were actually filed. Of these claims, only 180,000 filed the notices in a timely manner and returned the court questionnaire.

At the time that this aspect of the case arose, Robins was challenging the validity and amount of the claims. None of the claims had been estimated for a value amount, thus none had been allowed by the district court as a payable claim. In addition, the final reorganization plan had not been filed. In the meantime, the Official Committee of Equity Securities Holders (The Equity Committee) had been appointed by the district court to represent Robins's public shareholders. Common stock for the Robins Company is traded on the New York Stock Exchange, with more than 20 million shares outstanding.

In August 1986, the district court appointed Mabey as an examiner to evaluate a plan of reorganization. He, together with Robins, the Dalkon Shield Claimants' Committee, and the future claimants' representative created the concept of an emergency treatment fund that would provide payment for surgery or cash payments to qualified women. In May 1987, the district

Case 13.5
OFFICIAL COMMITTEE OF EQUITY SECURITY HOLDERS v. MABEY
United States Court of Appeals, Fourth Circuit, 1987.
832 F.2d 299.

court ordered Robins to establish the fund and to fund it with $15 million. The Equity Committee appealed this order.

Judge CHAPMAN
* * * *

The May 21, 1987, order of the district court approving the Emergency Treatment Fund makes no mention of its authority to establish such a fund prior to the allowance of the claims of the women who would benefit from the fund, and prior to the confirmation of a plan of reorganization of Robins. However, in its order denying The Equity Committee's motion for a stay pending appeal of the May 21, 1987, order, the district court relied upon the "expansive equity power" of the court. [The court stated that it:]
* * * recognizes that the establishment of an emergency treatment fund is unusual and, indeed, may be unprecedented. Nevertheless, the Code provides the Court * * * with an expansive equity power to "issue any order, process or judgment that is necessary or appropriate to carry out the provisions of this title." The dire circumstances of this case required the Court to invoke its power under Section 105(a) and take those steps needed to treat these claimants equitably. *See also Midlantic Nat'l Bank v. New Jersey Dept. of Env'tl Protection.*
We have searched *Midlantic* without finding any reference to the equitable powers and we find such decision has no relevance to the issues presently before us. While equitable powers are quite important in the general bankruptcy scheme, and while such powers may encourage courts to be innovative, and even original, these equitable powers are not a license for a court to disregard the clear language and meaning of the bankruptcy statutes and rules. * * *
* * * * *

The Bankruptcy Code does not permit a distribution to unsecured creditors in a Chapter 11 proceeding except under and pursuant to a plan of reorganization that has been properly presented and approved. * * * The clear language of * * * the Bankruptcy Rules * * * does not authorize the payment in part or in full, or the advance of monies to or for the benefit of unsecured claimants prior to the approval of the plan of reorganization. The creation of the Emergency Treatment Program has no authority to support it in the Bankruptcy Code and violates the clear policy of Chapter 11 reorganizations by allowing piecemeal, preconfirmation payments to certain unsecured creditors. Such action also violates [the] Bankruptcy Rule which allows distribution to creditors only after the allowance of claims and the confirmation of a plan.

DECISION AND REMEDY *The creation of the emergency treatment fund was premature. The fund was created prior to the district court allowing the claims for payment and prior to the confirmation of Robins's plan for reorganization. The district court order was in violation of the Bankruptcy Code, and the district court had no other basis of authority to create the fund.*

Chapter 13: Adjustment of Debts of an Individual with Regular Income The former Bankruptcy Act provided for the formulation of wage-earner plans as a means of allowing wage earners to pay off their debts free from the harassment of creditors. Under these plans, the wage earner avoided the stigma of being adjudicated a "bankrupt." Today, Chapter 13 of the Bankruptcy Code provides for "Adjustment of Debts of an Individual with Regular Income."

Who May File Individuals (not partnerships or corporations) with regular income who owe unsecured debts of less than $100,000 and secured debts of less than $350,000 may take advantage of Chapter 13. The act includes individual busi-

Ethical Considerations

Do You Have to Have Credit Life Insurance?

You negotiate for the purchase of a new automobile. You need to borrow the money for the purchase. As you read through the contract, you notice a provision for credit life and credit disability insurance. The lender informs you that you must provide him or her with insurance coverage. In case you die or are disabled, the monthly payments will continue to be paid from the insurance proceeds. What you do not know is that the lender earns more money from the sale of credit life and disability policies than from lending money.

Can the lender ethically require you to provide insurance coverage so that if you are disabled or if you die, the loan will be paid? Can the lender require you ethically to purchase these types of insurance contracts through him or her, or should you be free to shop around for the best premium rate?

---

ness proprietors and individuals on welfare, social security, fixed pension, or investment income. Many small-business debtors have the choice of filing a plan under either Chapter 11 or Chapter 13.

Several advantages come with filing a Chapter 13 plan, among them the fact that it is less expensive and less complicated than a Chapter 11 proceeding or a Chapter 7 liquidation. A Chapter 13 case can only be initiated by the voluntary filing of a petition by the debtor. Any eligible debtor, who is presently in a Chapter 7 or Chapter 11 bankruptcy proceeding, can convert to a Chapter 13 case.

Bankruptcy Proceedings When a debtor files a Chapter 13 petition, the automatic stay previously discussed takes effect.

The debtor may propose a plan that provides for either full payment or partial payment of the debts. A Chapter 13 plan must provide for the turnover of future earnings or income of the debtor to the trustee as is necessary to carry out the plan. Full payment of all claims entitled to priority must be included in the plan. The full payment is made by paying smaller amounts over a longer time period than would have been allowed under the original creditor-debtor agreement. Each claim within a particular class must be treated equally; each secured debt, for example, must be paid in the same method as all other secured debts. The time for payment under the plan may not exceed three years unless the court approves an extension. The plan with extension may not exceed five years.

The plan must be confirmed by the court as long as all of the debtor's projected disposable income will be applied to making payments. Disposable income is all income less amounts needed to support the debtor (and dependents) and/or those needed to meet ordinary expenses to continue operation of a business.

The debtor is required to make "timely payments." Payments must begin under the proposed plan within 30 days after the plan has been filed. Failure of the debtor to make timely payments or to commence payments within the 30-day period will allow the court to convert the case to a Chapter 7 liquidation or to dismiss the petition.

After completion of all payments under a Chapter 13 plan, the court grants a discharge of all debts provided for by the plan. Taxes, alimony, and child support debts cannot be discharged. Because there are fewer nondischargeable debts under Chapter 13, the discharge is even greater than that provided for in a Chapter 7 liquidation.

Even if the debtor does not complete the plan, a hardship discharge may be granted if the failure to complete the plan was due to circumstances beyond the debtor's control and if the property distributed by the plan was greater than would have been paid in a Chapter 7 liquidation. For example, if the debtor is seriously injured in an accident and is permanently disabled, the debtor's

International Considerations

Consumer Credit Protection In Foreign Countries

No direct equivalents to the consumer protections set out in this chapter have been adopted in the international setting. The Organization for Economic Cooperation and Development (OECD) in 1977 recognized the importance of consumer credit. A recommendation was made to its member countries to adopt internal legislation that includes the following protections.

Consumers should be provided with credit information through advertisements—a recommendation that is very similar to the Truth-in-Lending Act. Full disclosure of all the credit terms should be clearly spelled out in the documents. The consumer's privacy should be respected and protected through legislation. Regulation of door-to-door sales, abolishment of the consumer holder-in-due-course concept, prohibition of unfair trade practices, and regulation of debt collection agencies are a few of the consumer protections recommended by the OECD. Notice that most of these provisions are already a part of the United States' Consumer Credit Protection Act.

income would be severely reduced, and he or she would be unable to complete the plan. In such a case, a discharge of the remaining debts may be granted.

Chapter 12: Adjustment of Debts of a Family Farmer with Regular Annual Income On November 27, 1986, the Family Farmer Bankruptcy Act became law. The new law defines a family farmer as one whose gross income is at least 50 percent farm-dependent and whose debts are at least 80 percent farm-related. The total debt must not exceed $1,500,000. A partnership or closely held corporation (at least 50 percent owned by the "farm family") can also take advantage of this law.

A Chapter 12 filing is very similar in procedure to a Chapter 13 filing. The farmer-debtor must file a plan not later than 90 days after the order of relief. The filing of the petition acts as an automatic stay against creditors and co-obligor actions against the estate.

The content and confirmation of the plan are basically the same as for a Chapter 13 filing. The plan can be modified by the farmer-debtor but, except for cause, must be confirmed or denied within 45 days of the filing of the plan. The plan must provide for payment of secured debts at the value of the collateral. If the secured debt exceeds the value of the collateral, the remaining debt is unsecured. For unsecured debtors, the plan must be confirmed if either the value of the property to be distributed under the plan equals the amount of the claim or if the plan provides that all of the debtor-farmer's disposable income received in a three-year period (longer by court approval) will be applied to making payments.

Disposable income is all income received less amounts needed to support the farmer-debtor and family and continue the farming operation. Completion of payments under the plan constitutes the discharge of all debts provided for by the plan.

FACING A LEGAL ISSUE   The Proper Way to Grant Credit

You are a manager of a medium-sized manufacturing firm that sells predominantly to retail consumers. Your average sale to a customer is $2,500, which makes it necessary for your firm to grant credit. Most of your consumers do not pay cash for your products.

No problems arise when your customers pay in accordance with your agreement, and normally your customers do pay on time. You, however, must plan ahead to give your company the best position possible under federal and state laws in the event that a customer does not pay.

First, before granting credit, you should obtain a detailed credit application that lists all the consumer's assets and liabilities. Included on this form are the names and addresses of creditors and relatives. The information about the relatives may help you find out what assets are available for attachment, execution, or garnishment, and may help you locate the debtor if he or she moves. You can ask for, but cannot require a social security number, although this information is helpful for identification purposes, especially when the consumer has a common name such as Brown, Smith, or Jones. With this application, you can verify credit with reporting agencies or with the creditors listed.

If you will be receiving more than four payments, you must comply with the truth-in-lending laws. Using the forms suggested by the Federal Reserve Board saves the time needed to draft forms and will prevent you from running afoul of the law. If you have a product that could be sold door to door, you must give the consumer a cooling-off period of three business days before you can regard the sale as irrevocable.

If you are selling personal property (goods), you must decide whether to secure your interest under the Uniform Commercial Code, Article 9. This procedure is covered in Chapter 12. Remember that you must have a written security agreement if the consumer-debtor has possession of the product. To protect your company's right fully, you must file a financing statement with the appropriate public office.

If an account becomes delinquent, what can your firm do to collect the monies owed? You should review the provisions of the Fair Debt Collection Practices Act. Keep in mind, first, that the collection agency you hire cannot harass or invade the right of privacy of an individual and, second, that there cannot be the threat of physical harm. Never threaten criminal prosecution, even if the debtor has committed a criminal act such as giving a bad check or committing fraud on the credit application. Such threatening could be considered duress in a civil action, and the threats themselves could result in you being charged with the crime of extortion.

Your firm should have a written policy as to the sequence of events that occurs when it is confronted with a bad debt. Remember that, if the consumer contests the bill, you must investigate and respond to his or her inquiry.

At times your firm will have to write off a debt as uncollectable and take a tax loss if that is allowed. The old saying that "you can't get blood out of a turnip" has application today. If the consumer has lost his or her job, is in prison, is disabled, or has suffered some other catastrophe, your firm should take the loss as soon as possible. In fact, if you do not have some losses on credit sales, it would indicate that your credit policies are too rigid. Your firm might be able to increase sales by relaxing those policies.

Lastly, you should be aware of the possibility of the debtor filing for bankruptcy. Having knowledge of the bankruptcy chapters available to the debtor and the ramifications for you as creditor under each chapter is important in establishing your credit policy.

Summary

This chapter has emphasized three areas of the law: consumer laws, creditors' rights, and bankruptcy.

The Consumer Credit Protection Act has five sections that apply directly to businesses and consumers. These sections may be summarized briefly as follows:

1. Truth-in-Lending Act: This statute requires the disclosure of the price owed, the finance charges, and the annual percentage rate of interest for the privilege of paying off the debt over a period of time. It also allows a three-day cooling-off period for credit transactions involving liens on residences (except first liens). The Federal Reserve Board has prepared forms that allow businesses to comply with this act. Under this act, a consumer cannot normally incur more than $50 of liability on a stolen or lost credit card for its unauthorized use.

2. The Fair Credit Reporting Act establishes certain rights for consumers. First, only information from the last seven years may be maintained, and information regarding bankruptcies over ten years old must be deleted from the record. The consumer can obtain the information contained in his or her credit records. In the event that the debtor contests this information, the reporting agency must investigate and correct misinformation and/or allow the debtor to file his or her explanation. Reports can only be used for legitimate credit or insurance purposes.

3. The Equal Credit Opportunity Act prohibits the creditor from discriminating against credit applicants based on race, color, religion, national origin, sex, marital status, age, or the receipt of income through public assistance.

4. The Fair Debt Collection Practices Act was adopted to protect consumers from overzealous collection agencies. Debt collectors must refrain from certain practices that would cause an invasion of privacy of the debtor and refrain from the intentional infliction of emotional distress, or duress.

5. The Fair Credit Billing Act was enacted to assist a debtor to correct a billing error. The law allows any debtor who believes a billing statement is in error to notify the creditor in writing explaining the error. The debtor does not have to pay the disputed amount at that time. The creditor must acknowledge receipt of the error inquiry and within 90 days correct the account or inform the debtor by explanation that the amount is correct.

Creditors use three judicial methods to try to collect on judgments owed them: writ of attachment, writ of execution, and writ of garnishment. Writs of attachment and execution are directed against nonexempt property in the possession of the debtor, while a writ of garnishment is directed against the debtor's property that is in the possession of a third party.

Chapters 7, 11, 12, and 13 of the Bankruptcy Code are of major importance to businesses. Chapter 11 provides for reorganization, while Chapter 7 allows a discharge of most debts. Chapters 12 and 13 permit family farmers and individuals to readjust their debts with a pay-out plan over a three- to five-year period. Some debts are not dischargeable by bankruptcy. In addition, there are certain assets that are exempt from bankruptcy by law; thus, the debtor may keep these assets.

Key Terms

annual percentage rate (316)
automatic stay (333)
bankruptcy law (332)
Consumer Credit Cost
    Disclosure Act (316)
Consumer Credit Protection
    Act (316)
Consumer Leasing Act (317)

discharge (334)
Equal Credit Opportunity Act
    (316)
exempt property (329)
Fair Credit Billing Act (316)
Fair Credit Reporting Act
    (316)
Fair Debt Collection Practices

Act (316)
finance charge (316)
garnishment (328)
homestead exemption (332)
judicial sale (329)
mortgagee (331)
mortgagor (331)
reaffirm (334)

Real Estate Settlement
   Procedures Act (**328**)
straight bankruptcy (**333**)
Truth-in-Lending Act (TILA)
   (**316**)

Uniform Consumer Credit
   Code (**328**)
usury (**328**)
writ of attachment (**329**)
writ of execution (**320**)

Questions and Case Problems

1. The East Bank was a secured party on a loan of $5,000 that it made to Sally. Sally later got into financial difficulty, and creditors other than the East Bank petitioned her into Chapter 7 involuntary bankruptcy. The value of the secured collateral had substantially decreased; on sale, the debt to East Bank was reduced only to $2,500. Sally's estate consisted of $100,000 in exempt assets and $2,000 in nonexempt assets. After the bankruptcy costs and back wages to Sally's employees were paid, nothing was left for unsecured creditors. Sally received a discharge in bankruptcy. Six years later she decided to go back into business. By selling a few exempt assets and getting a small loan, she would be able to buy a small but profitable restaurant. She went to East Bank for the loan. East Bank claimed that the balance of its secured debt was not discharged in bankruptcy. Sally agreed and signed an agreement to pay East Bank the $2,500, as the bank was not a party to the petitioning of Sally into bankruptcy. Because of this, East Bank made the new unsecured loan to Sally.
a. Discuss East Bank's claim that the balance of its secured debt was not discharged in bankruptcy.
b. Discuss the legal effect of Sally's agreement to pay East Bank $2,500 after the discharge in bankruptcy.
c. If, one year later, Sally went into voluntary bankruptcy, what effect would the bankruptcy proceedings have on the new unsecured loan?

2. Green receives two new credit cards on May 1. One was solicited from the King Department Store, and the other was unsolicited from the Flyways Airline. During the month of May, Green makes numerous credit card purchases from King, but she does not use the Flyways Airline card. On May 31, a burglar breaks into Green's home and, along with other items, steals both credit cards. Green notifies the King Department Store of the theft on June 2, but she fails to notify Flyways Airline. Using the King credit card, the burglar makes a $500 purchase on June 1 and a $200 purchase on June 3. The burglar then charges a vacation flight on the Flyways Airline card for $1,000 on June 5. Green receives the bills for these charges and refuses to pay them. Discuss Green's liability in these situations.

3. Prior to filing for bankruptcy, Bray was making loan payments to his company's credit union through payroll deductions. Bray's employer continued to deduct the loan payments from Bray's paychecks after being notified of the bankruptcy petition. Is this a violation of the Bankruptcy Code? [In re Bray, 17 B.R. 152 (Bkrtcy.N.D.Ga. 1982)]

4. Roseman resigned as an insurance agent after an audit revealed shortages in his account. A credit report prepared after his resignation contained the following information: "He resigned due to discovery of discrepancies in his accounts amounting to $314.84. This was all repaid by Roseman." Roseman brought an action to remove this information from his file. Should this information be removed? Discuss why or why not. [Roseman v. Retail Credit Co., 428 F.Supp. 643 (1977)]

5. John Yee earned more than $16,000 a year in his position with CBS. Prior to working for CBS he obtained a degree in accountancy from Bernard M. Baruch College of the City University of New York. He obtained this degree through the assistance of the National Student Direct Loan, to which he owed $2,583. His other debts totaled $10,790, and he had no assets. John Yee filed a Chapter 13 plan wherein he proposed to pay a total of $918 over 36 months on all of his loans. Do you think the court should accept this plan? Was it made in good faith? [In re Yee, 7 B.R. 747 (Bkrtcy.E.D.N.Y. 1980)]

6. Harold Grey signed an installment contract as payment for membership in European Health Spas Club, Inc. The disclosure documents that accompanied the installment loan contract were printed in regular type, with the exception of the following words, which were printed in capital letters: "FINANCE CHARGE," "ANNUAL PERCENTAGE RATE," and "MEMBER ACKNOWLEDGES THAT HE HAS READ AND RECEIVED A FILLED-IN SIGNED COPY OF THIS AGREEMENT." In addition, at the top of the disclosure statement, the words "NOTICE TO BUYER" were printed. Under federal truth-in-lending regulations, the words "finance charge" and "annual percentage rate" must be printed conspicuously in the truth-in-lending disclosure statements; otherwise, the creditor is deemed in violation of the act. Has the requirement of conspicuousness been met? [Grey v. European Health Spas, Inc., 428 F.Supp. 841 (D.Conn. 1977)]

7. In the summer of 1972, Robert Martin applied for and was issued an American Express card. Approximately three years later, in April 1975, Martin gave his card to E. L. McBride, a business associate, and orally authorized McBride to charge up to $500 on the card. He also wrote to American Express requesting that charges on his account be limited to $1,000. In June 1975, however, Martin received a statement from American Express indicating that the amount owed on his card account was approxi-

mately $5,300. Under the Truth-in-Lending Act, for how much will Martin be liable to American Express? [Martin v. American Express, Inc., 361 So.2d 597 (Ala.App. 1978)]

8. Telecredit is a computerized check authorization and purchase service. It purchases on average 608,959 dishonored checks a year. A customer writes a check to a merchant who then verifies with Telecredit whether the customer previously has written bad checks. If the customer's record is clean, Telecredit authorizes acceptance of the check. If the check then is dishonored, Telecredit purchases the check and attempts collection of it. Holmes had written a bad check for $315. Telecredit purchased the check and used various means to collect from Holmes. These procedures possibly violated the Fair Debt Collection Practices Act. Telecredit argued that it owned the check and thus was not subject to the act. Is Telecredit subject to the act? Discuss why or why not. [Holmes v. Telecredit Service Corp., 736 F.Supp. 1289 (D.Del. 1990)]

Chapter 14   Consumer Protection

Caveat emptor: *Let the buyer beware.*

Latin maxim

OUTLINE

Introduction

In earlier chapters we have seen how the law attempts to protect the interests of consumers. Certain business practices have been outlawed after they have been determined by courts, administrative agencies, or legislatures to be unfair or deceptive. In this chapter we will discuss laws that attempt to control unfair and deceptive trade practices, to prevent misleading advertising, and to encourage the development of safe products.

Consumer protection statutes promote both safety and fair dealing. They try to prevent injury to a person's body or damage to his or her property or economic well-being. Although some statutes provide a specific remedy if the consumer suffers an injury, the aim of consumer protection is to eliminate the harm itself, and many of these statutes do not have remedies for injured consumers. Redress for injuries suffered usually involves another area of the law, such as tort or contract law (covered in Chapters 8–11).

Costs are associated with consumer protection: Businesses bear the cost of complying with government regulation; these costs, in turn, are passed on to consumers in the form of higher prices for goods and services.

For every consumer protection statute, society poses three questions:

1. From what harm does the statute protect consumers?
2. Whom does the statute protect?
3. What is the cost of this protection?

Exhibit 14–1 lists statutes and regulations designed to protect consumers. Complete coverage of all of them would be impossible in a book of this length. This chapter will familiarize you with the nature and existence of some of the important statutes. Chapter 13, on credit regulation, explored the most significant legislation applicable to consumer financing.

Federal Trade Commission

Consumer protection, as we know it today, originated with the **Wheeler-Lea Act** of 1938. The 1938 law amended the **Federal Trade Commission Act,** which was originally passed in 1914 to supplement such statutes as the Sherman Antitrust Act. The Wheeler-Lea amendment gave the Federal Trade Commission Act a dual focus: to regulate anticompetitive business behavior and to provide consumer protection. Prior to 1938, courts aided only a few purchasers who sued sellers of defective goods by finding that the seller had breached a contract, had breached a warranty, or had violated a duty to the purchaser. As pointed out in Chapter 11, these claims are often difficult to prove.

The Wheeler-Lea amendment, through its prohibition of "**unfair or deceptive acts or practices,**" enabled the Federal Trade Commission (FTC) to focus its attention on direct protection of the consumer. The FTC was also given the authority to monitor deceptive advertising practices. Under this amendment, the FTC does not have to prove to the court that the practice had any effect on the competition. The definitions of "unfair" and "deceptive" are left to the FTC. In general, any practice that would tend to mislead consumers is unfair or deceptive.

As a result of this amendment, the FTC has two bureaus: the Bureau of Competition and the Bureau of Consumer Protection. The antitrust activities of the FTC are handled by the Bureau of Competition. The Bureau of Consumer Protection monitors advertising and labeling practices, investigates complaints, and prosecutes cases involving alleged unfair practices. Exhibit 14–2 shows the organizational structure of the FTC.

Trade Regulation Rules

As an administrative agency, the FTC is able to adopt trade regulation rules. A **trade regulation rule** is a statement by the agency that has general applicability, and the effect of the rule is to implement the law, policy, or practice of the agency. In other words, a rule has the force of law.

An FTC trade regulation rule applies to an entire industry rather than to a particular seller. The commission has the authority to focus on an industry and can formulate standards to which all businesses within that industry must conform. In the past, the FTC has investigated household detergents, appliances, office copiers, the title in-

Exhibit 14–1 Consumer Protection Statutes and Regulations

DATE	POPULAR NAME	PURPOSE
ADVERTISING		
1938	Wheeler-Lea Act	Amends Federal Trade Commission Act (1914); prohibits deceptive and unfair trade practices
1950	Oleomargarine Tax Repeal Act	Prohibits advertising that oleomargarine is a dairy product
1969	Public Health Cigarette Smoking Act	Prohibits advertising of cigarettes on television
1973	FTC Rules of Negative Options	Regulates advertisements for book and record clubs
INSPECTION AND CERTIFICATION		
1906	Meat Inspection Act	Provides for inspection of meat
1967	Wholesome Meat Act	Amends Meat Inspection Act
1938	Food, Drug, and Cosmetic Act	Provides for inspection and regulation of food, drugs, and cosmetics
1958	Food Additive (Delaney) Amendment to Food, Drug, and Cosmetic Act	Requires that food additives not cause cancer and be safe
1966	Hazardous Substances Act	Regulates hazardous substances
1968	Poultry Inspection Act	Provides for inspection of poultry
1969	Child Protection and Toy Safety Act	Amends Hazardous Substances Act; bans toys that pose electrical, mechanical, or thermal hazards
1972	Odometer Act	Regulates odometers
1976	Medical Device Amendments	Requires premarket clearance of medical devices
LABELING		
1939	Wool Products Labeling Act	Requires accurate labeling of wool products
1951	Fur Products Labeling Act	Prohibits misbranding of fur products
1953	Flammable Fabrics Act	Sets standards and requires labeling for flammable fabrics and products
1958	Textile Fiber Products Identification Act	Requires accurate labeling of textiles
1960	Hazardous Substances Labeling Act	Requires accurate labeling of hazardous substances
1966	Fair Packaging and Labeling Act	Requires accurate names, quantities, and weights to be reported on packages
1966	Child Protection Act	Requires childproof devices and special labeling
1966	Cigarette Labeling and Advertising Act	Requires labels warning of possible health hazards
1986	Smokeless Tobacco Act	Requires conspicuous warnings
SALES AND WARRANTIES		
1968	Interstate Land Sales	Requires full disclosure in interstate land sales
1973	FTC Rule on Door-to-Door Sales	Regulates door-to-door sales contracts
1975	Magnuson-Moss Warranty Act	Regulates warranties
1976	Real Estate Settlements Procedures Act	Requires disclosure of home-buying costs
1980	FTC Rule on Vocational and Correspondence Schools	Regulates contracts with these types of schools
1984	FTC Rule on Used Cars	Regulates warranties in used car sales

Exhibit 14–2 Federal Trade Commission

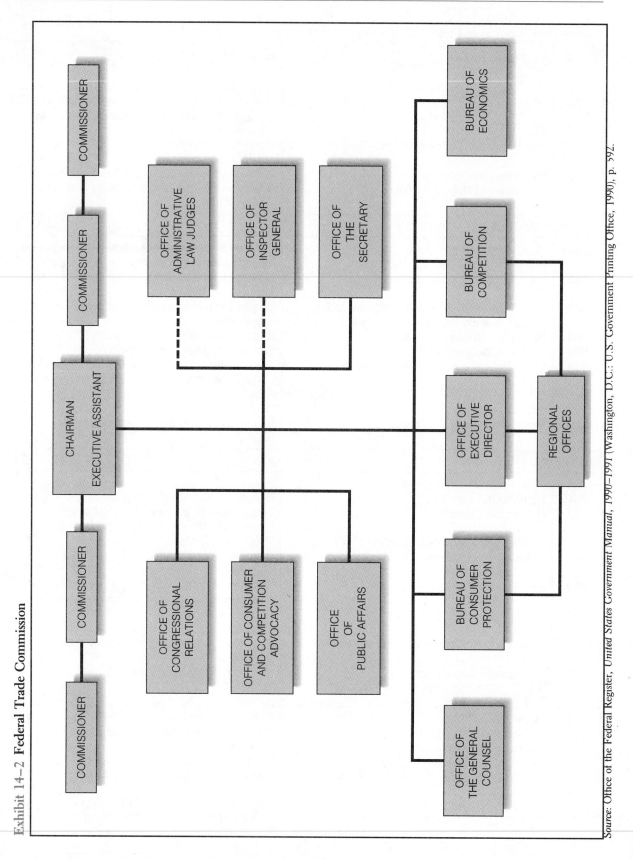

Source: Office of the Federal Register, *United States Government Manual, 1990–1991* (Washington, D.C.:: U.S. Government Printing Office, 1990), p. 592.

surance business, the funeral industry, and car rental agencies. Other investigations include such industries as transportation, health care facilities, nursing homes, agriculture, and energy.

The FTC can bring an action against an alleged wrongdoer either in its administrative law court or in federal court. The FTC tries first to force a seller to stop an unfair or deceptive practice. Most cases are settled by a **consent decree.** The seller consents to an order restraining the activity that the FTC has found unfair or deceptive. This agreement is then finalized in the form of a consent decree. The FTC may also force a defendant-seller to compensate injured buyers when the seller has violated an FTC rule or order.

The FTC can also seek to obtain a **cease and desist order.** This ruling, issued by the administrative law court, orders the defendant to cease its activities and desist from committing those activities in the future. This type of order forces the seller to correct its business operations. The FTC can also obtain court injunctions to restrain or prohibit a particular practice. Fines for violations may amount to $10,000 per day. Any person or firm subject to an FTC order or rule may seek review of the FTC's action in a United States court of appeals.

Additional remedies and forceful orders that the FTC can issue include affirmative disclosure orders, corrective advertising orders, and multiple product orders. By issuing an **affirmative disclosure order,** the FTC requires the defendant to place in future advertisements affirmative disclaimers in order to remedy the past deceptive advertisements. For example, the FTC required the J. B. Williams Company to state in its future advertisements for Geritol that it would not be of any benefit to the great majority of people who suffer from tiredness. Geritol had advertised that it was effective for any illness that had tiredness as a symptom. The advertising was deceptive according to the FTC because tiredness is a symptom of many illnesses including cancer and diabetes, for which Geritol had no effect.

A **corrective advertising order** is very similar in nature to affirmative disclaimers, but it takes the remedy one step further. This order requires the defendant to place in the advertisements a statement to the effect that its past advertisements were false. The FTC can order the words "contrary to prior advertising" to be placed in future advertisements if the defendant had engaged in egregious and intentional deception. A corrective advertising order is one of the issues at stake in *Warner-Lambert Co. v. FTC* (Case 14.3), found later in this chapter.

Generally, if the FTC finds deceptive advertising, it will require the firm to refrain from making any further deceptive advertisements. In cases where a firm sells multiple products, such an order may have little effect. If the FTC finds not only deceptive advertising but also a history of false advertising, the FTC has the power to issue a **multiple product** (or multiproduct) **order.** This order requires all future advertisements for all of the firm's products (or for all of the products in a certain category) to be accurate, not just advertisements for the product that was originally falsely advertised. In the following case, the court of appeals reviews the power of the FTC to issue a multiple product order.

BACKGROUND AND FACTS   *Sears, Roebuck and Company directly petitioned the court of appeals after Sears was issued an order by the Federal Trade Commission. The case questioned the validity of a multiple product order that was the result of the use by Sears of certain alleged unfair and deceptive advertising practices to sell one of the products in a product group.*

In the early 1970s, Sears had formulated a plan to increase sales of its top-of-the-line Lady Kenmore dishwasher. The plan did not call for reengineering of the dishwasher or for any other mechanical improvement. Rather, the plan fostered a change of image for the Lady Kenmore, or in sales jargon, Sears sought to "reposition" the machine in the marketplace. The objective was to change the consumer image from a "price" brand to a superior product at a reasonable price. The machine was to move from market leadership to market dominance as the market share increased.

Case 14.1
SEARS, ROEBUCK AND CO. v. FEDERAL TRADE COMMISSION
United States Court of Appeals, Ninth Circuit, 1982.
676 F.2d 385.

Sears knew that a machine that actually performed the entire job of washing dishes, eliminating the need to prerinse and prescrape dishes, would attract new customers and command a premium price. It also knew that a machine's ability to clean dishes on the upper rack as thoroughly as those on the bottom rack would be a further attraction for new customers.

Based on this knowledge, Sears prepared advertisements claiming that the Lady Kenmore "completely eliminated" the need for prescraping and prerinsing and characterizing the machine as the "freedom maker." Advertisements for the Lady Kenmore appeared in print and on television throughout the country over a four-year-period at a cost to Sears of roughly $8 million. During the first three years, Lady Kenmore unit sales rose 300 percent. The value of the company's total dishwasher sales rose from $73,470,000 in 1971 to $94,500,000 in 1973.

The "no scraping, no prerinsing" claim was not true. Sears had no reasonable basis for asserting the claim, and the owner's manual that customers received after they had purchased the dishwasher contradicted the claim. A 1973 survey conducted for Sears found that more than half of recent Lady Kenmore purchasers disagreed with the proposition that the Lady Kenmore did not require prerinsing.

The FTC began an investigation of the advertisements in 1975. In 1977 the FTC issued a complaint, charging Sears and its advertising agency, J. Walter Thompson Company, with disseminating deceptive and unfair advertisements. After an extensive administrative hearing, the administrative law judge held Sears liable for deceptive and false advertising. The remedy ordered was that Sears was not to make any performance claims for any major home appliances without first possessing a reasonable basis consisting of competent and reliable tests. Sears was to keep records for three years.

Judge REINHARDT
*   *   *   *

A judgment regarding "reasonable relation" in multi-product order cases "depends upon the specific circumstances of the case." "[T]he ultimate question is the likelihood of the petitioner committing the sort of unfair practices [the order] prohibit[s][.]" We answer that question by first examining the specific circumstances present in a particular case. Then, giving due deference to the Commission's expertise and judgment, we determine whether there is a "reasonable relation" between those circumstances and the concern regarding future violations manifested by the Commission's order.

Where a fair assessment of an advertiser's conduct shows a ready willingness to flout the law, sufficient cause for concern regarding further, additional violations exists. Two factors or elements frequently influence our decision—the deliberateness and seriousness of the present violation, and the violator's past record with respect to unfair advertising practices. Other circumstances may be weighed, including the adaptability or transferability of the unfair practice to other products. The weight given a particular factor or element will vary. The more egregious the facts with respect to a particular element, the less important it is that another negative factor be present. In the final analysis, we look to the circumstances as a whole and not to the presence or absence of any single factor.
*   *   *   *

*   *   * Sears states that advertisements concerning the other covered products, e.g., microwave ovens and trash compactors, are *never* related to those promoting dishwashers since dishwashers do not perform work similar to the work performed by the microwave ovens or trash compactors, and that, therefore, an order covering these functionally unrelated machines is inherently unreasonable. This argument misses the fundamental point that the Commission is concerned not with how machines work, but with how machines are sold. Thus, the correct question is not whether the machines function in similar ways but whether the machines could be sold with similar techniques. * * *

* * * *

* * * Under [the specific] circumstances, Sears' advertising campaign demonstrates "blatant and utter disregard" for the law. The Commission also considered petitioner's compliance record and concluded that it was "a wash." We see no reason to find otherwise.

Sears' advertisements were no accident or "isolated instance." Rather, they were part of an advertising strategy, with attendant slogans, adopted without regard to the actual performance of the advertised machines. As the Commission pointed out, the covered machines are major ticket items generally purchased infrequently by any particular person. For that reason, their profitability does not depend on repeat purchases as is the case with frequently purchased, low-cost items. A selling strategy based on this purchasing fact, *e.g.*, the making of false and unsubstantiated performance claims as to a major ticket item, would be effective for a considerable period of time, with great benefit to the merchant but at great cost to consumers. This selling strategy could readily be transferred to the marketing of other machines in the home appliance category.

The prevention of "transfers" of unfair trade practices is a fundamental goal of the Commission's remedial work. Justice Brandeis, a draftsman of the 1914 legislation which created the Commission, made this point in *Federal Trade Comm'n v. Gratz[.]* Objecting to the Court's attempt to narrow the Commission's remedial authority, he expressed a view which has since become law:

> The purpose of Congress [in creating the Commission] was to prevent any unfair method which may have been used by any concern in competition from becoming its general practice. It was only by stopping its use before it became general practice that the apprehended effect of an unfair method . . . could be averted.

It is not only pretermitting a "general practice" which is important here, however. The "transfer" to any other single major home appliance could well cause substantial damage to consumers prior to the time that the Commission could again investigate the facts and obtain the evidence necessary to prove that a similar violation had occurred. By that time, it would be too late to protect the large number of consumers who, in reliance on the truthfulness of the advertised claims, had purchased a major home appliance which they expected to perform the advertised work for many years. This danger is particularly acute where national brands, like Sears' major home appliances, are involved and the advertising campaigns are both widespread and intensive.

In addition, if we were to deny "transfer prevention" authority to the Commission under these circumstances, unscrupulous merchandisers (and we do not imply that Sears falls in that category) might be encouraged to transfer unlawful but successful advertising techniques from product to product, leaving the Commission the job of instituting separate proceedings to secure new orders for each unlawfully advertised product. Because so drastic a limitation on the Commission's enforcement procedure would conflict with the Congressional intent described by Justice Brandeis, would consume enormous resources, and would afford no particular protection to lawful advertisements and little protection to consumers, the Commission need not wait until a "transfer" occurs before issuing multi-product orders in cases like the one before us. It may issue and enforce such orders to avert an "apprehended effect."

To prevent the false and unsubstantiated performance claims strategy from being used in connection with another major home appliance or from becoming Sears' general practice with respect to such appliances, the Commission deemed a broad order necessary. A judgment of this nature depends on detailed knowledge of the major home appliances business and its related advertising techniques. "[D]eceptive advertising cases necessarily require 'inference and pragmatic judgment.' " This sort of knowledge of the commercial world and the ability to make the type of judgment required lie in the realm of the Commission's greatest expertise.

We note one other important fact. * * * [T]he order before us is not an all-products order. It is a limited order that applies only to 14 major ticket items. These 14 items constitute a small proportion of the total number of products sold by Sears.

In light of the flagrant and egregious nature of the violation found and the other circumstances present here, and given the Commission's conclusions the required "great weight," we find no basis for substituting our judgment for the Commission's regarding the necessity for this multi-product order. We hold that the multi-product order is reasonably related to the petitioner's conduct, that a multi-product order is appropriate, and that the inclusion of the "performance claims" provision in that order is supported by the record before us and does not render the order overbroad.

DECISION AND REMEDY *The court of appeals upheld the validity of the FTC's multiproduct order covering all of the major home appliances from Sears, including clothes washers, clothes dryers, disposals, trash compactors, refrigerators, freezers, ranges, stoves, ovens, and stereophonic consoles. As the court pointed out, the FTC's fundamental goal is to prevent the "transfer" of unfair trade practices from one product to another. Congress created the FTC to stop unfair practices before they became a general practice; thus, the FTC has the power to issue multiproduct orders.*

Exemptions to FTC Regulation

The major exemptions to FTC trade regulation activities are those firms or industries that are regulated by local, state, or other federal authorities. For example, public utilities are regulated by state authorities; thus, few public utilities have been subjected to the FTC's authority.

Industries directly regulated by federal agencies are also outside the scope of FTC investigations. For example, the securities markets are regulated by the Securities and Exchange Commission. Some exceptions exist where both the FTC and another federal agency have the power from Congress to investigate the same industry. For example, the FTC enforces some credit protection statutes even though the Federal Reserve Board, the Federal Home Loan Bank Board, and other federal agencies regulate credit. Another example is where both the FTC and the Food and Drug Administration regulate labeling of food and drugs.

These agencies have interagency agreements that set out the specific duties of each agency and indicate which one will have primary investigation and enforcement powers. Thus, only one federal

agency will handle the aspects of any given case, rather than two or more federal agencies competing against each other and wasting resources by repeating the same investigation and enforcement procedures.

Deceptive Advertising

Through its focus on advertising, the FTC can intervene before there is an injury to consumers. If an advertiser challenges an FTC administrative court ruling in a judicial court, the FTC needs only to prove that the advertisement could deceive consumers, not that it actually did so. Evidence of consumer understanding of the claims made in the advertisement is usually not offered.

In 1983, the FTC adopted a policy statement that set out the guidelines as to what constitutes deceptive advertising. First, the advertising must contain a representation, omission, or practice. Second, the act or omission must be found likely to mislead consumers acting reasonably under the circumstances. Third, the representation, omission, or practice must be material (or significant). The act or practice must be likely to mislead; an actual deception need not occur.

Advertisements are most frequently challenged based on one of the following:

1. False statements or claims
2. Failure to disclose important facts
3. Statements that are less than the whole truth
4. Unsupported claims.

False Statements or Claims

Misrepresentations about the quality, composition, origin, character, or availability of products are illegal. Such misrepresentations need not involve an explicit false statement or claim. An advertisement that creates a false impression is deceptive; no verbal or written statement is required. For example, a cosmetic company advertises a "rejuvenescence cream" that would rejuvenate and restore youth or the appearance of youth to the skin. Unfortunately, virtually nothing is known to medical science that could bring about a restoration of youthfulness to the skin. This type of advertising is false and deceptive.

Failure to Disclose Important Facts

Silence may be considered deceptive when it represents a failure to disclose important facts. Some facts known to the seller are so important that these facts should be communicated to prospective buyers. While the FTC does not require that every negative fact about a product must be revealed, instances exist when the FTC will force an advertiser either to include additional information or to stop its advertising program. Even if state law permits a practice (that is, a certain type of advertising or certain wording used in advertising), an FTC ruling will preempt the state's determination of legality. In the following case, the FTC required the disclosure of certain facts within the advertisements.

BACKGROUND AND FACTS   *The defendants (petitioners) operated a weight-loss clinic in California. The FTC issued a cease and desist order prohibiting their continued use of an advertisement that failed to indicate that a drug used by the clinic was new and had not been approved for such use by the Food and Drug Administration (FDA).*

The clinics utilized the Simeon method of weight reduction. After an initial physical examination by a licensed physician, patients were put on a four- or six-week treatment program, which generally included a 500-calorie-per-day diet, daily medical counseling, and daily injections of human chorionic gonadotropin (HCG)—a prescription drug derived from the urine of pregnant women. The FDA declared that HCG was a new drug and approved it for some uses, but not for the treatment of obesity because it found that there was no substantial evidence that HCG was safe or effective for such use.

As one of the principal means of promoting the business of their weight-reduction clinics, the petitioners placed advertisements in newspapers, magazines, and other media. These advertisements represented that the treatment program the clinics utilized was safe, effective, and medically approved. The advertisements did not mention HCG or that the injection of a drug would be part of the treatment program.

The clinics were registered under the Health Plan Act that had been passed by the California legislature. The act required the clinics' advertisements to be reviewed by the state attorney general's office prior to dissemination.

The FTC commenced administrative proceedings against the clinics. The advertisements were challenged as deceptive, unfair, and false because they

Case 14.2
SIMEON MANAGEMENT CORP. v. FEDERAL TRADE COMMISSION
United States Court of Appeals, Ninth Circuit, 1978.
579 F.2d 1137.

failed to disclose that the treatments offered involved injections of HCG and that HCG was not approved by the FDA as safe and effective for use in weight control.

Judge BURNS

*   *   *   *

Petitioners *   *   * contend that we should set aside the cease and desist order because, after reviewing the advertisements pursuant to the Knox-Mills Health Plan Act, the California Attorney General did not disapprove of their nature and contents. Petitioners argue that this failure to disapprove constitutes a prima facie determination that the advertisements are representative, fair and legal. They also argue that FTC regulation of their advertisements impermissibly interferes with the state regulation.

These contentions lack merit. Whether a state official has approved the advertisements or not is irrelevant to the operation of the federal regulatory scheme set forth in the [Federal Trade Commission Act (FTCA)]. That scheme does not impermissibly intrude upon state regulation.

Petitioners contend that the FTC has no jurisdiction to encroach upon the confidential relationship between a physician and patient. They argue that, because HCG is administered by or under the supervision of a physician as part of the weight reduction program, the Commission has no jurisdiction to regulate the advertising used in promoting the clinics.

This contention also lacks merit. The Commission's order does not pretend to affect the right of a physician to prescribe or administer HCG for his or her patients as part of a course of weight reduction treatments. The order prevents petitioners from advertising their clinics and weight reduction program in a way which fails to disclose that the FDA has not approved HCG for such use and that there is no substantial evidence that HCG is effective in the treatment of obesity. The order in no way impinges upon the traditional physician-patient relationship.

*   *   *   *

The Commission found that (1) some consumers will reasonably believe that the government exercises control over the promotion and use of prescription drugs; (2) this belief is intensified by the advertisements' representations that the weight loss treatments are safe, effective and medically approved; and (3) the representations may therefore reasonably lead consumers into the mistaken belief that the claims of safety and effectiveness are based, not on the advertiser's own opinion, but on a determination by the FDA. It further found that, in view of the public's belief that the government strictly regulates drugs, the fact that the treatments involve administration of a drug lacking FDA approval for such use may materially affect a consumer's decision to undergo the treatment. Accordingly, the Commission declared that the failure to disclose that the weight reduction treatments involve injection of a drug lacking FDA approval for such use renders the advertisements deceptive and thus in violation of § 5 of the FTCA.

*   *   *   *

The need for the courts to defer to the Commission's judgment results in part from the statutory scheme and in part from the weight of accumulated agency expertise. The generality of the § 5 proscriptions "necessarily gives the Commission an influential role in interpreting § 5 and in applying it to the facts of particular cases arising out of unprecedented situations." Determining whether a particular advertisement is deceptive requires a familiarity with the expectations and beliefs of the public, especially where the alleged deception results from an omission of information instead of a statement. The Commission has been engaged in making such determinations since 1938, when its jurisdiction was extended to include the prevention of unfair or deceptive acts or practices in commerce. As a result, the Commission has accumulated extensive experience and is therefore generally in a better position than the courts to determine when a practice is deceptive within the meaning of the FTCA.

*   *   *   *

Once the Commission has found an advertisement to be deceptive, it is authorized, within the bounds of reason, to infer that the deceptive information would be a material factor in the consumer's decision to buy. The Commission found that the fact that the advertised treatments involve administration of a drug lacking FDA approval for such use might materially affect the consumer's decision to obtain such treatments. Again, in view of the extent of governmental regulation in this area, we cannot say that this determination is unreasonable.

*   *   *   *

For the foregoing reasons, we hold that the Commission's determination that the petitioners' advertisements are deceptive in violation of § 5 of the FTCA is supported by substantial evidence on the record as a whole and is not arbitrary, capricious, an abuse of discretion or otherwise not in accordance with law.

The Commission is authorized, and indeed required, to prevent such deceptive advertising by issuing a cease and desist order.

The court of appeals upheld the FTC order preventing the petitioners' use of the advertisements because they were deceptive and in violation of Section 5 of the Federal Trade Commission Act. **DECISION AND REMEDY**

This case did not stop the use of HCG for possible weight reduction, but it did require more disclosures by providers of this product to the consumer. **COMMENT**

Statements That Are Less Than the Whole Truth

This form of deception, stating less than the whole truth, is the counterpart to failing to disclose important facts. Instead of omitting a material fact, the advertiser uses true statements out of context or in a way that is deliberately misleading. A product that is "guaranteed for life" usually means for the life of the consumer, not for the life of the product. The FTC restrained the Parker Pen Company from making such guarantees after Parker revealed that it was referring to the life of its pens.

Ocean Spray Cranberry Juice was required by a consent order to explain in future advertisements its statement that "Cranberry Juice Cocktail has more food energy than orange juice or tomato juice." Ocean Spray was using "food energy" not to mean vitamins or minerals but calories.

Unsupported Claims

Reasonable, scientific evidence is required to substantiate advertising claims; otherwise the advertisement is making unsupported claims. If a product is claimed to be faster or safer than similar products, sufficient testing must prove the validity of the claim. Certain statements are merely considered puffing and are not deceptive advertising. "Puffing" means an affirmative expression of opinion by the seller of goods. For example, a manufacturer's statement that his or her product is "the best" would not be regarded as a product claim but merely as puffing. On the other hand, a statement that a product lasts three times longer than comparable products must be supported by reasonable evidence. During the 1950s, one of the major cigarette companies advertised that their cigarettes were "just what the doctor ordered." To-day this advertisement would be a violation of the law.

The next case demonstrates the requirement that a product must live up to the claims made about it.

Case 14.3
WARNER-LAMBERT CO. v. FEDERAL TRADE COMMISSION
United States Court of Appeals, District of Columbia Circuit, 1977.
562 F.2d 749.

BACKGROUND AND FACTS   *Warner-Lambert manufactures Listerine mouthwash. The Federal Trade Commission issued a cease and desist order to prevent Warner-Lambert from advertising that Listerine prevented, cured, or alleviated the common cold. The FTC also required the seller to undertake corrective advertising by including in future advertisements the information that "contrary to prior advertising" Listerine would not help prevent colds or sore throats or lessen their severity. Warner-Lambert petitioned the court of appeals for review of the FTC order.*

Judge WRIGHT
*   *   *   *

The order under review represents the culmination of a proceeding begun in 1972, when the FTC issued a complaint charging petitioner with violation of Section 5(a)(1) of the Federal Trade Commission Act by misrepresenting the efficacy of Listerine against the common cold.

Listerine has been on the market since 1879. Its formula has never changed. Ever since its introduction it has been represented as being beneficial in certain respects for colds, cold symptoms, and sore throats. Direct advertising to the consumer, including the cold claims as well as others, began in 1921.
*   *   *   *

The first issue on appeal is whether the Commission's conclusion that Listerine is not beneficial for colds or sore throats is supported by the evidence. The Commission's findings must be sustained if they are supported by substantial evidence on the record viewed as a whole. We conclude that they are.
*   *   *   *

First, the Commission found that the ingredients of Listerine are not present in sufficient quantities to have any therapeutic effect. This was the testimony of two leading pharmacologists called by Commission counsel. The Commission was justified in concluding that the testimony of Listerine's experts was not sufficiently persuasive to counter this testimony.

Second, the Commission found that in the process of gargling it is impossible for Listerine to reach the critical areas of the body in medically significant concentration. The liquid is confined to the mouth chamber. Such vapors as might reach the nasal passage would not be in therapeutic concentration. Petitioner did not offer any evidence that vapors reached the affected areas in significant concentration.

Third, the Commission found that even if significant quantities of the active ingredients of Listerine were to reach the critical sites where cold viruses enter and infect the body, they could not interfere with the activities of the virus because they could not penetrate the tissue cells.
*   *   *   *

Petitioner contends that even if its advertising claims in the past were false, the portion of the Commission's order requiring "corrective advertising" exceeds the Commission's statutory power. The argument is based upon a literal reading of

Section 5 of the Federal Trade Commission Act which authorizes the Commission to issue "cease and desist" orders against violators and does not expressly mention any other remedies. The Commission's position, on the other hand, is that the affirmative disclosure that Listerine will not prevent colds or lessen their severity is absolutely necessary to give effect to the prospective cease and desist order; a hundred years of false cold claims have built up a large reservoir of erroneous consumer belief which would persist, unless corrected, long after petitioner ceased making the claims.

*　　*　　*　　*

Having established that the Commission does have the power to order corrective advertising in appropriate cases, it remains to [be] consider[ed] whether use of the remedy against Listerine is warranted and equitable. We have concluded that part 3 of the order should be modified to delete the phrase "Contrary to prior advertising." With that modification, we approve the order.

*　　*　　*　　*

We turn next to the specific disclosure required: "Contrary to prior advertising, Listerine will not help prevent colds or sore throats or lessen their severity." Petitioner is ordered to include this statement in every future advertisement for Listerine for a defined period. In printed advertisements it must be displayed in type size at least as large as that in which the principal portion of the text of the advertisement appears and it must be separated from the text so that it can be readily noticed. In television commercials the disclosure must be presented simultaneously in both audio and visual portions. During the audio portion of the disclosure in television and radio advertisements, no other sounds, including music, may occur.

These specifications are well calculated to assure that the disclosure will reach the public. It will necessarily attract the notice of readers, viewers, and listeners, and be plainly conveyed. Given these safeguards, we believe the preamble "Contrary to prior advertising" is not necessary. It can serve only two purposes: either to attract attention that a correction follows or to humiliate the advertiser. The Commission claims only the first purpose for it, and this we think is obviated by the other terms of the order. The second purpose, if it were intended, might be called for in an egregious case of deliberate deception, but this is not one. While we do not decide whether petitioner proffered its cold claims in good faith or bad, the record compiled could support a finding of good faith. On these facts, the confessional preamble to the disclosure is not warranted.

The court of appeals upheld the FTC order prohibiting the advertising of Listerine as a cure for colds but modified the corrective advertising that the FTC sought.

DECISION AND REMEDY

Warner-Lambert, in the next $10 million of advertising of Listerine, placed the statement that "Listerine will not help prevent colds or sore throats or lessen their severity."

COMMENT

Other Deceptive Practices

Every year complaints flow into the Federal Trade Commission office. By categorizing the complaints, the FTC can determine if a pattern of behavior has developed. Once a pattern of deception evolves, the FTC may issue rules to curb this practice. The following are a few of the more important regulations that the FTC has developed in order to protect the public.

Bait and Switch

In some cases, the Federal Trade Commission has promulgated specific rules to govern advertising. One of its more important rules is called "Guides on Bait Advertising." This rule is designed to prohibit bait-and-switch advertisements that specify a very low price for a particular item. The low price is the bait to lure the consumer into the store. The salesperson then tries to switch the consumer to some other more expensive item. According to the FTC guidelines, bait advertising occurs if the seller refuses to show the advertised item, fails to have adequate quantities of it available, fails to promise or deliver the advertised item within a reasonable time, or discourages employees from selling the item.

The following case illustrates the difference between negotiation and bait and switch.

Case 14.4
GOLDBERG v.
MANHATTAN FORD
LINCOLN-MERCURY,
INC.
Supreme Court of New York,
1985.
492 N.Y.S.2d 318.

BACKGROUND AND FACTS *Goldberg alleged that he went to the Manhattan Ford Lincoln-Mercury showroom in New York City to purchase a 1985 Lincoln Town Car, proposing to trade in his 1981 Volvo as part of the deal. Manhattan originally agreed to give a $10,000 trade-in allowance, subject to appraisal and sales manager approval. Goldberg was to keep his Volvo until the Lincoln was ready. There was slight damage to the Volvo, and the trade-in allowance was reduced to $8,500. Goldberg insisted that the Volvo should not be subject to mechanical inspection at the time of delivery. Manhattan's sales manager refused to sign such a provision. The deal ended. Goldberg sued, claiming that each of these stages in negotiation for the used car constituted a "deceptive practice," and he sought damages.*

Justice GREENFIELD
*   *   *   *

The practice of modifying proposed terms of a contract as the negotiations proceed is not at all analogous to "bait and switch" selling. The recognized deceptive practice of "bait and switch" involves an advertisement and offer of a product which is not bona fide because what the merchant actually has on hand and intends to sell is significantly different from that which drew the potential customer in. The technique, which is essentially a variant of false advertising, involves luring prospective purchasers through the "bait" of a desirable item, and then talking the customer into or steering him over to a less desirable item, presumably with greater profit margin for the seller. The trick is to lure the prospective "sucker" and then overwhelm him with glib salesmanship. The essence of this practice is that the seller really has no intention of delivering the product advertised. *   *   *

In this case, there can be no question but that the Ford Lincoln-Mercury showroom advertised Lincolns, sold Lincolns and had many in stock or available on order. The customer was not being lured by the promise of a Lincoln and then switched over to a 1928 DeSoto.

The ultimate trade-in deal that was offered was, of course, less than what was prospectively described over the telephone, but the appraisal was reduced after an actual inspection of the vehicle had demonstrated body damage. Plaintiff was free to accept or reject what was being offered for his used car. He twice indicated that he would accept the reduction in appraised value, but the deal fell through when the sales manager indicated that he would not approve.

DECISION AND
REMEDY

The court found that Manhattan engaged strictly in negotiations and that its conduct constituted neither a deceptive trade practice nor a bait-and-switch operation.

Deceptive Comparisons

Deceptive comparative advertising is subject to the **Lanham Act** of 1946. This statute prohibits false descriptions about products or services when people are likely to be damaged by these deceptive comparative advertisements. An inaccurate comparative advertisement is one in which the defendant makes false statements about either the quality or the price of its own product as compared to the competitors'.

The FTC has ruled that several forms of pricing are deceptive. Stating the price of goods in a way that causes consumers to believe they are getting a bargain or a good deal when in fact they are not is unlawful. If the seller compares the current sales price to a higher regular price, the goods must actually have been offered by that seller at the higher price in the recent past. It is deceptive to compare the retail price of goods to a "manufacturer's list price" that is not the usual and customary retail price in the area.

The FTC has issued guidelines for the offer of "free" merchandise. If goods are offered "two for the price of one" or "buy one, get one free," the price charged for the two items must not exceed the regular price for the same single item. The seller cannot immediately recover the cost of the free item by marking up the regular price of the item to be purchased or by substituting inferior merchandise.

In the case that follows, Vidal Sassoon, Inc., charged Bristol-Myers Company with inaccurate comparative advertising for a shampoo product that competed with Sassoon's.

BACKGROUND AND FACTS *In the spring of 1980, Bristol-Myers Company (Bristol), the defendant, decided to wage an aggressive new advertising campaign on behalf of its shampoo product, Body on Tap, so named because of its high beer content. In June 1980, Bristol began to broadcast on national television a commercial using Cristina Ferrare, a well-known model. In the advertisement she claimed that, "in shampoo tests with over 900 women like me, Body on Tap got higher ratings than Prell for body. Higher than Flex for conditioning. Higher than Sassoon for strong, healthy-looking hair." Prell, Flex, and Sassoon are shampoo competitors of Body on Tap.*

Bristol had had tests conducted by an independent market research firm, Marketing Information Systems, Inc. (MISI). In fact, 900 women, after trying both or all shampoos, did not make a product-to-product comparison between Body on Tap and its competitors. Rather, groups of 200 women tested one shampoo and rated it. Bristol instructed the marketing agency to have the women who tested Sassoon use it contrary to Sassoon's own instructions. Bristol also allowed the women during the testing period to use other brands while they were testing Sassoon. The propriety of this type of testing for the purpose of comparative advertising claims is in doubt.

At trial, Sassoon submitted, along with other evidence, a consumer perception study by ASI Market Research, Inc. (ASI). This study showed that viewers thought that the 900 women had tested two or more brands. Sassoon sued and was granted a preliminary injunction for a violation of Section 43(a) of the Lanham Act. Bristol appealed the injunction.

Case 14.5
VIDAL SASSOON, INC. v. BRISTOL-MYERS CO.
United States Court of Appeals, Second Circuit, 1981.
661 F.2d 272.

Judge KAUFMAN
* * * *

Bristol asserts that the misrepresentations alleged by Sassoon are only misstatements concerning the test results and the manner in which the tests were conducted, not the "inherent quality," of Body on Tap. Misleading statements regarding consumer test methodology, Bristol argues, do not fall within § 43(a). We agree that

Bristol has not in so many words falsely described the quality of Body on Tap. It has not, to give a hypothetical example, baldly stated that the shampoo smells like roses when it in fact does not. The inaccuracies alleged concern the number and age of the women in the tests, how the comparisons were made, and how the results were tabulated. After a careful review of cases interpreting the Lanham Act and its legislative history, however, we are persuaded that § 43(a) does prohibit the misrepresentations alleged here.

*   *   *   *

One of the principal purposes of the 1946 revisions of the Lanham Act was "[t]o modernize the trade-mark statutes so that they will conform to legitimate present-day business practice." We are therefore reluctant to accord the language of § 43(a) a cramped construction, lest rapid advances in advertising and marketing methods outpace technical revisions in statutory language and finally defeat the clear purpose of Congress in protecting the consumer. The language of § 43(a) is indeed very broad: "Any person who shall . . . use *in connection with* any goods or services . . . any false description or representation . . . shall be liable" (emphasis supplied). Certainly the alleged untruths concerning the MISI tests were at least "in connection with" Body on Tap, and, as the ASI study reveals, they quite probably created the impression that Body on Tap was superior. Judge Stewart could appropriately find, moreover, that this view was probably false because, if the qualitative rating categories were combined in a different manner, there would be no significant statistical difference between Sassoon and Body on Tap. While we recognize that § 43(a) encompasses only misrepresentations with reference to the " 'inherent quality or characteristic' " of defendant's product, we are nevertheless convinced that Judge Stewart was correct in concluding that Sassoon would probably succeed in showing that the intent and total effect of the advertisements were to lead consumers into believing that Body on Tap was competitively superior, surely a representation regarding its "inherent quality."

In a case like this, where many of the qualities of a product (such as "body") are not susceptible to objective measurement, it is difficult to see how the manufacturer can advertise its product's "quality" more effectively than through the dissemination of the results of consumer preference studies. In such instances, the medium of the consumer test truly becomes the message of inherent superiority. We do not hold that every misrepresentation concerning consumer test results or methodology can result in liability pursuant to § 43(a). But where depictions of consumer test results or methodology are so significantly misleading that the reasonably intelligent consumer would be deceived about the product's inherent quality or characteristics, an action under § 43(a) may lie.

Finally, we believe that Sassoon made an adequate showing of the possibility of irreparable injury. Although the likelihood of injury and causation cannot be presumed, Judge Stewart properly concluded that Sassoon had offered "proof providing a reasonable basis for the belief that . . . [it] is likely to be damaged as a result of the false advertising." Sassoon and Body on Tap compete in the same market, and it is quite likely that the apparently effective suggestions of competitive superiority, if repeatedly communicated to consumers, would eventually result in loss of sales to Sassoon. Although Sassoon offered no evidence of actual sales loss directly traceable to the alleged misrepresentations, proof of diversion of sales is not required for an injunction to issue pursuant to § 43(a). *   *   *

DECISION AND REMEDY   *The injunction was upheld by the court of appeals. Bristol's own "Shampoo Tracking Study" revealed that awareness and purchases of Body on Tap among women ages 18 to 34 increased significantly shortly after the commencement of the "Ferrare–900 Women" advertising campaign. Sassoon did not have to suffer actual irreparable injury from the advertisements; it* *only had to show the likelihood of injury in order to be entitled to the preliminary injunction. Bristol's advertisements were removed from television and the print media.*

Deceptive Testimonials and Endorsements

From its inception, the FTC has proceeded with vigor against deceptive testimonials and endorsements used to promote products. This advertising technique is intended to make consumers believe that someone other than the seller believes in the benefits of the product. Film stars and athletes often endorse products. FTC guidelines require that the endorsements reflect the celebrity's honest opinion about the product. The endorser must be a user of the product.

If an advertisement represents that the endorser has superior expertise in making a judgment about the product, the endorser must have experience or training that qualifies her or him as an expert. If an advertisement represents that the person making the endorsement is a doctor, the endorser must have a medical degree. Some advertisements contain dramatizations of scenes involving purported doctors or scientists. Since the public recognizes that these people are actors, these advertisements have not been held to be endorsements.

Other Consumer Protection Laws

Over the years, Congress has passed laws that provide protection to consumers from abhorrent business practices. The following subsections examine the more significant of these statutes.

Fair Packaging and Labeling Act

The number of products that are prepackaged has increased significantly since 1950. The packaging often prevents the consumer from inspecting the product, so the label becomes the only source of information about the contents of the package. The **Fair Packaging and Labeling Act** (FPLA) was enacted by Congress in 1966, and it gave the Department of Commerce the authority to deal with this problem.

The FPLA applies to those who package or label any consumer commodity. The primary focus is on items sold in supermarkets. Four provisions of the FPLA are mandatory:

1. The label must contain the name and address of the manufacturer, packer, or distributor.
2. The net quantity must be indicated on the front panel.
3. The quantity must be listed in a specific manner.
4. If the quantity is stated as a specified number of servings, the size of each serving must be indicated.

These mandatory provisions enable the purchaser to compare competing products. The Department of Commerce, the Federal Trade Commission, and the Food and Drug Administration all promulgate rules under the FPLA.

Other federal statutes also apply to packaging and labeling. These acts include the Wool Products Labeling Act, the Fur Products Labeling Act, the Cigarette Labeling and Advertising Act, and the Flammable Fabrics Act.

Magnuson-Moss Warranty Act

Dissatisfaction with automobile warranties led Congress to pass the Magnuson-Moss Warranty Act of 1975. This act, also discussed in Chapter 12, establishes standards for consumer warranties. The Magnuson-Moss Warranty Act requires that every warranty disclosure contain certain information that is necessary for a consumer to determine the extent of the warranty and the method of enforcing it. If a warrantor refuses to honor the warranty, the consumer can bring a legal action in either a state or a federal court. The government may also bring a court action to prevent a manufacturer from continuing to issue deceptive warranties or for failing to comply with the act.

Food, Drug, and Cosmetic Act

The purpose of the Food and Drug Administration (FDA) is to protect the public from harm

Legal Highlight

Singing the Refund Blues

The singer Pat Boone appeared in many commercials endorsing Acne-Statin, advertised for the treatment of acne. Boone promoted the product on television and in printed advertisements, telling the public that all of his daughters had used Acne-Statin. Many people relied on his endorsement and purchased the product. When the product did not work as advertised, complaints were filed with the FTC.

An investigation revealed that, in fact, not all of Boone's daughters had used the product and, therefore, that these advertisements were unfair and deceptive. The FTC required Boone to contribute to a fund for making refunds to those purchasers who had relied on his endorsement.

Source: In the Matter of Cooga Mooga, Inc., 92 F.T.C. 310 (1978).

---

caused by food, drugs, cosmetics, therapeutic items, household substances, pesticides, poisons, and other consumer items. The FDA is part of the Department of Health and Human Services. Through its rule-making authority, the FDA attempts to ensure that food is safe, pure, and wholesome, that drugs and therapeutic items are safe and effective, that cosmetics are harmless, and that consumers are not exposed to excessive risks of injury.

The **Food, Drug, and Cosmetic Act** of 1938 prohibits the adulteration or misbranding of various items. The FDA informs the public through press releases about products that pose an imminent danger to health or products that grossly deceive the consumer. Warnings have involved soup, fish, cranberries, fireworks, and baby food.

Although numerous amendments to the act have been passed, none has been more important than the 1962 Drug Amendment. The amendment was adopted after a drug called thalidomide had been sold extensively in Europe. This drug caused numerous birth defects. The 1962 Drug Amendment requires the Food and Drug Administration to follow certain procedures in approving new prescription drugs for marketing.

The FDA has been severely criticized throughout its history. Many people contend that the agency takes too long to approve new drug applications, keeping the benefits of new scientific discoveries from the consumer for unreasonable periods of time. On the other hand, the FDA has now established a fast track to allow drugs that can be used to fight acquired immune deficiency syndrome (AIDS) to reach the market sooner than would ordinarily be possible.

The FDA can impose fines on those who violate its regulations, and violations of the Food, Drug, and Cosmetic Act can result in imprisonment. In addition, civil lawsuits for damages are frequently brought by plaintiffs who allege that they have suffered harm from an adulterated or misbranded product. These plaintiffs generally introduce evidence that the defendant has violated an FDA rule or regulation.

Despite many criticisms of the FDA's procedures, the courts defer to FDA determinations in most cases. In the following case, the Supreme Court upheld the FDA's authority to regulate drugs given to terminally ill patients.

Case 14.6
**UNITED STATES v.
RUTHERFORD**
Supreme Court of the United
States, 1979.
442 U.S. 544, 99 S.Ct. 2470,
61 L.Ed.2d 68.

BACKGROUND AND FACTS *Terminally ill cancer patients brought this action to enjoin the government from interfering with the interstate shipment and sale of Laetrile, a drug not approved for distribution under the Food, Drug, and Cosmetic Act. The district court concluded that Commissioner Rutherford of the Food and Drug Administration had infringed constitutionally protected privacy interests by denying cancer patients access to Laetrile. The court of appeals held that the act's safety and effectiveness*

standards have no reasonable application to terminally ill cancer patients.
The case was appealed to the Supreme Court.

Justice MARSHALL delivered the opinion of the Court.

*   *   *   *

In the Court of Appeals' view, an implied exemption from the Act was justified because the safety and effectiveness standards set forth in § 201 (p)(1) could have "no reasonable application" to terminally ill patients. We disagree. Under our constitutional framework, federal courts do not sit as councils of revision, empowered to rewrite legislation in accord with their own conceptions of prudent public policy. Only when a literal construction of a statute yields results so manifestly unreasonable that they could not fairly be attributed to congressional design will an exception to statutory language be judicially implied. Here, however, we have no license to depart from the plain language of the Act, for Congress could reasonably have intended to shield terminal patients from ineffectual or unsafe drugs.

A drug is effective within the meaning of § 201 (p)(1) if there is general recognition among experts, founded on substantial evidence, that the drug in fact produces the results claimed for it under prescribed conditions. Contrary to the Court of Appeals' apparent assumption, effectiveness does not necessarily denote capacity to cure. In the treatment of any illness, terminal or otherwise, a drug is effective if it fulfills, by objective indices, its sponsor's claims of prolonged life, improved physical condition, or reduced pain.

So too, the concept of safety under § 201 (p)(1) is not without meaning for terminal patients. Few if any drugs are completely safe in the sense that they may be taken by all persons in all circumstances without risk. Thus, the Commissioner generally considers a drug safe when the expected therapeutic gain justifies the risk entailed by its use. For the terminally ill, as for anyone else, a drug is unsafe if its potential for inflicting death or physical injury is not offset by the possibility of therapeutic benefit. Indeed, the Court of Appeals implicitly acknowledged that safety considerations have relevance for terminal cancer patients by restricting authorized use of Laetrile to intravenous injections for persons under a doctor's supervision.

Moreover, there is a special sense in which the relationship between drug effectiveness and safety has meaning in the context of incurable illnesses. An otherwise harmless drug can be dangerous to any patient if it does not produce its purported therapeutic effect. But if an individual suffering from a potentially fatal disease rejects conventional therapy in favor of a drug with no demonstrable curative properties, the consequences can be irreversible. For this reason, even before the 1962 Amendments incorporated an efficacy standard into new drug application procedures, the FDA considered effectiveness when reviewing the safety of drugs used to treat terminal illness. The FDA's practice also reflects the recognition, amply supported by expert medical testimony in this case, that with diseases such as cancer it is often impossible to identify a patient as terminally ill except in retrospect. Cancers vary considerably in behavior and in responsiveness to different forms of therapy. Even critically ill individuals may have unexpected remissions and may respond to conventional treatment. Thus, as the Commissioner concluded, to exempt from the Act drugs with no proved effectiveness in the treatment of cancer "would lead to needless deaths and suffering among . . . patients characterized as 'terminal' who could actually be helped by legitimate therapy."

It bears emphasis that although the Court of Appeals' ruling was limited to Laetrile, its reasoning cannot be so readily confined. To accept the proposition that the safety and efficacy standards of the Act have no relevance for terminal patients is to deny the Commissioner's authority over all drugs, however toxic or ineffectual, for such individuals. If history is any guide, this new market would not be long overlooked. Since the turn of the century, resourceful entrepreneurs have advertised a wide variety of purportedly simple and painless cures for cancer, including liniments of turpentine, mustard, oil, eggs, and ammonia; peat moss;

arrangements of colored floodlamps; pastes made from glycerine and limburger cheese; mineral tablets; and "Fountain of Youth" mixtures of spices, oil, and suet. In citing these examples, we do not, of course, intend to deprecate the sincerity of Laetrile's current proponents, or to imply any opinion on whether that drug may ultimately prove safe and effective for cancer treatment. But this historical experience does suggest why Congress could reasonably have determined to protect the terminally ill, no less than other patients, from the vast range of self-styled panaceas that inventive minds can devise.

DECISION AND REMEDY   *The Supreme Court determined that Laetrile was a new drug that could not be distributed in the United States without FDA approval because the Food, Drug, and Cosmetic Act also applies to drugs administered to terminally ill patients.*

COMMENT   *A moral dilemma developed as a result of the acquired immune deficiency syndrome (AIDS) crisis. Once a person has developed AIDS, the long-term prognosis is death, usually within one to five years after diagnosis. The pressure by various groups to make experimental drugs more widely available to these dying patients is becoming more intense. The FDA, on the other hand, is concerned with the fact that an experimental drug may cause death faster than the disease does. The* Rutherford *case only begins to touch on the ethical and moral issues involved in governmental monitoring and control of experimental drugs for terminally ill patients.*

Postal Fraud Statutes

Consumers purchase billions of dollars' worth of products through the mail each year. Two federal statutes prohibit mail fraud; one is criminal in nature and the other civil. The criminal statute provides for imprisonment and fines.

The civil statute allows the postmaster general to return all mail addressed to or mailed by a promoter who has made a false representation. This procedure of intercepting the fraudulent seller's mail is a very effective weapon in combating deceptive practices. In more serious cases, the postmaster can also confiscate the mail instead of returning it. The postal regulations also require unordered merchandise to have a clear and conspicuous statement that the merchandise is a free sample. No action can be taken to persuade the consumer to pay for the merchandise later.

Mail-Order Houses

Mail-order houses, a growing industry, have annual sales exceeding $80 billion. Consumers buying from mail-order houses have typically been given less protection than those who purchase items in stores. Many mail-order houses are in a different state from the purchaser, thus making it more costly for the customer who seeks redress for grievances. The FTC and the postal service share enforcement of the laws concerning mail-order houses.

Negative option plans used by book, record, videotape, and compact disc clubs are regulated. Such plans require the member to return a card if he or she does not wish the merchandise to be sent. A negative option plan must disclose all its terms, must send the notice of intent to send the product in enough time for the member to accept or reject, and must include a rejection form for use by the club member.

An FTC rule requires the mail-order house to ship the merchandise promptly. If the business is unable to ship the goods within 30 days, the buyer must be notified of his or her option either to cancel the order and receive a refund or to accept further delay of the shipment.

Interstate Land Sales Full Disclosure Act

During the 1950s and early 1960s, many older people invested their life savings in real estate, particularly in Florida and in the Southwest. Much of this land was marketed through advertisements in magazines and newspapers, through mail and

Legal Highlight

"Battlestar Galactica" and the Consumer Product Safety Commission

When the television program "Battlestar Galactica" was broadcast in the early 1980s, Mattel, Inc., had the contract to manufacture the "Battlestar Galactica" toy. Unfortunately, after the toy was placed on the store shelves, it became apparent that small children could swallow or

inhale the missiles. Mattel recalled the toys by sending 20,000 letters to store outlets, by mailing 1,400 mailgrams, and by placing advertisements in numerous newspapers, urging consumers to return these toys. Fortunately, no child died before the recall was completed. The CPSC became involved with this situation under the Child Protection and Toy Safety Act of 1969.

---

telephone solicitations, and by personal contact in booths set up near convention facilities. The purchasers rarely saw the parcel of land prior to signing the purchase contract and paying for the land. Later they discovered that the land they had purchased was underwater or was years away from being ready for development.

The **Interstate Land Sales Full Disclosure Act,** passed in 1968 and administered by the Department of Housing and Urban Development (HUD), is intended to decrease the opportunities for fraud and deception that are inherent in these "sight unseen" sales. The Office of Interstate Land Sales Registration within HUD now regulates the sale of undeveloped land for homesites. Regulations require developers to disclose fully their financial condition, and these rules also govern advertising and sales practices.

Developers must file a registration statement with the agency before commencing sales. If the Office of Interstate Land Sales Registration determines that the disclosure is adequate, the developer can solicit sales. If the disclosure is inadequate, the developer must file additional information in order to gain approval.

Purchasers must receive a copy of the property report before they sign a contract. The act applies to both sales and leases of property in subdivisions and to condominium units that will not be completed within two years of the date of purchase. Congress used its power under the interstate commerce clause to pass this legislation. If the developer fails to follow the statute, the purchaser may be entitled to a full refund.

Consumer Product Safety Act

The **Consumer Product Safety Act** was passed in 1972 to protect consumers from unreasonable risk of injury from hazardous products. The act is administered by the Consumer Product Safety Commission (CPSC). The CPSC has sweeping powers to regulate the production and sale of potentially hazardous consumer products. Consumer product safety legislation began earlier with a variety of statutes that sought to improve the safety standards in selected industries.

The act is very comprehensive. The CPSC is charged with regulating "any article, or component part thereof produced or distributed for sale to a consumer for use in or around a permanent or temporary household or residence, a school, in recreation or otherwise, or for the personal use, consumption or employment of a consumer." The authority to administer earlier consumer-oriented protection statutes was transferred to the CPSC. These acts include the Refrigerator Safety Act, the Flammable Fabrics Act, the Child Protection and Toy Safety Act, the Poison Prevention Packaging Act, and the Hazardous Substances Act.

Congress has charged the CPSC with conducting research on product safety and with maintaining a clearinghouse that collects, investigates, analyzes, and disseminates injury data relating to the causes and the possible prevention of death, injury, and illness associated with consumer products.

The commission has the authority to establish construction standards as well as performance

Ethical Considerations

Information Sharing from Warranty Cards

You purchase a television set that has a warranty card. You fill out the card and answer questions asking about your hobbies, salary, age, marital status, number of persons in the household, and other personal items. Unknown to you, this information is sold to companies that place it into their computer data banks. These lists of consumers and their demographics are in turn sold to direct-mail businesses. In this way, complete strangers become very knowledgeable

about your personal affairs, as more and more information is gathered about you from a variety of sources.

Is it ethical for a business to request this information on a warranty card when it knows that it will sell this information to others? Is it ethical for businesses to purchase this information? Should the consumer have the right to control the dissemination of this information? If the information is sold, should the consumer have a right to part of the proceeds?

---

standards for the finished product and to issue adequate warnings of danger. If the CPSC can isolate a consumer product that is extremely hazardous to consumers, the commission has the authority to ban the product from sale.

Door-to-Door Sales

Door-to-door sales are singled out for special treatment in the laws of most states and by FTC regulation. This type of business has a lengthy history of using high-pressure tactics (such as staying in the prospective customer's house all night) and other systematic consumer abuse (such as sending encyclopedias with blank or missing pages). The special treatment also stems in part from the nature of the sales transaction. A door-to-door seller has a captive audience because individuals are in their own home and are hesitant to ask people to leave.

Since repeat purchases are not as likely with door-to-door sales as they are in stores, the seller has little incentive to establish goodwill with the purchaser. Furthermore, the seller is unlikely to present alternative products and their prices. Thus, a number of states have rules that permit the buyers of goods sold door to door to cancel their contracts within a specified period of time, usually three days after the sale.

In addition, a Federal Trade Commission regulation makes it a violation for door-to-door sellers to fail to give consumers a notice of their right to cancel the sale within three days. This rule applies in addition to whatever rules are mandated by state statute so that consumers are given the most favorable benefits of the FTC rule and of their own state laws. Finally, the FTC rule requires that the notification be given in the same language in which the sale was negotiated.

Miscellaneous Consumer Protection Statutes

A variety of other consumer protection statutes exist that we are not able to examine in depth here. Various states have statutes that prohibit unfair or deceptive acts or practices (UDAP statutes). These state laws provide private remedies to fight the wide range of abuses of the consumer. Every state has at least one UDAP statute. Most of these statutes were adopted during the period from the mid 1960s to the mid 1970s. The following consumer areas are regulated by the FTC or another federal agency and/or by the states' UDAP statutes.

Statutes cover subject matter ranging from automobiles to funeral homes. For example, the federal Odometer Act prohibits odometers from being rolled back. The FTC Used Car Rule gov-

International Considerations

Self-Regulation by Foreign Corporations

Consumer protection proposals started first in Germany, the Netherlands, Sweden, and the United Kingdom before crossing the Atlantic to the United States. The debate over which is better, government regulation or business self-regulation, is a continuing one. Over the decades, the European Community has taken a leadership role in this area.

The International Chamber of Commerce, an independent organization, has promoted self-regulation by developing voluntary codes of marketing practices for businesses. The goal is to avoid governmental regulation. In 1976, the Organization of Economic Cooperation and Development (OECD) adopted the "Guidelines on Multinational Corporations." This document deals with issues of corporate disclosure and the liability of parent companies for their subsidiaries. No international organization to date specifically deals with consumer protection, however.

erns the sales of used cars. State laws regulate towing company charges (based on abuses in the past). Many other federal and state laws regulate such areas as mobile home sales, private vocational schools, insurance sales, solar energy equipment, hearing aids, and carpet sales.

These statutes and regulations only hint at the volume of consumer protection in force today from both the federal and the state governments. As a direct result of the abuse of consumers by a few businesses, all businesses and consumers are now paying the price for this protection.

FACING A LEGAL ISSUE

Operating a Mail-Order Business

After much consideration, you decide to start a new business. You believe that it should initially be the type of business that will have limited overhead. After reviewing numerous business opportunities, you decide to operate a mail-order business. You can operate it from your home during your spare time, thus limiting overhead expense.

The big expense in the mail-order business is advertising through magazines, catalogs, and brochures. You learn that, to be successful, you need repeat sales from satisfied customers based on your promotional materials. You also need to offer products that are not readily available in local stores. You decide to offer a line of "how-to" books that describe how to construct different pieces of furniture, how to refinish furniture, and how to make general household repairs. You prepare your advertisements to be placed in magazines and newspapers of general interest, such as *Better Homes & Gardens* and *Reader's Digest*. You also prepare a small catalog offering 32 different books or plans.

If you do not think that your business has any major involvement with federal or state laws, you are wrong. First, you must be in compliance with the regulations of the United States Postal Service. You cannot advertise in a fraudulent manner by misrepresenting your products. If you do, the postal service will return your customers' mail, and the Department of Justice may bring criminal charges against you. You cannot make claims that you cannot prove. For example, if you use testimonials from customers, they must be from real customers, and you must be able to prove this to the postal service authorities should they

inquire. If you offer a money-back guarantee, any customer who is dissatisfied with your product must be given a full and prompt refund.

The actual mailing of your product is another problem. The postal service offers a book rate that is considerably lower than the first-class postal rate. At the book rate, however, you cannot include with the book any advertisements for your other products. The book offered must be a book and not merely plans for the construction of certain products. If you fail to follow the postal service rules, your mailing will be returned to you or, worse, confiscated.

The rules of the Federal Trade Commission also must be followed. Your promotional material is not completely honest if false claims are made, if important facts are not disclosed, if the whole truth is not stated, or if unsupported claims are made. The FTC and the postal service cooperate in their investigations if fraudulent materials are involved.

If you had decided to sell other products through the mail, you would be required to comply with the regulations of other administrative agencies. For example, you would have to comply with the Fair Packaging and Labeling Act if your product had a label. The label must disclose at least the minimum required information. If you sell cosmetics through the mail, you will have to comply with the regulations of the Food, Drug, and Cosmetic Act.

As you can see, a simple business operated from your home can involve compliance with many federal laws and regulations. Some states have similar legal provisions. These laws are intended to protect the consumers, even though the laws may be troublesome and costly for business.

Summary

This chapter has emphasized the importance of consumer law and the protection of the consumer from both financial and bodily harm. Costs are associated with this protection, and these costs are eventually paid by the consumer in the form of higher prices.

The Federal Trade Commission has the primary duty to prohibit "unfair or deceptive acts or practices." The Bureau of Consumer Protection carries out this responsibility by obtaining consent decrees or cease and desist orders and by issuing trade regulations that apply to entire industries.

The FTC regulates advertising that either makes false statements or claims, fails to disclose important facts, does not relate the whole truth, or makes unsupported claims. The FTC also has rules against bait-and-switch advertisements. These advertisements entice a consumer to respond by offering an alleged bargain; then the salesperson attempts to switch the consumer to a more expensive product.

Other statutes that protect consumers include the Fair Packaging and Labeling Act, which requires certain information to be disclosed on any package that does not allow the consumer to inspect the product. The Food, Drug, and Cosmetic Act ensures that goods are safe, pure, and wholesome and that pharmaceutical products are therapeutic and not experimental. The United States Postal Service has the power to return or confiscate any mail that makes a false representation. The Interstate Land Sales Full Disclosure Act controls the sale of unimproved lots through interstate commerce. Finally, the Consumer Product Safety Act ensures the safety of products that are sold to the public.

Key Terms

affirmative disclosure order (347)
cease and desist order (347)
consent decree (363)
Consumer Product Safety Act (363)
corrective advertising order (347)

Fair Packaging and Labeling Act (359)
Federal Trade Commission Act (344)
Food, Drug, and Cosmetic Act (360)
Interstate Land Sales Full

Disclosure Act (363)
Lanham Act (357)
multiple product order (347)
trade regulation rule (344)
unfair or deceptive acts or practices (344)
Wheeler-Lea Act (344)

Questions and Case Problems

1. Harry's Home-Sweet-Home Rocking Chair Company advertised in the newspaper a special sale price of $159 on machine-caned rocking chairs. In the advertisement was a drawing of a natural wood rocking chair with a caned back and seat. The average person would not be able to tell from the drawing whether the rocking chair was machine-caned or hand-caned. Hand-caned rocking chairs were selling for $259. John and Joanne Wolf went to Harry's because they had seen the advertisement for the machine-caned rocking chair and were very interested in purchasing one. The Wolfs arrived the morning that the sale began. Harry said the only machine-caned rocking chairs he had were painted lime green and were priced at $159. He immediately turned the Wolfs' attention to the hand-caned rocking chairs, praising their workmanship and pointing out that, for the extra $100, the hand-caned chair was a better value. The Wolfs, preferring the natural wood, machine-caned rocking chair for $159 as pictured in the advertisement, said they would like to order one, but Harry told them that this was not possible. Discuss fully whether Harry has violated any consumer protection laws.

2. Joyce made toys at home. She began a new line of homemade dolls. These stuffed dolls were especially appealing because they had real glass marbles for eyes. Three-year-old Samantha received one of these marble-eyed dolls for her birthday. Samantha was captivated by the shiny marble eyes. Unfortunately, after a month of use, the

glue holding the marbles on the face of the doll disintegrated to the point that Samantha was able to pull the marbles off, put one in her mouth, swallowed it, and then choked on it. She was rushed to the hospital where her stomach was pumped. Can Joyce, as the manufacturer, be regulated by a federal agency? If so, which agency would regulate and under what act? What will the agency be able to do to regulate the marble-eyed dolls?

3. Monty advertises a fuel-saving device for automobile engines. The advertisement claims that the device is "an important unique invention," that "every car needs one," and that a typical driver will realize a significant improvement in fuel economy. Jane buys the device and installs it on her automobile. After six months, she checks her maintenance records, and she finds that she has not realized any savings in fuel economy. Discuss fully any rights that Jane may have under consumer protection laws.

4. IRONMED advertises that it can cure "tired blood." One television advertisement states, "If you often have a tired and run-down feeling and if you take vitamins and still feel worn out, remember your trouble may be due to iron-poor blood. Vitamins alone can't build up your iron-poor blood. But IRONMED can. Just two tablets daily contain seven vitamins, plus twice the iron in a whole pound of calves' livers. IRONMED starts strengthening your iron-poor blood in 24 hours."

Ron begins to take IRONMED daily. After six months, he feels the same—worn out and tired. Ron hears that most people feel tired not as a result of iron-deficiency anemia but for a variety of other reasons that only medical tests can detect. Discuss fully the rights Ron has under consumer protection laws. Is there any federal agency that regulates IRONMED's actions? If so, discuss fully.

5. Baby Food, Inc. makes and sells a baby formula from which it has removed all the salt. Ann feeds her baby the infant formula, but she notices that the baby is sick and weak after being on the formula for a while. Although she takes the baby to a pediatrician, the baby dies in six weeks from a lack of salt. Ann checks the label on the formula and sees that one of the ingredients is salt.

Later she learns through a magazine article that Baby Food, Inc. had removed the salt from the infant formula two years before her baby was born. The American Academy of Pediatrics Committee on Nutrition has found that salt is absolutely necessary for a baby's nutrition. Discuss fully the rights Ann may have under consumer protection laws. Is there any federal agency that regulates Baby Food's actions? If so, discuss fully.

6. At one time, *Reader's Digest* used large bulk mailings that contained simulated checks for readers to win big prizes. The FTC thought that this practice was deceptive, and *Reader's Digest* accepted a consent decree. Years later, *Reader's Digest* used simulated cash-convertible bonds and travel checks in the same type of promotion. The federal district court found that *Reader's Digest* had violated the consent decree by mailing more than 17 million of these items. The court assessed a $1,750,000 fine. Was this the proper method of determining damages or were there only two violations? If the latter, what might have been the penalty? [United States v. Reader's Digest Association, Inc., 662 F.2d 955 (3d Cir. 1981)]

7. In the past, it was common for used automobile dealers to turn back the odometers on used cars. The federal Odometer Act allows a penalty in the amount of $1,500 for each occurrence. The attorney general of Ohio brought action against Hughes Motors. The defense was based on the grounds that (1) the attorney general did not have standing without making the consumers part of the lawsuit, and (2) there could not be a judgment entered unless there was proof of actual loss. Was the defendant successful in its legal position? [Celebrezze v. Hughes, 18 Ohio 3d 71, 479 N.E.2d 886 (1985)]

8. All-State produced aluminum siding and storm windows. It featured in advertisements "ADV," a lower-cost aluminum, but All-State's salespeople, following the training manual, always attempted to sell "PRO" grade, which was better quality, to customers. The salespeople did not receive a commission if ADV was sold, but they received a substantial commission if PRO was sold. Was this an unfair trade practice? Please explain. [All-State Industries of North Carolina, Inc. v. Federal Trade Commission, 423 F.2d 423 (1970)]

9. The Consumer Product Safety Commission proposed safety standards that mandated placing a warning on swimming pool slides. It was shown that there was one chance in 10 million that a spinal injury could occur when using a pool slide. Would you consider a warning standard reasonably necessary and that the use of a pool slide constitutes an "unreasonable risk" of bodily harm? [Aqua Slide N Dive Corp. v. Consumer Product Safety Commission, 569 F.2d 831 (1978)]

10. American Home Products sold one of its products under the trade name Anacin. The company promoted Anacin by claiming that it consisted of a unique pain-killing formula far superior to that of similar products. In reality Anacin was only aspirin. The FTC issued a cease and desist order after finding this claim to be deceptive. American Home Products appealed the decision. Was this trade puffing, or was it deceptive advertising? [American Home Products Corp. v. FTC, 695 F.2d 681 (1982)]

Chapter 15 Property Law and Computer Law

> *Property, or the dominion of man over external objects, has its origin from the Creator, as his gift to mankind.*
>
> **William Blackstone,**
> *Commentaries: Book II, 1765*

OUTLINE

Introduction

In our culture, individual rights and property rights are so interwoven with one another that any discussion of one must include both. We place a premium on individual rights, but property rights are also protected whenever they do not conflict with individual rights.

If property rights were not recognized, we could not have the economic system that exists today. Our business community could not exist without the concept of property rights and the law that protects these rights. Business organizations own or control property that, with the addition of labor, produces a final product or service. The end result of any successful business is a profit based on the sale of these products or services. Property rights are the foundation of our free enterprise system.

Property rights are specifically recognized and protected by the Constitution. The Fifth Amendment provides that "[n]o person shall be * * * deprived of life, liberty, or property, without due process of law; nor shall private property be taken for public use, without just compensation." Similar language is found in the Fourteenth Amendment: "No State shall * * * deprive any person of life, liberty, or property, without due process of law * * *."

Property use is regulated under the **police power** of government. This power is the inherent power of any government or sovereign to govern itself. In our country, police power is controlled and limited by the above constitutional provisions.

It is important to study the distinction between real property and personal property because different laws apply to each category. In particular, the law of taxation and the methods of property transfer will vary depending on whether property is real or personal. Thus, in this chapter we will study: (1) the classifications of property, (2) property rights and ownership title, (3) real property, (4) how we acquire ownership over personal property, (5) bailments, and (6) property law as it affects computers.

Classifications of Property

Property is divided into these classifications: real or personal, tangible or intangible, and fixtures.

Real and Personal Property

Real property (sometimes called real estate or realty) means the land surface, the air space, those materials that are underneath the surface, and those items that are permanently attached to the land. Everything else is **personal property.** Real property is conveyed by a **deed.** Personal property is sold by the use of a **bill of sale.**

The same article may at different times be both real and personal property. For example, a growing tree would be considered real property. When it is cut down and turned into lumber, the tree becomes personal property. The tree becomes real property again when it is transformed into the framing of a house. In other words, if an item is not land or permanently attached to land, it is personal property.

Tangible and Intangible Property

All property is classified as being either tangible or intangible. **Tangible property** is visible and has physical existence, such as land, cattle, buildings, sheep, automobiles, or computers. **Intangible property** has an invisible value, such as annuities, checks, copyrights, patents, common stock, debts, or bonds. The value of any of these properties is invisible and is represented by a piece of paper stating that it is a bond, copyright, and so forth. The rights these pieces of paper represent are recognized by the law.

Fixtures

Certain personal property can become so closely associated with the real property to which it is attached that the law views it as real property. Such property is known as a **fixture**—a thing affixed to realty. Personal property becomes a fixture when the personal property is attached to the realty by roots, embedded in it, or permanently attached by means of cement, plaster, bolts, nails, or screws. Gravity can even be the method of attachment if the item is large enough; a two-ton statue, for example, qualifies as a fixture. The fixture can be physically attached to real property, can be attached to another fixture, or can even be without any actual physical attachment to the land as long as the owner intends the property to be a fixture.

Fixtures are included in the sale of land unless the sales contract provides otherwise. The sale of a house includes the land and the house and garage on it, as well as the cabinets, plumbing, and windows. Since these items are permanently affixed to the property, they are considered a part of it. Unless otherwise agreed, the curtains and throw rugs are not included. Items such as drapes, metal storage units, and window-unit air-conditioners are difficult to classify. A contract for the sale of a house or commercial realty should indicate which items are included in the sale.

In order to determine whether a certain item is a fixture, we must examine the intention of the party who placed it on the property. If the facts indicate that the person intended the item to be a fixture, it will be treated as a fixture. The following case emphasizes some of the problems surrounding fixtures.

BACKGROUND AND FACTS *In 1973 Van Sickle moved his double-wide mobile home to a plot of land in Silver City, Iowa. He had the real estate landscaped, a foundation poured, concrete blocks set, and steel girders aligned on the blocks. After removing hitches and wheels, the mobile home was set on the foundation by a crane. The mobile home and the foundation were then hooked together. Over time, Van Sickle substantially modified his residence. It could not be moved as one unit except by a house mover.*

Jedlicka owned the land. In 1977 Ford purchased the land from Jedlicka for $3,350. In 1982 Venard attempted to enforce a judgment against Van Sickle by attaching and forcing execution on the home. Ford brought this suit, claiming he owned Van Sickle's home. He requested an injunction to restrain Venard from executing on it.

Justice HARRIS

*   *   *   *

The first question is whether the mobile home was a fixture included under the terms of the land contract between Jedlicka and Ford. We think it plainly was. Under our common law rule personal property becomes a fixture when:

(1) it is actually annexed to the realty, or to something appurtenant thereto;
(2) it is put to the same use as the realty with which it is connected; and
(3) the party making the annexation intends to make a permanent accession to the freehold.

*   *   * The intention of the party annexing the improvement is the "paramount factor" in determining whether the improvement is a fixture. *   *   * Physical attachment of the structure to the soil or to an appurtenance thereto is not essential to make the structure a part of the realty. *   *   * On the other hand, a building which cannot be removed without destruction of a substantial part of its value becomes almost unavoidably an integral part of the real estate. *   *   *

The court held that Van Sickle's home was an integral part of the real property. The home had become attached to the land. It could only be removed from its present location in the same way that any permanent home could be.

Case 15.1
FORD v. VENARD
Supreme Court of Iowa, 1983.
340 N.W.2d 270.

DECISION AND REMEDY

Property Rights and Ownership Title

Property can be viewed as a bundle of rights. Some of these rights include:

1. The right of possession
2. The right of disposition by sale, by gift, by leasing, and by will.

More than one person can hold the same rights at one time. You may own, with another person, either personal or real property in one of the four types of concurrent ownerships:

1. Tenancy in common
2. Joint tenancy with right of survivorship, commonly called joint tenancy
3. Tenancy by the entirety
4. Community property.

Tenancy in Common

Tenancy in common is co-ownership in which two or more persons own an undivided (equal or unequal) fractional interest in the property but, on one tenant's death, that interest passes to his or her heirs. For example, brother and sister, Michael and Laura, own a farm as tenants in common. Should Michael die before Laura, Michael's interest in the farm would become the property of Michael's heirs. If Michael sold his interest to Patricia before he died, Patricia and Laura would be co-owners as tenants in common. If Patricia died, her interest in the property would pass to her heirs and they in turn would own the property with Laura as tenants in common.

Joint Tenancy with Right of Survivorship

In a **joint tenancy with right of survivorship,** two or more people own an undivided interest in either personal or real property. If a joint tenant dies, his or her interest is transferred to the remaining joint tenants, not to his or her heirs. If Michael and Laura are joint tenants and Michael dies before Laura, the entire farm becomes the property of Laura. Michael's heirs receive absolutely no interest in the real estate. If, prior to Michael's death, he sells his interest to Patricia, Patricia and Laura become tenants in common. Michael's sale terminates the joint tenancy. Joint tenancy with

right of survivorship can be terminated any time by gift or by sale before the joint tenant's death. If either Patricia or Laura dies, her interest passes to her heirs.

Tenancy by the Entirety

Tenancy by the entirety is less common today than it used to be. Only a husband and wife can own property in tenancy by the entirety. Typically, it is created by a husband and wife purchasing property. It is distinguished from joint tenancy with right of survivorship because neither spouse can transfer separately his or her interest during his or her life without the consent of the other. Generally, the two must sell the property together. A divorce will end a tenancy by the entirety and, depending on the state in which the property is located, will usually turn the estate into a tenancy in common.

Community Property

This type of ownership applies in Arizona, California, Idaho, Louisiana, Nevada, New Mexico, Texas, Washington, and Wisconsin. The **community property** laws apply only to the property of married couples. Each spouse owns an undivided one-half interest in most property acquired during the marriage. Under this type of ownership, when a spouse dies, he or she can give his or her one-half community property interest to someone other than the other spouse through a last will and testament. The deceased cannot deprive the other spouse of his or her own one-half interest.

Several exceptions do exist. Property acquired prior to the marriage or property obtained by gift or inheritance during the marriage is not usually classified as community property, but rather as "separate property."

Real Property

Real property consists of land, buildings, plants, trees, subsurface and air rights, and fixtures. Whereas personal property is movable, real property is immovable.

Air and Subsurface Rights

The owner of real property has relatively exclusive rights to the air space. Until 80 years ago, the right to use air space was not significant. Today, cases involving air rights present questions such as the right of air space for high-rise buildings, the right of individuals and governments to seed clouds and produce artificial rain, and the right of commercial and private airplanes to fly over property. Flights over private land do not normally violate the property owners' rights unless the flights are low and frequent, causing a direct interference with the enjoyment and use of the land.

In many states, the owner of the surface of a piece of land is not the owner of the subsurface; hence, the land ownership may be separated. Subsurface rights can be extremely valuable, as these rights include the ownership of minerals and, in most states, oil and natural gas. Water rights are also extremely valuable, especially in the West. When the ownership is separated into surface and subsurface rights, each owner can pass title to what he or she owns without the consent of the other.

Ownership Interest in Real Property: Estates in Land

Ownership of property is an abstract concept that does not exist independently of the legal system. No one can actually possess or hold a piece of land, the air above, the earth below, and all the water contained on it. The legal system therefore recognizes certain rights and duties that constitute the ownership interest in real property. Rights of ownership in real property are called estates and are classified according to their nature, interest, and extent. Interests in real property are divided into two classifications: freehold estates and non-freehold estates.

Freehold Estates   A **freehold estate** is one in which the owner has the right to the land for an undetermined time period. The two classes of freehold estates are estates in fee and life estates.

Estates in Fee   The three major categories of estates in fee are **fee simple absolute** (the title to the land is held by the owner with virtually no limitations), **fee simple defeasible** (the title to the land is taken away automatically from the owner under certain conditions), and **fee simple subject to a condition subsequent** (the title to the land may be taken away by the original owners if a specified event occurs).

A fee simple absolute (generally called a fee simple) encompasses the greatest aggregation of rights, privileges, and power possible. The owner of a fee simple absolute has the right to use the land for whatever purpose he or she sees fit, subject to two restrictions. First, laws prevent the owner from unreasonably interfering with another person's land. Second, the owner is subject to applicable zoning, building, and other regulations. A person can own a fee simple absolute for an indefinite period of time, but he or she can dispose of it by deed, by will, by gift, or by sale.

The owner of a fee simple defeasible or of a fee simple subject to a condition subsequent has less rights than the owner of a fee simple absolute. With a fee simple defeasible or a fee simple subject to a condition subsequent, the right of ownership can be taken away if specific conditions set out in the deed either occur or fail to occur.

For example, a conveyance from Lincoln "to Tex and his heirs as long as the land is used for a church" creates a fee simple defeasible. In this type of conveyance, Lincoln retains a partial ownership interest. As long as the specified condition occurs (the land is used for a church), Tex has all other ownership rights. If the specified condition does not occur (the land ceases to be used for a church), the land reverts (returns) to the original owner, Lincoln, or, if he is not alive, to his heirs. The interest that Lincoln retains is called a *future interest* since, *if* it arises, it will arise in the future.

In the following case, a conveyance was made for a courthouse and jail. The deed included the phrase "and shall be used for no other purpose." The Arizona Supreme Court had to interpret these words of conveyance in reaching its decision.

BACKGROUND AND FACTS   *The plaintiff's father deeded in 1898 certain property to the County of Navajo, Territory of Arizona, under a deed that stated the following:*

> The title to which said foregoing described tract or lot of land shall vest in said County of Navajo, Territory of Arizona at any time, said county shall or may begin

Case 15.2
LACER v. NAVAJO COUNTY
Arizona Supreme Court, 1983.
141 Ariz. 396, 687 P.2d 404.

the erection [sic] of a courthouse and jail for use of said county, on said tract or lot of land and shall be used for no other purpose.

The property ceased to be used as the county courthouse in 1976. The plaintiff brought this action to obtain the real estate, arguing that, since the property was not used as a county courthouse, the land reverted to her, as the only heir of her father.

Judge KLEINSCHMIDT
*   *   *   *

The deed did not grant a fee simple determinable [defeasible]. A fee simple determinable is created by any limitation in a conveyance which creates an estate in fee simple and then provides that the estate shall automatically expire upon occurrence of a stated event. Such an intent is usually manifested by a limitation which contains the words "until," "so long as," or "during." The conveyance must express the intent of the grantor that the estate will automatically expire upon the happening of an event and a mere statement as to the purpose of the grant is not sufficient.
*   *   *   *

A fee simple subject to a condition subsequent is created by an effective conveyance in fee simple which provides that upon the occurrence of a stated event the grantor or his successor shall have the power to terminate the estate created. The reversion is not automatic but depends upon a decision on the part of the grantor to re-enter. The instrument of conveyance must manifest the conditional nature of the deed and must contain some provision demonstrating the grantor's power to re-enter and terminate. Since forfeitures are not favored the intent must be clear.
*   *   *   *

*   *   * The deed "grants," "sells," and "conveys" in return for consideration recited and speaks of title vesting in the county when construction of the courthouse is begun. *   *   * Everything in the record, including the grantor's disclaimer of any remainder interest in the land at the time he was going through bankruptcy, points to an outright conveyance of the fee *   *   *.

DECISION AND REMEDY *The court found that the conveyance to Navajo County, Arizona, was not a fee simple subject to a condition subsequent nor a fee simple defeasible but an outright conveyance of the fee (that is, a fee simple absolute).*

COMMENT *In order to create a fee simple defeasible, the words used in the deed must be conditional words. The magic words are* until, so long as, *and* during. *In this case, if the deed had contained one of these words, the property would have automatically reverted back to the plaintiff. The deed could have read as follows:*

> *The title to which said foregoing described tract or lot of land shall vest in said County of Navajo, Territory of Arizona at any time, said county shall or may begin the erection [sic] of a courthouse and jail for use of said county, on said tract or lot of land and so long as the said county shall use the tract or lot of land for no other purpose, then title shall remain vested in said county.*

Similarly, to create a fee simple subject to a condition subsequent, the deed must clearly state its conditional nature and contain a provision demonstrating the grantor's power to take the land away from the current owner by doing something affirmative to regain it. The deed could have read as follows:

> *The title to the said foregoing described tract or lot of land shall vest in said County of Navajo, Territory of Arizona, but if the tract or lot of land shall be used for any*

purpose other than that of a county courthouse and jail, the grantor or his heirs shall have the right to re-enter and repossess the land.

The law does not favor forfeitures and thus requires that the original owner's intent be made very clear and be written in very specific language.

Life Estates   A **life estate** is one in which the duration of the estate is measured by the life of one or more human beings. A life estate may be created, for example, by a conveyance of the land by the owner to another person to occupy and use the land during his or her lifetime. The person granting the life estate has designated someone else (or the owner himself or herself) as the future owner of the land who holds the land in fee simple absolute after the life tenant. During the life estate, however, the life tenant has the same rights as a fee simple owner except that he or she must preserve the value of the land for the holder of the future interest.

Nonfreehold Estates   A **nonfreehold estate** occurs when a person has the right to possess real estate but does not own the property. This type of estate is generally treated as a personal interest and not as an interest in real property. Nonfreehold estates are commonly called leases or tenancies. Leases are classified as: (1) tenancy for years, (2) tenancy from period to period, or (3) tenancy at will.

Another tenancy is called tenancy by sufferance, but it is not actually an estate, as we will see shortly.

Landlord-Tenant Relationship   Before looking at these types of tenancies, we need to define the landlord-tenant relationship. Most owners of real property do not use that property themselves. Instead, others, called **tenants,** occupy and use the property under a **lease.** A lease is a contract by which the **landlord**—the owner—grants the tenant an exclusive right to use and possess the land, usually for a specific period of time. The tenant is under an obligation to pay rent and to return the premises in good condition at the end of the lease period.

The landlord has a duty to ensure that the tenant is able to possess the property at the time the lease period begins. Thus, the landlord must

not have rented the premises to others or allow others to occupy and remain on the premises. The tenant, while in possession, is entitled to possess the premises in peace and without disturbance. Whether the landlord is under an obligation to maintain and repair the premises is usually determined by the lease. In absence of agreement, generally the tenant is liable for maintenance and normal repairs and the landlord for major repairs and improvements.

Types of Tenancies   A tenancy for years, tenancy from period to period, and tenancy at will involve the transfer of the right to possession from the landlord (lessor) to a tenant (lessee) for a specified period of time. In every lease, the tenant has a qualified right to exclusive possession (qualified by the right of the landlord to enter the premises for limited purposes, such as emergency repairs). The tenant can make appropriate use of the land—for example, to grow crops—but cannot injure the land by such activities as cutting down timber for sale or pumping gas or oil.

A **tenancy for years** is created by express contract (which can sometimes be oral) in which the property is leased for a specified period of time. For example, signing a one-year lease to rent an apartment creates a tenancy for years. At the end of the period specified in the lease, the lease ends (without notice) and the right to possession of the apartment returns to the lessor.

A **tenancy from period to period** is created by a lease that does not specify how long it is to last but does specify that rent is to be paid at certain intervals. This type of tenancy is automatically renewed for another rental period unless *properly* terminated.

Suppose a landlord rents an apartment to a tenant "for as long as both agree." In such a case, the tenant receives a leasehold estate known as a **tenancy at will.** At common law, either party can terminate the tenancy without notice. This type of estate usually arises when a tenant who has been under a tenancy for years retains possession,

Legal Highlight

Whose House Is This?

Edna Snowden of Sunset Beach, California, thought life estates were wonderful. She was the beneficiary of one.

In 1928, Edna moved in with Mrs. Mary Jane McKinley as live-in housekeeper and companion. When Mrs. McKinley died in 1946, her two sons inserted a clause into the deed that gave Edna a life estate. She was to live in the house rent free,

and the owners were to maintain all the utilities and provide whatever work was necessary to keep the place livable at no cost to her. She was 68 years old at that time. When she died in the early 1980s, over 100 years old, she had outlived the two sons and six more owners. The last owner, a schoolteacher, was the first owner to be able to live in the house in almost 40 years.

---

with the landlord's consent, after the termination date of that tenancy. Sometimes no rent is paid, but the tenant acknowledges that the landlord does own the property. Quite often this tenancy is converted to a tenancy from period to period, which then is automatically renewed and proper notice of termination is required.

A **tenancy by sufferance** is not a true tenancy; it is the mere possession of land without right. A tenancy by sufferance is not an estate, since it is created by a tenant wrongfully retaining possession of property. Whenever a tenancy for years, tenancy from period to period, or tenancy at will ends and the tenant retains possession of the premises without the owner's permission, a tenancy by sufferance is created. The tenant is subject to immediate eviction.

Exhibit 15–1 summarizes the forms of ownership described in this section.

Transfer of Ownership

A number of methods exist by which the ownership of real property can pass from one person to another. These methods include: (1) inheritance or will, (2) eminent domain, (3) adverse possession, and (4) conveyance by deed (which includes transfer by sale and by gift).

Transfer by Inheritance or Will   Property that is transferred on an owner's death is passed to the

beneficiaries or heirs either by will or by inheritance. When the owner of land dies with a will, the land passes according to the terms of the will. When the owner dies without a will, the land passes according to state statutes that set out who will inherit the property. Joint tenancy with right of survivorship overrides any will provisions.

Eminent Domain   Even where ownership in real property is fee simple absolute, a superior ownership may limit that fee simple absolute. Called **eminent domain,** it is part of the police power of the government to condemn land in order to convert it to public use. The government has a right to acquire real property in the manner authorized by the Constitution and by the laws of the state whenever the public interest requires it.

For example, when a new public highway is to be built, the government must decide where to build it and how much land to condemn. The power of eminent domain is generally invoked through condemnation proceedings. After the government determines that a particular parcel of land is necessary for public use, it brings a judicial proceeding to obtain title to the land. Then, in another proceeding, the court further determines the fair value of the land, which is usually approximately equal to its market value. Under the Fifth Amendment, private property may not be taken for public use without just compensation.

Exhibit 15–1 Forms of Ownership of Real Property

FORMS OF OWNERSHIP	TYPES AND DEFINITIONS

Freehold Estate (Held indefinitely)	1. Estate in Fee—
	  a. *Fee simple absolute*—Most complete form of ownership.
	  b. *Fee simple defeasible*—Ownership ends automatically if specified condition occurs or fails to occur; land reverts to original owner.
	  c. *Fee simple subject to a condition subsequent*—Ownership may end if the specified condition occurs or fails to occur; ownership continues in the current owner; original owner must take affirmative action to reacquire the land.
	  d. *Life estate*—A person owns the property during his or her lifetime; upon death the property reverts back to the grantor or to someone the grantor has selected.

Nonfreehold Estates (Possessory interests held for a specified period of time)	1. *Tenancy for years*—Lasts for period of time stated by express contract. 2. *Tenancy from period to period*—Period determined by frequency of rent payments; automatically renewed unless proper notice is given. 3. *Tenancy at will*—For as long as both parties agree; no notice of termination required. 4. *Tenancy by sufferance*—Possession of land without legal right.
Concurrent Ownership (Jointly held ownership)	1. *Tenancy in common*—Each tenant owns an undivided fractional share of the property. Such interest can be conveyed without consent and, upon death, pass to tenant's heirs. 2. *Joint tenancy* (with right of survivorship)—Each tenant owns an undivided share of the property. Such interest can be conveyed without consent, converting the interest to a tenancy in common. Upon death, interest passes to surviving joint tenant, not heirs. 3. *Tenancy by the entirety*—A joint tenancy with right of survivorship between husband and wife. 4. *Community property*—Most property acquired during marriage by either or both spouses is owned equally by each spouse.

In the following case, the United States Supreme Court had to decide whether an ordinance temporarily restricting the use of land was a taking of property that required compensation to be paid by Los Angeles County, California.

BACKGROUND AND FACTS   *First English Evangelical Lutheran Church operated a retreat and recreational area for handicapped children. In 1978, a flood destroyed the buildings. Afterward, the County of Los Angeles adopted an ordinance prohibiting any construction of buildings within the area. Shortly after passage of this ordinance, the church filed an action claiming damages in inverse condemnation. Inverse condemnation is an indirect taking of property by the government without compensation. The trial court granted a motion to dismiss that was upheld by the California Court of Appeals. The United States Supreme Court took jurisdiction of the case.*

Case 15.3
FIRST ENGLISH EVANGELICAL LUTHERAN CHURCH v. COUNTY OF LOS ANGELES
Supreme Court of the United States, 1987.
482 U.S. 304, 107 S.Ct. 2378, 96 L.Ed.2d 250.

Chief Justice REHNQUIST delivered the opinion of the Court.
*   *   *   *

Consideration of the compensation question must begin with direct reference to the language of the Fifth Amendment, which provides in relevant part that "private property [shall not] be taken for public use, without just compensation." As its language indicates, and as the Court has frequently noted, this provision does not prohibit the taking of private property, but instead places a condition on the exercise of that power. This basic understanding of the Amendment makes clear that it is designated not to limit the governmental interference with property rights per se, but rather to secure *compensation* in the event of otherwise proper interference amounting to a taking. Thus, government action that works a taking of property rights necessarily implicates the "constitutional obligation to pay just compensation."

We have recognized that a landowner is entitled to bring an action in inverse condemnation as a result of " 'the self-executing character of the constitutional provision with respect to compensation. . . .' " [It] has been established at least since *Jacobs v. United States* that claims for just compensation are grounded in the Constitution itself:

"The suits were based on the right to recover just compensation for property taken by the United States for public use in the exercise of its power of eminent domain. *That right was guaranteed by the Constitution.* The fact that condemnation proceedings were not instituted and that the right was asserted in suits by the owners did not change the essential nature of the claim. The form of the remedy did not qualify the right. It rested upon the Fifth Amendment. Statutory recognition was not necessary. A promise to pay was not necessary. Such a promise was implied because of the duty imposed by the Amendment. *The suits were thus founded upon the Constitution of the United States.*" (Emphasis added.)

Jacobs, moreover, does not stand alone, for the Court has frequently repeated the view that, in the event of a taking, the compensation remedy is required by the Constitution.

*   *   *   *

*   *   * While the typical taking occurs when the government acts to condemn property in the exercise of its power of eminent domain, the entire doctrine of inverse condemnation is predicated on the proposition that a taking may occur without such formal proceedings. *   *   *

*   *   *

*   *   * It is axiomatic that the Fifth Amendment's just compensation provision is "designed to bar Government from forcing some people alone to bear public burdens which, in all fairness and justice, should be borne by the public as a whole." In the present case the interim ordinance was adopted by the county of Los Angeles in January 1979, and became effective immediately. Appellant filed suit within a month after the effective date of the ordinance and yet when the Supreme Court of California denied a hearing in the case on October 17, 1985, the merits of appellant's claim had yet to be determined. The United States has been required to pay compensation for leasehold interests of shorter duration than this. The value of a leasehold interest in property for a period of years may be substantial, and the burden on the property owner in extinguishing such an interest for a period of years may be great indeed. Where this burden results from governmental action that amounted to a taking, the Just Compensation Clause of the Fifth Amendment requires that the government pay the landowner for the value of the use of the land during this period. Invalidation of the ordinance or its successor ordinance after this period of time, though converting the taking into a "temporary" one, is not a sufficient remedy to meet the demands of the Just Compensation Clause.

*   *   *   *

Nothing we say today is intended to abrogate the principle that the decision to exercise the power of eminent domain is a legislative function, " 'for Congress and Congress alone to determine.' " Once a court determines that a taking has occurred, the government retains the whole range of options already available—amendment of the regulation, withdrawal of the invalidated regulation, or exercise of eminent domain. We hold that where the government's activities have already worked a taking of all use of property, no subsequent action by the government can relieve it of the duty to provide compensation for the period during which the taking was effective.

*   *   * We realize that even our present holding will undoubtedly lessen to some extent the freedom and flexibility of land-use planners and governing bodies of municipal corporations when enacting land-use regulations. But such consequences necessarily flow from any decision upholding a claim of constitutional right; many of the provisions of the Constitution are designed to limit the flexibility and freedom of governmental authorities and the Just Compensation Clause of the Fifth Amendment is one of them. As Justice Holmes aptly noted more than 50 years ago, "a strong public desire to improve the public condition is not enough to warrant achieving the desire by a shorter cut than the constitutional way of paying for the change."

Here we must assume that the Los Angeles County ordinance denied appellant all use of its property for a considerable period of years, and we hold that invalidation of the ordinance without payment of fair value for the use of the property during this period of time would be a constitutionally insufficient remedy. The judgment of the California Court of Appeals is therefore reversed, and the case is remanded for further proceedings not inconsistent with this opinion.

The United States Supreme Court held that, under the Fifth Amendment, where the government has denied the owner all use of its property, even if only temporarily, a taking has occurred for which compensation must be paid by the government.   **DECISION AND REMEDY**

Adverse Possession   **Adverse possession** is a means of obtaining title to land without a deed being delivered. Essentially, one person must possess the property of another in an open, hostile, notorious manner and for an uninterrupted statutory period of time (ranging from three to 30 years, with ten years being most common). Called an adverse possessor, that person acquires title to the land and cannot be removed from the land by the original owner.

For example, Bill and Karen find an unoccupied house in the woods. They decide to occupy the house, find the owner, and buy it. After six months, they cannot find the owner, and since the land has two years of back taxes owed they assume the owner has abandoned the property. Bill and Karen pay the back taxes, and for ten years live on the property, fence in the property, remove trespassers, pay taxes and utilities, have mail and other items delivered to it, and invite community guests to the house. Suddenly, the recorded title owner, Jerry Foster, appears and demands that Bill and Karen vacate the premises. If Bill and Karen have possessed the property con-

tinuously for the required statutory period (assume ten years), they will be able successfully to claim title by adverse possession. Their possession was open, it was exclusive as to others (hostile), and they were living on the premises without the permission of Jerry Foster.

After all statutory requirements have been met, the adverse possessor must file a **quiet title** action in court in order to have the recorded title placed in his or her name. A quiet title action is just what the name implies: an action that will decide who has title to the property, thus settling a dispute over the title and placing the title in the name of the true owner. The adverse possessor is vested with a perfect title just as if there had been a conveyance by deed.

Conveyance by Deed   Possession and title to land are generally passed from person to person by means of a deed—the written instrument of conveyance of real property. A deed is signed by an owner of property in order to transfer title to it to another person. Deeds must meet certain requirements, such as being delivered from the grantor to the grantee and containing a full description of the property as well as, in some states, an acknowledgment of the grantor's signature by a notary public.

Several types of deeds are used today. The first is a **general warranty deed.** This type of deed gives the buyer the most protection against defects in the title to the land. The seller is warranting, first, that he or she has the right and power to convey the title to the land; second, that no liens or interests exist, or if there are liens or interests, that they are listed and/or known to the buyer (liens and interests include mortgages, tax liens, mechanic's liens, and easements); third, that the buyer will have "quiet enjoyment" of the property—in other words, that no one will come in with a better title than the seller to force the buyer from the property.

A second type of deed is the **special warranty deed.** The seller warrants only that he or she has not previously done anything to lessen the value of the real estate. The third type of deed is called the **quitclaim deed** and conveys less than other types of deeds. This deed conveys to the buyer whatever interest the grantor (who is not necessarily the seller) has, if any. For example, a piece of realty is held in the name of the husband. The husband and wife have separated. A prospective buyer of the property may want a warranty deed from the seller husband and a quitclaim deed from the wife. If the prospective buyer pays a nominal amount of money, the wife will sign a quitclaim deed transferring any interest she may have in the property, including any homestead rights.

Recording Statutes   Every state has a **recording statute.** The purpose of these statutes is to provide prospective buyers with a way to check the history of the property and to determine what outstanding interests, liens, judgments, or taxes have been placed against the title to the property. Recording a deed (or a lien) gives notice to the world that a certain person is now the owner of a particular parcel of real estate and notice that a "cloud" may be on the title.

Anything recorded against the property can act as a cloud on its title for persons interested in purchasing or lending money on it. For example, by recording your deed you are placing everyone on notice as to who the true owner is. Thus, in the case of recorded deeds, former owners are

prevented from fraudulently conveying the land to other purchasers, and in the case of recorded liens, owners are prevented from selling their land without paying what is owed to creditors who have a lien on the property.

Nonpossessory Interests

Some interests in land do not include any rights of possession. One important nonpossessory interest is an **easement.** An easement is the right to make limited use of another person's real property without actually possessing it. Often an easement is called a "right-of-way." The right to drive across another's property and the right to place water and sewage pipes, electrical or telephone wires, or cables on another's property are examples of easements. Easements can be created by deed, will, contract, or law.

Acquiring Ownership of Personal Property

The ownership of personal property can be acquired in a variety of ways. Rights can be acquired by possession, purchase, production, gift, will or inheritance, accession, and confusion.

Possession

Possession is exactly what the word implies: If you have possession, you normally have ownership. A familiar adage is "Possession is nine-tenths of the law." In reality, this concept of ownership is limited in its application. Possession is important in the following situations: wildlife, lost or mislaid property, and abandoned property. One example of acquiring ownership by possession is the capture of wild animals. Wild animals belong to no one in their natural state, and the first person to take possession of a wild animal normally owns it. The killing of a wild animal amounts to assuming ownership of it. A commercial fishing captain, for example, acquires ownership over fish caught in the open seas.

Mislaid and Lost Property   Property that has been placed somewhere by the owner voluntarily and then inadvertently forgotten is **mislaid property.**

Whenever mislaid property is found, the finder does not obtain title to or possession of the goods. Instead, the owner of the place where the property was mislaid becomes the caretaker of the property because it is highly likely that the true owner will return. Suppose you leave your textbook under your chair after class. The textbook is mislaid property, and if a school employee finds it, the school is entrusted with the duty of reasonable care for the goods.

Property that is not voluntarily left but is forgotten is **lost property**. In absence of a statutory provision, a finder of lost property can claim title to the property against everyone in the whole world, except the true owner. If the true owner demands that the lost property be returned, the finder must do so. If a third party attempts to take possession of lost property from a finder, the third party cannot assert a better title than the finder.

Abandoned Property   Property that has been discarded by the true owner with no intention of claiming title to it is **abandoned property;** for example, garbage qualifies as abandoned property. Someone who finds abandoned property acquires title to it, and such title is good against everyone in the whole world, including the original owner. The owner of lost property who eventually gives up any further attempt to find the lost property is frequently held to have abandoned the property.

Purchase

Purchase is one of the most common means of acquiring and transferring ownership of personal property. The purchase or sale of personal property (called goods) is covered in Chapter 11.

Production

Production—the fruits of labor—is another means of acquiring ownership of personal property. Nearly everyone in the United States today is involved in some sort of production. For example, writers, inventors, and manufacturers all produce personal property and thereby acquire title to it. If you are employed to produce an item, however, your employer will own the item.

Gifts

A **gift** is another fairly common means of both acquiring and transferring ownership of personal property. A gift is essentially a voluntary transfer of property ownership. It is not supported by legally sufficient consideration to make a contract since the very essence of a gift is giving without consideration. A gift must be transferred or delivered in the present rather than in the future, and the donor must intend to make a gift.

For example, suppose that your aunt, the donor, tells you, the donee, that she is going to give you a new Mercedes-Benz for your next birthday. This is simply a promise to make a gift. It is not considered a gift until the Mercedes-Benz is delivered to you. Once the gift has been unconditionally delivered, it is irrevocable.

Will or Inheritance

The law in our society requires that, on the death of a person, title to the decedent's property must vest in (deliver full possession to) someone. The decedent can direct the passage of property after his or her death through the legal instrument known as a will, subject to certain limitations imposed by the state. If the person dies without a will, he or she is said to have died intestate, and state law determines the distribution of his or her property among next of kin. If no kin can be found, the property escheats (title is transferred) to the state.

In addition, a person can transfer property through a trust. The owner (settlor) of the property transfers legal title to a trustee, who has a duty imposed by law to hold the property for the use or benefit of another (the beneficiary).

Accession

Accession means addition or increase, or coming into possession of a right. In property law, accession refers to someone's adding value to a piece of personal property (owned by another) by either labor or materials. Generally no dispute exists about who owns the improved property after accession has occurred, especially when the accession is accomplished with the owner's consent.

For example, Michio takes his Corvette to Corvette Customizing Garage. Michio wants a unique bumper placed on his Corvette. Michio simply pays the customizer for the value of the labor for improving his automobile, and he retains title to the Corvette with the unique bumper.

Confusion

Confusion occurs when you mix property of the same type, otherwise known as **fungible goods.** Fungible goods are identical goods (the equivalent of other like units) by nature or usage of trade. For example, a farmer takes his or her wheat crop to the grain elevator. Once the wheat is mixed with other farmers' wheat of like grade and quality, there is a change in ownership. The farmers become owners of the grain as tenants in common. The farmer now owns a percentage of the wheat in the grain elevator. Because the goods are fungible, there is no way or reason to separate the farmer's original grain from the other farmers' grain. Thus, title can pass without the grain being removed from the grain elevator.

Bailments

Virtually every individual and business is affected by the law of bailments at one time or another (and sometimes even on a daily basis). When individuals deal with bailments, whether they realize it or not, they are subject to the obligations and duties that arise from the bailment relationship. A **bailment** is formed by the delivery of personal property, without transfer of title, by one person, called a **bailor,** to another, called a **bailee,** usually under an agreement for a particular purpose (for example, loan, storage, repair, or transportation). On completion of the purpose, the bailee is obligated to return the bailed property to the bailor or a third person, or to dispose of it as directed.

Most bailments are created by agreement but not necessarily by contract, because in many bailments not all of the elements of a contract, such as mutual assent or consideration, are present. For example, if you mislay your textbook, its finder and subsequent possessor is a bailee, but not by contract, because there is no legal consideration. Similarly, if you loan your textbook to a friend so your friend can read tomorrow's assignment, a bailment is created, but not by contract, because again there is no consideration. On the other hand, many commercial bailments, such as the delivery of your suit or dress to the cleaners for dry cleaning, are based on contract.

A bailment is distinguished from a sale or a gift in that, in a bailment, possession is transferred without passage of title or without intent to transfer title. In a sale or gift, on the other hand, title is transferred from the seller or donor to the buyer or donee.

Once a bailment is created, the bailee has certain duties and rights concerning the bailed property. Exhibit 15–2 summarizes these rights and duties.

Computer Law

A distinction must be made between **software** and **hardware** when discussing computer law. By software, we mean the programming involved with a computer system. The two basic kinds of software are system programs, which coordinate the operation of the computer, and application programs, which solve particular user problems, such as word-processing programs or spread-sheet programs. Some authorities believe that software encompasses the programming plus the advice, assistance, and counseling in loading a machine for a certain program.

The hardware is the equipment itself. In most cases, the general principles of contract, sales, and leasing law will suffice when discussing hardware. The unique aspect of computer law really involves software and semiconductor chips. In particular, it becomes necessary to understand the creation and protection of programs, the transfer of programs, and the use of them.

Contract Law Versus the Sale of Goods

As noted in Chapter 9, the Uniform Commercial Code (UCC) has been adopted in part by all jurisdictions. Article 2 of the UCC applies to the sale of goods. The question is whether there is a sale of goods or a sale of service when there is a sale of a computer program. The importance of this determination is that Article 2 gives very specific rights and obligations to both the buyer and seller. If Article 2 does not apply, basic contract law will apply. Article 2 is more protective of the buyer, while common law tends to give more protection to the seller, such as under the doctrine of *caveat emptor* (let the buyer beware).

The courts have uniformly held that, when software is sold with or given with the sale of

Legal Highlight

Faxes and Computers

New technology forces the law to recognize new methods of conducting business. Fax machines, available for decades, have only recently become popular because of low prices. As electronic data speed back and forth through the telephone lines, the old questions concerning contracts arise: When did the persons complete the negotiations and enter into a contract? Are faxed signatures valid? Virtually no cases exist on this issue. This is probably because courts treat the fax documents as the writing. These documents can be entered into evidence.

But what about contracts made through computers that are hooked together through networks? The "documents" may not be reduced to paper as are faxed materials; instead, they may still be in an electronic state on disk. And what about signatures? The traditional signature is not used commonly on computer transmissions, although new technology allows people to use an electronic pen on the computer screen; this can send the writing on the screen to other computers in the network. Will this electronic signature be recognized by courts?

Interactive television programs hooked either to cellular telephones or to personal computers are available. How will the courts decide contract cases when problems arise? Will today's standard rules meet the challenge of tomorrow's technology?

Exhibit 15–2 **Rights and Duties of a Bailee**

BAILEE	BASIC RULES
Rights	1. A bailee has the right to be compensated or reimbursed for keeping bailed property. This right is based in contract or quasi-contract.
	2. Unpaid compensation or reimbursement entitles the bailee to a lien (usually possessory) on the bailed property and the right of foreclosure.
	3. A bailee has the right to limit his or her liability. An ordinary bailee can limit risk or monetary amount or both, provided proper notice is given and the limitation is not against public policy. In special bailments, limitations on types of risk are usually not allowed, but limitations on the monetary amount at risk are permitted by regulation.
	4. The right of possession allows actions against third persons who damage or convert the bailed property and allows actions against the bailor for wrongful breach of the bailment.
	5. The right to an insurable interest in the bailed property allows the bailee to insure and recover under the insurance policy for loss or damage to the property.
Duties	1. A bailee must exercise reasonable care over property entrusted to him or her. A common carrier (special bailee) is held to a standard of care based on *strict liability* unless the bailed property is lost or destroyed due to (a) an act of God, (b) an act of a public enemy, (c) an act of a governmental authority, (d) an act of a shipper, or (e) the inherent nature of the goods.
	2. Bailed goods in a bailee's possession must be returned to the bailor or disposed of according to bailor's directions.
	3. A bailee cannot use or profit from bailed goods except by agreement or in situations where the use is implied to further the bailment purpose.

hardware, a sale of goods occurs. Thus, Article 2 of the UCC applies. The problem occurs when only software is sold. The courts tend to treat it as a sale of goods when the software is purchased from a store because it is sold under a sales contract, but what happens when a program is written for a specific use, not for common usage? Is this a sale of goods or the provision of a service?

The cases are divided on this issue. Logic dictates that this transaction would be considered a sale of a specialty good. After all, there is a transfer of a tape or disk. Under the law, the definition of goods is very broad and should encompass the sale of software. Some cases hold, however, that it is a transaction involving service and not a sale of goods. In those jurisdictions, the general principles of contract law will be applied, and the protection given to buyers by Article 2 of the UCC will not be applicable.

Another problem arises with the application of Article 2 to the transfer of computer programs. Many of the statutory provisions cover the sale of goods but not other transactions in goods. A large segment of the computer software business involves transfer by either a lease or a license but not by a sale.

In general, three legal theories exist that grant the UCC Article 2 protection to licenses and leases. First, the transaction is treated as a sale if the lease allows the user to purchase the program or hardware. Second, a theory known as the third-party beneficiary doctrine applies when a financing company purchases the items and then leases the program to the user. Under this doctrine, the user can utilize the same legal rights as the purchaser. Third, the courts can extend the coverage of Article 2 to leases or licenses.

In a few years, the need to extend Article 2 by theory to leases will disappear in most states. The Permanent Editorial Board of the UCC has approved a codification of the law with respect to leases of goods. This codification, entitled Article 2A of the UCC, is substantially similar in content to the present Article 2 (except, of course, that it relates only to leases). It is presently being considered for adoption by a number of states. Thus, Article 2 and Article 2A of the UCC will cover both the sales and leases of goods.

Software Warranties

If we assume that the UCC applies to the transfer (sale or lease) of software, then specific warranties apply. In particular, the UCC defines an express warranty, the implied warranty of merchantability, and the implied warranty of fitness for a particular purpose. These warranties are covered in Chapter 11. Warranties give the buyer-user specific rights that are not available from the common law.

Protection of Property Rights

Although the computer was developed prior to World War II,[1] the real expansion of the market occurred in the late 1970s and 1980s with the development and refinement of semiconductor chips and integrated circuits. The law has evolved slowly, while the pace of technology has accelerated. Congress has amended patent, copyright, and trademark laws and passed new laws dealing with legal issues surrounding computer technology.

Patent Law   In 1981, the Supreme Court held that a "claim containing a mathematical formula implements or applies that formula in a structure or process, which when considered as a whole, is performing a function which the patent laws were designed to protect (e.g., transforming or reducing an article to a different state or thing), then the claim satisfies the [patent laws]."[2] This case set the stage for software to be patented.

Computer software is now patentable with the United States Patent and Trademark Office (PTO). A patent gives the patent holder the exclusive right to make, use, and market the invention for a non-renewable period of seventeen years. Although the PTO accepts patents for software, these patents are subject to challenge and are difficult to defend.

The algorithm used in software is not patentable because an algorithm is like a law of nature and cannot be the subject of a patent. The software process itself may be patented even though some steps, such as the use of the algorithms within the software, are not novel or independently eligible for patent protection. The software must be viewed as a whole to show it is performing a function designed to be protected by the patent laws. Although patents of many computer programs are hard to defend, those who patent computer games

---

1.   The first analog computer was built in 1930, and the first digital computer was completed in 1944.
2.   *Diamond v. Diehr*, 450 U.S. 175, 192; 101 S.Ct. 1048, 1059; 67 L.Ed.2d 155, 169 (1981).

have an easier time because it is the game that is unique.

Copyright Law The Copyright Act of 1976 gives protection to original works. A copyright is valid for the life of the author plus 50 years. In 1980, Congress for the first time specifically included computer programs as a type of work entitled to copyright protection. The courts recognize that the source code and object code of a computer program are protected under the Copyright Act. In the following case, the appellate court, in examining whether the copyright law had been infringed, disagreed with the district court in its interpretation of the phrase *literary works* as it applies to source code and object code.

Case 15.4
APPLE COMPUTER, INC. v. FRANKLIN COMPUTER CORP.
United States Court of Appeals, Third Circuit, 1983.
714 F.2d 1240.

BACKGROUND AND FACTS *Apple Computer, Inc., the plaintiff, is one of the leading manufacturers of personal computers and computer programs. Apple had sold over 400,000 Apple II computers, distributed over 150 programs (of which fourteen were the subject of the lawsuit), employed approximately 3,000 people, and had annual sales of $335 million for the fiscal year 1981.*

Franklin Computer Corporation employed about 75 people and manufactured the ACE 100 personal computer that could use the Apple software. Fewer than 1,000 ACE 100 computers had been sold. Franklin's copying of Apple's operating system was the reason this action was filed. Franklin did not dispute that it had copied the Apple programs. Apple made a motion for a preliminary injunction to enjoin Franklin from infringing the copyrights on Apple's computer programs. The motion was denied because the district court found that the object code, as distinguished from the source code, may not be the proper subject of a copyright.

Two footnotes from the case have been retained in this edited version because the information contained in them adds to the understanding of the case. The original footnote numbers, numbers 3 and 7, from the case have been retained.

Judge SLOVITER
* * * *

There are three levels of computer language in which computer programs may be written. High level language, such as the commonly used BASIC or FORTRAN, uses English words and symbols, and is relatively easy to learn and understand (e.g., "GO TO 40" tells the computer to skip intervening steps and go to the step at line 40). A somewhat lower level language is assembly language, which consists of alphanumeric labels (e.g., "ADC" means "add with carry"). Statements in high level language, and apparently also statements in assembly language, are referred to as written in "source code." The third, or lowest level computer language, is machine language, a binary language using two symbols, 0 and 1, to indicate an open or closed switch (e.g., "01101001" means, to the Apple, add two numbers and save the result). Statements in machine language are referred to as written in "object code."

The CPU [central processing unit] can only follow instructions written in object code. However, programs are usually written in source code which is more intelligible to humans. Programs written in source code can be converted or translated by a "compiler" program into object code for use by the computer. Programs are generally distributed only in their object code version stored on a memory device.

A computer program can be stored or fixed on a variety of memory devices, two of which are of particular relevance for this case. The ROM (Read Only Memory) is an internal permanent memory device consisting of a semi-conductor "chip" which is incorporated into the circuitry of the computer. A program in object code is embedded on a ROM before it is incorporated in the computer. Information stored on a ROM can only be read, not erased or rewritten.[3] The ACE 100 apparently contains EPROMS (Erasable Programmable Read Only Memory) on which the stored information can be erased and the chip reprogrammed, but the district court found that for purposes of this proceeding, the difference between ROMs and EPROMs is inconsequential. The other device used for storing the programs at issue is a diskette or "floppy disk," an auxiliary memory device consisting of a flexible magnetic disk resembling a phonograph record, which can be inserted into the computer and from which data or instructions can be read.

Computer programs can be categorized by function as either application programs or operating system programs. Application programs usually perform a specific task for the computer user, such as word processing, checkbook balancing, or playing a game. In contrast, operating system programs generally manage the internal functions of the computer or facilitate use of application programs. The parties agree that the fourteen computer programs at issue in this suit are operating system programs.

*   *   *   *

[Court's discussion of the copyrightability of a computer program expressed in object code]

The 1980 amendments [to the Copyright Act] added a definition of a computer program:

A "computer program" is a set of statements or instructions to be used directly or indirectly in a computer in order to bring about a certain result.

*   *   *   *

We considered the issue of copyright protection for a computer program in *Williams Electronics, Inc. v. Artic International, Inc.,* and concluded that "the copyrightability of computer programs is firmly established after the 1980 amendment to the Copyright Act." *   *   *

The district court here questioned whether copyright was to be limited to works "designed to be 'read' by a human reader [as distinguished from] read by an expert with a microscope and patience." *   *   *

Under the statute, copyright extends to works in any tangible means of expression *"from which they can be perceived,* reproduced, or otherwise communicated, either directly or *with the aid of a machine or device."* ([E]mphasis added). Further, the definition of "computer program" adopted by Congress in the 1980 amendments is "sets of statements or instructions to be used *directly or indirectly* in a computer in order to bring about a certain result." ([E]mphasis added). As source code instructions must be translated into object code before the computer can act upon them, only instructions expressed in object code can be used "directly" by the computer. *   *   *

The defendant in *Williams* had also argued that a copyrightable work "must be intelligible to human beings and must be intended as a medium of communication to human beings." We reiterate the statement we made in *Williams* when we rejected that argument: "[t]he answer to defendant's contention is in the words of the statute itself."

The district court also expressed uncertainty as to whether a computer program in object code could be classified as a "literary work."[7] However, the category of "literary works," one of the seven copyrightable categories, is not confined to literature in the nature of Hemingway's *For Whom the Bell Tolls.* The definition of "literary works" in section 101 includes expression not only in words but also "numbers, or other . . . numerical symbols or indicia," thereby expanding the common usage of "literary works." *   *   * Thus, a computer program, whether in object code or source code, is a "literary work" and is protected from unauthorized copying, whether from its object or source code version.

*   *   *   *

[Court's discussion of copyrightability of a computer program embedded on a ROM]

Just as the district court's suggestion of a distinction between source code and object code was rejected by our opinion in *Williams* issued three days after the district court opinion, so also was its suggestion that embodiment of a computer program on a ROM, as distinguished from in a traditional writing, detracts from its copyrightability. In *Williams* we rejected the argument that "a computer program is not infringed when the program is loaded into electronic memory devices (ROMs) and used to control the activity of machines." Defendant there had argued that there can be no copyright protection for the ROMs because they are utilitarian objects or machine parts. We held that the statutory requirement of "fixation," the manner in which the issue arises, is satisfied through the embodiment of the expression in the ROM devices. Therefore we reaffirm that a computer program in object code embedded in a ROM chip is an appropriate subject of copyright.

3. In contrast to the permanent memory devices a RAM (Random Access Memory) is a chip on which volatile internal memory is stored which is erased when the computer's power is turned off.

7. The district court stated that a programmer working directly in object code appears to think more as a mathematician or engineer, that the process of constructing a chip is less a work of authorship than the product of engineering knowledge, and that it may be more apt to describe an encoded ROM as a pictorial three-dimensional object than as a literary work. The district court's remarks relied in part on a quotation about "microcode"; Apple introduced testimony that none of the works in suit contain "microcode." Moreover, Apple does not seek to protect the ROM's architecture but only the program encoded upon it.

The court found that Franklin's argument that computer operating systems were not copyrightable was not valid. In fact, the court found that Congress intended computer software programs to be protected by copyright laws.

DECISION AND REMEDY

Congress in 1984 passed the **Protection of Semiconductor Chip Products Act.** Products in this field, called **mask work,** were allowed to be copyrighted. A mask work is a series of related images, fixed or encoded, in a three-dimensional pattern on the chip that are layered in a series, so that each image has a pattern. Imagine a film negative which is black on clear plastic. As it is processed into a picture, various layers of plastic with images are placed on top of one another. Eventually the final product, a colored photograph, is produced. Mask work is a similar process. This application of copyright law is designed to protect the manufacturer from counterfeiters, a prevalent problem in the industry.

The law also gave authority to the secretary of commerce to issue orders extending protection under this act to foreign governments. It is expected that treaties and other agreements will be used to achieve international consensus in this area. President Reagan in 1985 issued an executive order extending this protection against unauthorized duplication of semiconductor chip products to foreign countries.

The Copyright Act was further amended by the **Computer Software Rental Amendments Act** of 1990. This act allows the copyright holder of a computer program to control the rental, leasing, or lending of the computer program after the first sale. Prior to the passage of this act, the exclusive right to sell a copy extended only to the first sale of the copy. After the first sale of a copy, the copyright owner did not have any control over the conditions of future sales.

The following case contains an in-depth examination of copyright law and computers. The court reviewed the question of whether the computer spread-sheet program, Lotus 1-2-3, was copyrightable and if so, whether VP-Planner had infringed on that copyright.

Case 15.5
**LOTUS DEVELOPMENT
CORPORATION v.
PAPERBACK
SOFTWARE
INTERNATIONAL**
United States District Court,
1990.
740 F.Supp. 37 (D.Mass.)

BACKGROUND AND FACTS   *Lotus sued Paperback Software for copyright infringement, alleging that Lotus's computer spread-sheet program, Lotus 1-2-3, had been wrongfully copied by Paperback Software's VP-Planner. In a 50-page opinion, the judge reviewed the constitutional constraints, background of computers, the congressional mandates and judicial interpretation, and the legal test for copyrightability.*

District Judge KEETON
*   *   *   *

Thus, a statement of the most significant elements of the legal test for copyrightability [is]:

FIRST, in making a determination of "copyrightability," the decisionmaker must focus upon alternatives that counsel may suggest, or the court may conceive, *along the scale from the most generalized conception to the most particularized*, and choose some formulation—some conception or definition of the "idea"—for the purpose of distinguishing between the idea and its expression.
*   *   *   *

SECOND, the decisionmaker must focus upon whether an alleged expression of the idea is limited to elements essential to expression of *that* idea (or is one of only a few ways of expressing the idea) or instead includes identifiable elements of expression not essential to every expression of that idea.

THIRD, having identified elements of expression not essential to every expression of the idea, the decisionmaker must focus on whether those elements are a substantial part of the allegedly copyrightable "work."
*   *   *   *

The fact that some of these specific command terms are quite obvious or merge with the idea of such a particular command term does not preclude copyrightability for the command structure taken as a whole. If particular characteristics not distinctive individually have been brought together in a way that makes the "whole" a distinctive expression of an idea—one of many possible ways of expressing it—then the "whole" may be copyrightable. The statutory provisions regarding "compilation" *   *   * are not essential to this conclusion, but do reinforce it. A different total structure may be developed even from individual components that are quite similar and limited in number. To determine copyrightability, a court need not—and, indeed, should not—dissect every element of the allegedly protected work. Rather, the court need only identify those elements that are copyrightable, and then determine whether those elements, *considered as a whole*, have been impermissibly copied. *   *   *
*   *   *   *

I conclude that a menu command structure is capable of being expressed in many if not an unlimited number of ways, and that the command structure of 1-2-3 is an original and nonobvious way of expressing a command structure. *   *   * Accordingly, the menu structure, taken as a whole—including the choice of command terms, the structure and order of those terms, their presentation on the screen, and the long prompts—is an aspect of 1-2-3 that is not present in every expression of an electronic spreadsheet. It meets the requirements of the second element of the legal test for copyrightability.

Finally, I consider the third element of the legal test—whether the structure, sequence, and organization of the menu command system is a substantial part of the alleged copyrighted work—here Lotus 1-2-3. That the answer to this question is "yes" is incontrovertible. The user interface of 1-2-3 is its most unique element, and is the aspect that has made 1-2-3 so popular. That defendants went to such trouble to copy that element is a testament to its substantiality. Accordingly, evaluation of the third element of the legal test weighs heavily in favor of Lotus.

Taking account of all three elements of the legal test, I determine that copyrightability of the user interface of 1-2-3 is established.

DECISION AND REMEDY *The court held that Lotus did have a copyrightable program in Lotus 1-2-3. Paperback Software was liable for the copyright infringement.*

Trademarks Trademark law established the federal Principal Register where trademarks may be registered. A trademark had to be used in order to be registered, until 1988 when Congress passed the Trademark Law Revision Act. This act allows a person to register a trademark prior to use. The importance of this amendment to the computer field was tremendous. For the first time, businesses that make the effort and spend the time and money to develop a product can have legal protection for a proposed trademark.

The Ever-Developing Field

In an ever-changing society, the concept of personal property is expanding to take into account new types of such property. Often after a new type of property is developed, the courts and legislature must resolve problems that arise from it. For example, it is now a crime to make illegal duplicate tapes of records, audio tape recordings, video tape recordings, computer programs, and compact discs. The next question is: Is the law broad enough to cover the developing problems of personal property in outer space, in space laboratories, or during long-term space flights?

Ethical Considerations

What the Computer Knows About You

In two seconds you can now communicate anywhere in the world, thanks to computers and satellites. In the past, you left a trail of paperwork as a result of your daily activities. Today you leave an electronic wave of information as your daily activities are monitored by various computers. At the job site, your arrival time in the electronically controlled parking lot is noted; the time you turn on the computer at your workstation is logged in; your telephone calls are monitored not only for the content of your conversation but also for the length of time spent, down to the second. Your pay is electronically deposited into your bank account, which in turn automatically debits your account as preauthorized bills are paid.

Your travel agent's computer knows you are taking a trip. It knows your name, address, telephone numbers, arrival and departure times, destination and arrival, whether you are traveling round trip or one way, whether you have excess luggage or are bringing your pet along, and what your meal preferences are. It knows the rates charged and time used in rental automobile and hotel arrangements, your driver's license information, perhaps your social security number, and any special requests. The computer also knows your credit card issuer, your card number, expiration date, who is authorized to sign, and the number of credit cards you have. It knows your passport number and where you have been outside the United States.

Which information did you voluntarily disclose and which information was gathered with little knowledge or thought on your part? How long does this information stay in the various computer banks? What happens to the information? Is it destroyed or archived? Who has access to this information: competitors who may gain access lawfully by purchasing it? Or the government, which may request information and seek the cooperation of the parties who have control over it? What are the ethical considerations of businesses that handle this sensitive information? Should Congress investigate and regulate this area?

International Considerations

Protecting Your Assets and Ideas in Foreign Countries

Investments in businesses and property are controlled by the laws of the host country. Many countries restrict foreigners from owning a majority interest in domestic businesses. Under the **Exon-Florio** provision of the **Omnibus Trade and Competitiveness Act** of 1988, the President can prevent the purchase by a foreign business of any U.S. firm, such as airline companies, telecommunications businesses, or defense industries, if the purchase threatens national security.

Some countries require foreign investors to go through a preapproval procedure. The potential investor must submit a proposal to a host country's government for evaluation. The proposal will be reviewed by various agencies, occasionally going through up to 100 agencies, to determine if the potential investor meets all the government requirements. At times this procedure may take months, if not years. Ownership in private property is allowed only through a trust by which the foreign corporation owns up to 49 percent, while a domestic corporation owns the remaining 51 percent. Usually these trusts have a limited period of ten years, after which time the trust must end or be renewed.

Other countries are encouraging investments by offering preferences and incentives, particularly for high-technology industries. The former Eastern European countries are encouraging investments to bolster sagging economies. For example, Hungary in 1988 adopted the Investments of Foreigners in Hungary Act. This act encourages investments by streamlining an approval procedure, allowing profits to flow out of the country, providing contract guarantees, and allowing foreign managers. Russia allows private land ownership by foreign corporations. Tax and other incentives are being used to encourage investment in Russia.

There are now ways for a business to protect its intellectual property, such as copyrights and patents, at the international level. The United States signed the **Universal Copyright Convention** in 1952 and the **Berne Convention of the Protection of Literary and Artistic Works** in 1988. The Universal Copyright Convention grants an author copyright protection in every country that has signed when he or she first publishes the work in one of the countries with the prescribed notice. Each country is bound to protect the work according to its laws. The Berne convention is very similar in nature. Any country that has signed provides the citizens of any other member country the same rights it provides its own citizens.

As early as 1883, the United States and others were signatories to a treaty that provided the citizens of the other countries the same rights to obtain a patent as were granted to the country's own citizens. This early treaty established the principle of right of priority. If a person applied for a patent in his or her own country and within a year applied for a patent in one of the other countries, the later application was considered as having been made on the same date as the one made in his or her own country.

The **Paris Convention for the Protection of Industrial Property** is attempting to achieve uniformity in the patent area by having countries adopt a universal system of granting and recognizing patents. This convention also recognizes the principle of right of priority.

FACING A LEGAL ISSUE

Protecting Real Property

You decide to purchase a specific parcel of real property. It consists of several vacant buildings located in a suburban area on twenty acres of land. Because the property is rather isolated, numerous illegal intrusions into the buildings have been made by transients in order to stay a night or two and by youths for parties. These individuals have caused considerable damage to the buildings.

You are considering several alternatives to deal with these occurrences, namely: (1) placing guard dogs on the premises, (2) hiring a night watchperson, (3) setting up shotguns that would be triggered by a person touching a string close to the floor, or (4) simply letting these people use the premises until you find a tenant to lease the property.

You check with an attorney to find out which alternative is best. You are told that the first alternative is not allowed. Many states, including yours, have adopted laws that the owner of a dog is liable for any bites caused when the owner knows the dog is vicious. The second alternative is possible: The use of a night watchperson is proper as long as he or she does not use a firearm against trespassers. No one has the right to shoot mere trespassers. Before a

person can use deadly force, a clear danger to the person or another person must exist.

The third alternative is the worst choice and should not be considered. The owner of the property who sets up this type of gun arrangement is liable for criminal and civil charges if anyone is injured. According to longtime English and American laws, no one has the right to protect property by this method.

The fourth alternative is not the best solution either. If a person, even though a trespasser, is injured on your property by falling into a hole or tripping on debris, you may be liable. As the owner of the property, you have certain legal duties toward them. Many states require that you act as a reasonable and prudent person would under the same or similar circumstances. Other states require you to make the premises reasonably safe once you are aware that other people are using them.

What should you do? First, make sure you have sufficient liability insurance covering the property. Second, you should post "No Trespassing" signs. Third, you should board up the buildings, making them very difficult for anyone to enter. Fourth, you should inform the police department about the situation and have them watch the premises. These alternatives are the safest ones that an owner of real estate may exercise.

Summary

Property rights are of prime importance to our society. In fact, property rights are protected by the United States Constitution.

These classifications of property are recognized: real or personal, tangible or intangible, and fixtures. All property constitutes either real estate or personal property. Tangible property has physical existence, while intangible property consists of rights. Fixtures are items that are installed in real estate and that become part of the land.

A person may own real property with another person. These joint forms of ownership are ten-

ancy in common, joint tenancy with right of survivorship, tenancy by the entirety, and community property. To own an interest in either tenancy by the entirety or community property, the joint owners must be husband and wife.

The seven ways to obtain ownership of personal property are by possession, purchase, production, gift, will or inheritance, accession, and confusion.

Bailments concern the transfer of possession of personal property without transfer of title from the "owner" to another person. The bailment can be based on a contract, or it can be gratuitous.

Different interests in real property are found in freehold and nonfreehold estates. A freehold estate provides a person ownership for an indefinite period. Among freehold estates are the fee simple absolute, fee simple defeasible, fee simple subject to a condition subsequent, and life estates. The nonfreehold estates are leases that govern possessory rights to real property in the relationship between a landlord and a tenant.

Eminent domain is the right of the government to take a person's property. The government must pay just compensation to the owner, even if the taking is temporary. The government may control an owner's use of real property through zoning laws.

Transferring an interest in real property occurs by deed, by will, by operation of law, or by adverse possession. Adverse possession means obtaining title to land (without a deed) by the adverse use of real property for a specified period of time.

Computer law is a unique branch of the law that is still developing. An important question in computer law is whether there is a sale of goods or of service when a computer program is transferred.

Under recent legislative changes adopted by the United States Congress, the law of patents, copyrights, and trade secrets now applies to computer hardware and software.

Key Terms

abandoned property (381)
accession (381)
adverse possession (382)
bailee (382)
bailment (382)
bailor (382)
Berne Convention of the Protection of Literary and Artistic Works (391)
bill of sale (370)
community property (372)
Computer Software Rental Amendments Act (387)
confusion (382)
deed (370)
easement (380)
eminent domain (376)
Exon-Florio (391)
fee simple absolute (373)
fee simple defeasible (373)
fee simple subject to a condition subsequent (373)

fixture (370)
freehold estate (373)
fungible goods (382)
general warranty deed (380)
gift (381)
hardware (382)
intangible property (370)
joint tenancy with right of survivorship (372)
landlord (375)
lease (375)
life estate (375)
lost property (381)
mask work (387)
mislaid property (380)
nonfreehold estate (375)
Omnibus Trade and Competitiveness Act (391)
Paris Convention for the Protection of Industrial Property (391)
personal property (370)

police power (370)
production (381)
Protection of Semiconductor Chip Products Act (387)
purchase (381)
quiet title (379)
quitclaim deed (380)
real property (370)
recording statute (380)
software (382)
special warranty deed (380)
tangible property (370)
tenancy at will (375)
tenancy by sufferance (376)
tenancy by the entirety (372)
tenancy for years (375)
tenancy from period to period (375)
tenancy in common (372)
tenants (375)
Universal Copyright Convention (391)

Questions and Case Problems

1. Sally goes into Meyer's Department Store to do some Christmas shopping. She becomes engrossed in looking over a number of silk blouses when she suddenly realizes she has a dinner engagement. She hastily departs from the store, inadvertently leaving her purse on a sales counter. Julie, a sales clerk at the store, notices the purse on the counter but leaves it there, expecting Sally to return for it. Later, when Sally returns, the purse is gone. Sally files an action against Meyer's Department Store for the loss of her purse. Discuss the probable outcome of her suit.

2. Goodman contracts to lease an apartment near the campus from landlord Lopez for one year, with the monthly rent due and payable on the first of each month. At the end of the year, Goodman does not vacate the apartment, and Lopez does not object. Goodman continues to pay

the rent on the first day of the month and it is accepted by Lopez. Six months later, Lopez informs Goodman that the apartment has been leased to Green and that Goodman must vacate the premises by the end of the week. Goodman refuses to leave, and Lopez threatens eviction proceedings. Discuss the rights of the parties under these circumstances.

3. Bill Heise is a janitor for the First Mercantile Department Store. While walking to work, Bill discovers an expensive watch lying on the curb. Later that day, while Bill is cleaning the aisles of the store, he discovers a wallet containing $500 but no identification. Bill turns over the wallet to his superior, Joe Frances. Bill gives the watch to his son Gordon. Two weeks later, Martin Avery, the owner of the watch, discovers that Bill found the watch and demands it back from Gordon. Bill decides now to claim the wallet with its $500, but Joe refuses to turn it over, saying that Bill is not the true owner and that the money is really the property of the store. Discuss who is entitled to the watch and who is entitled to the wallet containing $500.

4. Harold was a wanderer until 22 years ago. At that time, he decided to settle down on a vacant three-acre piece of land, which he did not own. People in the area indicated to him that they had no idea who owned it. Harold built a house on the land, got married, and raised three children while living there. He fenced the land, placed a gate with a sign, "Harold's Homestead," above it, and had trespassers removed. Harold is now confronted by Joe Moonfeld, who has a deed in his name as owner of the property. Moonfeld orders Harold and his family off the property, claiming his own title ownership. Discuss who has best "title" to the property.

5. Lee owns and operates a service station. Walter's car needs some minor repairs. Walter takes his car to Lee's station. Lee tells Walter that he will be unable to do the work until the next day and that Walter can either bring the car back at that time or leave it overnight. Walter leaves the car with Lee. The next afternoon Walter comes to pick up his car. Lee presents Walter with a bill for $220 and refuses to return the car until he has been paid. On inspecting the car, Walter discovers that the mileage indicator shows 150 more miles on the car than when he brought it in. Lee claims that he was allowed by law to let one of his employees road test the car by taking it home and driving it during the previous evening. Applying bailment law, discuss Walter's and Lee's legal rights under these circumstances.

6. The owners of the Seven Palms Motor Inn decided that their motel was in need of renovation. Accordingly, they ordered a large quantity of bedspreads, curtain rods, and drapes from Sears, Roebuck and Company. Thereafter, Seven Palms Motor Inn failed to pay its bill, which amounted to approximately $8,000, including installa-

tion. Under Missouri law, a supplier of fixtures can establish a lien on the land and the building to which the fixtures become attached. Sears sought to establish such a lien to make it easier to recover the debt that Seven Palms owed it. Which, if any, of the above-named items will Sears be able to argue are fixtures? [Sears, Roebuck & Co. v. Seven Palms Motor Inn, Inc., 530 S.W.2d 695 (Mo. 1975)]

7. A mortgage was placed on a parcel of land. Afterward, a grain storage facility was constructed. It consisted of a number of steel structures bolted into concrete slabs that were partially embedded into the ground and that included 50 to 60 feet of underground tubing. Air was electronically pumped through the tubing in order to move grain from the dryer to several storage bins. To remove these structures would take about two weeks. The owner of the facility defaulted on the mortgage, leading the mortgage creditor to file an action to regain the property. The mortgage creditor argued that this facility was a fixture and should remain on the land. Do you agree? Please explain your answer fully. [Metropolitan Life Insurance Co. v. Reeves, 223 Neb. 299, 389 N.W.2d 295 (1986)]

8. Paul was the owner of real estate located in Putnam County, Florida. In 1982, while Paul was living with Lucille, he executed a deed conveying the property to himself and Lucille as joint tenants with right of survivorship. In 1985, Paul and Lucille stopped living together, and three months later Lucille conveyed her interest in the property to her daughter, Sandra. What type of interest does Sandra possess in the property, and why? [Foucart v. Paul, 516 So.2d 1035 (Fla.Dist.Ct.App. 1987)]

9. Danny Smith and his brother discovered a sixteen-foot boat lying beside a roadway in Alabama. Danny Smith informed the police, who immediately impounded the boat and stored it in a city warehouse. Although Smith acquiesced to the police action, he told the police that if the true owner did not claim the boat he wanted it. When the true owner did not come forward, the police department refused to relinquish the boat to Smith and instead told Smith that it planned to auction it to the highest bidder on behalf of the city. Smith sued for custody of the boat. Since Smith never physically held the boat, but rather allowed the police to take possession, should Smith succeed in his claim to title as finder? Could Smith defeat a claim if the true owner sought to retake the boat? [Smith v. Purvis, 474 So.2d 1131 (Ala.Civ.App. 1985)]

10. A bank installed bank vault doors, night depository equipment, drive-up teller window equipment, and remote transaction systems. The City of Lansing taxed these improvements as real property. The bank took the position that it never intended these items to become part of the real estate. Who should win and why? [Michigan National Bank, Lansing v. City of Lansing, 293 N.W.2d 626 (1980)]

UNIT III BUSINESS FORMATION

Chapter 16   Agency and Private Employment Law

Employment gives health, sobriety, and morals. Constant employment and well-paid labor produce, in a country like ours, general prosperity, content, and cheerfulness.

Daniel Webster (1782–1852)

OUTLINE

Introduction

Agency law is important because its rules permeate the entire legal system. Agency law defines the relationship between two parties in which one of them, called the **agent,** agrees to represent or act for the other, called the **principal.** The principal has the right to control the agent's conduct in matters entrusted to the agent.

The actual rules are relatively simple and straightforward, although the application of the rules to a specific problem is not always easy. Both agency law and its counterpart, employment law, have evolved over the centuries, but the basic concepts have not really changed that much. In this chapter we will discuss agency law and the private employment relationship.

Background

The forerunners of agency law were the legal principles developed during Roman times that related to the ownership of slaves. Even in ancient times, an owner was financially liable for the torts of his or her slaves. The reasoning was that, if a person was able to increase his or her wealth through the services of slaves, he or she should be responsible for the slaves' acts.

This concept continued to develop through the Middle Ages. Eventually a body of law governing the relationship of master and servant evolved. A master could be held liable for the servant's acts committed within the **scope of employment**—in other words, within the time and area of the work assignment. A servant could not make contracts on behalf of the master. The normal liability of a master was, therefore, limited to tort law. For example, the master would be held liable if a servant negligently harnessed a carriage and this resulted in damages or injuries to another person. Today the same concept is applied to the employer-employee relationship. Employers are responsible for the harm caused by the torts of their employees who were acting within the scope of their employment.

The Industrial Revolution, which started in the mid 1700s, created the need for many contractual relationships. The owners of new industrial plants had to enter into many contracts at any given time in order to keep the plant operating. The owner had to purchase raw materials in volume from several sources and also had to sell the manufactured products over a wide territory to many people. No longer would the majority of contracts be between the individual who produced an item and another individual who would purchase the item.

People who owned industrial plants began to delegate the responsibility to enter into these contracts to individuals known as agents. By using agents, the owner (or principal) could conduct multiple business operations simultaneously in various locations. In addition, the owner of the industrial plant incurred liability on the contracts made on his or her behalf by the agents. Thus, the concept of agency law developed.

The underlying concept of the employer-employee and principal-agent legal relationship is summarized by a Latin phrase, *qui facit per alium facit per se,* which means "he [or she] who acts through another acts through himself [or herself]. This phrase summarizes the theory that has been the foundation of agency law from Roman times through today: If a person increases business profits through the use of other people, he or she should be liable for the actions of those people.

Formation of the Agency Relationship

Generally, no formalities are required to create an agency. The agency relationship can arise by one of several methods: agreement, ratification, or estoppel.

Agency by Agreement

Agency is a consensual relationship. The agency relationship is based on some affirmative indication that the principal agrees to have the agent act on behalf of the principal and that the agent agrees to act for the principal. Most agency relationships are created in this manner.

Many agency relationships are based on express agreements that are oral. Good business practice, however, dictates that the agreement should be in writing. Because the agency relationship is normally a contractual one, contract rules apply, including the statute of frauds (see Chapter 10). This statute requires certain types of contracts to be in writing if they are to be enforceable in a court. For example, the sale of any interest in real estate must be in writing. Thus, real estate listing agreements between the seller (principal) and the real estate broker (agent) are required to be in writing.

Agency by Ratification

On occasion, a person, who is not in fact an agent or who is acting outside the scope of his or her authority as an agent, may make a contract on behalf of a purported principal. No authority from the principal, either express or implied, is present when the unauthorized contract or act is made. If the principal later approves or affirms that contract by word or by action, an agency relationship is created by **ratification.** Ratification is a question of intent, and intent can be expressed by either words or conduct.

Ratification binds the principal to the agent's acts and treats the agent's acts or contracts as if they had been authorized by the principal from the beginning. Thus, the principal must be aware of all material facts; otherwise, the ratification is not effective. The principal's ratification can be either express or implied from the words or conduct of the principal. The creation of the agency by ratification "relates back" to the time of the unauthorized act. By his or her acceptance, the principal acknowledges all the advantages and disadvantages of this agency and that this contract started at the time of the unauthorized act.

The following case looks at whether silence on the part of a purported principal can be construed as ratification.

BACKGROUND AND FACTS *In 1974, Mrs. Crawford executed a power of attorney naming her daughter, Mrs. Howe, as her agent. Mrs. Howe and her husband operated a dairy farm. Mrs. Crawford took no part in the management of the dairy business and received no benefits from it.*

In 1980, the Howes experienced severe financial difficulties in the operation of their farm, and they needed to refinance their debt. A few days before the new loan closed, Mrs. Howe advised the attorney handling the transaction that she would like to sign the loan instruments as agent for her mother under the 1974 power of attorney so that her mother would not have to come to town for the closing. The attorney examined the power of attorney, approved it, and the loan papers were prepared. Mrs. Howe acted as an agent for Mrs. Crawford in this matter without Mrs. Crawford's knowledge or consent. Mrs. Crawford testified at the trial that she knew nothing about the loan transaction. Mrs. Howe testified that she told her mother something about it sometime, approximately a month after the loan was closed, but her testimony as to what she told her mother was very vague and indefinite.

Mr. and Mrs. Howe were unable to pay the debt and went into bankruptcy. The bank sued Mrs. Crawford to collect the loan, alleging that Mrs. Crawford had ratified the agreement. The trial court entered a judgment for Mrs. Crawford.

Case 16.1
FIRST NATIONAL BANK OF SHREVEPORT v. CRAWFORD
Court of Appeals of Louisiana, 1984.
455 So.2d 1209.

Judge HALL
❖   ❖   ❖   ❖

The bank argues that Mrs. Crawford, by her silence and inaction after being informed of the bank transaction, ratified the action of her agent in executing the note and mortgage, and is bound thereby regardless of the agent's original authority.

The concept of ratification by a principal of an agent's unauthorized acts is recognized in two articles of the Civil Code:

[1] "The attorney can not go beyond the limits of his procuration; whatever he does exceeding his power is null and void with regard to the principal, unless ratified by the latter, and the attorney is alone bound by it in his individual capacity."

[2] "The principal is bound to execute the engagements contracted by the attorney, comformably to the power confided to him.

"For anything further he is not bound, except in so far as he has expressly ratified it."

The applicable principles are well expressed in *Bamber Contractors v. Morrison Engineering*:

"Ratification, in the law of agency, is the adoption by one person of an act done on his behalf by another without authority. Ratification amounts to a substitute for prior authority. The burden of proving ratification is on the party asserting it and to find ratification of an unauthorized act, the facts must indicate a clear and absolute intent to ratify the act, and no intent will be inferred when the alleged ratification can be explained otherwise. Ratification will occur when the principal, knowing of the contract, does not repudiate it but accepts its benefits."

The bank did not prove by a preponderance of the evidence that Mrs. Crawford knew and understood what her agent had done in this case. Mrs. Crawford denied knowing anything about the transaction until this suit was filed. Mrs. Howe's testimony was vague and indefinite as to what she told her mother about the transaction and when she told her. A clear intent to ratify the [loan] * * * cannot be inferred from the facts of this case. Ratification was not established.

DECISION AND REMEDY   *The court of appeal affirmed the trial court's judgment for Mrs. Crawford. Ratification must be proved by the plaintiff; there must be a clear and absolute intent to ratify the unauthorized act. Under these circumstances, where Mrs. Crawford's knowledge of the loan had not been proved, mere silence did not amount to ratification.*

Agency by Estoppel

When a principal leads a third person to believe that another person is her or his agent and the third person deals with the supposed agent, the principal cannot deny the agency relationship. In other words, the principal is not allowed to claim that no agency relationship exists. In these situations, the principal's actions create the appearance of an agency that does not in fact exist.

For example, Kona is in the insurance business and hires McGant as an agent to solicit and sell insurance. Kona advertises to the general public that McGant is his agent. After a period of time, Kona discovers that McGant is keeping some of the premiums paid in cash. Obviously, McGant is dishonest and probably has committed a criminal act. McGant is fired immediately, but he still has the appearance, through the advertisements, of being Kona's agent. If McGant should contract with an innocent third party after he was fired, Kona will be estopped from denying that McGant was Kona's agent. Kona has represented McGant to the public as his agent, and an innocent purchaser has relied on this representation. Kona is, therefore, not allowed to claim a lack of an agency relationship. To avoid possible future liability, Kona might publish notice that McGant is no longer Kona's agent and personally notify all previous customers who dealt with McGant.

Agency Relationships

Three types of agency relationships exist:

1. Principal-agent, including professional agents
2. Employer-employee
3. Employer's or principal's relationship with an independent contractor.

The legal principles developed under either employer-employee law or agency law have similar applications. Moreover, a person can be both an employee and act as a servant or as an agent at the same time. For example, a business may employ a person full time to analyze the real estate market and that person could also have the authority to negotiate the price of and to purchase or sell specific pieces of land. Because these two areas can easily be intertwined, a clear application of separate legal principles is not always possible.

Relationship Between the Principal and Agent

A principal cannot be everywhere to transact his or her own business. The agent acts on behalf of and instead of the principal to negotiate, conduct, and contract business with third persons. The agent has **derivative authority**—that is, he or she derives the authority to carry out the principal's business from the principal and not from his or her own acts. The principal is liable to the third party for the acts of the agent based on that contract.

Say that Staid Corporation, for example, hires Fast Freddy, a booking agent, to negotiate and contract with the Hot Rappers, the latest rap group, for a series of appearances and television commercials endorsing Staid's products. Contracts made by Fast Freddy, the agent, within his authority are binding and legally enforceable by Staid Corporation, the principal. The Hot Rappers, the third party, may also enforce the contract against Staid Corporation. If Fast Freddy had no authority to represent Staid Corporation, he cannot on his own bind Staid to a contract with the Hot Rappers. The authority must come from the principal. A principal cannot be held liable for acts of another unless the principal hires an agent or otherwise satisfies or acts in such a way as to create an agency relationship.

Scope of Agent's Authority A principal's liability in a contract with a third party arises from the authority given the agent to enter legally binding contracts on the principal's behalf. An agent's authority to act stems from one of the following sources:

1. Actual authority
   a. Express (or specific)
   b. Implied
2. Apparent authority.

3, emergency authority

Even if an agent contracts outside the scope of his or her authority, the principal may still be liable by ratifying the contract, as discussed earlier.

Actual Authority An agent who acts on behalf of the principal either by agreement or by oper-

ation of law will have **actual authority.** Actual authority can be either express or implied.

Express authority offers the agent specific instructions on matters germane to the agency. Express authority can be granted orally or in writing. A principal who writes out express instructions that establish the agent's authority is engaging in good business practice. A well-drafted instrument allows both the principal and the agent to be clear about their relationship.

Even in the best instruments giving an agent express authority, however, many of the agent's responsibilities are not covered. These responsibilities are part of the agent's **implied authority.** Often implied authority is conferred by virtue of the customary practices of that particular agency. Implied authority may be inferred from the position the agent occupies. For example, in a department store, the manager of the men's clothing section has the implied authority to discount a shirt that has a spot on it.

Implied authority can also be claimed for an act that is reasonably necessary in order for the agent to carry out what he or she has been expressly authorized to do. For example, Cherri is employed by Dolly's Clothing to manage one of its stores. Dolly's Clothing has not expressly stated Cherri's authority to contract with third persons, but the authority to manage a business implies the authority to do what is reasonably required in order to operate the business. Thus, Cherri's implied authority includes the ability to make contracts with employees, buy merchandise and equipment, and advertise the products sold in the store.

Apparent authority can only come from Principle

Apparent Authority A principal, by either word or action, makes a third party reasonably believe that a particular person has the authority to act on the principal's behalf. If the third party relies on the appearance of authority that the principal has given that person, the person is said to be an agent by **apparent authority.** This agency is based on the principles of estoppel. That is, apparent authority is a substitute for implied authority when the principal has instructed the agent not to perform certain duties. The principal is stopped from saying the person did not have any authority to act on the principal's behalf, even though the agent has no express or implied authority.

Apparent authority is often considered to be *title authority*—that is, the authority exists by virtue of the person's business title—general manager, assistant manager, sales manager, and so on. It also depends on the size and scope of the business. For example, not all radio station managers have the authority to promote other station personnel. In a small station, the owner may retain the right to promote personnel, while in larger stations, the general manager may have that authority.

The following case discusses the creation of an agency relationship based on the concept of apparent authority.

Case 16.2
BILL McCURLEY CHEVROLET, INC. v. RUTZ

Court of Appeals of Washington, 1991. 808 P.2d 1167.

BACKGROUND AND FACTS *On April 14, 1987, McCurley Chevrolet sold a new Camaro to Ms. Rutz. Four days later she was involved in a collision and the automobile was towed back to McCurley Chevrolet. Rutz requested a written estimate for the repairs but was never given one. A written estimate, however, was submitted to the insurance adjuster, who issued a check made payable to both Rutz and McCurley Chevrolet in the amount of $7,114.48. The Camaro was in the shop until June. Rutz was not satisfied with the work and brought the vehicle back numerous times until November. Finally, McCurley Chevrolet brought this action to recover compensation for the work on the Camaro. Rutz, who had kept the insurance check, turned it over to the court. McCurley Chevrolet was awarded $3,657.24. Rutz made this appeal.*

Chief Judge GREEN
*   *   *   *

First, the Rutzes contend McCurley Chevrolet failed to comply with the provisions of the automotive repair act, *   *   * which requires a written estimate of the repair costs be given the customer prior to commencing the work. Consequently, they claim the matter should have been dismissed. We disagree. *   *   *

The Automotive Repair Act is a consumer protection statute designed to foster fair dealing and to eliminate misunderstandings in a trade replete with frequent instances of unscrupulous conduct. *   *   * The act is strictly construed. *   *   * Consequently, in those cases where a repairman provided only an oral estimate, the repairman was precluded from recovering the repair costs.

Here, Ms. Rutz's insurer was provided with a written estimate and the repairs were done with her knowledge and approval. In these circumstances, the question is whether Ms. Rutz's insurer was acting as her agent when it accepted the written estimate, or whether she waived her right to assert a violation of the act. Although this theory was not raised at trial, we may affirm the trial court on any theory which is established by the pleadings and supported by the proof.

A principal may be liable because of the apparent or ostensible authority of its agent. Apparent authority can only be inferred from the acts of the principal, not from the acts of the agent, and there must be evidence the principal had knowledge of the agent's acts. *   *   * Apparent authority exists when, although authority is not actually granted, "the principal knowingly permits the agent to perform certain acts, or where he holds him out as possessing certain authority." *   *   * Even if an agent acts without the principal's authority, the principal may nevertheless ratify the agent's act by acting with full knowledge of the act, accepting the benefits of the act or intentionally assuming the obligation imposed without inquiry. *   *   *

Although the question of an agency relationship is generally one of fact, when the facts are not disputed and susceptible of only one interpretation, the relationship becomes a question of law. *   *   * Here, the undisputed facts reflect Ms. Rutz and her father permitted the work to be undertaken without objection and regularly visited McCurley Chevrolet to check on the progress of the repairs. Additionally, Ms. Rutz accepted the insurance check without objecting to the written estimate. McCurley Chevrolet had no reason to believe Ms. Rutz had any objection to the

Legal Highlight

Whose Agent Are You, Anyway?

Television advertisements for insurance may leave you with the impression that the insurance agent is your (the customer's) agent. Legally this is not true. The agent represents the insurance company, not you. The company is the principal, and the insurance agent is an agent of the insurance company, not your agent. The agent is paid by the insurance company, not by you.

The same is true of travel agents. The travel agent is selling a travel package to you, the third party, on behalf of his or her principal, such as a hotel or airlines. The travel agent represents and is paid by the hotel or airline, not by you. If you have a travel agent make reservations at a hotel and something goes wrong and if, as you are standing at the counter, the clerk tells you that "your travel agent" made a mistake, you might gently inform the clerk that the travel agent is the hotel's agent, not yours. As the principal, the hotel is responsible for the acts of its agent.

estimate and, in fact, was told by her that she was going to endorse the check. Thus, we conclude in the context of the facts presented here the insurance carrier was the agent for Ms. Rutz as a matter of law and its acceptance of the written estimate complied with the act.

The court found that the insurance adjuster was an agent of Rutz. This decision was primarily based upon the apparent authority of the adjuster as the agent of Rutz, the principal. The court indicated that the principles of ratification were also applicable to this factual situation.

DECISION AND REMEDY

Professional Agents A **professional agent** is in a business that handles contracts in a particular field. Professional agents are often licensed by the state government to represent principals in contracts in those fields. Examples of professional agents are insurance agents, real estate brokers, travel agents, attorneys, and entertainment agents.

For example, real estate brokers are licensed to represent a person who wants to sell his or her real estate. The real estate broker, then, is the professional agent; the "real estate agent" is actually a subagent of the real estate broker and cannot represent anyone except through his or her employer, the real estate broker. You must learn the lines of authority in a particular business in order to determine what each person is authorized to do.

Relationship Between the Employer and Employee

The law defines an employee as one employed by the employer to perform services; the employee's conduct is controlled by the employer. Agency law also applies to the employer-employee relationship. The rules governing the employer-employee relationship arose out of the impact of the Industrial Revolution and, more recently, social legislation. We examine the impact of social legislation in Chapters 21 and 22.

The employer-employee relationship is included in this chapter because frequently an employee is also an agent for his or her employer-principal. For example, Ruby is employed by a large department store as a clerk in the jewelry section. When she is stocking or straightening inventory, she is a servant. When Ruby sells a bracelet, she is an agent who is contracting with a customer on behalf of her employer, who is also the principal. In both cases, she is an employee. On the other hand, a person employed as an electrician in the department store is strictly a servant and does not have any authority to transact business on behalf of the employer. The employer is liable, however, for any torts that the electrician commits on the job.

Preemployment Practices

In Chapter 13 we discussed credit reports and procedures to correct erroneous information that might be in a credit file. A credit report is a major tool on which businesses rely when considering hiring a new employee. Employers believe that how a person handles his or her personal finances indicates how honest and dependable he or she is. When a person is having serious financial problems, he or she may be more likely to take advantage of the employment situation and abscond with cash, inventory, or trade secrets. Employers believe this even though no studies have ever shown that this belief is justified.

Some credit firms specialize in providing relevant information. Stores Protective Association (SPA) assists many of the large retailers. It maintains records based on both its subscribers' information and public records. A record is kept of all persons who are terminated for dishonesty by a subscriber. A copy of any written confession signed by the employee is preserved. If no written confession exists, the event causing the termination must be videotaped or witnessed by at least two individuals. Any convictions obtained from public records for felonies or criminal misdemeanors are placed in an individual's file. SPA keeps the records for seven years, the maximum time allowed under the federal Fair Credit Reporting Act.

Persons must keep a good credit rating and not be involved in any criminal behavior. Information to the contrary can easily stop a career.

Independent Contractors

An **independent contractor** is not an employee but may be an agent. A person who hires an independent contractor is said to have "employed" the independent contractor. Thus, when the term *employment* is used in connection with an independent contractor, it is not used in the legal context of employer-employee. The employer of an independent contractor does not have control over all the details of the performance of the independent contractor. Because the employer does not control the independent contractor, the employer is not normally responsible for the torts of the independent contractor.

Restatement, Second, Agency, Section 2, defines an independent contractor as:

> * * * a person who contracts with another to do something for him but who is not controlled by the other nor subject to the other's right to control with respect to his physical conduct in the performance of the undertaking. He may or may not be an agent.

The courts review many elements to determine whether a relationship is one of employer-employee or of employer and independent contractor. Some factors considered by the courts are:

1. The extent of control exercised by the employer over the details of the work
2. The type of job, business, or occupation involved and the amount of skill required to perform the job
3. Who supplies the tools or equipment
4. The length of employment
5. The method of payment
6. The tax return filed by both parties.

The construction industry is a good example of an employer-independent contractor relationship. Say that an owner of raw land wants to build an office building. She or he hires a general contractor who is responsible for building the office complex. The general contractor in turn hires subcontractors, such as electrical subcontractors or plumbing subcontractors, who are responsible for specific portions of the building. The general contractor is an independent contractor, and the property owner does not control the acts of this professional. The property owner does not have any contractual relationship with the subcontractors

Exhibit 16–1 **Legal Relationships in Agency Law**

TYPES OF LEGAL RELATIONSHIPS	DEFINITIONS
Principal-Agent	An agent acts on behalf of, and instead of, the principal, and uses a certain degree of his or her own discretion.
Employer-Employee	An employee's (servant's) physical conduct is controlled or subject to control by an employer. An employee can also be an agent.
Principal– or Employer– Independent Contractor	The contractor is not an employee and the employer, or principal, has no control over the details of physical performance. Except for professional agencies, the contractor is usually not an agent.

who are hired by the general contractor, and thus the owner is not responsible for the acts of the subcontractors. Today there is a whole area of the law governing the construction industry, but these general concepts are still applicable.

If the property owner in this example hires a real estate broker to negotiate a sale of the property, the owner not only has contracted with an independent contractor (the real estate broker) but also has established an agency relationship for the specific purpose of finding a third party who will enter into a contract to purchase the property.

A person retaining the services of an independent contractor is normally not responsible for its tortious acts because of the lack of control over the independent contractor. An employer is responsible for the acts of an independent contractor, however, if the independent contractor is per-

forming one of the employer's duties, as established by law. For example, a department store cannot avoid its liability if it has hired an independent security agency to supply security and a security officer makes an illegal arrest for shoplifting. The store, along with the security agency, is liable for the victim. An employer is also liable for acts of independent contractors if the activity involves ultrahazardous conduct, such as handling explosives.

Exhibit 16–1 summarizes the types of agency relationships recognized by law. Throughout the rest of this chapter, we will use the terms *principal* and *agent* to include the terms *employer* and *employee*, unless otherwise stated.

The following case discusses the employer-employee relationship versus the relationship between an employer and an independent contractor.

BACKGROUND AND FACTS *Robert Bartholomew, the plaintiff, was injured on October 30, 1984, while working on an offshore production platform on the outer continental shelf off the Louisiana coast. He was employed by Booker Drilling Company. Booker was working as an independent contractor for the defendant, CNG Producing Company (CNG), which owned the platform.*

CNG reserved the right to inspect the work being performed. Bartholomew and others were putting pipe in the well hole when he slipped because of a wet and muddy floor. The fall resulted in serious injuries. The district court awarded a $325,000 judgment for Bartholomew against CNG.

Case 16.3
BARTHOLOMEW v. CNG PRODUCING CO.
United States Court of Appeals,
Fifth Circuit, 1987.
832 F.2d 326.

Judge JOHNSON
* * * *

The Bartholomews brought this negligence suit against CNG, asserting that CNG was negligent (1) in ordering Bartholomew's employer, Booker, to engage in an unsafe work practice and (2) in contracting with Booker for an inadequate number of floor hands to operate the equipment safely. In defense, CNG argues that as a principal which exercised no operational control over its independent contractor, Booker, CNG was insulated from liability in this case. Because we find that some evidence exists to support a finding by the jury that CNG expressly authorized an unsafe work practice on the platform, we reject CNG's arguments and affirm the district court's judgment without addressing the claim that CNG was negligent in failing to contract for adequate personnel.

It is well established that a principal is not liable for the activities of an independent contractor committed in the course of performing its duties under the contract. However, two notable exceptions exist to this general rule. First, a principal may not escape liability arising out of ultrahazardous activities which are contracted out to an independent contractor. Second, and of importance to the instant case, a principal is liable for the acts of an independent contractor if he exercises operational control over those acts or expressly or impliedly authorizes an unsafe practice.

Where an available safe method, which includes the taking of adequate precautions, will render it at least ordinarily safe, and the work is done in an unsafe manner, the employer will be liable if he has expressly or impliedly authorized the particular manner which will render the work unsafe, and not otherwise.

*   *   *   *

Bartholomew testified at trial that the company man, J. T. Madison, expressly told the driller, Perry Gill, not to wash the rig floor until after the operation was completed. Bartholomew also testified that the driller was fearful for his job. As a floor hand, Bartholomew took his orders directly from the driller. Bartholomew's testimony was not directly contradicted by any of CNG's witnesses. In fact, the Booker tool pusher testified that he had heard of some company men ordering the driller to speed up the operations and not to wash down the rig. Emmett Farrar, the other company man for CNG, who was independently employed, testified that he did not know whether or not Madison had ever issued such an order to the driller. Thus, the question was one of Bartholomew's credibility. The jury was entitled to make that credibility determination and did so. On the record before us, we conclude that some evidence supported a finding by the jury that CNG, through its representative on the rig, J. T. Madison, expressly authorized the unsafe practice of failing to wash down the rig floor which eventually caused Bartholomew's accident.

It is submitted by CNG that because Madison possibly gave him [an] order not to wash down the floor two days prior to the accident, CNG was not exercising operational control at the time of the accident and therefore was not liable. Without determining who the company man was at the time of the accident, we conclude that whether Madison was on duty at the time of the accident or whether he gave the order two days prior to the accident is not dispositive. An employee does not stop obeying his employer's orders merely because the employer is no longer present. It is not unrealistic to expect the driller, as well as the floor hands, to continue to conduct operations without washing down the floor, in light of Madison's previous order to do so. Since there was some evidence to support a finding by the jury that CNG expressly authorized an unsafe work practice, we affirm the district court's judgment.

DECISION AND REMEDY

The decision of the district court was affirmed. The court of appeals concluded that some evidence existed to support the trial court's judgment that CNG had expressly authorized unsafe practices by telling the driller not to wash down the rigging floor until after operations were completed. The principal (CNG, the employer of Booker, the independent contractor) is liable for damages sustained by an employee (Bartholomew) of the independent contractor when the principal-employer expressly authorizes unsafe working conditions.

Duties of Agents and Principals

Once the principal-agent relationship has been created, both parties have duties that govern their conduct. The principal-agent relationship is **fiduciary**—that is, it is one based on trust. In it, each party owes the other the duty to act with the utmost good faith. Neither party may keep from the other information that has any bearing on their agency relationship.

The Agent's Duty to the Principal

The duties that an agent owes to a principal are set out in the agency agreement or arise by operation of law. The duties are also implied from the agency relationship itself and exist between the principal and the agent whether or not the identity of the principal is disclosed to a third party. Generally, the agent owes the principal the following five duties: performance, notification, loyalty, obedience, and accounting.

The Duty of Performance   An implied condition in every agency contract is the agent's agreement to use reasonable diligence and skill in performing the work. When an agent fails to perform the work in this manner, liability for breach of contract will occur. In addition, the principal may be liable to a third party for any negligent act of the agent that occurs within the context of the contract.

For example, a principal hires a real estate broker to sell her house. A potential buyer asks how many square feet the house has. The real estate broker negligently answers 2,700 square feet because he is too lazy to look up the precise footage and he thinks he is good at guessing. When the buyer finds out that the actual amount is 2,500 square feet, the principal is liable for the agent's negligent conduct because it is within the context of the contract. Of course, the agent is in turn liable to the principal if the buyer successfully collects money for damages against the principal.

The degree of skill or care required of an agent is usually that expected of a reasonable person under similar circumstances. Although this standard is usually interpreted to mean "ordinary care," if an agent has presented herself or himself as possessing special skills (such as those of an accountant or an attorney), the agent is expected to exercise the skill claimed. Even if the agent is not paid, she or he must exercise the same degree of skill or care as a paid agent. Failure to do so constitutes a breach of the agent's duty. When an agent performs carelessly or negligently, the agent can also be liable in tort.

The Duty of Notification   A maxim in agency law is that "all the agent knows, the principal knows." This refers to the duty of notification. The agent is required to notify the principal of all matters that come to his or her attention concerning the subject matter of the agency and is within the scope of the agency. The common law has adopted the **legal fiction** that knowledge to the agent is the same as knowledge to the principal. A legal fiction is an assumption in law; regardless of what actually happened, the law treats this assumption as if it had occurred. Thus, even if the agent has not told the principal something he or she should have, the law will assume that the principal knew what the agent knew and will hold the principal liable. The agent is liable to the principal for failing to fulfill the duty of notification.

The Duty of Loyalty   Loyalty is one of the most fundamental duties in a fiduciary relationship. Basically stated, the agent has the duty to act solely for the benefit of his or her principal and not in the interest of the agent or a third party. Under common law, this fiduciary duty is owed only in one direction: from the agent to the principal. For example, International Business Machines (IBM) has the right to appoint two sales agents to the same territory—unless IBM has specifically contracted with one agent for an exclusive territory. On the other hand, the IBM sales agent does not have the right to represent more than one computer manufacturer.

Numerous obligations result from this duty. First, the agent has a duty not to represent two principals in the same transaction unless both principals know of the dual capacity and consent to it. For example, a real estate broker cannot represent both the seller and the buyer in the sale of a house. After all, the seller wants to sell at the highest price, and the buyer wants to buy at the lowest price. The real estate broker's commission is a percentage based on the sale price and is paid out of the proceeds due the seller; thus, ordinarily it is the seller who lists the house with a real estate broker.

Often a buyer also seeks the assistance of a real estate broker, however. Although the buyer may at first believe that this broker is representing him or her, in fact it is the seller who pays the broker's commission. In most states, the ethical code of the state real estate association requires that the broker inform the buyer of this conflict. Once both the buyer and the seller have full knowledge of the role of the real estate broker, they can authorize him or her to proceed with the representation.

Another concept states that an agent cannot have any dealings with himself or herself that involve his or her principal. An agent employed by a principal to purchase property cannot buy that property for himself or herself and then turn around and sell the property to the principal.

On the other hand, an agent employed to sell property cannot purchase the property without the principal's consent. In short, the agent's loyalty must be undivided. The agent's actions must be strictly for the benefit of the principal and must not result in any secret profit for the agent.

The Duty of Obedience   When an agent is acting on behalf of the principal, the agent has a duty to obey all lawful and clearly stated instructions of the principal. The agent violates this duty whenever he or she deviates from those instructions. If the circumstances merit it—for example, during emergency situations when the principal cannot be consulted—the agent may deviate from such instructions without violating this duty. Whenever instructions are not clearly stated, the agent can fulfill the duty of obedience by acting in good faith and in a reasonable manner under the circumstances.

The Duty of Accounting   The agent has a duty to the principal to keep and make available an accounting of all property and money received and paid out on behalf of the principal. The principal is entitled to receive all gifts from third persons collected by the agent. For example, an airline gives the agent a gift for qualifying as a frequent flyer. The agent accumulated the mileage while traveling on business for the principal. The gift received by the agent belongs to the principal.

Commingling of personal and agency funds is not allowed. The agent has a duty to maintain separate accounts, one for her or his own personal funds and another for the principal's funds. Whenever a licensed professional, such as an at-

torney, real estate broker, or insurance agent, violates the duty to account, she or he may be subject to disciplinary proceedings by the appropriate regulatory institution. These proceedings are in addition to the agent's liability to the principal for failure to account.

Principal's Duties to the Agent

The principal's duties to the agent are compensation, reimbursement and indemnification, cooperation, and safe working conditions. These duties may be set out in a contract or the duties may be implied by law.

The Duty of Compensation   The principal must pay for his or her agent's services unless it is a **gratuitous agency** relationship. Such a relationship occurs when the agent performs services without any compensation. Even though the agent may not be paid, she or he still owes the principal the duties of care and loyalty as discussed in the previous section.

The principal and agent must agree to compensate the agent for her or his services before the agent is entitled to remuneration. When the amount of compensation is agreed on by the parties, the principal owes the duty to compensate the agent on completion of the specified activities. If no amount is agreed on, the principal owes the agent the customary compensation for such services. For example, in the auction of horses, the auctioneer normally takes 10 percent commission. If no amount is established either by custom or by law, the principal owes the agent the reasonable value of her or his services.

The Duty of Reimbursement and Indemnification   When an agent enters into a contract with a third party to purchase something, it is the principal who has the ultimate duty to pay the third party, not the agent. The principal may use one of several methods to pay the third party. The principal may arrange with the third party to pay her or him directly, the principal may advance the funds to the agent to pay the third party, or the agent may pay the third party out of his or her own pocket. In the last case, the principal then has the duty to reimburse the agent for expenses that the agent has incurred while performing his or her job for the principal. Thus, if an agent pays for other necessary expenses in the course of reasonable performance of agency duties, the principal has the duty to reimburse the agent.

The principal has an overlapping duty to indemnify the agent for any losses that the agent suffers while performing her or his duties for the principal. For example, if the agent loses money while performing a contract, the principal must compensate the agent for those losses.

Agents cannot recover for expenses or losses incurred by their own misconduct or negligence. For example, if an agent has the principal's money on hand to pay a bill on time but negligently fails to pay it, the late penalty must be paid by the agent, and the principal does not have a duty to reimburse the agent.

The Duty of Cooperation A principal has a duty both to cooperate with and to assist an agent in performing his or her duties. The principal must do nothing to prevent such performance. For example, a seller hires a real estate broker to sell a house. The broker finds a buyer who is willing, able, and ready to buy the house. The seller-principal must cooperate with the agent, must sign the papers in a timely manner, and must not do anything that would cause the buyer not to proceed with the purchase.

The Duty to Provide Safe Working Conditions The common law requires the principal to provide safe premises, equipment, and conditions for all agents and employees. The principal has a duty to inspect working conditions and to warn agents and employees about any unsafe areas. If the agent is also an employee (as in the case of a department store clerk, for example), the employer's liability is frequently covered by workers' compensation insurance, which is the primary remedy for an employee's injury on the job.

Liability of Principals and Agents to Third Parties

Once the principal-agent relationship is created, attention often focuses on the rights of third persons who deal with the agent. Both the agent and the principal may become liable to a third person based either on contract or tort law.

Principal's and Agent's Liability for Contracts

Principals are classified as disclosed, partially disclosed, or undisclosed. A **disclosed principal** is a principal whose identity is known by the third party at the time the contract is made by the agent. A **partially disclosed principal** is a principal whose identity is not known by the third party, but the third party knows that the agent is acting for a principal at the time the contract is made. An **undisclosed principal** is a principal whose identity is totally unknown by the third party, and the third party has no knowledge that the agent is acting in an agency capacity at the time the contract is made.

Liability of Disclosed Principals If an agent acts within the scope of her or his authority, a disclosed principal is liable to a third party for a contract made by the agent. In these situations, an agent has no contractual liability for the nonperformance of the principal or of the third party.

Liability of Partially Disclosed or Undisclosed Principals In most states, if the principal is partially disclosed, the principal and agent are both treated as parties to the contract, and the third party can hold either liable if the contract is not performed.

The third party is deemed to be dealing directly with the agent personally if neither the fact of agency nor the identity of the principal is disclosed. Thus, for an undisclosed principal, the agent is liable as a party on the contract.

For example, Walt Disney Company decides to build another amusement park. Research shows that, in a specific prime tourist area, the needs for the new park will be met if Disney can purchase five parcels of land. Disney, however, knows that if word gets out that it plans to purchase land, the price of the land will be higher. Disney hires five different agents to make the five different land purchases. Naturally, Disney is the undisclosed principal. The five agents make the respective purchases over the period of a year. Each agent has purchased the land in his or her own name, and the sellers have relied on the respective agent's credit and reputation and not on that of Disney.

On the other hand, since each agent has acted within the scope of his or her authority, the undisclosed principal, Disney, is fully bound to perform just as if it had been fully disclosed to each seller at the time the purchase contract was made. Moreover, Disney, even though an undisclosed principal, can enforce the contract against each seller.

Warranties of the Agent

Occasionally the agent will lack authority for an action or will exceed the scope of her or his authority. When this situation occurs, the agent, not the principal, is liable to the third party. The agent's liability to the third party is based on a breach of **implied warranty of authority**, not on breach of the contract itself.

The agent can breach the implied warranty of authority by committing an intentional breach of the warranty or by a good-faith mistake. The agent is liable if the third party relied on the agent's status. On the other hand, when the third party knows at the time the contract is made that the agent is mistaken or if the agent indicates to the third party uncertainty about the extent of his or her authority, the agent is not personally liable for breach of warranty. In these situations, the third party knew something was amiss and should have checked further about the agent's authority.

Tort Liability

An agent or employee is always liable for his or her own torts and crimes. A principal or employer also becomes liable for the negligent torts of the person hired if the torts are committed within the scope of the agency or the scope of employment. This liability is known as the doctrine of *respondeat superior*.

The principal or employer is rarely liable in common law for the intentional torts of the employed person. In some states, however, a statute may exist that places liability on the employer or principal. In the following discussion, most references will be made to the employer-employee context, but the same rules apply to the principal-agent relationship. Three areas will be examined: negligence and the doctrine of *respondeat superior*, misrepresentation, and strict liability.

Negligence and the Doctrine of *Respondeat Superior* The theory of liability based on the **doctrine of *respondeat superior*** imposes strict liability on the employer. Liability is imposed without regard to the personal fault of the employer for negligent torts committed by an employee in the course of employment. For example, an employee works for a construction company and part of his or her job is to drive the company pickup truck from one job site to another. One day the employee has a traffic accident by negligently turning left in front of an oncoming automobile. The employee is liable because he or she was negligent, but the company is also liable under the doctrine of *respondeat superior*.

Also, an employer who knows or should know that an employee has a propensity for committing tortious acts is liable for the employee's acts even if they would not ordinarily be considered within the scope of employment.

When an employee goes on a frolic of his or her own—that is, departs from the employer's business to take care of personal affairs—is the employer liable? It depends. If the employee's activity is a substantial departure akin to an utter abandonment of the employer's business, the employer is not liable.

For example, Clint, a traveling salesperson, is driving his employer's automobile to call on a customer for a possible sales order. On the way to the customer's place of business, Clint deviates one block from his usual route to mail a letter at the post office. As Clint approaches the post office, Clint negligently runs into a parked vehicle owned by Doug. Clint's departure from the employer's business to take care of a personal affair is not substantial. Clint is still within the scope of his employment, and his employer is liable to Doug.

If Clint decided to pick up a few friends for cocktails in another city and in the process negligently ran the vehicle into Doug, Doug normally could not hold Clint's employer liable; only Clint would be liable in this case.

The court considers the following general factors in determining whether an agent's particular tort occurred within the course or scope of employment:

1. Was the act authorized by the employer?
2. What was the time, place, and purpose of the act?
3. Was the act one commonly performed by employees on behalf of their employers?

4. What was the extent to which the employer's interest was advanced by the act?
5. What was the extent to which the private interests of the employee were involved?
6. Did the employer furnish the means or instrumentality (for example, a truck or a machine) that caused the injury?
7. Did the employer have reason to know that the employee would do the act in question, and had the employee ever done it before?
8. Did the act involve the commission of a serious crime?

The following case involves problems of defining the scope of employment.

Case 16.4
CLOVER v. SNOWBIRD SKI RESORT
Supreme Court of Utah, 1991.
808 P.2d 1037.

BACKGROUND AND FACTS *Zulliger was employed by Snowbird as a chef at the Plaza Restaurant located at the base of the ski resort. The Mid–Gad Restaurant was located halfway to the top of the mountain. Zulliger's father was head chef at both restaurants. Zulliger was instructed by his father to make periodic trips to the Mid–Gad to monitor its operations. Prior to the accident, Zulliger had made several inspection trips to the Mid–Gad. On one occasion, he was paid for the trip.*

Snowbird preferred that their employees knew how to ski because it made it easier for them to get to and from work. As part of Zulliger's compensation, he received season ski passes. On the date of the accident, Zulliger was asked to inspect the operation of the Mid–Gad prior to beginning work at the Plaza at 3 P.M. Zulliger stopped at the Mid–Gad in the middle of his first run down the mountain. At the restaurant he inspected the kitchen, talked to the personnel for twenty minutes, and ate a snack. He skied four runs before heading down the mountain to begin work. On his final run, Zulliger decided to jump off a crest on the side of an intermediate run, a jump he had taken many times before. From this jump, a skier will become airborne because of the steep drop-off. It is impossible for skiers above the crest to see skiers below the crest. The jump was well known to Snowbird. Snowbird ski patrol often instructed people not to jump off the crest, and a sign was posted instructing skiers to ski slowly at this point in the run. Zulliger ignored the sign and skied over the crest at a significant speed. Clover, who had just entered the same ski run from a point below the crest, was in his path. As Zulliger went over the jump, he collided with Clover, who was hit on the head and severely·injured. Clover brought claims against Zulliger and Snowbird. The trial court, in a summary judgment, dismissed the claims against Snowbird by finding that as a matter of law Zulliger was not acting within the scope of his employment at the time of the collision.

Chief Justice HALL
*   *   *   *

Under the doctrine of respondeat superior, employers are held vicariously liable for the torts their employees commit when the employees are acting within the scope of their employment. Clover's respondeat superior claim was dismissed on the ground that as a matter of law, Zulliger's actions at the time of the accident were not within the scope of his employment. In a recent case, *Birkner v. Salt Lake County*, this court addressed the issue of what types of acts fall within the scope of employment. In *Birkner*, we stated that acts within the scope of employment are " 'those acts which are so closely connected with what the servant is employed to do, and so fairly and reasonably incidental to it, that they may be regarded as methods, even though quite improper ones, of carrying out the ob-

jectives of the employment.' " The question of whether an employee is acting within the scope of employment is a question of fact. * * * In *Birkner*, we observed that the Utah cases that have addressed issues of whether an employee's actions, as a matter of law, are within or without the scope of employment have focused on three criteria. First, an employee's conduct must be of the general kind the employee is employed to perform. * * * Second, the employee's conduct must occur substantially within the hours and ordinary spatial boundaries of the employment. Third, the employee's conduct must be motivated at least in part, by the purpose of serving the employer's interest. Under specific factual situations, such as when the employee's conduct serves a dual purpose or when the employee takes a personal detour in the course of carrying out his employer's directions, this court has occasionally used variations of this approach. These variations, however, are not departures from the criteria advanced in *Birkner*. Rather, they are methods of applying the criteria in specific factual situations. * * * The difficulty, of course, arises from the fact that Zulliger did not return to the Plaza after he finished inspecting the facilities at the Mid–Gad. Rather, he skied four more runs and rode the lift to the top of the mountain before he began his return to the base. Snowbird claims that this fact shows that Zulliger's primary purpose for skiing on the day of the accident was for his own pleasure and that therefore, as a matter of law, he was not acting within the scope of his employment. In support of this proposition, Snowbird cites *Whitehead v. Variable Annuity Life Insurance. Whitehead* concerned the dual purpose doctrine. Under this doctrine, if an employee's actions are motivated by the dual purpose of benefiting the employer and serving some personal interest, the actions will usually be considered within the scope of employment. However, if the primary motivation for the activity is personal, even though there may be some transaction of business or performance of duty merely incidental or adjunctive thereto, the [person] should not be deemed to be in the scope of his employment. In situations where the scope of employment issue concerns an employee's trip, a useful test in determining if the transaction of business is purely incidental to a personal motive is whether the trip is one which would have required the employer to send another employee over the same route or to perform the same function if the trip had not been made.
* * * *

The instant case is distinguishable from *Whitehead* in that the activity of inspecting the Mid–Gad necessitates travel to the restaurant. Furthermore, there is evidence that the manager of both the Mid–Gad and the Plaza wanted an employee to inspect the restaurant and report back by 3 P.M. If Zulliger had not inspected the restaurant, it would have been necessary to send a second employee to accomplish the same purpose. Furthermore, the second employee would have most likely used the ski lifts and ski runs in traveling to and from the restaurant.
* * * *

Under the circumstances of the instant case, it is entirely possible for a jury to reasonably believe that at the time of the accident, Zulliger had resumed his employment and that Zulliger's deviation was not substantial enough to constitute a total abandonment of employment.

DECISION AND REMEDY *The court found that it was for a jury to decide whether Zulliger was within the scope of his employment. His actions were not, as a matter of law, outside the scope of his employment with Snowbird. Clover will have her day in court.*

Misrepresentation Whenever a third person sustains losses because of the agent's misrepresen-

tation, the principal is exposed to tort liability. The key to a principal's liability is whether the agent was actually or apparently authorized to make representations and whether such representations were made within the scope of the agency.

When a principal has placed an agent in a position to defraud a third party, the principal is liable for the agent's fraudulent acts. For example, Harmon is a loan officer for State Employees Credit Union. In the ordinary course of her job, Harmon approves and services loans and has access to the credit records of all customers. Harmon calls Lopez, a member of the credit union who has an outstanding loan. Harmon falsely represents to Lopez that the credit union believes that Lopez is about to default on his loan and will call in the loan (meaning that Lopez must pay the loan in full) unless he provides additional collateral such as stocks and bonds. Lopez gives Harmon numerous stock certificates that Harmon keeps in her own possession. She later uses them to make personal investments, and she loses money on all these investments. The credit union is liable to Lopez for losses sustained on the stocks, even though the credit union had no direct role or knowledge of the fraudulent scheme.

The principal (the credit union) placed the agent (Harmon) in a position that conveys to third persons (such as Lopez) the impression that Harmon had the authority to make statements and perform acts consistent with the ordinary duties of the position. When an agent appears to be acting within the scope of the authority that the position of agency confers but is actually taking advantage of a third party, the principal who placed the agent in that position is liable. For example, if a security guard had told Lopez that the credit union required additional security for a loan, Lopez would not be justified in relying on that person's authority to make that representation. Lopez could reasonably expect, however, that the loan officer was telling the truth.

Intentional Torts   The employer may be liable for intentional torts of the employee committed within the scope of employment. In this area, the employer's liability is very limited. For example, an employer may be liable in some states for an employee's intentional torts, such as assault and battery or false imprisonment, committed while acting within the time and work space of his or her employment and while he or she is trying to further the employer's business.

For example, Duffy's Tavern employs Vicious Vic as a bouncer, knowing that he has a history of arrests for assault and battery. While he is working one night within the scope of his employment, he viciously attacks a patron who "looks at him funny." Duffy's Tavern will bear the responsibility for Vicious Vic's assault and battery because it knew he had a propensity for committing such acts and because he committed this tort during the normal course of his job.

Termination of the Agency Relationship

An agency can be terminated either by an act of the parties or by operation of law. Once the relationship between the principal and agent has ended, the agent no longer has the right to bind the principal. The principal must notify third persons when the agency has been ended in order to stop an agent's apparent authority.

Termination by Act of the Parties

Often the agency agreement sets out the time period during which the agency relationship will exist. The agency ends when that time expires. If no definite time is stated, the agency continues for a reasonable time and can be terminated at will by either party. A reasonable time depends on the circumstances and the nature of the agency relationship.

An agent can be employed to accomplish a particular objective, such as the purchase of a computer system for a business. In this case, the agency relationship automatically ends after the computer system has been purchased.

Parties can cancel (rescind) a contract by mutually agreeing to terminate the contractual relationship. For example, Leslie no longer wants Cisco to be her agent, and Cisco does not want to work for Leslie any longer. Either Leslie or Cisco can communicate with the other the intent to end the relationship. Agreement to terminate the agency relationship effectively relieves each party of the rights, duties, and powers inherent in the relationship.

Termination by Operation of Law

The general rule is that death or insanity of either the principal or the agent automatically and immediately terminates the ordinary agency relationship. Knowledge of the death is not required. For example, Cassie sends Marcia to Mexico to purchase a rare coin. Before Marcia makes the purchase, Cassie dies. Marcia's status as an agent ends at the moment of death, even though Marcia does not know that Cassie has died.

An exception to this rule applies to banks. UCC 4-405 allows banks to honor checks up to ten days after the death of their customers. A bank cannot honor payment of notes or drafts after death, however.

When the specific subject matter of an agency is destroyed or lost, the agency terminates. For example, Priscilla employs Mark to sell her house. Prior to any sale, the house is destroyed by a hurricane. Mark's agency and authority to sell Priscilla's house are both ended. In addition, when it is impossible for the agent to perform the agency's responsibilities lawfully because of war or because of a change in the law, the agency is terminated.

When an event occurs that has such an unusual effect on the subject matter of the agency that the agent can reasonably infer that the principal will not want the agency to continue, the agency terminates. Priscilla hires Aaron to sell a tract of land for $1 million. Subsequently, Aaron learns that the soil is contaminated with toxic substances, and the land is now worth $50,000. The agency and Aaron's authority to sell the land for $1 million are both terminated.

Notice Required for Termination

When an agency terminates by operation of law because of death, insanity, or some other unforeseen circumstance, no duty exists to notify third persons. If, however, the parties themselves have terminated the agency, the principal has the duty to inform any third parties who knew of the existence of the agency that it has been terminated.

The principal is expected to notify directly any third person whom the principal knows has dealt with the agent. For third persons who have heard about the agency but have not dealt with the agent, constructive notice is sufficient. In other words, a notice should be published in a newspaper within the general area or in commercial journals for technical employees, stating that the agent is no longer employed by the principal. Until notice is

given, the agent retains apparent authority for a reasonable length of time.

Regulation of the Employer-Employee Relationship

Many statutory provisions adopted at both the federal and the state levels control the employer-employee relationship. A body of common law, however, also exists that has direct application to this relationship.

Employment Contracts

Employer-employee relationships are generally created by a contract. The contract basically gives the employer the right to control the employee's conduct, workplace, work habits, and the benefits enjoyed within the scope of the employee's employment.

An employment contract is a mutual agreement between the employer and the employee. Basic contract rules apply. The parties can include any contract terms they desire, as long as these terms are not in violation of a statute or against public policy. For example, a contract today for an hourly wage of $1.00 is in violation of the minimum wage rate set by the Fair Labor Standards Act and is illegal.

In some employment contracts, an employee agrees that, should she or he ever leave her or his employment for whatever reason, she or he will not accept employment with a competitor. This clause in the employment contract is called a *covenant not to compete*. If the scope of the prohibition is reasonable in geographic area and duration, the covenant is generally enforceable.

Modern View on Termination of Employees

If termination of the employment breaches the employment contract, the employee can seek damages, but most employment situations are created without a written employment contract and are called "employment at will." In this case, a person can be terminated at any time and has no course of action against the employer.

This situation has led to abuses by employers. In some states, specific statutes have been passed to protect an employee from an arbitrary termination after she or he has been employed for a specified period of time. Specific grounds must be set out before a person can be fired.

Other states without statutory provisions have attempted through the courts to create certain rights for employees. For example, an employee manual given to all employees has been interpreted to be the employment contract in the absence of a contract. If an employer establishes certain procedures in the manual, these procedures must be followed before an employee can be fired, or the employer will be held liable for breach of contract.

Many states recognize that in every employment contract there is an implied covenant of good faith and fair dealing. The courts find this covenant even in states that recognize the doctrine of employment at will. In other words, the law requires a business to treat its employees fairly.

An employer cannot terminate an employee for failing to follow instructions that would force the employee to break the law. In the following case, the court grants damages for termination of employment because the plaintiff refused to break the law.

BACKGROUND AND FACTS *Wagenseller was employed by the Scottsdale Memorial Hospital from March 1975 until November 1979. Her supervisor was Kay Smith. She was promoted over the years and received very favorable comments from Smith in her reviews until May 1979.*

In May, both Smith and Wagenseller joined a group of personnel from other hospitals for an eight-day camping and rafting trip down the Colorado River. Smith and others during the trip engaged in public urination, heavy drinking, "grouping up" with other rafters, staging a parody of the song "Moon River" that concluded with members of the group "mooning" the audience, and other similar activities. The "Moon River" skit was allegedly performed twice at the hospital after the trip. Wagenseller refused to participate in any of these activities. After the trip, the relationship between Wagenseller and Smith deteriorated, and finally Wagenseller was terminated. Wagenseller was an at-will employee.

The trial court entered a summary judgment in favor of the hospital. The appellate court affirmed in part and reversed in part that decision. Wagenseller then appealed to the Arizona Supreme Court.

Case 16.5
WAGENSELLER v. SCOTTSDALE MEMORIAL HOSPITAL
Arizona Supreme Court, 1985.
147 Ariz. 370, 710 P.2d 1025.

Justice FELDMAN
* * * The issues we address are:
1. Is an employer's right to terminate an at-will employee limited by any rules which, if breached, give rise to a cause of action for wrongful termination?
2. If "public policy" or some other doctrine does form the basis for such an action, how is it determined?
3. Did the trial court err * * * when it determined as a matter of law that the terms of Scottsdale Memorial Hospital's personnel policy manual were not part of the employment contract?
* * * * *

As early as 1562, the English common law presumed that an employment contract containing an annual salary provision or computation was for a one-year term. Originally designed for the protection of seasonal farm workers, the English rule expanded over the years to protect factory workers as well. Workers were well protected under this rule, for the one-year presumption was not easy to overcome. English courts held an employer liable for breaching the employment contract if he terminated an employee at any time during the year without "reasonable cause to do so." To uphold an employer's discharge of an employee without a showing of "good cause," the courts required a clear expression of a contrary intent as evidenced either on the face of the contract or by a clearly defined custom of the industry.

In the early nineteenth century, American courts borrowed the English rule. The legal rationale embodied in the rule was consistent with the nature of the predominant master-servant employment relationship at the time because it reflected the master's duty to make provision for the general well-being of his servants. In addition, the master was under a duty to employ the servant for a term, either a specified or implied time of service, and could not terminate him strictly at will. The late nineteenth century, however, brought the Industrial Revolution; with it came the decline of the master-servant relationship and the rise of the more impersonal employer-employee relationship. In apparent response to the economic changes sweeping the country, American courts abandoned the English rule and adopted the employment-at-will doctrine. This new doctrine gave the employer freedom to terminate an at-will employee for any reason, good or bad.

   *   *   *   *

The trend has been to modify the at-will rule by creating exceptions to its operation. Three general exceptions have developed. The most widely accepted approach is the "public policy" exception, which permits recovery upon a finding that the employer's conduct undermined some important public policy. The second exception, based on contract, requires proof of an implied-in-fact promise of employment for a specific duration, as found in the circumstances surrounding the employment relationship, including assurances of job security in company personnel manuals or memoranda. Under the third approach, courts have found in the employment contract an implied-in-law covenant of "good faith and fair dealing" and have held employers liable in both contract and tort for breach of that covenant.   *   *   *

*   *   *   *

We therefore adopt the public policy exception to the at-will termination rule. We hold that an employer may fire for good cause or for no cause. He may not fire for bad cause—that which violates public policy. *   *   *

*   *   *   *

In the case before us, Wagenseller refused to participate in activities which arguably would have violated our indecent exposure statute. She claims that she was fired because of this refusal. *   *   *

While this statute may not embody a policy which "strikes at the heart of a citizen's social right, duties and responsibilities" as clearly and forcefully as a statute prohibiting perjury, we believe that it was enacted to preserve and protect the commonly recognized sense of public privacy and decency. The statute does, therefore, recognize bodily privacy as a "citizen's social right." *   *   *

*   * Arizona is among the jurisdictions that have recognized the implied-in-fact contract term as an exception to the at-will rule. In *Leikvold v. Valley View Community Hospital*, * * * this court held that a personnel manual can become part of an employment contract and remanded the cause for a jury determination as to whether the particular manual given to Leikvold had become part of her employment contract with Valley View.

*   *   *   *

*   * Employers are certainly free to issue no personnel manual at all or to issue a personnel manual that clearly and conspicuously tells their employees that the manual is not part of the employment contract and that their jobs are terminable at the will of the employer with or without reason. Such actions, either not issuing a personnel manual or issuing one with clear language of limitation,

instill no reasonable expectations of job security and do not give employees any reason to rely on representations in the manual. However, if an employer does choose to issue a policy statement, in a manual or otherwise, and, by its language or by the employer's actions, encourages reliance thereon, the employer cannot be free to only selectively abide by it. Having announced a policy, the employer may not treat it as illusory.

The Arizona Supreme Court adopted the "public policy" exception to the at-will termination rule. The court found that Scottsdale Memorial Hospital possibly had illegally terminated the plaintiff because she refused to participate in conduct that would have been a violation of law. Because of this possibility, Wagenseller was entitled to a jury trial in which she could try to show that her termination was caused by her refusal to perform some act contrary to public policy. An issue also existed as to whether the employee manual could form the basis of an employment contract when there is no other written contract. The court held that she had a right to have this issue tried before a jury.

DECISION AND REMEDY

Government Regulation of Employment Law

Employment law today has many aspects that are controlled by government regulation. Federal and state laws govern the relationship between management and labor. Discrimination on the basis of sex, race, national origin, religious beliefs, and other invidious classifications are forbidden by statutes. We examine the government's role in employment law in Chapters 21 and 22.

Ethical Considerations

Employee Leasing

A fast-growing business is supplying workers to large businesses on a contract basis. A person may work at a Motorola or at a Ford plant but be hired and paid by a company that is in the business of leasing employees to major companies.

Profits are the driving force behind this arrangement. A large organization can obtain bids from several companies to supply certain types of personnel. Generally, the employment company does not have any retirement, medical insurance, or other type of benefits. Businesses that hire the leased employee do not include these leased employees in their benefit package, nor do they have to pay unemployment insurance, workers'

compensation insurance, or social security insurance. Although these last costs are paid by the employment company, the workers can be hired for less money because no benefits are paid. Leasing employees is also a method of avoiding unions and collective bargaining.

Is the employment of leased workers, who may work for years at the same company and at the same job, ethical? Is the avoidance of a federal right granted to employees, the right to organize, ethical? Most people plan for their retirement income by relying on the company's pension plan and social security. Is the avoidance of paying benefits, such as pension plans and medical coverage, ethical?

International Considerations

Decision Making By Employees

American companies operate in a fairly free environment concerning employee relations. Employees rarely are on boards of directors or have input into the business decision-making process. Other countries, especially European countries and Japan, have a different attitude toward employees.

In other industrialized countries, a distinctive management style exists. Often a two-tiered board of directors governs the corporation. One level supervises the day-to-day activities, while the other deals with long-range planning. There is a requirement for substantial employee representation on the supervisory board of directors. Both boards of directors must agree to the layoff of employees.

American companies that invest in overseas businesses must adhere to the host countries' traditional and legal procedures affecting the rights of employees. Knowledge of those arrangements is essential to doing business overseas.

FACING A LEGAL ISSUE

Do You Have to Pull the Trigger?

You are hired at Lucky Lasso, Inc., a restaurant with a western theme, to work as a waiter. The hours are long and the pay is minimal. The restaurant is not attracting enough customers. Your boss and the owner of the restaurant decide to obtain more visibility by using a huge advertising balloon and having their employees present a show that requires the use of guns. Assume both of these actions are illegal under state and local law: The use of guns in public is a felony, and the use of the balloon constitutes an advertising sign in violation of the local zoning laws.

At first, you and your coworkers decide not to participate in the show, but you are informed that any employee who refuses to take part will be fired. You need the job, so you agree to participate. During one show, live ammunition is used accidentally instead of the usual blanks. A spectator is shot. He falls over and knocks a candle off the table, igniting a bale of hay and causing a fire that destroys the restaurant and the building next door. The local newspapers and television news programs decide to emphasize the show and accident. The police arrest all employees who were onstage during the show for assault with a deadly weapon.

Because of the publicity, the restaurant prospers. Your employer retains a lawyer for all of the employees, but you are all found guilty of a reduced charge. Having never been arrested before, you do not want a repeat conviction on your record. You decide not to take part in future performances and are fired. Shortly afterward, you are sued by the spectator with a civil complaint for his injuries, which add up to $150,000 in medical and hospital bills and $300,000 for pain and suffering. You are also sued by the owner of the destroyed building for damages in the amount of $250,000.

These facts are ones with which an employee could be confronted. An employer can create a situation where the employee is required to commit a crime for which, if apprehended, he or she could be prosecuted and found guilty. In addition, the employee can be held liable in a civil lawsuit. Following your employer's directions is not a legal defense in criminal or civil lawsuits, and it does not matter whether you were instructed to violate the law in the manner described in this example or whether you were asked to violate the antitrust laws, to pay off corrupt officials, or to commit any other crime. Similarly, you are liable for civil damages as a result of your own torts whether your employer also is liable or not.

In this case, because the injuries and damages were caused by a gun, you would probably be liable under strict liability rules. In other words, you would be held liable if you were the one who pulled the trigger, despite the fact that you did not intend to harm anyone. Liability insurance would not be applicable because the use of guns and other ultrahazardous activities are normally excluded from coverage.

Based on the facts in this case and the case of *Wagenseller v. Scottsdale Memorial Hospital*, you may have a valid claim for future wages because of your illegal termination. Even though you were an at-will employee, the modern trend is to allow recovery when an employee relationship is terminated because the employee refused to follow instructions that would constitute violations of the state law.

Summary

This chapter emphasizes the private relationship of the employment sphere. This body of law has its origins in the legal principles concerning the ownership of slaves. During the Middle Ages, the principles were expanded to cover the master-servant relationship. With the Industrial Revolution, the law developed the concepts of principal and agent. The distinction between master-servant and principal-agent is that a servant does not enter into contracts on behalf of his or her employer while an agent does enter into contracts on behalf of his or her principal. Basically, the same rules apply whether it is a master-servant or principal-agent relationship.

The concept underlying these relationships is summarized by this phrase: "He [or she] who acts through another acts through himself [or herself]." The theory is that, if a company increases its business through the use of employees, the company should be responsible for the acts of those employees. The company, however, should not be liable if it cannot control the acts of an individual, unless the company has a legal duty to ensure such control. The general rule is that a company is not liable for acts of independent contractors unless the company has delegated one of its own legal duties to that contractor.

An agency relationship can be created by agreement, by ratification, or by estoppel. The most common means is by agreement. Ratification occurs when an agent who has no authority acts in the name of a principal or when an agent exceeds his or her limited authority, and the principal lets the action stand. Apparent authority applies when an agent is terminated but continues to act for the former principal.

The agent owes certain duties to the principal. The agent must not act in a negligent manner, must notify the principal of important facts, owes a high degree of loyalty and obedience, and must account to the principal for all property that is in the control of the agent. The principal owes a duty to compensate the agent, to reimburse the agent for expenditures incurred in the performance of the agency, to cooperate with the agent, and to provide safe working conditions.

Both the principal and agent can be held liable to third persons. An agent has either express or apparent authority. A principal is liable for any torts or contract concluded within this authority. An agent is normally not responsible for contracts unless she or he has exceeded the authority granted or is acting for a partially disclosed or an undisclosed principal. An agent is always responsible for her or his own torts, even if the principal is also liable under the doctrine of *respondeat superior*.

An agency relationship may be terminated when the date stated in the employment contract is reached, when the purpose is achieved, by mutual agreement or whenever either party decides to terminate, by death or insanity of either party, by impossibility or illegality, and by bankruptcy of the principal. On termination, notice should be given to anyone dealing with the agency, and a notice of termination should be published to inform anyone who has never dealt with the agency.

Most employment involves employment at will. Historically, an employer could terminate an employee for any reason. This doctrine has changed. The law now gives employees some rights; in particular, a person cannot fire an employee for refusing to violate the law.

Key Terms

actual authority (401)	express authority (401)	partially disclosed
agency law (398)	fiduciary (407)	principal (409)
agent (398)	gratuitous agency (408)	principal (398)
apparent authority (401)	implied authority (401)	professional agent (403)
derivative authority (401)	implied warranty of	ratification (399)
disclosed principal (409)	authority (410)	scope of employment (398)
doctrine of *respondeat*	independent contractor (404)	undisclosed principal (409)
superior (410)	legal fiction (407)	

Questions and Case Problems

1. Roy makes deliveries for a local pizza restaurant. Roy drives the company car with the restaurant's telephone number printed on the side. One day, after a delivery but while still on duty, Roy picks up three of his friends who

need a ride into the next town. Figuring that the restaurant is so busy that he won't be missed, he agrees to take them. While in the next town, Roy accidentally backs into Mr. Phillip's truck, putting a small dent in the truck's bumper. Because it is such a small dent and because Roy needs to get back to work, he leaves without writing a note to the truck's owner. When he arrives back at work, Tony, the owner of the restaurant, is waiting for him. Mr. Phillips had been watching his truck from a window in his apartment; he saw the accident and the telephone number on the side of the car. When he called the telephone number, he reached Tony. Who is responsible for the cost of fixing Mr. Phillip's bumper? Discuss fully.

2. Able is hired by Peters as a traveling salesperson. Able not only solicits orders but also delivers the goods and collects payments from his customers. Able places all payments in his private checking account and at the end of each month withdraws sufficient cash from his bank to cover the payments made. Peters is totally unaware of this procedure. Because of a slowdown in the economy, Peters tells all his salespeople to offer 20 percent discounts on orders. Able solicits orders, but he offers only 15 percent discounts, pocketing the extra 5 percent paid by customers. Able has not lost any orders by this practice, and he is rated one of Peters's top salespeople. Peters now learns of Able's actions. Discuss fully Peters's rights in this matter.

3. Mark is a pilot for the Big Canyon Tour Company. He flies passengers into the canyon to photograph the view. Over the past few years, he has been honored with all but one of Big Canyon's employee awards for outstanding service. The state legislature has passed a law that prohibits all aircraft from flying below the rim of the canyon. Wayne, the owner of Big Canyon Tour Company, has told all the pilots to ignore the new law because the quality of the view available without flying below the rim of the canyon is poor. Mark has refused to break this law even though he has been threatened with losing his job if he does not follow company orders. Mark, an at-will employee, is fired. Is Mark entitled to damages of any kind? Discuss fully.

4. Anne is an agent for Fish Galore, Inc. She has express authority to solicit orders and receive payments in advance of shipment. She is well known as an agent in the region. Seafood Quality has been a regular customer of hers for five years, has usually made large orders, and has always paid Anne in advance to get the discount offered by Fish Galore. Fish Galore learns that Anne has incurred large gambling debts and has recently used some of the customers' payments to pay off these debts. When Anne cannot reimburse Fish Galore, she is fired. Fish Galore hires a new agent and publishes in the regional newspapers that the new agent will be covering the territory. Desperately in need of cash, Anne solicits a large order from Seafood Quality and receives payment. Then she calls on a new customer, Catfish Heaven, who also gives Anne an order and payment. Anne absconds with the money. Fish Galore refuses to honor either order. Seafood Quality and Catfish Heaven claim Fish Galore is in breach of contract. Discuss fully their claims.

5. Douglas was hired as an agent by Aztec Petroleum. He was to receive $5,000 along with a royalty. Aztec sent Douglas a $5,000 payment in advance and two checks in the total amount of $124,180 to pay for oil leases. Douglas obtained most of the leases. He spent the rest of the money on two cars, a boat, and personal expenses. He sent Aztec a photocopy of each check but altered the payee to indicate that a lessor had received the money that he had spent on himself. During the final accounting, Douglas sent bogus receipts to show that other checks sent by Aztec had been paid to the lessors. Aztec discovered Douglas's spending spree and refused to pay the royalty. Douglas sued Aztec. Aztec counterclaimed and was awarded by the trial court $107,000 in actual damages and $100,000 in punitive damages. Douglas appealed. Who prevails on appeal and why? [Douglas v. Aztec Petroleum Corp., 695 S.W.2d 312 (1985)]

6. Sargent, a former bank auditor, was fired for refusing to destroy or alter a report to the audit committee of Central Bank. Several statutes existed that prohibited the acts that his superiors had allegedly urged him to commit. Sargent brought an action to recover for wrongful discharge. Who prevails and why? [Sargent v. Central National Bank & Trust Co., 809 P.2d 1298 (Okl. 1991)]

7. During the course of the administration of the estate of Baldwin M. Baldwin, it became necessary to sell a vast apartment complex owned by the estate, known as Baldwin Hills Village. Lemby, a real estate broker doing business as Skyline Realty, was commissioned to make the sale. A number of prospective purchasers were contacted, and they were present at the private sale of Baldwin Hills Village. On a number of prior occasions, Lemby had indicated to the executors of Baldwin's estate that he was interested in purchasing the property. At the private sale, Lemby outbid all others and bought Baldwin Hills Village. Lemby then sought his commission on the sale from the Baldwin estate. Will anything in agency law prevent Lemby from recovering? Discuss fully. [In re Estate of Baldwin, 34 Cal.App.3d 596, 110 Cal.Rptr. 189 (1973)]

8. Hohenberg Brothers was a Memphis-based cotton merchandiser, and Killebrew was a Mississippi cotton farmer. Both parties were represented by D. T. Syle, Jr., a cotton agent. In February 1973, Killebrew signed and delivered to Syle a one-page purchase and sales agreement form covering the sale of Killebrew's 1973 cotton crop. All of the blanks in this document were completed, except for the name and signature of the purchaser, who was still unknown. On March 2, Syle secured an oral commitment that Hohenberg would purchase Killebrew's crop at the prices set forth in the one-page contract. Hohenberg

immediately sent Syle its standard three-page purchase and sales agreement, the terms of which were identical to Killebrew's one-page document. Syle signed Killebrew's name and returned it to Hohenberg. Has Syle acted beyond the scope of his agency in signing Killebrew's name? Discuss fully. [Hohenberg Brothers Co. v. Killebrew, 505 F.2d 643 (5th Cir. 1974)]

9. Alaska Mack Trucks of Fairbanks is a dealer and franchisee of Mack, Inc., of Allentown, Pennsylvania. As part of the franchise agreement, Mack allowed Alaska Mack to use the name "Mack"; Alaska Mack was listed in the telephone directory under the heading "MACK TRUCKS"; the Mack bulldog was displayed on the Alaska Mack building; and the Mack logo was on Alaska Mack's posters, printed Mack brochures, and promotional materials. Further, a distributorship agreement existed between Alaska Mack and Mack, Inc.; Mack provided training for the distributorship's employees; Mack engaged in national advertising programs and in joint advertising with the distributor; and Mack established sales quotas and required reports as to the use of the vehicles sold.

The city of Delta Junction, Alaska, entered into a contract with Alaska Mack Trucks for a fire truck. The truck was modified by Alaska Mack to carry a 5,000-gallon tank on it. After delivery, the truck exceeded the specifications for total gross weight, and it was dangerous to drive. The city brought action against Alaska Mack and Mack, Inc. Did Alaska Mack have apparent authority to act as an agent for Mack, Inc., and did the act of modifying the truck exceed the possible limits of any apparent authority? Discuss fully. [City of Delta Junction v. Mack Trucks, Inc., 670 P.2d 1128 (Alaska 1983)]

Chapter 17　Business Enterprises: Sole Proprietorships and Partnerships

It is a socialist idea that making profits is a vice. I consider the real vice is making losses.

Sir Winston Churchill (1874–1965)

OUTLINE

Introduction

Many people consider owning a business at some point in their lives. A common belief is that, when people are in business for themselves, they set their own hours, are their own boss, and make a comfortable living. Although this belief has some validity, the sad truth is that most small businesses fail.

Many reasons exist for the large number of failures among small businesses. They include lack of planning, of financing, of effective marketing strategies, of good management structures, and of consideration of the legal issues. If a business employs fewer than twenty employees, there is almost a 91 percent chance of failure in the first ten years.

This chapter will examine three different forms of businesses: **sole proprietorships, partnerships,** and **limited partnerships.** This chapter also includes a discussion of the Bulk Sales Act.

A sole proprietorship is a business owned by one person. A partnership is a business that is run for profit in which two or more people have an undivided (and sometimes unequal) ownership interest. In a limited partnership two or more people own the business, and at least one person, called the **general partner,** has unlimited liability, while the **limited partner** has limited liability. This type of business entity is often used as an investment vehicle and for tax benefits.

Comparing Business Enterprises

Knowing the different forms of business entities can help you make the proper decisions when starting a business. The four entities most often considered are a sole proprietorship, a general partnership, a limited partnership, and a corporation. A corporation is by far the most complex of any business entity. Corporations are discussed in detail in Chapter 18.

In deciding which form to adopt, you should take into consideration the following factors, among many others:

- Difficulty of forming the organization
- Liability
- Tax considerations
- Continuity of existence and ability to transfer ownership

- Management and control
- Financing and licenses
- Location

Each of these factors has legal as well as business ramifications. Decisions on each of these issues help determine which business form best suits the needs of the owners, since each type of business organization has its own advantages and disadvantages.

Difficulty of Forming the Organization

Some business organizations are easier to create than others. A sole proprietorship is the easiest because a person merely starts doing business. The person may have to obtain a business license from the city or county before starting, but no legal formalities are demanded by the state. If the person is going to use a business name other than his or her own, he or she may be required to make a **fictitious name filing**. This consists of filing with the state a simple form that gives the proprietor's real name and address and the name under which business will be conducted. This notifies the public that a particular person is participating in this business.

A general partnership is similarly easy to form. Two or more people simply conduct a business for profit. A person may even be in a partnership without realizing it. Again, besides obtaining a business license or filing for the use of a fictitious name, no legal formalities are required. All states, however, have legal requirements that must be met before a limited partnership or a corporation can do business. Although a limited partnership is created initially by agreement, to form a limited partnership the parties must execute a certificate of limited partnership, and the certificate must be filed in the appropriate state office (in most states with the secretary of state).

Liability

A businessperson may be financially liable to a variety of people, such as customers, guests on the property, and at times even trespassers. Financial liability may stem from a negligent act of the businessperson, such as failure to keep the business premises free of hazards, or from a product liability case (discussed in Chapter 11). Sole proprietors and general partners have unlimited liability. This means that, if the sole proprietor or partnership (or partner) is successfully sued, the person who has obtained a judgment may seek to have the judgment paid out of the assets of the business *and* out of the personal assets of the sole proprietor or general partner.

Personal liability is limited in the case of a limited partner or an owner of a corporation. A limited partner, for example, is liable generally to the extent of his or her investment in the limited partnership. With a corporation, the owners are the shareholders, and their liability generally is limited to their investment in the shares.

Tax Considerations

The federal and state tax laws must be considered in deciding on a type of business organization, and the income tax law is usually the most important. No tax advantages are available to a business operated as a sole proprietorship. Because it is not a legal entity separate from the owner, it does not file any tax returns. The sole proprietor reports and pays taxes on the income earned.

Partnerships and limited partnerships are not subject to income tax. Each must file with the government an informational return. The income or deductions are passed from the partnership to the individual partner, who is subject to income tax laws.

A corporation is taxed as an entity on its income. In addition, stockholders who are paid dividends are subject to individual income tax laws. Depending on the current tax laws and the amount of income involved, the income tax rates for individuals may be higher or lower than the tax rates for corporations (called C corporations in the federal tax laws). Federal tax laws currently allow corporations that meet specific guidelines to qualify for various tax breaks. Called S corporations, they are discussed in more detail in Chapter 18. Some states have more favorable tax laws for businesses than other states.

Continuity of Existence and Ability to Transfer Ownership

A sole proprietorship usually exists as long as the owner is able to work. Once the person becomes incapacitated or dies, the business ends, and any

sale of the business normally takes place only after a probate case has been opened in court. Even if the person is alive and well, the business may be hard to sell for any number of reasons, including whether there is a market for this type of business. Often only the assets of the business are salable. If the sale includes inventory, the Bulk Sales Act provisions of the Uniform Commercial Code discussed later in this chapter must be followed.

A partnership is dissolved whenever a new partner is added or a current partner dies or otherwise leaves the business. Although the partnership is technically dissolved, the business may continue under the new partnership formed by the change in personnel. Selling a partnership interest may be difficult, again depending on the market. The same holds true for a limited partnership.

Corporate ownership is usually sold by the selling of the owner's shares of stock. If a corporation's shares are listed on a major stock exchange, the transfer of the shares is relatively easy because a structured market exists. For a corporation that does not have its shares sold on a stock exchange, selling the stock may be difficult or nearly impossible. In this situation, people are often willing to buy the physical assets of the corporation but not an ownership interest in the corporation. A purchaser may be reluctant to buy an ownership interest because of an outstanding liability that the corporation may have. For example, an employee is at fault in an accident with a company automobile in January 1993. The corporation is sold in July 1993. A lawsuit is filed against the corporation in December 1993. The corporation is found liable in an amount that bankrupts it. If the person had purchased only the corporation's assets, he or she would not be liable for the harm caused by the automobile accident.

Management and Control

A sole proprietor has total management and control over his or her business. With a general partnership arrangement, in absence of agreement, each partner has as much management and control as the other partners. Thus, each partner has one vote in management matters regardless of the proportionate size of his or her interest in the partnership. This can lead to major problems if the partners do not agree on the same business strategy. In a limited partnership, the general partners have the responsibility of management and control.

In a corporation, the shareholders elect a board of directors, who in turn hire officers to manage the activities of the corporation. Therefore the shareholders, through the election of the board of directors, control and manage the corporation.

Financing

A sole proprietor obtains loans based on her or his personal worth, which includes the assets of the business. The same may be true of general partnerships unless the partnership has a lengthy business record; then the loans may be made on the strength of the partnership's assets and business abilities, rather than on the creditworthiness of the individual partners. Since a limited partner's liability is generally limited to his or her capital investment in the partnership, loans are made more on the basis of the value of the limited partnership assets.

Corporations raise money by selling shares. A corporation may also obtain loans based on the strength of its assets and business record. A lending institution, however, that is dealing with a new corporation or one with few shareholders may require the individual shareholders or officers to be personally liable for the corporate loans in case the corporation fails. For example, a ten-year-old corporation is owned by a family. The bank may require each shareholder to guarantee personally the corporation's $15 million operating line of credit.

Licenses

A businessperson must consider which licenses are needed in order to conduct business. Almost all states require some type of sales or use tax license, since a business is required to collect taxes to be remitted to the state from its customers. In addition, many businesses are subject to specific regulations. For example, licenses are required for insurance agents, real estate brokers, contractors, exterminators, sellers of regulated products such as alcohol, guns, or explosives, and operators of such businesses as pawnshops, funeral homes, nursing homes, day-care centers, and food preparation businesses. Most regulated businesses must obtain a specific license.

The importance of having a license cannot be overemphasized, especially when the purpose of the licensing statute is to regulate and not to raise revenues. Any contract entered into by an unlicensed individual whose business is required to have a license may be void if the purpose of the statute is to regulate the business or profession. In addition, if an individual should conduct business without a license under these circumstances, it may result in criminal prosecution and civil liability, including the inability to collect amounts owed on contracts that the business has completed.

The following case reviews the reasons why a license is required and what happens when a person fails to obtain one.

Case 17.1
GROSS v. BAYSHORE LAND CO.
Supreme Court of Alaska, 1985.
710 P.2d 1007.

BACKGROUND AND FACTS   *Bayshore was a corporation in the business of subdividing land and selling lots, primarily to builders. Gross was a self-employed general contractor in the business of building houses. Gross had used the name Creative Builders, Inc., for many years.*

Gross entered into a contract with Bayshore Land Company to purchase nine lots. Part of the contract required Gross to construct houses on them. Gross did not hold a contractor's license at the time of entering into the contract, but had held one prior to that time. Bayshore required payment of one-half of the money down, with the other half being due once the homes were completed and sold. Gross obtained a loan commitment from the Alaska Bank of Commerce in order to purchase the lots, on the condition that the bank would have a first lien on the property and Bayshore would have a second lien interest.

Bayshore refused to be a second lien holder. It sent a letter to Gross canceling the Gross contract prior to the closing of the nine lots—that is, before the title to the nine lots was put in Gross's name. Gross filed a lawsuit against Bayshore for breach of contract. Among other defenses that Bayshore used, it claimed that Gross had failed to comply with the Alaskan registration requirements and that therefore the contract was void.

The trial court found for Bayshore on other grounds. Gross appealed to the state supreme court. There, Bayshore argued that, even if Bayshore were not correct in any of its other arguments, Gross was barred from filing a lawsuit since he had failed to comply with Alaska's Construction Contractors Registration Act.

Justice BURKE

*   *   *   *

A person acting in the capacity of a contractor who is unregistered at the time of contracting is barred from bringing an action in state court for breach of contract. A critical issue in this case is whether the trial court erred in holding *   *   * that registration as a contractor was not required.

*   *   *   *

A contractor who has not registered at all, not filed the required surety bond, nor obtained insurance has not substantially complied with the registration requirements of [the statute]. The burden of compliance is solely the responsibility of the unlicensed contractor.

*   *   *   *

Gross has not substantially complied with the construction contractor's registration requirements because Gross' failure to register at all prevented the public from ascertaining his status. In fact, state records available to the public at the time of the contract's formation would have shown that Gross had not been registered since 1978, and that Creative Builders was involuntarily dissolved in September 1980. Gross' registration did not lapse for a short period. *   *   * On the contrary, Gross has not been registered since 1978. Two months before signing the contract, Gross filed and then withdrew his application for registration. Consequently, he was well aware of his non-registered status at the time of contract formation.

*   *   *

*   *   * The purchase agreement is a contract for which registration is required. Bayshore is within the class the legislature intended to protect under the contractor's licensing act. Gross was therefore required to register as a contractor. Gross did not substantially comply with the registration requirements because he did not afford the public or Bayshore the same protection which strict compliance would offer.

DECISION AND REMEDY

The trial court's judgment was affirmed. The purchase agreement was a contract for which registration was required. Bayshore was within the class of businesses that the legislature intended to protect under the contractor's licensing act. Gross was, therefore, required to register as a contractor before he could bring a lawsuit.

COMMENT

In most states, a person must have a contractor's license to construct residential homes. The lack of a license may result in the contractor not being able to bring a lawsuit for any breach of contract committed by others.

Location

The location of the new business is an important decision regardless of the form you adopt. There are numerous legal restrictions that may determine your choice of location. When reviewing a prospective location, an owner should consider the visibility of the business, including signs that promote it. Many local ordinances control the size, location, and type of signs that can be used. The owner must make certain that the zoning regulations allow his or her type of business, along with the appropriate signs, to be established in a particular location. Obtaining **use permits** and/or **variances** from local governmental bodies may be required. A use permit grants permission to operate a given type of business, while a variance allows an exception to the zoning laws. Chapter 15 discussed other legal issues concerning property that are relevant to businesses.

Partnerships

All but two states have officially adopted the major provisions of the **Uniform Partnership Act** (UPA). If a partnership agreement exists, but is silent on certain matters, the UPA supplies the missing provisions. Most sections of the UPA have no application when the partners have made provisions in the agreement addressing that particular area.

A general partnership is defined as "an association of two or more persons to carry on as co-owners a business for profit" [UPA Section 6]. A partnership agreement is a contract. Although most partnerships are formed pursuant to a partnership agreement among the parties, a partnership may also arise as a result of the conduct of the parties. A sharing of profits from a business, for example, raises a presumption of a partnership [UPA Section 7(4)]. In addition, if the conduct of the parties leads third parties to believe that a partnership exists, a partnership may be found to exist legally. This is known as a **partnership by estoppel** [UPA Section 16].

No law requires a partnership agreement to be in writing. If two or more people decide to operate a business as co-owners for profit, that is all that is required in order for a court to find that a partnership exists. Even though it is not legally required, a written document should be prepared whenever the partnership form of business organization is used. Partners are in a very close relationship that it not unlike a marriage; both relationships are based on trust, confidence, and mutual reliance. Misunderstandings, frustrating situations, and disagreements are bound to occur. Through a written partnership agreement, many of these problems can be resolved before they have a chance to escalate.

The statute of frauds (discussed in Chapter 10) requires the agreement to be in writing if the partnership is to last more than one year. Without a written agreement, the partnership is at will, which means that it can be dissolved by a partner at any time.

A partnership is treated as a legal entity for certain purposes. For example, partnership property can be held and transferred in the partnership name [UPA Section 8]. In most situations, the partnership is treated as an "aggregate" of individuals. Thus, property can be held and transferred in the name of an individual partner [UPA Section 10], partners can individually be sued [UPA Section 15], and partners have unlimited individual liability.

Capital Requirements and Funding of a Partnership

A partnership is generally funded through the capital contributions of each partner. The partnership may also be able to obtain credit and loans based on the creditworthiness of all of the partners, plus the creditworthiness of the business itself. In addition, the partners may make loans to the partnership.

Partnership Management and Control

Each partner has an equal right to manage and control the partnership [UPA Section 18(e)] and to use partnership property for an appropriate purpose [UPA Section 25(2)(a)]. These rights can be altered by an agreement among the partners. Each partner is an agent for the partnership and for every other partner [UPA Section 9]. Thus, each partner is in a fiduciary relationship with the other partners, and this relationship imposes a responsibility on each partner to act in good faith for the benefit of the partnership and to consider the mutual welfare of all partners in partnership activities. For

Legal Highlight

The Uniform Partnership Act of 1914

The National Conference of Commissioners on Uniform State Laws (NCC) first discussed the desirability of a uniform act on partnership law in 1902 at their annual meeting. The Committee on Commercial Law was instructed at that time to oversee the preparation of a draft on partnership law, and during the following decade a number of drafts were prepared.

A major problem for the drafters of the act was determining which theory of partnership should be employed. Under common law, the partnership was interpreted as an *aggregate* of individuals associated in business—this was the theory commonly used in most of the states. An alternate theory regarded the partnership as an *entity*. In order to make the best determination, the committee invited to a 1910 conference in Philadelphia "all the teachers of, and writers on, partnerships, besides several other lawyers known to have made a special study of the subject"—a meeting that, needless to say, would be inconceivable today! At the conclusion of this meeting, the assembled experts recommended

that the act be based on the aggregate, or common-law, theory. Thus, the committee requested that the partnership act be drafted on this basis.

At the 1914 meeting of the NCC, the eighth and final draft of the act was reported to the conference, which passed a resolution recommending the act for adoption by the legislatures of all the states. After a decade of drafting and deliberation, the Uniform Partnership Act (UPA) became a reality.

The UPA contains 45 sections and is divided into seven parts. Its laws are applied by the courts whenever a partner or a partnership is involved in a dispute in an area not covered by the express agreement of the partners. All of the law affecting partnerships is not contained in the UPA; it therefore provides that the law of agency and the law of estoppel be followed where applicable, and it further states that, in situations not covered by the act, common law and equity will govern.

The first state to adopt the UPA was Pennsylvania, in 1914; other states followed, and today all of the states except Georgia and Louisiana have adopted the UPA.

---

example, unless an agreement states otherwise, a partner cannot engage in outside activities that involve the partnership's time.

The partners are not generally entitled to compensation for their management of the partnership's business [UPA Section 18(f)]. The profit of the business is their compensation. In the absence of an agreement, profits are shared equally and losses are shared in the same proportion as profits, or, if an agreement exists, they are shared in the proportion that this agreement sets out [UPA Section 18(a)]. The amount of capital contributions by the partners has no application in the sharing of profits and losses unless a contrary agreement has been made.

Although the partners may agree to delegate day-to-day management responsibilities to one or more of the partners, generally each partner has one vote in management matters regardless of his

or her capital contribution, and a majority vote is usually required for such partnership decisions [UPA Section 18(b)]. The unanimous consent of all the partners, however, is required in matters significantly altering the nature of the partnership business or property. Other actions requiring the consent of all of the partners include an act by a partner that makes it impossible to carry on the business of the partnership in the usual way; the disposition of the goodwill of the business; and the submission of a partnership dispute to arbitration [UPA Section 9(3)].

Any act of any partner that apparently carries on the business of the partnership in the usual way binds the partnership to that act. This principle does not apply if the partner has in fact no authority and if the person with whom the partner is dealing knows that there is no authority [UPA Section 9(1)].

Liability of Partners

Each partner is personally liable for the entire amount of the partnership's debts. A partner is liable for any act by another partner, even if the act is wrongful, that results in liability for the partnership [UPA Section 13]. This liability exists because, when a partner acts, he or she acts as an agent for the partnership. Such liability can result from either a contract or a tort [UPA Section 15]. A partner is not liable for other partners' debts that are not connected with the business.

In satisfying their claims based on partnership liabilities, creditors can look to the assets of the individual partners after the partnership assets have been exhausted. If a person joins an existing partnership, her or his capital contribution is subject to the claims of prior creditors, but she or he is not personally liable for the prior debts of the partnership [UPA Section 17]. The new partner is personally liable for debts incurred after she or he joins the partnership, just as an original partner would be.

Duration and Termination of the Partnership

A partnership has indefinite duration unless the partnership agreement states a specific time period. The members of the partnership may change, but no person can become a partner without the consent of all of the existing partners, unless the partnership agreement states otherwise [UPA Section 18(g)].

Ending a partnership is a three-step process: **dissolution, winding up**, and **termination**. A new partner, a transfer of a partner's interest in the partnership, a partner's decision to withdraw, or unanimous consent by all the partners will dissolve the original partnership. A partnership is also dissolved if the business of the partnership becomes unlawful; if the business can only be carried on at a loss or if it becomes bankrupt; if a partner

dies, becomes mentally ill, or becomes bankrupt; or if a court orders a dissolution [UPA Sections 31 and 32].

Dissolution does not mean that the business is automatically terminated [UPA Section 30]. Depending on the circumstances, the business may continue, but it is conducted by a new partnership entity. When a partnership dissolves, each partner is a co-owner with the other partners of the partnership property.

When dissolution occurs and a new partnership is not going to be formed, then winding up of the business takes place. All the partners must be notified. At this point, the partners can no longer create any new liabilities on behalf of the partnership. The only authority they have is to complete the transactions begun but not yet finished at the time of the dissolution and to wind up the business [UPA Section 35]. Winding up includes collecting and preserving partnership assets, paying debts, and accounting to each partner for the value of her or his partnership interest.

Both creditors of the partnership and creditors of the individual partners can make claims on the partnership's assets. In general, partnership creditors have priority on the partnership assets, and individual creditors have priority on the personal assets of the partners.

When the business has been wound up, it is then terminated. The assets, if any, are distributed in the following order:

1. Debts owed to creditors other than partners
2. Debts owed to partners for loans made to the partnership
3. Debts owed to partners for capital
4. Debts owed to partners as profits [UPA Section 40].

The following case discusses some of the problems that can arise when a partnership is dissolved. Notice that the business continued after dissolution.

Case 17.2
LANGE v. BARTLETT
Court of Appeals of Wisconsin,
1984.
121 Wis.2d 599,
360 N.W.2d 702.

BACKGROUND AND FACTS　*Lange was a partner in a business known as Pool Boys that installed swimming pools. Art Lange and Bert Bartlett had worked together installing pools for several years on a part-time basis. In 1972, they verbally agreed to form the partnership "Pool Boys" and began operating the business full time. This arrangement continued until April of*

1975 when Lange told Bartlett that he no longer wanted to participate in the partnership.

Bartlett eventually offered Lange $3,000 in payment for Lange's share of the partnership; Lange refused this offer. Neither Bartlett or Lange obtained an accounting, nor was Lange paid any money. Subsequently, in 1978, Lange sued to recover his interest in the partnership, claiming he was entitled to one-half of both the assets and the profits from the business subsequent to April 1975. The trial court entered a judgment that gave him only one-half of the assets. Lange appealed, asserting that he was also entitled to one-half of the profits. The judge in the trial court had seemed confused about whether a wind-up had occurred, first deciding that it had, then changing his mind and holding that there was a continuation of the business.

Presiding Judge BROWN
* * * *

Before discussing the trial court's decision after trial, it is important for a clear understanding of this case to review the basic tenets of partnership law.

When a partner dies or retires, the partnership is dissolved. However, the partnership is not terminated upon dissolution; it continues until the wind-up of the partnership affairs are completed.

It is at this juncture, the point of dissolution, that the retiring partner makes an election. He can either force the business to "wind-up" and take his part of the proceeds, sharing in profits and losses after dissolution, or he can permit the business to continue and claim as a creditor the value of his interest at dissolution. The determination of whether the retiring partner consented to or acquiesced in the continuation of the business is a question of fact.

Thus, the first task for a trial court faced with making a settlement of a former partner's account after dissolution is to determine what election the retiring partner made at the point of dissolution. Every partnership dissolution causes a wind-up rather than a continuation unless the outgoing partner "consents" to a continuation. Distinguishing in the first instance whether a wind-up or a continuation is at hand is critical simply because the settlement of the former partner's account differs depending on whether it is a wind-up or a continuation.

For instance, if a trial court determines that a business was engaged in a wind-up, the former partner receives the value of his or her interest at the date of liquidation or final settlement. *   *   * In other words, the outgoing partner shares in both profits *and losses* until termination. The former partner, therefore, does not take as a creditor. The outgoing partner gets a share of the profits, if any, only after all of the other creditors have been paid and only until termination. Termination is the point in time when all of the partnership affairs are wound up.

Continuation, however, effects a totally different settlement of the former partner's account. The outgoing partner can agree, at the time of dissolution, that the business will be continued. If the outgoing partner elects to allow the business to continue, then that partner has a second election—to receive either interest or profits from the date of dissolution—in addition to the value of his or her interest in the partnership. This "second election" can be made only by the former partner; it cannot be made by either the continuing partner or the trial court. The profits garnered from continuation are different from the profits at wind-up simply because, in a continuation, the outgoing partner is not responsible for the debts of the continuing partnership. The outgoing partner, instead, takes as a creditor.
*   *   *   *

Having analyzed the basic law, we now turn to the trial court's decision, which we hold is inconsistent with these tenets. The trial court found that a wind-up had taken place rather than a continuation. It then determined the worth of the assets at the date of dissolution and divided the value of those assets equally between the two parties. Instead of determining the value of the assets at the time of dissolution, it should have determined profits and losses from the date of dissolution to the date of the hearing. This would assume that the assets have been sold as part of the wind-up and the income derived therefrom added to the amount to be divided or that the trial court place a market value on the assets as if sold. It did not, and this alone is error.

Moreover, the trial court's decision is inconsistent with an earlier decision it made following a pretrial motion by Lange. At the conclusion of that earlier hearing, the trial court held that a continuation had taken place, not a wind-up.

*   *   *   *

Finally, we reach a contention by Bartlett which is found to be a common complaint in partnership dissolution in our research of cases across the country. Bartlett strenuously argues that the business has greatly expanded since Lange left in 1975. He claims it is not the intent of the statutes to allow Lange to reap profits from aspects of the business which were not operating at the time of the partnership dissolution. Bartlett is incorrect. [The statute] states that the retiring partner may opt, in lieu of interest, for "profits attributable *to the use of his right in the property of the dissolved partnership.* *   *   *" (Emphasis added.) This figure may differ from year to year depending upon Bartlett's use of partnership property. Lange's partnership property includes not only the tangible assets but also any goodwill in the "Pool Boys" name and reputation prior to dissolution that would have contributed to the success of Bartlett's sauna, spa and hot tub business.

However, we understand Bartlett's concerns, and they can be addressed by compensating Bartlett for his efforts. Although authorities are not in accord regarding the problem of compensation to continuing partners in the absence of a specific agreement, we feel the better reasoned view is that one who continues a partnership business after dissolution and contributes substantial labor and management services is entitled to compensation for that effort.

We conclude that regardless of the expended effort on behalf of Bartlett, Lange is still entitled to a share of the partnership profit from the day of dissolution. However, a court can take into account the substantial labor and management services made by the continuing partner and deduct that amount before arriving at the figure of what profit is due the former partner.

DECISION AND REMEDY   *The trial court's judgment was reversed, and the case was remanded for a new trial. Whenever a partner withdraws from a partnership, a determination must be made as to whether the partnership is in the stage of winding up with the expectation of termination or whether it is being continued. This is a question of fact to be determined based on the conduct of all partners.*

COMMENT   *When a person is involved with a partnership that is dissolved because one partner is leaving, the partner winding up the partnership should insist on an accounting and a determination as to what the retiring partner's interest is worth. Otherwise, the remaining partner or partners are left open to great liability. If the business fails, the remaining partners will have to pay the retiring partner his or her investment. If the business is a success after the partner leaves, the retiring partner must be paid a share of the profits even though he or she did not take part in making the business a success.*

Limited Partnerships

A limited partnership is used when one or more partners want to manage the day-to-day activities of the business while the other partners merely want to make an investment in it. The investing partners find a limited partnership attractive for two reasons: A limited partnership limits the liability of its limited partners to the amount of their contributions, and tax advantages exist. Although the 1986 Tax Reform Act curtailed many of these tax benefits, enough incentives still exist, especially in certain industries, such as oil and lumber, to make limited partnerships an inviting investment.

A limited partnership must have at least one general partner and one or more limited partners. The limited partners, as such, are not bound by the obligations of the partnership and cannot have any day-to-day management responsibilities. The general partner or partners have total responsibility for management of the partnership and unlimited liability for all of its debts.

A limited partnership is a statutory creation and must comply with all statutory requirements to be formed. Failure to comply may change the limited partnership into a general partnership. The **Uniform Limited Partnership Act** (ULPA) of 1916 and the **Revised Uniform Limited Partnership Act** (RULPA) of 1976 contain the current law on limited partnerships. The original ULPA was updated in the RULPA to resolve current problems with limited partnerships. All states, except Louisiana, have adopted either the ULPA or the RULPA.

The ULPA and the RULPA require the limited partnership to file a certificate (see Exhibit 17–1) that becomes part of the public record. The certificate is similar to the articles of incorporation for a corporation. A partnership certificate contains basic information, such as the name, location, and business of the partnership; the name and residence of each partner, general or limited; the term for which the partnership will exist; and the amount of cash and property contributed by each limited partner.

In addition to the certificate of limited partnership, the partners often enter into a more detailed partnership agreement that is not filed as part of the public record but that covers such items as the share of the profits to which each partner is entitled.

Limited partnership interests are considered to be securities (like stock certificates or corporate bonds). First, there is money paid from one person (the limited partner) to another (the general partner). Second, the money is invested in a common enterprise from which the investor is led to expect profits. Third, the profits arise primarily from the effort of people other than the investor. Thus, the issuance, sale, and transfer of a limited partner's interest are subject to federal and state securities laws (discussed in detail in Chapter 19).

Sources of Funding for Limited Partnerships

The general and the limited partners contribute to the capital of the limited partnership and may also make loans to it. The partnership agreement may provide for additional contributions and voluntary or involuntary assessments of the partners after formation of the partnership. Since the liability of the limited partners is restricted to the amount of their contributions, the ability of the partnership to obtain loans from third parties will be based on the partnership's assets and the creditworthiness of the general partner or partners, who have unlimited liability.

Liability in Limited Partnerships

A limited partnership must have at least one general partner who has unlimited liability. Most states now allow the general partner to be a corporation, as well as a natural person.

Generally speaking, the limited partners' liability is limited to their capital contributions. This includes the amount of capital that limited partners have pledged to contribute but that they have not yet actually paid.

Limited partners can lose their limited liability if they participate in the management and control of the partnership's business. Certain state statutes specify that the right of a limited partner to demand that the general partner be expelled from the partnership will not be considered as taking part in the control of the business.

The following case examines the question of whether the limited partner had lost his limited liability status. This case was decided under the ULPA.

Exhibit 17–1 **Sample Certificate of Limited Partnership**

CERTIFICATE OF LIMITED PARTNERSHIP

The undersigned, desiring to form a Limited Partnership under the Uniform Limited Partnership Act of the State of _____, make this certificate for that purpose.

§ 1. Name. The name of the Partnership shall be "_____ _____."

§ 2. Purpose. The purpose of the Partnership shall be to [describe].

§ 3. Location. The location of the Partnership's principal place of business is _____ _____ County, _____.

§ 4. Members and Designation. The names and places of residence of the members, and their designation as General or Limited Partners are:

_____	[Address]	General Partner
_____	[Address]	General Partner
_____	[Address]	Limited Partner
_____	[Address]	Limited Partner

§ 5. Term. The term for which the Partnership is to exist is indefinite.

§ 6. Initial Contributions of Limited Partners. The amount of cash and a description of the agreed value of the other property contributed by each Limited Partner are:

[Name]	[Describe]
[Name]	[Describe]

§ 7. Subsequent Contributions of Limited Partners. Each Limited Partner may (but shall not be obliged to) make such additional contributions to the capital of the Partnership as may from time to time be agreed upon by the General Partners.

§ 8. Profit Shares of Limited Partners. The share of the profits which each Limited Partner shall receive by reason of his contribution is:

[Name]	_____ %
[Name]	_____ %

Signed_____, 19_____

_____
_____
_____
_____

Signed and sworn before me, the undersigned authority, this_____ _____, 19_____.

Notary Public

_____ County, _____

BACKGROUND AND FACTS *Gonzalez was hired by Chalpin to be the superintendent and maintenance worker at Excel's apartment building. Excel was a limited partnership that had one individual general partner, Lipkin; one corporate general partner, Tribute Music, Inc., a valid corporation; and one limited partner, Chalpin. Chalpin was also the president, sole shareholder, and director of Tribute. Gonzalez was not paid for much of the work he performed. He sued Chalpin individually, as well as Excel Associates and its limited and general partners, for breach of contract.*

Case 17.3
GONZALEZ v.
CHALPIN
Court of Appeals of New York,
1990.
564 N.Y.S.2d 702.

Judge BELLACOSA
* * * *

The general restriction on the liability of limited partners is not controlling here because, if the partner in addition to the exercise of [the partner's] rights and powers as a limited partner takes part in the control of the business, the limited partner becomes liable as a general partner * * *. Chalpin cannot challenge the trial court's affirmed factual determination that he took part in the control of Excel's business. Instead, he attempts to skirt the individual and general responsibility imposed [by the law] by claiming that he acted at all times solely in his capacity as an officer of Tribute.

Irrefutably, individual liability should not be imposed on a limited partner merely because that person happens also to be an officer, director and/or shareholder of a corporate general partner * * *. But that is not this case. Moreover and conversely, a limited partner who takes part in the control of the limited partnership's business should not automatically be insulated from individual liability merely by benefit of status as an officer and sole owner of the corporate general partner. That is this case.

A limited partner who assumes such a dual capacity rightly bears a heavy burden when seeking to elude personal liability. For once a plaintiff meets the threshold burden of proving that a limited partner took an active individual part in effectuating the limited partnership's interests * * *, the fulcrum shifts. The limited partner in such a dual capacity must then, at least, prove that any relevant actions taken were performed solely in the capacity as officer of the general partner.

Defendant in this case failed to adjust to the shift and did not overcome the proof of involvement and responsibility for his actions undertaken in his individual capacity.

The court rejected Chalpin's limited liability defense. He had failed to prove that he acted only as an officer of the general partnership; thus, he was held individually liable to Gonzalez.

DECISION AND REMEDY

Control of the Limited Partnership

The control and management of the limited partnership is vested in the hands of the general partner. Thus, control does not necessarily follow ownership interest, as it does in a corporation. A general partner may have a very small ownership interest yet still retain the right to control the entity. Unless there is an agreement to the contrary, the general partner will have absolute discretion as to when distributions of profits are made.

The general partner has all of the rights and powers and is subject to all of the restrictions and liabilities of a partner in a general partnership. The general partner does not have authority to act in a manner that contravenes the partnership certificate.

A limited partner has the same rights as any general partner to access partnership books and records; to have an accounting of the partnership business; to have a dissolution and winding up of the partnership by court order; to receive the share

of profits or compensation stipulated in the partnership certificate; and to have a return of his or
her contribution on dissolution and distribution
of the partnership assets, subject to the rights of
creditors.

Exhibit 17–2 illustrates the basic comparisons
of general partnerships and limited partnerships
under both the ULPA and the RUPLA.

Tax Consequences for a Limited Partnership

The taxation of a limited partnership is the same
as that of a general partnership. The partnership
makes an informational filing, reporting the allocation of profits and losses and other tax items
to the various partners. Individual partners, lim-

ited and general, report on their own tax returns
their allocated profits or losses. The partnership
itself is not a taxable entity, and profits and losses
pass through to the individual partners.

Since limited partnerships have been used extensively as tax shelters, their tax status as partnerships has often been challenged by the Internal
Revenue Service. For federal income tax purposes, the Internal Revenue Service regulations
provide that a limited partnership will be classified
as a "partnership" rather than as "an association
taxable as a corporation," as long as it does not
possess more corporate than noncorporate characteristics.

The characteristics that, according to the regulations, distinguish a corporation from a partnership are the following: continuity of life, lim-

Exhibit 17–2 **Basic Comparison of Partnerships**

CHARACTERISTIC	GENERAL PARTNERSHIP	LIMITED PARTNERSHIP	REVISED LIMITED PARTNERSHIP
Creation	By agreement of two or more persons to carry on a business as co-owners for profit.	By agreement of two or more persons, under the laws of the state, having one or more general partners and one or more limited partners to carry on a business as co-owners for profit. Filing of certificate in appropriate state office is required.	Same as limited partnership, except filing of certificate with secretary of state is required.
Sharing of profits and losses	By agreement, or in absence thereof, profits are shared equally by partners and losses are shared in same ratio as profits.	Profits are shared as required in certificate agreement, and losses shared likewise, except limited partners share losses only up to their capital contribution.	Same as limited partnership, except in absence of provision in certificate agreement, profits and losses are shared on basis of percentages of capital contributions.
Liability	Unlimited personal liability of all partners.	Unlimited personal liability of all general partners; limited partners only to extent of capital contributions.	Same as limited partnership.
Capital contribution	No minimal or mandatory amount; set by agreement.	Set by agreement; may be cash, property, or any obligation except services.	Same as limited partnership; contribution of services is allowed.

Exhibit 17–2 **Basic Comparison of Partnerships**—*continued*

CHARACTERISTIC	GENERAL PARTNERSHIP	LIMITED PARTNERSHIP	REVISED LIMITED PARTNERSHIP
Management	By agreement, or in absence thereof, all partners have an equal voice.	General partners by agreement, or else each has an equal voice. Limited partners have no voice, or else subject to liability as general partners.	Same as limited partnership, except limited partner involved in partnership management is liable as a general partner *only* if third party has knowledge of such involvement. Limited partner may act as agent or employee of partnership, and vote on amending certificate or sale or dissolution of partnership.
Duration	By agreement, or can be dissolved by action of partner (withdrawal), operation of law (death or bankruptcy), or court decree.	By agreement in certificate, or by withdrawal, death, or insanity of general partner in absence of right of other general partners to continue the partnership. Death of a limited partner, unless he or she is only remaining limited partner, does not terminate partnership.	Same as limited partnership, except it enlarges class of activities by general partner that result in termination.
Priorities (order) upon liquidation	1. Outside creditors. 2. Partner creditors. 3. Capital contribution of partners. 4. Profits of partners.	1. Outside creditors. Limited partner creditors. 2. Profits to limited partners. 3. Limited partner capital contributions. 4. General partner creditors. 5. Profits to general partners. 6. Capital contributions to general partners.	1. Outside creditors. Partner creditors. 2. Amounts before withdrawal to which partners are entitled as might be stated in an agreement. 3. Capital contributions—limited and general partners. 4. Profits—limited and general partners.

ited liability, free transferability of interest, and centralization of management. If an entity lacks any two of these corporate characteristics, it will be classified as a partnership rather than as a corporation for tax purposes.

Since all limited partnerships have the characteristic of centralized management in the hands of the general partner or partners, a limited part-nership agreement will often impose restrictions on transferability of interest in order to avoid the corporate characteristic of free transferability.

In addition, to avoid the corporate characteristic of limited liability, a general partner must have sufficient net worth so that the theoretical unlimited liability of the general partner is not in reality limited by a lack of assets. An individual general partner must have substantial assets and must not be acting as a "dummy" agent of the limited partners. The regulations do not provide any clear-cut guidance as to what constitutes substantial assets.

Bulk Sales: Buying a Going Business

When a person decides to go into business, he or she will often purchase an existing business. If the business being purchased sells merchandise (not just services), the bulk sales provisions of the Uniform Commercial Code, Article 6, usually apply. The UCC changed Article 6 from the "Bulk Transfer Act" to the "Bulk Sales Act," altering many provisions. A **bulk sale** is defined as any transfer of more than one-half of the seller's inventory not made in the ordinary course of the seller's business [UCC 6-102].

No problems exist if all the creditors of the seller are paid in full at the time that the business is transferred to the buyer. The problems occur when the seller's creditors are not paid. The creditors have certain rights against the buyer if the provisions of the Bulk Sales Act are not followed.

The buyer is responsible for complying with the Bulk Sales Act. Some of the requirements that must be met to *protect the buyer* from the former creditors of the seller are:

1. The buyer must obtain a list of all the names and addresses the seller has used for the last three years [UCC 6-104(1)(a)];
2. Three days prior to the notice of sale being sent to all creditors, the buyer must obtain from the seller a sworn list of the names, addresses, and amounts owed to the current creditors [UCC 6-104(1)(b)];
3. The buyer and seller must prepare a schedule showing how the proceeds from the sale will be distributed and give the list to the creditors [UCC 6-104(c)]; and
4. Notice of the proposed bulk sale must be given by the buyer to each creditor at least 45 days prior to the sale [UCC 6-105].

If the buyer follows the provisions set out in the Act, the bulk sale will comply with the statutory requirements. The buyer acquires title to the goods free of all claims of the creditors of the seller.

The buyer must give *written notice to the creditors*. This written notice must include

1. A statement that a bulk sale is about to be made
2. The current names and addresses of the seller and the buyer
3. All other names and addresses used by the seller during the past three years
4. The date on which more than ten percent of the assets will be transferred and which specific assets are being sold, and
5. A copy of the schedule of distribution of the proceeds that will accompany the notice to the creditors [UCC 6-105].

When the requirements of the Bulk Sales Act are not complied with, the buyer is personally liable to the creditors. This liability is reduced by the amount the creditor would not have been able to receive if the buyer had complied with the Act. Further, this liability could be twice the purchase price, but is reduced by any amount the buyer paid to the seller or other creditors [UCC 6-107]. For example, Mary purchases a business for $100,000. She pays $25,000 down to the seller and agrees to pay the balance over the next five years. She did not comply with the Bulk Sales Act. Rodney was owed $50,000 by the seller. Mary's potential liability is $200,000 less than the $25,000 she had paid. In other words, she is liable to Rodney for the $50,000. She can deduct this amount she owes the seller. If she is able to prove that Rodney would have received less than $50,000 if she had fully complied with the Act, she would owe Rodney the lesser amount.

Any legal actions must be taken within one year after the discovery by creditors that the bulk sale has taken place [UCC 6-110]. Failure to comply with the statute does not make the sale ineffective, void, or voidable. In other words, the sale cannot be set aside [UCC 6-107(8)].

In the following case, the court was faced with a bulk transfer of the assets of a business but without any notice to a creditor being given. The issue before the court was whether the six-month period began with the date of the transfer of possession of the assets to the buyer or with the date of the possession of the assets to the buyer or with the date of the creditor's discovery of the transfer. This case was decided under the old law which had only a six-month statute of limitations. The new law now allows a one year period to bring actions against a purchaser of a business.

BACKGROUND AND FACTS *The plaintiff, Columbian Rope Company, extended credit to the defendants, Rinek Cordage Company and its president, Jerome Brose. The defendants confronted serious financial problems and owed the plaintiff $22,683.48. Rinek Cordage Company also owed Rinek Rope Company $17,588.55. Rinek Cordage and Rinek Rope operated out of the same address, both used the Rinek name, and Brose was not conscientious in maintaining the corporate identity of each company. Rinek Cordage Company transferred its entire inventory to Rinek Rope Company; thus, the debt of $17,588.55 was canceled.*

This transaction, on April 1, 1974, constituted a bulk sales transfer. The complaint by Columbian Rope Company was not filed until November 12, 1976, but this was within six months of its discovery of the transfer. The lower court dismissed the action based on the six-month statute of limitations.

Case 17.4
COLUMBIAN ROPE CO. v. RINEK CORDAGE CO.
Pennsylvania Superior Court, 1983.
314 Pa.Super. 585,
461 A.2d 312.

Judge HOFFMAN
Appellant, a creditor, contends that the lower court erred in denying its claim against Jerome Brose, the former president of a debtor corporation, and against Rinek Rope Co. [Rope], which received the debtor's remaining assets in a bulk transfer. We find the claim against Brose was properly denied. However, because the bulk transfer to Rope was "concealed," * * * the six-month statute of limitations did not begin running until appellant discovered the bulk transfer. Accordingly, we reverse the lower court's order dismissing appellant's claim against Rope, and remand for findings of fact as to whether appellant commenced its action within six months of discovering the bulk transfer.
* * * *

Appellant contends that Rope's complete failure to give notice of the bulk transfer constituted a concealment of the bulk transfer, and thus the statute of limitations did not begin to run against it until its discovery of the transfer. We agree. The Uniform Commercial Code, Article 6, concerning bulk transfers, * * * is designed to remedy the "major bulk sales risk" of the merchant, owing debts, who sells away virtually all his stock in trade and disappears leaving his creditors unpaid. The statute's basic mechanism is to require the prospective transferee to give advance notice to the transferor's creditors of the impending bulk sale. The transferee must also take steps to insure that the proceeds are applied to the benefit of the transferor's creditors. The prior notice affords the creditors an opportunity to participate in structuring the transfer or commence legal action against their debtor, the transferor, before the assets are sold away. To promote compliance, the statute establishes three alternative time limitations for creditor actions against the transferee. First, if the transferee gives the statutory notice and otherwise complies with the statute, the bulk transfer will be "effective" against any creditor of the transferor. The complying transferee will be shielded immediately upon the transfer from the creditors' actions. Creditors will therefore be required to act expeditiously against their debtor, the transferor, within the ten or more days between the statutory notice and the transfer or they will effectively lose their opportunity to collect their debt. Second, if the transferee does not give the required notice, the transfer will be "ineffective" against the transferor's creditors, who may then commence actions for the transferor's debts against the transferee within the six months following the transfer. Third, if the transferee's failure to give notice is not simply noncompliance with the statute but amounts to "concealment" of the bulk transfer, the transferee is subject to actions by the transferor's creditors commenced within six months of when the creditor discovers the concealed bulk transfer. The question we face here is whether a completely undisclosed bulk transfer should be treated as "concealed" for purposes of the U.C.C.'s statute of limitations.

Case law is divided upon what constitutes concealment of a bulk transfer. No prior Pennsylvania appellate decision has interpreted this statutory term. Some courts have required "active" or "affirmative" concealment. Others have held that "*complete* failure to comply with the notice provisions of [UCC] Article 6 . . . was tantamount to a concealment of a transfer of assets * * *." We find that the complete failure to give notice of the impending bulk transfer is not merely non-compliance, but "concealment."

* * * *

Applying these principles, the record reveals that the bulk transfer here was wholly undisclosed, and thus concealed. No notice, formal or informal, was sent to Cordage's two outstanding creditors, apparently because Rope's and Cordage's officers did not think it necessary. The circumstances in no way revealed to creditors

Ethical Considerations

Refinancing Your Home: What Should the Bank Tell You?

You purchased your house for $85,000 several years ago. Advertisements on television and in the newspapers explain the benefits of a home equity loan. Benefits range from low interest rates that are tax deductible to putting your hidden wealth—that is, the equity—to good use now. You locate a small business that you think would be a good investment. You apply for a home equity loan in order to purchase this business. The appraisal places the value of the house at $235,000. According to the advertisement, the bank will lend you 100 percent of the equity at a 10 percent rate of interest. You decide to borrow $150,000.

You go to the bank and fully disclose that you intend to use this money to purchase a small business. You are not asked to provide the bank with a business plan. Even without this plan, it agrees to lend you the money. You sign a negotiable note agreeing to repay the $150,000 at 10 percent over twenty years and place a second mortgage on your house to secure the loan. When signing the loan papers, the loan officer rushes you through the transaction, and you fail to read all the documents. In them are the disclosures required to be made by the bank under the federal home equity loan amendments to the Truth-in-Lending Act.

Over the next few years, on your federal income tax return you deduct the interest paid on the $150,000 along with the interest on the first mortgage. After you are audited, you find that only the interest paid on the first $100,000 of the home equity loan was deductible. Worse, after the first two years you find that the interest rate has jumped from 10 percent to 14 percent. The terms of the note allow the interest rate to be raised after the first 24 months.

Does a financial institution in the business of making loans have any ethical considerations when it knows that most small businesses will fail? What are the ethics of advertising that fails to fully disclose tax rules and that uses a low interest rate to attract inquiries by the public? Should there be any regulation on how you choose to spend the equity loan? Does the government have any interest in whether you have the equity in your home available for the expenses of your senior years, so you will not be on welfare? Does the government have any interest in how you spend the equity loan, such as limiting the proceeds to be used only for medical expenses or for educational expenses? Should funds from equity loans be available for a capitalistic venture? If these funds are not available, where does a person obtain funds to start or purchase a small business?

that the transfer had occurred. Both transferor and transferee operated out of the same business address, with Cordage owning the premises and Rope leasing space. Both used the "Rinek" name. Even after the transfer, Cordage's president was not scrupulous in differentiating between the two entities. Letter from Jerome Brose to Michael Hole, April 25, 1974 ("I have completed refinancing of the *Rinek* real estate" (emphasis added)). Moreover, although Rope had existed separately since 1971, and used stationery showing its own name—Rinek Cordage forms with "Cordage" blacked-out and "Rope" rubber-stamped above—such a precaution did not reveal the fact of the bulk transfer on April 1, 1974. Accordingly, even though the record contains no proof of deceptive intent, the bulk transfer was effectively "concealed" from creditors by the complete nondisclosure. We thus reverse the lower court's dismissal of the action against Rope, and remand for findings of fact to determine whether appellant commenced action within six months of its discovering the bulk transfer.

DECISION AND REMEDY

The court found that, because the transfer was concealed until a creditor discovered that a bulk transfer had occurred, the six-month statute of limitations had not begun. The complete failure to comply with the bulk transfer provisions, including the failure to give the creditor notice, constituted concealment. Therefore, the innocent creditor was not precluded from exercising its rights even though six months had passed from the date the buyer took possession.

The new Bulk Sales Act now is very clear that the statute of limitations does not begin to run until the bulk sale is discovered by the creditor [UCC 6-110]. The court's position was confirmed when the law was rewritten.

International Considerations

Different Attitudes on Entrepreneurships

The collapse of the communist economic systems offers business opportunities. Capitalism, however, is still not viewed favorably by many citizens in the remnants of the former Union of Soviet Socialist Republics. After all, the government provided employment and other basic necessities for 70 years. No incentive was given to managers and workers to follow the basic capitalistic rule of minimizing expenses and maximizing profits. In fact, profits were not used to encourage investments and no one individual benefited from a financially successful government project.

The concepts of profits and entrepreneurship, for example, are perceived differently than in a capitalistic country. Let's say a young man living and working in Moscow purchases a truck. Now he is able to drive to the Ukraine, purchase fresh vegetables, and return to Moscow to sell the produce. Businesspersons in capitalistic countries would call him an entrepreneur. But many Russians in Moscow would call him a greedy, opportunistic person who makes money at the expense of hungry people. The few people left in Russia with any experience in the free enterprise system are now 80 to 90 years old. The Russian experience has been one of government and economic regulation. It will be interesting to witness the change in attitude towards entrepreneurship in the coming years.

FACING A LEGAL ISSUE

Drafting a Partnership Agreement

You and a friend decide to go into partnership to sell a new product. The following are some of the considerations to be included in your written partnership agreement:

1. Names and addresses of the general partners and the designation of partnership status
2. Name of the partnership and address of the principal place of business
3. Character of the business
4. Duration of the partnership
5. Contributions of the partners
   a. Form of contribution
   b. Interest on contribution
   c. Additional contribution requirements
6. Assets of the partnership
   a. Identification of the assets
   b. Valuation of the assets
   c. Control of the assets and accountability for them
   d. Distribution of the assets
7. Duties of the partners
8. Distribution of profits and losses
9. Compensation, benefits, and expenses of the partners
10. Policy and management of the business
11. Accounting practices and procedures
12. Liability and insurance requirements
13. Indemnity clause (to compensate for loss or to reimburse expenses)
14. Changes in the partners by withdrawal, retirement, death, mental illness, bankruptcy, or admission of additional partners
15. Sale or assignment of the partnership interest
16. Arbitration provisions
17. Amendment provisions
18. Dissolution, winding up, and termination of the partnership
19. Date of the agreement
20. Signatures of the partners

With a well-drafted agreement, you should also be able to answer these questions, which frequently arise:

1. What happens if one of you fails to spend the necessary amount of time in the business? For example, what happens if your partner goes to Europe for a six-month vacation?
2. What happens if one of you should become disabled or die?
3. How will the profits and losses be shared?
4. What happens if the business requires additional capital?
5. How much time should each partner spend doing partnership business?
6. Who should sign the checks and make the deposits?
7. What happens if one partner decides to leave the partnership? How does the partnership end?

Summary

Four principal forms of business organization exist: sole proprietorship, general partnership, limited partnership, and corporation. Concerns in selecting a type of business entity include the difficulty in forming it, limited liability, tax considerations, continuity of existence, transferability, management, control, financing, licenses, and location.

The sole proprietorship is the most informal business organization. The sole owner of a business has unlimited liability, and the business may cease to operate on the death or incapacity of the owner. No tax advantages exist for this form of ownership, but it does give maximum control of the business to the owner.

The general partnership allows people to join together to operate a business. No formal requirements exist for its organization. If a partner should die, become incapacitated, or otherwise leave the partnership, a dissolution of the partnership will occur. Assuming a dissolution occurs, the remaining partners should buy out the withdrawing partner's interest as soon as possible. Just as with a sole proprietorship, there are no real tax advantages to a partnership. In the absence of an agreement among the partners, most business decisions are based on majority vote and not the amount of capital contribution.

The limited partnership must be organized in accordance with statutory provisions. All limited partnerships must have at least one general partner and one limited partner. The general partner manages the operation of the business. If a limited partner takes an active role in managing, that limited partner assumes unlimited liability for the debts of the business. Otherwise, a limited partner's only liability is his or her capital contribution. The death of a limited partner will not cause a dissolution of the partnership. In the past, there were major tax advantages for a limited partnership; the Tax Reform Act of 1986 greatly reduced these advantages.

Corporations are the fourth form of business organization; they are covered in the next chapter.

When a person purchases a going business, compliance with the bulk sales provisions of the Uniform Commercial Code may be required. Any purchase of a business that sells merchandise must comply with the act.

Key Terms

bulk sale (438)
dissolution (430)
fictitious name filing (424)
general partner (424)
limited partners (424)
limited partnership (424)
partnership by estoppel (428)

partnerships (424)
Revised Uniform Limited
    Partnership Act (433)
sole proprietorships (424)
termination (430)
Uniform Limited Partnership

Act (433)
Uniform Partnership Act
    (428)
use permits (428)
variances (428)
winding up (430)

Questions and Case Problems

1. Lisa, Amy, and Mary are college graduates. Lisa has an idea for a new product that she believes could make the three of them very wealthy. Her idea is to manufacture beer dispensers for home use, and her goal is to market them to consumers throughout the Midwest. Lisa's personal experience qualifies her to be both first line supervisor and general manager of the new firm. Amy is a born salesperson. Mary has little interest in sales or management but would like to invest a large sum of money that she has inherited from her aunt. What should Lisa, Amy, and Mary consider in deciding which form of business organization to adopt?

2. Assume that Mary, in problem 1, is willing to put her inherited money into the business but that she does not want any further liability should the beer dispenser manufacturing business fail. The bank is willing to lend capital at a 9 percent interest rate, but it will do so only if certain restrictions are placed on management decisions. This is not satisfactory to Amy or Lisa, and the two decide to bring Mary into the business. Under these circumstances, discuss the types of business organizations best suited to meet the needs of Mary.

3. The limited liability aspect of the corporation or limited partnership is one of the most important reasons that firms choose to organize as corporations or limited partnerships rather than as general partnerships or sole proprietorships. Limited liability means that, if a corporation or limited partnership is not able to meet its obligations with corporate or partnership assets, creditors will not be allowed to look to the owners (stockholders) of the corporation or the limited partners to satisfy their claims. Assume that Lisa and Amy (from problem 1) do not have a wealthy friend like Mary who wants to go into business with them and that, therefore, they must borrow money to start their business. Lisa and Amy decide to incorporate. What do you think a lender will ask them when they seek a loan? What effect does this have on the "advantage" of limited liability under corporations?

4. Able, Baker, and Carlton have formed a twenty-year partnership to purchase land, develop it, manage it, and then sell the property. The partnership agreement calls for the partners to devote full time to the business. Assume one of the following events takes place:

a. After two years, Baker and Carlton agree that the working hours of the partnership will be from 8:00 A.M. to 6:00 P.M., rather than the previously established schedule of 9:00 A.M. to 5:00 P.M. Able refuses to come to work before 9:00 A.M. and quits promptly at 5:00 P.M.
b. After two years, Able quits the partnership.
c. After two years, Able becomes insolvent.
d. After two years, Able dies.
Discuss fully which of these acts constitutes a dissolution

and whether there is any ensuing liability for Able.

5. Rosemary and George have formed a partnership. At the time of formation, Rosemary's capital contribution was $10,000, and George's was $15,000. Later Rosemary made a $10,000 loan to the partnership when it needed working capital. The partnership agreement provides that profits are to be shared, with 40 percent for Rosemary and 60 percent for George. The partnership is dissolved by George's death. At the end of the dissolution and winding up of the partnership, the partnership's assets are $50,000, and the partnership's general creditor debts are $8,000. Discuss fully how the assets will be distributed.

6. Able and Baker form a limited partnership with Able as the general partner and Baker as the limited partner. Baker puts up $15,000, and Able contributes some office equipment that he owns. A certificate of limited partnership is properly filed, and business is begun. One month later Able becomes ill. Instead of hiring someone to manage the business, Baker takes over complete management himself. While Baker is in control, he makes a contract with Thomas involving a large sum of money. Able returns to work. Because of other commitments, the Thomas contract is breached. Thomas contends that he can hold Able and Baker personally liable if the amount owed him cannot be satisfied out of the assets of the limited partnership. Discuss this contention.

7. Diversified Properties was organized as a limited partnership with Weil as the only general partner. After one year of operation, it was hard pressed for cash. At a partnership meeting, Weil offered to discontinue his salary and close up the partnership office. Weil's proposal was accepted, and two of the limited partners were selected to manage the properties on a commission basis. Weil went to work for a real estate company. The limited partners were involved in business transactions to keep the business going. Creditors demanded payment and looked to Weil. Weil sued to have the limited partners declared general partners so that they would also be liable for the limited partnership's debts. Who prevails and why? [Weil v. Diversified Properties, 319 F.Supp. 778 (1970)]

8. Oddo and Ries entered into a partnership agreement in March 1978 to create and publish a book describing how to restore F-100 pickup trucks. Oddo was to write the book, and Ries was to provide the capital. Oddo supplied Ries with the manuscript, but Ries was dissatisfied and hired someone else to revise the manuscript. Ries published the book containing substantial amounts of Oddo's work. Did Ries's actions constitute a dissolution of the partnership, and can Oddo require Ries to account formally for the profits on the book? [Oddo v. Ries, 743 F.2d 630 (9th Cir. 1984)]

9. Robert retired from an accounting partnership and entered into a liquidation agreement requiring the partnership to pay him a fixed sum over a ten-year period. Three years later, another partner, Shepard, withdrew from the partnership. The remaining partners did not purchase Shepard's partnership interest, and he was forced to file suit to recover. While the suit was pending, the partnership was sold to Jerry. Robert died leaving Jean his widow. Shepard prevailed in his lawsuit and was awarded the value of his partnership less his share of the remaining obligation owed to Robert. Payments to Jean ceased, and she filed suit against all the partners including Shepard to collect the remaining balance owed. All the partners except Shepard filed for bankruptcy. Who prevails and why? [Belt v. Shepard, 808 P.2d 907 (Kan.App. 1991)]

10. Paramount Steamship Company owned the *Courtney D*, a seagoing vessel. Paramount Petroleum Corporation was in the oil business. Both companies were owned by the same shareholders, operated out of the same address, had the same accountant, and when the telephones were answered, the person would say "Paramount." The *Courtney D* required extensive repairs. Taylor Rental Center extended credit on equipment to make these repairs. When Taylor was not paid, it sued both Paramount corporations. Can both Paramount corporations be held liable under the theory of partnership by estoppel? Discuss fully. [Paramount Petroleum Corp. v. Taylor Rental Center, 712 S.W.2d 534 (Tex. Ct. App. 1986)]

Chapter 18 Corporate Law and Franchising Law

A corporation is an artificial being, invisible, intangible, and existing only in contemplation of law.

Chief Justice John Marshall
Dartmouth College v. Woodward,
17 U.S. (4 Wheat.) 518, 4 L.Ed. 629 (1819).

OUTLINE

Introduction

The corporate form of organization is the most important type of business organization in the United States. Corporations are the most formal kind of business organization, but they offer many advantages over other types of business entities.

A **corporation** is a separate legal entity that is owned by shareholders. Although many exceptions exist, corporations, generally speaking, are characterized by centralized management, continuity of existence, limited liability of the shareholders, and freely transferable shares.

The corporate organizational structure is well suited to a public offering of securities and a listing on a stock exchange. Any publicly offered securities are subject to federal and/or state securities laws, which are discussed in detail in Chapter 19.

Ease of Formation

Corporations are formed under state law. While the Model Business Corporation Act has been adopted or is followed by a majority of states, the state corporate codes are not entirely uniform.

Incorporators are the people who start the corporation. They have a choice of states in which to charter their corporation. Most states allow a business to incorporate in one state but to locate its principal place of business elsewhere, as long as the corporation maintains a registered office in the state where it is incorporated. A corporation is a **domestic corporation** in the state in which it originally incorporated. A corporation files as a **foreign corporation** in all other states in which it will do business.

Incorporators look for favorable state corporate and tax codes and also consider the state's case law interpreting its corporate code. The more developed the state's law, the more certain the corporation can be about the legal consequences of its actions.

Incorporators frequently hire a **promoter,** who makes contacts for and takes preliminary steps in organizing the corporation. Unless a promoter specifically limits his or her liability in the contract by requiring parties to look to the corporation yet to be formed, the promoter has personal liability for all preincorporation contracts. These contracts can include the purchase or lease of land, contracts to construct buildings, purchase of equipment and inventory, and even financing agreements with third parties. Even after the corporation is formed, the promoter remains personally liable until the corporation, through its board of directors, assumes responsibility for the contracts by adopting them as contracts of the corporation.

Articles of Incorporation

The creation of a corporation requires a formal public filing. As part of the initial incorporation process, the incorporators must file **articles of incorporation** with a designated state office, usually the office of the secretary of state. The articles provide basic information about the corporation and are the primary source of authority for its future operations. The articles of incorporation are analogous to a constitution for the corporation.

While specific requirements vary somewhat from state to state, basically the articles of incorporation include:

1. The name of the corporation
2. The purpose of the corporation, which may be stated in a general way in order to include all lawful business
3. The duration of the corporation, which is almost always perpetual
4. The date and time of the commencement of corporate existence, which usually starts with the filing of the articles with the secretary of state or which may be set by statute
5. The number of shares that the corporation has the authority to issue, which often includes a list of the various classes of shares and their rights and limitations and any minimum capital invested to start business
6. The address of the corporation's registered office and the name of its registered agent in the state
7. The number of members on and, where required, the names and addresses of the first board of directors and the name and address of each incorporator
8. The right (if such is desired) for shareholders to have preemptive rights (the rights of existing shareholders to purchase newly issued stock to maintain their position of control and financial interest in the corporation).

In many states only one incorporator is required, and the incorporator may be a natural person, a corporation, a partnership, a limited partnership, or an association. The corporation's name must include the word *corporation, incorporated, company, limited,* or an abbreviation of one of these words.

Exhibit 18–1 shows sample articles of incorporation.

Bylaws

After the charter has been issued and the corporation has been formed, the incorporator(s) elect the board of directors; then the initial board meets and, among other things, adopts the corporation's **bylaws.** In many states the board of directors may consist of only one person. The bylaws cannot conflict with the state corporate code or the articles of incorporation.

If the articles of incorporation are considered equivalent to a constitution, the bylaws are equivalent to statutes. Just as the constitution (articles of incorporation) is the basic governing document and is hard to change, statutes (bylaws) carry out the guidelines of the constitution and are easier to change.

The bylaws set forth the internal rules of management for the corporation, typically including what constitutes a quorum (minimum number of members who must be present at a meeting in order to take valid actions), voting requirements for shareholders and directors, the requirements for election of the directors and officers and the terms for which they will serve, the duties of the officers, and similar provisions.

Exhibit 18–1 Sample Articles of Incorporation

ARTICLE ONE: Name
The name of the corporation is Private Investigators, Inc.

ARTICLE TWO: Time Period
The period of its duration is perpetual.

ARTICLE THREE: Purpose
This corporation is organized for the purpose of transacting any or all lawful business for which corporations may be incorporated under the laws of the State of Nevada, including private investigations.

ARTICLE FOUR: Shares
The aggregate number of shares that the corporation shall have authority to issue is 1,000 of the par value of $10 each (or without par value).

ARTICLE FIVE: Capital
The amount of stated capital is $10,000.

ARTICLE SIX: Address
The address of the corporation's registered office is 1 Avenida de Estrellas, Hot Desert, Nevada, and the name of its registered agent at such address is Ron Kilgore.

ARTICLE SEVEN: Directors
The number of initial directors is one and the name and address of the director is Ron Kilgore, 1 Avenida de Estrellas, Hot Desert, Nevada.

ARTICLE EIGHT: Incorporator
The name and address of the incorporator is Ron Kilgore, 1 Avenida de Estrellas, Hot Desert, Nevada.

(signed) _____
                                    (Incorporator)

Sworn to before me on _____ by the above named incorporator.
                              (date)

_____
Notary Public, Thornhill County, Nevada

My Commission expires _____, 19 _____.   (Notary Seal)

Legal Highlight

The Model Business Corporation Act and the Revised Model Business Corporation Act

The Model Business Corporation Act (MBCA) is a codification of modern corporation law. A "model" statute is created with the understanding that it may need amendments or changes in order to reflect local interests, needs, or problems, but it is presented for various jurisdictions to draw upon in forming their decisions concerning corporate law.

The MBCA was first published in its complete form in 1933 by the Committee on Corporate Laws of the American Bar Association. It was patterned after the Illinois Business Corporation Act of 1933. The act was drafted, in part, in response to the tumultuous history of corporations in the United States prior to that time. While the corporate form of business organization is common today, it was rare until after the Civil War. Until the late 1800s, the corporate privilege was granted sparingly, and only when the grant seemed necessary to procure some specific benefit for the community.

The reason the corporate form was limited was because people feared that the sheer size of a corporate enterprise, along with its concentration of economic power and its separation of ownership from control, would have disastrous effects on the economic life of the community. It was believed that corporations could easily swallow up individual businesspersons and could virtually enslave labor and thus dominate the state. Even when the use of the corporate structure was eventually permitted for more general business purposes, the states placed severe restrictions on the size and scope of its use. The states also limited the scope of the business corporation's powers and activities, established a maximum duration for corporate franchises, and required state residence as a prerequisite to incorporation.

Because of the growing interest in the corporate form of business by the turn of the century, however, a number of states removed these safeguards from their incorporation statutes in order to capture the significant revenue to be obtained by granting corporate charters. For example, a New York corporation would be permitted to incorporate under the more permissive laws of New Jersey and yet continue to operate principally in New York. The consequent rivalry between states vying for revenues and control incident to domestic incorporation created notable inconsistencies in corporate law among the states and substantial confusion in the courts.[a] The need for some kind of uniformity in corporate law was evident—a need filled by the Model Business Corporation Act (MBCA). Since 1933 the act has undergone several changes and was last revised and renumbered in 1969.

The Revised Model Business Corporation Act (RMBCA), as approved in June of 1984, was drafted as a convenient guide for revision of state business corporation acts. It was designed for use by both publicly held and closely held corporations and includes provisions for the rights and duties of shareholders, management, and directors. Already a number of states have amended their corporation laws, to a limited degree, based on the RMBCA.

Neither the revised and renumbered 1969 act nor the 1984 act has been totally adopted by any state in its current form. The 1969 act, however, has been influential in the codification of corporate statutes in more than 37 states and in the District of Columbia. It should be kept in mind that there is considerable variation among the state statutes based on the MBCA; therefore, those individual statutes should be relied upon rather than the MBCA.

a.   The intense competition among the states to attract corporate charters is vividly described by Justice Brandeis in *Louis K. Liggett Co. v. Lee*, 288 U.S. 517, 548–564, 53 S.Ct. 483, 490–496, 77 L.Ed. 929 (1933).

Source of Funding

A corporation can raise money in several different ways. The two most common ways are (1) to sell a part ownership in the corporation by issuing **equity securities** and (2) to borrow money by issuing **debt securities.**

A corporation commonly acquires funds by accepting offers to buy an interest in it. The corporation gives pieces of paper—stock—representing that ownership interest to the purchaser. This ownership interest in a corporation, represented by stock, is known as an equity security.

A corporation may also raise money by borrowing it. Often a corporation will issue **bonds** (which represent a long-term secured debt) or **debentures** (which represent an unsecured debt), and these are known as debt securities. Each represents a debt of the corporation.

Equity Securities Versus Debt Securities

Differences exist between equity securities (shares in the corporation) and debt securities (evidence of borrowed money). With an equity security, if the value of the shares increases, the holder of the shares is able to profit from the increased valuation as an owner of the corporation. If the value of the shares decreases, the shareholder loses the equity and may even lose her or his entire investment.

A debt security is treated like any loan. With a debt security, the holder knows that he or she will receive interest paid at a specific rate, such as 10 percent, on the loan. If the corporation is dissolved, the debt holders always have a higher priority for repayment than the equity holders when the assets are divided up.

Equity Securities

Common Stock   The owners of **common stock** generally have voting rights in the election of directors, in the amendment of articles and bylaws, and in other major corporate matters. Common stock is an equity security. The shareholder also has a right to a share of the corporation's profits, proportionate to the number of shares owned, if a dividend is declared by the board of directors. Common stock generally does not have a fixed dividend rate and does not carry with it any inherent right to have a dividend declared, even when the corporation is profitable.

On dissolution and liquidation of a corporation, the shareholders have a right to a proportionate share of the assets after the creditors' claims have been satisfied. Unless stock is redeemed (repurchased) by the corporation, the shares have an indefinite duration.

Preferred Stock   Although **preferred stock** is generally considered an equity security, from an investment standpoint it also bears certain similarities to a debt security. Preferred stock offers various designated preferences that are set by the articles of incorporation. Generally, preferred stock carries a preference in payment of dividends before dividends are paid to common stockholders and often pays dividends at a fixed rate. Also upon corporate dissolution and liquidation of assets, preferred shareholders often have priority over common shareholders. If the corporation is not profitable and preferred dividends cannot be paid, some preferred stock carries the right to accumulate the unpaid dividend. This means that if, in the future, a dividend is declared, the preferred stockholder must receive the previous unpaid dividend before any payment of dividends is made to the common stockholders. These shares are called **cumulative preferred stock.**

Preferred stockholders may or may not have voting rights on corporate issues. Most often voting rights are reserved strictly for common stockholders. On liquidation, the debt securities and other debts of the corporation are paid first; then, depending on provisions in the articles of incorporation, the value of the preferred stock may be paid to its holder before any payments are made to holders of common stock. Preferred stock dividends paid by the corporation are not deductible as an interest expense (treated as an equity security) for corporate income tax purposes.

Exhibit 18–2 illustrates the numerous types and definitions of stock.

Exhibit 18–2 Types and Definitions of Stock

TYPES	DEFINITIONS
Common Stock	Owners of common stock receive the lowest priority with respect to dividends paid and to the distribution of assets upon dissolution of the corporation.
Preferred Stock	Shares of stock that have priority over common stock shares as to payment of dividends and distribution of assets upon corporate dissolution. Dividend payments are usually a fixed percentage of the face value of the share.
Cumulative Preferred Stock	Preferred stock for which required dividends not paid in a given year must be paid in a subsequent year before any common stock dividends are paid.
Participating Preferred Stock	Owners of preferred stock first receive agreed-to dividends and then receive the same distribution of dividends that is paid on common stock.
Convertible Preferred Stock	Preferred stock giving holders the option to convert their shares into a specified number of common shares either in the issuing corporation or, sometimes, in another corporation.
Redeemable or Callable Preferred Stock	Preferred shares issued with the express condition that the issuing corporation has the right to repurchase the shares as specified.
Authorized Shares	Shares allowed to be issued by the articles of incorporation.
Issued Shares	Shares that are actually transferred to shareholders.
Outstanding Shares	Authorized and issued shares still held by shareholders.
Treasury Shares	Shares that are authorized and issued but are not outstanding (reacquired by the corporation).
No Par Value Shares	Shares issued with no stated value. The price is usually fixed by the board of directors or shareholders.
Par Value Shares	Shares issued and priced at a stated value per share.

A corporation must be careful not to sell more stock than is authorized in its articles of incorporation. In the following case, the officers and directors of the corporation were found liable when the corporation issued too many shares of stock.

Case 18.1
AGOSTA v.
SOUTHWEST
BREEDERS, INC.
Court of Appeals of Oklahoma,
1991.
810 P.2d 377.

BACKGROUND AND FACTS   *The articles of incorporation for Southwest Breeders allowed the corporation to issue no more than 50,000 shares of its stock at $1.00 per share. In March 31, 1986, Agosta purchased 15,000 shares. Agosta later discovered that on December 27, of the previous year, the officers and directors of Southwest Breeders had issued to themselves 1,370,000 shares at below-par value; these shares were clearly in excess of the amount allowed by the articles of incorporation. Sometime after March 31, Southwest Breeders filed an amendment to its articles of incorporation with the secretary of state, which authorized it to increase the number of shares from 50,000 to 50 million and an amended certificate of incorporation was issued.*

Agosta filed suit to rescind the contract, seeking $6,000 in damages for purchase of the overissued stock. The trial court determined that the sale of the overissued stock to Agosta constituted a sale of nonexistent stock for which the directors were personally liable.

Chief Judge HUNTER
*   *   *   *

A corporation whose capital is limited by its charter either in amount or in the number of shares, cannot issue valid certificates in excess of the limit prescribed. *   *   * Certificates of stock issued in violation of statute are wholly valueless and void, without regard to the intent of the parties to the overissue.
*   *   *   *

Generally, officers of a corporation are not liable to third persons for corporate acts where they do not purport to bind themselves. *   *   * However, it is also true that officers and agents of the corporation may be held personally liable by the purchaser for a fraudulent issue of stock or stock issued in violation of the law. 18A [American Jurisprudence, 2d] Corporations, section 515, states, in part:

> It is said that in authenticating and issuing certificates the officers represent that the stock is not spurious and is not invalid by reason of fraudulent or known acts or omissions of such officers, and such representations are addressed to whoever should thereafter purchase the certificate.

> In this case, the participation of these officers by their acts in negotiating the sale of the stock and by signing the certificates represented to Agosta that the stock was valid and bound them by their false representations.

The court found the officers were personally liable for the stock issued which was later found to be invalid.

DECISION AND REMEDY

Debt Securities

Different forms of debt exist, including bonds and debentures. A bond is a long-term commitment, and repayment to the creditor is secured by property. A debenture is unsecured by any property; the loan is made to the corporation based on its ability to repay the debt. A bond or debenture does not carry with it any right to control the management of the corporation and usually does not offer any voting rights on other matters.

Bonds and debentures earn interest at a fixed rate that is payable regardless of the corporation's profitability. The bonds or debentures mature at a specified date when the principal must be paid. Generally, bond and debenture holders have first claim against the assets of the corporation on its liquidation.

Liability

The corporate form of business entity is favored because liability is limited for shareholders, directors, and officers. Liability may stem from creditors' claims or from a judgment against the corporation. The limit on liability offered by a corporation is not, however, absolute.

Liability of Shareholders

If a creditor has a claim against the corporation, the claim must be satisfied from corporate assets. As a general rule, the shareholder has limited liability to the extent of her or his investment in the corporation; in other words, the shareholder can lose the amount she or he had invested in stock, but her or his personal assets are insulated from the liabilities of the corporation.

In some circumstances, especially with smaller corporations, when the corporation obtains a loan or enters into a contract, the creditor may require, in addition to the corporation's liability, a personal guarantee from the shareholders or officers. This means, of course, that the guarantor will have his or her personal assets at risk if the corporation does not meet its obligations.

In some circumstances, a court may **pierce the corporate veil** (ignore the corporate structure) and look to the shareholders' personal assets to satisfy corporate obligations. The corporate veil may be pierced for a number of reasons. First, the shareholder may have ignored the existence of the corporation by failing to comply with the corporate formalities, such as holding meetings of the board of directors or keeping corporate minutes. Second, the shareholder may have com-

Legal Highlight

Some Costs of Businesses

Starting a business is not cheap. Consider the following costs, but remember that these are only the basic ones:

1. Lawyers' fees—Fees can range from a minimum of $250 to $25,000 or more if the business is a corporation that must meet securities law requirements in its issue of stock.
2. Filing fees—The fees for filing the incorporation papers can range from a few dollars to several hundred dollars. Often businesses other than corporations (such as limited partnerships) also must pay fees associated with the filing of appropriate forms in various state or federal offices.

Once a business has been established, the ongoing costs are significant. A few of these costs include:

1. Unemployment insurance taxes—Payment of state unemployment insurance taxes for all employees is mandatory in all states.
2. Employer's contribution to social security—Payment of the nonrefundable employer's contribution to the federal social security system for all employees is mandatory. A self-employed person must pay the equivalent of the employer's plus the employee's contributions to social security.

3. Annual legal and accounting fees—Businesses must keep accurate books both for tax purposes and as a good business practice. The books should be audited by a certified public accountant (CPA). Audit costs can range from several hundred dollars to thousands of dollars. Various forms must be filed on a monthly, quarterly, and annual basis. Corporate records and minute books must be maintained, usually by an accountant or a lawyer. Annual fees for such services can run into many hundreds or thousands of dollars.

4. Insurance plans—Some states require a business to provide a health plan for all its employees.

5. Retirement plans—Although no state requires a business to provide retirement plans for its employees, if such a plan is adopted, the business must comply with the federal and state requirements.

---

mingled personal and corporate assets. Thus the corporation may be regarded as merely the alter ego (that is, one cannot distinguish between the shareholder and the corporation) of the shareholder. Third, the shareholder may have undercapitalized the corporation to such an extent that creditors are unable to collect against the corporation. Fourth, he or she, rather than putting money in as capital, may make a loan and take a security interest in the corporate assets. Finally, any evidence that the corporation was used to perpetuate a fraud, to circumvent the law, or to accomplish some illegal objective may lead a court to disregard the corporate existence.

In the following case, the court had to decide whether to disregard the corporate entity (pierce the corporate veil) and hold the shareholder personally liable.

Case 18.2

AMFAC FOODS, INC. v. INTERNATIONAL SYSTEMS & CONTROLS CORP. AND FLODIN, INC.

Supreme Court of Oregon, 1982.
294 Or. 94, 654 P.2d 1092.

BACKGROUND AND FACTS

is a food-processing firm that manufactures potato products. Through another party, Amfac entered into a contract with Flodin, Inc., to build and install certain machinery. Flodin is solely owned by International Systems and Controls Corporation (ISC). Flodin had limited assets, but its parent corporation was financially secure. The equipment supplied was not constructed properly. Amfac brought this action to hold ISC liable for breach of contract. Amfac won a jury verdict in the trial court, and that decision was upheld by the court of appeals. ISC then petitioned the supreme court of Oregon to review the case.

Justice PETERSON

   *   *   * This case involves the question whether a corporate shareholder, by exercising control over the affairs of a corporation of which it is the sole shareholder, may lose the limitation of liability which corporate shareholders normally enjoy and become liable to creditors of the corporation.
*   *   *   *

Limited shareholder liability was extended to corporate shareholders to encourage risk capital investments. *   *   *

The corporate form was not intended to be a device by which persons could engage in business without obligation or risk. The privilege of limited liability of the shareholders of a business corporation carries with it the obligation to conduct business as a corporation, and abuse of the privilege may create personal liability for the act of the corporation.

It soon became apparent that the benefits of limited shareholder liability could lead to corporate abuses. The turn of the century saw the rise of numerous claims against corporate shareholders by creditors of insolvent corporations. A body of common law was created, denying shareholder limited liability when the corporation was being used for an improper purpose. *   *   *
*   *   *   *

The disregard of a legally established corporate entity is an extraordinary remedy which exists as a last resort, where there is no other adequate and available remedy to repair the plaintiff's injury. Inasmuch as it is an extraordinary remedy, the doctrine is limited by conditions and limitations which are inapplicable to other remedies. Accordingly, when a plaintiff seeks to impose liability upon a stockholder of a defaulting corporation, the plaintiff and the court must be careful to keep the theories of recovery scrupulously segregated.

The statements of the exceptions have taken many forms. Courts' opinions often described results more than rules, saying that the shareholder would be held liable "to prevent injustice," "to prevent fraud," to prevent "evasion of just responsibility," to prevent the "distortion or hiding of the truth," to prevent a public wrong, to protect the rights of innocent parties where recognition of corporate separateness would result in "a manifest absurdity," or to prevent the avoidance of a legal obligation or duty.
*   *   *   *

Analysis of the opinions reveals that in many cases shareholder immunity was upheld even though the defendant was the sole owner of the stock and controlled the day-to-day operations of the company. Though control is an element in the formula, we are convinced that if one does not look beyond the element of control (adding "domination" to "control" does not aid the analysis), hopeless confusion will be the result of an inductive effort to derive a legal rule which can be applied to attain predictable results.
*   *   *   *

We state the exception to the rule as follows: When a plaintiff seeks to collect a corporate debt from a shareholder by virtue of the shareholder's control over the debtor corporation rather than on some other theory, the plaintiff must allege and prove not only that the debtor corporation was under the actual control of the shareholder but also that the plaintiff's inability to collect from the corporation resulted from some form of improper conduct on the part of the shareholder. This causation requirement has two implications. The shareholder's alleged control over the corporation must not be only potential but must actually have been exercised in a manner either causing the plaintiff to enter the transaction with the corporation or causing the corporation's default on the transaction or a resulting obligation. Likewise, the shareholder's conduct must have been improper either in relation to the plaintiff's entering the transaction or in preventing or interfering with the corporation's performance or ability to perform its obligations toward the plaintiff.

Conduct which has been held to be "improper" under the foregoing rule has included:

Inadequate capitalization: It has been held that gross undercapitalization of the debtor corporation, by itself, may suffice to hold the shareholder liable to a creditor who is unable to collect against the corporation because it was inadequately capitalized.

Milking: Shareholders have been held liable for a corporation's debt because they have milked a corporation by payment of excessive dividends.

Misrepresentation, commingling and holding out: Misrepresentations which may not be sufficient to constitute fraud would support a recovery against a shareholder on a misrepresentation theory. In some number of cases, shareholders have been held liable for corporate debts because of misrepresentations by the shareholder to the creditor, or because the respective enterprises were not held out to the public as separate enterprises.

Violation of Statute: In a number of cases involving regulations, courts have enjoined conduct of parent corporations which, in order to evade federal or state regulation, were doing business by means of wholly-owned subsidiaries.

The foregoing examples are just that, examples. This case is being remanded for a new trial. The plaintiff will have the opportunity to plead and prove the specific acts of ISC which are claimed to result in its loss of shareholder immunity. This case was tried on the "injustice" theory referred to above, and the evidence in the record of the specific instances of shareholder misconduct apart from proof of an agency relationship is not notably specific or in detail. Setting forth the precise evidence upon which the plaintiff relied to prove its case against ISC would only add to the length of the opinion and we see no need to do so. * * *

DECISION AND REMEDY *The supreme court of Oregon reversed the decision of the court of appeals and remanded the case to the trial court to be retried.*

COMMENT *It is unusual for a shareholder to be liable for the debts of a corporation. This case listed factors to be considered by a court when it is asked to pierce the corporate veil in order to hold the shareholder liable. The opinion emphasizes that control by the shareholder alone will not result in personal liability. The plaintiff must show that it cannot collect from the debtor corporation because of improper conduct by the shareholder. A causal relationship between any shareholder misconduct and the fact that the creditor's claim cannot be paid must exist.*

Liability of Directors and Officers

The **directors** and **officers** of a corporation are fiduciaries of the corporation and of its shareholders. A fiduciary relationship is based on trust and confidence. Directors are elected by the shareholders to the **board of directors.** The board of directors is responsible for the overall policy and management of the corporation. The board of directors (and in rare instances the shareholders) hires officers to implement the management's policy and oversee the daily operations of the corporation.

Directors and officers are required to perform their duties in good faith and in a manner that they reasonably believe to be in the best interest of the corporation. While the officers and directors of the corporation are not guarantors of its success, they cannot ignore their obligation to perform their duties. In performing their duties, they are entitled to rely on information presented by officers or employees of the corporation whom they reasonably believe to be reliable and competent in the matters presented. Directors of corporations that must register with the Securities and Exchange Commission (SEC) have a greater exposure to liability because they are ultimately responsible for compliance with the SEC rules.

Directors may not rely on information provided by officers and employees if the directors have knowledge or expertise that would make such a reliance unwarranted. Directors are required to be diligent in seeking information. They must act with the care that a reasonably prudent person in a comparable position would use under similar circumstances. If they perform their duties as directors in compliance with this standard, they will have no liability based simply on their being, or having been, directors of the corporation.

While the law imposes on directors and officers a duty to deal honestly and in good faith in steering the corporation, it gives them wide latitude in making valid business decisions. The law will not hold directors and officers liable for honest errors in business decisions if these decisions have been made with the correct motives and in good faith. This is referred to as the **business judgment rule.** The decisions must be within the powers of the corporation, and the resulting actions must be exercised with due care. The test of the decisions is objective: The directors and officers must exercise the same degree of care that reasonably prudent people use in the conduct of their own business affairs to avoid personal liability.

Directors must act in the best interests of the corporation as a whole, rather than on behalf of any individual or group of shareholders. Because they are fiduciaries, the directors and officers of a corporation may not usurp business opportunities that legitimately belong to the company itself. When a business opportunity would be of interest to the company, the directors or officers, in good faith, may take advantage of the opportunity only if the company is unable to and only if the directors or officers are not in direct competition with the company.

The business judgment rule has been reexamined by several courts because of mergers and buyouts of large corporations. The following case applied the business judgment rule.

BACKGROUND AND FACTS   *In the early 1980s, Time's executive board began considering expansion of Time's operations into the entertainment industry. By 1987, Time had established a special committee to consider and propose corporate strategies for the 1990s. First, Time wanted better control over quality and price of the film products delivered to its subsidiaries, Home Box Office and Cinemax. Second, Time was concerned with the increasing globalization of the world economy. By late spring 1987, representatives from Time and Warner Brothers met to discuss the possibility of a joint venture. In July 1988, Time's board of directors met to consider the expansion into the entertainment industry on a global scale and heard the profiles of Warner, Disney, 20th Century Fox, Universal, and Paramount.*

The strategic plan for Time's expansion was approved by the board, and the board gave management the right to continue discussions with Warner about a possible merger. After extensive negotiations, on March 3, 1989, Time's board unanimously approved a stock-for-stock merger with Warner and a new name, Time-Warner, Inc.

On June 7, 1989, Paramount made a surprise all-cash offer to purchase all outstanding shares of Time for $175 per share. Time's stock rose the next day from $126 to $170 per share. After many meetings and negotiations, Time's board on June 16 formally rejected Paramount's offer. At the same meeting, Time's board decided to acquire Warner as follows: all cash for 51 percent of Warner's outstanding stock at $70 per share. This action did not require shareholder approval. To provide the funds, Time agreed to assume $7–10 billion worth of debt.

Case 18.3
PARAMOUNT COMMUNICATIONS, INC. v. TIME INC.
Supreme Court of Delaware, 1990.
571 A.2d 1140.

On June 23, Paramount raised its all cash offer to $200 per share. On June 26, Time's board formally rejected this second offer. The board believed that Paramount's offer was inadequate and that the Warner transaction offered a greater long-term value for the stockholders. It also perceived in Paramount's offer a threat to the "Time Culture" and its editorial freedom because Time would be the acquired company. During all the negotiations with Warner and with Paramount, Time was adamant about preserving the "Time Culture" and its editorial freedom.

Paramount and some of Time's shareholders instituted this lawsuit. In the lower court, the chancellor (judge) wrote a 50-page opinion in which he refused to enjoin Time's purchase of Warner's stock; Paramount appealed.

Justice HORSEY
*   *   *   *

The principal ground for reversal, asserted by all plaintiffs, is that Paramount's June 7, 1989 uninvited all-cash, all-shares, "fully negotiable" (though conditional) tender offer for Time triggered duties under *Unocal Corp. v. Mesa Petroleum Co.*, and that Time's board of directors, in responding to Paramount's offer, breached those duties. As a consequence, plaintiffs argue that in our review of the Time board's decision of June 16, 1989 to enter into a revised merger agreement with Warner, Time is not entitled to the benefit and protection of the business judgment rule.
*   *   *   *

We turn now to plaintiffs' *Unocal* claim. We begin by noting, as did the Chancellor, that our decision does not require us to pass on the wisdom of the board's decision to enter into the original Time-Warner agreement. That is not a court's task. Our task is simply to review the record to determine whether there is sufficient evidence to support the Chancellor's conclusion that the initial Time-Warner agreement was the product of a proper exercise of business judgment.
*   *   *   *

In *Unocal*, we held that before the business judgment rule is applied to a board's adoption of a defensive measure, the burden will lie with the board to prove (a) reasonable grounds for believing that a danger to corporate policy and effectiveness existed; and (b) that the defensive measure adopted was reasonable in relation to the threat posed. Directors satisfy the first part of the *Unocal* test by demonstrating good faith and reasonable investigation. We have repeatedly stated that the refusal to entertain an offer may comport with a valid exercise of a board's business judgment.
*   *   *   *

Plaintiffs' position represents a fundamental misconception of our standard of review under *Unocal* principally because it would involve the court in substituting its judgment as to what is a "better" deal for that of a corporation's board of directors.

The usefulness of *Unocal* as an analytical tool is precisely its flexibility in the face of a variety of fact scenarios. *Unocal* is not intended as an abstract standard; neither is it a structured and mechanistic procedure of appraisal. Thus, we have said that directors may consider, when evaluating the threat posed by a takeover bid, the inadequacy of the price offered, nature and timing of the offer, questions of illegality, the impact on constituencies other than shareholders, the risk of nonconsummation, and the quality of securities being offered in the exchange.
*   *   *   *

We turn to the second part of the *Unocal* analysis. The obvious requisite to determining the reasonableness of a defensive action is a clear identification of the nature of the threat. As the Chancellor correctly noted, this "requires an evaluation of the importance of the corporate objective threatened; alternative methods of protecting that objective; impacts of the 'defensive' action, and other relevant factors." It is not until both parts of the *Unocal* inquiry have been satisfied that the business judgment rule attaches to defensive actions of a board of directors. As applied to the facts of this case, the question is whether the record evidence supports the Court of Chancery's conclusion that the restructuring of the Time-Warner transaction, including the adoption of several preclusive defensive measures, was a *reasonable response* in relation to a perceived threat. * * * Delaware law confers the management of the corporate enterprise to the stockholders' duly elected board representatives. The fiduciary duty to manage a corporate enterprise includes the selection of a time frame for achievement of corporate goals. That duty may not be delegated to the stockholders. Directors are not obliged to abandon a deliberately conceived corporate plan for a short-term shareholder profit unless there is clearly no basis to sustain the corporate strategy.

* * * *

We affirm the Chancellor's rulings as clearly supported by the record. Finally, we note that although Time was required, as a result of Paramount's hostile offer, to incur a heavy debt [$7–10 billion] to finance its acquisition of Warner, that fact alone does not render the board's decision unreasonable so long as the directors could reasonably perceive the debt load not to be so injurious to the corporation as to jeopardize its well being.

DECISION AND REMEDY

Time prevailed in this case. The court found that Paramount's tender offer was reasonably perceived by Time's board to pose a threat to Time and that the board's response to that threat was reasonable. The court rejected the argument that the only corporate threat posed by an all-shares, all-cash offer was the possibility of inadequate value. The threat was to the very life of "Time Culture" and editorial freedom.

Control

In theory, one of the characteristics of a corporation is centralized management. Directors set policy for the corporation and hire the officers to run the corporation on a day-to-day basis. An officer can also be a director of the corporation. The usual officers are the president, at least one vice president, the secretary, and the treasurer. Under the MBCA a person may have more than one office but cannot serve as both president and secretary. Corporate officers can be removed by the board of directors at any time with or without cause (without shareholder approval). A wrongful dismissal could result in breach of contract liability, however.

Shareholders' Control

The shareholders elect the directors and have voting rights on major corporate matters, such as amending the articles of incorporation or bylaws, deciding to merge or consolidate with another corporation, opting to sell all or substantially all of the corporate assets, or dissolving the corporation.

Controlling, or majority, shareholders also have a fiduciary duty to the corporation and to minority shareholders when transferring their shares, a duty similar to that of officers and directors. While a controlling shareholder is free to dispose of his or her stock and to receive a premium price for the ability to control, the controlling shareholder may not sell control of the corporation if a reasonably prudent person would foresee the possibility of mismanagement by the purchaser.

Generally, in the absence of extraordinary circumstances, such as fraud or detriment to the corporation, courts have held that directors, officers, and controlling shareholders are free to buy and sell their shares without including or even making disclosures to minority shareholders. Minority shareholders can receive some protection through bylaws or restrictions stamped on the stock certificate. This protection may include requiring a majority shareholder or officer or director to give notice of sale or purchase to minority sharehold-

Voting Techniques

Once a quorum is present, a majority vote of the shares represented at the meeting is usually required to pass resolutions and elect members of the board of directors. Most states permit or require shareholders to elect directors by cumulative voting, a method designed to allow minority shareholders representation on the board of directors. Cumulative voting operates in the following way: The number of members of the board to be elected is multiplied by the number of voting shares held by the shareholder. The result equals the number of votes a shareholder has, and this total can be cast for one or more nominees for director. All nominees running for the elective board seats to be filled stand for election at the same time. Where cumulative voting is not required either by statute or under the articles of incorporation, the entire board can be elected by a majority of shares at a shareholders' meeting.

For example, say that a corporation has 10,000 shares issued and outstanding. The minority shareholders hold only 3,000 shares, and the majority shareholders hold the other 7,000. Three members of the board are to be elected. The majority shareholders' nominees are Anne, Betty, and Charlene. The minority shareholders' nominee is Diane. Can Diane be elected by the minority shareholders?

If cumulative voting is allowed, the answer is yes. The minority shareholders have 9,000 votes among them: The number of directors to be elected (3) times the number of shares (3,000) equals the number of votes (9,000). All of these votes can be cast to elect Diane. The majority shareholders have 21,000 votes (3 times 7,000 equals 21,000), but these votes have to be distributed among their three nominees. Under the principle of cumulative voting, no matter how the majority shareholders cast their 21,000 votes, they will not be able to elect all three directors, if the minority shareholders decide as a unit to cast all of their 9,000 votes for Diane.

---

ers, or providing the right of first refusal (to be discussed later) to the minority shareholders or the corporation to purchase the shares being sold.

Close Corporation Control

A **close corporation** has its shares closely held by members of a family or by relatively few persons. Close corporations are often referred to as *closed, closely held, family,* or *privately held* corporations. The members know each other personally, and because the number of shareholders is so small, frequently no trading market exists for these shares. In practice, these corporations operate more like a partnership.

In a close corporation, the question of who controls the business is very important. It is often said that a person should always try to obtain 51 percent ownership, accept 50 percent, but never accept 49 percent or less common-stock owner-

ship. In a close corporation, the board of directors can be one person. That person controls the corporation because the board of directors appoints officers and establishes the budget, including the amount to be paid in salaries and the types of fringe benefits.

Directors' Control

The board of directors is authorized to exercise all of the corporate powers, to manage the business, and to set the policy of the corporation. The directors' responsibilities include the declaration and payment of dividends to shareholders. The board also fixes the compensation of the officers and directors.

In larger corporations, the directors will often select an executive committee from among the board members to handle management decisions between meetings of the board. Often officers are also directors of the corporation and sit on many of the executive committees created by the board of directors. The board of directors delegates much of the responsibility for day-to-day management to the officers. However, major policy, financial, and contract decisions involving the management of a corporation cannot be delegated by the board of directors to the corporation's officers.

Transferability of Interest

Another characteristic of corporations is the free transferability of shares. The law generally recognizes the right of an owner to transfer property unless there are valid restrictions on its transferability. Some restrictions are imposed by securities laws if the shares are registered with the Securities and Exchange Commission or if, for example, insiders, such as directors, officers, or controlling shareholders of the corporation who may have access to inside information trade their securities on the basis of this information. Other restrictions may be imposed by contract, articles of incorporation, or bylaws.

Restrictions for Close Corporations

Within a close corporation, the need to provide restrictions on the transfer of common shares is greater than in other types of corporations. The interpersonal relationship of the principal shareholders of the close corporation is very intense; in many close corporations, a person spends more time with fellow shareholders than with his or her own family. This commitment requires mutual respect, trust, and understanding among the shareholders. The possibility is always present that one of the principal shareholders may die, may obtain a divorce, or may decide to leave the corporation or retire from the business. Without restrictions on the transferability of shares, a remaining shareholder might find himself or herself in business with the former associate's ex-spouse, heirs, or even some stranger. The shareholder may find it impossible to work with and to be closely associated with these new parties.

One method of restricting transfer of shares in a close corporation is providing for the option of *right of first refusal* when any member's shares are being transferred. The articles of incorporation or bylaws normally will provide that the shares to be transferred must first be offered for sale to the remaining shareholders and often to the corporation itself. These shareholders or the corporation has the first right either to buy the shares or the right to refuse to buy the shares. It is extremely important that there be a procedure established to determine the price of the stock and that the corporation or remaining shareholders have the capability to buy the shares. For example, the articles of incorporation, the bylaws, or a shareholder agreement could give the corporation or remaining shareholders a right to purchase the stock upon the death of a shareholder with the value of the shares to be determined by an independent appraiser. Funds for the purchase of the stock on the death of the shareholder could be provided by a life insurance policy taken out and paid for by the corporation on the shareholder's life.

Notice of Restrictions

Any restrictions on transferability (including right of first refusal) must be placed on the stock certificate, but they should also at least be contained in the bylaws; in some states, they must be included in the articles of incorporation. The common law does not like restrictions on transferability; because of this, the restrictions must be written in very specific language and follow the state law exactly.

Taxes

The corporation, as a separate entity, is also a separate taxpayer. The corporation pays taxes on its earnings in the year earned. When the earnings are distributed to the shareholders as dividends, the shareholders are also taxed. Unlike a partnership, however, the shareholders are not taxed until they actually receive the distribution in the form of dividends. Losses are also deducted by the corporation; they offset corporate income rather than passing through to the shareholders to be deducted from their income for tax purposes.

One means of avoiding the double taxation where the shareholders are also officers or employees of the corporation is by paying salaries to them rather than dividends. The salaries will be a deduction for the corporation and are therefore not taxed at the corporate level. This deduction may be disallowed, however, by the Internal Revenue Service (IRS) if the salaries are held to be excessive or unreasonable.

Avoidance of Taxes

Shareholders can also avoid double taxation by means of their capital structure. Rather than contributing all of their money to the capital of the corporation, a portion of it is given as a loan. The interest on the loan is a deductible item for the corporation and therefore is not taxable. Again, the IRS pays close attention to undercapitalization of corporations. Generally, a debt-to-equity ratio greater than three to one may be challenged by the IRS. This type of undercapitalization also endangers the limited liability of shareholders.

As long as the corporation's earnings are not distributed to the shareholders as dividends, no tax is paid by the shareholder. Often the corporation will accumulate earnings rather than distributing them. The IRS, however, has rules that will impose a tax on the corporation for excessive accumulated earnings. The IRS rules encourage the distribution of earnings to shareholders rather than the retention of those earnings that are not needed for the business.

S Corporation

The label **S Corporation** refers to the tax status of a corporation and not to a type of corporation. S Corporation refers to the IRS statutes that set out the qualifications for and the advantages of meeting the S Corporation requirements. S Corporation is a voluntary tax status for a close corporation. In other words, the shareholders must elect to adopt the S Corporation status.

This status allows the corporation to be taxed as a partnership (yet retain the advantages of a corporation, such as limited liability) and to have all losses and gains passed through to the individual shareholders without taxation at the corporate level. In an S Corporation, the profit is passed through to the shareholders for tax purposes regardless of whether it is actually distributed to them in the form of dividends.

To qualify, an S Corporation may not have more than 35 shareholders, and no more than 25

percent of its income may be earned from passive investments such as rentals, interest, royalties, and dividends. An S Corporation is allowed to have only one class of stock. Only domestic corporations can qualify for this status. Many technical requirements must be met for a corporation to become an S Corporation, and the IRS may retroactively revoke the S Corporation status if these conditions are not met. If the shareholders want to maintain the S Corporation status, the shareholders' agreement must provide that their shares can be transferred only to qualified shareholders (corporations, partnerships, and many trusts cannot be shareholders).

Duration

Unless otherwise specified in the articles of incorporation, a corporation has perpetual existence. In theory, the death of a shareholder, officer, or director has no effect on the corporate entity. As a practical matter, in many close corporations, the death of the major shareholder, who is also a director or an officer, effectively brings an end to the business, if not the corporation. In such instances, the estate of the deceased shareholder may attempt to find a buyer for the corporation's shares who will continue the operation. If a buyer cannot be found, the corporation may have to be dissolved.

Dissolution

Under most state statutes, a corporation may be dissolved following adoption by the board and a majority of the shareholders of a resolution called the **articles of dissolution.** The corporation may then either proceed with its own liquidation of the business and its assets, or it may apply to the court to supervise the liquidation. The court has the power to appoint a receiver who, with the powers and duties specified by the court, will proceed to liquidate the assets and the business.

After the business and assets have been liquidated, all the liabilities of the corporation are paid. If there are any remaining assets, they will be distributed to shareholders according to their respective rights and interests. Finally, the articles of dissolution are filed with the state and the existence of the corporation ceases. In most states, for a period of years following the filing of the articles of dissolution, claims that existed prior to the dissolution may be made against the corporation and its directors, officers, or shareholders.

The dissolution of a corporation does not extinguish its debts or terminate its contracts. Under some circumstances, a corporation may be held liable for failure to perform a contract if the corporation has been dissolved voluntarily.

Dissolution can also occur by means other than the voluntary filing of the resolution for articles of dissolution. For example, any of the following may result in dissolution:

1. An act of the legislature in the state of incorporation (such as making the activities of the corporation illegal)
2. Expiration of the time of existence specified in the charter or statute without a renewal
3. By a court decree through an action brought by the state attorney general when the actions of the corporation justify dissolution (such as procurement of the charter by fraud, abuse of corporate powers, abandonment of operations, and continued violation of criminal statutes)
4. By merger (a legal combination of two or more corporations by which one corporation is absorbed into the surviving corporation, thus dissolving the other corporation)
5. By consolidation (a combination of two or more corporations by which the corporations are joined to form a new corporation, dissolving the original corporations).

Franchising

The Federal Trade Commission defines a **franchise** as an arrangement between a **franchisor**, who is the owner of a trademark, a trade name, or a copyright, and another person known as the **franchisee**. The franchisor licenses the franchisee (the holder of the franchise) to use the trademark, trade name, or copyright in marketing the goods or services under specified conditions or limitations. Most franchisees are corporations, but ownership is not limited to the corporate form.

The franchise system has also been described as an organization composed of distributive units established and administered by a supplier as a means of expanding and controlling the market for its products. Each franchise dealer is a legally independent but economically dependent unit of the integrated business system. The individual franchisee operates as an independent business, yet it obtains the advantages of affiliation with the regional or national organization, which supplies the products, advertising, and other services.

The use of franchises has expanded rapidly in recent years. Between 1910 and 1940, franchising was used primarily in the automobile industry, sports, and the soft-drink bottling industry. Now franchises account for about 34 percent of all retail sales. The franchise pattern of business development is a particularly appealing form of capitalist enterprise, as it enables groups of individuals with small amounts of capital to become entrepreneurs.

Types of Franchises

The three types of franchises are **distributorship, business format,** and **manufacturing or processing plant.**

1. Distributorship—A manufacturing concern (the franchisor) licenses a dealer (the franchisee) to sell its product. The franchise outlets serve merely as conduits through which the trademarked goods of the franchisor flow. The trademark in a distributorship franchise represents the end product marketed by the system. Often, a distributorship covers an exclusive territory. Two diverse examples of this type of franchise are an automobile dealership and a Baskin-Robbins Ice Cream Company franchise.
2. Business format—This franchise is the typical chain-style business. The franchisor merely provides the trademark, and the franchisee is responsible for the manufacture and sale of the end product. The franchisee operates under the franchisor's trade name and is identified as a member of a select group of dealers that engages in the franchisor's business. The franchisee is generally required to follow standardized methods of operations. Often the franchisor requires that minimum prices and quality standards be maintained. Examples of this type of franchise are McDonald's and most other fast-food chains.
3. Manufacturing or processing plant—The franchisor transfers to the franchisee the essential ingredients or formula to make a particular product.

The franchisee then markets it either wholesale or retail in accordance with the franchisor's standards. Examples of this type of franchise are Coca-Cola and other soft-drink corporations.

The Law of Franchising

The growth in franchise operations has outdistanced the law of franchising. No solid body of franchise law has been developed. Because of the absence of law precisely addressed to franchising, the courts tend to apply general common-law principles and federal or state statutes when appropriate. Although the franchise agreement itself is a contract, the franchise relationship has characteristics associated with agency law and employment law, as well as ordinary contract law.

Disclosure Protection   A franchise purchaser can suffer substantial losses if the franchisor has not provided complete information regarding the franchisor-franchisee relationship, as well as the details of the contract under which the business will be operated.

Only a few of the states that have enacted legislation concerning franchising have included disclosure provisions. California was the first state to enact a franchise disclosure law, and it has served as a model for other disclosure statutes. The California Franchise Investment Law sets out 22 items that must be disclosed in a registration filed with the state. Some of the items of disclosure include:

1. The name and business address of the franchisor
2. The business experience of any people affiliated with the franchisor
3. Whether any person associated with the franchisor has been convicted of a felony
4. A recent financial statement
5. A typical franchise agreement
6. A statement of all fees that the franchisee is required to pay
7. Other information that the commissioner of corporations may reasonably require.

When misrepresentation permeates the initial sale of a franchise operation, the common-law remedy of fraud does not provide adequate relief. In most cases, the franchisee has already paid the franchise purchase price and may also have incurred substantial losses in the initial operating phases of the business. The elements of fraud are exceedingly difficult to prove. The franchisee has a great burden to show that the franchisor's original offer was fraudulent.

The FTC Franchise Rule of 1978 was promulgated in response to widespread evidence of deception and unfair practices in connection with the sale of franchises and business opportunity ventures. This rule requires that, within a specified time, franchisors and franchise brokers must furnish the information that prospective franchisees need in order to make an informed decision about entering into a franchise relationship. The rule sets forth the circumstances under which a franchisor or broker can make claims about the projected sales income or profits of existing or potential outlets. The rule also imposes requirements that concern the establishment and termination of the franchise relationship.

The Franchise Agreement

The relationship between the franchisor and the franchisee is defined by a contract. Each franchise relationship and each industry have their own characteristics, so it is difficult to describe the broad range of details that a franchising contract may include. The following sections, however, will define the essential characteristics of the franchise relationship.

Payment for Franchise   The franchise ordinarily pays an initial fee or lump-sum price for the franchise license (the privilege of being granted a franchise). This fee is separate from the various products that the franchisee purchases from or through the franchisor. In some industries, the franchisor relies heavily on the initial sale of the franchise in order to realize a profit. In other industries, the continued dealing between the parties brings profit to both.

In most situations, the franchisor will receive a stated percentage of the annual sales or annual volume of business done by the franchisee. The franchise agreement may also require the franchisee to pay a percentage of advertising costs and certain administrative expenses incurred throughout the franchise arrangement.

Location and Business Organization Typically, the franchisor will determine the territory to be served. The franchise agreement can specify whether the premises for the business must be leased or purchased outright. In some cases, construction of a building is necessary to meet the terms of the franchise agreement.

In addition, the agreement will specify whether the franchisor supplies equipment and furnishings for the premises or whether this is the responsibility of the franchisee. When the franchise is a service operation such as a motel, the contract often provides that the franchisor will establish certain standards for the facility and will make inspections to ensure that the standards are being maintained in order to protect the franchise name and reputation.

The business organization of the franchisee is of great concern to the franchisor. Depending on the terms of the franchise agreement, the franchisor may specify particular requirements for the form and capital structure of the business. The

franchise agreement can provide that certain standards of operation, such as sales quotas, quality considerations, or record keeping, must be met by the franchisee.

Furthermore, a franchisor may want to retain stringent control over the training of personnel involved in the operation and over administrative aspects of the business. Although the day-to-day operation of the franchise business is normally left up to the franchisee, the franchise agreement can provide for whatever amount of supervision and control the parties desire.

One area of franchises that causes a great deal of conflict is the *territorial exclusivity* of the franchise. Many franchise agreements, while they do define the territory allotted to a particular franchise, specifically state that the franchise is nonexclusive. Nonexclusivity allows the franchisor to establish multiple franchises in the same territory. The following case illustrates a situation where the franchise agreement did not guarantee exclusivity in a specific territory.

BACKGROUND AND FACTS *In early 1976, the plaintiff, Imperial Motors, Inc., and Flynn, who owned the dealership, entered into direct dealer agreements for Chrysler and Plymouth dealerships with the defendant, Chrysler Corporation. The direct dealer agreements explicitly provided that Imperial would not have the exclusive right to purchase for resale defendant's cars in a four-town area of South Carolina. The Chrysler district manager, however, orally told Flynn that Imperial's Chrysler-Plymouth dealership would be the only one in these four towns.*

In August of 1976, Chrysler allowed another Chrysler-Plymouth dealer, Carroll Motors, to move into a new showroom seven miles from Imperial's location. Imperial claimed that Chrysler had violated the Automobile Dealers' Day in Court Act (a federal statute governing written franchise agreements between auto manufacturers and auto dealers) by approving the relocation of Carroll Motors. Chrysler moved for summary judgment contending that the plaintiff had not established a cause of action for the lawsuit.

Case 18.4
IMPERIAL MOTORS, INC. v. CHRYSLER CORP.
United States District Court, District of Massachusetts, 1983.
559 F.Supp. 1312.

Judge ZOBEL
* * * *

Defendant's motion for summary judgment is proper as to that part of plaintiffs' claim which alleges that defendant's approval of Carroll's relocation was a violation of the [Automobile Dealers' Day in Court Act]. The Act covers only those actions of a franchisor which amount to a "failure . . . to act in good faith in performing or complying with any of the terms or provisions of the franchise, or in terminating, cancelling, or not renewing the franchise with a dealer." Good faith is narrowly defined as "the duty of each party . . . to act in a fair and equitable manner toward each other so as to guaranty the one party freedom from coercion, intimidation or threats of coercion or intimidation by the other party. The failure to abide by the terms of a franchise agreement cannot by itself constitute a violation of the act. Moreover, the Act explicitly defines a franchise as a "written agreement"; accordingly, oral promises are not part of a franchise agreement and cannot form the basis of a claim of bad faith.

DECISION AND REMEDY *Chrysler's motion for summary judgment was granted. The court held that granting a franchise to Carroll in the same area as Imperial was not a violation of the franchise agreement or of the Automobile Dealers' Day in Court Act because the promise was oral, not written.*

COMMENT *The franchisee in this case was left unprotected by the franchise agreement as far as territorial exclusivity was concerned. The same denial of relief resulted under the Unfair Trade Practices Act when a Ford automobile dealer (with a nonexclusive franchise agreement) filed suit after Ford Motor Company had granted a franchise to another Ford Dealership in close proximity to his own. [See McLaughlin Ford, Inc. v. Ford Motor Company, 192 Conn. 558, 473 A.2d 1185 (1985).]*

Price and Quality Controls Franchises provide the franchisor with an outlet for the firm's goods and services. Depending on the nature of the business, the franchisor may require the franchisee to purchase products from the franchisor at an established price. Of course, a franchisor cannot set the prices at which the franchisee will resell the goods, as this is a violation of state or federal antitrust laws. A franchisor can suggest retail prices but cannot insist on them.

Although a franchisor can require franchisees to purchase supplies from it, requiring a franchisee to purchase *exclusively* from the franchisor may violate state or federal antitrust laws. The implications of antitrust violations on territorial restrictions, restrictions on products sold, resale price fixing, and price discrimination are discussed in Chapter 20.

As a general rule, no question exists as to the validity of a provision permitting the franchisor to enforce certain quality standards. Since the franchisor has a legitimate interest in maintaining the quality of the product or service in order to protect its name and reputation, it can exercise greater control in this area than would otherwise be tolerated.

Termination of the Franchise Arrangement

The duration of the franchise is a matter to be determined between the parties. Generally, a franchise will start out for a short period, such as a year, so that the franchise and the franchisor can determine whether they want to stay in business with one another. The franchise agreement will usually specify that termination must be for cause, such as death or disability of the franchisee, insolvency of the franchisee, breach of the franchise agreement, or failure to meet specified sales quotas. Most franchise contracts provide that notice of termination must be given.

Much franchise litigation has arisen over termination provisions. Since the franchise agreement is normally a "form" contract prepared by the franchisor and since the bargaining power of the franchisee is rarely equal to that of the franchisor, the termination provisions of contracts are generally more favorable to the franchisor. The lack of statutory law and case law in this area affects the franchisee most keenly. Franchisees in automobile dealerships and gasoline stations have some statutory protection under the Automobile Dealers' Day in Court and Petroleum Marketing Practices Acts.

Ethical Considerations

Should Business Be Able to Influence Politicians?

Sir Edward Coke in the early seventeenth century observed that corporations are different from natural persons because corporations "cannot commit treason, nor be outlawed nor excommunicated, for they have no souls." A wealthy corporation can influence the election of candidates and other political issues by spending large sums to purchase television and radio advertising time. Are there ethical problems when these expenditures, which are made either directly or through political action committees (PACs), are not limited? Are there any correlations between a corporation's political ideas and those of the public? Should a corporation not have the right to speak out on public issues? What are the effects of congressional and state regulations in this area?

The franchisee normally invests a substantial amount of time and money in the franchise operation to make it successful. Despite this fact, the franchisee may receive little or nothing for the business on termination. The franchisor owns the trademark and hence the business.

Franchisee's Relationship to Franchisor: Agent or Independent Contractor?

The mere licensing of a trade name does not create an agency relationship. The courts have determined that certain other factors in the franchisor-franchisee relationship may indicate the existence of an agency relationship:

1. The terms of the agreement create an agency relationship.
2. The franchisor exercises a high degree of control over the franchisee's activities.
3. A third person looking at the relationship between the franchisor and the franchisee would reasonably believe that there is an agency relationship.
4. The franchisor derives an especially great benefit from the franchisee's activities. The greater the benefit, the more likely an agency relationship will be found.

If these factors show a very close relationship between the franchisor and the franchisee, their relationship will be deemed to be that of an employer-employee or principal-agent in dealings with third parties. If the factors show a high degree of independence between the franchisee and franchisor, the franchisee will be deemed an independent contractor.

The characterization of the relationship has tax implications and implications for the regulatory treatment of the business organization. In addition, if an agency relationship is found, the franchisor is liable for the franchisee's improper actions or injuries to third parties both in tort and in contract.

International Considerations

How To Expand Without Investing

American corporations often do business overseas through the use of licensing or franchising agreements. Licensing agreements can be divided into two categories: patent licensing and know-how licensing. With a patent license, the foreign licensee has access to and use of the patent, while the American licensor receives the royalties. With know-how licensing, the American licensor has a trade secret or knows how to use certain technology that no one else knows how to use. The American business gives the foreign licensee the right to use the trade secret or know-how.

Franchising is a specialized form of licensing. The franchisor (supplier) licenses the franchisee (foreign firm) to use the franchisor's marketing knowledge, product, and services in exchange for fees. This agreement allows the franchisee to use the trademark and copyrights of the franchisor. Examples include the International Hilton Hotel chain, McDonald's, and Coca-Cola.

Foreign companies are, of course, able to do business in the United States under the same arrangements. Examples include foreign automobile dealerships and distributorships of electronic equipment, such as computers, video cameras, and compact disc players.

Choosing the Best Form of Business Organization

A friend has developed a new oil filter for use in internal combustion engines that enables the engine to use the same oil up to ten times as long as is currently possible. She believes there is a market for such a product, but, being totally unfamiliar with business matters, she comes to you for advice.

After reviewing the materials she has developed to explain the product, you believe that the project is worth pursuing. The two of you would like to begin a business to produce and sell the product.

Good business practice would suggest that you consult an attorney before proceeding with your plans. A good business lawyer can discuss with you your goals, alternative courses of action to meet those goals, and the probable consequences of each alternative.

To take maximum advantage of the time spent with your attorney, you should prepare certain information. What assets will be part of the business? In whose name are those assets held now? You may be transferring real property to the business, or your friend may be transferring patent or other rights, and you will need to discuss the tax consequences of those transfers.

Each of you will also want to collect information on your individual financial and tax statuses that may enter into the decision as to what form of business entity is appropriate for you. How much money will you need to bring

to your business in order to carry it through the first year? You should have some idea of how you will raise this money. Can you and your friend provide it personally from your savings or through a bank loan, or will you bring in other equity investors?

If you bring in other investors, the questions of liability and control of the business will become more complex. Even if you and your friend provide all of the capital, however, the issues of liability and of control of day-to-day operations and long-term policy are critical and will be an important element in choosing the form of business entity.

You must also consider how freely ownership interests in your business can be transferred. Your friend may have implicit trust in your business judgment, but would she want to be in business with your heirs if you should die? Would you want to proceed if she were to sell her interest in the business to a stranger without her technical skills? Perhaps both of you will want the option to buy the other's interest in the business in case of death, or you both may want a right of first refusal if one of you decides to transfer your interest during your lifetime.

Obviously, the answers to all of these questions have an impact on what form of business organization you should use. By considering these questions in advance and bringing with you cash-flow projections, as well as tax and other relevant information, your attorney will be better able to assist you in starting your business.

Summary

A corporation is the most formal type of business entity. The first step in formalizing a corporation is to file articles of incorporation with the appropriate state agency. Among the items included in this document are the name, address, and general purpose of the corporation, its duration, the num-

ber and class of shares, the number of directors, and the names of the incorporators.

The next step is the adoption of bylaws. The bylaws control the internal operation of the business. In addition, any business must have funds with which to operate. Funds are obtained by issuing securities. The two broad classes of securities are equity securities and debt securities.

The most frequently used equity security is common stock. This form of security generally offers voting rights in the election of the board of directors and other major corporate matters. Common stock does not have a fixed dividend rate. On dissolution, the shareholders have a right to a proportionate share of the assets after payment of all other parties.

Closely akin to common stock is preferred stock. It is considered an equity security, but it bears great similarity to a debt obligation. Normally, preferred shareholders have a preference for dividends that are paid at a fixed rate. During dissolution, preferred stock is paid ahead of common stock but after corporate debt obligations.

Debt financing is used by all businesses and is usually represented by a bond or debenture. These debts will pay a fixed interest rate whether or not the corporation is profitable. On dissolution, debt securities are paid ahead of equity securities. Generally, in the absence of a personal guarantee, shareholders are immune from liability for the debts of the corporation. If the corporation is not properly conducted, however, the courts may allow a piercing of the corporate veil in order to hold shareholders liable.

As long as directors and officers do not breach their fiduciary duties, they are likewise not personally liable for the debts of the corporation. They can, however, be held liable for mismanagement in carrying out their responsibilities. They are protected from legal actions based on losses brought about by their making honest errors in business decisions (the business judgment rule).

The shareholders own the corporation. They elect the board of directors. The board of directors sets corporate policy and appoints the officers. All corporations must have officers who conduct the day-to-day activities of the corporation. These officers include a president, at least one vice president, a secretary, and a treasurer. The same person may occupy several positions, except for president and secretary.

A corporation can limit the transferability of securities. These restrictions must be reasonable, and the limitations must be known (placed on the security) to the holder and prospective purchaser.

Whenever a business decision is made, its effects on taxes must be considered. This is especially true when selecting a corporate form of organization. Special tax advantages occur if S Corporation status is selected instead of the normal tax status of a corporation. All losses and profits are passed through the corporation to the shareholders if a corporation elects to be taxed under the S Corporation provisions of the Internal Revenue Code.

The law of franchising is developing through cases and through state and federal statutes. A franchise exists when there is a contract in which one party owns a trademark, trade name, or copyright and he or she allows another party to use this right under specified conditions or limitations. Three different types of franchises have been developed: (1) distributorship, (2) business format, and (3) manufacturing or processing plant.

The franchise agreement establishes the rights of the franchisor and franchisee. Among the items included in this document may be the payments required, the location of the business, pricing and quality control provisions, and how the franchise may be terminated.

The franchise industry is facing increasing controls from both the state and federal governments. This is due in part to prior negative conduct on the part of franchisors. Among these controls are the Federal Trade Commission's disclosure rules, which specify information that must be given to all franchisees before they sign franchise agreements. This information enables franchisees to analyze the potential business success of the venture.

Key Terms

articles of dissolution (460)	board of directors (454)	business format franchise
articles of incorporation (446)	bonds (449)	(461)

Questions and Case Problems

1. Blake is interested in becoming a service station dealer. He contacts Esco Oil Corporation and obtains a franchise contract in which Esco agrees to furnish Blake all gasoline, oil, and related products necessary to run the service station. In addition, Esco provides Blake with Esco signs and promotional materials. A sign reading "Blake's Esco Service" is provided for the front of the station. In return for supplying all the necessary products, promotional materials, signs, and other services, Esco is to receive a percentage of receipts on all products sold. Esco advertises that it stands behind its dealers. The relationship between Blake and Esco is challenged. Discuss whether the association is strictly a franchisor-franchisee relationship or whether it is a principal-agent (employer-employee) relationship.

2. Morad, Thomson, and Coupounas were officers, directors, and shareholders of Bio-Lab. While serving as officers and directors of Bio-Lab, Morad and Thomson incorporated and operated a competing business, Med-Lab. Coupounas brought a suit on behalf of Bio-Lab against Morad, Thomson, and Med-Lab, alleging that they had usurped a corporate opportunity of Bio-Lab. Who prevails and why? [Morad v. Coupounas, 361 So.2d 6 (1978)]

3. The Boston Athletic Association (BAA) is responsible for organizing the Boston Marathon. This activity is the principal business of the corporation. The president, Cloney, was granted the authority by the board of directors to negotiate and execute agreements to promote the marathon. Cloney entered into a contract with International Marathons, Inc. (IMI), as the exclusive promoter of the Boston Marathon. IMI was granted all rights, title, and interest to the exclusive use of the Boston Marathon and its logo. The board later learned of the exclusive contract. It brought a lawsuit to declare the contract void based on improper delegation of the board's authority. Should this contract be declared null and void? Why or why not? [Boston Athletic Assoc. v. International Marathons, Inc., 467 N.E.2d 58 (1984)]

4. Klinicki and Lundgren formed Berlinair, a closely held Oregon corporation, to provide air transportation out of West Germany. Klinicki, who owned 33 percent of the company stock, was the vice president and a director. Lundgren and his family owned 66 percent of Berlinair, and Berlinair's attorney owned the last 1 percent of stock. One of the goals of Berlinair was to obtain the contract with BFR, a West German consortium of travel agents, to provide BFR with air charter service. Later Lundgren learned that the BFR contract might become available. Lundgren then incorporated Air Berlin Charter Company, of which he was the sole owner, and bid for the BFR contract. Lundgren won the BFR contract for Air Berlin while using Berlinair working time, staff, money, and facilities without the knowledge of Klinicki. When Klinicki learned of the BFR contract, he filed a suit, as a minority stockholder, against Lundgren and Air Berlin for usurping a corporate opportunity. Should Klinicki recover against Air Berlin? If so, what should Klinicki be awarded as damages? [Klinicki v. Lundgren, 67 Or.App. 160, 678 P.2d 1250 (1984)]

5. Salem Tent & Awning Company was a corporation in the business of renting awnings and tents. Dusty Schmidt came into the office to rent seven tents to use as covers for his Christmas trees during the four weeks before Christmas. Although Dusty and another owned Western Oregon Christmas Trees, Inc., he signed the prepared invoice without indicating that he was part owner of this corporation or that the tents were for the business. The invoice stated, "Renter is Responsible for Damages." Dusty gave Salem Tent a $2,000 down-payment check on which was printed "Western Oregon Christmas Trees." No indication was made that a corporation existed. Dusty received the tents and began to use them. A sudden storm destroyed several of the tents. When Dusty refused to pay for the damaged tents, Salem Tent sued for damages. Are both Western Oregon Christmas Trees, Inc., and Dusty Schmidt liable for this loss, or is just one of them liable? [Salem Tent & Awning Co. v. Schmidt, 79 Or.App. 475, 719 P.2d 899 (1986)]

6. Atlantic Properties, Inc., had only four shareholders, each of whom owned 25 percent of the capital stock. The

bylaws required an 80 percent affirmative vote of the shareholders on all actions taken by the corporation. This provision had the effect of giving any of the four original shareholders a veto in corporate decisions. One shareholder refused for seven years to vote for any dividends, although he was warned that his actions might expose the corporation to Internal Revenue Service penalties for unreasonable accumulation of corporate earnings and profits. The Internal Revenue Service did impose such penalties on the corporation. Can the dissenting shareholder be held personally liable for these penalties? [Smith v. Atlantic Properties, Inc., 12 Mass.App.Ct. 201, 422 N.E.2d 798 (1981)]

7. Harvey's is a group of New York corporations. Five of these corporations entered into an agreement with Flynt Distributing Company for Flynt to distribute their magazines. Following this agreement, Harvey failed to pay Flynt or to ship their magazines to Flynt, causing Flynt injury. Two of Harvey's shareholders converted the assets of the five corporations to their own use, which left the corporations undercapitalized. Discuss if this conduct amounts to an abuse of corporate business, allowing Flynt to pierce the corporate veil. [Flynt Distributing Co. v. Harvey, 734 F.2d 1389 (9th Cir. 1984)]

8. Pacific Development, Inc., was incorporated in the District of Columbia for the purpose of international brokerage consulting. Pacific's founder, president, and sole shareholder was Tongsun Park, a South Korean who was on close terms with South Korea's president, Park Chung Hee. The government alleged that Park's main purpose was to influence Congress to give economic and military aid to South Korea. The IRS assessed $4.5 million in back taxes against Park in 1977. It then seized the assets of Pacific Development, Inc., claiming that the company was a mere alter ego of Park. Valley Finance, Inc., was another of Park's wholly owned corporations. It had loaned money to Pacific Valley Finance, and it held a second deed of trust on the real property that the IRS had seized. Both Pacific Development and Valley Finance attempted to obtain the return of Pacific Development's assets. The plaintiffs claimed that the IRS had improperly pierced the corporate veil of Pacific. Discuss whether you agree with the plaintiffs. [Valley Finance, Inc. v. United States, 629 F.2d 162 (D.C. Cir. 1980)]

UNIT IV   BUSINESS AND GOVERNMENT REGULATION

Chapter 19 Securities Regulation

[Corporations] cannot commit treason, nor be outlawed nor excommunicated for they have no soul.

Sir Edward Coke,
Case of Sutton's Hospital (1625)

OUTLINE

Introduction

This chapter covers the regulation of transactions involving securities. Only in this century did any governmental body consider establishing statutory or administrative laws to regulate this area of business. The first such law was adopted in 1911 by the state of Kansas. This statute and subsequent state legislation regulated the sale of securities within the state (intrastate transactions). To pass the initial legislation, a member of the Kansas legislature claimed that promoters were so shrewd that they could sell anyone a "piece of the blue sky itself." Since then, statutes that regulate the sales of securities within a state have been known as **blue sky laws.**

This chapter defines securities and looks in detail at the major laws that regulate these transactions.

What Is a Security?

Securities are created by the issuing party; they can be issued in unlimited amounts, at relatively little cost, because securities are nothing more than pieces of paper that represent a financial interest. Securities are not used or consumed; rather, they are a type of currency, traded in what is called the "secondary market." Securities in the secondary market are bought and sold by people who normally are not the issuers of the security.

Securities are more vulnerable to price fluctuation than other types of investments, such as automobiles or real estate, because the value of a security may rise or fall on the basis of information concerning the entity; true, false, and misleading information all influence the stock price. This distinctive feature of securities makes it very easy for individuals or brokerage firms to misrepresent the value of an investment. Securities laws attempt to protect investors in two ways: by mandating disclosure and by prohibiting fraud.

What constitutes a security? Stocks and bonds are two types of securities. The definition of a security, set out in the Securities Act of 1933, is very broad, and the exact definition is not clear. The courts have interpreted this language expansively. In addition to the traditional stocks and bonds, investment contracts have been found to be securities. An investment contract is defined as: (1) an investment of money or other consideration, (2) in a common enterprise, (3) with the investor expecting a profit, and (4) the profit is derived primarily through the efforts of a promoter or a third party other than the investor.

To meet the criteria of an investment contract, the investor must turn money over to another individual for investment purposes, and the capital must be pooled with the capital of other investors so that each individual owns an undivided interest in the whole. The investor does not have any day-to-day control over the enterprise. The owner of a security is passive. An officer or employee who owns stock in his or her company is always considered to be a passive investor.

Securities laws have been applied to various transactions that have not traditionally been thought of as securities. Examples of these transactions include the sale of interest in land involving orange groves and pecan groves, the sale of limited partnership interests, and investments in mink and chinchilla farms. The possibility that a business venture may be termed a security must be considered in every transaction, as the legal ramifications of engaging in the buying and selling of securities are far reaching. The next case illustrates this point.

Case 19.1
REVES v. ERNST & YOUNG
Supreme Court of the United States, 1990.
494 U.S. 56, 110 S.Ct. 945, 108 L.Ed.2d 47.

BACKGROUND AND FACTS *Farmer's Cooperative of Arkansas and Oklahoma (Co-op) is a 23,000-member agricultural cooperative. In order to raise money, it sold promissory notes payable on demand by the holder. The notes were not backed with any collateral, nor were they insured. The Co-op marketed the notes as an investment program, advertising that more than $11 million in assets stood behind these investments. The Co-op filed for bankruptcy, leaving 1,600 people holding notes worth a total of $10 million.*

This litigation was instituted against the accounting firms for over-evaluating a gasohol plant that was one of the biggest assets. The plaintiffs obtained a $6.1 million judgment in the trial court; this judgment was overturned by the U.S. Eighth Circuit Court of Appeals on the basis that these demand notes were not covered by the 1934 Securities and Exchange Act. The act excluded, among other things, "any note . . . which has a maturity at the time of issuance of not exceeding nine months." In other words, the debt, evidenced by a promissory note, must be paid before the end of nine months.

Justice MARSHALL delivered the opinion of the Court.

*   *   *   *

This case requires us to decide whether the note issued by the Co-Op is a "security" within the meaning of the 1934 Act. Section 3(a)(10) of that Act is our starting point:

"The term 'security' means any . . . but shall not include currency or any note, draft, bill of exchange, or banker's acceptance which has a maturity at the time of issuance of not exceeding nine months." *   *   *

The fundamental purpose undergirding the Securities Acts is to eliminate serious abuses in a largely unregulated securities market.

*   *   *   *

In discharging our duty, we are not bound by legal formalisms, but instead take account of the economics of the transaction under investigation. *   *   * Congress' purpose in enacting the securities laws was to regulate *investments*, in whatever form they are made and by whatever name they are called.

*   *   *   *

First, we examine the transaction to assess the motivations that would prompt a reasonable seller and buyer to enter into it. If the seller's purpose is to raise money for the general use of a business enterprise or to finance substantial investments and the buyer is interested primarily in the profit the note is expected to generate, the instrument is likely to be a "security." If the note is exchanged to facilitate the purchase and sale of a minor asset or consumer good, to correct for the seller's cash-flow difficulties, or to advance some other commercial or consumer purpose, on the other hand, the note is less sensibly described as a "security." *   *   * Second, we examine the plan of distribution of the instrument to determine whether it is an instrument in which there is common trading for speculation or investment. Third, we examine the reasonable expectations of the investing public: The Court will consider instruments to be "securities" on the basis of such public expectations, even where an economic analysis of the circumstances of the particular transaction might suggest that the instruments are not "securities" as used in that transaction. Finally, we examine whether some factor such as the existence of another regulatory scheme significantly reduces the risk of the instrument, thereby rendering application of the Securities Acts unnecessary. *   *   *

We conclude, then, that in determining whether an instrument denominated a "note" is a "security," courts are to apply the version of the "family resemblance" test that we have articulated here: a note is presumed to be a "security," and that presumption may be rebutted only by a showing that the note bears a strong resemblance (in terms of the four factors we have identified) to one of the enumerated categories of instrument. If an instrument is not sufficiently similar to an item on the list, the decision whether another category should be added is to be made by examining the same factors.

Respondent's contention that the demand notes fall within the "plain words" of the statute rests entirely upon the premise that Arkansas' statute of limitations for suits to collect demand notes is determinative of the "maturity" of the notes,

as that term is used in the *federal* Securities Acts. The "maturity" of the notes, however, is a question of federal law. To regard States' statutes of limitations law as controlling the scope of the Securities Acts would be to hold that a particular instrument is a "security" under the 1934 Act in some States, but that the same instrument is not a "security" in others. *   *   * We are unpersuaded that Congress intended the Securities Acts to apply differently to the same transactions depending on the accident of which State's law happens to apply.
*   *   *   *

Neither the law of Arkansas nor that of any other State provides an answer to the federal question, and as a matter of federal law, the words of the statute are far from "plain" with regard to whether demand notes fall within the exclusion. If it is plausible to regard a demand note as having an immediate maturity because demand *could* be made immediately, it is also plausible to regard the maturity of a demand note as being in excess of nine months because demand *could* be made many years or decades into the future. *   *   * [S]hort-term notes are, as a general rule, sufficiently safe that the Securities Acts need not apply. As we have said, however, demand notes do not necessarily have short terms. In light of Congress' broader purpose in the Acts of ensuring that investments of all descriptions be regulated to prevent fraud and abuse, we interpret the exception not to cover the demand notes at issue here. *   *   *

For the foregoing reasons, we conclude that the demand notes at issue here fall under the "note" category of instruments that are "securities" under the 1933 and 1934 Acts. We also conclude that, even under a respondent's preferred approach to § 3(a)(10)'s exclusion for short-term notes, these demand notes do not fall within the exclusion.

DECISION AND REMEDY   *Whether a promissory note is a security depends on how it was issued. The Court set out four factors to be considered in making this determination and concluded that the notes in this case were securities.*

Major Securities Laws

The devastating effects of the Great Depression led Congress to hold hearings. These investigations tried to search out the causes of the collapse of the financial system in 1929 so that legislation could be adopted to prevent another such disaster. Some of the laws eventually adopted were specifically aimed at the regulation of financial markets. Some of the statutes regulated practices, while others regulated specific industries. As a result of congressional action at that time and over the intervening decades, two major pieces of legislation, along with their amendments, were adopted to regulate securities and to control insider trading of securities.

Securities Act of 1933

The first statute enacted by Congress was the **Securities Act of 1933,** which is often referred to as

the "Truth in Securities" law. Full and truthful disclosure is required by companies issuing securities. The securities must be registered before they are offered or sold to the public. The 1933 act was designed to protect the investing public through full disclosure of information about the securities. The act also forbids fraud and deceit in the distribution of the securities, even those that are not required to be registered.

Securities Exchange Act of 1934

A year later, Congress adopted the **Securities Exchange Act of 1934.** Divided into six major parts, this statute created the **Securities and Exchange Commission** (SEC). Second, it requires that all national securities exchanges, such as the New York Stock Exchange and the American Exchange, and all broker-dealers who have interstate operations, be registered with the SEC. Third, in order to monitor the activities of the various se-

Legal Highlight

Earthworms and Salvador Dali Are Securities?

Earthworms and Securities

Allen J. Gross solicited buyer-investors to raise earthworms. In a newsletter, Gross promised that he would give any buyer growing instructions that would ensure a profitable farm, that the time required would be similar to that of raising a garden, that the earthworms double in quantity every 60 days, and that he would buy back all baitsize worms produced for $2.25 per pound. Gross told Smith that success was guaranteed because Gross agreed to repurchase Smith's production.

In reality, worms multiply at a maximum of eight rather than 64 times per year. The price of $2.25 per pound was ten times greater than the true market conditions. The only way for Smith to make a profit was to sell the worms for $2.25. This qualified as a "common enterprise" since the fortune of the Smiths was interwoven with and dependent on the efforts and success of Gross. The efforts of those other than the investor were undeniably significant: Smith was promised that the effort necessary to raise worms was minimal, and the promised income could only occur if

Gross purchased the worms. As a result, the court found the sale of the earthworm farms to be an investment security. [*Smith v. Gross*, 604 F.2d 639 (9th Cir. 1979)]

Salvador Dali and Securities

Some art galleries had been selling fake Salvador Dali prints to customers for several years. Some of these sales were boiler-room operations where the seller placed calls to people, telling them that they could own an affordable Dali print. The print, purchased by the seller for $25 to $50 was sold to the victim for $1,500 to $2,500. The only problem was that the print was really a reproduction and not a genuine limited-edition lithograph. The "fake" Dali prints were prints but were neither authorized nor supervised reproductions by Dali of his own works.

Although each victim was overcharged a relatively small sum, the total amount was staggering. In New York, a boiler-room operation was convicted of deceiving investors out of $1.3 million. Because the owners of this operation had sold the Dali prints to victims over the telephone as investments, they were convicted of securities fraud.

curities markets, the SEC is required to maintain surveillance of them, which it does now through the use of computers.

Fourth, like the 1933 act, the 1934 act establishes a registration and disclosure requirement that applies to corporations whose securities are listed on any national securities exchange and that covers the exchange of these securities. A fifth section regulates the solicitation of proxies (written authorization given by a shareholder to a third party to vote the shareholder's stock). Finally, insider trading is prohibited under two sections of the statute: Section 16 and Section 10(b).

The Securities and Exchange Commission is an independent regulatory agency. Congress delegated to the SEC administrative rule-making

powers and the responsibility for administering all federal securities law. The SEC is composed of five members who serve staggered five-year terms. They are appointed by the president, but no more than three members may be from the same political party.

The Securities Investor Protection Act of 1970

A series of stockbrokerage houses failed in the 1960s, leading Congress to amend the 1934 act to protect the consumer. The amendment created the **Securities Investor Protection Corporation** (SIPC). This corporation manages a fund that protects investors from the financial harm caused when stockbrokerage houses fail. The fund is similar to the fund administered by the Federal Deposit Insurance Corporation (FDIC), which protects depositors in banks.

Foreign Corrupt Practices Act

The **Foreign Corrupt Practices Act** (FCPA) of 1977 also amended the 1934 act. Although part of the FCPA applies to corporations doing business in other countries, the rest of the act applies to all corporations registered with the SEC, whether or not they are engaged in foreign business.

This act requires, for the first time, public corporations to keep and maintain records that accurately reflect their financial activities. All corporations reporting to the SEC under the 1934 act must comply, even if they only operate in the United States and have no international business relations. Further, the FCPA requires all corporations reporting under the 1934 act to have an internal accounting system in order to ensure accurate records.

This act attempts to prevent the concealment of illegal activities. The type of illegal actions that Congress discovered in its hearings ranged from the purchasing of castles in Ireland for top management to the paying of millions to foreign officials in order to ensure lucrative contracts. These millions of dollars in payment were not disclosed to the shareholders or to the SEC. Some of the activities were criminal acts even prior to the adoption of the FCPA.

Insider Trading Sanctions Act of 1984

The **Insider Trading Sanctions Act** (ITSA) of 1984 gives additional power to the SEC for violations of insider trading. The SEC is allowed to recover up to three times the profit made in these situations. Any recovery goes to the government and not to the parties who may have been injured by such activity. In 1988, this act was amended by the **Insider Trading and Securities Fraud Enforcement Act.** The amendment enlarged the scope of persons who would have civil liability under the act, gave the SEC authority to reward informants in insider trading cases, gave the SEC rule-making authority to require specific policies and procedures to prevent insider trading, and increased criminal penalties (increased maximum

jail terms from five to ten years, and criminal fines for individuals from $100,000 to $1 million and for corporations and partnerships from $500,000 to $2.5 million). The amendment also provided for the award of treble damages against securities firms for failing to maintain a proper system of supervision to prevent and detect insider trading violations by employees.

The Securities Act of 1933

The Securities Act of 1933 was designed to prohibit various forms of fraud and to stabilize the securities industry by requiring that all essential information concerning the issuing of securities be made available to the investing public. The 1933 act is basically a disclosure requirement. Every new issue of securities must be registered with the SEC under the 1933 act, unless the securities qualify for an exemption from being registered.

Requirements of the Registration Statement

Corporations issuing a security, unless exempt, must file a registration statement with the SEC. The security must be registered before it is offered to the public. In addition, investors must be provided with a **prospectus,** which is the document that is utilized to sell the security. In principle, the registration statement and prospectus supply sufficient information to enable unsophisticated investors to evaluate the financial risk involved.

The registration statement must be signed by the corporation's principal executive officer, principal accounting officer, principal financial officer, and at least a majority of the members of the board of directors. Signing the registration statement makes a person potentially liable if there are any errors or material omissions in it.

The SEC does not attempt to determine whether an investment is a good one. The only thing demanded is that sufficient information be available to a potential investor so that he or she can make an intelligent decision.

Requirements of the Registering Corporation

Before filing the registration statement and prospectus with the SEC, the corporation is allowed to obtain an underwriter who will monitor distribution of the new issue. A twenty-day waiting period after registration is mandated before any sale can take place. This period may be extended by the SEC, or the registration statement may require amendments that start the twenty-day period over again. During this period, oral offers between interested investors and the issuing corporation concerning the purchase and sale of the proposed securities may take place, but the securities cannot be legally bought or sold.

During the waiting period, written advertising is allowed in the form of a **tombstone advertisement.** This advertisement is so named because the format resembles a tombstone and is outlined in black. Such advertisements simply tell the investor where and how to obtain a prospectus. Normally, any other type of advertising is prohibited.

At this time, a **red herring prospectus** (or preliminary prospectus) may be distributed. It gets its name from the red legend printed across it, stating that the registration has been filed but has not become effective. The red legend indicates that the prospectus is not final and not yet approved by the SEC.

Misrepresentations in Registering with the SEC

A registration statement that contains material untruths or omissions makes the issuer (such as a corporation) liable for violation of the securities laws. In addition, all individuals who signed, were named, or participated in drafting the registration statement are liable. Several defenses are available to those who sign a false statement. For example, the defendants will not be held liable if there is proof that the plaintiff knew the statement was untrue. Also, a defendant who exercised "due diligence" in verifying the truth of the statement may also escape liability for false statements made to the SEC. The **due diligence defense** is available to all defendants except the issuer.

In the following case, the court found that the registration statement contained material false statements of fact and material omissions, and the court imposed liability on the individuals who were involved in the issuance of new securities.

BACKGROUND AND FACTS *This lawsuit was brought by purchasers of BarChris debentures under Section 11 of the Securities Act of 1933. The plaintiffs alleged that the registration statement filed with the Securities and Exchange Commission, which became effective on May 16, 1961, contained material false statements and material omissions.*

The defendants fell into three categories: (1) the people who signed the registration statement, (2) the underwriters (consisting of eight investment banking firms), and (3) BarChris's auditors—Peat, Marwick, Mitchell & Co. Included in the group of defendants who signed the registration statement were (1) BarChris's nine directors, (2) BarChris's controller, (3) one of BarChris's attorneys, (4) two investment bankers who were later named as directors of the BarChris Corporation, and (5) numerous other people participating in the preparation of the registration statement.

BarChris grew out of a business started in 1946 as a bowling-alley building company. The introduction of automatic pin-setting machines in 1952 sparked rapid growth in the bowling industry. BarChris benefited from this increased interest in bowling, and its construction operations expanded rapidly. It was estimated that in 1960 BarChris installed approximately 3 percent of all bowling lanes built in the United States. BarChris's sales increased dramatically between 1956 and 1960, and the company was recognized as a significant factor in the bowling construction industry.

BarChris was in constant need of cash to finance its operations, a need that grew more and more pressing as the operations expanded. In 1959,

Case 19.2
ESCOTT v. BARCHRIS CONSTRUCTION CORP.
United States District Court, Southern District of New York, 1968.
283 F.Supp. 643.

BarChris sold over a half-million shares of its common stock to the public. By early 1961 it needed additional working capital, and this time it decided to sell debentures.

BarChris filed a registration statement of the debentures with the SEC and received the proceeds of the financing. Nevertheless, it experienced increasing financial difficulties, which in time became insurmountable. By early 1962, it was painfully apparent that BarChris was beginning to fail. In October BarChris filed a petition for an arrangement under the Bankruptcy Act, and it defaulted on the interest due on the debentures in November.

The plaintiffs challenged the accuracy of the debenture registration statement and charged that the text of the prospectus—including many of the figures—was false and that material information had been omitted. The federal district court reviewed all of the figures and statements included in the prospectus.

Judge McLEAN
*   *   *   *

Materiality

It is a prerequisite to liability under Section 11 of the Act that the fact which is falsely stated in a registration statement, or the fact that is omitted when it should have been stated to avoid misleading, be "material."
*   *   *   *

The average prudent investor is not concerned with minor inaccuracies or with errors as to matters which are of no interest to him. The facts which tend to deter him from purchasing a security are facts which have an important bearing upon the nature or condition of the issuing corporation or its business.

Judged by this test, there is no doubt that many of the misstatements and omissions in this prospectus were material.
*   *   *   *

The "Due Diligence" Defenses

Section 11(b) of the Act provides that:
   "*   *   * no person, other than the issuer, shall be liable *   *   * who shall sustain the burden of proof—

      *   *   *

      (3) that (A) as regards any part of the registration statement not purporting to be made on the authority of an expert *   *   * he had, after reasonable investigation, reasonable ground to believe and did believe, at the time such part of the registration statement became effective, that the statements therein were true and that there was no omission to state a material fact required to be stated therein or necessary to make the statements therein not misleading."

Kircher

Kircher was treasurer of BarChris and its chief financial officer. He is a certified public accountant and an intelligent man. He was thoroughly familiar with BarChris's financial affairs. He knew the terms of BarChris's agreements. *   *   * He knew of the customers' delinquency problem. *   *   * He knew how the financing proceeds were to be applied and he saw to it that they were so applied. He arranged the officers' loans and he knew all the facts concerning them.
*   *   *   *

As to the rest of the prospectus, knowing the facts, he did not have a reasonable ground to believe it to be true. On the contrary, he must have known that in part it was untrue. Under these circumstances, he was not entitled to sit back and place the blame on the lawyers for not advising him about it.

Kircher has not proved his due diligence defenses.

Trilling

Trilling's position is somewhat different from Kircher's. He was BarChris's controller. He signed the registration statement in that capacity, although he was not a director.

Trilling was not a member of the executive committee. He was a comparatively minor figure in BarChris. The description of BarChris's "management" on page 9 of the prospectus does not mention him. He was not considered to be an executive officer.

Trilling may well have been unaware of several of the inaccuracies in the prospectus. But he must have known of some of them. As a financial officer, he was familiar with BarChris's finances and with its books of account.
* * * *

As far as appears, he made no investigation. He did what was asked of him and assumed that others would properly take care of supplying accurate data as to the other aspects of the company's business. This would have been well enough but for the fact that he signed the registration statement. As a signer, he could not avoid responsibility by leaving it up to others to make it accurate. Trilling did not sustain the burden of proving his due diligence defenses.

Birnbaum

Birnbaum was a young lawyer, admitted to the bar in 1957, who, after brief periods of employment by two different law firms and an equally brief period of practicing in his own firm, was employed by BarChris as house counsel and assistant secretary in October 1960. Unfortunately for him, he became secretary and a director of BarChris on April 17, 1961, after the first version of the registration statement had been filed with the Securities and Exchange Commission. He signed the later amendments, thereby becoming responsible for the accuracy of the prospectus in its final form.

Although the prospectus, in its description of "management," lists Birnbaum among the "executive officers" and devotes several sentences to a recital of his career, the fact seems to be that he was not an executive officer in any real sense. He did not participate in the management of the company. As house counsel, he attended to legal matters of a routine nature.

It seems probable that Birnbaum did not know of many of the inaccuracies in the prospectus. He must, however, have appreciated some of them. In any case, he made no investigation and relied on the others to get it right. * * * As a lawyer, he should have known his obligations under the statute. He should have known that he was required to make a reasonable investigation of the truth of all the statements in the unexpertised portion of the document which he signed. Having failed to make such an investigation, he did not have reasonable ground to believe that all these statements were true. Birnbaum has not established his due diligence defenses. * * *

Auslander

Auslander was an "outside" director, i.e., one who was not an officer of BarChris. He was chairman of the board of Valley Stream National Bank. * * * In February 1961 [he was asked] to become a director of BarChris. * * *
* * * *

Auslander was elected a director on April 17, 1961. The registration statement in its original form had already been filed, of course without his signature. On May 10, 1961, he signed a signature page for the first amendment to the registration statement which was filed on May 11, 1961. This was a separate sheet without any document attached. Auslander did not know that it was a signature page for a registration statement. He vaguely understood that it was something "for the SEC."

Auslander attended a meeting of BarChris's directors on May 15, 1961. At that meeting he, along with the other directors, signed the signature sheet for the second amendment which constituted the registration statement in its final form. Again, this was only a separate sheet without any document attached.

It is true that Auslander became a director on the eve of the financing. He had little opportunity to familiarize himself with the company's affairs. *   *   *

Section 11 imposes liability in the first instance upon a director, no matter how new he is. He is presumed to know his responsibility when he becomes a director. He can escape liability only by using that reasonable care to investigate the facts which a prudent man would employ in the management of his own property. In my opinion, a prudent man would not act in an important matter without any knowledge of the relevant facts, in sole reliance upon representations of persons who are comparative strangers and upon general information which does not purport to cover the particular case. To say that such minimal conduct measures up to the statutory standard would, to all intents and purposes, absolve new directors from responsibility merely because they are new. This is not a sensible construction of Section 11, when one bears in mind its fundamental purpose of requiring full and truthful disclosure for the protection of investors.

I find and conclude that Auslander has not established his due diligence defense.

Peat, Marwick

*   *   *   *

Berardi was then about thirty years old. He was not yet a C.P.A. He had had no previous experience with the bowling industry. This was his first job as a senior accountant. He could hardly have been given a more difficult assignment.

*   *   *   *

Berardi had no conception of how tight the cash position was. He did not discover that BarChris was holding up checks in substantial amounts because there was no money in the bank to cover them. He did not know of the loan from Manufacturers Trust Company or of the officers' loans. Since he never read the prospectus, he was not even aware that there had ever been any problem about loans from officers.

*   *   *   *

Accountants should not be held to a standard higher than that recognized in their profession. I do not do so here. Berardi's review did not come up to that standard. He did not take some of the steps which Peat, Marwick's written program prescribed. He did not spend an adequate amount of time on a task of this magnitude. Most important of all, he was too easily satisfied with glib answers to his inquiries.

This is not to say that he should have made a complete audit. But there were enough danger signals in the materials which he did examine to require some further investigation on his part. Generally accepted accounting standards required such further investigation under these circumstances. It is not always sufficient merely to ask questions.

[T]he burden of proof is on Peat, Marwick. I find that that burden has not been satisfied. I conclude that Peat, Marwick has not established its due diligence defense.

DECISION AND REMEDY   *BarChris Corporation itself, all the signers of the registration statement for the debentures, the underwriters, and the corporation's auditors were held liable.*

Exemptions

A corporation can avoid the high cost and complicated procedures associated with registration by taking advantage of certain exemptions to the registration requirement. Two general types of exemptions are allowed: **exempt transactions** and **exempt securities.**

Exempt Transactions   The three exempt trans-actions allowed by the 1933 act are **small offering exemptions, intrastate offering exemptions,** and **private offering exemptions.** These exemptions are available only for the current transaction and do not cover future transactions. The next trans-action must either be registered or must be exempt from registration in its own right.

Small Offering Exemptions   The SEC rules out-line three different types of small offering exemp-tions. These offerings by an issuer are not large enough for the federal government to regulate: (1) certain types of bank loans, (2) privately ne-gotiated sales of securities to large institutional investors, and (3) business-venture promotions by a few closely related persons.

Regulation D of the 1933 act creates the dis-tinction between an **accredited investor** and an **unaccredited investor.** The accredited investor is not likely to need government protection in mak-ing its investment determinations. An accredited investor is one of the following:

1. An institutional investor, such as an insurance company, bank, credit union, or pension fund
2. The seller's directors and officers
3. An individual investor who has had an annual income of over $200,000, or a husband and wife with annual income in excess of $300,000, for two consecutive years
4. An individual with a net worth of over $1 million
5. Any corporation or charitable organization with total assets of over $5 million.

An unaccredited investor does not meet these requirements. Regulation D has three rules cover-ing exemptions, some of which are concerned with unaccredited investors.

Under Regulation D, **Rule 504,** a seller can sell up to $1 million in securities during any twelve-month period without registration if no general solicitation or advertising is used. Any amount over $500,000 however, must be registered under a state securities registration law. Although reg-istration is not required, a notice must be filed with the SEC. Resale of these issues is restricted. This exemption is for small businesses which are not reporting to the SEC under the Securities Exchange Act of 1934.

Under **Rule 505** of Regulation D, the seller may sell up to $5 million in securities during any

twelve-month period if there are no more than 35 unaccredited investors. These transactions are ex-empt if no general solicitation or advertising is used. The number of accredited investors is un-limited. If the sale involves any unaccredited investors, all investors must be given material in-formation about the offering company, its busi-ness, and the securities before the sale. The issuer is not required to believe that each unaccredited investor "has such knowledge and experience in financial and business matters that he [or she] is capable of evaluating the merits and the risks of the prospective investment." A notice must be filed with the SEC. This exemption applies to corpo-rations even if they are covered by the 1934 act.

Under SEC **Regulation A,** a seller is allowed to sell up to $1.5 million in a one-year period with a simplified registration process. No limit is placed on the number of purchasers, and disclo-sure is not required if the offering is under $100,000. Any offering above $100,000 must have an of-fering circular that discloses material information regarding the investment. The circular must be filed with the SEC ten days prior to the sale of the securities.

Intrastate Offering Exemptions   The federal government allows each state to regulate securities offerings that are within its boundaries. An in-trastate offering must be made only to resident investors in one state by a seller that resides within that state. The seller must have its principal office located in the state, have 80 percent of its assets and 80 percent of its gross revenues in the state, and 80 percent of the proceeds of the offering must be used within the state. One effect of an offer to an out-of-state resident would be the cancellation of this exemption.

Private Offering Exemptions   The federal gov-ernment is not interested in offerings that are pri-vately made, since the protection of the public is the goal of the 1933 act.

Under **Rule 506** of Regulation D, businesses, including the ones covered by the 1934 act, may offer an unlimited amount of securities if the se-curities are not generally solicited or advertised. An unlimited number of accredited investors can participate, but there can be no more than 35 unaccredited investors and the seller must deter-mine that each unaccredited investor has enough knowledge and experience in financial and business matters to be able to evaluate the merits and the risks of the prospective investment. If there are any unaccredited investors, the issuer must provide to all purchasers material information about itself, its business, and the securities before the sale. A notice must be filed with the SEC.

Thus, Rule 506 differs from Rule 505 in that it requires material information to be given to unaccredited investors, and it requires the seller to verify that the unaccredited investor has sufficient knowledge or experience to evaluate the risks and merits of the issue.

Rule 412, Shelf Registration Corporations with stock having a minimum value of $150 million may register a new security but need not sell all issues of it at one time. Falling under **Rule 412,** popularly called **shelf registration,** these securities are put "on the shelf" to be sold at a later time. Once the registration is approved by the SEC, the only requirement is for the company to amend its registration if there are any major changes. This rule aids efficiency by reducing legal, accounting, and printing costs.

Exempt Securities In addition to the exempt transactions, some types of securities are exempt from registration under the 1933 Act. These include securities issued by governments (state and federal), banks, savings and loan associations, charitable organizations, and common carriers that are regulated by other federal laws. Securities distributed as stock dividends or in stock splits are also exempt.

The Securities Exchange Act of 1934

The primary purposes of the Securities Exchange Act are to ensure the integrity of stock and securities sold through national stock exchanges and over-the-counter markets, to inform the investing public of the financial condition of a business and to protect the public from fraudulent activity. The act provides for the regulation and registration of security exchanges, brokers, dealers, and national securities associations, such as the National Association of Securities Dealers (NASD). It regulates the markets in which securities are traded by maintaining a continuous disclosure system for all

corporations with securities on the securities exchanges and for those companies that have assets in excess of $5 million and 500 or more shareholders. The SEC is allowed by the 1934 act to engage in market surveillance in order to regulate such undesirable market practices as fraud, market manipulation, and misrepresentation.

Proxy Requirement

The act regulates proxy solicitation for voting. A **proxy** is a written authorization to cast a shareholder's vote. A person can solicit proxies from a number of shareholders in an attempt to concentrate voting power. The SEC reviews the procedures used in obtaining proxies, and the SEC's rules require that proposed proxy material be filed in advance for examination. In any solicitation there must be clear disclosures on all matters on which stockholders are to vote and the stockholder must be afforded the right to vote on a simple yes or no on each matter.

Forms That Must Be Filed

Publicly held corporations are required to update their registration periodically with annual and quarterly reports. The annual report, Form 10-K, is filed at the end of the fiscal period, and it must include audited financial statements, the present status of the business, and its securities holdings.

Form 10-Q is the quarterly report that reflects any financial changes that have occurred since the last reporting period. In addition, any time a material event occurs, such as a change in control or bankruptcy, Form 8-K must be filed. The legal definition of a material event is any occurrence that a reasonably prudent investor would want to know about in order to reevaluate his or her investment.

Insider Trading and Fraud

One of the most important parts of the 1934 act relates to **insider trading.** Because of their positions, corporate directors, officers, and key employees often obtain advance inside information that can affect the future market value of the corporate stock. Obviously, their positions can give them a trading advantage over the general public and shareholders. Another important part of the

Crime and Punishment

Starting in the mid 1980s, federal prosecutors, acting mainly on tips, unearthed some of the largest insider trading scandals in American history. Americans and Wall Street were shocked by the numerous revelations of insider trading that resulted in the prosecution of some of the most successful traders. The following is a partial list of these people and their activities and ages at the time of sentencing.

PAUL THAYER, 65. *History:* Thayer was a corporate director with a number of major corporations. During the time he served on those boards, he leaked inside information to his girlfriend and a stockbroker, who, in turn, earned $3 million from the tips. Thayer did not make any money. The SEC brought civil and criminal charges. He pleaded guilty to obstructing justice by lying to the SEC.

Sentence: In May 1985, Thayer was sentenced to four years in prison and fined $5,000. He also paid the government $550,000 as a fine for the profits earned by others through his tips.

DENNIS B. LEVINE, 34. *History:* Levine was an investment banker who worked on Wall Street. Through his contacts, he set up an information network of Wall Street sources at investment banks and law firms. He traded on insider information through an offshore bank account from which he earned $12.6 million on stock trades. He pleaded guilty to insider trading, perjury, and tax violations. He was given a lighter sentence in view of his cooperation with authorities, which led SEC investigators to Ivan Boesky and others.

Sentence: In February 1987, Levine was sentenced to two years in prison and fined $362,000. He has repaid $11.6 million.

ILAN K. REICH, 32. *History:* Reich is a lawyer who gave Levine information about his law firm's corporate clients who were planning major corporate moves. He stopped giving Levine information on two occasions. Despite this, Levine set aside $300,000 for Reich, who never claimed the money. He pleaded guilty to charges of securities fraud.

Sentence: In January 1987, Reich was sentenced to one year and a day in prison and five years' probation. He has paid $485,000 to the SEC.

IVAN BOESKY, 55. *History:* Boesky was known as Mr. Arbitrage on Wall Street. He is by far the biggest investor to be caught trading with insider information. Much of his information came from Dennis Levine. After cooperating with the SEC, he pleaded guilty to one felony count.

Sentence: In November 1987, Boesky was sentenced to three years in prison. He had previously paid the government $50 million in illegal profits, had paid $50 million in civil penalties, and had agreed to withdraw permanently from the securities business.

MICHAEL MILKEN, 43. *History:* An employee of Drexel Burnham Lambert, Inc., Milken assisted Boesky by keeping fraudulent records to hide securities that Boesky owned. He failed to disclose to Drexel the true price of stocks purchased and sold, with the profits going to his junk bond operation. He pleaded guilty to six felonies.

Sentence: In November 1990, he was sentenced to spend ten years in prison and to pay $200 million in fines to the government and $400 million in restitution to defrauded investors. He has been barred for life from the securities industry.

DREXEL BURNHAM LAMBERT, INC. *History:* An established Wall Street firm, it hired Michael Milken, who eventually took over the junk bond operation. By 1988, Milken and Drexel had half of the $140 billion junk bond market. Drexel and Boesky agreed covertly to defraud clients by driving up the price of certain stocks. Drexel pleaded guilty to six felony counts of securities fraud.

Sentence: In December 1988, Drexel was ordered to pay $680 million in fines and restitution and agreed to fire Milken.

1934 act is to promote investor protection by prohibition of fraud. Several provisions of the 1934 act deal with insider trading and prohibition of fraud, specifically **Section 16** and **Section 10(b)**, together with SEC **Rule 10b-5.**

Section 16   Section 16 covers directors, officers, and owners of more than 10 percent of the shares of any one class of stock of a company registered under the 1934 act. These people are designated as "insiders," and they must file reports of their holdings and transactions with the SEC.

If these people make a purchase and sale or sale and purchase of stock within a six-month period that results in a profit, that profit is illegal and may be forfeited to the issuer of the stock. Called an "illegal short-swing profit," liability is *automatic* because Congress decided not to require the SEC to prove that the person had used insider information for personal gain. For stock owned longer than six months, it must be proved that these people made a profit based on insider information. If the case is proved, they can be forced to return the illegal profit to the corporation.

Section 10(b) and Rule 10b-5   One of the basic tools employed by the SEC to provide and promote investor protection is the prohibition of fraud. The most widely applied section is Section 10(b) of the 1934 act, along with SEC Rule 10b-5. Section 10(b) makes it unlawful "to use or employ, in connection with the purchase or sale of any security . . . any manipulative or deceptive device or contrivance, in contravention of such rules and regulations as the [SEC] may prescribe. . . ." Rule 10b-5 makes it "unlawful for any person, directly or indirectly, by use of any means or instrumentality of interstate commerce, or of the mails, or of any facility of any national securities exchange to defraud or mislead anyone in the purchase or sale of any security."

The antifraud rule applies to the purchase or sale of any security, regardless of how small or large the amount of the transaction is or of whether it is a public or private offering. The exemptions discussed earlier apply only to registration, not to the antifraud provisions. Therefore, the rule covers virtually every transaction involving a security. Furthermore, the act does not specify what constitutes an offense of fraud or misrepresentation. As a result, the SEC rules and the courts have broadly defined this offense and the criteria for a violation of Rule 10b-5. Violations generally fit into two categories: insider trading cases, and claims arising out of corporate misstatements or omissions (such as knowingly inflating earning projections or manipulating financial records to show profits rather than a real loss) and out of fraud and manipulation by brokers and dealers in the trading of stock.

Disclosure Under Rule 10b-5   Any material omission or misrepresentation of material facts in connection with the purchase or sale of a security may violate Section 10(b) and Rule 10b-5. The key to liability is whether the insider's information is material.

Some examples of material facts calling for a disclosure under the rule have included a new ore discovery, fraudulent trading in the company stock by a broker-dealer, a dividend change (whether up or down), a contract for the sale of corporate assets, a new discovery (of a process or a product), a significant change in the firm's financial condition, or a takeover bid by another firm or individual.

The Supreme Court in the following case expressly adopts the standard of materiality applicable to Section 10(b) and Rule 10b-5. According to this standard, an omitted fact is material if there is a substantial likelihood that its disclosure would have been considered significant by a reasonable investor. This case is a private class-action lawsuit; the SEC was not involved in this case.

Case 19.3
**BASIC INC. v.
LEVINSON**
Supreme Court of the United
States, 1988.
485 U.S. 224, 108 S.Ct. 978,
99 L.Ed.2d 194.

BACKGROUND AND FACTS   *Basic Incorporated was a publicly traded company primarily engaged in manufacturing chemical refractories for the steel industry. Combustion Engineering, Inc., was a company that produced alumina-based refractories. Combustion was interested in acquiring Basic. In 1976, representatives from the two companies conferred concerning the possibility of a merger. During 1977 and 1978, Basic made three public* *statements denying that it was engaged in merger negotiations (October 21, 1977, September 25, 1978, and November 6, 1978).*

On December 18, 1978, Basic asked the New York Stock Exchange to suspend trading in its shares and issued a release stating that it had been "approached" by another company concerning a merger. On December 19, Basic's board of directors endorsed Combustion's offer and the following day announced its approval of Combustion's offer for all outstanding shares.

The plaintiffs were former Basic shareholders who had sold their stock after Basic's first public statement of October 21, 1977, and before the suspension of trading on December 18, 1978. The class action against Basic and its directors asserted that the defendants had issued three false or misleading public statements that violated Section 10(b) and Rule 10b-5. The shareholders were harmed by selling Basic shares at artificially depressed prices in a market affected by Basic's misleading statements.

The district court found that the alleged misstatements were immaterial and granted a summary judgment in favor of Basic. The court of appeals reversed the summary judgment and found that information concerning otherwise insignificant developments becomes material solely because of an affirmative denial of the existence of these developments. The United States Supreme Court granted certiorari.

Justice BLACKMUN delivered the opinion of the Court.
* * * *

The application of [the] materiality standard to preliminary merger discussions is not self-evident. Where the impact of the corporate development on the target's fortune is certain and clear, the * * * materiality definition admits straightforward application. Where, on the other hand, the event is contingent or speculative in nature, it is difficult to ascertain whether the "reasonable investor" would have considered the omitted information significant at the time. Merger negotiations, because of the ever-present possibility that the contemplated transaction will not be effectuated, fall into the latter category.
* * * *

We * * * find no valid justification for artificially excluding from the definition of materiality information concerning merger discussions, which would otherwise be considered significant to the trading decision of a reasonable investor, merely because agreement-in-principle as to price and structure has not yet been reached by the parties or their representatives.
* * * *

Whether merger discussions in any particular case are material therefore depends on the facts. Generally, in order to assess the probability that the event will occur, a factfinder will need to look to indicia of interest in the transaction at the highest corporate levels. Without attempting to catalog all such possible factors, we note by way of example that board resolutions, instructions to investment bankers, and actual negotiations between principals or their intermediaries may serve as indicia of interest. To assess the magnitude of the transaction to the issuer of the securities allegedly manipulated, a factfinder will need to consider such facts as the size of the two corporate entities and of the potential premiums over market value. No particular event or factor short of closing the transaction need be either necessary or sufficient by itself to render merger discussions material.
* * * *

* * * The courts below accepted a presumption * * * that persons who had traded Basic shares had done so in reliance on the integrity of the price set by the market, but because of petitioners' material misrepresentations that price had been fraudulently depressed. Requiring a plaintiff to show a speculative state of facts, i.e., how he would have acted if omitted material information had been disclosed, or if the misrepresentation had not been made, would place an unnecessarily unrealistic evidentiary burden on the Rule 10b-5 plaintiff who has traded on an impersonal market.

* * * The presumption of reliance employed in this case is consistent with, and, by facilitating Rule 10b-5 litigation, supports, the congressional policy embodied in the 1934 Act. * * *

DECISION AND REMEDY
The United States Supreme Court reversed the judgment of the court of appeals and sent the case back to the district court for further proceedings. Materiality depends on the facts in each particular case, and, therefore, the decision whether a violation of Rule 10b-5 has occurred must be made on a case-by-case basis. The statements must be misleading as to a material fact.

Timing of Disclosure Under Rule 10b-5   Courts have struggled with the problem of when information becomes public knowledge. Clearly, when inside information becomes public knowledge, all insiders should be allowed to trade without disclosure. The courts have suggested that insiders should refrain from trading for a reasonable waiting period when the news is not readily translatable into investment action. Presumably, this time period gives the news time to filter down and to be evaluated by the investing public. What constitutes a reasonable waiting period is not at all clear.

The following is one of the landmark cases interpreting Section 10(b) and Rule 10b-5. The SEC sued Texas Gulf Sulphur for issuing a misleading press release. The release underestimated the magnitude and value of a mineral discovery. The SEC also sued several of Texas Gulf Sulphur's directors, officers, and employees under Rule 10b-5 after these people had purchased large amounts of the corporate stock prior to the announcement of the corporation's rich ore discovery.

Case 19.4
SECURITIES AND EXCHANGE COMMISSION v. TEXAS GULF SULPHUR CO.
United States Court of Appeals, Second Circuit, 1968.
401 F.2d 833.

BACKGROUND AND FACTS   *Texas Gulf Sulphur Co. (TGS) drilled a hole on November 12, 1963, near Timmins, Ontario. It appeared to yield a core with exceedingly high mineral content. Since TGS did not own the mineral rights in the surrounding regions, it maintained secrecy about the results of the core sample. Evasive tactics were undertaken to camouflage the drill site, and a second hole was drilled. TGS completed an extensive land acquisition program and then began drilling this lucrative site. Rumors began to spread, and, by early April 1964, a "tremendous staking rush [was] going on."*

On April 11, 1964, an unauthorized report of the extraordinary mineral find hit the papers. On April 12, TGS issued a press release that played down the discovery and stated that it was too early to tell whether the ore finding would be significant. Charles Fogarty, executive vice president of TGS, had already purchased 1,700 shares of stock during the month of November 1963 and an additional 300 shares in December. In March 1964 he bought 400 shares, and in April he bought 300 shares. Other TGS officials had also purchased stock. They had accepted stock options on February 20, 1964.

The Securities and Exchange Commission filed suit against TGS and several of its officers, directors, and employees to prevent TGS's continued violation of the Securities Exchange Act of 1934 and to compel the individual defendants to rescind the securities transactions they had made. The complaint alleged that, on the basis of material inside information concerning the results of TGS's drilling, the defendants either personally or through agents had purchased TGS stock, while the information concerning the drill site remained undisclosed to the investing public. The SEC further charged that certain of the defendants (tippers) had divulged information to certain others (tippees) for their use in purchasing TGS stock before the information was disclosed to the public or to other sellers. In addition, certain defendants had accepted options to purchase TGS stock without disclosing material information about the progress of the drilling to either the stock option committee or the TGS board of directors. Finally, the complaint charged that TGS had issued a deceptive press release on April 22, 1964.

The deceptive press release should be the focus in reading the following case. The trial court judge held that the issuance of the press release was lawful because it was not issued for the purpose of benefiting the corporation, and there was no evidence that any insider had used the information in the press release to personal advantage. Thus, it was not "misleading or deceptive on the basis of the facts then known." The trial court went on to find that most of the defendants had not violated Rule 10b-5. The case was appealed.

Judge WATERMAN
*   *   *   *

I. THE INDIVIDUAL DEFENDANTS
*   *   *   *

In each case, *   *   * whether facts are material within Rule 10b-5 when the facts relate to a particular event and are undisclosed by those persons who are knowledgeable thereof will depend at any given time upon a balancing of both the indicated probability that the event will occur and the anticipated magnitude of the event in light of the totality of the company activity. Here, *   *   * knowledge of the possibility, which surely was more than marginal, of the existence of a mine of the vast magnitude indicated by the remarkably rich drill core located rather close to the surface (suggesting mineability by the less expensive open pit method) within the confines of a large anomaly (suggesting an extensive region of mineralization) might well have affected the price of TGS stock and would certainly have been an important fact to a reasonable, if speculative, investor in deciding whether he should buy, sell, or hold. After all, this first drill core was "unusually good and *   *   * excited the interest and speculation of those who knew about it."
*   *   *   *

Finally, a major factor in determining whether the *   *   * discovery was a material fact is the importance attached to the drilling results by those who knew about it. In view of other unrelated recent developments favorably affecting TGS, participation by an informed person in a regular stock-purchase program, or even sporadic trading by an informed person, might lend only nominal support to the inference of the materiality of the *   *   * discovery; nevertheless, the timing by those who knew of it of their stock purchases and their purchases of short-term calls—purchases in some cases by individuals who had never before purchased calls or even TGS stock—virtually compels the inference that the insiders were influenced by the drilling results. *   *   *
*   *   *   *

We hold, therefore, that all transactions in TGS stock or calls by individuals apprised of the drilling results *   *   * were made in violation of Rule 10b-5. Inasmuch as the visual evaluation of that drill core (a generally reliable estimate though less accurate then a chemical assay) constituted material information, those advised of the results of the visual evaluation as well as those informed of the chemical assay traded in violation of law. * * *

* * * *

II. THE CORPORATE DEFENDANT

* * * *

At 3:00 P.M. on April 12, 1964, evidently believing it desirable to comment upon the rumors concerning the Timmins project, TGS issued the press release quoted in pertinent part [as follows:

[Recent drilling on one property near Timmins has led to preliminary indications that more drilling would be required for proper evaluation of this prospect. The drilling done to date has not been conclusive, but the statements made by many outside quarters are unreliable and include information and figures that are not available to TGS.]

[The work done to date has not been sufficient to reach definite conclusions and any statements as to size and grade of ore would be premature and possibly misleading. When we have progressed to the point where reasonable and logical conclusions can be made, TGS will issue a definite statement to its stockholders and to the public in order to clarify the Timmins project.]

* * * *

* * * It does not appear to be unfair to impose upon corporate management a duty to ascertain the truth of any statements the corporation releases to its shareholders or to the investing public at large. Accordingly, we hold that Rule 10b-5 is violated whenever assertions are made, as here, in a manner reasonably calculated to influence the investing public, e.g., by means of the financial media, if such assertions are false or misleading or are so incomplete as to mislead irrespective of whether the issuance of the release was motivated by corporate officials for ulterior purposes. It seems clear, however, that if corporate management demonstrates that it was diligent in ascertaining that the information it published was the whole truth and that such diligently obtained information was disseminated in good faith, Rule 10b-5 would not have been violated.

* * * *

We conclude, then, that, having established that the release was issued in a manner reasonably calculated to affect the market price of TGS stock and to influence the investing public, we must remand to the district court to decide whether the release was misleading to the reasonable investor and if found to be misleading, whether the court in its discretion should issue the injunction the SEC seeks.

DECISION AND REMEDY

The appellate court's judgment was favorable to the SEC. The information contained in the press release was material, and the transactions, in stock by the insiders who knew of it, had violated Rule 10b-5. Thus, the options of the individual defendants were rescinded. However, the questions of whether the press release was misleading and what remedies should be imposed were remanded to the trial court for decision. A trial court is bound to apply the law as enunciated by the court of appeals in making this type of decision.

COMMENT

Texas Gulf Sulphur Company was not only sued by the SEC but numerous civil actions for damages were also brought against it by plaintiff-investors who had sold their TGS stock as a result of the deceptively gloomy press release regarding the corporation's mineral exploration. All these suits were settled in 1972. In a federal lawsuit filed against TGS some two years after the initial case, a court of appeals held that investors who had sold stock relying on the representations in the press release could recover damages from the corporation and the officers who had drafted the release. The court went on to state that the proper measure of damages was the difference between the selling price and the price at which the investors could have reinvested within a reasonable period of time after they became aware of TGS's curative press release announcing the 25-million-ton strike.

The court held that a diligent and reasonable investor could have known the information within four days of TGS's curative press release. The investors, who sold their stock more than four days after the second press release was made, could not recover under the Securities Exchange Act by claiming that they had relied on the earlier, deceptive release.

Scienter *Requirement Under Rule 10b-5* The elements of a Section 10(b) and Rule 10b-5 violation are the use of a manipulative or deceptive device in connection with the purchase or sale of a security, where a material fact has been misrepresented or omitted. In addition, the act must have been committed with **scienter** (guilty knowledge that is greater than simple negligence). The additional requirement of *scienter* limited the broad application of Section 10(b) after the *Texas Gulf Sulphur* case. The first case to establish this criterion was the following case.

BACKGROUND AND FACTS *Ernst & Ernst, a Chicago accounting firm, was retained by First Securities Company, a brokerage firm, to audit its books. In addition to the auditing, Ernst & Ernst prepared and filed the necessary reports of First Securities with the SEC. The president of First Securities, Leston B. Nay, manipulated a fraudulent scheme of investment in which Hochfelder and several others invested their money. The scheme involved interest rates on low-risk escrow accounts. These accounts never existed, and, for over twenty years, Hochfelder continued unknowingly to place money into the nonexistent account.*

Nay took the money for his own use. The escrow accounts never appeared in Ernst & Ernst's audits. Nay committed suicide and left information describing the fraud. Hochfelder then filed a complaint against Ernst & Ernst for aiding and abetting Nay's fraud. The district court granted Ernst & Ernst a summary judgment, the court of appeals reversed the decision, and the United States Supreme Court reviewed the issue.

Case 19.5
ERNST & ERNST v. HOCHFELDER
Supreme Court of the United States, 1976.
425 U.S. 185, 96 S.Ct. 1375, 47 L.Ed.2d 668.

Justice POWELL delivered the opinion of the Court.

The issue in this case is whether an action for civil damages may lie under Section 10(b) of the Securities Exchange Act of 1934, and Securities and Exchange Commission Rule 10b-5, in the absence of an allegation of intent to deceive, manipulate, or defraud on the part of the defendant.

Petitioner, Ernst & Ernst, is an accounting firm. From 1946 through 1967 it was retained by First Securities Company of Chicago (First Securities), a small brokerage firm and member of the Midwest Stock Exchange and of the National Association of Securities Dealers, to perform periodic audits of the firm's books and records. In connection with these audits Ernst & Ernst prepared for filing with the Securities and Exchange Commission (Commission) the annual reports required of First Securities. It also prepared for First Securities responses to the financial questionnaires of the Midwest Stock Exchange (Exchange).

Respondents were customers of First Securities who invested in a fraudulent securities scheme perpetrated by Leston B. Nay, president of the firm and owner of 92 percent of its stock. Nay induced the respondents to invest funds in "escrow" accounts that he represented would yield a high rate of return. Respondents did so from 1942 through 1966, with the majority of the transactions occurring in the 1950s. In fact, there were no escrow accounts as Nay converted respondents' funds to his own use immediately upon receipt.

This fraud came to light in 1968 when Nay committed suicide, leaving a note that described First Securities as bankrupt and the escrow accounts as "spurious." Respondents subsequently filed this action for damages against Ernst & Ernst * * *. As revealed through discovery, respondents' cause of action rested on a theory of negligent nonfeasance. The premise was that Ernst & Ernst had failed to utilize "appropriate auditing procedures" in its audits of First Securities, thereby failing to discover internal practices of the firm said to prevent an effective audit. The practice principally relied on Nay's rule that only he could open mail addressed to him at First Securities or addressed to First Securities to his attention, even if it arrived in his absence. Respondents contended that if Ernst & Ernst had conducted a proper audit, it would have discovered this "mail rule." The existence of the rule then would have been disclosed in reports to the Exchange and to the Commission by Ernst & Ernst as an irregular procedure that prevented an effective audit. This would have led to an investigation of Nay that would have revealed the fraudulent scheme. Respondents specifically disclaimed the existence of fraud or intentional misconduct on the part of Ernst & Ernst.
*   *   *   *

We granted *certiorari* to resolve the question whether a private cause of action for damages will lie under Sec. 10(b) and Rule 10b-5 in the absence of any allegation of "scienter"—intent to deceive, manipulate, or defraud. We conclude that it will not and therefore we reverse.
*   *   *   *

Section 10 of the 1934 Act makes it "unlawful for any person . . . [t]o use or employ, in connection with the purchase or sale of any security . . . any manipulative or deceptive device or contrivance in contravention of such rules and regulations as the Commission may prescribe as necessary or appropriate in the public interest or for the protection of investors." *   *   *

Although Sec. 10(b) does not by its terms create an express civil remedy for its violation, and there is no indication that Congress, or the Commission when adopting Rule 10b-5, contemplated such a remedy, the existence of a private cause of action for violations of the statute and the Rule is now well established. *   *   *

Section 10(b) makes unlawful the use or employment of "any manipulative or deceptive device or contrivance" in contravention of Commission rules. The words "manipulative or deceptive" used in conjunction with "device or contrivance" strongly suggest that Sec. 10(b) was intended to proscribe knowing or intentional misconduct.
*   *   *   *

*   *   * When a statute speaks so specifically in terms of manipulation and deception, and of implementing devices and contrivances—the commonly understood terminology of intentional wrongdoing—and when its history reflects no more expansive intent, we are quite unwilling to extend the scope of the statute to negligent conduct.

DECISION AND REMEDY

The United States Supreme Court reversed the court of appeals and held that, in the absence of scienter, *no cause of action for fraud exists under Section 10(b).*

COMMENT

Scienter *is generally defined as a mental state embracing the intent to deceive, manipulate, or defraud. The more difficult question is whether recklessness is enough to satisfy the* scienter *requirement. In certain areas of*

*the law, recklessness is considered a form of intentional conduct if the conduct
is so careless as to evince a total disregard for the welfare of others and will
create liability.*

Ethical Considerations

Information for the Small Investor

Both the 1933 and the 1934 federal securities acts
were adopted to protect investors from fraudulent
activities ranging from actual fraud to the use of
insider information. The federal law, however,
allows many exemptions to these securities laws,
such as the small offering and private offering
exemptions. But why should any exemptions
exist? Is it not just as important to protect the
small investor who is purchasing any type of
security? State laws sometimes fill the void when
a federal exemption exists.

Persons Who Have a Duty Under Rule 10b-5
The SEC will prosecute insiders who, based on
nonpublic information, trade a security to their
financial benefit. The reasoning behind this rule
is that an insider should not use nonpublic information to his or her gain because such actions
are unfair to the individual investors who are not
privy to such information and have no equal means
of acquiring the information. Thus, the courts
and the SEC prohibit insiders from trading unless
information is first disclosed to the general public.

Insider trading rules cover not only corporate
officers, directors, and majority shareholders but
also generally anyone having access to or receiving
information of a nonpublic nature from an insider
on which trading is based. Those people to whom
the material information is given are known as
tippees.

State Securities Laws

All states have their own corporate securities laws
that regulate the offer and sale of securities within
individual state borders. Since the adoption of the
1933 and 1934 acts, the state and federal governments have regulated securities concurrently. Indeed, both acts specifically allow state securities
laws. Certain features are common to all state blue
sky laws. For example, they all have antifraud
provisions, many of which are patterned after the
federal law, and most state corporate securities
laws regulate securities brokers and dealers.

Typically, these laws provide for the registration or qualification of securities offered or issued
for sale within the state. Unless an applicable exemption from registration is found, issuers must
register or qualify their stock with the appropriate
state official, often called a corporations commissioner.

A difference in philosophy exists among the
state statutes. Many statutes are similar to the Securities Act of 1933 and mandate certain disclosures before the registration is effective; they may
also require a permit to sell the securities. Other
statutes have fairness standards that a corporation
must meet in order to offer or sell stock in the
state. A few states require a **merit registration,**
whereby the states review the registration for its
merits and are not restricted to reviewing the registration for disclosures only. The Uniform Securities Act (adopted in part by several states) was
drafted to be acceptable to states with differing
regulatory philosophies.

International Considerations

Attitudes toward Securities Regulations

Right this minute, in some country around the world, a stock market is open, doing business, and can be monitored from homes via personal computers and television. Each market is operated in accordance with the laws of its host country. No international agreements have been made regarding stock markets.

American law has criminalized violations of the heavily regulated securities markets. Computers monitor the markets to ensure compliance with the laws. Other countries have different attitudes toward securities regulation.

Japan has legislation prohibiting securities violations, but the government rarely enforces these laws. In the past, some large Japanese stockbrokerage houses reimbursed large traders in the stock market for losses they had incurred on recommended investments. This public revelation eventually led to a change in the government and promises by the stockbrokers not to treat large investors differently from small investors.

Members of the European Community (EC) have different views of insider trading. Denmark, France, Great Britain, and Switzerland have insider trading prohibitions, while the rest of the member nations do not. Large profits have been made on international stock markets. "Caveat emptor" is applicable to any American investor in the overseas market.

FACING A LEGAL ISSUE

Making a Public Offering

You have decided to go into business for yourself. You are interested in types of businesses requiring considerable initial capital for buildings and equipment. You have tried to raise this capital from family members, local banks, and other local financial institutions, as well as from the Small Business Administration, but without success.

A classmate of yours has joined the investment banking firm of Smart, Tight, and Moresight. In the past, this firm has been very conservative, only involving itself with extremely profitable corporations. Recently, however, they have promoted a person to partner whose financial philosophy is to assist new ventures that will offer the investment firm greater profits but higher risks. Your friend works for this new partner.

One day you meet your friend for lunch. You explain your predicament in not being able to raise capital and ask for any suggestions. Your friend recommends that you seek capital in the form of equity funds from the open market. This will require a public offering.

You must be concerned with both federal and state regulatory laws. The first thing you must remember when going public is that all material facts must be disclosed and presented in an honest format. The problem lies in deciding what is material. A material fact that is omitted can result in liability just as much as misstating a fact within a disclosure statement can. It is better to err on the side of giving more information than necessary than to neglect to disclose something that is material.

Normally, audited financial statements and an attorney's opinion letter must be filed with the registration statement. To obtain this information can be expensive and time consuming. You must bear the costs because you are the issuer. Your investment banking friend may assist you by overseeing the information, but such a firm normally does not advance funds to allow you to obtain this information. Going public also requires intensive work with your investment banker (the underwriter), lawyers, and accountants. All three advisers will make comments that will require changes to your prospectus. This procedure can take a long time; it may be months before you can file your legal documents with the appropriate governmental agency.

Because you do not have a financial record, you might be better off concentrating your efforts on locating a small corporation that has gone public. These types of firms have already become duly registered with state and federal authorities, and they already have a history of financial transactions. You can obtain control of one of these firms by purchasing a controlling interest of its common stock or through some form of merger or consolidation.

As you can see from this simple example, it is difficult and time consuming to start a business venture by yourself when you seek funding from the general public. If you take this approach, you will need the backing of good professional individuals along with a lot of perseverance.

Summary

This chapter has emphasized the regulation of securities by both federal and state authorities. A security can be something other than a stock or bond. It is any financial transaction in which an investor exchanges money for an interest in a common enterprise with the expectation of making a profit through the endeavors of the promoter or third party. Two primary federal statutes have been adopted: the Securities Act of 1933 and the Securities Exchange Act of 1934.

The 1933 act regulates new issues of securities and requires, prior to issuance, a full disclosure of all material facts. This information is presented in a prospectus, which is based on the registration statement. The registration statement is filed with the SEC and must be signed by the corporation's principal executive officer, principal accounting officer, and financial officer and by a majority of the members of the board of directors. Any person signing the registration statement is personally liable if there has not been a full and truthful disclosure of all material facts. Certain transactions and securities are exempt from the registration requirements of the 1933 act.

The Securities Exchange Act of 1934 regulates securities that are traded on national exchanges and ones extensively traded over the counter. In addition, this statute established the Securities and Exchange Commission.

Both acts prohibit fraud in the issuance of securities and in the disclosure of information available to the investing public.

Under Rule 10b-5 no individual may generally take advantage of insider information whether a situation involves new securities or ones actively traded. Most insiders are either directors, officers, key employees, or owners of 10 percent or more of the common stock. Rule 10b-5 applies, however, to both insiders and tippees. Any profits realized from inside information will belong to the corporation, and substantial criminal penalties can be assessed.

Key Terms

accredited investor (483)
blue sky laws (474)
due diligence defense (479)
exempt securities (482)
exempt transactions (482)
Foreign Corrupt Practices Act (478)
insider trading (484)
Insider Trading Sanctions Act (478)
Insider Trading and Securities Fraud Enforcement Act (478)
intrastate offering exemptions (483)

merit registration (493)
private offering exemptions (483)
prospectus (478)
proxy (484)
red herring prospectus (479)
Regulation A (483)
Regulation D (483)
Rule 10b-5 (486)
Rule 412 (484)
Rule 504 (483)
Rule 505 (483)
Rule 506 (483)
scienter (491)
Section 10(b) (486)

Section 16 (486)
Securities Act of 1933 (476)
Securities and Exchange Commission (476)
Securities Exchange Act of 1934 (476)
Securities Investor Protection Corporation (477)
shelf registration (484)
small offering exemptions (483)
tippees (493)
tombstone advertisement (479)
unaccredited investor (483)

Questions and Case Problems

1. Maresh, an experienced geologist, owned certain oil and gas leases covering land in Nebraska. To raise money for the drilling of a test well, he undertook to sell fractional interests in the leases. He approached Garfield, a man with whom he had done business in the past. Garfield had mentioned that he would be interested in investing in some of Maresh's future oil ventures. Garfield had wide business experience in the stock market and in oil stocks. He felt that the investment in Maresh's gas leases could be lucrative. Based on Garfield's promise to wire the money promptly, Maresh began drilling. Soon after, when Maresh realized that the land was dry, Garfield claimed that he could rescind the agreement to invest since the investment offered by Maresh was a security within the meaning of the Securities Act of 1933, and it had not been registered. Did Maresh offer a security within the meaning of the 1933 act? [Garfield v. Strain, 320 F.2d 116 (10th Cir. 1963)]

2. The Howey Company owned large tracts of citrus acreage in Lake County, Florida. For several years, the company planted about 500 acres annually, keeping half of the groves itself and offering the other half to the public to help finance additional development. Howey-in-the-Hills Service, Inc., was a service company engaged in cultivating and developing these groves, including the harvesting and marketing of the crops. Each prospective cus-

tomer was offered both a land sales contract and a service contract, after being told that it was not feasible to invest in a grove unless service arrangements were made. Of the acreage sold by Howey, 85 percent was sold with a service contract with Howey-in-the-Hills Service, Inc. Must Howey register the sales of these parcels of citrus groves with the Securities and Exchange Commission? [Securities and Exchange Comm'n v. W. J. Howey Co., 328 U.S. 293, 66 S.Ct. 1100, 90 L.Ed. 1244 (1946)]

3. Chiarella was a printer who handled announcements of corporate takeover bids. Even though the documents concealed the identity of the target corporations, he was able to deduce the names of the target companies. He purchased stock in target companies and sold the shares immediately after the takeover attempts were made public. He realized a gain of slightly more than $30,000 over fourteen months. The SEC investigated. He was convicted of insider trading. He appealed his conviction. What was the result and why? [Chiarella v. United States, 445 U.S. 222, 110 S.Ct. 1108, 63 L.Ed.2d 348 (1980)]

4. On September 1, 1971, the Ecological Science Corporation issued a press release stating, in part, that it had renegotiated the terms of approximately $14 million in loans from its prime lender and that, under the renegotiated agreement, $4 million was due on demand and the remainder on a specified date. The press release, however, failed to mention that, on the same date as the renegotiated loan agreement, an insurance and annuity association had refused to provide the corporation with the $4 million loan that it had planned to use to repay the demand loan. Moreover, while discussing its European prospects in the press release, Ecological Science Corporation failed to mention the proposed transfer of voting control among its European subsidiaries. Has Ecological Science Corporation violated any of the provisions of the Securities Exchange Act of 1934? [Securities and Exchange Comm'n v. Koenig, 469 F.2d 198 (2d Cir. 1972)]

5. Emerson Electric Company owned 13.2 percent of Dodge Manufacturing Company's stock. Within six months of the purchase of this stock, Emerson sold enough shares to a broker to reduce its holding to 9.96 percent of its former Dodge holdings. One week later (but still less than six months after Emerson's initial purchase), Emerson sold its remaining shares of Dodge stock. The sole purpose of Emerson's initial sale of just over 3 percent of its Dodge stock was to avoid liability under Section 16 of the Securities Exchange Act of 1934, which prohibits short-swing trading. Assuming Emerson made no profit on the initial sale of stock but made substantial profits when it sold the remaining 9.96 percent of Dodge stock, must it return the profits it made on the sale? [Reliance Electric Co. v. Emerson Electric Co., 404 U.S. 418, 92 S.Ct. 596, 30 L.Ed.2d 575 (1972)]

6. American Breeding Herds (ABH) offered a cattle-breeding plan for which Ronnett contracted to buy 36 Charolais cows at $3,000 per head and a one-quarter interest in a Charolais bull at $5,000, totaling $113,000. The ABH agreement described itself as a "tax shelter program . . . unlike the purchase of securities such as stocks and bonds." Ronnett entered into the agreement after receiving investment advice from Shannon, an investment counselor. The cows were tagged and sent to an ABH-approved breeding ranch. Ronnett signed a maintenance agreement and paid a monthly maintenance fee. Was the ABH plan a security, and should it have been registered under the securities law? [Ronnett v. American Breeding Herds, Inc., 124 Ill.App.3d 842, 464 N.E.2d 1201, 80 Ill.Dec. 218 (1984)]

7. Dirks advised institutional investors as to the financial merits of different insurance companies. A former officer of Equity Funding of America told Dirks that Equity Funding had fraudulently overstated many assets in its financial reports. While investigating this information, Dirks openly discussed the matter with reporters and a number of his clients. He did not own any shares. Some of his clients sold their stock based on information received from Dirks. The stock fell from about $26 a share to $15 a share in two weeks. Dirks was censured by the SEC, contending that he was an insider or a tippee of an insider. Was the SEC correct to censure Dirks? Discuss fully. [Dirks v. Securities and Exchange Comm'n, 463 U.S. 646, 103 S.Ct. 3255, 77 L.Ed.2d 911 (1983)]

8. Adams devised a plan to sell "rabbit kits." For $7,200 per kit, a person would receive twelve female and two male rabbits that should produce 720 breeding females within a year. Part of the sales promotion was that Adams would be available for consultation. Also, Adams requested all buyers to join an association that would purchase all of the buyers' pelts. Membership in the association was not part of the "rabbit kit." The association was controlled by Adams. The state of Florida claimed that Adams was selling an unlicensed security. Was Adams selling securities that should have been registered? Discuss fully. [Adams v. State, 443 So.2d 1003 (Fla. Dist. Ct. App. 1983)]

9. MAI was in the business of financing computer installations through sale and lease-back agreements. In this type of agreement, MAI would purchase the computer and lease it back to the original owner. As part of the lease, MAI was required to maintain and repair the computers. MAI did not have the facilities or capacity to perform maintenance services. MAI entered into a contract with IBM to service the machines. Subsequently, MAI learned that IBM would substantially increase its maintenance charges, and the monthly net earnings of MAI would decrease by 75 percent. When this information became public, the price of MAI stock fell from $28 to $11. Prior to this information becoming public, two officers of MAI had sold their stock. A lawsuit was filed against them by the shareholders on behalf of the cor-

poration claiming the two officers' actions violated Rule 10b-5 and Section 10(b) of the Securities Exchange Act. Are the two officers liable to the corporation for profits resulting from the sale? Discuss fully. [Diamond v. Oreamuno, 24 N.Y.2d 494, 248 N.E.2d 910, 301 N.Y.S.2d 78 (1969)]

10. Apple Computer developed and marketed the Lisa line of computers. The company promoted this new line of computers as if it would take over the computer market. This was publicized in the major journals with the fol-lowing quotation: "Lisa is going to be phenomenally suc-cessful in the first year out of the chute." Many critics pointed out that Lisa was not IBM compatible, that there were problems with software suppliers, and that Lisa was very expensive. Lisa turned out to be a complete failure, causing a 75 percent drop in Apple stock. Purchasers of Apple stock brought an action for failure to disclose prob-lems with Lisa. Who prevails and why? [In re Apple Com-puter Securities Litigation, 886 F.2d 1109 (9th Cir. 1989)]

Chapter 20   Antitrust Law

*Every agreement concerning trade, every regulation of trade,
restrains. To bind, to restrain, is of their very essence. The true test of
legality is whether the restraint imposed is such as merely regulates
and perhaps thereby promotes competition or whether it is such as
may suppress or even destroy competition.*

Justice Brandeis,
*Board of Trade of the City of Chicago
v. United States,*
246 U.S. 231, 38 S.Ct. 242, 62 L.Ed. 683 (1918).

OUTLINE

Introduction

A trust is a legal entity in which a trustee holds title to property for the benefit of another. The trustee manages the property, and the beneficiaries of the trust are entitled to the income from the property. Most trusts are legal, and their use flourishes today, particularly in estate planning.

In the past, this form of organization was used to restrain trade. After the Civil War, trusts were used by groups of corporations to eliminate competition. Corporations that were engaged in the same type of business transferred their stock to a trustee and in return received trust certificates. The trustee made decisions that fixed prices, controlled production, and determined the control of exclusive geographical markets for the entire industry. Corporations participating in a trust no longer competed with each other. The trusts wielded such power that corporations outside the trusts were unable to affect the market.

States attempting to control such monopolistic restraints in trade behavior enacted statutes to outlaw the use of trusts. That is why laws that regulate economic competition are referred to as **antitrust laws.** The purpose is to prevent monopolists from controlling the economy through restraints. The federal government recognized that monopolies were a national problem and in 1887 passed the **Interstate Commerce Act** and in 1890 enacted the **Sherman Antitrust Act.** These laws and subsequent ones prohibited anticompetitive behavior and are based on the belief that competition lowers prices, encourages innovation, and provides for equitable distributions of wealth between producers and consumers.

This chapter discusses the major antitrust statutes that are enforced by the Department of Justice and the Federal Trade Commission. It also focuses on various contractual and business actions that affect competition, and discusses possible defenses to claims of antitrust conduct.

Trusts and Common Law in the United States

American common law protected every person's freedom to enter a market and his or her rights to trade, but the common law was inadequate to deal with the giant corporations and trusts that developed in the latter half of the nineteenth century. The power of the railroads, for example, exceeded the power of the courts to deal with them. The railroads refused to serve sparsely populated areas, charged high rates to some shippers, and offered rebates to others. Several states regulated railroad rates and service to overcome these problems, but state regulations could not solve interstate trade abuses.

In the second half of the nineteenth century, the Standard Oil Company and other trusts gained control of several major industries—oil, cotton, whiskey, sugar, and linseed oil. Their activity constituted a monopoly in each geographical area. For example, Standard Oil would sell kerosene at a price below its own costs in order to drive competitors out of business. Once its monopoly position was assured, Standard Oil would raise prices to recoup the losses and reap monopoly profits.

Similar activity was found in other business areas. The public became concerned that the trusts were controlling an increasing number of industries and using unfair methods to gain this control. Congress had to find a way to destroy the trusts without destroying free enterprise.

The Sherman Antitrust Act was the response, and its purpose was to promote competition within the United States economy. The author of the legislation, Senator John Sherman, argued that the Sherman Act did not announce a new principal of law but simply applied well-recognized principles of the common law. The Sherman Act was an attempt by Congress to make the federal courts create a common body of federal antitrust law.

Sherman Antitrust Act

Sections 1 and 2 contain the main provisions of the Sherman Act:

> Sec. 1: Every contract, combination in the form of trust or otherwise, or conspiracy, in restraint of trade or commerce among the several States, or with foreign nations, is hereby declared to be illegal [and is a felony punishable by fine and/or imprisonment]. * * *
>
> Sec. 2: Every person who shall monopolize, or attempt to monopolize, or combine or conspire

with any other person or persons, to monopolize any part of the trade or commerce among the several States, or with foreign nations, shall be deemed guilty of a felony [and is similarly punishable].

*   *   *

Sections 1 and 2 Compared

Both provisions are relatively vague and cover different commercial activity. Congress left it to the courts to determine what constituted a violation of this act. The courts have continued to consider the meaning of these two provisions through the intervening decades.

These two main sections are quite different from each other. Section 1 requires action by two or more people, since a person cannot combine or conspire alone. The essence of the illegal activity is the act of joining together. Section 2 applies to both an individual person and to several people because it states, "[e]very person who *   *   *." Thus, conduct by one person can result in a violation of Section 2.

The cases brought to court under Section 1 of the Sherman Act differ from those brought under Section 2. Section 1 cases are often concerned with finding an agreement (written, oral, or based on conduct) that leads to a restraint of trade. Section 2 cases deal with the structure of a monopoly that exists in the marketplace.

Section 1 focuses on agreements that are restrictive—that is, agreements that have a wrongful purpose—while Section 2 looks at the misuse of monopoly power in the marketplace. Both sections seek to curtail commercial practices that result in undesired pricing, collusion, and other restraints of trade. Any case brought under Section 2, however, must be one in which the threshold or necessary amount of monopoly power already exists.

The Sherman Act does not regulate how a business should act. The statute sets out how a business should not act. In this sense, the statute is proscriptive rather than prescriptive. It is the basis for policing rather than regulating business conduct.

Two doctrines are used in deciding Sherman Act cases: the rule of reason and per se illegality.

The Rule of Reason

The most important early case involved Standard Oil Company of New Jersey. The Supreme Court found the oil company guilty of violations of both Sections 1 and 2. Having determined that Congress could not have intended a literal interpretation of every restraint of trade in Section 1, the Court used a standard of reasonableness to analyze the conduct of the oil company.

The **rule of reason** is still used to determine which anticompetitive acts violate the antitrust laws. The rule requires a court to review all the circumstances of a case in order to decide whether the effect of the defendant's practice was an unreasonable restraint on competition. Certain conduct is conclusively presumed to be unreasonable; as we will discuss later, this means that the conduct is illegal per se and is not subject to the rule of reason. When reading the following case, try to determine when the rule of reason should be applied.

BACKGROUND AND FACTS   *Standard Oil Company of New Jersey and 33 other corporations, John D. Rockefeller, William Rockefeller, and five other individual defendants were the appellants in this case. They attempted to reverse a decree holding that they were conspiring "to restrain the trade and commerce in petroleum, commonly called 'crude oil,' in refined oil, and in the other products of petroleum, among several States and Territories of the United States and the District of Columbia and with foreign nations, and to monopolize the said commerce." The conspiracy was alleged to have been formed around 1870 by three of the individual defendants—John D. Rockefeller, William Rockefeller, and Henry M. Flagler.*

The government charged that the individual defendants organized the Standard Oil Corporation of Ohio and soon afterward became participants in an illegal plan to acquire substantially all of the oil refineries located in

Case 20.1
STANDARD OIL CO. OF NEW JERSEY v. UNITED STATES

Supreme Court of the United States, 1911.
221 U.S. 1, 31 S.Ct. 502, 55 L.Ed. 619.

Cleveland, Ohio. Therefore, the government charged the original owners of the company with being in an illegal combination for the restraint and monopolization of all interstate commerce in petroleum products.

In addition, the government charged that there was a trust agreement in which the stock of over 40 corporations, including Standard Oil of Ohio, was held for the benefit of the members of the combination. The court voided the trust agreement because it was in restraint of trade, and the trust was ordered dissolved. It is questionable whether the trust was actually dissolved as required by the decree, because the stock held by the trust was apparently shifted around, and control of the companies was preserved in the same hands.

In the third phase of its case, the government charged that the individual defendants operated a holding company through Standard Oil Company of New Jersey. This company acquired the majority of stock in various other corporations engaging in the purchasing, transporting, refining, shipping, and selling of oil in the United States, the District of Columbia, and foreign nations. In short, the government attacked the Standard Oil Trust, the Standard Oil Company, and the Standard Oil Company of New Jersey because the net effect of these organizations was to create a monopoly and restrain trade. The government sought an injunction to prevent the defendants from continuing their control over the subsidiary corporations.

Chief Justice WHITE delivered the opinion of the Court.
*   *   *   *

Let us consider the language of the first and second sections, guided by the principle that where words are employed in a statute which had at the time a well-known meaning at common law or in the law of this country they are presumed to have been used in that sense unless the context compels to the contrary.

As to the first section, the words to be interpreted are: "Every contract, combination in the form of trust or otherwise, or conspiracy in restraint of trade or commerce *   *   * is hereby declared to be illegal." As there is no room for dispute that the statute was intended to formulate a rule for the regulation of interstate and foreign commerce, the question is, What was the rule which it adopted?

In view of the common law and the law in this country as to restraint of trade, which we have reviewed, and the illuminating effect which that history must have under the rule to which we have referred, we think it results:

a. That the context manifests that the statute was drawn in the light of the existing practical conception of the law of restraint of trade, because it groups as within that class, not only contracts which were in restraint of trade in the subjective sense, but all contracts or acts which theoretically were attempts to monopolize, yet which in practice had come to be considered as in restraint of trade in a broad sense.

b. That in view of the many new forms of contracts and combinations which were being evolved from existing economic conditions, it was deemed essential by an all-embracing enumeration to make sure that no form of contract or combination by which an undue restraint of interstate or foreign commerce was brought about could save such restraint from condemnation. The statute under this view evidenced the intent not to restrain the right to make and enforce contracts, whether resulting from combination or otherwise, which did not unduly restrain interstate or foreign commerce, but to protect that commerce from being restrained by methods, whether old or new, which could constitute an inference that is an undue restraint.

c. And as the contracts or acts embraced in the provision were not expressly defined, since the enumeration addressed itself simply to classes of acts, those classes being broad enough to embrace every conceivable contract or combination which could be made concerning trade or commerce or the subjects of such commerce, and thus caused any act done by any of the enumerated methods anywhere in the whole field of human activity to be illegal if in restraint of trade, it inevitably follows that the provision necessarily called for the exercise of judgment which required that some standard should be resorted to for the purpose of determining whether the prohibitions contained in the statute had or had not in any given case been violated. Thus not specifying but indubitably contemplating and requiring a standard, it follows that it was intended that the standard of reason which had been applied at the common law and in this country in dealing with subjects of the character embraced by the statute, was intended to be the measure used for the purpose of determining whether in a given case a particular act had or had not brought about the wrong against which the statute provided.

* * * *

* * * The merely generic enumeration which the statute makes of the acts to which it refers, and the absence of any definition of restraint of trade as used in the statute, leaves room for but one conclusion, which is, that it was expressly designed not to unduly limit the application of the act by precise definition, but, while clearly fixing a standard, that is, by defining the ulterior boundaries which could not be transgressed with impunity, to leave it to be determined by the light of reason, guided by the principles of law and the duty to apply and enforce the public policy embodied in the statute, in every given case whether any particular act or contract was within the contemplation of the statute.

* * * *

Recurring to the acts done by the individuals or corporations who were mainly instrumental in bringing about the expansion of the New Jersey corporation during the period prior to the formation of the trust agreements of 1879 and 1882, including those agreements, not for the purpose of weighing the substantial merit of the numerous charges of wrongdoing made during such period, but solely as an aid for discovering intent and purpose, we think no disinterested mind can survey the period in question without being irresistibly driven to the conclusion that the very genius for commercial development and organization which it would seem was manifested from the beginning soon begot an intent and purpose to exclude others which was frequently manifested by acts and dealings wholly inconsistent with the theory that they were made with the single conception of advancing the development of business power by usual methods, but which on the contrary necessarily involved the intent to drive others from the field and to exclude them from their right to trade and thus accomplish the mastery which was the end in view. * * *

The Supreme Court agreed with the lower court and affirmed the decree. Standard Oil was forbidden to engage in any future combinations in violation of the Sherman Antitrust Act. In addition, the decree attempted to neutralize the effect of the monopoly that Standard Oil had created by commanding the dissolution of the combination (the trust) and causing the New Jersey corporation to divest itself of the numerous shares of stock that it controlled.

DECISION AND REMEDY

The Court in *Standard Oil* reasoned that Congress had intended the Sherman Act to apply only to unreasonable restraints on trade that would achieve monopolization. This is what is meant by the rule of reason. The Court rejected the idea that the act should reach every restraint, regardless of its reasonableness. If the Court had not interpreted the act in this way, every conceivable business practice would have violated the Sherman Act.

Per Se Rule

Certain types of restrictive agreements are deemed to be inherently anticompetitive and are an unreasonable restraint on trade. Many of these agreements normally are subject to the **per se rule** (no evidence beyond the fact that the agreement existed is required to prove the illegality). Four types of agreements generally are per se illegal: **price-fixing, horizontal restraints, vertical restraints,** and **group boycotts.**

Price-Fixing Price-fixing is one of the practices to which courts apply the per se standard rather than the rule of reason. Price-fixing occurs when competitors conspire to fix the price of an item or service.

The following case established the principle that price-fixing agreements are unlawful per se. *Standard Oil Co. of New Jersey v. United States* is the classic case on the rule of reason, and *United States v. Socony-Vacuum Oil Co.* is the classic case on the per se doctrine.[1]

---

1. Socony-Vacuum Oil Company was one of the companies in the Standard Oil Trust. Socony-Vacuum Oil Company and Standard Oil of New York are now Mobil Oil Company.

Case 20.2
UNITED STATES v. SOCONY-VACUUM OIL CO.

Supreme Court of the United States, 1940.
310 U.S. 150, 60 S.Ct. 811,
84 L.Ed. 1129.

BACKGROUND AND FACTS *During the Great Depression, more oil was refined into gasoline than consumers demanded at the then-current market price. The major oil refiners had ample storage facilities and the capacity to distribute gasoline to retailers. Smaller, independent refiners lacked storage facilities and sold their gasoline at distressed prices on the spot market for immediate delivery to retailers. Prices on the spot market affected prices throughout the industry, and the glut of gasoline available in the spot market drove prices down.*

The major oil companies embarked on a program of purchasing and storing the "distressed oil." Each major company agreed to buy from a particular independent. Although it appeared that the bidding and buying were based on the market price, the major companies through their bidding established a floor for gasoline prices that enabled them to prevent prices on the spot market from falling any lower.

Justice DOUGLAS delivered the opinion of the Court.
*   *   *   *

The elimination of the so-called competitive evils is no legal justification for such buying programs. The elimination of such conditions was sought primarily for its effect on the price structures. Fairer competitive prices, it is claimed, resulted when distress gasoline was removed from the market. But such defense is typical of the protestations usually made in price-fixing cases. Ruinous competition, financial disaster, evils of price cutting and the like appear throughout our history as ostensible justifications for price-fixing. If the so-called competitive abuses were to be appraised here, the reasonableness of prices would necessarily become an issue in every price-fixing case. In that event the Sherman Act would soon be emasculated; its philosophy would be supplanted by one which is wholly alien to a system of free competition; it would not be the charter of freedom which its framers intended.

The reasonableness of prices has no constancy due to the dynamic quality of business facts underlying price structures. Those who fixed reasonable prices today would perpetuate unreasonable prices tomorrow, since those prices would not be subject to continuous administrative supervision and readjustment in light of changed conditions. Those who controlled the prices would control or effectively dominate the market. And those who were in that strategic position would have it in their power to destroy or drastically impair the competitive system. But the thrust of the rule is deeper and reaches more than monopoly power. Any combination which tampers with price structures is engaged in an unlawful activity. Even though the members of the price-fixing group were in no position to control the market, to the extent that they raised, lowered, or stabilized prices they would be directly interfering with the free play of market forces. The Act places all such schemes beyond the pale and protects that vital part of our economy against any degree of interference. Congress has not left with us the determination of whether or not particular price-fixing schemes are wise or unwise, healthy or destructive. It has not permitted the age-old cry of ruinous competition and competitive evils to be a defense to price-fixing conspiracies. It has no more allowed genuine or fancied competitive abuses as a legal justification for such schemes than it has the good intentions of the members of the combination. If such a shift is to be made, it must be done by Congress. Certainly Congress has not left us with any such choice. Nor has the Act created or authorized the creation of any special exception in favor of the oil industry. Whatever may be its peculiar problems and characteristics, the Sherman Act, so far as price-fixing agreements are concerned, establishes one uniform rule applicable to all industries alike. There was accordingly no error in the refusal to charge that in order to convict the jury must find that the resultant prices were raised and maintained at "high, arbitrary and noncompetitive levels." The charge in the indictment to that effect was surplusage.

*   *   *   *

Under the Sherman Act a combination formed for the purpose and with the effect of raising, depressing, fixing, pegging, or stabilizing the price of a commodity in interstate or foreign commerce is illegal *per se*. *   *   *

The Supreme Court affirmed the judgment of the trial court. Each corporation was fined $5,000; each individual, $1,000. It was held that it is illegal to try to fix prices even though the prices seem to be reasonable. Any attempt to fix prices is an illegal per se violation of the Sherman Act.

DECISION AND REMEDY

Horizontal Restraints   Dividing a market for the sale of a specific product among competitors is a per se violation. Market division can be accomplished in many ways, all of which are illegal. Competitors cannot allocate among themselves exclusive territories, products, or customers. Even though such agreements might seem reasonable, they eliminate competition. Whether price-fixing and other restraints on trade are part of the plan to divide a market is irrelevant.

These activities among competitors are referred to as horizontal restraints when the competitors are on the same basic level of business operation—for example, retailers, manufacturers, or producers. The parties involved may be sellers of the same brand, suppressing intrabrand competition, or of different brands, suppressing interbrand competition. Franchise agreements seem to be the only exception, but they are subject to the rule of reason.

Trade Associations   Businesspeople in certain types of associations must be careful not to engage in actions that might be considered in violation of the antitrust laws.

For example, competitors often organize into **trade associations** in order to pursue common interests. These associations disseminate information, represent the members' business interests before governmental bodies, initiate joint advertising campaigns, and attempt to police their own industry. These exchanges of information among related businesses pose special antitrust problems. Trade association activities are, by their very nature, joint actions, and they are subject to the antitrust laws.

Professional Associations   For many years, professionals were thought to be outside the scope of the antitrust laws because their activities did not involve trade or commerce. This is not so today. The impact that professional services have on the economy has been used to impose antitrust liability on **professional associations.** For example, a minimum fee schedule mandated by a bar association was held to be price-fixing,[2] while a maximum fee plan set by a medical association was also held to be price-fixing.[3]

Other Types of Horizontal Restraints   There are other types of horizontal restraints that violate antitrust laws. One type is the **concerted refusals to deal.** Sellers of goods and services generally have the right to select customers, provided that such a selection is not based on a customer's religious beliefs, color, sex, or national origin. When two or more sellers act in concert to refuse to sell to a particular buyer or class of buyers, however, the courts have generally found such acts unlawful under either the Sherman Act or the Clayton Act, or both. The provisions of the Clayton Act are discussed later in this chapter.

Another type of horizontal restraint is the **territorial and customer divisions.** It is a Section 1 violation of the Sherman Act for competitors to divide up territories or customers. For example, manufacturers A, B, and C compete against each other in the states of Kansas, Nebraska, and Iowa. By agreement, A sells products only in Kansas, B sells only in Nebraska, and C sells only in Iowa. This concerted action reduces costs and allows all three (assuming there is no other competition) to raise the price of the goods sold in their respective states.

The same violation would take place if A, B, and C had simply agreed that A would sell only to institutional purchasers (school districts, universities, state agencies and departments, cities, and so on) in the three states, B only to wholesalers, and C only to retailers.

Vertical Restraints   Trade practices involving firms at different levels of the production and distribution processes may violate the antitrust laws. When they do, they are referred to as vertical restraints of trade. Vertical relationships are more complex than horizontal ones, and they vary to such a degree that it is sometimes difficult even to define the typical vertical arrangement. The most common vertical restraints are discussed here.

Resale Price Maintenance   A manufacturer or wholesaler would like to keep control of the price of the product being sold and resold. In the past, a **resale price maintenance agreement** would be made between the seller, such as a manufacturer, and the buyer, such as a retailer; this agreement would dictate the price at which the product must be resold. These types of agreements are per se violations of Section 1 of the Sherman Act.

Restrictions in the Distribution Process   The methods by which manufacturers market their products vary greatly. A manufacturer may sell directly to retailers or to wholesale distributors, who in turn sell to retailers. The manufacturer may enter into franchise agreements that permit retailers to present themselves to the public as dealers of the manufacturer's product. The manufacturer may even own the retail outlets where its products are sold.

Regardless of the arrangement selected, both the manufacturer and the retailer are seeking maximum profits. Some of the methods that increase profits violate the antitrust laws; others do not. The manufacturer will often impose territorial restrictions on each of its retailers in order to prevent the retailers from competing with each other. This creates a sales advantage for each retailer, since the desired product cannot be purchased anywhere else in the immediate area. Thus, selling goods of the same make under territorial restrictions results in less competition.

The manufacturer or distributor may also require the retailer not to sell the products of competing firms. This is an **exclusive dealing contract.** Conversely, individual firms can refuse to sell their products to certain buyers. As long as it is an individual decision and not a concerted refusal to deal (a boycott) by a group of firms, such action is legal.

Manufacturers may attempt to prohibit wholesalers or retailers from reselling the products to certain classes of buyers, such as competing retailers; therefore, these actions constitute consumer restrictions. Territorial and customer restrictions are lawful unless their use unreasonably restricts trade.

---

2.   *Goldfarb v. Virginia State Bar*, 421 U.S. 773, 95 S.Ct. 2004, 44 L.Ed.2d 572 (1975).
3.   *Arizona v. Maricopa County Medical Society*, 457 U.S. 332, 102 S.Ct. 2466, 73 L.Ed.2d 48 (1982).

Group Boycotts Concerted refusals to deal, usually called boycotts, are a per se offense. A boycott generally involves two different levels of business operation rather than competitors on the same basic level. Traders on one level coerce traders on another level not to deal with certain parties. For example, a group of wholesalers may refuse to buy from a supplier who sells to a particular wholesaler. Or the group of wholesalers may refuse to sell to retailers who buy from a specified wholesaler. The group undertaking the boycott seeks to protect itself from competition by depriving the excluded party of trade relationships. The boycotting group threatens to stop dealing with any

business that sells to or buys from a business that is not a group member.

Concerted refusals to deal violate the Sherman Act only when their purpose is to drive out competitors or to prevent their entry into business. For example, boycotts to prevent the sale of copies of designer clothing and the boycott by car dealers to prevent General Motors from selling cars to discount outlets were per se violations of the antitrust laws.

Illegal boycotts are not restricted to businesses dealing with goods. As you will see in the next case, illegal boycotts may also involve services.

BACKGROUND AND FACTS *Members of the Superior Court Trial Lawyers Association represented indigent defendants before the District of Columbia Superior Court. The members wanted an increase in their statutorily fixed fees, which were set in 1970 at $20 per hour for out-of-court time and at $30 per hour for in-court time. In order to obtain higher fees, they agreed among themselves to refuse to accept new clients. About 90 percent of the regular District of Columbia Criminal Justice Act (CJA) lawyers took part in this boycott. Within two weeks the criminal justice system was on the brink of collapse. The city agreed to an immediate temporary fee increase to $35 per hour for all work with a subsequent permanent increase to $45 an hour for out-of-court work and $55 for in-court time. The Federal Trade Commission filed a complaint against the association and four officers, alleging that they had entered into an agreement that amounted to restraint of trade. The initial hearing was held in front of an administrative law judge (ALJ) whose decision was appealed to the full Federal Trade Commission. The case was appealed to the Second Circuit Court of Appeals and eventually to the Supreme Court of the United States.*

Case 20.3
FEDERAL TRADE COMMISSION v. SUPERIOR COURT TRIAL LAWYERS ASSOCIATION
Supreme Court of the United States, 1990.
493 U.S. 411, 110 S.Ct. 768, 107 L.Ed. 851.

Justice STEVENS delivered the opinion of the Court.
* * * *

As the ALJ, the FTC, and the Court of Appeals all agreed, respondents' boycott constituted a classic restraint of trade within the meaning of Section 1 of the Sherman Act. As such, it also violated the prohibition against unfair methods of competition in § 5 of the FTC Act. Prior to the boycott CJA lawyers were in competition with one another, each deciding independently whether and how often to offer to provide services to the District at CJA rates. The agreement among the CJA lawyers was designed to obtain higher prices for their services and was implemented by a concerted refusal to serve an important customer in the market for legal services and, indeed, the only customer in the market for the particular services that CJA regulars offered. "This constriction of supply is the essence of 'price-fixing,' whether it be accomplished by agreeing upon a price, which will decrease the quantity demanded, or by agreeing upon an output, which will increase the price offered." The horizontal arrangement among these competitors was unquestionably a "naked restraint" on price and output.
* * * *

The lawyers' association argues that if its conduct would otherwise be prohibited by the Sherman Act and the Federal Trade Act, it is nonetheless protected by the First Amendment rights recognized in NAACP v[.] Claiborne Hardware. That case arose after black citizens boycotted white merchants in Claiborne County, Miss. The white merchants sued under state law to recover losses from the boycott. We found that the right of the States to regulate economic activity could not justify a complete prohibition against a nonviolent, politically motivated boycott designed to force governmental and economic change and to effectuate rights guaranteed by the Constitution itself. We accordingly held that the nonviolent elements of petitioners' activities are entitled to the protection of the First Amendment.

The lawyers' association contends that because it, like the boycotters in Claiborne Hardware, sought to vindicate constitutional rights, it should enjoy a similar First Amendment protection. It is, of course, clear that the association's efforts to publicize the boycott, to explain the merits of its cause, and to lobby District officials to enact favorable legislation—like similar activities in Claiborne Hardware—were activities that were fully protected by the First Amendment. But nothing in the FTC's order would curtail such activities, and nothing in the FTC's reasoning condemned any of those activities.

The activity that the FTC order prohibits is a concerted refusal by CJA lawyers to accept any further assignments until they receive an increase in their compensation; the undenied objective of their boycott was an economic advantage for those who agreed to participate. It is true that the Claiborne Hardware case also involved a boycott. That boycott, however, differs in a decisive respect. Those who joined the Claiborne Hardware boycott sought no special advantage for themselves. They were black citizens in Port Gibson, Mississippi, who had been the victims of political, social, and economic discrimination for many years. They sought only the equal respect and equal treatment to which they were constitutionally entitled. They struggled to change a social order that had consistently treated them as second class citizens. * * *

The same cannot be said of attorney's fees. As we recently pointed out, our reasoning in Claiborne Hardware is not applicable to a boycott conducted by business competitors who "stand to profit financially from a lessening of competition in the boycotted market."

DECISION AND REMEDY   *The lawyers' boycott produced a crisis in the administration of criminal justice in Washington, D.C. The Court found a conspiracy to set prices in violation of the antitrust laws. The Court further found that there need not be a monopoly in order for a violation of antitrust laws to exist.*

Structural Analysis of Monopoly Power

Courts are not always concerned with concerted activity among competitors; they may be confronted with an alleged monopoly, for example. Courts must decide when a firm has **monopoly power,** as antitrust statutes do not define the term *monopoly*. Consequently, a judicial review is concerned with whether the firm has **market power.** Is the power of the firm so great that it can force its decisions on others? The courts must also ask whether the firm has obtained monopoly power with the wrongful intent of acquiring that power.

Although various methods for assessing market power could be used, courts today employ the structural analysis advanced by Judge Learned Hand in the following case. Stated simply, the structural analysis of market power involves the following two steps:

1. Define the market in which the firm's power should be evaluated
2. Measure the extent of the firm's share of that market.

Structural analysis involves more than identifying the firms within a market and comparing their sales. Structural analysis is not exact; it is a tool used by the courts to support the inference that monopoly power exists. After defining the **relevant product market** and the **relevant geographic market,** the court compares the sales of the firms within these markets. In addition to the firm's market share, the court considers any barriers to entry that may exist and whether acceptable substitutes are available for the firm's product. The following case illustrates how the courts analyze whether a firm has an illegal monopoly.

BACKGROUND AND FACTS *The United States charged Aluminum Company of America (Alcoa) with monopolizing interstate and foreign commerce in the manufacture and sale of "virgin" aluminum ingot. Alcoa was the sole producer of virgin ingot in the United States, and the government contended that that fact alone made Alcoa an unlawful monopoly. Alcoa contended that it was subject to competition from imported virgin ingot and from "secondary" ingot (recycled aluminum) and therefore did not have monopoly power. The district court found that Alcoa had a 33 percent share of the market, which included both the secondary material that had been salvaged from scrap and the new ingot. The lower court found for Alcoa. The court of appeals computed the market share differently and found that Alcoa had 90 percent of the virgin ingot market.*

Case 20.4
UNITED STATES v. ALUMINUM COMPANY OF AMERICA (ALCOA)
United States Court of Appeals, Second Circuit, 1945.
148 F.2d 416.

Judge HAND
*   *   *   *

From 1902 onward until 1928 "Alcoa" was making ingot in Canada through a wholly owned subsidiary; so much of this as it imported into the United States it is proper to include with what it produced here. In the year 1912, the sum of these two items represented nearly ninety-one percent of the total amount of "virgin" ingot available for sale in this country. *   *   * The effect of such a proportion of the production upon the market we reserve for the time being, for it will be necessary first to consider the nature and uses of "secondary" ingot, the name by which the industry knows ingot made from aluminum scrap. *   *   *

There are various ways of computing "Alcoa's" control of the aluminum market—as distinct from its production—depending upon what one regards as competing in that market. The judge figured its share—during the years 1929–1938, inclusive—as only about thirty-three percent; to do so he included "secondary," and excluded that part of "Alcoa's" own production which it fabricated and did not therefore sell as ingot. If on the other hand, "Alcoa's" total production, fabricated and sold, be included, and balanced against the sum of imported "virgin" and "secondary," its share of the market was in the neighborhood of 64% for that period. The percentage we have already mentioned—over 90—results only if we both include all "Alcoa's" production and exclude "secondary." That percentage is enough to constitute a monopoly; it is doubtful whether sixty or sixty-four percent would be enough; and certainly thirty-three percent is not. Hence it is necessary to settle what we shall treat as competing in the ingot market. That part of its production which "Alcoa" itself fabricates, does not of course ever reach the market as ingot. *   *   * [T]he ingot fabricated by "Alcoa," necessarily had a direct effect upon the ingot market. All ingot—with trifling exceptions—is used to fabricate intermediate, or end, products; and therefore all intermediate, or end, products which "Alcoa" fabricates and sells, pro tanto reduce the demand for ingot itself. The situation is the same, though reversed, as in *Standard Oil Co. v. United States,* where the court answered the defendants' argument that they had no control over the crude oil by saying that "as substantial power over the crude product was the inevitable result of the absolute control which existed over the refined product, the monopolization of the one carried with it the power to control the other." We cannot therefore agree that the computation of the percentage of "Alcoa's" control over the ingot market should not include the whole of its ingot production.

＊　　＊　　＊　　＊

We conclude therefore that "Alcoa's" control over the ingot market must be reckoned at over ninety percent, that being the proportion which its production bears to imported "virgin" ingot. If the fraction which it did not supply were the product of domestic manufacture, there could be no doubt that this percentage gave it a monopoly—lawful or unlawful, as the case might be. The producer of so large a proportion of the supply has complete control within certain limits.

＊　　＊　　＊

＊　　＊　　＊　　＊

DECISION AND   *The court of appeals found Alcoa had monopolized the aluminum industry*
REMEDY   *by having a 90 percent share of the virgin ingot market along with having*
                   an intent to acquire a monopoly of this market.

Defining the Relevant Market

One of the most important questions facing the courts in monopoly cases is this: What is the relevant market for measuring monopoly power? Over time, the courts have narrowed the definition of the relevant market by considering more information about the characteristics of the product, its substitutes, and the geographic area where the product is sold. Because the market share is extremely sensitive to the definition of relevant market, both sides in these cases take considerable care in assembling and presenting evidence to help determine the market.

The importance of determining the market share was well illustrated in the *Alcoa* decision. If the relevant market consisted only of those who bought virgin ingot, Alcoa was the sole producer at that time. The secondary market was not considered because it would not exist except for the sale of virgin ingot. Another definition of the relevant market included those who bought secondary aluminum, which is an almost perfect substitute for virgin ingot; this definition significantly broadened the relevant market and lowered the measure of Alcoa's share. And when the market was further broadened to include fabricated and secondary aluminum, the measure of Alcoa's share fell roughly to 33 percent of the aluminum production market.

Product Market   Substitutes are available for most products. If General Motors raised the prices for its cars significantly, consumers would purchase more Fords or other brands. If the question arose as to whether General Motors' Cadillac division had monopoly power, courts would have to determine the relevant product market. Should all cars sold in the United States be included in the computation of Cadillac's market share? Should only luxury cars be included? Do Japanese imports compete with Cadillacs for sales? Although General Motors is the sole producer of Cadillacs, it will not have monopoly power as long as there are substitute products, since market forces will keep the price of Cadillacs competitive with the price of substitute products.

Courts determine the relevant product market by defining the products that can be substituted for the product that is alleged to be dominating the market to the exclusion of competitors. In some cases, the product market will be extremely wide. Including all cars sold in the United States makes Cadillac's market share relatively small. Measuring Cadillac sales against the combined sales of cars and trucks decreases Cadillac's share even further. If only luxury cars are considered, Cadillac has a larger share of the market. Whenever monopoly power is alleged, courts must decide which products offer competition to the dominant product.

Geographic Market   The relevant geographic market is usually less difficult to determine than the relevant product market. If sellers within an area can raise prices or reduce the supply of products without quantities of lower-priced goods quickly flowing into the area, the sellers have a separate geographic market for their products.

Geographic markets may be local, regional, or national. The mobility of both competing sellers and of purchasers must be considered. The courts consider whether a buyer can easily go outside the immediate area to purchase the goods at a lower price or whether a seller in another geographic area can easily ship goods into the area. Because consumers are willing to travel greater distances to make major purchases than to buy everyday necessities, the geographic market will be defined more broadly for sales of automobiles than for sales of milk.

Determining the Market Share

After defining the relevant product and geographic markets, the court can determine the percentage of the market held by any one firm. This percentage is the firm's market share—the comparison of one firm's position to the positions of all other firms with which it competes. Monopoly power is a matter of degree. In the *Alcoa* case, 90 percent of the relevant market was sufficient for the court to conclude that Alcoa had a monopoly.

Courts have found there was no monopoly where the firms have controlled less than 65 percent of their relevant markets. The court in *Alcoa* said that two-thirds of the relevant market would be a questionable case, but one-third of the market would not be a monopoly situation. What the courts actually attempt to determine is whether a firm has such substantial power that it can engage in actions not associated with natural growth to exclude competitors and control prices. Market share is the measurement used to make that determination objectively.

Clayton Act

In 1914 Congress attempted to strengthen federal antitrust laws by adopting the **Clayton Act**, which was aimed at specific monopolistic practices. The important sections of the Clayton Act are Sections 2, 3, 7, and 8.

Section 2, as originally passed, was very weak. Thus, Congress passed the **Robinson-Patman Act,**

which strengthened Section 2. The objective of Section 2 is to promote economic equality in the purchasing and selling of goods. In other words, Section 2 deals with price discrimination. The Robinson-Patman Act does not apply to services.

A seller of goods cannot obtain an unfair advantage over its competitors by giving a better price (and thus discriminating) between different buyers of like goods where the effect will be to lessen competition substantially or where it may create a monopoly. For example, Flour Mill offers flour to all the big bakeries in the state at a lower price than it sells flour to small bakeries. Big bakeries all purchase from Flour Mill. Competitors of Flour Mill are either driven out of business or end up with a smaller share of the market because they sell only to the smaller bakeries.

The reverse is also prohibited: Buyers cannot use their economic power to obtain better prices from the seller in order to gain an economic advantage over their competitors.

Section 3 prohibits exclusive dealing agreements and tying arrangements when their effect is to lessen competition substantially or tend to create a monopoly. Under an exclusive dealing agreement, the seller of goods requires the buyer to promise not to handle products of any competitors of the seller. Tying arrangements are prohibited by a court decision that interpreted Section 3. Under a tying arrangement, the buyer must purchase one item in order to purchase the tied product. The item required to be purchased might not even be wanted by the buyer. Tying arrangements and exclusive dealing contracts are also violations of Section 2 of the Sherman Act. Under the Sherman Act, both goods *and* services are covered, while the Clayton Act covers only goods. Tying arrangements were once treated as per se illegal, but recently courts have required the seller to have economic power in the market for the tying product in order for such dealings to be illegal.

For example, Fast-Food Franchise requires its franchisees to purchase from it not only its secret recipe mix but also all paper products, such as paper boxes, paper bags, and paper napkins. The franchisee cannot purchase any paper products elsewhere; otherwise it will lose the franchise. This requirement is an illegal tying arrangement under Section 3, since the franchisee must purchase the paper products in order to buy the tied product, the secret recipe mix. Paper products have nothing to do with Fast-Food Franchise and can be purchased at lower prices from others. On the other hand, remember that franchise agreements may allocate geographical areas. Thus, these provisions are subject to the rule of reason.

Section 7 was also weak; in 1950, Congress passed the **Celler-Kefauver Act,** which strengthened and expanded this section. Corporations are prohibited from merging with another corporation if the merger may lessen competition or tend to create a monopoly. Corporate mergers are legally tested under this section.

Section 8 prohibits interlocking directorships. A person cannot be a director of two or more competing businesses where one of them has capital and profits exceeding $10 million. This amount will be increased or decreased based upon the national gross product index. This index is now called the national domestic product index.

The Sherman Act proscribed activities that eliminated competition or resulted in monopoly power, but it did not reach activities that merely *reduced* competition or *could* lead to monopoly power. The Clayton Act declares these specific activities to be illegal, even though these practices might not constitute the contract, combination, or conspiracy in restraint of trade necessary for a Sherman Act violation. Actual monopolization is unnecessary under the Clayton Act as is any attempt to monopolize. The act does not require that an injury to competition be demonstrated; therefore, the burden of proof for violations of the Clayton Act is less than for violations of the Sherman Act. In short, the Clayton Act reaches practices before a monopoly is actually created.

Federal Trade Commission Act

In 1914 Congress also passed the Federal Trade Commission Act, which created the Federal Trade Commission (FTC), a bipartisan, independent administrative agency headed by five commissioners. No more than three commissioners can be from the same political party. The act gives the FTC broad powers to prevent "unfair methods of competition in or affecting commerce, and unfair or deceptive acts or practices in or affecting commerce." The Magnuson-Moss Act of 1975,

which amended the Federal Trade Commission Act, broadened the commission's powers.

The FTC has the authority to conduct investigations relating to alleged violations of antitrust statutes. In addition, the FTC makes reports and recommendations to Congress regarding legislation. More important, the FTC can promulgate interpretive rules and general statements of policy with respect to unfair or deceptive acts or practices. The FTC can also adopt trade regulation rules that define particular unfair or deceptive acts or practices, including requirements whose purpose is to prevent such acts or practices. The FTC has no power to enforce the Sherman Act, but it does have authority to bring civil actions under the Clayton Act, and it enforces the Federal Trade Commission Act.

Exhibit 20–1 lists the major antitrust laws and gives a brief summary of each.

Mergers

A **merger** is the combination of two or more businesses into one. Mergers, whether horizontal or vertical, result in one business gaining greater control of the market. Accordingly, the antitrust laws apply to mergers and are used to prevent consolidations that would substantially lessen competition.

Section 7 of the Clayton Act is the principal statute that applies to horizontal and vertical mergers. It prohibits one "person" (corporations, partnerships, sole proprietorships, and so on) from acquiring another if the merger would tend to lessen competition substantially or to create a monopoly.

Horizontal Mergers

Section 7 of the Clayton Act was enacted because Congress feared that concentration by merger or consolidation would potentially facilitate collusion among sellers in the market and that such collusion would be difficult to detect. In general, the FTC and the Antitrust Division of the Justice Department determine the legality of **horizontal mergers** by looking at the degree of concentration or market shares of merging firms.

If a merger facilitates horizontal collusion without increasing production or marketing effi-

Exhibit 20–1 Major Antitrust Statutes and Amendments

DATE	NAME	DESCRIPTION	ENFORCEMENT	CIVIL	CRIMINAL
1890	**Sherman Act** Section 1	Bans contracts, combinations, and conspiracies in restraint of trade	Justice Department, state attorney general, private parties	Civil: Treble damages; costs and attorneys' fees Equitable: injunction; divestiture; asset distribution	Individuals: $350,000 and/or three years in prison Corporation: $10,000,000
	Section 2	Bans monopolies, attempts to monopolize, and conspiracies			
1914 1936	**Clayton Act** Section 2 Robinson-Patman Act	Price discrimination: bans sellers from charging different customers different prices for the same goods where effect may be to lessen competition substantially	Same	Same	Directors and officers liable if they had intent and knowledge and the action taken has an anticompetitive effect; $5,000 and/or one year (misdemeanor)
	Section 3	Bans exclusive dealing and tying arrangements that may substantially lessen competition	Same	Same	
1950	Section 7 Celler-Kefauver Act	Bans mergers that may substantially lessen competition	Same	Same	
	Section 8	Prohibits interlocking directors and officers (corporation: $10,000,000 subject to Gross Domestic Product)			
1914	**Federal Trade Commission Act**	Created the Federal Trade Commission	Federal Trade Commission	Civil: same Equitable: same Administrative: cease and desist	None
1938	Section 5 Wheeler-Lea Act	Bans unfair methods of competition, unfair or deceptive trade practices, false advertising	Same		None
1975	Magnuson-Moss Act	Strengthened FTC mandate			
1976	Section 7 Hart-Scott-Radino Antitrust Improvement Act	Premerger notification requirements	FTC, Justice Department		

ciencies, it will be declared unlawful. Mergers will be permitted when they enhance consumer welfare by increasing efficiency, as long as they do not increase the probability of horizontal collusion. Mergers that facilitate collusion *and* increase efficiency must be evaluated according to the relative magnitude of these two facts.

Vertical Mergers

Vertical mergers occur when a company at one stage of distribution acquires a company at a higher or lower stage of distribution. Thus, the acquisition of a tire plant by an automobile manufacturer would constitute a backward vertical integration, while acquisition of a car-renting agency would constitute a forward vertical integration. The government's approach to vertical mergers depends on a number of factors, including definition of the relevant product and geographic markets as well as the characteristics identified as impeding competition.

The government will attack any vertical merger that keeps competitors of either party from a segment of the market that otherwise would be open to them. The law's current theory of injury to competition in vertical mergers is contained in the concept of foreclosure. For example, a manufacturer can acquire a retailer and force the new retail subsidiary to sell the manufacturer's product. This acquisition would foreclose rival manufacturers from the market. The FTC has found that "foreclosure manifests a particularly anticompetitive character when it occurs as part of a trend toward forward integration in a concentrated market."

Conglomerate Mergers

A **conglomerate merger** is the consolidation of two or more firms dealing in unrelated products and operating in markets not horizontally or vertically linked. For example, a firm that operates motion picture theaters acquires a firm that manufactures automobile parts. Sometimes the products of the merged firms are complementary, and a merger permits the marketing of additional products at very little expense.

The Department of Justice (along with the FTC) has guidelines that determine whether a proposed merger should be consummated. The guidelines look at the concentration of the relevant market and the increase in concentration resulting from the merger. The department also looks at nonmarket considerations, such as how easy an entry is into the type of business and the competitive strength of the merged firms. In determining this, the department uses a statistical formula called the Herfindahl-Hirschman Index. After considering the other factors and implementing this index, the department will determine whether a merger is likely to be challenged. (The index is featured in the Legal Highlight.)

Defenses and Exemptions

Congress and the courts have created certain defenses and exemptions to the antitrust laws.

Defenses

Several defenses have been upheld by the courts for businesses confronted with allegations of creating an illegal monopoly or conspiring to restrain trade. The subsections that follow describe some defenses that the courts have accepted.

Price Discrimination   Section 2(a) of the Clayton Act, as amended by the Robinson-Patman Act, makes it illegal for any seller to discriminate in the prices charged for *goods* of the same quality to different purchasers. Sales at differing prices must have an anticompetitive effect for there to be a violation of the act. The courts view any two sales at different prices among competitors as a discrimination under Robinson-Patman.

Section 2(a) of the Clayton Act fortifies Section 2 of the Sherman Act by making **price discrimination** unlawful even when the firm engaging in it does not have and is not seeking monopoly power.

To have a violation of the Robinson-Patman Act, the seller must be engaged in interstate commerce and must sell goods of like grade and quality

Legal Highlight

Herfindahl-Hirschman Index

In June 1984, the Justice Department modified merger guidelines that had originally been issued in 1982. These guidelines are based on what is called the Herfindahl-Hirschman Index (HHI). The underlying theme of the guidelines is that mergers should not be permitted to create or enhance market power or to facilitate its exercise. A market is defined as "a product or group of products and a geographic area in which it is sold such that a hypothetical, profit-maximizing firm, not subject to price regulation, that was the only present and future seller of those products in that area would impose a 'small but significant and nontransitory' increase in price above prevailing or likely future levels."

The Justice Department basically asks whether the merger will tend to create a monopoly. The department determines the answer through the use of the index. If the index is less than 1,000 points, the merger normally will not be questioned. If the index is between 1,000 and 1,800 points, it likewise will not be challenged if the index increases by 100 or less after the merger. The same is true above 1,800 if the index increases by 50 points or less. If it is 1,800 and above and increases more than 50 points after

the merger, it will be challenged in most circumstances.

The index is obtained by squaring the market shares and then adding all industry shares together. The Justice Department does not like decimals so they are multiplied by 100. The following is an example:

FIRM	MARKET SHARE	MARKET SHARE × 100	MARKET SHARE SQUARED
A	.30	30	900
B	.10	10	100
C	.40	40	1600
D	.05	5	25
E	.15	15	225

The Herfindahl-Hirschman Index: 2850

Based on guidelines, a proposed merger of any two firms among those listed would not be allowed. For example if D and E were to merge, the new market share would be (5 + 15) 20. This, squared, would result in a market share of 400. Since the market share of D and E before merger would be 250 (25 + 225), the difference of (400 − 250) 150 would be greater than 50 points on an HHI index that exceeds 1,800. This merger would be challenged.

to different purchasers resulting in one suffering a competitive injury.

The three defenses to price discrimination under Section 2 of the Clayton Act are **meeting competition, cost justification,** and **changing market conditions.**

The Meeting-Competition Defense The statutory provisions of the Clayton Act allow the reduction of a price made "in good faith to meet an equally low price of a competitor." The meeting-competition defense allows a business to sell at a lower price to some customers if it is really necessary to meet a competitor's price. But this price must be lowered in order to meet but not to beat

a competitive price. The lowering cannot be made with intent to drive the competitor out of business. Also, the lower price must be for goods of similar quality to those of the competitor. Finally, the lower price to these customers must be temporary so as not to result in a competitive injury to other customers of the seller. As long as these three conditions are met, a business may sell at a lower price to certain customers to meet competition.

The Cost-Justification Defense It may be less expensive to manufacture and sell a thousand units of an item instead of ten units. A due allowance in pricing is permitted for these savings due to a particular customer's purchase. The seller must carry the burden of proof when using a cost-justification defense. A large-volume purchase by itself does not mean that the seller can give that purchaser a lower price. The seller must prove that it obtains savings from such a large purchase, such as lower transportation costs, and then the seller can pass these savings on to a buyer who orders a carload, planeload, and the like. Actual evidence of these savings must be shown. It is sometimes very difficult to determine the proper allocation of overhead and other expenses in order to demonstrate these savings.

The Changing-Market-Conditions Defense The changing-market-conditions defense to price discrimination allows a business to discontinue a product or product line, have fire or bankruptcy sales, and the like. In doing so, the business may sell the product at a reduced price. This defense allows a business to discount prices on seasonal goods or goods that will deteriorate.

The Colgate Doctrine The **Colgate doctrine** comes from *United States v. Colgate & Co.*[4] The United States Supreme Court allowed Colgate to refuse unilaterally to deal with retailers who did not follow its suggested retail prices. This refusal to deal was a vertical restraint. The Court emphasized that a firm can deal with whomever it desires.

The Thrust-Upon Defense A business that has a monopoly can use the **thrust-upon defense** by showing that the monopoly itself was thrust upon it. Such a monopoly might have been created by the production of a superior product, by better business practices, or by events, such as owning the only restaurant in an area where all the other restaurants have closed as a result of economic conditions. For this defense, there must exist no wrongful intent to create the monopoly.

The Failing-Company and Inadequate-Resources Defenses The courts have allowed a merger, even if it violates antitrust guidelines, when a company is confronting complete failure and there are no other prospective purchasers. This is known as the **failing-company defense.** Closely akin to this doctrine is the **inadequate-resources defense.** If a

company does not have the financial resources to be a competitor, the courts will allow a merger with another competing company, even though the result violates antitrust guidelines.

Exemptions

Congress's attention to the antitrust laws since passing the Clayton Act has focused primarily on creating exceptions from the coverage of the Sherman Act.

Labor The Norris-LaGuardia Act of 1932 and the National Labor Relations Act of 1935 protected unions from antitrust legislation. Today, unions can lawfully engage in actions that are normally prohibited as long as they act in their own self-interest and do not conspire or combine with nonlabor groups to accomplish their goals.

Agriculture and Baseball Likewise, the Clayton Act exempts agricultural organizations from the Sherman Antitrust Act. Although most commercial sport activities are subject to the antitrust laws, there is an exception. Baseball remains untouched by the antitrust laws. The U.S. Supreme Court held early in the 1900s that baseball was not commerce. Baseball's exemption is anomalous, especially since no other professional sport receives such treatment.

Insurance The **McCarran-Ferguson Act,** enacted in 1945, exempted from the antitrust laws all activities that are in the business of insurance. The primary element of the insurance business is the spreading and underwriting of policyholder risk. Thus, strict insurance activities are exempted from the antitrust laws by the McCarran-Ferguson Act. An agreement between an insurance company and pharmacies setting the profit margin in prescription drugs, however, is subject to the antitrust laws.

Exports Sometimes a decision to exempt certain activities from antitrust actions is made in the belief that certain goals can be better achieved through cartelization—that is, a banding together of competing firms. For example, the **Webb-Pomerene Act** exempts acts or agreements made in the course of export trade by associations of producers formed solely for the purpose of engag-

---

4.   250 U.S. 300, 39 S.Ct. 465, 63 L.Ed. 992 (1919).

ing in export trade. Cartelization promotes an increased national investment in the covered activities, thereby aiding the nation's balance of payments.

Political Activities The **Noerr-Pennington Doctrine** was derived from two United States Supreme Court cases. Basically, the Court held that "the Sherman Act does not prohibit two or more persons from associating together in an attempt to persuade the legislature or the executive to take particular action with respect to a law that would produce a restraint or a monopoly." In other words, businesses are allowed to work with Congress in order to pass appropriate, favorable laws.

In general, actions taken by state, local, and other public jurisdictions are exempt from antitrust laws. In 1978 it was held, however, that the doctrine of "state action unity" does not exempt all government entities from federal antitrust laws. Thus, unauthorized anticompetitive practices by state bodies are subject to antitrust laws.

Enforcement of Antitrust Laws

Enforcement of the various antitrust laws is handled by the Federal Trade Commission, private parties, and the Department of Justice. All three, however, do not have the right to enforce all the laws. The Department of Justice is the only federal department authorized to bring criminal charges, and only the Sherman Act has criminal provisions.

Enforcement by the Federal Trade Commission

The Federal Trade Commission has the authority to enforce the FTC Act and the Clayton Act under civil charges. Neither the Justice Department nor any private party has the right to enforce the Federal Trade Commission Act. When the Federal Trade Commission has jurisdiction, the usual procedure is for the FTC to issue a cease and desist order (an order to stop certain activities or practices), prohibiting the individual or corporation from further violating the law. If the cease and desist order is ignored, the Justice Department seeks to impose criminal sanctions.

The FTC investigates business conduct and holds administrative hearings. A cease and desist order issued by the FTC may be appealed; it is then reviewed by an appellate court. Businesses that violate an FTC cease and desist order are subject to fines of up to $10,000 per day for each day of continued violation.

The Federal Trade Commission Act overlaps with a number of other antitrust statutes, including the Sherman Act, the Clayton Act, and other laws designed to reduce unfair methods of competition. The FTC initiates investigations and issues cease and desist orders particularly for violations of the Clayton Act, as amended by the Robinson-Patman Act, and for other acts.

Enforcement by Private Parties

Private parties can also sue for up to three times their damages and for other remedies. They may bring action under either the Sherman or Clayton Acts but not under the Federal Trade Commission Act. The courts have determined that the test of ability to sue depends on the directness of the injury suffered by the purported plaintiff. Thus, a person wanting to sue under the Sherman Act must prove (1) that the antitrust violation either directly caused or was at least a substantial factor in causing the injury that was suffered and (2) that the unlawful actions of the purported defendant affected business activities of the plaintiff that were protected by the antitrust laws.

Enforcement by the Department of Justice

Any person violating either Section 1 or 2 of the Sherman Act is subject to criminal prosecution for a felony by the Department of Justice. Currently, on conviction, a person can be fined up to $350,000, imprisoned for three years, or both. A corporation can be fined $10 million.

The Department of Justice can simultaneously institute civil proceedings to restrain the conduct that is in violation of the act. The various remedies that the Justice Department has asked the court to impose include confiscation of goods in interstate commerce; divestiture, dissolution, and divorcements; and the demand that a company give up one of its operating functions. A group of meat packers, for example, can be forced to divorce

Ethical Considerations

Trade Association Issues

Trade associations assist their business members in reaching goals that no single firm could reach by itself. Goals include encouraging proper conduct by drafting ethical guidelines for members to follow; exchanging ideas to better their industry; hiring lobbyists to meet legislative goals; and improving the image of the industry in the eyes of the public.

Thousands of these trade associations exist, representing diverse groups from funeral directors to retail grocers. Associations date back to the Middle Ages when craftspeople would gather together in guilds. Two major goals of guilds were to set prices for the members' work and to keep the number of craftspeople low by allowing into the trade only a certain number of apprentices a year. Anticompetitive in nature, these goals are in violation of United States antitrust laws, but they are still encouraged in many other nations.

Where does one draw the line between an exchange of information that takes place at trade association meetings and antitrust violations? For example, a trade association is formed to promote the sale of milk products. After monthly meetings, the members have dinner. The normal conversation revolves around milk products, their costs and prices, and their sale. What information can be exchanged at these dinners?

What if the information exchanged includes prices contained in a bid for government contracts, such as the bid to supply milk to schools? What if the conversation includes the suggestion of a rotation of bids so that each dairy will receive a school contract? The sharing of bid information is unethical and, indeed, is a criminal act. But where does one draw the line between discussions of items of general interest, which are ethical, and discussions that slip into unethical and perhaps even illegal behavior?

themselves from controlling or owning butcher shops.

The Antitrust Division of the Department of Justice settles most cases before the trial stage. These out-of-court settlements, however, must receive court approval. In order to gain approval, the court must find that the settlement is in the national interest. Because the issues in antitrust cases are extremely complex and sometimes take years to litigate, settlements reduce the cost of enforcement. Probably one of the best examples of such a settlement is the divestiture and breakup of American Telephone and Telegraph.

A high percentage of these cases are settled through the use of ***nolo contendere*** pleas in crim-

inal cases and consent decrees in civil cases. A *nolo contendere* plea does not admit guilt, but a court may treat the plea as if the defendant had pleaded guilty and may impose the same penalty as for a guilty plea. With a consent decree, the defendant allows the court to impose remedial measures aimed at correcting the anticompetitive effects of the defendant's actions. Such remedial measures include ordering the defendant to divest itself of the stock of another company, to cancel a contract, to refrain from a particular type of conduct, or to dissolve itself and go out of business.

International Considerations

European Community and Antitrust Laws

The United States has had antitrust laws on the books for 100 years, while many nations currently have cartels that are sponsored by their governments. The United Nations and the drafters of the General Agreement on Tariffs and Trade (GATT) have not yet adopted an internationally accepted set of antitrust laws that would effectively prohibit restrictive trade practices. Many cultural differences must be overcome in order to reach such an agreement.

Articles 85 and 86 of the Treaty of Rome, which created the European Community (EC), are modeled after Sections 1 and 2 of the Sherman Antitrust Act. Article 85 prohibits concerted anticompetitive conduct, such as price-fixing and limiting markets. Article 86 is aimed at monopolistic practices and market domination.

Articles 85 and 86 of the treaty are implemented through an EC regulation. The regulation is concerned with whether a concentration of a product creates or strengthens a dominant position as the result of effective competition. The question is whether the product concentration significantly impedes the common market or whether it is incompatible with the common market. This regulation applies internally to the EC members and not externally to the EC's trading practices.

FACING A LEGAL ISSUE

Avoiding Antitrust Violations

You are the marketing director of a firm that has just patented a revolutionary product similar to plastic but with the strength of steel, the breathing ability of leather, the smoothness of silk, and the flexibility of rubber. Your business goal is to maximize profits but not to run afoul of the antitrust laws.

In preparing a detailed marketing plan to reach your goal, you have one large benefit granted by federal law. Assuming that your product is patentable, you will have an automatic exemption to the antitrust laws in the event that your product creates a monopoly. This does not mean that other antitrust aspects can be ignored. For example, you cannot sell this product at a different price to different competing distributors, unless you obtain cost savings in filling large orders. Also, you cannot require the distributors to sell at a given price unless you have retained title to the product. These are several examples of how a business must be concerned with antitrust violations even when the law grants it the right to create a monopoly.

Summary

This chapter has introduced you to antitrust law. Even in early common law, the court of England found certain agreements that restricted competition to be illegal. This basic theory has been carried forward through the federal laws adopted in the United States.

The major antitrust statutory provisions are found in the Sherman Act. The first provision of this law makes it illegal to enter into any contract, combination, or conspiracy in restraint of trade or commerce. The second section makes it illegal to monopolize or attempt to monopolize any trade or commerce. Any criminal violation of this act may result in a felony conviction.

The major defense to this act is that the conduct is subject to the rule of reason. Certain conduct, however, is conclusively presumed to be in violation of this act under the *per se* rule.

The second major act to be adopted that involves antitrust law is the Clayton Act. This statute makes illegal certain specified actions such as price discrimination, exclusive dealing, and tying arrangements, certain types of mergers, and interlocking directorates.

The Federal Trade Commission Act is the third major legislation. Establishing the Federal Trade Commission, the FTC Act authorizes the FTC to investigate and to issue cease and desist orders when it finds unfair or deceptive acts or practices, including antitrust violations.

A number of exemptions to the antitrust laws exist: labor unions, agriculture organizations, baseball, insurance, certain foreign trade groups, and certain activities conducted by individual states.

Several defenses to possible violations of the antitrust laws can be used. Among them are the defenses of meeting competition, cost justification, and changing market conditions; the *Colgate* doctrine; the thrust-upon defense; the failing-company doctrine; and the inadequate-resources doctrine.

In enforcing antitrust laws, the Department of Justice is the only one that can bring criminal cases. The Federal Trade Commission may issue cease and desist orders, and private persons may bring action for three times the actual damages.

Key Terms

antitrust laws (500)
Celler-Kefauver Act (512)

changing-market-conditions
defense (515)

Clayton Act (511)
Colgate doctrine (516)

concerted refusals to deal (506)
conglomerate merger **(514)**
cost-justification defense **(515)**
exclusive dealing contract (506)
failing-company defense **(516)**
group boycotts **(504)**
horizontal merger **(512)**
horizontal restraint **(504)**
inadequate-resources defense (516)
Interstate Commerce Act (500)
market power **(508)**

McCarran-Ferguson Act **(516)**
meeting-competition defense (515)
merger **(512)**
monopoly power **(508)**
Noerr-Pennington Doctrine (517)
nolo contendere **(518)**
per se rule **(504)**
price discrimination **(514)**
price-fixing **(504)**
professional association **(506)**
relevant geographic market (509)
relevant product market **(509)**

resale price maintenance agreement **(506)**
Robinson-Patman Act **(511)**
rule of reason **(501)**
Sherman Antitrust Act **(500)**
territorial and customer division **(506)**
thrust-upon defense **(516)**
trade association **(505)**
vertical merger **(514)**
vertical restraint **(504)**
Webb-Pomerene Act **(516)**

Questions and Case Problems

1. Discuss fully whether each of the following situations is in violation of the Sherman Act:

a. Genovese Foods, Inc., is the leading seller of frozen Italian foods in the northeastern United States. The various retail outlets that sell Genovese products are in close competition, and customers are very price conscious. Genovese has conditioned its sales to retailers on the agreement that the retailer will not sell below a minimum price or above a maximum price. Except for these limits, the retailer is allowed to set any price the retailer feels appropriate.

b. Zimmermann, Inc., Hicks, Inc., and Micro, Inc., are competitors in the manufacture and sale of microwave ovens sold primarily on the West Coast. As a patriotic gesture and to assist the unemployed, the three competitors agree to lower their prices on all microwave models by 20 percent for a three-month period, which includes July Fourth and Labor Day.

c. Best Beer, Inc., sells beer to distributors all over the United States. Best Beer sends to each of its distributors a recommended price list, explaining that past records indicate that beer sold at these prices should ensure the distributor a reasonable rate of return. The price list clearly states that the sale of the beer by Best Beer, Inc., to the distributor is not conditioned on the distributor reselling the beer at the recommended price, and the distributor is free to set the price.

2. Innovative Appliance Store is a new retail seller of appliances in Sunwest City. Innovative's different sales techniques and financing have caused a substantial loss of sales for the appliance department of Depressed Department Store. Depressed is a large department store and is part of a large chain with substantial buying power. Depressed told a number of appliance manufacturers that, if they continued to sell to Innovator, Depressed would discontinue its large volume of purchases from these man-

ufacturers. The manufacturers immediately stopped selling appliances to Innovator. Innovator files suit against Depressed and the manufacturers, claiming their actions constitute an antitrust violation. Depressed and the manufacturers can prove that Innovator is a small retailer with a small portion of the market, and, since the relevant market was not substantially affected, they claim they are not guilty of restraint of trade. Discuss fully whether there is an antitrust violation.

3. Assume the following event takes place: The partnership of Montoya and Marsh is engaged in the oil wellhead service industry in the states of New Mexico and Colorado. They presently have about 40 percent of the market for this service. The firm of West, Williams, and Wilson, Inc., is engaged in competition with the Montoya-Marsh partnership in the same geographic area. The West corporation has approximately 35 percent of the market. Montoya and Marsh acquire the stock and assets of West. Discuss which antitrust law has been primarily violated, if any.

4. Harcourt Brace Jovanovich Legal and Professional Publications (HBJ) is the nation's largest provider of bar review materials and lecture services. From 1976–1979 HBJ offered a Georgia bar review course in direct competition with BRG of Georgia, Inc. (BRG). In early 1980, both companies entered into an agreement that gave BRG an exclusive license to market HBJ's material in Georgia. Both agreed that HBJ would not compete with BRG in Georgia and that BRG would not compete with HBJ outside of Georgia. Under the agreement, HBJ received $100 per student enrolled by BRG and 40 percent or all revenues over $350. The price of BRG's course was increased from $150 to $400 after the agreement. After being sued by persons enrolled in the bar review course, both companies defended on the grounds that no per se violation occurred under a geographic market allocation theory,

because they had not divided the relevant market in which they had previously competed. Who should prevail and why? [Palmer v. BRG of Georgia, 498 U.S. _____ , 111 S.Ct. 401, 112 L.Ed.2d 349 (1990)]

5. The plaintiff, Edwin G. Hyde, a certified anesthesiologist, applied for a position on the medical staff of the defendant, East Jefferson Parish Hospital. The hospital handled 30 percent of the patients in the area. Because the hospital had entered into a contract in which all anesthesiological services required by the hospital's patients were to be performed by a professional medical corporation, it denied the plaintiff's application. The plaintiff subsequently brought an action, alleging that the contract violated Section 1 of the Sherman Act. Does this contract provision constitute a per se violation of Section 1 of the Sherman Act, since every patient undergoing surgery at Jefferson Hospital must use the services of one firm of anesthesiologists? (Remember that tying arrangements are subject to the per se rule.) [Jefferson Parish Hospital District No. 2 v. Hyde, 466 U.S. 2, 104 S.Ct. 1551, 80 L.Ed.2d 2 (1984) remanded to Hyde v. Jefferson Parish Hosp. Dist. No. 2, 764 F.2d 1139 (5th Cir. 1985)]

6. Febco, Inc., manufactured lawn and turf equipment. The Colorado Pump and Supply Company was a wholesale distributor of such equipment in the Colorado area. An important item that Colorado Pump distributed was a control device for sprinkling systems. Although Febco manufactured one of the better sprinkler controls, a number of other manufacturers competed in the field with competitively priced and satisfactory substitutes for the Febco controllers. In an agreement between Febco and Colorado Pump under which Colorado Pump was given the right to distribute Febco products, Colorado Pump was required to stock a complete line of Febco products. Industry data proved that, in this line of goods, it was important for distributors to protect the "goodwill" of manufacturers by carrying a complete line of a manufacturer's goods or none at all. Does the requirement by Febco that Colorado Pump stock an entire line of Febco products constitute an illegal tying arrangement? [Colorado Pump and Supply Co. v. Febco, Inc., 472 F.2d 637 (10th Cir. 1973)]

7. Sylvania sold its televisions directly to franchised retailers. Sylvania limited the number of franchises granted for any given area and required each franchise to sell the Sylvania products from only the locations of the franchise. A franchise did not constitute an exclusive territory, and Sylvania retained sole discretion to increase the number of retailers in an area, depending on the success or failure of existing retailers in developing their market.

Continental T.V., a Sylvania franchisee, withheld all payments owed for Sylvania products after a dispute over additional locations sought by Continental. John P. Maguire & Company, the finance company that handled the credit arrangements between Sylvania and its franchisees, sued Continental T.V. for payment and for return of secured merchandise (the televisions). In turn, Continental T.V. claimed that Sylvania had violated Section 1 of the Sherman Act by entering into and by enforcing franchise agreements that allowed the sale of Sylvania products only in specified locations. Was this a violation of the Sherman Act? [Continental T.V., Inc., v. GTE Sylvania, Inc., 433 U.S. 36, 97 S.Ct. 2549, 53 L.Ed.2d 568 (1977)]

8. American Oil Company was a producer and distributor of oil, gas, and related products. Olson was engaged in bulk distribution and retail sales of oil products. Early in 1967, American decided to acquire control of Olson's bulk distribution operations, and it purchased substantially all of Olson's assets. Thereafter, American hired Lawrence McMullin to assume control of the Olson operation for American. Under the agreement, McMullin was to take charge of the Olson plant and was to be paid on a commission basis in lieu of salary for the bulk petroleum sales that he procured. In addition, the contract between American and McMullin imposed certain territorial limitations and price restrictions on sales by the operations that McMullin was to control. Could the agreement between McMullin and American Oil imposing price restrictions and territorial controls on the operations of which McMullin took charge constitute a violation of Section 1 of the Sherman Antitrust Act? Explain. [American Oil Co. v. McMullin, 508 F.2d 1345 (10th Cir. 1975)]

9. The National Collegiate Athletic Association (NCAA) plays an important role in regulating amateur collegiate sports. As a result of various surveys and reports, the NCAA concluded that television adversely affects college football game attendance and, further, that the telecasting of such games seriously threatens the athletic system in the United States. The NCAA subsequently imposed regulations that restrained the ability of member colleges to negotiate and contract for the telecasting of college football games. Some member colleges began to assert that colleges with major football programs deserved to have greater input in the formulation of football television policy than they presently had in the NCAA. In addition, when some member colleges proceeded to enter into a television agreement with NBC on their own, NCAA announced that it would take disciplinary action against any member that complied with this contract. Has there been a Sherman Act violation here? If so, does the rule of reason or per se analysis apply to the NCAA's television plan? [National Collegiate Athletic Association v. Board of Regents of the University of Oklahoma, 468 U.S. 85, 104 S.Ct. 2948, 82 L.Ed.2d 70 (1984)]

Chapter 21 Legislative Control Over Labor and Labor Relations

Labor disgraces no man; unfortunately you occasionally find men disgrace labor.

Ulysses S. Grant
Speech at Midland International Arbitration Union, Birmingham, England (1877)

OUTLINE

Introduction

In the past, the freedom to contract, as applied to employment, gave rise to perceived inequities in the employer-employee relationship and resulted in such abuses as child labor camps, dangerous working conditions, and worker discrimination. These abuses produced two major responses in the United States. First, the federal government passed national legislation that covered working standards, discrimination, and safety. Second, the workers began to unionize in an attempt to gain a more powerful position in bargaining with management.

The earliest attempts by Congress to set employment standards were ruled unconstitutional on grounds that the laws infringed on an individual's right to contract. Over time, though, the courts began to limit the employers' power in employment contracts and to recognize Congress's constitutional power to regulate employment practices under the commerce clause.

Today, unions make up less than 20 percent of the American work force; governmental employees, both federal and state, comprise 15 percent; and 65 percent of all American workers are employed at will (without a written contract). Regardless of the contractual category of the worker, the employer must meet certain minimum standards with reference to pay, hours, and working conditions. This chapter discusses the legislation that protects employees; then it looks at the rights of employees to form unions and describes what unions can and cannot accomplish.

Fair Labor Standards Act

The **Fair Labor Standards Act (FLSA)** of 1938 established a minimum wage, overtime standards, record-keeping requirements, and child labor prohibitions. The act affects more than 70 million full-time and part-time workers. These fundamental standards are applicable to people employed in private industry, government, and unions. In addition, the FLSA spells out the administrative procedures of enforcing and complying with these standards.

Who Is Covered?

The FLSA is an extensive statute that is based on the commerce clause of Article I of the Consti-

tution. Generally, the FLSA applies to employees: (1) who are engaged in commerce, (2) who are engaged in the production of goods to be placed in commerce, or (3) who are employed in an enterprise engaged in commerce.

The first two types of coverage involve the "employee test" that looks at the nature of the employee's work, not the nature of the business. In the third category, the controlling factor is the nature of the business. If the enterprise is covered, all the employees are covered, regardless of the relationship between their duties and commerce.

The FLSA explains which actions by an employer constitute a punishable violation of the statute and the rules promulgated under it. Understanding the meaning of "employer" for purposes of the act is key to determining which actions will be considered violations.

The FLSA's definition of the term *employer* is extremely broad: An employer "includes any person acting directly or indirectly in the interest of an employer in relation to an employee." An individual, such as a corporate officer, who actively participates in the running of a business, including the employment practices of the business, is an employer within the meaning of the statute. Such an individual will be personally liable, along with the corporation, for any violations of the act, and, therefore, will be liable for the payment of any fines under the act.

An employer who violates the FLSA is liable in a civil action to the employee, who may recover from the employer unpaid wages, overtime compensation, liquidated damages, and reasonable attorneys' fees. The statute also empowers a court to issue an injunction restraining further violations. The employer may be criminally prosecuted by the federal government and, if found guilty, may be punished by a fine of up to $10,000 for the first offense and a fine of up to $10,000 plus imprisonment for up to six months for subsequent violations.

Exempt Employees

Because of the nature of certain industries, it would be impossible to operate some businesses under the FLSA. In order to accommodate these businesses, Congress allowed exemptions to the act. Each exemption is narrowly defined by the statute.

The employer asserting the exemption must meet each element of the statutory requirement for exemption. Some of the classes of industries

Legal Highlight

Exemptions and Requirements Under the Minimum-Wage and Overtime Laws

Certain employees are exempt from both the minimum-wage and overtime provisions. Some of these exemptions include:

1. Executive, administrative, and professional employees, including teachers in elementary or secondary schools
2. Employees of certain enterprises, if the annual gross income of the business is under $500,000
3. Employees of seasonal amusement or recreational businesses
4. Employees of small newspapers that have a circulation of less than 4,000
5. Switchboard operators of small telephone companies with less than 750 stations
6. Sailors employed on foreign vessels
7. Employees engaged in fishing operations
8. Certain farm workers
9. Casual baby-sitters and people employed as companions to the elderly or infirm.

Employees subject to both minimum-wage and overtime provisions must have on file for each employee the following items:

1. Personal information, including name, home address, occupation, sex, and birth date
2. Hour and day when the work week begins
3. Total hours worked each work week and workday
4. Total daily or weekly straight-time earnings
5. Regular hourly pay rate for any week when overtime is worked
6. Total overtime pay for the work week
7. Deductions from or additions to wages
8. Total wages paid each pay period
9. Date of payment and pay period covered.

whose workers are exempt from the FLSA include agriculture, commercial fishing, some retail service businesses, and domestic services. In addition, many white-collar positions are not included under the act, because it is believed that these individuals are able to protect themselves from the employer abuses that the FLSA prohibits.

Wage and Hour Requirements

Both state and federal statutes govern the minimum-wage and maximum-hour requirements for workers. For the most part, state laws are congruent with the FLSA. Since most businesses are subject to the federal act, the FLSA is the most important guarantee of proper treatment for employees.

Wages   The minimum wage was initially $0.25 an hour in 1938. Periodically, this amount has been increased. In 1991, the minimum wage was raised to $4.25 an hour. The increases in the minimum wage over the years are shown in Exhibit 21–1.

The FLSA provides for an exception to the minimum wage in the case of tipped employees. The statute defines tipped employees as those who customarily and regularly receive more than $30 a month in tips. In such a case, the employer may consider the tips as part of the wages, but the wage

Exhibit 21–1 Federal Minimum-Wage Chart

YEAR	MINIMUM WAGE
1938	$0.25
1945	0.40
1950	0.75
1960	1.15
1965	1.25
1970	1.60
1975	2.10
1980	3.10
1981	3.35
1990	3.80
1991	4.25
Training wage, paid for a maximum 180 days	3.61

credit (tips) must not exceed 40 percent of the minimum wage.

Hours An employee must be paid for all hours worked in a week; however, what constitutes working time is not completely clear. Generally, the hours worked—those for which an individual must be paid at least the minimum wage and which must be included when computing total hours worked in order to determine overtime hours—encompass all the time that an employee is actually at work or is required to be on duty and that the employee is not free to use for his or her own purposes.

For example, all police officers are regularly required to be at work twenty minutes ahead of the hour (say, at 7:40) in order to change into their uniforms and be in formation by 8:00. The officers must be paid for those twenty minutes in addition to their eight-hour shifts.

The calculation and payment of overtime wages can be confusing and is usually the source of many employee-employer misunderstandings. Violations of FLSA's requirement for overtime wages can easily happen because the formulas for determining overtime pay are complex and appear at times to be unfair and illogical.

The FLSA stipulates that, when an employee has worked in excess of 40 hours for one work week, that employee must be paid no less than one and one-half times her or his regular hourly rate for any hours worked in excess of 40. Overtime is not one and one-half times minimum wage but one and one-half times the employee's regular wages.

Investigation and Enforcement Procedures The Wage and Hour Division (WHD) of the Department of Labor has the primary responsibility for enforcing and administering the FLSA. The WHD has officers throughout the United States who conduct investigations and gather data on wages, hours, and other employment conditions.

The FLSA provides several methods for recovering unpaid wages. The methods include supervision by the WHD of the employer's payment of back wages; court action by the secretary of labor to collect unpaid wages; a lawsuit by the employee for unpaid wages and for attorneys' fees; and an injunction obtained by the secretary of labor to restrain employers from further violation of the FLSA.

Child Labor Laws

The provisions of the FLSA that govern child labor are simple, yet the penalties for violating these standards are severe and should not be ignored by the private businessperson. The child labor laws are part of public policy; they are intended to ensure that each minor has the opportunity to attend school, and they prohibit the employment of children in hazardous jobs or under working conditions that are dangerous to their health or well-being.

An individual who is over seventeen years of age does not fall under the child labor provisions of the statute. Minors between the ages of sixteen and seventeen are allowed to be employed, but there are restrictions. Certain industries are considered to be dangerous and, therefore, off limits for sixteen- and seventeen-year-olds. In addition, children between fourteen and fifteen years of age may be employed only in specially approved jobs; these jobs include retail stores, restaurants, and service stations.

Children under the age of fourteen are prohibited from working except in certain occupations, such as agricultural employment, and are subject to FLSA regulations requiring school obligations. Young actors, actresses, and performers are also exempt, when certain conditions are met, from the FLSA prohibitions against child labor.

Retirement and Income Security

Federal and state governments participate in programs of insurance to cover the financial impact on employees of retirement, disability, death, hospitalization, and unemployment. The key federal law in this area is the **Social Security Act** of 1935.

Social Security

Social Security is more formally known as **Old Age, Survivors, and Disability Insurance (OASDI)**. Both employers and employees must contribute under the **Federal Insurance Contributions Act (FICA)** to help fund Social Security. The employee's contribution is a percentage of his or her annual wage base (the annual wage base is the

Legal Highlight

Checking on Your Social Security Account

Before any social security benefits can be paid, you must have credit for a certain amount of work. Measured in "quarters of coverage," you can earn a maximum of four quarters a year (obviously, three months per quarter). If your job is covered by the Social Security Act, you have an individual lifetime earnings record established at the Social Security Administration headquarters in Baltimore, Maryland. Your earnings are reported under your name and social security number. You should check on your social security account every three years to ensure that your record is properly credited.

How do you check on your record? You can call the Social Security Administration at 1-800-

SSA-1213 (1-800-772-1213). Or you can obtain a form entitled "Request for Statement of Earnings" from your local Social Security Administration office, fill it out, and send it in. Within six weeks, a summary of your account will be returned. It will list the last three years individually. If there is a mistake, you can correct it immediately (yes, by sending in *another* form along with your W-2 forms). Otherwise, if the mistake is left in your record, your social security check at retirement may be reduced because your account does not accurately reflect the amount of money you have really earned. Even if there is a mistake, however, your checks will not be reduced if you are receiving the minimum amount allowed to be collected.

maximum amount of an employee's wages that are subject to the tax).

A health insurance program, **Medicare** is administered by the Social Security Administration for people 65 years of age and older and for those under 65 who are disabled. It has two parts, one pertaining to hospital costs and the other to non-hospital medical costs, such as doctors' office visits. People who have Medicare hospital insurance can obtain additional federal medical insurance if they pay small monthly premiums that increase as the cost of medical care increases.

Private Retirement Plans

Significant legislation now regulates retirement plans set up by employers. These plans are used to supplement Social Security benefits. The major piece of legislation of this type is the **Employee Retirement Income Security Act (ERISA)** of 1974. ERISA covers the financing, vesting, and administration of pension plans for workers in private business and industry. The Department of Labor, through the Pension Benefit Guaranty Corporation and the Labor Management Services Admin-

istration, and the treasury department enforce ERISA's provisions.

Unemployment Compensation

Unemployment insurance is funded by employers who pay into the fund; the proceeds are paid out to qualified unemployed workers. The major piece of federal legislation concerning unemployment is the **Federal Unemployment Tax Act (FUTA)**, which became law in 1954. This act established a state system that provides **unemployment compensation** to eligible individuals—those who worked a certain minimum number of weeks, earned wages in a certain amount, and are involuntarily out of work. The cost of administering the unemployment insurance program is paid by the federal government out of part of the tax collected. This is not a welfare program. The unemployed person does not have to show a need to receive benefits; the decision to grant or deny benefits is based on whether the individual is willing and able to work. The following case concerns whether a person is entitled to benefits when she quits her job.

Case 21.1
**STEFFEN v. DAVISON,
COPPLE, COPPLE &
COPPLE**
Supreme Court of Idaho, 1991.
814 P.2d 29.

BACKGROUND AND FACTS *Donna Steffen, an experienced legal secretary, began working as a secretary for the Davison, Copple, Copple & Copple law firm on March 27, 1989, on a probationary status and continued employment until May 5, 1989. Prior to working for the law firm, she had been receiving unemployment benefits based on wages earned from a previous employer. Within one week after Steffen was hired, another secretary was terminated. Steffen became concerned that she could not perform adequately to satisfy the attorneys, and she perceived some instability in the secretarial staff. On May 4, Steffen found a handwritten note on her desk that her supervising attorney had made the night before while talking with a client. When Steffen asked the attorney about the note, he wadded it up and laughingly told her that he did those things to make her think she was losing her mind and that he might ask her to find a file that does not exist. Steffen became upset as a result of this incident and believed the attorney was intentionally attempting to make her job more difficult. Steffen quit her job on May 5.*

Steffen was paid unemployment benefits for the period of May 6 through September 23. When she filed her unemployment benefit claim for the weeks ending April 29 and May 6, she did not report any wages earned or employment even though she had worked during that period of time. The State of Idaho, Department of Employment, served her with notice of overpayment. The appeals examiner found that she voluntarily quit without good cause and ordered her to repay the benefits.

Justice BOYLE.

*   *   *

Unemployment benefits may be awarded if:

His unemployment is not due to the fact that he left his employment voluntarily without good cause connected with his employment, or that he was discharged for misconduct in connection with his employment.

Idaho law in this regard is well established and clearly provides that claimant Steffen is eligible for unemployment compensation benefits, although she voluntarily terminated her employment, if she did so with "good cause" *   *   * and explored all viable options prior to terminating her employment. *   *   * In order to constitute good cause, *   *   * the circumstances which compel the decision to leave employment must be real, not imaginary, substantial, not trifling, and reasonable, not whimsical; there must be some compulsion produced by extraneous and necessitous circumstances, and the standard of what constitutes good cause is the standard of reasonableness as applied to the average man or woman. *   *   * We have held that the test used to determine good cause is whether a reasonable person would consider the circumstances resulting in a claimant's unemployment to be real, substantial and compelling.

*   *   *

Thus, in the present case, Steffen has the burden to prove that the conduct of her supervising attorney created good cause for her to voluntarily leave her employment and that she pursued all reasonable alternatives prior to terminating her employment. After hearing the evidence, the appeals examiner found that Steffen voluntarily left her employment with respondent law firm without good cause and that there was continuing work available to her. The decision of the appeals examiner contains a thorough recitation of the factual background and a thoughtful analysis and application of the law to the facts.

*   *   *

The case presented at the hearing level involves an interpretation and resolution of conflicting evidence. Based on the conflicting evidence submitted, the appeals examiner was not persuaded that Steffen left her employment for good cause. Accordingly, Steffen was found to have received an overpayment of $2,504.00 which must be repaid. * * * Based on the evidence presented at the hearing level, claimant Steffen did not prove or establish to the satisfaction of the finder of fact that a reasonable person under those circumstances would terminate employment.

The appeals examiner expressly found that Steffen willfully failed to report material information to the Department of Employment in her application for unemployment benefits. Our review of the record, and particularly the continued claim report form for the April 29 and May 6, 1989 period where item 8(c) was not completed * * *, satisfies us that the finding of willful failure to report a material fact is supported by the evidence.

The Supreme Court of Idaho affirmed the decision of the appeals examiner who found that Steffen did not have good cause to terminate her employment. Steffen was required to repay the overpaid unemployment benefits to the Employment Security Fund.

DECISION AND REMEDY

Legal Highlight

All for the Want of a Penny

The Place: Yuma, Arizona
The Time: 1987
The Parties: Immaculate Conception
          Church and the
          Internal Revenue Service

The Immaculate Conception Church underpaid its quarterly federal employment withholding tax for 29 employees by one penny. Once the error was discovered, the church sent a check in the amount of one cent to the Internal Revenue Service, but it was too late. The church was assessed $453.60 worth of penalties—in other words, a 45,360 percent penalty. The Internal Revenue Service waived the penalty several months later when the matter was brought to its attention.

Other Statutes for Employee Protection

Numerous state statutes are designed to protect employees and their families from the risk of accidental injury, death, or disease resulting from their employment. This section covers state workers' compensation laws and the Occupational Safety and Health Act of 1970.

State Workers' Compensation Acts

Workers' compensation laws are usually administered by a state agency that has quasi-judicial powers. All rulings of these agencies are subject to review by the courts. These laws are not based on federal law.

The right to recover under workers' compensation laws is given to the injured employee without regard to the existence of negligence or fault of the employer. Rather, the right to recovery is predicated on the employment relationship and the fact that the injury arose out of the employment. Basically, employers are under a system of strict liability. This is similar to the strict liability used in product liability cases, which we discussed in Chapter 11. Few, if any, defenses exist for them.

The simple, two-pronged test for determining whether an employee can receive workers' compensation consists of these questions:

1. Was the injury accidental?
2. Did the injury arise out of and in the course of employment?

Intentionally inflicted self-injuries are not considered accidental and are not covered. In the past, heart attacks or other medical problems arising out of preexisting disease or physical conditions were not covered, but recently the courts have started to treat these medical problems as covered under the act. Some states have limited by legislation the recovery possible when an employee has a heart attack.

The following case discusses the question of injuries caused by asbestos that was used in the work environment. The major question presented is whether an employee can seek workers' compensation while filing a separate lawsuit. The lawsuit alleged that the employer was liable for the injuries because the employer did not fully inform the employee of the dangers of asbestos and did not protect the employee from those dangers.

Case 21.2
JOHNS-MANVILLE PRODUCTS CORP. v. CONTRA COSTA SUPERIOR COURT
Supreme Court of California, 1980.
27 Cal.3d 465,
612 P.2d 948,
165 Cal.Rptr. 858.

BACKGROUND AND FACTS *Reba Rudkin, the real plaintiff in this case, brought this action against Johns-Manville, his employer for 29 years. The defendant had been in the business of manufacturing asbestos for many years. Rudkin alleged in his complaint that, as a result of his exposure to asbestos, he developed pneumoconiosis, lung cancer, and other asbestos-related illnesses.*

Rudkin also alleged that Johns-Manville had known since 1924 that long exposure to asbestos or the ingestion of that substance is dangerous to health, yet it had concealed this knowledge from the plaintiff and had advised him that it was safe to work in close proximity to asbestos. It failed to provide him with adequate protective devices, and it did not operate the plant in accordance with state and federal regulations governing dust levels.

Johns-Manville filed an answer alleging that the action was barred. It requested the trial court to take judicial notice of an application filed by the plaintiff seeking workers' compensation benefits for disability caused by "[e]xposure to asbestos." The defendant moved for judgment on the pleadings. The trial court denied the motion. The defendant appealed to the California Supreme Court.

Justice MOSK
*   *   * [T]he Labor Code provides that an employer is liable for injuries to its employees arising out of and in the course of employment, and *   *   * declares that where the conditions of workers' compensation exist, the right to recover such compensation is the exclusive remedy against an employer for injury or death of an employee. The issue to be decided in this proceeding is whether an employee is barred by these provisions from prosecuting an action at law against his employer for the intentional torts of fraud and conspiracy in knowingly ordering the employee to work in an unsafe environment, concealing the risk from him, and, after the employee had contracted an industrial disease, deliberately failing to notify the state, the employee, or doctors retained to treat him, of the disease and its connection with the employment, thereby aggravating the consequences of the disease.

We conclude that while the workers' compensation law bars the employee's action at law for his initial injury, a cause of action may exist for aggravation of the disease because of the employer's fraudulent concealment of the condition and its cause.

*   *   *   *   *

Prior to 1917, the law allowed an employee a choice of remedies if an injury was caused by an employer's gross negligence or willful misconduct. He could either claim workers' compensation benefits or maintain an action at law for damages. In that year, however, this provision was deleted and a new section added specifying a one-half increase in compensation in the event of serious and willful misconduct by the employer. This history, contends defendant, demonstrates that the right to seek additional compensation for injuries caused by the serious and willful misconduct of the employer was intended by the Legislature as a substitute for the right to seek damages in an action at law for such conduct.

We find the historical background cited by defendant to be persuasive. The clear implication is that the addition in 1917 of the "exclusive remedy" limitation and the provision for a penalty for the willful misconduct of the employer was a substitute for the previous right of an employee to bring an action at law.

* * * *

Thus, if the complaint alleged only that plaintiff contracted the disease because defendant knew and concealed from him that his health was endangered by asbestos in the work environment, failed to supply adequate protective devices to avoid disease, and violated governmental regulations relating to dust levels at the plant, plaintiff's only remedy would be to prosecute his claim under the workers' compensation law.

But where the employer is charged with intentional misconduct which goes beyond his failure to assure that the tools or substances used by the employee or the physical environment of a workplace are safe, some cases have held that the employer may be subject to common law liability. A physical assault by the employer upon the employee has been held to justify an action at law against the employer. In *Ramey v. General Petroleum Corporation*, it was held that an action for fraud could be maintained against an employer who made misrepresentations regarding the employee's right to medical care and conspired with a third party to conceal from the employee that his injuries, which occurred while he was working, were caused by the third party against whom he had resource. And in *Unruh v. Truck Insurance Exchange*, we allowed an action at law against an insurer for assault, battery, and intentional infliction of emotional distress, based upon its deceitful conduct in investigating a workers' compensation claim.

* * * *

We conclude the policy of exclusivity of worker's compensation as a remedy for injuries in the employment would not be seriously undermined by holding defendant liable for the aggravation of this plaintiff's injuries, since we cannot believe that many employers will aggravate the effects of an industrial injury by not only deliberately concealing its existence but also its connection with the employment. Nor can we believe that the Legislature in enacting the workers' compensation law intended to insulate such flagrant conduct from tort liability. Finally, although plaintiff filed an application for workers' compensation and may receive an award in that proceeding, double recovery may be avoided by allowing the employer a set-off in the event plaintiff is awarded compensation for the aggravation of his injury in that proceeding and in the present case as well.

DECISION AND REMEDY

Johns-Manville could not escape civil liability if the trial court should determine that the plaintiff's allegations were correct. The plaintiff was entitled to both workers' compensation benefits and additional damages if his employer had intentionally concealed the danger of asbestos. To avoid a double recovery, however, the court could offset the amount of workers' compensation benefits awarded to compensate the plaintiff for the aggravation of his injury against any damages awarded for the same purpose.

Health and Safety Protection

The main federal legislation for employee health and safety protection is the **Occupational Safety and Health Act** of 1970. This act was passed to ensure safe and healthful working conditions for practically every employee in the country. The act created the **Occupational Safety and Health Administration (OSHA)**, the Occupational Safety and Health Review Commission, and the National Institute for Occupational Safety and Health. OSHA promulgates and enforces workers' safety and health standards, as well as conducting inspections and investigations, requiring employers to keep detailed records of worker injuries and illnesses, and conducting research.

OSHA's enforcement policy is twofold: First, it deals with egregious, violation-by-violation citations; second, it enforces settlements at the corporate, rather than the plant, level. Both policies allow OSHA to seek large penalties. In addition to civil penalties, OSHA has the power to close a plant.

OSHA first employed the egregious citation strategy against Union Carbide in 1986 after finding flagrant disregard for record-keeping requirements. Violation-by-violation citations and the corresponding penalties were issued for each of the hundreds of instances of the alleged record-keeping infractions. OSHA sought penalties for alleged violations ranging from $4 million from John Morrell Corp. for health violations in its meat-packing plants to $7 million from USX Corporation steel plants for safety violations.

In most instances, an employee will make a written complaint requesting an OSHA inspection. OSHA will generally protect the identity of the complaining employee. As an added protection, OSHA prohibits the discharge of or any discrimination against an employee who, by submitting a formal complaint against an employer, exercises his or her rights under the statute. The act stipulates that an employee who believes that she or he has been discriminated against for bringing possible violations to the attention of OSHA may file a complaint with the secretary of labor. The secretary will conduct an investigation and, if appropriate, seek relief for the employee in federal court. The next case is an example of such an occurrence.

Case 21.3
**WHIRLPOOL CORP. v.
MARSHALL**
Supreme Court of the United
States, 1980.
445 U.S. 1, 100 S.Ct. 883,
63 L.Ed.2d 154.

BACKGROUND AND FACTS *Whirlpool has a plant that produces appliances. Within the plant, the machines are transported on conveyors. In order to protect the employees below the conveyor belt from appliances that occasionally fall, Whirlpool installed high guard screens. As part of their routine duties, maintenance employees were required to remove fallen parts from the screens. In order to do so, the workers had to walk on the screens. Starting in 1973, Whirlpool began replacing the screen material with heavier gauge mesh. Several workers had fallen through the old screen, and, on June 28, 1974, a maintenance employee had fallen to his death through the mesh in a section where stronger gauge mesh had not yet been installed.*

Subsequently, Whirlpool made some repairs and issued a general order to clean the screens without walking on them. Two weeks after the death, two employees asked for the local OSHA officer's phone number. The next night they were ordered onto the screens: they refused. As a result, the employees were not allowed to work their shift and were issued written reprimands that were placed in their files.

The secretary of labor filed suit against Whirlpool for suspending and reprimanding the employees in violation of rules promulgated under OSHA by the Department of Labor. The secretary sought to have the employees' reprimands expunged from their records and to recover the pay lost due to the disciplinary action. The trial court denied the request. The appellate court reversed and granted relief to the employees. Whirlpool appealed to the United States Supreme Court, challenging the regulation promulgated by the secretary of labor.

Justice STEWART delivered the opinion of the Court.

The Occupational Safety and Health Act of 1970 (Act) prohibits an employer from discharging or discriminating against any employee who exercises "any right afforded by" the Act. The Secretary of Labor (Secretary) has promulgated a regulation providing that, among the rights that the Act so protects, is the right of an employee to choose not to perform his assigned task because of a reasonable apprehension of death or serious injury coupled with a reasonable belief that no less drastic alternative is available. The question presented in the case before us is whether this regulation is consistent with the Act.

* * * *

The regulation clearly conforms to the fundamental objective of the Act—to prevent occupational deaths and serious injuries. The Act, in its preamble, declares that its purpose and policy is "to assure so far as possible every working man and woman in the Nation safe and healthful working conditions and to *preserve* our human resources. . . ." (Emphasis added.)

To accomplish this basic purpose, the legislation's remedial orientation is prophylactic in nature. The Act does not wait for an employee to die or become injured. It authorizes the promulgation of health and safety standards and the issuance of citations in the hope that these will act to prevent deaths or injuries from ever occurring. It would seem anomalous to construe an Act so directed and constructed as prohibiting an employee, with no other reasonable alternative, the freedom to withdraw from a workplace environment that he reasonably believes is highly dangerous.

Moreover, the Secretary's regulation can be viewed as an appropriate aid to the full effectuation of the Act's "general duty" clause. That clause provides that "[e]ach employer * * * shall furnish to each of his employees employment and a place of employment which are free from recognized hazards that are causing or are likely to cause death or serious physical harm to his employees." As the legislative history of this provision reflects, it was intended itself to deter the occurrence of occupational deaths and serious injuries by placing on employers a mandatory obligation independent of the specific health and safety standards to be promulgated by the Secretary. Since OSHA inspectors cannot be present around the clock in every workplace, the Secretary's regulation ensures that employees will in all circumstances enjoy the rights afforded them by the "general duty" clause.

The regulation thus on its face appears to further the overriding purpose of the Act, and rationally to complement its remedial scheme. In the absence of some contrary indication in the legislative history, the Secretary's regulation must, therefore, be upheld, particularly when it is remembered that safety legislation is to be liberally construed to effectuate the congressional purpose. * * *

The Supreme Court held that the secretary's regulation must be upheld. The regulation was made in accordance with the congressional statutory scheme. Employees may refuse to perform work under certain circumstances when confronted with hazardous job conditions.

DECISION AND REMEDY

Plant Closing Law

In 1988 Congress passed a law that applies to businesses employing more than 100 employees. Such businesses are required to give notice if a plant will be closed down. Notice must be given to the workers 60 days in advance of the closure. Similarly, businesses must give workers advance notice of a mass layoff, which includes more than one-third of the company's employees.

Unions and Collective Bargaining

Government regulation of employment and labor relations is very much present in our society. Businesses must operate within the confines established by these regulating statutes. Over the years, legislation has greatly affected the rights and liabilities of employees, as well as employers.

Until the early 1930s, laws at the federal and state levels generally favored management. Collective activities such as unions were discouraged, sometimes forcibly, by employers. Early legislation and agencies protecting the rights of employees, such as the National War Labor Board that operated during World War I, were often temporary. In addition, the legislation was frequently restricted to a particular industry, such as the Railway Labor Act of 1926, which required railroads and their employees to attempt to make employment agreements through representatives chosen by each side. Beginning in 1932, however, a number of statutes were enacted that greatly increased employees' rights to join unions and to engage in collective bargaining.

Norris-LaGuardia Act

Congress protected peaceful strikes, picketing, and boycotts in 1932 with the **Norris-LaGuardia Act.** The statute restricted the power of federal courts to issue injunctions against unions engaged in peaceful strikes. In effect, the act declared a national policy permitting employees to organize.

National Labor Relations Act

The **National Labor Relations Act (Wagner Act)** of 1935 established the rights of employees to engage in collective bargaining and to strike. The Wagner Act created the **National Labor Relations Board (NLRB)** to oversee elections and to prevent employers from engaging in unfair and illegal antiunion activities and unfair labor practices.

The act defined a number of practices by employers as unfair to labor:

1. Interference with the efforts of employees to form, join, or assist labor organizations
2. An employer's domination of a labor organization or contribution of financial or other support to it
3. Discrimination in the hiring or awarding of tenure to employees based on union affiliation
4. Discrimination against employees for filing

charges under the act or giving testimony under the act
5. Refusal to bargain collectively with the duly designated representative of the employees.

Until this act was passed, an employer could refuse to bargain with a union. Now, an employer is required to recognize the union as a bargaining power if the employees so decide by a neutral election.

The **Labor-Management Relations Act (Taft-Hartley Act)** of 1947 amended the Wagner Act. This act contains provisions protecting employers as well as employees. The act was bitterly opposed by organized labor groups because it provided a detailed list of unfair labor activities that unions as well as management are now forbidden to practice. Moreover, a free speech amendment allowed employers to propagandize against unions prior to any National Labor Relations Board election.

Both the Wagner and the Taft-Hartley acts affected certain types of businesses known as closed shops and union shops. A **closed shop** is a firm that requires union membership from its workers as a condition of employment. Closed shops were made illegal under the Taft-Hartley Act because they put the unions, rather than the employers, in charge of hiring.

A **union shop** does not require membership as a prerequisite for employment but can, and usually does, require that workers join the union after a specified amount of time on the job. In an **agency shop,** membership in a union is not a prerequisite to be hired, and workers are not required to join the union after they have been hired. Workers, however, can be required to pay initiation fees and union dues, the theory being that these people are enjoying the benefits of the union.

The Taft-Hartley Act allowed individual states to pass their own **right-to-work laws.** A right-to-work law makes it illegal for union membership to be required for continued employment in any establishment. Thus, union shops are technically illegal in states with right-to-work laws.

One of the most controversial aspects of the Taft-Hartley Act was the 80-day cooling-off period. This provision allows federal courts to issue injunctions against strikes that would create a national emergency. The president of the United

States can obtain such a court injunction that will last 80 days. For example, President Eisenhower applied the 80-day injunction to striking steelworkers in 1959, President Nixon applied it to striking longshoremen in 1971, and President Carter applied it to striking coal miners in 1978.

Labor-Management Reporting and Disclosure Act of 1959

The **Labor-Management Reporting and Disclosure Act (Landrum-Griffin Act)** of 1959 instituted an employee bill of rights as well as reporting requirements for union activities. This act regulates internal union business, such as union elections. Elections of officers must be regularly scheduled, and secret ballots must be used. Ex-convicts and members of the Communist party are precluded from holding union office. Union officials are accountable for union property and for union funds. Members have the right to attend and to participate in union meetings, to nominate officers, and to vote in most union proceedings.

The National Labor Relations Board

The National Labor Relations Board enforces all of these statutes. The NLRB consists of five members who are appointed by the president with the advice and consent of the Senate. The board members have staggered five-year terms and may be removed only for neglect of duty or malfeasance.

The board has the usual administrative powers and is charged with supervising secret elections in which the employees determine whether a union will represent them in collective bargaining. The board then certifies the union selected by the majority of employees as the collective bargaining agent. Charged with preventing and remedying unfair labor practices, the board hears and rules on charges of unfair labor practices by unions and employers.

The Taft-Hartley Act transferred the investigative and prosecutorial roles of the board to a general counsel who is also appointed by the president with the advice and consent of the Senate. The general counsel supervises the NLRB's 31 regional offices and is responsible for the conduct of union representative elections. Individual charges of unfair labor or antiunion practices are filed with one of the NLRB's regional offices. The regional director may, at her or his discretion, file a complaint after investigating the charges.

Complaints filed by regional directors are heard initially by administrative law judges who have delegated authority from the NLRB. If appealed, the administrative law judge's decision serves as a recommendation to the board. Board decisions may be appealed to the court of appeals and from there to the Supreme Court of the United States.

Remedies

The NLRB has broad discretionary authority to fashion appropriate remedies whenever it finds unfair labor practices. The courts have held that the board's orders will not be overturned unless it can be shown that the remedies ordered cannot fairly be said to effectuate the policies of the NLRA, as amended.

The board may issue cease and desist orders and may also require a person to take an action designed to carry out the purposes of the act. The board may order reinstatement of an employee who is wrongfully discharged, along with the payment of back wages and the restoration of seniority. When union election results are contested, the board may order new elections if unfair labor practices are deemed to have influenced the outcome, or it may, in certain instances, require an employer to bargain with the appropriate union without holding a new election.

The Collective Bargaining Agreement

The NLRA requires both employers and the unions who represent their employees to bargain in good faith. This obligation requires the employer and union to meet at reasonable times and to confer in good faith with respect to wages, hours, and other terms and conditions of employment. The obligation to bargain in good faith does not require the parties to come to an agreement. But the purpose behind the statute is to encourage parties to negotiate enforceable contracts. The following case involves the enforceability of a collective bargaining agreement that contained a no-strike provision.

Case 21.4
**JACKSONVILLE v.
INTERNATIONAL
LONGSHOREMEN
ASSOCIATION**
Supreme Court of the United
States, 1982.
457 U.S. 702, 102 S.Ct. 2672,
72 L.Ed.2d 327.

BACKGROUND AND FACTS *President Carter announced an embargo of certain goods that were to be shipped to the Soviet Union because of its intervention in Afghanistan. The respondent, the International Longshore-men's Association, announced that its members would not handle any cargo bound to or coming from the Soviet Union. When an affiliated local union refused to load any goods, including goods not contained in the presidential embargo, bound for the Soviet Union, the petitioners, Jacksonville, brought suit in federal district court against the international union pursuant to the Labor-Management Relations Act.*

Jacksonville alleged that the union's work stoppage violated the terms of a collective bargaining agreement that contained a no-strike clause and a provision requiring arbitration of disputes. The court ordered the union to arbitrate the question of whether the work stoppage violated the collective bargaining agreement, and it granted a preliminary injunction pending arbitration. The court reasoned that the political motivation behind the work stoppage rendered inapplicable the Norris-LaGuardia Act. This act prohibits injunctions against strikes "in any case involving or growing out of any labor dispute." The trial court decided this was not a labor dispute.

The court of appeals affirmed the district court's order insofar as it required arbitration, but it disagreed with the conclusion that the Norris-LaGuardia Act was not applicable.

Justice MARSHALL delivered the opinion of the Court.
In this case, we consider the power of a federal court to enjoin a politically motivated work stoppage in an action brought by an employer pursuant to § 301(a) of the Labor Management Relations Act (LMRA) to enforce a union's obligations under a collective-bargaining agreement. We first address whether the board anti-injunction provisions of the Norris-LaGuardia Act apply to politically motivated work stoppages. Finding these provisions applicable, we then consider whether the work stoppage may be enjoined under the rationale of *Boys Markets, Inc. v. Retail Clerks,* pending an arbitrator's decision on whether the strike violates the collective-bargaining agreement.
*   *   *   *

Section 4 of the Norris-LaGuardia Act provides in part:
"No court of the United States shall have jurisdiction to issue any restraining order or temporary or permanent injunction in any case involving or growing out of any labor dispute to prohibit any person or persons participating or interested in such dispute *   *   * from doing, whether singly or in concert, any of the following acts:
    "(a) Ceasing or refusing to perform any work or to remain in any relation of employment."
Congress adopted this broad prohibition to remedy the growing tendency of federal courts to enjoin strikes by narrowly construing the Clayton Act's labor exemption from the Sherman Act's prohibition against conspiracies to restrain trade. This Court has consistently given the anti-injunction provisions of the Norris-LaGuardia Act a broad interpretation, recognizing exceptions only in limited situations where necessary to accommodate the Act to specific federal legislation or paramount congressional policy.
At the outset, we must determine whether this is a "case involving or growing out of any labor dispute" within the meaning of § 4 of the Norris-LaGuardia Act. Section 13(c) of the Act broadly defines the term "labor dispute" to include "any

controversy concerning terms or conditions of employment."

* * * *

The language of the Norris-LaGuardia Act does not except labor disputes having their genesis in political protests. Nor is there any basis in the statutory language for the argument that the Act requires that *each* dispute relevant to the case be a labor dispute. The Act merely requires that the case involve "any" labor dispute. Therefore, the plain terms of § 4(a) and § 13 of the Norris-LaGuardia Act deprive the federal courts of the power to enjoin the Union's work stoppage in this * * * action, without regard to whether the Union also has a nonlabor dispute with another entity.

* * * *

The attempts by the Solicitor General and the Employer to characterize the underlying dispute as arbitrable do not withstand analysis. The "underlying" disputes concerning the management-rights clause or the work-conditions clause simply did not trigger the work stoppage. To the contrary, the applicability of these clauses to the dispute, if any, was triggered by the work stoppage itself. Consideration of whether the strike intruded on the management-rights clause or was permitted by the work-conditions clause may inform the arbitrator's ultimate decision on whether the strike violates the no-strike clause. Indeed, the question whether striking over a nonarbitrable issue violates other provisions of the collective-bargaining agreement may itself be an arbitrable dispute. The fact remains, however, that the strike itself was not over an arbitrable dispute and therefore may not be enjoined pending the arbitrator's ruling on the legality of the strike under the collective-bargaining agreement.

* * * *

In conclusion, we hold that an employer's * * * action to enforce the provisions of a collective-bargaining agreement allegedly violated by a union's work stoppage involves a "labor dispute" within the meaning of the Norris-LaGuardia Act, without regard to the motivation underlying the union's decision not to provide labor. Under our decision in *Boys Markets* * * * when the underlying dispute is not arbitrable, the employer may not obtain injunctive relief pending the arbitrator's ruling on the legality of the strike under the collective-bargaining agreement.

The Supreme Court held that the parties still had to arbitrate whether the strike violated the collective bargaining agreement. An injunction prohibiting a strike cannot be issued under the Norris-LaGuardia Act, even though this involved a political and not an economic issue.

DECISION AND REMEDY

Duty of Fair Representation

Both in negotiating and in administering a collective bargaining agreement, a union has an implied duty of fair representation for the employees it represents. A union must act fairly, impartially, and in good faith. The right to determine eligibility for its own membership remains with the union, but it is, nevertheless, obligated in collective bargaining to represent nonunion or minority union members without hostile discrimination and fairly, impartially, and in good faith.

The union has the power to exercise its discretion in contract negotiations in order to draw reasonable distinctions among groups of employees based on differences relevant to the authorized purposes of the contract, such as differences in seniority, type of work performed, competence, and skill. The following is a case in which a labor union sought to end a long strike by negotiating three alternatives for its members.

Case 21.5
**AIR LINE PILOTS
ASSOCIATION,
INTERNATIONAL v.
O'NEILL**

Supreme Court of the United
States, 1991.
499 U.S. ——,
111 S.Ct. 37,
113 L.Ed.2d 51.

BACKGROUND AND FACTS   *This case arose out of a bitter confrontation between Continental Airlines, Inc., and the union representing its pilots, the Air Line Pilots Association, International (ALPA). In 1983 Continental filed a petition for reorganization under the Bankruptcy Code and, with the approval of the bankruptcy court, repudiated its collective bargaining agreement with ALPA and unilaterally reduced its pilots' salaries and benefits by more than half. ALPA responded by calling a strike that lasted for over two years. Of the approximately 2,000 pilots employed by Continental, all but 200 supported the strike. By trimming its operations and hiring about 1,000 replacements, Continental continued in business. By August 1985, 1,600 pilots had returned to work, leaving 1,000 strikers.*

Continental used a "system bid" procedure for assigning pilots to new positions. Under this system, bid notices were posted well in advance in order to allow time for necessary training. Any pilot could submit a bid. Vacant positions were awarded on the basis of seniority. On September 9, 1985, Continental posted its "Supplementary Base Vacancy Bid 1985–5," which covered an unusually large number of anticipated vacancies: over 400 positions. Pilots were given nine days to submit their bids.

Fearing that this bid might effectively lock the striking pilots out of jobs for the indefinite future, ALPA authorized the strikers to submit bids. Although Continental initially accepted bids from both strikers and nonstrikers, it later announced that all the positions had been awarded to working pilots. At this point, ALPA intensified its negotiations for a complete settlement. ALPA and Continental reached an agreement that was entered as an order by the Bankruptcy Court. The agreement ended the strike, disposed of all the pending litigation from the past two years, and reallocated the positions covered by the bid.

The agreement offered the striking pilots three options. First, pilots who settled all outstanding claims with Continental were eligible to bid on the open positions. Second, the strikers could accept a lump-sum severance package. The third option was to retain the individual claims against Continental, but the pilots would not be eligible to return to work until all the first-option pilots had been reinstated. The pilots from the third option brought this action on the theory that the union had breached its duty of fair representation in negotiating and accepting this settlement, since it discriminated against striking pilots.

Justice STEVENS delivered the opinion of the Court.
*   *   *   *

We granted certiorari to clarify the standard that governs a claim that a union has breached its duty of fair representation in its negotiation of a back-to-work agreement terminating a strike. *   *   * [T]he rule *   *   * —that a union breaches its duty of fair representation if its actions are either "arbitrary, discriminatory, or in bad faith"—applies to all union activity, including contract negotiation. We further hold that a union's actions are arbitrary only if, in light of the factual and legal landscape at the time of the union's actions, the union's behavior is so far outside a "wide range of reasonableness" as to be irrational.
*   *   *   *

The duty of fair representation is thus akin to the duty owed by other fiduciaries to their beneficiaries. For example, some Members of the Court have analogized the duty a union owes to the employees it represents to the duty a trustee owes to trust beneficiaries. Others have likened the relationship between union and employee to that between attorney and client. The fair representation duty also parallels the responsibilities of corporate officers and directors toward shareholders. Just as these fiduciaries owe their beneficiaries a duty of care as well as a duty of loyalty, a union owes employees a duty to represent them adequately as well as honestly and in good faith.

* * * *

For purposes of decision, we may assume that the Court of Appeals was correct in its conclusion that, if ALPA had simply surrendered and voluntarily terminated the strike, the striking pilots would have been entitled to reemployment in the order of seniority. Moreover, we may assume that Continental would have responded to such action by rescinding its assignment of all of the 85–5 bid positions to working pilots. After all, it did rescind about half of those assignments pursuant to the terms of the settlement. Thus, we assume that the union made a bad settlement—one that was even worse than a unilateral termination of the strike.

Nevertheless, the settlement was by no means irrational. A settlement is not irrational simply because it turns out *in retrospect* to have been a bad settlement. Viewed in light of the legal landscape at the time of the settlement, ALPA's decision to settle rather than give up was certainly not illogical. At the time of the settlement, Continental had notified the union that all of the 85–5 bid positions had been awarded to working pilots and was maintaining that none of the strikers had any claim on any of those jobs.

* * * *

At the very least, the settlement produced certain and prompt access to a share of the new jobs and avoided the costs and risks associated with major litigation. Moreover, since almost a third of the striking pilots chose the lump-sum severance payment rather than reinstatement, the settlement was presumably more advantageous than a surrender to a significant number of striking pilots. In labor disputes, as in other kinds of litigation, even a bad settlement may be more advantageous in the long run than a good lawsuit. In all events, the resolution of the dispute over the 85–5 bid vacancies was well within the "wide range of reasonableness" that a union is allowed in its bargaining.

The Court reaffirmed public policy favoring the peaceful settlement of labor disputes. The Court found the settlement to be a rational compromise and one that did not violate the union's duty of fair representation. **DECISION AND REMEDY**

Strikes

Two types of strikes are authorized under labor-management laws: *economic strikes* and *unfair labor practices strikes*. Most strikes are economic in nature—that is, the employees strike for higher wages and benefits. Management may permanently replace economic strikers. The strikers, however, are entitled to priority when management starts to rehire after the strike, and management cannot discriminate against these strikers.

In Case 21.5, you can see how the union felt pressure to settle the strike. If the strike had not ended, Continental could have hired over 400 permanent replacements; if the strike had ended after these new people had been hired, the strikers would have had to wait a long time for new vacancies to open up.

Unfair labor practices strikes occur when management has violated the law. Earlier in the chapter we discussed unfair labor practices. When this type of strike ends, management must give the job back to the striking employee. If the law were the same here as for an economic strike, management would effectively be rewarded for illegal practices.

Ethical Considerations

Retirement Benefits

The 1980s saw a major decrease in the amount of benefits offered by corporations to their employees. Health insurance benefits were slashed or eliminated. Likewise, pension plans were curtailed or eliminated, and by the mid 1980s over half of all workers were not covered by any pension plan. When these plans were abolished, the employers normally increased the hourly rate paid to employees. Many employees, for whatever reason, did not save the increase for retirement or health insurance.

Nearly all employees pay into the social security trust fund and count on it as part of their retirement income. Today, as the population ages, the average number of years between retirement and death increases. In 1934, when social security was enacted, the retirement age was set at 65. Then, less than 4 percent of the population was 65 or older. If the social security benefits were to be paid to the same percentage of aged population today, benefits would start at 90 years of age.

What will happen when employees reach retirement age? Social security was never planned to be the bulk of a person's retirement income, but a supplement to it. In 1992, the maximum annual benefit paid was $12,804, an amount received only by the persons who paid the maximum amount into social security. The average social security benefit was far less and was not sufficient to support a person beyond a very minimum standard of living. As a result, as economic costs have increased, many senior citizens have been forced into welfare and thus have become an economic drain on taxpayers.

What ethical responsibilities does a business have for making provisions for employee retirement and health plans? Should employees have the option to receive either higher pay or fringe benefits? What responsibilities do employees have to save the increase provided by employers when the retirement and health plans are eliminated in order to provide for their own retirement and health care?

International Considerations

International Considerations

The Western European countries have each developed an independent administrative court system that handles problems concerning labor. These courts hear cases ranging from unemployment compensation and workers' compensation to union contracts and social security benefits. Many of these courts have an attorney as the presiding official; skilled representatives, appointed by the employee and the employer, sit on the panel with the lawyer.

Under international agreements, many industries are moving their production facilities from developed nations to countries that have cheap labor. The workers generally found in underdeveloped countries are not provided with the protections and benefits normal for workers in developed nations. Such benefits as health and safety protections, union contracts, social security, workers' compensation, and unemployment benefits are not available. Some countries even use prison labor to produce products cheaply. These products are then sent overseas to developed countries and sold at a price below domestic manufacturing costs. If this practice is detected, international agreements allow for the confiscation of the illegally imported items.

In most of the developed world, an employee has a vested right to his or her job. This practice has been recognized by the 1982 International Labor Organization's Convention on Termination at the Initiative of the Employer. The United States is not a signatory to this convention, although most of the Western European countries have ratified it. The convention recognizes that an employee cannot be terminated except for cause.

The philosophical belief of the United States is that the employer controls all costs, including that of labor. Thus, an employer is allowed to terminate employees in cost-cutting measures aimed at maintaining competitiveness. An employee may be terminated with cause based on the employee's performance or without any cause so long as the employer does not have a bad motive.

Unfair Labor Practices

Although you have asked your employees not to discuss their salaries with each other, you learn that one of your employees has not only been talking about what he makes, but has also been encouraging others to do so.

You have called the employee into your office. "Listen, Mark," you begin, "you knew when I hired you what the rule was. All you're going to do is cause jealousy by comparing salaries. I can justify the differences in various employees' pay, but if I have to explain to a worker why he is not as good as the next, he's not going to believe it anyway and it's just going to hurt morale."

But Mark tells you, "We have no way of knowing if you're treating us fairly unless we talk about what we all make. The secrecy only benefits you by keeping us from being able to negotiate with you to pay all of us what you should."

Your immediate response may be to fire this employee. After all, he understood when he was hired that you expected employees to refrain from comparing salaries, and he implicitly agreed to this when he accepted the job. Federal labor laws, however, may prohibit you from firing him.

Section 7 of the National Labor Relations Act safeguards the right of employees to engage in concerted activities "for the purpose of collective bargaining or other mutual aid or protection." While most cases under Section 7 involve strikes or other activities by unions, the language of the section protects not only union activities but also activities of all workers. The comparing of salaries by your workers could be viewed as their gathering information in order to obtain more equitable pay scales. Thus, although your employees are not organized as a union, their discussions could be construed to fall under the protection of Section 7, and your firing of the employee could be an unfair labor practice.

Even if Mark's attempts to instigate salary discussions with the other employees had been unsuccessful, his own activities would still be protected, and as long as he does not engage in threats or violence, he may not be fired. You could fire Mark if he were insubordinate, disloyal, or disobedient, as long as these behaviors were not part of protected activities of organizing workers.

Summary

This chapter has covered statutory regulation of labor and labor unions. We have seen that federal law has had a significant impact in both areas.

The Fair Labor Standards Act establishes a minimum wage of (currently) $4.25 per hour, overtime provisions requiring time-and-a-half pay for any work over 40 hours per week, certain record-keeping requirements, and child labor protection. Some employees are exempt under this act, but the great majority of American businesses are bound by its terms. The act is enforced by the Wage and Hour Division of the Department of Labor.

Federal acts govern other labor-related concerns. Social security provisions include Old Age, Survivors, and Disability Insurance and Medicare. Unemployment compensation is handled through both federal and state funding. State workers' compensation laws cover employees injured while on the job. For an injury to be covered by these laws, the only questions asked are whether the injury was accidental and whether it arose in the course of employment.

Federal law also attempts to ensure safe and healthful working conditions for practically every employee in the country through the Occupational Safety and Health Act.

Employees have the right to organize unions and to participate in collective bargaining. These rights are protected by federal statutory provisions. The National Labor Relations Act of 1935 is the cornerstone of protection for the labor movement. This act has been amended several times to reflect changing attitudes toward the labor movement.

Certain activities are illegal under the NLRA. It outlaws the closed shop in which a person must be a union member in order to be employed. A union shop requires a person to join a union after employment has started. An agency shop requires a person to pay initiation fees and dues, but the person is not required to join the union. These agreements are legal in the absence of a state right-to-work law.

The National Labor Relations Board (NLRB) was established by the 1935 act. It is charged with supervising union elections and with determining when an unfair labor practice has occurred. Both unions and employers have certain specified rights when there is an election, and each has a duty to bargain in good faith with the other.

Key Terms

agency shop (534)
closed shop (534)
Employee Retirement Income
  Security Act (ERISA)
  (527)
Fair Labor Standards Act
  (FLSA) (524)
Federal Insurance
  Contributions Act (FICA)
  (526)
Federal Unemployment Tax
  Act (FUTA) (527)
Labor-Management Relations
  Act (Taft-Hartley Act)
  (534)

Labor-Management Reporting
  and Disclosure Act
  (Landrum-Griffin Act)
  (534)
Medicare (527)
National Labor Relations Act
  (Wagner Act) (534)
National Labor Relations
  Board (NLRB) (534)
Norris-LaGuardia Act (534)
Occupational Safety and
  Health Act (532)
Occupational Safety and
  Health Administration
  (OSHA) (532)

Old Age, Survivors, and
  Disability Insurance
  (OASDI) (526)
right-to-work laws (534)
Social Security Act (526)
unemployment compensation
  (527)
union shop (534)
workers' compensation laws
  (529)

Questions and Case Problems

1. Workers' compensation statutes cover the injuries, disease, or death of employees while at work. Professor Able is employed by a private university in California. He is attending a professional meeting. Prior to traveling, he requested permission and travel money to attend the meeting. He was granted permission but was not granted the travel money. After the meeting, but three hours prior to his airplane trip to return home, he visited a cathedral that is noted for its beauty. When he emerged from the cathedral, he stumbled down the stairs and injured himself. He was taken by ambulance to the hospital where he was seen by the emergency room physician. He was treated and released in time to catch the return flight. Are his injuries covered by workers' compensation? Did the injuries occur while at work?

2. Hamburger Joint is a nationwide franchise fast-food outlet. The management is very interested in teenage un-

employment. Consequently, it creates a program for hiring teens. The program would hire 50 people in each age bracket. The fourteen-year-olds would be janitors, the fifteen-year-olds would work at the counter taking orders, the sixteen-year-olds would learn to cook the various foods, and the seventeen-year-olds would drive the company vehicles and deliver the food orders. Do you see any violations of the child labor laws in this program?

3. Joseph owns an interstate business engaged in manufacturing and selling boats. Joseph has 500 nonunion employees. Representatives of these employees approach Joseph seeking a four-day, ten-hours-per-day work week. Joseph is concerned that this proposal will require him to pay his employees time and a half after eight hours per day. Discuss fully which federal act concerns Joseph and whether the proposal will require Joseph to pay time and a half.

4. Yeshiva University is a private university. The faculty association, acting as a bargaining agent for the full-time faculty members, filed a petition with the NLRB. The university opposed this on the basis that faculty members are managerial personnel and are not under the jurisdiction of the NLRB. Do you think college professors are managers or workers? [NLRB v. Yeshiva University, 444 U.S. 672, 100 S.Ct. 856, 63 L.Ed.2d 115 (1979)]

5. Gary Segler was employed by Caterpillar Tractor Company. About 25 feet from his work was a large industrial oven that had a conveyor system going through it. Molds for parts were placed on the conveyor belt and sent through the oven. One day the conveyor belt was not operating, and Segler placed a pie inside the oven. As he was retrieving it, the conveyor system started functioning, which resulted in a mold striking him, causing serious injuries. The corporation took the position that the injuries were not work related and therefore Segler was not covered by workers' compensation. Were they correct? [Segler v. Industrial Commission, 81 Ill.2d 125, 406 N.E.2d 542 (1980)]

6. Jiffy June Farms had properly paid overtime to its employees. It entered into a collective bargaining agreement that purportedly exempted it from paying time and a half for overtime but that increased basic wages considerably. The lower court found that this was a willful violation of the FLSA. Do you agree? [Coleman v. Jiffy June Farms, 458 F.2d 1139 (5th Cir. 1972)]

7. Local 165, a labor union, went on strike against Illinois Bell Telephone Company. A labor picket line was established, which Bradley, a union member, ignored. The union gave notice to him that a union trial board would conduct a hearing in order to determine if he had crossed the picket line. He failed to attend the hearing. At the hearing, he was found guilty and assessed $1,357 in fines and was barred from union membership for five years. He failed to pay the fine and the union sued him in small-claims court. Who prevails and why? [Local 165, International Brotherhood of Electric Workers v. Bradley, 149 Ill.App.3d 193, 499 N.E.2d 577 (1986)]

8. James Brown was a union member and worked for City Disposal Systems, Inc. He was ordered to drive a truck that he thought had faulty brakes. Because of this, he refused to drive and was discharged. He filed an unfair labor practice charge that challenged his dismissal. What was the result? [NLRB v. City Disposal Systems, Inc., 465 U.S. 822, 104 S.Ct. 1505, 79 L.Ed.2d 839 (1984)]

9. At an REA shipping terminal, a conveyor belt was inoperative because an electrical circuit had shorted out. The manager called a licensed electrical contractor. When the contractor arrived, REA's maintenance supervisor was in the circuit breaker room. The floor was wet, and the maintenance supervisor was using sawdust to try to soak up the water. While the licensed electrical contractor was attempting to fix the short circuit, standing on the wet floor, he was electrocuted. Simultaneously, REA's maintenance supervisor, who was standing on a wooden platform, was burned and knocked unconscious. OSHA wanted to fine REA Express $1,000 for failure to furnish a place of employment free from recognized hazards. What was the result? [REA Express, Inc. v. Brennan, 495 F.2d 822 (2d Cir. 1974)]

Chapter 22 Employment Law and Equal Opportunity

Laborin' man an' laborin' woman
    Hev one glory an' one shame;
Ev'y thin' thet's done inhuman
    Injers all on 'em the same.

The Biglow Papers,
Series 1, No. 1, Stanza 10, (1848).
James Russell Lowell (1819–1891)

OUTLINE

Introduction

At common law, both employment and membership in labor unions were considered private contractual matters. Little or no protection was provided against arbitrary and discriminatory actions by employers or labor unions. Not until the National Labor Relations Act of 1935 did employees gain some statutory protection against discrimination. Under the act, employers are prohibited from discriminating against employees or applicants because of union or organizational activity. Within a decade after the act, the United States Supreme Court prohibited certain forms of racial discrimination by unions.

This chapter looks first at the federal laws that prohibit discrimination and then discusses affirmative action.

The Civil Rights Act of 1964, Title VII

Title VII of the **Civil Rights Act** of 1964 prohibits discrimination in all areas of employment on the basis of race; color; religion; national origin; or on the basis of gender, including pregnancy, childbirth, or abortion. Title VII does not prohibit discrimination based on physical disability or age because these areas are covered by other federal statutory provisions. Title VII coverage extends to state and local governments as well as the specified federal employees.

Limitations of Title VII

Title VII covers employers with at least fifteen workers, labor unions with at least fifteen members, and employment agencies that obtain workers for an employer covered by the law. In order for Title VII to apply, the activities of the employer, labor union, or employment agency must be part of or must affect interstate commerce, which is interpreted very broadly.

Noncovered Employment Situations

Title VII exempts religious associations and religious educational institutions from the prohibition against discrimination on the basis of religion. Whenever these organizations are employers, they are prohibited from discriminating on the basis of gender, race, or national origin. Congress has exempted itself not only from Title VII, but also from all of the Civil Rights Act of 1964. Except for specified federal employers, the federal government is exempt from Title VII, since it is prohibited from discriminating on the basis of race, color, religion, gender, and national origin under other acts and executive orders. Indian tribes and departments of the District of Columbia are also exempt.

Theories of Discrimination Under Title VII

Two basic, but not mutually exclusive, theories of discrimination are covered under Title VII: **disparate impact** and **disparate treatment**. Often both disparate treatment and disparate impact claims are combined in the same case.

Disparate Impact   Sometimes employment practices may appear neutral on the surface, but they nonetheless adversely affect a protected class. This is the nature of disparate impact discrimination cases. With such cases, statistics on the impact of the practice or device on a protected class are not only relevant but are also often the only way to establish a *prima facie* case that the practice has a disproportionately adverse effect on a protected class. A *prima facie* case means that the evidence presented will prove the case until contradicted and overcome by other evidence. In the following case, the Supreme Court reviews an employment practice that appeared neutral but in fact had a disparate impact on African-American employees.

Case 22.1
GRIGGS v. DUKE POWER CO.

Supreme Court of the United States, 1971.
401 U.S. 424, 91 S.Ct. 849, 28 L.Ed.2d 158.

BACKGROUND AND FACTS   *Thirteen African-American employees of Duke Power Company brought this class-action suit against their employer. Prior to July 2, 1965, the effective date of the Civil Rights Act of 1964, the company had hired African Americans in only one of its five departments, the Labor Department; there, the highest-paying jobs paid less than the lowest-paying jobs in the other departments in which only whites were em-*

ployed. In 1955 the company had instituted a policy of requiring a high school diploma for initial assignment to any department except labor. When the company abandoned its policy of restricting African Americans to the Labor Department in 1965, completion of high school was made a prerequisite for transfer from labor to any other department.

In 1965, the company added a further requirement for new employees in all departments other than labor—satisfactory scores on two professionally prepared aptitude tests. Completion of high school alone continued to render employees eligible for transfer to the more desirable departments if they had been employed by Duke Power prior to the time the testing requirement was instituted. Employees who lacked a high school education could qualify for transfer to other departments by passing the two aptitude tests.

The district court found that the company had followed a policy of overt racial discrimination prior to enactment of the Civil Rights Act of 1964 but that its discriminatory conduct had ceased. The court of appeals concluded that there was no showing of a discriminatory purpose in the adoption of the diploma and test requirements and, therefore, no violation of the Civil Rights Act. The Supreme Court then reviewed the case to determine whether such requirements were unlawful under Title VII if they were not shown to be job related.

Justice BURGER delivered the opinion of the Court.

The objective of Congress in the enactment of Title VII is plain from the language of the statute. It was to achieve equality of employment opportunities and remove barriers that have operated in the past to favor an identifiable group of white employees over other employees. Under the Act, practices, procedures, or tests neutral on their face, and even neutral in terms of intent, cannot be maintained if they operate to "freeze" the status quo of prior discriminatory employment practices.

The Court of Appeals' opinion, and the pretrial dissent, agreed that, on the record in the present case, "whites register far better on the Company's alternative requirements" than Negroes. This consequence would appear to be directly traceable to race. Basic intelligence must have the means of articulation to manifest itself fairly in a testing process. Because they are Negroes, petitioners have long received inferior education in segregated schools and this Court expressly recognized these differences in *Gaston County v. United States.* There, because of the inferior education received by Negroes in North Carolina, this Court barred the institution of a literacy test for voter registration on the ground that the test would abridge the right to vote indirectly on account of race. Congress did not intend by Title VII, however, to guarantee a job to every person regardless of qualifications. In short, the Act does not command that any person be hired simply because he was formerly the subject of discrimination, or because he is a member of a minority group. Discriminatory preference for any group, minority or majority, is precisely and only what Congress has proscribed. What is required by Congress is the removal of artificial, arbitrary, and unnecessary barriers to employment when the barriers operate invidiously to discriminate on the basis of racial or other impermissible classification.

Congress has now provided that tests or criteria for employment or promotion may not provide equality of opportunity merely in the sense of the fabled offer of milk to the stork and the fox. On the contrary, Congress has now required that the posture and condition of the job-seeker be taken into account. It has—to resort again to the fable—provided that the vessel in which the milk is proffered be one all seekers can use. The Act proscribes not only overt discrimination but also practices that are fair in form, but discriminatory in operation. The touchstone is business necessity. If an employment practice which operates to exclude Negroes cannot be shown to be related to job performance, the practice is prohibited.

DECISION AND REMEDY   *The judgment of the court of appeals was reversed. The Supreme Court held that diploma and test requirements had to be job related. Duke Power must prove that the test and degree requirements were necessary for the job.*

The Civil Rights Act of 1991 reaffirmed this decision. Codified into federal law are the terms *business necessity* and *job related*. The act provides statutory guidelines for disparate impact lawsuits. An unlawful employment practice occurs when the employer uses a particular practice that results in a disparate impact on the basis of race, religion, sex, or national origin. The employer has the burden of proving that the challenged practice is job related and consistent with business necessity. The employee may show that an alternative practice exists that meets the goals of the business without the disparate impact but that the business refuses to adopt it.

Prior to the 1991 act, there was confusion on whether a business could use race-norming tests. To race-norm a test meant that different cutoff scores were used based on the person's race, religion, sex, or national origin. This practice is now illegal under the 1991 act.

Disparate Treatment The simplest form of discrimination involves treating a member of one class differently from other employees or other applicants. The plaintiff-employee must establish a *prima facie* case of discrimination. Once shown, the defendant-employer now has the burden of proving legitimate, nondiscriminatory reasons for the applicant not being hired or the employee's failure to be promoted or given a salary increase.

If the defendant is successful in rebutting the *prima facie* case, the plaintiff, in the next stage of a disparate treatment case, must prove that the reason articulated by the employer is not legitimate but is rather a pretext to cover up discrimination.

Patterns of Discrimination

The government can bring suit through the **Equal Employment Opportunity Commission (EEOC)** against an employer when a pattern of discrimination is evident. These cases can be brought by the EEOC on the basis of disparate treatment or disparate impact. The government in these "pattern and practice" cases, nonetheless, bears the initial burden of establishing a *prima facie* case of discrimination. More than the mere occurrence of isolated, accidental, or sporadic discriminatory acts must be proved.

The government must show that a protected class is suffering from discrimination because of a company's standard operating procedure. For example, the government can make out a *prima facie* case by showing large statistical disparities between the racial composition of the general work force and that of the more specialized employment positions. The government can strengthen its case by presenting evidence of specific instances of discrimination.

Specific Applications of Title VII

Employees' grievances about various types of discrimination represent important concerns. Title VII has been applied to cases involving sex discrimination, pregnancy discrimination, sexual harassment, pension and life insurance, and discrimination based on religion, national origin, or race.

Sex Discrimination Discrimination based on sex is prohibited under Title VII. Title VII, however, does not prohibit discrimination based on sexual or affectional preferences, nor does it protect transsexuals. Since its enactment, Title VII has been used to strike down protective state legislation, such as laws that prevented women from undertaking jobs deemed too dangerous or strenuous by the state. In reality, such "protective" state legislation often prevented women from obtaining higher-paying jobs. Under EEOC guidelines, state statutes may not be used as a defense to a charge of illegal sex discrimination.

Sex-plus discrimination has been made illegal by Title VII. This discrimination involves discrimination based on sex, plus an additional element. For example, women with preschool-age children have been refused employment. Now it is illegal for an employer to refuse to hire these women if the employer accepts men with preschool-age children. An employer may not require that female employees be single if male employees may be married. EEOC guidelines forbid advertising jobs in publications as male or female, unless sex is a bona fide occupational qualification (BFOQ) for the particular job.

Pregnancy Discrimination   Title VII was amended in 1978 by the **Pregnancy Discrimination Act.** This act redefined sex discrimination to include discrimination based on pregnancy, childbirth, or related medical conditions. Based on this amendment, health and disability insurance plans must cover pregnancy, childbirth, or related medical conditions in the same way that they cover any other temporary disability.

An employer must provide leaves of absence for pregnant women on the same terms and conditions as those provided to any other worker for any other temporary disability. A woman who is pregnant cannot be forced to take a maternity leave for any specified period of time. As long as she is capable of performing her duties, she must be allowed to work. The 1978 amendment applies both to married and unmarried women and to any aspect of employment.

The following case involves disparate treatment, sex discrimination prohibitions, and pregnancy discrimination prohibitions under the 1964 Civil Rights Act and the Pregnancy Discrimination Act.

BACKGROUND AND FACTS   *Johnson Controls manufactures batteries. In the manufacturing process, the element lead is a primary ingredient. Occupational exposure to lead entails health risks, including the risk of harm to any fetus carried by a female employee. Before the Civil Rights Act of 1964, Johnson Controls did not employ any women in the battery-manufacturing job. In June 1977, the company adopted a policy of warning any woman of childbearing age of the potential hazards of working in such a job and then had the woman sign a statement that she had been advised of the risks. Between 1979 and 1983, eight women became pregnant while maintaining blood lead levels at what the Occupational Safety and Health Administration (OSHA) noted to be a critical level.*

In 1982 Johnson Controls shifted from a policy of warning to a policy of exclusion. In 1984 the International Union, United Automobile, Aerospace, and Agricultural Implement Workers of America, United Automobile Workers, and others filed a class action challenging Johnson Controls' fetal-protection policy as sex discrimination that violated Title VII of the Civil Rights Act of 1964.

Case 22.2
**AUTOMOBILE
WORKERS v.
JOHNSON
CONTROLS, INC.**
Supreme Court of the United
States, 1991.
499 U.S. ___ , 111 S.Ct. 1196,
113 L.Ed.2d 158.

Justice BLACKMUN delivered the opinion of the Court.
*   *   *   *

In this case we are concerned with an employer's gender-based fetal-protection policy. May an employer exclude a fertile female employee from certain jobs because of its concern for the health of the fetus the woman might conceive?
*   *   *   *

The bias in Johnson Controls' policy is obvious. Fertile men, but not fertile women, are given a choice as to whether they wish to risk their reproductive health for a particular job. [T]he Civil Rights Act of 1964 prohibits sex-based classifications in terms and conditions of employment, in hiring and discharging decisions, and in other employment decisions that adversely affect an employee's status. Respondent's fetal-protection policy explicitly discriminates against women on the basis of their sex. The policy excludes women with childbearing capacity from lead-exposed jobs and so creates a facial classification based on gender.

*   *   *   *

First, Johnson Controls' policy classifies on the basis of gender and childbearing capacity, rather than fertility alone. Respondent does not seek to protect the unconceived children of all its employees. Despite evidence in the record about the debilitating effect of lead exposure on the male reproductive system, Johnson Controls is concerned only with the harms that may befall the unborn offspring of its female employees. *   *   * Johnson Controls' policy is facially discriminatory because it requires only a female employee to produce proof that she is not capable of reproducing.

Our conclusion is bolstered by the Pregnancy Discrimination Act of 1978 (PDA) in which Congress explicitly provided that, for purposes of Title VII, discrimination "on the basis of sex" includes discrimination because of or on the basis of pregnancy, childbirth, or related medical conditions. The Pregnancy Discrimination Act has now made clear that, for all Title VII purposes, discrimination based on a woman's pregnancy is, on its face, discrimination because of her sex. In its use of the words "capable of bearing children" in the 1982 policy statement as the criterion for exclusion, Johnson Controls explicitly classifies on the basis of potential for pregnancy. Under the PDA, such a classification must be regarded, for Title VII purposes, in the same light as explicit sex discrimination. Respondent has chosen to treat all its female employees as potentially pregnant; that choice evinces discrimination on the basis of sex.

We concluded above that Johnson Controls' policy is not neutral because it does not apply to the reproductive capacity of the company's male employees in the same way as it applies to that of females. Moreover, the absence of a malevolent motive does not convert a facially discriminatory policy into a neutral policy with a discriminatory effect. Whether an employment practice involves disparate treatment through explicit facial discrimination does not depend on why the employer discriminates but rather on the explicit terms of the discrimination.

*   *   *   *

*   *   * We hold that Johnson Controls' fetal-protection policy is sex discrimination forbidden under Title VII unless respondent can establish that sex is a "bona fide occupational qualification."

The wording of the BFOQ defense contains several terms of restriction that indicate that the exception reaches only special situations. The statute thus limits the situations in which discrimination is permissible to "certain instances" where sex discrimination is "reasonably necessary" to the "normal operation" of the "particular" business. Each one of these terms—certain, normal, particular—prevents the use of general subjective standards and favors an objective, verifiable requirement. But the most telling term is "occupational"; this indicates that these objective, verifiable requirements must concern job-related skills and aptitudes.

*   *   *   *

[H]istory counsels against expanding the BFOQ to allow fetal-protection policies. *   *   * [E]mployers may not require a pregnant woman to stop working at any time during her pregnancy unless she is unable to do her work. Employment late in pregnancy often imposes risks on the unborn child, but Congress indicated that the employer may take into account only the woman's ability to get her job done. With the PDA, Congress made clear that the decision to become pregnant or to work while being either pregnant or capable of becoming pregnant was reserved for each individual woman to make for herself.

We conclude that the language of both the BFOQ provision and the PDA which amended it, as well as the legislative history and the case law, prohibit an employer from discriminating against a woman because of her capacity to become pregnant unless her reproductive potential prevents her from performing the duties of her job. We reiterate our holdings in [prior cases] that an employer must direct its concerns about a woman's ability to perform her job safely and efficiently to those aspects of the woman's job-related activities that fall within the "essence" of the particular business.

The Court found that the policy was discriminatory on its face by requiring only women to prove that they were not capable of reproducing. The decision to work is that of the employed woman, not that of the employer.

DECISION AND REMEDY

Sexual Harassment By the late 1970s, the federal courts began ruling that sexual harassment constituted illegal sex discrimination under Title VII. Today, under EEOC guidelines, all unwelcome sexual advances, requests, or other physical or verbal conduct of a sexual nature are illegal sexual harassment if submission is a condition of employment or a basis of pay, promotion, or of other employment decisions. If this unwanted conduct interferes with an employee's job performance or creates an intimidating, hostile, or offensive environment, the conduct is illegal. The employer under some restricted circumstances also may be held liable for illegal sexual harassment perpetrated by supervisors in the company.

Pension and Life Insurance Because women have a longer life expectancy than men, virtually all pension and annuity plans used to require either that women pay a higher annual amount to re-

ceive the same yearly retirement benefits or that women pay the same annual amount but retire with fewer annual benefits. Today, employers are required to treat employees as individuals rather than as a class of men or of women. Even though women as a class do live longer than men, many women do not live as long as the average man, and many men outlive the average woman.

Discrimination Based on Religion Pursuant to Title VII, employers must make reasonable accommodations to an employee's or a prospective employee's religious practices, beliefs, or observances, as long as the employer is able to do so without undue hardship in the conduct of her or his business. The following case shows what a court may consider in determining undue hardship for a business that is confronted with an employee who desires a certain day off.

BACKGROUND AND FACTS *Angeline Protos was employed by Volkswagen of America, Inc. She was terminated when she refused to work on Saturdays because of her religious beliefs. She brought this action under Title VII of the Civil Rights Act.*

Case 22.3
PROTOS v. VOLKSWAGEN OF AMERICA
United States Court of Appeals, Third Circuit, 1986.
797 F.2d 129.

Judge ADAMS

Under Title VII of the Civil Rights Act of 1964, employers are required to make reasonable accommodation for the religious practices of their employees. In this case, the district court ruled that Volkswagen had violated the statute by refusing to accommodate the request of an assembly line employee to be excused from overtime work on Saturday, her Sabbath. This appeal requires us to consider whether the trial judge erred in determining that accommodation of the request would not cause the company undue hardship.

Angeline S. Protos is a member of the Worldwide Church of God. Under the tenets of that church, the Sabbath lasts from sunset Friday to sunset Saturday. Work is prohibited during this time, and failure to observe the Sabbath is cause for excommunication.
*   *   *   *

The principal issue before the district court was the degree of hardship that accommodating Protos's request for Saturdays off would have imposed on Volkswagen. Finding that "defendant suffered no economic loss" because of Protos's absence, and that the "efficiency, production, quality and morale" of her segment of the Trim Department and the entire assembly line remained intact without her, the district court ruled that Volkswagen could have accommodated her "without undue hardship and at no cost." Thus, the company was held to have violated the statute.

Section 703(a)(1) of the Civil Rights Act of 1964, Title VII, makes it an unlawful employment practice to "discharge *   *   *, or otherwise to discriminate against any individual with respect to his compensation, terms, conditions or privileges of employment, because of such individual's race, color, religion, sex, or national origin." Section 701(j) of the Act, added by Congress in a 1972 amendment, elaborated on this provision by defining religion:

> The term 'religion' includes all aspects of religious observance and practice, as well as belief, unless an employer demonstrates that he is unable to reasonably accommodate an employee's or prospective employee's religious observance or practice without undue hardship on the conduct of the employer's business.

*   *   *   *

*   *   * [S]everal courts of appeals have set forth guidelines to use in evaluating a religious accommodation case: those guidelines are modeled after the shifting burdens of proof employed in race and gender discrimination suits under Title VII. A plaintiff must first establish a *prima facie* case, by showing: "(1) he or she has a bona fide religious belief that conflicts with an employment requirement; (2) he or she informed the employer of this belief; (3) he or she was disciplined for failure to comply with the conflicting employment requirement."

Once a plaintiff establishes a *prima facie* case, the burden then shifts to the employer to produce evidence showing that it cannot reasonably accommodate the worker without incurring undue hardship.

In the case at hand, the district judge followed these guidelines in considering the evidence. His determination that Protos established a *prima facie* case is not disputed on appeal. Volkswagen agrees that Protos's religious beliefs are sincere, and it is clear that her religion forbade her to work on Saturdays. It is also evident that she informed her employer of her beliefs and was disciplined for failure to work on Saturdays.

Thus, the primary issue is whether the district court erred in determining that the company would not have to incur even a *"de minimis* cost" to accommodate Protos. *   *   *

Here, the question of hardship was vigorously disputed at trial. The evidence showed that Volkswagen regularly maintained, along with employees assigned to specific posts on the assembly line, a crew of roving absentee relief operators (ARO) to be deployed as substitutes for absent employees. Protos introduced witnesses who testified that her job was easily learned, and that the line operated as efficiently when an ARO served in her stead as when she performed the job. Volkswagen's witnesses, by contrast, testified that the line operated with diminished efficiency in Protos's absence.

The court resolved this conflict in favor of Protos, finding that "plaintiff's witnesses were more credible than the witnesses presented by the defendant," and that "the efficiency, production, quality and morale of Trim 15 and the entire assembly line remained intact during her absence." While Volkswagen argues that plant-wide absenteeism was especially high on Saturdays, and that Protos's absence therefore was felt more than it would otherwise have been, evidence supporting this contention was presented to the district court, and rejected as unpersuasive.
*   *   *   *

To summarize, we hold that the district court did not err in ruling that Volkswagen could have accommodated Protos without "undue hardship," and that Title VII's religious accommodation requirement does not violate the Establishment Clause.

The court found that Protos had been discriminated against based on her religious views. In doing so, the court stated that the following three factors must be established to have a prima facie *case: (1) The employee has a bona fide religious belief that conflicts with an employment requirement; (2) he or she informed the employer of this belief; (3) he or she was disciplined for failure to comply with the conflicting employment requirement. Once a plaintiff has established a* prima facie *case, the burden then shifts to the employer to produce evidence showing that the company cannot reasonably accommodate the worker without incurring undue hardship.*

DECISION AND REMEDY

Discrimination Based on National Origin While prohibiting discrimination based on national origin, Title VII does not define the term. By case law, national origin refers to the country where a person is born or from which his or her ancestors came. In 1980, the EEOC issued guidelines that defined national origin discrimination to include denial of equal employment opportunity because of an individual's, or his or her ancestors', place of origin, or because an individual has the physical, cultural, or linguistic characteristics of a national origin group.

The question of discrimination against aliens is a thorny one, but Title VII does not prohibit discrimination against aliens. Such discrimination may, however, violate the Civil Rights Act of 1866 (discussed in the next subsection), or it may violate a union's duty of fair representation. The Civil Rights Act of 1866 made it illegal to discriminate, contractually or otherwise, based on race.

Title VII's prohibition of national origin discrimination forbids a foreign corporation doing business in the United States from discriminating in favor of its own nationals. This prohibition is waived if such discrimination is permitted specifically by a treaty.

Discrimination Based on Race Discrimination in employment on the basis of race has existed in this country for over 300 years. Over the last 100 years, serious attempts have been made to live up to the words in the Declaration of Independence "We hold these truths to be self-evident, that all

Men are created equal[.]" The Civil Rights Acts of 1866, 1871, 1875, and 1964, along with the Thirteenth, Fourteenth, and Fifteenth Amendments (called the Civil War Amendments) to the Constitution, have been applied to outlaw racial discrimination. Congress has not only forbidden racial discrimination by the government but has also directly legislated that private individuals cannot violate the constitutional rights of other individuals.

Today, Title VII is the cornerstone of employment antidiscrimination law. **Affirmative action** is used to give work opportunities to those who have been deprived of employment based on race or other nonwork-related criteria. Affirmative action consists of a set of programs, some of which are required by court decrees, some by national and state legislation, and some by administrative regulation.

Title VII's protection has always applied to nonwhite classes. Recent court decisions have concluded that Title VII prohibits racial discrimination against the white class (called **reverse discrimination**) based on the same standards applicable to nonwhites.

The Administration and Enforcement of Title VII

The Equal Employment Opportunity Commission is a five-member administrative agency created by the 1964 Civil Rights Act to administer Title VII. Members are appointed by the president with the advice and consent of the Senate. No more than three members may be of the same political party. Each serves a five-year term.

The EEOC can issue interpretive guidelines and regulations that do not, however, have the force of law. Rather, they give notice of the commission's enforcement policy. The EEOC also has been charged with investigatory powers. It has broad authority to require the production of documentary evidence, to hold hearings, and to subpoena and examine witnesses under oath. The EEOC may also require the covered parties to keep statistics and records of employment and employment practices.

When an aggrieved person files charges or when the commission members determine that a pattern or practice of illegal discrimination exists, the commission can litigate. Nonetheless, the commission must have the opportunity to attempt conciliation between the parties prior to filing the suit.

EEOC Procedures   Any person claiming to be aggrieved may file a charge of discrimination with the EEOC. A member of the EEOC or others acting on behalf of an aggrieved person may likewise file a charge. Generally speaking, the charge must be filed within 180 days after the discriminatory action. Whenever a state or local fair employment practices agency exists, the commission will defer to it for 60 days. If, at the end of 60 days, the dispute has not been resolved, the EEOC will take over.

Within ten days of the filing of a charge with the EEOC (or within ten days of the EEOC taking over), the agency must notify the employer. Once notified, the employer is prohibited from retaliation against the charging employee. Once the employer has been notified, the EEOC investigates the charge. If it finds reasonable cause to believe that Title VII has been violated, it will attempt to resolve the dispute by informal means.

Even when both the EEOC and the company are willing to accept a settlement, if the charging party does not accept it, his or her right to go to court to seek more favorable results cannot be prejudiced. If, on the other hand, the EEOC does not find reasonable cause to believe a violation has occurred, it will notify the charging party and inform him or her of the right to pursue the matter in court. When informal means do not result in a settlement, the EEOC may bring an action 30 days after the charge is filed.

Statutory Defenses   Title VII's prohibitions against discrimination are subject to three main statutory exceptions:

1. **Bona fide occupational qualifications (BFOQs)**
2. **Bona fide seniority or merit systems**
3. **Professionally developed ability tests.**

Bona Fide Occupational Qualifications   This defense allows discrimination in hiring and referrals where sex, religion, or national origin (but not race) is a "bona fide occupational qualification reasonably necessary to the normal operation of that particular business." Such a defense has been very narrowly interpreted by the courts. For example, the BFOQ defense is allowed in situations where sex or national origin is inherently part of the qualification for the job, such as for a wet nurse, or is necessary for authenticity, such as for actors or actresses.

The burden is on the defendant to establish a BFOQ defense. To do so, the defendant must show that the alleged discrimination is a business necessity. Customer preference does not make a particular sex, religion, or national origin a BFOQ.

Bona Fide Seniority Systems   It is not unlawful for there to be differences in the terms, conditions, or privileges of employment based on a bona fide seniority (or merit) system. The differences, however, cannot be the result of an intent to discriminate. Most collective bargaining agreements include detailed seniority systems. Indeed, such seniority systems are one of the most important aspects of collective bargaining agreements.

In order for the seniority system to qualify as an exception to Title VII, the system must be bona fide. Four factors are necessary for a seniority system to be bona fide:

1. The system must apply equally to all persons.
2. The seniority units (that is, occupational groupings for purposes of hiring, promoting, and terminating) must follow industry practices, and the units must constitute separate collective bargaining units.
3. The seniority system must not have its genesis in racial discrimination.
4. The system must be maintained free from any illegal racial purpose.

Professionally Developed Ability Tests Employers may give and act on the results of any professionally developed ability test. An ability test, its administration, and the actions based on the results must not be intended to discriminate in any prohibited way. The employer must meet the burden of proving that the particular test is job related if the test has the effect of eliminating a disproportionate number of members of a protected class. Job relation ordinarily must be proved by validation studies meeting professional standards.

Immigration Acts

The **Immigration Reform and Control Act** of 1986 makes it illegal for an employer knowingly to hire unauthorized aliens. The statute defines an unauthorized alien as an individual who is not admitted as a permanent United States resident or who is not eligible to work in the United States.

Verification of newly hired employees, through documentation supplied by each employee, is now required. An employee may comply in two ways: First, the employee may prove his or her identity and employment authorization through various documents. The employer cannot refuse to honor documents that on their face reasonably appear to be genuine. Nor can the employer request an applicant to present more or different documents than are required by law. For an employer to have different requirements is an unfair employment practice.

Once employment eligibility has been established, an employer on an individual basis may legally prefer a United States citizen or national over an *equally qualified* alien to fill a specific position. An employer may not adopt a blanket policy of always preferring a qualified citizen over a qualified alien, however, as this practice violates the antidiscrimination laws. The employer must fill out Form I-9, which records the employee's documents. This must be done within 24 hours after hiring. This form must be kept by the business for three years from the date of employment.

The **Immigration Act** of 1990 was the first comprehensive overhaul of legal immigration in 25 years. The previous law favored immigration based on family ties with U.S. citizens or nationals. The new law favors immigrants based on their potential ability to contribute to the economy. Managers, professionals, and skilled laborers have preference under this law.

Americans with Disabilities Act

The **Americans with Disabilities Act (ADA)** of 1990 gives federal civil rights protection to people with disabilities. Congress has set a national mandate to prohibit discrimination in business and public settings against people with disabilities.

Employers with 25 or more employees may no longer discriminate against a *qualified* applicant who happens to be disabilitied. By 1994, the number of employees drops to fifteen. The act defines a person with disabilities as any person who (1) has a physical or mental impairment that *substantially* limits one or more of the person's major life activities; (2) has a record of such an impairment; or (3) is regarded as having such an impairment. This protection extends to persons who have recovered from earlier disabilities, such as a person whose cancer is in remission and who is currently cancer free; in the past, this person would not have been hired. The act also extends protection to persons with Acquired Immune Deficiency Syndrome (AIDS).

Employers must make "reasonable accommodations" to facilitate the employment of people with disabilities. These accommodations include making facilities accessible; restructuring jobs; accommodating work schedules; and providing training policies and materials to *qualified* applicants. Employers may show *undue hardship* and thus be excused from making reasonable accommodations. The defense of undue hardship means that significant difficulty or expense is involved in making reasonable accommodations; it includes a review of the overall financial resources of the employer.

Equal Pay Act

The **Equal Pay Act** of 1963 was enacted as an amendment to the Fair Labor Standards Act of 1938. The act is administered by the Equal Employment Opportunity Commission, and it concerns only gender-based discrimination and ques-

What's In a Name?

The National Organization for Women threatened in October 1982 to file charges against a local police department in Palm Beach County, Florida. The patrol cars were emblazoned with the word *patrolman*, and the local group believed that this discouraged women from applying for police jobs.

Such concern with language may seem at first to be misplaced. But language is an important barometer of the society that uses it. For example, if a language contains phrases like *lady lawyer* or *woman doctor*, you can be sure that women are new to these fields in that society. Language also directs and limits what we can think about. When you hear the word *fireman* or *policeman*, it is hard to think of a woman in uniform. But a firefighter or police officer is something any youngster could grow up to be.

Under Title VII, employers may not use advertisements that indicate, through language or otherwise, any preference in hiring for a particular race, color, religion, gender, or national origin (except when a BFOQ exists). Similarly, the Age Discrimination in Employment Act forbids want ads that imply that older workers need not apply. An advertisement for a "girl Friday" or for an "ambitious young salesman," for example, might be unacceptable on both counts.

Are prospective applicants really deterred by these language cues and other indications, such as listing certain help-wanted ads under sex-segregated columns that are headed "Jobs—Male Interest"? Some studies show this to be the case. In one study,[a] 52 women were asked to rate their willingness to apply for each of 32 jobs. When the jobs were separated and labeled by gender, less than half of the women were as likely to apply for "male-interest" as for "female-interest" jobs. When the same ads were listed alphabetically with no reference to sex, more than 80 percent of the women preferred the "male-interest" jobs—not a surprising result in at least one respect: These jobs averaged higher pay.

[a]Testimony of Sandra L. Bem and Daryl J. Bem, then of the Department of Psychology at Carnegie-Mellon University, reproduced in Hearings on Section 805 of H.R. 16098, pp. 892–894, Special Subcommittee on Education of the House Committee on Education and Labor, July 31, 1970.

tions of pay. Basically, it prohibits discrimination in wages paid for equal work on jobs that require equal skills, effort, and responsibility and that are performed under similar conditions. Job content rather than job description controls in all cases.

For the equal pay requirements to apply, the act requires that male and female employees must work at the same establishment. The issue is not the equivalence of the employees' skills and training. The issue is whether the jobs performed by the two employees are substantially equal or not. Small differences in job content do not justify higher pay for one gender. The courts look to primary duties involved in the two jobs. For example, a barber and a beautician are considered to do essentially equal work. So, too, are a tailor and a seamstress.

Enforcement

The government or private parties may bring suit under the Equal Pay Act. If, however, the government sues on behalf of a particular employee, that employee's right to sue is cut off unless, of course, the employee has already brought suit. All suits must be commenced within two years of the violation or three years if the violation is willful. Each payday is a new violation. No employer may retaliate against an employee bringing suit or in any other way attempting to enforce her or his rights under the act.

Employers may not reduce the wages of men in order to be in compliance with the act; rather, the wages of women must be increased. Back pay for up to two years (three years if the violation is willful) is available to the successful employee. Liquidated damages equal to the amount of back pay will be awarded as a penalty unless there were reasonable grounds for the employer to form a good-faith belief that he or she was actually acting lawfully. A successful plaintiff may also recover attorneys' fees.

Exceptions

Specific exceptions are provided in the Equal Pay Act. Whenever pay differentials are based on seniority systems, merit systems, piecework, production bonus systems, or on any considerations other than sex, they are allowed. These systems must be created in good faith and not created with the intention of specifically avoiding the act.

Bona fide training programs may justify pay discrimination. As with the seniority or merit system, the training program must be formal, communicated to employees, and have an articulated training goal. If, however, women employees are excluded from a training program, payment of a premium to male trainees is not defensible.

For example, shift differentials or bonuses paid because of job training would not violate the act as long as the jobs or bonuses were available to both males and females. The issue as to shift differentials is confronted in the following case.

BACKGROUND AND FACTS *Corning Glass Works, the petitioner, paid a higher base wage to male night shift inspectors than it paid to female inspectors performing the same tasks on the day shift. In two suits arising under the Equal Pay Act, two separate courts of appeals reached different conclusions as to whether Corning's actions violated the principle of equal pay for equal work regardless of gender. The Supreme Court resolved the conflict between the two appellate court decisions.*

Case 22.4
CORNING GLASS WORKS v. BRENNAN
Supreme Court of the United States, 1974.
417 U.S. 188, 94 S.Ct. 2223, 41 L.Ed.2d 1.

Justice MARSHALL delivered the opinion of the Court.
*   *   *   *

Congress' purpose in enacting the Equal Pay Act was to remedy what was perceived to be a serious and endemic problem of employment discrimination in private industry—the fact that the wage structure of "many segments of American industry has been based on an ancient but outmoded belief that a man, because of his role in society, should be paid more than a woman even though his duties are the same."
*   *   *   *

The Act also establishes four exceptions—three specific and one a general catchall provision—where different payment to employees of opposite sexes "is made pursuant to (i) a seniority system; (ii) a merit system; (iii) a system which measures earnings by quantity or quality of production; or (iv) a differential based on any other factor other than sex." Again, while the Act is silent on this question, its structure and history also suggest that once the Secretary has carried out his burden of showing that the employer pays workers of one sex more than workers of the opposite sex for equal work, the burden shifts to the employer to show that the differential is justified under one of the Act's four exceptions. All of the many lower courts that have considered this question have so held, and this view is consistent with the general rule that the application of an exemption under the Fair Labor Standards Act is a matter of affirmative defense on which the employer has the burden of proof.

The contentions of the parties in this case reflect the Act's underlying framework. Corning argues that the Secretary has failed to prove that Corning ever violated the Act because day shift work is not "performed under similar working conditions" as night shift work. The Secretary maintains that day shift and night shift work are performed under "similar working conditions" within the meaning of the Act. Although the Secretary recognizes that higher wages may be paid for night shift work, the Secretary contends that such a shift differential would be based upon a "factor other than sex" within the catchall exception to the Act and that Corning has failed to carry its burden of proof that its higher base wage for male night inspectors was in fact based on any factor other than sex.

*   *   *   *

While a layman might well assume that time of day worked reflects one aspect of a job's "working conditions," the term has a different and much more specific meaning in the language of industrial relations. As Corning's own representative testified at the hearings, the element of working conditions encompasses two subfactors: "surroundings" and "hazards." "Surroundings" measures the elements, such as toxic chemicals or fumes, regularly encountered by a worker, their intensity, and their frequency. "Hazards" takes into account the physical hazards regularly encountered, their frequency, and the severity of injury they can cause. This definition of "working conditions" is not only manifested in Corning's own job evaluation plans but is also well accepted across a wide range of American industry.

Nowhere in any of these definitions is time of day worked mentioned as a relevant criterion. The fact of the matter is that the concept of "working conditions," as used in the specialized language of job evaluation systems, simply does not encompass shift differentials. Indeed, while Corning now argues that night inspection work is not equal to day inspection work, all of its own job evaluation plans, including the one now in effect, have consistently treated them as equal in all respects including working conditions.

*   *   *   *

We agree with Judge Friendly that "in light of this apparent congressional understanding, we cannot hold that Corning, by allowing some—or even many—women to move into the higher paid night jobs, achieved full compliance with the Act. Corning's action still left the inspectors on the day shift—virtually all women—earning a lower base wage than the night shift inspectors because of a differential initially based on sex and still not justified by any other consideration; in effect, Corning was still taking advantage of the availability of female labor to fill its day shift at a differentially low wage rate not justified by any factor other than sex."

DECISION AND REMEDY   *The Supreme Court ruled that Corning had discriminated against female employees through the use of different base wages for night and day workers. The company's attempt to show that the wage differential was based on a neutral factor other than gender was unsuccessful. The wage differential operated to perpetuate the company's prior illegal practice of paying women less than men for equal work.*

Affirmative Action

Affirmative action can be defined as the remedial step taken to improve work opportunities for women, for racial and ethnic minorities, and for other people considered to have been deprived of job opportunities in the past.

Great attention has been paid to establishing goals under numerous affirmative action programs. No less important, however, are the identification and elimination of artificial barriers to equal employment. In addition, a work-force analysis may be undertaken to determine if women and protected minority men are being discriminated against, and goals and timetables may be developed to correct any substantial disparities. Note that these goals and timetables are not quotas. If an employer makes a good-faith effort to meet goals and timetables, the requirements of affirmative action are met.

It is the employer's responsibility to publicize the existence of affirmative action programs, both internally and externally. Supervisors and managers must be advised of the company's policy and of their responsibilities in implementing it. Recruitment sources must also be advised of the company policy. The company must take active steps to expand its traditional recruitment sources to include those sources likely to result in a higher flow of protected minority and female applicants. Finally, the employer must establish a procedure for monitoring the success of the program.

Affirmative action has been criticized as causing reverse discrimination. A person with better qualifications will be denied a job opportunity when a less-qualified individual from a protected class is hired or promoted. The person with the lesser qualifications must be minimally qualified for the job opportunity. This issue of reverse discrimination has now been decided by the United States Supreme Court in the following case.

BACKGROUND AND FACTS *The Santa Clara County Transportation Agency voluntarily adopted an affirmative action plan for hiring and promoting minorities and women in 1978. The plan provided that, in making promotions to jobs that had been traditionally segregated, the person's sex and ethnicity could be considered. The plan set short-range goals and annually adjusted these goals so that they could serve as a realistic guide for actual employment decisions. The long-term goal was to have a work force whose composition reflected the proportion of minorities and women in the local area's general work force.*

In 1979, the agency announced a vacancy for a road dispatcher. Twelve employees applied for the promotion, including Joyce, a woman, and Johnson, a man. Both were deemed qualified for the job after their applications had been reviewed by two panels. Johnson was tied for second, while Joyce was ranked next lower by two points. At the time, the agency had never employed a woman as a road dispatcher. Johnson was recommended to be promoted by a panel who reviewed both records.

The agency's affirmative action coordinator had the responsibility of keeping the director of the agency informed of opportunities for the agency to accomplish its objectives under the plan. The coordinator recommended that Joyce be hired for the job after he had also reviewed both applications with their respective qualifications, test scores, expertise, and background and had taken affirmative action matters into consideration.

The director accepted the recommendation of the coordinator and promoted Joyce. He considered the two-point difference in her ranking to be insignificant as he looked at the whole picture.

Johnson filed a complaint with the Equal Employment Opportunity Commission. He received a right-to-sue letter from the EEOC. The district court held for Johnson, but that decision was overturned by the Ninth Circuit Court of Appeals.

Case 22.5
JOHNSON v. TRANSPORTATION AGENCY
Supreme Court of the United States, 1987.
480 U.S. 616, 107 S.Ct. 1442, 94 L.Ed.2d 615.

Justice BRENNAN delivered the opinion of the Court.

*   *   *   *

As a preliminary matter, we note that petitioner bears the burden of establishing the invalidity of the Agency's Plan. Only last term in *Wygant v. Jackson Board of Education*, we held that "[t]he ultimate burden remains with the employees to demonstrate the unconstitutionality of an affirmative-action program," and we see no basis for a different ruling regarding a plan's alleged violation of Title VII.
*   *   * Once a plaintiff establishes a *prima facie* case that race or sex has been taken into account in an employer's employment decision, the burden shifts to the

employer to articulate a nondiscriminatory rationale for its decision. The existence of an affirmative action plan provides such a rationale. If such a plan is articulated as the basis for the employer's decision, the burden shifts to the plaintiff to prove that the employer's justification is pretextual and the plan is invalid.

The first issue is therefore whether consideration of the sex of applicants for skilled craft jobs was justified by the existence of a "manifest imbalance" that reflected underrepresentation of women in "traditionally segregated job categories." In determining whether an imbalance exists that would justify taking sex or race into account, a comparison of the percentage of minorities or women in the employer's work force with the percentage in the area labor market or general population is appropriate in analyzing jobs that require no special expertise.

Where a job requires special training, however, the comparison should be with those in the labor force who possess the relevant qualifications. The requirement that the "manifest imbalance" relate to a "traditionally segregated job category" provides assurance both that sex or race will be taken into account in a manner consistent with Title VII's purpose of eliminating the effects of employment discrimination, and that the interests of those employees not benefitting from the plan will not be unduly infringed.

It is clear that the decision to hire Joyce was made pursuant to an Agency plan that directed that sex or race be taken into account for the purpose of remedying underrepresentation. The Agency Plan acknowledged the "limited opportunities that have existed in the past" for women to find employment in certain job classifications "where women have not been traditionally employed in significant numbers." As a result, observed the Plan, women were concentrated in traditionally female jobs in the Agency, and represented a lower percentage in other job classifications than would be expected if such traditional segregation had not occurred.

* * * *

We next consider whether the Agency Plan unnecessarily trammeled the rights of male employees or created an absolute bar to their advancement. In contrast to the plan in [another case] which provided that 50% of the positions in the craft training program were exclusively for blacks, and to the consent decree upheld last term in *Firefighters v. Cleveland*, which required the promotion of specific numbers of minorities, the Plan sets aside no positions for women. The Plan expressly states that "[t]he 'goals' established for each Division should not be construed as 'quotas' that must be met." Rather, the Plan merely authorizes that consideration be given to affirmative action concerns when evaluating qualified applicants. As the Agency Director testified, the sex of Joyce was but one of numerous factors he took into account in arriving at his decision. The Plan thus resembles the "Harvard Plan" which considers race along with other criteria in determining admission to the college. "In such an admission program, race or ethnic background may be deemed a 'plus' in a particular applicant's file, yet it does not insulate the individual from comparison with all other candidates for the available seats." Similarly, the Agency Plan requires women to compete with all other qualified applicants. No persons are automatically excluded from consideration; all are able to have their qualifications weighed against those of other applicants.

In addition, petitioner had no absolute entitlement to the road dispatcher position. Seven of the applicants were classified as qualified and eligible, and the Agency Director was authorized to promote any of the seven. Thus, denial of the promotion unsettled no legitimate firmly rooted expectation on the part of the petitioner. Furthermore, while the petitioner in this case was denied a promotion, he retained his employment with the Agency, at the same salary and with the same seniority, and remained eligible for other promotions.

* * * *

We therefore hold that the Agency appropriately took into account as one factor the sex of Diane Joyce in determining that she should be promoted to the road dispatcher position. The decision to do so was made pursuant to an affirmative action plan that represents a moderate, flexible, case-by-case approach to effecting a gradual improvement in the representation of minorities and women in the Agency's work force. Such a plan is fully consistent with Title VII, for it embodies the contribution that voluntary employer action can make in eliminating the vestiges of discrimination in the workplace.

The judgment of the court of appeals was affirmed. The agency had appropriately taken into account Joyce's sex as one factor in determining that she should be promoted. The Supreme Court found that the agency's plan was moderate and flexible and that it provided a case-by-case approach to reaching the long-term goal of improvement in the representation of minorities and women in the agency's work force.

DECISION AND REMEDY

Legal Highlight

Posting of Labor Laws

Specific employee information notices must be posted at every separate business location. The federal government requires information to be posted on the Employee Polygraph Protection Act, Equal Employment Opportunity Act, Americans with Disabilities Act, and the federal minimum wage, as well as job safety and health protection information. Failure to do so may result in federal penalties being assessed. Is your employer in compliance with these requirements?

Additional Statutory Provisions

The 1991 Civil Rights Act gives workers additional rights to recover compensatory and punitive damages if there is harassment or other intentional discrimination based on sex, religion, or disability. Before money damages will be awarded, the act requires that the employee demonstrate that the employer engaged in a discriminatory practice with malice or reckless indifference. The act sets limits on the combined compensatory and punitive damages based on a sliding scale: for companies hiring 14 to 100 employees, $50,000; 101 to 200 employees, $100,000; 201 to 500 employees, $200,000; and over 501 employees, $300,000.

The 1991 Civil Rights Act does limit remedies when hiring is at issue. An applicant can obtain an injunction, attorneys' fees, and court costs if there is discrimination based upon race, religion, sex, or national origin. The applicant cannot recover back pay but will be hired.

The 1991 Civil Rights Act, Title VII of the Civil Rights Act of 1964, and the Americans with Disabilities Act apply also to U.S.-based companies operating in foreign nations. Businesses are exempted from compliance if such companies would violate a foreign country's laws.

Privacy Rights of Employees

In 1928, the United States Supreme Court established the right of privacy. Justice Louis D. Brandeis wrote that it is "the right to be let alone— the most comprehensive of rights and the right most valued by civilized man." The Court based this right on the Fourth Amendment's proscriptions against illegal searches and seizures by the government.

The right of privacy is used to oppose Acquired Immune Deficiency Syndrome (AIDS) testing. The

Ethical Considerations

Genetic Testing

Medical biotechnology can now determine genetic information from minute bits of blood and tissue samples. Genetic information can point out certain characteristics in an individual that may lead to a disease process, such as colon cancer, or an inherited disease, such as Huntington's chorea. Carrying a genetic characteristic is not a disability unless it later develops into a physical disease.

Cases exist where people have been discriminated against on the basis of results from genetic testing. Is it ethical for a business to discriminate against a person who has the potential of becoming ill, possibly in 30 years? When people donate blood and have routine blood tests, they do not expect the samples to be further analyzed to determine what genetic problems may exist. Do people have any right to privacy when blood or tissue samples are taken? Should employers have access to this information if the tests are conducted at their expense, such as in a company physical examination? Can an employer ethically require this information?

right is also used to limit the distribution of information contained in an employee's record of employment.

Polygraphs

For many years, both the government and private businesses used polygraph tests as a condition for employment, retention, or promotion. These tests presented one major problem: They had to be subjectively interpreted by an individual; therefore, the validity of the test was based upon the training and knowledge of the interviewer. Many innocent persons were denied employment based upon inaccurate interpretations of their polygraph tests.

To rectify this situation, Congress adopted the **Employee Polygraph Protection Act** of 1988. This act makes it unlawful to use a polygraph except under restricted conditions. Among these exceptions are (1) national defense, (2) ongoing investigations, (3) drug security, drug theft, or drug diversion investigations, and (4) armored car and security personnel. The major exception is that of ongoing investigations. To terminate an employee under this exemption, there must be additional supporting evidence establishing that the employee was involved in a theft, embezzlement, or other unlawful activity against the employer.

Drug Testing

An employer has a right to test an applicant for drugs prior to hiring. The 1991 Civil Rights Act exempts from disparate impact challenges employers' efforts to screen out drug abusers. In addition, an employer has a right to test an employee if the employer thinks the employee is under the influence of alcohol or drugs. Employees who hold very sensitive jobs, such as national security employees, are tested at random. Persons involved with aviation, railroads, trucking, or other jobs involved with public safety are also subject to drug testing.

The real problem lies in the area of random drug testing in nonsensitive areas. The states are split on this issue, and Congress has not set a public policy. Some courts have found that random testing does violate an individual's reasonable and legitimate expectation of privacy because of the personal information obtainable from a person's body fluids.

Employee Records

Two legal theories apply to the use and distribution of information contained in an employee's personnel file: defamation and invasion of the right to privacy. A defamation case is founded on an

International Considerations

Progress Against Discrimination

In the 1960s, the United States started to develop its antidiscrimination laws, and the process has continued as further discrimination patterns have become apparent. Most countries have not developed laws as stringent as those in the United States. Few countries provide any protection for alien workers, prevent discrimination based on religious beliefs, or provide help to those of a different race or color. Still, progress in this area is being made, although it is slow.

The European Community (EC) has adopted nonbinding legislation prohibiting sexual harassment. The code is a guide for employers and unions in all twelve member countries of the EC. Until this legislation was adopted, individual countries had no laws specifically prohibiting sexual harassment. The EC has, however, laws requiring equal pay for work of equal value for women. In addition, EC members have laws providing mandatory paid parental leave and requiring management to hold open a position until a woman returns from maternity leave. Child care is provided for by a combination of government, management, and union programs.

Older workers are protected from discrimination in the United States. The benefits of hiring and continuing to employ older workers are being discovered by management around the world. For example, a firm in Great Britain, annoyed at the high turnover of its younger workers, decided to hire workers over age 55. Much to the surprise of the firm, the benefits were immediate. Absenteeism dropped dramatically, losses from employee theft were down, employee turnover dropped, and fewer workers' compensation claims were reported. Customer satisfaction went up and business increased. The older workers took more interest in knowing the products and explaining them to customers. These workers' politeness was very much appreciated by the customers. The experiment was such a success that the firm plans to hire more older workers in its other stores.

---

employer communicating harmful information about a current or prior employee. Most of these communications are granted a limited privilege. As long as an employer is communicating with a prospective new employer, there is no major problem unless it can be proved that the first employer's comments are made with malice. To limit a claim that the information was released with the intent of harming a former employee, only the basic employment history should be disclosed. This information would be limited to job title, dates of employment, and ending salary.

If, on the other hand, an employer communicates to current employees that the terminated employee was fired on the basis of moral or other reasons, this can give rise to legal problems. These statements could go beyond the limited privilege that the law grants. Further, this can be considered an invasion of the right to privacy, even if what is disclosed is true.

Discriminatory Questions

One of the more important business procedures is the hiring of new employees. Before an individual is hired, most businesses have standard employment applications or questions. Some of the information sought may be considered discriminatory in nature. Questions that can be discriminatory sometimes take forms like these:

1. What was your maiden name?
2. How old are your children? How old is your youngest child?
3. What is your birth date?
4. Have you ever declared bankruptcy?
5. Are you married? (Single? Divorced? Separated? Widowed?)
6. (A more subtle form of the same question): Is there anyone in your life who strongly influences your decisions?
7. Who will care for your children while you are working?
8. How long have you lived at your present address?
9. What is your father's name?
10. Have you ever had your wages garnished?
11. Where do you bank? Do you have any loans outstanding?
12. Do you own or rent your home?
13. Were you ever arrested?
14. What religious group do you belong to? What is the name of your priest? (Rabbi? Minister?)
15. Where does your husband (wife, father, mother) work?
16. How did you learn to speak Spanish (German, Russian, and so on)?
17. List for me all the societies, clubs, and lodges you belong to.

Thinking through these questions before they come up will help an applicant to handle them in the best way. They may never come up. If they do, though, there are options.

Answering militantly ("I'll see you in court for asking me that!") is a no-win choice. Answering something like "Legally I do not have to provide you with that information" is not the best option either.

Try to answer so as to: (1) deflect that line of questioning courteously, (2) give the interviewer some useful, helpful information, and (3) not put him or her in the wrong. Suppose the interviewer has asked, "How will you have your children cared for while you work?" One way to answer is "If you'll show how this question is related to my ability to do a good job for you, I'll be glad to answer." Or applicants can say child care is all taken care of and then refer to their record of low absenteeism in their current job, despite family responsibilities.

Another way is to try to think why the interviewer is asking a particular question—why he or she is worried about how you will have your children cared for—and *restate the question behind the question*. You might say, "If by asking me that question you really mean, 'Will I be on the job every day, on time, and ready to give my full attention and energy to the job?,' the answer is most definitely 'Yes.'"

A third option is a little riskier but some-times effective. *If* the rapport up until that question has been pleasant and *if* you are pretty sure you are not talking to an ogre, you might be able to laugh pleasantly and say, "I'll bet you didn't really mean to ask me that question, did you?"

Most often, interviewers will back away from the "don't-ask" questions if the applicants show in a low-key and courteous way that they want to answer only questions directly related to their qualifications for the job. If the interviewer does not back away, the applicant might reconsider whether he or she really wants to work for this type of organization. Worse than not being hired is being hired by an organization where you would be unhappy.

Before the interview, then, think through all the possible questions, good and bad, that you might be asked, and determine how you will respond. Update your research on the company, too, because the third part of the interview usually consists of the interviewer's question: "Now what questions do you have that I can answer?"

■ *Source: Business Correspondence for Today*, by J. W. Gilsdorf. Copyright © 1989. Reprinted by permission of John Wiley & Sons, Inc.

Summary

This chapter has emphasized laws that seek to prevent discrimination in employment. The major federal statutory provisions are Title VII of the Civil Rights Act of 1964 and the Equal Pay Act of 1963. There are also other acts that have attempted to restrict discrimination in the workplace based on age or physical disabilities.

Title VII prohibits discrimination for employment based on race, sex, color, religion, or national origin. It covers employers with fifteen or more employees, labor unions with fifteen or more members, and employment agencies. Certain exemptions are based on religious or ethnic grounds.

Two basic legal theories underlie actions based on Title VII: the disparate treatment theory, which involves treatment of any individual that differs from treatment of other employees based on his or her background or sex, and the disparate impact theory, in which, although on the surface a certain practice is not discriminatory, its effect is to discriminate against a protected class. Under either theory, the employer can be found liable.

Under Title VII, sex discrimination is illegal, but this does not cover discrimination based on sexual preference. It does, however, cover sexual harassment and discrimination based on sex in pension and life insurance plans.

The Equal Employment Opportunity Commission (EEOC) is charged with the enforcement of Title VII. A person files a charge with the EEOC, which then attempts to settle, through conciliation procedures, the potential dispute. The employer has three statutory defenses to any action under Title VII: (1) bona fide occupational qualifications (BFOQs), (2) bona fide seniority or merit system, and (3) professionally developed ability tests.

The other major federal statutory provision is the Equal Pay Act of 1963, which is also administered by the EEOC. It prohibits discrimination on the basis of gender in wages paid for equal work on jobs that require equal skills, effort, and responsibility and that are performed under similar conditions. Some exemptions to the act allow different payment because of the job situation, such as shift differentials.

Affirmative action is the process of improving work opportunities for women and others who have in the past been discriminated against. The idea behind affirmative action plans is that, if a member of a protected class has the necessary requirements for an employment position, that individual should be given the job over a person who is not a member of a protected class. Although it might seem that a person is being discriminated against because he or she is not within the protected class, the United States Supreme Court has approved these plans.

Key Terms

affirmative action (553)
Americans with Disabilities
    Act (555)
bona fide occupational
    qualifications (BFOQs)
    (554)

bona fide seniority or merit
    systems (554)
Civil Rights Act, Title VII
    (546)
disparate impact (546)
disparate treatment (546)

Employee Polygraph
    Protection Act (562)
Equal Employment
    Opportunity Commission
    (EEOC) (548)
Equal Pay Act (555)

Immigration Act (555)
Immigration Reform and
 Control Act (555)

Pregnancy Discrimination Act
 (549)
professionally developed

ability tests (554)
reverse discrimination (553)

Questions and Case Problems

1. Discuss fully which of the following constitutes a violation of the 1964 Civil Rights Act, Title VII, as amended.
a. Causeway, Inc., is a consulting firm and has ten employees. These employees travel on consulting jobs in seven states. Causeway has an employment record of hiring only white males.
b. Filmtex, Inc., is making a film about Africa. Filmtex needs to employ approximately 100 extras for this picture. Filmtex advertises in all major newspapers in Southern California for the hiring of these extras. The ad states that only African Americans need apply.
c. Green is a major processor of cheese sold throughout the United States. Green employs 100 employees at its principal processing plant. The plant is located in Windward City, whose population is 50 percent white, 25 percent African American, and the balance Hispanic, Asian, and so on. Green requires a high school diploma as a condition of employment on its cleanup crew. Three-fourths of the white population complete high school, as compared to only one-fourth of the minority population. Green has an all-white cleaning crew.

2. Four women were employed to guard female prisoners. They were paid less than male guards who guarded male prisoners. The County of Washington argued that the jobs were not substantially equal because the men supervised ten times as many prisoners per guard as did the female guards. The women argued that the pay discrepancy was attributable to intentional sex discrimination. Who prevails and why? [County of Washington, v. Gunther, 452 U.S. 161, 101 S.Ct. 2242, 68 L.Ed.2d 751 (1981)]

3. The state of Connecticut required the passing of a written examination before a person could be considered for a supervisor position. Those taking the tests had a 79 percent passing rate for whites and a 34 percent passing rate for African Americans. The state of Connecticut showed, however, that more African Americans than whites were promoted from the eligibility list. The state argued that this "bottom line" was a defense to the discrimination suit. Was this a valid defense? [Connecticut v. Teal, 457 U.S. 440, 102 S.Ct. 2525, 72 L.Ed.2d 130 (1982)]

4. The city of Memphis, Tennessee, implemented an affirmative action plan. In 1981 the city was confronted by severe deficits and had to lay off a considerable number of employees. The city announced that it would follow the last-hired first-fired rule. This was contrary to the city's

affirmative action plan and would cause a large number of African Americans to be terminated. The district court ordered the city to modify the layoff plan so that it would not adversely affect so many African Americans. The case was appealed to the United States Supreme Court. The issue presented was whether a seniority plan that was not intentionally discriminatory would be upheld when the effect was to lay off large numbers of African Americans. What do you think the court held? [Firefighters Local Union No. 1784 v. Stotts, 467 U.S. 561, 104 S.Ct. 2576, 81 L.Ed.2d 483 (1984)]

5. Elizabeth Hishon was employed as an associate attorney for a large law firm in Atlanta, Georgia. The firm had more than 100 lawyers but had never made a woman a partner in the firm. The district court held that Title VII was not applicable to the selection of partners in a law firm. Do you think that the district court was correct? [Hishon v. King & Spalding, 467 U.S. 69, 104 S.Ct. 2229, 81 L.Ed.2d 59 (1984)]

6. Western Airlines required all of its pilots to retire at age 60. This rule was implemented because the Federal Aviation Administration (FAA) had regulations that required retirement at age 60. Criswell was physically fit and wanted to continue flying past the age of 60. When he was required to retire, he instituted action. Was this age requirement a valid BFOQ? [Western Airlines v. Criswell, 472 U.S. 400, 105 S.Ct. 80, 86 L.Ed.2d 321 (1985)]

7. Mantolete was an epileptic who applied for employment with her local post office. She was not hired because the post office was afraid she would have a seizure on the job while operating certain equipment. She brought action based on the theory that she was discriminated against solely by reason of her handicap. Was she successful? [Mantolete v. Bolger, 767 F.2d 1416 (9th Cir. 1985)]

8. Five employees, white and African American, were terminated by Omni Georgia and replaced by five people of Korean origin. The supervisor who terminated the employees was of Japanese origin. Action was brought by the five terminated employees based on violation of Title VII. Was the law violated? [Bullard v. Omni Georgia, 640 F.2d 632 (5th Cir. 1981)]

9. Hasselman was required to wear a "revealing and provocative" uniform while working as a lobby attendant in a large office complex. She was subjected to repeated sexual harassment by different people. Finally, she refused

to wear the uniform and was terminated. Was her termination a violation of Title VII? [EEOC v. Sage Realty Corp., 507 F.Supp. 599 (S.D.N.Y. 1981)]

10. Velva Wise was employed by Mead Corporation. She and another employee were involved in a fight. Prior to this fight, four other reported fights among employees had occurred. Only one person had been fired because of fighting, and this was a male who had been involved in two out of the four fights. Velva Wise claimed she was discriminated against when she was terminated. Was she correct? [Wise v. Mead Corp., 614 F.Supp. 1131 (M.D. Ga. 1985)]

Chapter 23 Environmental Law

To waste, to destroy, our natural resources, to skin and exhaust the land instead of using it so as to increase its usefulness, will result in undermining in the days of our children the very prosperity which we ought by right to hand down to them amplified and developed.

President Theodore Roosevelt,
Message to Congress,
December 3, 1907

OUTLINE

Introduction

Bhopal, *Exxon Valdez*, Chernobyl—each name spells an environmental disaster. Scientific research has discredited traditional beliefs that air, water, and land can absorb and cleanse waste products without being harmed. As our society and the world have become more urbanized, concern about the degradation of the environment has grown.

Economic growth, greater wealth, and the proliferation of synthetic products that resist decomposition have motivated policymakers to seek strategies to clean up, then reduce, and finally prevent pollution. Focusing on protecting nature and restraining the people whose activities upset the earth and its delicate life-sustaining ecosystems, environmental laws regulate human pollution of air, water, and land.

This chapter covers how we have handled pollution problems in the past and how state and local governments regulate the environment. The chapter emphasizes relatively recent federal legislation that covers such items as clean air, water, noise, and toxic substances. Most of these federal laws are implemented by administrative agencies through regulations and by criminal prosecutions.

Historical Background

Concerns about the environment are not new. The English parliament passed a number of laws that regulated the burning of soft coal in medieval England. In the United States, through the common-law doctrine of **private nuisance,** property owners historically were given relief from pollution in situations where the individual could identify a distinct harm to himself or herself separate from that affecting the general public. A nuisance occurred when a person used his or her property in such a manner as to affect adversely the neighbor's property. Thus, if a factory polluted the air and killed a farmer's crops, the farmer could recover damages from the factory.

Nuisance suits granting specific relief for individuals were inadequate when the harm from pollution could not be identified as affecting specific groups separate from the public at large. Under the common law, citizens were denied access to the courts unless specific harm could be shown. Thus, a group of citizens who wanted to stop a new development that would cause significant water pollution would be denied access to the courts on the ground that the harm to them did not differ from the harm borne by the general public. In these types of cases, only a public authority could sue for a **public nuisance.**

Another common-law cause of action is trespass. This action is defined as the intentional or unintentional going upon another's land uninvited, regardless of whether any physical damage is done. Traditionally, to bring an action under trespass successfully, the landowner had to prove a direct physical invasion of the land, such as dumping dirt or debris on the property. In today's world, trespass occurs many times in a more subtle fashion—for example, through radiation pollution or through permeation by a harmful invisible gas. These types of invasions may hurt plant life or destroy animals, and recovery for such losses is possible under the doctrine of trespass. Today, courts often merge nuisance and trespass, requiring the plaintiff to show both invasion and harm.

In addition to the torts of nuisance and trespass, injured parties may file a common-law negligence action. The basis for the allegation of negligence is the business's failure to use reasonable care toward the individual whose injury was foreseeable and was caused by the company. Failure to use pollution controls may give rise to an action for negligence when contamination of the air produces respiratory illnesses in employees and neighboring residents.

Courts have allowed injured parties to recover under the theory of strict liability in tort. Businesses that engage in ultrahazardous activities, such as blasting operations or transporting radioactive materials, are liable for injuries that these activities cause even if the utmost care was exercised. With strict liability, the injured party does not need to prove that the damages resulted from the fault (failure to use care) of the party.

There are problems in pursuing any of these remedies. Historically, the common law limited relief from pollution in situations where the harm was caused by two or more independent sources. For example, if a number of firms were polluting the air, a harmed individual could sue any individual firm; however, until early in the twentieth century, the plaintiff was not able to sue all of the factories simultaneously. Thus, specific proof of damages in individual actions was often impossible.

These difficulties in seeking relief in pollution cases, coupled with the fact that tort theory initially only allowed for money damages and thus was not effective in preventing environmental harms, ultimately gave rise to the federal and state legislation that today regulates and controls activities affecting the environment.

Regulation by State Government

State government has some authority in regulating the environment. The private tort actions just noted take place under state laws. Recent federal legislation permits direct state or local governmental control of the environment. Many states have statutes against polluting the air, water, and the general environment.

These laws range from restricting the amount of emissions from motor vehicles, requiring environmental impact statements for developments above a certain size or amount, and restricting the disposal of toxic material. These laws also vary from one state to another because each state has its own unique problems. State environmental laws will influence decisions made by a business. Many of these state statutes have been passed under pressure from the federal government.

Several states, for example, have attempted to regulate dumping of bottles and cans through the use of what are commonly called "bottle bills." The following case illustrates the implementation of one of the first statutes of this kind of regulation.

BACKGROUND AND FACTS *The state of Oregon adopted a law prohibiting the use of nonreturnable containers for beer and carbonated beverages. The law also prohibited the sale of metal beverage containers that used detachable pull-top opening devices. The American Can Company instituted an action against the Oregon Liquor Control Commission attacking the validity of the statute, claiming violation of equal protection and due process clauses of the Fourteenth Amendment and the Commerce Clause of the United States Constitution. The trial court upheld the law, and American Can Company appealed.*

Case 23.1
AMERICAN CAN CO. v. OREGON LIQUOR CONTROL COMMISSION
Court of Appeals, Oregon, 1973.
15 Or.App. 618, 517 P.2d 691.

Judge TANZER
*   *   *   *

The primary legislative purpose of the bottle bill is to cause bottlers of carbonated soft drinks and brewers to package their products for distribution in Oregon in returnable, multiple-use deposit bottles toward the goals of reducing litter and solid waste in Oregon and reducing the injuries to people and animals due to discarded "pull tops."
*   *   *   *

*   *   * [T]he introduction of any new circumstance affecting competition will cause economic winners and economic losers throughout the industry as it readjusts to that new circumstance. The evidence is that plaintiffs expect to be among the losers, unless, of course, they are able to make marketing adjustments.

Economic loss restricted to certain elements of the beverage industry must be viewed in relation to the broader loss to the general public of the state of Oregon which the legislature sought, by enactment of the bottle bill, to avoid. The availability of land and revenues for solid waste disposal, the cost of litter collection on our highways and in our public parks, the depletion of mineral and energy resources, the injuries to humans and animals caused by discarded pull tops, and the esthetic blight on our landscape, are all economic, safety and esthetic burdens of great consequences which must be borne by every member of the public. The legislature attached higher significance to the cost to the public than they did to the cost to the beverage industry and we have no cause to disturb that legislative determination.

The bottle bill is not discriminatory against interstate commerce and is not intended to operate to give Oregon industry a competitive advantage against outside firms. The ban on pull tops and the deposit-and-return return provisions apply equally to all distributors and manufacturers whether Oregon-based or from out of state. According to plaintiffs' testimony, the economic burden of the industry's adjustment to the change will be shared by Oregon businesses as well as non-Oregon businesses. *   *   *
*   *   *   *

Plaintiffs' *   *   * constitutional challenges having failed, we hold the bottle bill to be a valid exercise of Oregon's police power. In doing so, we acknowledge having had the benefit of an able analysis by the trial court.

**DECISION AND
REMEDY**   *The appellate court affirmed the trial court's ruling that Oregon had legitimately exercised its state police power in passing laws concerning solid waste disposal. The additional cost to the beverage industry was recognized, but the court would not accept it as a justification for overturning a legislative enactment. Hence, the bottle bill was upheld.*

Regulation by Local Government

County and municipal local governments have control over certain aspects of the environment. Zoning laws adopted by local governments control the usage of land. Many communities have adopted ordinances controlling the appearance of buildings. Both usage and appearance regulations have a direct impact on the local government.

Currently, Americans generate about 160 million tons of solid waste per year. Packaging is one form of solid waste that is rapidly increasing. Compact discs, for example, are placed in larger containers in order to prevent theft, while food is packaged in individual servings to provide convenience and to lessen food waste. Both types of packaging result in increased solid wastes. Cities and counties have the primary responsibility for disposing of this and other types of garbage. Landfills take 85 percent of the solid wastes, while 8 percent is incinerated, and the rest, including glass, newspapers, and cans, is recycled.

Ordinances controlling outdoor billboards, antinoise laws prohibiting certain levels of noise from being heard beyond the business premises, and laws banning smoking indoors are examples of local government regulations. Political decisions in these areas are often hard to make. If smoking is banned in restaurants, will the patrons go to restaurants in the next city? Less patronage will mean less income for businesses, which in turn can lead to fewer taxes collected by the local

government and thus less money available for a variety of programs.

Private Litigation

Private parties continue to recover damages or obtain injunctions for environmental harms under a combination of statutory and common-law provisions. The Clean Air Act, the Clean Water Act, and the Noise Control Act, for example, authorized private lawsuits for violations of air, water, and noise pollution standards.

Some federal statutes give the government exclusive rights to filing lawsuits for violations of environmental protection regulations. For example, the Environmental Protection Agency has the exclusive right to bring suits for violations of the Federal Water Pollution Control Act.

Regulation by the Federal Government

The congressional attitude toward the environment has changed over the decades. In the first stage, described in the section titled "Historical Background," little was done to prevent environmental damage or to control pollution. The second stage began in the 1960s when Congress enacted statutes that basically regulated the cleanup of the environment. The third stage is now under way. Congress continues to be interested in cleaning up the environment, but it now also focuses on methods of preventing pollution from being created in the first place. Keep in mind that all the federal statutes described in the sections that follow represent a financial or health cost to someone: the government, business, or the individual.

National Environmental Policy Act

The **National Environmental Policy Act** (NEPA) of 1969 created the **Environmental Protection Agency (EPA)**. The EPA makes the regulatory rules for the various federal environmental acts.

NEPA also mandated **environmental impact statements (EIS)**. The EIS is undertaken by the particular federal agency that proposes to build a project. For example, the Federal Bureau of Investigation (FBI) needs to construct a new building to house its fingerprinting center. The FBI must file an EIS that analyzes the impact on the environment. Every proposed major *federal* project or *federally* funded project must have an EIS. The EIS has become an instrument for private citizens, businesses, and the federal agencies to help shape the final outcome of federal projects.

The EIS must contain: (1) the environmental impact of the proposed action, (2) any adverse effects to the environment along with alternative actions that might be taken, and (3) what irreversible effects the action might create.

Air Pollution

Federal involvement with air pollution goes back to the 1950s when Congress authorized funds for air pollution research. In 1963 Congress passed the **Clean Air Act,** which focused on multistate air pollution and provided assistance to states for implementation of antipollution measures. Various amendments over the years have strengthened the government's authority to regulate the quality of the air. In 1990 Congress passed a sweeping overhaul of the Clean Air Act that included stronger cleanup provisions and formulated prevention measures.

Air pollution silently damages human and animal health, vegetation, lakes, and forests. The original act distinguished between two types of air pollutants. The first type causes death or serious illness at low levels. This type will be discussed in the subsection titled "Air Toxics." The second type are "criteria" pollutants, so named because the EPA must issue criteria documents identifying the effects of each pollutant. Criteria pollutants are discussed in the subsection titled "National Ambient Air Quality."

Although both types of pollutants were included in the original Clean Air Act, the 1990 amendments gave the EPA more authority over them. In 1989 Congress found over 150 million people still living in areas that did not meet the air quality standards. The reasons for the failure to achieve healthy air are diverse.

For example, the 1970 and 1977 Clean Air Act amendments required the states to adopt **state implementation plans** (SIPS). Each state was to inventory the various sources of pollution. But the states' inventories of air polluters understated the problem, and the EPA approved these inadequate reports. Some states failed to implement an SIP. When failure to achieve projected emission reductions was evident, additional controls were not immediately implemented by Congress or the EPA. At the same time, while the demands on the EPA grew during the 1980s, EPA programs decreased. The failure to achieve the goals of the original Clean Air Act resulted in the 1990 amendments.

State Implementation Plans   The amendments require the states to reformulate their SIPs. Each state must take a complete emissions inventory of all polluters, designating them as stationary or mobile. Although this sounds like a relatively easy task, sometimes the source of an emission is elusive; dust sources, particularly in arid areas of the western United States, are one example. At other times, the emissions migrate over state lines and national boundaries. For example, air pollution, generated by American-owned as well as Mexican-owned plants in Mexico, is pushed by wind patterns into the United States.

National Ambient Air Quality   Funding for research in controlling and preventing the deterioration of air quality increased tremendously under the 1990 act. The act specifies that uniform, nationwide ambient air quality standards will be established by the EPA. *Primary ambient standards* are based on the impact of air quality on human health. These standards will be determined by

Outer Continental Shelf Activities?

Air pollution comes from unlikely sources. As only Congress can put it, outer continental shelf (OCS) activities—translated, this term refers to offshore drilling and to ships—cause emissions in excess of 500 tons of oxides of nitrogen (NO_x) annually. The emissions from constructing one platform is 350 tons of NO_x, while drilling a single exploration well can exceed 100 tons of NO_x. A major offshore oil project easily exceeds the air pollution caused by 100,000 automobiles that meet 1988 California emission standards, each traveling 10,000 miles. The 1990 Clean Air Act marks the beginning of regulation of outer continental shelf activities. The standards for controlling this source of pollution are the same as those for "corresponding onshore areas."

identifying the lowest level of pollution at which an effect on health is observed and then setting a margin of safety. *Secondary ambient standards* protect against adverse impacts on human welfare, such as visibility, vegetation, animals, wildlife, materials, and property. The EPA and the states are responsible for meeting primary air quality standards and deadlines set out in the act. Secondary standards are to be attained within a reasonable time period.

The six criteria pollutants for which ambient standards have been set are ozone, lead, sulfur dioxide, particulates, nitrogen dioxide, and carbon monoxide. Let's look at three pollutants: ozone, carbon monoxide, and particulates.

Ozone is fatal at high concentrations. Once breathed in, 90 percent of the ozone is never exhaled. It reacts rapidly with the cells and irritates and inflames the lungs. Nearly 58 million people in the United States live in areas that have high ozone concentrations.

Carbon monoxide is more readily absorbed into the blood than is oxygen. Carbon monoxide displaces oxygen and threatens bodily functions. In high concentrations, it, too, is fatal. Since it poses particular harm to fetal development, pregnant women are especially at risk. Nearly 1.4 million pregnant women live in areas of high concentration of carbon monoxide. Motor vehicles are the single largest source of ozone and carbon monoxide pollution. As a result, the 1990 act imposes an annual $2 fee on motor vehicle registration in those areas where the air quality does not meet the standards.

Particulate matter measuring less than ten microns (a unit of length equal to one millionth) in diameter (PM-10) can produce a range of effects from temporary lung dysfunction to death. Particulates come from wood stoves, power station emissions, exhausts from diesel vehicles, and common dust. Particulates impair visibility so much that the National Park Service has reported that scenic views are visually impaired 90 percent of the time. People in the United States spend $40 billion per year in additional health care costs because of particulate matter. Legislators hope that if the new air quality standards are met by the year 2003, the amount saved in health costs will offset the plan's estimated $2.79 billion in pollution control costs.

Air Toxics   Hazardous air pollutants are toxic and generally are cancer-causing substances. Toxic releases from major manufacturing facilities amount to approximately 2.7 billion pounds. Cancer incidences may be as high as 500,000 fatal cases for Americans alive in 1992.

In 1985, in Institute, West Virginia, the Union Carbide plant had a toxic release one year after the Bhopal incident. An Occupational Safety and Health Administration (OSHA) investigation discovered 221 safety and health violations. OSHA imposed a fine of $1.38 million for willful disregard of health and safety.

Accidental releases of extremely hazardous substances during a recent four-year period caused 309 deaths, 11,341 injuries, and the evacuation of 464,677 people from homes and jobs.

Seventy percent of the events occurred at stationary facilities while 30 percent were related to transportation.

As a result of the harm caused by air toxics, the EPA established a list of hazardous air pollutants that can be amended over the years. A national air toxics clearinghouse was established to coordinate and disseminate information.

Acid Rain   Acid rain is extremely corrosive and can damage humans and materials. It can dissolve heavy metals and destroy such materials as stone, rubber, zinc, steel, leather, and paint. Congress has convened a task force to investigate acid rain and to study the impact of acid rain on bodies of water, forests, and crops.

Ozone Layer and Climate Protection   The earth's main shield against the sun's harmful ultraviolet radiation is the ozone layer. Some scientific evidence shows that this layer is being destroyed. At the same time, a global warming, commonly called the greenhouse effect, has been detected. The national goal is to correct these two problems: first, by eliminating the emissions that destroy the ozone layer—for example, the gas in aerosol cans will no longer be allowed—and second, by reducing as much as possible the emissions that have led to and that perpetuate the warming of the climate. If the ozone layer can be saved, it will be one step toward slowing the climate warming.

Enforcement   The EPA has the authority to issue administrative citations for which the penalties can go up to $200,000 in any given case. Criminal liability can be imposed for unlawful releases of toxic pollutants, including negligent releases. The EPA now must issue certificates of compliance. These certifications, with limitations on specific emissions, will give the agency more control over polluters.

Suits filed by private citizens may be brought to compel action by the EPA. Civil penalties obtained in citizen suits will be deposited in a separate fund to be used by the EPA for further air pollution control activities.

The EPA also has reporting requirements with which businesses must comply. These reporting requirements are far reaching, as we see in the next case.

BACKGROUND AND FACTS   *In 1985 the United States Navy contracted with Hugo Key and Son, Inc., a general contractor, to demolish four buildings. Hugo Key hired Asbestos Removal and Consulting Company, Inc. (ARCON), to perform the asbestos removal work. ARCON developed an asbestos removal plan that required that the removal take place within sealed-off buildings, which would be off limits to all personnel not directly involved in the removal process.*

The boilers in the buildings were insulated with asbestos. Before ARCON could remove the asbestos insulation from the boilers, Hugo Key demolished two buildings and lifted the asbestos-covered boilers out of the rubble with a backhoe without taking any precautions to contain the asbestos material. Chunks of dry asbestos material were stripped from the boiler, and asbestos was emitted into the air. When the EPA heard about this event, it requested information from Hugo Key about the release of asbestos and demanded that a response be filed within ten days. Hugo Key failed to respond.

Case 23.2
UNITED STATES v. HUGO KEY AND SON, INC.
United States District Court, District of Rhode Island, 1989. 731 F.Supp. 1135.

District Judge PETTINE.
* * * *

The legislative history of the 1977 amendments to the Clean Air Act makes clear that Congress intended that the Act and the asbestos NESHAP [National Emission Standards for Hazardous Air Pollutants] provide strict liability for civil violations of their provisions. Federal courts have consistently adhered to the legislative intent of the Act to provide for strict liability.
* * * *

The stationary source of emissions in a demolition or renovation operation is, by definition, the operation itself. Therefore, the demolition of buildings conducted by Hugo Key at the Naval Base was a "demolition operation." The "owner or operator" of a demolition operation is any person who "owns, leases, operates, controls or supervises" the demolition operation. Hugo Key was the contractor of the demolition operation and supervised the job. Moreover, the demolition contractor is, by definition, the owner or operator of the demolition operation. Therefore, this Court finds that Hugo Key was the "owner or operator" of the "demolition operation" within the meaning of the Act and the asbestos NESHAP.

*   *   *   *

The United States claims in the first count of its complaint that Hugo Key failed to respond in a timely manner to EPA's reporting requirement seeking information on the demolition operation in violation of the Act. EPA is authorized *   *   * to seek information from any person who owns or operates an emission source in order to establish compliance with the Act. The information obtained by EPA pursuant to this broad investigatory power is vital to its ability to establish violations of the Act and the asbestos NESHAP. Violations of reporting requirements and compliance orders are reviewed under the strict liability standard of the Act.

DECISION AND REMEDY   *Hugo Key was a person within the meaning of the act and thus was required to file a report concerning asbestos contamination. The EPA is authorized to bring an action against a person who fails to make the required report.*

Water Pollution

Federal regulations governing the pollution of water can be traced back over a century to the **Rivers and Harbors Act** of 1886, amended in 1890 and in 1899. These regulations required a permit for discharging or depositing refuse in navigable waterways. The courts have determined that even hot water can be considered refuse because it affects the fish and aquatic plant life.

Clean Water Regulation The most important and comprehensive legislation plan to eliminate pollution in our waters took place in 1972. The 1972 **Clean Water Act** established these goals: (1) to make waters safe for swimming, (2) to protect fish and wildlife, and (3) to eliminate the discharge of pollutants into the water. Specific time schedules dating from the 1972 act were extended by amendments in 1977 and 1987. Regulations for the most part specify that businesses and governments install the best available technology.

The act requires both municipal and industrial dischargers to apply for permits before they discharge wastes into the nation's navigable waters. Finally, the act establishes legal standing for citizens (or organizations) whose interests have been affected by parties who violate EPA or state standards and orders. Both injunctive relief and damages can be sought through claims under the act.

Oil Pollution In 1990 the **Oil Pollution Act** was signed into law. The act is a result of the *Exxon Valdez* oil spill off the Alaskan shore and other spills during the same period into the Delaware River, the Arthurkill, Montana's Whitefish Lake, the Southern California coast, and Galveston Bay. The strict liability limit was increased eightfold. For a spill equivalent to that of the *Exxon Valdez*, the liability cap has been increased from $14.3 million to $114 million under the act. This is in addition to damages that may be awarded under other theories. Liability now covers cleanup costs, natural resource damages, losses to subsistence resources, and costs to local government. The $1 billion Oil Pollution Liability Trust Fund established under the act will be financed by oil companies. In the future, all new oil tankers must be double-hulled, phasing out single-hulled tankers by 2010. The statute also established the Oil Spill Recovery Institute, a research center.

Quality Standards Millions of gallons of waste water daily flow into effluent treatment plants, are cleaned, and returned to navigable streams. Today the quality standard for the water leaving the treatment plants is higher than that applied to drinking water supplied to homes. A higher cleaning standard has also been imposed for water containing toxic wastes than for water with normal pollutants.

Wetlands   Throughout much of the United States is land designated as wetlands. This is the land that lies between solid land and open bodies of water, such as lakes, large rivers, or the ocean. Often underwater, wetlands are home to wildlife and birds. In the past, wetlands were filled in by developers, and homes and businesses were built on the landfill. Today wetlands cannot be filled in unless a permit has been issued by the Army Corps of Engineers. The following case involves a landowner whose land became wetlands because of actions taken by governmental agencies.

BACKGROUND AND FACTS   *A dispute arose over 153 acres of undeveloped land south of San Francisco, called the Newark Coyote Property, owned by Leslie Salt. The land abuts the San Francisco National Wildlife Refuge and lies approximately one-quarter mile from the Newark Slough, a tidal arm of the San Francisco Bay.*

The condition of the property in 1985 was the result of many artificial changes over the last 100 years. Starting out as pastureland, it was excavated for salt until 1959. The salt pits remained and were temporarily filled with water during the winter rainy season. Fish lived in the ponds, and migratory birds used the pits as habitat during the winter and spring. An endangered species, the salt marsh harvest mouse, also used the property as habitat.

The California Department of Transportation (Caltrans) constructed culverts adjacent to Leslie's land. Caltrans and the Fish and Wildlife Service breached the levee on the wildlife refuge adjacent to Leslie's property, and this allowed water to flow through the culverts onto Leslie's land. Caltrans and the Fish and Wildlife Service failed to place effective floodgates on the culverts. Over time, wetlands conditions were created.

In 1985 Leslie started to dig a ditch in order to drain the land and to fill it in. The Army Corps of Engineers (the Corps) became aware of this activity and issued a cease and desist order pursuant to its authority under the Clean Water Act. The Corps claimed jurisdiction over the majority of the property, which Leslie then challenged. The trial court found for Leslie.

Circuit Judges FARRIS, PREGERSON, *and* RYMER.
*   *   *   *

The Corps claims that the *   *   * property [is] wetlands within its jurisdiction. The district court denied the Corps jurisdiction for three reasons: (1) the wetland conditions were caused by the government, (2) the conditions were not "normal," *   *   * and (3) the property was not adjacent to waters of the United States.
*   *   *   *

The fact that third parties, including the government, are responsible for flooding Leslie's land is irrelevant. The Corps' jurisdiction does not depend on how the property at issue became a water of the United States. Congress intended to regulate local aquatic ecosystems regardless of their origin.
*   *   *   *

If the Corps' regulations under Clean Water Act jurisdiction harm a landowner, her appropriate response is to seek damages through inverse condemnation proceedings, not to restrict the scope of Corps jurisdiction. *   *   *

The district court's second rationale for denying Corps jurisdiction over the *   *   * property was a Corps regulation that defines wetlands as an area that

Case 23.3
LESLIE SALT CO. v. UNITED STATES
United States Court of Appeals, Ninth Circuit, 1989.
896 F.2d 354.

"under normal circumstances" supports wetland vegetation.

*   *   *   *

The phrase "under normal circumstances" is meant to exclude those areas which are not aquatic, but experience an "abnormal presence of aquatic vegetation." According to the district court's findings, the southern fringes of the parcel are aquatic areas. The fact that these wetlands are man-made does not make them "abnormal." Whether the wetlands are artificially or naturally created is irrelevant to this determination.

We disagree with the district court's third alternative holding, that this wetland is not adjacent to waters of the United States. In reaching this conclusion, the district court again relied on its decision to exclude from consideration any consequences of the backflow through the culverts created by Caltrans and the Fish and Wildlife Service. In the absence of this erroneous holding, the southern portions of the property are adjacent to waters of the United States—the water in the culvert, which is directly connected to the Newark Slough.

*   *   *   *

The southern portions of Leslie's property meet both the statutory and regulatory requirements for the Corps to exert Clean Water Act jurisdiction over them. The fact that the government in part caused the inundation of the property is not of consequence. Similarly, the government's actions do not affect the normalcy or adjacency requirements of the regulations.

DECISION AND REMEDY   *The Corps had jurisdiction over the property, even though the wetlands were man-made. The effect of this decision was that Leslie lost the ability to use its land. The court, however, allowed Leslie to bring another action for inverse condemnation.*

Other Regulations   In 1972, through the **Marine Protection, Research, and Sanctuaries Act,** Congress established a system of permits that regulates the discharge and introduction of materials into coastal waters and continuous marine areas. The **Safe Drinking Water Act** of 1974 established additional regulations governing drinking water standards. The rules, which are similar to those of the Clean Water Act, provide that states assume the primary responsibility for complying with national standards. The federal government assumes responsibility where states fail to institute or enforce drinking water standards. In most cases, explicit penalties are imposed on parties that pollute the water. The polluting party can also be required to clean up pollution or to pay the cost of doing so.

Nuclear Wastes

Millions of pounds of nuclear waste, in both liquid and solid form, are generated each year. Most of this waste is radioactive and will remain dangerous for thousands of years. In 1982 Congress passed the **Nuclear Waste Policy Act** (NWPA).

This act required the building of a permanent repository for the disposal of spent nuclear fuel and high-level wastes. In the meantime, Congress provided that a monitored retrievable storage (MRS) facility could be built as a temporary measure until the permanent site was developed.

Shore Protection

In the 1980s, medical wastes, such as needles and bandages, washed ashore on New Jersey beaches crowded with bathers. Soon there were other reports of such garbage washing ashore, and the local governments reacted quickly by closing the beaches. Congress now has forbidden the indiscriminate disposal into the oceans of potentially infectious medical waste. New regulations provide for proper disposal.

Similarly, Congress has passed a statute, entitled **Shore Protection Act** of 1988, that controls the disposal of solid wastes in oceans and lakes. A permit system has been created to track and control the solid waste as it is transported to its final place of disposal. The law also provides for

Safe Drinking Water?

Do you know anyone who has died of typhoid fever or cholera? Probably not. Once the killer diseases were traced to the water supply, experiments proved that chlorine would stop the spread of them. From the 1900s to the 1970s, chlorinated water was thought to be safe. Now it turns out that the chlorine reacts with organic material in the water to form new chemicals. Chlorine additives now are highly suspected of being carcinogenic—that is, of causing cancer. Drinking chlorinated water doubles the risk of having bladder cancer, and 40,000 cases of this disease are diagnosed annually. What else is in the water?

Water from rainstorms flows into rivers and lakes, routinely bringing fertilizers, animal wastes, pesticides, herbicides, and industrial pollution with it. Lead finds its way into the water supply through old lead pipes, which still service parts of the nation. Leaking underground storage tanks filled with chemicals, gas, oil, and hazardous wastes, as well as industrial discharges, find their way into the groundwater supply from which drinking water is eventually taken. Naturally occurring poisons, such as arsenic and radon gas, also find their way into the drinking water supply. In its 1974 statutes, Congress envisioned a safe drinking water supply. Unfortunately this has not been achieved. Drinking water pollution is one of the four top environmental concerns.

study and recommendations as this problem continues to grow.

Noise Pollution

In 1972, Congress prescribed standards and regulations for the control of aircraft noise, including sonic booms, and the control of emissions of railroad and motor vehicles involved in interstate commerce. The **Noise Control Act** of 1972 established the goal of creating an environment free from noise that is injurious to the health and welfare of the public. The courts have ruled that local control of noise is preempted when state regulations conflict with those established by federal statutes.

Regulations promulgated by the Noise Control Act are administered by the Federal Aviation Administration, the Environmental Protection Agency, and the Department of Transportation. The EPA, for example, is authorized to establish noise emission levels for equipment, motors, and engines. It also reviews production processes, verifies reports for compliance with the law, conducts audit tests, and makes inspections of manufacturers' records.

Toxic Substances

The **Toxic Substances Control Act** was passed in 1976 to regulate chemicals and chemical compounds that are known to be toxic and to institute investigation of any possible harmful effects from new chemical compounds. The regulations authorize the Environmental Protection Agency to require that manufacturers, processors, and other organizations planning to use chemicals first determine their effect on human health and the environment. The EPA also has the authority to regulate substances that potentially create a hazard or an unreasonable risk of injury.

Pesticide and Herbicide Control

The use of chemical pesticides to kill insects and herbicides to kill weeds has significantly increased agricultural productivity. On the other hand, there is a growing body of evidence that residuals from these chemicals have not been absorbed by the environment. In some cases, buildups of residuals have killed animals, and some potential long-term effects detrimental to the public have also been identified.

The original regulations governing pesticides were established by the **Federal Insecticide, Fungicide, and Rodenticide Act** of 1947, as amended in 1972 by the **Federal Environmental Pesticide Control Act.** The Environmental Protection Agency has been given the authority to control the introduction of pesticides into the environment.

Pesticides must be (1) registered before they can be sold, (2) certified and used only for approved applications, and (3) used in amounts that meet established limits when they are applied to crops that provide food for animals or people. The EPA also has the right to inspect manufacturing establishments. In some situations, the supply of pesticides is controlled to keep hazardous chemicals off the market. Those substances that are identified as harmful are subject to suspension and cancellation of registration.

Waste Disposal

Waste disposal can occur on land, in the water, or in the air; thus, regulations protecting these resources from pollution also apply to waste disposal. In 1965 Congress passed the **Solid Wastes Disposal Act,** an act designed to reduce solid waste disposal by encouraging the recycling of waste and the reuse of materials by society. The act encourages the development and use of technology that converts garbage into useful products.

The EPA also carries out the provisions of the **Resource Conservation and Recovery Act** (RCRA) of 1976, as amended in 1984, which governs EPA studies and recommendations on solid waste disposal, ranging from glass and plastic waste to airport landfill. The RCRA provides a cradle-to-grave (from creation to disposal) tracking system of *hazardous* waste. Both the federal and state governments are granted authority to regulate companies that generate, store, transport, dispose, or handle at any time those wastes deemed hazardous. The EPA issues permits for and conducts on-site inspections of hazardous waste facilities.

In 1980, Congress passed the **Comprehensive Environmental Response, Compensation, and Liability Act** (CERCLA), commonly known as the Superfund. This act provides that when a release or threatened release from a hazardous waste site occurs, the EPA may clean up the site to correct the problem. The government may then recover its cleanup costs from (1) the person who generated the wastes disposed at the site; (2) the person who transported wastes to the site; (3) the person who owned or the tenant who operated the site at the time of the waste disposal; (4) the current owner and operator of the site; or (5) a lending institution if it had management control over the property. Many companies may thus be liable for their past actions in waste disposal.

Moreover, Superfund mandates a harsh standard of liability. Strict liability applies by statute. In addition, liability among multiple defendants may be held to be joint and several. *Joint and several liability* means that one or more of the responsible parties may be sued. If a money judgment is rendered on behalf of the plaintiff, the money may be collected from one or all of the wrongdoers. Usually, the defendants jointly pay their respective share of the judgment. At other times, a company that is responsible for only a fraction of the share of the judgment may be held liable to pay for all of the judgment. This result happens when the other co-defendants are unable to pay their share of the judgment.

The practical effect of this law is seen in the purchase of real property. Whoever owns the land is liable under the act and is required to clean up the land. Cleanup costs may range from a few hundred dollars to millions. Heavy use of pesticides, leaking underground storage tanks, and general disposal of waste have made real property subject to cleanup. Today, before a lending institution will repossess any property, it will verify that no environmental problems exist. Residential property is exempted from this rule.

Three defenses exist: (1) act of God; (2) act of war; and (3) act of a third party (an innocent purchaser can use this defense.) An owner of property will not be liable if someone dumps hazardous waste on the property without permission. The innocent purchaser defense occurs when a person purchases property without knowledge or without reason to know of the hazardous waste already on the property. In the following case, a current owner of land seeks damages from the prior owner under the Superfund provisions.

BACKGROUND AND FACTS *In 1977 Amoco wanted to purchase certain property from Borden. The parties discussed two prices: $1.8 million for the site "as is," or $2.2 million if Borden removed the phosphogypsum. Amoco accepted the "as is" option. The Texas Department of Water Resources informed Amoco that phosphogypsum is radioactive. Amoco hired several consultants to measure the radioactivity. The consultants' reports revealed the various elevated radiation levels throughout the site in the form of radium-226. The site was unused and was secured with fences and guards to prevent access. Amoco claimed cleanup costs would be between $11 million and $17 million.*

Amoco sued Borden on a number of counts, including sharing liability under the Superfund (CERCLA). Borden's primary defenses against liability were (1) that the property was sold "as is" and that this fact and the doctrine of caveat emptor precluded a finding of liability and (2) that the levels of radiation emanating from the site were not high enough to be considered a release of a hazardous substance within the meaning of CERCLA.

Case 23.4
AMOCO OIL COMPANY v. BORDEN, INC.
United States Court of Appeals,
Fifth Circuit, 1989.
889 F.2d 664.

Circuit Judges BROWN, REAVLEY, and HIGGINBOTHAM.
*   *   *   *

Radium–226, the primary radioactive waste on the property, decays to form a gas, radon–222. *   *   * Radon and its products are considered radionuclides, which are defined as "any nuclide that emits radiation." The term hazardous substance includes any element, compound, mixture, solution, or substance designated pursuant to *   *   * [CERCLA], [and] any hazardous air pollutant listed under the Clean Air Act. The EPA has designated radionuclides as hazardous substances under CERCLA. Additionally, the regulations promulgated by the EPA under the Clean Air Act, list radionuclides as a hazardous air pollutant.

The plain statutory language fails to impose any quantitative requirement on the term hazardous substance and we decline to imply that any is necessary. Radionuclides meet the listing requirements and therefore the radioactive materials on Amoco's property are hazardous substances within the meaning of CERCLA.
*   *   *   *

The term "release" is defined to mean: any spilling, leaking, pumping, pouring, emitting, emptying, discharging, injecting, escaping, leaching, dumping, or disposing into the environment (including the abandonment or discarding of barrels, containers, and other closed receptacles containing any hazardous substance or pollutant or contaminant).
*   *   *   *

Borden's actions met the release requirement in two ways. First, it did so by disposing of the phosphogypsum and highly radioactive wastes on the property. *   *   * Second, the gas emanating from the radionuclides constitutes a release within the meaning of the statute. *   *   *

To establish a prima facie case of liability in a CERCLA cost recovery action, a plaintiff must prove: (1) that the site in question is a "facility;" *   *   * (2) that the defendant is a responsible person; *   *   * (3) that a release or a threatened release of a hazardous substance has occurred; and (4) that the release or threatened release has caused the plaintiff to incur response costs. *   *   * If the plaintiff establishes each of these elements and the defendant is unable to establish the applicability of one of the defenses, the plaintiff is entitled to summary judgment on the liability issue. This is true even when there is a genuine issue as to appropriate damages. *   *   *

A plaintiff may recover those response costs that are necessary and consistent with the National Contingency Plan ("NCP").

*   *   *   *

It is undisputed that Amoco's property falls within the statutory definition of a "facility"; that Borden is a responsible party within the meaning of CERCLA, and that the statutory defenses to liability are inapplicable. The question of liability centers around the determination of whether a release of a hazardous substance has occurred.

*   *   *   *

The hazard on the property constitutes an indivisible harm. As an owner of a facility that continues to release a hazardous substance, Amoco shares joint and several liability for remedial actions with Borden. When one liable party sues another to recover its equitable share of the response costs, the action is one for contribution, which is specifically recognized under CERCLA. *   *   *
Under that provision a court has considerable latitude in determining each party's equitable share. After deciding the appropriate remedial action, the court will have to determine each party's share of the costs. Possible relevant factors include: the amount of hazardous substances involved; the degree of toxicity or hazard of the materials involved; the degree of involvement by parties in the generation, transportation, treatment, storage, or disposal of the substances; the degree of care exercised by the parties with respect to the substances involved; and the degree of cooperation of the parties with government officials to prevent any harm to public health or the environment. Additionally, the circumstances and conditions involved in the property's conveyance, including the price paid and discounts granted, should be weighed in allocating response costs.

Borden *   *   * claim[s] that the equities in this case require Amoco to bear the full cost of cleanup. However, because both parties are liable under CERCLA, this is a question more properly decided by the district court, after it has determined the proper scope of the cleanup efforts.

DECISION AND REMEDY   *The case was sent back to the trial court to decide the equitable share that each party must pay. CERCLA imposes responsibility on every owner of real property that contains hazardous materials. CERCLA creates joint and several liability in these situations.*

Judicial Limits

In the first half of the 1970s, federal and state legislators enacted many statutes that regulate environmental quality. Judicial interpretations of these statutes have generally given broad discretionary powers to the administrate agencies that carry out their directives. Beginning in the mid 1970s, however, the courts began to place stricter limits on administrative discretion. Court decisions imposed a **cost-benefit standard** on administrative decisions. Under the cost-benefit standard, courts will consider the cost of an action and compare it with the benefit that may result from the action.

Generally, the economic and technological infeasibility and/or cost-benefit considerations are not defenses in and of themselves to the charge of noncompliance with these acts. They are only factors courts *may* consider. For example, in *Union Electric Co. v. Environmental Protection Agency*,[1] the utility claimed it would cost $500 million to comply with the Clean Air Act and that this sum could not be obtained through financial markets. The United States Supreme Court turned down this argument and held that the clean air regu-

---

1. 427 U.S. 246, 96 S.Ct. 2518, 49 L.Ed.2d 474 (1976).

lations are of "technology-forcing character and are expressly designed to force regulated sources to develop pollution control devices that might at the time appear to be economically or technologically infeasible."

The conflict between the cost of maintaining the quality of our environment and the economic benefit of technological advances is one the courts face when deciding environmental questions, as the next case clearly indicates.

BACKGROUND AND FACTS *The Endangered Species Act of 1973 authorizes the secretary of the interior to declare a species "endangered." The secretary listed a small fish, popularly known as the snail darter, as an endangered species under this act. The snail darter lived in a portion of the Little Tennessee River in which the Tellico Dam was under construction. More than $100 million had already been expended.*

The secretary ordered all federal agencies to take action to ensure that the critical habitat of the snail darter was not modified or destroyed. An association of scientists, a conservation group, and citizens of the Little Tennessee Valley brought this suit to enjoin completion of the dam, claiming that impoundment of the waters would violate the act by causing the snail darter's extinction.

Case 23.5
TENNESSEE VALLEY AUTHORITY v. HILL
Supreme Court of the United States, 1978.
437 U.S. 153, 98 S.Ct. 2279, 57 L.Ed.2d 117.

Chief Justice BURGER delivered the opinion of the Court.
*   *   *   *

We begin with the premise that operation of the Tellico Dam will either eradicate the known population of snail darters or destroy their critical habitat. Petitioner does not now seriously dispute this fact. In any event, under the Act, the Secretary of the Interior is vested with exclusive authority to determine whether a species such as the snail darter is "endangered" or "threatened" and to ascertain the factors which have led to such a precarious existence. Congress has authorized— indeed commanded—the Secretary to "issue such regulations as he deems necessary and advisable to provide for the conservation of such species." As we have seen, the Secretary promulgated regulations which declared the snail darter an endangered species whose critical habitat would be destroyed by creation of the Tellico Reservoir. Doubtless petitioner would prefer not to have these regulations on the books, but there is no suggestion that the Secretary exceeded his authority or abused his discretion in issuing the regulations. Indeed, no judicial review of the Secretary's determinations has ever been sought and hence the validity of his actions are not open to review in this Court.

Starting from the above premise, two questions are presented: (a) would TVA [Tennessee Valley Authority] be in violation of the Act if it completed and operated the Tellico Dam as planned? (b) if TVA's actions would offend the Act, is an injunction the appropriate remedy for the violation? For the reasons stated hereinafter, we hold that both questions must be answered in the affirmative.

It may seem curious to some that the survival of a relatively small number of three-inch fish among all the countless millions of species extant would require the permanent halting of a virtually completed dam for which Congress has expended more than $100 million. The paradox is not minimized by the fact that Congress continued to appropriate large sums of public money for the project, even after congressional appropriations committees were apprised of its apparent impact upon the survival of the snail darter. We conclude, however, that the explicit provisions of the Endangered Species Act require precisely that result.

One would be hard pressed to find a statutory provision whose terms were any plainer than those of the Endangered Species Act. Its very words affirmatively command all federal agencies "to insure that actions *authorized, funded, or carried out* by them do not *jeopardize* the continued existence" of an endangered species or "result in the destruction or modification of habitat of such species. . . ." (Emphasis added.) This language admits of no exception. Nonetheless, petitioner urges, as do the dissenters, that the Act cannot reasonably be interpreted as applying to a federal project which was well under way when Congress passed the Endangered Species Act of 1973. To sustain that position, however, we would be forced to ignore the ordinary meaning of plain language. It has not been shown, for example, how TVA can close the gates of the Tellico Dam without "carrying out" an action that has been "authorized" and "funded" by a federal agency. Nor can we understand how such action will "insure" that the snail darter's habitat is not disrupted. Accepting the Secretary's determinations, as we must, it is clear that TVA's proposed operation of the dam will have precisely the opposite effect, namely the *eradication* of an endangered species.

*   *   *   *

Concededly, this view of the Act will produce results requiring the sacrifice of the anticipated benefits of the project and of many millions of dollars in public funds. But examination of the language, history, and structure of the legislation under review here indicates beyond doubt that Congress intended endangered species to be afforded the highest of priorities.

*   *   *   *

*   *   * Our system of government is, after all, a tripartite one, with each branch having certain defined functions delegated to it by the Constitution. While "[i]t is emphatically the province and duty of the judicial department to say what the law is," it is equally—and emphatically—the exclusive province of the Congress not only to formulate legislative policies and mandate programs and projects, but also to establish their relative priority for the Nation. Once Congress, exercising its delegated powers, has decided the order of priorities in a given area, it is for the Executive to administer the laws and for the courts to enforce them when enforcement is sought.

Here we are urged to view the Endangered Species Act "reasonably," and hence shape a remedy "that accords with some modicum of common sense and the public will." But is that our function? We have no expert knowledge on the subject of endangered species, much less do we have a mandate from the people to strike a balance of equities on the side of the Tellico Dam. Congress has spoken in the plainest of words, making it abundantly clear that the balance has been struck in favor of affording endangered species the highest of priorities, thereby adopting a policy which it described as "institutionalized caution."

*   *   *   *

DECISION AND REMEDY   *The United States Supreme Court enforced the Endangered Species Act by enjoining completion of the Tellico Dam.*

COMMENT   *Scientists found that snail darters could live in another area of the Little Tennessee River that would be unaffected by the dam. The snail darters were moved at government expense, making it possible to complete the Tellico Dam.*

Ethical Considerations

Economic and Environmental Concerns

Everyone is in favor of protecting the environment. Everyone is in favor of earning an honest living. But what happens when these two values come into conflict with one another? This conflict is played out when environmentalists clash with the logging industry. In the Northwest, for example, the loggers are pitted against those who want to protect old-growth forests and spotted owls.

The logging industry either owns the land it logs or leases the land from the federal or state government and then operates under permits to log the forest. This work creates employment and thus a tax base, and the monies earned by employees support other private industries, such as grocery and furniture stores, as well as taxes paid to the local and federal government. Since the 1920s, many logging companies have cooperated with the Save-the-Redwoods League and the Sierra Club.

If the spotted owl, along with the Harris's hawk, Henslow's sparrow, loggerhead shrike, seaside sparrow, snowy plover, and vermilion flycatcher, is placed on the endangered species list, this would effectively stop all logging. The designation would protect 1.5 million acres of old-growth forest from future logging. Since the pilgrims arrived in the early 1600s, over 90% of the original woodland in the United States been destroyed.

Is it ethical to protect birds and forests over the jobs of people who are generally second-and third-generation loggers? As mentioned before, these people contribute to the economic basis of the community.

Most old-growth wood is shipped overseas for use in other countries. Should this be allowed? Would it make any difference if the old-growth wood was used in the United States?

Destruction of habitat poses the greatest threat to the survival of wild species. Birds, animals, and plants have evolved over centuries to survive in specific environments. Destruction of the old-growth forests would mean the destruction of some species. Each species plays a part in the delicate balance of the ecosystem. Is it ethical to allow these wild species to perish?

International Considerations

Global Anti-Pollution Actions

Pollution knows no international boundaries. The radioactive pollution from Chernobyl was detected over a weekend by Sweden and Norway before it was reported by the former Union of Soviet Socialist Republics (USSR). The radioactivity eventually encircled the earth and led to the ban of agricultural products from some countries because such products as milk contained radioactive elements.

The more developed nations have passed legislation similar to the laws of the United States. The European Community (EC) passed the Single Europe Act, which requires it to issue a comprehensive regulatory scheme to protect the environment. Adopted in 1987, this program contains laws similar to those of the United States.

The third-world countries are not as interested in protecting the environment. They want and need industrial development and are willing to accept pollution in order to obtain that goal. Slowly, ecological progress is being made by these countries. For example, in 1985, the **Association of Southeast Asian Nations (ASEAN)** entered into the **Agreement on the Conservation of Nature and Natural Resources.** Each signatory recognized its responsibility in controlling pollution and preventing it from migrating to other countries.

One of the few international treaties that is global is the **Montreal Protocol on Substances that Deplete the Ozone Layer,** which was signed by 24 nations in 1987. This treaty is unique in that its goal is to prevent pollution rather than simply to provide cleanup measures. The treaty requires all nations to reduce both production and consumption of chemicals that deplete the ozone layer. By 1998, each nation is supposed to achieve at least a 50 percent reduction in the use and release of these chemicals.

The **United Nations Convention on the Law of the Sea** imposes on signatory members the duty not to pollute the oceans from land or from vessels, including the dumping of raw wastes from ships. The **Law of the Navigational Uses of International Watercourses** has an article in draft form that provides for exchange of information between states if water-related hazards occur. Another draft article requires nations to take all measures to prevent harmful conditions, such as toxic chemical spills.

The United Nations Educational, Scientific, and Cultural Organization (UNESCO) is attempting to control pollution. It has been particularly successful in compiling data and arranging for regional agreements to stop pollution. In addition, the World Bank requires pollution controls as part of each applicant's business plan before it will make a loan for industrial purposes.

FACING A LEGAL ISSUE

Considerations When Purchasing Real Property

A person must be very careful when purchasing real property. In the past, one had to consider zoning laws, financing, and engineering studies of the land and any projected buildings. Today a purchaser must take into consideration the various federal statutes concerning the environment. As we have seen, if an environmental hazard exists on the property, it is up to the property owner to correct it. In reality, there is only one defense a person can use: that of the innocent purchaser. Auditing can help a purchaser establish this defense.

The EPA has issued a policy statement on auditing. An environmental audit usually has two parts: (1) a surface analysis (phase I); (2) a technical subsurface study (phase II); and, if necessary, a cleanup of the property (phase III). A phase II study is very expensive and is not normally necessary if phase I does not reveal an environmental problem. Neither audit is legally required, but without it, the EPA takes a hard stand against a purchaser claiming no knowledge. Without an audit, it is almost impossible to meet the innocent purchaser defense.

A phase I analysis should be done by a professional known as an environmental consultant. The public records of ownership for at least the last 50 years must be reviewed. The names in the public record may reveal the type of business activities in which previous owners, such as an oil company, engaged. The public record will also show existing environmental cleanup liens.

The consultant will review aerial photographs that might show prior use of the property. He or she will examine federal, state, and local records to look for building permits and reports or environmental records of previous land use. A visual inspection of the property and of the adjacent property is also necessary because hazardous materials may have migrated from an adjoining property on to the property for sale.

The phase II audit includes physical sampling and testing. The soil and groundwater are sampled to identify and isolate the type and extent of the contamination. A phase II audit is accomplished only when a phase I audit indicates environmental problems. Phase III occurs when the property is cleaned up. Today, potential purchasers and their lending institutions should always perform a phase I audit before purchasing raw land; otherwise, they may be held liable.

Summary

This chapter has discussed the private and public regulation of various activities in an attempt to protect our environment. The private regulations focus on the tort theories of nuisance, trespass, negligence, and strict liability. Most of these private actions face legal defenses that hinder a private party from successfully restricting activity that has or might harm the environment.

The local government has a direct effect on the environment through the adoption of statutes

or ordinances covering such areas as zoning, building design, and noise.

Because of the problems associated with private actions and because of limited control at the local level, legislative bodies have passed legislation for the protection of the environment. On both the state and federal levels, administrative agencies play an important role in implementing this legislation. In particular, the Environment Protection Agency (EPA) was created by the federal government to monitor numerous federal statutes for environmental protection. One of the effective tools that this agency uses is the environmental impact statement (EIS). Most projects using federal funds must prepare an EIS in order to ascertain the project's effect on the environment. Many states have similar statutory provisions for projects they fund or that affect their environments.

Numerous federal statutes have been adopted for specific problem areas. The Clean Air Act promotes standards for pollution control. The Rivers and Harbors Act, Federal Water Pollution Control Act, and the Clean Water Act were adopted to clean up our rivers, lakes, and ocean beaches.

Even noise control has been attempted through regulations covering airplanes and sonic booms, as well as railroad and motor vehicles and the amount of noise they may emit. Toxic substances and pesticides are controlled by the EPA. Waste disposal is covered by the Solid Wastes Disposal Act, which attempts to reduce solid waste disposal by encouraging the recycling of waste and the reuse of materials. The federal government has even provided funds under the Comprehensive Environmental Response, Compensation, and Liability Act (Superfund) to clean up dangerous hazardous waste disposal sites.

The courts have attempted to balance the adverse effect of certain activities on the environment and on society with the cost of rectifying these problems. The courts recently have tended to interpret legislation in the light of whether benefits bear a reasonable relationship to the standards' demonstrably high costs.

Key Terms

Agreement of the Conservation of Nature and Natural Resources (586)
Association of Southeast Asian Nations (ASEAN) (586)
Clean Air Act (573)
Clean Water Act (576)
Comprehensive Environmental Response, Compensation, and Liability Act (580)
cost-benefit standard (582)
environmental impact statement (EIS) (573)
Environmental Protection Agency (EPA) (573)
Federal Environmental

Pesticide Control Act (580)
Federal Insecticide, Fungicide, and Rodenticide Act (580)
Law of the Navigational Uses of International Watercourses (586)
Marine Protection, Research, and Sanctuaries Act (578)
Montreal Protocol on Substances That Deplete the Ozone Layer (586)
National Environmental Policy Act (NEPA) (573)
Noise Control Act (579)
Nuclear Waste Policy Act (578)

Oil Pollution Act (576)
private nuisance (570)
public nuisance (570)
Resource Conservation and Recovery Act (580)
Rivers and Harbor Act (576)
Safe Drinking Water Act (578)
Shore Protection Act (578)
Solid Wastes Disposal Act (580)
state implementation plans (SIPs) (573)
Toxic Substances Control Act (579)
United Nations Convention on the Law of the Sea (586)

Questions and Case Problems

1. Oakhill is a development-home building corporation that primarily develops retirement communities. Washington Feeds owns several feedlots in Buckeye. Oakhill purchased 20,000 acres of farmland in the same area and began building and selling homes on this acreage. In the meantime, Washington Feeds continued to expand its feedlot business, and eventually only 500 feet separated the two operations. Because of the odor and flies from the feedlots, Oakhill found it difficult to sell the homes in its development. Oakhill wants to enjoin Washington

Feeds from operating its feedlots in the vicinity of the retirement home development. Under what theory would Oakhill file this action? Discuss fully.

2. Flylight, Inc., is a manufacturer of a new 250-seat passenger airplane that is fuel efficient and that travels at a cruising speed of 900 miles per hour. The plane would only be cost effective for flights of 1,000 miles or more. Traveling at 900 miles per hour creates a sonic boom lasting for no more than five seconds. The sound measured during the five-second period exceeds aircraft noise levels established by the EPA. Discuss fully whether Flylight, Inc., aircraft can be banned from flying over the United States.

3. Atlantic Richfield Company (ARCO) had an accidental oil spill that was reported to the Coast Guard in accordance with the law. ARCO cleaned up the oil spill to the satisfaction of the Coast Guard. The Coast Guard assessed a civil penalty for this accidental discharge. ARCO refused to pay, claiming it had cleaned up the spill and that the spill was accidental. ARCO also argued that such penalties are criminal in nature. The federal government sued to collect the penalty. What was the result and why? [United States v. Atlantic Richfield Co., 429 F.Supp. 830 (E.D.Pa., 1977)]

4. The Government Services Administration (GSA) entered into an agreement with a private individual under which the individual was to construct a building to GSA's specifications and lease it to the GSA. Under the contemplated lease provision, GSA would have use of the entire building for a five-year (renewable) period. As many as 2,300 government employees would be assigned to the building, and most would commute by automobile. The cost of the lease was approximately $11 million. GSA proceeded with its plans for the building without preparing any environmental impact statement. Was a statement necessary? [S.W. Neighborhood Assembly v. Eckard, 445 F.Supp. 1195 (D.D.C. 1978)]

5. Citizens Against Toxic Sprays, Inc., was an organization established to challenge the use of toxic sprays in places where they could be harmful to humans, animals, or vegetation. The group sought to enjoin the United States Forest Service from using the herbicide TCDD because of its hazardous effect on people who breathed it. TCDD was used only in national forests, not in any residential areas. Citizens Against Toxic Sprays alleged that some of its members were affected by the use of TCDD in two of the national forests because they lived near them, worked in them, or used them for recreational activities. Does Citizens Against Toxic Sprays have the

standing to sue the United States Forest Service? [Citizens Against Toxic Sprays, Inc. v. Bergland, 428 F.Supp. 908 (1977)]

6. Virginia Dalsis, the owner of a small store in the city of Olean, New York, brought a suit to enjoin the construction of a mall because of its projected size. Dalsis alleged that the large size of the shopping center would have an adverse environmental effect on the downtown area, causing economic blight and deterioration of the section in which her business was located. Dalsis, however, did not bring the suit until three months after construction of the shopping mall had begun, even though she was aware of the mall's potential size almost a year before construction started. Should Dalsis be allowed to enjoin the construction of the shopping mall under the National Environmental Policy Act? [Dalsis v. Hills, 424 F.Supp. 784 (W.D.N.Y. 1976)]

7. Judy Godwin began construction of her home. At about the same time, Exxon began construction of a "separation" plant 700 feet north of the homesite. The residence and plant were completed about the same time. The plant emitted noise, vibration, and sulfurous odors around the clock. These caused Godwin headaches, and because of the odor, she would not bring her friends to her residence. What legal theories could she use against Exxon? What result would be obtained under them? [Exxon Corp., U.S.A. v. Dunn, 474 So.2d 1269 (Fla. Dist.Ct.App. 1985)]

8. Interpretation of the language in environmental statutes is very important. Section 505(a) of the Clean Water Act authorizes private citizens to commence a civil action for injunctive relief and/or the imposition of civil penalties in federal district court against any person "alleged to be in violation" of the conditions of a National Pollutant Discharge Elimination System (NPDES) permit. Between 1981 and 1984, Smithfield repeatedly violated the conditions of its NPDES permit by exceeding authorized effluent limitations. Because of the installation of new equipment, Smithfield's last reported violation occurred in May 1984. Nevertheless, in June 1984, having given notice of their intent to sue to the Environmental Protection Agency and to state authorities, as required by Section 505(b) of the act, Chesapeake Bay Foundation filed a Section 505(a) suit alleging that Smithfield "has violated . . . [and] will continue to violate its NPDES permit." Smithfield filed a motion to dismiss, alleging that the federal statute required that he be in violation of the act at the time the action was filed. What was the result? [Gwaltney of Smithfield v. Chesapeake Bay Foundation, 484 U.S. 49, 108 S.Ct. 376, 98 L.Ed.2d 306 (1987)]

Chapter 24 International Business Law

The manufacturer who waits in the woods for the world to beat a path to his door is a great optimist. But the manufacturer who shows his "mousetraps" to the world keeps the smoke coming out of his chimney.

O. B. Winters

OUTLINE

Introduction

Since World War II, business has become increasingly multinational in character. It is not uncommon for a United States corporation to have investments or manufacturing plants in a foreign country or for a foreign country to have operations in the United States. Because the exchange of goods, services, and ideas on a global level is now a common phenomenon, it is important for the businessperson to have some familiarity with the laws pertaining to these international business transactions.

International law consists of a body of laws that are considered to be legally binding among otherwise independent nations. Although no sovereign nation can be compelled, against its will, to obey a law external to itself, nations can and do voluntarily agree to be governed in certain respects by international law for the purpose of facilitating international trade and commerce as well as civilized discourse. A nation's laws fundamentally control the relationship between the international business activities (conducted within its borders or conducted by the nation's businesses outside its borders) and the international agreements that the nation has signed.

This chapter explores the sources of international law, the sources of American international law, the statutes affecting international business, the agencies responsible for implementing those laws, and international business transactions. The "International Considerations" at the end of each chapter provide further information.

Sources of International Law

Businesses engaged in international commerce are regulated by international, regional, and national laws. International law has evolved in three ways: through international customs, through agreements that have the force of law, and through international organizations and conferences. Agreements or treaties are developed either by the nations themselves gathering together or by international agencies to which various nations belong.

International Customs

International customs have evolved among nations in their relations with one another. The United

Nations International Court of Justice defines international custom as "evidence of a general practice accepted as law." Customary law serves as an independent form of law. The application of this definition, however, is subject to challenge on a case-by-case basis. The courts must decide, for example, when a particular custom has evolved into a general practice that constitutes a law.

Agreements

Instruments used to bring about an international agreement include a treaty or compact, a convention, a protocol, or an executive agreement. A **treaty** is an agreement, or **compact**, between two or more nations that is authorized by the supreme power of each nation. When a country is a party to multiple treaties, conflicts may arise. Under the auspices of the United Nations, the **Vienna Convention on the Law of Treaties** was adopted in 1969 and became legally enforceable in 1980. The entire body of the law of treaties is codified by this convention. It covers issues such as the legal difference between treaties and other types of agreements, constitutional limitations on treaty-making powers, terminology, legal designation of parties, and general rules to be applied when interpreting treaties.

A **convention** is a code adopted by an international organization, such as the United Nations. The code is circulated among the members of the organization who, the drafters hope, will adopt it.

A **protocol** is an official agreement, but it does not have the force of a treaty. The document reflects the issues agreed upon by the diplomats.

The last important type of international agreement is the executive agreement. An **executive agreement** is not provided for in the United States Constitution, but it has a long history in the diplomatic world. A head of state reaches an executive agreement with another head of state. This process is faster than that of concluding a treaty, which is used for more complicated problems.

These agreements have an effect on international business and cover a multitude of areas, such as exporting, importing, quotas, and tariffs. **Exporting** is the selling of goods manufactured in and sent (exported) from the domestic country to a foreign country. **Importing** is the opposite; it is the buying of goods manufactured in a foreign country, which are then brought (imported) into the domestic country.

A **quota** places limits on the goods to be imported. For example, the United States at one time had a quota on the number of automobiles that could be imported from Japan. Other items subject to quotas are silicon chips and high-technology electronic equipment.

A **tariff** is a tax placed on imported goods. No equivalent tax exists for the same type of domestic goods. A tariff is generally assessed on either an *ad valorem* basis or a flat-rate basis. An *ad valorem* tariff is a percentage of the value of the imported goods. A flat-rate tariff is a unit item, such as each barrel of oil, or is based on weight, such as a tariff assessed on each ton of material that is imported.

International Organizations

Over 3,100 governmental international organizations can be found around the world, of which over 300 are concerned with economic matters. These organizations are normally formed by one of the international agreements we just examined.

The organizations or agreements fall into six classifications. First, the United Nations has an array of organizations whose duties range from keeping the peace to addressing health concerns. The United Nations operates out of three locations. It is headquartered in New York City, while the U.N.'s International Court of Justice is located at The Hague in the Netherlands. The United Nations' European office and a number of specialized agencies operate out of Geneva, Switzerland.

The second type includes economic organizations or agreements, such as the World Bank, the International Monetary Fund (IMF), the General Agreement on Tariffs and Trade (GATT), and the Organization for Economic Cooperation and Development (OECD). Third are the regional organizations, such as the European Community (EC),[1] Association of Southeast Asian Nations (ASEAN),[2] Andean Common Market (AN-COM),[3] and the Gulf Cooperation Council.[4]

Fourth, specialized commodity agreements exist for products like jute, sugar, or cotton. Fifth, specialty agreements and organizations exist that are very narrow in scope. Examples include the Customs Cooperation Council, located in Brussels, Belgium, which works with GATT on customs problems; the World Intellectual Property Organization, which deals with copyright and patent issues; and the American-Mexican Boundary Treaty Act of 1972. Sixth are bilateral economic agreements, such as the United States–Canada Free-Trade Agreement.

General Agreement on Tariffs and Trade (GATT) After World War II, the United States and other nations saw the need to reduce tariffs as one way to avoid the economic mistakes made between the two world wars. These negotiations eventually resulted in the General Agreement on Tariffs and Trade (GATT). GATT was completed by 1947 and originally was to be a multilateral treaty, not an organization. Today, it is an organization that administers GATT agreements. GATT has been very successful in reducing tariff levels.

Tariff and trade negotiations sponsored by GATT are called *rounds*,[5] and these negotiations take years to complete. The last round, the Tokyo Round, lasted from 1973–1979 and has 99 signatories, called contracting parties. The Uruguay Round, started in 1986, is expected to be concluded in the early 1990s.

The GATT round does not conclude in one agreement. In addition to the tariff reduction protocols, the Tokyo Round resulted in nine special agreements and four "understandings." Special agreements were reached concerning "trade in civil aircraft" and an "international dairy arrangement." An understanding was reached concerning a "declaration on trade measures taken for balance-of-payments purposes." Each special agreement is a treaty and is binding only on those contracting parties that have signed it. An understanding is not well defined, but it sets out goals for the contracting parties.

GATT has two nondiscrimination principles: the most-favored-nation (MFN) principle and na-

---

1. The twelve member states are Belgium, Denmark, France, Greece, Ireland, Italy, Luxembourg, the Netherlands, Portugal, Spain, United Kingdom, and West Germany.
2. The six member states are Brunei, Indonesia, Malaysia, the Philippines, Singapore, and Thailand.
3. The five member states are Bolivia, Colombia, Ecuador, Peru, and Venezuela.
4. The six member states are Bahrain, Kuwait, Oman, Qatar, Saudi Arabia, and the United Arab Emirates.

---

5. Since 1947, seven rounds have been completed. The Tokyo and Uruguay Rounds are named after the places where the round talks started. Over the years, the negotiations have been held in a variety of places.

tional treatment. The **most-favored-nation** condition does not mean especially favorable treatment but rather equal treatment to the other countries granted MFN status. The importing country must treat imported goods from a most favored nation as favorably as it treats goods from other MFN countries.

National treatment means the importing country must treat foreign goods just as it treats domestic goods, once the imported goods have cleared customs and have become part of the domestic commerce. GATT requires that if one nation grants a trade advantage to another country, it must be given to all other members which have signed the treaty.

United States Law Affecting International Business

This section looks at the United States governmental agencies concerned with international law and at the federal laws that apply to this area.

Federal Lawmaking Authority

The Constitution divides the lawmaking authority concerning international relations between the Congress and the president. Article I, Section 8, gives Congress the power "[t]o regulate Commerce with foreign Nations, and among the several States." Over the past two centuries, the Supreme Court has reaffirmed Congress's authority to establish economic policy. Congress has the power to impose and collect taxes and duties. Section 9, however, specifically forbids export taxes. Article II, Section 2, gives to the president the constitutional right to make treaties, but the Senate must ratify them by a two-thirds vote. During this last century, the president has been predominant in dealing with international affairs.

Agencies Regulating International Trade

Trade policy and trade disputes are handled by four federal agencies and one special court.

Office of the United States Trade Representative   Originally established in 1963, the **United States trade representative** (USTR) is a cabinet-level official with the rank of ambassador, directly responsible to the president. The formulation of trade policy for the United States starts in the office of the USTR. The USTR is responsible for all bilateral and multilateral trade negotiations. The USTR is the chief representative of the United States in all activities concerning the General Agreement on Tariffs and Trade.

United States Customs Service   The **United States Customs Service,** established in 1789, is housed in the Department of the Treasury. The customs service assesses and collects customs duties, excise taxes, fees, and penalties owed on imported merchandise. It detects and apprehends persons engaged in fraudulent practices designed to circumvent customs. The customs service also enforces copyright, patent, trademark, and maskwork provisions; quotas; and marking requirements for imported merchandise. International trade statistics are collected by the service. It also cooperates with other foreign customs services.

International Trade Administration   The **International Trade Administration** (ITA) is found in the Department of Commerce. Created in 1980 by the secretary of commerce, the ITA promotes world trade and strengthens the international trade and investment position of the United States. The ITA supports the trade policy negotiation efforts of the United States trade representative. This office promotes export trading companies and issues them certificates that provide limited exemptions from liability under the antitrust laws. We will return to this later in this chapter.

International Trade Commission   The **International Trade Commission** (ITC) is an independent agency created in 1916. The ITC imposes tariff adjustments and import quotas for industries. Adjustment assistance to workers and firms in industries adversely affected by imports can be authorized.

The ITC has broad investigatory powers concerning (1) the volume of importation in comparison with domestic production and consumption; (2) the conditions, causes, and effects relating to competition of foreign industries with those of the United States; and (3) all other factors affecting competition between domestically produced articles and imported articles. The commission advises the president as to the probable economic effect on the domestic industry of any proposed trade agreement involving the increase, reduction, or elimination of a tariff.

The ITC, upon petition by a harmed group, conducts investigations to determine whether an article is being imported in such increased quantities as to comprise or pose the threat of a serious injury to a domestic industry that produces a competitive article. If the commission finds that this situation, called dumping (examined later in this chapter) exists, it recommends to the president the action that would redress the injury.

United States Court of International Trade Established in 1890 and formerly known as the United States Tariff Commission, the **Court of International Trade** (CIT) became a court in 1980. The court has all the powers in law and equity of a federal district court. It reviews agency decisions involving dumping and countervailing duty matters. A countervailing duty is imposed when the importing nation determines that the exporting country is subsidizing the product. All civil actions against the United States arising from laws governing import transactions are heard by the CIT. Civil actions commenced by the United States that seek penalties and allege fraud or negligence are also within the exclusive jurisdiction of the court.

Statutes Regulating International Trade

The following subsections look at some of the federal statutes that govern international trade.

Export Administration Act The **Export Administration Act** restricts the export of goods and technology in the military field when it would be detrimental to the United States. The Export Enhancement Act of 1988 liberalized what could be exported, penalties were stiffened if the statute was violated, and enforcement was increased.

First, an exporter must determine whether any products may be shipped to the specific country where the exporter hopes to do business. Currently, exports to Cuba, Vietnam, North Korea, and Iraq are prohibited. If trade is permitted to a specific country, the exporter must determine whether a license is required.

Two types of licenses exist: general and validated. The **general license** is really a misnomer. Many goods can be shipped to specific countries without any official license. The general license is more of a general authority to ship than an actual license. The Department of Commerce classifies the foreign countries, and that list determines whether the goods being exported to a specific country require a general license.

A **validated license** normally covers goods involved with high technology. This license prohibits certain types of goods from being shipped to countries that may pose a military threat to the United States. Goods such as computers were not allowed to be sent to the former Union of Soviet Socialist Republics (USSR), for example.

A validated license is also used to aid the United States in its foreign policy objectives. A validated license is required for exports to Libya or Iran, for example, countries that have previously supported terrorism.

Finally, the act attempts to keep products within this country when there is a short supply. During the Korean conflict when copper was in short supply, its export was restricted.

In the following case, the court was confronted with implementing a provision of the Export Administration Act and supporting the foreign policy objectives of the United States. Two of the objectives were to support Israel and to refrain from supporting any boycott not sanctioned by the United States.

BACKGROUND AND FACTS *In December 1954, the League of Arab States approved a resolution calling for an economic boycott of Israel. The boycott was not confined to actual trade with Israel but also applied to companies blacklisted for activities deemed to be inconsistent with the resolution. A firm was blacklisted if it traded with Israel or if it dealt with a firm that traded with Israel.*

Israel is a country friendly to the United States and is not itself the object of any form of boycott pursuant to United States law or regulation. In the mid 1970s, Congress became concerned about Arab efforts to pressure

Case 24.1
BRIGGS & STRATTON CORPORATION v. BALDRIGE
United States District Court,
E.D. Wisconsin, 1982.
539 F.Supp. 1307.

American companies into participating in the boycott. Congress enacted antiboycott amendments to the Export Administration Act.

Briggs & Stratton makes internal combustion engines that are incorporated as power components in the end products of other manufacturers. Briggs does not manufacture or sell end products but only supplies components to end-product manufacturers. The customers usually manufacture their products in large quantities using assembly-line techniques. Briggs products are designed for a particular engine model, and the design is not readily alterable.

Manufacturers located around the world sell products powered by Briggs & Stratton engines. The Arab countries were a minor segment of this worldwide market in terms of volume. Syria requested information about Briggs's dealings with Israel. The antiboycott amendments made it illegal for Briggs to supply this information. Briggs was blacklisted and could not transact business in Syria or other Arab states, nor could it do business with companies that incorporated Briggs & Stratton engines into their products that were in turn sold to Arab countries. The volume of sales involved exceeded $15 million and meant the employment of over 100 people in the United States.

Because Briggs was blacklisted, a number of customers notified Briggs that they would no longer purchase its engines as components of products that they would be shipping not only to Arab countries but to all other countries as well. Foreign manufacturers have sufficient capacity to supply the foreign market with engines. Briggs brought this action against the federal government, challenging the constitutionality of the antiboycott provisions of the Export Administration Act. Malcolm Baldrige was then secretary of commerce.

District Judge GORDON

*   *   *   *

This litigation focuses on specific provisions of the anti-boycott legislation and the regulations implementing it. The crucial portion of the statute reads:

"(a)(1) . . . [T]he President shall issue regulations prohibiting any United States person, with respect to his activities in the interstate or foreign commerce of the United States, from taking or knowingly agreeing to take any of the following actions with intent to comply with, further, or support any boycott fostered or imposed by a foreign country against a country which is friendly to the United States and which is not itself the object of any form of boycott pursuant to United States law or regulation."

*   *   *   *

The plaintiffs primarily object to the regulations promulgated by the Commerce Department on the issue of intent. These regulations read:

"(e) 'Intent'. (1) Part 369 prohibits a United States person from taking or knowingly agreeing to take certain specified actions with intent to comply with, further, or support an unsanctioned foreign boycott.

"(2) A United States person has the intent to comply with, further, or support an unsanctioned foreign boycott when such a boycott is at least one of the reasons for that person's decision whether to take a particular prohibited action. So long as that is at least one of the reasons for his action, a violation occurs regardless of whether the prohibited action is also taken for non-boycott reasons. Stated differently, the fact that such action was taken for legitimate business reasons does not remove that action from the scope of this part if compliance with an unsanctioned foreign boycott was also a reason for the action.

*   *   *   *

The plaintiffs argue that the effect of the regulations on intent is at odds with the premises of the act. The anti-boycott provisions amended the Export Administration Act; the plaintiffs argue that the overall act stresses the importance of United States exports. To that end, the President must, prior to the imposition of export controls for foreign policy or national security purposes, consider whether the same goods are available from foreign suppliers; if they are, the President must specifically find that the controls are necessary.

While the promotion of the export of American goods is certainly one goal of the EAA, it is not the only one. Congress included a detailed "declaration of policy" in the act. Congress stated that it is the policy of the United States

"... to encourage and, in specified cases, require United States persons engaged in the export of goods or technology or other information to refuse to take actions, including furnishing information or entering into or implementing agreements, which have the effect of furthering or supporting the restrictive trade practices or boycotts fostered or imposed by any foreign country against a country friendly to the United States or against any United States person." *   *   *

The Commerce Department regulations are consistent with this express policy to require persons to refuse to furnish information which would have the effect of furthering a boycott against a nation friendly to the United States. Thus the regulations are not inconsistent with the policies of the act.

DECISION AND REMEDY

The court upheld the antiboycott amendments even though they had the effect of restricting Briggs & Stratton from exporting goods to the Arab states. The government could forbid an exporter from providing information that would assist in the boycott of a friendly nation.

COMMENT

At the time the case was heard, Briggs had been taken off the blacklist, and its products were being accepted throughout the nations of the Arab League. Briggs never supplied the information originally requested that had led to its being temporarily blacklisted.

Interestingly, the Export Administration Act controls exports even when the final product is not produced in the United States. The key question is whether the final goods are manufactured either with technical data developed in the United States or with parts originating in the United States. For example, a computer made in South Korea from component parts or based on technical information from the United States must have a validated license when sold by the Korean company to a buyer in the Republic of China. Export laws, thus, have extraterritorial applications.

One major problem is knowing whether there will be a diversion of the products from one country to another. A United States exporter sells a product to Nigeria. Unknown to the exporter, the Nigerian business ships the product to Iraq. An exporter can be held liable if it should have known that the product could be sent to an embargoed area.

The penalties for violating this act are substantial. Fines can equal up to five times the value of the exports or $1 million, whichever is greater, if it is a willful violation. The businessperson faces five years in prison, plus a $250,000 fine. The law allows for forfeitures of property, civil penalties, and revocation of export license privileges.

The following case illustrates the implementation of this act when the defendant was involved in a diversion of goods to a banned country.

Case 24.2
**UNITED STATES v.
ELKINS**
United States Court of Appeals,
Eleventh Circuit, 1989.
885 F.2d 775.

BACKGROUND AND FACTS *This prosecution arose out of an investigation into the 1985 shipment of two Lockheed L-100-30 aircraft to Libya. At the time, Libya was subject to strict export controls. Export licenses were required for the export of these two jets; because of government restrictions on trade with Libya, no export licenses would have been granted to export these planes to Libya.*

Elkins owned a company called Armaflex, Inc. He negotiated with Lockheed as a representative of Contrust, a West German oil exploration subsidiary controlled by Badir, a Libyan dealer. Lockheed preferred to sell to Armaflex rather than Contrust. Elkins created a new corporation, AFI Int'l, which represented Contrust in the negotiations. In negotiations with Lockheed, Elkins maintained that the airplanes were destined for the West African country of Benin. When Lockheed learned of Badir's involvement, Lockheed canceled the negotiations.

Elkins assured Lockheed that Badir represented a legitimate West German concern and that Badir was a Libyan expatriate antagonistic to the Libyan government. With this news, Lockheed resumed negotiations. Elkins never told Lockheed that the planes were to be modified with midair refueling capability and were to be used by the Libyan Air Force. Elkins and Lockheed agreed on the sale of two L-100-30 planes and parts to AFI. The contract provided that AFI had the sole responsibility to obtain a valid export license. Elkins made a net profit of $7 million.

Lockheed officials accompanied Elkins to the Department of Commerce to obtain an export license. The government officials knew that Contrust was owned by Libyans. Elkins explained that the planes were destined for Benin. At no time did Elkins tell the government officials of the planned refueling modification. The Department of Commerce approved the export license. Lockheed delivered the planes to Benin. They were never seen in Benin again. One plane was found in Cairo, Egypt. The plane's radio signal and operations manual indicated that the plane had been used by the Libyan Air Force.

Elkins, along with several other individuals, was indicted as a result of an investigation. Elkins was convicted of violating export restrictions. He received a fifteen-year prison sentence and was fined $6.6 million. He also had a $100 special assessment imposed. Elkins appealed.

Circuit Judge JACKSON
*   *   *   *

An indictment must set forth the elements of the offense in a manner which fairly informs the defendant of the charges against him and enables him to enter a plea which will bar future prosecution for the same offense. In this case, the indictment charged defendant with conspiracy to commit four substantive offenses against the United States. Although the fraud was charged as the object of the substantive offense of wire fraud rather than as the object of the conspiracy, defendant had clear notice that violations of the substantive offenses constituted fraud against the government. Conspiracy to violate the substantive offenses *is* conspiracy to defraud the government. Reading the indictment as a whole, we conclude that the indictment adequately charged defendant with conspiring to deprive the United States of its ability to control its foreign policy by concealing material facts from responsible government agencies.

We also conclude that the district court adequately charged the jury on conspiracy to defraud the United States. *   *   *
*   *   * The district court clarified and repeated this instruction as follows:

> What must be proved beyond a reasonable doubt is that the accused planned knowingly and willfully to devise or intending—to devise a scheme to defraud the United States of America and its executive agencies out of the right to implement its foreign policy and to conduct its affairs free from stealth, false statement, and fraud and that the use of the interstate wire or foreign wire communications were to be closely related to the scheme.

*   *   * Conspiracy to commit wire fraud against the United States contains all of the elements of conspiracy to defraud the United States. Conspiracy to commit wire fraud contains the additional element of use of wire transmission services in furtherance of the scheme to defraud.
*   *   *   *

Defendant was sentenced to five years' imprisonment on the conspiracy conviction, and to a consecutive term of ten years' imprisonment and a $6.6 million fine on the export control violation conviction. Defendant also received a special assessment of $50 on each count. Defendant eventually makes one argument that his sentence violated the Eighth Amendment: "Because the harshness of Appellant's sentence far exceeds the sentences imposed in similar export prosecutions in the Northern District of Georgia and elsewhere, Appellant respectfully submits this Court should conclude that his sentence is unconstitutionally disproportionate." A sentence is disproportionate for Eighth Amendment purposes if the punishment is grossly disproportionate when compared with the nature of the crime. *   *   *

In a variety of situations, life sentences with the possibility of parole have been held not to violate the Eighth Amendment. These sentences, five years for conspiracy and ten years for violating export control laws, certainly are not grossly excessive compared to the nature of the crime. Additionally, the ten-year sentence imposed for violating export control regulations is not grossly disproportionate to the sentences imposed in other federal jurisdictions for violations of the same federal laws. Defendant unlawfully sold $57 million worth of high technology aircraft equipment to an unfriendly nation. Although his sentence may have been longer than the sentences normally imposed for this offense, that fact alone does not mean it was grossly disproportionate. *   *   *

Defendant also challenges the fine imposed on count two. There may be circumstances where an excessive fine constitutes cruel and unusual punishment in violation of the Eighth Amendment. We need not identify those circumstances in this case. Defendant made a gross profit of $13,049,474, a net profit of $7,336,233, and an after-tax profit of $3,368,917 from the sale of these aircraft. Defendant's fine of $6.6 million was less than his gross profit and less than his net profit from the sale of these planes. Although a large amount, we hold that a fine representing an amount less than the net profit of an illegal transaction does not violate the Eighth Amendment absent a showing of severe, particularized hardship suffered by defendant.

Elkins's conviction for conspiracy against the United States in violation of the Export Administration Act was upheld.   **DECISION AND REMEDY**

Omnibus Trade and Competitiveness Act In 1988 Congress passed an act to enhance the competitiveness of American industry. The **Omnibus** Trade and Competitiveness Act (OTCA) has four purposes: (1) to authorize the negotiation of reciprocal trade agreements; (2) to strengthen United

States trade laws; (3) to improve the development and management of United States trade strategy; and (4) through these actions, to improve standards of living in the world.

Under this act, Congress made it the highest priority to pursue a broad array of domestic and international policies. Future declines in the United States economy and standards of living will be stemmed. National policy established the importance of maintaining the vitality of the technological, industrial, and agricultural base of the United States. Congress resolved that it is in the national interest of the United States to remain a world leader. Working with the president, Congress through the OTCA strengthened an existing procedure called a *fast-track* procedure when dealing with other governments.

Fast-Track Procedures In the past, the president would make a trade agreement with a foreign government, send it to Congress to be approved, and if approved, the bill would then be returned to the president for his or her signature. The trade agreement was then binding on the United States, although it was not part of the domestic statutes.

Occasionally, it was politically embarrassing when a president made a trade agreement but Congress refused to adopt it. Foreign nations viewed it as "two shakes of the dice." When Congress failed to approve an agreement and insisted on other provisions, the president was forced to re-open negotiations. Foreign countries took a dim view of this process when the original commitment was not honored. To remedy this problem, Congress enacted fast-track procedures for adopting trade agreements.

Both the 1974 **Trade Act** and the 1988 Omnibus Trade and Competitiveness Act contain procedures allowing the president to fast-track a trade agreement into law. Prior to concluding a trade agreement, the president notifies Congress of his or her intention to enter into the trade agreement. A draft is sent to Congress for review. Public notice of the anticipated trade agreement is published in the *Federal Register*. If Congress approves, the trade agreement is enacted into law when the president concludes the negotiations.

This procedure reassures foreign governments that the president is able to deliver on promises made. When negotiations began in 1986 between Canada and the United States to create a free-trade agreement, Canada insisted on the use of the fast-track procedure for the negotiation results. The North American Free Trade Agreement (NAFTA) to establish a North American free-trade zone among Canada, Mexico, and the United States also will be adopted through the use of the fast-track procedure.

Export Trading Company Act The **Export Trading Company Act** of 1982 was the result of legal difficulties concerning violations of antitrust laws by companies dealing internationally. The act allows a business to file an application for a certificate of antitrust immunity with the International Trade Administration. The application contains information based on the company's business plans. Once the certificate is granted and as long as the company follows its business plan, the company will be immune from antitrust prosecution by the Department of Justice.

Foreign Sales Corporation The Revenue Act of 1971 provides tax benefits when a firm markets its products overseas through a **foreign sales corporation.** The foreign sales corporation must be located outside the United States, although it may be based in a United States possession, such as Puerto Rico. If it is located in a foreign country, the country must be a party to an information exchange agreement with the United States.

Export-Import Bank The **Export-Import Bank (Eximbank)** provides financial assistance to exporting and importing firms. The primary type of assistance offered consists of the credit guarantees that Eximbank gives to commercial banks. Based on those guarantees, the commercial banks, in turn, make direct loans to exporting companies.

Other Exporting and Importing Statutes All nations prohibit the import of goods perceived to be harmful to it. The **Trading with the Enemy Act** of 1917 restricts imports from nations designated as enemies of the United States. Other laws prohibit the importation of cocaine, which is an illegal drug, and of agricultural products that pose a danger to domestic crops or animals. For example, cattle infected with hoof-and-mouth disease may not be imported into the United States.

Unfair Practices

Several unfair import practices can occur. The following subsections examine four types of unfair practices: (1) dumping; (2) infringement of copyright, trademark, and patent laws; (3) government financing of products, called subsidizing; and (4) the sale of gray-market goods.

Dumping   **Dumping** is the practice of selling goods in a buyer country below the price charged for them in the seller's country. The purpose is to drive out competition in the buyer's country. When material injury is sustained by a domestic industry, GATT allows additional duties to be added to equal the discrepancy in prices.

The **Trade Agreements Act** of 1979, which adopted the GATT Antidumping Code, regulates dumping in the United States. The International Trade Administration protects domestic industries against economic injury caused by the sale of foreign merchandise at less than fair value in the United States.

The International Trade Administration ascertains the type of goods most likely to be sold at less than fair value. If a business believes itself to be injured, it may file a complaint with the ITC. The International Trade Commission determines whether a threat of or actual material injury to the business exists because the imports are being subsidized or sold at less than fair value. If the ITC finds that dumping has occurred, import duties are assessed against the merchandise. The duties can remain in effect for three to five years after violations of the act have ceased.

Infringement   The ITC is likewise charged with investigating unfair methods of competition including infringement of copyright, patent, trademark, and maskwork laws. For example, a business located in a less-developed country makes copies of music tapes from famous U.S. performers. This copying is done without permission and without paying any royalties to the copyright holders. These tapes can be seized by the United States Customs Service upon request from the ITC.

Over $430 million in royalties are lost annually because copyrighted works are copied by businesses in China. China and the United States reached an agreement that China would adopt laws making it illegal to copy copyrighted work. Thus, China avoided the potential imposition of penalties in the amount of $430 million. If the penalties had been imposed on China, businesses in Hong Kong would have suffered, since nearly 80 percent of Chinese exports go through Hong Kong.

Subsidies   The third unfair practice occurs when a government grants subsidies to local exporters. Subsidies may take different forms, such as low-interest or interest-free loans, rebates on taxes earned from sales to foreign countries, or price guarantees so that the local business is not subject to international currency fluctuations.

Any subsidy distorts the true movement of trade in the international community. The ITA is charged with protecting American businesses from subsidies when they constitute a material injury to an industry. Countervailing duties are imposed on the imports. A **countervailing duty** is an import tax equal to the grant extended to an exporter by its home country to encourage exportation or used to assist the exporter in meeting competition. Countervailing duties are intended to eliminate the competitive advantage gained by government subsidization of foreign exporters.

The following case concerns whether Mexico gave financial assistance to businesses. The question is whether a countervailing duty should be imposed, and if so, how much it should be.

BACKGROUND AND FACTS   *Carbon black is produced from carbon black feedstock, natural gas, and water. Carbon black feedstock is made early in the petroleum refining process. Crude oil is heated to cause it to break down into its constituent parts, gas oil and heavy gas oil. Further refinement results in a "catalytic cracker."*

In the typical catalytic cracking process, a catalyst is introduced into the heating of gas oil. At extremely high temperatures and pressures, the gas

Case 24.3
**CABOT CORPORATION
v. UNITED STATES**
United States Court of
International Trade, 1985.
620 F.Supp. 722.

oil breaks down—that is, cracks—and yields gasoline. Besides gasoline,
another product results from catalytic cracking: carbon black feedstock. This
process represents the major cost of producing the final product, carbon black.
Primarily used in the rubber industry, carbon black is also used in paints,
inks, plastics, and carbon paper.

In the Mexican carbon black industry, the two carbon black producers,
Hules Mexicanos and Negromex, use the carbon black feedstock available
from Petroleos Mexicanos (PEMEX), the government-owned petroleum com-
pany of Mexico. During the period investigated, both firms purchased carbon
black feedstock from PEMEX at a price substantially below the world market
price. Both firms received natural gas at a deeply discounted rate.

Cabot Corporation, a United States producer of carbon black, petitioned
the International Trade Administration (ITA) to make a countervailing duty
determination. The ITA found some benefits required the imposition of a
countervailing duty while other action did not. Cabot made a motion to
the Court of International Trade (CIT) to review the ITA's final order.

Judge CARMAN
*   *   *   *

Plaintiff first challenges the ITA final determination that Mexico did not confer
a countervailable bounty or grant, within the meaning of the Tariff Act of 1930,
by providing carbon black feedstock and natural gas to Hules Mexicanos and
Negromex at below "world market prices." Plaintiff contends that the term "bounty
or grant" is to be broadly construed and includes essentially every governmental
program which "bestow[s] an unfair competitive advantage on a foreign company
as against U.S. producers of the products." Defendant opposes this proposition,
arguing that programs or benefits which are generally available within the exporting
country are not countervailable. *   *   * In response, plaintiff secondarily argues
that the Mexican carbon black feedstock and natural gas programs are as a factual
matter not generally available.

In reviewing the countervailing duty law, the Court determines that 19 U.S.C.
§ 1303 applies to this investigation. Section 1303 clearly delineates those elements
that, if present, require the assessment of countervailing duties. The elements are:

(1) Any county, dependency, colony, province, or other political subdivision of
government, person, partnership, association, cartel, or corporation that

(2) pays or bestows

(3) any bounty or grant

(4) upon the manufacture or production or export of any article or merchandise
manufactured or produced in such country, and

(5) the importation of such article or merchandise into the United States.

The element of bounty or grant is further defined by the case law and [by] Congress.
First, a bounty or grant is a benefit which gives rise to a "competitive advantage."

Second, in the case of domestic subsidies, the benefit must be conferred upon
"a specific enterprise or industry or group of enterprises or industries."

Congress in enumerating some examples of countervailable subsidies, explicitly
stated that the list is not inclusive. The determination of whether a bounty or grant
has been bestowed must therefore be made upon the facts of each case. Since the
enactment of section 1303 courts have recognized that they must examine the
actual results or effects of assistance provided by foreign governments and not the
purposes or intentions. Nor is section 1303 concerned with the nominal availability
of a governmental program. The question is what aid or advantage has actually
been received "regardless of whatever name or in whatever manner or form or for
whatever purpose" the aid was provided.

The ITA applied the incorrect "generally available" test to the question of
whether the provision of industrial inputs at government-set prices constitutes a

countervailable bounty or grant; therefore the case must be remanded for further investigation. The ITA is directed to apply the test as set forth above to the facts of this case and accordingly investigate whether or not the provision of carbon black feedstock and natural gas in Mexico at government-set prices should be countervailed.

The Court of International Trade took the position that any assistance given an exporter by a foreign government must be reviewed by the International Trade Administration (ITA) to determine if a countervailing duty should apply. The ITA must evaluate the results of that assistance when these products are imported into the United States.

DECISION AND REMEDY

Gray-Market Goods   The term **gray-market goods** refers to foreign-manufactured goods for which a valid United States trademark has been registered. The goods are legally purchased abroad and imported into the United States but without the consent of the American trademark holder. The term *gray market*, which is at times used unfairly, implies a nefarious undertaking by the importer. A more accurate term for the goods is *parallel import*. This term is devoid of negative connotations. But "gray-market," for better or for worse, has become the commonly accepted term for such goods.

The following case discusses some of the issues involved with parallel imports.

BACKGROUND AND FACTS   *Weil Ceramics and Glass, Inc., was the wholly owned subsidiary of Lladro Exportadora, S.A., a Spanish corporation. Weil is a New York corporation in the business of importing and selling fine porcelain and glassware and was the exclusive distributor in the United States of LLADRO porcelain. Weil obtained a valid United States registration for the LLADRO trademark.*

Jalyn Corporation began importing LLADRO porcelain. Jalyn legally obtained the porcelain in Spain from distributors of Lladro, S.A., and sold it in the United States without the consent of Weil. Weil filed a lawsuit against Jalyn contending that Jalyn's import and sale of LLADRO porcelain was an infringement of Weil's exclusive right to use the trademark.

The court relied heavily on the reasoning of K-Mart v. Cartier, Inc.,[a] *a case decided just prior to this one by the United States Supreme Court.*

Case 24.4
WEIL CERAMICS AND GLASS, INC. v. DASH
United States Court of Appeals, Third Circuit (1989).
878 F.2d 659.

Circuit Judge HIGGINBOTHAM
*   *   *   *

In its analysis [of *K-Mart v. Cartier, Inc.*], the Court identified three general case scenarios in which the gray-market goods issue is presented. *   *   * The case 1 scenario, which the Court described as prototypical, involves a domestic company—that is independent of the foreign manufacturer—which purchases the right from the foreign company to register and use that company's trademark in the United States. The case 2 scenario involves a domestic company that registers a trademark for a good produced by a foreign manufacturer with which the domestic company shares a corporate affiliation. This scenario has three variations: a foreign company that has an incorporated subsidiary in the United States which distributes its product domestically (case 2a); a domestic company that incorporates a subsidiary

---

a.   486 U.S. 281, 108 S.Ct. 1811, 100 L.Ed.2d 313 (1988).

manufacturing company abroad and then imports its goods (case 2b); or a domestic company that establishes an unincorporated manufacturing division abroad and then imports the foreign manufactured product into the United States (case 2c). The case 3 scenario involves a domestic trademark holder that authorizes an independent foreign manufacturer to use its trademark. * * *

The opinion of the Court, written by Justice Kennedy, was founded upon different majorities for each of the holdings announced in its separate parts. Significantly, however, that opinion stated the unanimous judgment of the Court * * * to the scenario in which a domestic subsidiary is the trademark holder for foreign manufactured goods that are produced by its foreign parent. * * * ("All Members of the Court are in agreement that the agency may interpret the statute to bar importation of gray-market goods in what we have denoted case 1 and to *permit the imports under case 2(a)."*) (emphasis added). The Court concluded that the term "owned by" * * * "is sufficiently ambiguous, in the context of the statute, that it applies to situations involving a foreign parent, which is case 2a." The Court noted further that "[t]his ambiguity arises from the inability to discern, from the statutory language, which of the two entities involved in case 2a can be said to 'own' the U.S. trademark if, as in some instances, the domestic subsidiary is wholly owned by its foreign parent."

The case before us most closely resembles the case 2(a) scenario. Weil is the wholly owned subsidiary of the foreign manufacturer and, consistent with the Supreme Court's decision regarding that scenario, * * * excludes the goods imported by Jalyn from * * * prohibition[s] of parallel imports.

Weil argues that *K-Mart* does not preclude it from protection against parallel importation * * * because Weil has demonstrated factually that it is the *independent* owner of the United States LLADRO trademark even though Weil is not independent of the foreign manufacturer, Lladro, S.A. It reads *K-Mart* as affirming only * * * instances of sham incorporation, in which a foreign manufacturer incorporates a shell domestic corporation so that it can control the distribution of its product in the United States without competition. * * * Accordingly, [Weil] can demonstrate factually that it was not a sham incorporation by Lladro, S.A., and that it independently owns the LLADRO trademark. * * *

Although Weil is not a subsidiary that was incorporated by its parent, its affiliation with Lladro, S.A. enables it nonetheless to enjoy every benefit that inheres in the corporate relationship that the Supreme Court described in the case 2(a) scenario. More significantly, that relationship also provides the opportunity for the foreign manufacturer's control of the United States market [that the trademark act intended to preclude]. Thus, although Weil was not a "sham" incorporated by Lladro with the specific intent to benefit from the protections of the trademark act, its present relationship with Lladro nonetheless presents the potential for undesired monopoly of the domestic market. * * *

DECISION AND REMEDY   *Because Weil was a wholly owned subsidiary of the manufacturer, Jalyn was allowed to purchase and import for resale the products manufactured by the parent company, Lladro Exportadora, S.A.*

COMMENT   *If an independent business entity had owned the trademark, the results of this case would have been different. If a business is not related to the manufacturer and owns the trademark in the United States on imported goods, it has the authority to stop another company from buying those goods overseas and importing them for resale into the U.S.*

Transacting Business Internationally

Whether a company is in the importing or exporting business, a fundamental need exists for a contract. As with all commercial contracts, the transnational (international) business contract should be in writing.

Provisions Within a Contract

Contracts should be negotiated first until all the details are understood. The contract should be drafted by attorneys familiar with the business involved and with international law. The drafts should be reviewed before reducing the contract to final form. The following subsections cover some provisions that should be considered in the formation of any international contract.

Choice of Law
The parties can write into the contract a choice-of-law clause. A **choice-of-law clause** designates the forum where the case will be heard and which substantive law will be applied in the event of any disputes.

Many countries recognize the validity of the choice-of-law clause and will enforce it in their courts. It is of critical importance, however, that, before entering into a transnational business contract, both parties be familiar with the laws of the foreign country involved.

Official-Language Clause
The contract should also contain a clause that designates the official language to be used in interpreting the terms of the contract. This clause promotes a clear and precise understanding of the terms of the contract by each of the parties.

For example, in a sale of goods contract, the basic contract of sale should include a legal definition of terms, the price and manner of payment, and a provision specifying the acceptable currency for payment. A *force majeure* clause, which protects the parties from forces beyond their control, such as acts of God, is also advisable.

Risk-of-Loss Clause
Transacting international business involves peculiar risks since buyers and sellers are often separated by thousands of miles. Sellers want to avoid delivering goods for which they might not be paid. Buyers do not want to pay the sellers until there is evidence that the goods have been shipped. Specific clauses can dictate the exact moment when risk of loss passes from the seller to the buyer. In addition, to limit the risks of nonpayment for goods shipped or of payment for goods not shipped, the parties frequently use letters of credit to facilitate international business transactions.

A Sample International Business Transaction

In most international business transactions, three separate contracts are involved. The first contract is the purchase/sell agreement between the buyer and the seller. The second contract is between the bank and the buyer, establishing that the bank will extend credit to the buyer. The third contract involves the **letter of credit,** which guarantees payment and is issued by the bank to the seller.

Each contract is separate. The bank's obligations under the letter of credit are not involved with the purchase/sell contract between the buyer and seller. The bank's duty is to make sure the documents presented by the seller comply with the terms of the letter of credit.

Businesses often use the next two documents in connection with letters of credit: bills of exchange and bills of lading. The **bill of exchange** is normally called a draft. A check is a form of draft. The difference is that a check is always drawn on a bank. Bills of exchange are normally drawn upon the buyer of the goods. A **bill of lading** is initially issued by a common carrier, such as a railroad, a trucking firm, an airline, or a steamship company. The bill of lading controls who is entitled to possession of the goods.

The common carrier delivers the bill of lading to the seller. Prior to shipment, the buyer obtains a letter of credit from its bank. In the meantime, the seller (drawer) prepares a bill of exchange naming the buyer as the drawee. The payee normally is the seller's bank.

The bill of lading, the bill of exchange, and the letter of credit are sent to the seller's bank, which transmits all three documents to the buyer's bank. The buyer's bank then pays the bill of exchange under the terms of the letter of credit and provides the buyer with the bill of lading. The

Legal Highlight

The Life Cycle of a Letter of Credit

Although the letter of credit appears quite complex at first, it is not difficult to understand. It merely involves the exchange of documents (and money) through intermediaries. The following steps depict the letter-of-credit procurement cycle:

Step 1: The buyer and seller agree upon the terms of sale. The sales contract dictates that a letter of credit is to be used to finance the transaction.

Step 2: The buyer completes an application for a letter of credit and forwards it to his or her bank, which will issue the letter of credit.

Step 3: The issuing buyer's bank then forwards the letter of credit to a correspondent bank in the seller's country.

Step 4: The correspondent bank relays the letter of credit to the seller.

Step 5: Having received assurance of payment, the seller makes the necessary shipping arrangements.

Step 6: The seller prepares the documents required under the letter of credit and delivers them to the correspondent bank.

Step 7: The correspondent bank negotiates the documents. If it finds them in order, it sends them to the issuing bank and pays the seller in accordance with the terms of the letter of credit.

Step 8: The issuing bank, having received the documents, examines them. If they are in order, the issuing bank will charge the buyer's account and send the documents on to the buyer or his or her customs broker. The issuing bank will also reimburse the correspondent bank.

Step 9: The buyer or broker receives the documents and picks up the merchandise from the shipper (carrier).

Source: National Association of Purchasing Management.

---

buyer's bank is bound to pay the seller through the seller's bank when the seller has complied with the terms of the letter of credit. The seller looks to the buyer's bank, not to the buyer, to be paid when the seller presents the documents required by the letter of credit.

The buyer takes the bill of lading to the transport company that has possession of the goods. With the bill of lading, the buyer obtains possession of the goods.

A letter of credit assures the seller of payment and at the same time assures the buyer that payment will not be made until the seller has complied with the terms of the letter of credit. The letter of credit protects both the buyer and the seller. If the documents presented by the seller comply with the terms of the letter of credit, the bank must honor the letter. The letter of credit is a key financial document in international trade.

The United Nations Convention on International Bills of Exchange and Promissory Notes now provides rules in this area. The convention provides guidance and ensures uniformity in the creation, interpretation, and performance of bills of exchange and promissory notes. The U.N. agreement entitled "Uniform Customs and Practices for Documentary Credits" provides rules covering letters of credit.

Ethical Considerations

What Products Should Be Sold Internationally?

American businesses must consider the effects that their products may have when sold in foreign markets. A product appropriate to the American market may not be acceptable in other countries. Marketing techniques should always be directed so that a company is not exploiting a foreign economy. The following are some examples.

In the United States and the rest of the industrialized world, the consumption of tobacco has decreased in recent years. Meanwhile, the use of tobacco is increasing in third-world countries. The governments of these countries are very involved in the sale of tobacco, either through their ownership of the distributor or through their taxation of the tobacco products. Because this involvement provides these governments with a positive revenue flow, the governments do not discourage the use of tobacco.

After the 1964 surgeon general's report, United States tobacco companies moved abroad. They entered into marketing arrangements with foreign firms through business agreements and made direct investments in production facilities. In addition, United States trade policy has pressured countries like Japan to open their markets for more tobacco products. This was done to assist in the balance of trade between the United States and countries such as Japan. U.S. tobacco companies are now competing for a share of the Japanese markets.

Do you think it was ethical conduct by the tobacco companies to move their production overseas or to try to open new markets for tobacco? Is it up to the foreign governments to regulate this area? Isn't the foreign nation most

able to decide what is good for its own citizens? But is it ethical for the governments of the poorer nations to use valuable foreign exchange on a product that poses serious health hazards? Would it not be better for them to purchase the products that would assist in improving standard health care? Should the United States government be involved in assisting the sale of tobacco to these countries for the purposes of balancing foreign trade and assisting U.S. producers?

While the use of tobacco presents a clear health hazard, other products marketed overseas to third-world countries would not seem to create a problem at first glance. An example is baby formula. In this country, no real problems have developed from the use of this product. In the third-world countries, serious problems arose. These problems centered on three issues.

First, the majority of people in these countries cannot read or write. The consumer could not read, let alone understand, the directions on the side of the box or package. Second, the foreign consumer weakened the formula. As a result, babies were undernourished. If these babies had been kept on their mother's milk, no malnourishment would have occurred. Third, formula is made by adding water. In many of these countries, the water supply is of poor quality. By using this water, the infant was exposed to additional health hazards.

Should American companies sell their products to underdeveloped countries? In these examples, the products themselves were not defective. What do you think a business should do with these types of products?

The Gray-Market for Automobiles

Many people would like to acquire one of those special automobiles manufactured by Rolls Royce, Mercedes-Benz, Porsche, BMW, and other prestigious companies. The cost of these vehicles is very high. This is particularly true if you make your purchase through a dealer who is authorized to sell the vehicles within the United States.

Considerable sums of money can be saved in a variety of ways. One is to take a trip to Europe and purchase a vehicle there. The current import tax on a vehicle is 2.5 percent of what you pay overseas. You might be able to negotiate a good price for the automobile and thus save on both original price and import duty. Or you can bypass the authorized dealers and purchase the automobile in what is commonly called the "gray market" through an unauthorized dealer here. This market offers both new and used vehicles.

Two major problems exist, however, with either approach. First, you must recognize that federal law requires certain equipment on all vehicles, such as antipollution devices, steel reinforcement in the doors, and side lights. The European countries do not have these

requirements. It costs an estimated $5,000 to equip a European automobile to meet United States standards.

When a vehicle is imported to the United States, a bond of three times the value must be posted to guarantee that it will meet all federal standards. The owner has 90 days to bring the vehicle up to those standards, but he or she can obtain a 30-day extension. If the automobile does not meet the standards within 120 days, it must be either exported or destroyed, and the bond is forfeited. Each time the vehicle is tested by the federal government, it costs $1,000. As you can see, importing and testing can be very expensive. Automobiles manufactured prior to 1968 do not have to have this equipment.

The second problem involves the possibility of purchasing a stolen vehicle. There have been cases where a vehicle has been stolen in Europe, then imported and sold through the gray market in the United States. Months later, the United States Customs Service office of enforcement has contacted the new owner and repossessed the vehicle on behalf of the European owner. This does not occur frequently, but it does occur.

After considering these factors, you may decide just to purchase this type of vehicle from an authorized United States dealer.

Summary

The growth in international business relations has led in turn to the development of international law. International law consists of a body of laws that are considered to be legally binding among otherwise independent nations. This legal area has developed through two methods: international customs and agreements that have the force of law. International customs consist of the relationship that nations have developed over years with one another on particular legal matters. Agreements are reached either by nations acting inde-

pendently, as in the signing of treaties, or through international organizations and conferences.

The United States Constitution grants authority to Congress and the president to regulate commerce with foreign nations. Several administrative agencies and one court assist in this regulation. Several statutory provisions have been adopted to control import and export activities. The Export Administration Act restricts exports to certain countries and requires licenses to other countries for certain products. Violations of this act can result in long prison terms and substantial damages against the defendant.

The 1988 Omnibus Trade and Competitiveness Act encourages exports. It strengthened the fast-track procedure to expedite the ratification of trade agreements.

Three unfair trade practices can result in either forfeiture of goods or additional import duties. These practices are dumping; infringement of copyright, patent, trademark, and maskwork laws; and government subsidizing.

The Export Trading Company Act, Export-Import Bank, and Trading with the Enemy Act all relate to import and export benefits for the United States. Special tax benefits are given to foreign sales corporations, which are normally established outside the United States.

Key Terms

bill of exchange (605)
bill of lading (605)
choice-of-law clause (605)
compact (592)
convention (592)
countervailing duty (601)
Court of International Trade (595)
dumping (601)
executive agreement (592)
Export Administration Act (595)
Export-Import Bank (Eximbank) (600)
exporting (592)
Export Trading Company Act (600)

foreign sales corporation (600)
general license (595)
gray-market goods (603)
importing (592)
international customs (592)
international law (592)
International Trade Administration (594)
International Trade Commission (594)
letter of credit (605)
most favored nation (594)
national treatment (604)
Omnibus Trade and Competitiveness Act (599)

protocol (592)
quota (593)
tariff (593)
Trade Act (600)
Trade Agreements Act (601)
Trading with the Enemy Act (600)
treaty (592)
United States Customs Service (594)
United States trade representative (594)
validated license (595)
Vienna Convention on the Law of Treaties (592)

Questions and Case Problems

1. Arnold Roth, a United States wholesaler, enters into an agreement to purchase widgets from Manufacturers, Inc., a Colombian manufacturer. Roth secures an irrevocable letter of credit from Sunnydays Bank, a U.S. bank. When Manufacturers, Inc., places the 60 crates of widgets on board a steamship, it receives in return the invoices required under the letter of credit. The invoices are being forwarded to Sunnydays Bank for payment. The purchaser, Arnold Roth, subsequently learns that Manufacturers, Inc., has filled the 60 crates with rubbish, not widgets. Given the fact that an issuer's obligation under a letter of credit is independent of the underlying contract between the buyer and seller, will the issuer be required to pay the letter of credit? (See UCC 5-114(2)(a).)

2. XYZ, Inc., desires to import goods from Nigeria. It wants to make certain that the goods are the ones desired and that they are received in good condition. Nigeria desires to be paid if the goods are shipped. Describe what procedures should be followed.

3. The federal law on gray-market goods is found in both statutory and administrative rules. The statutory provisions prohibit importing into the United States any merchandise if it bears a trademark owned by an American trademark holder that has been registered with the Patent and Trademark Office. The owner of the trademark may give written permission for someone to import marked merchandise.

One of the regulations states that the articles of the foreign manufacturer must bear a recorded trademark or trade name applied for under authorization of the United States owner. The effect of this regulation is to allow goods to be imported into the United States when the U.S. owner of the trademark permits the foreign business to use the trademark outside of the United States. In other words, could a business purchase trademarked goods in a foreign country, then import them into the United States for resale without the permission of the owner of the United States trademark? Is this regulation valid under these statutory provisions? Why or why not? [K-Mart Corporation v. Cartier, Inc., 486 U.S. 281, 108 S.Ct. 1811, 100 L.Ed.2d 313 (1988)]

4. A letter of credit was issued by North Carolina National Bank for its customer, Adastra Knitting Mills, Inc. The credit was to cover Adastra's purchases of acrylic yarn from Courtaulds, an Alabama corporation, the beneficiary. Under the letter of credit, Courtaulds was to present a draft accompanied by a commercial invoice stating that it covers 100 percent acrylic yarn. When Courtaulds presented the draft, the accompanying invoices stated that the goods were "Imported Acrylic Yarn." The packing lists, however, disclosed that the packages contained 100 percent acrylic yarn. The bank refused to honor the draft, claiming the invoices did not meet the requirements of the letter of credit. Should the bank be liable to Courtaulds for the amount of the draft? Discuss. [Courtaulds North America, Inc. v. North Carolina National Bank, 528 F.2d 802 (4th Cir. 1975)]

5. The plaintiffs represented the domestic prestressed concrete steel wire strand industry. They believed the wire strand manufactured in Spain, France, and Brazil was being subsidized and that imports from the United Kingdom were also being sold at less than fair value. Prior to the court's ruling, the plaintiffs' production increased steadily over several years, and employment in the industry likewise increased. The International Trade Commission (ITC), based on this information, found that the actions of the importers did not create a material injury to the domestic producers. The ITC did not apply the antidumping and countervailing duty provisions. The plaintiffs argued that their net profits had decreased because of the subsidies and sales at less than fair value. Should the court reverse the findings of the ITC based on reduced profits? Support your reasons. [American Spring Wire Corporation v. United States, 590 F.Supp. 1273 (Court of International Trade, 1984)]

6. Harris Corporation, the plaintiff, entered into a contract with the defendant, National Iranian Radio and Television (NIRT), to manufacture and deliver 144 FM broadcast transmitters to Teheran, Iran. Due to the revolution in Iran, the plaintiff was unable to complete delivery of the transmitters. NIRT attempted to collect on a letter of credit that had been set up to guarantee performance. The plaintiff subsequently brought an action against the defendant seeking to enjoin receipt of payment on the letter of credit. Bank Melli Iran, the issuer, was also made a defendant. Both defendants alleged that the district court lacked jurisdiction over them under the Foreign Sovereign Immunities Act (FSIA). From 1969 to 1982, Melli maintained an office in New York City where it carried out significant business transactions. Moreover,

NIRT entered into this contract that required performance by Harris in the United States and also required the training of NIRT personnel in the United States. Discuss whether this action falls under the FSIA. [Harris Corp. v. National Iranian Radio, Etc., 691 F.2d 1344 (11th Cir. 1982)] (See Chapter 5 for Foreign Sovereign Immunities Act and act of state doctrine).

7. Charles T. Main International brought an action to recover assets that had been lost due to the overthrow of the Shah in Iran. To obtain the release of hostages, President Carter had signed an agreement to submit all claims by either Iran or the United States to binding arbitration. The plaintiff wanted to recover from Iran assets that had been frozen in the United States. Main claimed the president's agreement freezing Iranian assets exceeded the president's authority and violated its constitutional rights as a taking of its property without just compensation. What was the result? [Charles T. Main International v. Khuzestan Water and Power Authority, 651 F.2d 800 (1st Cir. 1981)]

8. Mitsubishi and Soler Chrysler-Plymouth entered a contract that required binding arbitration. A dispute occurred, and Mitsubishi wanted to arbitrate it. Soler Chrysler-Plymouth claimed that Mitsubishi had violated the antitrust laws of the United States, which made the parties' contract illegal and thus not subject to arbitration. Who prevailed in this case? [Mitsubishi Motor Corp. v. Soler Chrysler-Plymouth, 473 U.S. 614, 105 S.Ct. 3346, 87 L.Ed.2d 444 (1985)] (See Chapter 4 concerning arbitration).

9. Nigeria contracted for the purchase of millions of tons of cement from Texas Trading and Milling Corp. and others. It overbought, resulting in the country's docks becoming clogged. Unable to accept the cement, Nigeria repudiated many of its cement contracts. Legal action was instituted by Texas Trading in the United States. Nigeria claimed its sovereign immunity under the Foreign Sovereign Immunities Act. Discuss the result. [Texas Trading and Milling Corp. v. Federal Republic of Nigeria, 647 F.2d 300 (2d Cir. 1981)] (See Chapter 5 for Foreign Sovereign Immunities Act and act of state doctrine).

10. Chisholm & Co. and the Bank of Jamaica agreed that Chisholm & Co. would arrange lines of credit from various banks and procure from Eximbank credit insurance. Unknown to Chisholm & Co., the Bank of Jamaica dealt directly with Eximbank and excluded Chisholm & Co. from receiving any benefit from the credit insurance. Chisholm & Co. brought an action, alleging that the Bank of Jamaica was enriched at the expense of Chisholm & Co. The Bank of Jamaica took the position that its actions were protected by sovereign immunity and the act of state doctrine. Was this position correct? [Chisholm & Co. v. Bank of Jamaica, 643 F.Supp. 1393 (S.D. Fla. 1986)] (See Chapter 5 for Foreign Sovereign Immunities Act and act of state doctrine).

Appendix A The Constitution of the United States of America

We the People of the United States, in Order to form a more perfect Union, establish Justice, insure domestic Tranquility, provide for the common defence, promote the general Welfare, and secure the Blessings of Liberty to ourselves and our Posterity, do ordain and establish this Constitution for the United States of America.

ARTICLE I

Section 1. All legislative Powers herein granted shall be vested in a Congress of the United States, which shall consist of a Senate and House of Representatives.

Section 2. The House of Representatives shall be composed of Members chosen every second Year by the People of the several States, and the Electors in each State shall have the Qualifications requisite for Electors of the most numerous Branch of the State Legislature.

No Person shall be a Representative who shall not have attained to the Age of twenty five Years, and been seven Years a Citizen of the United States, and who shall not, when elected, be an Inhabitant of that State in which he shall be chosen.

Representatives and direct Taxes shall be apportioned among the several States which may be included within this Union, according to their respective Numbers, which shall be determined by adding to the whole Number of free Persons, including those bound to Service for a Term of Years, and excluding Indians not taxed, three fifths of all other Persons. The actual Enumeration shall be made within three Years after the first Meeting of the Congress of the United States, and within every subsequent Term of ten Years, in such Manner as they shall by Law direct. The Number of Representatives shall not exceed one for every thirty Thousand, but each State shall have at Least one Representative; and until such enumeration shall be made, the State of New Hampshire shall be entitled to chuse three, Massachusetts eight, Rhode Island and Providence Plantations one, Connecticut five, New York six, New Jersey four, Pennsylvania eight, Delaware one, Maryland six, Virginia ten, North Carolina five, South Carolina five, and Georgia three.

When vacancies happen in the Representation from any State, the Executive Authority thereof shall issue Writs of Election to fill such Vacancies.

The House of Representatives shall chuse their Speaker and other Officers; and shall have the sole Power of Impeachment.

Section 3. The Senate of the United States shall be composed of two Senators from each State, chosen by the Legislature thereof, for six Years; and each Senator shall have one Vote.

Immediately after they shall be assembled in Consequence of the first Election, they shall be divided as equally as may be into three Classes. The Seats of the Senators of the first Class shall be vacated at the Expiration of the second Year, of the second Class at the Expiration of the fourth Year, and of the third Class at the Expiration of the sixth Year, so that one third may be chosen every second Year; and if Vacancies happen by Resignation, or otherwise, during the Recess of the Legislature of any State, the Executive thereof may make temporary Appointments until the next Meeting of the Legislature, which shall then fill such Vacancies.

No Person shall be a Senator who shall not have attained to the Age of thirty Years, and been nine Years a Citizen of the United States, and who shall not, when elected, be an Inhabitant of that State for which he shall be chosen.

The Vice President of the United States shall be President of the Senate, but shall have no Vote, unless they be equally divided.

The Senate shall chuse their other Officers, and also a President pro tempore, in the Absence of the Vice President, or when he shall exercise the Office of President of the United States.

The Senate shall have the sole Power to try all Impeachments. When sitting for that Purpose, they shall be on Oath or Affirmation. When the President of the United States is tried, the Chief Justice shall preside: And no Person shall be convicted without the Concurrence of two thirds of the Members present.

Judgment in Cases of Impeachment shall not extend further than to removal from Office, and disqualification to hold and enjoy any Office of honor, Trust, or Profit under the United States: but the Party convicted shall nevertheless be liable and subject to Indictment, Trial, Judgment, and Punishment, according to Law.

Section 4.   The Times, Places and Manner of holding Elections for Senators and Representatives, shall be prescribed in each State by the Legislature thereof; but the Congress may at any time by Law make or alter such Regulations, except as to the Places of chusing Senators.

The Congress shall assemble at least once in every Year, and such Meeting shall be on the first Monday in December, unless they shall by Law appoint a different Day.

Section 5.   Each House shall be the Judge of the Elections, Returns, and Qualifications of its own Members, and a Majority of each shall constitute a Quorum to do Business; but a smaller Number may adjourn from day to day, and may be authorized to compel the Attendance of absent Members, in such Manner, and under such Penalties as each House may provide.

Each House may determine the Rules of its Proceedings, punish its Members for disorderly Behavior, and, with the Concurrence of two thirds, expel a Member.

Each House shall keep a Journal of its Proceedings, and from time to time publish the same, excepting such Parts as may in their Judgment require Secrecy; and the Yeas and Nays of the Members of either House on any question shall, at the Desire of one fifth of those Present, be entered on the Journal.

Neither House, during the Session of Congress, shall, without the Consent of the other, adjourn for more than three days, nor to any other Place than that in which the two Houses shall be sitting.

Section 6.   The Senators and Representatives shall receive a Compensation for their Services, to be ascertained by Law, and paid out of the Treasury of the United States. They shall in all Cases, except Treason, Felony and Breach of the Peace, be privileged from Arrest during their Attendance at the Session of their respective Houses, and in going to and returning from the same; and for any Speech or Debate in either House, they shall not be questioned in any other Place.

No Senator or Representative shall, during the Time for which he was elected, be appointed to any civil Office under the Authority of the United States, which shall have been created, or the Emoluments whereof shall have been increased during such time; and no Person holding any Office under the United States, shall be a Member of either House during his Continuance in Office.

Section 7.   All Bills for raising Revenue shall originate in the House of Representatives; but the Senate may propose or concur with Amendments as on other Bills.

Every Bill which shall have passed the House of Representatives and the Senate, shall, before it become a Law, be presented to the President of the United States; If he approve he shall sign it, but if not he shall return it, with his Objections to the House in which it shall have originated, who shall enter the Objections at large on their Journal, and proceed to reconsider it. If after such Reconsideration two thirds of that House shall agree to pass the Bill, it shall be sent together with the Objections, to the other House, by which it shall likewise be reconsidered, and if approved by two thirds of that House, it shall become a Law. But in all such Cases the Votes of both Houses shall be determined by Yeas and Nays, and the Names of the Persons voting for and against the Bill shall be entered on the Journal of each House respectively. If any Bill shall not be returned by the President within ten Days (Sundays excepted) after it shall have been presented to him, the Same shall be a Law, in like Manner as if he had signed it, unless the Congress by their Adjournment prevent its Return in which Case it shall not be a Law.

Every Order, Resolution, or Vote, to which the Concurrence of the Senate and House of Representatives may be necessary (except on a question of Adjournment) shall be presented to the President of the United States; and before the Same shall take Effect, shall be approved by him, or being disapproved by him, shall be repassed by two thirds of the Senate and House of Representatives, according to the Rules and Limitations prescribed in the Case of a Bill.

Section 8.   The Congress shall have Power To lay and collect Taxes, Duties, Imposts and Excises, to pay the Debts and provide for the common Defence and general Welfare of the United States; but all Duties, Imposts and Excises shall be uniform throughout the United States;

To borrow Money on the credit of the United States;

To regulate Commerce with foreign Nations, and among the several States, and with the Indian Tribes;

To establish an uniform Rule of Naturalization, and uniform Laws on the subject of Bankruptcies throughout the United States;

To coin Money, regulate the Value thereof, and of foreign Coin, and fix the Standard of Weights and Measures;

To provide for the Punishment of counterfeiting the Securities and current Coin of the United States;

To establish Post Offices and post Roads;

To promote the Progress of Science and useful Arts, by securing for limited Times to Authors and Inventors the exclusive Right to their respective Writings and Discoveries;

To constitute Tribunals inferior to the supreme Court;

To define and punish Piracies and Felonies committed on the high Seas, and Offenses against the Law of Nations;

To declare War, grant Letters of Marque and Reprisal, and make Rules concerning Captures on Land and Water;

To raise and support Armies, but no Appropriation of Money to that Use shall be for a longer Term than two Years;

To provide and maintain a Navy;

To make Rules for the Government and Regulation of the land and naval Forces;

To provide for calling forth the Militia to execute the Laws of the Union, suppress Insurrections and repel Invasions;

To provide for organizing, arming, and disciplining the Militia, and for governing such Part of them as may be employed in the Service of the United States, reserving to the States respectively, the Appointment of the Officers, and the Authority of training the Militia according to the discipline prescribed by Congress;

To exercise exclusive Legislation in all Cases whatsoever, over such District (not exceeding ten Miles square) as may, by Cession of particular States, and the Acceptance of Congress, become the Seat of the Government of the United States, and to exercise like Authority over all Places purchased by the Consent of the Legislature of the State in which the Same shall be, for the Erection of Forts, Magazines, Arsenals, dock-Yards, and other needful Buildings;—And

To make all Laws which shall be necessary and proper for carrying into Execution the foregoing Powers, and all other Powers vested by this Constitution in the Government of the United States, or in any Department or Officer thereof.

Section 9. The Migration or Importation of such Persons as any of the States now existing shall think proper to admit, shall not be prohibited by the Congress prior to the Year one thousand eight hundred and eight, but a Tax or duty may be imposed on such Importation, not exceeding ten dollars for each Person.

The privilege of the Writ of Habeas Corpus shall not be suspended, unless when in Cases of Rebellion or Invasion the public Safety may require it.

No Bill of Attainder or ex post facto Law shall be passed.

No Capitation, or other direct, Tax shall be laid, unless in Proportion to the Census or Enumeration herein before directed to be taken.

No Tax or Duty shall be laid on Articles exported from any State.

No Preference shall be given by any Regulation of Commerce or Revenue to the Ports of one State over those of another: nor shall Vessels bound to, or from, one State be obliged to enter, clear, or pay Duties in another.

No Money shall be drawn from the Treasury, but in Consequence of Appropriations made by Law; and a regular Statement and Account of the Receipts and Expenditures of all public Money shall be published from time to time.

No Title of Nobility shall be granted by the United States: And no Person holding any Office of Profit or Trust under them, shall, without the Consent of the Congress, accept of any present, Emolument, Office, or Title, of any kind whatever, from any King, Prince, or foreign State.

Section 10. No State shall enter into any Treaty, Alliance, or Confederation; grant Letters of Marque and Reprisal; coin Money; emit Bills of Credit; make any Thing but gold and silver Coin a Tender in Payment of Debts; pass any Bill of Attainder, ex post facto Law, or Law impairing the Obligation of Contracts, or grant any Title of Nobility.

No State shall, without the Consent of the Congress, lay any Imposts or Duties on Imports or Exports, except what may be absolutely necessary for executing its inspection Laws: and the net Produce of all Duties and Imposts, laid by any State on Imports or Exports, shall be for the Use of the Treasury of the United States; and all such Laws shall be subject to the Revision and Controul of the Congress.

No State shall, without the Consent of Congress, lay any Duty of Tonnage, keep Troops, or Ships of War in time of Peace, enter into any Agreement or Compact with another State, or with a foreign Power, or engage in War, unless actually invaded, or in such imminent Danger as will not admit of delay.

ARTICLE II

Section 1. The executive Power shall be vested in a President of the United States of America. He shall hold his Office during the Term of four Years, and, together with the Vice President, chosen for the same Term, be elected, as follows:

Each State shall appoint, in such Manner as the Legislature thereof may direct, a Number of Electors, equal to the whole Number of Senators and Representatives to which the State may be entitled in the Congress; but no Senator or Representative, or Person holding an Office of Trust or Profit under the United States, shall be appointed an Elector.

The Electors shall meet in their respective States, and vote by Ballot for two Persons, of whom one at least shall not be an Inhabitant of the same State with themselves. And they shall make a List of all the Persons voted for, and of the Number of Votes for each; which List they shall sign and certify, and transmit sealed to the Seat of the Government of the United States, directed to the President of the Senate. The President of the Senate shall, in the Presence of the Senate and House of Representatives, open all the Certificates, and the Votes shall then be counted. The Person having the greatest Number of Votes shall be the President, if such Number be a Majority of the whole Number of Electors appointed; and if there be more than one who have such Majority, and have an equal Number of Votes, then the House of Representatives shall immediately chuse by Ballot one of them for President; and if no Person have a Majority, then from the five highest on the List the said House shall in like Manner chuse the President. But in chusing the President, the Votes shall be taken by States, the Representation from each State having one Vote; A quorum for this Purpose shall consist of a Member or Members from two thirds of the States, and a Majority of all the States shall be necessary to a Choice. In every Case, after the Choice of the President, the Person having the greater Number of Votes of the Electors shall be the Vice President. But if there should remain two or more who have equal Votes, the Senate shall chuse from them by Ballot the Vice President.

The Congress may determine the Time of chusing the Electors, and the Day on which they shall give their Votes; which Day shall be the same throughout the United States.

No person except a natural born Citizen, or a Citizen of the United States, at the time of the Adoption of this Constitution, shall be eligible to the Office of President; neither shall any Person be eligible to that Office who shall not have attained to the Age of thirty five Years, and been fourteen Years a Resident within the United States.

In Case of the Removal of the President from Office, or of his Death, Resignation or Inability to discharge the Powers and Duties of the said Office, the same shall devolve on the Vice President, and the Congress may by Law provide for the Case of Removal, Death, Resignation or Inability, both of the President and Vice President, declaring what Officer shall then act as President, and such Officer shall act accordingly, until the Disability be removed, or a President shall be elected.

The President shall, at stated Times, receive for his Services, a Compensation, which shall neither be increased nor diminished during the Period for which he shall have been elected, and he shall not receive within that Period any other Emolument from the United States, or any of them.

Before he enter on the Execution of his Office, he shall take the following Oath or Affirmation: "I do solemnly swear (or affirm) that I will faithfully execute the Office of President of the United States, and will to the best of my Ability, preserve, protect and defend the Constitution of the United States."

Section 2.   The President shall be Commander in Chief of the Army and Navy of the United States, and of the Militia of the several States, when called into the actual Service of the United States; he may require the Opinion, in writing, of the principal Officer in each of the executive Departments, upon any Subject relating to the Duties of their respective Offices, and he shall have Power to grant Reprieves and Pardons for Offenses against the United States, except in Cases of Impeachment.

He shall have Power, by and with the Advice and Consent of the Senate to make Treaties, provided two thirds of the Senators present concur; and he shall nominate, and by and with the Advice and Consent of the Senate, shall appoint Ambassadors, other public Ministers and Consuls, Judges of the supreme Court, and all other Officers of the United States, whose Appointments are not herein otherwise provided for, and which shall be established by Law; but the Congress may by Law vest the Appointment of such inferior Officers, as they think proper, in the President alone, in the Courts of Law, or in the Heads of Departments.

The President shall have Power to fill up all Vacancies that may happen during the Recess of the Senate, by granting Commissions which shall expire at the End of their next Session.

Section 3.   He shall from time to time give to the Congress Information of the State of the Union, and recommend to their Consideration such Measures as he shall judge necessary and expedient; he may, on extraordinary Occasions, convene both Houses, or either of them, and in Case of Disagreement between them, with Respect to the Time of Adjournment, he may adjourn them to such Time as he shall think proper; he shall receive Ambassadors and other public Ministers; he shall take Care that the Laws be faithfully executed, and shall Commission all the Officers of the United States.

Section 4.   The President, Vice President and all civil Officers of the United States, shall be removed from Office on Impeachment for, and Conviction of, Treason, Bribery, or other high Crimes and Misdemeanors.

ARTICLE III

Section 1.   The judicial Power of the United States, shall be vested in one supreme Court, and in such inferior Courts as the Congress may from time to time ordain and establish. The Judges, both of the supreme and inferior Courts, shall hold their Offices during good Behaviour, and shall, at stated Times, receive for their Services a Compensation, which shall not be diminished during their Continuance in Office.

Section 2. The judicial Power shall extend to all Cases, in Law and Equity, arising under this Constitution, the Laws of the United States, and Treaties made, or which shall be made, under their Authority;—to all Cases affecting Ambassadors, other public Ministers and Consuls;—to all Cases of admiralty and maritime Jurisdiction;—to Controversies to which the United States shall be a Party;—to Controversies between two or more States;—between a State and Citizens of another State;—between Citizens of different States;—between Citizens of the same State claiming Lands under Grants of different States, and between a State, or the Citizens thereof, and foreign States, Citizens or Subjects.

In all Cases affecting Ambassadors, other public Ministers and Consuls, and those in which a State shall be a Party, the supreme Court shall have original Jurisdiction. In all the other Cases before mentioned, the supreme Court shall have appellate Jurisdiction, both as to Law and Fact, with such Exceptions, and under such Regulations as the Congress shall make.

The Trial of all Crimes, except in Cases of Impeachment, shall be by Jury; and such Trial shall be held in the State where the said Crimes shall have been committed; but when not committed within any State, the Trial shall be at such Place or Places as the Congress may by Law have directed.

Section 3. Treason against the United States, shall consist only in levying War against them, or, in adhering to their Enemies, giving them Aid and Comfort. No Person shall be convicted of Treason unless on the Testimony of two Witnesses to the same overt Act, or on Confession in open Court.

The Congress shall have Power to declare the Punishment of Treason, but no Attainder of Treason shall work Corruption of Blood, or Forfeiture except during the Life of the Person attainted.

ARTICLE IV

Section 1. Full Faith and Credit shall be given in each State to the public Acts, Records, and judicial Proceedings of every other State. And the Congress may by general Laws prescribe the Manner in which such Acts, Records and Proceedings shall be proved, and the Effect thereof.

Section 2. The Citizens of each State shall be entitled to all Privileges and Immunities of Citizens in the several States.

A Person charged in any State with Treason, Felony, or other Crime, who shall flee from Justice, and be found in another State, shall on Demand of the executive Authority of the State from which he fled, be delivered up, to be removed to the State having Jurisdiction of the Crime.

No Person held to Service or Labour in one State, under the Laws thereof, escaping into another, shall, in Consequence of any Law or Regulation therein, be discharged from such Service or Labour, but shall be delivered up on Claim of the Party to whom such Service or Labour may be due.

Section 3. New States may be admitted by the Congress into this Union; but no new State shall be formed or erected within the Jurisdiction of any other State; nor any State be formed by the Junction of two or more States, or Parts of States, without the Consent of the Legislatures of the States concerned as well as of the Congress.

The Congress shall have Power to dispose of and make all needful Rules and Regulations respecting the Territory or other Property belonging to the United States; and nothing in this Constitution shall be so construed as to Prejudice any Claims of the United States, or of any particular State.

Section 4. The United States shall guarantee to every State in this Union a Republican Form of Government, and shall protect each of them against Invasion; and on Application of the Legislature, or of the Executive (when the Legislature cannot be convened) against domestic Violence.

ARTICLE V

The Congress, whenever two thirds of both Houses shall deem it necessary, shall propose Amendments to this Constitution, or, on the Application of the Legislatures of two thirds of the several States, shall call a Convention for proposing Amendments, which, in either Case, shall be valid to all Intents and Purposes, as part of this Constitution, when ratified by the Legislatures of three fourths of the several States, or by Conventions in three fourths thereof, as the one or the other Mode of Ratification may be proposed by the Congress; Provided that no Amendment which may be made prior to the Year One thousand eight hundred and eight shall in any Manner affect the first and fourth Clauses in the Ninth Section of the first Article; and that no State, without its Consent, shall be deprived of its equal Suffrage in the Senate.

ARTICLE VI

All Debts contracted and Engagements entered into, before the Adoption of this Constitution shall be as valid against the United States under this Constitution, as under the Confederation.

This Constitution, and the Laws of the United States which shall be made in Pursuance thereof; and all Treaties made, or which shall be made, under the Authority of the United States, shall be the supreme Law of the Land; and the Judges in every State shall be bound thereby, any Thing in the Constitution or Laws of any State to the Contrary notwithstanding.

The Senators and Representatives before mentioned, and the Members of the several State Legislatures, and all executive and judicial Officers, both of the United States and of the several States, shall be bound by Oath or Affirmation, to support this Constitution; but no religious Test shall ever be required as a Qualification to any Office or public Trust under the United States.

ARTICLE VII

The Ratification of the Conventions of nine States shall be sufficient for the Establishment of this Constitution between the States so ratifying the Same.

AMENDMENT I [1791]

Congress shall make no law respecting an establishment of religion, or prohibiting the free exercise thereof; or abridging the freedom of speech, or of the press; or the right of the people peaceably to assembly, and to petition the Government for a redress of grievances.

AMENDMENT II [1791]

A well regulated Militia, being necessary to the security of a free State, the right of the people to keep and bear Arms, shall not be infringed.

AMENDMENT III [1791]

No Soldier shall, in time of peace be quartered in any house, without the consent of the Owner, nor in time of war, but in a manner to be prescribed by law.

Amendment IV [1791]

The right of the people to be secure in their persons, houses, papers, and effects, against unreasonable searches and seizures, shall not be violated, and no Warrants shall issue, but upon probable cause, supported by Oath or affirmation, and particularly describing the place to be searched, and the persons or things to be seized.

AMENDMENT V [1791]

No person shall be held to answer for a capital, or otherwise infamous crime, unless on a presentment or indictment of a Grand Jury, except in cases arising in the land or naval forces, or in the Militia, when in actual service in time of War or public danger; nor shall any person be subject for the same offence to be twice put in jeopardy of life or limb; nor shall be compelled in any criminal case to be a witness against himself, nor be deprived of life, liberty, or property, without due process of law; nor shall private property be taken for public use, without just compensation.

AMENDMENT VI [1791]

In all criminal prosecutions, the accused shall enjoy the right to a speedy and public trial, by an impartial jury of the State and district wherein the crime shall have been committed, which district shall have been previously ascertained by law, and to be informed of the nature and cause of the accusation; to be confronted with the witnesses against him; to have compulsory process for obtaining witnesses in his favor, and to have the Assistance of Counsel for his defence.

AMENDMENT VII [1791]

In Suits at common law, where the value in controversy shall exceed twenty dollars, the right of trial by jury shall be preserved, and no fact tried by jury, shall be otherwise re-examined in any Court of the United States, than according to the rules of the common law.

AMENDMENT VIII [1791]

Excessive bail shall not be required, nor excessive fines imposed, nor cruel and unusual punishments inflicted.

AMENDMENT IX [1791]

The enumeration in the Constitution, of certain rights, shall not be construed to deny or disparage others retained by the people.

AMENDMENT X [1791]

The powers not delegated to the United States by the Constitution, nor prohibited by it to the States, are reserved to the States respectively, or to the people.

AMENDMENT XI [1798]

The Judicial power of the United States shall not be construed to extend to any suit in law or equity, commenced or prosecuted against one of the United States by Citizens of another State, or by Citizens or Subjects of any Foreign State.

AMENDMENT XII [1804]

The Electors shall meet in their respective states, and vote by ballot for President and Vice-President, one of whom, at least, shall not be an inhabitant of the same state with themselves; they shall name in their ballots the person voted for as President, and in distinct ballots the person voted for as Vice-President, and they shall make distinct lists of all persons voted for as President, and of all persons voted for as Vice-President, and of the number of votes for each, which lists they shall sign and certify, and transmit sealed to the seat of the government of the United States, directed to the President of the Senate;—The President of the Senate shall, in the presence of the Senate and House of Representatives, open all the certificates and the votes shall then be counted;—The person having the greatest number of votes for President, shall be the President, if such number be a majority of the whole number of Electors appointed; and if no person have such majority, then from the persons having the highest numbers not exceeding three on the list of those voted for as President, the House of Representatives shall choose immediately, by ballot, the President. But in choosing the President, the votes shall be taken by states, the representation from each state having one vote; a quorum for this purpose shall consist of a member or members from two-thirds of the states, and a majority of all states shall be necessary to a choice. And if the House of Representatives shall not choose a President whenever the right of choice shall devolve upon them, before the fourth day of March next following, then the Vice-President shall act as President, as in the case of the death or other constitutional disability of the President.—The person having the greatest number of votes as Vice-President, shall be the Vice-President, if such number be a majority of the whole number of Electors appointed, and if no person have a majority, then from the two highest numbers on the list, the Senate shall choose the Vice-President; a quorum for the purpose shall consist of two-thirds of the whole number of Senators, and a majority of the whole number shall be necessary to a choice. But no person constitutionally ineligible to the office of President shall be eligible to that of Vice-President of the United States.

AMENDMENT XIII [1865]

Section 1.   Neither slavery nor involuntary servitude, except as a punishment for crime whereof the party shall have been duly convicted, shall exist within the United States, or any place subject to their jurisdiction.

Section 2.   Congress shall have power to enforce this article by appropriate legislation.

AMENDMENT XIV [1868]

Section 1.   All persons born or naturalized in the United States, and subject to the jurisdiction thereof, are citizens of the United States and of the State wherein they reside. No State shall make or enforce any law which shall abridge the privileges or immunities of citizens of the United States; nor shall any State deprive any person of life, liberty, or property, without due process of law; nor deny to any person within its jurisdiction the equal protection of the laws.

Section 2.   Representatives shall be apportioned among the several States according to their respective numbers, counting the whole number of persons in each State, excluding Indians not taxed. But when the right to vote at any election for the choice of electors for President and Vice President of the United States, Representatives in Congress, the Executive and Judicial officers of a State, or the members of the Legislature thereof, is denied to any of the male inhabitants of such State, being twenty-one years of age, and citizens of the United States, or in any way abridged, except for participation in rebellion, or other crime, the basis of representation therein shall be reduced in the proportion which the number of such male citizens shall bear to the whole number of male citizens twenty-one years of age in such State.

Section 3.   No person shall be a Senator or Representative in Congress, or elector of President and Vice President, or hold any office, civil or military, under the United States, or under any State, who having previously taken an oath, as a member of Congress, or as an officer of the United States, or as a member of any State legislature, or as an executive or judicial officer of any State, to support the Constitution of the United States, shall have engaged in insurrection or rebellion against the same, or given aid or comfort to the enemies thereof. But Congress may by a vote of two-thirds of each House, remove such disability.

Section 4.   The validity of the public debt of the United States, authorized by law, including debts incurred for payment of pensions and bounties for services in suppressing insurrection or rebellion, shall not be questioned. But neither the United States nor any State shall assume or pay any debt or obligation incurred in aid of insurrection or rebellion against the United States, or any claim for the loss or emancipation of any slave; but all such debts, obligations and claims shall be held illegal and void.

Section 5.   The Congress shall have power to enforce, by appropriate legislation, the provisions of this article.

AMENDMENT XV [1870]

Section 1.   The right of citizens of the United States to vote shall not be denied or abridged by the United States or by any State on account of race, color, or previous condition of servitude.

Section 2.   The Congress shall have power to enforce this article by appropriate legislation.

AMENDMENT XVI [1913]

The Congress shall have power to lay and collect taxes on incomes, from whatever source derived, without apportionment among the several States, and without regard to any census or enumeration.

AMENDMENT XVII [1913]

[1] The Senate of the United States shall be composed of two Senators from each State, elected by the people thereof, for six years; and each Senator shall have one vote. The electors in each State shall have the qualifications requisite for electors of the most numerous branch of the State legislatures.

[2] When vacancies happen in the representation of any State in the Senate, the executive authority of such State shall issue writs of election to fill such vacancies: *Provided*, That the legislature of any State may empower the executive thereof to make temporary appointments until the people fill the vacancies by election as the legislature may direct.

[3] This amendment shall not be so construed as to affect the election or term of any Senator chosen before it becomes valid as part of the Constitution.

AMENDMENT XVIII [1919]

Section 1. After one year from the ratification of this article the manufacture, sale, or transportation of intoxicating liquors within, the importation thereof into, or the exportation thereof from the United States and all territory subject to the jurisdiction thereof for beverage purposes is hereby prohibited.

Section 2. The Congress and the several States shall have concurrent power to enforce this article by appropriate legislation.

Section 3. This article shall be inoperative unless it shall have been ratified as an amendment to the Constitution by the legislatures of the several States, as provided in the Constitution, within seven years from the date of the submission hereof to the States by the Congress.

AMENDMENT XIX [1920]

[1] The right of citizens of the United States to vote shall not be denied or abridged by the United States or by any State on account of sex.

[2] Congress shall have power to enforce this article by appropriate legislation.

AMENDMENT XX [1933]

Section 1. The terms of the President and Vice President shall end at noon on the 20th day of January, and the terms of Senators and Representatives at noon on the 3d day of January, of the years in which such terms would have ended if this article had not been ratified; and the terms of their successors shall then begin.

Section 2. The Congress shall assemble at least once in every year, and such meeting shall begin at noon on the 3d day of January, unless they shall by law appoint a different day.

Section 3. If, at the time fixed for the beginning of the term of the President, the President elect shall have died, the Vice President elect shall become President. If the President shall not have been chosen before the time fixed for the beginning of his term, or if the President elect shall have failed to qualify, then the Vice President elect shall act as President until a President shall have qualified; and the Congress may by law provide for the case wherein neither a President elect nor a Vice President elect shall have qualified, declaring who shall then act as President, or the manner in which one who is to act shall be selected, and such person shall act accordingly until a President or Vice President shall have qualified.

Section 4. The Congress may by law provide for the case of the death of any of the persons from whom the House of Representatives may choose a President whenever the right of choice shall have devolved upon them, and for the case of the death of any of the persons from whom the Senate may choose a Vice President whenever the right of choice shall have devolved upon them.

Section 5. Sections 1 and 2 shall take effect on the 15th day of October following the ratification of this article.

Section 6. This article shall be inoperative unless it shall have been ratified as an amendment to the Constitution by the legislatures of three-fourths of the several States within seven years from the date of its submission.

AMENDMENT XXI [1933]

Section 1. The eighteenth article of amendment to the Constitution of the United States is hereby repealed.

Section 2. The transportation or importation into any State, Territory, or possession of the United States for delivery or use therein of intoxicating liquors, in violation of the laws thereof, is hereby prohibited.

Section 3. This article shall be inoperative unless it shall have been ratified as an amendment to the Constitution by conventions in the several States, as provided in the Constitution, within seven years from the date of the submission hereof to the States by the Congress.

AMENDMENT XXII [1951]

Section 1. No person shall be elected to the office of the President more than twice, and no person who has held the office of President, or acted as President, for more than two years of a term to which some other person was elected President shall be elected to the office of President more than once. But this Article shall not apply to any person holding the office of President when this Article was proposed by the Congress, and shall not prevent any person who may be holding the office of President, or acting as President, during the term within which this Article becomes operative from holding the office of President or acting as President during the remainder of such term.

Section 2. This article shall be inoperative unless it shall have been ratified as an amendment to the Constitution by the legislatures of three-fourths of the several States within seven years from the date of its submission to the States by the Congress.

AMENDMENT XXIII [1961]

Section 1. The District constituting the seat of Government of the United States shall appoint in such manner as the Congress may direct:

A number of electors of President and Vice President equal to the whole number of Senators and Representatives in Congress to which the District would be entitled if it were a State, but in no event more than the least populous state; they shall be in addition to those appointed by the states, but they shall be considered, for the purposes of the election of President and Vice President, to be electors appointed by a state; and they shall meet in the District and perform such duties as provided by the twelfth article of amendment.

Section 2.　The Congress shall have power to enforce this article by appropriate legislation.

Amendment XXIV [1964]

Section 1.　The right of citizens of the United States to vote in any primary or other election for President or Vice President, for electors for President or Vice President, or for Senator or Representative in Congress, shall not be denied or abridged by the United States, or any State by reason of failure to pay any poll tax or other tax.

Section 2.　The Congress shall have power to enforce this article by appropriate legislation.

Amendment XXV [1967]

Section 1.　In case of the removal of the President from office or of his death or resignation, the Vice President shall become President.

Section 2.　Whenever there is a vacancy in the office of the Vice President, the President shall nominate a Vice President who shall take office upon confirmation by a majority vote of both Houses of Congress.

Section 3.　Whenever the President transmits to the President pro tempore of the Senate and the Speaker of the House of Representatives his written declaration that he is unable to discharge the powers and duties of his office, and until he transmits to them a written declaration to the contrary, such powers and duties shall be discharged by the Vice President as Acting President.

Section 4.　Whenever the Vice President and a majority of either the principal officers of the executive departments or of such other body as Congress may by law provide, transmit to the President pro tempore of the Senate and the Speaker of the House of Representatives their written declaration that the President is unable to discharge the powers and duties of his office, the Vice President shall immediately assume the powers and duties of the office as Acting President.

Thereafter, when the President transmits to the President pro tempore of the Senate and the Speaker of the House of Representatives his written declaration that no inability exists, he shall resume the powers and duties of his office unless the Vice President and a majority of either the principal officers of the executive department or of such other body as Congress may by law provide, transmit within four days to the President pro tempore of the Senate and the Speaker of the House of Representatives their written declaration that the President is unable to discharge the powers and duties of his office. Thereupon Congress shall decide the issue, assembling within forty-eight hours for that purpose if not in session. If the Congress, within twenty-one days after receipt of the latter written declaration, or, if Congress is not in session, within twenty-one days after Congress is required to assemble, determines by two-thirds vote of both Houses that the President is unable to discharge the powers and duties of his office, the Vice President shall continue to discharge the same as Acting President; otherwise, the President shall resume the powers and duties of his office.

Amendment XXVI [1971]

Section 1.　The right of citizens of the United States, who are eighteen years of age or older, to vote shall not be denied or abridged by the United States or by any State on account of age.

Section 2.　The Congress shall have power to enforce this article by appropriate legislation.

Amendment XXVII [1992]

No law, varying the compensation for the services of the Senators and Representatives, shall take effect, until an election of Representatives shall have intervened.

Appendix B The Uniform Commercial Code (Excerpts)

Article 1
GENERAL PROVISIONS

§ 1—201. General Definitions.

Subject to additional definitions contained in the subsequent Articles of this Act which are applicable to specific Articles or Parts thereof, and unless the context otherwise requires, in this Act:

(6) "Bill of lading" means a document evidencing the receipt of goods for shipment issued by a person engaged in the business of transporting or forwarding goods, and includes an airbill. "Airbill" means a document serving for air transportation as a bill of lading does for marine or rail transportation, and includes an air consignment note or air waybill.

(15) "Document of title" includes bill of lading, dock warrant, dock receipt, warehouse receipt or order for the delivery of goods, and also any other document which in the regular course of business or financing is treated as adequately evidencing that the person in possession of it is entitled to receive, hold and dispose of the document and the goods it covers. To be a document of title a document must purport to be issued by or addressed to a bailee and purport to cover goods in the bailee's possession which are either identified or are fungible portions of an identified mass.

(19) "Good faith" means honesty in fact in the conduct or transaction concerned.

(20) "Holder" means a person who is in possession of a document of title or an instrument or a certificated investment security drawn, issued, or indorsed to him or his order or to bearer or in bank.

(45) "Warehouse receipt" means a receipt issued by a person engaged in the business of storing goods for hire.

§ 1—203. Obligation of Good Faith.

Every contract or duty within this Act imposes an obligation of good faith in its performance or enforcement.

§ 1—205. Course of Dealing and Usage of Trade.

(1) A course of dealing is a sequence of previous conduct between the parties to a particular transaction which is fairly to be regarded as establishing a common basis of understanding for interpreting their expressions and other conduct.

(2) A usage of trade is any practice or method of dealing having such regularity of observance in a place, vocation or trade as to justify an expectation that it will be observed with respect to the transaction in question. The existence and scope of such a usage are to be proved as facts. If it is established that such a usage is embodied in a written trade code or similar writing the interpretation of the writing is for the court.

(3) A course of dealing between parties and any usage of trade in the vocation or trade in which they are engaged or of which they are or should be aware give particular meaning to and supplement or qualify terms of an agreement.

(4) The express terms of an agreement and an applicable course of dealing or usage of trade shall be construed wherever reasonable as consistent with each other; but when such construction is unreasonable express terms control both course of dealing and usage of trade and course of dealing controls usage of trade.

(5) An applicable usage of trade in the place where any part of performance is to occur shall be used in interpreting the agreement as to that part of the performance.

(6) Evidence of a relevant usage of trade offered by one party is not admissible unless and until he has given the other party such notice as the court finds sufficient to prevent unfair surprise to the latter.

Article 2
SALES

§ 2—104. Definitions: "Merchant"; "Between Merchants"; "Financing Agency".

(1) "Merchant" means a person who deals in goods of the kind or otherwise by his occupation holds himself out as

having knowledge or skill peculiar to the practices or goods involved in the transaction or to whom such knowledge or skill may be attributed by his employment of an agent or broker or other intermediary who by his occupation holds himself out as having such knowledge or skill.

(2) "Financing agency" means a bank, finance company or other person who in the ordinary course of business makes advances against goods or documents of title or who by arrangement with either the seller or the buyer intervenes in ordinary course to make or collect payment due or claimed under the contract for sale, as by purchasing or paying the seller's draft or making advances against it or by merely taking it for collection whether or not documents of title accompany the draft. "Financing agency" includes also a bank or other person who similarly intervenes between persons who are in the position of seller and buyer in respect to the goods (Section 2—707).

(3) "Between merchants" means in any transaction with respect to which both parties are chargeable with the knowledge or skill of merchants.

§ 2—105. Definitions: Transferability; "Goods"; "Future Goods"; "Lot"; "Commercial Unit".

(1) "Goods" means all things (including specially manufactured goods) which are moveable at the time of identification to the contract for sale other than the money in which the price is to be paid, investment securities (Article 8) and things in action. "Goods" also includes the unborn young of animals and growing crops and other identified things attached to realty as described in the section on goods to be severed from realty (Section 2—107).

(2) Goods must be both existing and identified before any interest in them can pass. Goods which are both existing and identified are "future" goods. A purported present sale of future goods or of any interest therein operates as a contract to sell.

(3) There may be a sale of a part interest in existing identified goods.

(4) An undivided share in an identified bulk of fungible goods is sufficiently identified to be sold although the quantity of the bulk is not determined. Any agreed proportion of such a bulk or any quantity thereof agreed upon by number, weight or other measure may to the extent of the seller's interest in the bulk be sold to the buyer who then becomes an owner in common.

(5) "Lot" means a parcel or a single article which is the subject matter of a separate sale or delivery, whether or not it is sufficient to perform the contract.

(6) "Commercial unit" means such a unit of goods as by commercial usage is a single whole for purposes of sale and division of which materially impairs its character or value on the market or in use. A commercial unit may be a single article (as a machine) or a set of articles (as a suite of furniture or an assortment of sizes) or a quantity (as a bale, gross, or carload) or any other unit treated in use or in the relevant market as a single whole.

Part 2 Form, Formation and Readjustment of Contract

§ 2—201. Formal Requirements; Statute of Frauds.

(1) Except as otherwise provided in this section a contract for the sale of goods for the price of $500 or more is not enforceable by way of action or defense unless there is some writing sufficient to indicate that a contract for sale has been made between the parties and signed by the party against whom enforcement is sought or by his authorized agent or broker. A writing is not insufficient because it omits or incorrectly states a term agreed upon but the contract is not enforceable under this paragraph beyond the quantity of goods shown in such writing.

(2) Between merchants if within a reasonable time a writing in confirmation of the contract and sufficient against the sender is received and the party receiving it has reason to know its contents, it satisfies the requirements of subsection (1) against such party unless written notice of objection to its contents is given within ten days after it is received.

(3) A contract which does not satisfy the requirements of subsection (1) but which is valid in other respects is enforceable

(a) if the goods are to be specially manufactured for the buyer and are not suitable for sale to others in the ordinary course of the seller's business and the seller, before notice of repudiation is received and under circumstances which reasonably indicate that the goods are for the buyer, has made either a substantial beginning of their manufacture or commitments for their procurement; or

(b) if the party against whom enforcement is sought admits in his pleading, testimony or otherwise in court that a contract for sale was made, but the contract is not enforceable under this provision beyond the quantity of goods admitted; or

(c) with respect to goods for which payment has been made and accepted or which have been received and accepted (Sec. 2—606).

§ 2—204. Formation in General.

(1) A contract for sale of goods may be made in any manner sufficent to show agreement, including conduct by both parties which recognizes the existence of such a contract.

(2) An agreement sufficient to constitute a contract for sale may be found even though the moment of its making is undetermined.

(3) Even though one or more terms are left open a contract for sale does not fail for indefiniteness if the parties have intended to make a contract and there is a reasonably certain basis for giving an appropriate remedy.

§ 2—205. Firm Offers.

An offer by a merchant to buy or sell goods in a signed writing which by its terms gives assurance that it will be held open is not revocable, for lack of consideration, during the time stated or if no time is stated for a reasonable time, but in no event may such period of irrevocability exceed three months; but any such term of assurance on a form supplied by the offeree must be separately signed by the offeror.

§ 2—206. Offer and Acceptance in Formation of Contract.

(1) Unless otherwise unambiguously indicated by the language or circumstances

(a) an offer to make a contract shall be construed as inviting acceptance in any manner and by any medium reasonable in the circumstances;

(b) an order or other offer to buy goods for prompt or current shipment shall be construed as inviting acceptance either by a prompt promise to ship or by the prompt or current shipment of conforming or nonconforming goods, but such a shipment of nonconforming goods does not constitute an acceptance if the seller seasonably notifies the buyer that the shipment is offered only as an accommodation to the buyer.

(2) Where the beginning of a requested performance is a reasonable mode of acceptance an offeror who is not notified of acceptance within a reasonable time may treat the offer as having lapsed before acceptance.

§ 2—207. Additional Terms in Acceptance or Confirmation.

(1) A definite and seasonable expression of acceptance or a written confirmation which is sent within a reasonable time operates as an acceptance even though it states terms additional to or different from those offered or agreed upon, unless acceptance is expressly made conditional on assent to the additional or different terms.

(2) The additional terms are to be construed as proposals for addition to the contract. Between merchants such terms become part of the contract unless:

(a) the offer expressly limits acceptance to the terms of the offer;

(b) they materially alter it; or

(c) notification of objection to them has already been given or is given within a reasonable time after notice of them is received.

(3) Conduct by both parties which recognizes the existence of a contract is sufficient to establish a contract for sale although the writings of the parties do not otherwise establish a contract. In such case the terms of the particular contract consist of those terms on which the writings of the parties agree, together with any supplementary terms incorporated under any other provisions of this Act.

§ 2—209. Modification, Rescission and Waiver.

(1) An agreement modifying a contract within this Article needs no consideration to be binding.

(2) A signed agreement which excludes modification or rescission except by a signed writing cannot be otherwise modified or rescinded, but except as between merchants such a requirement on a form supplied by the merchant must be separately signed by the other party.

(3) The requirements of the statute of frauds section of this Article (Section 2—201) must be satisfied if the contract as modified is within its provisions.

(4) Although an attempt at modification or rescission does not satisfy the requirements of subsection (2) or (3) it can operate as a waiver.

(5) A party who has made a waiver affecting an executory portion of the contract may retract the waiver by reasonable notification received by the other party that strict performance will be required of any term waived, unless the retraction would be unjust in view of a material change of position in reliance on the waiver.

Part 3 General Obligation and Construction of Contract

§ 2—302. Unconscionable Contract or Clause.

(1) If the court as a matter of law finds the contract or any clause of the contract to have been unconscionable at the time it was made the court may refuse to enforce the contract, or it may enforce the remainder of the contract without the unconscionable clause, or it may so limit the application of any unconscionable clause as to avoid any unconscionable result.

(2) When it is claimed or appears to the court that the contract or any clause thereof may be unconscionable the parties shall be afforded a reasonable opportunity to present evidence as to its commercial setting, purpose and effect to aid the court in making the determination.

§ 2—305. Open Price Term.

(1) The parties if they so intend can conclude a contract for sale even though the price is not settled. In such a case the price is a reasonable price at the time for delivery if

(a) nothing is said as to price; or

(b) the price is left to be agreed by the parties and they fail to agree; or

(c) the price is to be fixed in terms of some agreed market or other standard as set or recorded by a third person or agency and it is not so set or recorded.

(2) A price to be fixed by the seller or by the buyer means a price for him to fix in good faith.

(3) When a price left to be fixed otherwise than by agreement of the parties fails to be fixed through fault of one party the other may at his option treat the contract as cancelled or himself fix a reasonable price.

(4) Where, however, the parties intend not to be bound unless the price be fixed or agreed and it is not fixed or agreed there is no contract. In such a case the buyer must return any goods already received or if unable so to do must pay their reasonable value at the time of delivery and the seller must return any portion of the price paid on account.

§ 2—306. Output, Requirements and Exclusive Dealings.

(1) A term which measures the quantity by the output of the seller or the requirements of the buyer means such actual output or requirements as may occur in good faith, except that no quantity unreasonably disproportionate to any stated estimate or in the absence of a stated estimate to any normal or otherwise comparable prior output or requirements may be tendered or demanded.

(2) A lawful agreement by either the seller or the buyer for exclusive dealing in the kind of goods concerned imposes unless otherwise agreed an obligation by the seller to use best efforts to supply the goods and by the buyer to use best efforts to promote their sale.

§ 2—307. Delivery in Single Lot or Several Lots.

Unless otherwise agreed all goods called for by a contract for sale must be tendered in a single delivery and payment is due only on such tender but where the circumstances give either party the right to make or demand delivery in lots the price if it can be apportioned may be demanded for each lot.

§ 2—308. Absence of Specified Place for Delivery.

Unless otherwise agreed

(a) the place for delivery of goods is the seller's place of business or if he has none his residence; but

(b) in a contract for sale of identified goods which to the knowledge of the parties at the time of contracting are in some other place, that place is the place for their delivery; and

(c) documents of title may be delivered through customary banking channels.

§ 2—309. Absence of Specific Time Provisions; Notice of Termination.

(1) The time for shipment or delivery or any other action under a contract if not provided in this Article or agreed upon shall be a reasonable time.

(2) Where the contract provides for successive performances but is indefinite in duration it is valid for a reasonable time but unless otherwise agreed may be terminated at any time by either party.

(3) Termination of a contract by one party except on the happening of an agreed event requires that reasonable notification be received by the other party and an agreement dispensing with notification is invalid if its operation would be unconscionable.

§ 2—310. Open Time for Payment or Running of Credit: Authority to Ship Under Reservation.

Unless otherwise agreed

(a) payment is due at the time and place at which the buyer is to receive the goods even though the place of shipment is the place of delivery; and

(b) if the seller is authorized to send the goods he may ship them under reservation, and may tender the documents of title, but the buyer may inspect the goods after their arrival before payment is due unless such inspection is inconsistent with the terms of the contract (Section 2—513); and

(c) if delivery is authorized and made by way of documents of title otherwise than by subsection (b) then payment is due at the time and place at which the buyer is to receive the documents regardless of where the goods are to be received; and

(d) where the seller is required or authorized to ship the goods on credit the credit period runs from the time of shipment but post-dating the invoice or delaying its dispatch will correspondingly delay the starting of the credit period.

§ 2—312. Warranty of Title and Against Infringement; Buyer's Obligation Against Infringement.

(1) Subject to subsection (2) there is in a contract for sale a warranty by the seller that

(a) the title conveyed shall be good, and its transfer rightful; and

(b) the goods shall be delivered free from any security interest or other lien or encumbrance of which the buyer at the time of contracting has no knowledge.

(2) A warranty under subsection (1) will be excluded or modified only by specific language or by circumstances which give the buyer reason to know that the person selling does not claim title in himself or that he is purporting to

sell only such right or title as he or a third person may have.

(3) Unless otherwise agreed a seller who is a merchant regularly dealing in goods of the kind warrants that the goods shall be delivered free of the rightful claim of any third person by way of infringement or the like but a buyer who furnishes specifications to the seller must hold the seller harmless against any such claim which arises out of compliance with the specifications.

§ 2—313. Express Warranties by Affirmation, Promise, Description, Sample.

(1) Express warranties by the seller are created as follows:

(a) Any affirmation of fact or promise made by the seller to the buyer which relates to the goods and becomes part of the basis of the bargain creates an express warranty that the goods shall conform to the affirmation or promise.

(b) Any description of the goods which is made part of the basis of the bargain creates an express warranty that the goods shall conform to the description.

(c) Any sample or model which is made part of the basis of the bargain creates an express warranty that the whole of the goods shall conform to the sample or model.

(2) It is not necessary to the creation of an express warranty that the seller use formal words such as "warrant" or "guarantee" or that he have a specific intention to make a warranty, but an affirmation merely of the value of the goods or a statement purporting to be merely the seller's opinion or commendation of the goods does not create a warranty.

§ 2—314. Implied Warranty: Merchantability; Usage of Trade.

(1) Unless excluded or modified (Section 2—316), a warranty that the goods shall be merchantable is implied in a contract for their sale if the seller is a merchant with respect to goods of that kind. Under this section the serving for value of food or drink to be consumed either on the premises or elsewhere is a sale.

(2) Goods to be merchantable must be at least such as

(a) pass without objection in the trade under the contract description; and

(b) in the case of fungible goods, are of fair average quality within the description; and

(c) are fit for the ordinary purposes for which such goods are used; and

(d) run, within the variations permitted by the agreement, of even kind, quality and quantity within each unit and among all units involved; and

(e) are adequately contained, packaged, and labeled as the agreement may require; and

(f) conform to the promises or affirmations of fact made on the container or label if any.

(3) Unless excluded or modified (Section 2—316), other implied warranties may arise from course of dealing or usage of trade.

§ 2—315. Implied Warranty: Fitness for Particular Purpose.

Where the seller at the time of contracting has reason to know any particular purpose for which the goods are required and that the buyer is relying on the seller's skill or judgment to select or furnish suitable goods, there is unless excluded or modified under the next section an implied warranty that the goods shall be fit for such purpose.

§ 2—316. Exclusion or Modification of Warranties.

(1) Words or conduct relevant to the creation of an express warranty and words or conduct tending to negate or limit warranty shall be construed wherever reasonable as consistent with each other; but subject to the provisions of this Article on parol or extrinsic evidence (Section 2—202) negation or limitation is inoperative to the extent that such construction is unreasonable.

(2) Subject to subsection (3), to exclude or modify the implied warranty of merchantability or any part of it the language must mention merchantability and in case of a writing must be conspicuous, and to exclude or modify any implied warranty of fitness the exclusion must be by a writing and conspicuous. Language to exclude all implied warranties of fitness is sufficient if it states, for example, that "There are no warranties which extend beyond the description on the face hereof."

(3) Notwithstanding subsection (2)

(a) unless the circumstances indicate otherwise, all implied warranties are excluded by expressions like "as is", "with all faults" or other language which in common understanding calls the buyer's attention to the exclusion of warranties and makes plain that there is no implied warranty; and

(b) when the buyer before entering into the contract has examined the goods or the sample or model as fully as he desired or has refused to examine the goods, there is no implied warranty with regard to defects which an examination ought in the circumstances to have revealed to him; and

(c) an implied warranty can also be excluded or modified by course of dealing or course of performance or usage of trade.

(4) Remedies for breach of warranty can be limited in accordance with the provisions of this Article on liquidation or limitation of damages and on contractual modification of remedy (Sections 2—718 and 2—719).

§ 2—317. **Cumulation and Conflict of Warranties Express or Implied.**

Warranties whether express or implied shall be construed as consistent with each other and as cumulative, but if such construction is unreasonable the intention of the parties shall determine which warranty is dominant. In ascertaining that intention the following rules apply:

(a) Exact or technical specifications displace an inconsistent sample or model or general language of description.

(b) A sample from an existing bulk displaces inconsistent general language of description.

(c) Express warranties displace inconsistent implied warranties other than an implied warranty of fitness for a particular purpose.

§ 2—318. **Third Party Beneficiaries of Warranties Express or Implied.**

Note: If this Act is introduced in the Congress of the United States this section should be omitted. (States to select one alternative.)

Alternative A

A seller's warranty whether express or implied extends to any natural person who is in the family or household of his buyer or who is a guest in his home if it is reasonable to expect that such person may use, consume or be affected by the goods and who is injured in person by breach of the warranty. A seller may not exclude or limit the operation of this section.

Alternative B

A seller's warranty whether express or implied extends to any natural person who may reasonably be expected to use, consume or be affected by the goods and who is injured in person by breach of the warranty. A seller may not exclude or limit the operation of this section.

Alternative C

A seller's warranty whether express or implied extends to any person who may reasonably be expected to use, consume or be affected by the goods and who is injured by breach of the warranty. A seller may not exclude or limit the operation of this section with respect to injury to the person of an individual to whom the warranty extends. As amended 1966.

§ 2—319. **F.O.B. and F.A.S. Terms.**

(1) Unless otherwise agreed the term F.O.B. (which means "free on board") at a named place, even though used only in connection with the stated price, is a delivery term under which

(a) when the term is F.O.B. the place of shipment, the seller must at that place ship the goods in the manner provided in this Article (Section 2—504) and bear the expense and risk of putting them into the possession of the carrier; or

(b) when the term is F.O.B. the place of destination, the seller must at his own expense and risk transport the goods to that place and there tender delivery of them in the manner provided in this Article (Section 2—503);

(c) when under either (a) or (b) the term is also F.O.B. vessel, car or other vehicle, the seller must in addition at his own expense and risk load the goods on board. If the term is F.O.B. vessel the buyer must name the vessel and in an appropriate case the seller must comply with the provisions of this Article on the form of bill of lading (Section 2—323).

(2) Unless otherwise agreed the term F.A.S. vessel (which means "free alongside") at a named port, even though used only in connection with the stated price, is a delivery term under which the seller must

(a) at his own expense and risk deliver the goods alongside the vessel in the manner usual in that port or on a dock designated and provided by the buyer; and

(b) obtain and tender a receipt for the goods in exchange for which the carrier is under a duty to issue a bill of lading.

(3) Unless otherwise agreed in any case falling within subsection (1)(a) or (c) or subsection (2) the buyer must seasonably give any needed instructions for making delivery, including when the term is F.A.S. or F.O.B. the loading berth of the vessel and in an appropriate case its name and sailing date. The seller may treat the failure of needed instructions as a failure of cooperation under this Article (Section 2—311). He may also at his option move the goods in any reasonable manner preparatory to delivery or shipment.

(4) Under the term F.O.B. vessel or F.A.S. unless otherwise agreed the buyer must make payment against tender of the required documents and the seller may not tender nor the buyer demand delivery of the goods in substitution for the documents.

§ 2—320. **C.I.F. and C. & F. Terms.**

(1) The term C.I.F. means that the price includes in a lump sum the cost of the goods and the insurance and freight to the named destination. The term C. & F. or C.F. means that the price so includes cost and freight to the named destination.

(2) Unless otherwise agreed and even though used only in connection with the stated price and destination, the term C.I.F. destination or its equivalent requires the seller at his own expense and risk to

(a) put the goods into the possession of a carrier at the port for shipment and obtain a negotiable bill or bills of lading covering the entire transportation to the named destination; and

(b) load the goods and obtain a receipt from the carrier (which may be contained in the bill of lading) showing that the freight has been paid or provided for; and

(c) obtain a policy or certificate of insurance, including any war risk insurance, of a kind and on terms then current at the port of shipment in the usual amount, in the currency of the contract, shown to cover the same goods covered by the bill of lading and providing for payment of loss to the order of the buyer or for the account of whom it may concern; but the seller may add to the price the amount of the premium for any such war risk insurance; and

(d) prepare an invoice of the goods and procure any other documents required to effect shipment or to comply with the contract; and

(e) forward and tender with commercial promptness all the documents in due form and with any indorsement necessary to perfect the buyer's rights.

(3) Unless otherwise agreed the term C. & F. or its equivalent has the same effect and imposes upon the seller the same obligations and risks as a C.I.F. term except the obligation as to insurance.

(4) Under the term C.I.F. or C. & F. unless otherwise agreed the buyer must make payment against tender of the required documents and the seller may not tender nor the buyer demand delivery of the goods in substitution for the documents.

§ 2—322. Delivery "Ex-Ship".

(1) Unless otherwise agreed a term for delivery of goods "ex-ship" (which means from the carrying vessel) or in equivalent language is not restricted to a particular ship and requires delivery from a ship which has reached a place at the named port of destination where goods of the kind are usually discharged.

(2) Under such a term unless otherwise agreed

(a) the seller must discharge all liens arising out of the carriage and furnish the buyer with a direction which puts the carrier under a duty to deliver the goods; and

(b) the risk of loss does not pass to the buyer until the goods leave the ship's tackle or are otherwise properly unloaded.

§ 2—324. "No Arrival, No Sale" Term.

Under a term "no arrival, no sale" or terms of like meaning, unless otherwise agreed,

(a) the seller must properly ship conforming goods and if they arrive by any means he must tender them on arrival but he assumes no obligation that the goods will arrive unless he has caused the nonarrival; and

(b) where without fault of the seller the goods are in part lost or have so deteriorated as no longer to con-

form to the contract or arrive after the contract time, the buyer may proceed as if there had been casualty to identified goods.

§ 2—326. Sale on Approval and Sale or Return; Consignment Sales and Rights of Creditors.

(1) Unless otherwise agreed, if delivered goods may be returned by the buyer even though they conform to the contract, the transaction is

(a) a "sale on approval" if the goods are delivered primarily for use, and

(b) a "sale or return" if the goods are delivered primarily for resale.

(2) Except as provided in subsection (3), goods held on approval are not subject to the claims of the buyer's creditors until acceptance; goods held on sale or return are subject to such claims while in the buyer's possession.

(3) Where goods are delivered to a person for sale and such person maintains a place of business at which he deals in goods of the kind involved, under a name other than the name of the person making delivery, then with respect to claims of creditors of the person conducting the business the goods are deemed to be on sale or return. The provisions of this subsection are applicable even though an agreement purports to reserve title to the person making delivery until payment or resale or uses such words as "on consignment" or "on memorandum". However, this subsection is not applicable if the person making delivery

(a) complies with an applicable law providing for a consignor's interest or the like to be evidenced by a sign, or

(b) establishes that the person conducting the business is generally known by his creditors to be substantially engaged in selling the goods of others, or

(c) complies with the filing provisions of the Article on Secured Transactions (Article 9).

(4) Any "or return" term of a contract for sale is to be treated as a separate contract for sale within the statute of frauds section of this Article (Section 2—201) and as contradicting the sale aspect of the contract within the provisions of this Article on parol or extrinsic evidence (Section 2—202).

§ 2—328. Sale by Auction.

(1) In a sale by auction if goods are put up in lots each lot is the subject of a separate sale.

(2) A sale by auction is complete when the auctioneer so announces by the fall of the hammer or in other customary manner. Where a bid is made while the hammer is falling in acceptance of a prior bid the auctioneer may in his discretion reopen the bidding or declare the goods sold under the bid on which the hammer was falling.

(3) Such a sale is with reserve unless the goods are in explicit terms put up without reserve. In an auction with reserve the auctioneer may withdraw the goods at any time until he announces completion of the sale. In an auction without reserve, after the auctioneer calls for bids on an article or lot, that article or lot cannot be withdrawn unless no bid is made within a reasonable time. In either case a bidder may retract his bid until the auctioneer's announcement of completion of the sale, but a bidder's retraction does not revive any previous bid.

(4) If the auctioneer knowingly receives a bid on the seller's behalf or the seller makes or procures such a bid, and notice has not been given that liberty for such bidding is reserved, the buyer may at his option avoid the sale or take the goods at the price of the last good faith bid prior to the completion of the sale. This subsection shall not apply to any bid at a forced sale.

Part 4   Title, Creditors and Good Faith Purchasers

§ 2—401. Passing of Title; Reservation for Security; Limited Application of This Section.

Each provision of this Article with regard to the rights, obligations and remedies of the seller, the buyer, purchasers or other third parties applies irrespective of title to the goods except where the provision refers to such title. Insofar as situations are not covered by the other provisions of this Article and matters concerning title become material the following rules apply:

(1) Title to goods cannot pass under a contract for sale prior to their identification to the contract (Section 2—501), and unless otherwise explicitly agreed the buyer acquires by their identification a special property as limited by this Act. Any retention or reservation by the seller of the title (property) in goods shipped or delivered to the buyer is limited in effect to a reservation of a security interest. Subject to these provisions and to the provisions of the Article on Secured Transactions (Article 9), title to goods passes from the seller to the buyer in any manner and on any conditions explicitly agreed on by the parties.

(2) Unless otherwise explicitly agreed title passes to the buyer at the time and place at which the seller completes his performance with reference to the physical delivery of the goods, despite any reservation of a security interest and even though a document of title is to be delivered at a different time or place; and in particular and despite any reservation of a security interest by the bill of lading

(a) if the contract requires or authorizes the seller to send the goods to the buyer but does not require him to deliver them at destination, title passes to the buyer at the time and place of shipment; but

(b) if the contract requires delivery at destination, title passes on tender there.

(3) Unless otherwise explicitly agreed where delivery is to be made without moving the goods,

(a) If the seller is to deliver a document of title, title passes at the time when and the place where he delivers such documents; or

(b) if the goods are at the time of contracting already identified and no documents are to be delivered, title passes at the time and place of contracting.

(4) A rejection or other refusal by the buyer to receive or retain the goods, whether or not justified, or a justified revocation of acceptance revests title to the goods in the seller. Such revesting occurs by operation of law and is not a "sale."

Part 5   Performance

§ 2—501. Insurable Interest in Goods; Manner of Identification of Goods.

(1) The buyer obtains a special property and an insurable interest in goods by identification of existing goods as goods to which the contract refers even though the goods so identified are nonconforming and he has an option to return or reject them. Such identification can be made at any time and in any manner explicitly agreed to by the parties. In the absence of explicit agreement identification occurs.

(a) when the contract is made if it is for the sale of goods already existing and identified;

(b) if the contract is for the sale of future goods other than those described in paragraph (c), when goods are shipped, marked or otherwise designated by the seller as goods to which the contract refers;

(c) when the crops are planted or otherwise become growing crops or the young are conceived if the contract is for the sale of unborn young to be born within twelve months after contracting or for the sale of crops to be harvested within twelve months or the next normal harvest season after contracting whichever is longer.

(2) The seller retains an insurable interest in goods so long as title to or any security interest in the goods remains in him and where the identification is by the seller alone he may until default or insolvency or notification to the buyer that the identification is final substitute other goods for those identified.

(3) Nothing in this section impairs any insurable interest recognized under any other statute or rule of law.

§ 2—509. Risk of Loss in the Absence of Breach.

(1) Where the contract requires or authorizes the seller to ship the goods by carrier

(a) If it does not require him to deliver them at a particular destination, the risk of loss passes to the buyer when the goods are duly delivered to the carrier even though the shipment is under reservation (Section 2—505); but

(b) if it does require him to deliver them at a particular destination and the goods are there duly tendered while in the possession of the carrier, the risk of loss passes to the buyer when the goods are there duly so tendered as to enable the buyer to take delivery.

(2) Where the goods are held by a bailee to be delivered without being moved, the risk of loss passes to the buyer.

(a) on his receipt of a negotiable document of title covering the goods; or

(b) on acknowledgment by the bailee of the buyer's right to possession of the goods; or

(c) after his receipt of a non-negotiable document of title or other written direction to deliver, as provided in subsection (4)(b) of Section 2—503.

(3) In any case not within subsection (1) or (2), the risk of loss passes to the buyer on his receipt of the goods if the seller is a merchant; otherwise the risk passes to the buyer on tender of delivery.

(4) The provisions of this section are subject to contrary agreement of the parties and to the provisions of this Article on sale on approval (Section 2—327) and on effect of breach on risk of loss (Section 2—510).

§ 2—510. Effect of Breach on Risk of Loss.

(1) Where a tender or delivery of goods so fails to conform to the contract as to give a right of rejection the risk of their loss remains on the seller until cure or acceptance.

(2) Where the buyer rightfully revokes acceptance he may to the extent of any deficiency in his effective insurance coverage treat the risk of loss as having rested on the seller from the beginning.

(3) Where the buyer as to conforming goods already identified to the contract for sale repudiates or is otherwise in breach before risk of their loss has passed to him, the seller may to the extent of any deficiency in his effective insurance coverage treat the risk of loss as resting on the buyer for a commercially reasonable time.

§ 2—513. Buyer's Right to Inspection of Goods.

(1) Unless otherwise agreed and subject to subsection (3), where goods are tendered or delivered or identified to the contract for sale, the buyer has a right before payment or acceptance to inspect them at any reasonable place and time and in any reasonable manner. When the seller is required and authorized to send the goods to the buyer, the inspection may be after their arrival.

(2) Expenses of inspection must be borne by the buyer but may be recovered from the seller if the goods do not conform and are rejected.

(3) Unless otherwise agreed and subject to the provisions of this Article on C.I.F. contracts (subsection (3) of Section 2—321), the buyer is not entitled to inspect the goods before payment of the price when the contract provides

(a) for delivery "C.O.D." or on other like terms; or

(b) for payment against documents of title, except where such payment is due only after the goods are to become available for inspection.

(4) A place or method of inspection fixed by the parties is presumed to be exclusive but unless otherwise expressly agreed it does not postpone identification or shift the place for delivery or for passing the risk of loss. If compliance becomes impossible, inspection shall be as provided in this section unless the place or method fixed was clearly intended as an indispensable condition failure of which avoids the contract.

Part 6   Breach, Repudiation and Excuse

§ 2—609. Right to Adequate Assurance of Performance.

(1) A contract for sale imposes an obligation on each party that the other's expectation of receiving due performance will not be impaired. When reasonable grounds for insecurity arise with respect to the performance of either party the other may in writing demand adequate assurance of due performance and until he receives such assurance may if commercially reasonable suspend any performance for which he has not already received the agreed return.

(2) Between merchants the reasonableness of grounds for insecurity and the adequacy of any assurance offered shall be determined according to commercial standards.

(3) Acceptance of any improper delivery or payment does not prejudice the aggrieved party's right to demand adequate assurance of future performance.

(4) After receipt of a justified demand failure to provide within a reasonable time not exceeding thirty days such assurance of due performance as is adequate under the circumstances of the particular case is a repudiation of the contract.

§ 2—615. Excuse by Failure of Presupposed Conditions.

Except so far as a seller may have assumed a greater obligation and subject to the preceding section on substituted performance:

(a) Delay in delivery or non-delivery in whole or in part by a seller who complies with paragraphs (b) and (c) is not a breach of his duty under a contract for sale if performance as agreed has been made impracticable by the occurrence of a contingency the nonoccurrence of which was a basic assumption on which the contract was made or by compliance in good faith with any applicable foreign or domestic governmental regulation or order whether or not it later proves to be invalid.

(b) Where the causes mentioned in paragraph (a) affect only a part of the seller's capacity to perform, he must allocate production and deliveries among his customers but may at his option include regular customers not then under contract as well as his own requirements for further manufacture. He may so allocate in any manner which is fair and reasonable.

(c) The seller must notify the buyer seasonably that there will be delay or non-delivery and, when allocation is required under paragraph (b), of the estimated quota thus made available for the buyer.

Part 7 Remedies

§ 2—708. Seller's Damages for Non-Acceptance or Repudiation.

(1) Subject to subsection (2) and to the provisions of this Article with respect to proof of market price (Section 2—723), the measure of damages for non-acceptance or repudiation by the buyer is the difference between the market price at the time and place for tender and the unpaid contract price together with any incidental damages provided in this Article (Section 2—710), but less expenses saved in consequence of the buyer's breach.

(2) If the measure of damages provided in subsection (1) is inadequate to put the seller in as good a position as performance would have done then the measure of damages is the profit (including reasonable overhead) which the seller would have made from full performance by the buyer, together with any incidental damages provided in this Article (Section 2—710), due allowance for costs reasonably incurred and due credit for payments or proceeds of resale.

§ 2—709. Action for the Price.

(1) When the buyer fails to pay the price as it becomes due the seller may recover, together with any incidental damages under the next section, the price

(a) of goods accepted or of conforming goods lost or damaged within a commercially reasonable time after risk of their loss has passed to the buyer; and

(b) of goods identified to the contract if the seller is unable after reasonable effort to resell them at a reasonable price or the circumstances reasonably indicate that such effort will be unavailing.

(2) Where the seller sues for the price he must hold for the buyer any goods which have been identified to the contract and are still in his control except that if resale becomes possible he may resell them at any time prior to the collection of the judgment. The net proceeds of any

such resale must be credited to the buyer and payment of the judgment entitles him to any goods not resold.

(3) After the buyer has wrongfully rejected or revoked acceptance of the goods or has failed to make a payment due or has repudiated (Section 2—610), a seller who is held not entitled to the price under this section shall nevertheless be awarded damages for non-acceptance under the preceding section.

§ 2—712. "Cover"; Buyer's Procurement of Substitute Goods.

(1) After a breach within the preceding section the buyer may "cover" by making in good faith and without unreasonable delay any reasonable purchase of or contract to purchase goods in substitution for those due from the seller.

(2) The buyer may recover from the seller as damages the difference between the cost of cover and the contract price together with any incidental or consequential damages as hereinafter defined (Section 2—715), but less expenses saved in consequence of the seller's breach.

(3) Failure of the buyer to effect cover within this section does not bar him from any other remedy.

§ 2—713. Buyer's Damages for Non-Delivery or Repudiation.

(1) Subject to the provisions of this Article with respect to proof of market price (section 2—723), the measure of damages for non-delivery or repudiation by the seller is the difference between the market price at the time when the buyer learned of the breach and the contract price together with any incidental and consequential damages provided in this Article (Section 2—715), but less expenses saved in consequence of the seller's breach.

(2) Market price is to be determined as of the place for tender or, in cases of rejection after arrival or revocation of acceptance, as of the place of arrival.

§ 2—715. Buyer's Incidental and Consequential Damages.

(1) Incidental damages resulting from the seller's breach include expenses reasonably incurred in inspection, receipt, transportation and care and custody of goods rightfully rejected, any commercially reasonable charges, expenses or commissions in connection with effecting over and any other reasonable expense incident to the delay or other breach.

(2) Consequential damages resulting from the seller's breach include

(a) Any loss resulting from general or particular requirements and needs of which the seller at the time of contracting had reason to know and which could not reasonably be prevented by cover or otherwise; and

(b) injury to person or property proximately resulting from any breach of warranty.

§ 2—716. Buyer's Right to Specific Performance or Replevin.

(1) Specific performance may be decreed where the goods are unique or in other proper circumstances.

(2) The decree for specific performance may include such terms and conditions as to payment of the price, damages, or other relief as the court may deem just.

(3) The buyer has a right of replevin for goods identified to the contract if after reasonable effort he is unable to effect cover for such goods or the circumstances reasonably indicate that such effort will be unavailing or if the goods have been shipped under reservation and satisfaction of the security interest in them has been made or tendered.

Article 3
COMMERCIAL PAPER

Part 1   Short Title, Form and Interpretation

§ 3—104. Form of Negotiable Instruments; "Draft"; "Check"; "Certificate of Deposit"; "Note".

(1) Any writing to be a negotiable instrument within this Article must

(a) be signed by the maker or drawer; and

(b) contain an unconditional promise or order to pay a sum certain in money and no other promise, order, obligation or power given by the maker or drawer except as authorized by this Article; and

(c) be payable on demand or at a definite time; and

(d) be payable to order or to bearer.

(2) A writing which complies with the requirements of this section is

(a) a "draft" ("bill of exchange") if it is an order;

(b) a "check" if it is a draft drawn on a bank and payable on demand;

(c) a "certificate of deposit" if it is an acknowledgment by a bank receipt of money with an engagement to repay it;

(d) a "note" if it is a promise other than a certificate of deposit.

(3) As used in other Articles of this Act, and as the context may require, the terms "draft", "check", "certificate of deposit" and "note" may refer to instruments which are not negotiable within this Article as well as to instruments which are so negotiable.

§ 3—105. When Promise or Order Unconditional.

(1) A promise or order otherwise unconditional is not made conditional by the fact that the instrument

(a) is subject to implied or constructive conditions; or

(b) states its consideration, whether performed or promised, or the transaction which gave rise to the instrument, or that the promise or order is made or the instrument matures in accordance with or "as per" such transaction; or

(c) refers to or states that it arises out of a separate agreement or refers to a separate agreement for rights as to prepayment or acceleration; or

(d) states that it is drawn under a letter of credit; or

(e) states that it is secured, whether by mortgage, reservation of title or otherwise; or

(f) indicates a particular account to be debited or any other fund or source from which reimbursement is expected; or

(g) is limited to payment out of a particular fund or the proceeds of a particular source, if the instrument is issued by a government or governmental agency or unit; or

(h) is limited to payment out of the entire assets of a partnership, unincorporated association, trust or estate by or on behalf of which the instrument is issued.

(2) A promise or order is not unconditional if the instrument

(a) states that it is subject to or governed by any other agreement; or

(b) states that it is to be paid only out of a particular fund or source except as provided in this section.

§ 3—106. Sum Certain.

(1) The sum payable is a sum certain even though it is to be paid

(a) with stated interest or by stated installments; or

(b) with stated different rates of interest before and after default or a specified date; or

(c) with a stated discount or addition if paid before or after the date fixed for payment; or

(d) with exchange or less exchange, whether at a fixed rate or at the current rate; or

(e) with costs of collection or an attorney's fee or both upon default.

(2) Nothing in this section shall validate any term which is otherwise illegal.

§ 3—107. Money.

(1) An instrument is payable in money if the medium of exchange in which it is payable is money at the time the

instrument is made. An instrument payable in "currency" or "current funds" is payable in money.

(2) A promise or order to pay a sum stated in a foreign currency is for a sum certain in money and, unless a different medium of payment is specified in the instrument, may be satisfied by payment of that number of dollars which the stated foreign currency will purchase at the buying sight rate for that currency on the day on which the instrument is payable or, if payable on demand, on the day of demand. If such an instrument specifies a foreign currency as the medium of payment the instrument is payable in that currency.

§ 3—108. Payable on Demand.

Instruments payable on demand include those payable at sight or on presentation and those in which no time for payment is stated.

§ 3—109. Definite Time.

(1) An instrument is payable at a definite time if by its terms it is payable

   (a) on or before a stated date or at a fixed period after a stated date; or

   (b) at a fixed period after sight; or

   (c) at a definite time subject to any acceleration; or

   (d) at a definite time subject to extension at the option of the holder, or to extension to a further definite time at the option of the maker or acceptor or automatically upon or after a specified act or event.

(2) An instrument which by its terms is otherwise payable only upon an act or event uncertain as to time of occurrence is not payable at a definite time even though the act or event has occurred.

§ 3—110. Payable to Order.

(1) An instrument is payable to order when by its terms it is payable to the order or assigns of any person therein specified with reasonable certainty, or to him or his order, or when it is conspicuously designated on its face as "exchange" or the like and names a payee. It may be payable to the order of

   (a) the maker or drawer; or

   (b) the drawee; or

   (c) a payee who is not maker, drawer or drawee; or

   (d) two or more payees together or in the alternative; or

   (e) an estate, trust or fund, in which case it is payable to the order of the representative of such estate, trust or fund or his successors; or

   (f) an office, or an officer by his title as such in which case it is payable to the principal but the incumbent of the office or his successors may act as if he or they were the holder; or

   (g) a partnership or unincorporated association, in which case it is payable to the partnership or association and may be indorsed or transferred by any person thereto authorized.

(2) An instrument not payable to order is not made so payable by such words as "payable upon return of this instrument properly indorsed."

(3) An instrument made payable both to order and to bearer is payable to order unless the bearer words are handwritten or typewritten.

§ 3—111. Payable to Bearer.

An instrument is payable to bearer when by its terms it is payable to

(a) bearer or the order of bearer; or

(b) a specified person or bearer; or

(c) "cash" or the order of "cash", or any other indication which does not purport to designate a specific payee.

§ 3—112. Terms and Omissions Not Affecting Negotiability.

(1) The negotiability of an instrument is not affected by

   (a) the omission of a statement of any consideration or of the place where the instrument is drawn or payable; or

   (b) a statement that collateral has been given to secure obligations either on the instrument or otherwise of an obligor on the instrument or that in case of default on those obligations the holder may realize on or dispose of the collateral; or

   (c) a promise or power to maintain or protect collateral or to give additional collateral; or

   (d) a term authorizing a confession of judgment on the instrument if it is not paid when due; or

   (e) a term purporting to waive the benefit of any law intended for the advantage or protection of any obligor; or

   (f) a term in a draft providing that the payee by indorsing or cashing it acknowledges full satisfaction of an obligation of the drawer; or

   (g) a statement in a draft drawn in a set of parts (Section 3—801) to the effect that the order is effective only if no other part has been honored.

(2) Nothing in this section shall validate any term which is otherwise illegal.

§ 3—113. Seal.

An instrument otherwise negotiable is within this Article even though it is under a seal.

§ 3—114. Date, Antedating, Postdating.

(1) The negotiability of an instrument is not affected by the fact that it is undated, antedated or postdated.

(2) Where an instrument is antedated or postdated the time when it is payable is determined by the stated date if the instrument is payable on demand or at a fixed period after date.

(3) Where the instrument or any signature thereon is dated, the date is presumed to be correct.

§ 3—115. Incomplete Instruments.

(1) When a paper whose contents at the time of signing show that it is intended to become an instrument is signed while still incomplete in any necessary respect it cannot be enforced until completed, but when it is completed in accordance with authority given it is effective as completed.

(2) If the completion is unauthorized the rules as to material alteration apply (Section 3—407), even though the paper was not delivered by the maker or drawer; but the burden of establishing that any completion is unauthorized is on the party so asserting.

§ 3—116. Instruments Payable to Two or More Persons.

An instrument payable to the order of two or more persons

(a) if in the alternative is payable to any one of them and may be negotiated, discharged or enforced by any of them who has possession of it;

(b) if not in the alternative is payable to all of them and may be negotiated, discharged or enforced only by all of them.

§ 3—118. Ambiguous Terms and Rules of Construction.

The following rules apply to every instrument:

(a) Where there is doubt whether the instrument is a draft or a note the holder may treat it as either. A draft drawn on the drawer is effective as a note.

(b) Handwritten terms control typewritten and printed terms, and typewritten control printed.

(c) Words control figures except that if the words are ambiguous figures control.

(d) Unless otherwise specified a provision for interest means interest at the judgment rate at the place of payment from the date of the instrument, or if it is undated from the date of issue.

(e) Unless the instrument otherwise specifies two or more persons who sign as maker, acceptor or drawer or indorser and as a part of the same transaction are jointly and severally liable even though the instrument contains such words as "I promise to pay."

(f) Unless otherwise specified consent to extension authorizes a single extension for not longer than the original period. A consent to extension, expressed in the instrument, is binding on secondary parties and accommodation makers. A holder may not exercise his option to extend an instrument over the objection of a maker or acceptor or other party who in accordance with Section 3—604 tenders full payment when the instrument is due.

Part 2   Transfer and Negotiation

§ 3—201. Transfer: Right to Indorsement.

(1) Transfer of an instrument vests in the transferee such rights as the transferor has therein, except that a transferee who has himself been a party to any fraud or illegality affecting the instrument or who as a prior holder had notice of a defense or claim against it cannot improve his position by taking from a later holder in due course.

(2) A transfer of a security interest in an instrument vests the foregoing rights in the transferee to the extent of the interest transferred.

(3) Unless otherwise agreed any transfer for value of an instrument not then payable to bearer gives the transferee the specifically enforceable right to have the unqualified indorsement of the transferor. Negotiation takes effect only when the indorsement is made and until that time there is no presumption that the transferee is the owner.

§ 3—202. Negotiation.

(1) Negotiation is the transfer of an instrument in such form that the transferee becomes a holder. If the instrument is payable to order it is negotiated by delivery with any necessary indorsement; if payable to bearer it is negotiated by delivery.

(2) An indorsement must be written by or on behalf of the holder and on the instrument or on a paper so firmly affixed thereto as to become a part thereof.

(3) An indorsement is effective for negotiation only when it conveys the entire instrument or any unpaid residue. If it purports to be of less, it operates only as a partial assignment.

(4) Words of assignment, condition, waiver, guaranty, limitation or disclaimer of liability and the like accompanying an indorsement do not affect its character as an indorsement.

§ 3—203. Wrong or Misspelled Name.

Where an instrument is made payable to a person under a misspelled name or one other than his own he may indorse in that name or his own or both; but signature in both names may be required by a person paying or giving value for the instrument.

§ 3—204. Special Indorsement; Blank Indorsement.

(1) A special indorsement specifies the person to whom or to whose order it makes the instrument payable. Any instrument specially indorsed becomes payable to the order of the special indorsee and may be further negotiated only by his indorsement.

(2) An indorsement in blank specifies no particular indorsee and may consist of a mere signature. An instrument payable to order and indorsed in blank becomes payable to bearer and may be negotiated by delivery alone until specially indorsed.

(3) The holder may convert a blank indorsement into a special indorsement by writing over the signature of the indorser in blank any contract consistent with the character of the indorsement.

§ 3—205. Restrictive Indorsements.

An indorsement is restrictive which either

(a) is conditional; or

(b) purports to prohibit further transfer of the instrument; or

(c) includes the words "for collection", "for deposit", "pay any bank", or like terms signifying a purpose of deposit or collection; or

(d) otherwise states that it is for the benefit or use of the indorser or of another person.

§ 3—206. Effect of Restrictive Indorsement.

(1) No restrictive indorsement prevents further transfer or negotiation of the instrument.

(2) An intermediary bank, or a payor bank which is not the depositary bank, is neither given notice nor otherwise affected by a restrictive indorsement of any person except the bank's immediate transferor or the person presenting for payment.

(3) Except for an intermediary bank, any transferee under an indorsement which is conditional or includes the words "for collection", "for deposit", "pay any bank", or like terms (subparagraphs (a) and (c) of Section 3—205) must pay or apply any value given by him for or on the security of the instrument consistently with the indorsement and to the extent that he does so he becomes a holder for value. In addition such transferee is a holder in due course if he otherwise complies with the requirements of Section 3—302 on what constitutes a holder in due course.

(4) The first taker under an indorsement for the benefit of the indorser or another person (subparagraph (d) of Section 3—205) must pay or apply any value given by him for or on the security of the instrument consistently with the indorsement and to the extent that he does so he becomes a holder for value. In addition such taker is a holder in due course if he otherwise complies with the

requirements of Section 3—302 on what constitutes a holder in due course. A later holder for value is neither given notice nor otherwise affected by such restrictive indorsement unless he has knowledge that a fiduciary or other person has negotiated the instrument in any transaction for his own benefit or otherwise in breach of duty (subsection (2) of Section 3—304).

§ 3—207. Negotiation Effective Although It May Be Rescinded.

(1) Negotiation is effective to transfer the instrument although the negotiation is

(a) made by an infant, a corporation exceeding its powers, or any other person without capacity; or

(b) obtained by fraud, duress or mistake of any kind; or

(c) part of an illegal transaction; or

(d) made in breach of duty.

(2) Except as against a subsequent holder in due course such negotiation is in an appropriate case subject to rescission, the declaration of a constructive trust or any other remedy permitted by law.

§ 3—208. Reacquisition.

Where an instrument is returned to or reacquired by a prior party he may cancel any indorsement which is not necessary to his title and reissue or further negotiate the instrument, but any intervening party is discharged as against the reacquiring party and subsequent holders not in due course and if his indorsement has been cancelled is discharged as against subsequent holders in due course as well.

Part 3   Rights of a Holder

§ 3—301. Rights of a Holder.

The holder of an instrument whether or not he is the owner may transfer or negotiate it and, except as otherwise provided in Section 3—603 on payment or satisfaction, discharge it or enforce payment in his own name.

§ 3—302. Holder in Due Course

(1) A holder in due course is a holder who takes the instrument

(a) for value; and

(b) in good faith; and

(c) without notice that it is overdue or has been dishonored or of any defense against or claim to it on the part of any person.

(2) A payee may be a holder in due course.

(3) A holder does not become a holder in due course of an instrument:

(a) by purchase of it at judicial sale or by taking it under legal process; or

(b) by acquiring it in taking over an estate; or

(c) by purchasing it as part of a bulk transaction not in regular course of business of the transferor.

(4) A purchaser of a limited interest can be a holder in due course only to the extent of the interest purchased.

§ 3—305. Rights of a Holder in Due Course.

To the extent that a holder is a holder in due course he takes the instrument free from

(1) all claims to it on the part of any person; and

(2) all defenses of any party to the instrument with whom the holder has not dealt except

(a) infancy, to the extent that it is a defense to a simple contract; and

(b) such other incapacity, or duress, or illegality of the transaction, as renders the obligation of the party a nullity; and

(c) such misrepresentation as has induced the party to sign the instrument with neither knowledge nor reasonable opportunity to obtain knowledge of its character or its essential terms; and

(d) discharge in insolvency proceedings; and

(e) any other discharge of which the holder has notice when he takes the instrument.

§ 3—306. Rights of One Not Holder in Due Course.

Unless he has the rights of a holder in due course any person takes the instrument subject to

(a) all valid claims to it on the part of any person; and

(b) all defenses of any party which would be available in an action on a simple contract; and

(c) the defenses of want or failure of consideration, non-performance of any condition precedent, non-delivery, or delivery for a special purpose (Section 3—408); and

(d) the defense that he or a person through whom he holds the instrument acquired it by theft, or that payment or satisfaction to such holder would be inconsistent with the terms of a restrictive indorsement. The claim of any third person to the instrument is not otherwise available as a defense to any party liable thereon unless the third person himself defends the action for such party.

Part 4 Liability of Parties

§ 3—401. Signature.

(1) No person is liable on an instrument unless his signature appears thereon.

(2) A signature is made by use of any name, including any trade or assumed name, upon an instrument, or by any word or mark used in lieu of a written signature.

§ 3—404. Unauthorized Signatures.

(1) Any unauthorized signature is wholly inoperative as that of the person whose name is signed unless he ratifies it or is precluded from denying it; but it operates as the signature of the unauthorized signer in favor of any person who in good faith pays the instrument or takes it for value.

(2) Any unauthorized signature may be ratified for all purposes of this Article. Such ratification does not of itself affect any rights of the person ratifying against the actual signer.

§ 3—405. Impostors; Signature in Name of Payee.

(1) An indorsement by any person in the name of a named payee is effective if

(a) an impostor by use of the mails or otherwise has induced the maker or drawer to issue the instrument to him or his confederate in the name of the payee; or

(b) a person signing as or on behalf of a maker or drawer intends the payee to have no interest in the instrument; or

(c) an agent or employee of the maker or drawer has supplied him with the name of the payee intending the latter to have no such interest.

(2) Nothing in this section shall affect the criminal or civil liability of the person so indorsing.

§ 3—407. Alteration.

(1) Any alteration of an instrument is material which changes the contract of any party thereto in any respect, including any such change in

(a) the number or relations of the parties; or

(b) an incomplete instrument, by completing it otherwise than as authorized; or

(c) the writing as signed, by adding to it or by removing any part of it.

(2) As against any person other than a subsequent holder in due course

(a) alteration by the holder which is both fraudulent and material discharges any party whose contract is thereby changed unless that party assents or is precluded from asserting the defense;

(b) no other alteration discharges any party and the instrument may be enforced according to its original tenor, or as to incomplete instruments according to the authority given.

(3) A subsequent holder in due course may in all cases enforce the instrument according to its original tenor, and when an incomplete instrument has been completed, he

may enforce it as completed.

§ 3—413. Contract of Maker, Drawer and Acceptor.

(1) The maker or acceptor engages that he will pay the instrument according to its tenor at the time of his engagement or as completed pursuant to Section 3—115 on incomplete instruments.

(2) The drawer engages that upon dishonor of the draft and any necessary notice of dishonor or protest he will pay the amount of the draft to the holder or to any indorser who takes it up. The drawer may disclaim this liability by drawing without recourse.

(3) By making, drawing or accepting the party admits as against all subsequent parties including the drawee the existence of the payee and his then capacity to indorse.

§ 3—414. Contract of Indorser; Order of Liability.

(1) Unless the indorsement otherwise specifies (as by such words as "without recourse") every indorser engages that upon dishonor and any necessary notice of dishonor and protest he will pay the instrument according to its tenor at the time of his indorsement to the holder or to any subsequent indorser who takes it up, even though the indorser who takes it up was not obligated to do so.

(2) Unless they otherwise agree indorsers are liable to one another in the order in which they indorse, which is presumed to be the order in which their signatures appear on the instrument.

§ 3—417. Warranties on Presentment and Transfer.

(1) Any person who obtains payment or acceptance and any prior transferor warrants to a person who in good faith pays or accepts that

(a) he has a good title to the instrument or is authorized to obtain payment or acceptance on behalf of one who has a good title; and

(b) he has no knowledge that the signature of the maker or drawer is unauthorized, except that this warranty is not given by a holder in due course acting in good faith

(i) to a maker with respect to the maker's own signature; or

(ii) to a drawer with respect to the drawer's own signature, whether or not the drawer is also the drawee; or

(iii) to an acceptor of a draft if the holder in due course took the draft after the acceptance or obtained the acceptance without knowledge that the drawer's signature was unauthorized; and

(c) the instrument has not been materially altered, except that this warranty is not given by a holder in due course acting in good faith

(i) to the maker of a note; or

(ii) to the drawer of a draft whether or not the drawer is also the drawee; or

(iii) to the acceptor of a draft with respect to an alteration made prior to the acceptance if the holder in due course took the draft after the acceptance, even though the acceptance provided "payable as originally drawn" or equivalent terms; or

(iv) to the acceptor of a draft with respect to an alteration made after the acceptance.

(2) Any person who transfers an instrument and receives consideration warrants to his transferee and if the transfer is by indorsement to any subsequent holder who takes the instrument in good faith that

(a) he has a good title to the instrument or is authorized to obtain payment or acceptance on behalf of one who has a good title and the transfer is otherwise rightful; and

(b) all signatures are genuine or authorized; and

(c) the instrument has not been materially altered; and

(d) no defense of any party is good against him; and

(e) he has no knowledge of any insolvency proceeding instituted with respect to the maker or acceptor or the drawer of an unaccepted instrument.

(3) By transferring "without recourse" the transferor limits the obligation stated in subsection (2) (d) to a warranty that he has no knowledge of such a defense.

(4) A selling agent or broker who does not disclose the fact that he is acting only as such gives the warranties provided in this section, but if he makes such disclosure warrants only his good faith and authority.

Part 5 Presentment, Notice of Dishonor, and Protest Necessary or Permissible

§ 3—502. Unexcused Delay; Discharge.

(1) Where without excuse any necessary presentment or notice of dishonor is delayed beyond the time when it is due

(a) any indorser is discharged; and

(b) any drawer or the acceptor of a draft payable at a bank or the maker of a note payable at a bank who because the drawee or payor bank becomes insolvent during the delay is deprived of funds maintained with the drawee or payor bank to cover the instrument may discharge his liability by written assignment to the holder of his rights against the drawee or payor bank in respect of such funds, but such drawer, acceptor or maker is not otherwise discharged.

(2) Where without excuse a necessary protest is delayed beyond the time when it is due any drawer or indorser is discharged.

§ 3—503. **Time of Presentment.**

(1) Unless a different time is expressed in the instrument the time for any presentment is determined as follows:

(a) where an instrument is payable at or a fixed period after a stated date any presentment for acceptance must be made on or before the date it is payable;

(b) where an instrument is payable after sight it must either be presented for acceptance or negotiated within a reasonable time after date or issue whichever is later;

(c) where an instrument shows the date on which it is payable presentment for payment is due on that date;

(d) where an instrument is accelerated presentment for payment is due within a reasonable time after the acceleration;

(e) with respect to the liability of any secondary party presentment for acceptance or payment of any other instrument is due within a reasonable time after such party becomes liable thereon.

(2) A reasonable time for presentment is determined by the nature of the instrument, any usage of banking or trade and the facts of the particular case. In the case of an uncertified check which is drawn and payable within the United States and which is not a draft drawn by a bank the following are presumed to be reasonable periods within which to present for payment or to initiate bank collection:

(a) with respect to the liability of the drawer, thirty days after date or issue whichever is later; and

(b) with respect to the liability of an indorser, seven days after his indorsement.

(3) Where any presentment is due on a day which is not a full business day for either the person making presentment or the party to pay or accept, presentment is due on the next following day which is a full business day for both parties.

(4) Presentment to be sufficient must be made at a reasonable hour, and if at a bank during its banking day.

§ 3—504. **How Presentment Made.**

(1) Presentment is a demand for acceptance or payment made upon the maker, acceptor, drawee or other payor by or on behalf of the holder.

(2) Presentment may be made

(a) by mail, in which event the time of presentment is determined by the time of receipt of the mail; or

(b) through a clearing house; or

(c) at the place of acceptance or payment specified in the instrument or if there be none at the place of business or residence of the party to accept or pay. If neither the party to accept or pay nor anyone authorized to act for him is present or accessible at such place presentment is excused.

(3) It may be made

(a) to any one of two or more makers, acceptors, drawees or other payors; or

(b) to any person who has authority to make or refuse the acceptance or payment.

(4) A draft accepted or a note made payable at a bank in the United States must be presented at such bank.

(5) In the cases described in Section 4—210 presentment may be made in the manner and with the result stated in that section.

§ 3—505. **Rights of Party to Whom Presentment Is Made.**

(1) The party to whom presentment is made may without dishonor require

(a) exhibition of the instrument; and

(b) reasonable identification of the person making presentment and evidence of his authority to make it if made for another; and

(c) that the instrument be produced for acceptance or payment at a place specified in it, or if there be none at any place reasonable in the circumstances; and

(d) a signed receipt on the instrument for any partial or full payment and its surrender upon full payment.

(2) Failure to comply with any such requirement invalidates the presentment but the person presenting has a reasonable time in which to comply and the time for acceptance or payment runs from the time of compliance.

§ 3—508. **Notice of Dishonor.**

(1) Notice of dishonor may be given to any person who may be liable on the instrument by or on behalf of the holder or any party who has himself received notice, or any other party who can be compelled to pay the instrument. In addition an agent or bank in whose hands the instrument is dishonored may give notice to his principal or customer or to another agent or bank from which the instrument was received.

(2) Any necessary notice must be given by a bank before its midnight deadline and by any other person before midnight of the third business day after dishonor or receipt of notice of dishonor.

(3) Notice may be given in any reasonable manner. It may be oral or written and in any terms which identify the instrument and state that it has been dishonored. A misdescription which does not mislead the party notified does not vitiate the notice. Sending the instrument bearing a stamp, ticket or writing stating that acceptance or

payment has been refused or sending a notice of debit with respect to the instrument is sufficient.

(4) Written notice is given when sent although it is not received.

(5) Notice to one partner is notice to each although the firm has been dissolved.

(6) When any party is in insolvency proceedings instituted after the issue of the instrument notice may be given either to the party or to the representative of his estate.

(7) When any party is dead or incompetent notice may be sent to his last known address or given to his personal representative.

(8) Notice operates for the benefit of all parties who have rights on the instrument against the party notified.

§ 3—603. Payment or Satisfaction.

(1) The liability of any party is discharged to the extent of his payment or satisfaction to the holder even though it is made with knowledge of a claim of another person to the instrument unless prior to such payment or satisfaction the person making the claim either supplies indemnity deemed adequate by the party seeking the discharge or enjoins payment or satisfaction by order of a court of competent jurisdiction in an action in which the adverse claimant and the holder are parties. This subsection does not, however, result in the discharge of the liability

(a) of a party who in bad faith pays or satisfies a holder who acquired the instrument by theft or who (unless having the rights of a holder in due course) holds through one who so acquired it; or

(b) of a party (other than an intermediary bank or a payor bank which is not a depositary bank) who pays or satisfies the holder of an instrument which has been restrictively indorsed in a manner not consistent with the terms of such restrictive indorsement.

(2) Payment or satisfaction may be made with the consent of the holder by any person including a stranger to the instrument. Surrender of the instrument to such a person gives him the rights of a transferee (Section 3—201).

§ 3—605. Cancellation and Renunciation.

(1) The holder of an instrument may even without consideration discharge any party

(a) in any manner apparent on the face of the instrument or the indorsement, as by intentionally cancelling the instrument or the party's signature by destruction or mutilation, or by striking out the party's signature; or

(b) by renouncing his rights by a writing signed and delivered or by surrender of the instrument to the party to be discharged.

(2) Neither cancellation nor renunciation without surrender of the instrument affects the title thereto.

Article 4
BANK DEPOSITS AND COLLECTIONS

Part 1   General Provisions and Definitions

§ 4—102. Applicability.

(1) To the extent that items within this Article are also within the scope of Articles 3 and 8, they are subject to the provisions of those Articles. In the event of conflict the provisions of this Article govern those of Article 3 but the provisions of Article 8 govern those of this Article.

(2) The liability of a bank for action or non-action with respect to any item handled by it for purposes of presentment, payment or collection is governed by the law of the place where the bank is located. In the case of action or non-action by or at a branch or separate office of a bank, its liability is governed by the law of the place where the branch or separate office is located.

Part 4   Relationship Between Payor Bank and Its Customer

§ 4—401. When Bank May Charge Customer's Account.

(1) As against its customer, a bank may charge against his account any item which is otherwise properly payable from that account even though the charge creates an overdraft.

(2) A bank which in good faith makes payment to a holder may charge the indicated account of its customer according to

(a) the original tenor of his altered item; or

(b) the tenor of his completed item, even though the bank knows the item has been completed unless the bank has notice that the completion was improper.

§ 4—402. Bank's Liability to Customer for Wrongful Dishonor.

A payor bank is liable to its customer for damages proximately caused by the wrongful dishonor of an item. When the dishonor occurs through mistake liability is limited to actual damages proved. If so proximately caused and proved damages may include damages for an arrest or prosecution of the customer or other consequential damages. Whether any consequential damages are proximately caused by the wrongful dishonor is a question of fact to be determined in each case.

§ 4—403. Customer's Right to Stop Payment; Burden of Proof of Loss.

(1) A customer may by order to his bank stop payment of any item payable for his account but the order must be received at such time and in such manner as to afford the bank a reasonable opportunity to act on it prior to any action by the bank with respect to the item described in Section 4—303.

(2) An oral order is binding upon the bank only for fourteen calendar days unless confirmed in writing within that period. A written order is effective for only six months unless renewed in writing.

(3) The burden of establishing the fact and amount of loss resulting from the payment of an item contrary to a binding stop payment order is on the customer.

§ 4—404. Bank Not Obligated to Pay Check More Than Six Months Old.

A bank is under no obligation to a customer having a checking account to pay a check, other than a certified check, which is presented more than six months after its date, but it may charge its customer's account for a payment made thereafter in good faith.

§ 4—405. Death or Incompetence of Customer.

(1) A payor or collecting bank's authority to accept, pay or collect an item or to account for proceeds of its collection if otherwise effective is not rendered ineffective by incompetence of a customer of either bank existing at the time the item is issued or its collection is undertaken if the bank does not know of an adjudication of incompetence. Neither death nor incompetence of a customer revokes such authority to accept, pay, collect or account until the bank knows of the fact of death or of an adjudication of incompetence and has reasonable opportunity to act on it.

(2) Even with knowledge a bank may for 10 days after the date of death pay or certify checks drawn on or prior to that date unless ordered to stop payment by a person claiming an interest in the account.

§ 4—406. Customer's Duty to Discover and Report Unauthorized Signature or Alteration.

(1) When a bank sends to its customer a statement of account accompanied by items paid in good faith in support of the debit entries or holds the statement and items pursuant to a request or instructions of its customer or otherwise in a reasonable manner makes the statement and items available to the customer, the customer must exercise reasonable care and promptness to examine the statement and items to discover his unauthorized signature or any alteration on an item and must notify the bank promptly after discovery thereof.

(2) If the bank establishes that the customer failed with respect to an item to comply with the duties imposed on the customer by subsection (1) the customer is precluded from asserting against the bank

(a) his unauthorized signature or any alteration on the item if the bank also establishes that it suffered a loss by reason of such failure; and

(b) an unauthorized signature or alteration by the same wrongdoer on any other item paid in good faith by the bank after the first item and statement was available to the customer for a reasonable period not exceeding fourteen calendar days and before the bank receives notification from the customer of any such unauthorized signature or alteration.

(3) The preclusion under subsection (2) does not apply if the customer establishes lack of ordinary care on the part of the bank in paying the item(s).

(4) Without regard to care or lack of care of either the customer or the bank a customer who does not within one year from the time the statement and items are made available to the customer (subsection (1)) discover and report his unauthorized signature or any alteration on the face or back of the item or does not within three years from that time discover and report any unauthorized indorsement is precluded from asserting against the bank such unauthorized signature or indorsement or such alteration.

(5) If under this section a payor bank has a valid defense against a claim of a customer upon or resulting from payment of an item and waives or fails upon request to assert the defense the bank may not assert against any collecting bank or other prior party presenting or transferring the item a claim based upon the unauthorized signature or alteration giving rise to the customer's claim.

Article 5
LETTERS OF CREDIT

§ 5—114. Issuer's Duty and Privilege to Honor; Right to Reimbursement.

(1) An issuer must honor a draft or demand for payment which complies with the terms of the relevant credit regardless of whether the goods or documents conform to the underlying contract for sale or other contract between the customer and the beneficiary. The issuer is not excused from honor of such a draft or demand by reason of an additional general term that all documents must be satisfactory to the issuer, but an issuer may require that specified documents must be satisfactory to it.

(2) Unless otherwise agreed when documents appear on their face to comply with the terms of a credit but a required document does not in fact conform to the warranties made on negotiations or transfer of a document of title (Section 7—507) or of a certified security (Section 8—306) or is forged or fraudulent or there is fraud in the transaction:

(a) the issuer must honor the draft or demand for payment if honor is demanded by a negotiating bank or other holder of the draft or demand which has taken the draft or demand under the credit and under circumstances which would make it a holder in due course (Section 3—302) and in an appropriate case would make it a person to whom a document of title has been duly negotiated (Section 7—502) or a bona fide purchaser of a certificated security (Section 8—302); and

(b) in all other cases as against its customer, an issuer acting in good faith may honor the draft or demand for payment despite notification from the customer of fraud, forgery or other defect not apparent on the face of the document but a court of appropriate jurisdiction may enjoin such honor.

(3) Unless otherwise agreed an issuer which has duly honored a draft or demand for payment is entitled to immediate reimbursement of any payment made under the credit and to be put in effectively available funds not later than the day before maturity of any acceptance made under the credit.

[(4) When a credit provides for payment by the issuer on receipt of notice that the required documents are in the possession of a correspondent or other agent of the issuer

(a) any payment made on receipt of such notice is conditional; and

(b) the issuer may reject documents which do not comply with the credit if it does so within three banking days following its receipt of the documents; and

(c) in the event of such rejection, the issuer is entitled by charge back or otherwise to return of the payment made.]

[(5) In the case covered by subsection (4) failure to reject documents within the time specified in subparagraph (b) constitutes acceptance of the documents and makes the payment final in favor of the beneficiary.]

Note: *Subsections (4) and (5) are bracketed as optional. If they are included the bracketed language in that last sentence of Section 5—112(1)should also be included.*

Article 6
BULK SALES

§ 6—102. Definitions and Index of Definitions.

(1) In this Article, unless the context otherwise requires:

(a) "Assets" means the inventory that is the subject of a bulk sale and any tangible and intangible personal property used or held for use primarily in, or arising from, the seller's business and sold in connection with that inventory, but the term does not include:

(i) fixtures (Section 9—313(1)(a)) other than readily removable factory and office machines;

(ii) the lessee's interest in a lease of real property; or

(iii) property to the extent it is generally exempt from creditor process under nonbankruptcy law.

(b) "Auctioneer" means a person whom the seller engages to direct, conduct, control, or be responsible for a sale by auction.

(c) "Bulk sale" means:

(i) in the case of a sale by auction or a sale or series of sales conducted by a liquidator on the seller's behalf, a sale or series of sales not in the ordinary course of the seller's business of more than half of the seller's inventory, as measured by value on the date of the bulk-sale agreement, if on that date the auctioneer or liquidator has notice, or after reasonable inquiry would have had notice, that the seller will not continue to operate the same or a similar kind of business after the sale or series of sales; and

(ii) in all other cases, a sale not in the ordinary course of the seller's business of more than half the seller's inventory, as measured by value on the date of the bulk-sale agreement, if on that date the buyer has notice, or after reasonable inquiry would have had notice, that the seller will not continue to operate the same or a similar kind of business after the sale.

(d) "Claim" means a right to payment from the seller, whether or not the right is reduced to judgment, liquidated, fixed, matured, disputed, secured, legal, or equitable. The term includes costs of collection and attorney's fees only to the extent that the laws of this state permit the holder of the claim to recover them in an action against the obligor.

(e) "Claimant" means a person holding a claim incurred in the seller's business other than:

(i) an unsecured and unmatured claim for employment compensation and benefits, including commissions and vacation, severance, and sick-leave pay;

(ii) a claim for injury to an individual or to property, or for breach of warranty, unless:

(A) a right of action for the claim has accrued;

(B) the claim has been asserted against the seller; and

(C) the seller knows the identity of the person asserting the claim and the basis upon which the person has asserted it; and
(States to Select One Alternative)

Alternative A

[(iii) a claim for taxes owing to a governmental unit.]

Alternative B

[(iii) a claim for taxes owing to a governmental unit, if:

(A) a statute governing the enforcement of the claim permits or requires notice of the bulk sale to be given to the governmental unit in a manner other than by compliance with the requirements of this Article; and

(B) notice is given in accordance with the statute.]

(f) "Creditor" means a claimant or other person holding a claim.

(g)(i) "Date of the bulk sale" means:

(A) if the sale is by auction or is conducted by a liquidator on the seller's behalf, the date on which more than ten percent of the net proceeds is paid to or for the benefit of the seller; and

(B) in all other cases, the later of the date on which:

(I) more than ten percent of the net contract price is paid to or for the benefit of the seller; or

(II) more than ten percent of the assets, as measured by value, are transferred to the buyer.

(ii) For purposes of this subsection:

(A) delivery of a negotiable instrument (Section 3—104(1)) to or for the benefit of the seller in exchange for assets constitutes payment of the contract price pro tanto;

(B) to the extent that the contract price is deposited in an escrow, the contract price is paid to or for the benefit of the seller when the seller acquires the unconditional right to receive the deposit or when the deposit is delivered to the seller or for the benefit of the seller, whichever is earlier; and

(C) an asset is transferred when a person holding an unsecured claim can no longer obtain through judicial proceedings rights to the asset that are superior to those of the buyer arising as a result of the bulk sale. A person holding an unsecured claim can obtain those superior rights to a tangible asset at least until the buyer has an unconditional right, under the bulk-sale agreement, to possess the asset, and a person holding an unsecured claim can obtain those superior rights to an intangible asset at least until the buyer has an unconditional right, under the bulk-sale agreement, to use the asset.

(h) "Date of the bulk-sale agreement" means:

(i) in the case of a sale by auction or conducted by a liquidator (subsection (c)(i)), the date on which the seller engages the auctioneer or liquidator; and

(ii) in all other cases, the date on which a bulk-sale agreement becomes enforceable between the buyer and the seller.

(i) "Debt" means liability on a claim.

(j) "Liquidator" means a person who is regularly engaged in the business of disposing of assets for businesses contemplating liquidation or dissolution.

(k) "Net contract price" means the new consideration the buyer is obligated to pay for the assets less:

(i) the amount of any proceeds of the sale of an asset, to the extent the proceeds are applied in partial or total satisfaction of a debt secured by the asset; and

(ii) the amount of any debt to the extent it is secured by a security interest or lien that is enforceable against the asset before and after it has been sold to a buyer. If a debt is secured by an asset and other property of the seller, the amount of the debt secured by a security interest or lien that is enforceable against the asset is determined by multiplying the debt by a fraction, the numerator of which is the value of the new consideration for the asset on the date of the bulk sale and the denominator of which is the value of all property securing the debt on the date of the bulk sale.

(l) "Net proceeds" means the new consideration received for assets sold at a sale by auction or a sale conducted by a liquidator on the seller's behalf less:

(i) commissions and reasonable expenses of the sale;

(ii) the amount of any proceeds of the sale of an asset, to the extent the proceeds are applied in partial or total satisfaction of a debt secured by the asset; and

(iii) the amount of any debt to the extent it is secured by a security interest or lien that is enforceable against the asset before and after it has been sold to a buyer. If a debt is secured by an asset and other property of the seller, the amount of the debt secured by a security interest or lien that is enforceable against the asset is determined by multiplying the debt by a fraction, the numerator of which is the value of the new consideration for the asset on the date of the bulk sale and the denominator of which is the value of all property securing the debt on the date of the bulk sale.

(m) A sale is "in the ordinary course of the seller's business" if the sale comports with usual or customary practices in the kind of business in which the seller is engaged or with the seller's own usual or customary practices.

(n) "United States" includes its territories and possessions and the Commonwealth of Puerto Rico.

(o) "Value" means fair market value.

(p) "Verified" means signed and sworn to or affirmed.

(2) The following definitions in other Articles apply to this Article:

(a)	"Buyer."	Section 2—103(1)(a).
(b)	"Equipment."	Section 9—109(2).
(c)	"Inventory."	Section 9—109(4).
(d)	"Sale."	Section 2—106(1).
(e)	"Seller."	Section 2—103(1)(d).

(3) In addition, Article 1 contains general definitions and principles of construction and interpretation applicable throughout this Article.

§ 6—104. Obligations of Buyer.

(1) In a bulk sale as defined in Section 6—102(1)(c)(ii) the buyer shall:

(a) obtain from the seller a list of all business names and addresses used by the seller within three years before the date the list is sent or delivered to the buyer;

(b) unless excused under subsection (2), obtain from the seller a verified and dated list of claimants of whom the seller has notice three days before the seller sends or delivers the list to the buyer and including, to the extent known by the seller, the address of and the amount claimed by each claimant;

(c) obtain from the seller or prepare a schedule of distribution (Section 6—106(1));

(d) give notice of the bulk sale in accordance with Section 6—105;

(e) unless excused under Section 6—106(4), distribute the net contract price in accordance with the undertakings of the buyer in the schedule of distribution; and

(f) unless excused under subsection (2), make available the list of claimants (subsection (1)(b)) by:

(i) promptly sending or delivering a copy of the list without charge to any claimant whose written request is received by the buyer no later than six months after the date of the bulk sale;

(ii) permitting any claimant to inspect and copy the list at any reasonable hour upon request received by the buyer no later than six months after the date of the bulk sale; or

(iii) filing a copy of the list in the office of the [Secretary of State] no later than the time for giving a notice of the bulk sale (Section 6—105(5)). A list filed in accordance with this subparagraph must state the individual, partnership, or corporate name and a mailing address of the seller.

(2) A buyer who gives notice in accordance with Section 6—105(2) is excused from complying with the requirements of subsections (1)(b) and (1)(f).

§ 6—105. Notice to Claimants.

(1) Except as otherwise provided in subsection (2), to comply with Section 6—104(1)(d) the buyer shall send or deliver a written notice of the bulk sale to each claimant on the list of claimants (Section 6—104(1)(b)) and to any other claimant of which the buyer has knowledge at the time the notice of the bulk sale is sent or delivered.

(2) A buyer may comply with Section 6—104(1)(d) by filing a written notice of the bulk sale in the office of the [Secretary of State] if:

(a) on the date of the bulk-sale agreement the seller has 200 or more claimants, exclusive of claimants holding secured or matured claims for employment compensation and benefits, including commissions and vacation, severance, and sick-leave pay; or

(b) the buyer has received a verified statement from the seller stating that, as of the date of the bulk-sale agreement, the number of claimants, exclusive of claimants holding secured or matured claims for employment compensation and benefits, including commissions and vacation, severance, and sick-leave pay, is 200 or more.

(3) The written notice of the bulk sale must be accompanied by a copy of the schedule of distribution (Section 6—106(1)) and state at least:

(a) that the seller and buyer have entered into an agreement for a sale that may constitute a bulk sale under the laws of the State of _____;

(b) the date of the agreement;

(c) the date on or after which more than ten percent of the assets were or will be transferred;

(d) the date on or after which more than ten percent of the net contract price was or will be paid, if the date is not stated in the schedule of distribution;

(e) the name and a mailing address of the seller;

(f) any other business name and address listed by the seller pursuant to Section 6—104(1)(a);

(g) the name of the buyer and an address of the buyer from which information concerning the sale can be obtained;

(h) a statement indicating the type of assets or describing the assets item by item;

(i) the manner in which the buyer will make available the list of claimants (Section 6—104(1)(f)), if applicable; and

(j) if the sale is in total or partial satisfaction of an antecedent debt owed by the seller, the amount of the debt to be satisfied and the name of the person to whom it is owed.

(4) For purposes of subsections (3)(e) and (3)(g), the name of a person is the person's individual, partnership, or corporate name.

(5) The buyer shall give notice of the bulk sale not less than 45 days before the date of the bulk sale and, if the buyer gives notice in accordance with subsection (1), not more than 30 days after obtaining the list of claimants.

(6) A written notice substantially complying with the requirements of subsection (3) is effective even though it contains minor errors that are not seriously misleading.

(7) A form substantially as follows is sufficient to comply with subsection (3):

Notice of Sale

(1) _____, whose address is _____, is described in this notice as the "seller."

(2) _____, whose address is _____, is described in this notice as the "buyer."

(3) The seller has disclosed to the buyer that within the past three years the seller has used other business names, operated at other addresses, or both, as follows:

_____.

(4) The seller and the buyer have entered into an agreement dated _____, for a sale that may constitute a bulk sale under the laws of the State of _____ .

(5) The date on or after which more than ten percent of the assets that are the subject of the sale were or will be transferred is _____, and [if not stated in the schedule of distribution] the date on or after which more than ten percent of the net contract price was or will be paid is _____.

(6) The following assets are the subject of the sale:

_____ .

(7) [If applicable] The buyer will make available to claimants of the seller a list of the seller's claimants in the following manner: _____.

(8) [If applicable] The sale is to satisfy $_____ of an antecedent debt owed by the seller to _____.

(9) A copy of the schedule of distribution of the net contract price accompanies this notice.

[End of Notice]

§ 6—107. **Liability for Noncompliance.**

(1) Except as provided in subsection (3), and subject to the limitation in subsection (4):

(a) a buyer who fails to comply with the requirements of Section 6—104(1)(e) with respect to a creditor is liable to the creditor for damages in the amount of the claim, reduced by any amount that the creditor would not have realized if the buyer had complied; and

(b) a buyer who fails to comply with the requirements of any other subsection of Section 6—104 with respect to a claimant is liable to the claimant for damages in the amount of the claim, reduced by any amount that the claimant would not have realized if the buyer had complied.

(2) In an action under subsection (1), the creditor has the burden of establishing the validity and amount of the claim, and the buyer has the burden of establishing the amount that the creditor would not have realized if the buyer had complied.

(3) A buyer who:

(a) made a good faith and commercially reasonable effort to comply with the requirements of Section 6—104(1) or to exclude the sale from the application of this Article under Section 6—103(3); or

(b) on or after the date of the bulk-sale agreement, but before the date of the bulk sale, held a good faith and commercially reasonable belief that this Article does not apply to the particular sale

is not liable to creditors for failure to comply with the requirements of Section 6—104. The buyer has the burden of establishing the good faith and commercial reasonableness of the effort or belief.

(4) In a single bulk sale the cumulative liability of the buyer for failure to comply with the requirements of Section 6—104(1) may not exceed an amount equal to:

(a) if the assets consist only of inventory and equipment, twice the net contract price, less the amount of any part of the net contract price paid to or applied for the benefit of the seller or a creditor; or

(b) if the assets include property other than inventory and equipment, twice the net value of the inventory and equipment less the amount of the portion of any part of the net contract price paid to or applied for the benefit of the seller or a creditor which is allocable to the inventory and equipment.

(5) For the purposes of subsection (4)(b), the "net value" of an asset is the value of the asset less (i) the amount of any proceeds of the sale of an asset, to the extent the proceeds are applied in partial or total satisfaction of a debt secured by the asset and (ii) the amount of any debt to the extent it is secured by a security interest or lien that is enforceable against the asset before and after it has been sold to a buyer. If a debt is secured by an asset and other property of the seller, the amount of the debt secured by

a security interest or lien that is enforceable against the asset is determined by multiplying the debt by a fraction, the numerator of which is the value of the asset on the date of the bulk sale and the denominator of which is the value of all property securing the debt on the date of the bulk sale. The portion of a part of the net contract price paid to or applied for the benefit of the seller or a creditor that is "allocable to the inventory and equipment" is the portion that bears the same ratio to that part of the net contract price as the net value of the inventory and equipment bears to the net value of all of the assets.

(6) A payment made by the buyer to a person to whom the buyer is, or believes he [or she] is, liable under subsection (1) reduces pro tanto the buyer's cumulative liability under subsection (4).

(7) No action may be brought under subsection (1)(b) by or on behalf of a claimant whose claim is unliquidated or contingent.

(8) A buyer's failure to comply with the requirements of Section 6—104(1) does not (i) impair the buyer's rights in or title to the assets, (ii) render the sale ineffective, void, or voidable, (iii) entitle a creditor to more than a single satisfaction of his [or her] claim, or (iv) create liability other than as provided in this Article.

(9) Payment of the buyer's liability under subsection (1) discharges pro tanto the seller's debt to the creditor.

(10) Unless otherwise agreed, a buyer has an immediate right of reimbursement from the seller for any amount paid to a creditor in partial or total satisfaction of the buyer's liability under subsection (1).

(11) If the seller is an organization, a person who is in direct or indirect control of the seller, and who knowingly, intentionally, and without legal justification fails, or causes the seller to fail, to distribute the net contract price in accordance with the schedule of distribution is liable to any creditor to whom the seller undertook to make payment under the schedule for damages caused by the failure.

§ 6—110. Limitation of Actions.

(1) Except as provided in subsection (2), an action under this Article against a buyer, auctioneer, or liquidator must be commenced within one year after the date of the bulk sale.

(2) If the buyer, auctioneer, or liquidator conceals the fact that the sale has occurred, the limitation is tolled and an action under this Article may be commenced within the earlier of (i) one year after the person bringing the action discovers that the sale has occurred or (ii) one year after the person bringing the action should have discovered that the sale has occurred, but no later than two years after the date of the bulk sale. Complete noncompliance with the requirements of this Article does not of itself constitute concealment.

(3) An action under Section 6—107(11) must be commenced within one year after the alleged violation occurs.

Article 9
SECURED TRANSACTIONS; SALES OF ACCOUNTS AND CHATTEL PAPER

Part 2 Validity of Security Agreement and Rights of Parties Thereto

§ 9—201. General Validity of Security Agreement.

Except as otherwise provided by this Act a security agreement is effective according to its terms between the parties, against purchasers of the collateral and against creditors. Nothing in this Article validates any charge or practice illegal under any statute or regulation thereunder governing usury, small loans, retail installment sales, or the like, or extends the application of any such statute or regulation to any transaction not otherwise subject thereto.

§ 9—203. Attachment and Enforceability of Security Interest; Proceeds; Formal Requisites.

(1) Subject to the provisions of Section 4—208 on the security interest of a collecting bank, Section 8—321 on security interests in securities and Section 9—113 on a security interest arising under the Article on Sales, a security interest is not enforceable against the debtor or third parties with respect to the collateral and does not attach unless:

(a) the collateral is in the possession of the secured party pursuant to agreement, or the debtor has signed a security agreement which contains a description of the collateral and in addition, when the security interest covers crops growing or to be grown or timber to be cut, a description of the land concerned;

(b) value has been given; and

(c) the debtor has rights in the collateral.

(2) A security interest attaches when it becomes enforceable against the debtor with respect to the collateral. Attachment occurs as soon as all of the events specified in subsection (1) have taken place unless explicit agreement postpones the time of attaching.

(3) Unless otherwise agreed a security agreement gives the secured party the rights to proceeds provided by Section 9—306.

§ 9—204. After-Acquired Property; Future Advances.

(1) Except as provided in subsection (2), a security agreement may provide that any or all obligations covered by the security agreement are to be secured by after-acquired collateral.

(2) No security interest attaches under an after-acquired property clause to consumer goods other than accessions

(Section 9—314) when given as additional security unless the debtor acquires rights in them within ten days after the secured party gives value.

(3) Obligations covered by a security agreement may include future advances or other value whether or not the advances or value are given pursuant to commitment (subsection (1) of Section 9—105).

Part 3 Rights of Third Parties; Perfected and Unperfected Security Interests; Rule of Priority

§ 9—302. When Filing Is Required to Perfect Security Interest; Security Interests to Which Filing Provisions of This Article Do Not Apply.

(1) A financing statement must be filed to perfect all security interests except the following:

(a) a security interest in collateral in possession of the secured party under Section 9—305;

(b) a security interest temporarily perfected in instruments or documents without delivery under Section 9—304 or in proceeds for a 10 day period under Section 9—306;

(c) a security interest created by an assignment of a beneficial interest in a trust or a decedent's estate;

(d) a purchase money security interest in consumer goods; but filing is required for a motor vehicle required to be registered; and fixture filing is required for priority over conflicting interests in fixtures to the extent provided in Section 9—313;

(e) an assignment of accounts which does not alone or in conjunction with other assignments to the same assignee transfer a significant part of the outstanding accounts of the assignor;

(f) a security interest of a collecting bank (Section 4—208) or in securities (Section 8—321) or arising under the Article on Sales (see Section 9—113) or covered in subsection (3) of this section;

(g) an assignment for the benefit of all the creditors of the transferor, and subsequent transfers by the assignee thereunder.

(2) If a secured party assigns a perfected security interest, no filing under this Article is required in order to continue the perfected status of the security interest against creditors of and transferees from the original debtor.

(3) The filing of a financing statement otherwise required by this Article is not necessary or effective to perfect a security interest in property subject to

(a) a statute or treaty of the United States which provides for a national or international registration or a national or international certificate of title or which specifies a place of filing different from that specified in this Article for filing of the security interest; or

(b) the following statutes of this state; [list any certificate of title statute covering automobiles, trailers, mobile homes, boats, farm tractors, or the like, and any central filing statute.]; but during any period in which collateral is inventory held for sale by a person who is in the business of selling goods of that kind, the filing provisions of this Article (Part 4) apply to a security interest in that collateral created by him as debtor; or

(c) a certificate of title statute of another jurisdiction under the law of which indication of a security interest on the certificate is required as a condition of perfection (subsection (2) of Section 9—103).

(4) Compliance with a statute or treaty described in subsection (3) is equivalent to the filing of a financing statement under this Article, and a security interest in property subject to the statute or treaty can be perfected only by compliance therewith except as provided in Section 9—103 on multiple state transactions. Duration and renewal of perfection of a security interest perfected by compliance with the statute or treaty are governed by the provisions of the statute or treaty; in other respects the security interest is subject to this Article.

Amended in 1972 and 1977.

§ 9—307. Protection of Buyers of Goods.

(1) A buyer in ordinary course of business (subsection (9) of Section 1—201) other than a person buying farm products from a person engaged in farming operations takes free of a security interest created by his seller even though the security interest is perfected and even though the buyer knows of its existence [subject to the Food Security Act of 1985 (7 U.S.C. Section 1631)].

(2) In the case of consumer goods, a buyer takes free of a security interest even though perfected if he buys without knowledge of the security interest, for value and for his own personal, family or household purposes unless prior to the purchase the secured party has filed a financing statement covering such goods.

(3) A buyer other than a buyer in ordinary course of business (subsection (1) of this section) takes free of a security interest to the extent that it secures future advances made after the secured party acquires knowledge of the purchase, or more than 45 days after the purchase, whichever first occurs, unless made pursuant to a commitment entered into without knowledge of the purchase and before the expiration of the 45 day period.

§ 9—312. Priorities Among Conflicting Security Interests in the Same Collateral.

(1) The rules of priority stated in other sections of this Part and in the following sections shall govern when applicable: Section 4—208 with respect to the security interests of collecting banks in items being collected, ac-

companying documents and proceeds; Section 9—103 on security interests related to other jurisdictions; Section 9—114 on consignments.

(2) A perfected security interest in crops for new value given to enable the debtor to produce the crops during the production season and given not more than three months before the crops become growing crops by planting or otherwise takes priority over an earlier perfected security interest to the extent that such earlier interest secures obligations due more than six months before the crops become growing crops by planting or otherwise, even though the person giving new value had knowledge of the earlier security interest.

(3) A perfected purchase money security interest in inventory has priority over a conflicting security interest in the same inventory and also has priority in identifiable cash proceeds received on or before the delivery of the inventory to a buyer if

(a) the purchase money security interest is perfected at the time the debtor receives possession of the inventory; and

(b) the purchase money secured party gives notification in writing to the holder of the conflicting security interest if the holder had filed a financing statement covering the same types of inventory (i) before the date of the filing made by the purchase money secured party, or (ii) before the beginning of the 21 day period where the purchase money security interest is temporarily perfected without filing or possession (subsection (5) of Section 9—304); and

(c) the holder of the conflicting security interest receives the notification within five years before the debtor receives possession of the inventory; and

(d) the notification states that the person giving the notice has or expects to acquire a purchase money security interest in inventory of the debtor, describing such inventory by item or type.

(4) A purchase money security interest in collateral other than inventory has priority over a conflicting security interest in the same collateral or its proceeds if the purchase money security interest is perfected at the time the debtor receives possession of the collateral or within ten days thereafter.

(5) In all cases not governed by other rules stated in this section (including cases of purchase money security interests which do not qualify for the special priorities set forth in subsections (3) and (4) of this section), priority between conflicting security interests in the same collateral shall be determined according to the following rules:

(a) Conflicting security interests rank according to priority in time of filing or perfection. Priority dates from the time a filing is first made covering the collateral or the time the security interest is first perfected, whichever is earlier, provided that there is no period thereafter when there is neither filing nor perfection.

(b) So long as conflicting security interests are unperfected, the first to attach has priority.

(6) For the purposes of subsection (5) a date of filing or perfection as to collateral is also a date of filing or perfection as to proceeds.

(7) If future advances are made while a security interest is perfected by filing, the taking of possession, or under Section 8—321 on securities, the security interest has the same priority for the purposes of subsection (5) with respect to the future advances as it does with respect to the first advance. If a commitment is made before or while the security interest is so perfected, the security interest has the same priority with respect to advances made pursuant thereto. In other cases a perfected security interest has priority from the date the advance is made.

Amended in 1972 and 1977.

Part 4   Filing

§ 9—402. Formal Requisites of Financing Statement; Amendments; Mortgage as Financing Statement.

(1) A financing statement is sufficient if it gives the names of the debtor and the secured party, is signed by the debtor, gives an address of the secured party from which information concerning the security interest may be obtained, gives a mailing address of the debtor and contains a statement indicating the types, or describing the items, of collateral. A financing statement may be filed before a security agreement is made or a security interest otherwise attaches. When the financing statement covers crops growing or to be grown, the statement must also contain a description of the real estate concerned. When the financing statement covers timber to be cut or covers minerals or the like (including oil and gas) or accounts subject to subsection (5) of Section 9—103, or when the financing statement is filed as a fixture filing (Section 9—313) and the collateral is goods which are or are to become fixtures, the statement must also comply with subsection (5). A copy of the security agreement is sufficient as a financing statement if it contains the above information and is signed by the debtor. A carbon, photographic or other reproduction of a security agreement or a financing statement is sufficient as a financing statement if the security agreement so provides or if the original has been filed in this state.

(2) A financing statement which otherwise complies with subsection (1) is sufficient when it is signed by the secured party instead of the debtor if it is filed to perfect a security interest in

(a) collateral already subject to a security interest in another jurisdiction when it is brought into this state, or when the debtor's location is changed to this state.

Such a financing statement must state that the collateral was brought into this state or that the debtor's location was changed to this state under such circumstances; or

(b) proceeds under Section 9—306 if the security interest in the original collateral was perfected. Such a financing statement must describe the original collateral; or

(c) collateral as to which the filing has lapsed; or

(d) collateral acquired after a change of name, identity or corporate structure of the debtor (subsection (7)).

(3) A form substantially as follows is sufficient to comply with subsection (1):

Name of debtor (or assignor) . . . .
Address . . . .
Name of secured party (or assignee) . . . .
Address . . . .
1. This financing statement covers the following types (or items) of property:
 (Describe) . . . .
2. (If collateral is crops) The above described crops are growing or are to be grown on:
 (Describe Real Estate) . . . .
3. (If applicable) The above goods are to become fixtures on *
*Where appropriate substitute either "The above timber is standing on . . . ." or "The above minerals or the like (including oil and gas) or accounts will be financed at the wellhead or minehead of the well or mine located on . . . ."
 (Describe Real Estate) . . . .
and this financing statement is to be filed [for record] in the real estate records. (If the debtor does not have an interest of record) The name of a record owner is
. . . .
4. (If products of collateral are claimed) Products of the collateral are also covered.

(use . . . .
whichever **Signature of Debtor (or Assignor)**
is . . . .
applicable) **Signature of Secured Party**
 (or Assignee)

(4) A financing statement may be amended by filing a writing signed by both the debtor and the secured party. An amendment does not extend the period of effectiveness of a financing statement. If any amendment adds collateral, it is effective as to the added collateral only from the filing date of the amendment. In this Article, unless the context otherwise requires, the term "financing statement" means the original financing statement and any amendments.

(5) A financing statement covering timber to be cut or covering minerals or the like (including oil and gas) or

accounts subject to subsection (5) of Section 9—103, or a financing statement filed as a fixture filing (Sectionfj9—313) where the debtor is not a transmitting utility, must show that it covers this type of collateral, must recite that it is to be filed [for record] in the real estate records, and the financing statement must contain a description of the real estate [sufficient if it were contained in a mortgage of the real estate to give constructive notice of the mortgage under the law of this state]. If the debtor does not have an interest of record in the real estate, the financing statement must show the name of a record owner.

(6) A mortgage is effective as a financing statement filed as a fixture filing from the date of its recording if

(a) the goods are described in the mortgage by item or type; and

(b) the goods are or are to become fixtures related to the real estate described in the mortgage; and

(c) the mortgage complies with the requirements for a financing statement in this section other than a recital that it is to be filed in the real estate records; and

(d) the mortgage is duly recorded.

No fee with reference to the financing statement is required other than the regular recording and satisfaction fees with respect to the mortgage.

(7) A financing statement sufficiently shows the name of the debtor if it gives the individual, partnership or corporate name of the debtor, whether or not it adds other trade names or names of partners. Where the debtor so changes his name or in the case of an organization its name, identity or corporate structure that a filed financing statement becomes seriously misleading, the filing is not effective to perfect a security interest in collateral acquired by the debtor more than four months after the change, unless a new appropriate financing statement is filed before the expiration of that time. A filed financing statement remains effective with respect to collateral transferred by the debtor even though the secured party knows of or consents to the transfer.

(8) A financing statement substantially complying with the requirements of this section is effective even though it contains minor errors which are not seriously misleading.

Note: *Language in brackets is optional.*

Note: *Where the state has any special recording system for real estate other than the usual grantor-grantee index (as, for instance, a tract system or a title registration or Tottens system) local adaptations of subsection (5) and Section 9—403(7) may be necessary. See Mass.Gen.Laws Chapter 106, Section 9—409.*

Part 5 Default

§ 9—501. Default; Procedure When Security Agreement Covers Both Real and Personal Property.

(1) When a debtor is in default under a security agreement, a secured party has the rights and remedies provided in this Part and except as limited by subsection (3) those provided in the security agreement. He may reduce his claim to judgment, foreclose or otherwise enforce the security interest by any available judicial procedure. If the collateral is documents the secured party may proceed either as to the documents or as to the goods covered thereby. A secured party in possession has the rights, remedies and duties provided in Section 9—207. The rights and remedies referred to in this subsection are cumulative.

(2) After default, the debtor has the rights and remedies provided in this Part, those provided in the security agreement and those provided in Section 9—207.

(3) To the extent that they give rights to the debtor and impose duties on the secured party, the rules stated in the subsections referred to below may not be waived or varied except as provided with respect to compulsory disposition of collateral (subsection (3) of Section 9—504 and Section 9—505) and with respect to redemption of collateral (Section 9—506) but the parties may by agreement determine the standards by which the fulfillment of these rights and duties is to be measured if such standards are not manifestly unreasonable:

(a) subsection (2) of Section 9—502 and subsection (2) of Section 9—504 insofar as they require accounting for surplus proceeds of collateral;

(b) subsection (3) of Section 9—504 and subsection (1) of Section 9—505 which deal with disposition of collateral;

(c) subsection (2) of Section 9—505 which deals with acceptance of collateral as discharge of obligation;

(d) Section 9—506 which deals with redemption of collateral; and

(e) subsection (1) of Section 9—507 which deals with the secured party's liability for failure to comply with this Part.

(4) If the security agreement covers both real and personal property, the secured party may proceed under this Part as to the personal property or he may proceed as to both the real and the personal property in accordance with his rights and remedies in respect of the real property in which case the provisions of this Part do not apply.

(5) When a secured party has reduced his claim to judgment the lien of any levy which may be made upon his collateral by virtue of any execution based upon the judgment shall relate back to the date of the perfection of the security interest in such collateral. A judicial sale, pursuant to such execution, is a foreclosure of the security interest by judicial procedure within the meaning of this section, and the secured party may purchase at the sale and thereafter hold the collateral free of any other requirements of this Article.

§ 9—503. Secured Party's Right to Take Possession After Default.

Unless otherwise agreed a secured party has on default the right to take possession of the collateral. In taking possession a secured party may proceed without judicial process if this can be done without breach of the peace or may proceed by action. If the security agreement so provides the secured party may require the debtor to assemble the collateral and make it available to the secured party at a place to be designated by the secured party which is reasonably convenient to both parties. Without removal a secured party may render equipment unusable, and may dispose of collateral on the debtor's premises under Section 9—504.

§ 9—504. Secured Party's Right to Dispose of Collateral After Default; Effect of Disposition.

(1) A secured party after default may sell, lease or otherwise dispose of any or all of the collateral in its then condition or following any commercially reasonable preparation or processing. Any sale of goods is subject to the Article on Sales (Article 2). The proceeds of disposition shall be applied in the order following to

(a) the reasonable expenses of retaking, holding, preparing for sale or lease, selling, leasing and the like and, to the extent provided for in the agreement and not prohibited by law, the reasonable attorneys' fees and legal expenses incurred by the secured party;

(b) the satisfaction of indebtedness secured by the security interest under which the disposition is made;

(c) the satisfaction of indebtedness secured by any subordinate security interest in the collateral if written notification of demand therefor is received before distribution of the proceeds is completed. If requested by the secured party, the holder of a subordinate security interest must seasonably furnish reasonable proof of his interest, and unless he does so, the secured party need not comply with his demand.

(2) If the security interest secures an indebtedness, the secured party must account to the debtor for any surplus, and, unless otherwise agreed, the debtor is liable for any deficiency. But if the underlying transaction was a sale of accounts or chattel paper, the debtor is entitled to any surplus or is liable for any deficiency only if the security agreement so provides.

(3) Disposition of the collateral may be by public or private proceedings and may be made by way of one or more contracts. Sale or other disposition may be as a unit or in parcels and at any time and place and on any terms but every aspect of the disposition including the method,

manner, time, place and terms must be commercially reasonable. Unless collateral is perishable or threatens to decline speedily in value or is of a type customarily sold on a recognized market, reasonable notification of the time and place of any public sale or reasonable notification of the time after which any private sale or other intended disposition is to be made shall be sent by the secured party to the debtor, if he has not signed after default a statement renouncing or modifying his right to notification of sale. In the case of consumer goods no other notification need be sent. In other cases notification shall be sent to any other secured party from whom the secured party has received (before sending his notification to the debtor or before the debtor's renunciation of his rights) written notice of a claim of an interest in the collateral. The secured party may buy at any public sale and if the collateral is of a type customarily sold in a recognized market or is of a type which is the subject of widely distributed standard price quotations he may buy at private sale.

(4) When collateral is disposed of by a secured party after default, the disposition transfers to a purchaser for value all of the debtor's rights therein, discharges the security interest under which it is made and any security interest or lien subordinate thereto. The purchaser takes free of all such rights and interests even though the secured party fails to comply with the requirements of this Part or of any judicial proceedings

> (a) in the case of a public sale, if the purchaser has no knowledge of any defects in the sale and if he does not buy in collusion with the secured party, other bidders or the person conducting the sale; or

> (b) in any other case, if the purchaser acts in good faith.

(5) A person who is liable to a secured party under a guaranty, indorsement, repurchase agreement or the like and who receives a transfer of collateral from the secured party or is subrogated to his rights has thereafter the rights and duties of the secured party. Such a transfer of collateral is not a sale or disposition of the collateral under this Article.

§ 9—505. Compulsory Disposition of Collateral; Acceptance of the Collateral as Discharge of Obligation.

(1) If the debtor has paid sixty per cent of the cash price in the case of a purchase money security interest in consumer goods or sixty per cent of the loan in the case of another security interest in consumer goods, and has not signed after default a statement renouncing or modifying his rights under this Part a secured party who has taken possession of collateral must dispose of it under Section 9—504 and if he fails to do so within ninety days after he takes possession the debtor at his option may recover in conversion or under Section 9—507(1) on secured party's liability.

(2) In any other case involving consumer goods or any other collateral a secured party in possession may, after default, propose to retain the collateral in satisfaction of the obligation. Written notice of such proposal shall be sent to the debtor if he has not signed after default a statement renouncing or modifying his rights under this subsection. In the case of consumer goods no other notice need be given. In other cases notice shall be sent to any other secured party from whom the secured party has received (before sending his notice to the debtor or before the debtor's renunciation of his rights) written notice of a claim of an interest in the collateral. If the secured party receives objection in writing from a person entitled to receive notification within twenty-one days after the notice was sent, the secured party must dispose of the collateral under Section 9—504. In the absence of such written objection the secured party may retain the collateral in satisfaction of the debtor's obligation. Amended in 1972.

§ 9—507. Secured Party's Liability for Failure to Comply with This Part.

(1) If it is established that the secured party is not proceeding in accordance with the provisions of this Part disposition may be ordered or restrained on appropriate terms and conditions. If the disposition has occurred the debtor or any person entitled to notification or whose security interest has been made known to the secured party prior to the disposition has a right to recover from the secured party any loss caused by a failure to comply with the provisions of this Part. If the collateral is consumer goods, the debtor has a right to recover in any event an amount not less than the credit service charge plus ten per cent of the principal amount of the debt or the time price differential plus 10 per cent of the cash price.

(2) The fact that a better price could have been obtained by a sale at a different time or in a different method from that selected by the secured party is not of itself sufficient to establish that the sale was not made in a commercially reasonable manner. If the secured party either sells the collateral in the usual manner in any recognized market therefor or if he sells at the price current in such market at the time of his sale or if he has otherwise sold in conformity with reasonable commercial practices among dealers in the type of property sold he has sold in a commercially reasonable manner. The principles stated in the two preceding sentences with respect to sales also apply as may be appropriate to other types of disposition. A disposition which has been approved in any judicial proceeding or by any bona fide creditors' committee or representative of creditors shall conclusively be deemed to be commercially reasonable, but this sentence does not indicate that any such approval must be obtained in any case nor does it indicate that any disposition not so approved is not commercially reasonable.

Appendix C Restatement of Torts, Second (Excerpts)

Section 402 A. Special liability of seller of product for physical harm to user or consumer.

(1) One who sells any product in a defective condition unreasonably dangerous to the consumer or to his property is subject to liability for physical harm thereby caused to the ultimate user or consumer, or to his property, if

(a) the seller is engaged in the business of selling such a product, and

(b) it is expected to and does reach the user or consumer without substantial change in the condition in which it is sold.

(2) The rule stated in Subsection (1) applies although

(a) the seller has exercised all possible care in the preparation and sale of his product, and

(b) the user or consumer has not bought the product from or entered into any contractual relation with the seller.

Section 402 B. Misrepresentation by seller of chattels to consumer.

One engaged in the business of selling chattels who, by advertising, labels, or otherwise, makes to the public a misrepresentation of a material fact concerning the character or quality of a chattel sold by him is subject to liability for physical harm to a consumer of the chattel caused by justifiable reliance upon the misrepresentation, even though

(a) it is not made fraudulently or negligently, and

(b) the consumer has not bought the chattel from or entered into any contractual relations with the seller.

Appendix D The Sherman Antitrust Act (Excerpts)

Section 1. Every contract, combination in the form of trust or otherwise, or conspiracy, in restraint of trade or commerce among the several States, or with foreign nations, is declared to be illegal. Every person who shall make any contract or engage in any combination or conspiracy hereby declared to be illegal shall be deemed guilty of a felony, and, on conviction thereof, shall be punished by fine not exceeding $10,000,000 if a corporation, or, if any other person, $350,000, or by imprisonment not exceeding three years, or by both said punishments, in the discretion of the court.

Section 2. Every person who shall monopolize, or attempt to monopolize, or combine or conspire with any other person or persons, to monopolize any part of the trade or commerce among the several States, or with foreign nations, shall be deemed guilty of a felony, and, on conviction thereof, shall be punished by fine not exceeding $10,000,000 if a corporation, or, if any other person, $350,000, or by imprisonment not exceeding three years, or by both said punishments, in the discretion of the court.

Appendix E The Clayton Act (Excerpts)

Section 2. Section 2 is also known as the Robinson-Patman amendment to Section 2 of the Clayton Act. (a) It shall be unlawful for any person engaged in commerce, in the course of such commerce, either directly or indirectly, to discriminate in price between purchasers of commodities of like grade and quality, . . . where such commodities are sold for use, consumption, or resale within the United States or any Territory thereof . . . and where the effect of such discrimination may be substantially to lessen competition or tend to create a monopoly in any line of commerce, or to injure, destroy, or prevent competition with any person who either grants or knowingly receives the benefit of such discrimination, or with customers of either of them: Provided, That nothing herein contained shall prevent differentials which make only due allowance for differences in the cost of manufacture, sale, or delivery resulting from the differing methods or quantities in which such commodities are to such purchasers sold or delivered: Provided, however, That the Federal Trade Commission may, after due investigation and hearing . . . fix and establish quantity limits, . . . as to particular commodities or classes of commodities, where it finds that available purchasers in greater quantities are so few as to render differentials on account thereof unjustly discriminatory or promotive of monopoly in any line of commerce; and the foregoing shall then not be construed to permit differentials based on differences in quantities greater than those so fixed and established: And provided further, That nothing herein contained shall prevent persons engaged in selling goods, wares, or merchandise in commerce from selecting their own customers in *bona fide* transactions and not in restraint of trade: And provided further, That nothing herein contained shall prevent price changes from time to time where in response to changing conditions affecting the market for or the marketability of the goods concerned, such as but not limited to actual or imminent deterioration of perishable goods, obsolescence of seasonal goods, distress sales under court process, or sales in good

faith in discontinuance of business in the goods concerned.

(b) Upon proof being made, at any hearing on a complaint under this section, that there has been discrimination in price or services or facilities furnished, the burden of rebutting the *prima facie* case thus made by showing justification shall be upon the person charged with a violation of this section, and unless justification shall be affirmatively shown, the Commission is authorized to issue an order terminating the discrimination: Provided, however, That nothing herein contained shall prevent a seller rebutting the *prima facie* case thus made by showing that his lower price or the furnishing of services or facilities to any purchaser or purchasers was made in good faith to meet an equally low price of a competitor, or the services or facilities furnished by a competitor.

(c) That it shall be unlawful for any person engaged in commerce, in the course of such commerce, to pay or grant, or to receive or accept, anything of value as a commission, brokerage, or other compensation, or any allowance or discount in lieu thereof, except for services rendered in connection with the sale or purchase of goods, wares, or merchandise, either to the other party to such transactions or to an agent, representative, or other intermediary therein where such intermediary is acting in fact for or in behalf, or is subject to the direct or indirect control, of any party to such transaction other than the person by whom such compensation is granted or paid.

(d) That it shall be unlawful for any person engaged in commerce to pay or contract for the payment of anything of value to or for the benefit of a customer of such person in the course of such commerce as compensation or in consideration for any services or facilities furnished by or through such customer in connection with the processing, handling, sale, or offering for sale of any products or commodities manufactured, sold, or offered for sale by such person, unless such payment or consideration is available on proportionally equal terms to all other customers competing in the distribution of such products or commodities.

(e) That it shall be unlawful for any person to discriminate in favor of one purchaser against another purchaser or purchasers of a commodity bought for resale, with or without processing, by contracting to furnish or furnishing, or by contributing to the furnishing of, any services or facilities connected with the processing, handling, sale, or offering for sale of such commodity so purchased upon terms not accorded to all purchasers on proportionally equal terms.

(f) That it shall be unlawful for any person engaged in commerce, in the course of such commerce, knowingly to induce or receive a discrimination in price which is prohibited by this section.

Section 3. It shall be unlawful for any person engaged in commerce, in the course of such commerce, to lease or make a sale or contract for sale of goods, wares, merchandise, machinery, supplies, or other commodities, whether patented or unpatented, for use, consumption, or resale within the United States or . . . other place under the jurisdiction of the United States, or fix a price charged therefor, or discount from, or rebate upon, such price, on the condition, agreement, or understanding that the lessee or purchaser thereof shall not use or deal in the goods, wares, merchandise, machinery, supplies, or other commodities of a competitor or competitors of the lessor or seller, where the effect of such lease, sale, or contract for sale or such condition, agreement, or understanding may be to substantially lessen competition or tend to create a monopoly in any line of commerce.

Section 4. [A]ny person who shall be injured in his business or property by reason of anything forbidden in the antitrust laws may sue therefor in any district court of the United States in the district in which the defendant resides or is found, or has an agent, without respect to the amount in controversy, and shall recover threefold the damages by him sustained, and the cost of suit, including a reasonable attorney's fee.

Section 4A. Whenever the United States is hereafter injured in its business or property by reason of anything forbidden in the antitrust laws it may sue therefor in the United States district court for the district in which the defendant resides or is found or has an agent, without respect to the amount in controversy, and shall recover threefold the damages by it sustained and the cost of suit.

Section 4B. Any action to enforce any cause of action under sections 4 or 4A shall be forever barred unless commenced within four years after the cause of action accrued. No cause of action barred under existing law on the effective date of this act shall be revived by this Act.

Section 4C. (a)(1) Any attorney general of a state may bring a civil action in the name of such State, as parens

patriae on behalf of natural persons residing in such State, in any district court of the United States having jurisdiction of the defendant, to secure monetary relief as provided in this section for injury sustained by such natural persons to their property by reason of any violation of the Sherman Act. The court shall exclude from the amount of monetary relief awarded in such action any amount of monetary relief (A) which duplicates amounts which have been awarded for the same injury, or (B) which is properly allocable to (i) natural persons who have excluded their claims pursuant to subsection (b)(2) of this section, and (ii) any business entity.

(2) The court shall award the State as monetary relief threefold the total damage sustained as described in paragraph (1) of this subsection, and the cost of suit, including a reasonable attorney's fee.

(b)(1) In any action brought under subsection (a)(1) of this section, the State attorney general shall, at such times, in such manner, and with such content as the court may direct, cause notice thereof to be given by publication. If the court finds that notice given solely by publication would deny due process of law to any person or persons, the court may direct further notice to such person or persons according to the circumstances of the case.

(2) Any person on whose behalf an action is brought under subsection (a)(1) may elect to exclude from adjudication the portion of the State claim for monetary relief attributable to him by filing notice of such election with the court within such time as specified in the notice given pursuant to paragraph (1) of this subsection.

(3) The final judgment in an action under subsection (a)(1) shall be res judicata as to any claim under section 4 of this Act by any person on behalf of whom such action was brought and who fails to give such notice within the period specified in the notice given pursuant to paragraph (1) of this subsection.

(c) An action under subsection (a)(1) shall not be dismissed or compromised without the approval of the court, and notice of any proposed dismissal or compromise shall be given in such manner as the court directs.

(d) In any action under subsection (a)—

(1) the amount of the plaintiffs' attorney's fee, if any, shall be determined by the court; and

(2) the court may, in its discretion, award a reasonable attorney's fee to a prevailing defendant upon a finding that the State attorney general has acted in bad faith, vexatiously, wantonly, or for oppressive reasons.

Section 6. The labor of a human being is not a commodity or article of commerce. Nothing contained in the antitrust laws shall be construed to forbid the existence and operation of labor, agricultural or horticultural organizations, instituted for the purposes of mutual help, and not having capital stock or conducted for profit, or to forbid or restrain individual members of such organizations from lawfully carrying out the legitimate objects thereof; nor shall such organizations or the members thereof, be held or construed to be illegal combinations or conspiracies in restraint of trade, under the antitrust laws.

Section 7. No person engaged in commerce . . . shall acquire, directly or indirectly, the whole or any part of the stock or other share capital and no person subject to the jurisdiction of the Federal Trade Commission shall acquire the whole or any part of the assets of another person engaged also in commerce . . . or in any activity affecting commerce in any section of the country, the effect of such acquisition may be substantially to lessen competition, or to tend to create a monopoly.

No person shall acquire, directly or indirectly, the whole or any part of the stock or other share capital and no person subject to the jurisdiction of the Federal Trade Commission shall acquire the whole or any part of the assets of one or more persons engaged in commerce, where in any line of commerce in any section of the country, the effect of such acquisition, of such stocks or assets, or of the use of such stock by the voting or granting of proxies or otherwise, may be substantially to lessen competition, or to tend to create a monopoly.

This section shall not apply to persons purchasing such stock solely for investment and not using the same by voting or otherwise to bring about, or in attempting to bring about, the substantial lessening of competition . . .

Section 8. (a)(1) No person shall, at the same time, serve as a director or officer in any two corporations (other than banks, banking associations, and trust companies) that are—

(A) engaged in whole or in part in commerce; and

(B) by virtue of their business and location of operation, competitors, so that the elimination of competition by agreement between them would constitute a violation of any of the antitrust laws;

if each of the corporations has capital, surplus, and undivided profits aggregating more than $10,000,000 as adjusted pursuant to paragraph (5) of this subsection.

(2) Notwithstanding the provisions of paragraph (1), simultaneous service as a director or officer in any two corporations shall not be prohibited by this section if—

(A) the competitive sales of either corporation are less than $1,000,000, as adjusted pursuant to paragraph (5) of this subsection;

(B) the competitive sales of either corporation are less than 2 per centum of that corporation's total sales; or

(C) the competitive sales of each corporation are less than 4 per centum of that corporation's total sales.

For purposes of this paragraph, "competitive sales" means the gross revenues for all products and services sold by one corporation in competition with the other, determined on the basis of annual gross revenues for such products and services in that corporation's last completed fiscal year. For the purposes of this paragraph, "total sales" means the gross revenues for all products and services sold by one corporation over that corporation's last completed fiscal year.

(3) The eligibility of a director or officer under the provisions of paragraph (1) shall be determined by the capital, surplus and undivided profits, exclusive of dividends declared but not paid to stockholders, of each corporation at the end of that corporation's last completed fiscal year.

(4) For purposes of this section, the term "officer" means an officer elected or chosen by the Board of Directors.

(5) For each fiscal year commencing after September 30, 1990, the $10,000,000 and $1,000,000 thresholds in this subsection shall be increased (or decreased) as of October 1 each year by an amount equal to the percentage increase (or decrease) in the gross national product, as determined by the Department of Commerce or its successor, for the year then ended over the level so established for the year ending September 30, 1989. As soon as practicable, but not later than October 30 of each year, the Federal Trade Commission shall publish the adjusted amounts required by this paragraph.

(b) When any person elected or chosen as a director or officer of any corporation subject to the provisions hereof is eligible at the time of his election or selection to act for such corporation in such capacity, his eligibility to act in such capacity shall not be affected by any of the provisions hereof by reason of any change in the capital, surplus and undivided profits, or affairs of such corporation from whatever cause, until, the expiration of one year from the date on which the event causing ineligibility occurred.

Appendix F The Federal Trade Commission Act (Excerpts)

Section 5. (a)(1) Unfair methods of competition in or affecting commerce, and unfair or deceptive acts or practices in or affecting commerce, are hereby declared unlawful.

(2) The Commission is empowered and directed to prevent persons, partnerships, or corporations . . . from using unfair methods of competition in or affecting commerce and unfair or deceptive acts or practices in or affecting commerce.

(l) Any person, partnership, or corporation who violates an order of the Commission after it has become final, and while such order is in effect, shall forfeit and pay to the United States a civil penalty of not more than $10,000 for each violation, which shall accrue to the United States and may be recovered in a civil action brought by the Attorney General of the United States. Each separate violation of such an order shall be a separate offense, except that in the case of a violation through continuing failure to obey or neglect to obey a final order of the Commission, each day of continuance of such failure or neglect shall be deemed a separate offense. In such actions, the United States district courts are empowered to grant mandatory injunctions and such other and further equitable relief as they deem appropriate in the enforcement of such final orders of the Commission.

Appendix G National Labor Relations Act (Excerpts)

Section 3. National Labor Relations Board. (a) The National Labor Relations Board (hereinafter called the "Board") . . . as an agency of the United States, shall consist of five . . . members, appointed by the President by and with the advice and consent of the Senate . . . for terms of five years each. . . . The President shall designate one member to serve as Chairman of the Board. Any member of the Board may be removed by the President, upon notice and hearing, for neglect of duty or malfeasance in office, but for no other cause.

Section 7. Rights of Employees. Employees shall have the right to self-organization, to form, join, or assist labor organizations, to bargain collectively through representatives of their own choosing, and to engage in other concerted activities for the purpose of collective bargaining or other mutual aid or protection, and shall also have the right to refrain from any or all of such activities except to the extent that such right may be affected by an agreement requiring membership in a labor organization as a condition of employment as authorized in section 8(a) (3).

Appendix H The Federal Civil Rights Laws (Excerpts)

42 U.S. Code, Section 1982. (1866)

All persons within the jurisdiction of the United States shall have the same right in every State and Territory to make and enforce contracts, to sue, be parties, give evidence, and to the full and equal benefit of all laws and proceedings for the security of persons and property as is enjoyed by white citizens, and shall be subject to like punishment, pains, penalties, taxes, licenses and exactions of every kind, and no other.

42 U.S. Code, Section 1982. (1866)

All citizens of the United States shall have the same right, in every State and Territory, as is enjoyed by white citizens thereof to inherit, purchase, lease, sell, hold and convey real and personal property.

42 U.S. Code, Section 1983. (1871)

Every person who, under color of any statute, ordinance, regulation, custom, or usage, of any State or Territory, subjects, or causes to be subjected, any citizen of the United States or other person within the jurisdiction thereof to the deprivation of any rights, privileges, or immunities secured by the Constitution and laws, shall be liable to the party injured in an action at law, suit in equity, or other proper proceeding for redress.

Title II of the Civil Rights Act of 1964—The Public Accommodations Section

Section 201. (a) All persons shall be entitled to the full and equal enjoyment of the goods, services, facilities, privileges, advantages, and accommodations of any place of public accommodation, as defined in this section, without discrimination on the ground of race, color, religion, or national origin.

(b) Each of the following establishments which serves the public is a place of public accommodation within the meaning of this title if its operations affect commerce, or if discrimination or segregation by it is supported by State action:

(1) any inn, hotel, motel, or other establishment which provides lodging to transient guests, other than an estab-lishment located within a building which contains not more than five rooms for rent or hire and which is actually occupied by the proprietor of such establishment as his residence;

(2) any restaurant, cafeteria, lunchroom, lunch counter, soda fountain. . . .

(3) any motion picture house, theater, concert hall, sports arena, stadium. . . .

Section 202. All persons shall be entitled to be free, at any establishment or place, from discrimination or segregation of any kind on the ground of race, color, religion, or national origin, if such discrimination or segregation is or purports to be required by any law, statute, ordinance, regulation, rule, or order of a State or any agency or political subdivision thereof.

Section 203. No person shall (a) withhold, deny, or attempt to withhold or deny, or deprive or attempt to deprive, any person of any right or privilege secured by section 201 or 202, or (b) intimidate, threaten, or coerce, or attempt to intimidate, threaten, or coerce any person with the purpose of interfering with any right or privilege secured by section 201 or 202, or (c) punish or attempt to punish any person for exercising or attempting to exercise any right or privilege secured by section 201 or 202.

. . . .

Title VII of the Civil Rights Act of 1964—The Employment Discrimination Section

Section 703. Unlawful Employment Practices. (a) It shall be an unlawful employment practice for an employer—

(1) to fail or refuse to hire or to discharge any individual, or otherwise to discriminate against any individual with respect to his compensation, terms, conditions, or privileges or employment, because of such individual's race, color, religion, sex, or national origin; or

(2) to limit, segregate, or classify his employees or applicants for employment in any way which would deprive or tend to deprive any individual of employment opportunities or otherwise adversely affect his status as an em-

ployee, because of such individual's race, color, religion, sex, or national origin.

(b) It shall be an unlawful employment practice for an employment agency to fail or refuse to refer for employment, or otherwise to discriminate against, any individual because of his race, color, religion, sex, or national origin, or to classify or refer for employment any individual on the basis or his race, color, religion, sex, or national origin.

(c) It shall be an unlawful employment practice for a labor organization—

(1) to exclude or to expel from its membership, or otherwise to discriminate against, any individual because of his race, color, religion, sex, or national origin;

(2) to limit, segregate, or classify its membership or applicants for membership, or to classify or fail or refuse to refer for employment any individual, in any way which would deprive or tend to deprive any individual of employment opportunities, or would limit such employment opportunities or otherwise adversely affect his status as an employee or as an applicant for employment, because of such individual's race, color, religion, sex, or national origin; or

(3) to cause or attempt to cause an employer to discriminate against an individual in violation of this section.

(d) It shall be an unlawful employment practice for any employer, labor organization, or joint labor-management committee controlling apprenticeship or other training or retraining, including on-the-job training programs to discriminate against any individual because of his race, color, religion, sex, or national origin in admission to, or employment in, any program established to provide apprenticeship or other training.

(e) Notwithstanding any other provision of this subchapter,

(1) it shall not be an unlawful employment practice for an employer to hire and employ employees, for an employment agency to classify, or refer for employment any individual, for a labor organization to classify its membership or to classify or refer for employment any individual, or for an employer, labor organization, or joint labor-management committee controlling apprenticeship or other training or retraining programs to admit or employ any individual in any such program, on the basis of his religion, sex, or national origin in those certain instances where religion, sex, or national origin is a bona fide occupational qualification reasonably necessary to the normal operation of that particular business or enterprise, and

(2) it shall not be an unlawful employment practice for a school, college, university, or other educational institution or institution of learning to hire and employ employees of a particular religion if such school, college, university, or other educational institution or institution of learning is, in whole or in substantial part, owned, supported, controlled, or managed by a particular religion or by a particular religious corporation, association, or society, or if the curriculum of such school, college, university, or other educational institution or institution of learning is directed toward the propagation of a particular religion.

(f) As used in this subchapter, the phrase "unlawful employment practice" shall not be deemed to include any action or measure taken by an employer, labor organization, joint labor-management committee, or employment agency with respect to an individual who is a member of the Communist Party of the United States or of any other organization required to register as a Communist-action or Communist-front organization. . . .

(g) Notwithstanding any other provision of this subchapter, it shall not be an unlawful employment practice for an employer to fail or refuse to hire and employ any individual for any position, for an employer to discharge any individual from any position, or for an employment agency to fail or refuse to refer any individual for employment in any position, or for a labor organization to fail or refuse to refer any individual for employment in any position, if—

(1) the occupancy of such position, or access to the premises in or upon which any part of the duties of such position is performed or is to be performed, is subject to any requirement imposed in the interest of the national security of the United States . . . and

(2) such individual has not fulfilled or has ceased to fulfill that requirement.

(h) Notwithstanding any other provision of this subchapter, it shall not be an unlawful employment practice for an employer to apply different standards of compensation, or different terms, conditions, or privileges of employment pursuant to a bona fide seniority or merit system, or a system which measures earnings by quantity or quality of production or to employees who work in different locations, provided that such differences are not the result of an intention to discriminate because of race, color, religion, sex, or national origin, nor shall it be an unlawful employment practice for an employer to give and act upon the results of any professionally developed ability test provided that such test, its administration or action upon the results is not designed, intended or used to discriminate because of race, color, religion, sex, or national origin. . . .

(j) Nothing contained in this subchapter shall be interpreted to require any employer, employment agency, labor organization, or joint labor-management committee subject to this subchapter to grant preferential treatment to any individual or to any group because of the race, color, religion, sex, or national origin of such individual or group on account of an imbalance which may exist with respect to the total number of percentage of persons of any race, color, religion, sex, or national origin employed by any employer, referred or classified for employment by any employment agency or labor organization, or admitted to, or employed in, any apprenticeship or other training program, in comparison with the total number or percentage of persons of such race, color, religion, sex, or national origin in any community, State, section, or other area, or in the available work force in any community, State, section, or other area.

. . . .

Section 704. Other Unlawful Employment Practices.

(a) It shall be an unlawful employment practice for an employer to discriminate against any of his employees or applicants for employment, for an employment agency, or joint labor-management committee controlling apprenticeship or other training or retraining, including on-the-job training programs, to discriminate against any individual, or for a labor organization to discriminate against any member thereof or applicant for membership, because he has opposed any practice made an unlawful employment practice by this subchapter, or because he has made a charge, testified, assisted, or participated in any manner in an investigation, proceeding, or hearing under this subchapter.

(b) It shall be an unlawful employment practice for an employer, labor organization, employment agency, or joint labor-management committee controlling apprenticeship or other training or retraining, including on-the-job training programs, to print or publish or cause to be printed or published any notice or advertisement relating to employment by such an employer or membership or any classification or referral for employment by such a labor organization, or relating to any classification or referral for employment by such an employment agency, or relating to admission to, or employment in, any program established to provide apprenticeship or other training by such a joint-labor-management committee, indicating any preference, limitation, specification, or discrimination, based on race, color, religion, sex, or national origin, except that such a notice or advertisement may indicate a preference, limitation, specification, or discrimination based on religion, sex or national origin when religion, sex, or national origin is a bona fide occupational qualification for employment.

The Federal Civil Rights Act of 1968, as Amended 1988

Section 803. It shall be unlawful—

(a) To refuse to sell or rent after the making of a bona fide offer, or to refuse to negotiate for the sale or rental of, or otherwise make unavailable or deny, a dwelling to any person because of race, color, religion, sex, familial status, or national origin.

(b) To discriminate against any person in the terms, conditions, or privileges of sale or rental of a dwelling, or in the provision of services or facilities in connection therewith, because of race, color, religion, sex, familial status, or national origin.

(c) To make, print, or publish, or cause to be made, printed, or published any notice, statement, or advertisement, with respect to the sale or rental of a dwelling that indicates any preference, limitation, or discrimination based on race, color, religion, sex, handicap, familial status, or national origin, or an intention to make any such preference, limitation, or discrimination.

(d) To represent to any person because of race, color, religion, sex, handicap, familial status, or national origin that any dwelling is not available for inspection, sale, or rental when such dwelling is in fact so available.

(e) For profit, to induce or attempt to induce any person to sell or rent any dwelling by representations regarding the entry or prospective entry into the neighborhood of a person or persons of a particular race, color, religion, sex, handicap, familial status, or national origin.

(f)(1) To discriminate in the sale or rental, or to otherwise make unavailable or deny, a dwelling to any buyer or renter because of a handicap of—

(A) that buyer or renter;

(B) a person residing in or intending to reside in that dwelling after it is so sold, rented, or made available; or

(C) any person associated with that buyer or renter.

(2) To discriminate against any person in the terms, conditions, or privileges of sale or rental of a dwelling, or in the provision of services or facilities in connection with such dwelling, because of a handicap of—

(A) that person; or

(B) a person residing in or intending to reside in that dwelling after it is so sold, rented, or made available; or

(C) any person associated with that person.

(3) For purposes of this subsection, discrimination includes—

(A) a refusal to permit, at the expense of the handicapped person, reasonable modifications of existing premises occupied or to be occupied by such person if such modifications may be necessary to afford such person full enjoyment of the premises except that, in the case of a rental, the landlord may where it is reasonable to do so condition permission for a modification on the renter agreeing to restore the interior of the premises to the condition that existed before the modification, reasonable wear and tear excepted;

(B) a refusal to make reasonable accommodations in rules, policies, practices, or services, when such accommodations may be necessary to afford such person equal opportunity to use and enjoy a dwelling; or

(C) in connection with the design and construction of covered multifamily dwellings for first occupancy after the date that is 30 months after September 13, 1988, a failure to design and construct those dwellings in such a manner that—

(i) the public use and common use portions of such dwellings are readily accessible to and usable by handicapped persons;

(ii) all the doors designed to allow passage into and within all premises within such dwellings are sufficiently wide to allow passage by handicapped persons in wheelchairs; and

(iii) all premises within such dwellings contain the following features of adaptive design:

(I) an accessible route into and through the dwelling;

(II) light switches, electrical outlets, thermostats, and other environmental controls in accessible locations;

(III) reinforcements in bathroom walls to allow later installation of grab bars; and

(IV) usable kitchens and bathrooms such that an individual in a wheelchair can maneuver about the space.

(a) Findings

The Congress finds that—

(1) some 43,000,000 Americans have one or more physical or mental disabilities, and this number is increasing as the population as a whole is growing older;

(2) historically, society has tended to isolate and segregate individuals with disabilities, and, despite some improvements, such forms of discrimination against individuals with disabilities continue to be a serious and pervasive social problem;

(3) discrimination against individuals with disabilities persists in such critical areas as employment, housing, public accommodations, education, transportation, communication, recreation, institutionalization, health services, voting, and access to public services;

(4) unlike individuals who have experienced discrimination on the basis of race, color, sex, national origin, religion, or age, individuals who have experienced discrimination on the basis of disability have often had no legal recourse to redress such discrimination;

(5) individuals with disabilities continually encounter various forms of discrimination, including outright intentional exclusion, the discriminatory effects of architectural, transportation, and communication barriers, overprotective rules and policies, failure to make modifications to existing facilities and practices, exclusionary qualification standards and criteria, segregation, and relegation to lesser services, programs, activities, benefits, jobs, or other opportunities;

(6) census data, national polls, and other studies have documented that people with disabilities, as a group, occupy an inferior status in our society, and are severely disadvantaged socially, vocationally, economically, and educationally;

(7) individuals with disabilities are a discrete and insular minority who have been faced with restrictions and limitations, subjected to a history of purposeful unequal treatment, and relegated to a position of political powerlessness in our society, based on characteristics that are beyond the control of such individuals and resulting from stereotypic assumptions not truly indicative of the individual ability of such individuals to participate in, and contribute to, society;

(8) the Nation's proper goals regarding individuals with disabilities are to assure equality of opportunity, full participation, independent living, and economic self-sufficiency for such individuals; and

(9) the continuing existence of unfair and unnecessary discrimination and prejudice denies people with disabilities the opportunity to compete on an equal basis and to pursue those opportunities for which our free society is justifiably famous, and costs the United States billions of dollars in unnecessary expenses resulting from dependency and nonproductivity.

(b) Purpose

It is the purpose of this chapter—

(1) to provide a clear and comprehensive national mandate for the elimination of discrimination against individuals with disabilities;

(2) to provide clear, strong, consistent, enforceable standards addressing discrimination against individuals with disabilities;

(3) to ensure that the Federal Government plays a central role in enforcing the standards established in this chapter on behalf of individuals with disabilities; and

(4) to invoke the sweep of congressional authority; including the power to enforce the fourteenth amendment and to regulate commerce, in order to address the major areas of discrimination faced day-to-day by people with disabilities.

Appendix I The Uniform Partnership Act (Excerpts)

Sec. 6. Partnership Defined

(1) A partnership is an association of two or more persons to carry on as co-owners a business for profit.

(2) But any association formed under any other statute of this state, or any statute adopted by authority, other than the authority of this state, is not a partnership under this act, unless such association would have been a partnership in this state prior to the adoption of this act; but this act shall apply to limited partnerships except in so far as the statutes relating to such partnerships are inconsistent herewith.

Sec. 8. Partnership Property

(1) All property originally brought into the partnership stock or subsequently acquired by purchase or otherwise, on account of the partnership, is partnership property.

(2) Unless the contrary intention appears, property acquired with partnership funds is partnership property.

(3) Any estate in real property may be acquired in the partnership name. Title so acquired can be conveyed only in the partnership name.

(4) A conveyance to a partnership in the partnership name, though without words of inheritance, passes the entire estate of the grantor unless a contrary intent appears.

Sec. 9. Partner Agent of Partnership as to Partnership Business

(1) Every partner is an agent of the partnership for the purpose of its business, and the act of every partner, including the execution in the partnership name of any instrument, for apparently carrying on in the usual way the business of the partnership of which he is a member binds the partnership, unless the partner so acting has in fact no authority to act for the partnership in the particular matter, and the person with whom he is dealing has knowledge of the fact that he has no such authority.

(2) An act of a partner which is not apparently for the carrying on of the business of the partnership in the usual way does not bind the partnership unless authorized by the other partners.

(3) Unless authorized by the other partners or unless they have abandoned the business, one or more but less than all the partners have no authority to:

    (a) Assign the partnership property in trust for creditors or on the assignee's promise to pay the debts of the partnership,

    (b) Dispose of the good-will of the business,

    (c) Do any other act which would make it impossible to carry on the ordinary business of a partnership,

    (d) Confess a judgment,

    (e) Submit a partnership claim or liability to arbitration or reference.

(4) No act of a partner in contravention of a restriction on authority shall bind the partnership to persons having knowledge of the restriction.

Sec. 10. Conveyance of Real Property of the Partnership

(1) Where title to real property is in the partnership name, any partner may convey title to such property by a conveyance executed in the partnership name; but the partnership may recover such property unless the partner's act binds the partnership under the provisions of paragraph (1) of section 9, or unless such property has been conveyed by the grantee or a person claiming through such grantee to a holder for value without knowledge that the partner, in making the conveyance, has exceeded his authority.

(2) Where title to real property is in the name of the partnership, a conveyance executed by a partner, in his own name, passes the equitable interest of the partnership, provided the act is one within the authority of the partner under the provisions of paragraph (1) of section 9.

(3) Where title to real property is in the name of one or more but not all the partners, and the record does not disclose the right of the partnership, the partners in whose name the title stands may convey title to such property,

but the partnership may recover such property if the partners' act does not bind the partnership under the provisions of paragraph (1) of section 9, unless the purchaser or his assignee, is a holder for value, without knowledge.

(4) Where the title to real property is in the name of one or more or all the partners, or in a third person in trust for the partnership, a conveyance executed by a partner in the partnership name, or in his own name, passes the equitable interest of the partnership, provided the act is one within the authority of the partner under the provisions of paragraph (1) of section 9.

(5) Where the title to real property is in the names of all the partners a conveyance executed by all the partners passes all their rights in such property.

Sec. 13. Partnership Bound by Partner's Wrongful Act

Where, by any wrongful act or omission of any partner acting in the ordinary course of the business of the partnership or with the authority of his co-partners, loss or injury is caused to any person, not being a partner in the partnership, or any penalty is incurred, the partnership is liable therefor to the same extent as the partner so acting or omitting to act.

Sec. 15. Nature of Partner's Liability

All partners are liable

(a) Jointly and severally for everything chargeable to the partnership under sections 13 and 14.

(b) Jointly for all other debts and obligations of the partnership; but any partner may enter into a separate obligation to perform a partnership contract.

Sec. 16. Partner by Estoppel

(1) When a person, by words spoken or written or by conduct, represents himself, or consents to another representing him to any one, as a partner in an existing partnership or with one or more persons not actual partners, he is liable to any such person to whom such representation has been made, who has, on the faith of such representation, given credit to the actual or apparent partnership, and if he has made such representation or consented to its being made in a public manner he is liable to such person, whether the representation has or has not been made or communicated to such person so giving credit by or with the knowledge of the apparent partner making the representation or consenting to its being made.

 (a) When a partnership liability results, he is liable as though he were an actual member of the partnership.

 (b) When no partnership liability results, he is liable jointly with the other persons, if any, so consenting to the contract or representation as to incur liability, otherwise separately.

(2) When a person has been thus represented to be a partner in an existing partnership, or with one or more persons not actual partners, he is an agent of the persons consenting to such representation to bind them to the same extent and in the same manner as though he were a partner in fact, with respect to persons who rely upon the representation. Where all the members of the existing partnership consent to the representation, a partnership act or obligation results; but in all other cases it is the joint act or obligation of the person acting and the persons consenting to the representation.

Sec. 17. Liability of Incoming Partner

A person admitted as a partner into an existing partnership is liable for all the obligations of the partnership arising before his admission as though he had been a partner when such obligations were incurred, except that this liability shall be satisfied only out of partnership property.

Sec. 18. Rules Determining Rights and Duties of Partners

The rights and duties of the partners in relation to the partnership shall be determined, subject to any agreement between them, by the following rules:

(a) Each partner shall be repaid his contributions, whether by way of capital or advances to the partnership property and share equally in the profits and surplus remaining after all liabilities, including those to partners, are satisfied; and must contribute towards the losses, whether of capital or otherwise, sustained by the partnership according to his share in the profits.

(b) The partnership must indemnify every partner in respect of payments made and personal liabilities reasonably incurred by him in the ordinary and proper conduct of its business, or for the preservation of its business or property.

(c) A partner, who in aid of the partnership makes any payment or advance beyond the amount of capital which he agreed to contribute, shall be paid interest from the date of the payment or advance.

(d) A partner shall receive interest on the capital contributed by him only from the date when repayment should be made.

(e) All partners have equal rights in the management and conduct of the partnership business.

(f) No partner is entitled to remuneration for acting in the partnership business, except that a surviving partner is entitled to reasonable compensation for his services in winding up the partnership affairs.

(g) No person can become a member of a partnership without the consent of all the partners.

(h) Any difference arising as to ordinary matters connected with the partnership business may be decided by a majority of the partners; but no act in contravention of any agreement between the partners may be done rightfully without the consent of all the partners.

Sec. 25. Nature of a Partner's Right in Specific Partnership Property

(1) A partner is co-owner with his partners of specific partnership property holding as a tenant in partnership.

(2) The incidents of this tenancy are such that:

(a) A partner, subject to the provisions of this act and to any agreement between the partners, has an equal right with his partners to possess specific partnership property for partnership purposes; but he has no right to possess such property for any other purpose without the consent of his partners.

(b) A partner's right in specific partnership property is not assignable except in connection with the assignment of rights of all the partners in the same property.

(c) A partner's right in specific partnership property is not subject to attachment or execution, except on a claim against the partnership. When partnership property is attached for a partnership debt the partners, or any of them, or the representatives of a deceased partner, cannot claim any right under the homestead or exemption laws.

(d) On the death of a partner his right in specific partnership property vests in the surviving partner or partners, except where the deceased was the last surviving partner, when his right in such property vests in his legal representative. Such surviving partner or partners, or the legal representative of the last surviving partner, has no right to possess the partnership property for any but a partnership purpose.

(e) A partner's right in specific partnership property is not subject to dower, curtesy, or allowances to widows, heirs, or next of kin.

Sec. 30. Partnership not Terminated by Dissolution

On dissolution the partnership is not terminated, but continues until the winding up of partnership affairs is completed.

Sec. 31. Causes of Dissolution

Dissolution is caused:

(1) Without violation of the agreement between the partners,

(a) By the termination of the definite term or particular undertaking specified in the agreement,

(b) By the express will of any partner when no definite term or particular undertaking is specified,

(c) By the express will of all the partners who have not assigned their interests or suffered them to be charged

for their separate debts, either before or after the termination of any specified term or particular undertaking,

(d) By the expulsion of any partner from the business bona fide in accordance with such a power conferred by the agreement between the partners;

(2) In contravention of the agreement between the partners, where the circumstances do not permit a dissolution under any other provision of this section, by the express will of any partner at any time;

(3) By any event which makes it unlawful for the business of the partnership to be carried on or for the members to carry it on in partnership;

(4) By the death of any partner;

(5) By the bankruptcy of any partner or the partnership;

(6) By decree of court under section 32.

Sec. 32. Dissolution by Decree of Court

(1) On application by or for a partner the court shall decree a dissolution whenever:

(a) A partner has been declared a lunatic in any judicial proceeding or is shown to be of unsound mind,

(b) A partner becomes in any other way incapable of performing his part of the partnership contract,

(c) A partner has been guilty of such conduct as tends to affect prejudicially the carrying on of the business,

(d) A partner willfully or persistently commits a breach of the partnership agreement, or otherwise so conducts himself in matters relating to the partnership business that it is not reasonably practicable to carry on the business in partnership with him,

(e) The business of the partnership can only be carried on at a loss,

(f) Other circumstances render a dissolution equitable.

(2) On the application of the purchaser of a partner's interest under sections 28 or 29 [should read 27 or 28];

(a) After the termination of the specified term or particular undertaking,

(b) At any time if the partnership was a partnership at will when the interest was assigned or when the charging order was issued.

Sec. 35. Power of Partner to Bind Partnership to Third Persons After Dissolution

(1) After dissolution a partner can bind the partnership except as provided in Paragraph (3).

(a) By any act appropriate for winding up partnership affairs or completing transactions unfinished at dissolution;

(b) By any transaction which would bind the partnership if dissolution had not taken place, provided the other party to the transaction

   (I) Had extended credit to the partnership prior to dissolution and had no knowledge or notice of the dissolution; or

   (II) Though he had not so extended credit, had nevertheless known of the partnership prior to dissolution, and, having no knowledge or notice of dissolution, the fact of dissolution had not been advertised in a newspaper of general circulation in the place (or in each place if more than one) at which the partnership business was regularly carried on.

(2) The liability of a partner under paragraph (1b) shall be satisfied out of partnership assets alone when such partner had been prior to dissolution

   (a) Unknown as a partner to the person with whom the contract is made; and

   (b) So far unknown and inactive in partnership affairs that the business reputation of the partnership could not be said to have been in any degree due to his connection with it.

(3) The partnership is in no case bound by any act of a partner after dissolution

   (a) Where the partnership is dissolved because it is unlawful to carry on the business, unless the act is appropriate for winding up partnership affairs; or

   (b) Where the partner has become bankrupt; or

   (c) Where the partner has no authority to wind up partnership affairs; except by a transaction with one who

   (I) Had extended credit to the partnership prior to dissolution and had no knowledge or notice of his want of authority; or

   (II) Had not extended credit to the partnership prior to dissolution, and, having no knowledge or notice of his want of authority, the fact of his want of authority has not been advertised in the manner provided for advertising the fact of dissolution in paragraph (1bII).

(4) Nothing in this section shall affect the liability under Section 16 of any person who after dissolution represents himself or consents to another representing him as a partner in a partnership engaged in carrying on business.

Sec. 40. Rules for Distribution

In settling accounts between the partners after dissolution, the following rules shall be observed, subject to any agreement to the contrary:

(a) The assets of the partnership are:

   (I) The partnership property,

   (II) The contributions of the partners necessary for the payment of all the liabilities specified in clause (b) of this paragraph.

(b) The liabilities of the partnership shall rank in order of payment, as follows:

   (I) Those owing to creditors other than partners,

   (II) Those owing to partners other than for capital and profits,

   (III) Those owing to partners in respect of capital,

   (IV) Those owing to partners in respect of profits.

(c) The assets shall be applied in the order of their declaration in clause (a) of this paragraph to the satisfaction of the liabilities.

(d) The partners shall contribute, as provided by section 18(a) the amount necessary to satisfy the liabilities; but if any, but not all, of the partners are insolvent, or, not being subject to process, refuse to contribute, the other partners shall contribute their share of the liabilities, and, in the relative proportions in which they share the profits, the additional amount necessary to pay the liabilities.

(e) An assignee for the benefit of creditors or any person appointed by the court shall have the right to enforce the contributions specified in clause (d) of this paragraph.

(f) Any partner or his legal representative shall have the right to enforce the contributions specified in clause (d) of this paragraph, to the extent of the amount which he has paid in excess of his share of the liability.

(g) The individual property of a deceased partner shall be liable for the contributions specified in clause (d) of this paragraph.

(h) When partnership property and the individual properties of the partners are in possession of a court for distribution, partnership creditors shall have priority on partnership property and separate creditors on individual property, saving the rights of lien or secured creditors as heretofore.

(i) Where a partner has become bankrupt or his estate is insolvent the claims against his separate property shall rank in the following order:

   (I) Those owing to separate creditors,

   (II) Those owing to partnership creditors,

   (III) Those owing to partners by way of contribution.

Appendix J Spanish Equivalents for Important Legal Terms in English

Abandoned property: bienes abandonados
Acceptance: aceptación; consentimiento; acuerdo
Acceptor: aceptante
Accession: toma de posesión; aumento; accesión
Accommodation indorser: avalista de favor
Accommodation party: firmante de favor
Accord: acuerdo; convenio; arregio
Accord and satisfaction: transacción ejecutada
Act of state doctrine: doctrina de acto de gobierno
Administrative law: derecho administrativo
Administrative process: procedimiento o metódo administrativo
Administrator (-trix): administrador (-a)
Adverse possession: posesión de hecho susceptible de proscripción adquisitiva
Affirmative action: acción afirmativa
Affirmative defense: defensa afirmativa
After-acquired property: bienes adquiridos con posterioridad a un hecho dado
Agency: mandato; agencia

Agent: mandatorio; agente; representante
Agreement: convenio; acuerdo; contrato
Alien corporation: empresa extranjera
Allonge: hojas adicionales de endosos
Answer: contestación de la demande; alegato
Anticipatory breach, or anticipatory repudiation: anuncio previo de las partes de su imposibilidad de cumplir con el contrato
Appeal: apelación; recurso de apelación
Appellate jurisdiction: jurisdicción de apelaciones
Appraisal right: derecho de valuación
Arbitration: arbitraje
Arson: incendio intencional
Articles of partnership: contrato social
Artisan's lien: derecho de retención que ejerce al artesano
Assault: asalto; ataque; agresión
Assignment of rights: transmisión; transferencia; cesión
Assumption of risk: no resarcimiento por exposición voluntaria al peligro
Attachment: auto judicial que autoriza el embargo; embargo

Bailee: depositario
Bailment: depósito; constitución en depósito
Bailor: depositante
Bankruptcy trustee: síndico de la quiebra
Battery: agresión; física
Bearer: portador; tenedor
Bearer instrument: documento al portador
Bequest or legacy: legado (de bienes muebles)
Bilateral contract: contrato bilateral
Bill of lading: conocimiento de embarque; carta de porte
Bill of Rights: declaración de derechos
Binder: póliza de seguro provisoria; recibo de pago a cuenta del precio
Blank indorsement: endoso en blanco
Blue sky laws: leyes reguladoras del comercio bursátil
Bond: título de crédito; garantía; caución
Bond indenture: contrato de emisión de bonos; contrato del empréstito
Breach of contract: incumplimiento de contrato
Brief: escrito; resumen; informe
Burglary: violación de domicilio

Business judgment rule: regla de juicio comercial
Business tort: agravio comercial

Case law: ley de casos; derecho casuístico
Cashier's check: cheque de caja
Causation in fact: causalidad en realidad
Cease and desist order: orden para cesar y desistir
Certificate of deposit: certificado de depósito
Certified check: cheque certificado
Charitable trust: fideicomiso para fines benéficos
Chattel: bien mueble
Check: cheque
Civil law: derecho civil
Close corporation: sociedad de un solo accionista o de un grupo restringido de accionistas
Closed shop: taller agremiado (emplea solamente a miembros de un gremio)
Closing argument: argumento al final
Codicil: codicilo
Collateral: garantía; bien objeto de la garantía real
Comity: cortesía; cortesía entre naciones
Commercial paper: instrumentos negociables; documentos a valores commerciales
Common law: derecho consuetudinario; derecho común; ley común
Common stock: acción ordinaria
Comparative negligence: negligencia comparada
Compensatory damages: daños y perjuicios reales o compensatorios
Concurrent conditions: condiciones concurrentes

Concurrent estates: condominio
Concurrent jurisdiction: competencia concurrente de varios tribunales para entender en una misma causa
Concurring opinion: opinión concurrente
Condition: condición
Condition precedent: condición suspensiva
Condition subsequent: condición resolutoria
Confiscation: confiscación
Confusion: confusión; fusión
Conglomerate merger: fusión de firmas que operan en distintos mercados
Consent decree: acuerdo entre las partes aprobado por un tribunal
Consequential damages: daños y perjuicios indirectos
Consideration: consideración; motivo; contraprestación
Consolidation: consolidación
Constructive delivery: entrega simbólica
Constructive trust: fideicomiso creado por aplicación de la ley
Consumer-protection law: ley para proteger el consumidor
Contract: contrato
Contracts under seal: contrato formal o sellado
Contributory negligence: negligencia de la parte actora
Conversion: usurpación; conversión de valores
Copyright: derecho de autor
Corporation: sociedad anómina; corporación; persona juridica
Co-sureties: cogarantes
Counterclaim, or cross-complaint: reconvención; contrademanda
Counteroffer: contraoferta
Course of dealing: curso de transacciones

Course of performance: curso de cumplimiento
Covenant: pacto; garantía; contrato
Covenant not to sue: pacto or contrato a no demandar
Covenant of quiet enjoyment: garantía del uso y goce pacífico del inmueble
Creditors' composition agreement: concordato preventivo
Crime: crimen; delito; contravención
Criminal law: derecho penal
Cross-examination: contrainterrogatorio
Cure: cura; cuidado; derecho de remediar un vicio contractual
Customs receipts: recibos de derechos aduaneros

Damages: daños; indemnización por daños y perjuicios
Debit card: tarjeta de débito
Debtor: deudor
Debt securities: seguridades de deuda
Deceptive advertising: publicidad engañosa
Deed: escritura; título; acta translativa de domino
Defamation: difamación
Delegation of duties: delegación de obligaciones
Demand deposit: depósito a la vista
Depositions: declaración de un testigo fuera del tribunal
Derivative suit: acción judicial entablada por un accionista en nombre de la sociedad
Devise: legado; deposición testamentaria (bienes inmuebles)
Directed verdict: veredicto según orden del juez y sin participación activa del jurado

Direct examination: interrogatorio directo; primer interrogatorio

Disaffirmance: repudiación; renuncia; anulación

Discharge: descargo; liberación; cumplimiento

Disclosed principal: mandante revelado

Discovery: descubrimiento; producción de la prueba

Dissenting opinion: opinión disidente

Dissolution: disolución; terminación

Diversity of citizenship: competencia de los tribunales federales para entender en causas cuyas partes intervinientes son cuidadanos de distintos estados

Divestiture: extinción premature de derechos reales

Dividend: dividendo

Docket: orden del día; lista de causas pendientes

Domestic corporation: sociedad local

Draft: orden de pago; letrade cambio

Drawee: girado; beneficiario

Drawer: librador

Duress: coacción; violencia

Easement: servidumbre

Embezzlement: desfalco; malversación

Eminent domain: poder de expropiación

Employment discrimination: discriminación en el empleo

Entrepreneur: empresario

Environmental law: ley ambiental

Equal dignity rule: regla de dignidad egual

Equity security: tipo de participación en una sociedad

Estate: propiedad; patrimonio; derecho

Estop: impedir; prevenir

Ethical issue: cuestión ética

Exclusive jurisdiction: competencia exclusiva

Exculpatory clause: cláusula eximente

Executed contract: contrato ejecutado

Execution: ejecución; cumplimiento

Executor (-trix): albacea

Executory contract: contrato aún no completamente consumado

Executory interest: derecho futuro

Express contract: contrato expreso

Expropriation: expropriación

Federal question: caso federal

Fee simple: pleno dominio; dominio absoluto

Fee simple absolute: dominio absoluto

Fee simple defeasible: dominio sujeta a una condición resolutoria

Felony: crimen; delito grave

Fictitious payee: beneficiario ficticio

Fiduciary: fiduciaro

Firm offer: oferta en firme

Fixture: inmueble por destino, incorporación a anexación

Floating lien: gravamen continuado

Foreign corporation: sociedad extranjera; U.S. sociedad constituída en otro estado

Forgery: falso; falsificación

Formal contract: contrato formal

Franchise: privilegio; franquicia; concesión

Franchisee: persona que recibe una concesión

Franchisor: persona que vende una concesión

Fraud: fraude; dolo; engaño

Future estate: bien futuro

Garnishment: embargo de derechos

General partner: socio comanditario

General warranty deed: escritura translativa de domino con garantía de título

Gift: donación

Gift *causa mortis:* donación por causa de muerte

Gift *inter vivos:* donación entre vivos

Good faith: buena fe

Good-faith purchaser: comprador de buena fe

Holder: tenedor por contraprestación

Holder in due course: tenedor legítimo

Holographic will: testamento ológrafico

Homestead exemption laws: leyes que exceptúan las casas de familia de ejecución por duedas generales

Horizontal merger: fusión horizontal

Identification identificación

Implied-in-fact contract: contrato implícito en realidad

Implied warranty: guarantía implícita

Implied warranty of merchantability: garantía implícita de vendibilidad

Impossibility of performance: imposibilidad de cumplir un contrato

Impostor: imposter

Incidental beneficiary: beneficiario incidental; beneficiario secundario

Incidental damages: daños incidentales

Indictment: auto de acusación; acusación

Indorsee: endorsatario

Indorsement: endoso

Indorser: endosante

Informal contract: contrato no formal; contrato verbal
Information: acusación hecha por el ministerio público
Injunction: mandamiento; orden de no innovar
Innkeeper's lien: derecho de retención que ejerce el posadero
Installment contract: contrato de pago en cuotas
Insurable interest: interés asegurable
Intended beneficiary: beneficiario destinado
Intentional tort: agravio; cuasi-delito intenciónal
International law: derecho internaciónal
Interrogatories: preguntas escritas sometidas por una parte a la otra o a un testigo
Inter vivos **trust:** fideicomiso entre vivos
Intestacy laws: leyes de la condición de morir intestado
Intestate: intestado
Investment company: compañia de inversiones
Issue: emisión

Joint tenancy: derechos conjuntos en un bien inmueble
Joint tenancy with right of survivorship: derechos conjuntos en un bien inmueble en favor del beneficiario sobreviviente
Judgment n.o.v.: juicio no obstante veredicto
Judgment rate of interest: interés de juicio
Judicial process: acto de procedimiento; proceso jurídico
Judicial review: revisión judicial
Jurisdiction: jurisdicción

Larceny: robo; hurto
Law: derecho; ley; jurisprudencia

Lease: contrato de locación; contrato de alquiler
Leasehold estate: bienes forales
Legal rate of interest: interés legal
Legatee: legatario
Less-than-freehold estate: menos de derecho de dominio absoluto
Letter of credit: carta de crédito
Levy: embargo; comiso
Libel: libelo; difamación escrita
Life estate: usufructo
Limited partner: comanditario
Limited partnership: sociedad en comandita
Liquidation: liquidación; realización
Lost property: objetos perdidos

Majority opinion: opinión de la mayoría
Maker: persona que realiza u ordena; librador
Mechanic's lien: gravamen de constructor
Mediation: mediación; intervención
Merger: fusión
Mirror-image rule: fallo de reflejo
Misdemeanor: infracción; contravención
Mislaid property: bienes extraviados
Mitigation of damages: reducción de daños
Moral hazard: riesgo moral
Mortgage: hypoteca
Motion to dismiss, or demurrer: excepción parentoria
Municipal law: derecho municipal
Mutual fund: fondo mutual

Negotiable instrument: instrumento negociable
Negotiation: negociación
Nominal damages: daños y perjuicios nominales

Novation: novación
Nuncupative will: testamento nuncupativo

Objective theory of contracts: teoria objetiva de contratos
Offer: oferta
Offeree: persona que recibe una oferta
Offeror: oferente
Order paper: instrumento o documento a la orden
Original jurisdiction: jurisdicción de primera instancia
Output contract: contrato de producción

Parol evidence rule: regla relativa a la prueba oral
Partially disclosed principal: mandante revelado en parte
Partnership: sociedad colectiva; asociación; asociación de participación
Past consideration: causa o contraprestación anterior
Patent: patente; privilegio
Pattern or practice: muestra o práctica
Payee: beneficiario de un pago
Penalty: pena; penalidad
Per capita: por cabeza
Perfection: perfeción
Performance: cumplimiento; ejecución
Personal defenses: excepciones personales
Personal property: bienes muebles
Per stirpes: por estirpe
Plea bargaining: regateo por un alegato
Pleadings: alegatos
Pledge: prenda
Police powers: poderes de policia y de prevención del crimen
Policy: póliza
Positive law: derecho positivo; ley positiva

Possibility of reverter: posibilidad de reversión
Precedent: precedente
Preemptive right: derecho de prelación
Preferred stock: acciones preferidas
Premium: recompensa; prima
Presentment warranty: garantía de presentación
Price discrimination: discriminación en los precios
Principal: mandante; principal
Privity: nexo jurídico
Privity of contract: relación contractual
Probable cause: causa probable
Probate: verificación; verificación del testamento
Probate court: tribunal de sucesiones y tutelas
Proceeds: resultados; ingresos
Profit: beneficio; utilidad; lucro
Promise: promesa
Promisee: beneficiario de una promesa
Promisor: promtente
Promissory estoppel: impedimento promisorio
Promissory note: pagaré; nota de pago
Promoter: promotor; fundador
Proximate cause: causa immediata o próxima
Proxy: apoderado; poder
Punitive, or exemplary, damages: daños y perjuicios punitivos o ejemplares

Qualified indorsement: endoso con reservas
Quasi-contract: contrato tácito o implícito
Quit-claim deed: acto de transferencia de una propiedad por finiquito, pero sin ninguna garantía sobre la validez del título transferido

Ratification: ratificación

Real defenses: defensas legitimas o legales
Real property: bienes immuebles
Reasonable doubt: duda razonable
Rebuttal: refutación
Recognizance: promesa; compromiso; reconocimiento
Recording statutes: leyes estatales sobre registros oficiales
Redress: reparación
Reformation: rectificación; reforma; corrección
Rejoinder: dúplica; contrarréplica
Release: liberación; renuncia a un derecho
Remainder: substitución; reversión
Remedy: recurso; remedio; reparación
Replevin: acción reivindicatoria; reivindicación
Reply: réplica
Requirements contract: contrato de suministro
Rescission: rescisión
Res judicata: cosa juzgada; res judicata
Respondeat superior: responsabilidad del mandante o del maestro
Restitution: restitución
Restrictive indorsement: endoso restrictivo
Resulting trust: fideicomiso implícito
Reversion: reversión; sustitución
Revocation: revocación; derogación
Right of contribution: derecho de contribución
Right of reimbursement: derecho de reembolso
Right of subrogation: derecho de subrogación
Right-to-work law: ley de libertad de trabajo
Robbery: robo

Rule 10b-5: Regla 10b-5

Sale: venta; contrato de compreventa
Sale on approval: venta a ensayo; enta sujeta a la aprobación del comprador
Sale or return: venta con derecho de devolución
Sales contract: contrato de compraventa; boleto de compraventa
Satisfaction: satisfacción; pago
Scienter: a sabiendas
S corporation: S corporación
Secured party: acreedor garantizado
Secured transaction: transacción garantizada
Securities: volares; titulos; seguridades
Security agreement: convenio de seguridad
Security interest: interés en un bien dado en garantía que permite a quien lo detenta venderlo en caso de incumplimiento
Service mark: marca de identificación de servicios
Signature: firma; rúbrica
Slander: difamación oral; calumnia
Sovereign immunity: immunidad soberana
Special indorsement: endoso especial; endoso a la orden de una person en particular
Specific performance: ejecución precisa, según los términos del contrato
Spendthrift trust: fideicomiso para pródigos
Stale check: cheque vencido
Stare decisis: acatar las decisiones, observar los precedentes
State exemption laws: leyes que exceptúan los estados
Statutory law: derecho estatutario; derecho legislado; derecho escrito

Stock: acciones
Stock split: fraccionamiento de acciones
Stock warrant: certificado para la compra de acciones
Stop-payment order: orden de suspensión del pago de un cheque dada por el librador del mismo
Strict liability: responsabilidad uncondicional
Summary judgment: fallo sumario

Tangible property: bienes corpóreos
Tenancy at will: inguilino por tiempo indeterminado (según la voluntad del propietario)
Tenancy by sufferance: posesión por tolerancia
Tenancy by the entirety: locación conyugal conjunta
Tenancy for years: inguilino por un término fijo
Tenancy in common: specie de copropiedad indivisa
Tender: oferta de pago; oferta de ejecución
Testamentary trust: fideicomiso testamentario
Testator (-trix): testador (-a)
Third-party-beneficiary contract: contrato para el beneficio del tercero-beneficiario
Tort: agravio; cuasi-delito

Totten trust: fideicomiso creado por un depósito bancario
Trade acceptance: letra de cambio aceptada
Trademark: marca registrada
Trade name: nombre comercial; razón social
Traveler's check: cheque del viajero
Trespass to land: ingreso no authorizado a las tierras de otro
Trespass to personalty: violación de los derechos posesorios de un tercero con respecto a bienes muebles
Trust: fideicomiso; trust

Ultra vires: ultra vires; fuera de la facultad (de una sociedad anónima)
Unanimous opinion: opinión unámine
Unconscionable contract or clause: contrato leonino; cláusula leonino
Underwriter: subscriptor; asegurador
Unenforceable contract: contrato que no se puede hacer cumplir
Unilateral contract: contrato unilateral
Union shop: taller agremiado; empresa en la que todos los empleados son miembros del gremio o sindicato
Usage of trade: uso comercial

Usury: usura

Valid contract: contrato válido
Venue: lugar; sede del proceso
Vertical merger: fusión vertical de empresas
Voidable contract: contrato anulable
Void contract: contato nulo; contrato inválido, sin fuerza legal
Voir dire: examen preliminar de un testigo a jurado por el tribunal para determinar su competencia
Voting trust: fideicomiso para ejercer el derecho de voto

Waiver: renuncia; abandono
Warranty of habitability: garantía de habitabilidad
Warranty of possession: garantía de posesión
Watered stock: acciones diluídos; capital inflado
White-collar crime: crimen administrativo
Writ of attachment: mandamiento de ejecución; mandamiento de embargo
Writ of *certiorari*: auto de avocación; auto de certiorari
Writ of execution: auto ejecutivo; mandamiento de ejecutión
Writ of mandamus: auto de mandamus; mandamiento; orden judicial

Glossary

A

abandoned property Property discarded by the true owner who has no intention of reclaiming it.

acceleration clause Clause in contract that allows payee or other holder of a time instrument to demand payment of the entire amount due with interest if a certain event, such as a default in the payment of an installment, occurs.

acceptance Voluntary act by word or by conduct of the offeree that shows assent or agreement to the terms of the offer.

accession Something added on, as in value added to a piece of personal property by labor or materials.

accord Agreement to discharge a claim by giving and accepting something different from or less than that to which the party agreeing to accept is entitled.

act of state doctrine Doctrine created by the judiciary that provides that the judicial branch of one country will not examine the validity of public acts committed by a recognized foreign government within its own territory.

actus reus Criminal conduct.

administrative agency Agency of the federal government created by the executive or legislative branch for a specific purpose; endowed with legislative, executive, and judicial powers, agency interprets and enforces congressional statutes and rules.

administrative law Body of law that governs the powers, procedures, and practices of administrative agencies.

Administrative Procedures Act of 1946 (APA) Federal statute that acts as a constitution for administrative agencies; provides standardized administrative agency practices and governs how an administrative agency conducts its business.

ad valorem **tariff** Tax on a percentage of the value of the imported good(s).

adverse possession Means of obtaining title to land without a deed being delivered. To establish title, the adverse possessor must prove nonpermissive use that is actual, open, notorious, exclusive, and adverse for the period prescribed by statute.

affirmative action Remedial step taken to improve work opportunities for women, racial and ethnic minorities, and other people considered to have been deprived of job opportunities in the past.

agency law Body of law that governs the relationship between two parties; one of them, the agent, agrees to represent or act for the other, the principal.

aggravated burglary Burglary with the use of a deadly weapon.

alternative dispute resolution Speedy and just means of resolving a dispute at a reasonable cost to both the parties and to the taxpayers; for example, arbitration, conciliation.

American Arbitration Association Private nonprofit organization established in 1926, whose purpose is to foster study of arbitration, to perfect the techniques of arbitration law, and to advance the science of arbitration for the prompt and economic settlement of disputes.

amicus curiae Friend of the court. A qualified person who is not a party to an action but who gives information to the court on a question of law involved in the case.

analytical school of law Approach to the study of law that uses logical analysis to extract the principles underlying a legal code.

ancillary restraint Trade restraint subordinate to the main lawful purpose of a transaction such as the sale of a business; generally, an ancillary restraint requires one party to refrain from competing with another for a specific period within a particular area.

annual percentage rate (APR) True rate of interest being charged on a yearly basis.

answer Document filed by defendant that answers a complaint and admits or denies the allegations stated in the complaint.

antitrust laws   Laws that regulate economic competition in order to prevent monopolists from controlling the economy.

appellate courts   Courts of appeal or courts of review; courts whose subject-matter jurisdiction is limited to hearing appeals.

arbitration   Procedure in which the parties to a dispute submit their case to an impartial third person (arbitrator).

arbitration clause   Clause in a contract that provides for arbitration in the event of a dispute; specifies the expertise of arbitrator, the forum, and the choice of law.

arbitrator   Person selected by the parties to a dispute to make a decision based on evidence submitted by both parties.

articles of incorporation   Initial incorporation process that provides basic information about the corporation and is the primary source of authority for future operation of the business.

assignment   A transfer of all or part of one's property, interest, or rights.

attachment   Court-ordered seizing and taking into custody of property that is in controversy over a debt.

automated clearinghouse   System of electronic signals that makes money transactions between banks; eliminates paper transfers.

B

bailment   Act of delivering personal property without transfer of title from one person (bailor) to another (bailee) under an agreement for a particular purpose on the completion of which the bailee must return the bailed property to the bailor or to a third person or dispose of it as directed.

bankruptcy fraud   Dishonesty with the bankruptcy court on the part of the person who has declared bankruptcy.

bilateral contract   Contract in which one person makes an offer and receives an acceptance from the offeree; most contracts are of this nature.

bilateral mistake   Mistake made by both of the contract parties.

Bill of Rights   First ten amendments to the United States Constitution; adopted in 1791; established specific protections for the individual against the federal government.

blank indorsement   Signature of the payee or of the person who was specified in a specific indorsement.

bona fide occupational qualification (BFOQ)   Job requirement that is unique and specific to a job but that could be discriminatory; for example, the requirement that a wet nurse be female is a BFOQ, and this fact would be a possible defense to an employment discrimination charge.

bond   Method of financing (as for a business) that is a long-term commitment in which the loan earns interest at a fixed rate, and repayment to the creditor is commonly secured by property.

breach of contract   Failure to perform what a party is under an absolute duty to perform based on an express or an implied-in-fact contract.

brief   Method of case analysis and summarization that contains the elements of case citation, facts, issue(s), holding, and reasoning.

burden of proof   Requirement that the plaintiff in a lawsuit must prove the truth of the allegations made against the defendant.

burglary   Act of entering into the building of another with the intent to commit a felony.

bylaws   Statutes of a corporation setting forth the internal rules of management for the corporation.

C

Celler-Kefauver Act   Section 7 of the Clayton Act, established in 1950; controls corporate mergers.

certificate of deposit (CD)   Acknowledgment by a bank of the receipt of money; carries an agreement to repay the money with interest.

certified check   Check that is recognized and accepted by a bank office as a valid appropriation of the specified amount drawn against the funds held by the bank.

chain-style business   Type of franchise that operates under a franchisor's trade name and is identified as a member of a select group of dealers engaging in the franchisor's business.

chattel   An article of personal property, as opposed to real property; any property other than freehold estates.

chattel real   Chattel that concerns real property, such as a lease.

check   Paper drawn on a bank, ordering it to pay a sum of money on demand.

choice-of-law clause   Clause in an international business contract that designates the forum in which adjudication will take place and the substantive law that will be applied in the event of any dispute.

civil law Body of law that establishes the legal rights and duties existing among individuals or between citizens and their governments.

Clayton Act Federal statute enacted in 1941 to strengthen federal antitrust laws; aimed at restraining specific monopolistic practices.

closed shop Firm that recognizes union membership by its workers as a condition for employment.

Colgate doctrine Rule that resulted from *United States v. Colgate* decision in which the U.S. Supreme Court allowed Colgate to refuse unilaterally to deal with retailers who did not follow suggested retail prices; that is, Colgate can deal with whomever it desires.

collateral note Written promise to pay secured by the payee-creditor in which the maker-debtor creates a lien against his or her personal property.

comity Deference that one nation gives to the laws and judicial decrees of another nation, based on respect.

commerce clause Clause in the U.S. Constitution that gives Congress the power "to regulate commerce with foreign nations, and among the several states, and with the individual tribes."

commercial law Body of law that governs commercial actions; business law.

common law Body of judge-made law comprised of principles and the rules of how these principles relate to the government and to the security of persons and property.

common stock Method of financing a business in which stock is held by a shareholder and carries voting rights and the right to a share of the profits of the business if a dividend is declared; has indefinite duration unless redeemed by the corporation.

community property Property of married couples in which each spouse owns an undivided half interest in any property acquired during the marriage.

comparable worth Pay equity; theory that equal pay should be received not just for equal work but also for work of comparable skill, effort, and responsibility.

compensatory damages Award to the injured party as a result of a lawsuit to make up for the monetary loss suffered because the other party breached the contract.

complaint Type of pleading issued by the plaintiff to the defendant that states the purpose of the lawsuit.

computer crimes Crimes committed by use of a computer; for example, electronic thefts of money through issuing an extra paycheck, shaving funds, or depositing funds in personal accounts.

concerted action Action that has been planned, agreed on, and settled between parties acting together pursuant to some scheme.

conciliation Process by which a third party successfully brings together the conflicting parties; this is the process used by the Better Business Bureau.

concurrent jurisdiction Power to hear a case held by both federal and state courts.

confiscation Taking property without proper public purpose or just compensation being awarded.

conglomerate merger Consolidation of two or more firms dealing in unrelated products and operating in markets not horizontally or vertically linked.

consequential damage Foreseeable damage that results when a party breaches a contract.

consideration Something of legal value given in exchange for a promise; essential element of a contract.

constitutional law Public law that involves questions of whether the government has the power to act.

constitutional tort Act by a government official that violates the constitutional rights of a person.

Consumer Credit Protection Act (CCPA) Federal statute that is the primary source of federal law covering credit transactions; enforced by several federal agencies.

contract Promise or set of promises for the breach of which the law gives a remedy, and the performance of which the law in some way recognizes as a duty.

contractual arbitration Arbitration established by contractual agreement entered into either before or after a dispute occurs.

contractual capacity Competence of the parties to a contract.

contributory negligence Negligence on the part of both parties; each party contributes to the negligence.

conversion Taking personal property from its rightful owner or possessor and placing it in the service of another; civil law side of stealing.

copyright Right granted by statute to the author or originator of certain literary or artistic productions.

corporate white-collar crime Crime committed by a complex organization.

corporation Separate legal entity that is owned by shareholders.

counterclaim   Claim in which the defendant sets forth allegations against the claims made by the plaintiff in a lawsuit.

counteroffer   Rejection of original offer and the simultaneous making of a new offer.

covenant not to compete   Clause in an employment contract in which the employee agrees that, if he or she leaves the employment for whatever reason, he or she will not accept employment with a competitor.

covenant running with the land   Agreement under which a landowner either acquires certain rights or is under certain obligations based on his or her ownership of the land that is bound by the covenant.

criminal law   Body of law that deals with violations of wrongs committed against society as a whole.

D

debenture   Form of bond that is unsecured.

debit card   Paperless transaction used to obtain a cash advance from an automatic teller machine; the amount is automatically debited from the customer's account.

debt securities   Bonds of debentures that represent a loan to the corporation.

deed   Writing signed by an owner of property by which title to the property is transferred to another.

defamation   Act of making any untrue statement or statements that harm the reputation of another person or corporation.

defamation by computer   Production by a computer of erroneous information about a person's credit standing or business reputation that may impair the person's ability to obtain further credit.

defamation of character   Act of wrongfully hurting a person's good reputation; results in the tort of slander if spoken or the tort of libel if written.

default   Failure to honor the conditions of a contract.

deficiency judgment   Award that represents the deficient amount (difference between the mortgage debt and the amount received from the proceeds of the foreclosure sale).

demurrer   Defendant's motion to dismiss the complaint, stating that, even if the facts are true, their legal consequences are such that there is no reason to go further with the lawsuit and no need for the defendant to present an answer.

deposition   Sworn oral testimony by opposing party or by witness(es) taken by interrogatories, not in open court.

derivative authority   Authority accorded the agent by the principal to carry out the principal's business.

discharge   To perform a contract fully.

disclosed principal   Principle whose identity is known by the third party at the time the contract is made by the agent.

discovery   Process of obtaining information from opposing party or from witnesses in a lawsuit.

disparagement of goods   False statement made about a person's product.

disparate impact   Employment discrimination practice that appears neutral on the surface but that actually affects a protected class adversely.

disparate treatment   Employment discrimination practice in which treatment of a certain class differs from the treatment of other employees or applicants.

distributorship relationship   Type of franchise where a manufacturing concern (franchisor) licenses a dealer (franchisee) to sell its products; for example, an automobile dealership.

district court   Federal trial court of general jurisdiction; the court of original jurisdiction for federal cases.

diversity of citizenship cases   Cases involving: (1) citizens of different states, (2) a foreign country as plaintiff and citizens of a state or different states, or (3) citizens of a state and citizens or subjects of a foreign country where the amount in controversy is greater than $50,000 and does not involve a federal question.

doctrine of laches   Rule that states that individuals who fail to look out for their rights until after a reasonable time has passed will not be helped.

doctrine of respondeat superior   Rule that makes the principal liable for the agent's torts if the torts are committed within the scope of the agency or the scope of employment.

doctrine of sovereign immunity   Rule that immumizes foreign nations from the jurisdiction of the United States.

draft   Unconditional written order; debt owed by the drawee to the drawer.

drawee   Debtor of the drawer.

drawer   One who creates or executes the order-to-pay instrument.

duress   Compulsion by threat; forcing someone to do something out of fear.

duty of fair representation Implied duty of a union to represent its membership fairly.

E

easement Right of a person to make limited use of another person's property without taking anything from the property.

economic school of law Approach to the study of law that holds that most laws may be evaluated in accordance with economic theory; developed by Richard A. Posner in the 1970s.

electronic funds transfer (EFT) Automatic payment or direct deposit using teller machines, point-of-sale systems, and automated clearinghouses.

eminent domain Power of government to condemn land in order to take it for public use.

employee One employed by the employer to perform services.

Employee Retirement Income Security Act of 1974 (ERISA) Federal statute that established a supplement to social security to be set up by employers for their employees.

employer One who provides a job, and, according to the Fair Labor Standards Act, any person acting directly or indirectly in the interest of an employer in relation to an employee.

employment contract Neutral agreement between employer and employee.

enabling act Congressional legislation that creates an administrative agency, determines its structure, and defines its powers.

Environmental Protection Agency (EPA) Federal agency created in 1970 that assembles various organizations responsible for environmental protection.

Equal Credit Opportunity Act Federal statute that forbids discrimination based on race, sex, religion, national origin, marital status, age, or person's income from public assistance in determinations of creditworthiness.

Equal Employment Opportunity Commission (EEOC) Five-member commission created in 1964 to administer Title VII; members are appointed by the president of the United States with consent of the Senate; issues interpretive guidelines and regulations but does not have force of law; investigates, holds hearings, keeps statistics.

Equal Pay Act of 1963 Amendment to the Fair Labor Standards Act of 1938, administered by the EEOC; prohibits discrimination in wages paid for equal work on jobs whose performance requires equal skills, effort, and responsibility and that are performed under similar conditions (job content rather than job description).

equal protection Legal right that holds that government must treat similarly situated individuals in a similar manner.

equity securities Shares of stock representing an ownership interest in a corporation.

estates Rights of ownership in real property.

exclusive dealing arrangement Legal vertical restraint of trade in which the manufacturer or distributor may require the retailer not to sell products of competing firms, provided there is no boycott but each decision is made on an individual basis.

exclusive jurisdiction Power to hear a case held by only a federal court (as in federal crimes, bankruptcy, patents, copyrights, and suits against the United States) or by only a state court (as in divorce, probate, and adoption cases).

executed contract Contract that is fully performed.

executive agreement Agreement made by the president of the United States without need for the consent of the Senate; used in making treaties with foreign countries.

executive branch Branch of the U.S. government that includes the president and is charged with enforcing the law; the powers of the president, as established in Article II of the Constitution.

executive immunity Doctrine that makes the president of the United States immune from certain lawsuits.

executive order Order or regulation issued under the presidential authority to make rules.

executive privilege Right of the president to keep certain secrets.

executory contract Contract that has not been performed.

express contract Contract in which the terms are stated exactly whether written or spoken.

express warranty Explicit statements made by the seller to the buyer regarding the condition or quality of the goods purchased.

expropriation Government seizure of a privately owned business or goods for a proper public purpose and with just compensation.

extension Increase in length of time (for example, the due date of a note).

extension clause Contract clause that allows the date of maturity to be extended into the future; reverse of acceleration clause.

extraterritorial Beyond the country's borders.

F

fact finding Investigative process by which a third party will investigate the issues and make findings of fact to present to the court or other body charged with ruling on the issues.

Fair Credit Billing Act Amendment to Truth-in-Lending Act (TILA) that requires creditors to correct errors promptly and without damage to a person's credit rating.

Fair Credit Reporting Act Title VI of the Consumer Credit Protection Act, which requires that consumers be informed of the nature and scope of a credit investigation, the kind of information that is being compiled, and the names of persons who will be receiving the report.

Fair Debt Collection Practices Act Part of the Consumer Credit Protection Act; adopted in 1977, it prohibits certain practices in the collection of consumer debt by debt collection agencies.

Fair Labor Standard Act of 1938 (FLSA) Federal statute that established minimum wage, overtime standards, record-keeping, and child labor prohibitions; provides for administrative procedures for the enforcement of and compliance with these standards as they apply to employees engaged in commerce, production of goods to be placed in commerce, or employees of an enterprise engaged in commerce.

false imprisonment Intentional confinement or restraint of another person without justification.

Federal Arbitration Act Federal statute favoring arbitration that withdraws from the states the power to require a judicial forum for the resolution of disagreements if the parties by contract have agreed to solve the problem by arbitration.

Federal Insurance Contribution Act Federal statute that provides funding for the social security program.

federalism System of government organization in which state governments and the federal government share powers.

Federal Trade Commission Bipartisan, independent administrative agency headed by five commissioners authorized to prevent unfair methods of competition in commerce and unfair or deceptive acts or practices in commerce.

Federal Trade Commission Act of 1914 Federal statute that created the Federal Trade Commission.

Federal Unemployment Tax Act (1954) (FUTA) Federal statute that established a state system of providing unemployment compensation to eligible individuals.

fee simple absolute Estate in property in which the owner has the greatest aggregation of rights, privileges, and power possible; is indefinite in duration.

felony Crime punishable by imprisonment in a federal or state penitentiary for more than one year, by fine, or by death.

finance charge Total amount of interest paid on a loan.

fixture Object affixed to realty by roots, embedded in it, or permanently attached by cement, nails, bolts, plaster, or screws.

flat rate tariff Tax on a unit item of goods entering or leaving a country.

force majeure **clause** Clause in a contract that protects parties from forces beyond their control.

foreclosure Legal procedure that mortgagee uses to obtain payment in a mortgage default.

Foreign Corrupt Practices Act of 1977 (FCPA) Federal statute that prohibits bribes given to foreign government officials by representatives of American companies and their directors, officers, shareholders, employees, or agents for the purpose of obtaining or retaining business for the American company.

Foreign Sovereign Immunities Act of 1976 (FSIA) Federal statute that codifies the law of sovereign immunity.

forgery Crime of obtaining goods by false pretenses.

formal contract Written contract between parties.

franchise Arrangement in which the owner of a trademark, a trade name, or copyright licenses another person under specified conditions or limitations to use the trademark, trade name, or copyright in marketing goods or services.

Freedom of Information Act of 1966 (FOIA) Amendment to the Administrative Procedures Act that makes all nonexempt information held by federal agencies available to the public.

freehold estate Estate in real property of uncertain duration.

G

garnishment Statutory procedure in which a person's property in possession of another is applied to payment of that person's debts.

general jurisdiction Power to hear almost any subject matter in a lawsuit; authority of the court of original jurisdiction.

general restraint Illegal restraint of trade used to eliminate competition.

general warranty deed Deed that provides the buyer protection against defects in the title to land.

geographic market Part of the structural analysis tool used by courts to determine whether a monopoly exists; considers whether sellers within an area can raise prices or reduce the supply of products without quantities of lower-priced goods quickly flowing into the regional, national, or local area.

gift Voluntary transfer of ownership of property.

good faith Honesty in a transaction.

government agency Administrative agency created by Congress to administer a quasi-business venture generating its own revenue; for example, U.S. Postal Service.

grand jury A body of people selected to conduct fact finding and based on their conclusions to issue indictments for criminal offenses.

group boycott *Per se* violation of the Sherman Act in which a group refuses to deal with some third party or parties.

H

hardware Computer equipment itself.

Herfindahl-Hirschman Index Statistical formula used by the Department of Justice to determine non-market considerations of a proposed merger, such as the ease of entry into the business and the resulting competitive strength of the merged firms.

historical school of law Approach to the study of law based on the origin and history of the legal system; looks to the past to discover what the principles of contemporary law should be.

holder Person who possesses negotiable instruments drawn, issued, or indorsed to his or her order or to the bearer or in blank.

holder in due course (HDC) Special-status transferee of a negotiable instrument.

homestead exemption Exemption of certain types of real and personal property from levy of execution or attachment in the event of mortgage default and deficiency judgment.

horizontal market division *Per se* violation of the Sherman Act that involves dividing a market for the sale of a specific product among competitors.

horizontal merger Merger of comparable companies.

I

implied-in-fact contract Contract formed in whole or in part from the conduct of the parties.

implied warranty Warranty derived from the facts of the case but not specifically stated.

implied warranty of fitness Warranty that arises when any seller knows the particular purpose for which a buyer will use the goods and knows the buyer is relying on the seller's skill and judgment to select suitable goods.

implied warranty of merchantability Warranty that goods are reasonably fit for the purpose for which they are sold, are properly packaged and labeled, and are of proper quality; arises in the sale of goods by a merchant who deals in goods of that kind.

incorporators People who start the corporation.

independent agency Administrative agency that is not under the control of the president or Congress but is freestanding; has a commission created by Congress and is headed by a commissioner.

independent contractor Person who contracts with another to do something for him or her but who is not controlled by the other or subject to the other's right to control with respect to his or her physical conduct in the performance of the undertaking.

indictment Formal charge of wrongdoing issued by a grand jury prior to trial.

indorsement Signature of the person known as the indorser written on the back of the instrument itself.

infliction of mental distress Intentional act that involves extreme and outrageous conduct and that results in severe emotional distress to another.

informal contract Written or oral contract.

informal rule making Rule making that consists of notice and comment; most commonly used by administrative agencies to promulgate rules.

injunction Equitable remedy in which an order is issued to a person or a business to refrain from doing wrongful act(s).

in personam **jurisdiction** Jurisdiction over the person.

in rem **jurisdiction** Jurisdiction over property.

intangible property Property that possesses an invisible value, such as an annuity, checks, or bonds, and is reported by a piece of paper with rights recognized by law.

intentional tort Intentional acts that cause injuries either against the person or against property.

interlocking directorship Situation in which one person is director of two or more competing businesses where one of them has a capital surplus exceeding $1 million.

international custom General practice among nations that is accepted as law.

international law Law considered legally binding among otherwise independent nations.

interpretive rule Statement by an administrative agency as to how it interprets the statute it is charged with administering; published in the Federal Register.

interrogatories Written questions sent to the opposing party that must be answered under oath.

intestate Dying without a will.

J

joint tenancy with right of survivorship Situation in which two or more persons own an undivided interest in either personal or real property, and, on the death of one of the joint tenants, his or her interest transfers to the remaining joint tenant, not to his or her heirs.

joint venture Undertaking in which two or more companies join together to conduct business.

judgment Verdict that has been signed by a judge and that states who won the case and the conditions of the award.

judicial arbitration Compulsory, court-mandated arbitration.

judicial branch Branch of the U.S. government that consists of the federal judicial system and its powers as established by Article III of the U.S. Constitution.

judicial review Process for deciding whether a law is in conflict with the mandates of the Constitution.

jurisdiction *Juris*: law + *diction*: to speak; the power to speak the law; the authority to interpret and apply the law, to hear cases.

jurisprudence Science or philosophy of law.

L

Labor Management Relations Act of 1947 Also known as the Taft-Hartley Act; amendment to the Wagner Act that provides protection for employers as well as employees in labor-related issues.

Labor Management Reporting and Disclosure Act of 1959 Also known as the Landrum-Griffith Act; statute that established an employee bill of rights and reporting requirements for union activities; regulates internal union business.

larceny Wrongful or fraudulent taking and carrying away by any person of the personal property of another.

law System that gives order to society; a system of moral conduct by which society achieves justice; a body of rules.

law merchant Rules resulting from the resolution of disputes and from transactions of merchants and other commercial traders; consists primarily of general customs of the trades that remain law unless displaced by specific statutes.

lease Transfer of real or personal property by landlord or lessor to the tenant or lessee for a period of time in exchange for a consideration (usually payment of rent); on termination, the property reverts to the lessor.

legal realists Those who stress the pragmatic and empirical sides of law; looking at how well the law meets the needs of society.

legislative branch Branch of the U.S. government that consists of Congress and its powers as established by Article I of the U.S. Constitution.

legislative immunity Doctrine that protects members of Congress from being held accountable for their acts and utterances that are part of their legitimate legal duties.

letter of credit Contract used in international business that assures the seller of payment while assuring the buyer that payment will not be made until all terms and conditions of the instrument are complied with.

license Revocable right of a person to come onto another person's land; for example, a ticket to attend the theater.

licensing power Authority of governmental body to grant a license to pursue a particular activity.

lien Type of tangible security beyond the mere promise to pay a debt; uses personal property held in the event of default.

limited jurisdiction Jurisdiction limited to certain subject matters.

line agency Administrative agency under the direct control of the president of the United States; for example, the Department of Labor.

liquidated damages Amount stipulated in a contract to serve as the measure of damages in case of a breach.

lobbyists Those who attempt to influence lawmakers in favor of certain legislation or special interests.

lost property   Property that is not voluntarily left and forgotten.

M

Magnuson-Moss Warranty Act   Federal statute designed to prevent deception in warranties by making them easier to understand; enforced by the Federal Trade Commission.

manufacturing or processing plant   Type of franchise in which the franchisor transfers to the franchisee essential ingredients or the formula to make a particular product.

market share   Part of the structural analysis employed by courts to determine whether a monopoly exists; considers the market positions of all other firms with which a business competes.

mask work   A series of related images, fixed or encoded, in a three-dimensional pattern on a silicon chip. The pattern is layered in a series, so that each image has a pattern. Similar to a film negative that is black on clear plastic. As it is processed into a picture, various layers of plastic with images are placed on top of one another. Eventually the final product, a colored photograph, is produced. May be copyrighted.

mediation   Process of promoting voluntary compromise or resolution of a dispute usually initiated before arbitration.

Medicare   Health insurance program administered by the Social Security Administration to people sixty-five years of age and older and for those under sixty-five years of age who are disabled.

mens rea   Criminal intent.

merger   Combination of two or more firms into one firm.

minor   Person less than the legal statutory age.

misdemeanor   Crime punishable by a fine or by confinement for up to a year; for example, tresspass or disorderly conduct.

mislaid property   Property that has been placed somewhere by the owner voluntarily and then inadvertently forgotten.

mortgagee   Creditor or lender; the beneficiary of the mortgage.

mortgage note   Type of collateral note used to buy a house.

mortgagor   Debtor or borrower who creates a mortgage on real estate.

mutual assent   Meeting of the minds of the offeror and the offeree; offer must be made by one person and accepted by another for the same item or service.

N

National Environmental Policy Act (NEPA)   Federal statute established in 1970 that created the Council of Environmental Quality and mandated that an environmental impact statement be prepared for every recommendation or report on legislation or major federal action significantly affecting the quality of the environment.

National Labor Relations Act   Also known as the Wagner Act; federal statute enacted in 1935 that established rights of employees to engage in collective bargaining and to strike.

National Labor Relations Board (NLRB)   Agency created by the Wagner Act to oversee union elections and to prevent employers from engaging in unfair and illegal union-labor activities and practices.

national law   Body of law that pertains to a particular nation.

natural law school   Approach to the study of law that holds ethics to be the source of legal authority; ethical values are used to make legal decisions.

negligence   Conduct that falls below the duty of care and that results in another's personal injury or property damage.

negotiation   Process in which two or more people meet to discuss their differences and attempt to arrive at a settlement that is acceptable to both.

nolo contendere   Plea by the defendant that does not admit guilt but that allows the court to impose the same penalty as for a guilty plea.

nominal damages   Damages awarded when there is a breach of contract and a technical injury has occurred, but where no actual damages are sustained.

nonfreehold estate   Chattel real; estate consisting of possession of land without possessing a freehold estate in it.

nonpossessory interests   Interests in land that do not include any rights of possession; for example, easements.

Norris-LaGuardia Act   Federal statute established in 1932 that permits employees to organize and restricts federal courts from issuing injunctions against unions engaged in peaceful strikes.

novation   Written agreement entered into by all the parties in which one party is substituted for another party; that is, one party is completely dismissed, and another party is substituted.

nuisance Improper activity that interferes with another's enjoyment or use of his or her property.

O

obligation to bargain in good faith Requirement of employers and unions to meet at reasonable times and to confer in good faith, but not necessarily to reach an agreement.

Occupational Safety and Health Act of 1970 Federal statute that requires health and safety protections for employees at their place of employment.

Occupational Safety and Health Administration (OSHA) Organization that promulgates and enforces workers' safety and health standards, conducts inspections and investigations, keeps records, and performs research.

occupational white-collar crime Crime committed by people through their work; for example, insider trading, bribes.

offeree Person receiving the offer.

offeror Person making the offer.

official language clause Clause in an international business contract that specifies the official language to be used in interpreting the terms of the contract.

order Decision of the administrative law judge; final disposition of a case between the government and a party in a lawsuit.

order to pay Document or instrument in which one party (drawer) orders another party (drawee) to pay money to a third party (payee).

P

partially disclosed principal Principal whose identity is not known by the third party but the third party knows that the agent is acting for a principal at the time the contract is made.

patent Grant from the government that conveys and secures to an inventor the exclusive right to make, use, and sell an invention for a period of seventeen years.

payee Bearer of an instrument.

perfection Legal process by which a secured creditor protects himself or herself against the claims of third parties who may want their debts satisfied out of the same collateral.

per se **illegality** Illegality that requires for proof only the fact that an agreement existed; for example, pricefixing.

personal property All property that is basically movable and is not real property.

petty offense Civil offense not classified as a crime, which is punishable by a fine, imprisonment, or both; for example, a traffic violation.

pleading Document written by one of the parties to a lawsuit and sent to the other parties and to the court to be included in the judge's case file; provides information to the other parties.

point-of-sale system Electronic system that allows the consumer to transfer his or her funds from his or her account to the merchant's in order to make a purchase through the use of a debit card.

preferred stock Equity security in a corporation that carries certain preferences, such as dividends at a fixed rate; may or may not carry voting rights and is entitled to preference over common stock in payment of assets in the event the corporation is liquidated.

price fixing Conspiracy among competitors to fix the price of an item or service.

Privacy Act 1974 amendment to the Administrative Procedures Act that protects individuals who are citizens or legal aliens from uncontrolled transfer of certain personal information to federal agencies for nonroutine uses.

private law Subdivision of substantive law; addresses direct dealings between persons.

private nuisance Tort that interferes with the property interest of a limited number of individuals.

privity Mutual or successive relationship to the same rights of property, or such an identification of interest of one person with another as to represent the same legal right (for example, a lessee is in privity with the lessor).

probable cause Reasonable ground for supposing that an individual has committed a crime.

procedural due process Guarantee granted to individuals that requires any government decision to take a person's life, liberty, or property to be made fairly.

procedural law Established methods or processes of enforcing the rights created by substantive law.

procedural rule Type of administrative agency rule that governs the internal practices of an agency.

process Document that is an order coming from the court, signed by the judge or representative; three stages of process exist: issued, served, filed.

professional agent One who handles contracts in a particular field; for example, real estate broker.

professional association Organized group of professionals with common interests; subject to antitrust laws.

promisee Person receiving the promise.

promisor Person making the promise.

promissory estoppel Doctrine that prevents the promisor from revoking the offer.

promissory note Written promise to pay made between two parties; payable at a definite time or on demand.

public law Subdivision of substantive law; addresses the relationship between individuals and their government.

public nuisance Crime that disturbs or interferes with the public.

punitive damages Damages awarded to punish a party for intentional and willful conduct that he or she knew at the time would harm someone.

purchase money security loan Security interest created as part of a purchase agreement.

Q

qualified fee estate Estate in property in which the owner has less rights than with fee simple; qualified, specific conditions exist to the ownership.

qualified indorsement Instrument of indorsement used by the indorser to disclaim or limit liability on the instrument.

quasi-contract Implied-in-law contract in which the parties did not make any promise by word or conduct but the law imposed a promise on the party who benefited.

quasi-executive function Administrative agency power to ensure compliance with the rules and to conduct investigations.

quasi-judicial function Administrative agency power to prosecute cases, render judgments, and impose penalties if violations occur.

quasi-legislative function Administrative agency power to promulgate rules that have the effect of law.

quitclaim deed Deed conveying to the buyer whatever interest the grantor had in the property, if any.

quota Limit, as on the number of goods that can be imported to a country.

R

Racketeer Influenced and Corrupt Organizations Act of 1970 (RICO) Amendment to the Organized Crime Control Act of 1970; designed to control the investment by organized crime into legitimate businesses and to force forfeiture of any profits made as a result of such criminal activity.

raising an affirmative defense Admitting the truth of the complaint but raising new facts that will result in the dismissal of the case.

ratification Express or implied conduct of the principal that binds the principal to the agent's acts and treats the agent's acts or contracts as if they had been authorized by the principal from the beginning.

real estate mortgage Lien that secures repayment of a note given to secure the purchase of real property.

Real Estate Settlement Procedures Act (RESPA) Federal statute that governs the purchase of a house and the borrowing of money to pay for it.

real property Land and the objects permanently attached to it.

reformation of the contract Rewriting of the contract because of errors in the written document.

Regulatory Flexibility Act 1980 amendment to the Administrative Procedures Act that requires an agency to publish in the Federal Register twice each year a special regulatory flexibility agenda.

release Giving up of a right, claim, or privilege by the person in whom it exists or to whom it accrues, to the person against whom it might have been enforced or demanded.

relevant market Part of the structural analysis used by the courts to determine whether a monopoly exists; considers the characteristics of the product, its substitutes, and the geographic area where the product is sold.

remedy Relief provided for an innocent party when the other party has breached a contract.

remedy at law Legal remedy awarded by the court; the harmed party could be awarded land, money, or items of value, or a combination of all three.

remedy in equity Legal remedy granted by the court; an appropriate remedy, based on fairness, justice, and honesty, is awarded to the harmed party in order to correct the situation.

reorganization Also known as Chapter 11 in a business bankruptcy filing; situation in which the creditors and debtors formulate a plan under which the debtor pays a portion of the debts and is discharged of the remainder, and the debtor is allowed to continue in business.

repossession Situation in which the secured party takes possession of the collateral covered by the security agreement in the event of default.

requirement contract Vertical restraint of trade in which either the buyer must purchase all his or her requirements of a particular product for a specific time from the seller or the seller must supply all of the product the buyer requests.

resale price maintenance Vertical restraint of trade in which the buyer and the seller agree to the price at which the buyer will resell the product.

rescission Remedy that cancels the agreement and returns the parties to the contract to the status quo; may be by mutual consent, by conduct, or by decree of a court of equity.

resolution Agreement reached mutually by the disputing parties.

Restatement, Second Body of law created by the judiciary and revised in 1979; covers the areas of law regarding contracts, property, trusts, and torts.

restitution Equitable remedy in which a person is restored to his or her original position prior to loss or injury, or is placed in the same position as if a breach had not occurred.

restrictive indorsement Indorsement on an instrument that requires the indorser to comply with certain instructions regarding the funds involved.

revocation Withdrawing of the offer by the offeror.

right-to-work law Statute making it illegal for union membership to be required for employment.

robbery Wrongful or fraudulent taking and carrying away by any person of the personal property of another, involving the use of fear or force.

Robinson-Patman Act Section 2 of the Clayton Act; promotes economic equality in the purchasing and selling of goods; prohibits price discrimination.

rule of reason Doctrine by which the court reviews all the circumstances of a case to decide whether the defendant's practice was an unreasonable restraint on trade.

S

satisfaction Tender of substitute performance in return for the relinquishment of the right of action on a prior obligation; accord is executed.

secured transaction Type of transaction secured by collateral.

service mark Mark used to distinguish the services of one person from those of another; the title, character names, or other distinctive features of radio and television programs may be registered as service marks.

shop right Employer's right to use invention developed during working hours by employee without payment of royalties.

sight (demand) draft Instrument payable on sight when the holder presents it for payment.

slander of title Defaming the title a person has to his or her property and possibly preventing the sale of the property.

Social Security Act of 1935 Federal statute that established a federal insurance program covering the financial impact of retirement, death, disability, hospitalization, and unemployment of a worker through contributions by a worker and his or her employer.

sociological school of law Approach to the study of law that seeks to discover, by observation through social science, what law will work.

software Programming involved with a computer system.

special indorsement Indorsement on an instrument that indicates a specific person to whom the indorser intends to make the instrument payable.

special warranty deed Deed in which the seller warrants that he or she has not previously done anything to lessen the value of the real estate for sale.

specific performance Equitable remedy in which the defendant is ordered to perform the act(s) promised in the contract.

stare decisis "Let the decision stand"; the practice of deciding a case with reference to former decisions.

statutory law Body of law enacted by state and federal legislatures.

stop-payment order Request made by a customer that his or her bank stop payment on an issued check.

straight bankruptcy Bankruptcy in which the debtor lists debts and turns his or her assets over to a trustee for settlement of the bankruptcy action.

strict liability Situation in which no defenses exist; applies to dangerous activities where all risk and responsibility for injury is assumed by the party involved or doing the hazardous activity.

structural analysis Tool used by the courts in determining whether monopoly power exists; involves defining the relevant product, geographic market, and market share.

sub judice Under or before a judge or court; under judicial consideration.

Subchapter S Voluntary tax status of a small corporation that allows the corporation to be taxed as a partnership; all losses and gains are passed through to the individual shareholders without taxation at the corporate level.

subpoena Process document that secures the attendance of a witness at a trial.

subpoena duces tecum Process document that requires evidence to be brought to court.

substantive due process Doctrine that holds that the content or substance of a piece of legislation must be in compliance with the Constitution.

substantive law Law that defines, describes, regulates, and creates legal rights and obligations of individuals with respect to each other.

substantive rule Administrative agency rule that is not procedural or interpretive in nature.

summary judgment Written request by either party to a lawsuit to the court to grant judgment on grounds that there is no genuine issue of material fact and the requesting party is entitled to judgment as a matter of law.

summons Process document that requires the defendant to defend against the claim of the plaintiff in a lawsuit.

sunset act Statute that establishes the automatic expiration date for an administrative agency.

Sunshine Act Amendment to the Administrative Procedures Act that prohibits administrative agencies from holding secret meetings.

supremacy clause Clause in the Constitution that governs the relationship between the states and the federal government.

Supreme Court of the United States Highest level of the federal court system, consisting of nine justices who serve for life, are appointed by the president, and are confirmed by the Senate; primarily an appellate court.

T

tangible property Visible property that has physical existence; for example, land, cattle, buildings, computers.

tariff Tax placed on imported goods based on either an *ad valorem* or a flat-rate basis.

tenancy by entirety Ownership where the husband and wife own property without separate transfer rights.

tenancy by sufferance Possession of land without right; not a true tenancy.

tenancy for years Nonfreehold estate created by express contract by leasing property for a specific period of time.

tenancy from period to period Nonfreehold estate created by a lease that does not specify length of time but states that rent is to be paid at certain intervals.

tenancy in common Co-ownership in which two or more persons can own an undivided fractional interest in the property, but, on one tenant's death, that interest passes to his or her heirs.

termination statement Statement showing that a debt has been paid.

time draft Draft that is payable at a definite future time.

Title VII of the Civil Rights Act of 1964 Federal statute that prohibits discrimination in all areas of employment on the basis of race, color, religion, national origin, sex, including pregnancy, childbirth, and abortion, to state, local, and federal agencies and employers of at least fifteen employees and involved in or a part of interstate commerce (the federal government is exempt); administered by the Equal Employment Opportunity Commission.

tort French word meaning "wrong"; wrongdoing for which a civil action in court is possible.

trade acceptance Draft frequently used with the sale of goods in which the purchaser becomes liable to pay the draft. Equivalent to note receivable of the seller and note payable of the buyer, a trade acceptance permits the seller to raise money on it before it is due.

trade association Group of organized competitors pursuing a common interest, such as dissemination of information, advertising campaigns, codes of conduct; subject to antitrust laws.

trademark Distinctive mark, motto, device, or implement that a manufacturer stamps, prints, or otherwise affixes to the goods it produces.

treaty Agreement or contract between two or more nations that must be authorized and ratified by the supreme power of each nation.

trespass to land Entering onto land, causing anything to enter onto land, remaining on land, or permitting anything to remain on land owned by another person.

trespass to personal property Unlawful injury to (or other interference with) the personal property of another that violates that person's exclusive possession and enjoyment of the property.

tribunal administrator   Person who manages the administrative matters and all communication between the parties and the arbitrator in an arbitration.

trust   Legal entity in which a trustee holds title to property for the benefit of another.

Truth-in-Lending Act (TILA)   Title I of the Consumer Credit Protection Act; deals with deceptive credit practices and requires notice and disclosure to prevent sellers and creditors from taking unfair advantage of consumers.

tying arrangement   Arrangement in which the buyer must purchase one item in order to purchase the tied product.

U

unconscionable contract or clause   Clause in a contract, or the entire contract, that is so one-sided as to be unjust after considering the needs of the particular case.

undisclosed principal   Principal whose identity is totally unknown by the third party and the third party has no knowledge that the agent is acting in an agency capacity at the time the contract is made.

Uniform Arbitration Act   It is designed to make legislation on arbitration more uniform throughout the country; has been adopted by 34 states and the District of Columbia.

Uniform Commercial Code (UCC)   Uniform act consisting of eleven articles that applies to both interstate and intrastate business transactions governing the conduct of business among individuals and businesses.

Uniform Consumer Credit Code (UCCC)   Comprehensive body of rules governing the most important aspects of consumer credit; has been adopted by only a few states.

unilateral contract   Contract in which a person makes a promise that requires in return an act (not a promise) by the other party; for example, a reward situation.

unilateral mistake   Mistake made by one of the contracting parties.

union shop   Business that does not require union membership of applicants in order to be hired but can and usually does require workers to join the union after a specific period of time on the job.

usury   Rate of interest that is above the amount allowed by statute; applies to cash loans only.

V

valid contract   Contract that meets all requirements of a contract to be enforced in a court.

venue   Particular geographic area within a judicial district where a suit should be brought.

verdict   Decision of the jury.

vertical merger   Merger of a company at one stage of production with another company at a higher or lower stage of production.

vertical restraint   Trade practice that involves firms at different levels of the production and distribution process and that violates antitrust laws.

voidable contract   Situation in which one party to a contract is bound by the other party may disaffirm it; for example, a contract by a minor.

voluntary arbitration   Arbitration entered into voluntarily based on a previous written agreement between the disputing parties to arbitrate when a dispute arises.

W

warranty   Seller's assurance to the buyer that the goods sold will meet certain standards.

warranty to title   Guarantee to the buyer that the goods are not stolen, have no lien against them, and do not infringe a patent or copyright.

white-collar crime   Monetary offense usually against a business; nonviolent crimes committed by corporations or by individuals against corporations.

will   Legal instrument that, on a person's death, directs how the person's property is to be distributed.

writ of *certiorari*   Order from the Supreme Court to a lower court to send the records of a case to the Supreme Court for review.

writ of attachment   Process document issued after judgment has been made by the court; may take the form of an order to take or seize property or persons to bring them under control of the court.

writ of execution   Process document issued after judgment has been made by the court; puts in force the court's decree or judgment.

writ of garnishment   Process document issued after judgment has been made by the court; garnishes the wages or property of the party at fault.

Z

zoning   Restrictions on land use imposed by the state or local government.

Table of Cases

The principal cases are in bold type. Cases cited or discussed are in roman type. Cases that can also be retrieved on West Publishing's LEGAL CLERK Research Software System are indicated by a color dot. To determine which of the three versions of LEGAL CLERK a particular case appears on, please turn to the text page cited and refer to the color coded computer symbol printed with the case citation.

A green computer symbol indicates that the case appears on *Uniform Commercial Code Article 2 Sales-Version 1.0*. A black computer symbol indicates that the case is on *Government Regulation and the Legal Environment of Business-Version 1.0*. A black computer symbol with a color background identifies the case as appearing on *Contracts-Version 1.0*.

Index